THE HISTORY

OF

ENGLISH LAW.

THE HISTORY

OF

ENGLISH LAW

BEFORE THE TIME OF EDWARD I

BY

SIR FREDERICK POLLOCK

AND

FREDERIC WILLIAM MAITLAND

SECOND EDITION

Reissued

with a new introduction and select bibliography by

S. F. C. MILSOM

VOLUME I

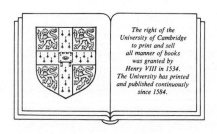

The right of the
University of Cambridge
to print and sell
all manner of books
was granted by
Henry VIII in 1534.
The University has printed
and published continuously
since 1584.

CAMBRIDGE UNIVERSITY PRESS

Cambridge

New York   New Rochelle   Melbourne   Sydney

Published by the Press Syndicate of the University of Cambridge
The Pitt Building, Trumpington Street, Cambridge CB2 1RP
32 East 57th Street, New York, NY 10022, USA
10 Stamford Road, Oakleigh, Australia 3166

Library of Congress catalogue card number: 69-21197

ISBN 0 521 07061 9 hard covers
ISBN 0 521 09515 8 paperback

First published 1895
Second edition 1898
Reprinted 1911 1923 1952
Reissued with a new introduction
and bibliography by
S. F. C. Milsom 1968
Reprinted 1978 1980 1988

Printed in Great Britain by
Woolnough Bookbinding, Irthlingborough, Northamptonshire

PREFACE TO THE SECOND EDITION.

IN this edition the first chapter, by Prof. Maitland, is new. In Book II., c. ii. § 12, on 'Corporations and Churches' (formerly 'Fictitious Persons'), and c. iii. § 8, on 'The Borough,' have been recast. There are no other important alterations: but we have to thank our learned critics, and especially Dr Brunner of Berlin, for various observations by which we have endeavoured to profit. We have thought it convenient to note the paging of the first edition in the margin.

F. P.

F. W. M.

PREFACE TO FIRST EDITION.

THE present work has filled much of our time and thoughts for some years. We send it forth, however, well knowing that in many parts of our field we have accomplished, at most, a preliminary exploration. Oftentimes our business has been rather to quarry and hew for some builder of the future than to leave a finished building. But we have endeavoured to make sure, so far as our will and power can go, that when his day comes he shall have facts and not fictions to build with. How near we may have come to fulfilling our purpose is not for us to judge. The only merit we claim is that we have given scholars the means of verifying our work throughout.

We are indebted to many learned friends for more or less frequent help, and must specially mention the unfailing care and attention of Mr R. T. Wright, the Secretary of the University Press.

Portions of the book have appeared, in the same words or in substance, in the *Contemporary Review*, the *English Historical Review* and the *Harvard Law Review*, to whose editors and proprietors we offer our acknowledgments and thanks.

F. P.
F. W. M.

Note. It is proper for me to add for myself that, although the book was planned in common and has been revised by both of us, by far the greater share of the execution belongs to Mr Maitland, both as to the actual writing and as to the detailed research which was constantly required.

F. P.

21 *Feb.* 1895.

CONTENTS.

PAGE

PREFACE TO THE SECOND EDITION v
PREFACE TO THE FIRST EDITION vi
TABLE OF CONTENTS vii
LIST OF ABBREVIATIONS xviii
LIST OF TEXTS xix
ADDENDA xxii
INTRODUCTION by Professor S. F. C. Milsom xxiii

I. The Place of *Pollock and Maitland* Today, xxiii; II. The Real Actions, xxvii; III. The Personal Actions, xlix; IV. Procedure, lxiv; V. A General View, lxxi.

SELECT BIBLIOGRAPHY AND NOTES by Professor S. F. C. Milsom   lxxv

I. (1) Original Sources: Ancent Laws and Law Books, lxxv; Records of Royal Courts to the late Thirteenth Century, lxxvi; Records of Local Courts to the early Fourteenth Century, lxxvii; Early Year Books, lxxviii. (2) Institutional Studies: General Accounts, lxxviii; Local and Private Courts and Officials, lxxix; Eyres, lxxx; Benches and Judicial Aspects of Exchequer, lxxx; Profession and Literature, lxxxi; Criminal Administration and Law, lxxxi; Jury Proceedings, lxxxii; Legislation, lxxxii; Ecclesiastical Jurisdiction, lxxxiii.

II. (1) The Real Actions: General and Background Discussions, lxxxiv; Background to the Actions, lxxxiv; Writ of Right, lxxxv; Mort D'Ancestor, lxxxvi; Seisin and Novel Disseisin, lxxxvi; Writs of Entry, lxxxviii; Other Actions, lxxxviii. (2) The Personal Actions: General Accounts, lxxxviii; Personal Actions in Local Courts, lxxxix; Contract in Royal Courts, lxxxix; Trespass, xc. (3) Procedure: General Accounts, xc; Writ and Plaint, xci; Procedure and Pleading, xci.

INTRODUCTION xciii

BOOK I.

SKETCH OF EARLY ENGLISH LEGAL HISTORY.

CHAPTER I.

THE DARK AGE IN LEGAL HISTORY, pp. 1—24.

The difficulty of beginning, 1. Proposed retrospect, 1. The classical age of Roman law, 2. The beginnings of ecclesiastical law, 2. **Century III.** Decline of Roman law, 3. **Century IV.** Church and State, 3. **Century V.** The Theodosian Code, 5. Laws of Euric, 5. **Century VI.** The century of Justinian, 6. The *Lex Salica*, 6. The *Lex Ribuaria*, and *Lex Burgundionum*, 7. The *Lex Romana Burgundionum*, 7. The *Lex Romana Visigothorum*, 8. The Edict of Theoderic, 9. The Dionysian collection of canons, 9. Justinian's books, 9. Justinian and Italy, 10. Laws of Æthelbert, 11. **Centuries VII and VIII.** Germanic laws, 12. System of personal laws, 13. The vulgar Roman law, 14. The latent Digest, 15. The capitularies, 16. Growth of canon law, 16. **Centuries IX and X.** The false Isidore, 17. The forged capitularies, 17. Church and State, 18. The darkest age, 18. Legislation in England, 19. England and the Continent, 20. **Century XI.** The Pavian law-school, 21. The new birth of Roman law, 22. The recovered Digest, 23. The influence of Bolognese jurisprudence, 24.

CHAPTER II.

Anglo-Saxon Law, pp. 25—63.

Imperfection of written records of early Germanic law, 25. Anglo-Saxon dooms and custumals, 27. Anglo-Saxon land-books, 28. Survey of Anglo-Saxon institutions, 29. Personal conditions : lordship, 29. The family, 31. Ranks : ceorl, eorl, gesíð, 32. Thegn, 33. Other distinctions, 34. Privileges of the clergy, 34. Slavery and slave trade, 35. Manumission, 36. Courts and justice, 37. Procedure, 38. Temporal and spiritual jurisdiction, 40. The king's jurisdiction, 40. The Witan, 41. County and hundred courts, 42. Private jurisdiction, 43. Subject-matter of Anglo-Saxon justice, 43. The king's peace, 44. Feud and atonement, 46. Wer, wíte and bót, 48. Difficulties in compelling submission to the courts, 49. Maintenance of offenders by great men, 50. Why no trial by battle, 50. Treason, 51. Homicide, 52. Personal injuries : misadventure, 53. Archaic responsibility, 55. Theft, 55. Property, 56. Sale and other contracts, 57. Claims for stolen goods : warranty, 58. Land tenure, 60. Book-land, 60. Lǽn-land, 61. Folk-land, 61. Transition to feudalism, 62.

CHAPTER III.

Norman Law, pp. 64—78.

Obscurity of early Norman legal history, 64. Norman law was French, 66. Norman law was feudal, 66. Feudalism in Normandy, 67. Dependent land tenure, 69. Seignorial justice, 72. Limits of ducal power, 73. Legal procedure, 74. Criminal law, 74. Ecclesiastical law, 74. The truce of God, 75. Condition of the peasantry, 76. Jurisprudence, 77. Lanfranc of Pavia, 77.

CHAPTER IV.

England under the Norman Kings, pp. 79—110.

Effects of the Norman Conquest, 79. No mere mixture of national laws, 79. History of our legal language, 80. Struggle between Latin, French and English, 82. The place of Latin, 82. Struggle between French and English, 83. Victory of French, 84. French documents, 85. French law-books, 87. Language and law, 87.

Preservation of old English law, 88. The Conqueror's legislation, 88. Character of William's laws, 89. Personal or territorial laws, 90. Maintenance of English land-law, 92. The English in court, 93. Norman ideas and institutions, 93. Legislation : Rufus and Henry I., 94. Stephen, 96. The law-books or *Leges*, 97. Genuine laws of William I., 97. The *Quadripartitus*, 98. *Leges Henrici*, 99. *Consiliatio Cnuti*, 101. *Instituta Cnuti*, 101. French *Leis* of William I., 101. *Leges Edwardi Confessoris*, 103. Character of the law disclosed by the *Leges*, 104. Practical problems in the *Leges*, 105. Practice of the king's court, 107. Royal justice, 108.

CHAPTER V.

ROMAN AND CANON LAW, pp. 111—135.

Contact of English with Roman and Canon law, 111. Cosmopolitan claims of Roman law, 112. Growth of Canon law, 112. Gratian, 113. *Decretales Gregorii*, 113. The Canonical system, 114. Relation of Canon to Roman law, 116. Roman and Canon law in England, 117. Vacarius, 118. English legists and canonists, 120. Scientific work in England, 120. The civilian in England, 122.

Province of ecclesiastical law, 124. Matters of ecclesiastical economy, 125. Church property, 126. Ecclesiastical dues, 127. Matrimonial causes, 127. Testamentary causes, 128. *Fidei laesio*, 128. Correction of sinners, 129. Jurisdiction over clerks, 130. *Miserabiles personae*, 131. The sphere of Canon law, 131. Influence of Canon upon English law, 131. English law administered by ecclesiastics, 133. Nature of canonical influence, 134.

CHAPTER VI.

THE AGE OF GLANVILL, pp. 136—173.

The work of Henry II., 136. Constitutions of Clarendon, 137. Assize of Clarendon, 137. Inquest of Sheriffs, 137. Assize of Northampton, 137. Henry's innovations. The jury and the original writ, 138. Essence of the jury, 138. The jury a royal institution, 140. Origin of the jury: The Frankish inquest, 140. The jury in England, 141. The jury and *fama publica*, 142. The inquest in the Norman age, 143. Henry's use of the inquest, 144. The assize *utrum*, 144. The assize of novel disseisin, 145. Import of the novel disseisin, 146. The grand assize, 147. The assize of mort d'ancestor, 147. The assize of darrein presentment, 148. Assize and jury, 149. The system of original writs, 150. The accusing jury, 151.

Structure of the king's courts, 153. The central court, 154. Itinerant justices, 155. Cases in the king's court, 156. Law and letters, 160. Richard Fitz Neal, 161. Dialogue on the Exchequer, 161. Ranulf Glanvill: his life, 162. *Tractatus de Legibus*, 163. Roman and Canon law in Glanvill, 165. English and continental law-books, 167.

The limit of legal memory, 168. Reigns of Richard and John, 169. The central court, 169. Itinerant justices, 170. Legislation, 170. The Great Charter, 171. Character of the Charter, 172.

CHAPTER VII.

THE AGE OF BRACTON, pp. 174—225.

Law under Henry III., 174. General idea of law, 174. Common law, 176. Statute law. The Charters, 178. Provisions of Merton, Westminster and Marlborough, 179. Ordinance and Statute, 181. The king and the law, 181. Unenacted law and custom, 183. Local customs, 184. Kentish customs, 186. Englishry of English law, 188. Equity, 189.

The king's courts, 190. The exchequer, 191. Work of the exchequer, 191. The chancery, 193. The original writs, 195. The chancery not a tribunal, 197. The two benches and the council, 198. Council and parliament, 199. Itinerant justices, 200. Triumph of royal justice, 202. The judges, 203. Clerical justices, 205.

Bracton, 206. His book, 207. Character of his work : Italian form, 207. English substance, 208. Later law books, 209. Legal literature, 210.

The legal profession, 211. Pleaders, 211. Attorneys, 212. Non-professional attorneys, 213. Professional pleaders, 214. Regulation of pleaders and attorneys, 215. Professional opinion, 217. Decline of Romanism, 217. Notaries and conveyancers, 218. Knowledge of the law, 220.

English law in Wales, 220. English law in Ireland, 221. English and Scottish law, 222. Characteristics of English law, 224.

BOOK II.

THE DOCTRINES OF ENGLISH LAW IN THE EARLY MIDDLE AGES.

CHAPTER I.

TENURE, pp. 229—406.

Arrangement of this book, 229. The medieval scheme of law, 229. The modern scheme, 230. Our own course, 231.

§ 1. *Tenure in General*, pp. 232—240.

Derivative and dependent tenure, 232. Universality of dependent tenure, 234. Feudal tenure, 234. Analysis of dependent tenure, 236. Obligations of tenant and tenement, 237. Intrinsec and forinsec service, 238. Classification of tenures, 239.

§ 2. *Frankalmoin*, pp. 240—251.

Free alms, 240. Meaning of 'alms,' 241. Spiritual service, 242. Gifts to God and the saints, 243. Free alms and forinsec service, 244. Pure alms, 245. Frankalmoin and ecclesiastical jurisdiction, 246. The assize *Utrum*, 247. Defeat of ecclesiastical claims, 248. Frankalmoin in cent. xiii., 250.

§ 3. *Knight's Service*, pp. 252—282.

Military tenure, 252. Growth and decay of military tenure, 252. Units of military service, 254. The forty days, 254. Knight's fees, 256. Size of knight's fees, 256. Apportionment of service, 257. Apportionment between king and tenant in chief, 258. Honours and baronies, 259. The barony and the knight's fee, 260. Relativity of the knight's fee, 261. Duty of the military tenant in chief, 262. Position of military sub-tenants, 263. Knight's service due to lords who owe none, 264. Scutage, 266. Scutage between king and tenant in chief, 267. Scutage and fines for default of service, 269. Scutage and the military sub-tenants, 271. Tenure by escuage, 272. The lord's right to scutage, 274. Reduction in the number of knight's fees, 275. Meaning of this reduction, 276. Military combined with other services, 277. Castle-guard, 278. Thegnage and drengage, 279. Tenure by barony, 279. The baronage, 280. Escheated honours, 281.

§ 4. *Serjeanty,* pp. 282—290.

Definition of serjeanty, 282. Serjeanty and service, 283. Types of serjeanty owed by the king's tenants in chief, 283. Serjeanties due to mesne lords, 285. Military serjeanties due to mesne lords, 286. Essence of serjeanty, 287. The serjeants in the army, 288. Serjeanty in Domesday Book, 288. Serjeanty and other tenures, 290.

§ 5. *Socage,* pp. 291—296.

Socage, 291. Types of socage, 291. Extension of socage, 293. Fee farm, 293. Meaning of 'socage,' 293. Socage in contrast to military tenure, 294. Socage as the residuary tenure, 294. Burgage, 295. Burgage and borough customs, 295. One man and many tenures, 296.

§ 6. *Homage and Fealty,* pp. 296—307.

Homage and fealty, 296. Legal and extra-legal effects of homage, 297. The ceremony of homage, 297. The oath of fealty, 298. Liegeance, 298. Vassalism in the Norman age, 300. Bracton on homage, 301. Homage and private war, 301. Sanctity of homage, 303. Homage and felony, 303. Feudal felony, 305. Homage, by whom done and received, 306. The lord's obligation, 306.

§ 7. *Relief and Primer Seisin,* pp. 307—318.

The incidents of tenure, 307. Heritable rights in land, 307. Reliefs, 308. Rights of the lord on the tenant's death, 310. Prerogative rights of the king, 311. Earlier history of reliefs, 312. Relief and heriot, 312. Heritability of fees in the Norman age, 314. Mesne lords and heritable fees, 315. History of the heriot, 316. Relief on the lord's death, 317.

§ 8. *Wardship and Marriage,* pp. 318—329.

Bracton's rules, 319. Wardship of female heirs, 320. Priority among lords, 320. What tenures give wardship, 321. Prerogative wardship, 321. The lord's rights vendible, 322. Wardship and the serjeanties, 323. The law in Glanvill, 323. Earlier law, 325. Norman law, 326. The Norman apology, 326. Origin of wardship and marriage, 327.

§ 9. *Restraints on Alienation*, pp. 329—349.

Historical theories, 329. Modes of alienation, 330. Preliminary distinctions, 331. Glanvill, 332. The Great Charter, 332. Bracton, 332. Legislation as to mortmain, 333. Alienation of serjeanties, 334. Special law for the king's tenants in chief, 335. Growth of the prerogative right, 336. *Quia emptores*, 337. Disputed origin of the prerogative right, 338. Summary of law after the Charter, 339. Older law, 340. Anglo-Norman charters, 340. Discussion of the charters, 341. Conclusions as to law of the Norman age, 343. Usual form of alienation, 345. General summary, 345. Gifts by the lord with his court's consent, 346. Alienation of seignories, 346. Law of attornment, 347. Practice of alienating seignories, 348.

§ 10. *Aids*, pp. 349—351.

Duty of aiding the lord, 349.

§ 11. *Escheat and Forfeiture*, pp. 351—356.

Escheat, 351. The lord's remedies against a defaulting tenant, 352. Action in the king's court, 352. Distress, 353. Proceedings in the lord's court, 354. Survey of the various free tenures, 355.

§ 12. *Unfree Tenure*, pp. 356—383.

Freehold tenure, 356. Technical meaning of 'freehold,' 357. Villeinage as tenure and as status, 358. Villein tenure : unprotected by the king's court, 359. Want of right and want of remedy, 360. Protection by manorial courts, 361. Evidence of the 'extents,' 362. Attempt to define villein tenure, 362. The manorial arrangement, 362. The field system, 364. The virgates, 364. Villein services, 365. A typical case of villein services, 366. Week work and boon days, 367. Merchet and tallage, 368. Essence of villein tenure, 368. The will of the lord, 370. Villeinage and labour, 370. Uncertainty of villein services, 372. Tests of villeinage, 372. Binding force of manorial custom, 376. Treatment of villein tenure in practice, 377. Heritable rights in villein tenements, 379. Unity of the tenement, 381. Alienation of villein tenements, 382. Villein tenure and villein status, 382.

§ 13. *The Ancient Demesne*, pp. 383—406.

The ancient demesne and other royal estates, 383. Immunities of the ancient demesne, 384. Once ancient demesne, always ancient demesne, 385. Peculiar tenures on the ancient demesne, 385. The little writ of right, 385. The *Monstraverunt*, 388. The classes of tenants, 389. Bracton's theory, 389. Theory and practice, 391. Difficulties of classification, 393. Sokemanry and socage, 394. Later theory and practice, 396. Why is a special treatment of the ancient demesne necessary ? 397. The king and the conquest settlement, 398. Royal protection of royal tenants, 400. Customary freehold, 401. No place for a tenure between freehold and villeinage, 404. The conventioners, 405. Conclusion, 406.

CHAPTER II.

THE SORTS AND CONDITIONS OF MEN, pp. **407—511.**

Law of personal condition, 407. Status and estate, 408.

§ 1. *The Earls and Barons*, pp. **408—411.**

The baronage, 408. Privileges of the barons, 409.

§ 2. *The Knights*, pp. **411—412.**

Knighthood, 412.

§ 3. *The Unfree*, pp. **412—432.**

The unfree, 412. General idea of serfage, 413. Relativity of serf-age, 415. The serf in relation to his lord, 415. Rightlessness of the serf, 416. Serfdom *de iure* and serfdom *de facto*, 417. Covenant between lord and serf, 418. The serf in relation to third persons, 419. The serf's property, 419. Difficulties of relative serfdom, 420. The serf in relation to the state, 421. How men become serfs, 422. Servile birth, 422. Mixed marriages, 423. Influence of the place of birth, 424. Villeins by confession, 424. Serfdom by prescription, 425. How serfdom ceases, 427. Manumission, 427. The freedman, 428. Modes of enfranchisement, 429. Summary, 429. Retrospect. Fusion of villeins and serfs, 430. The levelling process, 431. The number of serfs, 431. Rise of villeins, 432.

§ 4. *The Religious*, pp. **433—438.**

Civil death, 433. Growth of the idea of civil death, 433. Difficulties arising from civil death, 435. The monk as agent, 436. The abbatial monarchy, 437. Return to civil life, 437. Civil death as a development of the abbot's *mund*, 438.

§ 5. *The Clergy*, pp. **439—457.**

Legal position of the ordained clerk, 439. The clerk under temporal law, 439. Exceptional rules applied to the clerk, 440. Benefit of clergy, 441. Trial in the courts of the church, 443. Punishment of felonious clerks, 444. What persons entitled to the privilege, 445. What offences within the privilege, 446. The Constitutions of Clarendon, 447. Henry II.'s scheme, 448. Henry's scheme and past history, 449. Henry's allegations, 449. Earlier law: the Conqueror's ordinance, 449. The *Leges Henrici*, 450. Precedents for the trial of clerks, 450. Summary, 452. Henry's scheme and the Canon law, 454. The murderers of clerks, 456.

§ 6. *Aliens*, pp. 458—467.

The classical common law, 458. Who are aliens? 458. Disabilities of the alien, 459. Naturalization, 460. Law of earlier times, 460. Growth of the law disabling aliens, 461. The king and the alien, 462. The kinds of aliens, 464. The alien merchants, 464. The alien and the common law, 465. Has the merchant a peculiar status? 466. The law merchant, 467.

§ 7. *The Jews*, pp. 468—475.

General idea of the Jew's position, 468. The Exchequer of the Jews, 469. Relation of the Jew to the king, 471. Relation of the Jew to the world at large, 473. Law between Jew and Jew, 474. Influence of the Jew upon English law, 475.

§ 8. *Outlaws and Convicted Felons*, pp. 476—478.

Outlawry, 476. Condition of the outlaw, 477.

§ 9. *Excommunicates*, pp. 478—480.

Excommunication, 478. Spiritual leprosy, 478. Excommunication and civil rights, 480.

§ 10. *Lepers, Lunatics and Idiots*, pp. 480—481.

The leper, 480. The idiot, 481. The lunatic, 481.

§ 11. *Women*, pp. 482—485.

Legal position of women, 482. Women in private law, 482. Women in public law, 483. Married women, 485.

§ 12. *Corporations and Churches*, pp. 486—511.

The corporation, 486. Beginnings of corporateness, 487. Personality of the corporation, 488. The anthropomorphic picture of a corporation, 489. Is the personality fictitious? 489. The corporation at the end of the middle ages, 489. The corporation and its head, 491. The corporation in earlier times, 492. Gradual appearance of the group-person, 493. The law of Bracton's time, 494. The *universitas* and the *communitas*, 494. Bracton and the *universitas*, 495. No law as to corporations in general, 497.

Church lands, 497. The owned church, 497. The saints as persons, 499. The saint's administrators, 500. Saints and churches in Domesday Book, 500. The church as person, 501. The church as *universitas* and *persona ficta*, 502. The temporal courts and the churches, 503. The parish church, 503. The abbatial church, 504. The episcopal church, 505. Disintegration of the ecclesiastical groups, 506. Communal groups of secular clerks, 507. Internal affairs of clerical groups, 508. The power of majorities, 509. The ecclesiastical and the temporal communities, 509. The boroughs and other land communities, 510.

§ 13. *The King and the Crown*, pp. 511—526.

Is there a crown? 511. Theories as to the king's two bodies, 511. Personification of the kingship not necessary, 512. The king's rights as intensified private rights, 512. The king and other lords, 513. The kingship as property, 513. The king's rights can be exercised by him, 514. The king can do wrong but no action lies against him, 515. King's land and crown land, 518. Slow growth of a law of 'capacities,' 518. No lay corporations sole, 520. Is the kingdom alienable? 521. The king can die, 521. The king can be under age, 522. Germs of a doctrine of 'capacities,' 523. Personification of the crown, 524. Retrospect, 526.

CHAPTER III.

JURISDICTION AND THE COMMUNITIES OF THE LAND, pp. 527—532.

Place of the law of jurisdiction in the medieval scheme, 527. All temporal jurisdiction proceeds from the king, 528. The scheme of courts, 529. Division of the land, 529. The county court, 529. The hundred court, 530. The sheriff's turn, 530. Seignorial courts, 530. Feudal courts, 531. Franchise courts, 531. Leets, 532. Borough courts, 532. The king's courts, 532.

§ 1. *The County*, pp. 532—556.

The county, 532. The county officers, 533. The county community, 534. The county court, 535. Identity of county and county court, 536. Constitution of the county court, 537. Suit of court no right, but a burden, 537. Suit of court is laborious, 538. Sessions of the court, 538. Full courts and intermediate courts, 539. The suitors, 540. Suit is a 'real' burden, 541. 'Reality' of suit, 542. The vill as a suit-owing unit, 542. Inconsistent theories of suit, 543. The court in its fullest form, 544. The communal courts in earlier times, 545. Struggle between various principles, 546. Suit by attorney, 547. Representative character of the county court, 547. The suitors as doomsmen, 548. A session of the county court, 549. The suitors and the dooms, 550. Powers of a majority, 552. The *buzones*, 553. Business of the court, 553. Outlawry in the county court, 554. Governmental functions, 554. Place of session, 555.

§ 2. *The Hundred*, pp. 556—560.

The hundred as a district, 556. The hundred court, 557. Hundreds in the king's hands, 557. Hundreds in private hands, 558. Duties of the hundred, 558. The sheriff's turn, 559.

§ 3. *The Vill and the Township*, pp. 560—567.

England mapped out into vills, 560. Vill and parish, 560. Discrete vills, 561. Hamlets, 562. Vill and village, 562. Vill and township, 563. Ancient duties of the township, 564. Statutory duties, 565.

Contribution of township to general fines, 566. Exactions from townships, 566. Miscellaneous offences of the township, 566. Organization of the township, 567.

§ 4. *The Tithing*, pp. 568—571.

Frankpledge, 568. The system in cent. xiii., 568. Township and tithing, 568. The view of frankpledge, 570. Attendance at the view, 570. Constitution of tithings, 571.

§ 5. *Seignorial Jurisdiction*, pp. 571—594.

Regalities and feudal rights, 571. Acquisition of regalities, 572. Theories of royal lawyers, 573. Various kinds of franchises, 574. Fiscal immunities, 574. Immunities from personal service, 574. Immunities from forest law, 575. Fiscal powers, 575. Jurisdictional powers, 576. Contrast between powers and immunities, 577. Sake, soke, toll and team, 578. Sake and soke in cent. xiii., 579. View of frankpledge, 580. The leet, 580. The vill and the view, 581. The assize of bread and beer, 581. High justice, 582. High franchises claimed by prescription, 584. The properly feudal jurisdiction, 584. The feudal court is usually a manorial court, 585. Jurisdiction of the feudal court, 586. Civil litigation : personal actions, 587. Actions for freehold land, 587. Actions for villein land, 588. Litigation between lord and man, 588. Presentments, 589. Governmental powers and by-laws, 590. Appellate jurisdiction, 590. Constitution of the feudal court, 592. The president, 592. The suitors, 592.

§ 6. *The Manor*, pp. 594—605.

The manor, 594. 'Manor' not a technical term, 595. Indefiniteness of the term, 596. A typical manor, 596. The manor house, 597. Occupation of the manor house, 598. Demesne land, 599. The freehold tenants, 600. The tenants in villeinage, 601. The manorial court, 602. Size of the manor, 603. Administrative unity of the manor, 604. Summary, 604.

§ 7. *The Manor and the Township*, pp. 605—634.

Coincidence of manor and vill, 605. Coincidence assumed as normal, 606. Coincidence not always found, 607. Non-manorial vills, 608. Manors and sub-manors, 609. The affairs of the non-manorial vill, 610. Permanent apportionment of the township's duties, 610. Allotment of financial burdens, 611. The church rate, 612. Apportionment of taxes on movables, 615. Actions against the hundred, 616. Economic affairs of the non-manorial vill, 617. Intercommoning vills, 618. Return to the manorial vill, 620. Rights of common, 620. Rights of common and communal rights, 620. The freeholder's right of common, 621. The freeholder and the community, 622. Freedom of the freeholder, 623. Communalism among villeins, 624. The villein community, 624. Communalism and collective liability, 627. The community as farmer, 628. Absence of communal rights, 629. Communal rights disappear upon examination, 629. Co-ownership and corporate property, 630. The township rarely has rights, 632. The township in litigation, 632. Transition to the boroughs, 633.

§ 8. *The Borough,* pp. 634—688.

Cities and boroughs, 634. The vill and the borough, 634. The borough and its community, 635. Sketch of early history, 636. Borough and shire, 636. The borough as vill, 637. The borough's heterogeneity, 637. The borough and the king, 638. The borough and the gilds, 639. Transition to cent. xiii., 639.

Inferior limit of burgality, 640. Representation in parliament, 641. The typical boroughs and their franchises, 642. Jurisdictional privileges, 643. Civil jurisdiction, 644. Criminal jurisdiction, 644. Return of writs, 644. Privileged tenure, 645. Mesne tenure in the boroughs, 645. Seignorial rights in the boroughs, 646. Customary private law, 647. Emancipation of serfs, 648. Freedom from toll, 649. The *firma burgi*, 650. What was farmed, 650. The farm of the vill and the soil of the vill, 652. Lands of the borough, 652. Waste land, 653. The borough's revenue, 655. Chattels of the borough, 656. Elective officers, 656. Borough courts and councils, 657. By-laws and self-government, 660. Limits to legislative powers, 661. Enforcement of by-laws, 661. Rates and taxes, 662. The borough's income, 663. Tolls, 664. The gild merchant, 664. The formation of a gild, 664. The gild and the government of the borough, 665. Objects of the gild, 666. The gild and the burgesses, 667. The gild courts, 667. The borough as a franchise holder, 668.

Corporate character of the borough community, 669. Corporateness not bestowed by the king, 669. Gild-like structure of the community, 670. Admission of burgesses, 671. The title to burgherhood, 671. The 'subject' in the borough charters, 672. Discussion of the charters, 673. Charters for the borough, the county and the whole land, 674. Charters and laws, 674. The burgesses as co-proprietors, 676. The community as bearer of rights, 676. Inheritance, succession and organization, 677. Criminal liability of the borough, 678. Civil liability, 679. The communities in litigation, 680. Debts owed to the community, 682. The common seal, 683. The borough's property, 685. The borough's property in its tolls, 685. The ideal will of the borough, 686. The borough corporation, 686. The communities and the nation, 687.

LIST OF ABBREVIATIONS.

A.-S.	= Anglo-Saxon.
Bl. Com.	= Blackstone's Commentaries.
Co.	= Coke.
Co. Lit.	= Coke upon Littleton.
D. B.	= Domesday Book.
D. G. R.	= Deutsches Genossenschaftsrecht.
D. R. G.	= Deutsche Rechtsgeschichte[1].
E. H. R.	= English Historical Review.
Fitz. Abr.	= Fitzherbert's Abridgement.
Fitz. Nat. Brev.	= Fitzherbert's Natura Brevium.
Harv. L. R.	= Harvard Law Review.
Lit.	= Littleton's Tenures.
L. Q. R.	= Law Quarterly Review.
Mon. Germ.	= Monumenta Germaniae.
P. C.	= Pleas of the Crown.
P. Q. W.	= Placita de Quo Warranto.
Reg. Brev.	= Registrum Brevium.
Rep.	= Coke's Reports.
R. H.	= Hundred Rolls.
Rot. Cart.	= Charter Rolls.
Rot. Cl.	= Close Rolls.
Rot. Parl.	= Parliament Rolls.
Rot. Pat.	= Patent Rolls.
Sec. Inst.	= Coke's Second Institute.
Sel. Chart.	= Stubbs's Select Charters.
X.	= Decretales Gregorii IX.
Y. B.	= Year Book.

[1] The second edition of Schröder's D. R. G. is referred to.

LIST OF TEXTS USED [1].

[R = Rolls Series.   Rec. Com. = Record Commission.   Seld. = Selden Society.
Camd. = Camden Society.   Surt. = Surtees Society.]

Die Gesetze der Angelsachsen, ed. F. Liebermann, in progress.

Die Gesetze der Angelsachsen, ed. Reinhold Schmid, 2nd ed., Leipzig, 1858.

Ancient Laws and Institutes of England, 8vo. ed. (Rec. Com.).

Councils and Ecclesiastical Documents, ed. Haddan and Stubbs, vol. iii.
Oxford, 1871.

Quadripartitus, ed. F. Liebermann, Halle, 1892.

Consiliatio Cnuti, ed. F. Liebermann, Halle, 1893.

Leges Edwardi Confessoris, ed. F. Liebermann, Halle, 1894.

Instituta Cnuti, ed. F. Liebermann, Transactions of Royal Hist. Soc.
N. S. vol. vii. p. 77.

Collections of ancient laws and documents.

Codex Diplomaticus Ævi Saxonici, ed. J. M. Kemble (Eng. Hist. Soc.).

Diplomatarium Anglicum Ævi Saxonici, ed. B. Thorpe, London, 1865.

Cartularium Saxonicum, ed. W. de G. Birch, 1885 ff.

Placita Anglo-Normannica, ed. M. M. Bigelow, London, 1879.

Select Charters, ed. W. Stubbs, Oxford, 1881.

Chartes des Libertés Anglaises, ed. Ch. Bémont, Paris, 1892.

Statutes of the Realm, vol. i. (Rec. Com.), 1800.

Rolls of the King's Court, Ric. I. (Pipe Roll Soc.).

Rotuli Curiae Regis temp. Ric. I. et Joh., ed. Palgrave (Rec. Com.).

Placitorum Abbreviatio (Rec. Com.).

Select Pleas of the Crown, 1200–1225 (Seld.).

Select Civil Pleas, 1200–1203 (Seld.).

Pleas of the Crown for the County of Gloucester, 1221, ed. Maitland,
London, 1884.

Bracton's Note Book, ed. Maitland, Cambridge, 1887.

Three Assize Rolls for the County of Northumberland (Surt.).

Placita de Quo Warranto (Rec. Com.).

Somersetshire Assize Rolls (Somers. Record Soc.).

Judicial Records.

[1] For texts relating to Normandy see below, vol. i. pp. 64–5; and for texts relating to the English boroughs, see below, vol. i. pp. 642–3.

Select Cases from Coroners' Rolls (Seld.).
Rotuli Parliamentorum, vol. i. (official edition).
Memoranda de Parliamento, 1305 (R).

Select Pleas in Manorial Courts (Seld.).
The Court Baron (Seld.).
Durham Halmote Rolls (Surt.).
The Leet Jurisdiction in Norwich (Seld.).

Miscel-
laneous
Records.
Domesday Book (official edition).

Pipe Roll of 31 Henry I. (Rec. Com.).
Pipe Rolls of Henry II. (Pipe Roll Soc.).
Red Book of the Exchequer (R).
Liber Niger Scaccarii, ed. Hearne, Oxford, 1728.
Rotuli Literarum Clausarum, 1204–1227 (Rec. Com.).
Rotuli Literarum Patentium, 1201–1216 (Rec. Com.).
Rotuli Chartarum, 1199–1216 (Rec. Com.).
Rotuli de Oblatis et Finibus, temp. Joh. (Rec. Com.).
Excerpta e Rotulis Finium, 1216–1272 (Rec. Com.).
Fines, sive Pedes Finium, 1195–1215, ed. Hunter (Rec. Com.).
Feet of Fines, 1182–1196 (Pipe Roll Soc.).
Rotuli Hundredorum, Hen. III. et Edw. I. (Rec. Com.).
Parliamentary Writs (Rec. Com.).
Testa de Neville (Rec. Com.).
Documents illustrative of English History, ed. Cole (Rec. Com.).
Calendarium Genealogicum (Rec. Com.).

Foedera, Conventiones etc., ed. 1816 (Rec. Com.).
Prynne, Records, i.e. An exact Chronological Vindication...of the King's
    Supreme Ecclesiastical Jurisdiction, etc., London, 1655.

Munimenta Gildhallae (R), containing Liber Albus and Liber Custumarum.

Law-
books.
Bracton, Tractatus de Legibus, ed. 1569.
Bracton and Azo (Seld.).
Britton, ed. F. M. Nichols, Oxford, 1865.
Fleta, seu Commentarius Iuris Anglicani, ed. 1685.
Glanvill, Tractatus de Legibus, ed. 1604.
Hengham, Summae, printed at the end of Selden's ed. of Fortescue, De
    Laudibus.
The Mirror of Justices (Seld.).

Law
reports.
Year Books of 20–1, 21–2, 30–1, 32–3, 33–5 Edward I. (R).

Chronicles, Abbatum.   Gesta Abbatum Monasterii S. Albani (R).
Annals etc. Abingdon, Chronicon Monasterii de (R).
Anglo-Saxon Chronicle (R).
Annales Monastici (R).

Antiquis Legibus, Liber de (Camd.).
Becket.   Materials for the Life of Thomas Becket (R).
Benedictus Abbas.   See Gesta Henrici.
Brakelonda, Chronica Jocelini de (Camd.).
Burton, Annales de, in Annales Monastici, vol. i. (R).
Cambrensis.   See Giraldus.
Canterbury.   See Gervase.
Coggeshall, Radulphi de, Chronicon Anglicanum (R).
Cotton, Bartholomaei de, Historia Anglicana (R).
Diceto, Radulfi de, Opera Historica (R).
Dunstaplia, Annales Prioratus de, in Annales Monastici, vol. iii. (R).
Durham, Symeon of, The Historical Works of (R).
Eadmeri, Historia Novorum (R).
Edward I. and Edward II., Chronicles of (R).
Eveshamensis, Chronicon Abbatiae (R).
Flores Historiarum (R).
Franciscana, Monumenta (R).
Gervase of Canterbury, Works of (R).
Gesta Henrici Secundi (Benedict of Peterborough) (R).
Giraldus Cambrensis, The Works of (R).
Gloucester, Metrical Chronicle of Robert of (R).
Hemingburgh, Walteri de, Chronicon (Eng. Hist. Soc.).
Hovedene, Rogeri de, Chronica (R).
Hugonis, Magna Vita S. (R).
Huntendunensis, Henrici, Historia (R).
Liber de Antiquis Legibus (Camd.).
Malmesbiriensis, Willelmi, Gesta Regum (R).
Mapes, Gualterus, de Nugis Curialium (Camd.).
Melsa, Chronicon Monasterii de (R).
Monte, Roberti de, Chronica, in Chronicles of Stephen etc. vol. iv. (R).
Newborough, William of, in Chronicles of Stephen etc. vol. i. (R).
Parisiensis, Matthaei, Chronica Majora (R).
        „   „   Historia Anglorum (R).
Ramsey, Chronicle of the Abbey of (R).
Rishanger, Willelmi, Chronica et Annales (R).
Tewkesbury, Annals of, in Annales Monastici, vol. i. (R).
Torigneio, Roberti de, Chronica, in Chronicles of Stephen etc. vol. iv. (R).
Triveti, Nicholai, Annales (Eng. Hist. Soc.).
Waverleia, Annales de, in Annales Monastici, vol. ii. (R).
Wigorniensis, Florentii, Chronicon (Eng. Hist. Soc.).
Wykes, Thomae, Chronicon, in Annales Monastici, vol. iv. (R).
York, Historians of the Church of (R).

Academica, Munimenta (R).
Cantuarienses, Epistolae, in Chronicles etc. of Richard I., vol. ii. (R).   Letters, etc.
Cantuarienses, Literae (R).
Dunelmense, Registrum Palatinum (R).
Grosseteste, Letters of Bishop (R).

Lanfranci Opera, ed. Giles, Oxford, 1844.
Northern Registers, Historical Papers and Letters from (R).
Osmund, Register of St (R).
Peckham, Registrum Johannis (R).
Royal and other Historical Letters, Henry III. (R).
Saresberiensis, Joannis, Opera, ed. Giles, Oxford, 1848.

Cartu-laries.

Bath, Two Chartularies (Somerset Record Soc. 1893).
Battle, Cartulary (Camd.).
Brinkburn, Cartulary (Surt.).
Burton, Cartulary (Salt Society, 1884).
Gloucester, History and Cartulary (R).
Guisborough, Cartulary (Surt.).
Malmesbury, Register (R).
Newminster, Cartulary (Surt.).
Paul's, Domesday of St (Camd.).
Peterborough, Black Book of, at the end of Chronicon Petroburgense (Camd.).
Ramsey, Cartulary (R).
Rievaulx, Cartulary (Surt.).
Sarum, Charters and Documents of (R).
Selby, Coucher Book (Yorkshire Archaeological Soc. 1891–3).
Whalley, Coucher Book (Chetham Soc. 1847).
Whitby, Cartulary (Surt.).
Winchcombe, Landboc, vol. i., ed. D. Royce, Exeter, 1892.
Worcester, Register (Camd.).

Round, Ancient Charters (Pipe Roll Soc.).
Madox, Formulare Anglicanum, London, 1702.
Monasticon Anglicanum, ed. 1817 etc.

ADDITIONS AND CORRECTIONS.

p. 33, last lines. As to the *burh-geat* (not *burh-geat-setl*) see W. H. Stevenson, E. H. R. xii. 489 ; Maitland, Township and Borough, 209.

p. 118. Dr Liebermann has withdrawn the suggestion that Vacarius was the author of the tract on Lombard law. See E. H. R. vol. xiii. p. 297. The Summa de Matrimonio has been printed in L. Q. R. xiii. 133, 270.

p. 556, note 1. Add a reference to J. H. Round, The Hundred and the Geld, E. H. R. x. 732.

p. 663. As causes of municipal expenditure we ought to have mentioned the many presents, of a more or less voluntary kind, made by the burgesses to kings, magnates, sheriffs and their underlings. For these see the Records of Leicester, ed. Bateson, *passim.*

INTRODUCTION.

By S. F. C. Milsom.

I. *The Place of 'Pollock and Maitland' Today.*

MAITLAND, I think, would have been saddened by this re-issue of his book, and not only by the inadequacy of an introductory essay that is the sole addition to what last left his hands just seventy years ago. He felt sorry for those whose work became classical: it meant that vitality had been lost from the enterprise they had loved. Of course much has been done. Each generation has produced its handful of scholars from either side of the Atlantic, and from either shore of that other ocean dividing law and history. His own Selden Society has proved over and over again the richness of the surviving materials. It has become clearer than ever that we can hope to understand the growth of the common law, almost from its beginning as an intellectual system, in a detail unimaginable for its great rival in the western world. And yet, while every syllable of the Roman texts has attracted prolonged scrutiny, our own great stores of evidence are largely neglected. Workers are still few; the subscriptions of a private association are still a principal support of the work; and more than sixty years after Maitland died his book is reprinted, not as a dead masterpiece but as a still living authority.

Nor is it just that his book is still useful to scholars. In large part, the part that most interested him, it is still their starting-point. For the law itself, as opposed to legal institutions, they still rely upon his vision of the subject as a whole.

Their questions still take the form: was Maitland right? This is not true of institutions. What he had to say about these, mostly contained within the first volume, has indeed worn well. The general reader will get a picture which has been corrected and amplified in many details, but of which the broad outlines remain; and he will find it a livelier and more compelling picture than any produced since. But for the scholar it is superseded. Serious inquiry about our early courts or lawyers or their literature, though it cannot neglect *Pollock and Maitland*, does not begin there. These matters have all been the subject of more recent and more intensive study; and some of the work is listed in the first section of the bibliography which follows this essay.

The essay itself, however, will be devoted to what has not been done rather than to what has, to the area in which *Pollock and Maitland* remains the starting-point. Why is it that so much less progress has been made with the law than with its institutions? Largely it is because less has been attempted. Few lawyers venture into history, and few historians deal with the law on its own terms. To the beginner seeking a subject, the very bulk of the sources is discouraging. There is so much technicality to be mastered. This is true; but the calculation probably underestimates both what we can learn from technicalities and what force they can exert in their own day. To one who started as a lawyer and who stands uneasily between the two disciplines, there is visible a similarity between a traditional belief of historians and a newer belief among some lawyers: the law serves its day, and its reasoning, which can always be manipulated to produce a sensible, practical solution, does not matter. 'A sensible, practical solution it may be', wrote Maitland elsewhere, 'but legal principle avenges itself.'

The reality of this intellectual force may provide a different kind of explanation for the smaller progress made with the law itself than with its institutions. It is not only that less has been attempted: less success has been achieved in what has been done, and this may partly be due to the scale of the attempts. Maitland was of a generation which believed in great historical undertakings; and since his time scholarship has narrowed its vision, seeking to learn in greater detail about smaller areas. That this has been beneficial to institutional studies is proved by the results. But it may not suit legal studies. A fact found in a plea roll about a court, for example, can be picked up and handled as a thing in itself. But legal facts do not come away like that. They are parts of a pattern, and if we cut snippets away for examination we may not see even the detail of the design, because we look from the wrong angles.

But of course, when we rely upon Maitland's vision of the subject as a whole, we look from his angles; and when we ask whether Maitland was right, we ask his questions. I believe—and I do not know how to introduce one of the greatest works of English history otherwise than by a *credo*—that the very splendour of his achievement may have beguiled us into a too easy dependence. If he himself could have any wish for this reissue, I believe it would be that some reader would be stimulated to follow his example, to come to the sources without assumptions, and to make them indicate their own vantage-points and suggest their own questions.

This then will be an essay in heresy, pious heresy, intended to suggest the kind of doubt which it seems possible to have about Maitland's picture. To use a phrase familiar in thirteenth-century plea rolls, he wrote 'as one who saw and heard'. He seems to have seen a society and its law whole and to have heard its disputes singly. The voices arguing he heard indeed in his sources; and all the materials made available since his death have confirmed that he heard aright. What is difficult to realize is the extent to which the picture as a whole must have been his own creation, the extent to which any picture of early legal development must remain uncertain.

It is a property of legal sources, especially from the middle ages, that they will tell the investigator nearly everything except what he wants to know. Business documents are made for those who know the business; and the records of litigation, whether plea rolls which were the courts' minutes, or Year Books which were reports made for the professional or educational purposes of lawyers, are brusque in their unhelpfulness to outsiders. Charters and the like use words which we may not even recognize as terms of art, let alone guess at the volumes of meaning which it is the function of terms of art to import. Even legislative acts, even legal treatises, were addressed to an audience which knew something about the law and which lived in the society which the law regulated. We have to conjure up both. It is what was assumed that we need to know, not what was said.

One example of this inscrutability may serve to make the point. The earliest action of which we know for the recovery of land is called the writ of right, and it worked in this way. The demandant claiming the land made a formal declaration to the court asserting that a named ancestor had been seised in the reign of a named king, and then setting out the pedigree from that ancestor to himself. No other facts were alleged. The tenant, the man in possession against whom the action was brought, denied this declaration at large; and the court's business was to arrange a test which would indicate whether it was true or rather, in case truth seems too precise a concept, whether it was just. At first this test was always a battle, and what was directly tested was the oath of the demandant's champion, who made himself out to be a sort of hereditary witness. Later the tenant was allowed instead to choose the grand assize, a kind of jury; but even then, with exceptions that do not now matter, the plea roll recorded only an answer saying blankly that the one side or the other had the greater right.

About this legal process we know in great detail. It is described in the book known as Glanvill, written between 1187 and 1189; and there are countless examples in the plea rolls, the great series of which begins only a few years later. We know, for example, just what excuses the parties might make for not coming, and how often; we know that, if several parcels of land were at stake, arable had to be claimed before meadow, and meadow before marsh; we know what ceremonies the champions went through before fighting, and what oaths they swore; and we know what a demandant should do who wrongly guessed that his opponent would choose the grand assize and had not provided himself with a champion—when he saw the tenant returning to court with an armed man, he should instantly make off, lose by default and not by judgment, and so be free to start again. All this we know so well that with some rehearsal we could manage the law-suit ourselves. But we do not know what it was about, what 'the right' was. We do not even know what had happened: if the demandant's claim was just, how had the tenant come to the land? The law court is miraculously clear in our spotlight. The world around it, largely the world of fact and wholly the world of ideas, is in the dark.

II. *The Real Actions.*

HERESIES are not easily formulated. The suggestion underlying this and the following section is that Maitland did not sufficiently reckon with the law of courts other than the king's courts; and on the face of it this seems deeply unjust. There is much about other courts in this book; and elsewhere, especially in Selden Society editions, he did more than anybody to bring home their importance. But they are important in various ways. They are important to any picture of the life of ordinary people until long after the period covered by this book. They are important as the sources of custom from which the common law came. But they are also important to the interpretation of what we see in the king's courts themselves; and this is the point now in question. As is often the case with Maitland, attentive reading can sometimes detect suspicions. But he did not have time to follow them up. They did not much affect what he said, or at all affect what others have built upon his work. In the result, our picture of the early common law assumes that we can read its archives in isolation, and that although we shall get an incomplete picture of society we shall not thereby misunderstand the law itself. But we may misunderstand it by mistaking the original sense of its simplest words. To the extent that the king's courts were not inventing law but adopting customs enforced by other courts, their elementary concepts and categories must have been formed in those other courts; and the names by which they were known must have acquired their first meanings there. If we look only at materials from the king's courts, we may attribute to those names anachronistic meanings, narrowed or widened by later developments within the common law from an original and more elementary sense. The clearest example of this will be discussed in the next section: our picture of the personal actions has been distorted by paying insufficient attention to local jurisdictions. The present section will suggest that something similar may have happened with the real actions and feudal jurisdictions.

'Now were an examiner to ask who introduced the feudal system into England? one very good answer, if properly explained, would be Henry Spelman...If my examiner went on with his questions and asked me, when did the feudal system attain its most perfect development? I should answer, about the middle of the [eighteenth] century.' Maitland's joke ousted a great deal of legalistic history: perhaps too much. His account of the real actions and of seisin has been discussed more than any other part of his book: and the discussion has assumed Maitland's general picture and questioned details. Largely it has assumed his account of what happened and wondered about why. But it we stand back and look at the picture as a whole, the striking thing is the insignificant position occupied by the feudal relationship. Feudal jurisdiction is jurisdiction in our sense and no more: should a dispute go to this court or to that? And apart from jurisdiction, the system of actions is one that could have existed in ancient Rome, one that could have existed—and in some ghostly sense did exist—in nineteenth-century England.

The system is described in terms of possessory and proprietary remedies; and the Roman language, for which of course there is plenty of warrant in Bracton and some in Glanvill, was for Maitland and has ever since been a cause for doubt. But the chief doubt has been about the source of the idea of protection that can be called possessory, and there may be a prior doubt: in what sense was that the idea? There can be little question that it was the idea at the end of the period covered by this book. A tolerant Roman lawyer would then have allowed the real actions to be described in those terms, subject to two reservations. He might have felt that the principle behind the possessory remedies had manifested itself in a peculiarly English and *ad hoc* way. And he might have felt that the adjective 'proprietary' was being used in a peculiarly English and relative sense. But there was a range of remedies from the most obviously possessory, that for the ejected against his ejector, up to the most nearly proprietary, that which decided title as between the parties for ever. In the possessory remedies the question of right could not in general be raised. The ejected could not be met by an assertion of title in his ejector. The claimant seeking to retrieve land given to the present tenant's father by his own father, whom he alleges to have been mad when he gave it, could not be met by an assertion that his father's father had got the land in the first place only by ejecting some ancestor of the tenant. In a possessory remedy discussion could not go behind the facts alleged by the claimant, behind the possession from which his story started. And since by this time there was a possessory remedy for virtually every constellation of facts, and since they were all quicker, more convenient and more acceptable than the proprietary, the proprietary was becoming otiose, a little-used reserve.

In this scheme the actions are ranged up and down a single scale. A claimant can nearly always choose between the high point on that scale, the troublesome but conclusive proprietary remedy, or something lower down, based upon easily established facts, but inconclusive in that the loser can always begin a new action going higher into the right. This was the scheme which existed in the late thirteenth century, and which gave the common law its distinctive and sensible notion of relative title. But the question is, how it came into existence. For Maitland, the proprietary remedy, the writ of right, was primeval. The top of the scale came first. Then it was built up from the bottom, first the possessory assizes, and then the writs of entry which eventually reached up to the writ of right. Each stage offered the claimant a new alternative to the writ of right, and, since the possessory remedies were all royal, a new escape from feudal jurisdiction. From the point of view of the king, therefore, the desire to extend his jurisdiction may have been a motive. From the point of view of the claimant, however, and this is the proposition to be doubted, the whole development is seen as conducted in the same terms throughout: the writ of right, once the only remedy, would always cover his case, and he is offered an increasing range of more convenient possessory alternatives.

Taking first the writ of right, such work as has been done since Maitland's time has added only to our knowledge of its mechanics. In particular we know that the jurisdictional position was more complicated than he could see, and that the provision in Magna Carta about the writ *praecipe* was concerned with a genuine difficulty of legal administration and not with a straightforward attempt by the crown to steal jurisdiction. But it remains the case that early in the thirteenth century lords minded about their jurisdictional rights, though late in the century, when removal to the king's courts was regular, nobody much minded except litigants, to whom the matter was a nuisance.

But this decline of jurisdictional interest, which treats jurisdiction as the right to determine a case by applying to it the fixed rules of the common law and to take the profits of justice, looks like the last stage of a greater decline. Feudal jurisdiction had started as the power to decide, not just to declare a result reached by applying external criteria. And however much force we attribute to the customs of a lordship, there is a great difference between a lord and his court applying rules within their own control if within anybody's, and the same body applying royal rules. Seen from above the difference is that a lord's jurisdiction becomes a matter of dignity and cash, perhaps more trouble than it is worth. Real control is lost, the decisive step being one which later ideas would not even associate with jurisdiction: a tenant's dispositions become effective of their own force, and need no validation from above. Seen from below the same difference can be expressed only in the language of private law. The tenant's right has not only become larger and more secure; it has changed its nature. It now exists, not in the closed legal world of the lordship, but under an open Roman sky. The tenant has become an owner.

It was this abstract ownership that the demandant in a writ of right was in the thirteenth century claiming. But the logic of the action was inappropriate. What happened in court has already been described for the purpose of showing how reticent our voluble sources can be. There was the count based upon hereditary descent, the blank denial, and the test of battle or grand assize from which emerged a blank result.

It is easy, but wrong, to dismiss the whole process as archaic and therefore senseless. If we accept the premise of a divine test—and it seems to be the premise of all early law—even the battle answered a specific question. What was tested was an oath, in this case an oath by the demandant's champion that his own ancestor had seen the seisin upon which the claim rested, the seisin of the ancestor from whom the demandant traced his descent. The toss of the coin, if we choose to think in those terms, did not indicate just which party was to win: it indicated whether or not the demandant's count was true.

But the facts in the count, the ancestor's seisin and the hereditary descent, were in the thirteenth century irrelevant to any real question between the parties. The point can best be made by considering two cases which would in fact have been redressed by possessory actions; but on the received view it would be open to the demandant to bring a writ of right, and we shall suppose him to do so. First comes the claimant already postulated, who wishes to retrieve land granted away by his father when insane. In his count he will begin from the seisin of the most remote ancestor of whom he knows, and trace the descent to himself. His mad father is a name in the pedigree; and the fact mainly attested by the champion's oath, the ancestral seisin, is not even in dispute. That count went back beyond the true issue, and passed by without heeding it. In our second example, it does not reach it. Suppose that the demandant's father bought the land from one whose family had held it for generations, and suppose that the demandant has been ousted by one whose true claim is to have a better right than that family had. If he brings a writ of right, the demandant must count on the seisin of his father, and he cannot even mention the vendor's ancestral holding. It is about the seisin of the father that his champion must swear; and upon that the case somehow pointlessly turns.

Nor are these examples special. If land is considered as an object of ownership, capable of passing from hand to hand rightfully and wrongfully, then the range of possessory remedies in the later thirteenth century covers almost every imaginable dispute, every situation in which its passage from

one hand to another may have been wrongful. But in none of
them, except perhaps the situation covered by mort d'ancestor and its congeners, does the pattern of the writ of right
make other than mystical sense. The count and its denial
were incantations, not statements relevant to the dispute.
And when by the grand assize the dispute was put to human
determination, we can be sure that the facts to which the
knights applied themselves were not those in the count: they
were such as might in a writ of entry have been made the
basis of the claim, facts showing that the land had indeed
passed wrongfully from the demandant's line to the tenant's.

But the incantations of the thirteenth century were
probably meaningful statements in the twelfth; and they may
hint at the nature of the legal world in the dark time before
Glanvill. The logic of the action reflects a world in which land
was essentially inalienable, capable only of hereditary
descent. Nothing need be said of the way in which the land
has come into the tenant's hands, because that cannot
matter: if the count is true the demandant must be entitled.
If we neglect any possible feudal dimension, that can only be
a world of inalienable family land; and it may be that the
formulae of a count in the right, together with a distinction
between a man's freedom to dispose of his inherited and of
his acquired land, have ancient roots. Whether or not those
formulae had an earlier life, their immediate past was in a
feudal world; and the question is how completely the legal
ideas of land-holding were permeated by the feudal relationship. That it seems to play no part in the formulae themselves
is striking and important: this is what makes it conceivable
that they began in an essentially pre-feudal environment;
and this is what enabled them to survive, making no sense but
not making nonsense, into a post-feudal situation in which
they could be spoken indifferently in the king's court or in
the court of the lord.

But in the feudal world they were spoken in a feudal court,
addressed in some sense to the lord himself; and it is against
that background that we must interpret what is said and
what is not said. The proceedings were started by a writ to
the lord which, although it names the tenant, is really about
a relationship between the lord and the demandant. The lord

is required to do right to one who claims to hold the land of him by named services; and Glanvill has to explain that the lord must still do right, and seek other redress later, if the services named are less than those due. To use the inescapable Roman language, the right reflected in the writ is hardly *in rem* at all: it is a right against the lord to be the lord's tenant. Perhaps it was that polarized claim that was once made in the count: not 'this land is mine because my ancestor had it', which made the same sense in the king's court as in the lord's, but 'I am entitled to be your tenant because my ancestor was your tenant'. This is congruous with at least two of the three salient features of the count, namely its silence about the tenant and the claim by hereditary descent; and it may also be congruous with the ancestral seisin. These will be considered one by one.

The count in an action in the right is almost unique in putting an absolute claim in which, as in the writ, the tenant is no more than named. In every other action, except for such congeners of mort d'ancestor as aiel or its variants, the count tells a story involving both the two parties. But here the demandant does not say how the tenant came to the land, and, with a single exception to be mentioned below, the tenant's answer does not say this either. Perhaps it did not need saying in the feudal context, because the tenant was accepted as the lord's tenant of the land as well as tenant in what came to be the distinct sense of tenant to the action; and that acceptance was the only title he could have. At every point there are not two parties but three. The logic is not that of a dispute between two persons with rights generated or evidence by an abstract possession. It is that of a dispute between two donees, which the donor has to decide. But he is not just to choose: he is constrained from outside to honour his earlier gift.

The gift would have been a grant to one 'and his heirs' or the like. That formula has managed to outlive the heir himself, so proving more durable even than the formulae of a count in the right; but they lost their original sense together. When land became alienable by the tenant without reference to his lord or his heir, the words of grant inappropriately created something like ownership, and the formulae of an action in the right inappropriately protected it. But when the words of grant meant what they said, the count by hereditary descent would also be meaningful. The incongruities which we noted in the thirteenth century could not arise. The demandant's father could not have been grantee of anyone save the lord, could not have granted without the lord's consent and perhaps the heir's. The action in the right did not have to deal with the situations covered by the later possessory remedies: it did not have to cater for alienability. The count could always be the same because the facts were always the same: the lord, having given or been supposed to give the land to one 'and his heirs' has later let in another as tenant; and the demandant claims as heir to the first donee.

Curiously congruous with this view of the matter—it is impossible to use higher language than that of congruity—is the only concession ever made to a changing world by the formulae of an action in the right. A tenant putting himself upon the grand assize was in one situation permitted to embellish his denial with an explanation of his own coming to the land. This was when he claimed under a grant from the demandant or his ancestor. The relevance of the adjusted answer can most clearly be seen in terms of its earliest form: the tenant claims to be, not just a grantee of the demandant's ancestor, but a grantee by subinfeudation. He claims to be the demandant's tenant. The demandant is making a claim which looks upward to his lord, and his count goes to the proposition that he is entitled to hold of that lord. But this tenant is not disputing that, and he is not in through the demandant's lord. He wishes to make the demandant look downwards and accept that the tenant has a similar right against him. The alienability of land by the sole act of its holder has begun to deprive the count in the right of its sense.

But if alienability was to drive the writ of right out, heritability may have been what brought it in. A recent view has suggested a date near 1200 for the full heritability of the superior tenures, over a century after Maitland's. But neither the real nor the conceptual stages of the process are ever likely to be established. The customs of one lordship may have been clear, and different from the equally clear customs of another; and since lordships were at odds with geography,

we with our fragmentary evidence are sure to see confusion
even if contemporary eyes would have seen great precision.
Even within a single lordship the lord and his tenants formed
an almost sovereign body, so that for example an agreement
of which the lord was described as 'judge and witness' could
permanently exchange the rights of inheritance between the
brothers party to it. Against that background the decisive
event, if there was one, is likely to have been the control of
custom, not its hardening. Centuries later the unfree tenures
were first to get royal protection by a chancery decree
controlling the lord's will. The mere words of the great writ
of right look similar: the demandant is calling in the king's
law to coerce the lord's. The writ later becomes a mere
authorization to the lord without which he cannot make the
tenant answer; it can then plausibly be said not to interfere
with the lord's jurisdiction. But the words read like a great
interference with jurisdiction in a deeper sense: the lord's
control is itself controlled.

So far, then, the formalities of the action can be construed
in an intensely feudal light. The silence of writ and count
about how the tenant came to be in, the hereditary descent—
both these fall into place. But the third feature of the count,
the seisin of the ancestor, at first sight does not: it looks very
different from the allegation of a grant to the ancestor 'and
his heirs'. If, however, the writ was used to impose a uniform
heritability on lords, at a time when few grants were evi-
denced in writing, then mere ancestral possession would be
the necessary starting point. Nor, in the count as we know
it, was mere possession alleged: the ancestor was said to have
been seised 'as of fee' and later also 'as of right'; and the
former implies a relationship even more strongly than the
latter. Nor is it quite certain that to say that a man had been
seised would always have meant the same as saying that he
had been possessed.

Brevia Placitata, a thirteenth-century formulary, makes
the demandant in an action in the right assert more than that
his ancestor was seised: he was said to have been *vestu e seysi*.
If the first word represents some notion of investiture, and
is not merely tautologous, its fleeting appearance is at least
remarkable. But fleeting it was. The word does not appear

in later formularies or reported counts; and its equivalent is
not in the count in Glanvill. Either *Brevia Placitata* was
introducing some new feudal learning of its own; or, just
possibly, it was making explicit something old, something
that could no longer be assumed and that was probably no
longer real. *Saisina* as a noun was relatively recent, and
seems almost to have been coined to make a contrast with
rectum. Glanvill makes the contrast twice, once in those
words, once in the more Roman Latin of *possessio* and
proprietas. This equivalence may have helped the process by
which the right came to be seen as ownership; and, more
immediately relevant, the equation of *saisina* with *possessio*
may have swamped other connotations in the older verb,
the connotations of authoritative action. One can be possessed all by oneself; but is it certain that one could be
saisitus without somebody else to make him so? The past
participle is ambiguous, but all early appearances of the verb
do indeed describe an action; and it would be odd if the root
idea was the mere condition, for which no noun was in
use.

The action in the right, then, seems to make sense as part of
a truly feudal world. The framework of law-suits and dealings
concerning land was not the flat plane of more ancient or of
more modern times, upon which there moved just demandant
and tenant, just grantor and grantee: there was always a
third dimension. In that world, we must not think of a grant
to one 'and his heirs' as a once for all matter. When that
grantee died, his heir would become seised by the action of
the lord; and that was a new grant to the heir 'and his heirs',
even though the lord had bound himself to make it. There is
nothing remote or abstract about the right, and nothing
mystical about the count by which it was claimed. Those
qualities came as the feudal dimension collapsed.

In the flat framework left by that collapse, the framework
of Maitland's vision, the possessory actions all made perfect
sense. But it is possible that they too made a different sense
at their beginning, when the feudal dimension was a reality.
Of the two great assizes concerning land, mort d'ancestor
will be taken first. As what we should call a regular civil
action it may be marginally the older; and conceptually it is

the closer to the action in the right—or at least to the picture of the action in the right that has just been offered.

The assize was summoned to answer whether the claimant's ancestor had died seised of the land in question and whether the claimant was that ancestor's next heir. If yes to both these, and if the death had been within a limitation period, the claimant was put into the land. The ancestor had to be of close kin with the claimant; and a trio of later actions, aiel, besaiel and cosinage extended the principle to relations more remote. Alone of the possessory actions, these share with the action in the right the feature that nothing is said of how the tenant came to the land; and in the assize itself his part will appear as almost peripheral. The structural similarity is obvious, and if the right was not some abstract title but the polarized concept we have suggested, then this is indeed the possessory counterpart of the writ of right.

Maitland observed that the Assize of Northampton of 1176, which is believed to have created mort d'ancestor, was directed only at the lord; but he did not pursue the implications of this. When a freeholder dies, our text says, his heirs shall remain in seisin, and *postea* seek out the lord to satisfy him for his relief and other dues. If the heir is within age the lord shall take his homage and have his wardship; and it is clear that the taking of homage, accepting the infant as tenant, was meant to be a condition of having the wardship. 'And if the lord of the fee denies to the heirs of the dead man the seisin of that dead man which they demand, the justices of the lord king shall have recognition made by twelve lawful men concerning the nature of the seisin which the dead man had thereof on the day he was alive and dead; and as it is recognized, so shall they restore it to his heirs.'

If we give this its full value, mort d'ancestor began as a specific and not a general remedy. It was the sanction of a duty imposed upon lords to accept the heirs of their dead tenants at once. The lord may not take a real seisin even for the purpose of admitting the heir; and the heir's right will now look even more like an abstract ownership, existing independently of the lord and attributable to a single act of creation, a once-for-all grant to a man and his heirs.

How far the world was like that when the assize began is

another question. The legislation may have been made with a limited class of tenures in mind; and, although it is generally agreed that many early cases were in fact brought against lords, the action was probably from the beginning capable of a wider use. Since a lord would normally not keep the holding in hand but admit another, early use against third parties would be inevitable. Even when records begin, it is only from the pleading of exceptions that we get an occasional glimpse of the underlying facts: the entry of a mort d'ancestor is commonly as blank as that of an action in the right. In particular, if he says nothing against the holding of the assize, the tenant is named before the judgment only as part of the description of the land: 'which land such an one holds'. This accords with the writ, which names him at the end almost as an afterthought: 'And summon by good summoners such an one who holds the said land, so that he may be there to hear that recognition'. We cannot tell whether he is the dead man's lord, the lord's grantee, one with a genuine adverse claim independent of the lord, or a mere opportunist wrongdoer. One would expect that the last would be a relatively infrequent figure, and that the immediacy of the relationship would at first limit the scope for genuine dispute. But for all the reticence of individual entries, the plea rolls tell us one fact that must be accommodated: the assize was frequent. If in the case of the superior tenures it looks as though heritability was a fact before it was seen as an immutable principle, it is at least possible that at humbler levels it was resisted in fact after it was established in principle. Glanvill's exemplar for the great writ of right claims something of the order of a knight's fee: his mort d'ancestor claims one virgate. Against the heir of such a tenant, perhaps the lord still supposes that he can let in another at will.

The assize of novel disseisin is the greatest enigma in the history of the common law. Nobody since Maitland has attempted to trace the changes which enveloped the simple possessory remedy of the thirteenth century, although those changes are central to any understanding of litigation concerning land long after the other real actions were effectively dead. Our concern, however, is not with the future of the thirteenth century action but with its past. Did the assize indeed start as the simplest of possessory remedies in the sense generally accepted?

All the work done since Maitland died has assumed an affirmative answer to that question, and much of it has asked how far possessory protection was part of a conscious policy and how far the idea was of canonist and civilian origin. Other work has gone to the factual rather than the conceptual origins of the assize, and from this we shall take two points. First, Maitland knew that before the Assize of Clarendon in 1166, which is generally taken to have established novel disseisin, writs were sometimes issued bearing some general similarity to it; and a considerable mass of these has since been accumulated. The earlier simply order that somebody shall be seised or reseised of land, and they show three features of special interest: the order always uses the verb *saisire* and not the noun *saisina*; it seems to order executive action without any factual inquiry; and it may emanate from some lesser lord as well as from the king.

Secondly there is some reason to think that the Assize of Clarendon did not establish novel disseisin as, in our language, a regular civil process. It may have ordered that eyres should inquire into recent disseisins more in terms of criminal law, the local people being required to report them to the justices. If so, then the civil action is a later development, perhaps later than mort d'ancestor; and it represents a willingness by the king to allow the disseised themselves to take the initiative. Such a development would explain two features in the developed writ, the gratuitous '*questus est mihi*' with which it opens, and the unfortunate mode of limitation with which it was saddled; the original criminal inquiry would have had to fix a definite starting point. It would also accord with certain features of Glanvill's account. The parties are there described as *appellans* and *appellatus*, which would fit the private initiation of a process seen in criminal terms. Much more curious, however, if novel disseisin was ten years older than mort d'ancestor, is its position in Glanvill. It comes last of all the recognitions.

We may never penetrate the darkness behind Glanvill, but it is worth asking what was supposed to happen about a

disseisin before there was any assize. If one was ejected by a
mere wrongdoer, a thief of land, was he forced to choose
between self-help and the hazards of a writ of right? The
factual difficulty can be sharpened by supposing the victim
to be a newcomer, the first of his line to hold the land: there
is reason to think that a demandant in the right could not
count on his own seisin of land until well into the thirteenth
century. But that seeming oddity would follow from the logic
of an action in the right here suggested: and so would the
conclusion that that action was irrelevant to one ejected by
a wrongdoer, even if the victim was a holder in the twentieth
generation. The right, his right against his lord, was not in
question: it came into question only as against one accepted
by the lord as tenant of the land.

Against a mere wrongdoer the obvious remedy if the feudal
relationship was ever real was to seek more immediate aid
from the lord; and there may be reminiscences of this.
Bracton discusses 'the first remedy after disseisin', which is
self-help, in a passage which Maitland thought to represent
some old learning; and he explains that one can try to get
back himself before any resort to *superioris auxilium*, but
that after such resort there must be no return to self-help *in
praeiudicium superioris*. Only in the following chapter is
superioris auxilium identified in the famous *de beneficio
principis succurritur ei per recognitionem assisae novae
dissaisinae multis vigiliis excogitatam et inventam*....Another
reminiscence may be the middle member of a common trio of
seignorial undertakings: 'to warrant, defend and acquit'. In
the thirteenth century the first and last were well understood,
and enforced by well-known processes; but defence was a
mystery, the object of unlikely explanations and not reflected
in any known action. It is just possible, however, that we
have very ancient reflections in some of the early writs for
reseisin which appear to be mere orders for executive action.
If, to use an unreal contrast for the sake of emphasis, such
orders were at first seignorial rather than merely governmental in character, the absence of inquiry is intelligible.

But when once one begins to think in terms of seignorial
action and *superioris auxilium*, a different question about the
realities suggests itself. Was it indeed the third party wrong-

doer who was the ubiquitous villain? Mere anarchy might envelop the great, but at the level of the local community are we to think always of neighbour ousting neighbour? May not novel disseisin like mort d'ancestor have been in its inception a specific rather than a general remedy, and directed primarily against lords? Like mort d'ancestor, it from the beginning probably had a wider use; but the wording of the writ twice suggests a feudal orientation, and both phrases were to have curious effects in an essentially non-feudal world. The first comes in the question put to the assize: did the tenant disseise the plantiff *injuste et sine judicio*? It was through these words that general notions of wrongfulness were later imported, with the topsy-turvy result that in the fourteenth century novel disseisin came to be used for settling questions of title; and a topsy-turvy Year Book, the *Liber Assisarum*, shows how important were the questions of law that came to be raised at obscure country sittings designed for the mere ascertainment of fact. Even later, when such questions were raised in other actions and less directly, the unseen pivot was still that same *injuste et sine judicio*. The future of the phrase therefore depended upon its being given a generalized sense, what may be termed wrongfulness *in rem*. But in a feudal world it could have a more obvious and factual sense: had the holding been taken into hand or allotted to another without a judgment of the lord's court? Like the remedy, the reservation was perhaps not general but specific: distraint *per feodum* and other proper seignorial action, although probably a casualty of the assize in fact, was not intended to be so. It is sometimes pleaded in the earliest rolls.

The other phrase in the writ pointing in the same direction comes in the clause directing the summons of the disseisor: if he is not to be found, the sheriff is to summon his bailiff instead. This too had a future, though an odd rather than an important one. The bailiff in novel disseisin became a kind of informal attorney, and it took a statute in 1318 to allow the tenant to make an attorney in the ordinary way. Even then 'bailiffs' could still answer; and in the eyre of London three years later, for example, one of several charged with the disseisin of a rent may appear on behalf of all 'as bailiff', a pleasingly rural touch in so urban a dispute. But the oblique use later made of the word does not affect the possibility that at first it meant what it said, that the bailiff was the obvious representative because the lord was the obvious disseisor. If the lord was simply taking the holding into his own hand, indeed, the bailiff might play a more active part. But, as with mort d'ancestor, the man who actually came might be one to whom the lord had assigned it or whom he thought entitled. The use of the assize against third parties would inevitably follow, and so would its possessory relationship, not to some abstract title, but to the feudal right.

If that was the orientation of the assize in its earliest days, its eclectic scope may similarly be explained. After the basic writ, Glanvill has three forms which do not claim land as such, introduced by the statement that 'writs of novel disseisin may vary in a number of ways corresponding to the different kinds of tenement in which disseisins take place'. Two concern the raising or knocking down of a bank and the raising of the level of a mill pond; and though they do not use the word *dissaisire,* they were still sometimes called novel disseisin in the thirteenth century. In the third the plaintiff has been disseised of his common of pasture. This is an odd collection if the disputes were between neighbour and neighbour. But were they? Little can be proved against Glanvill's bank, but the mill and the common pasture were normally controlled by the lord.

As to the assize for pasture, a legislative mishap shows what one would anyway expect, namely that until much later it was typically brought by tenant against lord. In 1236 the Statute of Merton enabled a lord who had approved his waste to show that the plaintiff still had sufficient common; and only an afterthought in the Statute of Westminster II of 1285 allowed the same defence to be raised against one who was not the defendant's own tenant. Interesting in another way is a different provision of the latter statute. A general extension of the scope of novel dissesin included common rights other than pasture. But a few early cases had concerned turbary and the like, and their disappearance must reflect a restriction to the most central manorial rights. Even pasture itself came early to be excluded from mort d'ancestor, at any rate if it was claimed as belonging to a tenement which the demandant already had; and a new *beneficium principis* was needed, the writ *quod permittat*. This looks like a restriction of mort d'ancestor in such cases to its original purpose of securing the immediate recognition of the heir.

Glanvill's pasture, then, naturally continued to belong to a seignorial world. What happened to his mill-pond and his bank? They were joined by hedges, water-courses and ways as objects of an assize increasingly known as the assize of nuisance; and until a rationalization late in the fourteenth century they were contrasted with the so-called 'petty' nuisances which were for the sheriff. There are two puzzles of classification. Why did Registers of Writs continue to follow Glanvill in calling the former novel disseisin? And what distinguished those wrongs from the petty nuisances? Since petty nuisances were dealt with by courts whose records have not survived, we know little about them. But mostly at any rate they look like disputes between neighbour and neighbour, such as a smelly latrine or overlooked windows. The things covered by the assize on the other hand, though the list may have been arbitrarily closed to exclude for example the making of a new mill, look like manorial operations. Perhaps their original unity was in the protection of tenant against lord rather than neighbour against neighbour.

The same line of thought may help to explain the one notable and permanent exclusion from the scope of the assize; it was not available to the termor. The reason for this must have been as obvious at the time as it has been obscure ever since. Maitland had a Romanistic explanation which has fallen out of favour. It was based upon Bracton's analogy with the usufructuary, who did not have *possessio*. But even if we cannot accept that a dogma was wantonly transplanted, there may have been some underlying likeness which led to a like juridical result. Britton, rejecting Bracton's Roman law along with his Latin, says in effect that the subject-matter of a term is not the land but its yield; and this is not so very far from the economic kind of explanation which has been put forward to replace Maitland's. The difficulties may at least diminish if we suppose novel disseisin to have been first conceived, not as the protection *in rem* of something like possession but as the specific protection of a tenant against his lord. The termor was not in the feudal sense a tenant at all. Glanvill seems to classify both the gage and the letting as private agreements. Later rules about the interruption of a term by a wardship suggest that the lessor's lord was never affected; and it therefore seems likely that his consent was never required. Perhaps the 'tenement' of the assize was not just an object of property, but one side of a relationship first needing protection against the other.

If it is proper to think in terms of a sustained policy, the same policy may therefore lie behind novel disseisin, mort d'ancestor and the great writ of right itself, a policy of protecting tenants against their lords. On this view, all began as about the feudal relationship rather than about ownership and possession; and in the feudal dimension all looked upwards. A final suggestion about the real actions concerns the writs of entry. It is that these too began in that dimension, but that they looked downwards. The word itself may have had seignorial connotations. Consider the preamble to the great statute of 1290 which finally flattened out the framework of our land law: *Quia emptores terrarum...de feodis magnatum...in feodis suis sunt ingressi...*; or that of the Statute of Mortmain of 1279, echoing the Provisions of Westminster: *Cum dudum provisum fuisset quod viri religiosi feoda aliquorum non ingrederentur...* Or consider the hypothetical claim of a lord against his tenant's grantee, as refuted by Bracton: *Item si dicat quod iniuste ingressus sit feodum suum...* No earlier examples come to mind in which the word is so used of free tenures, unless we vouch the writs of entry themselves; but it is used earlier of the unfree. At common law a villein had no right and was nobody's heir; but he was allowed to 'enter' and normally made a payment to his lord *de ingressu*. Perhaps the word was not used differently when the villein purported to alienate, and the lord brought a *breve de ingressu* against the grantee. It denoted a mere fact, but the fact was being spoken about from above.

If so, it was a fact which in principle did not concern the speaker's lord; and here we come back to the proposition that the action in the right looked upward. One situation has been mentioned in which the tenant in a writ of right could relieve the customary blankness of his denial. If he put himself upon the grand assize he could say that he was in under a grant from the demandant's ancestor, in early examples a grant by subinfeudation. Two separate rights now featured in the case. The right asserted in the demandant's count was his hereditary right as against his lord. The tenant did not deny that: he asserted the existence of a similar right in himself as against the demandant. But for the settlement of that dispute, the action in the right was not appropriate. Suppose, to return indeed to our starting-point, that the demandant knew all about the grant, and his true case was that his ancestor had been mad when he made it. What was the use of a battle nominally about the seisin of some more remote and wholly irrelevant ancestor, about the wrong right?

In such a case the demandant came to have a writ claiming the land 'into which the tenant had no entry except through such an one to whom the demandant's father granted it when out of his mind', or the like. Although the writs of entry based upon disseisin, which are not the earliest, may have been conceived in terms of 'possessory' protection, those based upon defective or spent grants look like a response to the conceptual inappropriateness of the action in the right. But if so, we are obliged to ask what had created the need or made it apparent. One thing that may have created the need is the inhibition of direct seignorial action by novel disseisin and mort d'ancestor. The writ of escheat, for example, grew out of a writ of entry which itself does not seem to be early. Were lords making that most elementary claim by an action in the right which, on the view now proposed, was any way inappropriate? Were they not just taking back their lands? There was nothing new about the situation which that particular writ of entry came to remedy. But many of the situations must have been new in the sense that they depend upon alienability, upon the frequency with which it could happen that a grant was made about which the lord need not even know. The gage of land seems to have been a matter purely between the parties, and it may be significant that Glanvill's writ of gage was the earliest of the family of the writs of entry. But if battle had remained the only mode of trial, the inappropriateness of the action in the right might

still not have come into view. Although, to our loss, entries
of the grand assize just announce a finding for the one party
or the other, we know from Glanvill that the knights might
place the actual facts before the court; and it may have been
this that pre-disposed the royal officers to listen sym-
pathetically when a demandant sought a writ narrowing the
issue and excluding the question of right. He had more
reason than his own preference, a better argument than just
fairness, for excluding the battle which the tenant could
otherwise choose, and for avoiding the lord's court to which
the case would otherwise go. The right which the lord must
adjudicate and which the battle would test was not what was
in dispute.

Or at least, it was not what was in dispute on the demandant's account of the case; and the writ of entry decided no
more than the truth of that. But if the tenant was not in by
those means at all, or if he was, but there were yet earlier
facts—if for example the demandant's ancestor however
mad was only restoring what had been wrongfully taken—
then the tenant's title was probably independent of the
demandant's. The tenant could therefore lose a writ of entry
and still have a writ of right; and in Bracton's day he could
in suitable circumstances turn the writ of entry into the right.
If the entry alleged had been against an ancestor rather than
the demandant himself, the demandant had of course to trace
his descent from that ancestor; and if he incautiously counted
that the ancestor's seisin had been as of right, the tenant
could choose to answer as to an action in the right and avoid
issue on the entry.

A more puzzling feature of the relationship between writs
of entry and the right is the limitation of writs of entry to
the degrees. The arithmetic is not always easy to follow,
but Bracton could state the rule that a writ of entry would
not reach beyond the third hand since the alleged wrong.
Already in his day, however, there were doubts; and pressure
first voiced in the Provisions of the Barons of 1259 led to the
removal of the limit, and therefore to the effective end of the
writ of right. But the puzzle is at the beginning of the story,
not its end. Maitland, though he thought that rules about
warranty perhaps played some part, saw the limit as essenti-

ally political, an arbitrary line between 'possessory' and 'proprietary' to safeguard feudal jurisdiction; and he saw this explained or excused in terms of proof, of the limit of a jury's knowledge. But on the view here suggested, the lord's jurisdiction was not relevant to the claim being made. It is just possible that the matter of proof links rather with some relic of the evolution of heritability itself, some idea that a limited grant cannot be made for more than two or three lives, and that if a tenure has in fact lasted longer it cannot be recalled. A gift in *maritagium* lost its special character when the third heir entered. But there are many other reflections of a limit like that of the degrees; and there is still, as there was for Maitland, 'something to be discovered in this obscure region'.

An agreed obscurity is as good a place as any at which to turn from the real actions. But so large a heresy ought to be restated in the largest terms. It proceeds from a belief that the first century of English feudalism was indeed, at the levels which were to affect the king's courts, a feudal century, and that the world which Sir Frank Stenton saw cannot have changed abruptly into the world which Maitland saw. The juridical difference can only be expressed in the language of spatial dimensions. The world into which Maitland's real actions fit is essentially a flat world, inhabited by equal neighbours. Lordship is little more than a servitude over the land of another, and its content is fixed and economic. The services and incidents are important, but the law relating to them is self-contained, unrelated to other questions; and distress of chattels is all that is left of direct seignorial control. To the creation and protection of rights over land in general, the lord is fundamentally irrelevant. But in the earlier world he was relevant at every point; and transactions and litigation mainly happened in the vertical dimension.

There can be no doubt that by the end of the period covered by his book, the world was as Maitland saw it. The real actions then formed the continuous spectrum of his vision, vertical in a different sense: one could aim one's writ up a little, and go higher into the right. The suggestion is that the older world was still real when the actions began, and that in that world they formed a different system. 'If we

were free to write history out of our own heads...', I wonder
whether Maitland would so characterize this return from a
purely 'possessory' to a 'feudal' explanation of the beginnings of our property law. It can not rest upon the secure
foundation of the plea rolls. They never tell us about underlying assumptions, and we can not hope for direct evidence
of the nature of the right or of its relationship to an entry.
Even about facts they are meanly reticent. That mort
d'ancestor was provided for use against lords is something
we might never have guessed if we did not happen to know it.
As to novel disseisin, Glanvill's discussion of purprestures
shows its use between neighbours. By the time the rolls begin,
perhaps the lord himself was not often defendant. But the
rolls will not tell us even that, still less how often seignorial
action may lie behind a general verdict: late as it is, the
unique narrative of an assize in the *Consuetudines Diversarum
Curiarum* happens to show a disseisor relying upon his lord's
authority. Conversely the paralysis of seignorial action by
the assize itself may have led to its increasing use against
third parties, so that cases were unintentionally driven to
royal courts and not just attracted there. The hypothesis is
of a truly seignorial world; and it rests upon the belief of a
literal mind that legal forms at first mean what they say and
therefore reflect the society in which they were first spoken.
There is nothing new about the formalities of an action in
the right, the words of the Assize of Northampton, the
words of a writ of novel disseisin. The heresy seeks to
accommodate them at their face value.

One test of a changed view-point is whether you can see
more from it. For the general history of the period there are
implications in all this which others must judge. A particular
problem common to economic and legal historians may at
least look intractable in a new way: if novel disseisin and
mort d'ancestor were primarily conceived as remedies for
tenants against lords, their bearing upon villeinage becomes
very direct. More within the lawyers' frontier, the position of
the termor may be similarly affected; and the assize of
nuisance may even be provided with an explanation. If the
writs of entry can be seen as partly a replacement for direct
action by lords, itself inhibited by the assizes, then apparent

gaps in the real actions become less surprising: if escheats were simply taken, so perhaps were reversions after gifts in marriage; if grantors created remainders when remaindermen had no remedy, perhaps they assumed that they themselves would be there when the time came, law personified. Even well on in the thirteenth century, the law relating to dower may not be wholly intelligible unless an unexpectedly large part is allowed to seignorial action. And lastly there is seisin. For all that has been done, seisin is still the mystery of which Maitland wrote, the beatitude which can not be doubted but is no more explicable than the blessed word Mesopotamia. It is a possession contrasted with right, yet somehow imbued with it. In a Roman or a modern world, that is a contradiction. But in a feudal world it could make sense. For Glanvill to disseise means to dispossess. But much later royal disseisins may recall a world in which the seising and disseising of tenants were primarily actions by lords. Seisin would indeed be imbued with right when there was only the lord's law, and could later contrast with the right which the king's law might compel the lord's to do. There is no mystery about a contradiction when two voices may be speaking.

III. *The Personal Actions.*

COMPARED with relationships concerning land, other kinds of legal relationship, and in particular those which we talk about under the headings of contract and tort, were of little consequence. If therefore we allow the age to speak for itself, it will not have so much to say about them. And if we mainly allow the records of the king's courts to speak for the age, we shall hear relatively even less. Glanvill has already told us that private agreements were not for them, and the same will prove to be true of private wrongs.

But the legal historian plays a double part. As social historian he must observe the proportions allotted to things in the time of which he is writing. As historian of ideas he cannot forget what lay in the future, that this was to flourish and that was to fail; and he cannot avoid asking his records about matters that were of small concern to their makers.

There are two dangers. The records themselves are more than usually likely to give partial answers. And the inquirer is more than usually likely to ask anachronistic questions. About the latter danger, although no historian can hope to avoid it, Maitland was always conscious: 'We must not be wise above what is written or more precise than the lawyers of the age.' But the former danger he underestimated: he did not, at any rate, make clear to those who were to follow him how partial were the answers likely to be given by the records of the king's courts.

The difference that it makes is not a matter of social history. Nobody has ever doubted that most litigation in what we should call contract and tort took place in lesser courts than the king's, or that our picture was quantitatively incomplete. What matters is a distortion of ideas. The heresy is again about underlying assumptions, about the concepts behind the formalities, about the original sense of simple words. The word covenant became the name of an action in which, not long after the period covered by this book, a requirement was imposed by the king's courts that the plaintiff should have a document under seal. This requirement eventually infected the word itself, so that historians have unconsciously followed lawyers in assuming some formal concept akin to the Roman *stipulatio*. But outside the king's courts a deed was not required for actions called covenant; and there is no reason to think that the word became narrowed from its primary meaning of agreement, *conventio*, until relatively modern times. The word trespass similarly became the name of an action, or rather a group of actions, the common features of which were allegations of force and arms and breach of the king's peace; and these too infected the word itself, which came to denote some concept of direct physical injury. But that became the accepted definition only in a case which was on its way from the Somerset assizes to Westminster on the fifth centenary of Edward I's accession. In the thirteenth and fourteenth centuries all kinds of wrongs were being remedied in actions called trespass by courts other than the king's; and the point about the king's courts seems to have been that they would entertain only those wrongs which affected the king. Then and long after the word had its primary meaning of wrong, *transgressio*. For reasons that will appear we err, but we do not err hopelessly, if in Year Books we translate trespass into tort and covenant into contract. The main effect is on our understanding of events in the centuries after this book ends. For the formalistic development presented in Maitland's lectures on the forms of action, we can substitute another in which lawyers are heard to argue in terms of elementary legal ideas.

To take first the subject matter of what we call contract, the orthodoxy disputed is hardly due to Maitland himself. In Selden Society editions of local court records he had noted the wide usage of the word covenant; and he states it in this book, hedging the word only in precautionary inverted commas. Some work, though not enough, has been done on the subject of contract in local courts; and the rules that emerge go not to substantive questions like 'when is a promise binding?' but to matters of proof. That this was the original nature of the document under seal was also clearly stated by Maitland. The king's courts, moreover, were being practical and not formalistic when they came to insist upon it. The centralization of justice raised a dilemma over proof upon which contracts were particularly impaled. An agreement, however notoriously made, may be performed in private, or performed or broken in another place. But a jury's information could not reach into the minds of the parties, nor beyond the county boundary; and it was therefore necessary to preserve, for those actions in which the problem was allowed to arise, the ancient wager of law. This tested an oath by the defendant, whose knowledge was subject to neither limit. But geography had the last word. Wager would be effective in the court of a community, because the standing of all concerned would be at stake. But in Westminster, where oath helpers must soon have become hired strangers, all depended on the sole conscience of the defendant. With debt and detinue there was no escape, and sorry things happened. With account it became possible to insist on a jury when the defendant was charged as receiver from somebody other than the plaintiff: a jury could know of the receipt, and the resulting duty to account could not have been privately discharged. With covenant, there would have been constant dispute over the very terms of the agreement alleged to have been broken; and the insistence upon a deed, excluding questions of proof altogether unless its authenticity were denied, was a progressive step in its own time.

But at that time the king's courts would any way entertain only transactions large enough for such formalities to be reasonable. The mischief was to emerge much later, as forty shillings shrank to a level which could be reached by ordinary dealings. Then it would appear that the common law had crippled not just an action but the whole idea of contract by saddling it with an impracticable formality; and it was then that plaintiffs' lawyers turned finally to actions called trespass, to ideas that we should think proper to tort, and then that we can hear their opponents protesting that the matter sounds in covenant rather than in trespass.

Maitland himself might not have dissented from the proposition that the word covenant represents a concept of the same order as our contract. But at no time was the action of covenant common in the king's courts, except as a basis for levying fines, and something must be said of the reasons for this. There is more to it than that litigation was mostly going on in lesser courts, though that was most of the explanation in the period covered by this book. Nor is it just secular courts of which we must think. We have even more reason than did Maitland to suspect that the courts of the church, about which we know too little, may have been playing a substantial part, the king's writs of prohibition notwithstanding.

A different sort of consideration, and one which needs no new emphasis, is that much of the work done by contract in a modern society was done by rules growing out of proprietary relationships. To take an obvious example, agricultural labour presented itself as a matter of offences against manorial custom. To take a less obvious but striking example, the poor man who wished to buy himself what we should call an annuity with his land would create a tenure, reserving his guaranteed subsistence as the service; and by an ironical turn it was for this unlikely lord that legislation first introduced *cessavit*, a process by which a defaulting tenant could be made to forfeit his holding. What had once been an elementary ingredient of the feudal relationship was resurrected for a purpose more nearly contractual than feudal. A related point is best left in Maitland's words: '...the feeble law of contract is supplemented by a generous liberality in the creation of incorporeal things.' The treatment of corodies, rents, offices and the like as property was to him 'the most medieval part of medieval law', and he admired 'the daring fancy that created it, a fancy that was not afraid of the grotesque.' But for the most grotesque of these exploits, novel disseisin alone was responsible; and its versatility may have owed something to the almost random appearance of its range as the feudal orientation disappeared from view.

Even within the field of obligation, it is not easy to be sure when proprietary ideas may be at work. Maitland saw debt as a boundary of covenant, and vice versa, and was puzzled. There would indeed be a puzzle if both belonged to some concept akin to our contract, but it would be soluble in terms of a proposition to be made later. The common law writs were not fundamental in the sense generally understood, and the boundary between debt and covenant could be seen as one of form: the *praecipe* would demand money when money was due under the agreement, and performance when the agreement was for something other than a mere render. But the evidence all suggests that there was an elementary distinction.

Language has played some mean tricks. Consider the usual content of a franchise jurisdiction over civil pleas, 'trespasses, covenants and contracts'. The first two have already been translated into their rough modern equivalents. Tort had to become the generic term because trespass was annexed to a species, and the same happened with contract and covenant. But whereas tort did not have any specific sense to start with, contract did: generally it meant a transaction raising a debt, what the Year Books will tend to call a *duitie*. That the basis of this was different from agreement, *conventio*, is perhaps the only clear thing about it.

'We can not rethink the process which lies hidden away in the history of those two words *owe* and *own*.' Maitland's analysis of the relationship between debt and detinue will remain the starting point for English inquiry into a phenomenon which may be general among developing systems of law; and what follows differs only in focus. A source of confusion can best be taken up at a later period. In the fifteenth century detinue came to be pleaded in two ways, *sur bailment* and *sur trover*, the latter being a conventional form to denote that the defendant was not charged as bailee or privy. Maitland's discussion can be read as countenancing the possibility that was then new in substance. We have long known that it was not: the novelty was in pleading only, and detinue independent of any bailment can be carried back to the thirteenth century. But we do not have to postulate an original notion which would include the loan of money at one extreme, and at the other the claim for a chattel based only upon its earmark. In local courts the latter fell to the process *de re adirata*, an associate of the appeal of larceny. In royal courts there is no separate trace of this; and perhaps with the forty shilling limit there would be little need for it. But since the facts would be within the words of a writ of detinue, the likely explanation is that when the need did arise detinue was the writ issued. If so, detinue in the king's courts always covered two disparate ideas; and we can set the 'trover' situation on one side for a better reason than that we are not talking about it—Maitland was not often so arbitrary.

This leaves us to accommodate the *mutuum* and the *commodatum* with their variants. It is not only in Glanvill that they are not distinguished. They are not distinguished in the Statute of Wales or the printed Register of Writs; and so far as the formalities of the actions are concerned, there is still no clear test long after this book ends. If money is claimed, and if it is the original parties to the transaction who have gone to court, the writ will say that the defendant *debet*, and the action will clearly be debt. If barley is claimed, the writ will have only *detinet*. We are told that if the barley was specific, the action was detinue; if not, it was debt in the *detinet*. But there is no way of telling from the plea roll, and no way of knowing the facts. For the plea roll clerks in the fourteenth century detinue itself was no more an entity than it had been for Glanvill. Glanvill speaks only of debt: the clerks, when they have occasion to use a name instead of reciting the writ, for example when noting a formal appearance or the appointment of an attorney in detinue, say that it is *de placito debiti*.

The distinction never permeates the formalities of the action; but so long as the action could only be settled by the general denial and the wager or other test, it would never matter in a court. It would come to matter only when facts could emerge, and in particular when the borrower could plead that the thing was specific and that it had perished without his fault. The countryman of Glanvill's time to whom this happened might make his denial and wage his law, and hope he was not committing perjury; and the rarity of Year Book cases on the bailee's liability suggests that he stoutly went on doing so. What matters to us, however, is that his local court could have no occasion to ask the legal question. Glanvill's Roman learning compelled him to ask it: but the only English material for an answer was the identity of the writ, so he made the bailee strictly liable as a money debtor. Bracton took the other course and gave a Roman answer, depending upon fault. And Britton, our countryman turned lawyer, had no material but Bracton and made a hash of him; but it is a revealing hash. He repeats the proposition that loss without fault may be excusable, and then earnestly applies it to a money debt. The distinction was alien, not just because it was Roman, but because English law-suits were only now reaching the stage of development at which the question could arise.

It is questions arising that makes law; and in so doing it alters or refines the categories into which lawyers classify life. But even in a customary system, comprehensive categories must exist. Some writers have sought to dispose altogether of problems like that before us, to evade the dilemma that either the bailee 'owed' or the money creditor 'owned', by saying that for practical men the question did not arise. But lawyers can not be practical men in that sense, because classification is a practical need. When advice is sought, some such sentence as 'That is a case of...' is inevitable. For Glanvill, and for the system preserved in the plea roll forms, the bailor's was a case of debt, indistinguishable from that of the lender of money.

Maitland reviewed the features so clearly consonant with this, and in particular the bailee's liability and his exclusive right to sue third parties. But he shrank from the conclusion

that the bailor was a creditor for two main reasons. If the
bailee started as owner, how could ownership have come to
be transferred imperceptibly to the bailor? And 'to make the
bailor's right a mere right *ex contractu* is to throw upon the
nascent law of contract a weight that it will not bear.' So far
as the second is concerned, what was nascent was the law
relating to agreement, covenant. Contract in the medieval
sense looks like something distinct, very old, perhaps with the
same roots as the Roman contract *re*, and certainly very
strong. Was it obligation or property? 'We can not at will
displace from our minds the dilemma "*in rem* or *in personam*"
which seems to have been put there by natural law.' But if
we try, the single idea with which we are left is closer to a
right *in personam* than to a right *in rem*. Even the 'right' to
land, if the suggestions here made are acceptable, began as
an intensely personal thing. Rights were against people; and
if one had actually got an object there was no need to reflect
on his position as against the world. We can believe that the
bailee owed the chattel without being forced to conclude
that he owned it. He had it, the bailor wanted it, and that
was a question with which courts and lawyers had to deal.
They dealt with it in the same way as the loan of money, as
the seller's claim for his price or the buyer's claim for his
goods, resting the case on the transaction. For them the
bailee did owe. But only a Bracton would ask whether he
owned. What the bailee had, apart from the object itself, was
a question that indeed did not arise.

Contract in its original sense, covering a wide range of
obligations arising *re*, was therefore distinct from covenant,
of which the informing idea was agreement; and the only
situation in which a doubt about classification is imaginable
would be the mere promise to pay. We shall not consider the
analysis of a money bond: irrefutable evidence of indebted-
ness probably slid into dispositive magic. But the bond
became important outside its proper sphere, being responsible for the disuse of covenant. In the fourteenth century
lawyers took to advising clients to set up their agreements
indirectly. Instead of the desired performance being itself
promised by deed, it was made the condition of avoiding a
promise by deed to pay a penal sum. Sometimes the docu-

ments were deposited with a stakeholder, and litigation would be in detinue for the bonds. But in the straightforward case it would be in debt for the penalty, and would turn on satisfaction of the conditions. It may be added that the conditions were pleaded and entered verbatim; and since this remained the common form for important dealings until the sixteenth century, the rolls of the Common Pleas became rich in transcripts of every kind of agreement. That development and the reasons for it lie beyond the scope of this essay; but one factor may go to the initial framework of ideas.

Our first approximation was to identify covenant with the modern contract, noting only that most contracts would be for lesser courts and that many matters would be treated by rules arising from property. Then the medieval sense of contract was distinguished, and covenant identified with the enforcement of agreements as such. In local courts, subject to a point to be made later, that identification seems to work over its full width. But in royal courts, long before the document under seal narrowed the concept, there may have been some narrowing from another cause. The writ of covenant is a *praecipe*. The sheriff was to 'tell the defendant to keep to his agreement concerning' whatever it was; and the need for recital made the writ more variable than the *praecipes* for land or the writs of debt, detinue or account. So far as the words of the writ go, it is only in default of performance that the defendant was to be summoned to court. Broadly speaking the earlier common law writs were all *praecipes*, the later all in the form *ostensurus quare*. Some have seen this as a mere change of fashion. Some have explained the change in terms of a process of judicialization, royal writs beginning as mere executive commands, the developed *praecipe* having a judicial element tacked on, and the *ostensurus quare* being fully judicial. And some suspect that the change is associated by more than coincidence with the coming to the king's courts of a new kind of claim. *Praecipe* writs demand rights, *ostensurus quare* writs complain about wrongs.

If that is so, it tells us something about the early notion of covenant. But whether it is so or not, a literal mind will see the writ as contemplating specific performance, and therefore as appropriate to the case in which performance is still possible and desired, inappropriate to the case in which irreparable harm has already been done. The land that was promised can be handed over. The repair can be done to the mill, but what of the lost multure? And who wants just the small strengthening of the river wall when the land has been flooded and a harvest lost? Whether or not the form of the writ was more than a chronological accident, it would matter little so long as the only agreements important enough for the king's court were those about land; and in the thirteenth century covenant is overwhelmingly associated with the term of years. But it may have played its part in the later disuse of covenant. On the practical level, the lawyer who advised that an agreement be made by conditional bond perhaps guarded against a smiling locksmith coming to fix the stable door after the horse had gone. On the level of ideas, he perhaps felt that covenant was about the literal enforcement of agreements.

Even with land there was one situation that raised a question, namely the seller who agreed to convey to one and then conveyed to another. The Statute of Wales finds it necessary to explain that redress must be in money. Two centuries later this will be the chief situation in which *assumpsit* lies for what looks like the mere failure to carry out an agreement. Can we be sure that Year Book arguments at that time are formalistic or disingenuous when they say that such a case sounds in trespass rather than in covenant?

The wording of the covenant writ may therefore have helped bring about first its own virtual disuse and secondly that uncertainty about the conceptual boundary which was exploited by using trespass actions to get compensation for broken agreements. The earlier stages of that process seem to flow from yet another limitation on the original idea of covenant, and one which introduces trespass itself. The point can best be taken up in the king's courts a century after this book ends. The earliest *assumpsit* actions are also among the earliest actions of trespass on the case. Trespass on the case was not an invention of the king's courts at that time; it was no more than the result of a new willingness to entertain trespass actions, actions for wrongs, in which no royal interest was alleged. The surgeon who made his patient worse, the promisor who performed his promise badly, had not been immune before; he had been sued elsewhere. But when he is sued in the king's courts he repeatedly makes the same argument, that the case sounds in covenant; and the judges repeatedly hold against him that it is properly brought in trespass. This is an argument about classification: roughly, in our language, contract or tort. The defendant's motive for raising the question in the king's courts is clear: covenant there requires a seal. But our interest is in local courts where such actions had always hitherto been heard. There no seal was required in covenant, so that nothing more was at stake than the name by which the action was to be called. In fact it seems more often to have been called trespass. The king's judges in the late fourteenth century were following a majority opinion.

Even to the modern mind this may be the natural analysis; but for many misfeasances at any rate there was a more positive reason. Our first approximation with trespass was to equate it with tort; and this takes us further than carrying back its eighteenth-century sense of direct physical injury. But, rather after the manner suggested for the real actions, it leaves out a dimension. In the period covered by this book, contract and covenant may have been the only kinds of matter seen as truly private, truly disputes between neighbour and neighbour for which authority must provide but in which it had no other interest. In trespass, at any rate, authority had an interest, was in a sense a party. The wrong was a wrong to authority as well as to the private victim, if any. It follows that what was seen as a wrong to authority would be classified as a trespass, notwithstanding that some private dealing was involved. The city of London had no interest in a citizen's agreements with his surgeon, his tailor, his fishmonger. But it sought to control its surgeons, to maintain honest standards of workmanship among tailors, to punish fishmongers who sold bad fish. Its officials might initiate proceedings to these ends; and if they were initiated by the private victim, that did not alter the nature of the case. It was still a matter of trespass rather than covenant.

Again as with the real actions, but later, it was the collapse of this third dimension that left the categories of the common law with an arbitrary appearance. And the most arbitrary feature in the fourteenth century, when trespasses came to be seen as private matters between neighbour and neighbour, was the boundary dividing wrongs that could be brought before the king's courts from those that had to go to a county or other local court. Speaking roughly, the plaintiff had access to the royal courts if he could, without making obvious nonsense, allege that the wrong was committed *vi et armis* and *contra pacem regis*. If his horse had been deliberately killed, he could choose whether to make these allegations and sue in a royal court, or omit them and sue elsewhere. If he had been sold a dying horse warranted sound, he could not sensibly make the allegations and so could not come to a royal court. If his horse had died because of careless work by the smith, he could not come to a royal court openly saying that he had entrusted the horse to the smith, who had *vi et armis* and *contra pacem regis* worked badly so that the horse died: that was obvious nonsense. But he could and did bring the same general action that he would use against the stranger who deliberately killed his horse, and were it not for a few freaks which give us glimpses of the truth, we should have no means of knowing except that the defendant is so often a smith.

The artificiality of this position was ended in the late fourteenth century when the king's courts took to admitting trespasses in which no royal interest was alleged. This is the 'origin' of the action on the case; and for the general history of the common law that conclusion is the most important consequence of rejecting Maitland's view of trespass. For him trespass had always been the conceptual entity of his own day, 'a' tort, although a Protean one and with a criminal tinge. That entity was the 'fertile mother of actions', out of which there sprang the various kinds of trespass on the case; and these were to provide virtually all the law of tort that was not 'trespass' and, replacing the contractual actions we have considered, were to provide the modern law of contract and of personal property. All this development was seen by Maitland and by those who came after him in formalistic terms, terms which slowly came true in the minds of lawyers after the sixteenth century, but which did not reflect their thought in the middle ages. If that single assumption about the meaning of 'trespass' is abandoned, the development looks very different: the arguments suddenly become intelligible in elementary terms. Much therefore was at stake after the period covered by this book. But within that period, the adjustment required is not large, and it does not have important consequences outside itself.

To begin with the question of origin, Maitland saw trespass as the daughter of the appeal of felony in much the same way as he saw it as the mother of trespass on the case. Another writer, thinking in the same terms, saw it as coming from novel disseisin. Maitland's instinct about the appeal was almost certainly right; but the separation of the two from each other or from some common ancestor had gone far in local courts and in the dark time before records. In the thirteenth century, however, it was still true that the same set of facts might sometimes give rise to appeal or to trespass action at the plaintiff's choice, which would no doubt depend upon his willingness to face a battle. On the other hand Maitland probably supposed too simple a connection when he attributed the criminal aspect of trespass to its association with the appeal. The criminal aspect of trespass is the key to its beginning.

Trespasses, mere wrongs, were for local courts, for the courts whose law had been broken; and the immediate 'origin' of trespass in the king's courts was their taking jurisdiction when it was the king's special law that had been broken. This special law was the king's peace, the breach of which was a plea of the crown, for Glanvill a more serious matter than mere theft which was for the sheriff. And as a plea of the crown, it might reach the king's courts in the two ways in which any trespasses might reach their appropriate courts. Authority might act, in this case by inquiry of the local people; and when in later days linguistic confusion became intolerable, trespasses presented by indictment were translated as misdemeanours. Or the victim might act, might bring an action of trespass; but though his aim in doing so would be to get damages for himself, the convicted defendant still had to buy off the king's anger, and the case still had to

come to the king's justices. It was still a plea of the crown
and as such, as Magna Carta reaffirmed, outside the scope of
the sheriff.

The king's peace from which all this started was, of course,
something different from the modern peace which any affray
will break: it was more akin to protection. But as the persons,
the place, the season ceased to matter, so that there was only
the quality of the act to go on, the king's peace and the
sheriff's became indistinguishable. Then we can think of a
plaintiff choosing his court: the action becomes purely 'civil',
and the king's interest mainly important for the rapid process
by arrest that it entails. The fruitful decay has begun.

This had not been dated, and there may be no sign other
than statistics about actions brought or fines taken. It is in
the nature of writs, as is implicit in what has been said about
novel disseisin, that if the plaintiff's case is within the words
there is no way of denying him the benefit on the ground that
it is not within the spirit and intention. The writ-issuing
authority does not conduct a preliminary inquiry, and the
defendant can only plead Not Guilty. But the flow of actions
was increasing in the later years of Henry III, and the
Statute of Gloucester in 1278 sought to reverse it: trespasses,
it ordered, were to be heard as heretofore by sheriffs in their
counties. Even this may have done little more than increase
the vehemence of allegations. *Contra pacem regis* had been
almost invariable from the beginning, and in the last years of
the thirteenth century *vi et armis* suddenly becomes general
in trespass writs. The phrase seems first to have been at home
in novel disseisin: the assize finding that there had been a
disseisin would be asked whether it had been *vi et armis*; if
yes, the defendant was imprisoned, again until he bought off
the king's anger. In trespass the phrase was probably used by
way of emphasis, but not truthfully. Early in the fourteenth
century, awkward juries would find that the wrong had been
done but not *vi et armis*, and their rider had to be disregarded.
Not much later we find some very ludicrous counts, for
example the cask of wine that had been opened "with force
and arms, to wit with swords and bows and arrows". But
that case, heard in 1317, was of the degree of artificiality
which half a century later resulted in the allegations ceasing

to be compulsory: the plaintiff had bought the wine, and was really complaining that his seller had drawn some off and topped up with salt water so that the whole was undrinkable. This was a serious matter, but a far cry from Glanvill's breach of the king's peace.

If then we wish to get our conceptual bearings about the time of Edward I's accession, we must not identify trespass with our tort of trespass, nor with whatever we suppose to be our concept of tort; nor, if we think in terms of tort, must we attach conceptual significance to what we see coming before the king's justices. As to the element that we should call criminal, the procedural separation has probably already formalized the king's interest in, for example, an ordinary action for battery; but Edward I will by statute create several 'civil' writs of trespass with real and severe penal consequences. As to the scope of 'tort', what we are seeing in the king's courts is merely capricious. Very occasionally some quite different kind of wrong, perhaps purely economic, will find its way in to prove that 'trespass' can exist without '*contra pacem*'. And there is a small freshet of such oddities in the years immediately after the death of Henry III. His peace had died with him; and *contra pacem* could not now be alleged even of a truly violent wrong done while he lived. The confusion brought in cases in which it could never plausibly have been alleged, which ought not to have come to a royal court at all; and this may have been the proximate cause of the Statute of Gloucester's attempt to push trespasses back to the county courts. It is to county courts that we must chiefly look if we wish to see how far Englishmen are pro-texted against 'civil' wrongs. But today we look in vain. County court rolls of pleas were not kept in the preservative air of officialdom but by the sheriffs themselves; and although since Maitland wrote some fourteenth-century scraps have come to light to tantalize us, their general disappearance leaves one of the most serious gaps in our means of knowledge.

But in trespass and covenant alike, the records of other local courts seem to show us a world more modern by centuries than the one reflected from the king's courts. Of course the difference is an optical illusion: the formal contract and the physical wrong fit together into a lifelike picture of juristic backwardness. And of course, although he may have underestimated the part played by the idea of fraud, Maitland was not misled about the social realities. What is at stake is our understanding of the nature of later legal development.

IV. *Procedure.*

THE suggestions so far made come to this: that from a much earlier period than has been supposed the common law rested upon definite though shifting ideas. In turning to procedure we do not change the subject. Historians know how great an imaginative effort it takes to see an early law-suit in anything like a contemporary light; and Maitland, who joined Lincoln's Inn before the Judicature Acts were passed, was that much better placed than we to know how completely and how invisibly procedure pervades legal thinking. Perhaps it is our own greater distance, as well as new information, that makes it possible to think that he carried too far back in time, not just the meaning of certain words, but the manner of thought implicit in the 'forms of action'. It was a manner which does not belong to the period of this book, probably did not arise for long after.

Much turns on the position of the common law writs. From Glanvill on, those who tried to organize the material of the common law worked on the basis of the writs; and the writs became the groundwork of learning for a practitioner in the king's courts. In that practical sense they were always fundamental. But it was only as elementary words lost their meaning that the writs became fundamental in another sense, appearing to be the originals from which sprang not just actions but the law itself, a formalistic law.

Our knowledge of the commencement of actions has been extended in three principal respects. In the first place many of the ordinary returnable writs were probably even less than Maitland thought the product of definite acts of creation. Some have a long pre-history which may represent, as has been mentioned, a process of judicialization from executive commands. And although some are clear inventions, it appears that many evolved into common form through bargains for special treatment in individual cases. We cannot conclude from the appearance of a writ in a plea roll that a definite action and a definite piece of law 'existed' at that time.

Secondly, although Maitland knew that all sorts of actions might be heard by writ in county courts, he may have underestimated the scale and importance of this. Having no rolls, we know little even of the mechanism. But viscontiel writs seem to be important in the thirteenth and fourteenth centuries; and if, as seems likely, a common reason for their issue was the forty shilling or some other jurisdictional barrier, then we must suppose an underlying unity of ideas between a petty plaint in a local court and an action by writ in the king's court.

And this leads to the third and most important new fact. We now know that a considerable volume of litigation in the king's courts was initiated by plaint without writ, though the rule about freehold kept it mostly to personal actions. This discovery was first made in connection with the general eyre; and so much against nature did it seem for royal justices to act without writ, that they were taken to be acting above the course of the law. The justices in eyre were credited with an almost royal prerogative, with an equitable jurisdiction. But then it turned out that many cases were started without writ in the central courts, mainly, after the two benches had definitively separated, in the King's Bench. Within half a century of the end of the period covered by this book, the practice of hearing plaints about matters arising in the county where the court is, the eponymous ingredient of the later Bill of Middlesex, appears to be well established. All this, moreover, is on a larger scale than the plea rolls suggest. The entries of actions without writ were identified by verbal peculiarities. But the main peculiarity is that nothing was usually enrolled until the case was heard and finished. A writ, on the other hand, was a royal order, and every step taken under it had to be recorded. A single action by writ will therefore appear many times, an action by bill generally only once, and not at all if it is discontinued.

Looking forward from the end of this book, the chief importance of this is in the possibility of legal development which is partly concealed. Looking backward, what matters is that the writ system takes its proper place. Writs began as something exceptional, interferences with the ancient course of litigation. By a curious twist the Common Bench, which was to become the ordinary vehicle of royal justice, in principle needed individual warrant to hear each case: and this was what made procedure without writ appear extraordinary. But the most ancient part of a law-suit was not the writ, which started as something special and became red tape, but the count or plaint; and the appearance of plaints in royal courts without the formality of a writ is not an innovation but a survival. Procedurally it reflects no more than convenience and jurisdiction. The power of the justices in eyre derives from their commission. The power of the King's Bench is that of the king himself; and if the procedure is specially associated with the county in which the court is, that may reflect no more than ease of communication with the sheriff. As to matters of substance, there is nothing equitable about plaints. Nearly all cases begun by bill could have been begun by writ. And if we find a bill in eyre for which we think no returnable writ would have been issued, or if we find in the King's Bench some harbinger of an action which we think belongs to a later period—and in the fourteenth century the *Liber Assisarum* has such glimpses as the famour *Humber Ferry Case*—the revelation is only of royal judges dealing with a matter that the normal routine would leave to local courts. 'The law' is not bounded and defined by the Register of Writs, and does not spring from it. The forms of action which Maitland was to see buried had not yet been born.

Actionem dabo. Of course there are many common law writs of which the introduction can be compared to the sanctioning of a new formula. But the greatest importance of the writ system was administrative rather than legal. It was the clerical triumph that made workable the centralisation of English justice; and without it there would have been no other western system of law to set beside the Roman. Not long after this book ends, however, the writ system began its slow decay, and development was in spite of it rather than because of it. The writs on the case were still to come; but they were plaints transplanted from lesser courts. The real actions, even the writs of entry, ceased to perform their old functions; and their questions came to be raised by manipulating what happened in court, first in novel disseisin, and later in actions still more far-fetched. The future lay not with the clerks and their formulae but with the lawyers in court; and the true English counterpart of the formulary system is the process of pleading.

The clerks and their formulae were most strikingly left behind over debt and detinue: their failure to distinguish these has already been noted. Nor was there any reason for the lawyers to distinguish them so long as the ancient count was met by the ancient general denial. Bracton knew of a great difference between specific and unascertained goods, and knew that it mattered because specific goods could perish by accident. But the experience that had taught him this was not his own or English; and for his English readers it was a statement that could not be attached to any question that actually arose in a law-suit. Britton could not follow Bracton over this detail; and the English could not follow him more generally in his Roman answers, because they had not learnt to ask that kind of question.

Substantive law is the product of thinking about facts. What takes a legal system beyond the mere classification of claims is the adoption of a mode of trial which allows the facts to come out. In England, the starting point was the introduction of jury processes. So long as there was only wager of law, there was nobody but God to whom a bailee could explain about the accidental loss. In the action in the right, it was to the grand assize that a tenant could first say he was in under a grant from the demandant's ancestor; and it was the grand assize who probably first had to think about grants by the incapable. The intellectual beginnings of the common law are epitomized in a manuscript which begins as a copy of *Brevia Placitata* and ends as a Year Book. At first there is no more to a law-suit than the forms: writ; count; denial; test. Then answers other than the general denial are given. Then those other answers become so important that the old forms recede; and pleading, the subject-matter of the Year Books, is the core of the legal process. Later still pleas will themselves recede into mere forms: the important questions will come out before juries in the country, and ways will be devised to catch them there and bring them back to Westminster for discussion. The whole development can be seen as a chase after the facts, which seem to retreat because they are wanted in a refinement that eludes each succeeding mechanism.

But it was an unwilling chase, and the facts were not really wanted. We can see the introduction of rational trial as the opening of a door which led out into a modern world. At the time, perhaps only a Bracton, already accustomed to thinking in substantive terms, could even have looked out. Had lawyers passed through, willingly exploiting a fact-finding mechanism by putting forward the facts that told in their clients' favour, a modern system would have been instantly required; and perhaps it would have been taken off the Roman peg. But this is the speculation of hindsight. At the time a door was indeed seen to have opened, but it had opened to danger. What first seemed to matter about rational trial was that it was also fallible.

Pleading was not a direct but an indirect response. The pattern of claim and denial was not abandoned by choice, or at all. The defendant still denied at large, and the jury returned an answer as blank as any test of a comprehensive oath. But sometimes it was apparent that the particular facts could mislead them into giving the wrong blank answer. The danger generally arose when everything said on the plaintiff's behalf was true. The tenant in an action in the right who relied upon a grant from the demandant's father had reason for wishing to say so: a blank denial might seem to the knights of the grand assize to deny only the count, namely the seisin of some more remote ancestor. Unless their minds were directed to the grant, they might do injustice by giving the right answer to the wrong question. But it was the usual question in that action. The effect of the special circumstances was to make the usual question misleading.

In the period covered by this book the main development was in the raising of exceptions to novel disseisin and mort d'ancestor, and this is fully explained by Maitland. His first example, taken from Glanvill, is the analogue in mort d'ancestor of that just discussed in terms of a writ of right. Yes, the demandant's ancestor did die seised. Yes, the demandant is his nearest heir. But the assize ought not to

proceed, says the tenant, because the demandant indeed
entered into his inheritance, and then made a grant to the
tenant himself. The question in the writ is unalterable, but
the right answer to it will produce the wrong result. The
question must therefore not be asked; and the exception, a
submission that the assize should not be held at all, is
reasonably named. But the fact upon which it rests must
itself be verified; and the assize is sworn, is turned into a jury,
to answer that instead of the pre-determined question.

The word exception was for a time used in other actions,
and was not inappropriate. The writ did not formulate an
unalterable question; but the only final answer was the old
general denial, and it was this that might have to be avoided
on the same principle. Its application can most easily be seen
in the commonest kind of special plea, the justification in
trespass. Consider a defendant at the very end of the period
covered by this book who was sued for knocking the plaintiff's
house down *vi et armis.* He had knocked it down, and
deliberately: fire had engulfed neighbouring houses, and he
was trying to stop it spreading. He was permitted to plead
his facts specially because of the obvious peril in a bare denial.
But the result of his doing so was to raise, perhaps for the
first time in England, a legal question about the defence of
necessity. It was the raising of such questions that made the
common law.

But they could not be raised at will; and this is the point
of difference from Maitland's account. He thought that the
old denial in effect perished, and that the general issue was in
origin just a variety of exception. The matter is technical and
in itself small; but much turns on it for our understanding of
later development. In the plea rolls the defendant's answer to,
say, an action of trespass is enrolled in some such words as
these: 'The defendant comes and denies force and wrong
when etc. And he says that...'; and then there follows either
the general issue, 'he is not guilty', or a special plea such as
a justification. Maitland took the first sentence to be a fossil
vestige of the old denial, and thought that the second sentence, general issue as much as special plea, was a later
accretion derived from exceptions. On that view, what was
lost in the 'when etc.' with which the first sentence ends was

some reference to the event complained of. But we know from the French formularies, and from the rare zeal of early clerks, that there ought to be an 'etc.' before as well as after the 'when', which refers not to the past event but to the future proof. The unabbreviated sentence actually spoken in court was something more like this: 'The defendant comes and denies force and wrong now and he will deny where and when he ought to do so.' These were the words of court which had to be spoken at every continuance of the action. The defendant keeps alive his denial by offering to make the decisive denial, the one that will be tested, as and when the court declares that he should.

The general issue was in fact, though shortened, the old denial. It was not new, as were special pleas, and was not on the same level with special pleas. This is the point that matters. The pleader could not just choose whether he would plead his facts specially or deny at large. Had he been able to do so, the Year Books would reflect substantive law more directly than they do, and substantive law would have been made more directly than it was. Special pleas would have been freely advanced; demurrers to them would have shown unequivocally what the substantive law was thought to be; and their abandonment, frequent in the Year Books, would at least indicate the same. But the relationship between the pleadings and the law they were making was not so simple. The general issue remained primary. Special pleas could be made only when there was a clear possibility of injustice in the general issue. Discussion of a special plea is not necessarily about its substantive validity. The question is not 'Do these facts exonerate the defendant?' but 'Do they make it perilous to leave the general issue to a jury?' The spirit is still that of the exception. The Year Books are dark because still in the shadow of the old monolithic law-suit.

For the historian this is important in two ways: it affects his information; and it affects what happened. His information from the records of law-suits, both about the law and about life, is unexpectedly oblique: discussion is not about the effect of facts but about the propriety of treating them specially. It is also unexpectedly capricious: that propriety depends not upon their intrinsic importance but upon their capacity for misleading laymen. But for the same reasons, what actually happened, the course of legal development, was also oblique and capricious. The facts locked up in the general issue might be very important. But lawyers could not think about them until they were released; and methods for releasing them, such as the special verdict and the demurrer to evidence, were not regularized for centuries. The best example of both effects is the puzzle about the principles of liability in trespass. The defence of necessity is never very important; yet evidence has been mentioned from 1271. Accident is always important. But it will be more than three hundred years before we get good evidence; and that will be hesitant and amateurish, as though the question was then new. So it was, but not in the simple way that historians have tended to suppose. At first it was locked up in the judgment of God, and could not arise at all. In the king's courts with jury trial it could arise, but would first present itself in procedural terms: special plea or old general issue? Had the former been chosen, lawyers would have worked out an answer to the question that historians insist upon asking. There seems to have been hesitation soon after this book ends; but then the matter was consigned to the general issue. And there it remained until the general issue itself was broken open in the seventeenth century, out of sight for historians, out of mind for lawyers.

V. *A General View.*

So personal an essay as this must end personally. Maitland wrote not about rules and technicalities but about people and ideas, about an achievement. This is what makes his picture vivid and his book great. It has become the foundation of all that we know about the history of the common law, the basis of work on periods long after its own. But he has been followed in his answers, not in his kind of question, not in what may matter most, his sympathy. The rules and technicalities have been treated almost as living things, and few have listened for his Alan and Bernard, his circumspect Roger and blundering Ralph. Listening for them was the source of Maitland's strength, hearing them so consistently his unique gift.

This essay has suggested, not that he misheard, but that sometimes he misunderstood because he did not quite see how the speakers were placed. It is the framework of their discussion that is in issue, their factual and intellectual situation. How far can we understand the terms of a legal proposition, as we think we can today, unless we fix it not only in its society but in its procedural circumstances and in the court to which it was addressed?

Almost it is a question of what time was showing on some universal clock of legal development. If Maitland set his watch by any one source, it was by Bracton. But Bracton's Roman learning, good or bad, may have been chiefly important as vicarious experience enabling him to see with eyes not representative of his own time. Maitland's judgment of him is happily reprinted in the year of his seventh centenary. But it is true as well as trite that five of those seven centuries were to pass before a comparable book was written in England. Even longer on our clock might seem to lie backwards from Bracton to *Brevia Placitata*; but the calendar insists that they were contemporary. It is vain to ask whether the incongruity represents real possibilities, whether English law could have taken a short cut, a straight and Roman road to maturity. What the clerical tradition had actually given it was the opportunity to develop, and it developed in its own devious way. What Bracton did was to describe it, but from a view-point that its practitioners did not share. What the practititioners started from was *Brevia Placitata*.

This is to suppose a difference between Bracton and the practitioners more fundamental than the mere knowledge of some Roman rules, though even to Bracton that would have been the visible difference. It is also to attribute to book learning in legal matters a force greater than that seen by Bracton himself in his *Si insipiens et indoctus cathedram iudicandi ascenderit*, greater than that seen by Maitland himself when he spoke of the toughness of taught law. It is not a matter of knowledge nor of course, though Bracton was a giant, of intelligence or civilization in the obvious sense: it is a question of the terms in which a lawyer thinks. I believe that in some respects Maitland, working as it were backwards from Bracton, supposes too great a degree of general sophistication; and in particular, despite all his care, that he sometimes places highly abstract notions of property too early. For property in land a simpler and more immediate framework has been suggested. But it must be said again that even if Maitland's picture was not true to start with—and here the heretic is most disturbed by his own heresy—it came true; and what emerged from the confusion, if confusion it was, made lasting sense. All this goes to superstructure, to the extent to which we suppose ideas of substantive law to have come into existence. About the procedural substructure, the converse proposition is to be made. In *Brevia Placitata* we should not see the formalism of the later forms of action. It is what happens in court that refines ideas and concepts; but a classification of claims into headings of the same order as our tort and contract is an early and not a late thing. In that classification the boundaries of each heading are neither ours nor Roman, and were settled not by abstract analysis but by jurisdictional and other circumstances. But still they were legal abstractions that could be used in legal argument; and this, I think, Maitland missed.

But if all this is right, and if the modifications required now seem important, they are not important when compared with the original picture. Maitland himself would probably wish his work to be superseded. There is little sign that this will happen soon. When it does, the subject will still be his.

SELECT BIBLIOGRAPHY AND NOTES.

By S. F. C. Milsom.

This bibliography is confined to the field in which *Pollock and Maitland* remains the basis of studies, namely the early history of the common law. Even within that field it is in no way comprehensive.

The first section, which takes the form of lists, is in two parts. Part (1) sets out the main original sources of a strictly legal nature published since the second edition. Part (2) is a selection of studies in current use concerning courts and legal institutions.

The second section sets out in narrative form the main work done on the subjects treated in the second, third and fourth sections of the foregoing essay.

I.

(1) ORIGINAL SOURCES.

(Supplementing the rubrics 'Collections of ancient laws and documents', 'Judicial records', 'Law books' and 'Law reports', in the *List of Texts Used*, pp. xix ff., above)

ANCIENT LAWS AND LAW BOOKS.

Anglo-Saxon laws, etc.:

(a) F. Liebermann, *Die Gesetze des Angelsachsen* (Halle, 1903–1916), 3 vols.

(b) F. L. Attenborough, *The Laws of the Earliest English Kings* (Cambridge Univ. Press, 1922).

(c) A. J. Robertson, *The Laws of the Kings of England from Edmund to Henry I* (Cambridge Univ. Press, 1925).

Bracton:
(a) ed. G. E. Woodbine (Yale Univ. Press, 1915–1942), 4 vols.
(b) S. E. Thorne has an edition in progress, reprinting Woodbine's text but with a translation and other apparatus. It will be published by the Harvard Univ. Press in association with the Selden Society, and the first two volumes are expected shortly.
(c) For Bractonian studies see H. G. Richardson, *Bracton, The Problem of his Text* (Seld. Soc. Supp. Series, vol. 2, 1965), and its bibliography.
Brevia Placitata, ed. G. J. Turner and T. F. T. Plucknett (Seld. Soc., vol. 66 for 1947). See Professor Plucknett's preface for the story of this important volume, and for the reasons why Maitland was able to cite the earlier portions by page.
Casus Placitorum, ed. W. H. Dunham (Seld. Soc. vol. 69 for 1950).
'*Consuetudines Diversarum Curiarum*', ed. H. G. Richardson and G. O. Sayles in *Select Cases of Procedure without Writ under Henry III* (Seld. Soc., vol. 60 for 1941), Appendix II, text at pp. cxcv–cciii.
'*Exceptiones ad Cassandum Brevia*', ed. G. E. Woodbine, in *Four Thirteenth Century Law Tracts* (Yale Univ. Press, 1910).
'*Fer Asaver*', ed. G. E. Woodbine, in *Four Thirteenth Century Law Tracts* (Yale Univ. Press, 1910).
Fleta, ed. H. G. Richardson and G. O. Sayles (Seld. Soc., vol. 72 for 1953), Prologue and Books i and ii; remainder in progress.
Glanvill:
(a) ed. G. E. Woodbine (Yale Univ. Press, 1932); useful notes.
(b) ed. G. D. G. Hall (Nelson, in association with Seld. Soc., 1965); a definitive edition with translation.
Hengham, ed. W. H. Dunham (Cambridge Univ. Press, 1932).
'*Judicium Essoniorum*', ed. G. E. Woodbine, in *Four Thirteenth Century Tracts* (Yale Univ. Press, 1910).
'*Modus Componendi Brevia*', ed. G. E. Woodbine, in *Four Thirteenth Century Tracts* (Yale Univ. Press, 1910).
Novae Narrationes, ed. E. Shanks and S. F. C. Milsom (Seld. Soc., vol. 80 for 1963).
Placita Corone, ed. J. M. Kaye (Seld. Soc. Supp. Series, vol. 4, 1966).

RECORDS OF ROYAL COURTS TO THE LATE THIRTEENTH CENTURY.
Curia Regis Rolls (H.M.S.O., 1922–1961), vols i–xiv; work on further volumes in progress.
'*Curia Regis* Rolls for Hilary 7 Ric. I and Easter 9 Ric. I*', ed. R. Allen Brown, in *Memoranda Roll, 10 John* (Pipe Roll Soc., New Series, vol. xxxi, 1955), pp. 69–118.
Pleas before the King or his Justices, 1198–1212, ed. D. M. Stenton (Seld. Soc., vols 67 for 1948, 68 for 1949, 83 for 1966, 84 for 1967).
Rolls of the Justices in Eyre at Bedford, 1202, ed. G. H. Fowler (Publications of Bedfordshire Historical Record Soc., vol. 1 for 1913), pp. 133–247.

Earliest Lincolnshire Assize Rolls, 1202–1209, ed. D. M. Stenton (Lincoln Record Soc., vol. 22, 1926).

Earliest Northamptonshire Assize Rolls, 1202 and 1203, ed. D. M. Stenton (Northamptonshire Record Soc., vol. 5, 1930).

Rolls of the Justices in Eyre for Lincolnshire, 1218–1219, and Worcestershire, 1221, ed. D. M. Stenton (Seld. Soc. vol. 53 for 1934).

Rolls of the Justices in Eyre for Yorkshire, 1218–1219, ed. D. M. Stenton (Seld. Soc. vol. 56 for 1937).

Rolls of the Justices in Eyre for Gloucestershire, Warwickshire and Staffordshire [Shropshire], 1221, 1222, ed. D. M. Stenton (Seld. Soc., vol. 59 for 1940).

'Two Thirteenth Century Assize Rolls for the County of Durham' (27 and 53 Henry III), ed. K. C. Bayley, in *Miscellanea* (Surtees Soc., vol. 127, 1916), pp. 1–105.

Placita Coram Domino Rege, 1297, ed. W. P. W. Phillimore and E. A. Fry (British Record Soc., 1898).

A Lincolnshire Assize Roll for 1298, ed. W. S. Thomson (Lincoln Record Soc., vol. 36 for 1939).

Three Yorkshire Assize Rolls for the Reigns of King John and King Henry III, ed. C. T. Clay (Yorkshire Archaeological Soc., vol. 44 for 1910); in translation only.

Rolls of the Justices in Eyre at Bedford, 1227, ed. G. H. Fowler (Publications of Bedfordshire Historical Record Soc., vol. 3 for 1916), pp. 1–206; in translation only.

Crown Pleas of the Wiltshire Eyre, 1249, ed. C. A. F. Meekings (Wiltshire Archaeological Soc., Records Branch, vol. xvi for 1960); in translation only.

Select Pleas of the Forest, ed. G. J. Turner (Seld. Soc., vol. 13 for 1899).

Select Cases in the Exchequer of Pleas, ed. H. Jenkinson and B. Formoy (Seld. Soc., vol. 48 for 1931).

Select Cases of Procedure without Writ under Henry III, ed. H. G. Richardson and G. O. Sayles (Seld. Soc., vol. 60 for 1941).

Select Cases in the Court of King's Bench under Edward I, ed. G. O. Sayles (Seld. Soc., vol. 55 for 1936; vol. 57 for 1938; vol. 58 for 1939).

State Trials of Edward I, 1289–1293, ed. T. F. Tout and H. Johnstone (*Camden,* 3rd Ser. vol. ix, Royal Historical Soc., 1906).

RECORDS OF LOCAL COURTS TO THE EARLY FOURTEENTH CENTURY.

Alrewas Court Rolls, 1259–61, 1268–69, 1272–73, ed. W. N. Landor (Wm. Salt Archaeological Soc., New Series, vol. 10, 1907), pp. 245–293; (3rd ser. vol. for 1910), pp. 87–137.

Court Roll of Chalgrave Manor, 1278–1313, ed. M. K. Dale (Bedfordshire Historical Record Soc., vol. 28 for 1948).

Court Rolls of the Manor of Hales, 1270–1307, ed. J. Amphlett, S. G. Hamilton, R. A. Wilson (Worcestershire Historical Soc., Part I, 1910; Part II, 1912; Part III, 1933).

Court Rolls of the Manor of Wakefield, from 1274, ed. W. P. Baildon, J. Lister, J. W. Walker (Yorkshire Archaeological Soc., vol. 29 for

1900; vol. 36 for 1906; vol. 57 for 1917; vol. 78 for 1930; vol. 109 for 1944).

Court Rolls of the Manor of Ingoldmells, ed. W. O. Massingberd (Spottiswoode, 1902).

Court Rolls of the Abbey of Ramsey and of the Honor of Clare, ed. W. O. Ault (Yale Univ. Press, 1928).

'Extracts from Court Book' (St Albans), in A. E. Levett, *Studies in Manorial History* (Oxford Univ. Press, 1938), p. 300.

Records of the Barony and Honour of the Rape of Lewes, ed. A. J. Taylor (Sussex Record Soc., 1940).

Rolls of Highworth Hundred, 1275–1287, ed. B. Farr (Wiltshire Archaeological Soc., vol. xxi for 1965; vol. xxii for 1966.

Rolls from the Office of the Sheriff of Beds. and Bucks, 1332–1334, ed. G. H. Fowler (Bedfordshire Historical Record Soc., quarto memoirs vol. 3, 1929).

'Extracts from Rolls of County Court of Cornwall, 7 Ed. III', in W. A. Morris, *The Early English County Court* (Univ. of California Press, 1926), pp. 181 ff.

Calendar of County Court, City Court and Eyre Rolls of Chester, 1259–1297, ed. R. Stewart-Brown (Chetham Soc., New Series vol. 84, 1925).

Selected Rolls of the Chester City Courts, ed. A. Hopkins (Chetham Soc., 3rd Ser. vol. 2, 1950).

Calendar of Early Mayor's Court Rolls of the City of London, 1298–1307, ed. A. H. Thomas (Cambridge Univ. Press, 1924).

Calendar of Plea and Memoranda Rolls of the City of London, 1323–1364, ed. A. H. Thomas (Cambridge Univ. Press, 1926).

Select Cases on the Law Merchant, vol. i, ed. C. Gross (Seld. Soc., vol. 23 for 1908).

EARLY YEAR BOOKS.

Casus Placitorum, ed. W. H. Dunham (Seld. Soc., vol. 69 for 1950), contains two collections of cases of Year Book type from the early years of Edward I, some twenty years earlier than the earliest Year Books previously known. It contains also, pp. lxxv–lxxxiv, Latin notes under the title *Casus et Judicia*, largely made from plea rolls of 1252–1256; and, pp. lxxxv–lxxxix, extracts from a students' work-book of late Edward I.

Year Books of Edward II. The Selden Society Series, which now runs to twenty-five volumes and is still in progress, was started by Maitland, but not until this book was finished.

(2) INSTITUTIONAL STUDIES.

GENERAL ACCOUNTS.

C. T. Flower, *Introduction to the Curia Regis Rolls, 1199–1230* (Seld Soc., vol. 62 for 1944).

W. S. Holdsworth, *History of English Law*, vol. i (7th ed. 1956), with an introductory essay by S. B. Chrimes; vol. ii (4th ed., 1936).

T. F. T. Plucknett, *Concise History of the Common Law* (5th ed. Butterworth, 1956).

T. F. T. Plucknett, *Legislation of Edward I* (Oxford Univ. Press, 1949).

H. G. Richardson and G. O. Sayles, *The Governance of Medieval England* (Edinburgh Univ. Press, 1963).

H. G. Richardson and G. O. Sayles, *Law and Legislation* (Edinburgh Univ. Press, 1966).

D. M. Stenton, *English Justice between the Norman Conquest and the Great Charter* (American Philosophical Soc. and Allen & Unwin, 1965).

R. C. van Caenegem, *Royal Writs in England from the Conquest to Glanvill* (Seld. Soc., vol. 77 for 1958–1959).

F. J. West, *The Justiciarship in England* (Cambridge Univ. Press, 1966).

LOCAL AND PRIVATE COURTS AND OFFICIALS.

W. O. Ault, *Private Jurisdiction in England* (Yale Univ. Press, 1923).

H. M. Cam, *Studies in the Hundred Rolls* (Oxford Studies in Social and Legal History, vol. VI, Oxford Univ. Press, 1921).

H. M. Cam, *The Hundred and the Hundred Rolls* (Methuen, 1930).

H. M. Cam, *Liberties and Communities in Medieval England* (Cambridge Univ. Press, 1944; reprinted with some corrections, Merlin, 1963). A convenient collection of Dr Cam's major articles down to 1942.

H. M. Cam, *Law-Finders and Law-Makers in Medieval England* (Merlin, 1962). A collection of articles after 1942.

H. M. Cam, 'Shire Officials: Coroners, Constables and Bailiffs', in *The English Government at Work 1327–1336*, vol. III (Medieval Academy of America, 1950).

H. A. Cronne, 'The Office of Local Justiciar in England under the Norman Kings', *University of Birmingham Historical Journal*, VI (1957–58), p. 18.

J. P. Dawson, *A History of Lay Judges* (Harvard Univ. Press, 1960), pp. 178 ff.

N. Denholm-Young, *Seignorial Administration in England* (Oxford Univ. Press, 1937).

J. Goebel, *Felony and Misdemeanour* (Commonwealth Fund, 1937).

R. F. Hunnisett, *The Medieval Coroner* (Cambridge Univ. Press, 1961).

N. D. Hurnard, 'The Anglo-Norman Franchises', *English Historical Review*, LXIV (1949), pp. 289, 433.

G. T. Lapsley, 'Buzones', *English Historical Review*, XLVII (1932), pp. 177, 545; and in *Crown, Community and Parliament* (Blackwell, 1951), p. 63.

G. T. Lapsley, 'The Court, Record and Roll of the County in the Thirteenth Century', *Law Quarterly Review*, 51 (1935), p. 299.

W. A. Morris, *The Frankpledge System* (New York, 1910).

W. A. Morris, *The Early English County Court* (Univ. of California Press, 1926).

W. A. Morris, *The Medieval English Sheriff* (Manchester Univ. Press, 1927).

W. A. Morris, 'The Sheriff', in *The English Government at Work, 1327–1336*, vol. II (Medieval Academy of America, 1947).

H. G. Richardson and G. O. Sayles, *The Governance of Medieval England* (already cited).

H. G. Richardson and G. O. Sayles, *Law and Legislation* (already cited).

EYRES.

W. C. Bolland, *The General Eyre* (Cambridge Univ. Press, 1922).

W. C. Bolland, *The Eyre of Kent* (Seld. Soc., vol. 24 for 1909; vol. 27 for 1912; vol. 29 for 1913).

W. C. Bolland, *Select Bills in Eyre* (Seld. Soc., vol. 30 for 1914). But see below, p. xci, under 'Procedure'.

H. M. Cam, *Studies in the Hundred Rolls* (already cited).

H. M. Cam, 'The Marshalsy of the Eyre' and 'The General Eyres of 1329–30', reprinted in *Liberties and Communities* (already cited).

H. M. Cam: an edition of the Year Books and other sources relating to the eyre of London of 1321 will shortly be published by the Selden Society.

W. T. Reedy, 'The Origins of the General Eyre in the Reign of Henry I', *Speculum*, XLI (1966), p. 688.

H. G. Richardson and G. O. Sayles, *Select Cases of Procedure without Writ* (already cited), pp. xxvi ff.

H. G. Richardson and G. O. Sayles, *The Governance of Medieval England* (already cited).

H. G. Richardson, 'Richard fitzNeal and the Dialogus de Scaccario', *English Historical Review*, XLIII (1928), pp. 161, 321.

D. M. Stenton, *English Justice* (already cited).

D. M. Stenton, introductions to the editions of plea rolls listed under 'Original Sources' above, especially *Pleas before the King or his Justices*, vol. III (Seld. Soc., vol. 83 for 1966), Appendix I.

D. W. Sutherland, *Quo Warranto Proceedings in the Reign of Edward I* (Oxford Univ. Press, 1963).

F. J. West, *The Justiciarship in England* (already cited).

BENCHES AND JUDICIAL ASPECT OF EXCHEQUER.

H. Jenkinson and B. Formoy, *Select Cases in the Exchequer of Pleas* (Seld. Soc. vol. 48 for 1931).

N. Neilson, 'The Court of Common Pleas' in *The English Government at Work, 1327–1336*, vol. III (Medieval Academy of America, 1950), p. 259. There is no study of the Common Bench as such for an earlier period. For a later period see M. Hastings, *The Court of Common Pleas* (Cornell Univ. Press, 1947).

H. G. Richardson, *The Memoranda Roll for the Michaelmas Term of 1 John* (Pipe Roll Soc., New Series, vol. 21, 1943).

H. G. Richardson and G. O. Sayles, *Law and Legislation* (already cited).

G. O. Sayles, *Select Cases in the Court of King's Bench*, vol. I (Seld.

Soc., vol. 55 for 1936), pp. xi ff.; vol. II (Seld. Soc., vol. 57 for 1938), esp. pp. xxxiv ff.; vol. IV (Seld. Soc., vol. 74 for 1955), pp. xxvi ff.

D. M. Stenton, *English Justice* (already cited).

D. M. Stenton, *Pleas before the King or his Justices* (already cited), vols. I and III.

G. J. Turner, *Brevia Placitata* (already cited).

G. J. Turner, *Year Books 3 & 4 Edward II* (Seld. Soc., vol. 22 for 1907), pp. xxi ff.

F. J. West, *The Justiciarship in England* (already cited).

PROFESSION AND LITERATURE (*See also* ANCIENT LAWS AND LAW BOOKS *under* ORIGINAL SOURCES *above*).

H. Cohen, *History of the English Bar* (Sweet & Maxwell, 1929).

W. H. Dunham, *Casus Placitorum* (already cited). The introduction is concerned with the beginnings of reporting and refers to most other work about the origins of the Year Books.

W. S. Holdsworth, *History of English Law*, vol. II (4th ed. Methuen, 1936).

W. S. Holdsworth, *Sources and Literature of English Law* (Oxford Univ. Press, 1925).

S. F. C. Milsom, introduction to *Novae Narrationes* (already cited), pp. xxv ff.

T. F. T. Plucknett, *Early English Legal Literature* (Cambridge Univ. Press, 1958).

T. F. T. Plucknett, *The Medieval Bailiff* (Athlone Press, 1954), pp. 14–16.

G. O. Sayles, *Select Cases in the Court of King's Bench* (already cited), vol. I, esp. pp. xci ff.; vol. V, esp. pp. xxix ff.; vol. VI, esp. pp. xxvii ff.

D. M. Stenton, *English Justice* (already cited), esp. pp. 54 ff.

D. M. Stenton, *Pleas before the King or his Justices* (already cited), vol. III, pp. ccxcv ff.

S. E. Thorne, 'The Early History of the Inns of Court', *Graya*, 50 (1959), p. 79.

G. J. Turner, *Year Books 3 & 4 Edward II* (already cited), pp. xv ff., xli ff.

G. J. Turner, *Year Books 4 Edward II* (Seld. Soc., vol. 42 for 1925), pp. lvi ff.

P. H. Winfield, *The Chief Sources of English Legal History* (Harvard Univ. Press, 1925).

G. E. Woodbine, *Glanvill* (already cited), pp. 262 ff.

CRIMINAL ADMINISTRATION AND LAW (*See also* LOCAL AND PRIVATE COURTS etc., *above*).

E. de Haas, *Antiquities of Bail* (Columbia Univ. Press, 1940).

A. Harding, 'The Origins and Early History of the Keeper of the Peace', *Transactions of the Royal Historical Society*, 5th Ser. 10 (1960), p. 85. For the later development of the justices of the peace, the starting-point is B. H. Putnam, *Proceedings before the Justices of the Peace in the Fourteenth and Fifteenth Centuries* (Ames Foundation, 1938).

L. C. Gabel, *Benefit of Clergy in England in the later Middle Ages* (Smith College Studies in History, 1928–1929).

J. Goebel, *Felony and Misdemeanour* (already cited).

W. S. Holdsworth, *History of English Law* (already cited), vol. ii, pp. 43 ff.; vol. iii, pp. 276 ff.

R. F. Hunnisett, *The Medieval Coroner* (already cited).

N. D. Hurnard, 'The Jury of Presentment and the Assize of Clarendon', *English Historical Review*, lvi (1941), p. 374.

J. M. Kaye, *Placita Corone* (already cited).

C. A. F. Meekings, *Crown Pleas of the Wiltshire Eyre* (already cited).

T. F. T. Plucknett, *Edward I and Criminal Law* (Cambridge Univ. Press, 1960).

H. G. Richardson and G. O. Sayles, *The Governance of Medieval England* (already cited).

H. G. Richardson and G. O. Sayles, *Law and Legislation* (already cited).

G. O. Sayles, *Select Cases in the Court of King's Bench* (already cited), vol. ii, pp. xxxv ff.; vol. iii, pp. liv ff., lxxii ff., lxxvi ff.; vol. iv, pp. xxxv ff.

D. M. Stenton, *English Justice* (already cited).

D. M. Stenton, *Rolls of the Justices in Eyre for Lincolnshire and Worcestershire* (already cited), pp. lxix ff.

D. M. Stenton, *Rolls of the Justices in Eyre for Yorkshire* (already cited), pp. xl ff.

D. M. Stenton, *Rolls of the Justices in Eyre for Gloucestershire, Warwickshire and Staffordshire* (already cited), pp. lviii ff.

JURY PROCEEDINGS. (*The following references are in addition to those listed under* CRIMINAL ADMINISTRATION AND LAW, *above, and* THE REAL ACTIONS, *below.*)

C. T. Flower, *Introduction to the Curia Regis Rolls* (already cited).

W. S. Holdsworth, *History of English Law* (already cited), vol. i.

R. Lennard, 'Early Manorial Juries', *English Historical Review*, lxxvii (1962), p. 511.

T. F. T. Plucknett, *Concise History of the Common Law* (already cited), pp. 106 ff. The account of the jury was largely re-written for the 5th edition.

R. C. van Caenegem, *Royal Writs in England* (already cited).

LEGISLATION (*See also* ANCIENT LAWS AND LAW BOOKS, *above*).

J. C. Holt, *Magna Carta* (Cambridge Univ. Press, 1965).

T. F. T. Plucknett, *The Legislation of Edward I* (already cited).

T. F. T. Plucknett, *Statutes and their Interpretation in the First Half of the Fourteenth Century* (Cambridge Univ. Press, 1922).

H. G. Richardson and G. O. Sayles, 'The Early Statutes', *Law Quarterly Review*, 50 (1934), pp. 201, 540 (reprinted Stevens, 1934).

H. G. Richardson and G. O. Sayles, *The Governance of Medieval England* (already cited).

H. G. Richardson and G. O. Sayles, *Law and Legislation* (already cited).

G. O. Sayles, *Select Cases in the Court of King's Bench* (already cited), vol. III, pp. xi ff.

ECCLESIASTICAL JURISDICTION.

N. Adams, 'The Writ of Prohibition to Court Christian', *Minnesota Law Review*, 20 (1935–1936), p. 272.

N. Adams, 'The Judicial Conflict over Tithes', *English Historical Review*, LII (1937), p. 1.

N. Adams is working on a volume of cases in ecclesiastical courts, to be published by the Selden Society.

C. R. Cheney, 'The Punishment of Felonous Clerks', *English Historical Review*, LI (1936), p. 215.

G. B. Flahiff, 'The Use of Prohibitions by Clerics against Ecclesiastical Courts in England', *Mediaeval Studies* (Pontifical Institute of Toronto), iii (1941), p. 101.

G. B. Flahiff, 'The Writ of Prohibition to Court Christian in the Thirteenth Century', *Mediaeval Studies* (Pontifical Institute of Toronto), iv (1944), p. 261; vii (1945), p. 229.

C. T. Flower, *Introduction to the Curia Regis Rolls* (already cited), pp. 99 ff.

L. C. Gabel, *Benefit of Clergy in the Later Middle Ages* (already cited).

E. B. Graves, 'Circumspecte Agatis', *English Historical Review*, XLIII (1928), p. 1.

J. W. Gray, 'The *Ius Praesentandi* in England from the Constitutions of Clarendon to Bracton', *English Historical Review*, LXVII (1952), p. 481.

E. G. Kimball, 'The Judicial Aspects of Frank Almoign Tenure', *English Historical Review*, XLVII (1932), p. 1.

F. D. Logan, *Excommunication and the Secular Arm in Medieval England* (Pontifical Institute of Toronto, 1968).

S. F. C. Milsom in *Novae Narrationes* (already cited), pp. cxcviii ff.

M. M. Morgan, 'Early Canterbury Jurisdiction', *English Historical Review*, LX (1945), p. 392.

C. Morris, 'William I and the Church Courts', *English Historical Review*, LXXXII (1967), p. 449.

H. G. Richardson and G. O. Sayles, *The Governance of Medieval England* (already cited).

H. G. Richardson and G. O. Sayles, *Law and Legislation* (already cited).

G. O. Sayles, *Select Cases in the Court of King's Bench* (already cited), vol. III, p. lxxiv.

M. M. Sheehan, *The Will in Medieval England* (Pontifical Institute of Toronto, 1963).

S. E. Thorne, 'The Assize Utrum and Canon Law in England', *Columbia Law Review*, 33 (1933), p. 426.

B. L. Woodcock, *Medieval Ecclesiastical Courts in the Diocese of Canterbury* (Oxford Univ. Press, 1952).

II.

(1) THE REAL ACTIONS.

GENERAL AND BACKGROUND DISCUSSIONS.

General accounts published since Maitland's are: W. S. Holdsworth, *History of English Law* vol. III (Methuen, 5th ed. 1942); W. S. Holdsworth, *Historical Introduction to the Land Law* (Oxford Univ. Press, 1927); A. W. B. Simpson, *An Introduction to the History of the Land Law* (Oxford Univ. Press, 1961), replacing the last-named; and T. F. T. Plucknett, *Concise History of the Common Law* (5th ed., Butterworth, 1956). T. F. T. Plucknett, *Legislation of Edward I* (already cited) is also relevant at many points.

Any work touching the institutional, social or economic history of the period almost inevitably touches upon these matters. For the feudal background M. Bloch, *Feudal Society* (English ed. Routledge and Kegan Paul, 1961), and F. L. Ganshof, *Feudalism* (English ed. Longmans, Green, 1952) are important. For general studies of the factual background, the following seem specially illuminating: R. Lennard, *Rural England, 1086–1135* (Oxford Univ. Press, 1959); G. C. Homans, *English Villagers of the Thirteenth Century* (Harvard Univ. Press, 1941); E. A. Kosminsky, *Studies in the Agrarian History of England in the Thirteenth Century* (English ed. Blackwell, 1956); Levett, *Studies in Manorial History* (Oxford Univ. Press, 1938); H. S. Bennett, *Life on the English Manor* (Cambridge Univ. Press, 1937). Tenurial and related studies from various view-points include: Sir Frank Stenton, *The First Century of English Feudalism* (Ford Lectures, 1929; Oxford Univ. Press, 2nd ed. 1961); S. Painter, *Studies in the History of the English Feudal Barony* (Johns Hopkins Univ. Studies in Historical and Political Science, Series LXI, no. 3, 1943); D. C. Douglas, *The Social Structure of Medieval East Anglia* (Oxford Studies in Social and Legal History, vol. IX, Oxford Univ. Press, 1927); A. L. Poole, *Obligations of Society* (Oxford Univ. Press, 1946). N. Denholm-Joung, *Seignorial Administration in England* (Oxford Univ. Press, 1937); H. M. Chew, *Ecclesiastical Tenants in Chief and Knight-Service* (Oxford Univ. Press, 1932); E. G. Kimball, *Serjeanty Tenure in Medieval England* (Yale Univ. Press, 1936); W. O. Ault, *Private Jurisdiction in England* (Yale Univ. Press, 1923). There are also, of course, many studies of individual lordships. A recent study of Anglo-Saxon land holding, disputing received views, is E. John, *Land Tenure in Early England* (Leicester Univ. Press, 1964).

BACKGROUND TO THE ACTIONS.

Turning to the specific matters discussed in the essay, Maitland's picture of the development of the actions has been followed in its general outline. Even those who have been most concerned to show that he was too Roman in his thought have assumed that 'the right' and 'seisin', however closely related to each other and however different from *dominium* and *possessio*, were none the less concepts of the same order, somehow less abstract but still existing *in rem*. Concomitantly, the actions have all been seen to start from some archetype of the writ of right, into the scope of which the lesser remedies progressively encroached. For the suggestions made, therefore, which go to a different framework of thought, the only modern works that can be quoted are those which, while not addressing themselves to these questions at all, see a world in which seignorial control and jurisdiction are so dominant that the purely abstract concepts seem inappropriate. The most striking is Sir Frank Stenton's *The First Century of English Feudalism* (already cited), in which he expresses the belief that the king's courts must have owed much to the honour courts; but of course he was not concerned in any way with the terms of legal thinking. The chief attempt to accommodate strictly legal phenomena and ideas to the feudal framework is S. E. Thorne's important and controversial lecture 'English Feudalism and Estates in Land', [1959] *Cambridge Law Journal*, p. 193. The conclusion reached, about the late establishment of heritability, has been seen as raising difficulties. On this question see Simpson, *History of the Land Law* (already cited), pp. 46 ff.; R. H. C. Davis, 'What Happened in Stephen's Reign', *History*, XLIX (1964), pp. 1 ff. But Professor Thorne's lecture seeks only to work out in detail what must in principle have happened to produce the common law scheme of estates; and though again he cannot be quoted in support of the concept of 'the right' proposed in the foregoing essay, he does indeed consider the difficulties until a late date in attributing anything like 'ownership' to a tenant. The essay has suggested that an important step in the evolution of such a concept was that from heritability to alienability. For the mechanics of this, and for much else, reference should be made to S. J. Bailey, 'Warranties of Land in the Thirteenth Century', *Cambridge Law Journal*, 8 (1944), p. 274, *ibid.* 9 (1945), p. 82 and 'Warranties of Land in the Reign of Richard I', *ibid.* 9 (1946), p. 192.

WRIT OF RIGHT.

For the early history of the writ of right itself see *Royal Writs in England from the Conquest to Glanvill*, ed. R. C. van Caenegem (Seld. Soc. vol. 77 for 1958–1959), esp. pp. 206 ff. It may be appropriate to mention here that Professor van Caenegem is now editing for the Selden Society a comprehensive collection to replace Bigelow's *Placita Anglo-Normannica*; we shall know more about this and many other matters when that great task is completed. See also D. M. Stenton, *English Justice* (already cited) esp. pp. 26 ff. For the grand assize and the writ of peace see J. H. Round, 'The Date of the Grand Assize', *English Historical Review*, XXXI (1916), p. 268; H. G. Richardson, 'Glanville Continued', *Law Quarterly Review*, 54 (1938), p. 381, esp. pp. 384 ff.; H. G. Richardson and G. O. Sayles, *Law and Legislation* (Edinburgh Univ. Press, 1966), pp. 110 ff. For the nature of the difficulty over the writ *praecipe* see N. D. Hurnard, 'Magna Carta, Clause 34', in *Studies in Medieval History Presented to F. M. Powicke* (Oxford Univ. Press, 1948), p. 157; M. T. Clanchy, 'Magna

Carta, Clause Thirty-Four', *English Historical Review*, LXXIX (1964), p. 542. For the formalities in court on a writ of right see G. J. Turner in *Brevia Placitata* (Seld. Soc., vol. 66 for 1947), pp. lxix ff., lxxxv ff.; S. F. C. Milsom in *Novae Narrationes* (Seld. Soc., vol. 80 for 1963), pp. xxxi ff. The phrase *vestu e seysi* appears in the precedents in *Brevia Placitata*. See also *Casus Placitorum*, ed. W. H. Dunham (Seld. Soc., vol. 69 for 1950), p. 20/87; '*Consuetudines Diversarum Curiarum*' in *Select Cases of Procedure without Writ*, ed. H. G. Richardson and G. O. Sayles (Seld. Soc., vol. 60 for 1941), p. cxcv, at p. cc. If the phrase is indeed significant, Maitland may have been led to disregard it by one of his rare slips, apparently a misreading of his own work: in vol. II, p. 33, n. 1, is a reference to a thief 'vested and seised' of stolen goods; the case is *Bracton's Note Book*, p. 1539, and *Curia Regis Rolls*, vol. X, p. 105.

MORT D'ANCESTOR.

For the assize of mort d'ancestor see van Caenegem, *Royal Writs in England* (already cited), pp. 316 ff.; D. M. Stenton, *English Justice* (already cited), pp. 43 ff. Both writers emphasize the initial orientation of the assize as an interference between lord and tenant.

SEISIN AND NOVEL DISSEISIN.

On seisin and novel disseisin the principal literature, in chronological order, is: F. Joüon des Longrais, *La conception anglaise de la saisine* (Paris, 1924), reviewed by T. F. T. Plucknett in *Harvard Law Review*, 40 (1926–1927), p. 921; G. E. Woodbine in his edition of *Glanvill*, pp. 281 ff.; F. Joüon des Longrais, 'La portée politique des réformes d'Henry II en matière de saisine', *Revue historique de droit*, 4ᵉ serie, xv (1936), p. 540; S. E. Thorne, 'Livery of Seisin', *Law Quarterly Review*, 52 (1936), p. 345; H. G. Richardson and G. O. Sayles in *Select Cases of Procedure without Writ* (already cited), pp. cxxviii ff.; N. D. Hurnard, 'Did Edward I reverse Henry II's Policy upon Seisin?', *English Historical Review*, LXIX (1954), p. 529; R. C. van Caenegem, *Royal Writs in England* (already cited); a review by G. D. G. Hall in *English Historical Review*, LXXVI, p. 317; F. Joüon des Longrais, *Henry II and his Justiciars had they a Political Plan in their Reforms about Seisin?* (Limoges, 1962); D. M. Stenton, *English Justice* (already cited), pp. 23 ff., 33 ff.; G. D. G. Hall in his edition of *Glanvill*, p. 192; H. G. Richardson and G. O. Sayles, *Law and Legislation* (already cited), pp. 81 ff., 95, 112 ff. Royal orders for seisin and disseisin have also been considered in a quite different context by, e.g. J. E. A. Jolliffe, *Angevin Kingship* (A. & C. Black, 1955).

Any summary of the views of these writers could only lose the subtlety of thought involved; but the principal issues seem to be the following:

First, the suggestion that the legislation from which the assize immediately sprang was 'criminal' rather than 'civil' in emphasis has not been widely accepted. The direct evidence is small in quantity but telling; and it is congruous with Glanvill's account.

Secondly there is the question of the policy behind the assizes. Some have seen it as 'anti-feudal' in the sense of being directly aimed to enlarge royal jurisdiction. Others are content to think in terms of public order and good government. The suggestion made in the essay would see it as 'anti-feudal', not because of any jurisdictional scheming but in the sense of being directed against improper 'feudal' action; but also as intensely 'feudal' in that it was intended to compel that due process upon which the whole structure was thought to rest.

Thirdly, there is disagreement about the part played by civilian learning. The possibility of general influence must remain, although Maitland's specific canonist ancestry for novel disseisin has been rendered inadmissible by chronology. It would have accounted for *iniuste et sine iudicio*. Such phrases have been described as 'the small change of the legist'; but *sine iudicio* at least suggests authoritative action.

Fourthly, and most intractably, there are the conceptual problems. Everybody agrees that Roman ideas of *dominium* and *possessio* do not fit the English facts; and indeed those ideas may have been attributed too whole-heartedly to Maitland. Even the developed English 'right', although it is hard to deny it some of the properties of 'ownership', differs in obvious and important respects from *dominium* and could be defined only in terms of seisin. Beyond that it is not easy to see how far consensus goes. Most writers think that the establishment of the assize was responsible for a contrast between the right and seisin to which the language of possessory was not wholly inappropriate; and that this, the purely factual content of an assize verdict, and the use of Roman language all came together to turn seisin into something very like *possessio*. They think difficulties have arisen from a confusion between this and an earlier sense of seisin, which was an undifferentiated 'seisin-right'. But the nature of this earlier concept is not altogether clear. If there is law and the possibility of litigation, there must be ways of describing the position of the one who has the subject-matter and the one who thinks he has a better right to it. And if for example orders for reseisin could contemplate a subsequent adjudication of claims, it is hard to believe that some distinction like that between seisin and the right was not grasped. This seems to be the point at which Professor van Caenegem differs from the view, which in general terms he endorses, that the starting-point was a single idea. Although the undifferentiated seisin-right is presented in highly concrete terms, very much a relation between a person and a thing, the essay suggests that difficulty still arises from too abstract a mode of thought: the relationship between the person and the thing is seen to be or to generate a right *in vacuo* and existing against the world. In the feudal framework the lord who seises you is also the law that protects you; and against that background one could indeed suppose an undifferentiated idea to start with. On this view differentiation would mainly begin from the growth of the right to inherit, a claim that the lord should seise you; and the important jurisdictional event would be compulsion upon the lord to deal justly with this claim. On this view too the main consequence of the assize, of the Roman analogy, and of growing royal jurisdiction would be to make both seisin and the right appear to be things existing *in rem*; and this, combining with alienability at will, produced the idea that land was an object of property in more or less modern terms.

On the thirteenth century use and extension of novel disseisin, see Plucknett, *Legislation of Edward I* (already cited), pp. 85 ff. For an interesting example see D. W. Sutherland, 'Peytevin *v.* La Lynde', *Law Quarterly Review*, 83 (1967), p. 527.

WRITS OF ENTRY.

Individual writs of entry have attracted attention, mostly at a later period; and some attempt has been made to see how 'the degrees' worked out in practice. For this see S. F. C. Milsom in *Novae Narrationes* (already cited), pp. cxxxii ff. For the thirteenth-century relationship between writs of entry and writs of right see G. J. Turner in *Brevia Placitata* (already cited), pp. lxxvii ff. On the original place of the writs of entry in relation to other remedies see D. M. Stenton, *English Justice* (already cited), pp. 50 ff.; N. D. Hurnard, 'Did Edward I Reverse Henry II's Policy upon Seisin?' *loc. cit.*, p. 529.

OTHER ACTIONS.

For other actions concerning land, services, etc., see C. T. Flower, *Introduction to the Curia Regis Rolls* (already cited) and the introductions to *Brevia Placitata* and *Novae Narrationes* (both already cited). On formedon and the rise of the entail generally see: S. J. Bailey, 'Warranties of Land in the Thirteenth Century', *Cambridge Law Journal*, 9 (1945), pp. 91 ff., and 'The Countess Gundred's Lands', *ibid.* 10 (1948), p. 84; W. H. Humphreys, 'Formedon en Remainder at Common Law', *ibid.* 7 (1940), p. 238; T. F. T. Plucknett, *Legislation of Edward I* (already cited), pp. 125 ff.; S. F. C. Milsom, 'Formedon before *De Donis*', *Law Quarterly Review*, 72 (1956), p. 391; J. Updegraff, 'The Interpretation of Issue in *De Donis*', *Harvard Law Review*, 39 (1935), p. 200. On the relationship between maritagium and curtesy and on curtesy generally see G. L. Haskins, 'Curtesy at Common Law', *Boston University Law Review*, 29 (1949), p. 228; on dower generally see G. L. Haskins, 'The Development of Common Law Dower', *Harvard Law Review*, 62 (1948), p. 42; M. M. Sheehan, 'The Influence of Canon Law on the Property Rights of Married Women in England', *Mediaeval Studies* (Pontifical Institute of Toronto), xxv (1963), p. 109.

(2) THE PERSONAL ACTIONS

GENERAL ACCOUNTS.

Maitland's account in this book is supplemented by his posthumously published lectures on *The Forms of Action at Common Law* (first published with his lectures on *Equity*, Cambridge Univ. Press, 1909; published separately, Cambridge Univ. Press, 1936). Besides the general books, especially W. S. Holdsworth, *History of English*

Law (already cited), vol. III, and T. F. T. Plucknett, *Concise History of the Common Law* (already cited), the principal accounts since published are: C. H. S. Fifoot, *History and Sources of the Common Law: Tort and Contract* (Stevens, 1949); J. B. Ames, *Lectures in Legal History* (Harvard Univ. Press, 1913). Some of the material in the last-named was known to Maitland; and this is true also of much of the work gathered in *Select Essays in Anglo-American Legal History* (Little, Brown, 1907–1909), 3 vols.

PERSONAL ACTIONS IN LOCAL COURTS.

Since the essay stresses the importance of what was happening in local courts, so largely neglected since Maitland's day, it is right to draw attention to his own introduction to the rolls of the Bishop of Ely's court at Littleport in *The Court Baron* (Seld. Soc. vol. 4 for 1890), pp. 107 ff., esp. at pp. 115–118. He did not himself have time to follow up the thoughts there set out; and it is possible that the posthumous publication of *The Forms of Action* did something to obscure his own thought by giving too definitive a form to an exercise in simplification. So far as contract is concerned, the only general attempt since to consider what was happening in local courts is R. L. Henry, *Contracts in the Local Courts of Medieval England* (Longmans, Green, 1926). Much valuable material is collected in the two volumes of *Borough Customs*, ed. Mary Bateson (Seld. Soc. vols. 18 for 1904 and 21 for 1906), and in the first volume of *Select Cases Concerning the Law Merchant*, ed. C. Gross (Seld. Soc. vol. 23 for 1908). Particularly illuminating also are the London materials in *Calendar of Early Mayor's Rolls of the City of London, 1298–1307*, ed. A. H. Thomas (Cambridge Univ. Press, 1924) and in the successive *Calendars of Plea and Memoranda Rolls of the City of London* from 1323 on, the volumes for the years to 1437 being edited by A. H. Thomas, for subsequent years by P. E. Jones (Cambridge Univ. Press, 1926–1961).

CONTRACT IN ROYAL COURTS

Work on contract in the royal courts has mostly been concerned with the later story of the development of *assumpsit*, and the earlier actions have been subjected to little new scrutiny. The main exception is the action of account, not discussed in the essay. On this see T. F. T. Plucknett, *The Medieval Bailiff* (Creighton Lecture for 1953, Athlone Press, 1954), and *Legislation of Edward I* (Ford Lectures for 1947, Oxford Univ. Press, 1949), pp. 150 ff. A recent discussion with references to other literature is S. J. Stoljar, 'The Transformations of Account', *Law Quarterly Review*, 80 (1964), p. 203. Account and debt are both treated in R. M. Jackson, *The History of Quasi-Contract* (Cambridge Univ. Press, 1936). A survey of the early actions in general form the first part of W. T. Barbour, *The History of Contract in Early English Equity* (vol. IV of Oxford Studies in Social and Legal History, Oxford Univ. Press, 1914). The early writs are treated in R. C. van Caenegem, *Royal Writs in England* (already cited), pp. 254 ff. for debt, pp. 345 ff. for account. Although mainly concerned with later periods, there are relevant matters in A. W. B. Simpson, 'The Penal Bond with Conditional Defeasance', *Law Quarterly Review*, 82 (1966), p. 392; S. F. C. Milsom, 'Sale of Goods in the Fifteenth Century', *ibid.* 77 (1961), p. 257, and 'Account Stated in the Action of Debt', *ibid.* 82 (1966), p. 534. The language and concepts of both covenant and trespass are considered in S. F. C. Milsom, 'Reason in the Development of the Common Law', *Law Quarterly Review* 81 (1965), p. 496.

TRESPASS.

On the origins and development of trespass and case, which on the view taken in the essay should be considered together, there is a substantial literature: G. E. Woodbine, 'The Origins of the Action of Trespass', *Yale Law Journal*, 33 (1924), p. 799, and *ibid.* 34 (1925), p. 343; T. F. T. Plucknett, 'Case and the Statute of Westminster II', *Columbia Law Review*, 31 (1931), p. 778, commented upon by W. S. Holdsworth in *Law Quarterly Review*, 47 (1931), p. 334; P. A. Landon, 'Action on the Case and the Statute of Westminster II', *ibid.* 52 (1936), p. 68; T. F. T. Plucknett, 'Case and Westminster II', *ibid.* 52 (1936), p. 220; E. J. Dix, 'Origins of Trespass on the Case', *Yale Law Journal*, 46 (1937), p. 1142; *Select Cases of Procedure without Writ*, ed. H. G. Richardson and G. O. Sayles (already cited), pp. cviii ff.; A. K. R. Kiralfy, *The Action on the Case* (Sweet and Maxwell, 1951); S. F. C. Milsom, 'Not Doing is no Trespass', [1954] *Cambridge Law Journal*, p. 105; *Select Cases in the Court of King's Bench*, ed. G. O. Sayles, vol. IV (Seld. Soc., vol. 74 for 1955), pp. xxxvi ff., p. lxxi, n.; T. F. T. Plucknett, *Concise History of the Common Law* (5th ed. already cited), pp. 369 ff.; G. D. G. Hall, 'Some Early Writs of "Trespass"', *Law Quarterly Review*, 73 (1957), p. 65; S. F. C. Milsom, 'Trespass from Henry III to Edward III', *ibid.* 74 (1958), pp. 195, 407, 561. These discussions will not be summarized, but the principal issues raised are as follows: Assuming that trespass *vi et armis* was always a distinct entity, did it come from appeals of felony, novel disseisin, or from procedures in local courts, and did Roman law play any part in its development? Assuming that case was an entity derived from trespass *vi et armis*, was it through the *in consimili casu* clause of the Statute of Westminster II or in some other way? In either case, what part was played by proceedings by bill? And, lastly, was either trespass or case the entity supposed?

(3) PROCEDURE.

GENERAL ACCOUNTS.

For general accounts since Maitland's see W. S. Holdsworth, *History of English Law*, vol. III; T. F. T. Plucknett, *Concise History of the Common Law*, 5th ed.; and C. T. Flower, *Introduction to the Curia Regis Rolls*, pp. 335 ff. (all three already cited).

WRIT AND PLAINT.

On the evolution of writs concerning judicial procedure see *Royal Writs in England,* ed. R. C. van Caenegem; D. M. Stenton, *English Justice;* and *Brevia Placitata,* ed. G. J. Turner (all three already cited). See also G. O. Sayles in *Select Cases in Court of King's Bench,* vol. v (Seld. Soc., vol. 76 for 1957), pp. lxvii ff. The Selden Society will soon publish some early registers edited by E. de Haas and G. D. G. Hall.

On procedure by bill or plaint see *Select Bills in Eyre,* ed. W. C. Bolland (Seld. Soc., vol. 30 for 1914); E. F. Jacob, *Studies in the Period of Baronial Reform* (Oxford Studies in Social and Legal History, vol. VIII, Oxford Univ. Press, 1925); *Select Cases of Procedure without Writ,* ed. H. G. Richardson and G. O. Sayles (already cited); *Select Cases in the Court of King's Bench,* ed. G. O. Sayles, vol. IV (already cited), pp. lxvii ff.

PROCEDURE AND PLEADING.

See, generally, C. Johnson, 'Notes on Thirteenth Century Judicial Procedure', *English Historical Review,* LXII (1947), p. 508; D. W. Sutherland, 'Mesne Process upon Personal Actions in the Early Common Law", *Law Quarterly Review,* 82 (1966), p. 482; G. O. Sayles in *Select Cases in the Court of King's Bench,* vol. II (Seld. Soc., vol. 57 for 1938), pp. lxxiii ff.

For the rise of inquest procedure itself, see under 'Institutional Studies', sub-heading 'Jury' in Section I of this bibliography. There has been no extended study of the growth of exceptions and other special pleas, although much material is now in print. For the forms of count and defence see *Brevia Placitata* and *Novae Narrationes* (both already cited). For the changing pattern of litigation and the place of the general issue, see the introduction to *Novae Narrationes,* pp. xxv ff., xxxiv ff. For an attempt to examine the significance of the change, see S. F. C. Milsom, 'Law and Fact in Legal Development', *Toronto Law Journal,* XVII (1967), p. 1.

INTRODUCTION.

IN the First of the two Books into which our work is divided we have endeavoured to draw a slight sketch, which becomes somewhat fuller as time goes on, of the general outlines of that part of English legal history which lies on the other side of the accession of Edward I. In the Second Book we have tried to set forth at some length the doctrines and rules of English law which prevailed in the days of Glanvill and the days of Bracton, or, in other words, under Henry II., his sons and grandson. The chapters of our First Book are allotted to various periods of history, those of the Second to various branches of law. In a short Introduction we hope to explain why we have been guilty of what may be regarded as certain offences, more especially certain offences of omission.

It has been usual for writers commencing the exposition of any particular system of law to undertake, to a greater or less extent, philosophical discussion of the nature of laws in general, and definition of the most general notions of jurisprudence. We purposely refrain from any such undertaking. The philosophical analysis and definition of law belongs, in our judgment, neither to the historical nor to the dogmatic science of law, but to the theoretical part of politics. A philosopher who is duly willing to learn from lawyers the things of their own art is full as likely to handle the topic with good effect as a lawyer, even if that lawyer is acquainted with philosophy, and has used all due diligence in consulting philosophers. The matter of legal science is not an ideal result of ethical or political analysis; it is the actual result of facts of human nature and history. Common knowledge assures us that in every tolerably settled community there are rules by which men are expected to order their conduct. Some of these rules are not expressed in any authentic form, nor declared with authority by any person or body distinct from the community at large, nor enforced by any power constituted for that purpose. Others are declared by some person or body having permanently, or for the time being, public authority for that purpose, and, when so declared, are conceived as binding the members of the community in a special manner. In civilized states there are officers charged with the duty and furnished with the means of enforcing them. Of the former kind are the common rules of morals and manners, in so far as they do not coincide with rules of law. We shall find that in England, as elsewhere, and in times which must be called recent as compared with the known history of ancient civilization, many things were left to the rule of social custom, if not to private caprice or uncontrolled private force, which are now, as a matter of course, regulated by legislation, and controlled by courts of justice. By gradual steps, as singularly alike in the main in different lands and periods, at the corresponding stages of advance, as they have differed in detail, public authority has drawn to itself more and more causes and matters out of the domain of mere usage and morals; and, where several forms of public authority have been in competition (as notably, in the history of Christendom, the Church has striven with secular princes and rulers to enlarge her jurisdiction at their expense), we find that some one form has generally prevailed, and reigns without serious rivalry. Thus, in every civilized Commonwealth we expect to find courts of justice open to common resort, where judges and magistrates appointed in a regular course by the supreme governors of the Commonwealth, or, at least, with their allowance and authority, declare and administer those rules of which the State professes to compel the observance. Moreover, we expect to find regularly appointed means of putting in force the judgments and orders of the courts, and of overcoming resistance to them, at need, by the use of all or any part of the physical power at the disposal of the State. Lastly, we expect to find not only that the citizen may use the means of redress provided and allowed by public justice, but that he may not use others. Save in cases particularly excepted, the man who takes the law into his own hands puts himself in the wrong, and offends the community. "The law is open, and there are deputies; let them implead one another." Such are for the citizen, the lawyer, and the historian, the practical elements of law. When a man is acquainted with the rules which the judges of the land will apply to any subject of dispute between citizens, or to any act complained of as an offence against the common weal, and is further acquainted with the manner in which the decision of the competent court can be enforced, he must be said to know the law to that extent. He may or may not have opinions upon the metaphysical analysis of laws or legal duty in general, or the place of the topic in hand in a scientific arrangement of legal ideas. Law, such as we know it in the conduct of life, is matter of fact; not a thing which can be seen or handled, but a thing perceived in many ways of practical experience. Commonly there is no difficulty in recognizing it by its accustomed signs and works. In the exceptional cases where difficulties are found, it is not known that metaphysical definition has ever been of much avail.

It may be well to guard ourselves on one or two points. We have said that law may be taken for every purpose, save that of strictly philosophical inquiry, to be the sum of the rules administered by courts of justice. We have not said that it must be, or that it always is, a sum of uniform and consistent rules (as uniform and consistent, that is, as human fallibility and the inherent difficulties of human affairs permit) administered under one and the same system. This would, perhaps, be the statement of an ideal which the modern history of law tends to realize rather than of a result yet fully accomplished in any nation. Certainly it would not be correct as regards the state of English legal institutions, not only in modern but in quite recent times. Different and more or less conflicting systems of law, different and more or less competing systems of jurisdiction, in one and the same region, are compatible with a high state of civilization, with a strong government, and with an administration of justice well enough liked and sufficiently understood by those who are concerned.

Another point on which confusion is natural and may be dangerous is the relation of law to morality. Legal rules are not merely that part of the moral rules existing in a given society which the State thinks proper to enforce. It is easily recognized that there are, and must be, rules of morality beyond the commandments of law; no less is it true, though

less commonly recognized, that there are and must be rules of
law beyond or outside the direct precepts of morality. There
are many things for which it is needful or highly convenient to
have a fixed rule, and comparatively or even wholly indifferent
what that rule shall be. When, indeed, the rule is fixed by
custom or law, then morality approves and enjoins obedience to
it. But the rule itself is not a moral rule. In England men
drive on the left-hand side of the road, in the United States
and nearly all parts of the Continent of Europe on the right.
Morality has nothing to say to this, except that those who use
the roads ought to know and observe the rule, whatever it be,
prescribed by the law of the country. Many cases, again, occur,
where the legal rule does not profess to fulfil anything like
perfect justice, but where certainty is of more importance than
perfection, and an imperfect rule is therefore useful and
acceptable. Nay, more, there are cases where the law, for
reasons of general policy, not only makes persons chargeable
without proof of moral blame, but will not admit proof to the
contrary. Thus, by the law of England, the possessor of a
dangerous animal is liable for any mischief it may do, notwithstanding that he may have used the utmost caution for
its safe keeping. Thus, in our modern law, a master has to
answer for the acts and defaults of a servant occupied about his
business, however careful he may have been in choosing and
instructing the servant. Thus, again, there are cases where an
obviously wrongful act has brought loss upon innocent persons,
and no redress can be obtained from the primary wrong-doer.
In such cases it has to be decided which of those innocent
persons shall bear the loss. A typical example is the sale of
stolen goods to one who buys them in good faith. The
fraudulent seller is commonly out of reach, or, if within reach,
of no means to make restitution. Either the true owner must
lose his goods, or the purchaser must lose his money. This
question, simple enough as to the facts, is on the very
border-line of legal policy. Some systems of law favour the
first owner, some the purchaser, and in our English law itself
the result may be one way or the other, according to conditions
quite independent of the actual honesty or prudence of the
parties. In the dealings of modern commerce, questions which
are reducible to the same principle arise in various ways which
may be complicated to an indefinite extent. Evidently there

must be some law for such cases; yet no law can be made which will not seem unjust to the loser. Compensation at the public expense would, perhaps, be absolutely just, and it might be practicable in a world of absolutely truthful and prudent people. But in such a world frauds would not be committed on individuals any more than on the State.

Another point worth mention is that the notion of law does not include of necessity the existence of a distinct profession of lawyers, whether as judges or as advocates. There can not well be a science of law without such a profession; but justice can be administered according to settled rules by persons taken from the general body of citizens for the occasion, or in a small community even by the whole body of qualified citizens; and under the most advanced legal systems a man may generally conduct his own cause in person, if so minded. In Athens, at the time of Pericles, and even of Demosthenes, there was a great deal of law, but no class of persons answering to our judges or counsellors. The Attic orator was not a lawyer in the modern sense. Again, the Icelandic sagas exhibit a state of society provided with law quite definite as far as it goes, and even minutely technical on some points, and yet without any professed lawyers. The law is administered by general assemblies of freemen, though the court which is to try a particular cause is selected by elaborate rules. There are old men who have the reputation of being learned in the law; sometimes the opinion of such a man is accepted as conclusive; but they hold no defined office or official qualification. In England, as we shall see hereafter, there was no definite legal profession till more than a century after the Norman Conquest. In short, the presence of law is marked by the administration of justice in some regular course of time, place, and manner, and on the footing of some recognized general principles. These conditions appear to be sufficient, as they are necessary. But if we suppose an Eastern despot to sit in the gate and deal with every case according to the impression of the moment, recognizing no rule at all, we may say that he is doing some sort of justice, but we can not say that he is doing judgment according to law. Probably no prince or ruler in historical times ever really took upon himself to do right according to his mere will and pleasure. There are always points of accepted faith which even the strongest of despots dares not offend, points of custom which he dares not disregard.

At the same time the conscious separation of law from morals and religion has been a gradual process, and it has largely gone hand in hand with the marking off of special conditions of men to attend to religious and to legal affairs, and the development, through their special studies, of jurisprudence and theology as distinct sciences. If there be any primitive theory of the nature of law, it seems to be that laws are the utterance of some divine or heroic person who reveals, or declares as revealed to him, that which is absolutely right. The desire to refer institutions to a deified or canonized legislator is shown in England, as late as the fourteenth century, by the attribution to King Alfred of everything supposed to be specially national and excellent. In the extant Brahmanical recensions of early Hindu law this desire is satisfied with deliberate and excessive minuteness. Wherever and whenever such notions prevail, the distinction between legal and moral duty can at best be imperfectly realized. During the age of which we are to speak in this book a grand attempt was being made to reduce morality to legal forms. In the system of the medieval Church the whole of 'external' moral duty is included in the law of God and of Holy Church. Morality becomes a thing of arguments and judgments, of positive rules and exceptions, and even of legislative declaration by the authority supreme on earth in matters of faith and morals. Many things on which Protestants are accustomed to spend their astonishment and indignation are merely the necessary consequences of this theory. We shall often have to observe that the wide and flexible jurisdiction of the spiritual power was of great service in the middle ages, both in supplementing the justice of secular courts, and in stimulating them by its formidable competition to improve their doctrine and practice; but a discussion of the Church's penitential system will not be expected of us.

We have spoken but briefly of the law which prevailed in England before the coming of the Normans, and therefore we ought perhaps to say here that in our opinion it was in the main pure Germanic law. Question has been made at various times as to how much of ancient British custom survived the conquest of Britain by successive invaders, and became in-

corporated in English law. We are unable to assign any
definite share to this Celtic element. The supposed proofs of
its existence have, so far as we are aware, no surer foundation
than coincidence. Now the mere coincidence of particulars in
early bodies of law proves nothing beyond the resemblance of
all institutions in certain stages. There are, again, many
points of real organic connexion between Celtic and English law
even if there has been no borrowing from the Welshman on the
Englishman's part. If there be a true affinity, it may well go
back to a common stock of Aryan tradition antecedent to the
distinction of race and tongue between German and Celt. And
if in a given case we find that an institution or custom which
is both Welsh and English is at the same time Scandinavian,
Greek, Roman, Slavonic or Hindu, we may be reasonably
assured that there is nothing more specific in the matter. Or,
if there be a true case of survival, it may go back to an origin
as little Celtic or even Aryan as it is Germanic. Some local
usages, it is quite possible, may be relics of a prehistoric society
and of an antiquity now immeasurable, saved by their obscurity
through the days of Celt, Saxon and Norman alike. There is
no better protection against the stronger hand; bracken and
lichens are untouched by the storm that uproots oak and beech.
But this is of no avail to the Celtic enthusiast, or rather of
worse than none. Those who claim a Celtic origin for English
laws ought to do one of two things: prove by distinct historical
evidence that particular Celtic institutions were adopted by the
English invaders, or point out similar features in Welsh and
English law which can not be matched either in the laws of
continental Germany or in those of other Aryan nations.
Neither of these things, to the best of our knowledge, has ever
been effectually done. Indeed the test last named would be
hardly a safe one. The earliest documents of Welsh law known
to exist are in their present form so much later than the bulk
of our Anglo-Saxon documents that, if a case of specific
borrowing could be made out on the face of them, we should
need further assurance that the borrowing was not the other
way. The favourite method of partisans in this kind is, as has
been said, to enumerate coincidences. And by that method our
English medieval law could with little ado be proved to be
Greek, Slavonic, Semitic, or, for aught one knows, Chinese.
We can not say that no element derived from the Celtic

inhabitants of Britain exists in it, for there is no means of proving so general a negative. But there seems to be no proof nor evidence of the existence of that element in any such appreciable measure as would oblige us to take account of it in such a work as the present. Again, there is the possibility that Celtic details, assimilated in Gaul by French law during its growth, passed into England at the Norman Conquest. But it is not for us to discuss this possibility. On the other hand, no one can doubt that the English law stated and defined in the series of dooms which stretches from Æthelbirht to Cnut finds nearer kinsfolk in the law that prevailed in Saxony and Norway and on the Lombard plain than those that it finds among the Welsh or Irish.

Coming to the solid ground of known history, we find that our laws have been formed in the main from a stock of Teutonic customs, with some additions of matter, and considerable additions or modifications of form received directly or indirectly from the Roman system. Both the Germanic and the Romanic elements have been constituted or reinforced at different times and from different sources, and we have thus a large range of possibilities to which, in the absence of direct proof, we must attend carefully in every case before committing ourselves to a decision.

Taking first the Germanic material of our laws, we begin with the customs and institutions brought in by the English conquest of Britain, or rather by the series of conquests which led to the formation of the English kingdom. This is the prime stock; but it by no means accounts for the whole of the Germanic elements. A distinct Scandinavian strain came in with the Danish invasions and was secured by the short period of Danish sovereignty. A third of England, a populous and wealthy third, became known as the Danelaw. To some extent, but probably to no great extent, the Norman law and practice of William the Conqueror may have included similar matter. The main importance of the Norman contribution, however, was in other kinds. Much Anglo-Norman law is Germanic without being either Anglo-Saxon or Norse. Indeed of recent years it has become the fashion upon the Continent to speak of Anglo-Norman law as a daughter of Frankish law. The Frankish monarchy, the nearest approach to a civilized power that existed in Western Europe since the barbarian invasions, was in many things a pattern for its neighbours and for the states and principalities that rose out of its ruins. That we received from the Normans a contribution of Frankish ideas and customs is indubitable. It was, indeed, hardly foreign to us, being of kindred stock, and still not widely removed from the common root of Germanic tradition. We must not omit, however, to count it as a distinct variation. Neither must we forget that English princes had already been following in some measure the same models that the Dukes of the Normans copied. From the time of Charles the Great onward, the rulers of both Mercia and Wessex were in intimate relations with the Frankish kings.

Now each of these Germanic strains, the purely Anglo-Saxon, the Scandinavian, the Frankish, has had its champions. To decide between them is often a difficult, and sometimes in our opinion an impossible task. A mere 'method of agreement' is, as already said, full of dangers, and such is the imperfection of our record that we can seldom use a 'method of differences' in any convincing fashion. Even for the sake of these somewhat remote and obscure problems, the first thing needful seems to be that we should have a fairly full statement of the English law of the Angevin time. Before we speculate about hypothetical causes, we ought to know as accurately as possible the effect that has to be accounted for. The speculation we must leave for the more part to those who can devote their time to a close study of Anglo-Saxon, Scandinavian and Frankish law. The English law of the Angevin age is for the present our principal theme, though we have sometimes glanced at earlier and at later times also.

As to the Roman, or more properly Romanic, element in our English law, this also is a matter which requires careful distinction. It has been maintained at various times, and sometimes with great ingenuity, that Roman institutions persisted after Britain was abandoned by the Roman power, and survived the Teutonic invasions in such force as to contribute in material quantity to the formation of our laws. But there is no real evidence of this. Whether the invaders may not have learnt something in the arts of peace and war from those whom they were conquering, something of strategy, architecture, agriculture, is not here the question. We speak of law, and within the sphere of law everything that is Roman or Romanized can be accounted for by later importation. We know that the language and the religion of Rome were effaced. Roman Christianity had to make a fresh conquest of the English kingdom almost as if the British Church had never existed. The remnant of that Church stood aloof, and it would seem that Augustine did not think it entitled to much conciliation, either by its merits or by its importance[1]. It is difficult to believe that civil institutions remained continuous in a country where the discontinuity of ecclesiastical affairs is so pointedly marked, and in an age when the Church was far more stable and compact than any civil institution whatever. And, in point of fact, there is no trace of the laws and jurisprudence of imperial Rome, as distinct from the precepts and traditions of the Roman Church, in the earliest Anglo-Saxon documents. Whatever is Roman in them is ecclesiastical. The danger of arguing in these matters from a mere enumeration of coincidences has already been pointed out with reference to the attempt, in our opinion a substantially similar one, to attribute English law to a Celtic origin. This inroad of the Roman ecclesiastical tradition, in other words, of the system which in course of time was organized as the Canon Law, was the first and by no means the least important of the Roman invasions, if we may so call them, of our Germanic polity. We need not doubt the statement that English princes began to collect their customary laws in writing after the Roman example made known to them by Augustine and his successors[2].

Somewhat later the intercourse of English princes with the Frankish court brought in a fresh accession of continental learning and continental forms, in the hands of clerks indeed, but applicable to secular affairs. In this way the Roman materials assimilated or imitated by the Franks easily found their way into England at a second remove. Many, perhaps most, of the facts that have been alleged to show the per-

---

[1] The story that Augustine offended the Welsh bishops by not rising to receive them may be accepted as symbolically if not literally true.

[2] According to Bede (ii. 5) Æthelbirht of Kent set dooms in writing 'iuxta exempla Romanorum.' It is of course quite possible that a few of the more learned among the clergy may at times have studied some books of Roman Law. St Aldhelm (ob. 709) speaks as if he had done so in a letter printed by Wharton, Anglia Sacra, vol. ii. p. 6, and by Jaffé, Monumenta Moguntina, 32. On this see Savigny, Geschichte des römischen Rechts, c. 6, § 135.

sistence of Roman institutions in Britain are really of this kind. Such are for example the forms and phrases of the Latin charters or land-books that we find in the *Codex Diplomaticus.* A difficult question indeed is raised by these continental materials on their own ground, namely, what proportion of Germanic and Franco-Gallic usages is of Roman origin, and how far those parts that are Roman are to be ascribed to a continuous life of Roman institutions and habits in the outlying provinces of the empire, more especially in Gaul. Merovingian Gaul has been, and for a long time to come is likely to be, the battle-field of scholars, some of whom can see little that is Roman, some little that is Germanic. Interesting as these problems are, they do not fall within our present scope.

A further importation of more sudden and masterful fashion came with the Norman Conquest. Not only had the Normans learnt a Romance tongue, but the dukes of Normandy had adopted the official machinery of Frankish or French government, including of course whatever Roman elements had been taken up by the Franks. Here, again, a remoter field of inquiry lies open, on which we do not adventure ourselves. It is enough to say, at present, that institutions which have now-a-days the most homely and English appearance may nevertheless be ultimately connected, through the customs of Normandy, with the system of government elaborated in the latter centuries of the Roman Empire. The fact that this kind of Romanic influence operated chiefly in matters of procedure does not make it the less important, for procedure is the life of ancient law. But this, it need hardly be remarked, is a very different matter from a continuous persistence of unadulterated Roman elements. It may be possible to trace a chain of slender but unbroken links from the court of our William or Henry to that of Diocletian or Constantine. Such a chain, however, is by no means strengthened by the fact that Papinian was once at York, as it would in no way be weakened if that fact could be discredited.

Soon after the Norman Conquest a new and a different wave of Roman influence began to flow. The first ripple of it reached our shore when Lanfranc the lawyer of Pavia became the Conqueror's trusted adviser. In the middle of the next century it was streaming outwards from Bologna in full flood. Hitherto we have been speaking of a survival of Roman law in institutions and habits and customs; what we have now before us is of another kind, a scholarly revival of the classical Roman law that is to be found in Justinian's books. Of this we have spoken at some length in various parts of our work. For about a century—let us say between 1150 and 1250—this tide was shaping and modifying our English law; and we have tried to keep before the eyes of our readers the question—to our mind one of the central questions of English history—why the rapid and, to a first glance, overwhelming flow of Romanic learning was followed in this country by an equally rapid ebb.

At a later time yet other Roman elements began to make their way into our system through the equity administered by the chancellor. But of these we shall not speak in this book, for we shall not here bring down the story of our law beyond the time when Edward I. began his memorable reforms. Our reason for stopping at that moment we can give in a few words. So continuous has been our English legal life during the last six centuries, that the law of the later middle ages has never been forgotten among us. It has never passed utterly outside the cognizance of our courts and our practising lawyers. We have never had to disinter and reconstruct it in that laborious and tentative manner in which German historians of the present day have disinterred and reconstructed the law of medieval Germany. It has never been obliterated by a wholesale 're- ception' of Roman law. Blackstone, in order that he might expound the working law of his own day in an intelligible fashion, was forced at every turn to take back his readers to the middle ages, and even now, after all our reforms, our courts are still from time to time compelled to construe statutes of Edward I.'s day, and, were Parliament to repeal some of those statutes and provide no substitute, the whole edifice of our land law would fall down with a crash. Therefore a tradition, which is in the main a sound and truthful tradition, has been main- tained about so much of English legal history as lies on this side of the reign of Edward I. We may find it in Blackstone; we may find it in Reeves; we may find many portions of it in various practical text-books. We are beginning to discover that it is not all true; at many points it has of late been corrected. Its besetting sin is that of antedating the emergence of modern ideas. That is a fault into which every professional tradition is wont to fall. But in the main it is truthful. To this must be added that as regards the materials for this part of our history we stand very much where Blackstone stood. This we write to our shame. The first and indispensable preliminary to a better legal history than we have of the later middle ages is a new, a complete, a tolerable edition of the Year Books. They should be our glory, for no other country has anything like them : they are our disgrace, for no other country would have so neglected them.

On the other hand, as regards the materials which come from a slightly earlier time, we do not stand nearly where Blackstone stood. The twelfth and thirteenth centuries have been fortunate in our own age. Very many and some of the best and most authentic of the texts on which we have relied in the following pages were absolutely unknown to Blackstone and to Reeves. To the antiquaries of the seventeenth century high praise is due ; even the eighteenth produced, as it were out of due time, one master of records, the diligent Madox ; but at least half of the materials that we have used as sources of first-hand knowledge have been published for the first time since 1800, by the Record Commissioners, or in the Rolls Series, or by some learned society, the Camden or the Surtees, the Pipe Roll or the Selden. Even while our pages have been in the press Dr Liebermann has been restoring to us the law-books of the twelfth century. Again, in many particular fields of old English law—villeinage, for example, and trial by jury and many another—so much excellent and very new work has been done by men who are still living, by Germans, Frenchmen, Russians as well as Englishmen and Americans, and so much of it lies scattered in monographs and journals—we should be ungrateful indeed did we not name the Harvard Law Review— that the time seemed to have come when an endeavour to restate the law of the Angevin age might prosper, and at any rate ought to be made.

One of our hopes has been that we might take some part in the work of bringing the English law of the thirteenth century into line with the French and German law of the same age. That is the time when French law is becoming clear in Les Olim, in Beaumanoir's lucid pages, in the so-called Establishments of St Louis, in the Norman custumal and in many other books. It is also the classical age of German law, the age of the

Sachsenspiegel. We have been trying to do for English law what has within late years been done for French and German law by a host of scholars. We have often had before our minds the question why it is that systems which in the thirteenth century were so near of kin had such different fates before them. The answer to that question is assuredly not to be given by any hasty talk about national character. The first step towards an answer must be a careful statement of each system by itself. We must know in isolation the things that are to be compared before we compare them. A small share in this preliminary labour we have tried to take. Englishmen should abandon their traditional belief that from all time the continental nations have been ruled by 'the civil law,' they should learn how slowly the renovated Roman doctrine worked its way into the jurisprudence of the parliament of Paris, how long deferred was 'the practical reception' of Roman law in Germany, how exceedingly like our common law once was to a French *coutume*. This will give them an intenser interest in their own history. What is more, in the works of French and German medievalists they will now-a-days find many an invaluable hint for the solution of specifically English problems.

We have left to Constitutional History the field that she has appropriated. An exact delimitation of the province of law that should be called constitutional must always be difficult, except perhaps in such modern states as have written constitutions. If we turn to the middle ages we shall find the task impossible, and we see as a matter of fact that the historians of our constitution are always enlarging their boundaries. Though primarily interested in such parts of the law as are indubitably constitutional, they are always discovering that in order to explain these they are compelled to explain other parts also. They can not write about the growth of parliament without writing about the law of land tenure; 'the liberty of the subject' can only be manifested in a discourse on civil and criminal procedure. It may be enough therefore if, without any attempt to establish a scientific frontier, we protest that we have kept clear of the territory over which they exercise an effective dominion. Our reason for so doing is plain. We have no wish to say over again what the Bishop of Oxford has admirably said, no hope of being able to say with any truth what he has left unsaid. Besides, for a long time past, ever since the days of Selden and Prynne, many Englishmen have been keenly interested in the history of parliament and of taxation and of all that directly concerns the government of the realm. If we could persuade a few of them to take a similar interest in the history of ownership, possession, contract, agency, trust, legal proof and so forth, and if we could bring the history of these, or of some of these, matters within a measurable distance of that degree of accuracy and completion which constitutional history has attained in the hands of Dr Stubbs, we should have achieved an unlooked-for success. At the same time, we shall now and again discuss some problems with which he and his predecessors have busied themselves, for we think that those who have endeavoured to explore the private law of the middle ages may occasionally see even in political events some clue which escapes eyes that are trained to look only or chiefly at public affairs.

The constitutional is not the only department of medieval law that we have left on one side. We have said very little of purely ecclesiastical matters. Here again we have been compelled to draw but a rude boundary. It seemed to us that a history of English law which said nothing of marriage, last wills, the fate of an intestate's goods, the punishment of criminous clerks, or which merely said that all these affairs were governed by the law and courts of the church, would be an exceedingly fragmentary book. On the other hand, we have not felt called upon to speak of the legal constitution of the ecclesiastical hierarchy, the election and consecration of bishops, the ordination of clerks, the power of provincial councils and so forth, and we have but now and then alluded to the penitential system. What is still the sphere of ecclesiastical law we have avoided; into what was once its sphere we could not but make incursions.

At other points, again, our course has been shaped by a desire to avoid what we should regard as vain repetition. When the ground that we traverse has lately been occupied by a Holmes, Thayer, Ames or Bigelow, by a Brunner, Liebermann or Vinogradoff, we pass over it rapidly; we should have dwelt much longer in the domain of criminal law if Sir James Stephen had not recently laboured in it. And then we have at times devoted several pages to the elucidation of some question, perhaps intrinsically of small importance, which seemed to us difficult and unexplored and worthy of patient discussion, for such is the interdependence of all legal rules that the solution of some vital problem may occasionally be found in what looks at first sight like a technical trifle.

We have thought less of symmetry than of the advancement of knowledge. The time for an artistically balanced picture of English medieval law will come: it has not come yet.

BOOK I

SKETCH OF EARLY ENGLISH LEGAL HISTORY.

CHAPTER I.

THE DARK AGE IN LEGAL HISTORY.

SUCH is the unity of all history that any one who endeavours to tell a piece of it must feel that his first sentence tears a seamless web. The oldest utterance of English law that has come down to us has Greek words in it: words such as *bishop*, *priest* and *deacon*[1]. If we would search out the origins of Roman law, we must study Babylon: this at least was the opinion of the great Romanist of our own day[2]. A statute of limitations must be set; but it must be arbitrary. The web must be rent; but, as we rend it, we may watch the whence and whither of a few of the severed and ravelling threads which have been making a pattern too large for any man's eye. The difficulty of beginning.

To speak more modestly, we may, before we settle to our task, look round for a moment at the world in which our English legal history has its beginnings. We may recall to memory a few main facts and dates which, though they are easily ascertained, are not often put together in one English book, and we may perchance arrange them in a useful order if we make mile-stones of the centuries[3]. Proposed retrospect.

---

[1] Æthelb. 1.

[2] Ihering, Vorgeschichte der Indoeuropäer; see especially the editor's preface.

[3] The following summary has been compiled by the aid of Karlowa, Römische Rechtsgeschichte, 1885—Krüger, Geschichte der Quellen des römischen Rechts, 1888—Conrat, Geschichte der Quellen des römischen Rechts im früheren Mittelalter, 1889—Maassen, Geschichte der Quellen des canonischen Rechts, 1870—Löning, Geschichte des deutschen Kirchenrechts, 1878—Sohm, Kirchenrecht, 1892—Hinschius, System des katholischen Kirchenrechts, 1869 ff.—A. Tardif, Histoire des sources du droit canonique, 1887—Brunner, Deutsche Rechtsgeschichte, 1887—Schröder, Lehrbuch der deutschen Rechtsgeschichte, ed. 2, 1894—Esmein, Cours d'histoire du droit français, ed. 2, 1895—Viollet, Histoire du droit civil français, 1893.

The classical age of Roman law.

The beginnings of ecclesiastical law.

By the year 200 Roman jurisprudence had reached its zenith. Papinian was slain in 212[1], Ulpian in 228[2]. Ulpian's pupil Modestinus may be accounted the last of the great lawyers[3]. All too soon they became classical; their successors were looking backwards, not forwards. Of the work that had been done it were folly here to speak, but the law of a little town had become ecumenical law, law alike for cultured Greece and for wild Britain. And yet, though it had assimilated new matter and new ideas, it had always preserved its tough identity. In the year 200 six centuries and a half of definite legal history, if we measure only from the Twelve Tables, were consciously summed up in the living and growing body of the law.

Dangers lay ahead. We notice one in a humble quarter. Certain religious societies, congregations (*ecclesiae*) of non-conformists, have been developing law, internal law, with ominous rapidity. We have called it law, and law it was going to be, but as yet it was, if the phrase be tolerable, unlawful law, for these societies had an illegal, a criminal purpose. Spasmodically the imperial law was enforced against them; at other times the utmost that they could hope for from the state was that in the guise of 'benefit and burial societies' they would obtain some protection for their communal property[4]. But internally they were developing what was to be a system of constitutional and governmental law, which would endow the overseer (*episcopus*) of every congregation with manifold powers. Also they were developing a system of punitive law, for the offender might be excluded from all participation in religious rites, if not from worldly intercourse with the faithful[5]. Moreover, these various communities were becoming united by bonds that were too close to be federal. In particular, that one of them which had its seat in the capital city of the empire was winning a preeminence for itself and its overseer[6]. Long indeed would it be before

---

[1] Krüger, op. cit. 198; Karlowa, op. cit. i. 736.

[2] Krüger, op. cit. 215; Karlowa, op. cit. i. 741.

[3] Krüger, op. cit. 226; Karlowa, op. cit. i. 752.

[4] Löning, op. cit. i. 195 ff.; Sohm, op. cit. 75. Löning asserts that in the intervals between the outbursts of persecution the Christian communities were legally recognized as *collegia tenuiorum*, capable of holding property. Sohm denies this.

[5] Excommunication gradually assumes its boycotting traits. The clergy were prohibited, while as yet the laity were not, from holding converse with the offender. Löning, op. cit. i. 264; Hinschius, op. cit. iv. 704.

[6] Sohm, op. cit. 378 ff.; Löning, op. cit. i. 423 ff.

this overseer of a non-conformist congregation would, in the person of his successor, place his heel upon the neck of the prostrate Augustus by virtue of God-made law. This was not to be foreseen; but already a merely human jurisprudence was losing its interest. The intellectual force which some years earlier might have taken a side in the debate between Sabinians and Proculians now invented or refuted a christological heresy. Ulpian's priesthood[1] was not priestly enough[2].

The decline was rapid. Long before the year 300 juris- **Cent. III.** prudence, the one science of the Romans, was stricken with Decline of Roman sterility[3]; it was sharing the fate of art[4]. Its eyes were turned law. backwards to the departed great. The constitutions of the emperors now appeared as the only active source of law. They were a disordered mass, to be collected rather than digested. Collections of them were being unofficially made: the *Codex Gregorianus*, the *Codex Hermogenianus*. These have perished; they were made, some say, in the Orient[5]. The shifting eastward of the imperial centre and the tendency of the world to fall into two halves were not for the good of the West. Under one title and another, as *coloni, laeti, gentiles*, large bodies of untamed Germans were taking up their abode within the limit of the empire[6]. The Roman armies were becoming barbarous hosts. Constantine owed his crown to an Alamannian king[7].

It is on a changed world that we look in the year 400. **Cent. IV.** After one last flare of persecution (303), Christianity became a Church and State. lawful religion (313). In a few years it, or rather one species of it, had become the only lawful religion. The 'confessor' of yesterday was the persecutor of to-day. Heathenry, it is true, died hard in the West; but already about 350 a pagan sacrifice was by the letter of the law a capital crime[8]. Before the end of

---

[1] Dig. 1. 1. 1.

[2] The moot question (Krüger, op. cit. 203; Karlowa, op. cit. i. 739) whether the Tertullian who is the apologist of Christian sectaries is the Tertullian from whose works a few extracts appear in the Digest may serve as a mnemonic link between two ages.

[3] Krüger, op. cit. 260; Karlowa, op. cit. i. 932.

[4] Gregorovius, History of Rome (transl. Hamilton), i. 85.

[5] Krüger, op. cit. 277 ff.; Karlowa, op. cit. i. 941 ff. It is thought that the original edition of the Gregorianus was made about A.D. 295, that of the Hermogenianus between 314 and 324. But these dates are uncertain. For their remains see Corpus Iuris Anteiustiniani.

[6] Brunner, op. cit. i. 32–39.   [7] Ibid. 38.   [8] Löning, op. cit. i. 44.

the century cruel statutes were being made against heretics of all sorts and kinds[1]. No sooner was the new faith lawful, than the state was compelled to take part in the multifarious quarrels of the Christians. Hardly had Constantine issued the edict of tolerance, than he was summoning the bishops to Arles (314), even from remote Britain, that they might, if this were possible, make peace in the church of Africa[2]. In the history of law, as well as in the history of dogma, the fourth century is the century of ecclesiastical councils. Into the debates of the spiritual parliaments of the empire[3] go whatever juristic ability, and whatever power of organization are left among mankind. The new supernatural jurisprudence was finding another mode of utterance; the bishop of Rome was becoming a legislator, perhaps a more important legislator than the emperor[4]. In 380 Theodosius himself commanded that all the peoples which owned his sway should follow, not merely the religion that Christ had delivered to the world, but the religion that St Peter had delivered to the Romans[5]. For a disciplinary jurisdiction over clergy and laity the state now left a large room wherein the bishops ruled[6]. As arbitrators in purely secular disputes they were active; it is even probable that for a short while under Constantine one litigant might force his adversary unwillingly to seek the episcopal tribunal[7]. It was necessary for the state to protest that criminal jurisdiction was still in its hands[8]. Soon the church was demanding, and in the West it might successfully demand, independence of the state and even a dominance over the state: the church may command and the state must obey[9]. If from one point of view we see this as a triumph of anarchy, from another it appears as a

---

[1] Löning, op. cit. i. 97–98, reckons 68 statutes from 57 years (380–438).

[2] Hefele, Conciliengeschichte, i. 201. For the presence of the British bishops, see Haddan and Stubbs, Councils, i. 7.

[3] Sohm, op. cit. 443: 'Das ökumenische Koncil, die Reichssynode...bedeutet ein geistliches Parlament des Kaisertums.'

[4] Sohm, op. cit. 418. If a precise date may be fixed in a very gradual process, we may perhaps see the first exercise of legislative power in the decretal (A.D. 385) of Pope Siricius.

[5] Cod. Theod. 16. 1. 2.

[6] Löning, op. cit. i. 262 ff.; Hinschius, op. cit. iv. 788 ff.

[7] Löning, op. cit. i. 293; Karlowa, op. cit. i. 966. This depends on the genuineness of Constit. Sirmond. 1.

[8] Löning, op. cit. i. 305; Hinschius, op. cit. iv. 794.

[9] Löning, op. cit. i. 64–94.

triumph of law, of jurisprudence. Theology itself must become jurisprudence, albeit jurisprudence of a supernatural sort, in order that it may rule the world.

Among the gigantic events of the fifth century the issue of a statute-book seems small. Nevertheless, through the turmoil we see two statute-books, that of Theodosius II. and that of Euric the West Goth. The Theodosian Code was an official collection of imperial statutes beginning with those of Constantine I. It was issued in 438 with the consent of Valentinian III. who was reigning in the West. No perfect copy of it has reached us[1]. This by itself would tell a sad tale; but we remember how rapidly the empire was being torn in shreds. Already Britain was abandoned (407). We may doubt whether the statute-book of Theodosius ever reached our shores until it had been edited by Jacques Godefroi[2]. Indeed we may say that the fall of a loose stone in Britain brought the crumbling edifice to the ground[3]. Already before this code was published the hordes of Alans, Vandals and Sueves had swept across Gaul and Spain; already the Vandals were in Africa. Already Rome had been sacked by the West Goths; they were founding a kingdom in southern Gaul and were soon to have a statute-book of their own. Gaiseric was not far off, nor Attila. Also let us remember that this Theodosian Code was by no means well designed if it was to perpetuate the memory of Roman civil science in that stormy age. It was no 'code' in our modern sense of that term. It was only a more or less methodic collection of modern statutes. Also it contained many things that the barbarians had better not have read; bloody laws against heretics, for example.

We turn from it to the first monument of Germanic law that has come down to us. It consists of some fragments of what must have been a large law-book published by Euric for his West Goths, perhaps between 470 and 475[4]. Euric was a conquering king; he ruled Spain and a large part of southern Gaul; he had cast off, so it is said, even the pretence of ruling

Margin notes: Cent. V. The Theodosian Code. Laws of Euric.

---

[1] Krüger, op. cit. 285 ff.; Karlowa, op. cit. i. 944.

[2] The Breviary of Alaric is a different matter.

[3] Bury, History of the Later Roman Empire, 142: 'And thus we may say that it was the loss or abandonment of Britain in 407 that led to the further loss of Spain and Africa.'

[4] Zeumer, Leges Visigothorum Antiquiores, 1894; Brunner, op. cit. i. 320; Schröder, op. cit. 230.

in the emperor's name. Nevertheless, his laws are not nearly
so barbarous as our curiosity might wish them to be. These
West Goths who had wandered across Europe were veneered by
Roman civilization. It did them little good. Their later law-
books, that of Reckessuinth (652–672), that of Erwig (682),
that of Egica (687–701) are said to be verbose and futile
imitations of Roman codes. But Euric's laws are sufficient to
remind us that the order of date among these *Leges Barbarorum*
is very different from the order of barbarity. Scandinavian
laws that are not written until the thirteenth century will often
give us what is more archaic than anything that comes from
the Gaul of the fifth or the Britain of the seventh. And, on
the other hand, the mention of Goths in Spain should remind
us of those wondrous folk-wanderings and of their strange
influence upon the legal map of Europe. The Saxon of England
has a close cousin in the Lombard of Italy, and modern critics
profess that they can see a specially near kinship between
Spanish and Icelandic law[1].

Cent. VI.
The cen-
tury of
Justinian.

In legal history the sixth century is the century of Justinian.
But, in the west of Europe this age appears as his, only if we
take into account what was then a remote future. How powerless he was to legislate for many of the lands and races whence
he drew his grandiose titles—*Alamannicus, Gothicus, Francicus*
and the rest—we shall see if we inquire who else had been
publishing laws. The barbarians had been writing down their
customs. The barbarian kings had been issuing law-books for
their Roman subjects. Books of ecclesiastical law, of conciliar
and papal law, were being compiled[2].

The *Lex
Salica.*

The discovery of fragments of the laws of Euric the West
Goth has deprived the *Lex Salica* of its claim to be the oldest
extant statement of Germanic custom. But if not the oldest,
it is still very old; also it is rude and primitive[3]. It comes to
us from the march between the fifth and the sixth centuries;

[1] Ficker, Untersuchungen zur Erbenfolge, 1891–5; Ficker, Ueber nähere
Verwandtschaft zwischen gothisch-spanischem und norwegisch-isländischem
Recht (Mittheilungen des Instituts für österreichische Geschichtsforschung,
1888, ii. 456 ff.). These attempts to reconstruct the genealogy of the various
Germanic systems are very interesting, if hazardous.

[2] For a map of Europe at the time of Justinian's legislation see Hodgkin,
Italy and her Invaders, vol. iv. p. 1.

[3] Brunner, op. cit. i. 292 ff.; Schröder, op. cit. 226 ff.; Esmein, op. cit.
102 ff.; Dahn, Die Könige der Germanen, vii. (2) 50 ff.; Hessels and Kern, Lex
Salica, The ten texts, 1880.

almost certainly from the victorious reign of Chlodwig (486–511). An attempt to fix its date more closely brings out one of its interesting traits. There is nothing distinctively heathen in it; but (and this makes it unique[1]) there is nothing distinctively Christian. If the Sicambrian has already bowed his neck to the catholic yoke, he is not yet actively destroying by his laws what he had formerly adored[2]. On the other hand, his kingdom seems to stretch south of the Loire, and he has looked for suggestions to the laws of the West Goths. The *Lex Salica*, though written in Latin, is very free from the Roman taint. It contains in the so-called Malberg glosses many old Frankish words, some of which, owing to mistranscription, are puzzles for the philological science of our own day. Like the other Germanic folk-laws, it consists largely of a tariff of offences and atonements; but a few precious chapters, every word of which has been a cause of learned strife, lift the curtain for a moment and allow us to watch the Frank as he litigates. We see more clearly here than elsewhere the formalism, the sacramental symbolism of ancient legal procedure. We have no more instructive document; and let us remember that, by virtue of the Norman Conquest, the *Lex Salica* is one of the ancestors of English law.

Whether in the days when Justinian was legislating, the Western or Ripuarian Franks had written law may not be certain; but it is thought that the main part of the *Lex Ribuaria* is older than 596[3]. Though there are notable variations, it is in part a modernized edition of the *Salica*, showing the influence of the clergy and of Roman law. On the other hand, there seems little doubt that the core of the *Lex Burgundionum* was issued by King Gundobad (474–516) in the last years of the fifth century[4]. *The Lex Ribuaria and Lex Burgundionum.*

Burgundians and West Goths were scattered among Roman provincials. They were East Germans; they had long been Christians, though addicted to the heresy of Arius. They could *The Lex Romana Burgundionum.*

---

[1] However, there are some curious relics of heathenry in the *Lex Frisionum*: Brunner, op. cit. i. 342.

[2] Greg. Turon. ii. 22 (ed. Omont, p. 60): 'Mitis depone colla, Sicamber; adora quod incendisti, incende quod adorasti.'

[3] Brunner, op. cit. i. 303 ff.; Schröder, op. cit. 229; Esmein, op. cit. 107. Edited by Sohm in M. G.

[4] Brunner, op. cit. i. 332 ff.; Schröder, op. cit. 234; Esmein, op. cit. 108. Edited by v. Salis in M. G.

say that they had Roman authority for their occupation of
Roman soil. Aquitania Secunda had been made over to the
West Goths; the Burgundians vanquished by Aetius had been
deported to Savoy[1]. In their seizure of lands from the Roman
possessores they had followed, though with modifications that
were profitable to themselves, the Roman system of billeting
barbarian soldiers[2]. There were many *Romani* as well as many
barbari for whom their kings could legislate. Hence the *Lex
Romana Burgundionum* and the *Lex Romana Visigothorum.*
The former[3] seems to be the law-book that Gundobad promised
to his Roman subjects; he died in 516. Rules have been taken
from the three Roman *codices*, from the current abridgements of
imperial constitutions and from the works of Gaius and Paulus.
Little that is good has been said of this book. Far more
comprehensive and far more important was the Breviary of
Alaric or *Lex Romana Visigothorum*[4]. Euric's son, Alaric II.,
published it in 506 as a statute-book; among the *Romani* of
his realm it was to supplant all older books. It contained large
excerpts from the Theodosian Codex, a few from the *Gregorianus*
and *Hermogenianus*, some post-Theodosian constitutions, some
of the *Sententiae* of Paulus, one little scrap of Papinian and an
abridged version of the Institutes of Gaius. The greater part
of these texts was equipped with a running commentary
(*interpretatio*) which attempted to give their upshot in a more
intelligible form. It is thought now-a-days that this 'interpretation' and the sorry version of Gaius represent, not Gothic
barbarism, but degenerate Roman science. A time had come
when lawyers could no longer understand their own old texts
and were content with debased abridgements[5].

The West Goths' power was declining. Hardly had Alaric
issued his statute-book when he was slain in battle by the
Franks. Soon the Visigothic became a Spanish kingdom.
But it was not in Spain that the *Breviarium* made its permanent mark. There it was abrogated by Reckessuinth when he
issued a code for all his subjects of every race[6]. On the other
hand, it struck deep root in Gaul. It became the principal, if

The *Lex Romana Visigothorum.*

Import-
ance of the
Breviary.

---

[1] Brunner, op. cit. i. 50–1.   [2] Ibid. 64–7.

[3] Krüger, op. cit. 317; Brunner, op. cit. i. 354; Schröder, op. cit. 234.
Edited by v. Salis in M. G.

[4] Krüger, op. cit. 300; Brunner, op. cit. i. 358.   Edited by Hänel, 1849.

[5] Karlowa, op. cit. i. 976.   [6] See above, p. 6.

not the only, representative of Roman law in the expansive realm of the Franks. But even it was too bulky for men's needs. They made epitomes of it and epitomes of epitomes[1].

Then, again, we must remember that while Tribonian was busy upon the Digest, the East Goths were still masters of Italy. We recall the event of 476; one emperor, Zeno at Byzantium, was to be enough. Odovacer had ruled as patrician and king. He had been conquered by the East Goths. The great Theodoric had reigned for more than thirty years (493–526); he had tried to fuse Italians and Goths into one nation; he had issued a considerable body of law, the *Edictum Theodorici*, for the more part of a criminal kind[2]. *The Edictum Theodorici.*

Lastly, it must not escape us that about the year 500 there was in Rome a monk of Scythian birth who was labouring upon the foundations of the *Corpus Iuris Canonici*. He called himself Dionysius Exiguus. He was an expert chronologist and constructed the Dionysian cycle. He was collecting and translating the canons of eastern councils; he was collecting also some of the letters (decretal letters they will be called) that had been issued by the popes from Siricius onwards (384–498)[3]. This *Collectio Dionysiana* made its way in the West. Some version of it may have been the book of canons which our Archbishop Theodore produced at the Council of Hertford in 673[4]. A version of it (*Dionysio-Hadriana*) was sent by Pope Hadrian to Charles the Great in 774[5]. It helped to spread abroad the notion that the popes can declare, even if they can not make, law for the universal church, and thus to contract the sphere of secular jurisprudence. *The Collectio Diony siana.*

In 528 Justinian began the work which gives him his fame in legal history; in 534, though there were novel constitutions to come from him, it was finished. Valuable as the Code of imperial statutes might be, valuable as might be the modernized and imperial edition of an excellent but ancient school-book, *Justinian's books.*

---

[1] The epitomes will be found in Hänel's edition, Lex Romana Visigothorum, 1849.

[2] Brunner, op. cit. i. 365; Karlowa, op. cit. i. 947 ff. Edited by Bluhme in M. G.

[3] Maassen, op. cit. i. 422 ff.; Tardif, op. cit. 110. Printed in Migne, Patrologia, vol. 67.

[4] Haddan and Stubbs, Councils, iii. 119. See, however, the remarks of Mr C. H. Turner, E. H. R. ix. 727.

[5] Maassen, op. cit. i. 441.

the main work that he did for the coming centuries lies in the Digest. We are told now-a-days that in the Orient the classical jurisprudence had taken a new lease of life, especially in the school at Berytus[1]. We are told that there is something of a renaissance, something even of an antiquarian revival visible in the pages of the Digest, a desire to go back from vulgar practice to classical text, also a desire to display an erudition that is not always very deep. Great conqueror, great builder, great theologian, great law-giver, Justinian would also be a great master of legal science and legal history. The narrow escape of his Digest from oblivion seems to tell us that, but for his exertions, very little of the ancient treasure of wisdom would have reached modern times: and a world without the Digest would not have been the world that we know. Let us, however, remember the retrospective character of the book. The *ius*, the unenacted law, ceased to grow three hundred years ago. In time Justinian stands as far from the jurists whose opinions he collects as we stand from Coke or even from Fitzherbert.

Justinian
and Italy. Laws have need of arms: Justinian knew it well. Much depended upon the fortunes of a war. We recall from the Institutes the boast that Africa has been reclaimed. Little was at stake there, for Africa was doomed to the Saracens; nor could transient success in Spain secure a western home for the law books of Byzantium[2]. All was at stake in Italy. The struggle with the East Goths was raging; Rome was captured and recaptured. At length the emperor was victorious (552), the Goths were exterminated or expelled; we hear of them no more. Justinian could now enforce his laws in Italy and this he did by the pragmatic sanction *pro petitione Vigilii* (554)[3]. Fourteen years were to elapse and then the Lombard hordes under Alboin would be pouring down upon an exhausted and depopulated land. Those fourteen years are critical in legal history; they suffer Justinian's books to obtain a lodgement in the West. The occidental world has paid heavily for Code and Digest in the destruction of the Gothic kingdom, in the temporal power of the papacy, and in an Italy never united until our own day; but perhaps the price was not too high. Be that as it may, the coincidence is memorable. The Roman

---

[1] Krüger, op. cit. 319.   [2] Conrat, op. cit. i. 32.

[3] Krüger, op. cit. 354; Karlowa, op. cit. i. 938; Hodgkin, Italy and her Invaders, vi. 519.

empire centred in New Rome has just strength enough to hand
back to Old Rome the guardianship of her heathen jurisprudence, now 'enucleated' (as Justinian says) in a small compass,
and then loses for ever the power of legislating for the West.
True that there is the dwindling exarchate in Italy; true that
the year 800 is still far off; true that one of Justinian's successors, Constantine IV., will pay Rome a twelve days' visit
(663) and rob it of ornaments that Vandals have spared[1]; but
with what we must call Græco-Roman jurisprudence, with the
Ecloga of Leo the Isaurian and the Basilica of Leo the Wise,
the West, if we except some districts of southern Italy[2], has no
concern. Two halves of the world were drifting apart, were
becoming ignorant of each other's language, intolerant of each
other's theology. He who was to be the true lord of Rome, if
he loathed the Lombard, loved not the emperor. Justinian had
taught Pope Vigilius, the Vigilius of the pragmatic sanction,
that in the Byzantine system the church must be a department
of the state[3]. The bishop of Rome did not mean to be the head
of a department.

During some centuries Pope Gregory the Great (590–604) Laws of
is one of the very few westerns whose use of the Digest can be Æthelbert.
proved[4]. He sent Augustin to England. Then 'in Augustin's
day,' about the year 600, Æthelbert of Kent set in writing the
dooms of his folk 'in Roman fashion[5].' Not improbably he had
heard of Justinian's exploits; but the dooms, though already
they are protecting with heavy *bót* the property of God, priests
and bishops, are barbarous enough. They are also, unless
discoveries have yet to be made, the first Germanic laws that
were written in a Germanic tongue. In many instances the
desire to have written laws appears so soon as a barbarous race
is brought into contact with Rome[6]. The acceptance of the
new religion must have revolutionary consequences in the

---

[1] Gregorovius, History of Rome (transl. Hamilton), ii. 153 ff.; Oman, Dark
Ages, 237, 245.

[2] For Byzantine law in southern Italy see Conrat, op. cit. i. 49.

[3] Hodgkin, Italy and her Invaders, iv. 571 ff.: 'The Sorrows of Vigilius.'

[4] Conrat, op. cit. i. 8.

[5] Bede, Hist. Eccl., lib. 2, c. 5 (ed. Plummer, i. 90): 'iuxta exempla
Romanorum.' Bede himself (Opera, ed. Giles, vol. vi. p. 321) had read of
Justinian's Codex; but what he says of it seems to prove that he had never
seen it: Conrat, op. cit. i. 99.

[6] Brunner, op. cit. i. 283.

world of law, for it is likely that heretofore the traditional customs, even if they have not been conceived as instituted by gods who are now becoming devils, have been conceived as essentially unalterable. Law has been the old; new law has been a contradiction in terms. And now about certain matters there must be new law[1]. What is more, 'the example of the Romans' shows that new law can be made by the issue of commands. Statute appears as the civilized form of law. Thus a fermentation begins and the result is bewildering. New resolves are mixed up with statements of old custom in these *Leges Barbarorum.*

Centuries VII and VIII. Germanic laws. The century which ends in 700 sees some additions made to the Kentish laws by Hlothær and Eadric, and some others made by Wihtræd; there the Kentish series ends. It also sees in the dooms of Ine the beginning of written law in Wessex[2]. It also sees the beginning of written law among the Lombards; in 643 Rothari published his edict[3]; it is accounted to be one of the best statements of ancient German usages. A little later the Swabians have their *Lex Alamannorum*[4], and the Bavarians their *Lex Baiuwariorum*[5]. It is only in the Karolingian age that written law appears among the northern and eastern folks of Germany, the Frisians, the Saxons, the Angli and Warni of Thuringia, the Franks of Hamaland[6]. To a much later time must we regretfully look for the oldest monuments of Scandinavian law[7]. Only two of our 'heptarchic'

---

[1] The oldest Germanic word that answers to our *law* seems to be that which appears as A.-S. *ǽ*. This word lives on in our Eng. *ay* or *aye* (=ever, from all time). It is said to be cognate to Lat. *aevum*. See Brunner, op. cit. i. 109; Schröder, op. cit. 222; Schmid, Gesetze, 524; Oxf. Eng. Dict. s. v. *ay*. For *lagu*, see Brunner, loc. cit.; Schmid, 621. Hlothær and Eadric increase the *ǽ* of the Kentish folk by their dooms.

[2] Whether we have Ine's code or only an Alfredian recension of it is a difficult question, lately discussed by Turk, Legal Code of Ælfred (Halle, 1893) p. 42.

[3] Brunner, op. cit. i. 368; Schröder, op. cit. 236. Edited by Bluhme in M. G.

[4] Brunner, op. cit. i. 308; Schröder, op. cit. 238. Edited by Lehmann in M. G. There are fragments of a *Pactus Alamannorum* from circ. 600. The *Lex* is supposed to come from 717–9.

[5] Brunner, op. cit. i. 313; Schröder, op. cit. 239. Edited by Merkel in M. G. This is now ascribed to the years 739–48.

[6] Brunner, op. cit. i. 340 ff.; Schröder, op. cit. 240 ff. Edited by v. Richthofen and Sohm in M. G.

[7] K. Maurer, Ueberblick über die Geschichte der nordgermanischen Rechtsquellen in v. Holtzendorff, Encyklopädie.

kingdoms leave us law, Kent and Wessex, though we have reason to believe that Offa the Mercian (ob. 796) legislated[1]. Even Northumbria, Bede's Northumbria, which was a bright spot in a dark world, bequeaths no dooms. The impulse of Roman example soon wore out. When once a race has got its *Lex*, its aspirations seem to be satisfied. About the year 900 Alfred speaks as though Offa (circ. 800), Ine (circ. 700), Æthelbert (circ. 600) had left him little to do. Rarely upon the mainland was there any authoritative revision of the ancient *Leges*, though transcribers sometimes modified them to suit changed times, and by so doing have perplexed the task of modern historians. Only among the Lombards, who from the first, despite their savagery, seem to show something that is like a genius for law[2], was there steadily progressive legislation. Grimwald (668), Liutprand (713-35), Ratchis (746) and Aistulf (755) added to the edict of Rothari. Not by abandoning, but by developing their own ancient rules, the Lombards were training themselves to be the interpreters and in some sort the heirs of the Roman *prudentes*.

As the Frankish realm expanded, there expanded with it a wonderful 'system of personal laws[3].' It was a system of racial laws. The *Lex Salica*, for example, was not the law of a district, it was the law of a race. The Swabian, wherever he might be, lived under his Alamannic law, or, as an expressive phrase tells us, he lived Alamannic law (*legem vivere*). So Roman law was the law of the Romani. In a famous, if exaggerated sentence, Bishop Agobard of Lyons has said that often five men would be walking or sitting together and each of them would own a different law[4]. We are now taught that this principle is not primitively Germanic. Indeed in England, where there were no Romani, it never came to the front, and, for example, 'the Danelaw' very rapidly became the name for a tract of land[5]. But in the kingdoms founded by Goths and Burgundians the intruding Germans were only a small part of

System of personal laws.

---

[1] Alfred, Introduction, 49, § 9 (Liebermann, Gesetze, p. 46).

[2] Brunner, op. cit. i. 370; Schröder, op. cit. 235.

[3] Brunner, op. cit. i. 259; Schröder, op. cit. 225; Esmein, op. cit. 57.

[4] Agobardi Opera, Migne, Patrol. vol. 104, col. 116 : 'Nam plerumque contingit ut simul eant aut sedeant quinque homines et nullus eorum communem legem cum altero habeat.'

[5] Stubbs, Constit. Hist. i. 216. See, however, Dahn, Könige der Germanen, vii. (3), pp. 1 ff.

a population, the bulk of which was Gallo-Roman, and the
barbarians, at least in show, had made their entry as subjects
or allies of the emperor.   It was natural then that the Romani
should live their old law, and, as we have seen[1], their rulers
were at pains to supply them with books of Roman law suitable
to an age which would bear none but the shortest of law-books.
It is doubtful whether the Salian Franks made from the first
any similar concession to the provincials whom they subdued;
but, as they spread over Gaul, always retaining their own *Lex
Salica*, they allowed to the conquered races the right that
they claimed for themselves.   Their victorious career gave the
principle an always wider scope.   At length they carried it
with them into Italy and into the very city of Rome.   It would
seem that among the Lombards, the Romani were suffered to
settle their own disputes by their own rules, but Lombard law
prevailed between Roman and Lombard.   However, when
Charles the Great vanquished Desiderius and made himself
king of the Lombards, the Frankish system of personal law
found a new field.   A few years afterwards (800) a novel
Roman empire was established.   One of the immediate results
of this many-sided event was that Roman law ceased to be the
territorial law of any part of the lands that had become subject
to the so-called Roman Emperor.   Even in Rome it was reduced
to the level of a personal or racial law, while in northern Italy
there were many Swabians who lived Alamannic, and Franks
who lived Salic or Ripuarian law, besides the Lombards[2].   In
the future the *renovatio imperii* was to have a very different
effect.   If the Ottos and Henries were the successors of Augustus, Constantine and Justinian, then Code and Digest were
Kaiserrecht, statute law for the renewed empire.   But some
centuries were to pass before this theory would be evolved, and
yet other centuries before it would practically mould the law of
Germany.   Meanwhile Roman law was in Rome itself only the
personal law of the Romani.

The vulgar Roman law.
A system of personal laws implies rules by which a ' conflict
of laws' may be appeased, and of late years many of the international or intertribal rules of the Frankish realm have been
recovered[3].   We may see, for example, that the law of the slain,
not that of the slayer, fixes the amount of the wergild, and that
the law of the grantor prescribes the ceremonies with which land

[1] See above, p. 8.   [2] Brunner, op. cit. i. 260.   [3] Ibid. 261 ff.

must be conveyed. We see that legitimate children take their father's, bastards their mother's law. We see also that the churches, except some which are of royal foundation, are deemed to live Roman law, and in Italy, though not in Frankland, the rule that the individual cleric lives Roman law seems to have been gradually adopted[1]. This gave the clergy some interest in the old system. But German and Roman law were making advances towards each other. If the one was becoming civilized, the other had been sadly barbarized or rather vulgarized. North of the Alps the current Roman law regarded Alaric's *Lex* as its chief authority. In Italy Justinian's Institutes and Code and Julian's epitome of the Novels were known, and someone may sometimes have opened a copy of the Digest. But everywhere the law administered among the Romani seems to have been in the main a traditional, customary law which paid little heed to written texts. It was, we are told, *ein römisches Vulgarrecht*, which stood to pure Roman law in the same relation as that in which the vulgar Latin or Romance that people talked stood to the literary language[2]. Not a few of the rules and ideas which were generally prevalent in the West had their source in this low Roman law. In it starts the history of modern conveyancing. The Anglo-Saxon 'land-book' is of Italian origin[3]. That England produces no formulary books, no books of 'precedents in conveyancing,' such as those which in considerable numbers were compiled in Frankland[4], is one of the many signs that even this low Roman law had no home here; but neither did our forefathers talk low Latin.

In the British India of to-day we may see and on a grand scale what might well be called a system of personal laws, of racial laws. If we compared it with the Frankish, one picturesque element would be wanting. Suppose that among the native races there was one possessed of an old law-book, too good for it, too good for us, which gradually, as men studied it afresh, would begin to tell of a very ancient but eternally modern civilization and of a skilful jurisprudence which the lawyers of the ruling race would some day make their model. This romance of history will not repeat itself.

The latent Digest.

---

[1] Brunner, op. cit. i. 269; Löning, op. cit. ii. 284.   [2] Brunner, op. cit. i. 255.

[3] Brunner, Zur Rechtsgeschichte der römischen und germanischen Urkunde, i. 187.

[4] Brunner, D. R. G. i. 401; Schröder, op. cit. 254. Edited in M. G. by Zeumer; also by E. de Rozière, Recueil général des formules.

The capitularies.
During the golden age of the Frankish supremacy, the age which closely centres round the year 800, there was a good deal of definite legislation: much more than there was to be in the bad time that was coming. The king or emperor issued capitularies (*capitula*)[1]. Within a sphere which can not be readily defined he exercised a power of laying commands upon all his subjects, and so of making new territorial law for his whole realm or any part thereof; but in principle any change in the law of one of the folks would require that folk's consent. A superstructure of capitularies might be reared, but the *Lex* of a folk was not easily alterable. In 827 Ansegis, Abbot of St Wandrille, collected some of the capitularies into four books[2]. His work seems to have found general acceptance, though it shows that many capitularies were speedily forgotten and that much of the Karolingian legislation had failed to produce a permanent effect. Those fratricidal wars were beginning. The legal products which are to be characteristic of this unhappy age are not genuine laws; they are the forged capitularies of Benedict the Levite and the false decretals of the Pseudo-Isidore.

Growth of Canon law.
Slowly and by obscure processes a great mass of ecclesiastical law had been forming itself. It rolled, if we may so speak, from country to country and took up new matter into itself as it went, for bishop borrowed from bishop and transcriber from transcriber. Oriental, African, Spanish, Gallican canons were collected into the same book and the decretal letters of later were added to those of earlier popes. Of the *Dionysiana* we have already spoken. Another celebrated collection seems to have taken shape in the Spain of the seventh century; it has been known as the *Hispana* or *Isidoriana*[3], for without sufficient warrant it has been attributed to that St Isidore of Seville (ob. 636), whose *Origines*[4] served as an encyclopædia of jurisprudence and all other sciences. The *Hispana* made its way into France, and

---

[1] Brunner, op. cit. i. 374; Schröder, op. cit. 247; Esmein, op. cit. 116. Edited in M. G. by Boretius and Krause; previously by Pertz.

[2] Brunner, op. cit. i. 382; Schröder, op. cit. 251; Esmein, op. cit. 117.

[3] Maassen, op. cit. i. 667 ff.; Tardif, op. cit. 117. Printed in Migne, Patrol. vol. 84.

[4] For the Roman law of the Origines, see Conrat, op. cit. i. 150. At first or second hand this work was used by the author of our *Leges Henrici*. That the learned Isidore knew nothing of Justinian's books seems to be proved, and this shows that they were not current in Spain.

ıt seems to have already comprised some spurious documents before it came to the hands of the most illustrious of all forgers.

Then out of the depth of the ninth century emerged a book which was to give law to mankind for a long time to come. Its core was the *Hispana;* but into it there had been foisted besides other forgeries, some sixty decretals professing to come from the very earliest successors of St Peter. The compiler called himself Isidorus Mercator; he seems to have tried to personate Isidore of Seville. Many guesses have been made as to his name and time and home. It seems certain that he did his work in Frankland, and near the middle of the ninth century. He has been sought as far west as le Mans, but suspicion hangs thickest over the church of Reims. The false decretals are elaborate mosaics made up out of phrases from the bible, the fathers, genuine canons, genuine decretals, the West Goth's Roman law-book; but all these materials, wherever collected, are so arranged as to establish a few great principles: the grandeur and superhuman origin of ecclesiastical power, the sacrosanctity of the persons and the property of bishops, and, though this is not so prominent, the supremacy of the bishop of Rome. Episcopal rights are to be maintained against the *chorepiscopi*, against the metropolitans, and against the secular power. Above all (and this is the burden of the song), no accusation can be brought against a bishop so long as he is despoiled of his see: *Spoliatus episcopus ante omnia debet restitui.*

Closely connected with this fraud was another. Some one who called himself a deacon of the church of Mainz and gave his name as Benedict, added to the four books of capitularies, which Ansegis had published, three other books containing would-be, but false capitularies, which had the same bent as the decretals concocted by the Pseudo-Isidore. These are not the only, but they are the most famous manifestations of the lying spirit which had seized the Frankish clergy. The Isidorian forgeries were soon accepted at Rome. The popes profited by documents which taught that ever since the apostolic age the bishops of Rome had been declaring, or even making, law for the universal church. On this rock or on this sand a lofty edifice was reared[1].

Marginal notes: Centuries IX and X. The false Isidore. / The forged capitularies.

[1] The Decretales Pseudo-Isidorianae were edited by Hinschius in 1863. See also Tardif, op. cit. 133 ff.; Conrat, op. cit. i. 299; Brunner, op. cit. i. 384.

Church
and State.
And now for the greater part of the Continent comes the
time when ecclesiastical law is the only sort of law that is
visibly growing. The stream of capitularies ceased to flow;
there was none to legislate; the Frankish monarchy was going
to wreck and ruin; feudalism was triumphant. Sacerdotalism
also was triumphant, and its victories were closely connected
with those of feudalism. The clergy had long been striving to
place themselves beyond the reach of the state's tribunals.
The dramatic struggle between Henry II. and Becket has a
long Frankish prologue[1]. Some concessions had been won
from the Merovingians; but still Charles the Great had been
supreme over all persons and in all causes. Though his realm
fell asunder, the churches were united, and united by a
principle that claimed a divine origin. They were rapidly
evolving law which was in course of time to be the written
law of an universal and theocratic monarchy. The mass, now
swollen by the Isidorian forgeries, still rolled from diocese to
diocese, taking up new matter into itself. It became always
more lawyerly in form and texture as it appropriated sentences
from the Roman law-books and made itself the law of the only
courts to which the clergy would yield obedience. Nor was it
above borrowing from Germanic law, for thence it took its
probative processes, the oath with oath-helpers and the ordeal
or judgment of God. Among the many compilers of manuals
of church law three are especially famous: Regino, abbot of
Prüm (906-915[2]), Burchard, bishop of Worms (1012–1023)[3],
and Ivo, bishop of Chartres (ob. 1117)[4]. They and many
others prepared the way for Gratian, the maker of the church's
Digest, and events were deciding that the church should also
have a Code and abundant Novels. In an evil day for themselves the German kings took the papacy from the mire into
which it had fallen, and soon the work of issuing decretals
was resumed with new vigour. At the date of the Norman
Conquest the flow of these edicts was becoming rapid.

The
darkest
age.
Historians of French and German law find that a well-
marked period is thrust upon them. The age of the folk-laws

---

[1] Hinschius, op. cit. iv. 849 ff.

[2] Tardif, op. cit. 162. Printed in Migne, Patrol. vol. 132; also edited by
Wasserschleben, 1840.

[3] Ibid. 164. Printed in Migne, Patrol. vol. 140.

[4] Ibid. 170. See Fournier, Yves de Chartres, Paris, 1898.

and the capitularies, 'the Frankish time,' they can restore. Much indeed is dark and disputable; but much has been made plain during the last thirty years by their unwearying labour. There is no lack of materials, and the materials are of a strictly legal kind: laws and statements of law. This done, they are compelled rapidly to pass through several centuries to a new point of view. They take their stand in the thirteenth among law-books which have the treatises of Glanvill and Bracton for their English equivalents. It is then a new world that they paint for us. To connect this new order with the old, to make the world of 'the classical feudalism[1]' grow out of the world of the folk-laws is a task which is being slowly accomplished by skilful hands; but it is difficult, for, though materials are not wanting, they are not of a strictly legal kind; they are not laws, nor law-books, nor statements of law. The intervening, the dark age, has been called 'the diplomatic age,' whereby is meant that its law must be hazardously inferred from *diplomata*, from charters, from conveyances, from privileges accorded to particular churches or particular towns. No one legislates. The French historian will tell us that the last capitularies which bear the character of general laws are issued by Carloman II. in 884, and that the first legislative *ordonnance* is issued by Louis VII. in 1155[2]. Germany and France were coming to the birth and the agony was long. Long it was questionable whether the western world would not be overwhelmed by Northmen and Saracens and Magyars; perhaps we are right in saying that it was saved by feudalism[3]. Meanwhile the innermost texture of human society was being changed; local customs were issuing from and then consuming the old racial laws.

Strangely different, at least upon its surface, is our English story. The age of the capitularies (for such we well might call it) begins with us just when it has come to its end upon the Continent. We have had some written laws from the newly converted Kent and Wessex of the seventh century. We have

Legislation in England.

---

[1] We borrow *la féodalité classique* from M. Flach : Les origines de l'ancienne France, ii. 551.

[2] Esmein, op. cit. 487–8 ; Viollet, op. cit. 152. Schröder, op. cit. 624: 'Vom 10. bis 12. Jahrhundert ruhte die Gesetzgebung fast ganz...Es war die Zeit der Alleinherrschaft des Gewohnheitsrechtes.'

[3] Oman, The Dark Ages, 511.

heard that in the day of Mercia's greatness Offa (ob. 796), influenced perhaps by the example of Charles the Great, had published laws. These we have lost, but we have no reason to fear that we have lost much else. Even Egbert did not legislate. The silence was broken by Alfred (871—901), and then, for a century and a half we have laws from almost every king: from Edward, Æthelstan, Edmund, Edgar, Æthelred and Cnut. The age of the capitularies begins with Alfred, and in some sort it never ends, for William the Conqueror and Henry I. take up the tale[1]. Whether in the days of the Confessor, whom a perverse, though explicable, tradition honoured as a preeminent law-giver, we were not on the verge of an age without legislation, an age which would but too faithfully reproduce some bad features of the Frankish decadence, is a question that is not easily answered. Howbeit, Cnut had published in England a body of laws which, if regard be had to its date, must be called a handsome code. If he is not the greatest legislator of the eleventh century, we must go as far as Barcelona to find his peer[2]. He had been to Rome; he had seen an emperor crowned by a pope; but it was not outside England that he learnt to legislate. He followed a fashion set by Alfred. We might easily exaggerate both the amount of new matter that was contained in these English capitularies and the amount of information that they give us; but the mere fact that Alfred sets, and that his successors (and among them the conquering Dane), maintain, a fashion of legislating is of great importance. The Norman subdues, or, as he says, inherits a kingdom in which a king is expected to publish laws.

England and the continent.

Were we to discuss the causes of this early divergence of English from continental history we might wander far. In the first place, we should have to remember the small size, the plain surface, the definite boundary of our country. This

---

[1] As to the close likeness between the English dooms and the Frankish capitularies, see Stubbs, Const. Hist. i. 223. We might easily suppose direct imitation, were it not that much of the Karolingian system was in ruins before Alfred began his work.

[2] The Usatici Barchinonensis Patriae (printed by Giraud, Histoire du droit français, ii. 465 ff.) are ascribed to Raymond Berengar I. and to the year 1068 or thereabouts. But how large a part of them really comes from him is a disputable question. See Conrat, op. cit. i. 467; Ficker, Mittheilungen des Instituts für österreichische Geschichtsforschung, 1888, ii. p. 236.

thought indeed must often recur to us in the course of our work: England is small: it can be governed by uniform law: it seems to invite general legislation. Also we should notice that the kingship of England, when once it exists, preserves its unity: it is not partitioned among brothers and cousins. Moreover we might find ourselves saying that the Northmen were so victorious in their assaults on our island that they did less harm here than elsewhere. In the end it was better that they should conquer a tract, settle in villages and call the lands by their own names, than that the state should go to pieces in the act of repelling their inroads. Then, again, it would not escape us that a close and confused union between church and state prevented the development of a body of distinctively ecclesiastical law which would stand in contrast with, if not in opposition to, the law of the land[1]. Such power had the bishops in all public affairs, that they had little to gain from decretals forged or genuine[2]; indeed Æthelred's laws are apt to become mere sermons preached to a disobedient folk. However we are here but registering the fact that the age of capitularies, which was begun by Alfred, does not end. The English king, be he weak like Æthelred or strong like Cnut, is expected to publish laws.

But Italy was to be for a while the focus of the whole world's legal history. For one thing, the thread of legislation was never quite broken there. Capitularies or statutes which enact territorial law came from Karolingian emperors and from Karolingian kings of Italy, and then from the Ottos and later German kings. But what is more important is that the old Lombard law showed a marvellous vitality and a capacity of being elaborated into a reasonable and progressive system. Lombardy was the country in which the principle of personal law struck its deepest roots. Besides Lombards and Romani there were many Franks and Swabians who transmitted their law from father to son. It was long before the old question *Qua lege vivis?* lost its importance. The 'conflict of laws' seems to have favoured the growth of a mediating and

Century XI.
The Pavian law-school.

---

[1] Stubbs, Const. Hist. i. 263: 'There are few if any records of councils distinctly ecclesiastical held during the tenth century in England.'

[2] There seem to be traces of the Frankish forgeries in the Worcester book described by Miss Bateson, E. H. R. x. 712 ff. English ecclesiastics were borrowing and it is unlikely that they escaped contamination.

instructed jurisprudence. Then at Pavia in the first half of
the eleventh century a law-school had arisen. In it men were
endeavouring to systematize by gloss and comment the ancient
Lombard statutes of Rothari and his successors. The heads
of the school were often employed as royal justices (*iudices
palatini*); their names and their opinions were treasured by
admiring pupils. From out this school came Lanfranc. Thus
a body of law, which though it had from the first been more
neatly expressed than, was in its substance strikingly like, our
own old dooms, became the subject of continuous and professional
study. The influence of reviving Roman law is not to be
ignored. These Lombardists knew their Institutes, and, before
the eleventh century was at an end, the doctrine that Roman
law was a subsidiary common law for all mankind (*lex omnium
generalis*) was gaining ground among them; but still the law
upon which they worked was the old Germanic law of the
Lombard race. Pavia handed the lamp to Bologna, Lombardy
to the Romagna[1].

The new
birth of
Roman
law.

As to the more or less that was known of the ancient
Roman texts there has been learned and lively controversy in
these last years[2]. But, even if we grant to the champions of
continuity all that they ask, the sum will seem small until the
eleventh century is reached. That large masses of men in
Italy and southern France had Roman law for their personal
law is beyond doubt. Also it is certain that Justinian's Institutes
and Code and Julian's Epitome of the Novels were beginning
to spread outside Italy. There are questions still to be solved
about the date and domicile of various small collections of
Roman rules which some regard as older than or uninfluenced
by the work of the Bolognese glossators. One critic discovers

---

[1] Boretius, Preface to edition of Liber legis Langobardorum, in M. G. ;
Brunner, op. cit. i. 387 ff. ; Ficker, Forschungen zur Reichs- u. Rechtsgeschichte
Italiens, iii. 44 ff., 139 ff. ; Conrat, op. cit. i. 393 ff.

[2] It is well summed up for English readers by Rashdall, Universities of
Europe, i. 89 ff. The chief advocate of a maximum of knowledge has been
Dr Hermann Fitting in Juristiche Schriften des früheren Mittelalters, 1876, Die
Anfänge der Rechtsschule zu Bologna, 1888, and elsewhere. He has recently
edited a Summa Codicis (1894) and some Quaestiones de iuris subtilitatibus,
both of which he ascribes to Irnerius. See also Pescatore, Die Glossen des
Irnerius, 1888 ; Mommsen, Preface to two-volume edition of the Digest ; Flach,
Études critiques sur l'histoire du droit romain, 1890 ; Besta, L' Opera d' Irnerio,
1896 ; Ficker, op. cit. vol. iii. and Conrat, op. cit. passim.

evanescent traces of a school of law at Rome or at Ravenna
which others can not see. The current instruction of boys
in grammar and rhetoric involved some discussion of legal
terms. Definitions of *lex* and *ius* and so forth were learnt by
heart; little catechisms were compiled[1]; but of anything that
we should dare to call an education in Roman law there are few,
if any, indisputable signs before the school of Bologna appears
in the second half of the eleventh century. As to the Digest,
during some four hundred years its mere existence seems to
have been almost unknown. It barely escaped with its life.
When men spoke of 'the pandects' they meant the bible[2].
The romantic fable of the capture of an unique copy at the
siege of Amalfi in 1135 has long been disproved; but, if some
small fragments be neglected, all the extant manuscripts are
said to derive from two copies, one now lost, the other the
famous Florentina written, we are told, by Greek hands in the
sixth or seventh century. In the eleventh the revival began.
In 1038 Conrad II., the emperor whom Cnut saw crowned,
ordained that Roman law should be once more the territorial
law of the city of Rome[3]. In 1076 the Digest was cited in the
judgment of a Tuscan court[4]. Then, about 1100, Irnerius was
teaching at Bologna[5].

Here, again, there is room for controversy. It is said that The
he was not self-taught; it is said that neither his theme nor recovered
his method was quite new; it is said that he had a predecessor Digest.
at Bologna, one Pepo by name. All this may be true and is
probable enough: and yet undoubtedly he was soon regarded
as the founder of the school which was teaching Roman law to
an intently listening world. We with our many sciences can
hardly comprehend the size of this event. The monarchy of
theology over the intellectual world was disputed. A lay

[1] See E. J. Tardif, Extraits et abrégés juridiques des étymologies d'Isidore
de Séville, 1896.

[2] Conrat, op. cit. i. 65.

[3] M. G. Leges, ii. 40; Conrat, op. cit. i. 62.

[4] Ficker, Forschungen, iii. 126; iv. 99; Conrat, op. cit. 67. Apparently the
most industrious research has failed to prove that between 603 and 1076 any one
cited the Digest. The bare fact that Justinian had issued such a book seems to
have vanished from memory. Conrat, op. cit. i. 69.

[5] In dated documents Irnerius (his name seems to have really been
Warnerius, Guarnerius) appears in 1113 and disappears in 1125. The University of Bologna kept 1888 as its octocentenary.

science claimed its rights, its share of men's attention. It was a science of civil life to be found in the human, heathen Digest[1].

Influence of the Bolognese jurisprudence.   A new force had begun to play and sooner or later every body of law in western Europe felt it.   The challenged church answered with Gratian's Decretum (circ. 1139) and the Decretals of Gregory IX. (1234).   The canonist emulated the civilian and for a long while maintained in the field of jurisprudence what seemed to be an equal combat.   Unequal it was in truth. The Decretum is sad stuff when set beside the Digest and the study of Roman law never dies.   When it seems to be dying it always returns to the texts and is born anew.   It is not for us here to speak of its new birth in the France of the sixteenth or in the Germany of the nineteenth century; but its new birth in the Italy of the eleventh and twelfth concerns us nearly. Transient indeed but all-important was the influence of the Bologna of Irnerius and of Gratian upon the form, and therefore upon the substance, of our English law.   The theoretical continuity or 'translation' of the empire which secured for Justinian's books their hold upon Italy, and, though after a wide interval, upon Germany also, counted for little in France or in England.   In England, again, there was no mass of Romani, of people who all along had been living Roman law of a degenerate and vulgar sort and who would in course of time be taught to look for their law to Code and Digest.   Also there was no need in England for that *reconstitution de l'unité nationale* which fills a large space in schemes of French history, and in which, for good and ill, the Roman texts gave their powerful aid to the centripetal and monarchical forces.   In England the new learning found a small, homogeneous, well conquered, much governed kingdom, a strong, a legislating kingship.   It came to us soon; it taught us much; and then there was healthy resistance to foreign dogma.   But all this we shall see in the sequel.

[1] Esmein, op. cit. 347: 'Une science nouvelle naquit, indépendante et laïque, la science de la société civile, telle que l'avaient dégagée les Romains, et qui pouvait passer pour le chef-d'œuvre de la sagesse humaine...Il en résulta qu'à côté du théologien se plaça le légiste qui avait, comme lui, ses principes et ses textes, et qui lui disputa la direction des esprits avides de savoir.'   It is only by slow degrees that the Digest comes by its rights.   Throughout the middle ages the Code appears, as Justinian intended that it should appear, as the prominent book: it contains the new law.   See Fitting, Preface to the Summa of Irnerius.

CHAPTER II.

ANGLO-SAXON LAW.

[p.1]   THIS book is concerned with Anglo-Saxon legal antiquities, Scope of this chapter. but only so far as they are connected with, and tend to throw light upon, the subsequent history of the laws of England, and the scope of the present chapter is limited by that purpose. Much of our information about the Anglo-Saxon laws and customs, especially as regards landholding, is so fragmentary and obscure that the only hope of understanding it is to work back to it from the fuller evidence of Norman and even later times. It would be outside our undertaking to deal with problems of this kind[1].

    The habit of preserving some written record of all affairs of Imperfection of written records of early Germanic law. importance is a modern one in the north and west of Europe. But it is so prevalent and so much bound up with our daily habits that we have almost forgotten how much of the world's business, even in communities by no means barbarous, has been carried on without it. And the student of early laws and institutions, although the fact is constantly thrust upon him, can hardly accept it without a sort of continuing surprise. This brings with it a temptation of some practical danger, that of overrating both the trustworthiness of written documents and the importance of the matters they deal with as compared with other things for which the direct authority of documents is wanting. The danger is a specially besetting one in the early history of English law; and that inquirer is fortunate who is not beguiled into positive error by the desire of making his statements appear less imperfect. In truth, the manners, dress, and dialects of our ancestors before the Norman Conquest

---

[1] See Maitland, Domesday Book and Beyond, Cambridge, 1897.

are far better known to us than their laws. Historical inquiry must be subject, in the field of law, to peculiar and inevitable difficulties. In most other cases the evidence, whether full or [p.2] scanty, is clear so far as it goes. Arms, ornaments, miniatures, tell their own story. But written laws and legal documents, being written for present use and not for the purpose of enlightening future historians, assume knowledge on the reader's part of an indefinite mass of received custom and practice. They are intelligible only when they are taken as part of a whole which they commonly give us little help to conceive. It may even happen that we do not know whether a particular document or class of documents represents the normal course of affairs, or was committed to writing for the very reason that the transaction was exceptional. Even our modern law is found perplexing, for reasons of this kind, not only by foreigners, but by Englishmen who are not lawyers.

We can not expect, then, that the extant collections of Anglo-Saxon laws should give us anything like a complete view of the legal or judicial institutions of the time. Our Germanic ancestors were no great penmen, and we know that the reduction of any part of their customary laws to writing was in the first place due to foreign influence. Princes who had forsaken heathendom under the guidance of Roman clerks made haste, according to their lights, to imitate the ways of imperial and Christian Rome[1].

Although English princes issued written dooms with the advice of their wise men at intervals during nearly five centuries, it seems all but certain that none of them did so with the intention of constructing a complete body of law. The very

---

[1] The A.-S. laws were first printed by Lambard, Archaionomia, 1568. A second edition of his work was published by Whelock, Archaionomia, Cambridge, 1644.—This was followed in 1721 by Wilkins, Leges Anglo-Saxonicae.—In 1840 the Ancient Laws and Institutes of England were edited for the Record Commission by Price and Thorpe.—This was followed by Reinhold Schmid, Gesetze der Angelsachsen, 2nd ed. Leipzig, 1858, which superseded a first and incomplete edition of 1832.—A new edition by Dr F. Liebermann is in course of publication.— For detailed discussion see, besides Kemble's well-known works, the Glossary in Schmid's edition—Konrad Maurer, Angelsächsische Rechtsverhältnisse, in Kritische Ueberschau der deutschen Gesetzgebung, vol. i. ff. Munich, 1853, ff.— Essays in Anglo-Saxon Laws (Adams, Lodge, Young, Laughlin), 1876.—Full use has been made of the A.-S. documents by historians of German law, Brunner, Schröder, v. Amira and others.—For the Scandinavian side of the story, see Steenstrup, Danelag, Copenhagen, 1882.

slight and inconspicuous part which procedure takes in the written Anglo-Saxon laws is enough to show that they are mere superstructures on a much larger base of custom. All they do is to regulate and amend in details now this branch of customary law, now another. In short, their relation to the laws and customs of the country as a whole is not unlike that which Acts of Parliament continue to bear in our own day to the indefinite mass of the common law.

[p. 3]   Our knowledge of Anglo-Saxon law rests, so far as positive evidence goes, on several classes of documents which supplement one another to some extent, but are still far from giving a complete view. We have in the first place the considerable series of laws and ordinances of Saxon and English princes, beginning with those of Æthelbert of Kent, well known to general history as Augustine's convert, which are of about the end of the sixth century. The laws of Cnut may be said to close the list. Then from the century which follows the Norman Conquest we have various attempts to state the old English law. These belong to the second class of documents, namely, compilations of customs and formulas which are not known ever to have had any positive authority, but appear to have been put together with a view to practical use, or at least to preserve the memory of things which had been in practice, and which the writer hoped to see in practice again. Perhaps our most important witness of this kind is the tract or custumal called *Rectitudines singularum personarum*[1]. Some of the so-called laws are merely semi-official or private compilations, but their formal profession of an authority they really had not makes no difference to their value as evidence of what the compilers understood the customary law to have been. To some extent we can check them by their repetition of matter that occurs in genuine Anglo-Saxon laws of earlier dates. Apocryphal documents of this kind are by no means confined to England, nor, in English history, to the period before the Conquest. Some examples from the thirteenth century have found their way into the worshipful company of the Statutes of the Realm among the 'statutes of uncertain time.' It has been the work of more than one generation of scholars to detect

Marginal note: Anglo-Saxon dooms and custumals.

[1] Schmid, *Gesetze*, p. 371. The *Gerefa*, which seems to be a continuation of this tract, was published by Dr Liebermann, in *Anglia*, ix. 251, and by Dr Cunningham, *Growth of English Industry*, ed. 3, vol. i. p. 571 ff.

their true character, nor indeed is the work yet wholly done. From the existence and apparent, sometimes real, importance of such writings and compilations as we have now mentioned there has arisen the established usage of including them, together with genuine legislation, under the common heading of [p. 4] 'Anglo-Saxon laws.' As for the deliberate fables of later apocryphal authorities, the 'Mirror of Justices' being the chief and flagrant example, they belong not to the Anglo-Saxon but to a much later period of English law. For the more part they are not even false history; they are speculation or satire.

Charters. Another kind of contemporary writings affords us most valuable evidence for the limited field of law and usage which those writings cover. The field, however, is even more limited than at first sight it appears to be. We mean the charters or 'land-books' which record the munificence of princes to religious houses or to their followers, or in some cases the administration and disposition of domains thus acquired. Along with these we have to reckon the extant Anglo-Saxon wills, few in number as compared with charters properly so called, but of capital importance in fixing and illustrating some points. It was Kemble's great achievement to make the way plain to the appreciation and use of this class of evidences by his *Codex Diplomaticus.* We have to express opinions more or less widely different from Kemble's on several matters, and therefore think it well to say at once that no one who has felt the difference between genius and industrious good intentions can ever differ with Kemble lightly or without regret. Kemble's work often requires correction; but if Kemble's work had not been, there would be nothing to correct[1].

Chronicles, etc. Then we have incidental notices of Anglo-Saxon legal matters in chronicles and other writings, of which the value for this purpose must be judged by the usual canons of coincidence or nearness in point of time, the writer's means of access to contemporary witness or continuous tradition not otherwise preserved, his general trustworthiness in things more easily verified, and so forth. Except for certain passages of Bede, we

---

[1] The principal collections are:—Kemble, Codex Diplomaticus, 1839–48.— Thorpe, Diplomatarium, 1865.—Earle, Land Charters, 1888.—Birch, Cartularium, 1885 ff.—Napier and Stevenson, Crawford Charters, 1895.—Four volumes of facsimiles published by the British Museum, 1873 ff., and two volumes by the Ordnance Survey, 1877 ff.

do not think that the general literary evidence, so to call it, is remarkable either in quantity or in quality. Such as we have is, as might be expected, of social and economic interest in the first place, and throws a rather indirect light upon the legal aspect of Anglo-Saxon affairs.

Lastly, we have legal and official documents of the Anglo- Norman time, and foremost among them Domesday Book, which [p. 5] expressly or by implication tell us much of the state of England immediately before the Norman Conquest. Great as is the value of their evidence, it is no easy matter for a modern reader to learn to use it. These documents, royal and other inquests and what else, were composed for definite practical uses. And many of the points on which our curiosity is most active, and finds itself most baffled, were either common knowledge to the persons for whose use the documents were intended, or were not relevant to the purpose in hand. In the former case no more information was desired, in the latter none at all. Thus the Anglo-Norman documents raise problems of their own which must themselves be solved before we can use the results as a key to what lies even one generation behind them.

Anglo-Norman documents.

On the whole the state of English law before the Conquest presents a great deal of obscurity to a modern inquirer, not so much for actual lack of materials as for want of any sure clue to their right interpretation at a certain number of critical points. Nevertheless we cannot trace the history of our laws during the two centuries that followed the Conquest without having some general notions of the earlier period; and we must endeavour to obtain a view that may suffice for this purpose. It would be a barren task to apply the refined classification of modern systems to the dooms of Ine and Alfred or the more ambitious definitions of the *Leges Henrici Primi*. We shall take the main topics rather in their archaic order of importance. First comes the condition of persons; next, the establishment of courts, and the process of justice; then the rules applicable to breaches of the peace, wrongs and offences, and finally the law of property, so far as usage had been officially defined and enforced, or new modes of dealing with property introduced. The origin and development of purely political institutions has been purposely excluded from our scope.

Survey of Anglo-Saxon legal institutions.

As regards personal condition, we find the radical distinction, universal in ancient society, between the free man and the slave.

Personal conditions: lordship.

But in the earliest English authorities, nay, in our earliest
accounts of Germanic society, we do not find it in the clear-cut
simplicity of Roman law.   There is a great gulf between the
lowest of free men and the slave; but there are also differences
of rank and degrees of independence among free men, which
already prepare the way for the complexities of medieval society.
Some free men are lords, others are dependents or followers of
lords.   We have nothing to show the origin or antiquity of this [p. 6]
division; we know that it was the immemorial custom of Germanic chiefs to surround themselves with a band of personal
followers, the *comites* described by Tacitus, and we may suppose
that imitation or repetition of this custom led to the relation
of lord and man being formally recognized as a necessary part
of public order.   We know, moreover, that as early as the first
half of the tenth century the division had become exhaustive.
An ordinance of Æthelstan treats a ' lordless man ' as a suspicious
if not dangerous person; if he has not a lord who will answer
for him, his kindred must find him one; if they fail in this, he
may be dealt with (to use the nearest modern terms) as a rogue
and vagabond[1].   The term ' lord ' is applied to the king, in a
more eminent and extensive but at the same time in a looser
sense, with reference to all men owing or professing allegiance
to him[2].   Kings were glad to draw to their own use, if they
might, the feeling of personal attachment that belonged to
lordship in the proper sense, and at a later time the greater
lords may now and again have sought to emulate the king's
general power.   In any case this pervading division of free
persons into lords and men, together with the king's position as
general over-lord, combined at a later time with the prevalence
of dependent land tenures to form the more elaborate arrangements and theories of medieval feudalism.   It does not seem
possible either to assign any time in English history when some
free men did not hold land from their personal lords, or to
assign the time when this became a normal state of things.   In
the latter part of the ninth century there was already a considerable class of free men bound to work on the lands of others,
for an ordinance of Alfred fixes the holidays that are to be
allowed them; and we can hardly doubt that this work was

---

[1] Æthelst. II. 2. A man who was considerable enough to have only the king
above him required, of course, no other lord.

[2] A.-S. Chron. ann. 921.

incident to their own tenure[1]. At all events dependent land-
holding appears to have been common in the century before
the Norman Conquest. It was the work of the succeeding
century to establish the theory that all land must be 'held of'
some one as a fixed principle of English law, and to give to the
[p. 7] conditions of tenure as distinct from the personal status of the
tenant an importance which soon became preponderant, and
had much to do with the ultimate extinction of personal servitude under the Tudor dynasty[2].

Dependence on a lord was not the only check on the The family.
individual freedom of a freeborn man. Anglo-Saxon polity
preserved, even down to the Norman Conquest, many traces of
a time when kinship was the strongest of all bonds. Such a
stage of society, we hardly need add, is not confined to any one
region of the world or any one race of men. In its domestic
aspect it may take the form of the joint family or household
which, in various stages of resistance to modern tendencies and
on various scales of magnitude, is still an integral part of Hindu
and South Slavonic life. When it puts on the face of strife
between hostile kindreds, it is shown in the war of tribal
factions, and more specifically in the blood-feud. A man's
kindred are his avengers; and, as it is their right and honour
to avenge him, so it is their duty to make amends for his
misdeeds, or else maintain his cause in fight. Step by step, as
the power of the State waxes, the self-centred and self-helping
autonomy of the kindred wanes. Private feud is controlled,
regulated, put, one may say, into legal harness; the avenging
and the protecting clan of the slain and the slayer are made
pledges and auxiliaries of public justice. In England the
legalized blood-feud expired almost within living memory,
when the criminal procedure by way of 'appeal' was finally
abolished. We have to conceive, then, of the kindred not as
an artificial body or corporation to which the State allows
authority over its members in order that it may be answerable
for them, but as an element of the State not yielding precedence
to the State itself. There is a constant tendency to conflict
between the old customs of the family and the newer laws of
the State; the family preserves archaic habits and claims which
clash at every turn with the development of a law-abiding

---

[1] Ælf. 43.

[2] A solitary claim of villeinage is reported in the reign of James I.

commonwealth of the modern type. In the England of the tenth century[1], we find that a powerful kindred may still be a danger to public order, and that the power of three shires may be called out to bring an offending member of it to justice. At the same time the family was utilized by the growing institutions of the State, so far as was found possible. We [p.8] have seen that a lordless man's kinsfolk might be called upon to find him a lord. In other ways too the kindred was dealt with as collectively responsible for its members[2]. We need not however regard the kindred as a defined body like a tribe or clan, indeed this would not stand with the fact that the burden of making and the duty of exacting compensation ran on the mother's side as well as the father's. A father and son, or two half-brothers, would for the purposes of the blood-feud have some of their kindred in common, but by no means all.

The legal importance of the kindred continues to be recognized in the very latest Anglo-Saxon custumals, though some details that we find on the subject in the so-called laws of Henry I. fall under grave suspicion, not merely of an antiquary's pedantic exaggeration, but of deliberate copying from other Germanic law-texts. It is probable that a man could abjure his kindred, and that the oath used for the purpose included an express renunciation of any future rights of inheritance. We do not know whether this was at all a common practice, or whether any symbolic ceremonies like those of the Salic law were or ever had been required in England[3].

Ranks: ceorl, eorl, gesið.

Further, we find distinctions of rank among freemen which, though not amounting to fundamental differences of condition, and not always rigidly fixed, had more or less definite legal incidents. From the earliest times a certain pre-eminence is accorded (as among almost all Germanic people)[4] to men of noble birth. The ordinary freeman is a 'ceorl,' churl (there is no trace before the Norman Conquest of the modern degradation of the word); the noble by birth is an 'eorl.' This last word came later, under Danish influence, to denote a specific

---

[1] Æthelst. vi. (Iudicia civitatis Lundoniae) 8, § 2.

[2] Kemble, Saxons, i. 261. The A.-S. term for the kindred is 'mægð,' in Latin versions 'parentela.'

[3] Hen. 88, § 13; Schmid points out the strong resemblance to Lex Sal. 60, 'De eo qui se de parentilla tollere vult.'

[4] Brunner, D. R. G. i. 104 ff.

office of state, and our present 'earl' goes back to it in that sense. The Latin equivalent *comes* got specialized in much the same way. But such was not its ancient meaning. Special relations to the king's person or service produced another and somewhat different classification. 'Gesíð' was the earliest [p. 9] English equivalent, in practical as well as literal meaning, of *comes* as employed by Tacitus; it signified a well-born man attached to the king by the general duty of warlike service, though not necessarily holding any special office about his person. It is, however, a common poetic word, and it is not confined to men. It was current in Ine's time but already obsolete for practical purposes in Alfred's; latterly it appears to have implied hereditary rank and considerable landed possessions. The element of noble birth is emphasized by the fuller and commoner form 'gesíðcund.'

The official term of rank which we find in use in and after **Thegn.** Alfred's time is 'thegn[1]' (þegen, in Latin usually *minister*). Originally a thegn is a household officer of some great man, eminently and especially of the king. From the tenth century to the Conquest thegnship is not an office unless described by some specific addition (horsþegen, discþegen, and the like) showing what the office was. It is a social condition above [p. 10] that of the churl, carrying with it both privileges and customary duties. The 'king's thegns,' those who are in fact attached to the king's person and service, are specially distinguished. We may perhaps roughly compare the thegns of the later Anglo-Saxon monarchy to the country gentlemen of modern times who are in the commission of the peace and serve on the grand jury. But we must remember that the thegn had a definite legal rank. His wergild, for example, the fixed sum with which his death must be atoned for to his kindred, or which he might in some cases have to pay for his own misdoing, was six times as great as a common man's; and his oath weighed as much more in the curious contest of asseverations, quite different from anything we now understand by evidence, by which early Germanic lawsuits were decided. It is stated in more than one old document that a thegn's rights might be claimed by the owner of five hides (at the normal value of the hide, 600 acres) of land, a church and belfry, a 'burgh-gate-seat' (which may imply a private jurisdiction, or may only

---

[1] The modern form *thane* has acquired misleading literary associations.

signify a town house), and a special place in the king's hall.
The like right is ascribed to a merchant who has thrice crossed
'the wide sea' (the North Sea as opposed to the Channel) at
his own charges[1]. This may be suspected, in the absence of
confirmation, of being merely the expression of what, in the
writer's opinion, an enlightened English king ought to have
done to encourage trade, still it is not improbable. We have
no reason to reject the tradition about the five hides, which is
borne out by some later evidence. But this gives us no warrant
in any case for denying that a thegn might have less than five
hides of land, or asserting that he would forfeit his rank if he
lost the means of supporting it on the usual scale. However,
these details are really of no importance in the general history
of our later law, for they left no visible mark on the structure
of Anglo-Norman aristocracy[2].

Other distinctions. The last remark applies to certain other distinctions which [p. 11]
are mentioned in our authorities as well known, but never
distinctly explained. We read of 'twelf-hynd' and 'twy-hynd'
men, apparently so called from their wergild being twelve
hundred and two hundred shillings respectively. There was
also an intermediate class of 'six-hynd' men. It would seem
that the 'twelf-hynd' men were thegns, and the 'twy-hynd'
man might or might not be. But these things perhaps had no
more practical interest for Glanvill, certainly no more for
Bracton, than they have for us.

Privileges of clergy. In like manner, the privileges of clerks in orders, whether
of secular or regular life, do not call for close investigation
here. Orders were regarded as conferring not only freedom
where any doubt had existed, but a kind of nobility. There
was a special scale of wergild for the clergy; but it was a
question whether a priest who was in fact of noble birth should
not be atoned for with the wergild appropriate to his birth, if
it exceeded that which belonged to his ecclesiastical rank, and
some held that for the purpose of wergild only the man's rank
by birth should be considered.

It is well known that the superior clergy took (and with
good cause) a large part in legislation and the direction of
justice, as well as in general government. Probably we owe it

[1] Schmid, Gesetze, pp. 389, 397, 431.
[2] Little, Gesiths and Thegns, E. H. R. iv. 723; Maitland, Domesday
Book, 161.

to them that Anglo-Saxon law has left us any written evidences
at all.   But the really active and important part of the clergy
in the formation of English law begins only with the clear
separation of ecclesiastical and civil authority after the Conquest.

We now have to speak of the unfree class.

Slavery, personal slavery, and not merely serfdom or villein- Slavery.
age consisting mainly in attachment to the soil, existed, and
was fully recognized, in England until the twelfth century.
We have no means of knowing with any exactness the number
of slaves, either in itself, or as compared with the free population.   But the recorded manumissions would alone suffice to
prove that the number was large.   Moreover, we know, not
only that slaves were bought and sold, but that a real slave-
trade was carried on from English ports.   This abuse was
increased in the evil times that set in with the Danish
invasions.   Raids of heathen Northmen, while they relaxed
social order and encouraged crime, brought wealthy slave-
[p. 12] buyers, who would not ask many questions, to the unscrupulous
trader's hand.   But slaves were exported from England much
earlier.   Selling a man beyond the seas occurs in the Kentish
laws as an alternative for capital punishment[1]; and one obscure
passage seems to relate to the offence of kidnapping freeborn
men[2].   Ine's dooms forbade the men of Wessex to sell a
countryman beyond seas, even if he were really a slave or justly
condemned to slavery[3].

Selling Christian men beyond seas, and specially into bond- Slave-
age to heathen, is forbidden by an ordinance of Æthelred, trade.
repeated almost word for word in Cnut's laws[4].   Wulfstan,
archbishop of York, who probably took an active part in the
legislation of Æthelred, denounced the practice in his homilies[5],
and also complained that men's thrall-right was narrowed.
This is significant as pointing to a more humane doctrine,
whatever the practice may have been, than that of the earlier
Roman law.   It seems that even the thrall had personal rights
of some sort, though we are not able with our present information to specify them.   Towards the end of the eleventh century

---

[1] Wiht. 26.

[2] Hl. and E. 5; see Schmid thereon.   The slave-traders were often foreigners,
commonly Jews.   Ireland and Gaul were the main routes.

[3] In. 11.

[4] Æthelr. v. 2, vi. 9; Cn. ii. 3; cf. Lex Rib. 16; Lex Sal. 39 § 2.

[5] A. Napier, Berlin, 1883, pp. 129, *n.*, 158, 160–1.

the slave trade from Bristol to Ireland (where the Danes were then in power) called forth the righteous indignation of another Wulfstan, the bishop of Worcester, who held his place through the Conquest. He went to Bristol in person, and succeeded in putting down the scandal[1]. Its continued existence till that time is further attested by the prohibition of Æthelred and Cnut being yet again repeated in the laws attributed to William the Conqueror[2].

Manu-
mission.

Free men sometimes enslaved themselves in times of distress as the only means of subsistence; manumission of such persons after the need was past would be deemed a specially meritorious work, if not a duty[3]. Sometimes well-to-do people bought slaves, and immediately afterwards freed them for the [p. 13] good of their own souls, or the soul of some ancestor. At a later time we meet with formal sales by the lord to a third person in trust (as we should now say) to manumit the serf[4]. The Anglo-Saxon cases do not appear to be of this kind. Sometimes a serf 'bought himself' free. We may suppose that a freedman was generally required or expected to take his place among the free dependants of his former master; and the express licence to the freedman to choose his own lord, which is occasionally met with, tends to show that this was the rule. The lord's rights over the freedman's family were not affected if the freedman left the domain[5]. There is nothing to suggest that freedmen were treated as a distinct class in any other way. What has just been said implies that a bondman might acquire, and not unfrequently did acquire, money of his own; and, in fact, an ordinance of Alfred expressly makes the Wednesday in the four ember weeks a free day for him, and declares his earnings to be at his own disposal[6]. Moreover, even the earliest written laws constantly assume that a 'theow' might be able to pay fines for public offences.

---

[1] Will. Malm. Vita Wulstani, in Wharton, Anglia Sacra, ii. 258; quoted nearly in full, Freeman, Norman Conquest, iv. 386.

[2] Leges Willelmi, I. 41.

[3] Cod. Dipl. iv. 263 (manumission by Geatflæd of 'all the men whose heads she took for their food in the evil days'). This and other examples are conveniently collected at the end of Thorpe's Diplomatarium.

[4] L. Q. R. vii. 64.

[5] Wiht. 8: an archaic authority, but there is nothing to show any change.

[6] Ælf. 43 (as Schmid and the Latin version take it). Cp. Theod. Pen. xiii. 8 (Haddan and Stubbs, Councils, iii. 202).

On the whole the evidence seems to show that serfdom was much more of a personal bondage and less involved with the occupation of particular land before the Norman Conquest than after; in short that it approached, though it only approached, the slavery of the Roman law. Once, and only once, in the earliest of our Anglo-Saxon texts[1], we find mention in Kent, under the name of *læt*, of the half-free class of persons called *litus* and other like names in continental documents. To all appearance there had ceased to be any such class in England before the time of Alfred: it is therefore needless to discuss their condition or origin.

There are traces of some kind of public authority having been required for the owner of a serf to make him free as regards third persons; but from almost the earliest Christian times manumission at an altar had full effect[2]. In such cases a written record was commonly preserved in the later Anglo-Saxon period at any rate, but it does not appear to have been [p. 14] necessary or to have been what we should now call an operative instrument. This kind of manumission disappears after the Conquest, and it was long disputed whether a freed bondman might not be objected to as a witness or oath-helper[3].

We now turn to judicial institutions. An Anglo-Saxon court, whether of public or private justice, was not surrounded with such visible majesty of the law as in our own time, nor furnished with any obvious means of compelling obedience. It is the feebleness of executive power that explains the large space occupied in archaic law by provisions for the conduct of suits when parties make default. In like manner the solemn prohibition of taking the law into one's own hands without having demanded one's right in the proper court shows that law is only just becoming the rule of life. Such provisions occur as early as the dooms of Ine of Wessex[4], and perhaps preserve the tradition of a time when there was no jurisdiction save by consent of the parties. Probably the public courts

[Marginal notes: Slavery and serfage. Courts and justice.]

---

[1] Æthelb. 26.

[2] Wiht. 8: 'If one manumits his man at the altar, let him be folk-free.'

[3] Glanvill, ii. 6. Details on Anglo-Saxon servitude may be found in Kemble, Saxons, bk. i. c. 8, and Larking, Domesday Book of Kent, note 57. See also Maurer, Kritische Ueberschau, i. 410; Jastrow, Zur strafrechtlichen Stellung der Sklaven (Gierke's Untersuchungen, 1878); Brunner, D. R. G. i. 95.

[4] In. 9. The wording 'wrace dó' is vague: doubtless it means taking the other party's cattle.

were always held in the open air; there is no mention of
churches being used for this purpose, a practice which was
expressly forbidden in various parts of the continent when
court houses were built. Private courts were held, when practicable, in the house of the lord having the jurisdiction, as is
shown by the name *halimote* or hall-moot. This name may
indeed have been given to a lord's court by way of designed
contrast with the open-air hundred and county courts. The
manor-house itself is still known as a court in many places in
the west and south-east of England[1]. *Halimote* is not known,
however, to occur before the Norman Conquest.

So far as we can say that there was any regular judicial
system in Anglo-Saxon law, it was of a highly archaic type.
We find indeed a clear enough distinction between public
offences and private wrongs. Liability to a public fine or, in
grave cases, corporal or capital punishment, may concur with
liability to make redress to a person wronged or slain, or to his [p.15]
kindred, or to incur his feud in default. But neither these
ideas nor their appropriate terms are confused at any time.
On the other hand, there is no perceptible difference of authorities or procedure in civil and criminal matters until, within
a century before the Conquest, we find certain of the graver
public offences reserved in a special manner for the king's
jurisdiction.

The staple matter of judicial proceedings was of a rude and
simple kind. In so far as we can trust the written laws, the
only topics of general importance were manslaying, wounding,
and cattle-stealing. So frequent was the last-named practice
that it was by no means easy for a man, who was minded to
buy cattle honestly, to be sure that he was not buying stolen
beasts, and the Anglo-Saxon dooms are full of elaborate precautions on this head, to which we shall return presently.

Procedure.   As to procedure, the forms were sometimes complicated,
always stiff and unbending. Mistakes in form were probably
fatal at every stage. Trial of questions of fact, in anything like
the modern sense, was unknown. Archaic rules of evidence
make no attempt to apply any measure of probability to

---

[1] *E.g.* Clovelly Court, N. Devon. Cp. Rentalia et Custumaria, Somerset
Record Society, 1891, Glossary, s. v. *Curia.* For the *aula, haula, halla* of D. B.,
see Maitland, Domesday Book, 109 ff.

individual cases[1]. Oath was the primary mode of proof, an oath going not to the truth of specific fact, but to the justice of the claim or defence as a whole. The number of persons required to swear varied according to the nature of the case and the rank of the persons concerned. Inasmuch as the oath, if duly made, was conclusive, what we now call the burden of proof was rather a benefit than otherwise under ancient Germanic procedure. The process of clearing oneself by the full performance of the oath which the law required in the particular case is that which later medieval authorities call 'making one's law,' *facere legem.* It remained possible, in certain cases, down to quite modern times. An accused person who failed in his oath, by not having the proper number of oath-helpers[2] prepared to swear, or who was already disqualified from clearing himself by oath, had to go to one of the forms of [p. 16] ordeal. The ordeal of hot water appears in Ine's laws though until lately it was concealed from our view by the misreading of one letter in the text[3]. Trial by combat was to all appearance unknown to the Anglo-Saxon procedure[4], though it was formally sanctioned on the continent by Gundobad, king of the Burgundians, at the beginning of the sixth century and is found in the laws of nearly all the German tribes[5]. An apparently genuine ordinance of William the Conqueror enables Englishmen to make use of trial by battle in their lawsuits with Normans, but expressly allows them to decline it. This is strong to prove that it was not an English institution in any form[6] Permitted or justified private war, of which we do find considerable traces in England[7], is quite a different matter.

---

[1] Brunner, D. R. G. ii. 375.

[2] The usual modern term 'compurgator' was borrowed by legal antiquaries from ecclesiastical sources in much later times.

[3] This discovery is due to Dr Liebermann, Sitzungsberichte der berliner Akademie, 1896, xxxv. 829. The less common word *ceac* (a cauldron) was confused with *ceap* (buying) and the genuine reading was treated by the editors as an unmeaning variant.

[4] The appearance of *orest* (a correct Northern form=Eng. *eornest*) among the privileges of Waltham Abbey, Cod. Dipl. iv. 154, is probably due to a post-Norman scribe, for our text rests on a very late copy. At all events the charter is only a few years before the Conquest. However, trial by battle may well have been known in the Danelaw throughout the tenth century.

[5] Brunner, D. R. G. ii. 415.

[6] Leg. Will. ii. (Willelmes cyninges ásetnysse).

[7] Ælf. 42. Sir James Stephen's statement (Hist. Crim. Law, i. 61) that 'trial by battle was only private war under regulations' cannot be accepted.

The Anglo-Norman judicial combat belongs to a perfectly regular and regulated course of proceeding, is as strictly controlled as any other part of it, and has no less strictly defined legal consequences.

A 'fore-oath,' distinct from the definitive oath of proof, was required of the party commencing a suit, unless the fact complained of were manifest; thus a fore-oath was needless if a man sued for wounding and showed the wound to the court. A defendant who was of evil repute might be driven by the fore-oath alone to the alternative of a three-fold oath or the ordeal[1].

As regards the constitution of Anglo-Saxon courts, our direct evidence is of the scantiest. We have to supplement it with indications derived from the Norman and later times.

Union of temporal and spiritual jurisdiction.

One well-known peculiarity of the Anglo-Saxon period is that secular and ecclesiastical courts were not sharply separated, and the two jurisdictions were hardly distinguished. The bishop [p. 17] sat in the county court; the church claimed for him a large share in the direction of even secular justice[2], and the claim was fully allowed by princes who could not be charged with weakness[3]. Probably the bishop was often the only member of the court who possessed any learning or any systematic training in public affairs.

The king's justice not ordinary.

The most general Anglo-Saxon term for a court or assembly empowered to do justice is *gemót*. In this word is included all authority of the kind from the king and his witan[4] downwards. *Folc-gemót* appears to mean any public court whatever, greater or less. The king has judicial functions, but they are very far removed from our modern way of regarding the king as the fountain of justice. His business is not to see justice done in his name in an ordinary course, but to exercise a special and

---

[1] Cn. ii. 22, and the newly-printed gloss in Liebermann, Consil. Cnuti, p. 14. From this, so far as it may be trusted, it would seem that a triple fore-oath might put the 'credible' defendant to a stronger oath and the 'incredible' one to the severe 'three-fold' ordeal.

[2] Edg. iii. 5 (third quarter of tenth century); 'Institutes of Polity' in Thorpe, Ancient Laws, ii. 313.

[3] However, as to the manner in which justice was done in ecclesiastical causes and when clerks were accused extremely little is known. See Stubbs, Historical Appendix to Report of Eccl. Courts Comm. 1883, p. 23; Makower, Const. Hist. of the Church of England, 384 ff.

[4] 'Witenagemót' does not appear to have been an official term.

reserved power which a man must not invoke unless he has
failed to get his cause heard in the jurisdiction of his own
hundred[1]. Such failure of justice might happen, not from ill-
will or corruption on the part of any public officer, but from a
powerful lord protecting offenders who were his men[2]. In such
cases the king might be invoked to put forth his power. It is
obvious that the process was barely distinguishable from that
of combating an open rebellion[3].

After the Norman Conquest, as time went on, the king's
justice became organized and regular, and superseded nearly all
the functions of the ancient county and hundred courts. But
the king's power to do justice of an extraordinary kind was far
from being abandoned. The great constructive work of Henry
II. and Edward I. made it less important for a time. In the
fifteenth and sixteenth centuries it showed its vitality in the
hands of the king's chancellors, and became the root of the
modern system of equity[4]. Down to our own time that system
preserved the marks of its origin in the peculiar character of
the compulsion exercised by courts of equitable jurisdiction.
Disobedience to their process and decrees was a direct and
special contempt of the king's authority, and a 'commission of
[p. 18] rebellion' might issue against a defendant making default in a
chancery suit, however widely remote its subject-matter might
be from the public affairs of the kingdom[5].

We have many examples, notwithstanding the repeated *Jurisdic-*
ordinances forbidding men to seek the king's justice except *tion of witan.*
after failure to obtain right elsewhere, of the witan exercising
an original jurisdiction in matters of disputed claims to book-
land[6]. This may be explained in more than one way. Book-
land was (as we shall see) a special form of property which only
the king could create, and which, as a rule, he created with
the consent and witness of his wise men. Moreover, one or
both parties to such suits were often bishops or the heads of
great houses of religion, and thus the cause might be regarded
as an ecclesiastical matter fit to be dealt with by a synod rather
than by temporal authority, both parties doubtless consenting
to the jurisdiction.

---

[1] Edg. III. 2; repeated Cnut, II. 17.
[2] Æthelst. II. 3.   [3] Cf. Æthelst. VI. (Iud. Civ. Lund.) 8 §§ 2, 3.
[4] Blackstone, Comm. iii. 51.   [5] Blackstone, Comm. iii. 444.
[6] Cases collected in Essays in Anglo-Saxon Law, ad fin.

The charters that inform us of what was done, especially in
803 and 825, at the synods or synodal councils of Clovesho[1], that
'famous place' whose situation is now matter of mere con-
jecture[2], leave no doubt that on these occasions, at least, the
same assembly which is called a synod also acted as the witan.
The secular and spiritual functions of these great meetings
might have been discriminated by lay members not taking
part in the ecclesiastical business ; but it is by no means certain
that they were[3]. In any case it is highly probable that the
prohibitions above cited were never meant to apply to the
great men of the kingdom, or royal foundations, or the king's
immediate followers.

County and
hundred
courts.
　　　The ordinary Anglo-Saxon courts of public justice were the
county court and the hundred court, of which the county court
was appointed to be held twice a year, the hundred every four
weeks[4]. Poor and rich men alike were entitled to have right
done to them, though the need of emphasizing this elementary
point of law in the third quarter of the tenth century suggests
that the fact was often otherwise[5].

Thus the hundred court was the judicial unit, so to speak,
for ordinary affairs. We have no evidence that any lesser [p. 19]
public court existed. It is quite possible that some sort of
township meeting was held for the regulation of the common-
field husbandry which prevailed in most parts of England : and
the total absence of any written record of such meetings, or (so
far as we know) allusion to them, hardly makes the fact less
probable. But we have no ground whatever for concluding
that the township-moot, if that were its name, had any properly
judicial functions. 'Mark-moot,' which has been supposed to
be the name of a primary court, appears rather to mean a court
held on the marches of adjacent counties or hundreds, or
perhaps on the boundary dyke itself[6].

The ordinances which tell us of the times of meeting appointed for the county and hundred courts tell us nothing
whatever of their procedure. It may be taken as certain,

[1] Haddan and Stubbs, Councils, iii. 541, 596.
[2] Earle, Land Charters, 453.　　　　　　[3] Kemble, Saxons, ii. 247, 249.
[4] Edg. i. 1 (the ascription of this ordinance to Edgar is conjectural, but
serves to fix its earliest possible date, Schmid, p. xlviii.; Liebermann, Consil.
Cnuti, p. v.); Edg. iii. 5.
[5] Edg. iii. 1.
[6] Cf. Schmid, Glossar, s. v. *mearc*; Maitland, Domesday Book, 275.

however, that they had no efficient mode of compelling the attendance of parties or enforcing their orders. A man who refused to do justice to others according to the law could only be put out of the protection of the law, save in the cases which were grave enough to call for a special expedition against him. Outlawry, developed in the Danish period as a definite part of English legal process, remained such until our own time. All this is thoroughly characteristic of archaic legal systems in general. Nothing in it is peculiarly English, not much is peculiarly Germanic.

Thus far we have spoken only of public jurisdiction. But we know that after the Norman Conquest England was covered with the private jurisdictions of lords of various degrees, from the king himself downwards, holding courts on their lands at which their tenants were entitled to seek justice in their own local affairs, and bound to attend that justice might be done to their fellows. 'Court baron' is now the most usual technical name for a court of this kind, but it is a comparatively modern name. Further, we know that private jurisdiction existed on the continent much earlier, and that it existed in England in the early part of the eleventh century. It is a question not [p. 20] free from doubt whether the institution was imported from the continent not long before that time, or on the contrary had been known in England a good while before, perhaps as early as the date of our earliest Anglo-Saxon laws and charters, notwithstanding that it is not expressly and directly mentioned in documents of the earlier period. For our present purpose it is enough to be sure that private courts were well established at the date of the Conquest, and had been increasing in number and power for some time[1].

Private jurisdiction.

[p. 21] Proceeding to the subject-matters of Anglo-Saxon jurisdiction, we find what may be called the usual archaic features. The only substantive rules that are at all fully set forth have to do with offences and wrongs, mostly those which are of a violent kind, and with theft, mostly cattle-lifting. Except so far as it is involved in the law of theft, the law of property is almost entirely left in the region of unwritten custom and local usage. The law of contract is rudimentary, so rudimentary as to be barely distinguishable from the law of property. In fact people who have no system of credit and very little foreign

Subject-matter of Anglo-Saxon justice.

---

[1] Maitland, Domesday Book, 80 ff., 258 ff.

trade, and who do nearly all their business in person and by word of mouth with neighbours whom they know, have not much occasion for a law of contract. It is not our purpose to consider in this place the relation of Anglo-Saxon customs and ordinances to those of Germanic nations on the continent; to inquire, for example, why the Salic or the Lombard laws should present striking resemblances even in detail to the laws of Alfred or Cnut, but provide with equal or greater minuteness for other similar cases on which the Anglo-Saxon authorities are silent. In the period of antiquarian compilation which set in after the Norman Conquest, and of which the so-called laws of Henry I. are the most conspicuous product, we see not only imitation of the continental collections, but sometimes express reference to their rules[1]. But this kind of reference, at the [p. 22] hands of a compiler who could also quote the Theodosian code[2], throws no light whatever on the possibilities of continental influence at an earlier time. It is highly probable that Alfred and his successors had learned persons about them who were more or less acquainted with Frankish legislation if not with that of remoter kingdoms. But it suffices to know that, in its general features, Anglo-Saxon law is not only archaic, but offers an especially pure type of Germanic archaism. We are therefore warranted in supposing, where English authority fails, that the English usages of the Anglo-Saxon period were generally like the earliest corresponding ones of which evidence can be found on the continent.

The king's peace. Preservation of the peace and punishment of offences were dealt with, in England as elsewhere, partly under the customary jurisdiction of the local courts, partly by the special authority of the king. In England that authority gradually superseded all others. All criminal offences have long been said to be committed against the king's peace; and this phrase, along with 'the king's highway,' has passed into common use as a kind of ornament of speech, without any clear sense of its historical meaning. The two phrases are, indeed, intimately connected; they come from the time when the king's protection was not

---

[1] Leg. Hen. c. 87 § 10, 89 § 1, secundum legem Saligam; 90 § 4, secundum legem Ribuariorum solvatur.

[2] Leg. Hen. c. 33 § 4: 'de libro Theodosianae legis, iniuste victus infra tres menses reparet causam.' The quotation is really from an epitome of the Lex Romana Visigothorum.

universal but particular, when the king's peace was not for all
men or all places, and the king's highway was in a special
manner protected by it.   Breach of the king's peace was an act
of personal disobedience, and a much graver matter than an
ordinary breach of public order; it made the wrong-doer the
king's enemy.   The notion of the king's peace appears to have
had two distinct origins.   These were, first, the special sanctity
of the king's house, which may be regarded as differing only in
degree from that which Germanic usage attached everywhere
to the homestead of a free man; and, secondly, the special
protection of the king's attendants and servants, and other
persons whom he thought fit to place on the same footing.
In the later Anglo-Saxon period the king's particular protection
is called *grið* as distinct from the more general word *frið*.
Although the proper name is of comparatively recent introduc-
[p. 23] tion[1] and of Scandinavian extraction, the thing seems to answer
to the Frankish *sermo* or *verbum regis*, which is as old as the
Salic law[2].   The rapid extension of the king's peace till it
becomes, after the Norman Conquest, the normal and general
safeguard of public order, seems peculiarly English[3].   On the
continent the king appears at an early time to have been
recognized as protector of the general peace, besides having
power to grant special protection or peace of a higher order[4].

It is not clear whether there was any fixed name for the
general peace which was protected only by the hundred court
and the ealdorman.   Very possibly the medieval usage by which
an inferior court was said to be in the peace of the lord who
held the court may go back in some form to the earliest time
when there were any set forms of justice; and there is some
evidence that in the early part of the tenth century men spoke

The various peaces.

---

[1] See A.-S. Chron. ann. 1002.

[2] Fustel de Coulanges, Origines du système féodal, 300 ff.   Lex Sal. xiii.
6; lvi. 5.   Edict of Chilperic, 9.   To be out of the king's protection is to be
extra sermonem suum, foras nostro sermone.   In xiv. 4, *praeceptum* appears to be
the king's written protection or licence.   The phrase in Ed. Conf. 6 § 1
(cf. Brunner, D. R. G. ii. 42), *ore suo utlagabit eum rex*, or, as the second
edition gives it, *utlagabit eum rex verbo oris sui*, looks more like the confused
imitation of an archaizing compiler than a genuine parallel.

[3] For some further details see Pollock, Oxford Lectures, 1890, 'The King's
Peace,' 65.

[4] See Brunner, D. R. G. ii. §§ 65, 66, who calls attention (p. 42) to the
relative weakness of the crown in England before the Conquest.

of the peace of the witan[1]. We have not found English authority for any such term as *folk-peace*, which has sometimes been used in imitation of German writers. No light is thrown on early Anglo-Saxon ideas or methods of keeping the peace by the provision that every man shall be in a hundred and tithing, for it first appears in this definite form in the laws of Cnut[2], and both its history and meaning are disputable. This, however, is a matter of administrative mechanism rather than of the law itself. We shall have a word to say about this matter when hereafter we speak of frankpledge.

Feud and atonement. In Anglo-Saxon as well as in other Germanic laws we find [p. 24] that the idea of wrong to a person or his kindred is still primary, and that of offence against the common weal secondary, even in the gravest cases. Only by degrees did the modern principles prevail, that the members of the community must be content with the remedies afforded them by law, and must not seek private vengeance, and that, on the other hand, public offences cannot be remitted or compounded by private bargain.

Personal injury is in the first place a cause of feud, of private war between the kindreds of the wrong-doer and of the person wronged. This must be carefully distinguished from a right of specific retaliation, of which there are no traces in Germanic law[3]. But the feud may be appeased by the acceptance of a composition. Some kind of arbitration was probably resorted to from a very early time to fix the amount. The next stage is a scale of compensation fixed by custom or enactment for death or minor injuries, which may be graduated according to the rank of the person injured. Such a scale may well exist for a time without any positive duty of the kindred to accept the composition it offers. It may serve only the purpose of saving disputes as to the amount proper to be paid when the parties are disposed to make peace. But this naturally leads to the kindred being first expected by public opinion and then required by public authority not to pursue the feud if the proper composition is forthcoming, except in a

---

[1] Edw. ii. 1. Schmid, Gloss. s. v. *Friede*, considers the general peace to have been the king's peace in some sense. This lacks authority, but seems accepted as regards the continent: Brunner, D. R. G. ii. 42. It is nearer the truth than any talk about the 'folk-peace.'

[2] Cn. ii. 20.

[3] Ælf. Prolog. 19, copied from the book of Exodus, is of course no exception.

few extreme cases which also finally disappear. At the same
time, the wrong done to an individual extends beyond his own
family; it is a wrong to the community of which he is a
member; and thus the wrong-doer may be regarded as a public
enemy. Such expressions as 'outlaw against all the people' in
the Anglo-Saxon laws preserve this point of view[1]. The
conception of an offence done to the state in its corporate
person, or (as in our own system) as represented by the king,
is of later growth.

Absolute chronology has very little to do with the stage of
growth or decay in which archaic institutions, and this one in
particular, may be found in different countries and times. The
Homeric poems show us the blood-feud in full force in cases of
[p. 25] manslaying (there is little or nothing about wounding), tempered
by ransom or composition which appears to be settled by
agreement or arbitration in each case. In the classical period
of Greek history this has wholly disappeared. But in Iceland,
as late as the time of the Norman Conquest of England, we find
a state of society which takes us back to Homer. Manslayings
and blood-feuds are constant, and the semi-judicial arbitration
of wise men, though often invoked, is but imperfectly successful
in staying breaches of the peace and reconciling adversaries.
A man's life has its price, but otherwise there is not even any
recognized scale of compositions. In the Germanic laws both
of England and of the mainland we find a much more settled
rule some centuries earlier. Full scales of composition are
established. A freeman's life has a regular value set upon it,
called *wergild*, literally 'man's price' or 'man-payment[2],' or
oftener in English documents *wer* simply; moreover, for injuries
to the person short of death there is an elaborate tariff. The
modern practice of assessing damages, though familiar to Roman
law in the later republican period, is unknown to early Germanic
law, nor were there in Germanic procedure any means of
applying the idea if it had existed. Composition must generally
be accepted if offered; private war is lawful only when the
adversary obstinately refuses to do right. In that case indeed,
as we learn from a well-known ordinance of Alfred[3], the power

Tariff of composi-tions.

---

[1] Cp. Grettis Saga, c. 79.

[2] Brunner, D. R. G. i. 86. An archaic synonym *leód* occurs Æthelb. 22, 23,
cp. Grimm, 652.

[3] Ælf. 42.

of the ealdorman, and of the king at need, may be called in if
the plaintiff is not strong enough by himself; in other words
the contumacious denier of justice may be dealt with as an
enemy of the commonwealth. At a somewhat later time we
find the acceptance and payment of compositions enforced by
putting the obligation between the parties under the special
sanction of the king's peace[1]. But it was at least theoretically
possible, down to the middle of the tenth century, for a manslayer to elect to bear the feud of the kindred[2]. His own
kindred, however, might avoid any share in the feud by dis-
claiming him; any of them who maintained him after this, as
well as any of the avenging kinsfolk who meddled with any [p. 26]
but the actual wrong-doer, was deemed a foe to the king (the
strongest form of expressing outlawry) and forfeited all his
property.

Wer, wite, bót. We find the public and private aspects of injurious acts
pretty clearly distinguished by the Anglo-Saxon terms. *Wer*,
as we have said, is the value set on a man's life, increasing with
his rank. For many purposes it could be a burden as well as a
benefit; the amount of a man's own *wer* was often the measure
of the fine to be paid for his offences against public order.
Wite is the usual word for a penal fine payable to the king or
to some other public authority. *Bót* (the modern German
Busse) is a more general word, including compensation of any
kind. Some of the gravest offences, especially against the king
and his peace, are said to be *bótleás*, 'bootless'; that is, the
offender is not entitled to redeem himself at all, and is at the
king's mercy. The distinction between *wer* and *wite* must be
very ancient; it corresponds to what is told us of German
custom by Tacitus[3].

Punish-ment. The only punishments, in the proper sense, generally applicable to freemen, were money fines, and death in the extreme
cases where redemption with a money fine was not allowed. A
credible tradition preserved in the prologue to Alfred's laws
tells us that after the conversion of the English to Christianity

---

[1] Edm. ii. 7, and *Be Wergilde* (Schmid, App. vii.) § 4.

[2] Edm. ii. 1. Æthelr. ii. 6 § 1, suggests but hardly proves a change, leaving
the option with the slain man's kindred alone, though such is held to have been
the settled rule on the continent : Brunner, D. R. G. i. 163.

[3] Tac. Germ. c. 12. *Bót* is closely connected with 'better': the idea is
'making good.'

the bishops and wise-men 'for the mild-heartedness sake that Christ taught' sanctioned the redemption by fine of offences less than that of treason against one's lord[1]. Mutilation and other corporal punishments are prescribed (but with the alternative of redemption by a heavy fine) for false accusers, for habitual criminals, and for persons of evil repute who have failed in the ordeal[2].

Imprisonment occurs in the Anglo-Saxon laws only as a means of temporary security. Slaves were liable to capital and other corporal punishment, and generally without redemption. The details have no material bearing on the general history of the law, and may be left to students of semi-barbarous manners. Outlawry, at first a declaration of war by the commonwealth against an offending member, became a regular means of compelling submission to the authority of the courts, as in form it continued so to be down to modern times[3]. In criminal proceedings, however, it was used as a substantive penalty for violent resistance to a legal process or persistent contempt of court[4] Before the Conquest, outlawry involved not only forfeiture of goods to the king, but liability to be killed with impunity. It was no offence to the king to kill his enemy, and the kindred might not claim the wergild[5]. It was thought, indeed, down to the latter part of the sixteenth century, that the same reason applied to persons under the penalties appointed by the statutes of *praemunire*, which expressly included being put out of the king's protection[6].

[p. 27]

It would appear that great difficulty was found both in obtaining specific evidence of offences, and in compelling accused and suspected persons to submit themselves to justice, and pay their fines if convicted. This may serve to explain the severe provisions of the later Anglo-Saxon period against a kind of

Difficulties in compelling submission to courts.

---

[1] Ælf. Prolog. 49 § 7.

[2] In. 18; Ælf. 32; Cn. II. 16, 30. The 'folk-leasing' of Alfred's law must be habitual false accusation in the folk-moot, not private slander.

[3] It was formally abolished in civil proceedings only in 1879, 42 & 43 Vict. c. 59, s. 3. In criminal matters it is still possible. But it has not been in use for a generation or more.

[4] E. & G. 6 § 6; cp. Edg. I. 3; Æthelr. I. 1 § 9, and many later passages.

[5] E. & G. 6 § 7: the outlaw, if slain, shall lie *ǽgylde*, the exact equivalent of the Homeric νήποινος.

[6] Co. Litt. 130 a; Blackstone, Comm. iv. 118; 5 Eliz. c. 1.

persons described as 'frequently accused,' 'of no credit[1].' One
who had been several times charged (with theft, it seems we
must understand), and kept away from three courts running,
might be pursued and arrested as a thief, and treated as an
outlaw if he failed to give security to answer his accusers[2]. A
man of evil repute is already half condemned, and if he evades
justice it is all but conclusive proof of guilt. In communities
where an honest man's neighbours knew pretty well what he
was doing every day and most of the day, this probably did not
work much injustice. And English criminal procedure still held
to this point of view two centuries after the Conquest. It may
be said to linger even now-a-days in the theoretical power of
grand juries to present offences of their own knowledge.

Maintenance of offenders by great men.
Several passages, and those from a period of comparatively
settled government, show that great men, whose followers had
committed crimes, often harboured and maintained them in
open defiance of common right[3]. If it was needful for Æthelstan,
the victor of Brunanburh, to make ordinances against lawless- [p. 23]
ness of this kind, we can only think that weaker princes left it
without remedy, not because the evil was less in their days, but
because they had no power to amend it. The same thing was
common enough in the Scottish highlands as late as the early
part of the eighteenth century[4].

Why no trial by battle.
Putting together these indications of a feeble executive
power, we are apt to think that the absence of trial by battle
from Anglo-Saxon procedure can best be explained by the
persistence of extra-judicial fighting. Gundobad of Burgundy,
and other Germanic rulers after him, tempted their subjects
into court by a kind of compromise. It is hardly possible to
suppose that their ostensible reason of avoiding perjury was the
real one. Rather it was understood, though it could not be
officially expressed, that Burgundian and Lombard[5] freemen

---

[1] Eng. *tiht-bysig, folce ungetrȳwe*, Lat. *incredibilis*. The idea is the contradiction of *getrȳwe = homo probus* or *legalis*. *Folce* or *eallum folce* signifies merely notoriety: we cannot find in the text, as some writers have done, a doctrine of fealty to the people as a quasi-sovereign.

[2] Edg. iii. 7; Cn. ii. 33; cp. ib. 22.

[3] Æthelst. ii. 3, cp. 17; iv. 3. Cp. vi. 8, as to over-powerful clans.

[4] Cf. Baillie Nicol Jarvie on the state of the Highlands, Rob Roy, ii. ch. 12 (original edition).

[5] Liutprand openly regretted that trial by combat could not be abolished. Liutpr. c. 118: 'incerti sumus de iudicio dei, et multos audiuimus per pugnam

would submit to being forbidden to fight out of court on the terms of being allowed to fight under legal sanction, thus combining the physical joy of battle with the intellectual luxury of strictly formal procedure. It seems plausible to suppose that the mechanism of Anglo-Saxon government was not commonly strong enough to accomplish even so much. All this, however, is conjectural. There is no reason to doubt that among some Germanic tribes battle was recognized as a form of ordeal from very ancient times; we have no means of solving the ulterior question why those tribes did not include the ancestors of the Anglo-Saxons.

Offences specially dealt with in various parts of the Anglo-Saxon laws are treason, homicide, wounding and assault (which, however, if committed by free men, are more wrongs than crimes), and theft. Treason to one's lord, especially to the king, is a capital crime. And the essence of the crime already consists in compassing or imagining the king's death, to use the later language of Edward III.'s Parliament[1]. The like appears in other Germanic documents[2]. It seems probable, however, that this does not represent any original Germanic tradition, but is borrowed from the Roman law of *maiestas,* of which one main head was plotting against the lives of the chief magistrates[3]. No part of the Roman law was more likely to be imitated by the conquerors of Roman territory and provinces; and when an idea first appears in England in Alfred's time, there is no difficulty whatever in supposing it imported from the continent. Not that rulers exercising undefined powers in

Special offences
treason

[p. 29]

---

sine iustitia causam suam perdere: sed propter consuitutinem gentis nostrae langobardorum legem ipsam uetare non possumus'. Avitus, bishop of Vienne, protested against Gundobad's ordinance. At a later time Agobard of Lyons denounced it. See Lea, Superstition and Force, ed. 4, p. 409.

[1] Ælf. 4.

[2] Ed. Roth. 1 (L. Langob.) 'contra animam regis cogitaverit aut consiliaverit'; L. Sax. 24, 'de morte consiliatus fuerit'; so L. Baiuw. ii. 1; L. Alam. 23: 'in mortem ducis consiliatus fuerit'; cp. Brunner, D. R. G. ii. 688.

[3] The following words no doubt substantially represent the text of the lex Julia: 'Cuiusve opera *consilio* dolo malo *consilium initum erit* quo quis magistratus populi Romani quive imperium potestatemve habeat occidatur.' Dig. 48. 4. ad l. Iuliam maiestatis, 1 § 1. The *consiliaverit, consiliatus fuerit,* of the Germanic laws can hardly be an accidental resemblance. In Glanv. xiv. 1, the principal terms are *machinatum fuisse vel aliquid fecisse,* but *consilium dedisse* is there too.

a rude state of society needed the *Lex Julia* to teach them the importance of putting down conspiracies at the earliest possible stage. We are now speaking of the formal enunciation of the rule. On the other hand, the close association of treason against the king with treason against one's personal lord who is not the king is eminently Germanic. This was preserved in the 'petty treason' of medieval and modern criminal law.

The crime of treason was unatonable[1], and the charge had to be repelled by an oath adequate in number of oath-helpers, and perhaps in solemnity, to the wergild of the king or other lord as the case might be. If the accused could not clear himself by oath, and was driven to ordeal, he had to submit to the threefold ordeal[2], that is, the hot iron was of three pounds' weight instead of one pound, or the arm had to be plunged elbow-deep instead of wrist-deep into the boiling water[3].

Homicide.　　　Homicide appears in the Anglo-Saxon dooms as a matter for composition in the ordinary case of slaying in open quarrel. There are additional public penalties in aggravated cases, as where a man is slain in the king's presence or otherwise in breach of the king's peace. And a special application of the [p. 30] king's protection is made in favour of strangers; a matter of some importance when we remember that before the time of Alfred a Mercian was a stranger in Kent, and a Wessex man in Mercia. Two-thirds of a slain stranger's *wer* goes to the king. We find a rudiment of the modern distinction between murder and manslaughter, but the line is drawn not between wilful and other killing, but between killing openly and in secret. It would seem indeed that 'morð' at one time meant only killing by poison or witchcraft. The offence of 'morð' was unatonable,

---

[1] Cn. ii. 64; Leg. Hen. 12.

[2] Ælf. 4; Æthelst. ii. 4; Æthelr. v. 30, vi. 37; Cn. ii. 57. This last passage, in its literal terms, would not allow purgation by oath-helpers at all, but send the accused straight to the ordeal. So great a change of the previous law can scarcely have been intended. Æthelred's ordinance, vi. 37, requires the 'deepest oath,' whatever that was. Cp. Godwine's oath 'cum totius fere Angliae principibus et ministris dignioribus,' Flor. Wigorn. i. 195. Possibly Danish law may have been stricter than English. We hear of an oath of 48 thanes against the charge of robbing a corpse: *Be walreáfe*, Schmid, App. xv. in a document apparently of Danish extraction ; see Brunner, D. R. G. ii. 684. The Lex Ribuaria requires in some special cases an oath of 36 or even 72 men.

[3] Edg. i. 9; *Dóm be hátan isene and wætre*, Schm. App. xvi.

and the murderer, if ascertained, might be delivered over to the dead man's kindred[1].

An outlaw might, as we have seen, be slain with impunity; and it was not only lawful but meritorious to kill a thief flying from justice[2]. An adulterer taken *in flagrante delicto* by the woman's lawful husband, father, brother, or son, might be killed without risk of blood-feud. In like manner homicide was excusable when the slayer was fighting in defence of his lord, or of a man whose lord he was, or of his kinsman; but a man must in no case fight against his own lord[3]. A man who slew a thief (or, it would seem, any one) was expected to declare the fact without delay, otherwise the dead man's kindred might clear his fame by their oath and require the slayer to pay wergild as for a true man[4]. We do not find any formalities prescribed in the genuine dooms. The safest course would no doubt be to report to the first credible person met with, and to the first accessible person having any sort of authority[5].

Justifiable homicide.

Injuries and assaults to the person were dealt with by a minute scale of fixed compensations, which appears, though much abridged, as late as the Anglo-Norman compilations. But rules of this kind are not heard of in practice after the Conquest. It is worth while to notice that the contumelious outrage of binding a free man, or shaving his head in derision, or shaving off his beard, was visited with heavier fines than any but the gravest wounds[6]. In the modern common law compensation for insult, as distinct from actual bodily hurt, is arrived at only in a somewhat indirect fashion, by giving juries a free hand in the measure of damages. Accidental injuries are provided for in a certain number of particular cases. A man carrying a spear should carry it level on his shoulder in order to be free from blame if another runs upon the point. If the point is three fingers or more above the butt (so as to bring the point to the level of a man's face), he will be liable to pay *wer* in case of a fatal accident, and all the more if the point

Personal injuries: misadventure.

[p. 31]

---

[1] Cn. II. 56; Hen. 71, 92. See Schmid, Gloss. s. v. *morð*, and cp. the old Norse adage, 'Night-slaying is murder' (*Natt-vig er morð-vig*); also Lex Rib. 15.

[2] In. 35, cp. 28; Æthelst. VI. (Iud. Civ. Lund.) 7; cp. Ed. Conf. 36.

[3] Ælf. 42.   [4] In. 21.

[5] Hen. 83 § 6. The detailed instructions for laying out the slain man with his arms, etc., are curious but untrustworthy. The main object was to show that the killing was not secret.

[6] Ælf. 35. For continental analogies, see Brunner, D. R. G. ii. 674.

were in front (so that he could have seen the other's danger)[1]. This is rational enough; but in the case of harm ensuing even by pure accident from a distinct voluntary act, we find that the actor, however innocent his intention, is liable, and that the question of negligence is not considered at all. *Legis enim est qui inscienter peccat, scienter emendet,* says the compiler of the so-called laws of Henry I., translating what was doubtless an English proverb[2]. There is no earlier English authority, but such is known to have been the principle of all old Germanic laws. It seems to have extended, or to have been thought by some to extend, even to harm done by a stranger with weapons which the owner had left unguarded. Cnut's laws expressly declare, as if it were at least an unsettled point, that only the actual wrong-doer shall be liable if the owner can clear himself of having any part or counsel in the mischief[3]. Borrowing or stealing another man's weapons, or getting them by force or fraud from an armourer who had them in charge for repair, seems to have been a rather common way of obscuring the evidence of manslaying, or making false evidence; and it was a thing that might well be done in collusion. One man would be ready to swear with his oath-helpers, 'I did not kill him,' the other, with equal confidence, 'No weapon of mine killed him[4].' And in consequence, it would seem, of the general suspicion attaching to every one possibly concerned, an armourer [p 32] was bound to answer to the owner at all hazards (unless it were agreed to the contrary) for the safe custody and return of weapons entrusted to him[5], perhaps even for their return free from any charge of having been unlawfully used[6]. Such

---

[1] Ælf. 36 (probably enacted in consequence of some particular case in the king's court, or otherwise well known); cp. Hen. 88 §§ 1-3. The proviso as to holding the spear level is easily understood as referring to a spear of moderate length, which could not be well carried, like the long 16th–17th cent. pike, with the point so high up as to be wholly out of harm's way. The carriage of the 'puissant pike' was almost a special art when its time came.

[2] Hen. 88 § 6, 90 § 11. [þe] *brecht ungewealdes bete gewealdes,* in Germany *wer unwillig gethan muss willig zahlen*; see Heusler, Institutionen, ii. 263.

[3] Cn. ii. 75; cp. Hen. 87 § 2.

[4] See Ine 29; Ælf. 19.

[5] Ælf. 19 § 3; Hen. 87 § 3. A similar rule as to arms given in pledge still has the force of law in Montenegro: Code général des biens (tr. Dareste), Paris 1892, art. 176.

[6] The word *gesund* may well point to a warranty of this kind. Brunner, Forschungen, 520.

a charge might have involved the forfeiture of the weapon until quite modern times.

The extreme difficulty of getting any proof of intention, or of its absence, in archaic procedure is, perhaps, the best ex-planation of rules of this kind.   At all events, they not only are characteristic of early German law, but they have left their mark on the developed common law to a notable extent.   In modern times the principle of general responsibility for pure accidents arising from one's lawful act has been disallowed in the United States, and more lately in England.   But, as regards the duty of safely keeping in cattle, and in the case of persons collecting or dealing with things deemed of a specially dan-gerous kind, the old Germanic law is still the law of this land and of the greater part of North America. *Archaic principle of responsi-bility for accidents.*

Fire, which English law has regarded for several centuries as a specially dangerous thing in this sense, and which is dealt with in some of the early Germanic dooms, is not mentioned for this purpose in our documents[1].   Liability for damage done by dogs is on the other hand rather elaborately dealt with by a scale of compensation increasing after the first bite[2].

There are traces of the idea which underlay the Roman noxal actions, and which crops up in the medieval rule of deodand, that where a man is killed by accident, the immediate cause of death, be it animate or inanimate, is to be handed over to the avenger of blood as a guilty thing.   When men were at work together in a forest, and by misadventure one let a tree fall on another, which killed him, the tree belonged to the dead man's kinsfolk if they took it away within thirty days[3].   This kind of accident is still quite well known in the forest countries of Europe, as witness the rude memorial pic-tures, entreating the passer's prayers, that may be seen in any Tyrolese valley.   Also a man whose beast wounded another might surrender the beast as an alternative for money com-pensation[4].

[p. 33]   Theft, especially of cattle and horses, appears to have been by far the commonest and most troublesome of offences.   There is a solitary and obscure reference to 'stolen flesh' in the laws of Ine[5].   Perhaps this is to meet the case of a thief driving *Theft.*

---

[1] Ælf. 12 seems to relate only to wilful trespass in woods.
[2] Ælf. 23.   [3] Ælf. 13.   [4] Ælf. 24.   [5] In. 17.

cattle a certain distance and then slaughtering them, and hiding the flesh apart from the hides and horns, which would be more easily identified. If we are surprised by the severity with which our ancestors treated theft, we have only to look at the prevalence of horse-stealing in the less settled parts of the western American states and territories in our own time, and the revival of archaic methods for its abatement. Collusion with thieves on the part of seemingly honest folk appears to have been thought quite possible: Cnut required every man above twelve years to swear that he would be neither a thief nor an accomplice with thieves[1], and special penalties for letting a thief escape, or failing to raise, or follow, the hue and cry, point in the same direction[2]. Slavery was a recognized penalty when the thief was unable to make restitution. This, if it stood alone, might be regarded as handing over the debtor's person by way of compensation rather than a punishment in the modern sense. But moreover the offender's whole family might lose their freedom as accomplices. The harshness of this rule was somewhat relaxed if the thief's wife could clear herself by oath from having had any part in stolen cattle which had been found in his house[3]. But as late as the early part of the eleventh century, Wulfstan's homily[4] complains that 'cradle-children' are unjustly involved in the slavery of their parents. All this, however, belongs to social antiquities rather than to legal history. The common law of theft is wholly post-Norman. Nor is it needful to dwell on the Anglo-Saxon treatment of special and aggravated forms of theft, such as sacrilege[5]. Stealing on Sunday, in Lent, and on Christmas, Easter, or Ascension Day, was punishable with a double fine by the old Wessex law[6].

Property   In a modern system of law we expect a large portion of the whole to be concerned with the rules of acquiring, holding, and transferring property. We look for distinctions between land and movables, between sale and gift, between the acts completed among living persons and dispositions to take effect [p. 34] by way of inheritance. If the word *property* be extended to include rights created by contract, we may say that we

---

[1] Cn. ii. 21.   [2] Ib. 29.   [3] Ine 7, 57.

[4] Ed. Napier, Berlin, 1883, p. 158.

[5] As to robbing corpses, Schmid, App. xv. *Be Walreáfe.*

[6] Ælf. 5 § 5; the principle is reaffirmed, but so vaguely as to suggest that it had become obsolete in practice, in Cn. ii. 38.

contemplate under this head by far the greater and weightier
part of the whole body of legal rules affecting citizens in their
private relations.   But if we came with such expectations to
examine laws and customs so archaic as the Anglo-Saxon, we
should be singularly disappointed.   Here the law of property
is customary and unwritten, and no definite statement of it
is to be found anywhere, while a law of contract can hardly
be said to exist, and, so far as it does exist, is an insignificant appurtenance to the law of property.   But we must remember that even Hale and Blackstone, long after that view
had ceased to be appropriate, regarded contract only as a
means of acquiring ownership or possession.   Yet more than
this; it is hardly correct to say that Anglo-Saxon customs
or any Germanic customs, deal with ownership at all.   What
modern lawyers call ownership or property, the *dominium*
of the Roman system, is not recognized in early Germanic
ideas.   Possession, not ownership, is the leading conception; it
is possession that has to be defended or recovered, and to possess without dispute, or by judicial award after a dispute real
or feigned, is the only sure foundation of title and end of strife.
A right to possess, distinct from actual possession, must be
admitted if there is any rule of judicial redress at all; but it is
only through the conception of that specific right that ownership finds any place in pure Germanic law.   Those who have
studied the modern learning of possessory rights and remedies
are aware that our common law has never really abandoned
this point of view.

Movable property, in Anglo-Saxon law, seems for all prac- Sale and
tical purposes to be synonymous with cattle.   Not that there other
contracts
was no other valuable property; but arms, jewels, and the like,
must with rare exceptions have been in the constant personal
custody of the owners or their immediate attendants.   Our
documents leave us in complete ignorance of whatever rules
existed.   We may assume that actual delivery was the only
known mode of transfer between living persons; that the
acceptance of earnest-money and giving of faith and pledges
were customary means of binding a bargain; and that contracts
in writing were not in use.   There is no evidence of any regular
[p. 35] process of enforcing contracts, but no doubt promises of any
special importance were commonly made by oath, with the
purpose and result of putting them under the sanction of the

church. There is great reason to believe that everywhere or almost everywhere a religious sanction of promises has preceded the secular one[1], and that honourable obligation has been more effective than might be supposed in aiding or supplementing the imperfections of legality[2]. Apparently the earliest form of civil obligation in German law was the duty of paying wergild. Payment, when it could not be made forthwith, was secured by pledges, who no doubt were originally hostages. Gradually the giving of security sinks into the background, and the deferred duty of payment is transformed into a promise to pay. But our Anglo-Saxon authorities are of the very scantiest. We find the composition of a feud secured by giving pledges and the payment by instalments regulated[3]; and in Alfred's laws there is mention of a solemn kind of promise called 'god-borh'; if a suit is brought upon it, the plaintiff must make his fore-oath in four churches, and when that has been done, the defendant must clear himself in twelve, so that falsehood on either side would involve manifold perjury and contempt of the church and the saints[4]. Here we seem to have a mixture of secular and ecclesiastical sanctions, rendered all the easier by the bishop constantly being, as we have seen, the chief judicial officer of the shire. But this must have been a very special procedure, and probably confined to persons of high rank. And it is hard to tell what the subject-matter of these solemn undertakings can have been, unless it were marriages of the parties' children and what we now should call family settlements and, perhaps, reconciliation of standing feuds. We may guess, from what is known of the practice of local courts in the twelfth and thirteenth centuries, that before the Conquest the hundred courts did to some extent do justice in matters of bargain and promise in the ordinary affairs of life. But we have no direct [p. 36] information whatever.

Claims for stolen things: warranty.

On the other hand, there runs persistently through the Anglo-Saxon laws a series of ordinances impressing on buyers

[1] Muirhead, Private Law of Rome, 149, 163, 227 (origin of stipulation).

[2] The Roman words *credere*, *fides*, *spondere*, involve a whole history of this kind. Pernice, Labeo, i. 409; Pacchioni, Actio ex Sponsu, Bologna, 1888: *Ehrenverpfändung* in German formulas as late as 15th cent., see Kohler, Shakespeare vor dem Forum der Jurisprudenz, 1884, appx.

[3] Edm. ii. 7, and *Be Wergilde*, Schmid, App. vii.

[4] Ælf. 33. Cp. the provisions as to 'briduw' in the laws of Howel (10th cent.) ap. Haddan and Stubbs, Councils, i. 237, 271.

of cattle the need of buying before good witnesses. But this
has nothing to do with the validity of the sale between the
parties. The sole purpose, judging by the terms and context
of these enactments, is to protect the buyer against the subsequent claims of any person who might allege that the cattle
had been stolen from him. Difficulties of this kind were especially rife when the sale had been made (in the earlier times)
in another English kingdom, or up the country. Hlothær
and Eadric laid down the precautions to be observed by a
Kentish man buying cattle in London, then a Mercian town[1].
Evidently great suspicion attached to sales made anywhere out
of open market. Some ordinances require the presence of the
portreeve or other credible men at sales without the gates;
others attempt to prohibit selling altogether except in towns.
Afterwards witnesses are required in town and country alike[2],
and in the latest period we find the number of four witnesses
specified[3]. A buyer who neglected to take witness was liable
to eviction, if the cattle were claimed as stolen, without even
the chance of calling the seller to warrant him, and he might
also incur a forfeiture to the lord of the place, and be called on
to clear himself by oath of any complicity in the theft. If he
had duly taken witness, he still had to produce the seller, or, if
the seller could not be found, to establish his own good faith by
oath.

If the seller appeared, he had in turn to justify his possession, and this process might be carried back to the fourth
remove from the ultimate purchaser. These elaborate provisions for vouching to warranty (A.-S. *teám*)[4] or the custom on
which they were founded, persisted for some time after the
Norman Conquest[5], and are interesting by their analogy to the
doctrine of warranty in the law of real property, which after-
[p. 37] wards underwent a far more full and technical development,
and remained, long after it had been forgotten in practice, at
the foundation of many parts of modern conveyancing. The

---

[1] Hl. & E. 16. The supposed 'improbability of a Kentish king making a
law for purchases made in the Mercian city of London' (Thorpe's note *ad loc.*
is imaginary. The law applies to a claim made in Kent by a Mercian professing
to be the true owner, and it is to be executed wholly in Kent.

[2] Edg. IV. 6; Cn. II. 24.   [3] Leg. Will. I. 45.

[4] See Æthelr. II. 9, *Be teámum,* and Schmid's Glossary s. vv. *Käufe, Teám.*

[5] Glanv. x. 15–17.

dooms of Ine contain a curious archaic provision[1] for a buyer clearing himself by an oath taken over the stolen property at the seller's grave, in the case of the seller having died since the purchase of the slave, or other thing in dispute.

Land tenure. With regard to the tenure of land we have a considerable bulk of information, derived partly from charters and wills, partly from occasional passages in the laws, and partly from other documents, especially the tract known as *Rectitudines singularum personarum.* We have gone into the matter elsewhere[2], and we may confine ourselves here to a short statement of what is positively known.

Book-land. Our Anglo-Saxon charters or *books* are mostly grants of considerable portions of land made by kings to bishops and religious houses, or to lay nobles. Land so granted was called book-land, and the grant conferred a larger dominion than was known to the popular customary law. During the ninth century and the early part of the tenth the grant usually purports to be with the consent of the witan. *Alodium* (of which we have no English form) is, in documents of the Norman age, a regular Latin translation of book-land. There is great reason to believe that a grant of book-land usually made no difference at all to the actual occupation of the soil. It was a grant of lordship and revenues, and in some cases of jurisdiction and its profits. The inhabitants rendered their services and dues to new lords, possibly enough to the same bailiff on behalf of the new lord, and things went on otherwise as before. The right of alienating book-land depended on the terms of the original grant. They were often large enough to confer powers equivalent to those of a modern tenant in fee simple. Accordingly book-land granted by such terms could be and was disposed of by will, though it is impossible to say that the land dealt with in extant Anglo-Saxon wills was always book-land. Lords of book-land might and sometimes did create smaller holdings of the same kind by making grants to dependants. It is important to remember that book-land was a clerkly and exotic institution, and that grants of it owe their existence directly or indirectly to royal favour, and throw no light, save [p. 38] incidentally, on the old customary rules of land-holding.

---

[1] Ine 53.

[2] Pollock, The Land Laws, 3rd ed. Lond. 1896, chap. ii. and notes B, C and D; Maitland, Domesday and Beyond, 1897.

When the day of conquest was at hand, many of the tillers Inferior tenures: lǽn-land.
of the ground were dependent on a lord to whom they owed
rents and services substantially like those of which we have
ample and detailed evidence in later documents. A large
proportion of them were personally free men[1]; the homesteads
were several, and every free man was answerable for his own
fence[2]. There is little doubt that, except in the western counties,
common-field agriculture was general if not universal[3]; and
probably the scheme of distribution and the normal amount of
holdings was very like that which we find after the Conquest.
Free men sometimes held considerable estates under a lord, but
our authorities are too scanty to enable us to say on what
terms[4]. In the later Anglo-Saxon period, land held of a
superior, whether much or little, is called *lǽn-land*. It is not
clear whether this term extended to customary tenures (those
for example which would result from a grant of book-land as
between the new lord and the occupiers) or was limited to
interests created by an express agreement. In the latter case
it may be compared with the Gallo-Frankish *precarium*, from
which indeed it was perhaps derived[5].

Folk-land is a term which occurs only in a few documents, Folk-land.
and then without any decisive explanation. In the most
authoritative of these, a law of Edward the Elder, it is contrasted with book-land as if it included all land that was not
book-land. Spelman, so reading the passage, defined folk-land
as land held by common, that is customary law, without written
title. On this view an Englishman who was asked, 'What do
you mean by folk-land?' would have answered, 'Land held by
folk-right.' In 1830 John Allen put forth another view which
prevailed for two generations. He said[6] that 'folk-land, as the
word imports, was the land of the folk or people. It was the
property of the community.' The proposed analogy to the Latin
ager publicus was accepted as confidently as it was proposed,
[p. 39] and with singularly little discussion, by Kemble and almost

---

[1] Ine 3 § 2; Ælf. 43; Rect. S. P. 3.   [2] Ine 40.
[3] Ine 42 is a good illustration, though by itself not conclusive.
[4] Ine 63–67. We assume that the hide here spoken of is not materially
different from the normal hide of the Domesday period, *i.e.* 120 acres. Perhaps
these passages have to do with the settlement of a newly conquered district.
Maitland, Domesday Book, 237–8.
[5] See Fustel de Coulanges, Le bénéfice et le patronat, ch. iv–vii.
[6] Royal Prerogative, ed. 1849, p. 135.

every one who treated of Anglo-Saxon land tenures down to
1893. Difficulties occurred, however, in working out Allen's
theory, and were found to increase as one scholar after another
entered farther upon details. In particular, it was hard to
account for the number of free men, which must have been
considerable in the time of Edward the Elder at all events,
holding land which was not book-land. Various conjectural
names for that kind of holding were proposed by Kemble and
others, but for none of them was there any authority. If these
lands were included in folk-land, and *folc-land* meant *ager
publicus*, then every one who had not book-land was in name
and in law a mere tenant from the state. If not, there was no
evidence that land held by the most general and practically
important form of title had any proper name at all. Neither
conclusion could be deemed satisfying. In 1893 Mr Paul
Vinogradoff[1] pointed out that Allen's theory was really gratuitous. The documents do not by any means require it; the
analogy of other compounds in which the word *folc* occurs is
against it; and when it turns out to give rise to more difficulties
than it removes, it is better to fall back upon the older and
simpler explanation. Folk-land, then, appears to have been, as
Spelman said, land held without written title under customary
law. We have no right to assume that there were not varieties
of tenure within this general description, or that custom was
uniform even in the same kingdom. It is probable that the
alienation of folk-land was difficult, and we do not know to
what extent, if to any considerable extent, power to dispose of
it by will had been introduced. The problem of reconstructing
the old folk-right in detail belongs, however, rather to the
history of Germanic social antiquities than to that of the laws
of England; and our interpretation of the scanty evidence
available must depend in great measure on the manner in which
the fuller evidence of the two centuries after the Conquest is
interpreted[2].

**Transition
to Anglo-
Norman
feudalism.** After the Norman Conquest book-land preserved its name [p. 40]
for a time in some cases, but was finally merged in the feudal
tenures in the course of the twelfth century. The relations
of a grantee of book-land to those who held under him were

---

[1] Folk-land, E. H. R. viii. 1–17.

[2] It is now prudent rather than necessary to remind the reader that Kemble's
brilliant conjectures were premature and largely unwarranted.

doubtless tending for some considerable time before the Conquest to be practically very like those of a feudal superior; but Anglo-Saxon law had not reached the point of expressing the fact in any formal way. The Anglo-Saxon and the continental modes of conveyance and classification of tenures must have coalesced sooner or later. But the Conquest suddenly bridged a gap which at the time was still well-marked. After its work is done we find several new lines of division introduced and some old ones obliterated, while all those that are recognized are deeper and stronger than before. The king's lordship and the hands that gather the king's dues are everywhere; and where they have come the king's law will soon follow.

CHAPTER III.

NORMAN LAW[1].

OF the law of Normandy as it was on the eve of William's [p. 41]
expedition, little is known for certain. To illustrate the period
which had elapsed since the settlement of the Northmen in
Neustria, there are no written laws, no books on law and very
few charters, while the chroniclers have not much to tell about
the legal structure of the duchy, and what they tell is not
always trustworthy. The England of the same period supplies
us with the laws of Edward the Elder, Æthelstan, Edmund,
Edgar, Æthelred and Cnut; also with a large collection of
land-books and writs. Even in later days, after the duke of
the Normans had become king of the English, the duchy
was slow to follow the kingdom in the production of abiding
memorials of its law. It has nothing to set against Domesday

---

[1] The following brief sketch is based partly on the first-hand authorities for
Norman history, partly on the opinions expressed by Palgrave, Gneist, Stubbs,
Freeman in their well-known books.—Stapleton's editions of the Norman
Exchequer Rolls.—Brunner's account of the sources of Norman law given in his
Anglo-Normannisches Erbfolgesystem, his Entstehung der Schwurgerichte, and
his article upon this subject in Holtzendorff's Encyklopädie.—Waitz, Ueber die
Quellen zur Geschichte der Begründung der Normannischen Herrschaft in
Frankreich, Nachrichten von der Gesellschaft der Wissenschaften, Göttingen,
1866, pp. 69–95.—Steenstrup, Inledning i Normannertiden, Copenhagen, 1876,
of which the author gave a French translation in the Bulletin de la Société des
antiquaires de Normandie, vol. x. p. 185, under the title Études préliminaires
pour servir à l'histoire des Normands.—von Amira, Die Anfänge des Normannischen Reichs, Historische Zeitschrift, Neue Folge, vol. iii. p. 241.—
Delisle, Études sur la condition de la classe agricole en Normandie, Évreux,
1851, and the same writer's essays on Norman finance in the Bibliothèque de
l'École des chartes, ser. II. vol. 5; ser. III. vols. 1, 3.—The editions of the rolls
and custumals referred to below.—Luchaire, Institutions monarchiques de la
France sous les premiers Capétiens, 1883, and Luchaire, Manuel des institutions
françaises, 1892.

[p. 42] Book or against those law-books which we know as the *Leges* of the Confessor, the Conqueror and Henry the First. The oldest financial records[1], the oldest judicial records[2] that it has transmitted to us, are of much later date than the parallel English documents. Its oldest law-books, two small treatises now fused together and published under the title *Le très ancien Coutumier*[3], are younger and slighter than our Glanvill, and the *Grand Coutumier*, if not younger, is slighter than our Bracton[4]. Doubtless we have been more fortunate than our neighbours in the preservation of documents; still we have every reason to believe that the conquerors of England had little, if any, written law to bring with them. Hrolf, it is true, had gained the reputation of lawgiver; but our own history will show us that such a reputation might be easily gained by one who was regarded as the founder of a state or the representative of a race : Alfred was becoming, Edward the Confessor was to become, the hero of a legal myth. Hrolf may have published laws, in particular laws about theft, but what we hear of them will hardly dispose us to think that they would remain in force for long[5]. But not only had the Normans no written law of their own making; there was none that they could readily borrow from their French neighbours. Their invasions occurred in the very midnight of the legal history of France; indeed they brought the midnight with them. The stream of capitularies ceases to flow; no one attempts to legislate; and when the worst days are over, the whole structure of society has been so much changed, that the old written laws, the *Lex Salica*, the

---

[1] Magni Rotuli Scaccarii Normanniae sub Regibus Angliae, published by Stapleton, and reprinted in Mémoires de la Société des antiquaires de Normandie, vol. xv. A fragment of the roll of 1184 was published by Delisle, Caen, 1851.

[2] These are most accessible in Delisle's Recueil de jugements de l'échiquier de Normandie au xiiime siècle, Paris, 1864. A collection of judgments delivered in the assizes between 1234 and 1237 will be found in Warnkönig's Französische Staats- und Rechtsgeschichte, vol. ii. Urkundenbuch, pp. 48–69.

[3] Edited by E. J. Tardif, Rouen, 1881.

[4] This has been frequently printed. A recent edition by W. L. De Gruchy, Jersey, 1881, gives both the Latin and the French text. The Latin text has of late been admirably edited by E. J. Tardif under the title Somma de Legibus Normannie, 1896. He takes the Latin text to be the older and is inclined to date it in 1254–8.

[5] Dudo, Duchesne, p. 85. The story of Hrolf's legislation has been rejected as fabulous, but is defended by Steenstrup, Études préliminaires, pp. 351–391.

ordinances of Merovingian and Karlovingian kings, will no [p. 43] longer meet the facts.　When an Englishman of the twelfth century, the compiler of the *Leges Henrici*, strives to eke out the old English dooms with foreign texts and goes as far back as the *Lex Salica*, which was centuries old before Hrolf landed in Normandy, we know that he has no foreign texts at his command that are less obsolete.

Norman law was French.

The yet debated question, whether for a century or thereabouts after their settlement in Neustria, the law of the Northmen or Normans was mainly Frankish or mainly Scandinavian, we are not called upon to discuss.　It is now generally admitted that for at least half a century before the battle of Hastings, the Normans were Frenchmen, French in their language, French in their law, proud indeed of their past history, very ready to fight against other Frenchmen if Norman home-rule was endangered, but still Frenchmen, who regarded Normandy as a member of the state or congeries of states that owed service, we can hardly say obedience, to the king at Paris. Their spoken language was French, their written language was Latin, but the Latin of France; the style of their legal documents was the style of the French chancery; very few of the technical terms of their law were of Scandinavian origin. When at length the 'custom' of Normandy appears in writing, it takes its place among other French customs, and this although for a long time past Normandy has formed one of the dominions of a prince, between whom and the king of the French there has been little love and frequent war; and the peculiar characteristics which mark off the custom of Normandy from other French customs seem due much rather to the legislation of Henry of Anjou than to any Scandinavian tradition[1].

Norman law was feudal.

To say that the law of Normandy was mainly French is to say that it was feudal.　But *feudalism* is an unfortunate word. In the first place it draws our attention to but one element in a complex state of society and that element is not the most distinctive: it draws our attention only to the prevalence of [p. 44]

---

[1] This is frankly admitted by Steenstrup, Études préliminaires, p. 375: 'Les coutumes les plus anciennes de la Normandie datent du xiime siècle, et le droit qu'elles nous présentent est français, quoiqu'il y ait quelques restes des coutumes du Nord.　Il serait injuste d'enregistrer ces sources dans la législation scandinave; elles appartiennent à une législation spéciale, à la législation anglo-normande.'

dependent and derivative land tenure[1].   This however may well
exist in an age which can not be called feudal in any tolerable
sense.   What is characteristic of 'the feudal period' is not the
relationship between letter and hirer, or lender and borrower of
land, but the relationship between lord and vassal, or rather it
is the union of these two relationships.   Were we free to invent
new terms, we might find *feudo-vassalism* more serviceable than
feudalism.   But the difficulty is not one which could be solved
by any merely verbal devices.   The impossible task that has
been set before the word *feudalism* is that of making a single
idea represent a very large piece of the world's history, represent the France, Italy, Germany, England, of every century
from the eighth or ninth to the fourteenth or fifteenth.   Shall
we say that French feudalism reached its zenith under Louis
d'Outre-Mer or under Saint Louis, that William of Normandy
introduced feudalism into England or saved England from
feudalism, that Bracton is the greatest of English feudists or
that he never misses an opportunity of showing a strong anti-
feudal bias?   It would be possible to maintain all or any of
these opinions, so vague is our use of the term in question.
What would be the features of an ideally feudal state?   What
powers, for example, would the king have : in particular, what
powers over the vassals of his vassals?   Such a question has
no answer, for the ideal does not remain the same from century
to century, and in one and the same land at one and the same
time different men have different ideals: the king has his
opinion of what a king should be; his vassals have another
opinion.   The history of feudal law is the history of a series of
changes which leave unchanged little that is of any real
importance.

This, if true of the whole, is true of every element of feudalism, and true in the first place of that element whence it takes
its name.   In England from almost, if not quite, the earliest
moment of its appearance, the word *feodum* seems not merely
to imply, but to denote, a heritable, though a dependent right.
But if on the continent we trace back the use of this word, we
find it becoming interchangeable with *beneficium*, and if we go
[p. 45] back further we find *beneficium* interchangeable with *precarium*.
A tenancy at will has, we may say, become a tenancy in fee;
but we cannot speak of a tenancy at will and a tenancy in

Feudalism in Normandy.

---

[1] Waitz, D. V. G. vi. 1.

fee in one breath[1]. The Norman conquest of England occurs
at a particular moment in the history of this process. It
has already gone far; the words *feum, feudum, feodum* are fast
supplanting *beneficium;* the *feodum* is hereditary; men now
see little difference between the *feodum* and the *alodus* or
alodium, the fullest ownership that there can be. And yet a
trait of precariousness clings to the fee; it is easily forfeitable,
and the lord's rights in the land appear in the shape of reliefs
and wardships. So also with vassalism. Time was when the
vassus was an unfree man, though that time has long since
passed away, and some vassals of the king of the French are
apt to behave as sovereign princes. So again with that most
essential element of feudalism, jurisdiction in private hands,
the lord's court. Its growth, whether we have regard to
England or to the continent, seems the obscurest of all problems, for the law is rapidly shifting and changing just at the
time when it is leaving the fewest explicit memorials of its
shifts and changes. And it is so pre-eminently with the
political character of feudalism. Is the feudal tie the loose
bond—hardly other than an alliance between two sovereigns—
which binds the duke of the Normans to the king of the
French? Does the duke conceive that it is but a similar tie
that binds his viscounts and barons to him? Often enough
such questions must be solved by the sword; there is no
impartial tribunal for their solution. It is characteristic of
the time that rights of sovereignty shade off into rights of
property: the same terms and formulas cover them both: the
line between them is drawn by force rather than by theory.
This had been so in Normandy. Every moment at which the
duke was weak had been marked by rebellions. Duke William
had been stern and victorious and had reduced his vassals to
submission; but so soon as he was dead there was another era
of anarchy and private war. Indeed a first glance at the [p. 46]
Norman chronicles might induce us to say that the Normans
had little law beyond 'the good old rule, the simple plan.' But

---

[1] It seems to be now generally admitted that the Roman *precarium* is one of
the germs of feudalism; Waitz, D. V. G. ii. 229; Brunner, D. R. G. i. 211;
Fustel de Coulanges, Le bénéfice et le patronat. It has been pointed out that
even in the Digest, 43, 26, 14 (Paulus) the two words *precarium* and *beneficium*
are brought into contact; 'magis enim ad donationes et beneficii causam quam
ad negotii contracti spectat precarii conditio.' The belief that the *feudum* is in
any way connected with *emphyteusis* has long been exploded.

lawlessness is often a superficial phenomenon and whenever the
duke was strong enough to keep the peace then law revived.
We hear the same of England: times of 'unlaw' alternate with
times of law. At one moment prudent travellers journey in
parties of twenty, at the next a girl may go from end to end of
the realm and fear no harm. All depends upon the ruling man.
To say then of the Norman law of William's day that it was
feudal, is to say little; but it would be difficult for us to say
more without going beyond the direct and contemporary
evidence or repeating what has elsewhere been admirably said
of the history of feudalism in general. But a few traits may
be noted.

To the great generalization which governs the whole scheme *Dependent land tenure.*
of Domesday Book, the theory that every acre of land is
immediately or mediately 'held of' the sovereign lord, the
Normans in their own country may not have arrived. But
Domesday Book by itself would suffice to show that it was
not far from their minds, and in the Norman charters we
frequently discover the phenomena of dependent tenure. The
rich man who wishes to endow a religious house endows it with
land; but in many cases we see that he is not an absolute
owner of the land that he gives, or at all events is not the only
person interested in it. The land is held by tenants of divers
classes, *milites, vavassores, hospites, coloni, conditionarii, villani,
rustici,* and these tenants (that is to say, his rights over
these tenants) he gives to the church[1]. But further, if he has
subordinates who have rights in the land, he has also superiors
with rights in the land; he makes the gift with the consent of
his lord; that lord's confirmation is confirmed by the duke of
the Normans, perhaps it is even confirmed once more by the
duke or king of the French[2]. Of the *alodium* we often read,

---

[1] The term which occurs most often is *hospites,* a term which did not obtain
a permanent home in England, though it appears occasionally in Domesday,
e.g. D. B. i. 259 b. The Conqueror gives certain vills to the Abbey of Caen
'cum colonis et conditionariis seu liberis hominibus'; Gall. Christ. xi. Instrum.
p. 66; Neustria Pia, p. 626. In another charter he confirms 'dominium cum
militibus quod dedit Olilia'; Gall. Christ. xi. Instrum. p. 203.

[2] In 968 Duke Richard the Fearless grants Bretteville to Saint Denis with the
assent of his lord Hugh Duke of the French, 'cum assensu senioris mei Hugonis
Francorum Principis'; Bouquet, ix. 731. In 1006 King Robert confirmed a gift
made by Duke Richard the Good to Fécamp; Gall. Christ. xi. Instrum. p. 7.
Such transactions as these were probably exceptional; but instances in which
Norman lords confirm gifts made by their subordinates and in which the duke

and occasionally it is contrasted with the *beneficium,* the one [p. 47]
still meaning full ownership, the other dependent, and in some
degree precarious, tenure[1].   But the two are being fused
together.   Sometimes the *alodium* is held of a lord and the
alodial owner does not dispose of it, without his lord's consent; nay, the lord has rights over him and over it, and those
rights can be conveyed to a third person[2].   On the other hand,
the *beneficium* has gone half-way to meet the *alodium.*   The
viscounts and barons of Normandy held *beneficia, feoda, honores*
of the duke; in return they owed him military service, though
the precise amount of the service may not have been fixed[3].
We need not suppose that this had been so from the first, from [p. 48]
the day when, according to Norman tradition, Hrolf roped

confirms these confirmations are abundant.   See for example Orderic's account
of the gifts to Saint Evroul; ed. le Prevost, vol. ii. p. 16 ff.   Ralph Taisson,
when endowing an abbey, forbids any of his barons or other men to give or sell
any of their possessions to any other church; Gall. Christ. xi. Instrum. p. 63.

[1] Neustria Pia, 311: 'Ego Abbas Albertus Abbatiae SS. Stephani Protho-
martyris et Christi Confessoris Maximini......erat mihi quidam alodus ex
materna hereditate, non ex alicuius beneficio, quem S. Petro in Gemmetico
monasterio...dedi.   Est autem ipse alodus in pago Belismensi.'   Ibid. 217 in a
charter for Fécamp, Richard II. says that he is pleased to confirm 'ea quae
fideliter communi nostro (?) aut precario vel beneficiis quae nostri iuris erant
vel de hereditatibus quas paterno iure possidebant concessere.'   The first
words of this passage seem corrupt, but the *beneficium* is treated as something
that is not a *hereditas* and is brought into connexion with precarious tenure.
Rouen Cartulary (ed. Deville), 451: 'dedit S. Trinitati omnem decimam terrae
suae in alodio quam domini sui Rodolfi de Warenna tenebat beneficio.'
Neustria Pia, 634; the abbot of Caen 'emit allodium' and afterwards 'dedit
in feodo.'

[2] Neustria Pia, 627: William the Conqueror grants to the Abbey of Caen
'totum alodium quod tenent Osmundus, Aculeus, Richardus et Rogerius in
territorio Calvi Montis super Divam; et etiam totum illud quod tenent quicum-
que allodiarii infra leugam Pontis Divae.'   Ibid. 636: 'Rogerius de Rozel
vendidit Gisleberto Abbati [de Cadomo] concedente Normaniae Comite, pro
xv lib. census, allodium suum totum quod habebat in Rozel, tali conditione ut
eum de Sancto [Stephano] teneret per tale servitium quale antea ex eo Comiti
reddebat.'   In this case the alodiary does service for his land.

[3] It is thus, for example, that William of Jumièges (Duchesne, 250) speaks of
the relation between Duke Richard II. and his bastard brother William :—'Is
enim [Willelmus] fraterno contubernio Oximensem ab ipso [Ricardo] accipiens
munere comitatum ut inde exhiberet ei militiae statuta...dominium eius sprevit.'
William the Conqueror gives to the church of Lisieux 'terram de Fontaines...et
servitium militum...dominium cum militibus quod dedit Olilia'; Neustria Pia,
585; Gall. Christ. xi. Instrum. p. 203.   Richard son of Abp. Robert of Rouen
makes a gift to Saint Sauveur in these terms: 'apud A dedi totum quod in
dominio habebam excepto feodo militum'; Gall. Christ. xi. Instrum. p. 126,
where the date assigned is circ. 1060.

out the land and distributed it among his followers[1]. Whatever may have been the terms upon which Hrolf received Normandy from Charles the Simple—and the Norman tale was that he received it as the most absolute *alodium*[2]—his successors were conceived as holding a fief of the kings of the French in return for homage and service; and so, whatever may have been the terms on which Hrolf's followers acquired their lands, their successors were conceived as holding benefices or fiefs of the dukes of the Normans in return for homage and service. From the first the rights of the Norman nobles seem to have been hereditary. It may well be, however, that there was an element of precariousness in their tenure, an element which appears in later days in the shape of the duke's right to reliefs and wardships, and certainly their hold on the land was not sufficiently secure to prevent him from habitually having splendid fiefs to give away to his kinsfolk[3]. On the eve

[1] Dudo, Duchesne, 85: 'Illam terram suis fidelibus funiculo divisit.'

[2] According to Dudo, Duchesne 82–84, the grant was made 'in sempiternam per progenies progenierum possessionem...quasi fundum et alodium in sempiternum...in alodio et in fundo.'

[3] As regards the 'relief' the main proof is to be found in Domesday Book; *e.g.* on the first page of it we read that when a Kentish *alodiarius* dies 'rex inde habet relevationem terrae.' William of Jumièges, Duchesne, 250, says that Richard the Good gave to his brother William the county of Eu and a beautiful girl called Lescelina, the daughter of one Thurkill, a man of noble birth. The duke seems to be disposing of the hand of a vassal's daughter. So again Orderic (ed. le Prevost), ii. 409, speaking of the days of William the Conqueror, says: 'Guillelmus Gualterii de Falesia filius fuit et in militia nimium viguit, unde Guillelmus Princeps filiam Guidmundi cum toto ei honore Molinensi contulit.' It is not impossible that the king of the French had twice asserted a right to the wardship of an infant duke of the Normans. As to the case of Louis d'Outre-Mer and Richard the Fearless, see Palgrave, Hist. Normandy, ii. chs. 3, 4; Freeman, Norman Conquest, ch. iv. § 4; Kalckstein, Geschichte des französischen Königthums, i. 238–9. Dudo's romantic tale may be false enough, but the important point is, that not very long after the events the Normans believed that the king had asserted and abused a right of wardship. Then as to the minority of the Conqueror himself:—Henry of Huntingdon, p. 189, tells us that Harold son of Cnut banished his father's widow, the Norman Emma, and that she went to Flanders instead of to Normandy, 'Willelmo namque domino Normannorum adhuc in aetate puerili cum rege Francorum manente, Normannia fiscus regalis erat.' It is difficult to square this story with the known facts; still there seems to be a great deal in the behaviour of the king towards Normandy and its young duke that is best explained as an attempt of a lord to exercise rights over the land of an infant vassal. See the account of William's minority in Freeman, Norman Conquest, vol. ii. and see Luchaire, Institutions monarchiques sous les premiers Capétiens, i. 113–4; ii. 15.

of the conquest of England many of the great houses owed [p. 49] their greatness to some more or less legitimate relationship— legitimacy was a matter of degree—between them and the ducal family. Still the *feoda* were hereditary, and seemingly even women might inherit them. The *alodium* and the *beneficium* were meeting in the *feodum*. A new scheme of proprietary rights, of dependent proprietary rights, was being fashioned, and into that scheme every acre of a conquered kingdom might be brought[1].

Seignorial justice.

Some such scheme of dependent ownership is necessary if among the subjects of proprietary rights are to be reckoned justice and office. It can never be suffered that one who is not a sovereign prince should own a jurisdiction in the absolute sense in which he owns his flocks and herds. That in Normandy the right of doing justice and receiving the profits thereof had become heritable is plain. The *honores* of the Norman nobles comprised rights of jurisdiction; the viscounts were in name the successors of royal officials, of Frankish *vicecomites* whose offices had become hereditary[2]. Also the lands of the churches were defended by ducal grants of 'immunity,' grants [p. 50] modelled on Frankish precedents[3]. But the principles which regulated the existence and the competence of seignorial courts

---

[1] About the time of the Conquest the word *feodum* becomes very common in the Norman charters; but *beneficium* still appears. William of Jumièges, Duchesne, 259, tells how William of Bellême held the castle of Alençon 'beneficii iure' and tried to shake off 'serviminis iugum.' Luchaire, Institutions monarchiques sous les premiers Capétiens, i. 87, remarks that in the charters of the French kings *beneficium* is still common under Hugh Capet and Robert II. while *feodum* becomes usual under Henry I. and Philip I. He also, ii. 17, fixes the very moment of the Norman conquest of England as that at which the kings are finally forced to admit that the great fiefs have become hereditary, though practically they had been hereditary for a long time past. As to the inheritance of fiefs by females, the case of Mabel of Bellême is a capital instance. Women were inheriting fiefs in France from the end of the tenth century onwards; Luchaire, Manuel des institutions françaises, 167.

[2] Ord. Vit., vol. ii. p. 470: 'Hugo Paganus Crassa Lingua et Agnes uxor eius atque Guido filius eorum concesserunt S. Ebrulfo vicecomitatum, id est viariam, quantam habebant in Villariis Vastatis.'

[3] The early charter by which Richard the Fearless grants Bretteville to Saint Denis contains a full 'immunity'; Bouquet, ix. 731. Less explicit clauses of the same kind are found in the charters of Richard the Good for Fécamp and for Saint Michael of the Mount; Neustria Pia, 215-7, 377-8. Another instance is afforded by the charter of William of Bellême for Lonlai; Neustria Pia, 425. Observe also the words 'in pasnagio, in venationibus, in *placitis*' in the charter for Cérisi; Neustria Pia, 431.

are very dark to us. Whether the right to hold a court can only be conferred by the sovereign's grant, or whether it arises from the mere relation between lord and men, or between lord and tenants, is a question to which we get no certain answer for a long time after the conquest of England, whether we ask it of England or of Normandy. In good times, however, the duke's justice was powerful throughout his duchy. It is as supreme judge hearing and deciding the causes of all his subjects, the guardian of the weak against the mighty, the stern punisher of all violence, that his courtly chroniclers love to paint him[1], and we may doubt whether in his own country the Conqueror had ever admitted that feudal arrangements made by his men could set limits to his jurisdiction[2].

As to any constitutional restraints on the ducal power, the most opposite opinions have prevailed. The duke of the earliest period has been everything, from the most absolute of monarchs to a mere first among equals[3]. What we know is that when the time for the conquest of England is approaching, the duke consults, or professes to consult the great men of his realm, lay and spiritual, the *optimates,* the *proceres* of Normandy. He holds a court; we dare hardly as yet call it a court of his tenants in chief; but it is an assembly of the great men, and the great men are his vassals. Seemingly it is for them to make the judgments of the court[4], and just as the English [p.51] *witan* attest or confirm the king's grants, so the Norman *proceres* attest or confirm the charters of the duke[5]. In the lower courts also, so it would seem, the lord of the court is not the only judge; he is surrounded by doomsmen[6].

Limits to the ducal power.

---

[1] See in Dudo, Duchesne, 136–140, the panegyric on Richard the Fearless, also what William the Archdeacon of Lisieux, Duchesne, 193, says of the Conqueror.

[2] An argument to prove that the feudalization of justice had gone further in England than in Normandy, might be founded on the fact that the Normans in England when they wished to describe the rights of private jurisdiction, almost invariably employed the English terms *sake, soke* etc.

[3] The one extreme is marked by Palgrave, the other by Steenstrup.

[4] Thus in or about 1077 a suit came before William's court; he orders the Archbishop of Rouen, Roger de Beaumont 'and many other barons' to make a judgment 'ut facerent inde iudicium'; Mémoires de la Société des antiquaires de Normandie, vol. xv. pp. 196–7.

[5] See *e.g.* Richard II.'s grant to St Wandrille, his grant to St Michael of the Mount, the Conqueror's charter for Fécamp; Neustria Pia, 165–6, 377–9, 223–4.

[6] In 1086 a suit is heard in the court of Robert of Bellême; he presides, but

Legal
procedure.   Probably the ordinary procedure of the courts was much
the same in Normandy and in England. In neither country
had men passed the stage at which they look to the supernatural
for proof of doubtful facts. The means of proof are solemn
formal oaths and ordeals designed to elicit the judgment of God[1].
One ordeal the Normans recognized which had no place in
English law, namely, the ordeal of battle[2]. When immediately
after the Conquest we find this mode of proof in England, we
may say with some certainty that here we have a Norman
institution. The same may be said with great probability of a
far more important institution, of which we must speak at
length hereafter, namely the sworn inquest, the germ of the
jury.

Criminal
law.   Perhaps criminal law, or what served as such, had reached
a later stage of development in Normandy than in England.
The great need of the time was that the ancient system of
money compositions, of *bót* and *wer* and *wíte*, should give way
before a system of true punishments, and in Normandy the
alternations of rough anarchy and stern repression may have
hastened this desirable process. At any rate from Normandy
we hear little or nothing of the old money payments, though
at one time they had been familiar enough both to the Franks
and to the Norsemen, and in England the writers of the twelfth
century, who still know all about the *wer* of the West-Saxon,
the Mercian, the Dane, say no word of the Norman's *wer*
and show no acquaintance with any Norman or Frankish [p. 52]
criminal tariff[3].

Ecclesiasti-
cal law.   We may be more certain that in another direction Norman

three abbots, nine named laymen, and many others are the 'iudices huius
placiti'; Neustria Pia, 311.

[1] The ordeal of fire occurs in the legend of Rollo; Dudo, Duchesne, p. 85.
William Pantolf purged himself of the murder of Mabel of Bellême by carrying
the hot iron; Ord. Vit. (ed. le Prevost) ii. 432. The ordeal is also mentioned
in the statutes of the Council of Lillebonne; ibid. 322.

[2] See William's charter for St Wandrille, Neustria Pia, 168; the champions
being ready for battle William interferes and makes peace. This is an early
instance of a 'concordia per finem duelli.'

[3] In the Norman chronicles the crimes that we read of are chiefly the
rebellions of great men, and, when the rebel is brought to justice, his punishment is imprisonment or exile and disherison. The insurgent peasants were
punished by mutilation. In England the kinsfolk of the slain Norman receive
a certain part of the murder fine which falls on the hundred if the slayer be not
brought to justice; they receive six marks out of forty-six; the rest go to the
king; Leg. Henrici, 91 § 1; Edw. Conf. 15 § 6.

law had outstripped English law along what must seem to us a destined path of progress. It had come in sight of an ecclesiastical jurisprudence, of conflicts and compacts between church and state. Within our island church and state might still appear as but two phases of one organization; on the continent this could not be so. Long ago the claim of a 'supernational' church to jurisdiction had raised difficult problems and been satisfied for a while by complicated compromises—but only for a while, for the church was not easily satiable[1]. By the Conquest England was drawn into the mid-stream of a controversial torrent. Whatever else he might leave for the future, the Conqueror would have to define in precise terms his relation to the spiritual power in his new kingdom, and his definition would, if this were possible, be that which had come down to him from Norman dukes and Frankish kings. On the one hand, he would concede an ample room to 'the canons and episcopal laws;' on the other he would insist that the spiritual power should assume no right in England that it had not exercised in Normandy[2].

One ecclesiastical institution there was in Normandy, which, The truce so William might hope, would hardly be necessary in England: of God. the truce of God. In England the old family blood-feud was not dead, but it had not as yet developed into the feudal right of private warfare. In France a religious movement, which had its origin in the south, had been setting limits to this [p. 53] anarchical right by putting certain places and persons and seasons under the protection of the church and outside the limits of fair fighting. The truce of God had been received in Normandy; it reigned there after England had been conquered; but we only find very faint and uncertain traces in England either of it or of that tolerated private warfare which it presupposed[3].

---

[1] Hinschius, Kirchenrecht, iv. 797 ff; v. 402; Brunner, D. R. G., ii. 311 ff.

[2] Eadmer, Hist. Nov. p. 9, just before he makes his well-known statement about William's dealings with ecclesiastical matters, has said of him 'usus ergo atque leges quos patres sui et ipse in Normannia habere solebant in Anglia servare volens.' His edict (Leg. Will. iv.) establishing the ecclesiastical courts supposes that their proper province is known; it is that allowed to them in Normandy; it is that which will be made more definite by the Council of Lillebonne; see Ord. Vit. (ed. le Prevost) ii. 316.

[3] As to the *treuga Dei* in Normandy see Ord. Vit. (ed. le Prevost) ii. 316 and the editor's note; as to the truce generally see Hinschius, Kirchenrecht, v. 305. In the so-called Leges Edwardi Confessoris, c. 2, we read that the peace of God

Of the condition of the great mass of the inhabitants of
Normandy, the tillers of the soil, we know singularly little; the
chronicles have hardly a word to say about them, the charters
do little more than mention their existence. This we know,
that in the early years of Richard the Good there was a
formidable revolt of the Norman peasants, which was fiercely
suppressed. According to the chronicler, the insurgents showed
a high degree of organization; they sent representatives to a
central assembly[1]. This story, remarkable if true, is scarcely
less remarkable if false, but the mere rebellion will make us
believe that the Norman peasant was seldom a slave. It has
been said by high authority that there are few traces of
any serfage in Normandy even in the eleventh century, none [p. 54]
in the twelfth[2]. The charters of the Conqueror's day frequently speak of *hospites, coloni, rustici, villani*, rarely of *servi*,
though now and again we have hints that some men and some
lands are not deemed 'free'[3]. In later times Normandy was

prevails during certain holy seasons, *e.g.* from noon on Saturday throughout
Sunday, and that if anyone breaks this, the bishop has jurisdiction. This claim
of jurisdiction probably betrays French influence. The laws of Æthelred
v. 13–19; vi. 19–25, and of Cnut i. 15–17, forbid work and litigation during
certain holy seasons and vaguely add that during these seasons peace and
concord should prevail. Even this may betray the influence on England of the
great ecclesiastical movement which established the *treuga Dei*, but still we
have no English evidence of the truce itself prior to 1066, nor any of it after
that date, save in the untrustworthy Leges Edwardi. An allegation of a breach
of the peace of God became a common form in the pleadings of the thirteenth
century, but only as an untraversable ornament. The peace of God was then
conceived as existing always and everywhere. Of private warfare we shall speak
hereafter.

1 The only good authority is William of Jumièges (Duchesne, 249); and he
says very little; the poems of a later age cannot be trusted about such a
matter. See Delisle, Études sur la condition de la classe agricole, 121;
Freeman, Norman Conquest, i. 257 (ed. 3); Palgrave, Hist. Normandy, iii. 41;
Steenstrup, Études préliminaires, p. 346. These peasants have appeared in
every character, from that of Gallo-Romans reclaiming Roman liberties to that
of untamed Danes.

2 Delisle, op. cit. 17–19; Luchaire, Manuel des institutions, 295.

3 Thus in a charter of the Conqueror for Trinity Abbey at Caen: 'item in
insula de Gerzoi unum molendinum et terram duorum francorum hominum';
Neustria Pia, 659. So in a charter of the Conqueror for S. Stephen's Abbey at
Caen, Neustria Pia, 626: 'Trado igitur…villas iuris mei…cum colonis et
conditionariis seu liberis hominibus…Et homines quidem duarum premissarum
villarum videlicet C. et R. qui francam terram non tenent ad servitium ecclesiae
et monachorum…concedo.' Delisle, op. cit. 17, 18, gives a few instances of
servi in the eleventh century.

distinguished among the provinces of France by a singular
absence of serfage, and such evidence as we have tends to show
that the Conqueror left a land where there were few slaves for
one in which there were many, for one in which the slave was
still treated as a vendible chattel, and the slave-trade was
flagrant.

The Normans then had no written law to bring with them Juris-
to England, and we may safely acquit them of much that could prudence.
be called jurisprudence.   Not but that there were among them
men distinguished above others for their knowledge of the law.
The famous founder of the Abbey of Bec, Herlwin, who had
spent most of his life as layman and knight, was deeply learned
in the law of the land, and when he had become an abbot he
still gave opinions in temporal causes; but not until he was
near forty years of age did he learn the first rudiments of
letters[1].   His legal knowledge was probably the same in kind
as that attributed, as we shall read hereafter, to the English
bishop Æthelric and the monks of Abingdon, a knowledge of
the law to be evoked by concrete cases, not a body of doctrine
to be taught or written in a book.   But the mention of Herlwin Lanfranc
must remind us of Herlwin's prior, of Lanfranc the lawyer of lawyer.
Pavia, of Lanfranc the Conqueror's right-hand man.   Those who
tell us of the great theologian, of the great disciplinarian, never
forget to add that he was a lawyer of world-wide fame, the most
accomplished of pleaders.   Now, as we have already said, the
Lombard lawyers, especially the lawyers of Pavia, had been
[p. 55] engaged in a task well fitted to be an education for one who
was to be William's prime minister.   They had been har-
monizing, digesting and modernizing the ancient statutes of
the Lombard kings, a body of law very similar to our own old
English dooms[2].   Some Roman law they knew, and unless
Pavian tradition deceives us, we may still read the ingenious
arguments by which the youthful Lanfranc puzzled and abashed
his conservative opponents, arguments which derive their force
from the supposition that the dooms of King Liutprand and
the institutes of Justinian are or ought to be harmonious[3].

---

[1] Vita Herluini, Lanfranci Opera, ed. Giles, i. 270: 'Abbas peritus erat in
dirimendis causarum saecularium controversiis...Legum patriae scientissimus
praesidium suis erat contra iniquos exactores.' Ibid. 265: 'Prima litterarum
elementa didicit cum iam existeret annorum prope quadraginta.'

[2] See above, p. 22.

[3] Lanfranc's juristic exploits are chronicled in the Liber Papiensis, M. G.

Lanfranc, yet a layman, left Italy for Normandy and opened a
school, a secular school, at Avranches. What he taught there
we are not told; but he may have taught law as well as
grammar and rhetoric. He was remembered in Normandy as
one of the discoverers of Roman law[1]. If he taught law at
Avranches or at Bec[2], then we may say that the Normans were
being educated for their great exploit: when the time for
subduing England should come, the man at arms would have
the lawyer behind him. But, be this as it may, the very
existence of Lanfranc, who knew Lombard law and Roman law
and Canon law—when he was Archbishop the *decreta* and
canones were ever in his mouth[3]—who mastered English law so
thoroughly that he carried all before him even when the talk [p. 56]
was of *sake* and *soke*[4], must complicate the problem of any one
who would trace to its sources the English law of the twelfth
century. Who shall say that there is not in it an Italian
element? The Norman Conquest takes place just at a moment
when in the general history of law in Europe new forces are
coming into play. Roman law is being studied, for men are
mastering the Institutes at Pavia and will soon be expounding
the Digest at Bologna; Canon law is being evolved, and both
claim a cosmopolitan dominion.

Leges, iv. pp. xcvi., 402, 404, 566. See also Ficker, Forschungen zur Geschichte
Italiens, iii. 47, 458. It is not absolutely certain that this Lanfranc is our
Lanfranc, but the part here assigned to him, that of confuting his elders, agrees
well with what is said by Milo Crispin, Opera Lanfranci, ed. Giles, 291: 'Ado-
lescens orator veteranos adversantes in actionibus causarum frequenter revicit,
torrente facundiae accurate dicendo.'

[1] Robertus de Monte, ann. 1032, ed. Howlett, p. 25: 'Lanfrancus Papiensis
et Garnerius socius eius repertis apud Bononiam legibus Romanis, quas
Iustinianus imperator Romanorum...emendaverat, his inquam repertis, operam
dederunt eas legere et aliis exponere.' Savigny, Gesch. des röm. Rechts, cap.
xxvii. § 8, points out that the story cannot be true; Lanfranc must have left
Italy before the days of Irnerius.

[2] See Savigny, op. cit., cap. vi. § 135. Robert of Torigny (Robertus de
Monte), ann. 1117, ed. Howlett, p. 100, tells how Ivo of Chartres, the famous
canonist, had when a youth heard Lanfranc in the school at Bec 'de saecularibus et divinis litteris tractantem.'

[3] See Lanfranc's letters, especially No. 26, ed. Giles, in which he recommends
Bishop Herbert to mend his ways and read the canons: 'Postpositis aleis, ut
maiora taceam, ludisque saecularibus quibus per totam diem vacare diceris,
divinas litteras lege, decretisque Romanorum Pontificum sacrisque canonibus
praecipue studium impende.'

[4] See below, p. 93.

CHAPTER IV.

ENGLAND UNDER THE NORMAN KINGS.

[p. 57] THE Norman Conquest is a catastrophe which determines the whole future history of English law. We can make but the vaguest guesses as to the kind of law that would have prevailed in the England of the thirteenth century or of the nineteenth had Harold repelled the invader. We may for example ask, but we shall hardly answer, the question, whether the history of law in England would not have closely resembled the history of law in Germany, whether a time would not have come when English law would have capitulated and made way for Roman jurisprudence. But it is slowly that the consequences of the great event unfold themselves, and they are not to be deduced from the bare fact that Frenchmen subjugated England. Indeed if we read our history year by year onwards from 1066, it will for a long time seem doubtful whether in the sphere of law the Conquest is going to produce any large changes. The Normans in England are not numerous. King William shows no desire to impose upon his new subjects any foreign code. There is no Norman code. Norman law does not exist in a portable, transplantable shape. English law will have this advantage in the struggle :—a good deal of it is in writing.

Effects of the Norman conquest.

But then, the problem to which the historian must address himself should not be stated as though it were a simple ethnical question between what is English and what is French.

No mere mixture of two national laws.

[p. 58] The picture of two rivulets of law meeting to form one river would deceive us, even could we measure the volume and analyze the waters of each of these fancied streams. The law which prevails in the England of the twelfth century—this

one thing we may say with some certainty—can not be called
a mixture of the law which prevailed in England on the day
when the Confessor was alive and dead, with the law which
prevailed in Normandy on the day when William set sail from
Saint Valery. Nor can we liken it to a chemical compound
which is the result of a combination of two elements. Other
elements, which are not racial, have gone to its making.
Hardly have Normans and Englishmen been brought into
contact, before Norman barons rebel against their Norman
lord, and the divergence between the interests of the king and
the interests of the nobles becomes as potent a cause of legal
phenomena as any old English or old Frankish traditions can
be. Nor dare we neglect, if we are to be true to our facts, the
personal characters of the great men who accomplished the subjection of England, the characters of William and Lanfranc.
The effects, even the legal effects, of a Norman conquest of
England would assuredly have been very different from what they
were, had the invading host been led by a Robert Curthose.
And in order to notice just one more of the hundred forces
which play upon our legal history, we have but to suppose that
the Conqueror, instead of leaving three sons, had left one only,
and to ask whether in that case a charter of liberties would ever
have been granted in England. We have not to speak here of
all these causes; they do not come within the history of law;
only we must protest against the too common assumption that
the English law of later times must in some sort be just a
mixture, or a compound, of two old national laws.

History of
our legal
language.   If for a moment we turn from the substance to the
language of the law, we may see how slowly what we are apt to
think the most natural consequences of the Conquest manifest
themselves. One indelible mark it has stamped for ever on
the whole body of our law. It would be hardly too much to
say that at the present day almost all our words that have
a definite legal import are in a certain sense French words.
The German jurist is able to expound the doctrines of Roman
law in genuinely German words. On many a theme an English
man of letters may, by way of exploit, write a paragraph or a [p. 59]
page and use no word that is not in every sense a genuinely
English word; but an English or American lawyer who attempted this puritanical feat would find himself doomed to
silence. It is true, and it is worthy of remark, that within the

sphere of public law we have some old terms which have come
down to us from unconquered England. Earl was not displaced
by count, sheriff was not displaced by viscount; our king, our
queen, our lords, our knights of the shire are English; our
aldermen are English if our mayors are French; but our
parliament and its statutes, our privy council and its ordinances,
our peers, our barons, the commons of the realm, the sovereign,
the state, the nation, the people are French; our citizens are
French and our burgesses more French than English. So
too a few of the common transactions of daily life can be described by English verbs. A man may give, sell, buy, let, hire,
borrow, bequeath, make a deed, a will, a bond, and even be
guilty of manslaughter or of theft, and all this in English. But
this is a small matter. We will say nothing of the terms in
which our land law is expressed, estate, tenement, manor, mortgage, lease and the like, for though we have English freeholds
and half-English copyholds, this is a region in which we should
naturally look for many foreign terms. But let us look elsewhere and observe how widely and deeply the French influence
has worked. Contract, agreement, covenant, obligation, debt,
condition, bill, note, master, servant, partner, guarantee, tort,
trespass, assault, battery, slander, damage, crime, treason, felony,
misdemeanour, arson, robbery, burglary, larceny, property, possession, pledge, lien, payment, money, grant, purchase, devise,
descent, heir, easement, marriage, guardian, infant, ward, all are
French. We enter a court of justice: court, justices, judges,
jurors, counsel, attorneys, clerks, parties, plaintiff, defendant,
action, suit, claim, demand, indictment, count, declaration,
pleadings, evidence, verdict, conviction, judgment, sentence,
appeal, reprieve, pardon, execution, every one and every thing,
save the witnesses, writs and oaths, have French names. In
the province of justice and police with its fines, its gaols and its
prisons, its constables, its arrests, we must, now that outlawry is
a thing of the past, go as far as the gallows if we would find an
English institution. Right and wrong we have kept, and, though
we have received *tort*, we have rejected *droit*: but even law
[p. 60] probably owes its salvation to its remote cousin the French *lei*[1].

---

[1] The connexion between our *law* and the French *lei* or *loi* (Lat. *legem*) is
for the etymologist a remote one, and Henry I. knew what he was about when
he restored to us the *lagam* (not *legem*) *Eadwardi*. But the two words attracted
each other. We preserve the French *droit* in our 'droits of admiralty.'

Struggle
between
Latin,
French and
English.
But all this is the outcome of a gradual process; we can not
say that it is the necessary result of the conquest of England
by French-speaking men. Indeed for some time after the
conquest the English language seems to have a fair chance of
holding its own in legal affairs. In the first place, the combat
between English and French, if it must begin sooner or later,
can for a while be postponed or concealed, for there is a third
and a powerful rival in the field. Latin becomes the written
language of the law. It was a language understood and
written by the learned men of both races: it was the language
of such legal documents as the Normans knew, and, though it
was not the language of the English dooms or the English
courts, still it was the language of the English charters or
land-books. In the second place, English had long been a
written language, and a written language which could be used
for legal and governmental purposes, while French was as yet
hardly better than a vulgar dialect of Latin:—French would
become Latin if you tried to write it at its best. And so the
two languages which William used for his laws, his charters
and his writs were Latin and English[1]. Again, there were
good reasons why the technical terms of the old English law
should be preserved if the king could preserve them. They
were the terms that defined his royal rights. On the whole he
was well satisfied with the goodly heritage which had come to
him from his cousin King Edward. If only he could maintain
against his followers the rights of the old English kingship, he
would have done almost as much as he could hope to do. And
so his rights and their rights must be registered in the old
English terms. His clerks must still write, if not of *sacu and
socne*, still of *saca et soca*. Many foreign words have made
their way into Domesday Book, but many old English words
which had definite legal meanings were preserved[2].

Latin as a
legal
language.
During the century that follows, Latin keeps its pre- [p. 61]
eminence, and when, under Henry II. and his sons, the time
comes for the regular enrolment of all the king's acts and of all
the judgments of his court, Latin becomes the language of our

---

[1] The French set of *Leges Willelmi* will be mentioned below; it is private
work. The well-known passage about the English and French languages in the
would-be Ingulf's History of Croyland (Scriptores post Bedam, p. 512 b) is one
of that forger's clumsiest falsehoods.

[2] Maitland, Domesday Book, 8.

voluminous official and judicial records. From this position it is not dislodged until the year 1731, when it gives place to English[1]. It were needless to say that long before that date both French and English had been used for some very solemn, perhaps the solemnest legal purposes; but seemingly we may lay down some such rule as this, namely, that if a series of records goes back as far as the twelfth or the first half of the thirteenth century, it will until the reign of George II. be a series of Latin records. It is only in the newer classes of authoritative documents that either English or French has an opportunity of asserting its claims. French becomes the language of the privy seal, while Latin remains the language of the great seal. French expels Latin and English expels French from the parliament rolls and the statute rolls, but these rolls are new in Edward I.'s day[2]. In particular, Latin remains the language in which judicial proceedings are formally recorded, even though they be the proceedings of petty courts. In Charles I.'s day the fact that the Star Chamber has no proper Latin roll can be used as a proof that it is an upstart[3].

But, though throughout the middle ages some Latin could be written by most men who could write at all, and the lord of a manor would still have his accounts as well as his court rolls made up in Latin, still only the learned could speak Latin readily, and it could not become the language of oral pleading or of debate. Here was a field in which French and English might strive for the mastery. There could for a long while be no doubt as to which of these two tongues would be spoken in and about the king's court. The king spoke French, his barons French, his prelates French, and even when barons and prelates [p 62] were beginning to think of themselves as Englishmen, some new wave of foreign influence would break over the court; the new French queen brings with her a new swarm of Frenchmen. And 'the king's court' was not then a term with several meanings;

Struggle between French and English.

---

[1] Statute 4 Geo. II. c. 26.

[2] Our first parliament roll comes from 1290 and there is some French on the roll of 1293; Rot. Parl. i. 101. The very first entry on our statute roll as it now exists, the Statute of Gloucester 1278, is in French, and if, as seems probable, a membrane containing the Statute of Westminster 1275 has been lost, this also was covered with French writing.

[3] Stat. 16 Car. I. c. 10, abolishing the Star Chamber, solemnly recites the Statute 36 Edw. III. Stat. I. c. 15, which says that (despite the use of English as a medium for oral pleading) all pleas are to be enrolled in Latin.

the language of courtiers and courtliness was of necessity the language of business, discussion, pleading. All this might well have happened, however, and yet the English language, which was in the future to be the language even of courtiers, might have retained its stock of old and its power of engendering new legal terms. A French-speaking royal tribunal might have been merely superimposed upon an English substructure. But here what is perhaps the main theme of our legal history decides the fate of words. Slowly but surely justice done in the king's name by men who are the king's servants becomes the most important kind of justice, reaches into the remotest corners of the land, grasps the small affairs of small folk as well as the great affairs of earls and barons. This is no immediate and no necessary effect of the Norman Conquest. It would never have come about if the nobles who helped William to conquer England could have had their way; William himself can hardly have dared to hope for it. The destiny of our legal language was not irrevocably determined until Henry of Anjou was king.

Victory of French.   If we must choose one moment of time as fatal, we ought to choose 1166 rather than 1066, the year of the assize of novel disseisin rather than the year of the battle of Hastings. Then it was that the decree went forth which gave to every man dispossessed of his freehold a remedy to be sought in a royal court, a French-speaking court. Thenceforward the ultimate triumph of French law terms was secure. In all legal matters the French element, the royal element, was the modern, the enlightened, the improving element. The English stock of words is stricken with barrenness, the French stock can grow. The things of the law which have English names are things that are obsolete or obsolescent, *sake* and *soke*, *wer* and *wite* :— already men hardly know what these words mean[1]. It is difficult for us to believe that in the local courts, the suitors, who [p. 63] were for the more part peasants, pleaded their causes and rendered their judgments in French; still from the thirteenth century we get books of precedents for pleadings in manorial courts which are written in French, while we look in vain for

---

[1] Even the earliest and purest glossaries of A.-S. law terms, the *Expositiones Vocabulorum*, prove this ignorance. As to these glossaries, see Hall, Red Book of the Exchequer, vol. iii. Introduction.

any similar books written in English[1]. We may suspect that if the villagers themselves did not use French when they assailed each other in the village courts, their pleaders used it for them, and before the end of the thirteenth century the professional pleader might already be found practising before a petty tribunal and speaking the language of Westminster Hall[2]. Then in 1362 a statute, itself written in French, declared that as the French tongue was but little understood, all pleas should be 'pleaded, shown, defended, answered, debated and judged' in the English tongue[3]. But this came too late. It could not break the Westminster lawyers of their settled habit of thinking about law and writing about law in French, and when slowly French gave way before English even as the language of law reports and legal text-books, the English to which it yielded was an English in which every cardinal word was of French origin. How far this process had gone at the end of the thirteenth century we may learn from Robert of Gloucester's historical poem. He sets himself to translate into English verse the Constitutions of Clarendon, and in so doing he uses the terms which we now write as *custom, grant, lay fee, service, pleading, assize, judgment, traitor, chattels, felon, patron, advowson, court, plea, purchase, amendment, hold in chief, bailiff, homage, confirm, appeal, debt*[4]. Down to the end of the middle ages a few old English terms perdured which, at least as technical terms, we have since lost: English 'domesmen' might still 'deem dooms in a moot hall'; but the number of such terms was small and the blight of archaism was on them[5].

Meanwhile men had begun to write French and to write French documents. it for legal purposes. Legal instruments in French come to [p. 64] us but very rarely, if at all, from the twelfth century[6]; they

---

[1] The Court Baron (Seld. Society).

[2] The Court Baron, pp. 38, 42.   [3] 36 Edw. III. Stat. I. c. 15.

[4] Robert of Gloucester, lines 9650–9730.

[5] Wycliffite Translation of the Bible; Matth. vii. 1 'for in what dome ȝe demen, ȝe sculen ben demed'; Matth. xxvii. 19 'and while he [Pilat] sat for domesman'; Mark xv. 16 'the porche of the mote halle.'

[6] The volume of Sarum Charters (Rolls Series), p. 5, contains what at first looks like an early example, a French document executed by a bishop of Salisbury and apparently ascribed by a copyist of the fourteenth century to the year 1120. But there is some mistake here. A French charter of Stephen Langton entered on the Charter Roll of 10 John is given in facsimile by Hardy, Rot. Cart. p. xli.

become commoner in the thirteenth and yet commoner in the fourteenth, but on the whole Latin holds its own in this region until it slowly yields to English, and the instruments that are written in French seldom belong to what we may call the most formal classes; they are wills rather than deeds, agreements rather than charters of feoffment, writs under the privy seal, not writs under the great seal.

Language of Statute law.   From the royal chancery Latin is not to be driven. The example set by the Conqueror when he issued laws in English as well as in Latin was not followed; Latin is the language for laws and ordinances until the middle of the thirteenth century. Then for one brief moment the two vulgar tongues appear on an equality; in 1258 Henry III. declared both in French and in English his acceptance of the provisions which were forced upon him in the parliament at Oxford[1]. But while this English proclamation long remains unique, French forces its way to the front. It wrestles with Latin for the possession of the statute roll and the parliament rolls. By the end of Edward II.'s reign it has fairly won the statutes roll[2], and is fast gaining a mastery over the parliament rolls. For about two centuries, from the reign of Edward I. to the reign of Richard III., it is the usual language of the enacted law. Late in the fourteenth century English begins to make an insidious attack. Petitions to parliament are sometimes presented in English, and the English petition is sometimes put upon the roll without being translated. However, the middle ages are just at an end before the records of the English legislature are written mainly in English, and to this day, as all know, what a lawyer must regard as the most solemn of all our formulas is French—*La reine le veult*[3].

[1] The proclamations will be found in the Select Charters.

[2] The exceptions are rather apparent than real; *e.g.* the Ordinance for Ireland of 31 Edw. III., though on the statute roll, is in the form of letters patent, and is also on the patent roll.

[3] The transition from French to English statutes seems to occur suddenly at the accession of Richard III. and to be contemporaneous with a change in the method of enrolment. We pass at this date from the 'statute rolls' preserved at the Tower to 'enrolments of Acts of Parliament.' As early as 1386, and it may be earlier—for but few of the extant petitions are printed or dated—a petition to parliament might be written in English (Rot. Parl. iii. 225), and the English words which Henry IV. spoke when he met his first parliament are enrolled (iii. 423); then petitions in English appear on the roll; but on the whole it is not until 1425 or thereabouts that the parliament roll has much English on it. To the very last (1503) the formal parts of the roll are written either in French or in Latin.

[p. 65] Again, in the thirteenth century French slowly supplanted Latin as the literary language of the law. It is very possible that the learned Bracton thought about law in Latin; he wrote in Latin, and the matter that he was using, whether he took it from the Summa Azonis or from the plea rolls of the king's court, was written in Latin. But the need for French text-books was already felt, and before the end of the century this need was being met by the book that we call Britton, by other tracts[1], and by those reports of decided cases which we know as the Year Books. Thenceforward French reigns supreme over such legal literature as there is. We must wait for the last half of the fifteenth century if we would see English law written about in the English tongue, for the sixteenth if we would read a technical law-book that was written in English[2].

French law-books.

This digression, which has taken us far away from the days of the Norman Conquest, may be pardoned. Among the most momentous and permanent effects of that great event was its effect on the language of English lawyers, for language is no mere instrument which we can control at will; it controls us. It is not a small thing that a law-book produced in the England of the thirteenth century will look very like some statement of a French *coutume* and utterly unlike the *Sachsenspiegel*, nor is it a small thing that in much later days such foreign influences as will touch our English law will always be much rather French than German. But we have introduced in this place what must have been said either here or elsewhere about our legal language, because we may learn from it that [p. 66] a concurrence of many causes was requisite to produce some of those effects which are usually ascribed to the simple fact that the Normans conquered England[3].

Language and law.

---

[1] Court Baron (Seld. Society), p. 11. See also the *Brevia Placitata* which are now being edited by Mr Turner.

[2] The honour of being the first books concerning English law that were written in the English language must probably be given to some of Sir John Fortescue's treatises, but they cannot be called legal text-books. Before a deliberate judgment can be passed on the question as to which is our first English text-book, an intricate group of little tracts on pleading etc., some of which may not yet have been printed, must be examined.

[3] The French that is a literary language in England under Henry III. and Edward I. should not be called 'Norman-French'; Parisian French, the French of the Isle of France, is already its model; but there is some difference

Preserva-
tion of old
English
law.　　We may safely say that William did not intend to sweep
away English law and to put Norman law in its stead.　On the
contrary, he decreed that all men were to have and hold the law
of King Edward—that is to say, the old English law—but with
The Con-
queror's
legislation.　certain additions which he, William, had made to it[1].　So far
as we know, he expressly legislated about very few matters.
He forbad the bishops and archdeacons to hold in the hundred
courts pleas touching ecclesiastical discipline; such pleas were
for the future to be judged according to the canons and not
according to the law of the hundred; the lay power was to
aid the justice of the church; but without his leave, no canons
were to be enacted and none of his barons or ministers excommunicated[2].　He declared that his peace comprehended all men
both English and Normans[3].　He required from every free man
an oath of fealty[4].　He established a special protection for the
lives of the Frenchmen; if the slayer of a Frenchman was not
produced, a heavy fine fell on the hundred in which he was
slain.　He declared that this special protection did not extend
to those Frenchmen who had settled in England during the
Confessor's reign[5].　He defined the procedural rules which were
to prevail if a Frenchman accused an Englishman, or an Englishman a Frenchman[6].　He decreed that the county and hundred
courts should meet as of old.　He decreed that every free man
should have pledges bound to produce him in court[7].　He forbad
that cattle should be sold except in the towns and before
three witnesses.　He forbad that any man should be sold out of [p. 67]
the country.　He substituted mutilation for capital punishment[8].
This may not be an exhaustive list of the laws that he
published, nor can we be certain that in any case his very
words have come down to us; but we have good reason to
believe that in the way of express legislation he did these
things and did little more.

of opinion among philologists as to how far 'Anglo-French' is entitled to be
considered as a dialect which has a history of its own.　See Behrens in Paul's
Grundriss d. German. Philologie, i. 807.　To dignify with the name 'Norman-
French' the mere 'dog-French' that we find in law reports of the sixteenth
century is ridiculous.

1　Laws of William (Select Charters), c. 7.
2　Leg. Willelmi, iv.; Eadmer, Hist. Nov. p. 10.
3　Laws of William (Select Charters), c. 1.
4　Laws, c. 2; A.-S. Chron. an. 1086; Florence, ii. 19.
5　Laws, c. 3, 4; Leges Will. i. 22.　　　6　Laws, c. 6; Leges Will. ii.
7　Laws, c. 7, 8.　　　8　Laws, c. 5, 9, 10.

In the long run by far the most important of these rules will be that which secures a place in England for the canonical jurisprudence. And here we have a good instance of those results which flow from the Norman Conquest—a concrete conquest of England by a certain champion of Roman orthodoxy —which are in no wise the natural outcome of the mere fact that Englishmen were subjugated by Normans. For the rest, there are some rules which might have come from a king of the old race, could such a king have been as strong a ruler as William was. He would have had many precedents for attempting to prevent the transfer of stolen goods by prohibiting secret sales[1]. It was old, if disregarded, law that men were not to be sold over sea[2]. It was law of Cnut's day that every free man should be in pledge[3]. A wave of religious sentiment had set against capital punishment[4]. Whether the king could exact an oath of fealty from all men, even from the men of his men, was a question of power rather than of right[5]. Only two rules drew a distinction between French and English. We may doubt, however, whether the murder fine had not its origin in the simple principle that the lives of the Normans were to be as well protected in England as the lives of strangers were in Normandy; at any rate the device of making a district pay if a stranger was murdered in it and the murderer was not produced in court, was not foreign to Frankish nor yet to Scandinavian law. We are also told, though the tale comes from no good source, that Cnut had protected his Danes by a fine similar to that which was now to protect the Normans[6]. Again, [p. 68] the procedure in criminal cases is by no means unfavourable to the men of the vanquished race. The Englishman whom a Frenchman accuses has the choice between battle and ordeal.

---

[1] The precedents are collected in Schmid, Glossar, s.v. *Marktrecht.*

[2] Æthelred, v. 2; Cnut, II. 3.   [3] Cnut, II. 20.

[4] Æthelred, v. 3; VI. 10; Cnut, II. 2.

[5] Edmund, III. 1.

[6] Leg. Will. III. 3; Leg. Will. I. 22; Leg. Henr. 91; Leg. Edw. 15, 16; Bracton, f. 134 b. In Swedish laws it is common to find the hundred charged with a fine of forty marks (the exact sum that the Conqueror demands) if the manslayer be not produced, more especially if the slain man be a stranger; Wilda, Strafrecht, 217–218. Some similar liability seems to be indicated by an early capitulary added to the Lex Salica; Hessels, Lex Salica, p. 408; with which should be compared Leg. Henr. 92 § 8. Henry I. in his Coronation Charter, c. 9, seems to speak as though the murder fine was known to the *laga Eadwardi.* Liebermann, Leges Edwardi, p. 112, rejects the story about Cnut.

The Englishman who brings an accusation can, if he pleases, compel his French adversary to join battle; otherwise the Frenchman will be able to swear away the charge with oath-helpers 'according to Norman law.' Certainly we can not say that the legislator here shows a marked partiality for one class of his subjects. In this matter mere equality would not be equity, for English law has not known the judicial combat, and perhaps the other ordeals have not been much used in Normandy. As it is, the Englishman, whether he be accuser or accused, can always insist on a wager of battle if he pleases; he is the Norman's peer[1].

Personal or national law. In different ages and circumstances the pride of a conquering race will show itself in different forms. Now-a-days the victor may regard the conflict as one between civilization and barbarism, or between a high and a low morality, and force his laws upon the vanquished as the best, or the only reasonable laws. Or again, he may deliberately set himself to destroy the nationality of his new subjects, to make them forget their old language and their old laws, because these endanger his supremacy. We see something of this kind when Edward I. thrusts the English laws upon Wales. The Welsh laws are barbarous, barely Christian, and Welshmen must be made into [p.69] Englishmen[2]. In older and less politic days all will be otherwise. The conquerors will show their contempt for the conquered by allowing such of them as are not enslaved to live under their old law, which has become a badge of inferiority. The law of the tribe is the birthright of the men of the tribe,

---

[1] Laws of William, c. 6; Leges Willelmi, II. Had William said to the Englishman, 'If you accuse a Norman, you must adopt the Norman's law and offer battle,' even this could not have been regarded as a tyrannous decree; it would have been an application of the principle of 'personal law,' which would have looked plausibly equitable. As it is, the Norman has to purge himself even though the Englishman will not fight. He purges himself with 'an unbroken oath,' 'mid unforedan aðe,' 'sacramento non fracto.' This is a difficult phrase. Apparently a 'broken' or 'breaking' oath is an oath sworn 'in verborum observantiis,' and is an oath broken up into phrases, each of which must be repeated with punctilious accuracy by the swearer as it is dictated to him by his adversary. Dr Brunner sees in William's law a provision that the Norman need not swear in words dictated by an Englishman. Brunner, Zeitschrift d. Savigny-Stiftung, Germ. Abt. XVII., 128, and Pol. Science Quarterly, XI. 537; Forschungen, 328.

[2] Register of Abp. Peckham, i. 77: 'leges Howeli Da quae Decalogo dicuntur in diversis articulis obviare.'

and aliens can have no part or lot in it. Perhaps we should be
wrong were we to attribute any large measure of either of
these sentiments to the generality of the Norman invaders;
but probably they stood nearer to the old and tribal than to
the modern and political point of view. A scheme of 'personal
laws' would have seemed to them a natural outcome of the
conquest. The Norman will proudly retain his Norman law
and leave English law to the English. We have seen that in
matters of procedure William himself favoured some such
scheme, and to this idea of personal law may be due what is
apt to look like an act of gross iniquity. Roger of Breteuil and
Waltheof conspired against William; Waltheof was condemned
to death; Roger was punished 'according to the law of the
Normans' by disherison and perpetual imprisonment[1]. But it
was too late for a system of 'personal,' that is of racial laws.
Even in France law was becoming territorial, and a king of the
English who was but duke of the Normans was interested in
obliterating a distinction which stood in his way if he was to
be king of England. The rules which mark the distinction
between the two races rapidly disappear or are diverted from
their original purpose. Murder fines will swell the royal
treasure, and early in Henry I.'s reign it is already law that
every slain man is a Frenchman unless his Englishry can be
[p. 70] proved[2]. Outside the towns, Englishmen seem to have taken
to trial by battle very kindly, and already in the first years of
the twelfth century William's ordinance about procedure had
lost its force[3]. No doubt William and his sons distrusted

---

[1] Orderic (ed. le Prevost), ii. 264. Dr Stubbs, Const. Hist. i. 401, says of
Roger's punishment, 'The same penalty must have followed if he had been tried
by English law.' But under the old English law conspiracy against the king
was a capital crime; and Orderic (p. 262) makes Waltheof remark that this is
so. Roger, so it seems, is treated as a Norman who has rebelled and levied war
against the duke. Many examples of earlier and of later date show us that the
duke rarely puts a vassal to death for rebellion. We must remember that
William is merely duke or count of the Normans, while he is the crowned and
anointed king of the English. It may be that under the Conqueror's own
ordinance Waltheof should have been, not decapitated, but mutilated; but
'Interdico ne quis occidatur' does not bind the man who says it.

[2] Leg. Henr. 92 § 6.

[3] In Domesday Book Englishmen are offering proof by battle; Bigelow,
Placita Anglo-Normannica, 43, 60. The Leges Henrici no longer make any
distinction between the two races in this matter, though they still allow
Frenchmen and aliens to swear with less accuracy than would be required
of an Englishman: Leg. Hen. 64, § 3.

the English; even Henry would suffer no Englishman to be
abbot or bishop[1]. No doubt too the English were harshly and
at times brutally treated; but harshness and brutality are one
thing, an attempt to rule them by Norman law would have been
another.

Mainte-
nance of
English
land law.
Indeed the capital instance of harsh treatment consists in
an application of the theory that they have not been conquered
by foreign enemies, but, having rebelled against one who was
de iure king of the English, are to be lawfully punished for
their unlawful revolt. Those who fought by Harold's side
forfeited their lands, and so of course did those who resisted
William after he was crowned. These forfeitures, so far from
clearing the way for pure Norman land law, had the effect of
bringing even the Norman barons under English land law.
Here a combination might be made of all that was favourable
to the duke in the Norman, with all that was favourable to the
king in the English system. William's tenants in chief were to
owe him definite quantities of military service; the somewhat
vaguely territorialized scheme which had produced Harold's
army was to be superseded by a set of determinate contracts,
more determinate perhaps than any that had as yet been concluded in Normandy. On the other hand, the king was going
rigorously to exact the old English land tax, the danegeld.
With geld in view he achieved the most magnificent of all his
feats, the compilation of Domesday Book. It is very possible
that he purposed to reform the capricious assessment which had
come down to him from his ancestors. In the meantime, however, each Norman baron was to stand in the geld system just
where some one Englishman or some definite group of Englishmen had stood. For the purpose of taxation the Frenchman
succeeded to the duties of his English *antecessores*. Moreover, [p. 71]
what the Frenchman succeeded to was in many cases a superiority over free tenants of the soil. The rights of these tenants
might be left to the uncovenanted mercies of their new lord;
but the superiority often included rights of a jurisdictional kind,
rights of *sake* and *soke*, and in this matter the king had an
interest. The French lord was not to get other fines and forfeitures than those which his *antecessor* had received. For a long
time after the Conquest a serious attempt was made to maintain
the old law of *sake* and *soke* despite its archaisms.

[1] Eadmer, Hist. Nov. 224.

All this made English testimony and English tradition of The English in court. importance; the relative rights of the various Norman magnates were known only to Englishmen. Englishmen were mixed up with Frenchmen at the moots and often spoke the decisive word. The aged Æthelric, bishop of Chichester, 'a man very learned in the laws of the land,' was brought by the Conqueror's command to Penenden Heath that he might hear Lanfranc wax eloquent over *sake* and *soke* and *flymena-fyrmð*[1]. Eadric the steersman of the Confessor's ship, and Kineward who had been sheriff of Worcestershire, Siward of Shropshire, and Thurkill of Warwickshire were ready to attest the *sake* and *soke* which the church of Worcester had over Hamton and Bengeworth; but the abbot of Evesham dared not face them[2]. Godric, Godwin and Colswein were among the 'approved knights French and English' who heard the abbot of Ely's suit at Kentford, and that suit, in which many Normans were concerned, was decided under the king's command by a verdict of English jurors who knew how the disputed lands lay in the time of King Edward[3]. The abbot of Abingdon was protected in his possessions by the learning and eloquence of lawyerly English monks, whose arguments were not to be withstood[4].

On the other hand, it is not to be denied that the few Norman ideas and institutions. legal ideas and institutions which we can confidently describe [p. 72] as imported from Normandy, were of decisive importance. This is pre-eminently true of the transplanted Frankish inquest. It has in it the germ of all that becomes most distinctively English in the English law of the later middle ages, the germ of trial by jury and of a hard and fast formulary system of actions which will be tough enough to resist the attacks of Romanism. However, the fate of the inquest was still in the balance a century after the Conquest, and, but for the comprehensive ordinances of Henry II., it might have perished in England as it perished in its original home. Whether any definitely new idea is introduced into the English land law is a more disputable question, that cannot be here discussed, but

---

[1] Selden's Eadmer, 197; Plac. Anglo-Norm. 7.

[2] Heming's Cartulary, i. 82; Plac. Anglo-Norm. 18.

[3] Hamilton, Inquisitio Cantabr. pp. xvii, xviii; Plac. Anglo-Norm. 22.

[4] Hist. Abingd. ii. 2; Plac. Anglo-Norm. 30: 'sed et alii plures de Anglis causidici per id tempus in abbatia ista habebantur.' This does not imply the existence of men who are lawyers by profession.

undoubtedly the conquest, the forfeiture, the redistribution of
the land gave to the idea of dependent and derivative tenure a
dominance that it could not obtain elsewhere, and about that
idea in its Norman or French shape there clung traditions of
the old Frankish world, which in the subjugated country under
its foreign kings might bear fruit in a land law of unexampled
simplicity.   As to the institutes of private law we know much
too little to justify dogmatic ascriptions of this to an English
and that to a French origin; and when the French origin may
be granted, we are far from being able to say that here is
something which the Normans brought with them in the year
1066.   French influences had been at work in the court of
Edward the Confessor; Frankish influences had been at work
in the courts of much earlier kings; after the Conquest England
lay open for two centuries and more to the latest Parisian
fashions.   For example, the style of the English chancery—and
this in England becomes the model for all legal documents—
goes back by one path and another through the Frankish
chancery to Rome.   But the paths are very various.   Some of the
Conqueror's charters are very like those which Edward and Cnut
had issued, and very unlike those of Henry II[1].   We may say,
if we please, that the seal, of which our law made much in the
later middle ages, of which it makes much at the present day,
is French.   But the Confessor had a seal, and in all probability
but very few of the men who fought by the side of the Norman
duke had seals.   The chief result of the Norman Conquest in
the history of law is to be found not so much in the subjection [p. 73]
of race to race as in the establishment of an exceedingly strong
kingship which proves its strength by outliving three disputed
successions and crushing a rebellious baronage[2].

us.   During the whole Norman period there was little legislation.
We have spoken of the Conqueror's laws.   It seems probable
that Rufus set the example of granting charters of liberties to

[1] Stevenson, E. H. R. xi. 731: an important contribution to English
diplomatics.

[2] Dr Brunner, Zeitschrift d. Savigny-Stiftung, Germ. Abt. xvii. 125, in
reviewing the first edition of this book, says that in his opinion we have underestimated the influence of Norman law and somewhat overrated the originality
of Henry II.'s legislation.   It may be so.   The question is very difficult and we
fully admit that in any case our private law and law of procedure have many
French traits.   The English element is at its strongest in political structure,
e.g. in the non-feudal county court.

the people at large. In 1093, sick and in terror of death, he set his seal to some document that has not come down to us. Captives were to be released, debts forgiven, good and holy laws maintained[1]. Whatever promises he made, he broke. His claim upon the historians of English law is of another kind: for he surely built her an house to dwell in. Englishmen were proud of his work at Westminster. Search the wide world round, they said, there is no such hall for feast and plea.

> Aulam maiorem construxit Londoniarum,
> Orbis terrarum non optinet utiliorem
> Iudicibus legis, ac ad convivia regis,
> Regum regnorum flos est domus illa domorum[2].

The verses are rude but have the right ring in the ears of English lawyers.

Henry at his coronation, compelled to purchase adherents, granted a charter full of valuable and fairly definite concessions[3]. He was going back to his father's ways. The abuses introduced by his brother were to be abolished, abuses in the matter of reliefs, wardships, marriages, murder fines and so forth. Debts and past offences were to be forgiven. The demesne lands of the military tenants were to be free from the danegeld. Above all the *laga Eadwardi* as amended by William I. was to be restored. Though the king required that concessions similar to those which he made in favour of his barons should be made by them in favour of their tenants, we can hardly treat this charter as an act of legislation. It is rather a promise that the law disregarded by Rufus shall henceforth be observed. This promise in after times became a valuable precedent, but it could not be enforced against the king, and Henry did not observe it. The other great record of his reign, the Pipe Roll of his thirty-first year, shows that rightfully or wrongfully he was able to extend the rights of the crown beyond the limits that had been assigned to them in 1100, and the steady action of the exchequer under the direction of his able minister, Bishop Roger of Salisbury,

[margin note: Henry I.]

---

[1] Eadmer, Hist. Nov. pp. 31-2.

[2] These lines were probably written in John's day. They occur in a legal compilation discovered by Dr Liebermann: Leges Anglorum, Halle, 1894, p. 67.

[3] Charters of Liberties (Statutes of the Realm, vol. i.), p. 1; Select Charters. Liebermann, Trans. R. Hist. Soc. viii. 21, gives a critical text.

evolved a law for the tenants in chief which was perhaps the severest in Europe[1]. This was done in silence by the accumulation of precedent upon precedent. For the rest, we know that Henry, early in his reign, issued a writ declaring that the county [p. 74] and hundred courts should be held as they were held in the time of King Edward, straitly enjoining all men to attend them in the ancient fashion whenever royal pleas were to be heard, and in some measure defining the relation of these old tribunals to the feudal courts[2]. We are told that he legislated about theft, restoring capital punishment, that he issued severe laws against the utterers of bad money, that he prohibited the rapacious exactions of his courtiers, who had made the advent of his peripatetic household a terror to every neighbourhood, that he legislated about measures taking his own arm as the standard ell; but we depend on the chroniclers for our knowledge of these acts, and as yet they are not careful to preserve the words of the lawgiver[3]. We have, however, a writ in which he speaks of the 'new statutes' which he had made against thieves and false moneyers[4].

Stephen. Stephen on his accession conceded to his subjects in vague phrase 'all the liberties and good laws which King Henry had given and granted to them, and all the good laws and good customs which they had enjoyed in the time of King Edward[5]. Later on he had to promise once more that he would observe 'the good laws and just and ancient customs, as to murder fines,

---

[1] The Pipe Roll of 31 Henry I. was edited by Hunter for the Record Commissioners. We shall hereafter have more than one occasion to remark on the relation that it bears to the charter of 1100.

[2] The writ is given in the Select Charters; see Liebermann, Quadripartitus, p. 165.

[3] Legislation in 1108 about theft and coining: Florence, ii. 57; comp. A.-S. Chron. an. 1124, and Foedera, i. 12. Legislation against abuses of royal purveyance and against bad money: Eadmer, Hist. Nov. 192-3; Will. Malmesb. Gesta Regum, ii. 476. Legislation about wreck: Chron. de Bello, 65; Plac. Anglo-Norm. 144. Legislation about measures, Will. Malmesb. Gesta Regum, ii. 487; in this last passage it is said that towards the end of his reign Henry inclined rather to pecuniary mulcts than to corporal punishment. The enactment of other rules has been ascribed to Henry merely because they appear in the text-book known as *Leges Henrici*, of which hereafter.

[4] Historians of Church of York, iii. 22: 'et nova statuta mea de iudiciis sive de placitis latronum et falsorum monetariorum exequatur et finiat [archiepiscopus] per suam propriam iustitiam in curia sua.'

[5] Charters of Liberties (Statutes of the Realm, i.), p. 4; Select Charters; Stubbs, Const. Hist. i. 346.

pleas and other matters,' and that he would extirpate the
unjust exactions introduced by the sheriffs and others.   More
specific promises made to the church, besides the large and
dangerous promise that she should be 'free[1].'   In the ecclesiastical sphere there had been a good deal of legislation.   With
the assent of the king, stringent canons had been enacted and
enforced ; in particular, the rule of celibacy had been imposed
upon a reluctant clergy.   It was in the ecclesiastical council,
[p. 75] rather than the king's court, that the spirit of reforming legislation was once more active[2].

The best proof, however, of the perdurance of the old *The law-*
English law is given by what we may generically call the law- *books or*
'Leges.'
books of the Norman period.   The Conqueror had amended and
confirmed the *laga Eadwardi;* Henry I. had confirmed the
laga Eadwardi and his father's amendments of it.   Where
then could the law of Edward, that is to say, the law of
Edward's time, be found?   No doubt a good deal of it was
to be found in the code of Cnut and in the yet earlier dooms.
But the language in which they were written was unintelligible to Frenchmen, and was fast becoming unintelligible
even to Englishmen, for just at this time the English language
was undergoing a rapid change.   What is more, it was plain
that, despite the large words of the Norman kings, the old
dooms in their integrity could not fit the facts of the new age.
Thus what was wanted was no mere translation of ancient
texts, but a modernized statement of the old law, a practicable
laga Eadwardi.   Divers men in divers parts of the country
tried to meet this want.   The result of their efforts is a curious
and intricate group of writings, which even at the end of the
nineteenth century will hardly have been unravelled.   We
shall here speak very briefly of it, adopting what we believe to
be the soundest results of recent criticism[3].

In the first place, we may put on one side certain docu- *Genuine*
laws of
ments which profess to give us, not the old law, but the results *William L*
of William's legislation, the documents from which we have

---

[1] Charters of Liberties, p. 5; Select Charters; Stubbs, Const. Hist. i. 347.
As to the date of these charters, see Round, Geoffrey de Mandeville, 438.

[2] As to the ecclesiastical legislation, see Stubbs, Const. Hist. i. 404.

[3] Dr Liebermann has gradually been restoring the legal literature of this
period.   Lagam Eadwardi nobis reddit.   His forthcoming edition of the Anglo-
Saxon and Anglo-Norman laws will probably override some sentences in the
following brief summary.

already extracted our account of his edicts. We probably have in its original form, that of a writ sent into the various counties, the ordinance which severed the ecclesiastical from the temporal courts[1]. We have in English as well as in Latin the ordinance about criminal accusations brought by men of the one race against men of the other[2]. Lastly, we have a set of ten brief paragraphs dealing with the oath of fealty, the murder fine, the abolition of capital punishment and the other [p. 76] matters which have already come before us. These ten laws may not have been collected until some time after the Conqueror's death, and it is more than probable that we have not the words that he used; but the collection seems to have been made early in the twelfth, if not before the end of the eleventh century, and the result is trustworthy. At a much later date some one tampered with this set of laws, interpolated new matter into it and threw it into the form of a solemn charter[3].

The Quad-ripartitus. But we must pass to the attempts which were made to state the *laga Eadwardi.* In the reign of Henry I. some one set himself to translate the old dooms into Latin. To all seeming he was not an Englishman by race and English was not his natural tongue. He may have been a secular clerk living at Winchester and employed in the king's court or exchequer. He was closely connected by some tie or another with Archbishop Gerard of York. We have more than one edition of his work; these can be distinguished from each other by the author's increasing mastery of the English language, though to the end he could perpetrate bad mistakes. As the work went on, he conceived the project of adding to his Latin version of the ancient dooms three other books and calling the whole *Liber Quadripartitus.* The first book was to contain the old English

---

[1] This is Leges Willelmi IV. of Thorpe and Schmid.

[2] This is Leges Willelmi II. of Thorpe and Schmid.

[3] The set of ten laws is that printed by Dr Stubbs in his edition of Hoveden, vol. ii. p. ci, and again in the Select Charters. It may be conveniently referred to as *Hic intimatur.* It also appears with some variants in the text of Hoveden's Chronicle, vol. ii. p. 216, for Hoveden inserts it when, under the year 1180, he speaks of Glanvill's appointment to the justiciarship. Liebermann, Quadripartitus, p. 145, mentions the MSS. which give it and says that it was compiled after 1087 and before 1135. A French version of it from cent. xii. he gives in Zeitschrift für romanische Philologie, xix. 82. The expanded form of it is Leges Willelmi III. of Thorpe and Schmid. Dr Liebermann takes this to be the work of a Londoner of John's reign, who deliberately tampers with his documents: Ueber die Leges Anglorum, p. 32 ff.

laws done into Latin; the second was to contain some important state papers of his own day; the third was to be about legal procedure ; the fourth about theft. If the two last books were ever written, they have not come down to us. The first and second books we have. The second opens with the coronation charter of Henry I. Then apparently it purposes to give us the documents which relate to the quarrel about the investitures; but it gradually degenerates into a defence of Archbishop Gerard. The author seems to have been at his [p. 77] work between the years 1113 and 1118; but, as already said, he returned to it more than once.

Whatever grander projects he may at times have entertained, what he has left as a monument of English law is in the main a laborious but not very successful translation of the old dooms. He translated after his fashion most of the dooms that have come down to us, except the very ancient Kentish laws, and he translated a few which have not come down to us save through his hands. He translated for the more part without note or comment, translated honestly if unintelligently. But he aspired to be more than a mere translator. He put Cnut's code in the forefront ; this was the latest and most authoritative statement of English law ; the earlier dooms— they go back even to Alfred and to Ine—come afterwards as being of less practical value. He does not regard himself as a mere antiquarian[1].

Closely connected with the *Quadripartitus* is a far more *Leges* important book, the so-called *Leges Henrici*. It seems to have *Henrici.* been compiled shortly before the year 1118. After a brief preface, it gives us Henry's coronation charter (this accounts for the name which has unfortunately been given in modern days to the whole book), and then the author makes a gallant, if forlorn, attempt to state the law of England. At first sight the outcome seems to be a mere jumble of fragments ; rules brought from the most divers quarters are thrown into a confused heap. But the more closely we examine the book, the more thoroughly convinced we shall be that its author has undertaken a serious task in a serious spirit ; he means to state the existing law of the land, to state it in what he thinks to be a rational, and even a philosophical form. But the task

---

[1] We have here tried to sum up very briefly the results attained by Lieber-mann, Quadripartitus, Halle, 1892.

is beyond his powers. For one thing, his Latin is of the worst; he learnt it in a bad school and it will hardly suffer him to express his meaning; probably his mother tongue was French. Then the books from which he copies overweight him; he cannot adhere to any one plan or pursue any one line of thought. Nevertheless he is in earnest, and when he can leave his books alone and succeed in explaining himself, he tells us many things that are of great value. He had a good many books at his command. He took much from the code of Cnut and from some of the older dooms, but unless (this is [p. 78] not impossible) he himself was the author or projector of the *Quadripartitus,* he seems to have been dependent on the first book of that work for his text of these old English laws. His object being to state the *laga Eadwardi* as amended by the Conqueror and Henry I., he naturally made great use of this English matter; but he dipped at times into other springs. He had found a source of 'general jurisprudence' in Isidore's *Origines.* Ecclesiastical causes were no longer subject to native English law; the Conqueror had handed them over to the *canones,* and for the *canones* of the catholic church our author had to look to foreign books, in particular to that compiled by Burchard of Worms. He took a few passages from the venerable *Lex Salica,* from the *Lex Ribuaria,* from the Frankish capitularies; we may safely say that, had these ancient authorities been regarded by the Normans in England as practicable written law he would have taken more. He took one little sentence out of an epitome of the West Goth's version of the Theodosian Code[1]. But the most interesting parts of his work are those which we can trace to no remoter fount. If they paint English law as a wonderful confusion, they may yet be painting it correctly, and before we use hard words of him who wrote them, we should remember that he was engaged on an utterly new task, new in England,

---

[1] Leg. Henr. 33 § 4. He cites Liber Theodosianae Legis, but what he really has under that name seems to be the Epitome Aegidii; see Hänel, Lex Romana Visigothorum, p. 228. This citation, which may be the outcome of literary vanity, has been offered as proof of the prevalence of Roman law in England; but the fact that our author had a Roman book and took but one sentence from it, is really a strong testimony to the thoroughly un-Roman character of the English law of his day. It is quite possible that he had but a single volume of foreign temporal law. The *Salica* and *Ribuaria* occur in MS. along with epitomes of Alaric's Breviary.

new in Europe: he was writing a legal text-book, a text-book of law that was neither Roman nor Canon law. To have thought that a law-book ought to be written was no small exploit in the year 1118[1].

[p. 79] The writer of the *Leges Henrici* is in some sort the cham- The *Con-siliatio* and pion of West Saxon, or rather of Wessex law. Wessex is in his *Instituta Cnuti.* opinion the head of the realm, and in doubtful cases Wessex law should prevail[2]. Other attempts to state the old law were made elsewhere. In the early years of the twelfth century two Latin translations of Cnut's dooms, besides that contained in the *Quadripartitus,* were made, and in each case by one who tried to be more than a translator; he borrowed from other Anglo-Saxon documents, some of which have not come down to us, and endeavoured to make his work a practicable law-book. One of the most remarkable features of all these books is that their authors seem to be, at least by adoption and education, men of the dominant, not men of the subject race; if not Frenchmen by birth, they are Frenchmen by speech[3]. At a later date, some forest laws were concocted for Cnut, but to describe these we must use a harsh term; to all seeming they are the work of a forger, who was inventing a justification for the oppressive claims of those mighty hunters, the Norman kings[4].

Then we have another document which professes to give us *Les Leis Williame.* the old laws, the laws which King Edward held and which

---

[1] The preface can not have been written after 1118, since it treats Queen Matilda as living. The arguments of those who would give a later date to the body of the book seem to be sufficiently answered by Liebermann, Forschungen zur deutschen Geschichte (1876), vol. xvi. p. 582. His conclusion is accepted by Stubbs, Const. Hist. i. 533 (ed. 1883). Two mistakes should be avoided. (1) Our author is not forging laws for Henry I.; the title *Leges Henrici* refers only to the coronation charter with which he begins his book. (2) He is not pretending to set forth the *laga Eadwardi* as it stood in Edward's day; he states it in what he thinks to be its modern and practicable shape. The inference that he was a man of English race has been drawn from a passage, 92 § 10, in which he speaks of a French thief resisting capture 'more suo'; but he throws such phrases about in a hap-hazard way, and his knowledge of the old English language seems to have been small.

[2] Leg. Henr. 70 § 1; 87 § 5.

[3] These two tracts are Consiliatio Cnuti, published by Liebermann at Halle in 1893, and Instituta Cnuti aliorumque Regum Anglorum, communicated by him to the Royal Historical Society in the same year; Transactions, vii. 77.

[4] Constitutiones de Foresta, Schmid, p. 318. Liebermann, Ueber Pseudo-Cnuts Constitutiones de Foresta, Halle, 1894.

King William granted to the people of England. We have it both in French and in Latin, and to distinguish it from its fellows it has been called the bilingual code. We shall call it the *Leis Williame.* Its history is obscure and has been made the more obscure by contact with the forgeries of the false Ingulf. The Latin text is a translation of the French text, though not an exact translation of any version of the French text that has come down to modern times; but the French text may have been made from a Latin or from an English original. That we have here no authoritative code but mere private work will scarcely be disputed. It falls somewhat easily into three parts. The first seems to consist of certain rules of the old English law as they were understood under the Norman kings together with some of the Norman novelties. [p. 80] It is an intelligent and to all seeming a trustworthy statement. It harmonizes well with the ancient dooms, but is not made up of extracts from them. Its author may have been specially familiar with the Danelaw. The last part of the document is a pretty close translation of certain parts of the code of Cnut. Then between these two parts there come a few articles which betray the influence of Roman law. If the whole document comes from one man, we can not well suppose him to have done his work after the early years of the twelfth century; his statement of the old law seems too good to be of later date. We must further suppose that, having come to the end of the English rules that were known to him as living law, he taxed his memory for other rules and succeeded in remembering some half-dozen large maxims which had caught his eye in some Roman book, and that finally, being weary of trying to remember and to define, he took up the code of Cnut and translated part of it. The first section of his work is far from valueless; it is one more proof that attempts were being made to state the *laga Eadwardi* in a rational form. As to the middle section, it shows us how men were helplessly looking about for some general principles of jurisprudence which would deliver them from their practical and intellectual difficulties[1].

---

[1] The document in question is the Leges Willelmi I. of Thorpe and Schmid. For the history of the MSS. which gave the French version see the article in Quarterly Review, No. 67, p. 248, in which Palgrave exposed the Ingulfine forgery, also Liebermann's Ostenglische Geschichtsquellen. We are deeply indebted to Dr Liebermann for a valuable letter dealing with these *Leis.*

[p. 81]   Lastly, we have a book written in Latin which expressly *Leges Edwardi Confessoris.* purports to give us the law of Edward as it was stated to the Conqueror in the fourth year of his reign by juries representing the various parts of England[1]. However, the purest form in which we have it speaks of what was done in the reign of William Rufus[2], and probably was compiled in the last years of Henry I.[3]. It is private work of a bad and untrustworthy kind. It has about it something of the political pamphlet and is adorned with pious legends. The author, perhaps a secular clerk of French parentage, writes in the interest of the churches, and, it is to be feared, tells lies for them[4]. He professes to hate the Danes of the past and the Danelaw. According to him, William, being himself of Scandinavian

That the French text is the origin of the Latin is plain from several passages, in particular from c. 45 when compared with Cnut, II. 24 (the Latinist thinks that *voest* means 'let him see,' whereas it means 'let him vouch'). On this point see Liebermann, Quadripartitus, p. 54. The Latin version is sometimes exceedingly stupid; see *e.g.* the 'idoneos cultores' of c. 31. The text has 52 chapters. From c. 39 onwards we have a translation of Cnut. This, the third section of the work, is preceded by six articles, which, when taken together, seem to betray Roman influence:—c. 33, sentence of death on a pregnant woman is to be respited (Dig. 48, 19, 3); c. 35, a father may kill his daughter if he finds her committing adultery in his house or his son-in-law's house (Dig. 48, 5, 22); c. 36, a poisoner is to be killed or exiled for ever (Dig. 48, 8, 3 § 5); c. 37, a reminiscence of the *lex Rhodia de iactu* (Dig. 14, 2); c. 38, the eviction of one co-parcener does not prejudice the rights of the others, being *res inter alios acta* (Cod. 7, 56, 2). To these we may add c. 34, the division of an inheritance among all the children; this, unless *enfans* means *sons*, can hardly be English or Norman law, and is surrounded by romanesque sentences. Perhaps we ought to place the beginning of the middle section as far back as the very important c. 29; for c. 29–32 seem destined to define the position of the English peasants as being similar to that of the Roman *coloni*. Thus we are brought to the end of c. 28, where the only now extant MS. of the French version ends. As to the Danish traits of the earlier articles, see Steenstrup, Danelag, pp. 59, 306–319. The unauthoritative character of the document, if it be taken as a whole, is sufficiently proved by its style; see in particular c. 37, 38; but we shall not readily believe that even the first section of it comes from the Conqueror. As to the character of the French text, this must be left to philologists, but the result of recent discussions seems to be that, though the language has been much modernized by transcribers, it has some very ancient traits.

[1] This is the Leges Edwardi Confessoris of Thorpe and Schmid. See Liebermann, Leges Edwardi, Halle, 1896.

[2] Leges Edwardi Confessoris, c. 11.

[3] Liebermann, *op. cit.* p. 16.

[4] The exemption from Danegeld of ecclesiastical demesnes, as stated in c. 11, is, to say the least, exceedingly doubtful. See Round in Domesday Studies, i. 95–6.

race, was on the point of imposing the Danelaw upon the whole country, but at length was induced by the suppliant jurors to confirm the law of Edward. This, it is explained, was really the law of Edgar, but, from Edgar's death until the accession of the Confessor, law had slumbered in England— thus does this romancer strive to blacken the memory of Cnut, the great lawgiver. Little, if any, use is made of the Anglo-Saxon dooms; loose, oral tradition is the author's best warrant. Unfortunately, however, the patriotic and ecclesiastical leanings of his book made it the most popular of all the old lawbooks[1]. In the thirteenth century it was venerable; even Bracton quoted from it[2]. A second and more polished edition of it was soon made by its author's or another's hand; also there is a French version. And then men added to it other pious legends about the good old days when sheriffs were elective and the like. It has gone on doing its bad work down to our own time. It should only be used with extreme caution, for its statements, when not supported by other evidence, will hardly tell us more than that some man of the twelfth century, [p. 82] probably some man of Henry I.'s day, would have liked those statements to be true[3].

Character of the law disclosed by the Leges.

The picture that these law-books set before us is that of an ancient system which has received a rude shock from without

---

[1] Hoveden, ii. 218, takes it up into his chronicle.

[2] Bracton, f. 134 b. Liebermann, *op. cit.* 122.

[3] Dr Liebermann spoke of this work some time ago in his Einleitung in den Dialogus de Scaccario, pp. 72–7. He has lately written an exhaustive essay about it. It seems quite incredible that Glanvill had anything to do with the making of this book. The difference between the style of these Leges and the style of the treatise ascribed to Glanvill is the difference between darkness and light. The author of the Leges assumes the character of a patriotic Englishman as against the detested Danes, but Harold is for him an usurper, and he himself, if not French by race, seems to have regarded French as his natural tongue (c. 35 § 1) and may have known but little English. The account that he gives of 'the peace of God' (c. 2) seems to take us back rather to French than to English traditions. Liebermann thinks that he must have had access to the library of some cathedral, perhaps that of Coventry, and probably lived in or near Warwickshire. A French translation of the work exists in MS. but has not yet been printed. For specimens, see Liebermann, Zeitschrift für romanische Philologie, xix. 83. The story that the Conqueror caused a solemn statement of the *laga Eadwardi* to be made by juries is not very probable. Had such a statement been made, it would, like Domesday Book, have been officially preserved, and there would have been no room for such works as the Leges Henrici and the Leis Williame. Since the first edition of our book was published Dr Liebermann (Leges Edwardi, p. 45) has decisively rejected the tale.

while within it was rapidly decaying. The men who would state the existing law are compelled to take the old English dooms as the basis for their work, even though they can hardly understand the old English language. The old dooms are written law; they have not been abrogated; they have been confirmed; other written law there is none or next to none; Normandy has none; northern France has none, or none that is not effete. At a pinch a man may find something useful in the new science of the canonists, in the aged *Lex Salica*, in vague rumours of Roman law which come from afar. Any rule that looks authoritative and reasonable is welcome; we may say that it is law because it ought to be law. But in the main we must make the best of the dooms of Cnut and the older dooms. And the difficulty of making much that is good of them is not caused merely by the collision of two races, or by any preference of the Normans for laws that are not English. No doubt in the local courts confusion had been confounded by the influx of conquering Frenchmen; but there were causes enough of confusion which would have done their work even had there been no ethnical conflict to aid them. Everywhere in western Europe new principles of social and political order were emerging; new classes were being formed; the old laws, the only written laws, were becoming obsolete; the state was taking a new shape. If from the northern France or from [p. 83] the Germany of the first years of the twelfth century we could have a law-book, it would not be very simple or elegant or intelligible. As it is, our neighbours have little to show between the last of the capitularies and those feudal law-books which stand on a level with our own Glanvill. While the complex process which we call feudalism is transmuting the world, no one issues laws or writes about law. If in England it is otherwise, this seems to be chiefly due to two causes:—In England the age of the capitularies had not ended; but lately Cnut had legislated on a scale which for the eleventh century must be called magnificent. And then that very collision between two races which makes the law-books disorderly and obscure has made them necessary. The *laga Eadwardi* is confirmed. Even clerks of Norman race wish to know what the *laga Eadwardi* is.

These law-books have, we may say, one main theme. It is a very old theme. An offence, probably some violent offence, Practical problems in the Leges.

has been committed. Who then is to get money, and how much money, out of the offender? It is the old theme of *wer* and *wíte* and *bót*. But the criminal tariff has become exceedingly complex, and is breaking down under its own weight. In the first place the old tribal differences, which have become local differences, can not yet be disregarded. A text writer must still start with this, that England is divided between three laws, Wessex law, Mercian law, Danelaw. We must not make light of the few variances between these three laws which are expressly noticed by the books. If in the eleventh century a middle finger is more valuable than a first finger among the men of the Danelaw and less valuable among the men of Wessex, here is a difference which would have its equivalent in modern England if the law of Lancashire differed from the law of Yorkshire about the negotiable qualities of a bill of exchange, a difference fruitful of knotty problems. The law of Herefordshire, as settled by Earl William FitzOsborn, was that no knight should have to pay more than seven shillings for any offence[1]. Becket asserted even in the king's court that the heaviest amercement known to Kentish law was forty shillings[2]. But the country was becoming covered with small [p. 84] courts; every one who could was acquiring or assuming *sake* and *soke*. The courts rose one above the other; the great old tribal customs were breaking up into multitudinous petty customs. This introduced new complexities. We can see that for the writer of the *Leges Henrici* the grand central problem of the law is the question, Who in the myriad of possible cases has *sake* and *soke*, the right to hold a court for the offender and to pocket the profits of jurisdiction? The claims of the lords, the claims of the church, the claims of the king are adding to the number of the various fines and mulcts that can be exacted, and are often at variance with each other. Let us suppose that a man learned in the law is asked to advise upon a case of homicide. Godwin and Roger met and quarrelled, and Godwin slew Roger. What must be paid; by whom; to whom? Our jurist is not very careful about those psychical elements of the case which might interest us, but on the other hand he requires information about a vast number of particulars which would

---

[1] Will. Malm. Gesta Regum, ii. 314. Malmesbury says that in his own day FitzOsbern's rule still prevailed.

[2] Will. FitzStephen (Materials for Life of Becket, iii.), p. 62.

seem to us trivial. He can not begin to cast up his sum until he has before him some such statement as this:—Godwin was a free ceorl of the Abbot of Ely: Roger, the son of a Norman father, was born in England of an English mother and was a vavassor of Count Alan: the deed was done on the Monday after Septuagesima, in the county of Cambridge, on a road which ran between the land which Gerard a Norman knight held of Count Eustace and the land of the Bishop of Lincoln: this road was not one of the king's highways: Godwin was pursued by the neighbours into the county of Huntingdon and arrested on the land of the Abbot of Ramsey: Roger, when the encounter took place, was on his way to the hundred moot: he has left a widow, a paternal uncle and a maternal aunt. As a matter of fact, the result will probably be that Godwin, unable to satisfy the various claims to which his deed has given rise, will be hanged or mutilated. This, however, is but a slovenly, practical solution of the nice problem, and even if he be hanged, there may be a severe struggle over such poor chattels as he had. The old law consisted very largely of rules about these matters; but it is falling to pieces under the pressure of those new elements which feudalism has brought with it. For a [p. 85] while there must be chaos and 'unlaw'; every lord may assume what jurisdictional powers he pleases and will be able to find in the complicated tangle of rules some plausible excuse for the assumption. The Normans, hallowed and lay, have thrown themselves with all their native ardour into the warfare of litigation and chicane over rights which have old English names; 'nullus clericus nisi causidicus[1].'

Only to one quarter can we look hopefully. Above all local customs rose the custom of the king's court, 'the tremendous empire of kingly majesty[2].' Of the law that this court administered we know little, only we may guess that in a

Custom of the king's court.

---

[1] This famous phrase comes from a rhetorical passage in which William of Malmesbury is describing the days of Rufus; Gesta Regum, ii. 369: 'Nullus dives nisi nummularius, nullus clericus nisi causidicus, nullus presbyter nisi, ut verbo parum Latino utar, firmarius.' He has just called Ranulf Flambard 'invictus causidicus.' But, as noticed above, these *causidici* were not all of French race.

[2] Leg. Henr. 9 § 9: 'Legis enim Angliae trina est partitio; et ad eandem distantiam supersunt regis placita curiae, quae usus et consuetudines suas una semper immobilitate servat ubique.' Ibid. 6 § 2: 'Legis etiam Anglicae trina est partitio...praeter hoc tremendum regiae maiestatis titislamus (?) imperium.'

certain sense it was equity rather than strict law. On the
one hand, the royal tribunal cannot have held itself straitly
bound by the old English law; the men who sat in it were
Frenchmen, few of whom could understand a word of English.
On the other hand, it must often have happened that the
traditional Norman customs would not meet the facts, for
a Norman count and a Norman bishop would be quarrelling
over the titles of their English *antecessores*, and producing
English land-books. Besides, the king did not mean that
England should be another Normandy; he meant to have at
least all the rights that his cousin and predecessor had enjoyed.
The jurisprudence of his court, if we may use so grand a
phrase, was of necessity a flexible, occasional jurisprudence,
dealing with an unprecedented state of affairs, meeting new
facts by new expedients, wavering as wavered the balance of
power between him and his barons, capable of receiving
impressions from without, influenced by the growth of canon
law, influenced perhaps by Lombard learning, modern in the
midst of antique surroundings. In retrospect it would appear
to a statesman of Henry II.'s day as something so unlike the
laga Eadwardi, that it must be pronounced distinctively un-
English and therefore distinctively Norman, and Norman in a [p. 86]
sense it was[1]. It was not a jurisprudence that had been
transplanted from Normandy; but it had been developed by a
court composed of Frenchmen to meet cases in which Frenchmen were concerned; the language in which men spoke it was
French; and in the end, so far as it dealt with merely private
rights, it would closely resemble a French *coutume*.

Royal
justice.

The future was to make the jurisprudence of the king's
court by far the most important element in the law of England,
but we can hardly say that it was this during the reigns of
the Norman kings. In the main that court was a court only
for the great men and the great causes. It is true that these
foreign kings did not allow their justiciary powers to be limited
by any of those hedges which might have grown up in an
unconquered country and confined the scope of royal justice to

---

[1] Dialogus, lib. I. c. xvi.: 'Rex Willelmus...decrevit subiectum sibi populum
iuri scripto legibusque subicere. Propositis igitur legibus Anglicanis secundum
tripartitam earum distinctionem, hoc est Merchenelage, Denelage, West-
saxenelage, quasdam reprobavit, quasdam autem approbans, illas transmarinas
Neustriae leges, quae ad regni pacem efficacisimae videbantur, adiecit.'

certain particular fields. The list of the 'pleas of the crown' was long, disorderly, elastic[1]; the king could send a trusted baron or prelate to preside in the county courts; he could evoke causes into his own court[2]. But evocatory writs must be paid for and they were not to be had as matters of course. The local courts, communal and seignorial, were the ordinary tribunals for ordinary causes; the king's justice was still extraordinary, and even the pleas of the crown were for the more part heard by the sheriffs in the shiremoots[3]. Then, again, the king's court was not in permanent session. Under the two Williams the name *curia Regis* seems to be borne only by those great assemblages that collect round the king thrice a year when he wears his [p. 87] crown. It was in such assemblages that the king's justice was done under his own eye, and no doubt he had his way; still it was not for him to make the judgments of his court[4]. Under Henry I. something that is more like a permanent tribunal, a group of justiciars presided over by a chief justiciar, becomes apparent. Twice a year this group, taking the name of 'the exchequer,' sat round the chequered table, received the royal revenue, audited the sheriffs' accounts and did incidental justice. From time to time some of its members would be sent through the counties to hear the pleas of the crown, and litigants who were great men began to find it worth their while to bring their cases before this powerful tribunal. We can not say that these justiciars were professionally learned in English law; but the king chose for the work trusty barons and able clerks, and some of these clerks, besides having long experience as financiers and administrators, must have had a

---

[1] Leg. Henr. c. 10.

[2] Early instances of the king's *missi* presiding in the local courts are these:— the Bishop of Coutances presides at the famous session on Penenden Heath: Plac. Anglo-Norm. p. 7; he and others preside over the county court of Worcestershire: Ibid. p. 17; he and others preside over a combined moot of the eastern counties: Ibid. p. 24; Lanfranc presides at Bury over a combined moot of nine shires: Memorials of St. Edmund's Abbey, i. 65. The payments 'pro recto' recorded on the Pipe Roll of Henry I. were probably payments made for evocatory writs; see Plac. Anglo-Norm. 140-2.

[3] Apparently as a general rule the sheriffs hear the pleas of the crown, but the profits go to the king and are not, unless some special compact has been made, covered by the ferms of the counties; Leg. Henr. c. 10 § 3.

[4] Even Rufus in his rage respects this rule. Anselm is before the court; the magnates are reluctant to condemn him. 'Take heed to yourselves,' cries the king, 'for by God's face if you will not condemn him as I wish, I will condemn you.' Eadmer, Hist. Nov. 62.

tincture of the new canonical jurisprudence[1]. But, for all this, when Henry died little had yet been done towards centreing the whole work of justice in one small body of learned men. And then a disputed succession to the throne, a quarrel between the king and the officers of his exchequer, could impair, or for a while destroy, all such concentration as there was. In the woful days of Stephen, the future of English law looks very uncertain. If English law survives at all, it may break into a hundred local customs, and if it does so, the ultimate triumph of Roman law is assured[2].

[1] We have a life-like, though perhaps not an impartial, report of the trial of William of S*. Calais, bishop of Durham. There is a keen argument between the defendant, who knows his canon law, and Lanfranc, the great Lombardist, who presides over the court; but the barons are not silent, and Hugh de Beaumont gives judgment. See Symeon of Durham, i. 170. A little later Bishop William takes a leading part in what may perhaps be called the trial of Anselm; Eadmer, Hist. Nov. 60–2.

[2] As to the king's court and exchequer, see Stubbs, Const. Hist. c. xi., and Gneist, Geschichte, § 10.

CHAPTER V.

ROMAN AND CANON LAW.

[p. 88]   IN any case the restoration of order after the anarchy of Contact of English with Roman and canon law. Stephen's reign and the accession to the throne of a prince who would treat England as the buttress of a continental empire must have induced a critical period in the history of English law.   But we must add that in any case the middle of the twelfth century would have been critical.   Even had Harold held his own, had his sons and grandsons succeeded him as peaceful and conservative English kings, their rule must have come into contact with the claims of the cosmo-politan but Roman church, and must have been influenced, if only in the way of repulsion, by the growth of the civil and canon law.   Of all the centuries the twelfth is the most legal. In no other age, since the classical days of Roman law, has so large a part of the sum total of intellectual endeavour been devoted to jurisprudence.

[p. 89]   We have told above how Irnerius taught at Bologna[1].   Very Revival of Roman law. soon a school had formed itself around his successors.   The fame of 'the four doctors,' Bulgarus, Martinus, Jacobus, Hugo, had gone out into all lands; the works of Placentinus were copied at Peterborough.   From every corner of Western Europe students flocked to Italy.   It was as if a new gospel had been revealed.   Before the end of the century complaints were loud that theology was neglected, that the liberal arts were despised, that Seius and Titius had driven Aristotle and Plato from the schools, that men would learn law and nothing but

[1] See above, p. 23.

law[1]. This enthusiasm for the new learning was not soon spent; it was not spent until in the middle of the thirteenth century Accursius had summed up its results in the *Glossa Ordinaria* and Azo of Bologna had taught Bracton what a law-book should be.

Cosmopolitan claims of Roman law.
The keenest minds of the age had set to work on the classical Roman texts and they were inspired by a genuine love of knowledge. Still they were far from regarding their study as mere historical research; indeed for a critical examination of ancient history they were but ill prepared. The Roman law was for them living law. Its claim to live and rule was intimately connected with the continuity of the empire. A vast part, if not the whole, of the civilized world [p. 90] owed obedience to the Caesar for the time being. The German Henries and Fredericks were the successors of Augustus and the Antonines; the laws of their ancestors had not been repealed and therefore were in force. Even in those kingdoms in which it was impossible to press the claims of a German prince, the king might theoretically be regarded as holding the place of an emperor. Our own Henry I. was he not Gloriosus Caesar Henricus[2]? But, such theories apart, the Roman law demanded reverence, if not obedience, as the due of its own intrinsic merits. It was divinely reasonable.

Growth of canon law.
Another body of jurisprudence was coming into being. From humble beginnings the canon law had grown into a mighty system. Already it asserted its right to stand beside or above the civil law. The civil law might be the law of earth, *ius soli;* here was the law of heaven, *ius poli.* The time had now come when the Hildebrandine papacy could insist that, subject to small variations, the universal church had a common law. Many men had been endeavouring to state that law, but the fame of earlier labourers was eclipsed by that of [p. 91] Gratian[3]. A monk of Bologna, that city which was the centre of the new secular jurisprudence, he published between the years 1139 and 1142 (the work used to be ascribed to a somewhat later date) a book which he called *Concordia discordantium canonum,* but which was soon to become for all mankind simply

---

[1] See the passages collected by Holland, E. H. R. vi. 147-8.

[2] Quadripartitus, p. 149; Leg. Henr. preface.

[3] For the matter of this paragraph, see Schulte, Geschichte der Quellen des Canonischen Rechts.

the *Decretum Gratiani*, or yet more simply the *Decretum*[1]. It is a great law-book. The spirit which animated its author was not that of a theologian, not that of an ecclesiastical ruler, but that of a lawyer. One large section of his work is taken up with the discussion of hypothetical cases (*causae*); he states the various questions of law (*quaestiones*) that are involved in these cases; he endeavours to answer the questions by sorting and weighing the various 'authorities' (to use our English word) which bear upon them. These authorities consist of canons new and old, decretals new and old, including of course the Isidorian forgeries, principles of Roman law, passages from the fathers and the Bible. The Decretum soon became an authoritative text-book and the canonist seldom went behind it. All the same, it never became 'enacted law.' The canonist had for it rather that reverence which English lawyers have paid to Coke upon Littleton than that utter submission which is due to every clause of a statute. A sure base had now been found for the new science. Gratian became the master of a school, a school of lawyers well grounded in Roman law, many of them doctors *utriusque iuris*, who brought to bear upon the Decretum and the subsequent decretals the same methods that they employed upon Code and Digest. Legists and decretists alike looked to Italy for their teachers; but the papal system was even more cosmopolitan than the imperial; the sway of the Roman church was wider than that of the Roman empire. Gratian, Rufinus, Johannes Faventinus, Pillius, Hostiensis—these names we read in English books, to say nothing of those great canonists who attain to the papal throne, of Alexander III. and Innocent III., Gregory IX. and Innocent IV.

Gratian had collected decretals down to the year 1139. *The* But the time had now come when the popes were beginning to *Decretals.* pour out decretals for the whole of western Christendom in [p. 93] great abundance. Under Alexander III. and Innocent III. the flow was rapid indeed. From time to time compilations of these were made (*compilationes antiquae*) and Englishmen in Italy took part in this work[2]; but they were all set aside by a grand collection published by Gregory IX. in 1234. This was

---

[1] As to the date, see Schulte, i. 48.

[2] Schulte, i. 84, 85, 88, 187-9. Among the compilations which have been preserved are those of Alan and Gilbert, who seem to have been Englishmen, and that of Johannes Walensis, *i.e.* John the Welshman.

an authoritative statute book; all the decretals of a general import that had not been received into it were thereby repealed, and every sentence that it contained was law. It comprised five books. In 1298 Boniface VIII. added to these the 'Sext,' the Liber Sextus, a collection of those decretals issued since the Gregorian codification, which were to be in force for the future. Another collection of decretals known as the Clementines (they had proceeded from Clement V.) was added in 1317, and in 1500 the Corpus Iuris Canonici was completed by yet another collection—this had no statutory authority—known as the Extravagants; but by this time canon law had seen its best days. We must yet say a few more words of its vigorous maturity[1].

The canonical system.

It was a wonderful system. The whole of western Europe was subject to the jurisdiction of one tribunal of last resort, the Roman curia. Appeals to it were encouraged by all manner of means, appeals at almost every stage of almost every proceeding[2]. But the pope was far more than the president of a court of appeal. Very frequently the courts Christian which did justice in England were courts which were acting under his supervision and carrying out his written instructions. A very large part, and by far the most permanently important part, of the ecclesiastical litigation that went on in this country, came before English prelates who were sitting, not as English prelates, not as 'judges ordinary,' but as mere delegates of the pope commissioned to hear and determine this or that particular case[3]. When once the supreme pontiff has obtained seisin of a cause, that cause proceeds under his directions. He bids two or three English prelates try it, but he also tells them by what rules they are to try it, he teaches them, corrects them, reproves them, expresses in a fatherly way his surprise at their ignorance of law. Very many of the decretals are [p. 94]

---

[1] It may be well to explain that after the compilation of Gratian's work, the decretals not contained in it were known as *decretales extravagantes*, i.e. *quae vagabantur extra decretum.* Even after they had been collected by Gregory they were cited as *Extra* or *X.* Thus *Extra de rescriptis c. ex parte*, or *c.* 2. *X de rescript.* 1. 3, is a reference to the Gregorian collection. The Sext is referred to by *in* vi[to]; the Clementines by *Clem.*; the collection of Extravagants published in 1500 consists partly of Extravagantes Johannis XXII. (*Extrav. Joh.* XXII.), partly of Extravagantes Communes (*Extrav. Comm.*).

[2] We speak of the middle of the twelfth century; before its end even the popes perceive that limits must be set to the appeal.

[3] Maitland, Canon Law in England; E. H. R. vol. xii.

mandates issued to these judges delegate, mandates which deal with particular cases. Others are answers to questions of law addressed to the pope by English or other prelates. These mandates and these answers were of importance, not merely to the parties immediately concerned, but to all the faithful, for the canonist would treat as law in other cases the rules that were thus laid down. His science was to a great degree a science of 'case law,' and yet not of case law as we now understand it, for the 'dicta' rather than the 'decisions' of the popes were law; indeed when the decretals were collected, the particular facts of the cases to which they had reference, the *species facti*, were usually omitted as of no value. The pope enjoyed a power of declaring law to which but wide and vague limits could be set. Each separate church might have its customs, but there was a *ius commune*, a common law, of the universal church. In the view of the canonist, any special rules of the church of England have hardly a wider scope, hardly a less dependent place, than have the customs of Kent or the by-laws of London in the eye of the English lawyer[1]. During the time with which we are now dealing, the twelfth and thirteenth centuries, no English canonist attempts to write down the law of the English church, for the English church has very little law save the law of the church Catholic and Roman. When in the next century John de Athona wrote a commentary on the constitutions made by certain papal legates [p. 95] in England, he treated them as part and parcel of a system which was only English because it was universal, and brought to bear upon them the expositions of the great foreign doctors, Hostiensis, Durandus and the rest. On the other hand, a large portion of this universal system was in one sense specifically English. England seems to have supplied the Roman curia with an amount of litigation far larger than that which the mere size or wealth of our country would have led us to expect. Open the Gregorian collection where we will, we see the pope declaring law for English cases. The title *De filiis presbyterorum ordinandis vel non* has eighteen chapters; nine of these are addressed to English prelates. The title *De iure patronatus* has thirty-one chapters and at least fifteen of them are in this sense English. But if an English advocate made his

---

[1] This point has been argued at length in E. H. R. xi. 446, 641.

way to Rome, he was like to be told by the pope that his doctrine was the product of English beer, and might carry home with him a rescript which would give the English bishops a sound lesson in the law of prescription[1].

Relation of canon to Roman law.

The relation between the two great systems was in the twelfth century very close. The canon law had borrowed its form, its language, its spirit, and many a maxim from the civil law. Of course, however, it had to deal with many institutions which had never come within the ken of the classical Roman lawyers, or had been treated by them in a manner which the church could not approve. Thus, for example, the law of marriage and divorce, a topic which the church had made her own, had to be rewritten. Some elements which we may call Germanic had made their way into the ecclesiastical system; in penal causes the proof by compurgation was adopted, and, wherever the testamentary executor may come from, he does not come from the Roman law. Still the canonist's debt to the civilian was heavy; he had borrowed, for instance, the greater part of his law of procedure, and he was ever ready to eke out Gratian by an appeal to Justinian. In Richard I.'s day the monks of Canterbury went to law with the archbishop; a statement of their case has come down to us; probably it was [p 9C] drawn up by some Italian; it contains eighty citations of the Decretum, forty of the Digest, thirty of the Code. The works of the classical Roman jurists were ransacked to prove that the archbishop's projected college of canons would be an injury to his cathedral monastery[2]. In the thirteenth century the canon law began to think that she could shift for herself and to give herself airs of superiority. The bishops of Rome began to discourage a system which had only too much to say about the grandeur of emperors and hardly a word of popes. If they could have had their way, the civil law would have been but the modest handmaid of the canon law[3]. But in the days of our King Stephen the imperial mother and her papal daughter were fairly good friends. It was hand in hand that they entered England.

---

[1] Chron. Abb. de Evesham, p. 189: 'Pater sancte nos didicimus in scholis, et haec est opinio magistrorum nostrorum, quod non currit praescriptio contra iura episcopalia.' Et dominus papa, 'Certe et tu et magistri tui multum bibistis de cerevisia Anglicana quando haec didicistis.' The result is found in c. 15, X. 2. 26.

[2] Epistolae Cantuarienses, p. 520.   [3] See below, p. 122.

The history of law in England, and even the history of Roman and
canon
law in
England. English law, could not but be influenced by them.   Their action, however, hardly becomes visible until the middle of the twelfth century is at hand.   If the compiler of the *Leges Henrici* adopts a sentence which can be ultimately traced to the Theodosian Code through epitomes and interpretations, if the compiler of the *Leis Williame* seems to have heard a few Roman maxims, all this belongs to the pre-scientific era[1]. If William of Malmesbury, when copying a history of the Roman emperors, introduces into his work a version of the Breviary of Alaric, he is playing the part of the historian, not of the jurist[2].   It is remarkable enough that within a century after Lanfranc's death, within much less than a century after the death of Irnerius, a well-informed Norman abbot ascribed to them jointly the credit of discovering Justinian's books at Bologna[3].   The story is untrue, for Lanfranc had left Italy long before Irnerius began to teach ; still his name would never have been coupled with that of Irnerius had he known no Roman [p. 97] law.   Lanfranc's pupil Ivo of Chartres, the great canonist, knew much Roman law[4] and becomes of importance in English history; it was his legal mind that schemed the *concordat* between Henry I. and Anselm[5].   More to the point is it that from Burchard of Worms or some other canonist the author of our *Leges Henrici* had borrowed many a passage while as yet the *Decretum Gratiani* was unwritten.   Yet more to the point, that already in the reign of Rufus, William of St Calais, bishop of Durham, when accused of treason in the king's court, shows that he has the Pseudo-Isidorian doctrines at his fingers' ends, demands a canonical tribunal, formally pleads an *exceptio spolii*, appeals to Rome, and even—for so it would seem—brings a book of canon law into court[6].   When Stephen made his ill-

---

[1] See above, pp. 100, 102.

[2] Malmesbury's connexion with this work is discussed by Dr Stubbs in his introduction to the Gesta Regum, i. cxxxi ff.   The work itself is described by Hänel, Lex Romana Visigothorum, p. lv.   See also Conrat, Geschichte der Quellen des R. R., i. 232.

[3] See above, p. 78.

[4] Rob. de Torigny, p. 100; Savigny, Geschichte, cap. 15, § 106 ; Conrat, Geschichte, i. 378.

[5] Liebermann, Anselm von Canterbury, p. 41.

[6] Monasticon, i. 244–250: 'Christianam legem quam hic scriptam habeo testem invoco.'

advised attack on Roger of Salisbury and the other bishops, once more the *exceptio spolii* was pleaded, again the demand for a canonical tribunal was urged, and the king himself appealed to the pope[1]. The time when Gratian was at work on the Decretum, when the four doctors were flourishing at Bologna, was a time at which the English king had come into violent collision with the prelates of the church, and those prelates were but ill agreed among themselves.

Vacarius.

At this time it was that Archbishop Theobald, at the instance perhaps of his clerk Thomas,—Thomas who was himself to be chancellor, archbishop and martyr,—Thomas who had studied law at Bologna and had sat, it may be, at the feet of Gratian[2]—imported from Italy one Vacarius[3]. The little that we know of his early life seems to point to Mantua as his home and a short tract on Lombard law has been ascribed to him. It is not unlikely that Theobald availed himself of the help of this trained legist in his struggle with [p. 98] Stephen's brother, Henry bishop of Winchester, who, to the prejudice of the rights of Canterbury, had obtained the office of papal legate. That Vacarius taught Roman law in England there can be no doubt; a body of students looked up to him as their *magister* and reverently received his glosses[4]. That he taught in the archbishop's household, which was full of men who were to become illustrious in church and state, is highly probable. That he also taught at Oxford, where a school was just beginning to form itself, is not so plain, but is asserted by one who ought not to have made a mistake about such a matter[5]. That Stephen endeavoured to silence him and to

[1] William of Malmesbury, Gesta Regum, ii. 553. The legate says, 'Rex itaque faciat quod etiam in forensibus iudiciis legitimum est fieri, ut revestiat episcopos de rebus suis ; alioquin iure gentium dissaisiti non placitabunt.' The king's appeal occurs on the next page. As to the proceedings at Rome between Stephen and Matilda, see Round, Geoffrey de Mandeville, 250 ff.

[2] William Fitz Stephen, Materials for Life of Becket, iii. 17.

[3] Thomas's activity in this matter is made probable by Gervase of Canterbury, ii. 384. This passage, together with the words of Robert of Torigny (ed. Howlett), p. 159, and of John of Salisbury, Polycraticus, lib. viii. cap. 22, contains most what is known of the legal career of Vacarius. These passages are conveniently collected by Holland, Collectanea of Oxford Historical Society, ii. 139. In 1896 the whole story of Vacarius was put on a new footing by Liebermann, E. H. R. xi. 305, 514. We adopt his results.

[4] Wenck, Magister Vacarius, p. 134.

[5] Gervase of Canterbury, *loc. cit.* ; Liebermann, E. H. R. xi. 308; Rashdall, Universities, ii. 335 ff.

extirpate the books of civil and canon law we are told upon good authority[1]. We are told also, and may well believe, that the royal edict was ineffectual. Further, we know that Vacarius wrote a book and have some reason for ascribing this to the year 1149; he wrote it for the use of poor students who could not afford to purchase the Roman texts. That book still exists. It might be described as a condensed version of Justinian's Code illustrated by large extracts from the Digest[2]. It is a thoroughly academic book, as purely academic as would be any lectures on Roman law delivered now-a-days in an English university. In what of it has been printed we can see no practical hints, no allusions to English affairs[3]. Besides this, we have from Vacarius a christological pamphlet on the assumption of the manhood, and a little tract on the law of marriage in which he appears as an acute critic of the mischievous doctrine which the canonists and divines were evolving[4].

[p 99] Unless he had a namesake, he spent the rest of a long life in England, held some preferment in the northern province, was attached to Becket's rival, Archbishop Roger of York, and acted as Roger's compurgator when a charge of complicity in the murder of St Thomas was to be disproved[5]. We do not know that he took any part in the controversy between Henry and Becket; if he did, we must look for him rather among the king's than among the archbishop's legal advisers. Perhaps he lived until 1198 or 1200[6]; if so, he must have been a very young man when Theobald fetched him from Italy[7].

---

[1] Joh. Salisb. Polycr. *loc. cit.* This matter is discussed by Wenck, pp. 28-41. Liebermann, E. H. R. xi. 310.

[2] Large portions of the work were published in 1820 by Wenck, Magister Vacarius (Leipzig). Savigny discusses it, Geschichte, cap. 22, §174; cap. 36, §124. There is a MS. of it at Worcester, of which no full account has yet been given.

[3] There is just enough to show that some of those who glossed the work had English cases in their minds; *e.g.* Wenck, p. 189 : 'Argumentum pro decano Eboracensi.'

[4] Maitland, Magistri Vacarii Summa de Matrimonio, L. Q. R. 1897.

[5] Liebermann, E. H. R. xi. 312-4. Add to the references there given : Jessopp, E. H. R. xi. 747; Historians of the Church of York, iii. 81.

[6] Hoveden, iv. 75, and the note by Stubbs.

[7] In general as to Vacarius see Wenck's book; Stubbs, Const. Hist. §147; Stubbs, Lectures, 120, 137, 141, 301-3 ; Holland, E. H. R. vi. 243-4; Rashdall, Universities, ii. 335 ; Liebermann, E. H. R. xi. 305, 514.

From Stephen's reign onwards, the proofs that Roman and canon law are being studied in England become more frequent. The letters of Archbishop Theobald's secretary, John of Salisbury, the foremost scholar of the age, are full of allusions to both laws; many of these occur in relation to English ecclesiastical law-suits of which John is forwarding reports to the pope. In his *Polycraticus* he has given a sketch of civil procedure which drew high praise from Savigny[1]. The epistles ascribed to Peter of Blois, archdeacon of Bath and of London, are stuffed with juristic conceits. Giraldus Cambrensis is by way of lamenting that literature is being obliterated by law, while students of jurisprudence neglect its elements[2]. Maxims out of the Institutes or the Digest become part of the stock in trade of the polite letter writer, the moralist, and the historian. Manuscripts are being copied. Abbot Benedict of Peterborough has in his monastery the whole *Corpus Iuris Civilis* in two volumes, besides various parts of it, the Summa of Placentinus and the Summa—this, it is said, may be the work of a Norman or an Englishman—that is known as *Olim;* he has also the Decretum, a collection of Decretals and the canonical text-books of Rufinus and Johannes Faventinus[3]. Thomas of Marlborough, who became monk, prior, abbot at Evesham, had taught law at Oxford and, for so it would seem, at Exeter, and he brought with him to his monastery a collection of books *utriusque iuris*[4]. It is plain that a flourishing school of Roman and canon law had grown up at Oxford[5]. [p. 100]

But the Italians had been first in the field and easily maintained their pre-eminence. During the rest of the middle ages hardly a man acquires the highest fame as legist or decretist who is not Italian, if not by birth, at least by education. The second place must be conceded to the French universities; in particular to the school of Orleans. There are some signs of original work in England. The scholars of Vacarius glossed his glosses. Some manuals of procedure

---

[1] Geschichte, cap. 36, § 131.

[2] Opera, ii. 348; iv. 3. 7.

[3] Chronicles of Robert of Swafham, ed. Sparke, pp. 96-8. As to the Summa called *Olim* (it begins 'Olim edebatur'), see Caillemer, Le droit civil dans les provinces anglo-normandes, p. 32.

[4] Chron. Evesham, p. 267.

[5] Holland, Eng. Hist. Rev. vi. 247; Rashdall, Universities, ii. 338.

have been preserved which good critics have ascribed to the
England or the Normandy of the twelfth century[1]. Of these
the most interesting to us is one which has been attributed
to no less a man than William Longchamp. A clerk of
Norman race, he became for some years, as all know, King
Richard's viceroy and the true ruler of England. Even after
his fall he was still the king's chancellor[2]. Another lawyer
who for a while controls the destiny of our land is Cardinal
Guala Bicchieri[3], but it were needless to say that he was no
Englishman. Probably that one of our countrymen who gains
[p. 101] most fame in the cosmopolitan study is Ricardus Anglicus[4].
He has been somewhat hastily identified with Richard le Poore,
who became dean of Salisbury, bishop of Chichester, of Salisbury,
of Durham[5]. In the next century the most prominent name is
that of William of Drogheda, who taught at Oxford and wrote
a *Summa Aurea*[6]. But the Roman Catholicism—we need no
better term—of the canon law made against the development of
national schools. All the great cases, the *causes célèbres*, went to
Rome, and the English litigant, if prudent and wealthy, secured
the services of the best Italian advocates. In their dispute with
the archbishop, the monks of Canterbury retain the illustrious
Pillius and the illustrious Ugolino, who will be Gregory IX.[7]
Thomas of Marlborough, prior of Evesham, despite his having

---

[1] Caillemer, *op. cit.* pp. 15–50.

[2] Caillemer, *op. cit.* p. 50, prints the ʻPractica Legum et Decretorum edita a
Magistro W. de Longo Campo.ʼ Longchamp's career is described at length by
Stubbs in the Introduction to Hoveden, vol. iii. A manual known as the
Ordo Iudiciarius of the Bamberg MS. is attributed to England ; it was published
by Schulte in the Proceedings of the Vienna Academy (1872), vol. 70, p. 235.

[3] Chron. Evesham, p. 191: ʻdominum Gualam ...inter cardinales in iure
civili peritissimum.ʼ

[4] Schulte, Geschichte des canonischen Rechts, i. 183 ; Caillemer, *op. cit.*
33–4 ; Bethmann-Hollweg, Civil Prozess, vi. 105.

[5] In our first edition we said that the identification of the bishop with the
canonist might require reconsideration. See now Mr Blakiston's article *Poor,
Richard*, in Dict. Nat. Biog., which shows that the evidence of identity is very
slight. Schulte has collected a few particulars about English students and
teachers at Bologna—i. 151, a certain David, canon of St Paul's, who was a
master there in 1163 or thereabouts—i. 188, Gilbert, Alan, Johannes Walensis—
i. 211, Elias Anglicus. As to Master David, some entertaining stories are to be
found in Spicilegium Liberianum, p. 603. For some entries in a Bolognese
necrology relating to English masters, see Dublin Review, cxii. 78.

[6] Schulte, ii, 113 ; Bethmann-Hollweg, Civil Prozess, vi. 123–131 ; Delisle,
Littérature latine, p. 68 ; Maitland, E. H. R. vol. xii.

[7] Epist. Cantuar. pp. 68, 471, 476, 506.

taught law at Oxford, attended the lectures of Azo, 'master of all the masters of law,' before he trusted himself to plead the cause of his abbey at the threshold of the Apostles[1]. It was not from any English civilian but from Azo himself that our Bracton borrowed. Henry III. kept in his pay Henry of Susa, who was going to be cardinal bishop of Ostia, and who, for all [p. 102] men who read the law of the church, will be simply *Hostiensis*[2]. Edward I. had Franciscus Accursii at his side[3]. The great 'prizes of the profession' were beyond the reach of the Englishman; 'the leaders of the profession' whose books he had to read, whose opinions he had to quote, were Italians.

The civilian in England finds little to do.

As to Roman law, it led to nothing. For a while in their enthusiasm men might be content to study for its own sake this record of human wisdom, of almost superhuman wisdom, so it must have seemed to them. But it soon became plain that in England there would be no court administering Roman law, unless it were the court of a learned university. And then, as already said, the church, or at any rate a powerful party in the English church, began to look askance at the civilian. Theology was to be protected against law. Beneficed clerks were no longer to study the secular jurisprudence. In the year 1219 Honorius III. forbad that the civil law should be taught in the university of Paris[4], and when we read how in 1234 our Henry III. ordained that the *leges* should no longer be taught in the London schools—probably this refers to the schools of St Paul's Cathedral—it is by no means certain that we ought not to connect this with a movement in favour of ecclesiastical reform, rather than with that 'Nolumus leges Angliae mutare' which the barons were about to utter[5]. Matthew Paris has

---

[1] Chron. Evesham, pp. 147, 153, 168. Marlborough went to Bologna by the advice of the pope (Innocent III.) and Cardinal Ugolino. He employed as his counsel Magister Merandus Hispanus, who had argued the king's case against the Canterbury monks, and Bertrand, a knight of Pavia, who as a lawyer was second to none but Azo.

[2] Mat. Par. Chron. Maj. iv. 33, 286, 351–3; Schulte, ii. 123; Maitland, Canon Law in England; E. H. R. vol. xii.

[3] Stubbs, Const. Hist. § 179; Savigny, Geschichte, cap. 43, § 102.

[4] This by the bull *Super speculam*, of which divers portions are to be found in the Decretales Gregorii, in particular, c. 28, X. 5. 33; Denifle, Chartularium Universitatis Parisiensis, i. 80.

[5] Rot. Cl. 19 Hen. III. m. 16; Selden, Diss. ad Fletam, p. 525. Dr Stubbs, Lectures, p. 306, interprets the 'leges' of this writ as though it indicated the canon law; but surely it far more probably bears its usual sense, the sense in

handed down to us what purports to be the text of a papal
[p. 103] bull which goes much further[1]. Innocent IV., perhaps the
greatest lawyer among all the popes, is supposed to decree in
the year 1254 that in France, England, Scotland, Wales and
Hungary—in short almost everywhere save in Italy and Germany—the imperial laws shall not be read, unless the kings of
those countries will have it otherwise. In those countries, he
is made to say, the causes of the laity are decided, not by the
imperial laws, but by customs, while for ecclesiastical causes the
constitutions of the holy fathers will suffice. Strong reasons
have been shown for the condemnation of this would-be bull as
a forgery, or as the manifesto of English divines who will make
believe that the pope has done what he ought to do[2]. Genuine
or spurious, it is an instructive document, for it tells us that in
England the civilian is between two fires. The best churchmen
do not love him; ecclesiastical reformers are coming to the aid
of national conservatism. This did not destroy the study of the
Roman books. Oxford and Cambridge gave degrees as well in
the civil as in the canon law[3]. The one considerable work produced by an English canonist of the fourteenth century, the
gloss of John de Athona on the legatine constitutions, is full of
references to Code and Digest. But the civilian, if he was not
a canonist, had no wide field open to him in England. He might
become a diplomatist; there was always a call in the royal
chancery for a few men who would be ready to draw up treaties
and state-papers touching international affairs, and to meet

---

which it can be contrasted with 'decreta' or 'canones.' The question why this
bolt should be launched against the 'laws' in London while they are spared at
Oxford, is not unlike the much discussed question why Honorius struck at the
laws in Paris and only in Paris. The answer may be that these London schools
were primarily theological schools, and that the university of Paris was
the great theological school of the world. Or again, it seems possible that
Henry is protecting the Oxford law school against competition. That the
'leges' of this writ mean English law we can not believe; we shall hear nothing
of English law being taught for a long time to come. See Clark, Cambridge
Legal Studies, p. 40.

[1] Mat. Par. Chron. Maj. vi. 293–5.

[2] Digard, La papauté et l'étude du droit romain, Bibliothèque de l'École
des chartes, 1890, vol. 51, p. 381. Denifle, Chartularium Universitatis Parisiensis, i. 261, had already questioned the authenticity of this bull. Perhaps it
was originally no worse than an university squib; however, Matthew Paris
believed in it. Blackstone, Comm. i. 20, has strangely misunderstood the drift
of this document.

[3] Rashdall, Universities, ii. 451; Clark, Cambridge Legal Studies, 42–59.

foreign lawyers on their own ground. Nor must it be forgotten that so long as the English king was endeavouring to govern Guienne from Westminster, he was obliged to keep in his employ men who could write fluently about such romanesque institutions as *emphyteusis,* 'active and passive *testamenti factio*' and the like[1], for Guienne was in theory a country of the written law. But except as a diplomatist, a chancery clerk, or a teacher, the civilian would find little to do in England. The court of admiralty, the courts of the universities, even when they had come into existence, could not provide [p. 104] employment for many practitioners.

The history of Roman and canon law as studied and administered in England deserves to be written at length. We have said of it but enough to serve our immediate purpose; for we have now to note in the first place that a large tract in the field of law was made over to the ecclesiastical courts and their canonical jurisprudence, and secondly that this canonical jurisprudence affected the development of our English temporal law.

The province of ecclesiastical law.

The demarcation of the true province of ecclesiastical law was no easy task; it was not to be accomplished in England, in France, in Germany, without prolonged struggles[2]. The Conqueror, when he ordained that 'the episcopal laws' were not to be administered as of old in the hundred courts, left many questions open. During the first half of the twelfth century the claims of the church were growing, and the duty of asserting them passed into the hands of men who were not mere theologians but expert lawyers. Then, as all know, came the quarrel between Henry and Becket. In the Constitutions of Clarendon (1164) the king offered to the prelates a written treaty, a treaty which, so he said, embodied the 'customs' of his ancestors, more especially of his grandfather. Becket, after some hesitation, rejected the constitutions. The dispute waxed hot; certain of the customs were condemned by the pope. The murder followed, and then Henry was compelled to renounce, though in carefully guarded terms, all his innovations[3]. But his own assertion all along had been that he was

---

[1] See *e.g.* Memoranda de Parliamento of 33 Edward I. ed. Maitland, pp. 331, 335.

[2] Brunner, D. R. G. § 96 ; Fournier, Les officialités au moyen âge ; Luchaire, Manuel des institutions françaises, p. 121 ; Hinschius, Kirchenrecht, v. 373 ff.

[3] Gesta Henrici (Benedictus), i. 33.

no innovator; and though the honours and dishonours of the famous contest may be divided, the king was left in possession of the greater part of the field of battle. At two points he had been beaten :—the clerk suspected of felony could not be sentenced by, though he might be accused before, a lay court; appeals to Rome could not be prohibited, though in practice the king could, when he chose, do much to impede them. Elsewhere Henry had maintained his ground, and from his time onwards the lay courts, rather than the spiritual, are the [p. 105] aggressors and the victors in almost every contest. About many particulars we shall have to speak in other parts of our work; here we may take a brief survey of the province, the large province, which the courts Christian retain as their own.

The church claims cognizance of a cause for one of two reasons :—either because the matter in dispute is of an ecclesiastical or spiritual kind, or because the persons concerned in it, or some of them, are specially subject to the ecclesiastical jurisdiction[1].

I. (a) In the first place, she claims an exclusive cognizance of all affairs that can fairly be called matters of ecclesiastical economy, the whole law of ecclesiastical status, the ordination and degradation of clerks, the consecration of bishops, all purely spiritual functions such as the celebration of divine service, also the regulation of ecclesiastical corporations and the internal administration of their revenues. In this region the one limit set to her claims is the principle asserted by the state that the rights of the patrons (*advocati*) of churches are temporal rights, that the advowson (*advocatio ecclesiae*) is temporal property[2]. To start with, the majority of churches had been owned by the landowners who built them[3]. The spiritual power had succeeded in enforcing the rule that the 'institution' of the clerk lies with the bishop; the choice of the clerk still lay with the landowner. Henry II. maintained, Becket controverted, Alexander condemned this principle ; but, despite papal condemnation, it seems to have been steadily upheld by the king's court, which prohibited the courts Christian from interfering

Matters of ecclesiastical economy.

---

[1] An excellent statement will be found in Makower, History of the Church of England, 399 ; see further an interesting bull of Urban IV. in Chartae, Privilegia et Immunitates, Irish Rec. Com., p. 30.

[2] Const. Clarend. c. 1.

[3] Ulrich Stutz, Geschichte des kirchlichen Beneficialwesens, Berlin, 1895.

with the right of patronage[1]; and very soon we may find two prelates in litigation about an advowson before the royal justices[2]. In this instance the clergy seem to have given way somewhat easily[3]; both parties were at one in treating the advowson as a profitable, vendible right. Henry's victory at this point was of the utmost importance in after ages. It distinguishes England from other countries, and provides a base for anti-papal statutes[4]. As regards other matters falling under the present head there was little debate; but it behoves us to notice that our temporal lawyers were thus excluded from some fruitful fields of jurisprudence. The growth of our law of corporations is slow, because our courts have nothing to do with the internal affairs of convents and chapters—the only institutions, that is, which seem to require treatment as fictitious persons; and we might have come by a law of trusts sooner than we did, if the justices had been bound to deal with the administration of revenues given to prelates or convents as a provision for particular purposes, such as the relief of the [p. 106] poor or the maintenance of fabrics[5].

Church property.

(b) The ecclesiastical tribunals would much like to claim the decision of all causes which in any way concern those lands that have been given to a church, at all events if given by way of 'alms.' Henry himself was willing to make what may seem to us a large concession at this point. If both parties agreed that the land had been given in alms, litigation about it was to proceed in the ecclesiastical forum; if they did not agree, then the preliminary question, which would decide where the case should be tried, was to be settled by the verdict of a jury. Here he was successful and much more than successful. The courts of his successors insisted on their exclusive right to adjudge all questions relating to the possession or ownership of land, albeit given in alms; the spiritual judges could in this province do no more than excommunicate for sacrilege one who

---

[1] Glanvill, iv. 12–14.

[2] See *e.g.* Select Civil Pleas, i. pl. 245. Bracton's Note Book, pl. 551: in 1231 the bishop of London, in a suit for an advowson, accepts a wager of battle.

[3] Maitland, E. H. R. xi. 647.   [4] Maitland, E. H. R. xi. 649.

[5] To a small extent the lay courts were enabled to interfere with such matters by the doctrine that the services due from a 'tenant by divine service' could be exacted by distress or action; but on the whole the administration of pious gifts was left to the courts Christian.

invaded soil that had been devoted to God in the strictest sense
by being consecrated[1].

(c) The courts Christian claimed the exaction of spiritual Ecclesias-
tical dues.
dues, tithes, mortuaries, oblations, pensions.   The justice of the
claim was not contested, but it was limited by the rule that a
question about the title to the advowson is for the lay court.
From century to century there was a border warfare over tithes
between the two sets of lawyers, and from time to time some
curious compromises were framed[2].

(d) More important is it for us to notice that the church Matrimo-
nial causes.
claims marriage, divorce, and consequently legitimacy, as themes
of ecclesiastical jurisdiction.   This claim was not disputed by
Henry II. or his successors.   However, the church in the
twelfth century became definitely committed to the doctrine
that children who were born out of wedlock are legitimated by
the marriage of their parents[3].   As regards the inheritance of
[p. 107] land, a matter which lay outside the spiritual sphere, the king's
courts would not accept this rule[4].   The clergy endeavoured to
persuade the lay power to bring its law into harmony with the
law of the church, and then in the year 1236, as all know, the
barons replied with one voice that they would not change the
law of England[5].   Thenceforward the king's justices assumed
the right to send to a jury the question whether a person was
born before or after the marriage of his parents, and it might
well fall out that a man legitimate enough to be ordained or (it
may be) to succeed to the chattels of his father, would be a
bastard incapable of inheriting land either from father or from
mother.   But except when this particular question about the
retroactive force of marriage arose, it was for the ecclesiastical
court to decide the question of legitimacy, and, if this arose
incidentally in the course of a temporal suit, it was sent for
trial to the bishop and concluded by his certificate[6].

---

[1] Constitutions of Clarendon, c. 9.   We shall deal with this matter hereafter
when we speak of tenure by frank almoin.

[2] Mat. Par. Chron. Maj. iv. 614; Bracton, f. 402 b, 403; Circumspecte
Agatis (Statutes, i. 101), c. 3; Articuli Cleri (Stat. i. 171), c. 1.

[3] This was definitely settled by a mandate addressed by Alexander III. to the
bishop of Exeter, which appears in the Gregorian collection as c. 6, X. 4. 17.

[4] Glanvill, vii. 15.

[5] Stat. Merton, c. 9; Letters of Robert Grosseteste, pp. 76, 95; Bracton's
Note Book, i. pp. 104–116.

[6] It is for the ecclesiastical court to decide 'an issue of general bastardy,'

Testamentary causes.

(*e*) Yet more important to us at the present day was another claim of the church, which has had the effect of splitting our English law of property into two halves. She claimed as her own the testament, that 'last will' of a dead man which was intimately connected with his last confession. She claimed not merely to pronounce on the validity of wills, but also to interpret them, and also to regulate the doings of her creature the testamentary executor, whom she succeeded in placing alongside of the English heir. In the course of the thirteenth century the executor gradually becomes a prominent figure in the king's courts; he there sues the testator's debtors and is sued by his creditors; but the legatees who claim under the will must seek their remedies in the courts of the church. In this instance the common lawyers seem to have suffered the canonists to gradually enlarge a territory which was to be very valuable in the future. As a general rule, land could not be given by testament, and our king's court was concentrating its attention on land and crime. Meanwhile the church extends her boundaries[1], and at last succeeds in compassing the whole [p. 103] law of succession to movables *ab intestato*. The process whereby this was accomplished is very obscure; we shall speak of it upon another occasion; but here we may say that a notion prevailed that intestacy, if it be not exactly a sin[2], is often God's judgment on sin, for so closely is the last will connected with the last confession, that to die intestate is to die unconfessed[3]. And so 'the law of personal property' falls apart from 'the law of real property' and we at this day are suffering the consequences.

Pledge of faith.

(*f*) With great difficulty were the courts Christian prevented from appropriating a vast region in the province of contract. They claimed to enforce—at the very least by spiritual censures—all promises made by oath, or by 'pledge of faith.' The man who pledges his faith, pawns his Christianity,

---

while 'an issue of special bastardy' is tried by a jury. 'Is this man a bastard?' —that is an issue of general bastardy. 'Is this man a bastard because born before the marriage of his parents?'—that is an issue of special bastardy. Blackstone, Comm. iii. 335.

[1] Glanvill, vii. 7; xii. 17; Harvard Law Review, iii. 168; this matter will be discussed at greater length when we speak of the history of wills.

[2] Bracton, f. 60 b: 'nullam enim meretur poenam quis, quamvis decedat intestatus.'

[3] See in vol. ii. our section on Intestacy.

puts his hopes of salvation in the hand of another[1].   Henry II.
asserted his jurisdiction over such cases; Becket claimed at
least a concurrent jurisdiction for the church.   Henry was
victorious.   From his day onwards the royal court was always
ready to prohibit ecclesiastical judges from entertaining a
charge of breach of faith, unless indeed both parties to the
contract were clerks, or unless the subject-matter of the promise
was something that lay outside the jurisdiction of the temporal
forum[2].   All the same, there can be no doubt that during the
whole of the next century the courts Christian were busy with
breaches of faith.   Very often a contractor expressly placed
himself under their power and renounced all right to a prohibition.   Such a renunciation was not fully effectual, for the
right to issue the prohibition was the right of the king, not of
the contractor; still, as Bracton explains, a man commits an
[p. 109] enormous sin by seeking a prohibition when he has promised
not to seek one and may very properly be sent to prison[3].   In
practice ecclesiastical judges were quite willing to run the risk
of being prohibited; indeed the law of the church compelled
them to take this hazard.   A certain jurisdiction over marriage
settlements of money or movable goods, the church had as part
of its jurisdiction over marriage[4].

   (*g*)   There remains the indefinitely wide claim to correct Correction
the sinner for his soul's health, to set him some corporeal   of sinners.
penance.   The temporal courts put a limit to this claim by
asserting that, if the sin be also an offence which they can
punish, the spiritual judges are not to meddle with it.   There
are some few exceptions; the bodies of the clergy are doubly
protected; you may be put to penance for laying violent hands
upon a clerk besides being imprisoned for the breach of the
peace and having to pay damages for the trespass[5].   But,
even though this rule be maintained, much may be done for

---

[1] Cart. Riev. p. 164: 'et primum haec omnia sacramento firmavit, deinde
christianitatem in manu mea qua se obsidem dedit etc.'

[2] Glanvill, x. 1–3; Bracton's Note Book, pl. 50, 670, 683, 1361, 1464, 1671;
Bracton, f. 406 b.   We shall return to the *laesio fidei* hereafter in our section on
Contract.

[3] Bracton, f. 401 b, 402.

[4] The regular form of the prohibition relating to movables forbad the
ecclesiastical judge to meddle with chattels 'quae non sunt de testamento vel
matrimonio.'

[5] Circumspecte Agatis (Statutes, i. 101), c. 6, 11.

the correction of sinners. The whole province of sexual morality is annexed by the church; she punishes fornication, adultery, incest; and these offences are not punished by the king's court, though the old local courts are still exacting *legerwites* and *childwites*, fines for fornication. So also the province of defamation is made over to the spiritual jurisdiction, for, though the local courts entertain actions for slander and libel, the king's court, for some reason or another, has no punishment for the defamer, no relief for the defamed[1]. Usury is treated as a mere sin while the usurer is living; but if he dies in his sin, the king seizes his goods[2]. Simony naturally belongs to the church courts; perjury, not always well distinguished from the breach of a promissory oath, would come before them upon many occasions, though with perjured jurors the royal court could deal. Of heresy we need as yet say nothing, for England had hardly been troubled by heretics. No doubt the church courts were quite prepared to deal with heresy should it raise its head, and had they called upon the state to burn or other- [p. 110] wise punish the heretic, it is not likely that they would have called in vain[3].

Jurisdiction over clerks.

II. (*a*) But the church had opened a second parallel. She claimed cognizance of all personal causes, criminal or civil, in which a clerk was the accused or the defendant. The story of 'the benefit of clergy' we shall tell elsewhere. On the whole, save in one particular, the state had its way. The clerk accused of felony was to be tried in the ecclesiastical court and was to suffer no other punishment than that which the ecclesiastical court could inflict; it could inflict lifelong imprisonment. But whatever may have been the case in the twelfth century, the clerk of the thirteenth can be tried and punished for all his minor offences as though he were a layman. Then again, in Bracton's day the clerk has no privilege when he is defendant in a civil action, though in the past clerks have been allowed to sue each other for debts and the like in court Christian[4]. It should be well understood that 'the benefit of clergy' as allowed by English law was but a small part of that general

---

[1] Of this in our section on Trespasses.
[2] Glanvill, vii. 17.
[3] See in vol. ii. our section on Ecclesiastical Offences.
[4] Note Book, pl. 719, 808; compare Bracton, f. 401 b.

immunity from lay justice which was claimed for the ordained by canonists in England as well as elsewhere[1].

(*b*) On the continent of Europe the church often claimed as her own the suits of the *miserabiles personae*, as they were called, of widows and orphans[2]. Of any such claim we hear little or nothing in England, though some tradition of it may affect the later history of the Court of Chancery. In England it is the king who sets feudal rules aside in order that summary justice may be done to the widow[3]. Miserabiles personae.

Large then is the province of ecclesiastical law; but it might have been much larger. Despite the many advantages that Henry II. gave to his antagonists by his rages and his furies, he handed down to his successors a larger field of purely [p. 111] temporal justice than was to be found elsewhere[4]. Even in Normandy Richard had to consign to the ecclesiastical forum all questions about broken oath or broken faith[5]. But we are here concerned with the fact that from the middle of the twelfth century onwards a very large mass of litigation, of litigation too which in no very strict sense can be called ecclesiastical, was handed over to tribunals which administered the canon law, tribunals which were often constituted by a papal rescript, and from which there lay an appeal to the Roman curia. The sphere of canon law.

The canon law begins to affect our temporal law sometimes by way of repulsion, sometimes by way of attraction. It is in opposition to 'the canons and Roman laws[6]' that (if we may so speak) our English law becomes conscious of its own existence. In the Constitutions of Clarendon we have our first authoritative redaction of hitherto unwritten customs. If our *consuetudines* are to prevail against the *leges* and *canones*, they must be accurately formulated and set in writing. The 'Nolumus leges Influence of canon upon English law.

---

[1] Maitland, E. H. R. xi. 646. Gratian at the end of c. 47, C. 11, qu. 1, summed up the matter thus : 'Ex his omnibus datur intelligi, quod clericus ad publica iudicia nec in civili, nec in criminali causa est producendus, nisi forte civilem causam episcopus decidere noluerit, vel in criminali sui honoris cingulo eum nudaverit.'

[2] Schröder, D. R. G. 569 ; Fournier, Officialités, 79.

[3] Glanvill, vi. 14. The widow who has received no part of her dower may go straight to the king's court.

[4] Schröder, *op. cit.* 568 ; Fournier, *op. cit.* 64–94.

[5] Mat. Par. Chron. Maj. ii. 368.

[6] Glanvill, vii. 15 : 'secundum canones et leges Romanas.'

Angliae mutare' of 1236 is no announcement of a purely
abstract conservatism; our English rule is to be maintained
in opposition to the canons. Repulsion begets emulation.
Glanvill will have it that the English laws, at least those made
by the king with the counsel of his barons, are *leges*, just as
much *leges* as any that are studied at Bologna[1]. But this is
not all. In later days, in the fourteenth and fifteenth centuries,
the canon law can be administered in England without in-
fluencing our common law. The king's justices, the practitioners in the king's court, are in all probability profoundly
ignorant of the Digest and the Decretals. The learned doctors
who practise before the episcopal tribunals are not so ignorant
of the temporal law, for it sets limits to their sphere of action;
still they would not profess themselves masters of it. But in
the twelfth, and even in the thirteenth, century this was not
so. Henry's greatest, his most lasting triumph in the legal
field was this, that he made the prelates of the church his
justices[2]. Nothing could be less true than that he quarrelled
with the whole mass of bishops and clergy. No doubt his [p. 112]
bestowal of the great places of the church upon men who had
earned, or were to earn, them by fiscal and justiciary labours,
has an evil side as well as a good. We are here concerned with
its good side. English law was administered by the ablest,
the best educated, men in the realm; nor only that, it was
administered by the selfsame men who were 'the judges
ordinary' of the church's courts, men who were bound to be, at
least in some measure, learned in the canon law. At one
moment Henry has three bishops for his 'archjusticiars[3].' The
climax is reached in Richard's reign. We can then see the
king's court as it sits day by day. Often enough it was
composed of the archbishop of Canterbury, two other bishops,
two or three archdeacons, two or three ordained clerks who
were going to be bishops and but two or three laymen[4]. The

---

[1] Glanvill, Prologus; Bracton, f. 1.
[2] See the famous passage in Diceto, i. 434.   [3] Diceto, i. 435.
[4] Thus on 16th July, 1195, the court consists of Hubert Walter, abp. of
Canterbury, Godfrey Lucy, bp. of Winchester, Richard FitzNeal, bp. of London
(author of the *Dialogus*), Gilbert Glanville, bp. of Rochester (a distinguished
scholar), Richard Barre, archd. of Ely, Ralph Foliot, archd. of Hereford,
William of Chimelli, archd. of Richmond, William of Ste Mère l'Église,
afterwards bp. of London, Geoffrey FitzPeter, Simon Pateshull, Osbert
FitzHervy, Richard Heriet.

majority of its members might at any time be called upon to hear ecclesiastical causes and learn the lessons in law that were addressed to them in papal rescripts. Blackstone's picture of a nation divided into two parties, 'the bishops and clergy' on the one side contending for their foreign jurisprudence, 'the nobility and the laity' on the other side adhering 'with equal pertinacity to the old common law' is not true[1]. It is by 'popish clergymen' that our English common law is converted from a rude mass of customs into an articulate system, and when the 'popish clergymen,' yielding at length to the pope's commands, no longer sit as the principal justices of the king's court, the creative age of our medieval law is over. Very characteristic of our thirteenth century is it that when there is talk of legitimation *per subsequens matrimonium,* the champion of the common law is a canon of St Paul's, William Raleigh, who is going to be a bishop and somewhat of a martyr, whose name is to be joined with the names of Anselm and Becket[2]. These royal clerks have two sides; they are clerks, but they are royal. It would not surprise us to discover that [p. 113] Martin Pateshull, justice of the Bench, had prohibited Martin Pateshull, archdeacon of Norfolk, from meddling with lay fee. But as archdeacon he was bound to have a decent acquaintance with the canon law, and as justice he could not forget what he knew as archdeacon. In the second half of Richard's reign Hubert Walter, the chief justiciar of England, who sat day by day at Westminster, was also the archbishop of Canterbury. A spiteful tongue has told us that he was no great Latinist, that he could be guilty of 'Tres sunt species cautionis, fidei-iussoriam, iuratoriam, pignoraticiam' and the like[3]; still, though we can suppose that this busy primate of England was not deeply read in the Decretum, he must have heard a great deal of Decretum and Code and Digest, even before his prolonged struggle with the Canterbury monks and their Pillius and their Ugolino.

We attribute to these clerical justices in general no more than a superficial acquaintance with the canon law, an acquaint-ance with its main principles and with its methods. But this

English law administered by ecclesiastics.

---

[1] Blackstone, Comm. i. 19.

[2] Rob. Grosseteste, Epist. pp. 76, 95.

[3] Giraldus Cambrensis, ii. 344–5, iii. 27–8. Giraldus afterwards retracted his charges; see i. 426.

much we must attribute to them, and it means a great deal. Let us conceive a man, whose notion of law and the logic of law is that which is displayed in the *Leges Henrici*, coming upon a glossed version of the Decretum, or still better upon some Summa such as that attributed to William of Longchamp. His whole conception of what a law-book, what a judgment should be, of how men should state law and argue about law, must undergo a radical change. Viewed therefore from one point, the effect produced on English law by its contact with the romano-canonical learning seems immeasurable, or measurable only by the distance that divides Glanvill's treatise from the *Leges Henrici*.

Nature of the cano- nical in- fluence.

Law, it may be said, is one thing and the expression of law another. But we can hardly, even in thought, divorce the matter of law from its form. Old traditional rules must lose their old meaning so soon as men attempt to weave them into a reasonable system. English law, more especially the English law of civil procedure, was rationalized under the influence of the canon law. Here and there we may note a plain case in which the one system has borrowed a whole set of rules from [p. 114] the other. Thus Glanvill tells us that the 'exceptions,' or as we should say the 'challenges,' which can be made against jurors are the same as the exceptions which can be made against witnesses in the courts Christian[1]. Here a whole chapter of law, which in the hands of the canonists is already becoming a bulky chapter, is borrowed. Such instances, however, are rare, and this instance is typical and instructive. Our English jurors are already very unlike, and are becoming more unlike, the canonical *testes*; and they will not be made any more like the canonical *testes* by the application to them of these rules about exceptions or challenges. Another mass of rules is borrowed. The elementary outlines of the science of pleading can only be expressed in terms familiar to civilians and canonists. In any case we must begin by saying that 'of exceptions (special pleas) some are dilatory, while others are peremptory[2].' But in our lay courts a distinctive form is given to these rules by the mode of trial which prevails there, the

---

[1] Glanv. ii. 12.

[2] Will. de Longo Campo (Caillemer, p. 25): 'Sunt enim exceptiones aliae perpetuae, aliae dilatoriae.' Bract. f. 399 b: 'Exceptionum quaedam sunt dilatoriae, quaedam peremptoriae.' This from Inst. 4. 13. 8.

trial by jury, and before long the canonist will hardly be able
to understand the English lawyer's doctrine of special pleas.
The assize of novel disseisin is suggested by the *actio spolii;*
but it is not the *actio spolii.* Our English law shows itself
strong enough to assimilate foreign ideas and convert them to
its own use. Of any wholesale 'reception' of Roman law there
is no danger. From the day at Clarendon onwards it is plain
that we have many *consuetudines* which must be maintained in
the teeth of *leges* and *canones.* The king's justices, more
especially those of them who are clerks, become interested
in the maintenance of a system that is all their own. From
time to time the more learned among them will try to attain
a foreign, an Italian, standard of accuracy and elegance; they
will borrow terms and definitions, they will occasionally borrow
rules; but there must be no dictation from without. The
imperial laws as such have no rights in England; the canon
law has its proper province and should know its place.

CHAPTER VI.

THE AGE OF GLANVILL.

THE reign of Henry II. is of supreme importance in the [p. 115]
history of our law, and its importance is due to the action of
the central power, to reforms ordained by the king[1]. Still it
was rather as an organizer and governor than as a legislator
that Henry was active. He issued no code; we may even
doubt whether he published any one new rule which we should
call a rule of substantive law; but he was for ever busy with
new devices for enforcing the law. Much of what he did, much
that was to determine the fate of our law in after ages, was
done in an informal fashion without the pomp of legislation.
A few words written or but spoken to his justices might
establish a new mode of procedure. There would be nothing
to be proclaimed to the world at large, for in theory there was
no change in the law; and yet very surely the whole law of
England was being changed both in form and in substance.
To this administrative character of his reforms we may ascribe
our lamentable lack of documentary evidence. New laws demanding the obedience of all his subjects would have been
preserved; but a mere instruction given to his justices might
not be embodied in any formal instrument and might well
escape the notice of the most punctual chronicler. And so it
came about that in a very short time many of the results of
his activity were regarded, not as the outcome of ordinances,

---

[1] As to the constitutional side of Henry's reforms we have little to add to
what has been said by Dr Stubbs in the Introduction to the Gesta Henrici, voL.
ii, the Select Charters, and the Constitutional History.

[p. 116] but as part and parcel of the traditional common law. A few ordinances or 'assizes,' those which seemed most important to his contemporaries, found their way into the texts of the chroniclers; some have been recovered of late years out of almost unique manuscripts; but we have every reason to fear that others have been irretrievably lost.

The first great legal monument of the reign is, however, no ordinance. In 1164, when the dispute with Becket was waxing hot, Henry held a council at Clarendon and there caused a 'recognition and record' to be made of certain of those customs, liberties and dignities that his ancestors had enjoyed. He called upon his nobles to declare the law of the realm as to the matters that were in debate between church and state. Their declaration of the king's customs was put into a written document, known to us as 'the Constitutions of Clarendon,' and to this the bishops were required to append their seals[1]. Henry was not legislating; according to his own theory he was playing a conservative part and relying upon prescriptive right. He demands a definition of the old law and then tenders this to the prelates as a *concordat*. Not long afterwards, probably in the first months of 1166, he was again holding an assembly at Clarendon and 'by the counsel of all his barons' he issued an assize which made great changes in the administration of the criminal law. Whether this was intended to be a permanent measure or was merely to serve as an instruction for the justices who were just being sent out to hold an eyre, we cannot say for certain, but it was sufficiently new and stringent to require the consent of the magnates. We have, however, some reason for believing that on this same occasion Henry took another step which was to be of equal importance with that which is recorded by the words of our extant 'Assize of Clarendon,' that he issued—it may be merely by way of instruction to his justices—an Assize of Novel Disseisin which in course of time was to mould the whole history of our civil procedure and to cut deeply into the body of our land law. The words of this ordinance or instruction have not come down to us; very soon they were concealed from view by the case-law which had grown up around them. In 1170 Henry instituted a grand inquiry into the conduct of the sheriffs whom he had

Constitutions of Clarendon.

Assize of Clarendon.

Inquest of Sheriffs.

---

[1] The document that we have professes only to give 'a certain part' of the customs that were 'recognized and recorded.'

removed from their offices. The instruction for this 'Inquest of [p.117]
Sheriffs' we have : it is an early example of those articles of inquest by which, as time goes on, the whole machinery of justice

Assize of
Northamp-
ton.
is subjected to examination and amendment. At Northampton
in 1176 a fresh set of instructions was given to the itinerant
justices; the Assize of Clarendon was to be enforced, but in a
yet severer form. A brief clause in this Assize of Northampton
seems to be the origin of the possessory action of 'mort d'ancestor' which takes its place beside the 'novel disseisin[1].' An
Assize of Arms from 1181, an Assize of the Forest from 1184,
an Ordinance regulating the collection of the Saladin Tithe
from 1188, an Assize of Bread of an uncertain date,—these
seem to complete the list of the ordinances that have come
down to us[2]. For the rest, we may draw some inferences from
the sheriffs' accounts recorded in the annual pipe rolls, from the
works of Glanvill and Richard FitzNeal and from the stories
told by the chroniclers[3].

Henry's in-
novations.
The jury
and the
original
writ.
If we try to sum up in a few words those results of Henry's
reign which are to be the most durable and the most fruitful, we may say that the whole of English law is centralized
and unified by the institution of a permanent court of professional judges, by the frequent mission of itinerant judges
throughout the land, by the introduction of the 'inquest' or
'recognition' and the 'original writ' as normal parts of the
machinery of justice. We must speak briefly of each of these
matters, and will begin with that which modern Englishmen
will be apt to think the most distinctive—the inquest, the
recognition, trial by jury[4].

Essence of
the jury.
The essence of the jury—if for a while we use the term
'jury' in the widest sense that can be given to it—seems to be
this : a body of neighbours is summoned by some public officer
to give upon oath a true answer to some question. That

---

[1] Ass. Northamp. c. 4.

[2] The documents are printed in the Select Charters, except the Assize of
Bread, for which see Cunningham, English Industry and Commerce, ed. 3, i. 568.

[3] The most striking testimonies to Henry's governmental activity are collected by Stubbs, Const. Hist. §147. Ralph Niger says: 'Nullo quaestu satiatus,
abolitis legibus antiquis, singulis annis novas leges quas assisas vocavit edidit.'

[4] In the main we accept the results attained by Brunner in his Entstehung
der Schwurgerichte. These have already been adopted by Stubbs, Const. Hist.
§164. See also Brunner, D. R. G. ii. 522–7; Thayer, Development of Trial by
Jury, Boston, 1896.

[p. 118] question may take many different forms : it may or it may not be one which has arisen in the course of litigation ; it may be a question of fact or a question of law, or again what we should now-a-days call a question of mixed fact and law. What are the customs of your district ? What rights has the king in your district ? Name all the landowners of your district and say how much land each of them has. Name all the persons in your district whom you suspect of murder, robbery or rape. Is Roger guilty of having murdered Ralph ? Whether of the two has the greater right to Blackacre, William or Hugh ? Did Henry disseise Richard of his free tenement in Dale ?— The jury of trial, the jury of accusation, the jury which is summoned where there is no litigation merely in order that the king may obtain information, these all spring from a common root. On the other hand, we have to distinguish the jury from a body of doomsmen, and also from a body of compurgators or other witnesses adduced by a litigant to prove his case. A verdict, even though it may cover the whole matter that is in dispute between the litigants, even though it may declare that William has a better right to Blackacre than has Hugh, differs essentially from a judgment, a doom adjudging the land to William. Even though the form of the verdict and its conclusive force be such that the judgment must follow as mere matter of course, still between the sworn verdict and the judgment there is a deep gulf[1].

If what we were seeking for were a court in which at the bidding of its president, of some national or royal officer, ealdorman or reeve, the inhabitants of a district, or some selected group, perhaps twelve, of such inhabitants, deemed the dooms, we should have no difficulty in discovering the origin of trial by jury. Everywhere we might find such courts, for during the earlier middle ages it is the exception, rather than the rule, that the judgment should be made by the lord or president of the court or by a group of professional justices. But what the jurors or recognitors of our twelfth century

Jurors, doomsmen and witnesses.

---

[1] When both the jury and the body of doomsmen are already established institutions, the transformation of doomsmen into jurors may be possible, and this transformation may actually have taken place in our manorial courts. See Select Pleas in Manorial Courts (Selden Society), pp. lxvi–lxviii ; Vinogradoff, Villainage, 370–1. But that the jury should have originally grown out of a body of doomsmen seems almost impossible.

deliver is no judgment; they come to 'recognize,' to declare, [p. 119]
the truth: their duty is, not *iudicia facere*, but *recognoscere
veritatem.* No less deep is the gulf which separates them from
witnesses adduced by a litigant. If all that we wanted were
witnesses, if all that we wanted were a fixed number of witnesses,
for example, twelve, there would really be no problem before
us. But the witnesses of the old Germanic folk-law differ in
two respects from our jurors or recognitors:—they are summoned by one of the litigants, and they are summoned to swear
to a set formula. The jurors are summoned by a public officer
and take an oath which binds them to tell the truth, whatever
the truth may be. In particular, they differ from oath-helpers
or compurgators. The oath-helper is brought in that he may
swear to the truth of his principal's oath. Normally he has been
chosen by the litigant whose oath he is to support, and even
when, as sometimes happens, the law, attempting to make the
old procedure somewhat more rational, compels a man to choose
his oath-helpers from among a group of persons designated by
his adversary or by his judges, still the chosen oath-helper has
merely the choice between swearing to a set formula ('The
oath is clean that *A. B.* hath sworn') or refusing to swear at all.
On the other hand, the recognitor must swear a promissory
oath; he swears that he will speak the truth whatever the truth
may be.

The jury a royal institution.   Then on the face of our English history we seem to see
that the jury is intimately connected with royal power. Not
only do the king and his officers make the freest use of it in
the form of 'an inquest *ex officio*' for the purpose of obtaining
any information that they want about royal rights, local
customs or other matters in which the king has an interest,
but, as a part of legal procedure civil and criminal, the jury
spreads outwards from the king's own court. To the last,
trial by jury has no place in the ordinary procedure of our old
communal courts.

Origin of the jury. The Frankish inquest.   The English jury has been so highly prized by Englishmen,
so often copied by foreigners, that its origin has been sought
in many different directions. At the present day, however,
there can be little doubt as to the quarter to which we ought to
look. We must look to the Frankish *inquisitio*, the prerogative
rights of the Frankish kings. Not to the ordinary procedure of
the Frankish courts; that, like the procedure of our own ancient [p. 120]

communal courts, knows but such antique modes of proof as the ordeal and the oath with oath-helpers. But the Frankish king has in some measure placed himself outside the formalism of the old folk-law, his court can administer an equity which tempers the rigour of the law and makes short cuts to the truth[1]. In particular, imitating, it may be, the procedure of the Roman *fiscus*[2], he assumes to himself the privilege of ascertaining and maintaining his own rights by means of an inquest. He orders that a group of men, the best and most trustworthy men of a district, be sworn to declare what lands, what rights, he has or ought to have in their district. He uses this procedure for many different purposes. He uses it in his litigation:—he will rely on the verdict of the neighbours instead of on battle or the ordeal. He uses it in order that he may learn how he is served by his subordinates:—the neighbours are required to say all that they know about the misconduct of the royal officers. He uses it in order that he may detect those grave crimes which threaten his peace:—the neighbours must say whether they suspect any of murders or robberies. The procedure which he employs in support of his own rights he can and does grant as a favour to others. In particular, he will concede to a church that its lands shall, like his demesne lands, be protected by inquest, and that the bishop, if his title be attacked, may put himself upon the verdict of his neighbours instead of abiding the risk of a judicial combat. All this we see in the Frankish empire of the ninth century; we see it in the Neustria which the Normans are invading. Then the deep darkness settles down. When it lifts we see in the new states that have formed themselves no central power capable of wielding the old prerogatives. For a long time to come the sworn inquest of neighbours will not be an utterly unknown thing in France; it will only be finally overwhelmed by the spread of the romano-canonical procedure. Even in Germany it will appear from time to time. Yet on the whole we may say that, but for the conquest of England, it would have perished and long ago have become a matter for the antiquary.

Such is now the prevailing opinion, and it has triumphed in The jury in [p. 121] this country over the natural disinclination of Englishmen to England.

---

[1] Brunner, Schwurgerichte, pp. 74–5.
[2] Ibid. p. 87.

admit that this 'palladium of our liberties' is in its origin not English but Frankish, not popular but royal. It is certain that of the inquest of office or of the jury of trial the Anglo-Saxon dooms give us no hint, certain also that by no slow process of evolution did the doomsman or the oath-helper become a recognitor. The only doubt that there can be is as to the jury of accusation, the jury as an organ of *fama publica.*

The twelve thegns.

This species of the inquest is that which is the most likely to have penetrated beyond the limits of the empire, for within those limits it was adopted by the church for her own purposes. Just as the king might collect charges of crime, so the church might collect charges of sin. In the early part of the tenth century the canonist Regino of Prüm describes the bishop holding his synod, selecting a number of trustworthy men from among the assembled laity, administering to them an oath that they will tell the truth and conceal nothing for love or hate, reward or kinship, asking them to report their suspicions of their neighbours, and compelling to the ordeal or to compurgation those against whom bad tales are told[1]. It would not be wonderful if this procedure spread from the Frankish church to the English. In the days of Dunstan and Oswald the English church was borrowing ideas and institutions from the Frankish. But we have no direct proof that at any time before the Conquest the English church did use this system of sworn communal accusation. There is, however, one law which must cause some difficulty. It is a law of Æthelred the Unready, published, so it would seem, in the year 997 and applicable only to the Danish district[2]. In it we read how a moot is to be held in every wapentake, and how the twelve eldest thegns are to go out with the reeve and to swear upon the relic that he puts into their hands that they will accuse no innocent and conceal no guilty man. Certainly this looks like a jury of accusation; but the context will make us doubt whether we [p. 122]

---

[1] Regino Prumiensis de Eccles. Discipl. lib. 2, cap. 2 (Migne, Patrol. cxxxii. 282). Stubbs, Const. Hist. i. p. 662, remarks that the *iuratores synodi* 'do not present,' but 'only reply to the inquiry of the visiting bishop.' But there is no contrast here, for the English jurors by their presentments only reply to inquiries addressed to them by the royal officer. Cp. Burchardi Wormaciensis Decreta, lib. i. cap. 91 (Patrol. cxl. 571).

[2] Æthelred, III. 3. As to the Danish character of this ordinance see Schmid, Gesetze, p. li; Brunner, Schwurgerichte, p. 403; K. Maurer, Krit. Ueberschau, v. 389; Steenstrup, Danelag, p. 209.

have here a law of any generality[1]. There seem, however, to
be good reasons for believing that some of the Scandinavian
nations came by a route of their own to something that was
very like the jury[2]. The investigation of this matter is made
the more difficult by the comparatively recent date of the
Scandinavian law-books. No doubt there is here a field for
research, but it seems unlikely that any new discovery will
disturb the derivation of our English from the Frankish inquests. We can not say *a priori* that there is only one
possible origin for the jury, we can not even say that England
was unprepared for the introduction of this institution; but that
the Norman duke brought it with him as one of his prerogatives
can hardly be disputed[3].

Hardly had England been conquered, before the sworn
inquest of neighbours appeared as part of the system of government and royal justice. The great fiscal record known to us as
Domesday Book was compiled out of the verdicts of juries[4].
The king makes use of the same engine in his own litigation;
he can bestow the right to make use of it upon favoured
churches[5]; he can direct its employment in any particular
case[6]. We see too a close connexion between the jury of trial
and the protection of possession, a connexion which is to
become prominent hereafter. In the earliest case in which
there is to our knowledge anything that could be called a trial
by jury, the Conqueror directs his justiciars, Archbishop
Lanfranc, the count of Mortain and the bishop of Coutances,
to summon to one place the moots of several shires to hear a
plea between the abbot of Ely and divers other persons.
Certain of the English who know what lands were held by the
[p. 123] church of Ely on the day of the Confessor's death are to declare

The inquest in the Norman age.

---

[1] Brunner, Schwurgerichte, 402–3.

[2] K. Maurer, Das Beweisverfahren nach deutschen Rechten, Krit. Ueberschau, v. 332, 374.

[3] von Amira, Paul's Grundriss der German. Philologie II. ii. p. 198, contends
that the jury appears independently (1) in the Frankish king's court, (2) the
Danish king's court, and (3) the Icelandic courts.

[4] D. B. iv. 497 (Liber Eliensis.)

[5] See *e.g.* Henry II.'s charter for Rochester, Monast. i. 177: ʻOmnes
minutas terras...confirmo in perpetuum...in tantum et tam pleniter sicut proprii
ministri mei exquirere deberent.ʼ This should be compared with the Frankish
and Norman privileges. Brunner, Schwurgerichte, 92–95, 238–45.

[6] The principal cases are collected by Palgrave, Commonwealth, ii. p. clxxvi,
and Bigelow, Placita Anglo-Normannica.

their knowledge upon oath. This will be a verdict, not a judgment. The justices are to restore to the church, not all the lands that she had at the date thus fixed, but only such of them as no one claims under the Conqueror. A particular question, a question about possession at a given moment of time, is thus singled out as one that should be decided by a sworn inquest of neighbours[1]. Had the abbot of St Augustin's a ship free to cross the sea on the day when the king last went abroad? How many pigs free of pannage had the abbot of Abingdon in the time of Henry I.? Did this land belong of old to Bridton or to Bridport?—Such and such like are the questions about which verdicts are taken. Still throughout the Norman period trial by jury, the introduction of an inquest into the procedure of a law-suit, remains an exceptional thing. The *Leges Henrici* know nothing of it; the *iudices* who are there mentioned are not recognitors but doomsmen. Of the accusing jury on the other hand faint traces are to be found. We certainly cannot say that it was never used, but we read very little about it[2].

Henry's use of the inquest.

Under Henry II. the exceptional becomes normal. The king concedes to his subjects as a royal boon his own prerogative procedure. This is done bit by bit, now for this class of cases and now for that. It is probable that while not yet king he had done something of the same kind in Normandy[3].

The assize utrum.

It is by no means unlikely that the class of disputes which was the first to be submitted to a jury as a matter of common practice was one in which the claims of the church came into collision with the claims of the state. In the twelfth century the church was asserting and establishing the principle that all litigation about land that had been given by way of alms to

---

[1] Hamilton, Inquisitio Com. Cantab. p. xviii.

[2] On several occasions *iuratores* are mentioned on the Pipe Roll of 31 Henry I. See also Brunner, Schwurgerichte, pp. 465–6.

[3] Brunner, pp. 301–4. As to Scotland, there is no doubt that from the time of David I. onwards the kings made use of the inquest procedure. One passage in the laws ascribed to David (c. 35) speaks as though a whole system of writs of novel disseisin and mort d'ancestor was already in existence; but the mss. in which this passage is found seem to be few and late, and it is hardly in keeping with its surroundings. On the other hand, certain passages which point to inquests which decide subordinate questions in criminal cases (c. 6) may well be ancient. On the whole we take it that the jury has much the same history in Scotland and in England: it spreads outwards from the king; it is an 'assize,' an institution established by ordinance.

[p. 124] God and the saints should come before her courts. This principle was hardly disputed in Stephen's day; but of course in many cases the question would arise—'Is this land alms or is it lay fee?' To allow the case to go for good and all either to the temporal or to the spiritual forum, would be to beg this preliminary question. Church and state are at issue, and neither should be judge in its own cause. The voice of the countryside about this question—which can be regarded as a question of fact, 'Lay fee or alms?'—may be listened to; it comes, so to speak, from the outside and will be impartial. At any rate, Henry in the Constitutions of Clarendon claimed as one of the ancient customs of the realm that such a question should be decided by the oath of an inquest in the presence of his justiciar[1]. In this as in other instances we have some evidence that the king's claims were founded on past history. A story comes to us from the abbey of St Albans which describes a lawsuit of Stephen's day in which the question 'Lay fee or alms?' was submitted to a jury charged to tell the truth both by the king and by the bishop of the diocese[2]. Be this as it may, already in 1164 Henry asserted that a procedure which in after days was known as the *assisa utrum* was and ought to be a normal part of the machinery of justice. A 'recognition' by twelve lawful men was to decide whether (*utrum*) the land in question was alms or lay fee.

Some two years later, perhaps at the council held at Clarendon in the first months of 1166, Henry took a far more important step. He issued an ordinance and instituted a procedure: ordinance and procedure alike were known as the assize of novel disseisin (*assisa novae disseisinae*). At that council was published the edict known as the Assize of Clarendon, which deals with criminal matters and which served as instructions for the justices who were being sent out on a great eyre throughout the land. We fix this date as that of the assize of novel disseisin, because the next pipe roll, a roll which records the abundant profits reaped by the itinerant justices in the field of criminal law, gives us also our first

The assize of novel disseisin.

---

[1] Const. Clarend. c. 9.

[2] Gesta Abbatum, i. 113-5. The story is told with great particularity. In all probability the substance of it is true and comes from Stephen's reign; but apparently some mistakes have been made about the names of the various persons concerned in it, as a discussion of dates would show.

tidings of men being amerced for disseisin 'against the king's [p.125] assize'; from that moment onwards we get such tidings year by year[1].

Import of the novel disseisin.

Of this ordinance, which was in the long run to prove itself one of the most important laws ever issued in England, we have not the words. Bracton tells us that wakeful nights were spent over it[2], and we may well believe him, for the principle that was to be enforced was new and startling. It was this:— If one person is disseised, that is, dispossessed, of his free tenement unjustly and without a judgment, he is to have a remedy by royal writ: a jury is to be summoned; in the presence of the king's justices it is to answer this simple question about seisin and disseisin; if it gives the plaintiff a verdict he is to be restored to his possession. We may state the matter in two other ways: by the one we may show what is being done for our private, by the other what is being done for our public law. (1) Possession or seisin, as something quite distinct from ownership or best right, is to be protected by an unusually rapid remedy. (2) The seisin of a free tenement, no matter of what lord it be holden, is protected by the king. Hereafter in connexion with property law we may speak of the private side of this new remedy and of its relation to the *actio spolii* of the canon law; here we have but to notice the great principle of public law that the king has laid down. The ownership of land may be a matter for the feudal courts: the king himself will protect by royal writ and inquest of neighbours every seisin of a free tenement. It is a principle which in course of time can be made good even against kings. The most famous words of Magna Carta will enshrine the formula of the novel disseisin[3].

---

[1] Pipe Roll, 12 Hen. II. p. 65: 'pro dissaisina super assisam Regis'; 13 Hen. II. p. 134: 'pro dissaisina facta super assisam Regis'; 14 Hen. II. *passim*. No doubt there are writs of earlier date which in many respects resemble the writ of novel disseisin; see Bigelow, Placita, pp. 128, 130, 169, 170; Howlett, Chronicles of Stephen etc. vol. iii. p. xxxvii; but we cannot find anything which shows that the general ordinance or 'assize' was of earlier date than 1166.

[2] Bracton, f. 164 b: 'de beneficio principis succurritur ei per recognitionem assisae novae disseisinae multis vigiliis excogitatam et inventam.'

[3] Charter, 1217, c. 35: 'Nullus liber homo...dissaisietur de libero tenemento suo...nisi per legale iudicium parium suorum vel [=et] per legem terrae.' Compare the formula of the assize 'Si B. iniuste et sine iudicio dissaisivit A. de libero tenemento suo.'

At some time or another in his reign Henry went further The grand assize.
than this. He decreed that no man need answer for his free
[p. 126] tenement without royal writ[1]. He decreed also that in a
proprietary action for land, an action proceeding in the feudal
court, the defending party, the 'tenant' as he was called, might
have the action removed into the king's court and the whole
question of right determined by the verdict of neighbours. In
this case the inquest bears the name of 'the grand assize[2].' It
is a far more solemn affair than the assize of novel disseisin and
it speaks to the question of best right. The term 'grand assize'
would seem to point to some great ordinance; but the thought
cannot but occur to us that the three principles which we have
here stated may have been announced, and that the institutions
which were to maintain them may have been fashioned, at one
and the same time. In every case we see the royal protection
of possession. No one is to be disseised of his free tenement
unjustly and without a judgment; no one is to be disseised of
his free tenement even by a judgment unless he has been
summoned to answer by a royal writ; no one is to be forced
to defend his seisin of a free tenement by battle[3]. The
ordinance that instituted the grand assize was a one-sided
measure, a protection of possessors. The claimant had to offer
battle; the possessor, if he pleased, might refuse battle and put
himself upon the grand assize.

Then to all seeming the council held at Northampton in The assize of mort d'ancestor.
1176 instituted a second possessory assize, the assize of mort
d'ancestor (*assisa de morte antecessoris*[4]). Apparently we have
the words whereby this was accomplished, though the practice
of the courts soon left those words behind it. The principle of

---

[1] Glanvill, xii. 2, 25; Brunner, Schwurgerichte, 411.

[2] Glanvill, ii. 7.

[3] Bracton, f. 112: 'Et sicut non debet sine brevi respondere, ita nec debet
sine iudicio disseisiri.' Ibid. f. 161: 'Nemo debet sine iudicio disseisiri de
libero tenemento suo, nec respondere sine precepto domini Regis nec sine brevi.'
Rot. Pat. 76 : King John says to the people of Ireland, 'Nolumus...quod aliquis
...vos possit disseisire de liberis tenementis vestris iniuste aut sine iudicio, nec
quod in placitum ponamini per alicuius breve nisi per nostrum vel iusticiarii
nostri.' See Manorial Pleas (Selden Soc.), p. lv. We know from Glanvill (ii. 19)
that the grand assize was established by a written ordinance : 'poena autem
in hac assisa temere iurantium ordinata est et regali institutioni eleganter
inserta.'

[4] Ass. Northampt. c. 4.

the novel disseisin is that one man, even though he claims and [p. 127] actually has the ownership of the land, is not to turn another man out of possession without first obtaining a judgment. The principle of the mort d'ancestor is that if a man has died in seisin, that is, possession of a tenement, and was not holding it as a mere life-tenant, his heir is entitled to obtain possession of it as against every other person, no matter that such person claims and actually has a better right to the land than the dead man had. Such a right, if it exists, must be asserted in an action: it is not to be asserted by 'self-help,' by a seizure of the vacant tenement. Another and a heavy blow is thus struck at feudal justice, for the defendant in an assize of mort d'ancestor is very likely to be the dead tenant's lord, who will have seized the lands upon some pretext of making good his seignorial claims. Another use is found for the inquest of neighbours, for the questions whether the dead man died seised and whether the claimant is his heir will be decided by verdict.

The assize of darrein presentment. Scarcely less important than litigation about land is litigation about the advowsons of churches. Henry has here asserted as against the church that such litigation belongs to a temporal forum, and as against the feudatories that it belongs to the king's own court[1]. A proprietary action for an advowson must be begun in the king's court by royal writ, 'writ of right of advowson'; the claimant must offer battle; his adversary may choose between battle and the grand assize. Then at some time or another during his reign Henry gave a possessory action, the assize of darrein presentment (*assisa de ultima presentatione*), which stands to the writ of right of advowson in somewhat the same relation as that in which the novel disseisin stands to the writ of right for land. If the church is vacant and two persons are quarrelling about the advowson, it is very necessary that some provisional, some possessory judgment should be given. Especially necessary is this after the Lateran Council of 1179, for should the church remain vacant for a few months the diocesan bishop will fill up the vacancy[2]. The principle of the new assize is, simply stated, this: 'He who presented last time, let him present this time also; but this without prejudice to any question of right.' An inquest of

---

[1] Const. Clarend. c. 1.
[2] Gesta Henrici, i. 233; Hoveden, ii. 184.

[p. 128] neighbours is summoned to declare who it was that presented the last parson[1].

Thus the sworn inquest begins to make its way into our ordinary civil procedure. In a proprietary action for land or for advowson, the 'tenant,' the passive party, may, rejecting battle, 'put himself upon the grand assize of our lord the king,' and an inquest will then declare who has the better right. In four other cases a plaintiff may begin proceedings by obtaining a royal writ, which will direct that an inquest shall answer a particular question formulated in the writ. These four cases are the subject-matter of the four petty assizes, (1) the assize *utrum*, (2) the novel disseisin, (3) the mort d'ancestor, (4) the darrein presentment. It is probable that for a short while a few other cases were met in a similar fashion; but in a little time we have these four and only these four petty assizes. Only in these four instances does the writ which is the first step in the procedure, 'the original writ,' direct the empanelling of an inquest. Trial by jury, in the narrowest sense of that term, trial by jury as distinct from trial by an assize, slowly creeps in by another route. The principle from which it starts is simply this, that if in any action the litigants by their pleadings come to an issue of fact, they may agree to be bound by the verdict of a jury and will be bound accordingly. In course of time the judges will in effect drive litigants into such agreements by saying, 'You must accept your opponent's offer of a jury or you will lose your cause'; but in theory the jury only comes in after both parties have consented to accept its verdict. An assize, other than a grand assize, is summoned by the original writ; it is summoned at the same time that the defendant is summoned and before his story has been heard; a jury is not summoned until the litigants in their pleadings have agreed to take the testimony of 'the country' about some matter of fact. In course of time the jury, which has its roots in the fertile ground of consent, will grow at the expense of the assize, which has sprung from the stony soil of ordinance. Even an *assisa* when summoned will often be turned into a jury (*vertitur in juratam*) by the consent of the parties. But still trial by jury, if we use this term in a large sense, and neglect some technical details, is introduced by the ordinances [p. 120] of Henry II. as part of the usual machinery of civil justice.

Assize and jury.

---

[1] Glanvill, xiii. 18, 19.

Already before the end of his reign it fills a large space in Glanvill's text-book. The old modes of proof are not abolished; proof by battle we shall have with us until 1819[1], proof by oath-helpers until 1833[2]; but from this moment onwards they are being pushed into the background.

The system of original writs. Closely connected with the introduction of trial by inquest is the growth of that system of original writs which is soon to become the ground-plan of all civil justice. For a long time past the king at the instance of complainants has issued writs, which either bade their adversaries appear in the royal court to answer the complaint, or else committed their causes to the care of the sheriff or of the feudal lord and commanded that right should be done to them in the county court or the seignorial court. Such writs were wont to specify with some particularity the subject-matter of the complaint. The sheriff, for example, was not merely told to entertain a suit which the abbot of Abingdon was bringing against the men of Stanton: he was told to do full right to the abbot in the matter of a sluice which, so the abbot alleged, had been broken by the men of Stanton. As the king's interference becomes more frequent and more normal, the work of penning such writs will naturally fall into the hands of subordinate officials, who will follow precedents and keep blank forms. A classification of writs will be the outcome; some will be granted more or less as a matter of course, will be *brevia de cursu*, writs of course; those which are directed to a feudal lord will be distinguished from those which are directed to a sheriff; those which bid the sheriff do justice, from those which bid him summon the defendant to the king's own court; those which relate to the ownership of land from those which relate to debts. But the introduction of the possessory assizes gives to this system of writs a peculiar definiteness and rigidity. The new actions have a new procedure appropriate to them and are governed by carefully worded formulas. Thus the first writ issued in an assize of novel disseisin commands the sheriff to summon an inquest in order that one precise question may be answered:— Did *B* unjustly and without a judgment disseise *A* of his free [p. 130] tenement in *X* since the king's last journey into Normandy? At countless points an action thus begun will differ from

---

[1] Stat. 59 Geo. III. c. 46.
[2] Stat. 3 & 4 Will. IV. c. 42, sec. 13.

a proprietary action for land begun by a writ of right; both
of them will differ from an action of debt, and even between
the several possessory assizes many distinctions must be drawn,
in particular as to the number of 'essoins,' excuses for non-
appearance, that the litigants may proffer. Thus before the
end of Henry's reign we must already begin to think of
royal justice—and this is becoming by far the most important
kind of justice—as consisting of m⁻ y various commodities
each of which is kept in a different r ptacle. Between these
the would-be litigant must make his choice; he must choose
an appropriate writ and with it an appropriate form of action.
These wares are exposed for sale; perhaps some of them may
already be had at fixed prices, for others a bargain must be
struck. As yet the king is no mere vendor, he is a manu-
facturer and can make goods to order. The day has not yet
come when the invention of new writs will be hampered
by the claims of a parliament. But still in Glanvill's day the
officina iustitiae has already a considerable store of ready-made
wares and English law is already taking the form of a commentary upon writs.

The accusing jury also has become part of the ordinary The
mechanism of justice. The first definite tidings that we get of accusing jury.
it are somewhat puzzling. To all seeming Henry insisted, first
for Normandy in the year 1159, and then for England in the
year 1164, that the ecclesiastical courts ought to make use of
this institution. Laymen ought not to be put to answer in
those courts upon a mere unsworn suggestion of ill fame.
Either someone should stand forth and commit himself to a
definite accusation, or else the ill fame should be sworn to by
twelve lawful men of the neighbourhood summoned for that
purpose by the sheriff: in other words, the ecclesiastical judge
ought not to proceed *ex officio* upon private suggestions[1].

---

[1] Continuatio Beccensis, Howlett's edition of Robert of Torigny, p. 327:
'Rex Anglorum Henricus ad Natale Domini [1159] fuit apud Falesiam, et leges
instituit ut nullus decanus aliquam personam accusaret sine testimonio vicinorum circummanentium, qui bonae vitae fama laudabiles haberentur.' Const.
Clarend. c. 6: 'Laici non debent accusari nisi per certos et legales accusatores
et testes in praesentia episcopi...Et si qui tales fuerint qui culpantur, quod non
velit vel non audeat aliquis eos accusare, vicecomes requisitus ab episcopo faciet
iurare duodecim legales homines de vicineto, seu de villa, coram episcopo, quod
inde veritatem secundum conscientiam suam manifestabunt.' With this sho⁻ld
be compared Magna Carta, 1215, c. 38: 'Nullus ballivus ponat de cetero aliquem
ad legem simplici loquela sua, sine testibus fidelibus ad hoc inductis.'

Henry seems to be forcing this rule upon reluctant prelates, [p. 131]
and at the same time to be asserting that it is an ancient
rule. From this we may perhaps infer that the synodal jury,
described to us by Regino of Prüm, had been known in
Normandy—it may be, in England also—but that of late it
had been thrust aside by a laxer procedure which was less fair
to the laity. This part of the story must remain very obscure[1].
However in 1166 the accusing jury becomes prominent. In
every county twelve men of every hundred and four men of
every township are to swear that they will make true answer to
the question whether any man is reputed to have been guilty of
murder, robbery, larceny, or harbouring criminals since the
king's coronation. Those who are thus accused must go to the
ordeal. Even if they are successful there, even, that is to say,
though the judgment of God is in their favour, they must
abjure the realm. Ten years later at Northampton a sharper
edge was given to this new weapon; forgery and arson were
added to the list of crimes for which inquisition was to be
made; the criminal who failed at the ordeal was to lose a hand
beside that foot of which the earlier ordinance deprived him.
The new ordinance was to endure during the king's good
pleasure. Such inquests were to be taken before the itinerant
justices of the king; they were also to be taken by the sheriffs,
and here we may see the origin of those inquisitions into crime
which in later days the sheriff makes twice a year as he takes [p. 132]
his ' turn ' through the hundreds[2]. Every time that the justices
are sent on their rounds the king can at pleasure add to the

---

[1] In or about 1246 Robert Grosseteste made strict inquest as to the con-
tinence and morals of the laity. The king issued a prohibition to the effect
that he was not to take recognitions upon oath save in matrimonial or testamentary causes. See Prynne, Records, ii. 704-6. Matthew Paris, Chron. Maj.
iv. 579, speaks as though the bishop's proceedings were deemed both novel and
harsh. The writs preserved by Prynne tell the same tale. From this we may
infer that, in consequence of Becket's rejection of the Constitutions of Clarendon,
the church lost a right offered to her by Henry, namely, a right to demand that
the civil power should provide her with synodal juries. For the future she had
to rely upon her own powers, and the state seems even to have opposed such
endeavours as were made by Grosseteste to use the procedure of communal
accusation as a general means of detecting sins. As a matter of fact, this
procedure seems to have been chiefly used with reference either to purely
ecclesiastical matters, such as the repair of churches and attendance at church,
or to those sins of the flesh which admittedly lay within the province of
ecclesiastical jurisdiction.

[2] Select Pleas in Manorial Courts (Selden Soc.), pp. xxvii.–xxxviii.

list of questions that they are to put to the jurors; in the next century that list, the articles of the eyre (*capitula itineris*), will be long and will be constantly growing longer. Closely connected with the discovery of crimes is the ascertainment of the king's rights. Criminal justice is one source of revenue, but there are others, and the inquest may be used for their detection. From the verdicts of local juries the king collects whatever information he may require about his demesne lands, his feudal rights, the receipts of his sheriffs, the misconduct of his officers.

There can be no doubt that one result of these various measures was to increase at a rapidly accelerating rate the amount of judicial business that was transacted in the king's name. The functions of his court were changed and a corresponding change in its structure became necessary. It was no longer to be an extraordinary tribunal, a court for great men, for great causes, for matters that concerned the king; it was to become an ordinary tribunal for the whole realm. Many difficulties, however, meet us if we attempt to define the structural changes[1]. In the first place, we are tempted to use terms which are more precise than those that were current in the twelfth century. In particular we are wont to speak of *the* Curia Regis without remembering that the definite article is not in our documents. Any court held in the king's name by the king's delegates is Curia Regis. Thus the institution of what in course of time will be a new tribunal, a Court of King's Bench or a Court of Common Pleas, may be found in some small rearrangement, some petty technical change, which at the moment passes unnoticed. In the second place, the form which his court shall take, the mode in which it shall do justice, these are matters for the king; he is very free to decide them from day to day as he pleases, and this by a few spoken words. In the third place, we have direct evidence that Henry tried experiment after experiment[2]. He was keenly interested in the work of justice and learnt from year to year the lessons that experience taught him. Therefore it is but too possible that we may give undue weight to this or that passage in a chronicle. However, from the year 1178 we hear that the king

Structure of the king's court.

[p. 133]

---

[1] Stubbs, Introduction to Gesta Henrici, vol. ii., has discussed this matter at length. See also Round, Feudal England, 50J.

[2] Diceto, i. 434–5.

has chosen five men, two clerks and three laymen, who are not to depart from the king's court but are to hear all the complaints of the kingdom; questions that they can not decide are to be reserved for the king and his wise men[1]. We here see the definite selection of a small number of men who are to do justice habitually. The court that they are to hold is to be a permanent and a central court; but a reserve of justice is to remain in the king and his councillors. It is probable that we have here a measure of great permanent importance. From the following years we begin to get records which seem to put before us a tribunal which in the main is like that here described. It sits term after term; usually at Westminster, often at the exchequer. It is constituted by the king's most trusted advisers. There is Ranulf Glanvill who in 1180 became chief justiciar. There are the three famous clerks who have served Henry well during the fierce strife with Becket, Richard of Ilchester, now bishop of Winchester, John of Oxford, now bishop of Norwich, Geoffrey Ridel, now bishop of Ely. There is the treasurer, Richard son of Nigel, who is to be bishop of London. A little later there is Hubert Walter, who is rising to greatness. Some laymen there will be; but earls and powerful barons are conspicuously absent. We can not fix the number of the justices. Sometimes ten or twelve will be mentioned. But the court seems to have, as it were, a fringe; the chief justiciar, the treasurer, two or three bishops, will usually be sitting, while others come and go; some of them may be away upon circuits; others who are named may be not justices, but chamberlains or sewers; and the king is still making experiments, trying now one man and now another[2].

The central court.

However, we may say that before the end of the reign there is a permanent central tribunal of persons expert in the administration of justice—of sworn judges[3]. It can be distinguished from the courts held by the itinerant justices, for, [p. 134] though every such court is *curia Regis,* this is *capitalis curia*

---

[1] Gesta Henrici, ii. 207.

[2] See Eyton, Itinerary of Henry II. A good many 'final concords' from the last years of the reign are gradually being brought to light. See Round, The Earliest Fines, E. H. R. xii. 293.

[3] Mapes, De Nugis, p. 241: 'Habemus et nos censores sub serenissimo iudice, quorum iustitiam domini sui iustitia remordet, quia iurati coram ipso quod aequitate servata censebunt ut praedicti tres Plutonis arguti iudices.'

Regis[1]. It can be distinguished from the exchequer, for, though
it often sits at the exchequer, and though its principal justices
will be also the principal barons of the exchequer[2], it has a
seal of its own and may well sit away from Westminster,
while the fiscal business could hardly be transacted elsewhere[3]. It can be distinguished from those great councils of
prelates and nobles that the king holds from time to time;
questions too high for it are to be reserved for such councils[4].
Probably it is already getting the name of 'the bench' and
its justices are 'justices residing at the bench[5].' Though it is
curia Regis and *capitalis curia Regis* it is not necessarily held
coram ipso Rege. Apparently the writs that summon litigants
before it, bid them appear 'before the king or before his
justices,' that is to say, before the king if he happens to be in
England and doing justice, and if not, then before his justices[6].
No doubt when the king is in this country he will sometimes
preside in court, but whether the justices will then follow the
king in his progresses, we can not say for certain; as a matter
of fact during the last eight years of his reign the king's visits
to England were neither frequent nor long. Westminster seems
to be becoming the home of this tribunal; but as yet all its
arrangements are easily altered.

The visitation of the counties by itinerant justices has Itinerant
become systematic. From the early years of the reign we justices.
hear of pleas held on circuit by Richard Lucy the chief justiciar,
by Henry of Essex the constable, and by Thomas Becket the
chancellor. In 1166 the assize of Clarendon was enforced by
a party of justices headed by Richard Lucy and Earl Geoffrey
of Mandeville. In 1168 Richard of Ilchester, Guy the dean of
Waltham, William Basset and Reginald Warenne visited most
of the counties. In 1175 the north and east were perambulated
by Ranulf Glanvill and Hugh of Cressi, the south and west by
William of Lanvallei and Thomas Basset, while the king himself
seems to have been journeying with other justices in his suite[7].
[p. 135] In 1176 to execute the assize of Northampton eighteen justices

---

[1] Glanvill, viii. 5. A fine levied before the itinerant justices always purports
to be 'finalis concordia facta in curia domini Regis.' Such at least is the case
in later times; but see Round, E. H. R. xii. 297.

[2] Dialogus, lib. i., c. 4–6.   [3] Ibid. lib. i., c. 15.
[4] Gesta Henrici, ii. 207–8.   [5] Madox, Exchequer, i. 798–801.
[6] This is the usual form throughout Glanvill's book.
[7] Round, Feudal England, 513.

were employed and the country was divided into six circuits; in 1179 twenty-one justices were employed and the country was divided into four circuits; indeed from 1176 onwards hardly a year went by without there being a visitation of some part of England. These itinerant justices seem to have been chiefly employed in hearing the pleas of the crown (for which purpose they were equipped with the power of obtaining accusations from the local juries) and in entertaining some or all of the new possessory actions. The court that they held was, as already said, *curia Regis*; but it was not *capitalis curia Regis*, and probably their powers were limited by the words of a temporary commission. They were not necessarily members of the central court, and they might be summoned before it to bear record of their doings[1]; still it was usual that each party of justices should include some few members of the permanent tribunal. Also the counties were frequently visited for fiscal purposes, justices or barons of the exchequer being sent there to assess aids and tallages, while the chief justice of the forest often traversed the land and afflicted the people.

Cases in the king's court. No judicial rolls of the reign have come down to us, but during the last years of it such records were being compiled[2]. For our knowledge of what went on in the courts we have still to look to annalists and biographers, and they are apt to give us not the usual but the extraordinary. We dare not, for example, draw many general inferences about the constitution and procedure of the king's court from that famous scene in the castle of Northampton, in which Henry and Becket were the principal actors. We see, however, that, even though the king was angry and was striving to crush one who had become his enemy, he did not venture to pass judgment. To find the judgment at the king's request was the function of the assembled prelates and nobles, or, if the prelates would not aid in the work, then the lay barons would do it. Even the duty of pronouncing the judgment was delegated; it was committed to the justiciar, the Earl of Leicester[3].

Scenes in court. Another life-like, if not impartial, story tells of a great

---

[1] Glanvill, viii. 5.

[2] Select Pleas of the Crown (Selden Soc.), pp. xxvi–xxviii. The rolls of the itinerant justices spoken of in the Dialogus, lib. ii. c. 1, may have been mere lists of amercements.

[3] William FitzStephen (Materials for Life of Becket, iii.), p. 67.

[p. 136] suit between the abbot of Battle and the bishop of Chichester,
another of a similar suit between the abbot of St Albans
and the bishop of Lincoln. In both cases abbatial privileges
were urged against episcopal rights; in both the bishop
practically lost his cause; but in both papal claims were
involved, and the king, who had no mind to break with the
pope, succeeded in bringing about what was in form a
compromise; in neither case therefore was a judgment pronounced. In the one[1], which occurred in 1157, the king sat
in the chapter house of the monks at Colchester. Around him
were the two archbishops, three bishops, his chancellor (Becket),
the two chief justiciars (the Earl of Leicester and Richard
Lucy) and several other barons, while the hall was filled by no
small multitude of the people[2]. At times, it would seem, the
king retired with a few chosen councillors, the chancellor, the
two justiciars, the constables of England and Normandy, a
chamberlain and a clerk, and gave a private audience to one of
the parties. Some of the principal members of the court had
openly and warmly taken sides before the discussion began.
The justiciar Lucy was the abbot's brother, and played the part
of an advocate rather than of a judge; the chancellor also had
espoused the abbot's cause, and they and other members of the
court took counsel with the abbot while the case was proceeding. The dispute between the abbot of St Albans and the
bishop of Lincoln[3] was heard by the king in the chapel of St
Catherine at Westminster in the year 1163. He was surrounded
by the prelates and nobles; no less than thirteen bishops were
present. But again we see the king retiring to consult with a
much smaller body, which consisted of the Earl of Leicester,
Richard de Hommet the constable of Normandy, and that
expert clerk, Richard of Ilchester. Along with these he carefully perused the St Albans charters, and showed, so the monks
said, a wisdom comparable to that of Solomon[4], for he declared
that the unsealed land-books of the Anglo-Saxon kings were
as good as sealed since they were confirmed by a sealed charter
of Henry I. In vain another of the king's confidential clerks,

---

[1] Palgrave, Commonwealth, vol. ii. p. xxviii.
[2] Ibid. p. xlvii. : 'populique insuper multitudine non modica.'
[3] Gesta Abbatum, i. 150.
[4] Ibid. 151 : 'Quod in tam iuvene rege non minori sapientiae deputatum est
quod dixit, quam iudicium Salomonis inter meretrices altercantes.'

Geoffrey Ridel, disturbed this private session, and suggested [p. 137] defects in the abbot's title; the king turned him out of the room. The public session was resumed; the king delivered an opinion unfavourable to the bishop—'privileges prevail against prescription[1]'—but advised a compromise; the bishop confessed the immunity of the abbey and got some land in return for the confession. On another occasion the king sitting at Clarendon heard a suit between the abbot of Battle and Gilbert de Balliol[2]. The justiciar, Richard Lucy, was present, but Henry took a prominent part in the discussion, maintaining the validity of the royal charters produced by the abbot and swearing by God's eyes that such charters cost him dear. Still the judgment was given by the unanimous consent of the whole court. Short of proclaiming his own will to be the judgment of his court, there was little that he could not or would not do by way of controlling all the justice that was done in his name. During the early years of his reign, though he was abroad and though he had left a justiciar in England, he maintained this control. The abbot of St Albans sent all the way to Toulouse for a writ directing the justiciar to rehear a case, in which, in consequence of the abbot's default, certain lands had been adjudged to his adversary. He had to pay the heavy sum of a hundred pounds for that writ, and certainly it was of no ordinary kind, for he had scorned to appear in a court held by a mere justiciar[3]. But even for ordinary writs men had to go abroad.

The Anesty case.

The curious story told by Richard of Anesty has often been retold[4]. He was claiming as heir to his uncle certain lands of which Mabel of Francheville, whom he asserted to be illegitimate, was in possession[5]. He had to begin by sending to Normandy for the king's writ; soon after he had to send for another writ directed to the archbishop, since the question of bastardy would be transmitted to the ecclesiastical court. The litigation in the spiritual forum was tedious; he was adjourned from place to place, from month to month. The king summoned

[1] Gesta Abbatum, i. 154: 'Privilegia, ut credimus, praeiudicant praescriptioni.'

[2] Palgrave, Commonwealth, vol. ii. p. lxvii.; Bigelow, Placita, 175.

[3] Gesta Abbatum, i. 159–166.

[4] Palgrave, Commonwealth, vol. ii. pp. v.–xxvii.; Bigelow, Placita, 311; Hall, Court Life under the Plantagenets; Maitland, L. Q. R. xiii. 141.

[5] See Letters of John of Salisbury (ed. Giles), i. 124.

the army for the expedition to Toulouse; Richard had to go as
[p. 138] far as Gascony for yet another royal writ bidding the archbishop
proceed despite the war. The litigation went on for another
year, during which he appeared in the archbishop's court on
some ten different occasions. Once more he had to visit France,
for he required the king's licence for an appeal to the pope.
He sent his clerks to Rome and the pope appointed judges
delegate. Then his adversary appealed, and again he had to
send representatives to Rome. At length the pope decided
in his favour. Thereupon the case came back to the royal
court and week after week he had to follow it. The king
appointed two justices to hear his cause, and at length by the
king's grace and the judgment of the king's court he obtained
the wished for lands[1]. Many comments might be made upon
this story. It will not escape us that in these early years of
Henry's reign royal justice is still very royal indeed. Though
the king has left his justiciar in England, there is no one here
who can issue what we might have supposed to be ordinary
writs. A great change in this most important particular must
soon have taken place. The judicial rolls of Richard I.'s reign
are largely occupied by accounts of law-suits about very small
pieces of ground between men of humble station, men who
could not have laboured as Anesty laboured or spent money as
he spent it. But throughout his reign Henry took an active
share in the work of justice. Even when he had appointed
judges to hear a cause, they would advise the successful litigant
to wait until a judgment could be given by the king's own
mouth[2]. He was at heart a lawyer, quite competent to criticize
minutely the wording of a charter, to frame a new clause and
give his vice-chancellor a lesson in conveyancing[3]; quite willing
on the other hand to confess that there were problems that he
could not solve[4]. No doubt he sold his aid; he would take
gifts with both hands; he expected to be paid for his trouble.
He sold justice, but it was a better article than was to be
had elsewhere.

[1] Palgrave, p. lxxxiii.: 'et tandem gratia domini Regis et per iudicium
curiae suae adiudicata est mihi terra avunculi mei.'

[2] Bigelow, Placita, 170.

[3] Palgrave, p. lxxiii.; Bigelow, Placita, 222. Mapes, De Nugis, p. 227: 'In
legibus constituendis et omni regimine corrigendo discretus, inusitati occultique
iudicii subtilis inventor.'

[4] Bigelow, Placita, 239.

Walter Map has told us how in the exchequer a poor man obtained an expeditious judgment against a rich antagonist. Of this as of a marvellous thing he spoke to Ranulf Glanvill. [p. 139] Yes, said the justiciar, we are quicker about our business than your bishops are. Very true, replied Map, but you would be as dilatory as they are if the king were as far away from you as the pope is from the bishops. Glanvill smiled[1]. And then Map tells how all who had a good cause wished that it might come before the king himself, and he recalls a great day in the history of English law, the day when our king's court entertained a plea between the king of Castile and the king of Navarre[2]. Certainly this was no mean event; the kings of the south had acknowledged that there was excellent justice to be had in England, and if this was so, to Henry II. the praise is due[3]. In the middle of the next century Henry III. had quarrelled with Bracton's master and patron, Bishop William Raleigh, and a proposal was made that the dispute should be referred to the legal faculty at Paris. Raleigh rejected this plan, saying that there were good enough lawyers in England, and that time was when the greatest princes of the earth submitted their causes to English lawyers[4]. This boast was not baseless: Henry II. had made it true.

After many experiments he committed the ordinary work of justice to a court of experts, to a learned court. It was well leavened by laymen; a layman presided over it; there was no fear of its meekly accepting the romano-canonical system; but among its most active members were great clerks, and the high rank that they had won, for they had become bishops, would have made them influential members, even had they been less able than they were. But they were able. We speak of such men as Richard of Ilchester, John of Oxford and Geoffrey Ridel, who had lived in the large world, who had been in France, Germany, Italy, who had seen men and cities, pope and emperor, and had written the dispatches of a prince whose

---

[1] Mapes, De Nugis, p. 241.   [2] Ibid. p. 242.

[3] A full account of the case is given in Gesta Henrici, i. 138–154. We may say, if we will, that there was here an 'international arbitration'; still it was conducted with all the regularity of a law-suit, and the award was expressly based upon a rule of pleading. Each of the kings charged the other with having wrongfully dispossessed him of certain lands. Neither directly denied the charge. The judgment is that each must restore what he has taken.

[4] Prynne, Records, ii. 588, from Rot. Pat. 28 Hen. III.

policy was at work in every corner of Western Christendom. Very different were they from the English judges of the fourteenth century. Law and literature grew up together in the court of Henry II. Roger Hoveden the chronicler[1] and Walter Map the satirist[2] were among his itinerant justices. Law becomes the subject of literature in the Dialogue on the Exchequer and the treatise ascribed to Glanvill.

[p. 140]   The Dialogus de Scaccario is an anonymous book, but *Richard Fitz Neal.* there can be little doubt that we are right in ascribing it to Richard Fitz Neal: that is to say, to Richard the son of that Nigel, bishop of Ely, who was the nephew of Roger, bishop of Salisbury, the great minister of Henry I.[3] For three generations, first Roger, then Nigel, then Richard, held high offices in the king's court and exchequer. Richard himself became treasurer in or about the year 1158; in 1189 he became bishop of London, but he retained the treasurership until his death in 1198[4]. He was a well-educated man, knew something of the classical Latin literature, had heard of Aristotle and Plato, could make a hexameter upon occasion, and was fond of the technical terms of logic[5]; he acted as a royal justice; he wrote a history of his own time, the lost Tricolumnis[6]; but above all he was a financier and knew all that experience and tradition could teach about the history and practice of the exchequer. He seems to have set to work on his Dialogue in the year 1177, and to have finished it in 1179 or thereabouts, when already for twenty years he had been the king's treasurer[7].

The book stands out as an unique book in the history of *Dialogue on the Exchequer.* medieval England, perhaps in the history of medieval Europe. A high officer of state, the trusted counsellor of a powerful king, undertakes to explain to all whom it may concern the machinery of government. He will not deal in generalities, he will condescend to minute details. Perhaps the book was not meant for the general public so much as for the numerous clerks who were learning their business in the exchequer[8], but

---

[1] Hoveden, ed. Stubbs, i. p. xxi.

[2] Eyton, Itinerary, 265.

[3] The book has been fully discussed by Liebermann, Einleitung in den Dialogus de Scaccario. It is printed by Madox in his History of the Exchequer and by Stubbs in his Select Charters.

[4] Liebermann, pp. 33, 42, 54.   [5] Ibid. p. 31.

[6] Ibid. p. 65.   [7] Ibid. p. 10.

[8] Ibid. p. 96.

still that such a book should be written, is one of the wonderful things of Henry's wonderful reign. We may safely say that it was not published without the king's licence, and yet it exposes to the light of day many things which kings and ministers are wont to treat as solemn mysteries of state. We should know far more of the history of government than ever will be known, could we have a Dialogue on the Exchequer from every century; but we have one only, and it comes from the reign of Henry II. Henry was so strong that he had nothing to [p. 141] conceal; he could stand criticism; his will and pleasure if properly explained to his subjects would appear as reasonable, and at any rate would not be resisted[1]. And so his treasurer expounded the course of proceedings in the exchequer, the constitution of this financial board, its writs and its rolls, the various sources of royal income, the danegeld and the murder fine, the collection of the debts due to the king, the treatment of his debtors, and, coming to details, he described the chess-board and the counters, the tallies, the scales and the melting-pot. But for him, we should have known little of the ad-ministrative and fiscal law of his time or of later times—for the rolls of the exchequer sadly need a commentary—but, as it is, we may know much.

Ranulf Glanvill. What the treasurer's Dialogue did for administrative and fiscal law was done by another book for private and criminal law. That book has long been attributed to one who held a yet higher office than the treasurer's, to Ranulf Glanvill, the chief justiciar.

His life. Ranulf Glanvill[2] came of a family which ever since the Conquest had held lands in Suffolk; it was not among the wealthiest or most powerful of the Norman houses, but was neither poor nor insignificant. Probably for some time before 1163, when he was made sheriff of Yorkshire, he had been in the king's service; he had lately been one of those 'friends, helpers and pleaders' who had aided Richard of Anesty in his famous law-suit[3]. The shrievalty of Yorkshire was an office

---

[1] Dial. ii. c. 16: 'Huius autem rei causam, licet distorta modicum et regiae nimis utilitati serviens videtur, evidentem et satis iustam secundum patrias leges comprobabis.' Ibid. ii. c. 10: 'Propter solam regis assisam sic esse cognoscas; nec enim est qui regiae constitutioni, quae pro bono pacis fit, obviare presumat.'

[2] Dict. Nat. Biography.

[3] Palgrave, Commonwealth, ii. p. xxiii.

that Henry would not have bestowed upon an untried man;
Glanvill held it for seven years.   In 1174, being then sheriff of
Lancashire and custodian of the honour of Richmond, he did a
signal service to the king and the kingdom.   At a critical
moment he surprised the invading Scots near Alnwick, defeated
them and captured their king.   From that time forward he
was a prominent man, high in the king's favour, a man to be
employed as general, ambassador, judge and sheriff.   In 1180
[p. 142] he became chief justiciar of England, prime minister, we may
say, and viceroy.   Henry seems to have trusted him thoroughly
and to have found in him the ablest and most faithful of
servants.   Henry's friends had of necessity been Richard's
enemies, and when Henry died, Richard, it would seem, hardly
knew what to do with Glanvill.   He decided that the old
statesman should go with him on the crusade.   To Acre
Glanvill went and there in the early autumn of 1190 he died of
sickness.

   Whether he wrote the book that has long borne his name is *Tractatus*
a doubtful question.   Some words of the chronicler Roger *de Legi-*
Hoveden, his contemporary, may mean that he did write it; *bus.*
but they are obscure words[1].   On the other hand, the title
which it generally bears in the manuscripts seems to imply
that he did not write it.   It is called 'A Treatise on the Laws

---

[1] Hoveden (ii. 215) under the year 1180 says that Henry appointed as
justiciar Ranulf Glanvill 'cuius sapientia conditae sunt leges subscriptae quas
Anglicanas vocamus.'   On this there follow (1) one set of the Leges Willelmi
(*Hic intimatur*), (2) the Leges Edwardi, (3) a genealogy of the Norman dukes,
(4) an *Expositio Vocabulorum* or glossary of A.-S. legal words, (5) the treatise in
question, (6) certain assizes of Henry II.   We may regard it as certain that
Glanvill did not compose 1 or 2; also that the man who composed 5 did not
compose 2.   The question remains whether Hoveden's 'condidit leges' covers
all this legal stuff or is specially attributable to 5, the treatise on the *leges
Anglicanae*.   In the former case it must bear a very vague meaning; it can
mean little more than that Glanvill administered English law in accordance
with those documents which Hoveden is going to transcribe; the phrase is
hardly better than an excuse for the introduction of a mass of legal matter.   In
the latter case we still have to ask what Hoveden meant by 'condidit leges.'
This would be a strange phrase whereby to describe the compilation of a treatise.
In the contemporary Dialogue (ii. 14) it is used of a legislator.   The treatise
undoubtedly sets forth the law as administered by the royal court under
Glanvill's presidency.   Hoveden, so it seems to us, means no more than this.
It is fairly certain that Hoveden found 1, 2 and 3 already hitched together so as
to form a whole, which Dr Liebermann calls *Tripartita*, and not improbable that
the treatise known to us as Glanvill had already been tacked on to this
Tripartita.   See Liebermann in Zeitschrift für romanische Philologie, xix. 81.

and Customs of England composed in the time of King Henry the Second while the honourable (*illustris vir*) Ranulf Glanvill held the helm of justice'; but we can not be certain that this title is as old as the book. Such a title would sufficiently explain the fact that in the thirteenth century the book was already known as the 'Summa quae vocatur Glaunvile[1].' From internal evidence we infer that it was written before Henry's death, that is before the 6th of July, 1189, and yet that it was not completed before the month of November, 1187[2]. Certainly we can not say that Glanvill was incapable of writing [p. 143] it, for, though a book written by a layman would at this time have been an extremely rare thing, we know that Glanvill was not illiterate and could pass remarks on the illiteracy of the English gentry[3]. It is a more serious objection that during the stormy last years of Henry's reign the faithful and hard-worked justiciar can have had but little leisure for writing books[4]. To this we must add that the author of the treatise writes, not as a statesman, but as a lawyer. He speaks not as one in authority, but as one who is keenly interested in the problems of private law and civil procedure, and he is not ashamed to confess that he raises more questions than he can answer. He feels the impulse of scientific curiosity. No doubt Ranulf Glanvill was, like his master, a many-sided man, but his life was very busy, and we can not but think that such a book as this came from the pen of some clerk who had time for reading and for juristic speculations. We should not be surprised if it were the work of Glanvill's kinsman and secretary, Hubert Walter, who in his turn was to become a chief justiciar[5]. The question is interesting rather than important,

---

[1] Maitland, Glanvill Revised, Harvard Law Review, vi. 1.

[2] The king of the prologue is obviously Henry. In lib. viii. c. 3, reference is made to a record of 31 October, 1187.

[3] Mapes, De Nugis, p. 8.

[4] According to Eyton, Itinerary, 294–7, Glanvill was in France from March until June 1189; he then came to England to levy troops and was in France again in July.

[5] This suggestion is due to a passage in Bracton (f. 188 b). Half a century after Hubert Walter's death, Bracton, wishing to show how fatal it is for a pleader to make mistakes in names, chooses as examples his own name and that of Hubert Walter. Now the name 'Hubertus Walteri' was not merely an uncommon name, it was a name of an exceedingly uncommon kind. 'Hubertus filius Walteri' would of course be a name of the commonest kind, but the omission of the 'filius' is, among men of gentle birth, an almost distinctive

for, though we would gladly know the name of the man who wrote our first classical text-book, it is plain that he was one who was very familiar with the justice done in the king's court during the last years of Henry II. We may go further, we may safely say that it was not written without Glanvill's permission or without Henry's.

[p. 144] The writer knew something of Roman and of canon law. Perhaps he had read the Institutes; probably his idea of what a law-book should be had been derived from some one of the many small manuals of romano-canonical procedure that were becoming current[1]. He does not however adopt the arrangement of the Institutes as the plan of his treatise, and he can not have followed any foreign model very far. The first sentences of his book are a good example of his method:— ' Of pleas some are civil, some are criminal. Again, of criminal pleas some pertain to the crown of our lord the king, others to the sheriffs of the counties. To the king's crown belong these: the crime which in the [Roman] laws is called *crimen laesae maiestatis*,—as by slaying the king or by a betrayal of his person or realm or army,—the concealment of treasure trove, breach of his peace, homicide, arson, robbery, rape, forgery, and the like.' We have but to contrast these sentences with the parallel passages, if such we may call them, in the *Leges Henrici* to see the work of the new jurisprudence[2]. The dilemma 'criminal or civil' is offered to every plea. This is new and has been foreign to English law. In the disorderly list of the pleas of the crown a great simplification has been effected: homicide, for example, is now always a plea of the crown, and we can finish the list with a ' si quae sunt similia' which leaves scope for rationalism. And yet the materials that are used are ancient; the terms which describe the *crimen laesae maiestatis*

Roman and canon law in the Tractatus.

mark of a particular family, that to which the great archbishop belonged. Bracton therefore seems to be choosing the rare name of a man who has been dead these fifty years. May he not be coupling with his own name that of his only predecessor in English legal literature, whose book he has been constantly using? However this is no more than a suggestion. For arguments against Glanvill's claim to the treatise, see Hunter, Fines, i. p. xv; on the other side, Foss, Judges of England, i. 181; Liebermann, Einleitung, p. 73.

[1] Much first-hand knowledge of the Roman texts is not to be inferred from an imitation of the opening sentences of the Institutes, from the occurrence of such phrases as 'quod principi placuit,' 'melior est conditio possidentis,' or from occasional allusions to the ' leges et canones.'

[2] Leg. Hen. c. 10.

are rooted in the old law. And so throughout: we have no
reason to suspect that the writer is giving us his theories
instead of the practice of the king's court. What he has
borrowed from the new jurisprudence consists first of a few
general distinctions, such as that between criminal and civil
pleas, that between possessory and proprietary actions—distinctions which are already becoming well-marked outlines
in the procedure of the royal court,—and secondly a logical
method which we may call dilemmatic. We have to consider—
for naturally procedure is placed in the forefront—how an
action is carried on. The defendant is summoned. Either he [p 145]
appears or he does not appear. If he does not appear, either
he sends an excuse or he sends none. If he sends an excuse,
it must be of this kind or of that:—and so forth. And at
every turn the writer has to consider the wording of those
royal writs that are becoming the skeleton of English law.
Substantive law comes in incidentally, and we are allowed to
see that some very elementary problems are still unsolved,
for example, that simple problem in the law of primogenitary
inheritance which on King Richard's death will be raised between John and Arthur[1]. Again, there is a great deal of
customary law administered in the local courts of which he
professes his ignorance[2]. Old rules about *wer* and *wíte* and
bót may still be lurking in out-of-the-way places; but he says
nothing of them. He says nothing of the *laga Eadwardi* and
betrays no acquaintance with those books which have professed
to set forth that ancient system. He is concerned only with
the 'chief' or 'principal' court of our lord the king, and just
because that court is making a common law by way of commentary on royal assizes and royal writs and is not much
hampered by custom or even by precedent,—for as yet we
have no citation of precedents, no 'case law'—he is able to
write his lucid book. It became popular. Many manuscripts of
it are yet extant. Seventy years after it was written lawyers
were still using it and endeavouring to bring it up to date[3].
Someone was at pains to translate it from Latin into French[4].

---

[1] Glanvill, vii. 3.   [2] Glanvill, Prologus; xii. 6; xiv. 8.

[3] Maitland, Glanvill Revised, Harvard Law Review, vi. 1. A second MS. of
this revised Glanvill is preserved at Caius College.

[4] Brit. Mus. MS. Lansd. 467: the translator will give the text 'en un
commun romaunz sans ryme'; Camb. Univ. Ll. i. 16, f. 100. The version in
Camb. Univ. Ee. i. 1 is partly in Latin, partly in French.

A version of it known as *Regiam Maiestatem* became current in Scotland[1].

We may fairly say that under Henry II. England takes for [p. 146] a short while the lead among the states of Europe in the production of law and of a national legal literature. No other prince in Europe could have enforced those stringent assizes, and he could not have enforced them in all of his continental dominions. The most in the way of legislation that a king of the French could do, the most that an emperor could do in Germany, was to make for the maintenance of the peace rather a treaty with his vassals than a law for his subjects[2]. No one had been legislating since the last Carolingians issued the last capitularies; law had been taking the form of multitudinous local customs. The claims of the renovated, the scientific, Roman aw were unbounded; but north of the Alps it was only beginning to influence the practice of the temporal tribunals. We can not call Glanvill's treatise the earliest textbook of feudal jurisprudence, for parts at least of the *Libri Feudorum*, the work of Lombard lawyers, belong to the first half of the twelfth century, and some parts of the Assizes of Jerusalem, though not in the form in which they have come down to us, may be older than the English book; but in the production of such a book England stands well in advance of France and Germany[3]. Moreover it is noticeable that in France

English and continental literature.

---

[1] The *Regiam Maiestatem* is collated with Glanvill in vol. i. of the Acts of the Parliament of Scotland. Neilson, Trial by Combat, p. 104: 'Either the Regiam was compiled in the first half of the thirteenth century, say between 1200 and 1230...or it was compiled from materials of the law of that period.' Glanvill's Treatise was printed by Tottel without date about 1554; later editions were published in 1604, 1673, 1780; an English version by Beames in 1812. It will also be found in Houard's Coutumes anglo-normandes and in Phillips's Englische Rechtsgeschichte. A new edition is wanted.

[2] What is accounted the most ancient ordinance of a French king comes from Louis VII. in 1155: it establishes a 'peace' for ten years: Viollet, Histoire du droit civil français, p. 152; Esmein, Histoire du droit français, ed. 2, 488. From Germany also we have as yet merely *Landfriedensgesetze* which strive to set limits to private war: Schröder, D. R. G. p. 628.

[3] The *Libri Feudorum* in their present state are a composite work, some parts of which may even go back to the last years of the eleventh century: an edition by K. Lehmann is appearing in parts. See Lehmann, Das langobardische Lehnrecht, 1896; Schröder, *op. cit.* 668. The Assises for the Cour des Bourgeois were compiled, it is said, between 1173 and 1180, a few years before Glanvill's treatise: Viollet, p. 170; Brunner in Holtzendorff's Encyklopädie, p. 310. The Assises for the Haute Cour are of later date.

the provinces which are the first to come by written statements
of their law are those which have been under Henry's sway.
Foremost stands Normandy, which in or about the year 1200
has already a brief written custumal, Normandy where exchequer rolls are compiled and preserved, and where the judgments of the duke's court are collected by lawyers; and it is
not impossible that the second place must be conceded to
Touraine or Anjou[1].

The limit
of legal
memory.

It is a well-known doctrine not yet obsolete among us that [p. 147]
our legal memory is limited by the date of Richard I.'s coronation. The origin of this doctrine is to be found in certain
statutes of Edward I.'s reign[2]. Probably this date was then
chosen because it was just possible that a living man should
have been told by his father of what that father had seen in
the year 1189, and in a proprietary action for land the demandant's champion was allowed to speak of what his father
had seen. And yet had Edward and his parliament been
concerned to mark a boundary beyond which the history of
English law could not be profitably traced for practical purposes, they could hardly have hit upon a better date than the
3rd of September, 1189. The restless Henry had gone to his
rest; his reforms were beginning to take effect; our first
classical text-book had just been written; the strong central
court was doing justice term after term on a large scale; it was
beginning to have a written memory which would endure for

---

[1] The most notable French law books are (1) the first part (Brunner's Très
ancienne coutume) of (Tardif's) Très ancien coutumier de Normandie, compiled circ. 1200; (2) the second part of the same work, circ. 1220; (3) the
Grand coutumier de Normandie, circ. 1254-8 (see Tardif's edition); (4) a
custumal of Anjou, 1246; (5) a custumal of the Orléanais, from the first half of
the thirteenth century; (6) the so-called Établissements de Saint Louis (circ.
1273), a text-book which takes up into itself the works here designated as 4 and
5; (7) the Conseil de Pierre de Fontaines, circ. 1254-9, from the Vermandois,
highly romanized; (8) the Livre de Jostice et Plet from the Orléanais, circ. 1259;
(9) Beaumanoir's Custom of Clermont in the Beauvoisis, finished in 1283. See
Esmein, *op. cit.* 728-34; Viollet, *op. cit.* 177-88. In Germany the first
law-book is the Sachsenspiegel, 1215-35; Schröder, *op. cit.* 635 ff. This was
soon followed by the Deutschenspiegel and the so-called Schwabenspiegel. It is
by no means impossible that the development of French law in general was
quickened by the legislative or administrative activity of Henry, Duke of
Normandy and Count of Anjou; the practice of enrolling pleas seems to spread
outwards from Normandy and with it the assize of novel disseisin. Luchaire,
Manuel des institutions, p. 568: 'l'usage des rouleaux d'arrêts, d'origine anglo-
normande.' To the same effect, Esmein, *op. cit.* 742.

[2] Stat. West. I. (1275) c. 39; Statutes of Quo Waranto (1289-90).

all ages in the form of a magnificent series of judicial records. Our extant plea rolls go back to the year 1194, the great series of the 'feet of fines' (documents which tell us of the compromises, the final concords, made in the king's court) begins in 1195. The chancery then takes up the tale; all that goes on therein is punctually recorded upon the charter, patent, close and fine rolls. The historian of law and constitu-[p. 148] tion has no longer to complain of a dearth of authentic materials; soon he is overwhelmed by them[1].

Richard's reign, despite the exciting political struggles which filled its first years, was on the whole a time of steady if oppressive government, and the same may be said of so much of John's reign as had elapsed before he quarrelled with the church. The system created by Henry II. was so strong that it would do its work though the king was an absentee. Term after term, at least from 1194 onwards, a strong central court sat at Westminster. Until the middle of 1198 its president was the archbishop Hubert Walter, and shortly after he had resigned the justiciarship he became chancellor. During the autumn term of 1196, to take one example, we may see him presiding in court on October 13, 15, 17, 18, 19, 21, 22, 24, 28, 29, 30, November 4, 6, 12, 13, 14, 18, 20, 21, 22, 23, 27, 28, 29 and December 1, 2, 3, 4 and 6, until we wonder when he found time for the duties of his archiepiscopate[2]. As justiciar he was succeeded by a lay baron, Geoffrey Fitz Peter, who held the office until his death in 1213; he is one of the first of English laymen who is famed for his knowledge of law[3]. Another layman who comes to the front as a great judge is Simon Pateshull[4]; he may well have been the father of the yet more celebrated Martin Pateshull whom Bracton revered[5]. Already

Richard's reign and John's.

The central court.

---

[1] The earliest of the known plea rolls has lately been published by the Pipe Roll Society; others of Richard's and John's reigns have been published by the Record Commissioners and the Selden Society. The earliest charter rolls, patent rolls, close rolls have been published by the Record Commissioners.

[2] Feet of Fines, 7 & 8 Ric. I (Pipe Roll Soc.) p. 3 ff.

[3] Mat. Par. ii. 558: 'Erat autem firmissima regni columna, utpote vir generosus, legum peritus, thesauris, redditibus, et omnibus bonis instauratus, omnibus Angliae magnatibus sanguine vel amicitia confoederatus.'

[4] Mat. Par. iii. p. 296: 'qui quandoque habenas sane moderabatur totius regni iustitiarii.' Ibid. 542: 'cuius sapientia aliquando tota Anglia regebatur.'

[5] See Baker's History of Northamptonshire, i. 267; also Dict. Nat. Biog. He certainly was the father of Hugh Pateshull, who was for a while treasurer to Henry III. and became bishop of Lichfield. Simon had a clerk called Martin; Select Pleas of the Crown (Seld. Soc.), pl. 18.

in 1202 the king's justices are officially styled 'justices learned in the law[1].' But the court was still full of bishops, archdeacons and other clerks; for example, three successive bishops of London, Richard Fitz Neal, William of S. Mère Église, and Eustace of Fauconberg, were men who had done much justice for the king. During the reign of Richard, who paid but two brief visits to this country, it is of course an unusual thing to find the king presiding in person, though undoubtedly he did so while he was here; the court therefore shows no tendency to become two courts. But John liked to do justice, or what he called justice, and during his reign he was often travelling [p. 149] about the country with one party of judges in his train, while another party of judges headed by the chief justiciar was seated on the Bench at Westminster[2]. The permanent central tribunal is beginning to split itself into two tribunals, one of which follows the king, while the other remains at the Bench, and a series of small changes is completing the severance between the court and the exchequer. But at present all these arrangements are of a temporary character.

Itinerant justices.

The counties also were visited from time to time by itinerant justices. Apparently they were sometimes armed with ampler and sometimes with less ample powers. There was a great eyre in 1194, and the articles issued to the justices on that occasion are the most important edict of the period[3].

Legislation.

There was little that we could call legislation; an ordinance of 1195 enforced the ancient rules for the pursuit of malefactors[4]; in 1197 an assize of measures was issued[5], in 1205 an assize of money[6]. Richard's curious laws for the fleet of crusaders, under which thieves are tarred and feathered, deserve a passing word[7], and ordinances of John's reign began the extension of English law over those parts of Ireland which were subject to his power[8]. But it was rather by decisions of the courts and by writs penned in the chancery that English law was being constructed. A comparison of a collection of formulas which Henry III. sent to the Irish chancery in 1227 with Glanvill's treatise shows us that the number of writs which were to be

---

[1] Select Pleas of the Crown, pl. 34.　　[2] Ibid. pp. xii.—xvii.

[3] Stubbs, Select Charters; Rolls of the King's Court (Pipe Roll Soc.), vol. i.

[4] Select Charters, *Edictum Regium*; Hoveden, iii. 299.

[5] Hoveden, iv. 33.　　[6] Rot. Pat. Joh. p. 54.

[7] Gesta Henrici (Benedict), ii. 110.　　[8] Rot. Pat. Joh. p. 47.

had as of course, had grown within the intervening forty years[1]. A new form of action might be easily created. A few words said by the chancellor to his clerks—'Such writs as this are for the future to be issued as of course'—would be as effectual as the most solemn legislation[2]. As yet there would be no jealousy between the justices and the chancellor, nor would they easily be induced to quash his writs.

[p. 150]   It is not for us here to relate the events which led to the exaction and grant of the Great Charter, to repeat its clauses, or even to comment on all the general characteristics of that many-sided instrument. In form a donation, a grant of franchises freely made by the king, in reality a treaty extorted from him by the confederate estates of the realm, a treaty which threatens him with the loss of his land if he will not abide by its terms, it is also a long and miscellaneous code of laws[3]. Of course it is not long when compared with a statute of the eighteenth century; more words than it contains have often been spent upon some trifling detail. But, regard being had to its date, it is a lengthy document[4]. Every one of its brief sentences is aimed at some different object and is full of future law. The relative importance of its various clauses historians will measure by various standards. It is a great thing that the king should be forced to promise that no scutage shall be levied save by the common counsel of the realm, and that an attempt should be made to define the national assembly[5]. It is a great thing that he should be forced to say, 'No free man shall be taken or imprisoned or disseised or outlawed or exiled or in any wise destroyed, save by the

The Great Charter.

---

[1] This Irish Register of Writs is described in Harvard Law Review, iii. 110. The MS. is Cotton, Julius, D. 11.

[2] Rot. Claus. Joh. p. 32. A writ of 1205, which in technical terms is 'a writ of entry sur disseisin in the *per*,' has against it the note 'Hoc breve de cetero erit de cursu.'

[3] Charter 1215, c. 1: 'Concessimus etiam omnibus liberis hominibus regni nostri, pro nobis et heredibus nostris in perpetuum, omnes libertates subscriptas, habendas et tenendas eis et heredibus suis de nobis et heredibus nostris.' By c. 61 power is given the twenty-five barons to distrain the king 'per captionem castrorum, terrarum, possessionum et aliis modis quibus poterunt...salva persona nostra et reginae nostrae et liberorum nostrorum.'

[4] For an interesting discussion of a document professing to be a copy of an earlier charter of liberties, see E. H. R. vii. 288 (Round); ix. 117 (Prothero), 326 (Hall).

[5] Charter, 1215, c. 12, 14.

lawful judgment of his peers or the law of the land[1].' But
events will show that some of these celebrated clauses are
premature, while others are vague and can be eluded. In
the end the very definite promises about smaller matters—
promises which are also laws—are perhaps of greater value.
Precise limits are set to royal claims in strict terms of money,
time and space:—the relief for a knight's fee is not to exceed
one hundred shillings; the king will hold the felon's land for a
year and a day and no longer; all weirs in the Thames, in the
Medway or elsewhere in England, save along the coast of the
sea, shall be destroyed[2]. Such provisions can be enforced by
courts of law, which can hardly enforce against the king his [p. 151]
covenant that he will not sell or delay or deny justice, and that
he will appoint as judges only those who know the law[3].

Restora-
tive cha-
racter of
the charter.
On the whole, the charter contains little that is absolutely
new. It is restorative. John in these last years has been
breaking the law; therefore the law must be defined and set in
writing. In several instances we can prove that the rule that
is laid down is one that was observed during the early part of
his reign[4]. In the main the reforms of Henry II.'s day are
accepted and are made a basis for the treaty. So successful
have the possessory assizes been, that men will not now be
content unless four times in every year two royal justices come
into every county for the purpose of enforcing them[5]. In a few
cases there is even retrogression. Every class of men is to be
conciliated. The vague large promise that the church of England
shall be free is destined to arouse hopes that have been dormant
and can not be fulfilled[6]. The claims of the feudal lord to hold
a court which shall enjoy an exclusive competence in proprietary actions is acknowledged ; Henry II. would hardly have been
forced into such an acknowledgment, and it does immeasurable
harm to the form of English law, for lawyers and royal justices
will soon be inventing elaborate devices for circumventing a

---

[1] Charter, 1215, c. 39.   [2] Ibid. c. 2, 32, 33.   [3] Ibid. 215 c. 40, 45.

[4] For instance c. 54: 'Nullus capiatur nec imprisonetur propter appellum
feminae de morte alterius quam viri sui'; Select Pleas of the Crown, pl. 32
(1202): 'nullum est appellum eo quod femina non habet appellum versus
aliquem nisi de morte viri sui vel de rapo.' The rule was already law in
Henry II.'s day ; Glanvill, xiv, c. 1, 3, 6.

[5] Charter, c. 18.

[6] Ibid. c. 1: 'ecclesia Anglicana libera sit et habeat iura sua integra et
libertates suas illaesas.'

principle which they can not openly attack[1]. Even in the most famous words of the charter we may detect a feudal claim which will only cease to be dangerous when in course of time men have distorted their meaning :—a man is entitled to the judgment of his peers; the king's justices are no peers for earls or [p. 152] barons. Foreign merchants may freely come and go; they may dwell here and buy and sell; yes, but all cities and boroughs are to enjoy all their franchises and free customs, and often enough in the coming centuries they will assert that their dearest franchise is that of excluding or oppressing the foreigner[2]. And yet, with all its faults, this document becomes and rightly becomes a sacred text, the nearest approach to an irrepealable 'fundamental statute' that England has ever had. In age after age a confirmation of it will be demanded and granted as a remedy for those oppressions from which the realm is suffering, and this when some of its clauses, at least in their original meaning, have become hopelessly antiquated. For in brief it means this, that the king is and shall be below the law[3].

[1] Charter, c. 34 : ' Breve quod vocatur *Praecipe* de cetero non fiat alicui de aliquo tenemento unde liber homo amittere possit curiam suam.' Glanvill, i. 5, allows the king to issue this writ whenever he pleases. Had this prerogative been maintained, the horrible tangle of our 'real actions,' our 'writs of entry' and so forth, would never have perplexed us.   [2] Ibid. c. 41, 13.

[3] In after days it was possible for men to worship the words 'nisi per legale iudicium parium suorum vel per legem terrae' (cap. 39), because it was possible to misunderstand them. In passing, a commentator should observe that in medieval Latin *vel* will often stand for *and*. As the writer of the Dialogus (ii. 1) says, it can be used *subdisiunctive* (for which term see Dig. 50, 16, 124). Often it is like the *and* (*or*) of our mercantile documents. The wording of the clause leaves open the question whether a man can ever be imprisoned or disseised by the law of the land without having had the judgment of his peers. In the second place, it is now generally admitted that the phrase *iudicium parium* does not point to trial by jury. For a legal instrument to call the verdict of recognitors a judgment, would have been as gross a blunder in 1215 as it would be at the present time. See Select Pleas in Manorial Courts (Selden Soc.), p. lxvii. Thirdly, there can hardly be a doubt that this clause expresses a claim by the barons for a tribunal of men of baronial rank which shall try even the civil causes in which barons are concerned; we shall see hereafter that they certainly wished for such a tribunal. The spirit of the clause is excellently expressed by a passage in the laws ascribed to David of Scotland: Acts of Parliament, vol. i. p. 318: ' No man shall be judged by his inferior who is not his peer; the earl shall be judged by the earl, the baron by the baron, the vavassor by the vavassor, the burgess by the burgess; *but an inferior may be judged by a superior*.' Some of John's justices were certainly not of baronial rank. Just at this same moment the French magnates also were striving for a court of peers; Luchaire, Manuel des institutions, p. 560; they did not want trial by jury. For the history of the phrase *iudicium parium*, see Stubbs, Const. Hist. i. 578.

CHAPTER VII.

THE AGE OF BRACTON.

THE reign of Henry III. (1216–72) is in the history of our law an age of rapid, but steady and permanent growth. At the end of that period most of the main outlines of our medieval law have been drawn for good and all; the subsequent centuries will be able to do little more than to fill in the details of a scheme which is set before them as unalterable. It is difficult for any historian not to take a side in the political struggle which fills the reign, the simmering discontent, the loud debate and the open rebellion; and the side that he takes will probably not be that of the feeble, wilful and faithless king. But even at the worst of times law was steadily growing. Henry's tyranny was the tyranny of one who had a legal system under his control; it was enforced by legal processes, by judgments that the courts delivered, by writs that the courts upheld. And on the other side there was little lawlessness. Not only was it in the name of law that the nation rose against the king, but no serious attempt was made to undo the work of his courts and his chancery. If only the nation at large, the *universitas regni,* could obtain some share in the control over this great machine, its pressure might be patiently borne. But, leaving the political and constitutional events of the reign for others, we, placing ourselves at the end, will make a brief survey of what has been done in the realm of law.

General
idea of law. Our English lawyers have no philosophy of law, nor have they pursued very far the question, How does law, or a law, come into being? The opening chapters of Justinian's Institutes were

[p. 154] known. The sentences which define *iustitia, iurisprudentia, ius naturale, ius gentium, ius civile,* and so forth, were copied or imitated ; but, any real knowledge of Roman history being still in the remote future, these sentences served as a check upon, rather than as an incentive to, rational speculation. In practice there is no careful discrimination between *ius* and *lex* ; the whole mass of legal rules enforced by the English temporal courts can be indicated by such phrases as *ius regni*[1], *lex regni*[2], *lex terrae*[3], *ius et consuetudo regni*[4], *lex et consuetudo, leges et consuetudines, lei de la terre, lei et dreit de la terre*[5]. Of course *ius, lex* and *consuetudo* are not in all contexts exactly equivalent words ; *ius* and the French *dreit* often stand for 'a right'[6] ; *lex* and *lei* are technically used to signify the various modes of proof, such as the oath, the ordeal, the judicial combat[7]. Glanvill and Bracton make some apology for giving the name *leges* to the unwritten laws of England[8] ; Bracton can upon occasion contrast *consuetudo* with *lex*[9]. Of course too it is necessary at times to distinguish a new rule lately established by some authoritative act, from the old rules which are conceived as having been in force from time immemorial. The rule in question has its origin in a royal decree or edict, in a *novella constitutio* of the *princeps*[10], in

---

[1] Glanvill, vii. 1: 'secundum ius regni.'

[2] Charter, 1215, c. 45: 'qui sciant legem regni.'

[3] Ibid. 1215, c. 39: 'per legale iudicium parium suorum vel per legem terrae.' Bracton, f. 128 b: 'utlagatus rite et secundum legem terrae.' Ibid. f. 127 b: 'ante aetatem duodecim annorum non erit quis sub lege, et prius extra legem poni non poterit.' Ibid. f. 147: 'secundum legem Romanorum, Francorum et Anglorum.'

[4] Glanvill, vii. 12: 'secundum ius et consuetudinem regni.'

[5] Prov. Oxford (Select Charters): 'La haute justice a poer de amender les tors...solum lei et dreit de la tere. E les brefs seient pledez solum lei de la tere e en leus deues.'

[6] Thus in the count on a writ of right, 'Peto terram ut ius et hereditatem meam...pater meus fuit seisitus ut de iure...et de eo descendit ius...et quod hoc est ius meum offero probare.'

[7] Dialogus, ii. 7: 'leges candentis ferri vel aquae.' Glanvill, xiv. 2: 'per legem apparentem se purgare.' Charter, 1215, c. 38: 'Nullus ballivus ponat... aliquem ad legem simplici loquela sua.'

[8] Glanvill, Prologus: 'Leges namque Anglicanas, licet non scriptas, leges appellari non videtur absurdum.' Bracton, f. 1.

[9] Bracton, f. 1: 'Habent enim Anglici plurima ex consuetudine quae non habent ex lege.'

[10] Dialogus, ii. 21: 'Decrevit enim rex illustris.' Hoveden, iii. 299: 'Edictum regium.' Dialogus, ii. 1: 'ex novella constitutione, hoc est post tempora regis Henrici primi.' Glanvill, ii. 7: 'Est autem magna assisa regale quoddam beneficium, clementia principis de consilio procerum populis indultum...legalis

'provisions' made by the king with the common counsel of his [p. 155]
prelates and nobles, in an assize, or when we speak in English
in an 'isetnysse¹'—the word 'statute' is hardly yet in common
use²—we may even have to say of some unprinciped rule that
it is to be explained only by reference to the will of the legis-
lator³.　But as yet there is no definite theory as to the relation
between enacted and unenacted law, the relation between law
and custom, the relation between law as it is and law as it
ought to be.　The assizes of Henry II. have worked themselves
into the mass of unenacted law, and their text seems already
to be forgotten.　On the other hand, the writer of Edward I.'s
day, who is known to us as Britton, can represent the whole
law as statutory: it all proceeds from the king's mouth.　The
king's justices seem to claim a certain power of improving the
law, but they may not change the law⁴.　The king without the
consent of a national assembly may issue new writs which go
beyond the law, but not new writs which go against the law⁵.

Common
law.

　　The term *common law* (*ius commune, lex communis, commun
dreit, commune lei*) is not as yet a term frequent in the mouths
of our temporal lawyers.　On the other hand, *ius commune* is a
phrase well known to the canonists.　They use it to distinguish
the general and ordinary law of the universal church both from
any rules peculiar to this or that provincial church, and from
those papal *privilegia* which are always giving rise to ecclesiastical litigation.　Two examples may suffice.　Innocent III.
tells the bishops of London and Ely that the guardianship
of vacant churches in the diocese of Canterbury belongs to the
archdeacon, both by common law and by the general custom of
the English church⁶.　In 1218 papal delegates report that the

ista institutio [*al.* regalis ista constitutio].'　Bracton, f. 96: 'sed nova super-
veniente gratia et provisione.'

¹ Proclamation of the king's acceptance of the Provisions of Oxford (Select
Charters): 'and to werian þo isetnesses þæt beon imakede.'

² The laws of Merton and Marlborough, though they are retrospectively
called statutes, called themselves provisions.　However, Henry I. had spoken of
his *statuta.* See above, p. 96.

³ Dialogus, ii. 10: 'Propter solam regis assisam sic esse cognoscas; nec
enim est qui regiae constitutioni, quae pro bono pacis fit, obviare praesumat.'

⁴ Bracton, f. 1 b: the contrast is between *mutari* and *in melius converti.*

⁵ Bracton, f. 414 b: the contrast is between a writ which is *contra ius* and
one which is *praeter ius* but at the same time *rationi consonum et non iuri
contrarium.*

⁶ c. 32, X. 2. 20: 'tam de communi iure, quam de consuetudine generali
Anglicanae ecclesiae.'

[p.156] bishop of Salisbury asserts a right to the church of Malmesbury both under the common law and by virtue of a papal privilege[1]. But in truth the phrase was usual among the canonists, and they had warrant in ancient Roman texts for the use that they made of it[2]. From the ecclesiastical it would easily pass into the secular courts. A bishop of Salisbury in 1252 tells the pope how, acting as a papal delegate, he has decided that the common law makes in favour of the rector of one church and against the vicar of another. The common law of which he speaks is the common law of the catholic church; but this bishop is no other than William of York, who owes his see to the good service that he has done as a royal justice[3]. In connexion with English temporal affairs we may indeed find the term *ius commune* in the Dialogue on the Exchequer: the forest laws which are the outcome of the king's mere will and pleasure are contrasted with the common law of the realm[4]. A century later, in Edward I.'s day, we frequently find it, though *lex communis* (*commune lei*) has by this time become the more usual phrase. The common law can then be contrasted with statute law; still more often it is contrasted with royal prerogative; it can also be contrasted with local custom: in short it may be contrasted with whatever is particular, extraordinary, special, with 'specialty' (*aliquid speciale, especialté*)[5]. When Bracton speaks of common law or common right—and this he does but very rarely—it is to distinguish from rights which have

---

[1] Sarum Charters, p. 89.

[2] Thus in Cod. Theod. 16, 5, 23 is a constitution repealing an earlier law which had placed a certain class of heretics under disabilities. 'Vivant iure communi,' it says, and this we can best render by, 'They are to live under the common law,' *i.e.* the ordinary law. So in Cod. Theod. 2, 1, 10: Iudaei romano et communi iure viventes.'

[3] Sarum Charters, p. 320: 'Nos vero...ius commune pro ecclesia de Preschut faciens considerantes.'

[4] Dialogus, i. 11: 'Legibus quidem propriis subsistit; quas non communi regni iure, sed voluntaria principum institutione subnixas dicunt.' Ib. ii. 22: 'communis lex.'

[5] Thus Y. B. 21-2 Edw. I. contrasts common law with statute (pp. 55-6, 419), with local custom (pp. 213, 287), with prerogative (p. 406), with the law merchant (p. 459), with 'special law' (p. 71). P. Q. W. 681: 'videtur iusticiariis quod dominus Rex placitare potest per breve magis conveniens legi communi quam hoc breve.' Rot. Parl. i. 47 (1290): 'Perquirat sibi per legem communem.' Articuli super Cartas (28 Edw. I.): 'ou remedie ne fust avant par la commune ley...nul bref que touche la commune lei.' Y. B. 20-1 Edw. I. p. 55: 'You put forward no *espessyalté*.'

their origin in some specially worded contract or donation, those rights which are given to all men by the law of the land[1]. [p. 157] It is not until there is a considerable mass of enacted law, until the king's exceptional privileges are being defined, until the place which local custom is to have in the legal system is being fixed, that the term becomes very useful, and it is long before the lawyers of the temporal courts will bear the title 'common lawyers,' or oppose 'the common law' to 'the law of holy church[2].'

Statute law.

The mass of enacted law is as yet by no means heavy. As we have said above, the assizes of the twelfth century seem to be already regarded as part of the unenacted ancient law. No one is at pains to preserve their text. As to the Anglo-Saxon dooms, though men are still at times copying and tampering with the Latin versions of them, they are practically dead, and will remain almost unknown until in the sixteenth century William Lambard unearths them as antiquarian curiosities[3]. We have in manuscript many collections of statutes transcribed in the days of the two first Edwards: they seldom, if ever, go behind Magna Carta. That Charter takes its place as the first chapter of the enacted law; but, as is well known, its

The charters.

text is not exactly that which John sealed at Runnymead in 1215. Important changes were made when it was reissued in

---

[1] Bracton, f. 17 b: 'Modus enim legem dat donationi et modus tenendus est contra ius commune et contra legem, quia modus et conventio vincunt legem… Bene poterit donator…legem imponere donationi…contra legem terrae.' Ibid. 19 b: 'Item poterit conditio impedire descensum ad proprios heredes contra ius commune.' Ibid. 48 b: 'Item poterit donator ex speciali conventione contra ius commune conditionem suam meliorem facere in causa donationis.'

[2] Early instances of the use of the term in a more or less technical sense are these. Foedera, i. 266, a writ of 1246: 'Rex vult quod omnia brevia de communi iure quae currunt in Anglia similiter currant in Hibernia.' Provisions of Oxford (1259): 'de sectis autem quae…subtractae fuerunt currat lex communis (curge la commune lei)':—'habeat rationabilem summonitionem secundum communem legem terrae (solum la commune lei).' According to a story told in the Burton Annals, p. 210, when John asked the papal legates what they wanted, they replied, 'Nil nisi ius commune'; this seems to mean, 'Nothing but common justice.' See further as to the history of this phrase, Clark, Practical Jurisprudence, p. 70.

[3] The Leges Edwardi and one set of the Leges Willelmi (*Hic intimatur*) were still being amplified by imaginative persons, who wished to show how sheriffs were elected in the good old days, and how the Scots were subject to the English king. See Liebermann, Leges Anglorum, p. 28 ff. Bracton, f. 134 b, quotes historical matter from the Leges Edwardi; and in his work (f. 147) there is an *addicio* which seems to refer to some laws of Æthelstan.

1216; other important changes were made in 1217, and a
[p.158] few minor changes in 1225. The charter granted by Henry
in 1225, when he had lately attained his majority, became the
Magna Carta of future times[1]. He had to confirm it repeatedly.
These repeated confirmations tell us how hard it is to bind
the king by law. The pages of the chroniclers are full of
complaints that the terms of the charter are not observed.
These complaints, when they become specific, usually refer
to the articles which gave to the churches the right to elect
their prelates. If on the one hand the king is apt to regard
the charter as a mere promise from which, if this be necessary,
the pope will absolve him, on the other hand efforts are made
to convert every one of its clauses into a fundamental, irrepealable law. In 1253 with solemn ceremonial the anathema
was launched, not merely against all who should break the
charter, but also against all who should take any part whatever, even the humble part of mere transcribers, in making
or promulgating or enforcing any statutes contrary to the
sacred text[2]. This theoretical sanctity and this practical in-
security are shared with 'the Great Charter of Liberties' by
the Charter of the Forest, which was issued in 1217.

The first set of laws which in later days usually bears the *Provisions*
name of 'statute' is the Provisions of Merton issued by the *West-*
king with the consent of the prelates and nobles in 1236 on the *minster*
occasion of his queen's coronation: a few brief clauses amend *borough.*
the law about divers miscellaneous matters[3]. From the time
of storm and stress we have the Provisions of Westminster to
which the king gave a reluctant consent in 1259[4]. He did not
hold himself bound by them; they never became a well established part of the law of the land; but in 1267, when the
revolutionary period was at an end, almost all of them were
reenacted with the consent of great and small as the Provisions
or Statute of Marlborough[5]. These four documents, the two

---

[1] After 1225 but before Edward's confirmation in 1297 a change was made
in, or crept into, the clause which defines the amount of the relief; the baron's
relief was reduced from 100 pounds to 100 marks. See Bémont, Chartes des
libertés anglaises, pp. xxxi. 47–8. The text of the various editions can be
best compared in this excellent book.

[2] Statutes of the Realm, i. 6.

[3] Statutes, i. 1; Note Book, i. 104.

[4] Statutes, i. 8.

[5] Stat. Marlb. (Statutes, i. 19): 'convocatis discrecioribus eiusdem regni

Charters, the Provisions of Merton and of Marlborough, are the [p. 159] only documents of Henry's reign which are generally regarded in after ages as parts of the written law, though to these we may perhaps add the Dictum of Kenilworth issued in 1266 (an essentially temporary provision relating to the punishment of the insurgents[1]), and a writ of 1256, which has sometimes been dignified by the title 'the Statute of Leap Year'; it deals with a small matter, the computation of the 'excrescent' day of the bissextile[2]. But it is only in retrospect that the quantity of legislation that there has been appears so small. As yet there is no easily applicable external test by which we can distinguish the solemn statute from the less solemn ordinance. From Henry's reign we have neither a 'statute roll' nor any 'rolls of parliament'; and we have no reason to believe that any such records were kept[3]. Copies of the two charters were sent about the country; the only authoritative record that we have of the Provisions of Merton is a writ upon the close roll; the only authoritative records that we have of the Provisions of Westminster are writs upon the close and patent rolls, and upon those rolls and the judicial rolls of the king's court we find traces of other legislative acts, which for one reason or another did not permanently gain the character of statutes[4].

tam ex maioribus quam minoribus, provisum est et statutum ac concorditer ordinatum.' There seems no reason why we should any longer speak of Marlbridge when we mean Marlborough; 'Marlbridge' is but a stupid misrepresentation of the French form Marleberge.

[1] Statutes of the Realm, i. 12.

[2] Ibid. p. 7; Note Book, i. 43.

[3] The earliest statute roll now extant begins with the Statute of Gloucester, 1278. What is now its topmost membrane shows distinct signs of having been preceded by another membrane, which may have contained the Statute of Westminster I. (1275) and other matters. Our first parliament roll comes from 1290.

[4] Among these may be reckoned the ordinance of 1219 relating to the abolition of the ordeal, Foedera, i. 154; the 'constitution' of 1234 relating to the holding of the local courts, printed in Statutes of the Realm, i. 118; the ordinance of 1234 relating to special bastardy, which (see Bracton's Note Book, i. p. 104) is on the Coram Rege Roll; an ordinance of 1233 relating to the conservation of the peace, preserved on the Close Roll and printed in the Select Charters; a statute of limitation from 1237 which (see Note Book, i. p. 106) is usually but wrongly regarded as part of the Provisions of Merton; an ordinance about warranty made in 1251 on the dedication of the Abbey of Hailes and mentioned by Bracton, f. 382b; an ordinance of 1253 relating to watch and ward, preserved by Matthew Paris and printed in the Select Charters; an assize of bread, preserved in the Annals of Burton, p. 375, and elsewhere; lastly an

[p. 160] And if merely formal tests fail us, so also will more material Ordinance and Statute. tests. Of course we can not in dealing with Henry's day insist that a statute must be enacted with the consent of the three estates of the realm; we may be certain that the third estate was not represented at Merton, and may gravely doubt whether it was represented at Marlborough. On the other hand, we may take it as generally admitted that the king can not by his mere word make law. If he legislates, this must be by the counsel of the prelates and nobles; even if he ordains, this should be by the counsel, or at least with the witness, of his habitual counsellors[1]. But it is not easy to mark off the province of ordinances from the province of laws. In 1253 Henry issued an ordinance for the maintenance of the peace; it contained little, if anything, that was very new. Matthew Paris tells us that he wished to add to it something that was new, foreign, Savoyard. He wished to give to one who was robbed, an action against those whose duty it was to pursue the robbers; apparently he wished to do what his son did successfully by the statute of Winchester. Perhaps he desired to imitate an edict issued by his father-in-law Count Raymond of Provence in 1243[2]. But he had to withdraw this part of his decree, because so large a change in the law could not be made without the common assent of the baronage[3]. But between large changes and small, between changes and ameliorations, between laws and rules of procedure, no accurate lines could be drawn.

That the king is below the law is a doctrine which even a The king below the law.

important ordinance of 1255 against alienation, recently discovered on the Close Roll by Mr Turner and printed by him in L. Q. R. xii. 299. Besides all this Matthew Paris mentions a considerable number of acts of a legislative kind, *e.g.* vol. v. pp. 15, 18, an edict of 1248 relating to the coinage; p. 35, an edict relating to vengeance upon adulterers. The rolls of Henry's day have yet to be carefully searched for the remains of legislation.

[1] Rob. Grosseteste Epistolae, p. 96: Grosseteste to Raleigh: 'nec tam idiota sum quod credam ad alicuius suggestionem te vel alium sine principis et magnatum consilio posse leges condere vel commutare.'

[2] For this see Giraud, Histoire du droit français, ii. 24. It will be remembered that Henry's queen belongs to the house of Provence on her father's, to that of Savoy on her mother's side. Raymond himself may have copied what Matthew calls a *consuetudo Sabaudica*.

[3] The ordinance is printed in the Select Charters. Mat. Par. v. 369: 'praesertim cum tanta legis permutatio sine communi assensu barnagii constitui minime valuisset.'

royal justice may fearlessly proclaim[1]. The theory that in every
state there must be some man or definite body of men above the
law, some 'sovereign' without duties and without rights, would
have been rejected. Had it been accepted in the thirteenth
century, the English kingship must have become an absolute
monarchy, for nowhere else than in the person of the king could
the requisite 'sovereignty' have been found. But, for one thing,
nobody supposed that the king even with the consent of the [p. 161]
English prelates and barons could alter the common law of the
catholic church. If the theory of sovereignty popular among
Englishmen of our own day be pressed upon the reluctant
middle ages, the whole of Western Christendom must be
treated as one state[2]. Theology can be brought in to explain
or to conceal any difficulty that there may be in the conception
of a king, who though subject to no man, is subject to the
law:—God is subject to law, and has even made himself subject
to the law for man[3]. The practical question is whether there
is any mode in which the law can be enforced against the king.
That no ordinary process of his courts will touch him is admitted[4]. For a while men speculate as to whether in an extreme
case the Earl of Chester as count of the palace may not have
some coercive power over the king[5]. A more acceptable solution,
especially when these palatine counts have died out, is that the
incorporate realm represented by the baronage may judge the
king in his own court, if the worst come to the worst[6]. But
there is no established orderly method whereby this can be
accomplished, and the right to restrain an erring king, a king
who should be God's vicar, but behaves as the devil's vicar[7], is

---

[1] Bracton, f. 5 b, 107; Note Book, i. 29–33.

[2] Sidgwick, Elements of Politics, p. 21.

[3] Kingsford, Song of Lewes, pp. 103–4, 113–8.

[4] This matter will be discussed below when we speak of the King and the Crown.

[5] Mat. Par. iii. 337—8. At Henry's coronation the earl carries the sword of St. Edward 'in signum quod comes est palatii et regem si oberret habeat de iure potestatem cohibendi.' It seems not impossible that this theory, which can not have had any warrant in English precedents, was borrowed from Germany, where men were asserting that a court presided over by the Pfalzgraf might even adjudge the Emperor to death; Schröder, D. R. G., 468.

[6] Bracton, f. 171 b. The question whether the violent passage on f. 34 comes from Bracton has been discussed elsewhere; see Note Book, i. 29—33.

[7] Bracton, f. 107 b: 'Dum facit iustitiam, vicarius est Regis Eterni, minister autem diaboli dum declinat ad iniuriam.'

rather a right of revolution, a right to defy a faithless lord and
to make war upon him, than a right that can be enforced in
form of law.   The result of the barons' war is to demonstrate
that though the king is not above the law, the law has no means
of punishing him, and no direct means of compelling him to
make redress for the wrongs that he has done.

The unenacted part—and this is the great bulk—of the law   *Unenacted*
[p. 162] seems to be conceived as custom (*consuetudo*).   The most im-   *law and*
portant of all customs is the custom of the king's court.   The   *custom.*
custom may be extended by analogical reasoning; we may
argue from one case to another case which is similar though not
precisely similar[1].   On the other hand, we should be assigning
far too early a date for our modern ideas, if we supposed that the
law of the thirteenth century was already 'case-law,' or that a
previous judgment was regarded as 'a binding authority'; it
would but be an illustration of the custom of the court.
Bracton achieved the marvellous feat of citing some five
hundred cases from the judicial rolls.   But Bracton stands
quite alone; his successors Fleta and Britton abbreviate his
work by omitting the citations.   By some piece of good fortune
Bracton, a royal justice, obtained possession of a large number
of rolls.   But the ordinary litigant or his advocate would have
had no opportunity of searching the rolls, and those who know
what these records are like will feel safe in saying that even the
king's justices can not have made a habit of searching them for
principles of law.   Again, we may see that Bracton had not our
modern notions of 'authority.'   He has told us how he set
himself to peruse the ancient judgments of the just because his
ignorant and uneducated contemporaries were misrepresenting
the law; he appealed from them to the great men of the past,
to Martin Pateshull and William Raleigh[2].   On rare occasions

---

[1] Bracton, f. 1 b : 'Si autem aliqua nova et inconsueta emerserint et quae
prius usitata non fuerint in regno, si tamen similia evenerint, per simile
iudicentur, cum bona sit occasio a similibus procedere ad similia.   Si autem
talia nunquam prius evenerint, et obscurum et difficile sit eorum iudicium, tunc
ponantur iudicia in respectum usque ad magnam curiam, ut ibi per consilium
curiae terminentur.'   Thus in a quite unprecedented case the court may have
to declare for law what, as Bracton almost admits, has not as yet been law.
For this purpose the court should take the form of a great assembly of prelates
and barons.   In the above passage Bracton alludes to Dig. 1. 3. 13.

[2] Bracton, f. 1, 2.

specific precedents (*exempla*) may have been alleged in court[1]; in Edward I.'s day the pleaders are already citing and 'distinguishing' previous cases[2]; but as a general rule the judges, [p. 163] assisted by clerks, who were on their way to become judges, would regard themselves as having an implicit knowledge of the *consuetudo curiae* and would not feel bound to argue about past cases. The justices of the bench would often be fully justified in behaving thus; many of them were experienced men who had worked their way upwards through all the ranks of the king's court and chancery. And so even the knights who were employed to take assizes in their shires, though they had read no law, would believe that they knew the law and custom applicable to the cases that came before them. Every man who does his duty knows a great deal of law and custom: the difficulty is to persuade him that he does not know everything[3].

Local customs.

The custom of the king's court is the custom of England, and becomes the common law. As to local customs, the king's justices will in general phrases express their respect for them[4]. We see no signs of any consciously conceived desire to root them out[5]. None the less, if they are not being destroyed, their further growth is checked. Especially in all matters of procedure, the king's court, which is now obtaining a thorough control over all other courts, is apt to treat its own as the only just rules[6]. A heavy burden of proof is cast upon those

---

[1] Note Book, pl. 1213: the Earl of Chester appeals to cases concerning other palatine earls. Ibid. pl. 1227: in the exceedingly important case raising the question whether a palatinate can be partitioned, the magnates reject foreign precedents; 'nec voluerunt iudicare per exempla usitata in partibus transmarinis.' In 1291 the Earl of Gloucester, being concerned in a case which raised an unusual question, asked the king that the rolls of Pateshull (ob. 1229) and of later judges might be searched for precedents, and a precedent was produced from 1248; Rot. Parl. i. 66—7. Of course the rolls were often produced to show that a concrete question was *res iudicata*; but this is quite another matter.

[2] See *e.g.* Y. B. 21—2 Edw. I. p. 146. Occasionally the appeal to a precedent is entered on the roll as the substance of the plea: Northumberland Assize Rolls, p. 223.

[3] Bracton, f. 1 b: 'licet sint nonnulli qui de propria scientia praesumentes, quasi nihil iuris ignorent, nolunt alicuius consilium expetere.'

[4] Bracton, f. 1.

[5] For an instance of a custom that is declared to be unlawful, see Northumberland Assize Rolls, p. 353: 'illa consuetudo omnino est contra omnes leges.'

[6] Bracton, f. 329. The procedure of the feudal courts in respect of such matters as summons and essoins may differ from that of the king's court,

who would apply other rules; they must be prepared to show
not merely that a local tradition is in their favour, but that this
tradition has borne fruit in actual practice and governed the
decisions of the local courts[1].　The instances that we get of
[p.134] customs peculiar to counties or other wide tracts of land, such
as the episcopal barony of Winchester[2] or the honour of
Britanny[3], are of no great importance.　The law about frankpledge, the law about the presentment of Englishry, may
be somewhat differently understood in the various parts of
England; and in the north there prevail certain forms of land
tenure which are hardly to be found in the south:—but this is
a small matter.　The county courts are held under the presidency of sheriffs who will ask advice from Westminster when
difficult cases come before them[4].　Every manor will indeed
have its own customs, and to the unfree men these customs will
be very important; such rights as they have against their lords,
save the bare right to life and limb, will be but customary
and will not be acknowledged by the general law nor sanctioned by the king's court.　Still these manorial usages are
not so various as we might have expected them to be.　If a
custumal be put into our hands, only after a minute examination of it shall we be able to guess whether it comes from the
west or from the east, from Somersetshire or from Essex.　The
great estates of the great nobles have been widely dispersed;
the same steward has travelled throughout England holding all
his lord's courts, reducing their procedure to uniformity, and
completing in a humbler sphere the work of the king's itinerant
justices[5].　When the time comes for the king's courts to protect
that villein tenure which has become copyhold tenure, there will
be little difficulty about the establishment of a set of uniform

but as regards warranty, pleading, and battle the rules of the king's court must
be observed.

　[1] Bracton's Note Book, pl. 834.　The suitors of Havering are asked to
produce a precedent (*exemplum*) for a judgment that they have delivered; not
being able to do this, they are amerced.

　[2] Bracton, f. 85 b: 'licet in quibusdam partibus et per abusum observetur
in contrarium, sicut in episcopatu Wintoniae'; Note Book, pl. 282.

　[3] Note Book, pl. 623: 'talis est consuetudo in feodo Comitis Britanniae.'

　[4] Royal Letters, i. 103.　A difficult case having arisen in the county court of
Nottingham, the bailiff who held the court advises the sheriff to obtain the
opinion of the king's council.

　[5] Select Pleas in Manorial Courts, p. 3.

rules which will serve as a 'common law' for copyholds. Within
the walls of a chartered borough peculiar customs can grow
vigorously, for the charter will serve to protect them against
the meddling of the king's justices. The *consuetudo* of the
borough will be the *lex* of the borough, and sometimes it will be
solemnly committed to writing[1]. But even here there is less
variety than we might have looked for. The aspiring town was [p. 165]
often content to receive as a privilege the custom of some
famous borough, Winchester or Bristol or Oxford, and thenceforward in case of doubt it would send to its mother town for an
exposition of the rules that should guide it[2]. On the whole, the
local variations from the general law of the land are of no great
moment, and seldom, if ever, can we connect them with ethnical
differences or with remote history. We can no longer mark off
the Danelaw from Mercia or Wessex ; we hear of little that is
strange from Cornwall or from Cumberland. The strong central
power has quietly subdued all things unto itself. It has
encountered no resistance. No English county ever rebels for
the maintenance of its customary law.

Kentish
customs.
　　Kent is somewhat of an exception; it has a considerable
body of customs; there is a *lex Kantiae*[3]. In Edward I.'s day
a written statement of these customs was sanctioned by the
king's justices in eyre[4]. In the main they are concerned with
the maintenance of a peculiar form of land-tenure known as
gavelkind. The name seems to tell us that the chief characteristic of that tenure is or has been the payment of *gafol*,
of rent, as distinguished from the performance of military
service on the one hand and of agricultural labour on the
other[5]. There is in Kent a large class of landholders, who are
not knights, who are not gentle folk; they pay rent to their
lords; their tenure is protected by law; they are not burdened
with 'week work.' They are free men; indeed in Edward I.'s
day it is said that every one born in Kent is born free[6]. The
customs of Kent are, at least for the more part, the customs of
these gavelkinders; customs which fall within the province of

---

[1] More will be said of the borough customs in a later chapter.

[2] Gross, Gild Merchant, i. 259.

[3] Note Book, pl. 1644 : 'secundum legem Kantiae.'

[4] Statutes, i. 223.

[5] Elton, Tenures of Kent, p. 29. In the form *gavelingude* the word occurs
on our earliest plea roll ; Rolls of King's Court (Pipe Roll Soc.), p. 43.

[6] Statutes, i. 223 ; Y. B. 30—31 Edw. I. p. 163.

private law, which regulate the wife's dower and the husband's curtesy, which divide the dead tenant's land among all his sons, showing however a certain preference for the youngest, which determine the procedure that the lord must adopt if his rent be in arrear, and which, contrary to the general law, allow the sons of the hanged felon to inherit from him. Thus the task of [p. 166] accounting for the *lex Kantiae* is that of explaining a passage in the social and economic history of England, and a difficult passage. There is little in Domesday Book that marks off Kent from the surrounding counties, little indeed to make us think that at the date of the survey it was a peculiarly free county, that it was as free as the shires of the Danelaw[1]. We shall hardly find an answer to our question in the fact that the churches held wide lands in Kent: church lands are not the lands on which as a general rule we find many freeholders or many free men. No doubt some traits in the Kentish customs may be described as archaic—they enshrine old English proverbs, and a legend grew up telling how the men of Kent had made special terms with the Conqueror—but probably we shall do well in looking for the explanation of what has to be explained to the time which lies on this side of the Conquest[2]. Kent is no mountain home of liberty, no remote fastness in which the remnant of an ancient race has found refuge; it is the garden of England, of all English counties that which is most exposed to foreign influences. The great roads which join London to the seaboard are the arteries along which flows money, the destructive solvent of seignorial power. The tillers

---

[1] In Domesday Book and older charters Kent is distinguished by peculiar land measures, the *sulung* and the yoke (*iugum*). Also it had been lightly taxed; Maitland, Domesday Book, 466, 484. We can, however, find nothing in the record which in any way suggests that the numerous *villani* of Kent are in any respect better off than the *villani* of other counties or that they stand on a par with the *sokemanni* or the small *libere tenentes* of Norfolk and Suffolk. See however Kenny, Primogeniture, p. 29.

[2] Among the ancient features we may reckon the allotment of the 'aster' or hearth to the youngest son, and the peculiar nine-fold payment plus a wergild whereby a tenant can redeem land that he has lost by non-payment of rent. The proverb which sends 'the father to the bough and the son to the plough' seems corrupt. In the oldest versions of it the son goes to the 'lowe,' the fire, the hearth, the aster; Note Book, pl. 1644; Statutes, i. 223. The custumal ends with an assertion that the usages which it describes are older than the Conquest. As to the legend of the moving wood of Swanscombe, this first appears at a very late day; Freeman, Norman Conquest, iii. 539.

of Kentish soil can maintain their ancient or obtain new
liberties, because their lords have learnt to want money and
will rather have current coin than manorial rights. The gavelkinders are prosperous; they purchase a royal charter from
Henry III.[1]. There is general prosperity in Kent: even the
knights of the county are anxious that the *lex Kantiae* should
be observed[2]. All classes in the county seem to be bound [p. 167]
together by a tie of local patriotism. They feel that they are
better off than other Englishmen are[3]. In course of time there
must be 'treatises on gavelkind' and learned books on 'the
tenures of Kent,' for when once a district has established an
exemption from certain of the ordinary rules of law, the
number of the rules from which it is exempt will be apt to
grow[4]. But on the whole, the brief Kentish custumal of the
thirteenth century is only a small exception to the generality
of the common law.

Englishry
of English
law.
English law was by this time recognized as distinctively
English, and Englishmen were proud of it. From time to time
rumours went round that the king's detestable favourites were
going to introduce foreign novelties from Poitou or Savoy.
In a case for which no English precedent could be found our
king's court refused to follow foreign, presumably French,
precedents[5]. But the main contrast to English law was to be
found in the *leges et canones*. Bracton, having probably taken
some Italian legist at his word, entertained the belief that in
almost all countries the *leges scriptae* prevailed, and that only
England was ruled by unwritten law and custom[6]. This was
a mistake, for the Roman jurisprudence was but slowly pene-
trating into northern France and had hardly touched Germany;
but it served to make a great contrast more emphatic:
England was not governed by the *leges scriptae*. All men
know how at the Merton parliament the assembled barons
declared with one voice that they would not change the laws of

---

[1] Statutes, i. 225.　　　　　　　[2] Note Book, pl. 1338, 1644.

[3] Observe the first words of the custumal:—'These are the usages and
customs which *the community of Kent* claims to have in tenements of gavelkind
and gavelkind folk.'

[4] This is well shown by the establishment at a very late period of a custom
to devise gavelkind land by will, a matter fully discussed by Elton, Tenures of
Kent, 73—8.

[5] The case as to the partition of the Chester palatinate; see above, p. 184.

[6] Bracton, f. 1.

England[1]. Perhaps we do well to treat this as an outburst of nationality and conservatism. English law is to be maintained because it is English, for as to the specific question then at issue, namely, whether bastards should be legitimated by the [p. 168] marriage of their parents, we should hardly have suspected our barons of having a strong and unanimous opinion on so arguable a point. Curiously enough in the very next year the Norman exchequer decided to follow the church's rule, perhaps by way of showing that, despite King Henry's claims, the breach between Normandy and England was final[2]. But it is by no means impossible that the celebrated *Nolumus* expresses a professional as well as a national conservatism; at any rate it was no baron but a lawyer, an ecclesiastic, a judge, Bracton's master, William Raleigh, who had to meet the clerical forces and to stand up for English practice against the laws and canons and consensus of Christendom[3].

Of 'equity' as of a set of rules which can be put beside the rules of 'law,' or of courts whose proper function is the administration, not of law, but of equity, we shall hear nothing for a long time to come. We must however remember, first, that a contrast between *aequitas* and *rigor iuris* is already a part of what passes as philosophical jurisprudence, and secondly, that our king's court is according to very ancient tradition a court that can do whatever equity may require. Long ago this principle was asserted by the court of Frankish kings and, at all events since the Conquest, it has been bearing fruit in England[4]. It means that the royal tribunal is not so strictly bound by rules that it can not defeat the devices of those who would use legal forms for the purposes of chicane; it means

Equity.

---

[1] Note Book, i. pp. 104—115. We have no authoritative text of this famous resolution; but the last word of it seems to have been *mutare*, not *mutari*.

[2] Delisle, Recueil de jugements, p. 139: 'Judicatum est quod ille qui natus fuit ante sponsalia sive post est propinquior heres ad habendam hereditatem patris...si sancta ecclesia approbet maritagium.'

[3] Rob. Grosseteste Epistolae, 76—97. Grosseteste (p. 97) writes to Raleigh: 'Induxistis testimonium Ricardi de Luci; cuius testimonium quantam et qualem habeat comparationem ad testimonia divinae scripturae et canonicae contrarium testificantia, lippis patet et tonsoribus.' The arguments which Grosseteste adduces from the Bible and the law of nature are very curious; however, he seems to expressly disclaim the notion that the king's justices could desert their ungodly precedents in favour of divine and natural law until the law of England had been changed by king and magnates.

[4] Brunner, D. R. G. ii. 135—6.

also that the justices are in some degree free to consider all the circumstances of those cases that come before them and to adapt the means to the end. In the days of Henry II. and Henry III. the king's court wields discretionary powers such as are not at the command of lowlier courts, and the use of these powers is an exhibition of 'equity.' Often on the plea rolls we [p. 169] find it written that some order is made 'by the counsel of the court' (*de consilio curiae*). It is an order that could not be asked for as a matter of strict right; the *rigor iuris* does not dictate it—would perhaps refuse it; but it is made in order that the substantial purposes of the law may be accomplished without 'circuity of action[1].' The need of a separate court of equity is not yet felt, for the king's court, which is not as yet hampered by many statutes or by accurately formulated 'case law,' can administer equity.

The king's courts.　　In the middle of the thirteenth century the high courts that do justice in the king's name are rapidly taking what will long be their final form. When in 1875 a Supreme Court of Judicature once more absorbs them, the Court of King's Bench, the Court of Common Pleas, the Court of Exchequer and the Chancery will be able to claim some six centuries of existence as distinct and separate courts[2]. To fix precisely the exact moment at which one court became two or more courts, is perhaps impossible, for 'court,' as our modern statute book would amply prove, is a term that can not easily be defined. In dealing, however, with the thirteenth century and the later middle ages we might be justified in saying that each of the high courts of the realm must have a set of rolls that is its own and a seal that is its own. A continuous memory of all that it has done seems the essence of a court's identity, and this memory takes the shape of a continuous series of written records.

---

[1] Glanvill, vii. 1: 'aliquando tamen super hoc ultimo casu in curia domini Regis de consilio curiae ita ex aequitate consideratum est.' Note Book, pl. 273, 785, 786, 900, 940, 1376. Bracton, f. 1 b: unprecedented cases are to be decided 'per consilium curiae.' In the Year Books we may sometimes see a contrast between *rigor* and *aequitas*; Y. B. 30–1 Edw. I. 120.

[2] The exchequer plea rolls do not begin until far on in Henry III.'s reign; much business of a judicial character is noticed on the memoranda rolls of the remembrancers which begin with the beginning of the reign. There are also numerous sets of rolls which set forth the more purely financial business in the form of accounts.

At what we may call an early time the exchequer ceased to be a phase of the general governing body of the realm, and became a department, with a seal and many records of its own, a financial department[1]. In Bishop Richard's Dialogue we still see all the great ones of the kingdom seated round [p. 170] the chess-board. The chief justiciar is there and the chancellor of the realm. Gradually they withdraw themselves from the ordinary work of the board, though they may attend it on special occasions. The treasurer becomes its president; its seal is kept by the chancellor of the exchequer, an officer who first appears in Henry III.'s reign[1], and the writs that it issues are tested by the senior baron[2]; as yet there is no 'chief baron[3].' From the beginning of the reign onwards men are definitely appointed to be barons of the exchequer[4]. They are chosen from among the king's clerks, but they keep the old title and are sufficiently the 'peers' of the barons of the realm to enable them to inflict amercements on noble offenders. The treasurer is the head of the court whatever it may be doing. The position of the chancellor of the exchequer is subordinate; he keeps the seal of the court, and his accounts may serve to check the treasurer's, but apparently the acts of the court are always attributed to the treasurer and barons[5].

The exchequer.

The exchequer is called a *curia*[6]. In our view it may be a compound institution, in part a judicial tribunal, in part a financial bureau. The process which in course of time will divide a great 'government office' known as the treasury from the court of law held before a chief baron and other barons, has not as yet gone far. The duty of issuing the king's treasure is performed by the treasurer with the assistance of the deputy chamberlains—already the chamberlainships have become hereditary sinecures[7]—and in this matter he is not controlled by the barons. But then in this matter he has little discretion, for he dares issue no penny save in obedience to an order which comes to him under the great or the privy seal; even for

Work of the exchequer.

---

[1] Madox, Exchequer, ii. 51.
[2] Fleta, p. 82.
[3] Foss, Judges, iii. 196.
[4] Madox, Exchequer, ii. 54.
[5] Writs sent to the exchequer are addressed to the treasurer and barons, or, if they merely order the delivery of treasure or the like, to the treasurer and chamberlains.
[6] Fleta, p. 81: 'Habet etiam Rex curiam suam et iustitiarios suos in Scaccario apud Westmonasterium residentes.'
[7] Madox, Exchequer, ii. 295.

every payment of an annual salary he requires such a warrant
from above[1]. There was, however, some rivalry between the
two departments, and during some late years of Edward I.'s
reign the treasurer, rather than the chancellor, was the king's
first minister[2]. The main work of the court or board over
which he presides is that of collecting the king's revenue. It [p. 171]
receives and audits the accounts of the sheriffs and other col-
lectors; it calls the king's debtors before it, hears what they
have to say, investigates the truth of their allegations, grants
them an acquittance or issues process against them, 'according
to the customs and usages of the exchequer.' We may perhaps
call it an administrative tribunal. If questions of fact or questions of law arise, it ought to judge impartially between the
king and his subjects; but still its duty is to get in what is due
to the king, and to do this spontaneously without waiting for
any external impulse. It is a revenue board which hears and
decides. Then also it is often empowered to give relief against
the king. Not that a subject can bring an action against the
king either here or elsewhere, but when a man thinks that he
has a claim against the king, either in respect of some money
that the king owes him, or in respect of some land that the
king has seized, he will (this is the common practice of Edward
I.'s day) present a petition to the king and council, and a
favourable response to this petition will generally delegate the
matter to the treasurer and barons and bid them do what is
right[3]. If a question of general law is involved, they will often
be told to associate with themselves the justices of the two
benches, for they themselves are supposed to know rather 'the
course of the exchequer' than the common law of the land.
However, during our period we may see an irrepressible tendency at work which will give them a power to adjudicate in
personal actions between subject and subject. In Edward's reign
they are often forbidden to do this, but they do it; and in so
doing they may be rather striving to retain old powers, powers

---

[1] This is the theme of Lord Somers's magnificent judgment in The Banker's
case; State Trials, vol. xiv. p. 1. In course of time a practice of sending to the
exchequer 'current *liberates*,' or, as we might say, standing orders for the payment of periodical charges, was adopted.

[2] Hughes, The Parliament of Lincoln, Trans. Roy. Hist. Soc. ix. 41.

[3] Rolls of Parliament, vol. 1, *passim*. It would seem that most of those
matters which in after days would have been the subjects of 'petitions of right'
were in earlier days thus delegated to the exchequer.

that had been exercised by the exchequer when it was a phase of the as yet undifferentiated 'curia,' than to usurp a new function. We are at a loss to account on the one hand for the offence that they thus gave to the community of the realm, and on the other for the persistent recourse to their tribunal of creditors who might have gone elsewhere, unless it be that a creditor might thus obtain the advantage of some of those expeditious [p. 172] and stringent processes which had been devised for the collection of crown debts. In the end, as is well known, the exchequer triumphed under the cover of fictions; but this victory belongs to a later time than that of which we are speaking[1].

Men are beginning to speak of the chancery as a *curia*[2]; but even in Edward I.'s reign it is not in our view a court of justice; it does not hear and determine causes. It was a great secretarial bureau, a home office, a foreign office and a ministry of justice. At its head was the chancellor, who, when there was no longer a chief justiciar of the realm, became the highest in rank of the king's servants. He was 'the king's secretary of state for all departments[3].' Under him there were numerous clerks. The highest in rank among them we might fairly call 'under-secretaries of state'; they were ecclesiastics holding deaneries or canonries; they were sworn of the king's council; some of them were *doctores utriusque iuris*; they were graduates, they were 'masters'; some of them as notaries of the apostolic see were men whose 'authenticity' would be admitted all the

The chancery.

---

[1] The curious point is that in this matter the barons seem to have acted in defiance not merely of laws and ordinances but of the king's own interests. Whether the well-known phrase in the Charter ('Communia placita non sequantur curiam nostram sed teneantur in aliquo loco certo') was originally intended to deprive the exchequer of jurisdiction over common pleas is doubtful; but that intention was authoritatively attributed to it in Edward I.'s day. We find Edward laying down the prohibitive rule not merely in the Articuli of 1300 (Statutes, i. 138), some of which were won from him by pressure, but in a much earlier ordinance, the so-called Statute of Rhuddlan (i. 70), where he gives as his reason the delay of the exchequer's proper business. As to the motives which sent plaintiffs to the exchequer, we find that when the king by way of exceptional favour sanctions their going thither, he sometimes expressly says that they are to have the benefit of the processes appropriate to crown debts. See Madox, Exchequer, i. 209–214, ii. 73–6.

[2] Fleta, p. 66: 'Habet etiam [Rex] curiam suam in cancellaria sua.'

[3] Stubbs, Const. Hist. i. p. 381.

world over[1]. Very little was done by the king that was not
done by a document bearing the great seal; it was 'the key of
the kingdom[2].' The exchequer and the two benches had indeed [p. 173]
seals and could issue writs running in the king's name, writs,
for example, summoning juries, coercing contumacious litigants
or carrying judgments into effect; but the province of such
writs was not very wide, and it was a very general rule that no
action could be begun in the king's courts and that no action
touching freehold could be begun anywhere without an 'original'
or (as we might say) 'originating' writ, which proceeded from
the chancery and served as the justices' warrant for entertaining
that action[3]. During the course of Edward's reign writs under
the privy seal became common; but the king was constrained to
promise that no writ which concerned the common law should
issue under that seal[4], and very many of the writs thus authen-
ticated were addressed to the chancellor and did but bid him
set the great seal to some instrument which would be the final
expression of the king's will[5]. Confidential clerks or 'secretaries,'
(for this word was coming into use) were beginning to intervene
between the king and his chancellor, sending to him written, or
carrying to him oral messages[6]. The chancellor was now a man
of exalted rank, and, though theoretically the chancery 'followed
the king,' still as a matter of fact it often happened that the
king was at one place while the chancellor was at another[7]. In

---

[1] The term *magistri* when applied to the masters in chancery seems at first
merely to mark them as men with university degrees. But they were also
praeceptores, for in certain cases they had power to order that a writ should
issue; Fleta, p. 77. Apparently the class of writs known as *magistralia*
consists of those which must be settled by one of the *magistri*; Bracton, f. 413 b.
Edward I. had two apostolic notaries in his chancery, John Arthur of Caen
and John Busshe. The series of masters of the rolls goes back to the early
years of Edward's reign. The master of the rolls is the chancellor's principal
subordinate.

[2] Mat. Par. Chron. Maj. v. 130.

[3] Writs issued by the court in the course of litigation are *brevia iudicialia*;
they are sometimes said to 'issue out of the rolls of the court;' this means that
the order for the issue of the writ is on the court's roll.

[4] Articuli super cartas, 1300, c. 6 (Statutes, i. 139).

[5] The large collection of privy seal writs in the Record Office begins in
Edward I.'s reign.

[6] Maitland, Memoranda de Parliamento, 33 Edward I., p. xxxvii.

[7] The stages by which the chancery ceased as a matter of fact to be a
peripatetic office, following the king in his progresses, have never yet been
accurately ascertained; but it seems probable that Chancellor Burnel made
some noteworthy change in 1280: Annales Monastici, ii. 393, iv. 477.

its final form almost every message, order or mandate that came, or was supposed to come, from the king, whether it concerned the greatest matter or the smallest, whether addressed to an emperor or to an escheator, whether addressed to all the lieges or to one man, was a document settled in the chancery and sealed with the great seal.　Miles of parchment, close rolls and patent rolls, fine rolls and charter rolls, Roman rolls, Gascon rolls and so forth, are covered with copies of these documents[1], [p. 174] and yet reveal but a part of the chancery's work, for no roll sets forth all those 'original' writs that were issued 'as of course[2].'

The number of writs which were issued as of course for the purpose of enabling those who thought themselves wronged to bring their cases before the law courts, increased rapidly during the reign of Henry III.　A 'register of original writs' which comes from the end of that period will be much longer than one that comes from the beginning[3].　Apparently there were some writs which could be had for nothing; for others a mark or a half-mark would be charged, while, at least during Henry's early years, there were others which were only to be had at high prices.　We may find creditors promising the king a quarter or a third of the debts that they hope to recover[4].　Some distinction seems to have been taken between necessaries and luxuries.　A royal writ was a necessary for one who was claiming freehold; it was a luxury for the creditor exacting a debt, for the local courts were open to him and he could proceed there without writ.　Elaborate glosses overlaid the king's promise that he would sell justice to none, for a line between the price of justice and those mere court fees, which are demanded even in our own day, is not easily drawn[5].　That the poor should have their writs for nothing, was an accepted maxim[6].　The almost mechanical work of penning these ordinary writs was confided to clerks who stood low in the official hierarchy, to cursitors (*cursarii*); it consisted chiefly of

The original writs.

---

[1] The best introduction to them will be found in Bémont, Rôles Gascons (Documents inédits), Paris 1896.

[2] If an intending litigant has to pay for his original writ, then an entry will be made on the fine roll, but the nature of the writ will be but briefly described, *e.g.* as 'a writ of trespass,' 'an attaint' or the like. See Fleta, p. 77. The Record Office contains large stores of these writs.

[3] Harv. L. R., iii. 175.

[4] Excerpta e Rotulis Finium, i. 29, 49, 62, 68; Harv. L. R., iii. 12.

[5] Fleta, p. 77.　　　[6] Fleta, p. 77; Excerpta e Rotulis Finium, ii. 101.

filling with names and sums of money the blanks that were left
in the forms that they found in their registers; but some clerk
of a higher grade seems to have been responsible for every
writ[1]. No finality was as yet ascribed to the register; it was
not regarded as an exhaustive scheme of justice to which no
addition could be made save by definite legislation, though a
common form, when once settled, was not to be lightly tampered
with. New writs could be made, at all events if they were
'personal,' not 'real'—any innovation 'touching freehold' was a
more serious matter—and they were made somewhat freely[2]. [p.175]
To take the best example, towards the close of Henry's reign the
action of trespass, which is full of future history, becomes common
somewhat suddenly. The chancery had not yet fallen so far
apart from the courts of law that the justices could not get new
writs made if they wanted them. In manuscript registers we
find a group of new writs ascribed to William Raleigh who was
for a while the foremost judge in the king's court[3]. For
some years before the barons' war Henry attempted to govern
without a chancellor or with a chancellor who was such only in
name[4]; his chancery was no serious obstacle to his will and
pleasure, though now and again even a vice-chancellor might
resign rather than set the seal to a document that he regarded
as illegal[5]. Complaints against new and unaccustomed writs grew
loud[6]. The discontented prelates and barons demanded a real
chancellor and one sworn to issue no writs, save 'writs of course,'
without warrant from the baronial council[7]. Under Edward I.
two different causes tended to give stability and finality to the
cycle of original writs. On the one hand, it became apparent
that to invent new remedies was to make new laws, and events
were deciding that only in a parliament of the three estates
could new laws be made: even when the king was concerned,
the list of actions was to be a closed list[8]. On the other hand,

---

[1] Fleta, p. 77-8.   [2] Bracton, f. 413 b–414 b.

[3] Harv. L. R., iii. 173-4-6.

[4] Mat. Par. Chron. Maj. iii. 364, 491, 495, 530.

[5] Ibid. iii. 629 ; v. 594.

[6] This begins as early as 1244 ; ibid. iv. 363, 367 ; vi. 363.

[7] Ann. Burton, 448.

[8] Placita de Quo Warranto, 681, 686 : writs brought by the king are quashed
by the judges. Rolls of Parl. i. 52 : Edward complains to his council that a
particular case has occurred which is not exactly met by any of the three writs
of escheat current in the chancery.

chancery and chancellor had grown in dignity. There were
great chancellors who were usually the king's first ministers.
The chancery was by this time independent of the 'benches.'
The days when the chancellor would often sit among the justices
were passing away, the days for stiff official correspondence
between the courts and the chancery had come.

It is but rarely that we hear of the chancery or the chan- ^{The chan-}
cellor performing any work that can fairly be called judicial. ^{cery not a}
^{tribunal.}
The issuing of the 'original' writs was not judicial work, though
[p.176] we may learn from petitions addressed to the chancellor and
from other sources that it was not always done mechanically:
a friend of the chancellor might hope for a few words in
his writ that a stranger would hardly have obtained [1]. Of
any 'equitable jurisdiction' exercised in the chancery we hear
nothing; the king's justices still believe that they can do what
equity requires. But even of what afterwards became the
'common law jurisdiction' of the chancery, the jurisdiction of
its 'ordinary' or 'Latin side' we hear very little. In later
days that jurisdiction was concerned chiefly, though not solely,
with cases in which a subject required some relief against the
king[2]. In the latter half of the thirteenth century a subject
who has aught against the king has, at least as a general rule,
but one course open to him. He presents a petition to the
king or the king and his council. This may come before the
king himself, or before a full meeting of the council, or before a
select body of councillors assigned to deal with such petitions
as can be easily disposed of. If he gets a favourable answer,
this—since as yet he has shown but some plausible case for
relief—will in general send him before some tribunal which will
be instructed by a writ from the chancery to hear his claim
and do what is just. Commonly that tribunal is the exchequer,
which may be afforced for the occasion by the presence of the
chancellor and the justices; sometimes it is one of the benches.
Occasionally, but rarely, the chancellor is appointed to hear and
decide the cause[3].

---

[1] Royal Letters, i. 68, 276, 282; ii. 48.

[2] Hale, Jurisdiction of the House of Lords, 47; Blackstone, Comm. iii. 48.

[3] See Rolls of Parliament, vol. i. *passim*, and Maitland, Memoranda de
Parliamento, 33 Edward I. An instance of a case committed to the chancellor
occurs in Rolls of Parl. i. p. 60 : 'Veniant partes coram cancellario et ostendat
ei Adam quare ipsos eiecit ; et fiat eis iustitia.' Such a response as this is rare.
Already a practice obtained of acknowledging debts in the chancery, and when

[p. 177]

The two benches.

The king's court—to say no more of the exchequer and the chancery—has been slowly breaking up into three tribunals; there is a Common Bench, a King's Bench, and a yet higher court, which in the days of Edward I. we may indifferently call the King in Council or the King in Parliament. A cleft began to appear when Henry II. in 1178 appointed certain justices to sit permanently in his court and hear the complaints of all men, but reserved the more arduous cases for himself and the wise men of the realm[1]. It disappeared for a while under the absentee Richard; it reappeared under John, who travelled through the country with justices in his train while other justices remained on 'the bench' at Westminster[2]. Again it disappeared for a while during the minority of Henry III.; we can see no permanent, central tribunal save that held by 'the justices of the bench' who sit term after term at Westminster, though the council of regency may in some sort supervise their work. It begins to reappear and this time for good and all when Henry is of full age and does justice in person. From the year 1234 onwards—but the exact date can hardly be fixed—there are two different courts, each of which has its own set of rolls[3]. The one is held before the justices of 'the bench' who sit at Westminster, its records are the 'de banco rolls'; the other follows the king, its records are the 'coram rege rolls.' A litigant summoned before the one is told to come 'before our justices at Westminster'; if summoned before the other, he must appear 'before us wheresoever we shall be in England.' And then the Great Charter has decreed that 'common pleas' are not to follow the king, but are to be heard in some certain place[4]. Thus 'the bench' has become the appropriate tribunal for

this had been done, a writ of execution would issue from the chancery in the creditor's favour. Fleta, p. 76, mentions this as a case in which a 'judicial' writ issues from the chancery. But here originally there was little to be called jurisdiction, for the creditor who had a recognizance had in theory what was equivalent to a judgment in his favour, and execution would issue as a matter of course. It is probable that in dealing with the king's wards the chancery exercised something like jurisdiction, *e.g.* by deciding that full age had or had not been attained, by allotting dower to widows and making partition among co-heirs; but on the whole this (like much of the work done in the Chancery Division to this day) is the work of an administrative office rather than of a tribunal.

[1] Above, p. 153.

[2] Select Pleas of the Crown (Selden Soc.), pp. xiii–xix.

[3] Note Book, i. pp. 56–58.　　　　[4] Charter, 1215, c. **17**.

ordinary civil suits between subject and subject.   The comple-
mentary rule, which assigns the 'pleas of the crown' to the
court held *coram rege,* seems to grow up gradually and not to
be the outcome of legislation[1].   The court held *coram rege* is
superior to, for it can correct the errors of, 'the bench'[2].   Then
[p. 178] early in Edward I.'s reign 'the bench,' though in formal documents it will keep its old name and until 1875 be simply 'the
bench,' begins to be called the Common Bench, and the name
of King's Bench is given to the court that is held *coram rege,*
or rather to one offshoot of it[3].

We have to state the matter thus, for the court that during
Henry's reign is held *coram rege* breaks into segments.   For
ordinary purposes it is a court held by a few professional
justices; but at any moment it may become a fuller and
grander tribunal; the king may be there with his councillors;
all the prelates and barons of the realm may be assembled.
But whatever form it takes, it seems to be considered as
essentially but one tribunal, 'the court of our lord the king
held before the king himself.'   In modern terms we might say
that the court held before the king in parliament and the court
held before the king in council are the court of king's bench
raised to a higher power.   In Edward I.'s reign there comes a
further change.   The term 'king's bench' is brought into use
to signify the court held theoretically *coram rege* by the professional justices, and just about the same time a third set of
plea rolls begins to appear.   Besides the 'de banco rolls' and
the 'coram rege rolls' there are those records which we know

Council, parliament and benches.

---

[1] It is of comparatively late origin.   There are many criminal cases on the
de banco rolls of Edward I.

[2] Note Book, pl. 1166, 1189, 1190.

[3] In discussions of this obscure matter it has too often been forgotten that
so long as there was a Court of Common Pleas the most solemn title of its
justices was 'Justices of *the* Bench,' while in 1875 the justices of the Queen's
Bench were 'Justices assigned to hold pleas before the Queen herself.'   In
10 Edw. I. we have the King's Bench distinguished from the 'Great Bench';
Plac. Abbrev. p. 274.   About this time 'the justices of either bench' becomes a
common phrase.   Foss (ii. 160–186), viewing the matter from a biographer's
stand-point, may be right in fixing a late date for the final establishment of the
two courts, for until the end of Henry's reign the judges are easily moved
backwards and forwards between the two courts or divisions; but long before
this there are two parallel sets of rolls; and Bracton may serve as an instance of
a judge who, so far as we know, never sat at 'the bench,' but for several years
held pleas 'coram rege.'

as the 'parliament rolls'; the earliest extant roll comes from
the year 1290. For some time to come, however, the cleft is
not very deep; the same plea that is found on a parliament roll
may be found also on a *coram rege* roll[1]. For judicial purposes
the parliamentary sessions of the council can be conceived as
strengthened, as 'afforced,' sessions of the king's bench. All the
justices and all the chiefs of the great offices, all the masters [p. 179]
in chancery and so forth, are members of the council, and,
if they are not wanted elsewhere, will be summoned to those
plenary sessions of the council that are known as 'parliaments.'
There remain in suspense many questions as to the composition
and jurisdiction of this highest of all tribunals. Is that tribunal
to be the assemblage of prelates and barons, or is it to be the
king's council; is it to be but a court of second instance, or
is it to have any original jurisdiction? The fourteenth century
must answer these questions; the thirteenth leaves them open[2].

Itinerant
justices.

As to the courts held in the king's name by men who are
acting under temporary commissions, men who in a large
sense of the term are 'itinerant justices,' we must say but little,
though were we to descend to details much might be said, for
the king's power to issue commissions has hardly a limit in law,
but few limits in custom, and new needs are being ever and anon
met by new devices. But we may distinguish the main types
of these commissions. What seems treated as the humblest
is the commission to deliver a gaol. This in the latter part of
Henry III.'s reign is done very frequently; generally it is done
by some three or four knights of the shire, and thus, long before
the institution of justices of the peace, the country knights had
been accustomed to do high criminal justice[3]. In order to
dispose of the possessory assizes of novel disseisin and mort

---

[1] Hale, Jurisdiction of the House of Lords, p. 53.

[2] The problem for the fourteenth century is neatly raised by the words of
Fleta, p. 66: 'Habet enim Rex curiam suam *in concilio suo in parliamentis suis,*
praesentibus praelatis, comitibus, baronibus, proceribus et aliis viris peritis
[*corr.* iurisperitis].' Besides this the king has a court (King's Bench) of justices
'locum suum tenentes in Anglia'; also he has a court before the justices of
the (Common) Bench at Westminster. The parallel passage in Bracton (f. 105 b,
108) recognizes but two central courts, the Bench, and a higher court which is
more specifically the king's own court, where his 'chief justices' sit. See
Maitland, Memoranda de Parliamento, 33 Edw. I., Introduction, p. lxxix.

[3] Thus Cambridge gaol seems to have been delivered about twenty-four times
in seven years, beginning with 2 Edw. I., the deliverers being usually Cambridgeshire knights. Reports of Dep. Keeper, xliii–xlix.

d'ancestor, a vast number of commissions were issued in every
year. Early in Henry's reign this work was often entrusted to
four knights of the shire; at a later time one of the permanent
justices would usually be named and allowed to associate some
knights with himself. Apparently a justice of assize had often
to visit many towns or even villages in each county; his work
[p. 180] was not all done at the county town[1]. It must have been heavy,
for these actions were extremely popular. In the second year
of Edward's reign some two thousand commissions of assize
were issued[2]. Just at that time the practice seems to have
been to divide England into four circuits and to send two
justices of assize round each circuit; but a full history of the
circuits would be intricate and wearisome. Above all the other
commissions ranked the commission for an *iter ad omnia placita*,
or more briefly for an *iter* or eyre. An eyre was by this time a
long and laborious business. In the first place, if we suppose
an eyre in Cambridgeshire announced, this has the effect of
stopping all Cambridgeshire business in the bench. Litigants
who have been told to appear before the justices at Westminster
will now have to appear before the justices in eyre at Cambridge.
There is no business before the bench at Westminster if an eyre
has been proclaimed in all the counties[3]. Then, again, the
justices are provided with a long list of interrogatories (*capitula
itineris*) which they are to address to local juries. Every
hundred, every vill in the county must be represented before
them. These interrogatories—their number increases as time
goes on—ransack the memories of the jurors and the local
records for all that has happened in the shire since the last eyre
took place some seven years ago; every crime, every invasion of
royal rights, every neglect of police duties must be presented[4].
The justices must sit in the county town from week to week
and even from month to month before they will have got
through the tedious task and inflicted the due tale of fines and

---

[1] Bracton took Devonshire assizes at Exeter, Morchard, Molton, Torrington,
Chulmleigh, Barnstaple, Umberleigh; Note Book, i. p. 17.

[2] Calendar of Patent Rolls in 43rd Rep. of Dep. Keeper.

[3] During Henry's reign there seem to have been several years in which
no court was sitting at Westminster, eyres having been proclaimed in all or
most of the counties: Note Book, i. pp. 141-2.

[4] As to these articles see Select Pleas of the Crown (Selden Soc.), p. xxii.
More of them in our section on Trespasses.

amercements[1]. Three or four of the permanent judges will be
placed in the commission; with them will be associated some of
the magnates of the district; bishops and even abbots, to the
scandal of strict churchmen, have to serve as justices in eyre[2]. [p. 181]
Probably it was thought expedient that some of the great
freeholders of the county should be commissioned, in order that
no man might say that his judges were not his peers. An eyre
was a sore burden; the men of Cornwall fled before the face of
the justices[3]; we hear assertions of a binding custom that an
eyre shall not take place more than once in seven years[4].
Expedients were being adopted which in course of time would
enable the justices of assize to preside in the country over the
trial of actions which were pending before the benches; thus
without the terrors of an eyre, the trial of civil actions would
take place in the counties and jurors would no longer be called
to Westminster from their remote homes. But these expedients
belong for the more part to Edward's reign; under his father a
jury wearily travelling from Yorkshire or Devonshire towards
London must have been no very uncommon sight[5].

Triumph
of royal
justice.

The king's courts have been fast becoming the only judicial
tribunals of any great importance. Throughout the reign the
bulk of their plea rolls increased at a rapid rate. Every term
the bench at Westminster entertained a multitude of causes.
The litigants who came before it were often men of lowly rank
who were quarrelling about small parcels of land. Though we

[1] The proceedings of an eyre can be best studied in Page, Three Assize Rolls
for Northumberland (Surtees Society), and in the rolls which Mr Chadwyck
Healey is publishing for the Somersetshire Record Society.

[2] Bishops were largely employed in the first eyre of the reign. In 1236
the appointment of an abbot is a scandal; Rob. Grosseteste, Epistolae, pp. 105,
108.

[3] Ann. Dunst. p. 135 (1233): 'quorum metu omnes ad silvas fugerunt.'

[4] Ann. Wigorn. p. 446 (1261). Close Roll, Hen. III. No. 77, m. 9d: an
eyre in Norfolk is postponed as seven years have not elapsed since the last eyre.

[5] A 'nisi prius' clause was occasionally used as early as 1225; see Note
Book, pl. 721 and many other cases. The burden of jury service was not so
intolerable as it might seem, did we not remember (1) that by far the most
popular of all actions were the assizes of novel disseisin and mort d'ancestor;
(2) that these assizes were not as a general rule actions pending in the court at
Westminster, but were from the moment of their inception consigned to justices
of assize; (3) that 'trespass' did not become common until late in the reign;
(4) that jurors were seldom required for actions of debt or detinue or for actions
on prohibitions; (5) that a 'grand assize' was, or ought to have been, constituted of knights.

hear some bad stories of corrupt and partial judges[1], it is plain
that this powerful, central tribunal must have been well trusted
by the nation at large. Rich and poor alike would go to it
if they could. The local courts were being starved, and this
result we can not ascribe altogether to the ambition or greed
of the lawyers at Westminster. Of his own free will the small
[p. 182] freeholder passed by his lord's court and the county court on
his way to the great hall. He could there obtain a stronger and
better commodity than any that was to be had elsewhere, a
justice which, as men reckoned in those days, was swift and
masterful; he could there force his adversary to submit to a
verdict instead of finding that his claim was met by some
antique oath with oath-helpers. The voice of the nation, or
what made itself heard as such, no longer, as in 1215, demanded
protection for the seignorial courts[2]; it asked that the royal
court should be endowed with yet new and anti-feudal powers;
it was to be in all temporal causes supreme[3]. Men were fast
coming to the opinion that it ought to be, in Bentham's phrase,
'omnicompetent,' and that for every wrong there should be a
remedy in the court of their lord the king. This is not an idea
that is imposed from above upon an unwilling people. Bracton
himself, the royal judge, the professional lawyer, does not
thrust it forward as an obvious principle. He explains or even
apologizes for certain manifestations of kingly justice which
may seem to be at variance with feudal rules[4]. But still this
principle is at work: it is the king's business to provide a
competent remedy for every wrong[5].

The number of the justices whom Henry kept in his pay The judges
was never large. If there were some three or four in his train

---

[1] Mat. Par. v. 213, 223, 240, charges against Henry of Bath; v. 628, against
Henry de la Mare.

[2] Charter, 1215, c. 34.

[3] Petition of 1258, c. 29: the great lords are not to make their courts
tribunals of second instance. Provisions of Westminster, c. 9, 10, damages
are to be given in the assize of mort d'ancestor; c. 6, procedure in dower *unde
nihil habet* (an action which controverts feudal principles) is to be speedier;
c. 18, the royal control over all actions touching freehold is to be secured.
Stat. Marlb. c. 29: the scope of the writs of entry is to be extended at the
expense of the writ of right.

[4] Bracton, f. 106, a defence of dower *unde nihil habet;* f. 281, a defence of
the writ of cosinage; comp. Note Book, pl. 1215.

[5] Bracton, f. 414 b: 'pertinet enim ad regem ad quamlibet iniuriam com-
pescendam remedium competens adhibere.'

to hold the pleas *coram rege*, some four or five at 'the bench,' and three or four barons in the exchequer, this was enough. During the last years of the reign 'the bench' seems to have but three, or even but two, occupants[1]. These judges are very truly the king's servants; he can move them about as seems best to him or dismiss them at a moment's notice. By slow degrees the work of hearing and deciding causes is being disengaged from governmental business. The office of a chief [p. 183] justiciar who is both the king's prime minister and the president of the highest law court became extinct. Even Hubert de Burgh had hardly filled the place of Lucy and Glanvill, of Hubert Walter and Geoffrey Fitz Peter, for he seldom sat on the bench. For a short while after his fall in 1232 the justiciarship was committed to a lawyer, to Stephen Segrave; but from 1234, when Segrave was disgraced and dismissed, until 1258, when the time of revolution was at hand, the justiciarship was in abeyance. The title was then revived and borne for a season by Hugh Bigot, Hugh le Despenser and Philip Basset, whose names represent the alternating fortunes of contending factions. At last in 1268 Robert de Brus, the future 'competitor' for the crown of Scotland, was appointed 'chief justiciar to hold pleas before the king'; and the words thus added to the old title signified that only for judicial purposes was he to be chief justiciar[2]. With him began the new line of the chief justices of England who are but the presidents of a law court, and about the same time the presiding judge at 'the bench' or 'the common bench' began to be formally styled its chief justice[3]. It was no longer expected of the judge that he should be a statesman, or of the statesman that he should be expert in the law. We hear indeed complaints that the king puts unworthy and ignorant men upon the bench, men who will do

---

[1] Note Book, i. pp. 144–5.

[2] Foss, Judges, ii. 270. It is convenient to give the title of 'chief justice' to the series of presidents of the king's bench which begins at or about this point, reserving 'chief justiciar' for the line of first ministers or viceroys which is becoming extinct. But this is a modern artifice. The change of style was really a very small one; it consisted in adding to the old title 'Capitalis Justiciarius Angliae' the limiting words 'ad placita coram Rege tenenda.' So long as Latin is used, a justice is a *iusticiarius*, a chief justice is a *capitalis iusticiarius*. In the twelfth century *iustitia* had been the commoner title.

[3] Foss, Judges, iii. 142, makes Gilbert Preston the first chief justice of the common pleas.

just what he wants; but some of the judges of Henry's reign were known to their contemporaries merely as great lawyers and seem to have earned the respect of all parties in the state[1].

Many of them were ecclesiastics; among such we may reckon Martin Pateshull, William Raleigh, Robert Lexington, William of York, Henry of Bratton. Even Stephen Segrave seems to have had enough of the clerk about him to serve as a [p. 184] shield against temporal justice[2]. Bishops no longer steadily sat in the law courts, though they might now and again appear as justices in eyre; but canonries, deaneries and even bishoprics were still to be earned by good service on the bench; William Raleigh thus won the see of Norwich and William of York the see of Salisbury. However, all this was becoming somewhat scandalous; the clergy were being forbidden by the law of the church to study temporal law or decide temporal causes[3]. Before the end of the reign the lay element among the king's judges is beginning to outweigh the ecclesiastical; Thomas Multon and Roger Thurkelby are laymen who make names for themselves as learned justices[4]; but even of Edward I.'s justices not a few were clerks. This is no small change; it means that the study of English law is falling apart from all other studies. Just at the same time a class of advocates who practised in the king's courts was forming itself. Some of Edward's judges had practised at the bar of his courts; his father's judges seem for the more part to have worked their way upwards as clerks in the courts, in the exchequer, in the chancery[5]. The change brought good with it and evil. Our

---

[1] Note Book, i. pp. 24–5.   [2] Mat. Par. Chron. Maj. iii. 293.

[3] cc. 1, 2, 4, 5, 10, X. 3, 50. Ann. Burton. p. 308–9: Articles of inquiry into the life of the clergy; 'An aliqui sint...iustitiarii saeculares...An aliqui beneficiati audiant vel doceant leges saeculares.' Grosseteste, Epist. p. 266: Robert Lexington has piled irregularity upon irregularity by hearing criminal causes on Sunday. From another letter (p. 106) we learn that a clerical justice would salve his conscience by leaving the bench when a sentence of death was to be passed. The clerks who write the plea rolls have scruples about writing the word 'suspendatur':—'et ideo habeat iudicium suum,' or simply 'et ideo etc.' will be quite enough.

[4] Mat. Par. Chron. Maj. iv. 49: 'Thomas de Muletuna, miles in armis cum iuventus ei arridebat, et cum provectioris esset aetatis abundans possessionibus legisque peritus saecularis.' Ibid. v. 317: 'Rogerus de Thurkebi miles et literatus.'

[5] Laurence de Brok, who often represented Henry III. in litigation, seems to be one of the first men who climb to the judicial bench from the bar; Foss, Judges, ii. 267. It is by no means impossible that Martin Pateshull was clerk

judges became a little less dependent on the king than they had been; our law was protected against Romanism and our constitution against the monarchical doctrines that Romanism [p. 185] might have brought with it. On the other hand, law was divorced from literature; the age for law reports, for Year Books, had come; the age for a great exposition of English law had gone by. Happily in the fulness of the time the work had been done.

Bracton.   Bracton's book is the crown and flower of English medieval jurisprudence. What we know of its author has been written elsewhere, and may here be summed up very briefly[1]. His name was Henry of Bratton; he was a Devonshire man, and in all likelihood he began his career as William Raleigh's clerk. In 1245 he was already a justice in eyre and was holding a dispensation granted by Raleigh and confirmed by Innocent IV. for the tenure of three benefices. From 1248 until his death in 1268 he steadily took assizes in the south-western counties. From 1248 to 1257 or thereabouts he was among the justices who held pleas *coram ipso rege*: in other words, he was a justice of the nascent court of King's Bench, and the very highest places in church and state must have seemed to be open to him. We may see him witnessing the king's charters along with the great folk of the realm. Shortly after this, however, he appears to have retired or been dismissed from his position in the central court, though to his dying day he acted as a justice of assize. In 1259 he became rector of the Devonshire parish of Combe-in-Teignhead, in 1261 rector of Bideford, in 1264 archdeacon of Barnstaple, and in the same year chancellor of Exeter cathedral. Thus he seems to have left the king's court just at the time when the revolutionary movement that preceded the barons' war came to its first crisis; and just about the same time he was told to restore to the treasury the large store of plea rolls, those of Martin Pateshull and William Raleigh, which had been in his possession. Whether he was disgraced, and, if so, whether he had offended the king or the

to Simon Pateshull (see above, p. 1C9), that William Raleigh was Martin's clerk (Maitland, Gloucestershire Pleas of the Crown, p. xiii), that Bracton was Raleigh's clerk and thus inherited the rolls that he used. William of York had been a clerk in the chancery: 'I raised you from the depths; you were the scribbler of my writs, a justice and a hireling,' says King Henry; Mat. Par. Chron. Maj. v. 374.

[1] See Bracton's Note Book; also Bracton and Azo (Selden Soc.).

barons, we can not as yet decide. In the last year of his life,
in 1267, he appeared once more in a prominent place; he was
a member of a commission of prelates, magnates and justices
appointed to hear the complaints of 'the disinherited': that is,
of those who had sided with Simon de Montfort.

His is an unfinished book; we do not know that it was **His book**
published in his lifetime. The main part of it seems to have
been written between 1250 and 1258, the time when he had to
surrender the plea rolls; apparently he was still glossing and
annotating it at a later time; but at present we can not always
[p. 186] distinguish his own *addiciones* from those of later commentators. A 'note book' has come down to us which seems to
have been his. It contains some two thousand cases copied
from the rolls of Pateshull and Raleigh, over against some of
which marginal notes have been written; to all appearance they
came from Bracton's hand or from Bracton's head[1].

Romanesque in form, English in substance—this perhaps is **Character of Bracton's work**
the best brief phrase that we can find for the outcome of his
labours; but yet it is not very good[2]. He had at his command
and had diligently studied the works of the famous Italian
lawyer, Azo of Bologna; he also made some use at first hand of **Italian form.**
various parts of the Corpus Iuris Civilis, of the Decretum, and
of the Decretals, and he levied contributions from the canonist
Tancred. His general idea of a law book, of the method by
which law should be expounded and legal principles har-
monized, has been derived from these sources. He has
borrowed from them large maxims, such as might well be
conceived as parts of universal and 'natural' law; he has
borrowed some more specific rules, for the more part such as
deal with matters of rare occurrence in England; he is guilty
of a few classical pedantries and sometimes uses foreign terms
instead of those that were current in the courts. It is highly
probable that if many of his fellows on the bench had shared
his bent, the romano-canonical jurisprudence would have become a 'subsidiary law' in England: that is, a law to be
adduced when enacted law and customary law had no clear
answer for a question; but we can not treat his book as a

---

[1] Bracton's Note Book, vol. i. The discovery was due to Prof. Paul
Vinogradoff.

[2] See Güterbock, Henricus de Bracton; Scrutton, Roman Law in England;
Bracton and Azo (Selden Soc.).

proof that such was the case in his own day[1].　We do not know
that any of his fellows had more than that superficial acquaint- [p. 187]
ance with the law of the church which was common among
ecclesiastics : they might be archdeacons, they might hope to be
bishops, but the judicial functions of bishops and archdeacons
were by this time commonly delegated to their professionally
learned 'officials.'　But further, his own knowledge of Roman
law was by no means very deep when judged by the standard
of his time, and we have little reason for believing that he had
acquired it academically.　His neology leaves no mark on the
technical language of the courts; the 'tenant for term of years'
does not become an 'usufructuary'; and if upon a plea roll we
find a litigant made to talk about the *corpus* and *animus*
necessary for possession, we shall find that the roll is Bracton's
own[2].　Still Bracton's debt—and therefore our debt—to the
civilians is inestimably great.　But for them, his book would
have been impossible; but for them, as the fourteenth century
will show us, some beggarly collection of annotated writs would
have been the best that we should have had from him; we
should have missed not only the splendid plan, the orderly
arrangement, the keen dilemmas, but also the sacerdotal spirit
of the work[3].

English
substance.
On the other hand, the main matter of his treatise is genuine
English law laboriously collected out of the plea rolls of the

---

[1] The nearest approach to an admission that Roman law may be employed
to eke out English law is to be found on a roll of 1237–8, Note Book, pl. 1227.
The question is as to whether a palatinate can be partitioned among co-heirs;
the magnates, prelates and justices declare that they never heard of a similar
case, that they do not know whether there is anything about it in Magna
Carta, that they will not follow foreign precedents, and that they have seen no
such case *in iure scripto* (*i.e.* in Roman law); therefore they adjourn their
decision.　Any notion that this country was in any way subject to the empire
would have been scouted in England.　Just when Bracton was writing it had
become extremely probable that the Emperor for the time being would, when in
England, be a subject and vassal of the king of England.　Ricardus Rex
Alemanniae (he was *Rex Romanorum semper augustus*) was impleaded for a
novel disseisin; Placit. Abbrev. p. 145.

[2] Abbrev. Placit. p. 128: 'nunquam se dimisit de terra illa corpore nec
animo.'　This is from one of the rolls which record Bracton's doings as a
justice of assize.　They are to be edited by Mr Chadwyck Healey.　As to the
usufruct, see Note Book, i. p. 91–93.

[3] Bracton, f. 2 b, 3: 'Ius dicitur ars boni et aequi, cuius merito quis nos
sacerdotes appellat: iustitiam namque colimus et sacra iura ministramus.'
This old phrase (Dig. 1. 1. 1) is no cant in Bracton's mouth; he feels that he is
a priest of the law, a priest for ever after the order of Ulpian.

king's court.   He expressly cites some five hundred decisions,
and whenever we compare his treatise with the records—and
this can now be done at innumerable points—he seems to
be fairly stating the practice of the king's court.   No doubt
our modern, our very modern, conception of rigorous 'case law'
was far from his mind.   He assumed a much larger liberty of
picking and choosing his 'authorities' than would be conceded
now-a-days to an English text-writer.   But still his endeavour
is to state the practice, the best and most approved practice, of
the king's court, and of any desire to romanize the law we
must absolutely acquit him.   To take the most obvious instance,
in the controversy about the legitimation of bastards he is
as staunch an opponent of the *leges* and *canones* as the most
bigoted baron could be, and indeed we find some difficulty in
absolving him or his teachers from a charge of having falsified
[p. 188] history in order to secure a triumph for English law[1].   The few
political inclinations that we can detect in his book are those of
a royal justice; they are anti-feudal and anti-ecclesiastical
leanings.   He will maintain the state against the feudal lords,
the kingly power against seignorial justice, and pious churchman, dutiful son of the pope, though he be, he will maintain
the state against the church.   As to the flagrant disputes
between the king and the incorporate realm, the *universitas
regni,* perhaps his mind fluctuated; perhaps, though no courtier,
he sometimes said less than he thought; but at any rate
his Romanism has not made him an advocate of absolute
monarchy[2].

The book was successful.   Some forty or fifty manuscripts Later law
books.

---

[1] Note Book, i. 104–116.

[2] For the anti-feudal inclination see the argument in favour of free
alienation; Bracton, f. 45 b–46 b.   For the anti-ecclesiastical tendency see the
whole treatment of the writ of prohibition, f. 401–410, many sentences in which
flatly contradict claims which were being made by the high churchmen of the
day.   Bracton, however, if we mistake not, is within the ecclesiastical sphere a
thorough-going papalist.   He ascribes to the pope not merely a jurisdiction,
but an *ordinaria iurisdictio,* over all men.   As to his political opinions see Note
Book, i. pp. 29–33.   We can not decide what they were until some certain
answer has been found for the question whether he wrote the fiery words on
f. 34; but the moderate and unquestioned passage on f. 171 b is enough to
show that he was neither a courtly flatterer nor a champion of despotic
monarchy; this however is evident enough from many other passages,
including that (f. 107) in which he wilfully distorts (Note Book, i. p. 4) the 'sed
et quod principi placuit.'

of it will seem a sufficient body of witnesses to attest its popularity, especially when we remember that the text of some of our oldest Year Books has to be sought for in unique copies. It became the basis of the legal literature of Edward I.'s day. Gilbert Thornton, chief justice of the king's bench, made an epitome of it[1]. This we have lost, unless it be represented by some of those manuscripts of Bracton's work which omit his references to the plea rolls. About the year 1290 two other books were written which are to a great degree reproductions of the classical treatise[2]. The so-called 'Fleta' is little better than an ill-arranged epitome; what its author has not borrowed from Bracton he has for the more part borrowed from some of those little tracts on husbandry and the economic management of manorial affairs which were becoming popular[3]. The so-called 'Britton' has better claim [p. 189] to be called an original work. It is in French, and the whole law has been put into the king's mouth. It must have been useful, manuscripts of it are common; on the other hand, Fleta was to all appearance a failure. To these we might add some little tracts on procedure ascribed to Ralph Hengham, one of Edward I.'s chief justices. This however is not the place in which to speak at any length of these products of the Edwardian age; but to name them has been necessary since sometimes they will help us to discover the law of Henry III.'s reign when Bracton fails us. After all that has been done towards publishing the records of that reign, we shall still be dependent on Bracton; but enough has been published to prove that he is a guide who will not mislead us, if only we are careful to distinguish—and this is not very difficult—between his statement of English law and his cosmopolitan jurisprudence.

Other law
books of
Henry's
reign.

　　Of other law books of Henry's reign little is known and little need be said; the gap between them and Bracton's *Summa* is immense. Copies of the chancery's 'register of original writs' were pretty widely distributed; often a religious house had a copy; sometimes brief notes of an intensely practical character would be written in them. There is extant, and now in the press, an interesting book of precedents for the use of pleaders

---

1 Selden, Dissertatio ad Fletam, p. 456.

2 Nichols, Introduction to his edition of Britton.

3 Walter of Henley, ed. Lamond and Cunningham.

in the king's court which belongs to Henry's time[1], and from that time we begin to get precedents for the use of pleaders in the local courts, conveyancing precedents, and precedents for manorial accounts[2]; also brief disquisitions on rural economy which throw light on legal arrangements[3]. Once more we must mention—though they are not literature—the voluminous rolls of the two benches, the exchequer and the chancery. About the middle of the century these are being supplemented by the rolls of local courts[4], while much may be learnt from the manorial surveys or 'extents,' numerous examples of which have been preserved in the monastic cartularies and elsewhere.

[p. 190]   Before the end of the thirteenth century there already exists a legal profession, a class of men who make money by repre- senting litigants before the courts and giving legal advice. The evolution of this class has been slow, for it has been withstood by certain ancient principles[5]. The old procedure required of a litigant that he should appear before the court in his own person and conduct his own cause in his own words. For one thing, the notion of agency, the notion that the words or acts of Roger may be attributed to Ralph because Ralph has been pleased to declare that this shall be so, is not of any great antiquity. In the second place, so long as procedure is very formal, so long as the whole fate of a lawsuit depends upon the exact words that the parties utter when they are before the tribunal, it is hardly right that one of them should be represented by an expert who has studied the art of pleading:—John may fairly object that he has been summoned to answer not the circumspect Roger but the blundering Ralph; if Ralph can not state his own case in due form of law, he is not entitled to an answer. Still in yet ancient days a litigant is allowed to bring into court with him a party of friends and to take 'counsel' with them before he pleads. In the *Leges Henrici* it is already the peculiar mark of an accusation of felony that the accused is allowed no counsel, but must answer at once; in all other cases a man may have counsel[6]. What is more, it is by this time permitted that one

The legal profession.

Pleaders.

---

[1] Brevia Placitata, now being edited by Mr G. I. Turner.
[2] The Court Baron (Selden Soc.), Introduction.
[3] See the edition of Walter of Henley cited above.
[4] Select Pleas in Manorial Courts (Selden Soc.), Introduction.
[5] Brunner, Forschungen, p. 389; Brunner, D. R. G. ii. 349.
[6] Leg. Henr. 46, 47, 48, 49, 61 § 18, 19.

of those who 'are of counsel with him' should speak for him. The captiousness of the old procedure is defeating its own end, and so a man is allowed to put forward some one else to speak for him, not in order that he may be bound by that other person's words, but in order that he may have a chance of correcting formal blunders and supplying omissions. What the litigant himself has said in court he has said once and for all, but what a friend has said in his favour he may disavow[1]. The professional pleader makes his way into the courts, not as one [p. 191] who will represent a litigant, but as one who will stand by the litigant's side and speak in his favour, subject however to correction, for his words will not bind his client until that client has expressly or tacitly adopted them. Perhaps the main object of having a pleader is that one may have two chances of pleading correctly. Even in the thirteenth century we may see the pleader disavowed. One John de Planez, in pleading for William of Cookham, called Henry II. the grandfather instead of the father of King John; William disavowed the plea, and the advocate was amerced for his blunder[2]. And so, before any one is taken at his pleader's words, it is usual for the court to ask him whether he will abide by the plea[3]. Just because the pleader makes his appearance in this informal fashion, as a mere friend who stands by the litigant's side and provisionally speaks on his behalf, it is difficult for us to discover whether pleaders are commonly employed and whether they are already members of a professional class. The formal records of litigation take no notice of them unless they are disavowed[4].

Attorneys.   It is otherwise with the attorney, for the attorney represents his principal: he has been appointed, attorned (that is, turned to the business in hand), and for good and ill, for gain and loss

---

[1] Leg. Henr. 46 § 3: 'Bonum autem est, ut cum alicuius consilium in placito redditur, cum emendatione dicendum praedicatur, ut si forte perorator vel superadiecerit aliquid, vel omiserit, emendare liceat ei. Saepe enim fit, ut in sua causa quis minus videat quam in alterius, et in ore alterius plerumque poterit emendare quod in suo non liceret.'

[2] Note Book, pl. 298. So in pl. 131: 'deadvocat quod narrator suus pro eo narravit.' So in pl. 1106: 'Alanus de Waxtonesham qui narravit pro Eustachio in misericordia, quia Eustachius deadvocavit id quod pro eo narravit.'

[3] The Court Baron (Selden Soc.), p. 41. References to this practice may be found in the Year Books, *e.g.* Y. B. 33–5 Edw. I., pp. 297, 458.

[4] Mat. Par. Chron. Maj. iii. 124. It is noticed as somewhat strange that in 1227 the king's brother Earl Richard of Cornwall should urge his claims before the king 'sine aliquo advocato rationabiliter simul et eloquenter.'

(*ad lucrandum et perdendum*) he stands in his principal's stead. In England and in other countries the right to appoint an attorney is no outcome of ancient folk-law ; it is a royal privilege. The king, as is often the case, has put himself outside the old law : he appoints representatives to carry on his multitudinous law-suits, and the privilege that he asserts on his own behalf he can concede to others. Already in Glanvill's day every one who is engaged in civil litigation in the king's court enjoys this [p. 192] right of appointing an attorney, or rather, for the word *attorney* is hardly yet in use, a *responsalis*[1]. But the right is narrowly limited. The litigant must appear before the court in his proper person and must there put some one else in his stead to gain or lose in some particular plea. Whatever is more than this can only be accomplished by means of a royal writ. Thus it is only under a royal writ that a man can have a general prospective power of appointing attorneys to act for him in future litigation[2]. Such writs are by no means matters of course ; they usually recite some special reasons why an exceptional boon should be granted :—the grantee is going abroad on the king's business, or he is the abbot of a royal monastery and too old or infirm for laborious journeys[3]. In the communal courts a litigant could not appoint an attorney unless he had the king's writ authorizing him to do so[4].

The attorneys of the period which is now before us do not seem to be in any sense 'officers of the court,' nor do they as yet constitute a closed professional class. Probably every 'free and lawful' person may appear as the attorney of another ; even a woman may be an attorney[5], and a wife may be her husband's attorney[6]. A bishop will appoint one of his clerks, an abbot one of his monks, a baron will be represented by his steward or by one of his knights. Occasionally, however, as we look down the list of attorneys we see the same names repeating themselves, and draw the inference that there are some men who are holding themselves out as ready to represent whoever will employ them. A change comes in Edward I.'s day which

Attorneys not professional.

---

[1] Glanvill, lib. xi.

[2] See Stat. West. II. c. 10, which gave a general right to appoint an attorney to appear in all causes which should come before the justices in a given eyre.

[3] Registrum Brevium Originalium, ff. 20–22.

[4] Britton, vol. ii. p. 357.

[5] Select Civil Pleas, pl. 141.

[6] Note Book, pl. 342, 1361, 1507.

gives a new definiteness to the class of attorneys as well as to the class of counsellors.

Recurring for a moment to the class of counsellors, we observe that Richard of Anesty, when he prosecuted his tedious suit, followed the royal court in its peregrinations with a group of 'friends and helpers and pleaders' in his train[1]. For his litigation in the ecclesiastical courts he naturally required professional aid, and he had it from Italian lawyers resident in [p. 193] this country; among them was Master Ambrose, who was in every sense one of the first lawyers in England, first in time as well as first in learning[2]. But even in the king's court he was surrounded by friends and helpers and pleaders, and among them was Ranulf Glanvill[3]. For a long time, however, we hear very little of professional counsellors in the temporal courts. This is the more noticeable because Matthew Paris is full of complaints against the pack of bellowing legists whom the king employs and whom he lets slip whenever an episcopal election goes against his wishes[4]. They are not men skilled in English law; they are romanists and canonists; many of them are foreigners; one of the most infamous of them, if we judge them by Matthew's report, is the renowned Hostiensis[5]. The only persons who are mentioned as learned in English law are the king's justices[6], and they to all appearance have been selected, not out of a body of advocates seeking for employment from the

---

[1] See above, p. 158.

[2] Gesta Abbatum, i. 136: 'Robertus [Abbas S. Albani]......Magistrum Ambrosium, clericum suum, legis peritissimum, Italicum natione (de primis tempore, scientia et moribus, Angliae legis peritis) Romam...destinavit.' See also Liebermann, E. H. R. xi. 313–4.

[3] On 31 March, 1163, Glanvill appeared along with Anesty at Windsor; at Michaelmas in that year he became sheriff of Yorkshire.

[4] Mat. Par. Chron. Maj. iii. 111: 'Ricardus de Marisco Dunelmensis episcopus...cum tumultu valido reboantium legistarum.' Ibid. 531: 'Miserat enim [rex] ad curiam Romanam unum legistarum suorum, quorum magnam catervam retinuit, quasi venator canes venaticos, super electores praelatorum discopulandos, videlicet Simonem Normannum.' Ibid. 268, 'Rogerum de Cantelu legistam'; 483, 'Magister Odo [de Kilkenny] legista'; 491, 'legistas suas Romipedas'; 491, 'Simonem Normannum et Alexandrum Saecularem legistas conductitios'; iv. 266, 'Alexandrum legistam, cognomento Saecularem.'

[5] See above, p. 122.

[6] Thus, iii. 190, Pateshull is 'legum terrae peritus'; iii. 525, Raleigh is 'legum terrae peritissimus'; iv. 49, Multon is 'legis peritus'; iv. 537, William of York is 'legum regni peritissimus.'

general public, but from among the king's civil servants, the
clerks of his court and of his chancery and those laymen who
have done good work in subordinate offices.   However, when in
his account of the year 1235 Paris tells us how Henry sought to
crush the aged Hubert de Burgh with accusations, he represents
Hubert's faithful counsellor Lawrence of St Albans as having to
contend against ' all the advocates of the bench whom we com-
[p. 194] monly call countors¹.'   In 1268 'a countor of the bench'
assaulted a justice of the Jews in Westminster Hall; his fellow
countors interceded for him².   The king already seems to have
permanently retained a number of persons to plead his causes
for him; but whether these men are free to plead for other
people when the king's interests are not in question, and
whether they aspire to any exclusive right of audience we do
not know.   But lawyers seem to have rapidly taken possession
of the civic courts in London.   In 1259 the king was compelled
to concede to the citizens that in their hustings and other
courts they might plead their own causes without lawyers
(*causidici*), saving pleas of the crown, pleas of land, and pleas
of unlawful distraint³.   This looks as if in London there had
been an unusually rapid development of a professional caste.
By this time the practice of the ecclesiastical courts would
serve as an example.   The attorney is the temporal equivalent
for the canonical proctor, and the ' narrator' or ' countor' is the
temporal equivalent for the canonical advocate.   In 1237 the
legatine constitutions of Cardinal Otho had ordained that no
one was to serve as an advocate in an ecclesiastical court, except
in certain exceptional cases, until he had taken an oath before
his bishop to do his duty and not to pervert justice⁴.   Thus
a close body of professional advocates was formed, and this
would serve as a model for a similar body of professional
' countors.'

Then in Edward I.'s day we see that the king has retained Regulation
pleaders who are known as his servants or serjeants at law of pleaders
and attor-
neys.

---

¹ Mat. Par. Chron. Maj. iii. 619: 'licet Rex cum omnibus prolocutoribus
banci quos narratores vulgariter appellamus in contrarium niteretur.' The
Latin *narrator* and its French equivalent *contour* became technical terms. If
an English term was in use, it was perhaps *forspeaker*.

² Madox, Exchequer, i. 236.

³ Liber de Antiquis Legibus, 42–3.

⁴ Mat. Par. Chron. Maj. iii. 439–440; Joh. de Athona, p. 70.

(*servientes ad legem*). Already in 1275 it is necessary to threaten
with imprisonment 'the serjeant countor' who is guilty of
collusive or deceitful practice[1]. Also there seem to be about
the court many young men who are learning to plead, and whose
title of 'apprentices' suggests that they are the pupils of the
serjeants. We may infer that already before 1292 these
practitioners had acquired some exclusive right of audience.
In that year King Edward directed his justices to provide for
every county a sufficient number of attorneys and apprentices [p. 195]
from among the best, the most lawful and the most teachable,
so that king and people might be well served. The suggestion
was made that a hundred and forty of such men would be
enough, but the justices might, if they pleased, appoint a larger
number[2].

The two branches of the profession.
By this measure, which, however, may not have been the
first of its kind, 'both branches of the profession' were placed
under the control of the justices, and apparently a monopoly
was secured for those who had been thus appointed[3]. Some
twelve years earlier the mayor and aldermen of London had
been compelled to lament the ignorance and ill manners of the
pleaders and attorneys who practised in the civic courts, and to
ordain that none should habitually practise there who had not
been duly admitted by the mayor. They added that no countor
was to be an attorney, and thus sanctioned that 'separation of
the two branches of the profession' which still endures in
England ; but really, as we have already seen, these two branches
had different roots :—the attorney represents his client, appears
in his client's place, while the countor speaks on behalf of a
litigant who is present in court either in person or by attorney.
The civic fathers were further compelled to threaten with sus-
pension the pleader who took money with both hands or reviled
his antagonist[4]. It is from 1292 that we get our first Year
Book, and we see that already the great litigation of the realm,

---

[1] Stat. West. I. c. 29.

[2] Rolls of Parliament, i. 84.

[3] So early as 1253 the bishop of Rochester was impleaded by the archbishop
of Canterbury in the king's court, 'et Abell de S. Martino venit et narravit pro
episcopo et non fuit advocatus ; ideo in misericordia'; Placit. Abbrev. 137.
We can not be quite certain that the objection to Abel was that he was not a
member of the legal profession ; perhaps the bishop had given him no authority
to plead his cause.

[4] Liber Custumarum, i. 280 (A.D. 1280).

the litigation which is worthy to be reported, is conducted by a small group of men. Lowther, Spigornel, Howard, Hertpol, King, Huntingdon, Heyham—one of them will be engaged in almost every case. Nor is it only in the king's court and the civic courts that the professional pleader is found. Already in 1240 the Abbot of Ramsey ordained that none of his tenants was to bring a pleader into his courts to impede or delay his seignorial justice[1], and in 1275 we find one William of Bolton practising in partnership with other pleaders before the court [p. 196] of the fair of St Ives[2]. Many details are still obscure, but in Edward I.'s day it is that our legal profession first begins to take a definite shape. We see a group of counsel, of serjeants and apprentices on the one hand, and a group of professional attorneys on the other, and both of them derive their right to practise from the king either mediately or immediately[3].

So soon as there is a legal profession, professional opinion is Professional among the most powerful of the forces that mould the law, and opinion. we may see it exercising its influence directly as well as indirectly. In Edward I.'s day it is impossible to uphold a writ which 'all the serjeants' condemn, and often enough to the medieval law-reporter 'the opinion of the serjeants' seems as weighty as any judgment[4].

That the professional pleader of Edward I.'s day had learnt Decline of law as a science, had attended lectures or read books, we do not Romanism know; very probably his education had generally been of a purely empirical kind. Sometimes he was a legist. In 1307 a judge says to counsel, 'Passeley, you are a legist and there is a written law which speaks of this matter, *Cogi possessorem etc.*[5]' A certain knowledge of, and reverence for, the broader maxims of 'the written law' is apparent. 'Volenti non fit iniuria,' 'Melior est conditio possidentis,' 'Res inter alios acta,' such phrases as these can be produced in court when there is occasion

---

[1] Cart. Rams. i. 428.

[2] Pleas in Manorial Courts (Selden Soc.), 155, 159, 160.

[3] Walter of Hemingford (ed. Hearne), ii. 208, tells how in 1304 the Abp. of York was impleaded. 'None of his counsel nor any of all the pleaders (*narratores*) could or dared answer for him. So in his own person, like one of the people, and before all the people, he made his answer bareheaded:—for the men of the court did not love him.'

[4] See *e.g.* Y. B. 30–1 Edw. I. p. 107.

[5] Y. B. 33–5 Edw. I. p. 471. The allusion is to Cod. 3. 31. 11: 'Cogi possessorem ab eo, qui expetit, titulum suae possessionis dicere, incivile est.'

for them[1]. They could be easily found; the Decretals of Pope Boniface VIII. end with a bouquet of these showy proverbs[2]. When in any century from the thirteenth to the nineteenth an English lawyer indulges in a Latin maxim, he is generally, though of this he may be profoundly ignorant, quoting from the Sext. But we have only to look at manuscripts of Bracton's text to see that the influence of Roman law is on the wane, is already very slight. Transcribers who can copy correctly [p 197] enough good homely stuff about the assize of novel disseisin, make utter nonsense of the subtler discussions which Bracton had borrowed from Azo. A climax is reached when the *actio familiae herciscundae* has become an action about the family of the lady Herciscunda, or, since even her name is outlandish, the lady of Hertescombe, who probably had estates in Devonshire[3].

Notaries and conveyancers.

In England that Roman institution, the notarial system, never took deep root[4]. Our kings did not assume the imperial privilege of appointing notaries, nor did our law require that deeds or wills or other instruments in common use should be prepared or attested by professional experts. Now and again when some document was to be drawn up which would demand the credence of foreigners, a papal notary would be employed. It was a papal notary who framed the most magnificent record of King Edward's justice, the record of the suit in which the crown of Scotland was at stake[5]. But it is worthy of remark that, while in our temporal courts the art of recording pleas had been brought to a high degree of perfection, the English ecclesiastical courts seem to have borne among continental canonists a bad repute because of their careless and inartistic records. This we learn from an Italian notary, one

---

[1] Y. B. 33–5 Edw. I. p. 9; 30–1 Edw. I. p. 57; 21–2 Edw. I. 295.

[2] *De regulis iuris*, in vi[to].

[3] Britton (ed. Nichols), ii. 65.

[4] Constitutions of Otho (1237), Mat. Par. iii. 438; Joh. de Athona, p. 67: ‘Quoniam tabellionum usus in regno Angliae non habetur.’ See Selden, Titles of Honour, Works, ed. 1726, vol. iii. pp. 131–2, 467. A book of English precedents of the thirteenth century remarks that for a bond two witnesses with the tabellio or notary are enough; see L. Q. R. vii. 66. We must remember, however, that a mercantile bond should be so attested that it will be valid in foreign courts.

[5] Foedera, i. 784: ‘Ego Johannes Erturi de Cadomo apostolicae sedis auctoritate notarius.’ This John Arthur of Caen was a master of the chancery.

John of Bologna, who dedicated to Archbishop Peckham a
collection of judicial precedents, destined—so its author hoped
—to reform our slovenly insular documents[1]. In later days
there were always some apostolic notaries in England. In the
[p. 198] fourteenth century the testament of a prelate or baron will
sometimes take the form of a notarial instrument. But an
acquaintance with the law of the land sufficient to enable one
to draw a charter of feoffment, a lease, a mortgage, a will, was
in all likelihood a common accomplishment among the clergy,
regular and secular. If we closely scan the cartulary of any
rich religious house we shall probably infer that it had its own
collection of common forms. It is quite conceivable that some
instruction in conveyancing was given in the universities.
From the second half of the thirteenth century we begin to
get books of precedents, and sometimes the formulas of purely
temporal transactions will be mixed up with instruments destined to come before the ecclesiastical courts[2]. From the
Norman Conquest onwards the practice of using written instruments slowly spreads downwards from the king's chancery.
The private deeds (*cartae*) are for the more part very brief,
clear and business-like instruments; they closely resemble those
that were executed in northern France. The most elaborate
documents are those which proceed from the king's court. If
a man wishes to do with land anything that is at all unusual,
he does it by means of a fictitious action brought and compro-
mised in the king's court. The instrument which records this
compromise, this 'final concord' or 'fine,' will be drawn up
by the royal clerks, and one copy of it, the so-called 'foot of
the fine,' will remain with the court. By this means, before
the thirteenth century is out, some complex 'family settlements' are being made. Also the Lombard merchants have
brought with them precedents for bonds, lengthy, precise and

---

[1] Bethmann-Hollweg, Civilprozess, vi. 189, gives an account of this book.
The author says to the Archbishop: 'Cum solempnis vestra curia et regnum
Angliae quasi totum personis careat, quae secundum formam Romanae curiae
vel idoneam aliam qualemcunque intellectum et notitiam habeant eorum quae
ad artem pertinent notariae.' From the ignorance of the English scribes
'iudicibus obprobrium et partibus incommodum saepe proveniunt.' John of
Bologna seems to have been employed by Peckham and to have obtained a
benefice in Wales: Peckham's Register, i. 45, 278; iii. 1009.

[2] Maitland, A Conveyancer in the Thirteenth Century, L. Q. R. vii. 63; The
Court Baron (Selden Soc.), pp. 7, 12–14.

stringent forms, which they compel their English debtors to execute[1].

Knowledge of the law
On the whole it is hard for us to determine the degree to which knowledge of the law had become the exclusive property of a professional class. On the one hand, there were many things in Bracton's book which were beyond the comprehension of the laity—some things, we suspect, that were too refined for the ordinary lawyer—and it was fully admitted that the prudent litigant should employ a skilful pleader[2]. Even [p. 199] the writer of the *Leges Henrici* had observed that we better understand another person's cause than our own[3]. But the group of professional lawyers which had formed itself round the king's court was small; the king's permanent justices were few, the serjeants were few, and some seven score apprentices and attorneys seemed enough. A great deal of legal business was still being transacted, a great deal of justice done, by those who were not professional experts. The knight, the active country gentleman, would at times be employed as a justice of assize or of gaol delivery, besides making the judgments in the county court. The cellarer of the abbey would preside in its manorial courts and be ready to draw a lease or a will. The freeholders of the shire, besides attending the communal and the manorial courts, would have hard work to do as jurors; often would they be called to Westminster, and as yet the separation of matter of law from matter of fact was not so strict that a juror could afford to know nothing of legal rules. In one way and another the common folk were constantly receiving lessons in law; the routine of their lives often took them into the courts, even into courts presided over by a Pateshull, a Raleigh, a Bracton. This healthy co-operation of all sorts and conditions of men in the work of the law prevents the jurist from having it all his own way and making the law too fine a thing for common use.

English law in Wales.
English law was already spreading beyond the bounds of England. In 1272 the time had almost come when Wales would be subjugated and Edward's great *Statutum Walliae*[4], the most comprehensive code that any English legislator issues

---

[1] A good specimen is given in Mat. Par. iii. 329; but many may be found elsewhere.

[2] Y. B. 30–1 Edw.: 'Defaute de bon serjant fet B perdre ses deniers.'

[3] Leg. Henr. 46 § 3.　　　　　　　　　[4] Statutes, i. 55.

during the middle ages, would be promulgated.   Meanwhile in
the marches English and Welsh law had met; but the struggle
was unequal, for it was a struggle between the modern and
the archaic.   Welsh law had indeed a literature of its own,
but had hardly passed that stage which is represented in
England by the *Leges Henrici.*   No doubt there were those
who cherished the old tribal customs.   The men of Urchinfield,
a district within the English county of Hereford, tell the king's
justices that the manslayer may make his peace with the
[p. 200] kinsmen of the slain, and they ask that this ancient usage
may be observed[1].   On the other hand, the men of Kerry,
which lies within the modern county of Montgomery, petition
the king that they may live under English law, because that
law has suppressed the blood feud and does not punish the
innocent along with the guilty[2].   The old law of blood feud
and wergild, or *galanas* as the Welsh call it, will die hard in
Wales; still it is doomed to die, and along with it the tribal
system whence it springs.

Into Ireland Englishmen have carried their own law.   A
smaller England has been created across the Channel, with
chancery, exchequer, 'benches,' council, sheriffs, coroners, all
reproduced upon a diminished scale.   Statutes and ordinances
and 'the register of original writs' were sent from England into
Ireland; the king's English court claimed a supremacy over
his Irish tribunals, and multitudinous petitions from Ireland
came before the English council at its parliaments[3].   It is
probable however that, even in those parts of Ireland which
were effectually subject to English domination, the native Irish
were suffered to live under their old law so long as they would
keep the king's peace; but we may see Innocent IV. intervening to protect them against what seems to be an iniquitous

*English
law in
Ireland.*

---

[1] Note Book, pl. 1474.

[2] Royal Letters, Henry III., vol. ii. p. 353: 'Vestram rogamus regiam
dignitatem quatenus...leges terrarum vestrarum ubique per Walliam et per
Marchiam nobis concedere velitis, et hoc est, quod innocens non puniatur
pro nocente, nec etiam imputetur parentelae alicuius si aliquis de parentela
interfecerit aliquem vel furtum vel aliquam seditionem [fecerit] nisi ipsi
malefactori.'

[3] As to the transmission of the register, see Harv. L. R. iii. 110.   For
an early case in which an Irish judgment is corrected in England, see Rot.
Cl. p. 549; there are several other cases on the rolls of Edward I.   For Irish
petitions to the English council, see Memoranda de Parliamento, 33 Edw. I.
p. 232.

application of the system of 'personal law[1].' Individual Irishmen, like the men of the Welsh Kerry, petitioned that they might be allowed the benefits of English law; they probably meant by this that they wished their lives protected by a law which knew how to hang a manslayer instead of suffering him to purchase peace by wergild or 'eric' fine[2].

English and Scottish law.

Whether the king of Scotland was in any degree subject to the king of England, was a question about which Englishman and Scot would have disagreed in the year 1272 and about which they will hardly be brought to agree even now. Old precedents of homage and release from homage were being [p. 201] treasured on either side of the border and were soon to be brought into debate. But the utmost claimed for the English king was a feudal overlordship, and English law, as English law, had no power north of the Tweed. Nevertheless, we may doubt whether a man who crossed the river felt that he had passed from the land of one law to the land of another. In the first place, for some while he would have known himself to be under a law settled and put in writing by a joint committee of English and Scottish knights, the law of the marches, which decided that whenever a charge of felony lay between Englishman and Scot there must be trial by battle:—he would have known himself to be under a true international law[3]. But suppose him served with a writ. He might notice the name of Henry where he was accustomed to see Alexander, or the name of some Scottish burgh in the place of the familiar *Westmonasterium*; but nothing else in the writ would seem strange. If the proper names be omitted, we shall hardly now tell a Scottish charter of feoffment from an English, and the few Scottish records of litigation that have come down to us from the thirteenth century might have been written by the clerks of Robert Bruce, the chief justice of England. Of what went on beyond the Forth it is not for us to hazard a word, but for long ages past the law that prevailed between Forth

---

[1] Calendar of Papal Registers, i. 283 : Constitution (1253), whereby in the province of Cashel the evil custom of giving credence to an Englishman on his oath touching a theft, if supported by six Englishmen, while an Irishman, whose innocence is testified by thirty witnesses, has to make restitution, is abolished, and equal justice is ordered to be done between English and Irish.

[2] Memoranda de Parliamento, 33 Edw. I. pp. 253–4.

[3] Acts of Parliament of Scotland, i. 413 ; Neilson, Trial by Combat, 126.

and Tweed must have been very like the law that prevailed between Tweed and Humber. And then, if Frankish feudalism in the guise of a Norman army had conquered England, it had almost as effectually, though in more peaceful guise, conquered whatever of Scotland was worthy of conquest. On the whole, for a long time past the two nations, if two nations we must call them, had been good friends; the two kingly families had been closely allied. Many a great baron can hardly have known to which nation he belonged. The concentrated might [p. 202] of the English kingship, the imperious chancery, the exact and exacting exchequer, were ideals for the Scottish king; the English baron may well have yearned for franchises and regalities that were denied to him but enjoyed by his Scottish peers. The problem of the *Regiam Maiestatem*, the Scottish version of Glanvill's book, we must not try to solve; but it seems clear enough from abundant evidence that, at the outbreak of the war of independence, the law of Scotland, or of southern Scotland, was closely akin to English law[1]. That it had been less romanized than English law had been is highly probable: no Bracton had set it in order by the method of the *Summa Azonis*. That it was less uniform than was English law is also highly probable; the Scottish kingship was not so strong as was the English, and in Scotland there were ethnical differences impeding the progress of a common law. These seem to be the main causes which, when enforced, during the struggle for independence, by a loathing for all that was English, sever the stream of Scottish from that of English legal history. Romanism must come sooner or later; the later it comes the stronger it will be, for it will have gone half way to meet the medieval facts[2]. Uniformity, if it can not be evolved

---

[1] In Acts of Parliament of Scotland, vol. i., *Regiam Maiestatem* is collated with Glanvill. The present state of the question as to its date may be gathered from Neilson, Trial by Combat, pp. 99–104. Of all the various theories that have been started, that which ascribes this book to Edward I. will seem to an Englishman the most improbable. If Edward had attempted to foist an English law book on Scotland, that book would have been founded on Bracton or Britton and not on the antiquated Glanvill. The English law that is borrowed is distinctly law of the twelfth century.

[2] Schröder, D. R. G. 746. The Roman law that comes to England is the law of the early 'glossators.' The Roman law that wins victories in Scotland and Germany is the law of the later 'commentators' (Baldus, Bartolus and so forth) which has accommodated itself to practical needs.

from within, must be imported from without. Thus in the end Roman law is received in Scotland as subsidiary and academic law.

Precocious maturity of English law.

A comparison of the legal systems of various states as they were at some remote point of time will always be a difficult task, even for one who knows the history of each separate system. But if we could look at western Europe in the year 1272, perhaps the characteristic of English law which would seem the most prominent would be its precocity. Its substance was, to say the least, as modern and enlightened as was that of the systems with which it could be profitably compared. It had suppressed some archaisms which might still be found in France or at any rate in Germany. It knew nothing of the wergild save as a trait of Welsh barbarism; at the pope's bidding it had abolished the ordeal; it was rapidly confining the judicial combat and the oath with oath-helpers within very narrow limits. But we would speak rather of its form than of its matter. The great charter, the provisions of Merton and [p. 203] Marlborough, the minor ordinances, these in 1272 constituted what we must here call a large body of enacted law. And if in one sense England was never to be a 'country of the written law,' it had become preeminently the country of the written record. Every right, every remedy must be made definite by writing; if it can not find expression in some chancery formula, it must cease to exist. Then, again, English law is becoming the law of one court, or of a small group of intimately connected courts, the law of Westminster Hall, the law that in its full perfection is known only to some dozen men, the king's justices. Every right, every remedy, is being sharpened and hardened by the ceaseless activity of a court which in the course of a year decides thousands of cases, the greatest and the smallest, coming to it from all corners of the land.

Characteristics of English law.

Uniformity is thus secured, and even a certain simplicity, for some parts of our common law, notably the law of status, must, if we have regard to continental systems, be called surprisingly simple. Closely connected with its uniformity is another distinctive trait:—in England the law for the great men has become the law for all men, because the law of the king's court has become the common law. For example, the primogenitary rules of inheritance are rapidly spreading downwards from their native home among the military fees through all the subjacent strata, and the one 'formal contract' of English law can be made only by those who can write or hire others to write for them. Certainty also has been attained; Bracton's hands are far less free than are the hands of Philip Beaumanoir or Eike of Repgau; at every moment he must be thinking of the formulas in the chancery's register. English law is modern in its uniformity, its simplicity, its certainty; it is modern also in the amount of Romanism that it has absorbed. In Germany the theoretical sanctity of Justinian's texts has as yet borne little fruit in practice; in northern France the new Roman jurisprudence is still lying on the surface and hardly beginning to mix with the traditional customs, while in England it has already done a great work, and almost all the work that it will ever do. But all these modern excellences are being purchased at a price which may be heavy. The judges can no longer introduce much that is [p. 204] new; they know nothing of any system but their own; Roman law has lost its glamour. All now depends upon those who will wield the legislative power in this country, upon the 'sovereign one' or the 'sovereign many.' A vigilant, an enlightened, an expert legislator may be able to keep this rigid formulary system in harmony with the ever changing necessities of mankind, introducing new 'forms of action' and (for this will be equally necessary) ruthlessly abolishing all that is obsolete. But unless we are to have this continuous legislative activity— and we can hardly have it without despotism—the omens for the future of English law are not very favourable. It may easily become a commentary, an evasive commentary, on antique writs and statutes. It will circumvent by tortuous paths the obstacles that it can not surmount. Archaic institutions which the rationalism of the thirteenth century had almost destroyed, wager of battle, wager of law, will live on until the nineteenth, moribund but mischievous. It may become an occult science, a black art, a labyrinth of which the clue has been lost.

But now, having brought down our general sketch of the growth of English law to the accession of Edward I., 'the English Justinian,' we may turn to an examination of its rules and doctrines as we find them in the age of Glanvill and the age of Bracton.

BOOK II.

THE DOCTRINES OF ENGLISH LAW IN THE EARLY MIDDLE AGES.

CHAPTER I.

TENURE.

How best to arrange a body of medieval law for the use of modern readers, is a difficult question. Of the two obvious methods each has its disadvantages. On the one hand, if we were to adopt the arrangement which would be the best for a code or digest of our modern law, though we might possibly succeed in forcing the old rules into new pigeon-holes, we should run a great risk of ignoring distinctions which our ancestors saw, and a yet greater risk of insisting on distinctions which for them had no existence. On the other hand, were we to aim at such an arrangement as a medieval lawyer would have adopted, the result would be to hide those matters which interest us behind the intricate mass of procedural rules which interested him. The nature of both these dangers may be explained by a few words.

Arrangement of this book.

The arrangement of Bracton's treatise will for a moment seem one that is familiar enough to every lawyer; it is the most famous of all schemes. Following the Institutes, he treats of (1) Persons, (2) Things, (3) Actions. But if we may take the number of folios given to each of these topics as an indication of its importance in his eyes, we find that the relation between them may be expressed by the figures 7 : 91 : 356[1]. Nor is this all. It is to his 'law of actions' that we must often look for substantive English law. To a high degree in his treatment of 'persons,' to a less, but marked, degree in his treatment of 'things,' he is dependent on Azo and Roman Law. It is only as he approaches the law of

Possible methods of arrangement. (1) The medieval scheme of law.

---

[1] As to the arrangement of the treatise see Bracton and Azo, p. 14.

'actions' that we begin to know that he is giving us practicable [p. 208] English law and not speculative jurisprudence. As to Glanvill, the whole of his book is, we may say, devoted to the law of actions; he plunges at once into an account of the writ of right; and such arrangement as the *Leges Henrici* have, puts jurisdiction and procedure in the forefront. That characteristic mark of ancient jurisprudence, the prominent place given to what we sometimes speak of as 'adjective law,' the apparent subordination of rights to remedies, is particularly noticeable in our own case, and endures until modern times: and naturally, for our common law is the law of courts which gradually acquired their jurisdiction by the development and interpretation of procedural formulas. Still, though we shall have to say much about the 'forms of action,' we need not introduce the rules of property law as though they were but subsidiary to the law about assizes, writs of right and actions of trespass.

(2) The modern scheme.

The danger that would be run were we to follow the other of the two courses may be illustrated by reference to that division of law into 'public' and 'private' which seems eminently well suited to be among the first outlines of any institutional work on modern law. Bracton knew of the distinction and could notice it as a matter of scholastic learning; but he makes little use of it[1]. He could hardly have used it and yet dealt fairly with his materials. Feudalism, we may say, is a denial of this distinction. Just in so far as the ideal of feudalism is perfectly realized, all that we call public law is merged in private law: jurisdiction is property, office is property, the kingship itself is property; the same word *dominium* has to stand now for *ownership* and now for *lordship*. Again, the theory urged by a modern writer[2], that 'public law' is but [p. 209] a department of the 'law of persons,' however inapplicable to modern states, may sometimes be applied with advantage to the middle ages. Any such conception as that of 'the state'

---

[1] Bract. f. 3 b: 'Est autem ius publicum quod ad statum reipublicae (*al. cod.* rei Romanae) spectat...ius autem privatum est quod ad singulorum pertinet utilitatem principaliter et secundario pertinet ad rempublicam.' On the general ground that a copyist is more likely to have discarded than to have reintroduced the allusion to Rome, *rei Romanae* seems the preferable reading; it is also the reading of the best MSS. See Bracton and Azo, p. 27. A germ of the distinction between public and private law may be found in Bracton's treatment of suit of court, f. 37, and franchises, f. 55 b; but it is not prominent.

[2] Austin, Jurisprudence, i. 69–71.

hardly appears on the surface of the law; no line is drawn between the king's public and private capacities, or it is drawn only to be condemned as treasonable. The king, it is true, is a highly privileged as well as a very wealthy person; still his rights are but private rights amplified and intensified. He has greater rights than any other lord; but it is a matter of degree; many lords have some 'regalities'; the Earl of Gloucester has many, and the Earl of Chester more. Certainly it would be easy for us to exaggerate the approach made in any country, more especially in England, to the definite realization of this feudal ideal; but just in so far as it is realized, 'public law' appears as a mere appendix to 'real property law' modified in particular cases by a not very ample 'law of persons.'

Now albeit we can not adopt either of these two methods to the neglect of the other and must consider both medieval lawyers and modern readers, we need not work without a plan. In any body of law we are likely to find certain ideas and rules that may be described as elementary. Their elementary character consists in this, that we must master them if we are to make further progress in our study; if we begin elsewhere, we are likely to find that we have begun at the wrong place. Only some experience of the particular body of law that is in question will direct us to the proper quarter; but as regards the law of the feudal time we can hardly do wrong in turning to the law of land tenure as being its most elementary part. We shall begin therefore by speaking of land tenure, but in the first instance we shall have regard to what we may call its public side; its private side we may for a while postpone, though we must not forget that this distinction between the two sides of property law is one that we make for our own convenience, not one that is imposed upon us by our authorities. From land tenure we shall pass to consider the law of personal condition. The transition will be easy, for the broadest distinction between classes of men, the distinction between free men and men who are not free, is intricately connected with land tenure, in so much that the same word *villenagium* is currently used to denote both a personal status and a mode of tenure. Then we shall turn to the law of jurisdiction, for this again we shall find to be intertwined with the land law; and along with the law of jurisdiction we must examine 'the communities of the land.' Having dealt with these topics we shall, it is hoped, have said

Our own course.

[p. 210]

enough of political structure and public affairs, for those matters which are adequately discussed by historians of our constitution we shall avoid. Turning then to the more private branches of our law, we shall take as our chief rubrics, 'Ownership and Possession,' 'Contract,' 'Inheritance' and 'Family Law,' while our two last chapters will be devoted, the one to 'Crime and Tort,' the other to 'Procedure.' We are well aware that this arrangement may look grotesque to modern eyes; since, for example, it thrusts the law of persons into the middle of the law of property. Our defence must be that, after many experiments, we have planned this itinerary as that which will demand of us the least amount of repetition and anticipation, and therefore enable us to say most in the fewest words. We shall speak for the more part of the law as it stood in the period that lies between 1154 and 1272. This will not prevent us from making occasional excursions into earlier or later times when to do so seems advisable, nor from looking now and again at foreign countries; but with the age of Glanvill and the age of Bracton, we shall be primarily concerned. Again, we shall be primarily concerned with the evolution of legal doctrines, but shall try to illustrate by real examples some of the political and economic causes and effects of those rules that are under our examination. We have not to write a practical hand-book of medieval law, nor, on the other hand, have we to describe the whole of medieval life.—But an abstract discourse about method is seldom very profitable. Therefore, without more ado, we turn to the law of land tenure and begin with its fundamental dogma.

§ 1. *Tenure in General.*

Derivative and dependent tenure.

Every acre of English soil and every proprietary right therein have been brought within the compass of a single formula, which may be expressed thus:—*Z tenet terram illam de......domino Rege.* The king himself holds land which is in every sense his own; no one else has any proprietary right in it; [p. 211] but if we leave out of account this royal demesne, then every acre of land is 'held of' the king. The person whom we may call its owner, the person who has the right to use and abuse the land, to cultivate it or leave it uncultivated, to keep all

others off it, holds the land of the king either immediately or
mediately. In the simplest case he holds it immediately of
the king; only the king and he have rights in it. But it well
may happen that between him and the king there stand other
persons; *Z* holds immediately of *Y*, who holds of *X*, who holds
of *V*, who holds......of *A*, who holds of the king. Let us take
one real instance:—in Edward I.'s day Roger of St German
holds land at Paxton in Huntingdonshire of Robert of Bedford,
who holds of Richard of Ilchester, who holds of Alan of Chartres,
who holds of William le Boteler, who holds of Gilbert Neville,
who holds of Devorguil Balliol, who holds of the king of Scotland, who holds of the king of England[1]. A feudal ladder with
so many rungs as this has, is uncommon; but theoretically
there is no limit to the possible number of rungs, and practically,
as will be seen hereafter, men have enjoyed a large power, not
merely of adding new rungs to the bottom of the ladder, but of
inserting new rungs in the middle of it. The person who stands
at the lower end of the scale, the person who seems most like an
owner of the land, and who has a general right of doing what
he pleases with it, is said to hold the land in demesne; *Z tenet
terram in dominico*, or *in dominico suo*[2]. We suppose that he
holds it of *Y*; in that case *Y* is the lord (*dominus*) of *Z*, and *Z*
is the tenant (*tenens*) of *Y*. But *Y* again is said to hold the
land; he holds it however not in demesne but in service (*tenet
terram illam, non tamen in dominico sed in servitio*); and *Y*
again must hold it of someone—let us say of *X*—whose tenant
he will be, who will be his lord, and who also will be said
to hold the land in service. Ultimately we shall reach the
king; *A*, or some other person, will hold the land immediately
of the king and be his tenant in chief (*in capite*). Every person
[p. 212] who stands between the king and him who holds in demesne,
every *mesne lord* or *mesne*, is both lord and tenant, lord as
regards those who stand below him, tenant as regards those
who stand above[3].

[1] Rot. Hund. ii. 673.

[2] This statement will require some qualification hereafter when we speak of
the unfree tenures.

[3] In later days the term 'tenure in capite' was sometimes used as though it
were equivalent to 'tenure in capite of the crown' and even to 'tenure in capite
of the crown by knight's service.' In the Baronia Anglicana, Madox has sufficiently proved that this use of the term was an innovation. See also Hargrave's
notes to Co. Lit. 108 a. In the thirteenth century the term 'in capite' is

Universa-
lity of
dependent
tenure.

Before attempting to analyze this notion of dependent and derivative tenure, let us first observe how universally it has been applied[1]. Not only has every acre of land been brought within its scope, so that the English lawyer can not admit even a bare possibility of land being holden of no one, but the self-same formula has been made to cover relationships which have little in common. An Earl of Chester, who may at times behave like a sovereign prince, holds his county palatine of the king; the cottier, who like enough is personally unfree, holds his little croft of some mesne lord, or of the king himself. Even when of late a new mode of cultivating the soil has made its appearance and lords have let land to farmers for terms of years at substantial money rents, this new relationship has been brought within the old formula: the lessee holds the land of the lessor. Even when the tenant has no rent to pay, no temporal service to perform, even when the land has been devoted to God and the saints and is possessed by a religious house in free alms, still the formula has been found equal [p. 213] to the occasion: the religious community holds the land of the donor. We see at once therefore that the formula must be very elastic, that the notion of tenure must be in the highest degree an abstract notion. In England tenure is no mark of a class, and we may say the same of 'feudal' tenure.

Feudal
tenure.

The term *feodum*, which in Anglo-French is represented by *fe, fie, fee* and in English by *fee*, is one of the words which came

---

merely equivalent to 'immediately,' 'sine medio'; thus even a burgage tenant may have 'tenants in capite' holding of him: Ann. Dunstap. p. 173. Again, in the time of Henry I. Roger holds of Nigel, Nigel of the Earl of Chester; Nigel consents that Roger shall hold of the Earl 'in capite, ut vulgo loquitur': Hist. Abingd. ii. 67. See also Madox, Formulare, No. 22; but examples are plentiful. The term was in use in Normandy, where we find an equivalent and expressive phrase: 'Les fiefs sont tenus *nu à nu* [Lat. *immediate*] des seignurs quand il n'y a aulcune personne entre eulx et leurs tenants'; Ancienne Coutume (de Gruchy) c. 29. So too a tenant's 'capitalis dominus' is his immediate lord, not the lord who is chief above his other lords, but the lord who is nearest to him. See *e.g.* Petition of the Barons, 1258, [c. 29; Ann. Burton, p. 474, § 13. But perhaps this usage of the term 'chief lord' is not very consistently maintained; it was giving trouble in 1304; Y. B. 32–3 Edw. I., p. 39.

[1] We use the phrase 'dependent and derivative tenure' instead of saying merely 'tenure,' for though English lawyers have been wont to speak as though tenure of land were characteristic of feudalism, we ought to remember that long before there was any feudal tenure the verb *tenere*, sometimes in conjunction with *habere*, was currently used to describe the possession of land. What is characteristic of feudalism is not *tenere terram*, but *tenere terram de X*.

in with the Conqueror, and perhaps for a short while it carried
about with it a sense of military or noble tenure; but very soon
it was so widely used as to imply no more than heritability[1].
This is its settled sense in the thirteenth century.   To say of a
tenant that he holds in fee (*tenet in feodo*) means no more than
that his rights are inheritable.   He does not hold for life, he
does not hold for a term of years, he does not hold as guardian
of an heir, or as one to whom the land has been gaged
as security for money; he holds heritably and for his own
behoof[2].   But nothing more is implied as to the terms of his
holding, the relation between him and his lord.   His duties to
his lord may be onerous or nominal, noble or humble, military
or agricultural, but if his rights are heritable, then he holds in
fee and the land is *feodum suum,* at all events if his tenure has
about it no taint of villeinage[3].   Thus we can not, as continental writers do, treat feudal law as distinct from the ordinary
law of the land, a law to be administered by special courts, a
law which regulates some but not all of the proprietary rights
[p. 214] that men have in land.   We can hardly translate into English
the contrast which Germans draw between *Lehnrecht* and
Landrecht.   Our *Landrecht* is *Lehnrecht*; in so far as feudalism
is mere property law, England is of all countries the most
perfectly feudalized.   But this truth has another aspect:—
our *Lehnrecht* is *Landrecht*; feudal law is not a special law
applicable only to one fairly definite set of relationships, or
applicable only to one class or estate of men; it is just the

---

[1] There are two passages in the Leg. Henr. in which *feodum* seems to signify
rather inherited than heritable rights:—70, § 21, the eldest son is to inherit the
father's *feodum*, while the *emptiones* and *acquisitiones* the father may give to
whom he will; here the *feodum* seems to be the ancestral estate and is opposed
to lands acquired by purchase:—88, § 15, there seems a contrast drawn between
the *feodum* and the *conquisitum*, though the passage is not very plain as it
stands.   See also Maitland, Domesday Book, 152.

[2] Glanvill, xiii. 2: 'ut de feodo vel ut de vadio…ut de feodo vel ut de warda.'
Ibid. xiii. 24: land held by a church in free alms is *feodum ecclesiasticum.*
Where a church is tenant, there is of course no inheritance; but the church has
a perpetual right in its *feodum.*   The contrast between fee and gage disappears
when the gage takes the form of a conditional feoffment.

[3] Perhaps the tenant in villeinage was not yet spoken of as holding *in feodo.*
Demandants of customary land, while closely following the forms by which free
land was demanded, seem to avoid saying that their ancestors were seised 'of
fee,' while asserting that they were seised 'of right,' or 'of hereditary right';
Manorial Pleas (Seld. Soc.), i. 34, 39, 41.   On the other hand, among the sokemen on the ancient demesne we find seisin in fee freely asserted; Ibid., 123.

common law of England. That extensive application of the feudal formula (*Y tenet in feodo de X*) which is characteristic of England, and which perhaps was possible only in a conquered country, must have impaired its intensive force[1]. If it has to describe the relation between the king and the palatine earl, the relation (slight enough in England) between the pious founder and the religious house that he has endowed, the relation between the lord of a manor and the tenants who help to plough and reap his fields, the mere 'cash nexus' between a lessor and a lessee who has taken the land heritably at a full money rent, it can not mean very much. But this collection of the most diverse relationships under one head will have important effects; the lower 'tenures' will be assimilated to the higher, the higher to the lower; the 'feud' must lose half its meaning by becoming universal[2].

Analysis of dependent tenure. It is clear then that of dependent or of feudal tenure in general, little can be said: but still some analysis of it is possible. We may at least notice that it seems to be a complex of personal rights and of real rights. On the one hand, the lord has rights against his tenant, the tenant rights against his [p. 215] lord: the tenant owes services to his lord, the lord, at least normally, owes defence and warranty to his tenant. On the other hand, both lord and tenant have rights in the land, in the tenement, the subject of the tenure[3]. The tenant in demesne,

---

[1] Brunner, D. R. G., ii. 11: 'Wo jedes Grundeigentum sich in Lehn verwandelt, wird das Lehn, wie die Entwicklung des englischen Rechtes zeigt, schliesslich zum Begriff des Grundeigentums.'

[2] It is believed that the forms *feud* and *fief* appear in England but late in the day under the influence of foreign books; they never became terms of our law. It is noticeable also that *feodum* was constantly used in the sense that our *fee* has when we speak of a lawyer's or doctor's fee; payments due for services rendered, at least if they are permanent periodic payments, are *feoda*; the judges, for example, receive *feoda*, salaries. The etymological problem presented by the English *fee* seems no easy one, because at the Conquest the would-be Latin *feodum* or *feudum* (the *d* in which has puzzled philologists and does not always appear in Domesday Book) is introduced among a people which already has *feoh* as a word for property in general and cattle in particular. See Oxf. Eng. Dict. There are valuable remarks on this word in Flach, Origines de l'ancienne France, ii. 315.

[3] After a struggle in cent. xii. with other forms, such as *tenura, tenuitura*, the word *tenementum* has established itself in cent. xiii. as the proper word whereby to describe the subject of a tenure. Such a word is the more wanted because *terra* is often applied in a special sense to arable land; *tenementa* on the other hand will include houses, meadows, pastures, woods and the like, and will also comprise certain 'incorporeal things.'

the tenant on the lowest step of the feudal scale, obviously has
rights in the land, amounting to a general, indefinite right of
using it as he pleases.   But his lord also is conceived as having
rights in the land. We have not adequately described his position by saying that he has a right to services from his tenant.
Of him as well as of his tenant it may be said that he holds
the land, not indeed in demesne but in service, that the land
is his land and his fee, and even that he is seised, that is,
possessed of the land[1]. What has been said of the demesne
tenant's immediate lord, may be said also of that lord's lord;
he also has rights in the land and the land is in some sort
his. This, when regarded from the standpoint of modern jurisprudence, is perhaps the most remarkable characteristic of
feudalism:—several different persons, in somewhat different
senses, may be said to have and to hold the same piece of land.
We have further to conceive of the service due from the tenant
to his lord as being a burden on the tenement. It is service
owed by the tenement. This idea is so deeply engrained in
the law that the tenement is often spoken of as though it were
a person who could be bound by obligations and perform duties:
hides and virgates must send men to the war, must reap and
mow and do suit of court; 'these two half-hides ought to carry
the king's writs whenever they come into the county[2].' But
[p. 216] the vast liberty that men have enjoyed of creating new tenures
and sub-tenures gives us wonderful complications: the obligation of the tenement has to be kept distinct from the obligation
of the tenant. The tenement may be burdened with military
service, and yet, as between lord and tenant, the lord and not
the tenant may be bound to do it: all the same the land itself
is burdened with the duty and the lord's overlord may have his
remedy against the land.

To take a simple case:—The king has enfeoffed *A* to hold Obligations
of the
by military service; *A* can now proceed to enfeoff *B*, (whether tenant and
of the
he can do so without the king's leave is a question which we tenement.

---

[1] Phrases showing that the lord is conceived as holding the land are quite
common; see *e.g.* Bracton f. 432 b, 'Item cum petens totum petat in dominico,
tenens respondere potest et cognoscere quod totum non tenet in dominico, sed
partim in dominico et partim in servitio.' So also the lord is seised not merely
of the tenant's services but of the land; Bracton f. 81, 'nisi ipse vel antecessores
sui in seisina fuerint de tenemento illo in dominico vel servitio'; f. 392, 'antecessor obiit seisitus ut de feodo in dominico vel in servitio.'

[2] Testa de Neville, 71. See Gierke, Genossenschaftsrecht, ii. 92.

postpone) and may enfeoff *B* by some quite other service; *B* for example is to pay *A* a money rent. Now as regards the king, the land is burdened with and owes the military service; the king can enforce the service by distraining the land for its performance, that is, by seizing any chattels that are found on it, which chattels will probably belong to *B*, or (at least in some cases) by seizing the land itself. But *A* and *B* on the occasion of the feoffment, though they can not destroy the king's right or free the land from the military service, may none the less, as between themselves, settle the incidence of that service: *A* may agree that he will do it, or the bargain may be that *B* is to do it, besides paying his money rent to *A*. The terminology of Bracton's day and of yet earlier times neatly expresses the distinction between the service which the tenant owes to his immediate lord by reason of the bargain which exists between them, and the service which was incumbent on the tenement whilst it was in the lord's hand. The former is intrinsec service,

Intrinsec and forin-sec service. the latter forinsec service; the former is the service which is created by, which (as it were) arises within, the bargain between the two persons, *A* and *B*, whose rights and duties we are discussing; the latter arises outside that bargain, is 'foreign' to that bargain; nothing that the bargainers do will shift it from the land, though, as between themselves, they can determine its incidence. Suppose that *A* has undertaken to discharge this burden, then if the king attacks the land in *B*'s hand, *B* will have a remedy against *A*; there is a special form of action by which such remedy is sought, the action of mesne (*breve de medio*), very common in the thirteenth century; *A* who is mesne (*medius*) between the king and *B* is bound to 'acquit' *B* of this 'forinsec service,' to hold him harmless against the king's demands[1]. And then, if *B* enfeoffs *C*, the problem [p. 217] will reappear in a more complicated shape; some new service will perhaps be created; for instance *C*, who is a parson, is to pray for the soul of *B*'s ancestors; but there are two other services incumbent on the land, the rent that *B* owes to *A*, the military service that *A* owes to the king, and in one way or another those services must be provided for. As between them-selves, *B* and *C* can settle this matter by the terms of their bargain, but without prejudice to the rights of *A*, and of the

---

[1] The writ of *mesne* is not in Glanvill, but appears in very early Registers; Harv. L. R., iii. 113, 115. In Henry III.'s day it was in common use.

king. It is no impossibility that Edward should hold in villeinage of Ralph, who holds in free socage of the Prior of Barnwell, who holds in frankalmoin of Earl Alan, who holds by knight's service of the king[1]. Just as at the present day one and the same acre of land may be leasehold, copyhold and freehold—for there is no land without a freeholder—so in the past one and the same acre might be holden by many different tenures. It owed many and manifold services, the incidence of which, as between its various lords and tenants, had been settled by complicated bargaining[2].

[p. 218]   Little more could at this moment be said of tenure in general—an abstraction of a very high order. Efforts, however, had been made to classify the tenures, to bring the infinite modes of service under a few heads, and before the end of the

Classification of tenures.

---

[1] Y. B. 33–5 Edw. I., p. 377.

[2] See Bracton's explanation of the term 'forinsec service,' f. 35–7. This term had been in common use even in Richard's reign; see Fines, ed. Hunter, *passim*; and may be found in Domesday Book, i. 165 b. It seems constantly used as though it were equivalent, or almost equivalent, to 'royal service,' 'military service,' 'scutage,' insomuch that to say of a man that he owes forinsec service is almost the same as saying that his tenure is military, and therefore implies wardship and marriage; see Bracton's Note Book, pl. 33, 236, 288, 703, 795, 978, 1076, 1631; Y. B. 20–21 Edw. I., p. 133. Hence the notion put forward by Hale and supported by Hargrave (Co. Lit. 69 b, 74 a, *notes*) that forinsec service is so called because it is done in foreign parts. But this can hardly be true; the military tenants were constantly asserting that into foreign parts they were not bound to go. Besides, services which are not military are occasionally called 'forinsec,' services due from socage tenements, *e.g.* suit of court, landgafol, churchscot; Reg. Malm., ii. 51, 'salvo forinseco servicio pertinente ad liberum socagium quantum ad unam virgatam terrae'; Ibid. 52, 'salvo forinseco servicio pertinente ad unam virgatam terrae de libero socagio'; Ibid. 69, 'et pro chirchsote [*sic*] et omnibus aliis serviciis forinsecis.' And forinsec service is not necessarily due to the king; Whalley Coucher, i. 21: *A*'s tenant *B* has enfeoffed *C*; *A* releases to *C* 'omne forense servicium quod ad me pertinet'; the service due from *B* to *A* was forinsec as regards *C*. Thus the term is a relative one; what is 'intrinsec' between *A* and *B* is 'forinsec' as regards *C*. At the same time, it must be confessed that this use of the word, which has not been found in France, implies a considerable degree of abstraction, and it seems possible that as a matter of historic fact it is due to the legal development of a more concrete notion. In northern charters we sometimes read of the king's 'utware' just where we should expect to read of 'forinsec service.' Perhaps at first 'outside service' meant service done outside the tenement or outside the manor; but jurisprudence gave a new turn to the phrase, and there is hardly room for doubt that Bracton's explanation (f. 36) gives us the law of his time:—'forinsecum dici potest quia sit [*corr.* fit] et capitur foris sive extra servitium quod sit [*corr.* fit] domino capitali.' Observe that the tenant's 'dominus capitalis' is his *immediate* lord.

twelfth century the great outlines which were to endure for long ages had been drawn, though neither in Glanvill, nor even in Bracton, do we find just that scheme of tenures which became final and classical. In particular, 'fee farm' and 'burgage' threaten to be coordinate with, not subordinate to, 'free socage'; 'tenure by barony' is spoken of as something different from 'tenure by knight's service'; and in the north there are such tenures as 'thegnage' and 'drengage' which are giving the lawyers a great deal of trouble. Still, subject to some explanations which can be given hereafter, we may say that in Bracton's day tenures are classified thus:—they are either free or not free; the free tenures are (1) frankalmoin, (2) military service, (3) serjeanty, (4) free socage. In this order we will speak of them[1].

§ 2. *Frankalmoin.*

Frankal-
moin.

At the beginning of the thirteenth century an ever-increasing quantity of land was held by ecclesiastics, regular and secular, in right of their churches by a tenure commonly known as frankalmoin, free alms, *libera elemosina*. The service implied by this tenure was in the first place spiritual, as opposed to secular service, and in the second place it was an indefinite service. Such at least was the doctrine of later days[2]. We may take [p. 219] the second characteristic first. At all events in later days[3], if land was given to a churchman and there was a stipulation for some definite service albeit of a spiritual kind, (for example a stipulation that the donee should sing a mass once a year or should distribute a certain sum of money among the poor), the tenure thus created was called, not frankalmoin, but tenure by divine service; the tenant might perhaps be compelled to swear fealty to his lord, and the performance of the service might be exacted by distress or by action in the king's courts[4]. On the other hand, if the tenant held in frankalmoin, that is, if the

---

[1] The passage in Glanvill most important in this context is lib. ix. c. 4, where we read of 'barony,' 'knight's service,' 'serjeanty,' 'socage'; elsewhere 'burgage' and 'frankalmoin' appear; 'frankmarriage' will also demand attention, but at a later stage of our work.

[2] But in 13 Edw. I. (Fitz. Abr. *Counterple de voucher*, 118) it is said that frankalmoin is the highest and *most certain* of all services.

[3] Litt. sec. 133–8.

[4] See the writ *Cessavit de cantaria*, Reg. Brev. Orig. 237 b, 238.

terms of the gift (as was often the case) said nothing of service
or merely stipulated in a general way for the donee's prayers,
then no fealty was due; and only by ecclesiastical censures could
the tenant be compelled to perform those good offices for the
donor's soul that he had impliedly or expressly undertaken.
Perhaps this distinction was admitted during the later years
of the period with which we are now dealing; but we shall
hereafter see that in this region of law there was a severe
struggle between the temporal and the ecclesiastical courts,
and very possibly an attempt on the part of the former to
enforce any kind of service that could be called spiritual would
have been resented. The question is of no great importance,
because stipulations for definite spiritual services were rare
when compared with gifts in frankalmoin[1].

Here, as in France, the word *elemosina* became a technical
word, but it was not such originally. At first it would express
rather the motive of the gift than a mode of tenure that the
[p. 220] gift creates. And so in Domesday Book it is used in various
senses and contexts. In some cases a gift has been made by
the king *in elemosina*, but the donee is to all appearance a
layman; in one case he is blind, in another maimed; he holds
by way of charity, and perhaps his tenure is precarious. To
hold land 'in charity' might well mean to hold during the giver's
pleasure, and it may be for this reason that the charters of a
later day are careful to state that the gift has been made, not
merely in alms, but 'in perpetual alms[2].' Then, again, in some

Meaning of 'alms.'

---

[1] A few instances of such definite spiritual services may be found already in
Domesday, *e.g.* ii. 133, 133 b, a tenant has to sing three masses. Gifts for the
maintenance of lamps before particular altars and the like are not uncommon,
and often they expressly say that the land is frankalmoin, *e.g.* Reg. St Osmund
i. 234 (1220—5), a gift of land to the church of Sarum in pure and perpetual
alms to find a taper to burn before the relics on festivals. Sometimes it would
have been difficult to draw the line between 'certain' and 'uncertain' services,
as when land was given that its rents might be expended 'tam in reparanda
ecclesia quam in maioribus necessariis ecclesiae,' Reg. St Osmund, i. 350.

[2] D. B. i. 293: 'In W. tenet quidam cecus unam bovatam in elemosina de
rege.' Ibid. iv. 466: 'Tenuit Edritius mancus in elemosina de rege Edwardo.'
In Dorsetshire, under the heading 'Terra Tainorum Regis' (i. 84), we find
'Hanc terram dedit Regina Dodoni in elemosina.' In Devonshire, under the
like heading (118), we find 'Aluuard Mert tenet dim. virg....Regina dedit ei in
elemosina.' In Hertfordshire (137 b) we read how a manor was held by two
thegns, one of whom was the man of King Edward, the other was the man of
Æsgar; they could not sell 'quia semper iacuerunt in elemosina.' This would
seem to mean that they held precariously. See the curious entry, ii. 5 b, which

parts of the country it is frequently noted that the parish priest has a few acres *in elemosina*; in one case we learn that the neighbours gave the church thirty acres in alms[1]. There are, however, other cases in which the term seems to bear a more technical sense: some religious house, English or French, holds a considerable quantity of land in alms; we can hardly doubt that it enjoys a certain immunity from the ordinary burdens incumbent on landholders in general, including among such landholders the less favoured churches[2]. And so again in the early charters the word seems to be gradually becoming a word of art; sometimes we miss it where we should expect to find it, and instead get some other phrase capable of expressing a complete freedom from secular burdens[3]. In the twelfth century, the century of new monastic orders, of lavish endowments, [p. 221] of ecclesiastical law, the gift in free, pure, and perpetual alms has a well-known meaning[4].

Spiritual service.　　The notion that the tenant in frankalmoin holds his land by a service done to his lord seems to grow more definite in course of time as the general theory of tenure hardens and the church fails in its endeavour to assert a jurisdiction over disputes relating to land that has been given to God. The tenure

---

tells how Harold gave a hide to a certain priest of his, 'set hundret nescit si dedit liberae [*sic*] vel in elemosina'; seemingly the hundred did not know whether the priest's tenure was free or precarious.

[1] D. B. ii. 24 b; ii. 189 b: the parish church holds sixty acres of free land 'elemosina plurimorum.' See the survey of Suffolk, where the parish church generally holds some acres 'of free land' *in elemosina*.

[2] D. B. i. 25 b: 'Clepinges tenet Abbatia de Almanesches de Comite (Rogerio) in elemosina....se defendit pro xi. hidis....In eodem manerio tenet S. Marunus de Sais de Comite in elemosina xi. hidas.' Ibid. i. 58: 'Episcopus Dunelmensis tenet de Rege Waltham in elemosina.' Ibid. i. 166 b: 'Ecclesia de Cirecestre tenet de Rege duas hidas in elemosina et de Rege E. tenuit quietas ab omni consuetudine.'

[3] Thus when Henry I. makes gifts to the Abbey of Abingdon 'to the use of the alms of the said church,' we seem to get the term in a slightly different sense from that which becomes usual; he may well mean that the land is devoted to those pious works of the abbey which belong to the almoner's department; Hist. Abingd. ii. 65, 94.

[4] In comparatively late documents we may still find persons who are said to hold in frankalmoin but are not holding in right of any church. Thus in the Whalley Coucher, i. 43, William the clerk of Eccles gives land to his brother John, his heirs and assigns, to hold in pure and perpetual alms of the donor and his heirs, rendering yearly a pound of incense to God and the church of Eccles. William's tenure may have been frankalmoin, but according to modern notions John's could not be.

thus becomes one among many tenures, and must conform to the general rule that tenure implies service. Still this notion was very old[1]. In charters of the twelfth century it is common to find the good of the donor's soul and the souls of his kinsfolk, or of his lord, or of the king, mentioned as the motive for the gift: the land is bestowed *pro anima mea, pro salute animae meae.* Sometimes the prayers of the donees are distinctly required, and occasionally they are definitely treated as services done in return for the land[2]: thus, for example, the donor obliges himself to warrant the gift 'in consideration of the said service of prayers[3].' Not unfrequently, especially in the older charters, [p. 222] the donor along with the land gives his body for burial[4]; sometimes he stipulates that, should he ever retire from the world, he shall be admitted to the favoured monastery; sometimes he binds himself to choose no other place of retirement; often it is said that the donees receive him into all the benefits of their prayers[5].

We have spoken as though gifts in frankalmoin were made to men; but, according to the usual tenour of their terms, they were made to God. As Bracton says, they were made *primo et principaliter* to God, and only *secundario* to the canons or monks or parsons[6]. A gift, for example, to Ramsey Abbey would take the form of a gift 'to God and St Benet of Ramsey

Gifts to God and the saints.

---

[1] Already Bede, Hist. Eccl. iii. 24, tells how Oswy gave land to the church in order that prayers might be offered for the peace of his folk. The land, instead of providing for a *militia terrestris*, is devoted to a *militia caelestis.*

[2] Cart. Glouc. i. 197: 'habendum in liberam elemosinam...sine aliquo retinemento ad opus meum vel aliquorum heredum meorum nisi tantummodo orationes spirituales perpetuas.' Ibid. i. 199, 289, 335, ii. 10. Such phrases are common in the Whalley Coucher Book.

[3] Cart. Glouc. i. 307: 'Nos vero...praedictam terram...per praedictum servicium orationum warantizabimus.' The term 'consideration' is of course rather too technical, but still the prayers seem regarded as having a certain juristic value.

[4] Litigations over the right to bury benefactors may be found, *e.g.* Register of St Thomas, Dublin, p. 349, between the canons of St Thomas and the monks of Bective about the body of Hugh de Lacy; also struggles for the bodies of dying men, *e.g.* between the monks of Abingdon and the canons of St Frideswide, Hist. Abingd. ii. 175. See also a charter of John de Lacy in the Whalley Coucher, i. 33: 'Know ye that I have given and granted to the abbot and monks of Stanlaw after my death myself and my body to be buried.'

[5] For an elaborate agreement about masses and other spiritual benefits, see Newminster Cartulary, p. 120.

[6] Bracton, f. 12.

and the Abbot Walter and the monks of St Benet,' or simply
'to God and the church of St Benet of Ramsey,' or yet more
briefly 'to God and St Benet[1].' The fact that the land was
given to God was made manifest by appropriate ceremonies. Often the donor laid the charter of feoffment, or some
knife or other symbol of possession upon the altar of the
church[2]. Clauses denouncing excommunication and damnation
against all who should disturb the donee's possession did not go
out of use at the Norman Conquest, but may be found in
charters of the twelfth century[3], nor was it uncommon for a
religious house to obtain a papal bull confirming gifts already
made and thereafter to be made, and, whatever might be the
legal effect of such instruments, the moral effect must have
been great[4]. We are not entitled to treat these phrases which [p. 223]
seem to make God a landowner as of no legal value. Bracton
more than once founds arguments upon them[5], and they suggest
that land given in frankalmoin is outside the sphere of merely
human justice.

Free alms and forin-sec service. In later days the feature of tenure in frankalmoin which
attracts the notice of lawyers is a merely negative feature,
namely, the absence of any service that can be enforced by the
secular courts. But some distinctions must be drawn. The
king might give land to a religious house 'in free, pure, and
perpetual alms,' and in that case not only would no secular
service be due from the donee to the donor, but the land in the
donee's hand would owe no secular service at all. But tenure
in frankalmoin is by no means necessarily a tenure in chief of
the crown; indeed the quantity of land held in chief of the
crown by frankalmoin was never very large. It will be understood that an ecclesiastical person might well hold lands, and
hold them in right of his church, by other tenures. The ancient
endowments of the bishops' sees and of the greater and older
abbeys were held by knight's service; the bishop, the abbot,
held a barony. Beside this, we constantly find religious houses

---

[1] Cart. Ramsey, i. 159, 160, 255, 256.

[2] See *e.g.* Cart. Glouc. i. 164, 205; ii. 74, 86, 97.

[3] See *e.g.* Hist. Abingd. ii. 55; Whitby Cartulary, i. 200; Whalley Coucher,
i. 17, 113.

[4] See *e.g.* Bull of 1138, Hist. Evesham, 173; Bull of 1140, Cart. Ramsey, ii.
155; Bull of 1146, Hist. Abinga. ii. 191.

[5] Bracton, f. 12, 286 b.

taking lands in socage or in fee farm at rents and at substantial rents, and though a gift in frankalmoin might proceed from the king, it often proceeded from a mesne lord. In this case the mere gift could not render the land free from all secular service; in the donor's hand it was burdened with such service, and so burdened it passed into the hands of the donee[1]. If the donee wished to get rid of the service altogether, he had to go to the donor's superior lords and ultimately to the king for charters of confirmation and release. But, as between themselves, the donor and donee might arrange the incidence of this 'forinsec service' as pleased them best. The words 'in free, pure, and perpetual alms' seems to have implied that the tenant was to owe no secular service to his lord; but they did not necessarily imply that, as between lord and tenant, the lord was to do the forinsec service. And so we find the matter settled in various ways by various charters of donation:—sometimes it is stipulated that the tenant is to do the forinsec service[2], sometimes the lord burdens himself with this[3], often nothing is said, and apparently in such case the service falls on the lord.

[p. 224]

Another rule of interpretation appears, though somewhat Pure alms. dimly. In accordance with later books, we have spoken as though a gift in frankalmoin, in free alms, always implied that no secular service was due from the donee to the donor. But the words generally used in such gifts were 'free, pure, and perpetual alms,' and in Bracton's day much might turn on the use of the word 'pure[4].' Seemingly there was no contradiction between a gift in 'free and perpetual alms' and the reservation of a temporal service, and many instances may be found of such gifts accompanied by such reservations. This will give us cause to believe that the exemption from secular service had not been conceived as the core of tenure in frankalmoin; and if we find, as well we may, that a donor sometimes stipulates for

---

[1] Bracton, f. 27 b. Cf. Somma, p. 99.

[2] Fines, ed. Hunter, i. 200 (3 John): 'Ala dedit et concessit in puram et perpetuam elemosinam Deo et ecclesiae S. Marie de B...totam partem suam...ita quod praedictus prior et successores sui facient inde forinsecum servicium.' Cart. Glouc. i. 167: gift in frankalmoin, 'salvo tamen regali servicio.' Ibid. 187: gift in frankalmoin saving the landgafol due to the king. Ibid. 289: gift in free, pure and perpetual alms subject to a rent of pepper and to royal service.

[3] Cart. Glouc. ii. 17, 30, 98.

[4] Bracton, f. 27 b; Note Book, pl. 21.

secular service, though he makes his gift not only in free but even in pure alms, our belief will be strengthened[1].

Free alms
and eccle-
siastical
jurisdic-
tion.
The key to the problem is given by the Constitutions of Clarendon (1164). Freedom from secular jurisdiction rather than freedom from secular service has been the focus of frankalmoin. 'If,' says the famous document, 'a dispute shall arise between a clerk and a layman, or between a layman and a clerk, concerning any tenement which the clerk asserts to be *elemosina* and the layman asserts to be lay fee, it shall be determined by a recognition of twelve lawful men and the judgment of the chief justiciar whether (*utrum*) the tenement belongs to *elemo-* [p. 225] *sina* or belongs to lay fee. And if it be found to belong to *elemosina*, then the plea shall go forward in the ecclesiastical court: but if it be lay fee, then in the king's court, or, in case both litigants claim to hold of the same lord, then in the lord's court. And in consequence of such a recognition, the person who is seised is not to lose his seisin until it has been deraigned by the plea[2].' Let us observe how large a concession to the church the great Henry is compelled to make, even before the murder of Becket has put him in the wrong. This is all that those *avitae leges*, of which he talks so frequently, will give him, and he claims no more. The clergy have established this principle:—All litigation concerning land held in almoin belongs of right to the ecclesiastical courts. All that the king insists on is this: that, if there is dispute whether the land be almoin or no, this preliminary question must be decided by an assize under the eye of his justiciar. Thus the assize *Utrum* is established. It is a preliminary process; it will not even serve to give the claimant a possession *ad interim*; the possessor is to remain possessed; it decides not the title to land, but the competence of courts. Here then we find the essence of *almoin* as understood in the middle of the twelfth century:—the land is subject to no jurisdiction save that of the

---

[1] Rievaulx Cart. p. 29: gift by Bishop Hugh of Durham in free and perpetual alms at a rent of 60 shillings, payable to him and his successors. Ibid. pp. 80, 226, 249. Newminster Cart. p. 73: gift by Newminster Abbey to Hexham Priory in free, pure, and perpetual alms at a substantial rent. Bracton, f. 48, holds that in these cases the services must be done, but speaks with some doubt.

[2] Const. Clarend. c. 9. In the Gesta Abbatum, i. 114, the St Alban's chronicler gives an account of litigation in Stephen's reign in which something very like an *Assisa Utrum* takes place. See above p. 145.

tribunals of the church. Even to maintain his royal right to decide the preliminary question of competence was no easy matter for Henry. Alexander III. freely issued rescripts which ordered his delegates to decide as between clerk and layman the title to English land, or at least the possessory right in English lands: he went further, he bade his delegates award possession even in a dispute between layman and layman, though afterwards he apologized for so doing. The *avitae leges*, therefore, were far from conceding all that the clergy, all that the pope demanded [1].

[p. 226]　They conceded, however, more than the church could per- manently keep. If as regards criminous clerks the Constitutions of Clarendon are the high-water-mark of the claims of secular justice, as regards the title to lands they are the low-water-mark. In Normandy the procedure instituted by Henry, the *Breve de Feodo et Elemosina*, which was the counterpart, and perhaps the model, of our own *Assisa Utrum*, seems to have maintained its preliminary character long after Henry's son had forfeited the duchy: that is to say, there were cases in which it was a mere prelude to litigation in the spiritual forum [2]. In England it gradually and silently changed its whole nature; the *Assisa Utrum* or action *Juris Utrum* [3] became an ordinary proprietary action in the king's court, an action enabling the rectors of parochial churches to claim and obtain the lands of

The Assize Utrum.

---

[1] See the remarkable series of papal rescripts in the Rievaulx Cartulary, 189–197; see also c. 7, X. 4, 17, where the pope admits that he has gone too far in ordering his delegates to give possession in a dispute between laymen, which came into the ecclesiastical courts in consequence of a question having been raised about bastardy. See also in the Malmesbury Register, ii. 7, proceedings under letters of Innocent III. for the recovery from a layman of land improvidently alienated by an abbot. In the Gesta Abbatum, i. 159—162, there is a detailed account of litigation which took place early in Henry II.'s reign between the Abbot of St Alban's and a layman touching the title to a wood; the abbot procured letters from the pope appointing judges delegate.

[2] Somma, p. 295; Ancienne coutume, p. 288; Brunner, Entstehung der Schwurgerichte, 324–6; Brunner, Pol. Sci. Quarterly, xi. 538. Apparently, the Norman assize had from the first served as a petitory action; but if the recognitors could give no verdict, then the cause went to the ecclesiastical court.

[3] The term *Juris Utrum* seems due to a mistake in the expansion of the compendium *Jur'*; it should be *Jurata Utrum*, in French *Juré Utrum*; see *e.g.* Y. B. 14-15 Edw. III. (ed. Pike), p. 47; and see Bracton, f. 287, where the technical distinction between an *Assisa Utrum* and a *Jurata Utrum* is explained.

their churches: it became 'the parson's writ of right[1].' Between the time of Glanvill and the time of Bracton this great change was effected and the ecclesiastical tribunals suffered a severe defeat[2].

Defeat of the ecclesiastical claims.

The formal side of this process seems to have consisted in a gradual denial of the assize *Utrum* to the majority of the tenants in frankalmoin, a denial which was justified by the statement that they had other remedies for the recovery of their lands. If a bishop or an abbot thought himself entitled to lands which were withholden from him, he might use the [p. 227] ordinary remedies competent to laymen, he might have recourse to a writ of right. But one class of tenants in frankalmoin was debarred from this remedy, namely, the rectors of parish churches. Bracton explains the matter thus:—When land is given to a religious house, though it is in the first place given to God and the church, it is given in the second place to the abbot and monks and their successors, or to the dean and canons and their successors; so also land may be given to a bishop and his successors. If then a bishop or an abbot has occasion to sue for the land, he can plead that one of his predecessors was seised of it, just as a lay claimant might rely on the seisin of his ancestor. But with the parish parson it is not so; we do not make gifts to a parson and his successors; we make them to the church, *e.g.* 'to God and the church of St Mary of Dale[3].' True, that if the parson is ejected from possession, he may have an assize of novel disseisin, for he himself has been seised of a free tenement; but a proprietary (as opposed to possessory) action he can not bring. He can have no writ of right, for the land has not been given to a parson and his successors, it has been given to the church; he can

[1] Britton, ii. 207.

[2] According to Glanvill (xii. 25, xiii. 23, 24) the courts Christian are competent to decide an action for land between two clerks or between clerk and layman in case the person in possession is a clerk who holds in free alms. So late as 1206 an assize *Utrum* is brought by one monastic house against another and, on its appearing that the land is almoin, the judgment is that the parties do go to court Christian and implead each other there; Placit. Abbrev. p. 54 (Oxon.).

[3] This remark seems fairly well-supported by the practice of conveyancers in Bracton's time; thus *e.g.* a donor gives land 'to God and St Mary and St Chad and the church of Rochdale,' and contracts to warrant the land 'to God and the church of Rochdale,' saying nothing of the parson; Whalley Coucher, i. 162.

not therefore plead that his predecessor was seised and that on his predecessor's death the right of ownership passed to him; thus the assize *Utrum* is his only remedy of a proprietary kind[1].

In another context it might be interesting to consider the meaning of this curious argument; it belongs to the nascent law about 'corporations aggregate' and 'corporations sole.' The members of a religious house can already be regarded as constituting an artificial person; the bishop also is regarded as bearing the *persona* of his predecessors; the vast temporal possessions of the bishops must have necessitated the formation of some such idea at an early time. But to the parish parson that idea has not yet been applied. The theory is that the parish church itself is the landowner and that each successive parson (*persona ecclesiae*) is the guardian and fleeting representative of this invisible and immortal being[2]. It has been difficult to find a 'subject' who will bear the ownership of the lands appropriated to parish churches, for according to a view which is but slowly being discarded by the laity, the landowner who builds a church owns that church and any land that he may have devoted to the use of its parson[3]. However, our present point must be that legal argument takes this form— (1) No one can use the assize *Utrum* who has the ordinary proprietary remedies for the recovery of land; (2) All or almost all the tenants in frankalmoin, except the rectors of parish churches, have these ordinary remedies; (3) The assize *Utrum* is essentially the parson's remedy; it is *singulare beneficium,* introduced in favour of parsons[4]. This argument would naturally involve a denial that the assize could be brought by the layman against the parson. According to the clear words of the Constitutions of Clarendon, it was a procedure that was to be employed as

The parson and his land.

[p. 228]

---

[1] Bracton, f. 286 b, 287. This may have been the reasoning which caused a denial of the assize to the parson when that parson was a monastery, a denial which an ordinance of 1234 overruled; Note Book, pl. 1117.

[2] Bracton, f. 287 b. The parson has not only the assize of novel disseisin, but he may have a writ of entry founded on the seisin of his predecessor. This being so, the refusal to allow him a writ of right is already somewhat anomalous. But the writs of entry are new, and the law of the twelfth century (completely ignored by Bracton) was that the ecclesiastical court was the tribunal competent to decide on the title to land held in frankalmoin.

[3] Stutz, Geschichte des kirchlichen Benefizialwesens; Stutz, Die Eigenkirche.

[4] Bracton, f. 286 b.

well when the claimant was a layman as when he was a clerk.
But soon the doctrine of the courts began to fluctuate. Martin
Pateshull at one time allowed the layman this action; then he
changed his opinion, because the layman had other remedies;
Bracton was for retracing this step, because trial by battle and
the troublesome grand assize might thus be avoided[1]. One
curious relic of the original meaning of this writ remained
until 1285, when the Second Statute of Westminster gave an
action to decide whether a piece of land was the *elemosina* of
one or of another church[2]. The assize had originally been a
means of deciding disputes between clerks and laymen, or
rather of sending such disputes to the competent courts temporal or spiritual, and the Constitutions of Clarendon contain a
plain admission that if both parties agree that the land is
elemosina, any dispute between them is no concern of the lay
courts.

Meaning of frankalmoin in the thirteenth century.

We have been speaking of the formal side of a legal change,
but must not allow this to conceal the grave importance of the
matters that were at stake. The argument that none but
parochial rectors have need of the *Utrum*, and the conversion of [p. 229]
the *Utrum* from a preliminary procedure settling the competence
of courts, into a proprietary action deciding, and deciding
finally, a question of title to land, involve the assertion that
all tenants in frankalmoin (except such rectors) can sue and
be sued and ought to sue and be sued for lands in the temporal
courts by the ordinary actions. And this, we may add, involves
the assertion that they ought not to sue or be sued elsewhere.
The ecclesiastical courts are not to meddle in any way with the
title to land albeit held in frankalmoin. To prevent their so
doing, writs are in common use prohibiting both litigants and
ecclesiastical judges from touching 'lay fee' (*laicum feodum*)
in the courts Christian; and in Bracton's day it is firmly established that for this purpose land may be lay fee though it is
held in free, pure, and perpetual alms[3]. The interference of the
spiritual courts with land has been hemmed within the narrowest limits. The contrast to 'lay fee' is no longer (as in the
Constitutions of Clarendon) *elemosina*, but consecrated soil, the
sites of churches and monasteries and their churchyards, to

---

[1] Bracton, f. 285 b; Fleta, p. 332; Britton, ii. 207.
[2] Stat. 13 Ed. I., c. 24.
[3] Bracton, f. 407; Note Book, pl. 547, 1143.

which, according to Bracton, may be added lands given to churches at the time of their dedication[1]. The royal court is zealous in maintaining its jurisdiction; the plea rolls are covered with prohibitions directed against ecclesiastical judges[2]; and it is held that this is a matter affecting the king's crown and dignity—no contract, no oath to submit to the courts Christian, will stay the issue of a writ[3]. But the very frequency of these prohibitions tells us that to a great part of the nation they were distasteful. As a matter of fact, a glance at [p. 230] any monastic annals of the twelfth century is likely to show us that the ecclesiastical tribunals, even the Roman curia, were constantly busy with the title to English lands, especially when both parties to the litigation were ecclesiastics. Just when Bracton was writing, Richard Marsh at the instance of Robert Grosseteste was formulating the claims of the clergy:—

'He who does any injury to the frankalmoin of the church, which therefore is consecrated to God, commits sacrilege; for that it is *res sacra*, being dedicated to God, exempt from secular power, subject to the ecclesiastical forum, and therefore to be protected by the laws of the church[4].' It is with such words as these in our minds that we ought to contemplate the history of frankalmoin. A gift in free and pure alms to God and his saints has meant not merely, perhaps not principally, that the land is to owe no rent, no military service to the donor, but also and in the first place that it is to be subject only to the laws and courts of the church[5].

---

[1] Bracton, f. 407. Such lands constitute the church's *dos* or *dower*. See also f. 207 b.

[2] See Note Book *passim*. The writ of prohibition is found in Glanvill, xii. 21, 22. It is found in the earliest Chancery Registers. Bracton discusses its scope at great length, f. 402 ff.

[3] In the twelfth century the donor sometimes expressly binds himself and his heirs to submit to the church courts in case he or they go against the gift; see *e.g.* Rievaulx Cartulary, 33, 37, 39, 69, 159, 166. So in the Newminster Cartulary, 89, a man covenants to levy a fine and submits to the jurisdiction of the archdeacon of Northumberland in case he fails to perform his covenant. For a similar obligation undertaken by a married woman, see Cart. Glouc. i. 304. As to such attempts to renounce the right to a prohibition, see Note Book, pl. 678.

[4] Ann. Burton, p. 427. See also the protest of the bishops in 1257, Mat. Par. Chron. Maj. vi. 361.

[5] Viollet, Histoire du droit civil, p. 702: 'la franche aumône...un franc alleu ...échappant à toute juridiction civile.'

§ 3. *Knight's Service.*

We now turn to military tenure, and in the first place should warn ourselves not to expect an easy task. In some of our modern books military tenure has a definiteness and a stability which it never had elsewhere. An army is settled on the land, is rooted in the land. The grades in 'the service' correspond to, and indeed are, the grades of landholdership; the supreme landlord is commander-in-chief; each of his immediate tenants is the general of an army corps; the regiments, squadrons, companies, answer to honours or manors or knight's fees. All is accurately defined; each man knows his place, knows how many days he must fight and with what arms. This 'feudal system' is the military system of England from the Norman Conquest onwards throughout the middle ages; by means of it our land is defended and our victories are won in Wales and in Ireland, in Scotland and in France.—When however we look at the facts, all this definiteness, all this stability, vanish. We see growth and decay: we see decay beginning before growth is at an end. Before there is much law about military tenure it has [p. 231] almost ceased to be military in any real sense. We must have regard to dates. Every one knows that the military tenure of Charles I.'s reign was very different from the military tenure of Edward I.'s; but this again was very different from the military tenure of Henry I.'s or even of Henry II.'s reign.

Soon after the Conquest a process begins whereby the duty of service in the army becomes rooted in the tenure of land. This goes on for a century; but before it is finished, before the system of knight's fees has been well ordered and arranged, the kings are already discovering that the force thus created is not what they want, or is not all that they want. It may serve to defend a border, to harry Wales or Scotland for a few weeks in the summer, but for continuous wars in France it will not serve; the king would rather have money; he begins to take scutages. This, as we shall soon see, practically alters the whole nature of the institution. Another century goes by and scutage itself has become antiquated and unprofitable; another, and scutage is no longer taken. Speaking roughly we may say that there is one century (1066—1166) in which the military tenures are really military, though as yet there is little law about them;

that there is another century (1166—1266) during which these tenures still supply an army, though chiefly by supplying its pay; and that when Edward I. is on the throne the military organization which we call feudal has already broken down and will no longer provide either soldiers or money save in very inadequate amounts. However, just while it is becoming little better than a misnomer to speak of military tenure, the law about military tenure is being evolved, but as a part rather of our private than of our public law. The tenant will really neither fight nor pay scutage, but there will be harsh and intricate law for him about the reliefs and wardships and marriages that his lord can claim because the tenure is military. Thus in speaking of tenure by knight's service as it was before the days of Edward I., we have to speak not of a stable, but of a very unstable institution, and if of necessity we describe it in general terms, this should not be done without a preliminary protest that our generalities will be but approximately true. As to scutage, in the whole course of our history this impost was levied but some forty times, and we can not be certain that the method of [p. 232] assessing and collecting it remained constant. An English lawyer turning to study the history of these matters should remember that if Littleton had cared to know much about them, he would have had to devote his time to antiquarian research[1].

---

[1] There is only one half-century during which scutages are frequently imposed, namely that which lies between 1190 and 1240. The early history of scutage is now in the crucible. New materials have been rendered accessible by the publication of the Red Book of the Exchequer and some of the Pipe Rolls of Henry II.'s day. Two important tracts have come to our hands at the last moment, viz. (1) J. F. Baldwin, Scutage and Knight Service, Chicago, University Press, 1897; and (2) J. H. Round, The Red Book of the Exchequer (privately printed), 1898. Mr Round makes it fairly certain that our statement (*infra*, p. 267) as to the existence of scutage before the days of Henry II. is not strong enough, and he leaves us doubting whether at this point Henry did much that was new. Mr Baldwin has thrown light on many details. While agreeing with us in holding that in the last days of scutage the tenant in chief can not escape from the duty of military service at the cost of paying scutage, Mr Baldwin seems inclined to hold that in the earlier time the scutage was treated as a full equivalent of the service. His researches seem to show that Henry II.'s endeavour to charge the tenants in chief with the number of fees that they had created if it exceeded their old *servitium debitum* (*infra*, p. 266) was not permanently successful. Not the least interesting result of Mr Baldwin's essay is the proof that, as compared with other sources of revenue (*dona, auxilia, tallagia*), the importance of the scutages may easily be over-rated.

Units of
military
service.

By far the greater part of England is held of the king by knight's service (*per servitium militare*): it is comparatively rare for the king's tenants in chief to hold by any of the other tenures. In order to understand this tenure we must form the conception of a unit of military service. That unit seems to be the service of one knight or fully armed horseman (*servitium unius militis*) to be done to the king in his army for forty days in the year, if it be called for. In what wars such service must be done, we need not here determine; nor would it be easy to do so, for from time to time the king and his barons have quarrelled about the extent of the obligation, and more than one crisis of constitutional history has this for its cause. It is a question, we may say, which never receives any legal answer[1].

The forty
days.

Even the limit of forty days seems to have existed rather in [p. 233] theory than in practice, and its theoretic existence can hardly be proved for England out of any authoritative document[2]. But we hear of some such limit in Norman, French and German law, and attempts have been made to trace it back to the days of the Karlovingian emperors. From the Touraine of the thirteenth century we have a definite statement. 'The barons or men of the king are bound, if summoned, to follow him in his host and to serve at their own cost forty days and forty nights with as many knights as they owe him......And if the king will keep them more than forty days and forty nights at their cost, they need not stay unless they will; but if the king will keep them at his cost for the defence of the realm, they ought by rights to stay; but if the king would take them out of the realm, they need not go unless they like, after they have done their forty days and forty nights[3].' But the force of such a rule is

---

[1] Stubbs, Const. Hist. i. 563–4, ii. 132, 278. Already in 1198 the knights of the Abbot of St Edmund's asserted that they were not bound to serve outside the realm; Jocelin of Brakelond (Camd. Soc.), 63. Hugh, bishop of Lincoln, had just made a similar assertion; no service is due from the church of Lincoln outside the bounds of England; Vita Magna S. Hugonis, 249. See also the story of how the knights of Holderness refused to follow Edward into Scotland, Chron. de Melsa, ii. 107.

[2] What Littleton, sec. 95, has to say on this matter is little better than traditional antiquarianism.

[3] Viollet, Établissements, ii. 95–6; iii. 31, 352–3. In Germany also the rule seems to have been that the vassal was only bound to find provisions for six weeks; after this he served at his lord's cost; Schröder, D. R. G., 502. As to Normandy, see Somma, p. 69; Ancienne Coutume, p. 66, c. 25.

feeble; when in 1226 the Count of Champagne appealed to it
and threatened to quit the siege of Avignon, Louis VIII. swore
that if he did so his lands should be ravaged[1]. In England
when a baron or knight is enfeoffed, his charter, if he has one,
says no more than that he is to hold by the service of one
knight or of so many knights. When the king summons his
tenants to war, he never says how long they are to serve. The
exception to this rule is that they are told by John that they
are to serve for two quadragesims, eighty days, at the least[2].
Occasionally in the description of a military serjeanty, it is said
that the serjeant is to serve for forty days, but to this are often
added the words 'at his own cost,' and we are left to guess
[p. 234] whether he is not bound to serve for a longer time at his lord's
cost[3]. In 1198 Richard summoned a tenth part of the feudal
force to Normandy; nine knights were to equip a tenth; the
Abbot of St Edmunds confessed to having forty knights; he
hired four knights (for his own tenants had denied that they
were bound to serve in Normandy) and provided them with pay
for forty days, namely, with 36 marks; but he was told by the
king's ministers that the war might well endure for a year or
more, and that, unless he wished to go on paying the knights
their wages, he had better make fine with the king; so he made
fine for £100[4]. In 1277 the knights of St Albans served in a
Welsh campaign for eight weeks; during the first forty days
they served at their own cost; afterwards the king paid them
wages[5]. No serious war could be carried on by a force which
would dissipate itself at the end of forty days, and it seems probable that the king could and did demand longer service, and
was within his right in so doing, if he tendered wages, or if, as
was sometimes the case, he called out but a fractional part
of the feudal force[6]. We have to remember that the old duty
of every man to bear arms, at least in defensive warfare, was

---

[1] Mat. Par. Chron. Maj. iii. 116.

[2] Lords' Report on the Dignity of a Peer, App. i. p. 1. The summonses of
the feudal array are collected in this Appendix.

[3] Testa de Neville, *e.g.* 146–7.

[4] Chron. Jocelini de Brakelond (Camden Soc.), 63.

[5] Gesta Abbatum, i. 435.

[6] In 1212 John gives orders for the payment at his cost of the knights in
his service, from the time when the period shall have elapsed during which they
are bound to serve at their own cost; Rot. Cl. i. 117.

never—not even in France—completely merged in, or obliterated by, the feudal obligation[1]. Just when there seems a
chance that this obligation may become strictly defined by the
operation of the law courts, the king is beginning to look to
other quarters for a supply of soldiers, to insist that all men
shall be armed, to compel men of substance to become knights,
even though they do not hold by military tenure, and to issue
commissions of array.

Knight's
fees.

But these units of military service, however indeterminate
they may be, have become, if we may so speak, territorialized.
A certain definite piece of land is a knight's fee (*feodum militis*);
another tract is conceived as made up of five or ten knight's [p. 235]
fees; another is half, or a quarter, or a fortieth part of a knight's
fee, or, to use the current phrase, it is the fee of half, or a
quarter, or a fortieth part of one knight (*feodum quadragesimae
partis unius militis*)[2]. The appearance of small fractional parts
of a knight's fee could hardly be explained, were it not that the
king has been in the habit of taking money in lieu of military
service, of taking scutage or escuage (*scutagium*), a sum of so
much money per knight's fee. Without reference to this we
might indeed understand the existence of halves of knight's fees,
for practice has sanctioned the equation *duo servientes = unus
miles*, two serjeants will be accepted in lieu of one knight[3]; but
a fortieth part of the service of one knight would be unintelligible, were it not that from time to time the service of one
knight can be expressed in terms of money. Already in Henry
II.'s reign we hear of the twelfth, the twenty-fourth part of a
knight's fee[4]; in John's reign of the fortieth[5]; and we soon
hear of single acres which owe a definite quantum of military
service, or rather of scutage.

Varying
size of
knight's
fees.

To represent to ourselves the meaning and effect of this
apportionment is no easy matter. In the first place, we have

---

[1] As to France, see Viollet, Établissements, ii. 93; iii. 350. As to the
'retrobannus Normanniae,' see a charter granted by John to the Abp. of Rouen,
Rot. Cart. 69; also Somma, p. 69; Ancienne Coutume, p. 66.

[2] The Norman term *feodum loricae, fief de haubert*, occurs but rarely in
England, still it may be found; the Abbot of Tavistock holds fifteen and a half
fees *en fe de haubergh*; Rot. Hund. i. 81. Cf. Coronation Charter of Hen. I.
c. 11: 'Milites qui per loricas terras suas deserviunt.' It is also common to
speak of the knight's fee as a *scutum*, particularly in reference to taxation.

[3] See the muster rolls of Edw. I.; Parl. Writs, i. 197, 228.

[4] Liber Rubeus, i. 341.   [5] Hunter, Fines, i. 15.

to observe that the term 'knight's fee' does not imply any particular acreage of land. Some fees are much larger than others. This truth has long been acknowledged and is patent[1]. We may indeed see in some districts, for example among the knights of Glastonbury, many fees of five hides apiece[2]; but in a single county we may find a hide of land reckoned as a half, a third, a fourth, a fifth, and a sixth of a knight's fee[3]. In the north of England one baron holds sixteen carucates by the service of ten knights, while in another barony the single knight's fee has as many as fourteen carucates[4]. The fees held of the abbot of Peterborough were extremely small; in some cases [p. 236] he seems to have got a full knight's service from a single hide or even less[5]; on the other hand, a fee of twenty-eight carucates may be found[6]; and of Lancashire it is stated in a general way that in this county twenty-four carucates go to the knight's fee[7]. In one case, perhaps in other cases, the law had made some effort to redress this disparity : the fees of the honour of Mortain were treated as notoriously small; three of them were reckoned to owe as much service as was owed by two ordinary fees[8]. Perhaps a vague theory pointed to twenty librates of land as the proper provision for a knight; but even this is hardly proved[9].

Another difficulty arises when we ask the question, what was the effect of this apportionment, and in particular what persons did it bind? Modern lawyers will be familiar with the notion that an apportionment of a burden on land may be effectual among certain persons, ineffectual as regards others. Let us suppose that *A* owns land which is subject to a rent-charge of £100 in favour of *M* and a land-tax of £10 per annum; he sells certain acres to *X*; *A* and *X* settle as between themselves how the burdens shall be borne; they agree that each shall pay a half, or perhaps one of them consents to accept

Nature of the apportionment.

---

[1] Co. Lit. 69 a, 69 b (Hale's note); Stubbs, Const. Hist. i. 287; Round, Feudal England, 231 ff., 293 ff.; Hall, Liber Rubeus, vol. ii. p. clxiii.

[2] Glastonbury Inquests (Roxburgh Club), *passim.*

[3] Testa de Neville, 63–4.

[4] Liber Rubeus, i. 385, 431.

[5] Chron. Petroburg. 169.

[6] Kirkby's Inquest for Yorkshire (Surtees Soc.) 196–7.

[7] Testa de Neville, 408.　　　　　　[8] Madox, Exch. i. 649.

[9] Stubbs, Const. Hist. i. 288, and Round, Feudal England, 295, seem inclined to accept this theory. See also Hall, Lib. Rub. vol. ii. p. clxiv.

the whole burden. Now, allowing that this is an effectual agreement between them, we still have the question whether it can in any way affect the rights of *M* or of the king, who have hitherto been able to treat the whole land as subject to the whole rent-charge and the whole tax. It will not therefore surprise us if we find that the apportionment of military service was not absolute.

The apportionment between the king and his tenant in chief.
We may begin by considering the relation between the king and his tenants in chief. We have good reason to believe that the Conqueror when he enfeoffed his followers with tracts of forfeited land defined the number of knights with which they [p.237] were to supply him, and also that he defined the number of knights that were to be found by the cathedral and monastic churches whose land had not been forfeited. It would not be true to say that in this way the whole of England was, as between the king and his immediate tenants, cut up into knights' fees. From the Conquest onwards he had immediate tenants who held of him by frankalmoin, by serjeanty, in socage; still in this manner a very large part of England was brought within the scope of military contracts or what could be regarded as such. How definite these contracts were we can not say, for to all seeming they were not expressed in writing. The only documentary evidence that the great lord of the Conqueror's day could have produced by way of title-deed, was, in all probability, some brief writ which commanded the royal officers to put him in seisin of certain lands and said nothing about the tenure by which he was to hold them. And again, in the case of the churches, if we speak of a contract, we are hardly using the right word; it was in the king's power to dictate terms, and he dictated them. Whether in so doing he paid much or any regard to the old English law and the ancient land-books, is a question not easily decided, for we know little of the legal constitution of Harold's army. The result was capricious. The relative wealth of the abbeys of Peterborough, St Edmund's, St Albans and Ramsey can not have been expressed by the figures 60 : 40 : 6 : 4, which represented their fighting strength in the twelfth century; St Albans may have profited by a charter of King Offa, at which modern diplomatists have looked askance[1]. But, at any rate as regards the forfeited lands of the

---

[1] Mat. Par. Chron. Maj. vi. 1; Haddan and Stubbs, Councils, iii. 470.

English nobles, William had a free hand; he could stipulate for so many units of military service from this count and so many from that baron. Apparently he portioned out these units in fives and tens. The number of knights for which a great baron is answerable in the twelfth century is generally some multiple of five, such as twenty, or fifty. The total number of knights to which the king was entitled has been extravagantly overrated. It was certainly not 60,000, nor was it 32,000; we may doubt whether it exceeded 5,000. The [p. 238] whole feudal array of England would in our eyes have been but a handful of warriors. He was a powerful baron who owed as many as sixty knights. We are not arguing that William introduced a kind of tenure that was very new in England; but there seems to be no room for doubt that the actual scheme of apportionment which we find existing in the twelfth and later centuries, the scheme which as between king and tenant in chief makes this particular tract of land a fee of twenty or of thirty knights, is, except in exceptional cases, the work of the Conqueror[1].

At any rate in Henry II.'s day the allotment of military service upon the lands of the tenants in chief may be regarded as complete. It is already settled that this tenant in chief owes the king the service of one knight, while another owes the service of twenty knights. Historians have often observed that the tenants in chief of the Norman king, even his military tenants in chief, form a very miscellaneous body, and this is important in our constitutional history; a separation between the greater and the lesser tenants must be effected in course of time, and the king has thus a power of defining what will hereafter be the 'estate' of the baronage. In Henry II.'s day the king had many tenants each of whom held of him but one knight's fee, or but two or three knights' fees. On the other hand, there were nobles each of whom had many knights' fees; a few had fifty and upwards. Now to describe the wide lands held of the king by one of his mightier tenants, the terms *honour* and

Honours and baronies.

---

[1] This we regard as having been proved by Mr Round's convincing papers in E. H. R. vols. vi. vii., which are now reprinted in his Feudal England. Sometimes when land came to the king by way of escheat and was again granted out, new terms would be imposed on the new tenant; but in the main the settlement made in the Conqueror's day was permanent. As to the old English army, see Maitland, Domesday Book, 156 ff. 295, 308.

barony were used. Between these two terms we can draw no hard
line; *honour* seems to be generally reserved for the very largest
complexes of land, and perhaps we may say that every honour
was deemed a barony, while not every barony was usually called
an honour; but this seems a matter settled by fashion rather
than by law; for instance, it is usual to give the name *barony*,
not *honour*, to the lands which a bishop holds by military
service, though some of these baronies were very large[1]. To [p. 239]
mark the inferior limit of the honours and baronies is not easy.
We can not say that any particular number of knights' fees was
either necessary or sufficient to constitute a barony; in particular,
we can not accept the theory current in after times, that a
barony contains thirteen knights' fees and a third, and therefore
is to a knight's fee as a mark is to a shilling[2]. This equation
seems to have been obtained, not by an inductive process, but
by a deduction, which started with the rule that while the relief
paid for a single knight's fee was a hundred shillings, that paid
for a barony was a hundred marks. But neither can we make
the facts square with this theory, nor, as will be seen below, can
we treat the rule about reliefs as being so ancient as the constitution of baronies[3]. Nor must we think of the barony or
honour as surrounded by a ring-fence; fragments of it will
often lie scattered about in various counties, though there is
some castle or some manor which is accounted its 'head.'

The barony or honour as a complex of knights' fees.
　　　　　We find it said of a man not only that he holds a barony
(*tenet baroniam*), but also that he holds by barony (*tenet per
baroniam*). This phrase will deserve discussion hereafter; for
the present it is only necessary to notice that every military
tenant in chief of the king, whether he has a barony or no, is
deemed to owe the service of a certain number of knights. That
number may be large or small. Let us suppose that in a given
case it is fifty. Then in a sense this tenant may be said to hold
fifty knights' fees. But all the land, at least if all of it be held
by one title, and every part of it, is answerable to the king
for the fifty knights. This tenant may enfeoff some fifty

---

[1] The use of the term *honour* to signify none but the large estates can not be
traced back very far. But it seems to have borne this sense early in the twelfth
century; Leg. Hen. 55, § 1, where *honour* is contrasted with *manor*.

[2] Selden, Titles of Honour, pt. II., cap. v. sec. 26.

[3] The oldest versions of the Charter make the relief for the barony, not a
hundred marks, but a hundred pounds, so that were the argument sound, the
barony should contain twenty fees.

knights, making each of them liable to serve in the army; he may enfeoff more, giving each feoffee but a fractional part of a fee, that is to say, making him answerable for but a fractional part of one knight's service; he may enfeoff fewer, making each of them answerable for the service of several knights; he may retain much land in his own hand, and look to hiring [p. 240] knights when they are wanted. But, as between the king and himself, he has fifty knights' fees; he is answerable, and the land that he holds is answerable, for the production of fifty men. Every acre in the honour of Gloucester was liable to the king for the service of some two hundred knights and more. If the Earl of Gloucester makes default in providing the due number of knights, the king may distrain throughout the honour, or seize the honour into his hands. The exact nature of the power which a lord had of exacting service due to him from a tenement need not be here considered; but the main principle, which runs through the whole law on this subject, is that the service due from the tenant is due also from the tenement, and can be enforced against the tenement into whosesoever hands it may come, regardless of any arrangement that the tenant may have made with his sub-tenants.

This may be illustrated by the case of lands held in frank-almoin of a mesne lord, who himself holds by military service. In this case something like an exception was occasionally admitted. The canons of Wroxton held land in frankalmoin of John Montacute; the land was distrained for scutage; but on the petition of the canons, the sheriff was bidden to cease from distraining, 'because the frankalmoin should not be distrained for scutages so long as John or his heirs have other lands in the county whence the scutages may be levied.' This is an exception, and a carefully guarded exception; if the tenant has given land in frankalmoin, the king will leave that land free from distress, provided that there be other land whence he can get his service[1]. Thus, let us say that a baron holds twenty knights' fees, and has twenty knights each enfeoffed of a single fee; the boundaries between these fees in no way concern the king; the whole tract of land must answer for twenty knights. An early example of this may be given:—at some time before 1115

Relativity of the knight's fee.

---

[1] Madox, Exchequer, i. 670–1, where other cases of Henry III.'s reign are given. John had observed this rule: Rot. Pat. 52, writ in favour of the Abbot of Stanlaw.

the Bishop of Hereford gave Little Hereford and Ullingswick to Walter of Gloucester for the service of two knights; Walter gave Ullingswick as a marriage portion for his daughter Maud free from all knight's service, and thus, as between all persons claiming under him, the whole service of two knights was thrown on to Little Hereford. Thus really 'a knight's fee' is a relative [p. 241] term; what is two knights' fees as between C and B, is but part of two as between B and A[1]. In the time of Henry II. when the king was beginning to take stock of the amount of military service due to him, it was common for a tenant in chief to answer that he confessed the service of, for example, ten knights, that he had five knights enfeoffed each of a knight's fee, and that the other five he provided from his demesne[2]. In one case, even at the end of the thirteenth century, a lord had not carved out his land into geographically distinct knights' fees. Somehow or another the abbot of Ramsey held his broad lands by the service of only four knights, and we may therefore say that he had four knights' fees. But those fees were not separated areas; he had a number of tenants owing him military service; they chose the four who on any particular occasion should go to the war, and the others contributed to defray the expense by an assessment on the hide[3]. Thus the statement that a man holds a barony, or a parcel of knights' fees, of the king, tells us nothing as to the relationship between him and his tenants, and does not even tell us that he has any tenants at all.

Duty of the military tenant in chief.

The military tenant in chief of the crown was as a general rule bound to go to the war in person. If he held by the service of fifty knights, he was bound to appear in person with forty-nine. If he was too ill or too old to fight, he had to send not only a substitute but also an excuse[4]. Women might send

---

[1] Round, Ancient Charters, p. 19. In 1237, jurors are asked by what services Agnes de Wahull holds a number of manors: 'Servicium praedictorum maneriorum nesciunt separare, quia tota baronia de Wahulla respondet integre dom. Regi pro xxx. militibus': Note Book, pl. 1182.

[2] Liber Rubeus, *passim, e.g.* p. 368: 'Carta S. de Scaliers...Haec est summa; x. milites habeo feffatos et servitium v. militum remanet super dominium meum.'

[3] Select Pleas in Manorial Courts, pp. 48–51; Monast. ii. 578. But see Cart. Rams. iii. 48, 218, and Round, Feudal England, 298. Apparently the land had once been cut up into fees, and the arrangement under which it provided only four knights is not aboriginal.

[4] See the Muster Rolls of 1277 and 1282 in Parl. Writs, vol. i., *e.g.* p. 202:

substitutes and so might ecclesiastics[1]. The monks of St

[p. 242] Edmunds thought it a dangerous precedent when in 1193 Abbot Samson in person led his knights to the siege of Windsor[2]. How the nature of this obligation was affected by the imposition of scutage is a question that we are not as yet prepared to discuss.

We must first examine the position of a tenant who holds by knight's service of a mesne lord, and we will begin with a simple case. One *A* holds a mass of lands, it may be a barony or no, of the king in chief by the service of twenty knights, and *B* holds a particular portion of these lands of *A* by the service of one knight. Now in the first place, *B*'s tenement, being part of *A*'s tenement, owes to the king the service of twenty knights; it can be distrained by the king for the whole of that service. But, as between *A* and *B*, it owes only the service of one knight, and if the king distrains it for more, then *A* is bound to acquit *B* of this surplus service; this obligation can be enforced by an action of 'mesne'[3]. On the other hand, *B* has undertaken to do for *A* the service of one knight. The nature of this obligation demands a careful statement:—*B* is bound to *A* to do for *A* a certain quantum of service in the king's army. We say that *B* is bound to *A*; *B* is not bound to the king; the king it is true can distrain *B*'s tenement; but between *B* and the king there is no personal obligation[4]. The king can not by reason of tenure call upon *B* to fight; if somehow or other *A* provides his twenty knights, it is not for the king to complain that *B* is not among them[5]. None the less, the service that *B* is bound to do, is service in the king's army. Here we come upon a

Position of the military sub-tenant.

'Robertus de Markham infirmus, ut dicitur, offert servicium dimidii feodi militis in T. faciendum per W. de L. servientem.'

[1] This is often shown by the form of the summons; the lay man is told to come with his service; women and ecclesiastics are bidden to send their service.

[2] Jocelin of Brakelond (Camd. Soc.) 40.

[3] See above, p. 238.

[4] Thus, according to William Rufus, the knights of the archbishop of Canterbury appear in a Welsh war without proper armour; Rufus makes this the ground of a charge against Anselm. Freeman, Will. Ruf. i. 574, argues that even if the charge be true, it is not well founded in law; but we can not agree to this. Anselm may perhaps complain against his knights; but the king's complaint must be against Anselm.

[5] The king may compel *B* to do his service to *A*; see *e.g.* Rot. Cl. i. 117 (for Ralph Berners), 297 (for the abbot of Peterborough); but we must distinguish between what the king does as feudal lord and what he does as supreme judge and governor.

principle of great importance. According to the law of the king's court, no tenant is bound to fight in any army but the king's army, or in any quarrel but the king's quarrel. It might well have been otherwise; we may see that it nearly was otherwise; we may be fairly certain that in this respect the law was no adequate expression of the current morality; still [p. 243] we can not say that the law of England ever demanded private warfare[1]. Indubitably the military tenant often conceived himself bound to fight for his lord in his lord's quarrel; but the law enforced no such obligation. True, the obligation which it sanctioned was one that bound the man to the lord, and in a certain sense bound him to fight for his lord. It was at the lord's summons that the man came armed to the host, and if the lord had many knights, the man fought under the lord's banner; still he was only bound to fight in the king's army and the king's quarrel; his service was due to his lord, still in a very real sense it was done for the king and only for the king:— in short, all military service is *regale servitium.* It is the more necessary to lay stress upon this principle, for it had not prevailed in Normandy. The Norman baron had knights who were bound to serve him, and the service due from them to him had to be distinguished from the service that he was bound to find for the duke. The bishop of Coutances owed the duke the service of five knights, but eighteen knights were bound to serve the bishop. The honour of Montfort contained twenty-one knights' fees and a half for the lord's service; how many for the duke's service the jurors could not say. The bishop of Bayeux had a hundred and nineteen knights' fees and a half; he was bound to send his ten best knights to serve the king of the French for forty days, and, for their equipment, he took twenty Rouen shillings from every fee; he was bound to find forty knights to serve the duke of Normandy for forty days, and for their equipment he took forty Rouen shillings from every fee; but all the hundred and nineteen knights were bound to serve the bishop with arms and horses[2].

Knight's service due to a lord who owes none.

As a matter of fact, however, we sometimes find, even in England, that knight's service is due, at least that what is called knight's service is due, to a lord who owes no knight's service

---

[1] We shall discuss this matter more fully in connexion with homage.

[2] *Infeudaciones militum* in Red Book of the Exchequer, ii. 624 ff. ; Bouquet xxiii. 698.

to the king, or that more knight's service is due to the lord
than he owes to the king.   One cause of this phenomenon may
be that the lord is an ecclesiastic who has once held by military
service, but has succeeded in getting his tenure changed to
frankalmoin by the piety of the king or the negligence of the
[p. 214] king's officers.   The chronicler of the Abbey of Meaux tells us
how the abbot proved that he held all his lands in Yorkshire
by frankalmoin and owed no military service, and then how he
insisted that lands were held of him by military tenure and sold
the wardships and marriages of his tenants[1].   Since he was not
bound to find fighting men, his tenants were not bound to fight;
still their tenure was not changed; he was entitled to the profitable casualties incident to knight's service.   A similar result
might be obtained by other means.   The abbot of St Edmunds
held his barony of the king by the service of forty knights;
such at least was the abbot's view of the matter; but he had
military tenants who, according to his contention, owed him
altogether the service of fifty-two knights: or, to put it another
way, fifty-two knights' fees were held of him, though as between
him and the king his barony consisted of but forty[2].   The view
taken by the knights was that the abbot was entitled to the
service of forty knights and no more; the fifty-two fees had to
provide but forty warriors or the money equivalent for forty.
But in Richard I.'s day Abbot Samson, according to the admiring
Jocelin, gained his point by suing each of his military tenants
in the king's court.   Each of the fees that they held owed the
full contribution to every scutage and aid, so that when a
scutage of 20 shillings was imposed on the knight's fee, the
abbot made a clear profit of £12[3].   Bracton says distinctly that
the tenant in socage can create a military sub-tenure.   This,
however, seems to mean that a feoffor may, if he chooses, stipulate for the payment of scutage, even though the tenement

[1] Chron. de Melsa, ii. 210, 222–3.

[2] Liber Rubeus, i. 394.   But in Henry II.'s day the view taken at the
Exchequer was that the abbot owed aid for fifty-two fees.   Madox, Exch. i.
572.   See also in Testa de Neville, 415, the amusing letter in which the abbot
in Henry III.'s reign professes an absolute ignorance as to the whereabouts of
his fees:—'In what vills they are distributed and in what place they lie, God
knows.'

[3] Jocelin of Brakelond (Camd. Soc.), 20, 48.   See also Feet of Fines 7 & 8
Ric. I. (Pipe Roll Soc.), p. 53 ff., where are printed the documents which record
the abbot's victory.

owes none to the king. In such case the scutage may seem to us but a rent capriciously assessed, but apparently Bracton would call the tenure military, and it would serve to give the [p. 245] lord the profitable rights of wardship and marriage[1]. The extraordinary licence which men enjoyed of creating new tenures gave birth to some wonderful complications. If B holds a knight's fee of A, then A can put X between himself and B, so that B will hold of X and X of A; but further, the service by which X will hold of A need not be the service by which B has hitherto been holding of A and will now hold of X. In Richard's reign Henry de la Pomerai places William Briwere between himself and a number of tenants of his who altogether owe the service of $5\frac{5}{24}$ knights or thereabouts; but William is to hold of Henry by the service of one knight[2]. To 'work out the equities' arising between these various persons would be for us a difficult task: still no good would come of our representing our subject-matter as simpler than really it is. Lastly, as already hinted, we must not suppose that the barons or even the prelates of the Norman reigns were always thinking merely of the king's rights when they surrounded themselves with enfeoffed knights. They also had their enemies, and among those enemies might be the king. Still the only military service demanded by anything that we dare call English law was service in the king's host. It would further seem, that Henry II., not without some success, endeavoured to deduce from this principle the conclusion that if a tenant in chief enfeoffed more knights than he owed to the king, he thereby increased the amount of the service that the king could demand from him. Such a tenant in chief had, we may say, been making evidence against himself: this was the opinion of his royal lord[3].

Scutage.

The practice of taking scutages must have introduced into the system a new element of precision and have occasioned a downward spread of the tenure that was called military. The extent of the obligation could now be expressed in terms of pounds, shillings and pence; and tenants who were not really expected to fight might be bound to pay scutage. On the other hand, the history of scutage is full of the most perplexing difficulties. Before approaching these we will once more call to

---

[1] Bracton, f. 36. [2] Fines (ed. Hunter), ii. 51.
[3] Round, Feudal England, 242 ff.

mind the fact that scutage is an impost of an occasional kind, that there never were more than forty scutages or thereabouts.

[p. 246] We are wont to think of scutage as of a tax introduced by **Nature of scutage.** Henry II. in the year 1159, a tax imposed in the first instance on the military tenants in chief by way of commutation for personal service, a tax which they in their turn might collect from their sub-tenants. But it seems extremely probable that at a much earlier date payments in lieu of military service were making their appearance, at all events in what we may call the outer circles of the feudal system[1]. In no other way can we explain the existence, within a very few years after 1159, of small aliquot parts of knights' fees. When it is said that a man holds the twentieth part of a fee, this can not mean that he is bound to serve for two days in the army; it must mean that he and others are bound to find a warrior who will serve for forty days, and that some or all of them will really discharge their duty by money payments. We read too in very ancient documents of payments for the provision of knights[2] and of an *auxilium exercitus*, the aid for a military expedition[3]. In Normandy the equivalent for our scutage is generally known as the *auxilium exercitus*[4]. In England the two terms seem in course of time to have acquired different meanings; the lord exacted a scutage from his military, his nominally military tenants, while he took an 'army aid' from such of his tenants as were not military even in name[5]. But what we may call the natural development of a system of commutation and subscription between tenants in the outer circles of feudalism, was at once hastened and perplexed by a movement having its origin in the centre of the system, which thence spread outwards. The king began to take scutages. At this point we must face some difficult questions. **Scutage between the king and the tenant in chief.**

[p 247] In what, if any, sense is it true that the military service of

---

[1] Round, Feudal England, 268 ff.

[2] Charter of Abbot Faritius, Hist. Abingd. ii. 135.

[3] Ramsey Cart. i. 147; see also Henry II.'s Canterbury charter, Monast. i. 105.

[4] Somma, p. 70; Ancienne coutume, c. 25, where the *auxilium exercitus* seems the equivalent of scutage. In some Norman documents it appears as one of the three aids, along with those for knighting the son and marrying the daughter; Assisiae Normaniae, Warnkönig ii. 58; Très ancien coutumier, p. 39.

[5] See Rot. Cl. i. 570–1. Of these aids we shall speak in another section.

the tenants in chief was commuted into scutage? The king's ban goes forth summoning the host to a campaign. It says no word of scutage. Can the baron who owes twenty knights sit at home and say, 'I will not go to the war; and if I do not go, no worse can befall me than that I shall have to pay scutage for my twenty fees, and this indeed will be no heavy burden, for I shall be entitled to take a scutage from the knights whom I have enfeoffed'—can the baron say this? Even if he can, we must notice that his self-interested calculations involve one unknown quantity. It may be that on some occasions the king really did give the baron an option between leading his knights to battle and paying some fixed sum. But such was not the ordinary course, at all events in the thirteenth century. The rate at which the scutage was to be levied was not determined until after the defaulters had committed their defaults and the campaign was over; the baron therefore who stayed at home did not know whether he would have to pay twenty marks, or twenty pounds, or forty pounds. But as a matter of fact, we find that in Henry III.'s day and Edward I.'s the tenant in chief who does not obey the summons must pay far more than the scutage; he must pay a heavy fine. No option has been given him; he has been disobedient; in strictness of law he has probably forfeited his land; he must make the best terms that he can with the king. Thus in respect of the campaign of 1230, a scutage of three marks (£2) was imposed upon the knight's fee; but the abbot of Evesham had to pay for his 4½ fees, not £9, but £20; the abbot of Pershore for his 2 fees, not £4, but £10; the abbot of Westminster for his 15 fees, not 45 marks, but 100 marks[1]. In Edward I.'s day the fine for default is an utterly different thing from the scutage; in 1304 he announces that he will take but moderate fines from ecclesiastics and women, if they prefer to pay money rather than send warriors[2]. We hear of such fines as £20 on the fee when the scutage is [p. 248] but £2 on the fee[3]. Furthermore it seems evident that if an option had been given between personal service and scutage, every one would have preferred the latter and the king would have been a sad loser. Perhaps it is not absolutely impossible that Henry II. when he took two marks by way of scutage

[1] Madox, Exchequer, i. 660.
[2] See the writ in Lords' Report, iii. 165.
[3] Gesta Abbatum, ii. 94.

from each fee, took a sum which would pay a knight for forty days; in other words, that he could hire knights for eightpence a day[1]. But while the rate of scutage never exceeded £2 on the fee, the price of knights seems to have risen very rapidly as the standard of military equipment was raised and the value of money fell. In 1198 the abbot of St Edmunds hired knights for Normandy at the rate of three shillings a day[2]. In 1257 the abbot of St Albans put into the field an equivalent for his due contingent of six knights, by hiring two knights and eight esquires, and this cost him hard upon a hundred marks, while, as between his various tenants, the rule seems to have been that a knight, who was bound to serve, required two shillings a day for his expenses[3]. At about the same date the knights of Ramsey received four shillings a day from their fellow tenants[4]. We may be sure that the king did not take from the defaulting baron less than the market value of his military service.

Thus, so soon as our records become abundant, it seems plain that the tenant in chief has no option between providing his proper contingent of armed men and paying a scutage. The only choice that is left to him is that between obeying the king's call and bearing whatever fine the barons of the exchequer may inflict upon him for his disobedience. Therefore it seems untrue to say that as between him and the king there is any 'commutation of military service,' and indeed for a moment we may fail to see that the king has any interest in a scutage. If he holds himself strictly bound by principles that are purely feudal, the scutage should be nothing to him. From his immediate tenant he will get either military service or a heavy fine, and we may think that the rate of scutage will only determine the amount that can be extracted from the under-[p. 249] tenants by lords who have done their service or paid their fines. But this is not so. *The tenant in chief's service can not be discharged by scutage.*

We must speak with great diffidence about this matter, for it has never yet been thoroughly examined, and we are by no means sure that all scutages were collected on the same principle. But from the first the king seems to have asserted his right to collect a scutage from the 'tenant in demesne' *The scutage of under-tenants.*

---

[1] Round, Feudal England, 271.
[2] Jocelin (Camd. Soc.), 63.
[3] Mat. Par. Chron. Maj. vi. 374, 438.
[4] Select Pleas in Manorial Courts (Selden Soc.), 60–2.

who holds his land by knight's service. There are two conflicting elements in the impost; it is in part the equivalent for
a feudal, a tenurial service; it is in part a royal tax. The king
will regard it now as the one, and now as the other, as suits him
best. He refuses to be a mere lord of lords; he is also a king
of subjects. The undertenant of a mesne lord, if he owes
military service, owes a service that is to be done for the king;
the king will, if this seems profitable, deal directly with him
and excuse him from service on his paying money. And so in
the thirteenth century the king, while he is exacting military
service or fines from his tenants in chief, will also collect
scutage from their military tenants. Theoretically he is not
entitled to be paid for the same thing twice over. If a baron
has either produced the requisite number of knights or compounded for his breach of contract, it is he and not the king
who ought to receive scutage; in the one case he ought to get
a scutage from any military tenants of his who have disobeyed
his call to arms, in the other all his military tenants may have
to pay, though he has not given them a chance of going to the
war in person. That this ought to be so, seems to be admitted.
Such a baron, having proved that he fulfilled his contract or
paid his fine, will have a royal writ *de scutagio habendo*,
whereby the sheriff will be ordered to cause him to have the
scutage due from his tenants. Still, before he can get his
scutage, he has to obtain something that the king is apt to
treat as a favour. Meanwhile the sheriffs will be taking scutage
for the king's use from those who are in occupation of lands on
which military service is incumbent, and leaving the various
persons who are interested in those lands to settle the incidence
of the burden as best they may. What comes into the king's
hands generally stays there. But further, in Henry III.'s time,
the barons, assuming to act on behalf of the whole community, [p. 250]
will on occasion grant to the king a scutage in respect of some
military expedition that has taken place, and the meaning of
this, at least in some instances, seems to be that, in response to
the king's demands, they make over to him the right to collect
and to keep the scutages due from their undertenants, scutages
which the feudal principle would have brought into their own
coffers[1]. A national tax is imposed which the undertenants

---

[1] See in particular the writ of 27 Hen. III. in Madox, Exchequer, i. 681; also
Hall, Liber Rubeus, ii. p. clx.

pay to the king.   Much will remain obscure until the exchequer
rolls have been carefully analyzed; but this at least seems
clear, that the tenant in chief's duty of providing an armed
force is not commuted into a duty of paying scutage.   Indeed
the demand conceded by the Charter of 1215, namely, that no
scutage be imposed without the common counsel of the realm,
would be barely intelligible, if John had merely been giving his
tenants in chief an option between furnishing the due tale of
warriors and paying two marks for every fee[1].

We must now turn to a simple case and ask a simple ques-   The
tion.   What was the duty of a man who held by knight's service   military
of a mesne lord?   We will suppose him to hold a single knight's   tenants.
fee.   In the days before scutage his duty probably was to serve
in person if summoned by his lord to the king's host; only with
a good excuse might he send a substitute[2]; but women and
ecclesiastics would do their service by able-bodied representatives.   Failure to perform this duty would be punished by a forfeiture of the tenement[3].   But the practice of taking scutages
seems to have set up a change, and how far that change went it
is hard to decide.   The knights began to allege that they were
not bound to serve, but were only bound to pay a scutage, and
only to pay a scutage when their lords had obtained from the
king permission to levy it[4].   It would further seem that many

---

[1] Robert of Torigny (ed. Howlett), p. 202, in the classical passage which
describes the scutage of 1159 says that the king 'nolens vexare agrarios milites,
nec burgensium nec rusticorum multitudinem' took a sum of money from each
knight's fee, and, this done, 'capitales barones suos cum paucis secum duxit,
solidarios vero milites innumeros.'   The king does not give his *capitales barones*
an option between going to the war and paying scutage, but he absolves from the
duty of personal attendance their undertenants, many of whom, though in name
tenants by military service, are mere yeomen (*milites agrarii, burgenses, rustici*),
and instead he takes a scutage.   As Henry III. was bound by charter not to
collect scutage, except in accordance with the practice of Henry II., we might
seem entitled to draw inferences from the grandson's days to the grandfather's.
But more light is needed at this point.

[2] To the contrary Littleton, sec. 96, relying on Y. B. 7 Edw. III. f. 29
(Trin. pl. 23).   But Littleton knew nothing of knight's service as a reality.   See
Magna Carta, 1215, c. 29.

[3] Hist. Abingd. ii. 128 (temp. Hen. I.): an Abingdon knight fails to do
service; 'unde cum lege patriae decretum processisset ipsum exsortem terrae
merito debere fieri, etc.'

[4] Already in 1198 the knights of St Edmunds profess themselves willing
to pay scutage, but they will not serve in Normandy; Jocelin of Brakelond, 63.

of them made good this assertion by steady perseverance. The [p. 251]
lords were often compelled to hire soldiers because their knights
—their knights so called, for many a tenant by knight's service
was in habit but a yeoman—would not fight. It would even
seem that the tenants as a body got the better in the struggle,
and established the rule that if they did not choose to serve,
no worse could happen to them, than to be compelled to
pay a scutage at the rate fixed by royal decree, a sum much
less than they would have spent had they hired substitutes
to fill their places. In short, 'tenure by knight's service' of
a mesne lord, becomes first in fact, and then in law, 'tenure
by escuage[1].

Tenure by escuage.   The stages of this process we can not trace distinctly, but
it was closely connected with the gradual decline and fall of the
feudal courts. The lord who kept an efficient court of and for
his military tenants might in early days enforce a forfeiture of
the tenement for default of service; but the king's court seems
to have given him little or no assistance, and by degrees the
remedies afforded by the royal tribunal became the standard of
English law[2]. The process must have been hastened by the [p. 252]

Hear a groan from the Abbey of Evesham:—'Hic notantur milites et liberi
tenentes de Abbatia de Evesham, multi iniuste fefati, pauci vero iuste. Isti
nullum servitium faciunt ecclesiae nisi servitium Regis et hoc tepide.' (Quoted
by Wrottesley, Burton Cartulary, p. 2.)

[1] In Normandy by the middle of the thirteenth century the knights' fees had
become divisible into two classes; 'Quaedam feoda loricae servitium exercitus
debent dominis quod debet fieri Principi: quaedam vero auxilium exercitus':
Somma, p. 126; see also p. 70. It may be suspected that this really represents
the state of things that existed in England under Henry III.; some of the nominally military tenants had at least *de facto* established a right to do no more
than pay scutage. Then on the muster roll of 1277 we find this entry: 'Robert
of Lewknor says that he does not owe any service in the king's army, for he
holds a knight's fee and a half of the escheat of Laigle [an escheated barony]
and owes scutage when it is leviable for that knight's fee and a half': Parl.
Writs, i. 202. Then from Edward II.'s time we have this curious case:—*G.*
holds a knight's fee of the honour of *H.* which is in the king's hand; he asserts,
and as it seems successfully, that his obligation is merely to pay scutage and not
to serve in person; the king who fills the place of the lord of the honour can
only demand scutage; Madox, Exch. i. 652.

[2] It would not be safe to lay down a general rule. In 1257 the abbot of St
Albans, who had only to provide six knights, succeeded by a great effort in
forcing his military tenants to admit that they were bound to personal service.
He held a court for them under the great ash tree at St Albans and secured the
presence of one of the king's justices who had come there to deliver the gaol.
In 1277 they did their service in Wales, and, according to the chronicler, the
abbot profited thereby; for the total cost amounted to but 50 marks and almost

subdivision of knights' fees. We come across persons who hold
no more than aliquot parts of fees; we find them even in what
we may call the primary circle of feudalism, the circle of tenants
in chief; they are common in the secondary circle.   Sometimes
a fee preserves a notional integrity though it has become
divided into aliquot parts by subinfeudation or by partition
among coheiresses.   The abbot of St Albans confessed to
holding six *scuta* or knights' fees. Each of these *scuta* was
divided among several tenants holding of the abbot.   When
the king summoned his host, the various tenants of each *scutum*
had to meet and provide a knight; sometimes they did this by
hiring a knight, or two serjeants; sometimes they elected one
of their number to serve and contributed towards his expenses[1].
But we soon come upon small fractional parts, the twentieth
part or the fortieth part, of fees, which fees have no longer any
existence as integral wholes.   Such fractions could hardly have
come into being but for the practice of taking a scutage in lieu
of personal service, and the tenant's obligation is often expressed
in merely pecuniary terms; the charter of feoffment says, not
that he is to hold the fortieth part of a knight's fee, but that
when scutage is levied at the rate of 40 shillings on the fee he
is to pay a shilling[2].   When the holder of a knight's fee has
cut up a great part of it into little tenements each owing him
some small amount of scutage, the understanding probably is
[p. 253] that he is to do, or to provide, the requisite military service,
and is then to take scutage from his tenants.   All this must
have tended to change the true nature of the obligation even of
those tenants who held integral fees.   If to hold the fortieth
part of a fee merely meant that the tenant had to pay one
shilling when a scutage of two pounds per fee was exacted,
the tenant of a whole fee would easily come to the conclusion that a payment of forty shillings would discharge his
obligation.   Thus a permanent commutation into money of

---

all the prelates of England were compelled to pay as much as 50 marks per
knight's fee for default of service. However, soon after this even the abbot of
St Albans had to make fine for default of service, on one occasion with 120
marks, on another with £120. (Mat. Par. Chron. Maj. vi. 372–6, 437–9; Gesta
Abbatum, i. 435, ii. 94.)

[1] Mat. Par. Chron. Maj. vi. 437–9 ; Gesta Abbatum, ii. 45.

[2] See *e.g.* Note Book, pl. 795, where a tenement is said to owe 10 pence
scutage, when the rate is £2 on the knight's fee.

the personal service due from the subvassals seems to have taken place[1].

The lord's right to scutage. What is more, the right of a mesne lord to take scutage seems hardly to have been regarded, at least in the thirteenth century, as a right given by the common law. A lord who had done his service, or made fine for not doing it, could with some trouble to himself obtain a writ *de scutagio habendo*, which ordered the sheriff to collect for him the scutage from his knights' fees[2]. The king is said to grant to the lords their scutage; until the king has fixed the amount there is nothing that they can collect, and few if any of them attempted to collect it without obtaining the king's writs. Indeed it would seem that, at least in Henry III.'s day, they had no right to collect it. If they did not obtain a grant of scutage from the king, then the king himself took the scutage from their tenants for his own use[3]. As already said, there is in scutage an [p.254] element of royal and national taxation which is incompatible with purely feudal principles.

Service instead of scutage. Whether the tenant of a mesne lord could insist upon his right to do service in the army instead of paying scutage is a question that we are absolved from discussing, for perhaps

---

[1] The question 'whether escuage was a tenure distinct from knight service?' suggested by Littleton's text, has been learnedly discussed by Madox, Wright, Blackstone, Hargrave and others. The answer to it seems to be:—(1) From an early time there were many tenants, those of small aliquot parts of knights' fees, who were bound to pay scutage, but who can hardly, even in theory, have been bound to fight. (2) At a later date the great bulk of the military tenants of mesne lords seem certainly in fact, perhaps in theory also, to have been bound to do no more than pay scutage. (3) If a tenant was bound to pay scutage, he was deemed to hold *per servitium militare*, and his lord had the rights of wardship and marriage.

[2] The writ is in Reg. Brev. Orig. f. 88 (scutage of 1 Edw. III.). For earlier writs see Rot. Cl. i. 371 (1217), 377 (1218), 475 (1221), 571 (1223), 605–610 (1224). See also Madox, Exch. i. 675; Note Book, pl. 333, 1687, and Rolls of Parl. i. 166, where on the petition of the barons the king grants them their scutage. So in Normandy the 'auxilium exercitus' is defined as 'illud pecuniale quod concedit princeps Normanniae, facto exercitus per quadraginta dies servitio, baronibus et militibus de illis qui tenent de eis feodum loricale vel de tenentibus suis in feodo loricali: nec maius auxilium de suis tenentibus poterunt extorquere quam eis concessum fuerit a Principe Normannorum'; Somma, p. 70.

[3] Madox, Exch. i. 680–684; see especially the case on p. 682, note r. (27 Hen. III.): William de Hayrun is summoned before the Exchequer for having taken scutage from a military tenant of his, whereas it ought to have been paid to the sheriff.

it was never raised[1]. But as regards that duty of 'castle-guard' which was a common incident of military tenure, the Great Charter lays down the rule that, if the tenant is willing to do the service in person, he can not be compelled to pay money instead of doing it[2]. However, in the course of the thirteenth century this duty also seems to have been very generally commuted for money payments.

One more exceedingly obscure process must be noticed. Somehow or another in the second half of the thirteenth century the tenants in chief succeeded in effecting a very large reduction in the number of fees for which they answered to the king[3]. When, for example, Edward I. called out the feudal host in 1277, his ecclesiastical barons, who, according to the reckoning of the twelfth century, were holding about 784 fees, would account, and were suffered to account, for but little more than 100, while some 13 knights and 35 serjeants—two serjeants being an equivalent for one knight—were all the warriors that the king could obtain from the lands held by the churches. The archbishop of York had reduced his debt from twenty knights to five, the bishop of Ely from forty to six, the abbot of Peterborough from sixty to five. The lay barons seem to have done much the same. Humphry de Bohun offers three knights as due from his earldom of Essex; Gilbert of Clare, [p. 255] earl of Gloucester and Hertford, offers ten knights, with a promise that he will send more if it be found that more are due. While, however, the lay barons will generally send as many men as they professedly owe, the prelates do not even produce the very small contingents which they acknowledge to be due. Now these magnates were not cheating the king, nor endeavouring to cheat him. It was well known in the exchequer, notorious throughout Cambridgeshire[4], that the bishop

Reduction in the number of knights' fees.

---

[1] There is Norman authority from 1220 for an affirmative answer. Delisle, Recueil de jugements, p. 75: 'Iudicatum est...quod Abbas [mesne lord] non potest alium mittere in loco eiusdem P. [tenant by knight's service] ad faciendum servicium quod feodum dicti P. debet quando dominus rex debet seu vult capere servicium suum de Abbate, dum idem P. servicium quod debet de feodo suo in propria persona sua facere velit.'

[2] Charter of 1215, c. 29. A substitute may be sent, but only for reasonable cause.

[3] See the two muster rolls of the feudal host; Parliamentary Writs, i. 197, 228.

[4] Rot. Hund. ii. 441.

of Ely, who would confess to but six fees, had forty at the least. The king was not deceived. The bishop, having sent no knights at all, had to pay a fine of 240 marks, that is, 40 marks for each of the six fees. Some of the prelates, we are told, had to pay as much as 50 marks for every fee[1], and yet the scutage for this war was but two pounds, that is, three marks, on the fee. The reduction in the nominal amount of fees for which the baron is compelled to answer is accompanied by an at least proportional increase of the amount that he pays in respect of every fee.

Meaning of the change. This change seems to tell us three things. In the first place, it was impossible for the prelate to get military service out of his military tenants. The practice of subinfeudation, fostered by the king's court, had ruined the old system. His fees were now split up into small fractions, and they were in the hands of yeomen and small squires. Secondly, he was willing to pay a large sum rather than hire knights. The knight with his elaborate panoply had become a costly article. In the third place, the king by this time wanted money more than he wanted knights; if he had money, he could get soldiers of all sorts and kinds as pleased him best. And so he seems to have winked at the introduction of a new terminology, for really there was little else that was new. Provided that the bishop of Ely paid him £160 for his Welsh campaign, he did not care whether this was called a fine of six marks for each of forty fees, or a fine of forty marks for each of six fees; while the bishop, who would hardly find six tenants willing to fight, prefers the new set of phrases. But then, our already confused system is further confounded, for the bishop, who has but six fees for the king's service when the call is for warriors or a fine, [p. 256] will assuredly assert that he has, as of old, forty fees when the time comes for him to take a scutage from his tenants, and in this way he may, at the rate of three marks per fee, recover, if he is lucky and persistent, about half the sum that he has had to pay to the king. But in truth, the whole system is becoming obsolete. If tenure by knight's service had been abolished in 1300, the kings of the subsequent ages would have been deprived of the large revenue that they drew from wardships, marriages and so forth; really they would have lost little else[2].

---

[1] Gesta Abbatum, ii. 94.

[2] As regards the shape that scutage assumed at various periods, we have

We have next to observe that a lord when enfeoffing a Military tenant was free to impose other services in addition to that service combined military service which was incumbent on the land. Suppose with other services. that *B* holds a knight's fee of *A* ; *B* may enfeoff *C* of the fee, stipulating that *C* shall do the military service and also pay him a rent. Perhaps it was usual that a tenant who held a whole knight's fee should have no serious service to perform in addition to the military service, though, in such a case as we have put, *B* would often stipulate for some honorary rent, a pair of spurs, a falcon, or the like. But when we get among the holders of small plots, we constantly find that they must pay scutage while they also owe substantial rents[1]. A few entries on the Oxfordshire Hundred Roll will illustrate this. At Rycote, Adam Stanford holds the whole vill of the earl of Oxford for half a knight's fee ; he has a number of freeholders holding small plots ; they pay substantial rents and 'owe scutage' ; one has a virgate, pays 7s. 6d. a year and owes [p. 257] scutage ; another holds three acres for the rent of a penny and owes scutage[2]. Often it is said of the small freeholders that beside their rent they owe royal or forinsec service (*debent regale, debent forinsecum*)[3], and, at least in general, this seems to mean that they pay scutage and are nominally tenants by knight's service ; for Bracton's rule is clear, namely, that if the tenant owes but one hap'orth of scutage (*licet ad unum obolum*), his tenure is military, and this rule is fully borne out by

here dealt but superficially with a most difficult subject. We shall have done some good if we persuade others that there are yet many questions to be answered by a diligent study of the exchequer rolls. See Hall, Lib. Rub. vol. ii, Preface.

[1] The fines of Richard's and John's reigns present numerous instances of dispositions of both these classes:—thus (Fines, ed. Hunter, i., p. 22) a gift of half a hide to be held of the donor 'per forinsecum servicium quod ad tantum terrae pertinet'; (p. 31) a gift of a virgate to be held of the donor 'faciendo inde forinsecum servicium quantum pertinet ad illam virgatam terrae pro omni servicio'; (p. 91) a gift of a quarter of a virgate to be held of the donor by the service of one pound of pepper annually 'salvo forinseco servitio quod ad dominum Regem pertinet de eadem quarta parte virgatae terrae'; (p. 95) a gift of a messuage and seven virgates to be held of the donor by the service of 24 shillings annually 'salvo regali servicio scilicet servicio dimidii militis'; (p. 274) a gift of a messuage and three acres to be held of the donor at a rent of 12 pence, 'saving the king's service, namely, 3 pence to a scutage of 20 shillings and so in proportion.'

[2] Rot. Hund. ii. 756.

[3] Rot. Hund. ii. *e.g.* 733, 767, 769.

pleadings and decisions[1]. This point is important:—the division between tenants in socage and tenants by knight's service does not correspond, save in the roughest manner, to any political, social or economic division. The small yeoman often holds his little tenement by a tenure which is nominally and legally the same tenure as that by which the knight holds his manor[2].

Castle-
guard.

With the duty of attending the king in his wars was often coupled the duty of helping to garrison his castles; more rarely the latter duty appears without the former. The knights of the Abbey of Abingdon were bound to guard the king's castle of Windsor[3], the knights of the Abbey of Peterborough his castle of Rockingham[4], the knights of the Abbey of St Edmund his castle of Norwich. In Henry I.'s day the bishop of Ely purchased for his knights the privilege of doing ward within the isle instead of at Norwich[5]. Such service was well known in Normandy[6] and France[7], and is mentioned in Domesday Book[8]. The forty or fifty knights of St Edmunds were divided into four or five troops (*constabiliae*), each of which had [p. 258] to guard Norwich castle for three months in the year[9]. Often a tenement owed 'ward' to a far-off castle; thus in Cambridge-shire were lands held of the Count of Aumâle which owed ward to his castle of Craven[10], and lands held of the Count of Britanny which owed ward to his castle of Richmond[11]. We speak as though these castles belonged to their tenants in

---

[1] Bracton, f. 37. See the cases cited above, p. 239, note 2.

[2] It is rare, though not unknown, to find that a tenant in villeinage is said to pay scutage. Doubtless the weight of taxation often fell on the lowest class of tenants; but it might have been dangerous to exact scutage *eo nomine* from the villeins, as this might have encouraged them to assert that their tenure was free.

[3] Hist. Abingd. ii. 3.

[4] Rot. Cl. i. 297.

[5] Pipe Roll, 31 Hen. I., p. 44; Monast. i. 482.

[6] See the Assisiae Normaniae in Warnkönig's Französische Rechtsgeschichte, ii., *e.g.* p. 73 (A.D. 1208): 'apud Bellum Montem debebat servicium quinque militum per quadraginta dies ad custodiendum castellum ad custum domini de Bello Monte.'

[7] Viollet, Établissements, ii. 80.

[8] D. B. i. 151 b: 'De eodem Leuuino tenuit Radulfus Passaquam et inveniebat duos loricatos in custodia de Windesores.'

[9] This is a simplification of the story; the abbot and his knights differed as to the amount of the service to be done; Jocelin of Brakelond, 49, 135.

[10] Rot. Hund. ii. 548.

[11] Rot. Hund. ii. 580.

chief; but the kings were wont to regard all castles as in a sense their own, and the duty of castle-guard, like the duty of service in the host, though due to the lord, was to be done for the king. Before the end of the thirteenth century, however, payments in money had usually taken the place of garrison duty[1].

While the military system of feudalism is thus falling into decay there still may be found in the north of England scattered traces of an older military system. The Norman *milites* are already refusing to do the service to which their tenure binds them, but there are still in the ancient kingdom of Northumbria thegns holding in thegnage, drengs holding in drengage, thegns who are nominally bound to do the king's 'útware.' Were these tenures military or were they not? That was a puzzle for the lawyers. They had some features akin to tenure by knight's service, for thegns and drengs had been summoned to fight John's battles in Normandy; in other respects they were not unlike the serjeanties; they were sometimes burdened with services which elsewhere were considered as marks of villeinage; finally, as it would seem, they were brought under the heading of free socage. In truth they were older than the lawyers' classification, older than the Norman Conquest[2]. *[margin: Thegnage and drengage.]*

Above we have made mention of tenure by barony and passed it by with few words; and few seem needed. True, we may find it said of a man, not only that he holds a barony (*tenet baroniam*), but also that he holds by barony (*tenet per baroniam*), and this may look as though tenure by barony should be accounted as one of the modes of tenure[3]. But so far as the land law is concerned there seems no difference between tenure by barony and tenure by knight's service, save in one point, namely, the amount of the relief, about which we shall speak below. So far as regards the service due from the tenant, the barony is but an aggregate of knights' fees. There is no amount of military service that is due from a tenant by barony as such; but his barony consists of knights' fees; if it *[margin: Tenure by barony.]* *[margin left: [p. 259]]*

---

[1] Hall, Liber Rubeus, ii. p. ccxxxvi.

[2] See Maitland, Northumbrian Tenures, E. H. R. v. 625; Hall, Liber Rubeus, ii. p. ccxl. ff.

[3] Rot. Hund. ii. 18: 'Radulfus de Gaugy tenet feodum de Ellincham de dom. Rege in capite per baroniam per servicium trium militum.'

consists of twenty knights' fees he is answerable for the service
of twenty knights, if it consists of fifty knights' fees, then he
must produce fifty. And so, again, with the various incidents
of tenure, aids, wardship, marriage, escheat, all save relief;
there seem to be no special rules for tenure by barony or for
the tenure of a barony; it is but tenure by knight's service of
a certain number of knights' fees, unless indeed it be—and in
some cases it is—tenure by grand serjeanty. The fact that a
certain mass of lands is deemed a barony has some few legal
consequences of a subordinate kind. Always or generally some
castle or some manor is regarded as the head of the barony,
and it would seem that for some fiscal and administrative
purposes the whole barony was treated as lying in the county
that contained its head. Then, again, a widow is not to be
endowed with the *caput baroniae*, and the *caput baroniae* is not
to be partitioned among coheiresses[1]. Such rules as these may
necessitate an inquiry whether a certain manor is the head of a
barony or a single knight's fee held by a separate title[2]; but
they will not justify us in co-ordinating tenure by barony with
the other tenures, such as knight's service and serjeanty.

The baronage.
Of course, however, 'barony' can not be treated as a mere
matter of land tenure. The barons, together with the earls,
have become an estate of the realm, and to make a man a
member of this estate it is not sufficient that he should be a
military tenant in chief of the crown. A line has been drawn
which cuts the body of such tenants into two classes. The
question by what means and in accordance with what principle
that line was drawn has been much debated. We shall probably [p. 260]
be near the truth if, in accordance with recent writers, we
regard the distinction as one that is gradually introduced by
practice and has no precise theory behind it[3]. The heterogeneous mass of military tenants in chief could not hold together
as an estate of the realm. The greater men dealt directly with
the king, paid their dues directly to the exchequer, brought
their retainers to the host under their own banners, were summoned to do suit in the king's court by writs directed to them

[1] Bracton, f. 76 b, 93.

[2] Note Book, pl. 96.

[3] Hallam, Middle Ages, ed. 1837, vol. iii., p. 21; Stubbs, Const. Hist. i. 394,
605; ii. 181–184; Gneist, Verfassungsgeschichte, 237–8. For older theories,
see Madox, Baronia Anglicana, and Selden, Titles of Honour, pt. ii., cap. 5,
sec. 21.

by name; the smaller men dealt with the sheriff, paid their
dues to him, fought under his banner, were summoned through
him and by general writs. Then two rules emphasized the
distinction:—the knight's fee paid a fixed relief of 100 shillings,
the baron made the best bargain he could for his barony; the
practice of summoning the greater people by name, the smaller
by general writs was consecrated by the charter of 1215. The
greater people are *maiores barones,* or simply *barones,* the lesser
are for a while *barones secundae dignitatis,* and then lose the
title altogether; the estates of the greater people are baronies,
those of the smaller are not; but the line between great and
small has been drawn in a rough empirical way and is not the
outcome of any precise principle. The summons to court, the
political status of the baron, we have not here to consider,
while, as regards the land law, it is to all appearance the relief,
and the relief only, that distinguishes the barony from an aggregate of knights' fees, or makes it necessary for us to speak of
tenure by barony.

When, however, a certain territory had been recognized as **Escheated honours.**
a barony or an honour, this name stuck to it through all its
fortunes. Honours and baronies were very apt to fall into the
[p. 261] hands of the king by way of forfeiture or escheat owing to the
tenant's treason. When this happened they still kept their
names the honour of Wallingford might have escheated to the
king, but it was still the honour of Wallingford and did not lose
its identity in the general mass of royal rights. Nor was this a
mere matter of words. In the first place, the escheated honour
would probably come out of the king's hands; the general
expectation was that the king would not long keep it to
himself, but would restore it to the heir of its old tenant,
or use it for the endowment of some new family, or make it
an appanage for a cadet of the royal house[1]. But the continued existence of the honour had a more definite, and a legal
meaning. Normally, as we shall see hereafter, the military
tenant in chief of the king was subject to certain exceptional
burdens from which the tenants of mesne lords were free. A
tenant holds of the lord of the honour of Boulogne: that honour
escheats to the king; the tenant will now hold immediately
of the king; but is he to be subject to the peculiar burdens
which are generally incident to tenancy in chief? No, that

[1] Stubbs, Const. Hist. 433.

would be unfair, it would be changing the terms of his tenure.
This was recognized by the practice of the exchequer under
Henry II.[1], and the rule was confirmed by the Great Charter[2].
Thus it becomes necessary to distinguish between those tenants
in chief who are conceived as having always held immediately
of the king, and those who hold of the king merely because
a mesne lordship has escheated : in other words, between those
who hold of the king as of his crown (*ut de corona*) and those
who hold of him as of an escheated honour (*ut de escaeta, ut de
honore, ut de baronia*)[3]. On the other hand, the relief for a
barony having been fixed, two baronies do not become one
merely because they are held by one person; the honour of
Clare, the honour of Gloucester, the honour of St Hilary and
a moiety of Earl Giffard's honour meet in the hands of Earl
Gilbert; he has to pay for his three and a half honours a relief
of £350[4]. An honour or barony is thus regarded as a mass [p. 262]
of lands which from of old have been held by a single title[5].

§ 4. *Serjeanty.*

Difficulty of defining serjeanty. The idea of a serjeanty as conceived in the thirteenth
century is not easily defined. Here as elsewhere we find
several different classes of men grouped together under one
heading so that the bond that connects them is slight; also we
find it difficult to mark off serjeanty from knight's service on
the one hand and socage on the other. The tests suggested by
Littleton are inapplicable to the documents of this age[6]. We
can not say that the duty of serjeanty must be performed by
the tenant in his proper person, we can not say that 'petty
serjeanty' has necessarily any connexion with war, or that
one can not hold by serjeanty of a mesne lord, or that petty

---

[1] Dial. de Scac. ii. 24.

[2] Charter, 1215, c. 43.

[3] Madox, Baronia Anglicana, throughout; Hargrave, notes to Co. Lit. 108 a ;
Challis, Real Property, p. 4.

[4] Madox, Exch. i. 317.

[5] Madox, Bar. Ang., p. 27: 'I think there were not any honours created
de novo by feoffment in the reign of King Henry III. or perhaps of King
John.'

[6] See Britton, ii. 10, and the editor's note.

serjeanty is 'but socage in effect'[1]. Even the remark that
'*serjeantia* in Latin is the same as *servitium*'[2] is not strictly
true.

Here indeed lies the difficulty :—while every tenure implies Serjeanty
a service (*servitium*), it is not every tenure that is a serjeanty service.
(*seriantia, serianteria*): every tenant owes service, but not every
tenant is a servant or serjeant (*serviens*), still less of course is
every tenant a *servus*.   A single Latin stock has thrown out
various branches, the whole of medieval society seems held
together by the twigs of those branches.   Here we have to deal
with one special group of derivative words, not forgetting that
it is connected with other groups[3].

We may begin by casting our eye over the various 'ser- Types of
jeanties' known in the thirteenth century.   First we see those owed by
forms of service which are the typical 'grand serjeanties' of the king's
later days, 'as to carry the banner of the king, or his lance, or to chief.
lead his army, or to be his marshal, or to carry his sword before
him at his coronation, or to be his sewer at his coronation, or
his carver, or his butler, or to be one of the chamberlains of the
[p. 263] receipt of his exchequer[4].'   Some of the highest offices of the
realm have become hereditary; the great officers are conceived
to hold their lands by the service or serjeanty of filling those
offices.   It is so with the offices of the king's steward or
seneschal, marshal, constable, chamberlain; and, though the
real work of governing the realm has fallen to another set of
ministers whose offices are not hereditary, to the king's justiciar,
chancellor and treasurer, still the marshal and constable have
serious duties to perform[5].   Many of the less exalted offices of
the king's household have become hereditary serjeanties; there
are many men holding by serjeanties to be done in the kitchen,
the larder and the pantry[6].   Even some of the offices which have
to do with national business, with the finance of the realm, have
become hereditary; there are already hereditary chamberlains

---

[1] Lit. secs. 153–161.   [2] Lit. sec. 154.

[3] Some scribes, it is said, distinguish *seriantia*, the land, from *serianteria*,
the service or office.

[4] Lit. sec. 153.   [5] Stubbs, Const. Hist. i. 383.

[6] 'Seriantia W. M. pro qua debuit esse emptor coquinae dom. Regis,' Testa
de Neville, 78; 'Seriantia hostiariae dom. Regis,' Ib. 93; 'Seriantia pro qua
debuit custodire lardariam dom. Regis,' Ib. 146, 232.   We are compelled to cite
the bad but only edition of the Testa.   But see Hall, Lib. Rub. iii. 1305.
Mr Hall's index enables us to omit some citations given in our first edition.

of the exchequer who do their service by deputy[1]. We observe
that all these offices, if we regard only their titles, have something menial about them, in the old and proper sense of the
word 'menial'; their duties are *servitia mansionalia*, they are
connected with the king's household. It may be long since the
predecessors in title of these men really cooked the king's
dinner or groomed the king's horses: but they glory in titles
which imply, or have implied, that their duties are of this
menial kind; nor is it always easy to say when or whether the
duty has become honorary. When the Conqueror gives half a
hide of land in Gloucestershire to his cook[2], it were bold to
say that this tenant did not really roast and boil; and what
shall we say of the cook of the Count of Boulogne[3]? Then
scattered about England we find many men who are said to
hold by serjeanty and are bound by their tenure to do other
services, which are not so distinctly menial, that is to say, are
not so closely connected with the king's household. They are
bound to carry the king's letters, to act as the king's summoners
when the barons of the neighbourhood are to be summoned, to
aid in conveying the king's treasure from place to place, or the [p. 264]
like. Again, and this is very common, theirs is some serjeanty
of the forest, they are chief foresters, or under foresters. The
king's sport has given rise to numerous serjeanties; men are
bound by tenure to keep hounds and hawks for him, to find
arrows for him when he goes a-shooting; and we can not say
that these are honorary or particularly honourable services: to
find a truss of straw for the king's outer chamber when he stays
at Cambridge, this also is a serjeanty[4]. The carpenter, the mason,
or the gardener who holds land in the neighbourhood of some
royal castle in return for his work holds a serjeanty[5]. But, again,
many serjeanties are connected with warfare. The commonest
of all is that of finding a servant or serjeant (*servientem*) to do
duty as a soldier in the king's army. Sometimes he is to be
a foot-soldier, sometimes a horse-soldier (*servientem peditem,*

---

[1] Madox, Exch. ii. 295.

[2] D. B. 162 b.

[3] 'Robertus de Wilmiton tenet Wilmiton per sergeantiam de honore de
Bononia, et valet ij. marcas et debet esse cocus Comitis,' Testa de Neville, 217.

[4] Testa, 357; so to find litter for the king's bed and food for his horses at B.,
Ib. 237; so to meet the king when he comes into the rape of Arundel and give
him two capons, Ib. 229.

[5] Testa, 409, 118–9.

servientem equitem); often the nature of the arms that he is to bear is prescribed; often he is bound to serve for forty days and no more, sometimes only for a shorter period; often to serve only against the Welsh, sometimes to serve only within his own county. It would be a mistake to think that tenure supplied [p. 265] the king only with knights or fully armed horsemen; it supplied him also with a force, though probably a small force, of light horsemen and infantry, of bowmen and cross-bowmen. It supplied him also with captains and standard-bearers for the national militia; men were bound by their tenure to lead the infantry of particular hundreds[1]. It supplied him also with the means of military transport, with a baggage train; few serjeanties seem commoner than that of sending a 'serjeant' with horse, sack and buckle for the carriage of armour and the like[2]. It supplied him, to some small degree, with munitions of war; if one was bound by tenure to find lances, arrows or knives, this was reckoned a serjeanty.

A man may well hold by serjeanty of a mesne lord. Bracton speaks clearly on this point. The tenant of a mesne lord may be enfeoffed by serjeanty, and the serjeanty may be one which concerns the lord, or one which concerns the king. Thus, for example, he may be enfeoffed as a 'rodknight' bound to ride with his lord, or he may be bound to hold the lord's pleas, that is, to act as president in the lord's court, or to carry the lord's letters, or to feed his hounds, or to find bows and arrows, or to carry them: we can not enumerate the various possible serjeanties of this class. But there are, says Bracton, other serjeanties which concern the king and the defence of the realm, even though the tenant holds of a mesne lord; as if he be enfeoffed by the serjeanty of finding so many horse- or foot-soldiers with armour of such or such a kind, or of finding a man with horse, sack and buckle for service in the army[3].

Serjeanty of mesne lords.

All this is fully borne out by numerous examples. The grand serjeanties of the king's household were represented in [p. 266] the economy of lower lords. Thus John of Fletton held land at

Types of serjeanty owed to mesne lords.

---

[1] Testa, 58: Serjeanty to be constable of 200 foot-soldiers so long as the king is in Wales. Ib. 114: Serjeanty to carry a pennon in the king's army before the foot-soldiers of the hundred of Wootton. Ib. 119: 'Servicium portandi baneram populi prosequentis per marinam (?).'

[2] As to these 'sack and buckle men,' some references are given in Select Pleas in Manorial Courts (Selden Soc.) i. 186.

[3] Bracton, f. 35 b. Compare Fleta, p. 198.

Fletton in Huntingdonshire by the service of being steward in the abbot's hall at Peterborough[1]; at Cottesford in Oxfordshire John White is bound by tenure to hold the lord's court twice a year[2]; in the same county a tenant of the Earl of Lincoln must place the last dish before the earl, and shall have a rod from the earl like other free serjeants[3]. The abbot of Gloucester has tenants who spread his table, who hold towels and pour water on his hands[4]. In the twelfth century the stewardship of the Abbey of St Edmunds was hereditary in the family of Hastings, but was executed by deputy[5]. On the whole, however, the prelates and barons seem to have followed the policy of their royal master and seldom permitted substantial power to lapse into the hands of hereditary officers; the high steward of a monastery, like the high steward of the realm, was a man for pageants rather than for business[6]. Still such serjeanties existed. The service of carrying the lord's letters was not uncommon and may have been very useful[7]; the service of looking after the lord's wood was reckoned a serjeanty[8]. In various parts of England we find a considerable class of tenants bound to go a-riding with their lords or on their lord's errands, and doubtless, as Bracton suggests, we have here the *radchenistres* and *radmanni* of Domesday Book[9]; on some estates they are known as 'esquires,' and their tenure is a 'serjeanty of esquiry[10].'

Military serjeanties held of mesne lords. But again, there may, as Bracton says, be warlike service to be done. A tenant, for example, of the abbot of Ramsey is bound to find horse, sumpter saddle, sack and fastening pin to [p. 267] carry the harness of the knights bound for the Welsh war[11]; the prior of St Botolph at Colchester is bound to the same

[1] R. H. ii. 639.   [2] R. H. ii. 838.
[3] R. H. ii. 833.   [4] Cart. Glouc. ii. 207–9.
[5] Jocelin of Brakelond (Camd. Soc.) 20.
[6] The biographer of Abbot Samson of St Edmunds regards as a part of the prudent administration of his hero that he committed the affairs of the eight and a half hundreds belonging to the abbey to mere domestics, 'servientibus suis de mensa sua'; Jocelin, 21.
[7] See *e.g.* R. H. ii. 336, 539; Cart. Glouc. iii. 69.
[8] R. H. ii. 336.
[9] See Bracton's Note Book, pl. 758; Cart. Glouc. i. 356, ii. 101, 102, 207–9, iii. 149. The abbot of Ramsey has *ridemanni*, Manorial Pleas, i. 53.
[10] Cart. Glouc. ii. 207–9: 'debuerunt facere unum esquirerium nomine seriantiae.' Ib. iii. 149: 'per serianteriam......servitio esquierii.' Gesta Abbatum, i. 264: six *armigeri* are enfeoffed by the service of riding with the abbot of St Albans to his cell at Tynemouth and carrying his baggage.
[11] Select Pleas in Manorial Courts, i. 62, 63.

service by mesne tenure[1].   Again, the tenant may go to the
war in his lord's train to fight, not as a *miles* but as a *serviens*;
Reginald de Bracy is bound by the service of serjeanty to follow
William de Barentin as a *serviens* at William's cost[2].

Now it may be impossible to bring all these very miscella- Essence of
neous tenures under one definition which shall include them, serjeanty.
but exclude knight's service and socage.   However, the central
notion seems what we may call 'servantship'; we can not say
'service,' for that word is used to cover every possible return
which one man can make to another for the right of enjoying
land.   Obviously in many cases the tenant by serjeanty not
only owes 'service' in this large sense, but is a servant
(*serviens*); he is steward, marshal, constable, chamberlain, usher,
cook, forester, falconer, dog keeper, messenger, esquire; he is
more or less of a menial servant bound to obey orders within
the scope of his employment.   Modern efforts to define a
'servant' may illustrate old difficulties as to the limits of
'serjeanty'; it may be hard to draw the line between the duty
of habitually looking after the king's bed-chamber and that of
providing him with litter when he comes to a particular manor.
But the notion of servantship, free servantship, as opposed to
any form of serfdom, seems to be the notion which brings the
various serjeanties under one class name, and it points to one
of the various sources of what in the largest sense of the term
we call the feudal system.   One of the tributaries which swells
the feudal stream is that of menial service; it meets and
mingles with other streams, and in England the intermixture
is soon very perfect; still we can see that serjeanty has come
from one quarter, knight's service from another, socage from yet
a third, and we may understand how, but for the unifying,
generalizing action of our king's court, a special law of serjeanty might have grown up, distinct from the ordinary law of
land tenure[3].

---

[1] R. H. i. 157.   [2] R. H. ii. 767.

[3] In Germany the *servientes* or *ministeriales* became a powerful class. A
group of *servientes*, *e.g.* those of an abbey, had a court of its own and law of its
own (*Dienstrecht* as contrasted with *Lehnrecht, Hofrecht, Landrecht*), see Waitz,
v. 288–350, 428–442; Schröder, D. R. G. 667.   The nearest approach that
England in the thirteenth century can show to such a court of *servientes* is the
court of the king's household; but even this aims rather at a common law
jurisdiction over all that happens within the verge of the palace, than at
developing a special law for the king's *servientes*.   In England as in Germany

[p. 268]

The serjeants in the army.

　　As regards the military serjeanties we must remember that in the language of military affairs *serviens* had acquired a distinct meaning.　An army is largely made up of *milites* and *servientes*, of fully armed horsemen, and of men who, whether they serve on foot or on horse, have not the full knightly panoply[1].　Now when a tenant by serjeanty is bound to go to the war as a *serviens* with horse, purpoint, iron cap and lance, the difference between his tenure and knight's service seems to resolve itself into a mere difference between one kind of armour and another, or one position in the army and another; and it is possible that a certain ambiguity in the word *serviens*, which will stand for servant, and will stand for light armed soldier, may have attracted within the sphere of serjeanty certain tenures which had about them no strong trace of what we have called 'servantship.'　Still originally the *servientes* of the army were so called because they were attendants on the *milites*, whose shields they carried, and whose esquires they were—for the esquire (*scutifer, armiger*) of those times was one who carried the shield or arms of his lord.　Thus by one way or another we come back to the idea of 'servantship' as the core of serjeanty[2].

Serjeanty in Domesday Book.

　　Looking back towards the Norman Conquest we run no risk in seeing the predecessors of these tenants by serjeanty in the *servientes* of Domesday Book.　Near the end of the survey of a county we sometimes meet with a special section devoted to [p. 269] *Servientes Regis.*　Thus in Wiltshire after the *Terra Tainorum Regis* comes the *Terra Servientium Regis*[3]; it is so in Dorsetshire[4]; in Devonshire and Leicestershire the *Servientes Regis*

---

the duty of the *serviens* is frequently termed a *ministerium*; see *e.g.* Pipe Roll, 31 Hen. I., in which it is common to find a man making fine 'pro terra et ministerio patris sui.'　The word *magisterium* also occurs; *e.g.* Whitby Cart. i. 222: 'magisterium officii coquinae,' a hereditary office; Rot. Cart. 46: 'magistratum mariscalciae curiae nostrae.'

　　[1] Any contemporary account of warfare will illustrate this, *e.g.* Paris's account of the war in 1216-7 (Chron. Maj. iii. 6–23), '...quidam serviens strenuus...exierunt de castello milites et servientes...exierunt denuo milites et servientes...exierunt de castello quod Munsorrel appellatur milites et servientes... decem milites cum servientibus multis...capti sunt milites quadringenti praeter servientes equites et pedites, qui facile sub numero non cadebant.'　We do not however suggest that all these *servientes* were bound to fight by tenure.

　　[2] As to the military *servientes* see Selden, Titles of Honour, part ii. c. 5, § 47.

　　[3] D. B. i. 74 b.　　　　　　　　　　[4] D. B. i. 84 b.

have a special section[1]; in Oxfordshire we find *Terra Minis-trorum Regis*[2], and when elsewhere we meet with *Famuli Regis*[3] we may suppose that this is but another name for the *Servientes* and *Ministri*. We can tell something of their offices. Among the Wiltshire *Servientes* are three chamberlains (*camerarii*), a hoarder (*granetarius*) and a cross-bowman (*arbalistarius*); elsewhere are an archer, an usher, a goldsmith, a baker, a bedchamber man; near the end of the survey of Hampshire we find a treasurer, two chamberlains, a hunter, a marshal, a physician and a barber holding in chief of the king[4]. In some cases it is possible to trace the estates of these persons until we find them definitely held by serjeanty. Again, there can be little risk in finding the ancestors in law of Bracton's *rodknightes*[5] and the abbot of Ramsey's *ridemanni* in the *radchenistres* and *radmanni* of Domesday Book. It is true that in the western counties these *radchenistres* are occasionally found in large groups; there may be even twenty of them on a manor[6]; but in what was for Bracton the leading case on serjeanty the abbess of Barking asserted that she had full thirty tenants on one manor bound to ride about with her wherever she would[7]. However, the makers of Domesday Book were not concerned to specify the terms on which the tenants, especially the tenants of mesne lords, held their lands; of serjeanties we read little, just as we read little of knightly service. So soon, however, as any attempt is made to classify tenures, the serjeanties appear in a class by themselves. Glanvill, after defining the relief payable for knights' fees and for socage tenements, adds that as to baronies nothing has been definitely settled, the amount of the relief being at the will and mercy of the king; the same, he says, is true of serjeanties[8]. In 1198 [p. 270] the distinction was enforced by the great fiscal measure of that year; from the general land tax the *serianteriae* were excepted, but they were to be valued and the *servientes* who held them were to be summoned to meet the king at Westminster to hear and do his bidding[9].

[1] D. B. i. 117 b, 236 b.　　　　　　[2] D. B. i. 160 b.
[3] D. B. ii. 4 b, 98 b, 110 b.　　　　[4] D. B. i. 49.
[5] Bracton, f. 35 b.　　　　　　　　[6] Ellis, Introduction, i. 72.
[7] Note Book, pl. 758.　Maitland, Domesday Book, 305 ff.
[8] Glanvill, ix. 4.
[9] Hoveden, iv. 47.　Round, E. H. R. iii. 501, has shown that some of the returns made on this occasion are preserved in the Testa de Neville.

Other distinctions appear in course of time. Even in Bracton's day the amount of the relief for a serjeanty was not yet fixed; it was to be 'reasonable' but no more than this could be said[1]. In later days we find it fixed at one year's value of the land; but how or when this definition was arrived at we do not know[2]. That the serjeant's relief remains uncertain long after the reliefs of barons, knights and socagers are fixed is another fact which points to the peculiar nature of the relationship which had been involved in the tenure. It was not the mere relation between lord and tenant, or between lord and man, but was also the relation between master and servant, and, though a feoffment had been made to the tenant and his heirs, the law was slow to dictate the terms upon which the lord must receive the heir into his service. Again, we find that a tenement held by serjeanty is treated as inalienable and impartible. As regards alienation we shall be better able to speak hereafter, but will premise this much, that the king is rigorously enforcing the rule that his serjeants can not without his leave alienate their land, even by way of subinfeudation, at a time when he is not, or is not systematically, enforcing the same rule against his other tenants. We have some proof that so late as John's reign it was thought that a serjeanty could not be partitioned among coheiresses; the eldest daughter would take the whole[3]:—this also is an intelligible rule if we have regard to the 'serviential' character of the tenure; a serjeanty must not be 'lacerated'[4]. As to the wardship and marriage of tenants by serjeanty there was much dispute, and in course of time a line was drawn between what were called 'grand' and what were called 'petty' serjeanties. To this [p. 271] matter we must return; but by means of the rules to which allusion has here been made, tenure by serjeanty was kept apart from tenure by knight's service on the one hand and tenure by socage on the other, and even in the middle of the thirteenth century it still had an importance which is but faintly represented by the well-known sections of Littleton's book.

[1] Bracton, f. 84 b.

[2] It seems to be assumed in 1410, Y. B. 11 Hen. IV. f. 72 (Trin. pl. 9), and is stated by Littleton, sec. 154.

[3] Placit. Abbrev. p. 39 (Kent); compare p. 34 (Kent). Rot. Obl. p. 237: the eldest of several sisters claims the whole of her dead brother's land 'quia illa terra est de sergenteria.'

[4] Placit. Abbrev. p. 48 (Bedf.); Bracton, f. 395.

§ 5. *Socage.*

Any tenure that on the one hand is free and on the other
hand is not spiritual, nor military, nor 'serviential,' is called
tenure in free socage:—to this result lawyers are gradually
coming. Obviously therefore this term *socage* will cover a large
field ; it will include various relationships between men, which,
if we regard their social or economic or even their purely
legal aspects, seem very different from each other. We may
look at a few typical cases.

(*a*) The service which the tenant owes to his lord may be
merely nominal : he has no rent to pay or has to give but a rose
every year just by way of showing that the tenure exists. Such
a case may be the effect of one of various causes. It may ori-
ginate in what we should call a family settlement : a landowner
sometimes provides for a daughter or a younger son by a gift of
land to be held by a nominal service. Or again, the gift may
be a reward to some dependant for past services, or a retaining
fee for services to be rendered hereafter, which services however
are not defined and are not legally exigible. Or again, there
may well have been what in truth was a sale of the land : in
return for a gross sum a landowner has created a nominal
tenure. To have put the purchaser in the vendor's place might
have been difficult, perhaps impossible ; so the purchaser is
made tenant to the vendor at an insignificant rent.

(*b*) Such cases gradually shade off into others in which
a substantial rent has been reserved. We pass through the
very numerous instances in which the lord is to receive yearly
some small article of luxury, a sparrowhawk, a pair of gloves,
a pair of gilt spurs, a pound of pepper or of incense or of wax,
to other cases in which the rent, if we can not call it a 'rack
[p. 272] rent,' is 'the best rent that can reasonably be gotten.' We
thus enter the sphere of commerce, of rents fixed by supply
and demand.

Such tenures as these may be found in every zone of the
territorial system. The tenant may be holding of the king
in chief; the king has, as we should say, granted perpetual
leases at substantial rents of some of his manors, the lessees
being sometimes lay barons, sometimes religious houses[1]. Again,

---

[1] Thus *e.g.* the prior of Barnwell held of the king the ancient demesne
manor of Chesterton at a rent of £30; R. H. ii. 402.

from the Conquest onward, to say nothing of an earlier time, very great men have not thought it beneath them to hold church lands at easy rents[1]. It is an accusation common in monastic annals that the abbots of the Norman time dissipated the lands of their houses by improvident grants to their foreign kinsmen or by taking fines instead of reserving adequate rents. In such cases these tenants in socage may have other tenants in socage below them, who will pay them heavier rents. Ultimately we come to the actual occupant of the soil, whose rent will in many cases represent the best offer that his landlord could obtain for the land. Occasionally he may be paying more for the land than can be got from the villeins of the same village.

(*c*) Sometimes we find in charters of feoffment that the feoffee, besides paying rent, is to do or get done a certain amount of agricultural labour on his lord's land, so much ploughing, so much reaping. The feoffee may be a man of mark, an abbot, a baron, who will have many tenants under him and will never put his hand to the plough[2]. These cases are of importance because they seem to be the channel by which the term *socage* gradually spreads itself.

(*d*) Finally, within a manor there often are tenants bound to pay divers dues in money and in kind and bound to do or get done a fixed quantity of agricultural service for their lords. Their tenure is often regarded as very old; often they have no [p. 273] charters which express its terms[3]. Hereafter we shall see that it is not always easy to mark the exact line which separates them from the tenants in villeinage among whom they live and along with whom they labour for the lord's profit. Some of them are known as free sokemen (*sokemanni, sochemanni*); but this name is not very common except on 'the ancient demesne' of the crown. Of their position we must speak hereafter, for it can only be discussed in connexion with the unfree tenures.

---

[1] For early instances see Burton Cart. 30, 31. The Charter of 1215, c. 37, shows that the king has tenants in chief who hold in socage, burgage, fee farm.

[2] See *e.g.* in Cart. Glouc. i. 322 the elaborate labour services due from the abbot of Gloucester to the Templars. In the north of England among the tenants in thegnage and drengage it is common to find the lord of a whole vill bound to supply a number of ploughers and reapers for the assistance of his over-lord.

[3] Thus at Offord Cluny there is a group of *tenentes per cartam* and a much larger group of *tenentes per vetus feofamentum*; R. H. ii. 683.

Now to all appearance the term *socage*, a term not found in Normandy, has been extending itself upwards; a name appropriate to a class of cultivating peasants has begun to include the baron or prelate who holds land at a rent but is not burdened with military service. Of such a man it would seem natural to say that he holds at a rent (*tenet ad censum*), and for a century and more after the Norman Conquest it is rare to call his tenure socage. He is sometimes said to have *feodum censuale*; far more commonly he is said to hold 'in fee farm.' This term has difficulties of its own, for it appears in many different guises; a feoffee is to hold *in feofirma, in feufirmam, in fedfirmam*[1], *in feudo firmam, in feudo firma*[2], *ad firmam feodalem*[3], but most commonly, *in feodi firma*. The Old English language had both of the words of which this term is compounded, both *feoh* (property) and *feorm* (rent)[4]; but so had the language of France, and in Norman documents the term may be found in various shapes, *firmam fedium, feudifirmam*[5]. But, whatever may be the precise history of the phrase, to hold in fee farm means to hold heritably, perpetually, at a rent; the fee, the inheritance, is let to farm. This term long struggles to maintain its place by the side of *socage*; the victory of the latter is not perfect even in Bracton's day; the complete merger of fee farm in socage is perhaps due to a statute of Edward I., though the way towards this end had long been prepared[6].

As to the word *socage*, a discussion of it would open a series of difficult problems about the administration of justice in the days before the Conquest. These have been discussed elsewhere[7]. We must here notice two points. Bracton believed—

Gradual extension of the term socage.

Fee farm.

[p. 274]

Meaning of 'socage.'

---

[1] Burton Cart. 31, 37.   [2] Hist. Abingd. ii. 65, 128, 167.

[3] Reg. Malm. ii. 173; Rot. Obl. p. 12, 68.

[4] But the latter seems to be derived from Low Latin, in which *firma* has come to mean a fixed rent or tribute; Skeat, s.v. *farm*.

[5] Delisle, Études sur la condition de la classe agricole en Normandie, 45.

[6] For the co-ordination of fee farm and burgage with socage, see Magna Carta, 1215, c. 37: 'Si quis teneat de nobis per feodifirmam, vel per sokagium, vel per burgagium...occasione illius feodifirmae, vel sokagii vel burgagii.' Also Bracton, f. 85 b, 86, where as regards relief a distinction is drawn between socage and fee farm. The Statute of Gloucester (6 Edw. I. c. 4) seems in course of time to have generated the notion held by Coke that a rent is not 'a fee farm rent' unless it amounts to one-fourth of the annual value of the land; see 2nd Inst. 44, Co. Lit. 143 b, and the note in which Hargrave shows that neither in the statute nor in earlier history is there any warrant for this restriction of the term.

[7] Maitland, Domesday Book, 66 ff.

erroneously no doubt, but erroneous etymology is a force in the
history of the law—that socage had to do with *soc*, the French
word for a ploughshare[1]; tenants in socage therefore are
essentially agriculturists, and the duty of ploughing the lord's
demesne is the central feature of socage. In the second place,
if we turn to the true derivation, we come to much the same
result; socage is at starting the tenure of those *sokemen* of
whom we read in Domesday Book; *socage* is an abstract term
which describes their condition. Gradually it has been extended
and therefore attenuated until it is capable of expressing none
but negative characteristics:—socage is a tenure which is not
spiritual, not military, not serviential. No similar extension
has been given to the word *sokeman*; in the thirteenth century
many persons hold in socage who would be insulted were they
called sokemen; for the sokemen are a humble, though it may
be a well-to-do class[2].

Socage in
contrast
to military
tenure.
　　That they have been a numerous class we may gather as
from other evidence so from this, that socage becomes the
one great standing contrast to military tenure, and, as the [p. 275]
oppressive incidents of military tenure are developed, every
man who would free his holding from the burdens of wardship
and marriage is anxious to prove that he holds in socage.
To gain this end he is full willing to sink somewhat of dignity;
he will gladly hold by the peasant's tenure when the most
distinctive marks of that tenure are immunities—no scutage,
no wardship, no marriage[3].

Socage as
the re-
siduary
tenure.
　　Thus free socage, when that term has attained its full
compass, appears as the great residuary tenure, if we may so
speak; it is non-military, non-serviential, non-elemosinary. If,
however, we go back to the first half of the twelfth century, we
begin to doubt whether we can strictly insist on the most
characteristic of these negative attributes. The army is but
gradually taking its new shape; the sokemen of the abbot

---

[1] Bracton, f. 77 b: 'Et dici poterit sockagium a *socko*, et inde tenentes qui
tenent in sockagio sockemanni dici poterunt, eo quod deputati sunt ut videtur
tantummodo ad culturam.' As to the history of the Old French *soc* see
Skeat, s.v. *socket*. Apparently it occurs in Domesday Book, i. 167 b: 'unus
burgensis reddit iiij. soccos.'

[2] See Vinogradoff, Villainage, p. 196.

[3] In Glanvill, vii. 11, and even in Bracton, f. 87 b, the heirs who escape
wardship in chivalry are still the *heredes sokemannorum*. The term *socager*
seems to be of later date.

of Peterborough serve along with the knights[1].   In Edward I.'s
day the tradition among the Oxfordshire jurors was that the
ancestors of many of the bishop of Lincoln's socage tenants
were free sokemen or 'quasi sokemen' who served the king in
the war for forty days at their own cost with purpoints, lances
and iron caps[2].   It is not in the past that we must look for
clear definitions.

Tenure in burgage, if we examine but one specimen of it, *Burgage.*
may seem to differ in no essential from free socage[3].   The
service due from the tenant to his lord is very generally a
mere money rent, though there may be a little ploughing or the
like to be done.   But if we thus isolate a single tenant from
his fellows, the spirit of burgage escapes us.   The tenant is,
at least normally, a burgess, a member of a privileged community, which already aspires to become a municipal corporation.   This is not the place in which to discuss the history of
the boroughs, still we ought just to notice that tenure has been
an important element in it.   From a remote time there have
been in the greater and older boroughs men who paid rents for
their houses but did no other service.   Their tenure becomes
distinctive of the boroughs, and when in later days a manor is
to become a borough, the abolition of labour services and the
introduction of burgage tenure is one main feature of the
process[4].

[p. 276]   Regarded merely as a tenure, the chief characteristic of *Burgage
and
borough
customs.*
burgage is its subjection to local custom.   Other free tenures,
socage for example, may be affected by local custom, but
what is exceptional in their case is normal in the case of
burgage.   The lord has made over to the men of the borough
his court and the profits of his court; very frequently a royal
charter has conceded that actions for burgage tenements shall
not be tried except in the court of the borough; thus local
custom has room within which it can grow and is not liable to
be set aside in favour of common law.   It is chiefly within the
domain of private law, it is about such matters as inheritance

---

[1] Chron. Petroburg., p. 173, *e.g.* 'Sochemanni de Ailintona i. hidam et i.
virgam et serviunt cum militibus.'

[2] Rot. Hund. ii. 748–9.   These entries are very curious: 'set antecessores
eius solebant esse liberi quasi sokemanni et solebant facere servicium dom.
Regi in guerra,' etc.

[3] For the burgage of Normandy, see Somma, p. 98.

[4] More of this in our section on The Boroughs.

and dower, that the borough customs have their say. The point that most concerns us here is their tendency to treat the burgage tenement as an article of commerce; it is likened to a chattel; not only can it be disposed of by will, but 'it can be sold like a chattel.'

One man may hold by many tenures.

A man might hold of many different lords by many different tenures. This no one would deny; but some of the classical expositions of 'the feudal system' and 'the manorial system' are apt to make the texture of medieval society look simpler than really it was, and we think it part of our duty to insist that the facts which the lawyers of the thirteenth century had to bring within their theories were complicated. Therefore let us fix our eyes on one man, Sir Robert de Aguilon, and see what he held on the day of his death in 1286. He held lands at Greatham in Hampshire of the king at a rent of 18s.; he held lands at Hoo in Kent of the abbot of Reading at a money rent; he held lands at Crofton in Buckinghamshire of William [p. 277] de Say by some service that the jurors did not know; he held a manor in Norfolk of the bishop of Norwich by the service of a sixth part of a knight's fee and by castle-guard; he held a manor in Sussex of the earl of Warenne by the service of one knight; he held a manor in Hertfordshire of the king in chief by the serjeanty of finding a foot-soldier for forty days; he held tenements in London of the king in chief by socage and could bequeath them as chattels[1]. So we must not think that each man fills but one place in the legal structure of feudalism. In a remote past this may have been so; but it is not so in the age that defines the various tenures. Often enough the man who holds of the king in chief will hold also of other lords; he will hold by knight's service, by serjeanty, in fee farm, in socage and in burgage.

§ 6. *Homage and Fealty.*

Homage and fealty.

Very generally the mere bond of tenure is complicated with another bond, that of homage and fealty; the tenant either has done homage and sworn fealty, or is both entitled and compellable to perform these ceremonies. The right and the duty go together; in one particular case it may be the lord,

---

[1] Liber de Antiquis Legibus, pp. lxxi–lxxvi.

in another it may be the tenant, who will desire that these
solemnities should be observed, for each of them may thereby
gain something.

When we read what the law-books say of these matters, we Legal and
feel that they are dealing with institutions, the real importance extra-legal
effects of
of which lies but partly within the field of law. The law of homage.
homage as administered, or even as tolerated, by the king's
court of the thirteenth century is but a pale reflection of moral
sentiments which still are strong but have been stronger.
Glanvill and Bracton seem to lower their voices to a religious
whisper when they speak of homage; it is in this context that
Glanvill introduces a word very rare in English legal documents,
the antique word *vassallus*[1]. The ceremony of homage is as
solemn as ceremony can be.   But when we ask for the effects
of homage, we get on the one hand some rules of private law
[p. 278] about warranty and so forth, rules which may seem to us of no
great importance, and on the other hand some vague though
impressive hints that these legal rules express but a small part
of what is, or has been, the truth.

The ceremony of homage (in some of the older books *homi-* The cere-
nium, hominatio[2], but usually *homagium*) is much the same homage.
all Europe over[3]. According to Bracton, the tenant puts his
hands between the hands of the lord—this symbolical subjection seems from the first to have been the very essence of the
transaction[4]—and says: 'I become your man of the tenement
that I hold of you, and faith to you will bear of life and member
and earthly worship [*or, as some say*, of body and chattels and
earthly worship], and faith to you shall bear against all folk
[*some add*, who can live and die], saving the faith that I
owe to our lord the king.'[5]   Britton adds that the lord shall
then kiss his tenant[6]; Littleton adds that the lord sits, while
the tenant kneels on both knees, ungirt and with his head
uncovered; and these we may accept as ancient traits[7].

---

[1] Glanvill, ix. 1; for the use of this word before the Conquest, see Maitland,
Domesday Book, 293.

[2] D. B. i. 225 b: 'G. Episcopus clamat hominationem eorum.'

[3] Waitz, D. V. G. vi. 46; Schröder, D. R. G. 391; Warnkönig, Französische
Rechtsgeschichte, ii. 357.

[4] Waitz, D. V. G. vi. 47.

[5] Bracton, f. 80.   Cf. Glanvill, ix. 1; Statutes of the Realm, i. 227.

[6] Britton, ii. 37.

[7] Littleton, sec. 85.   Compare the details from French books in Warnkönig,
ii. 358.   The man must be without arms, or spurs, or mantle.

Everything seems done to tell us that the man has come helpless to the lord and has been received into the lord's protection.

The oath of fealty.

Homage is 'done,' fealty is 'sworn,' and it is worthy of observation that the oath is conceived as less solemn than the symbolic act and can be exacted in many cases in which homage is not exigible. The tenant now stands up with his hand on the gospels and says: 'Hear this my lord: I will bear faith to you of life and member, goods, chattels and earthly worship, so help me God and these holy gospels of God'; some add an express promise to do the service due for the tenement[1]. Bracton does not here mention any saving clause for the faith due to the king; but doubtless this was added[2]. The oath of fealty thus omits the words 'I become your man,' a significant omission. Fealty, of course, is the Latin *fidelitas*; but it is interesting to notice that on manorial rolls written [p. 279] by clerks who were no great Latinists, the word becomes *feodelitas* or *feoditas*, so close is the connexion between faith and fee.

Liegeance

The forms that have here been given are those of liege homage and of fealty sworn to a liege lord. The word *liege* seems to mean simple, unconditional, though very likely at a quite early time a false derivation from the Latin *ligare* (to bind) began to obscure this[3]. The man who has but one lord does unconditioned homage. If now he acquires a fee from another lord, his homage must be conditioned, he must save the faith that he owes to his first lord[4]. If tenements held of several lords descend to one heir, his liege homage seems due either to the lord from whom he claims his principal dwelling-place—*cuius residens et ligius est*[5]—or to that lord who made

---

[1] Bracton, f. 80. [2] Glanvill, ix. 1; Britton, ii. 39, 40.

[3] See Skeat, Dict. s.v. *liege*; Viollet, Histoire du droit civil français, 657; Esmein, Histoire du droit français, 199, where interesting passages are given from the canonist Durandus, which show that already in cent. xiii. there was some uncertainty about the import of this word. In the thirteenth century there was another context in which the word was commonly used, viz. a donor is said to have made a gift *in ligia potestate, i.e.* he was unconstrained, had full power; this phrase survived in Scots law in the form *liege poustie*; it is common in Bracton's Note Book, *e.g.* pl. 255, but is apt to degenerate into *in legitima potestate*.

[4] Britton, ii. 37, 38. Statutes of the Realm, i. 227.

[5] Leg. Hen. 43, § 6; Glanvill, ix. i. Comp. Statutes of the Realm, i. 227: 'de qi il tient son chief mesuage.'

the oldest of those feoffments under which he claims[1]. The
person to whom liege homage is done is by no means necessarily the king; but the king has been insisting with ever
greater success that there is a direct bond between him and
every one of his subjects; the growth of national feeling has
favoured this claim[2]. Not only has he insisted that in every
expression of homage or fealty to another there shall be a
saving for the faith that is due to him[3], but he has insisted
[p. 280] that every male of the age of twelve years shall take an oath of
fealty to him and his heirs, an oath 'to bear faith and loyalty
of life and limb, of body and chattels and of earthly honour,'
an oath which of course makes no reference to any tenement,
an oath which promises a fealty so unconditioned that it
becomes known as the oath of ligeance or allegiance (*ligeantia*)[4].
William the Conqueror, it would seem, had exacted, not only
an oath of fealty, but an act of homage from all the considerable tenants of his kingdom, no matter whose men they were,
for so we may fairly construe the words of the chronicler, 'they
bowed themselves and were this man's men'[5]; later kings as
well as earlier had exacted the oath of fealty from their subjects
in general. But this is a strong testimony to the force of
vassalism. It suggests that an oath is necessary in order to
constitute the relation between ruler and subject; it suggests
that the mere omission of a saving clause might make it a
man's duty to follow his lord even against the king; it makes

---

[1] Bracton, f. 79 b : 'feoffator primus propter primum feoffamentum.'

[2] Round, Ancient Charters, p. 8 : Henry I. gives the lordship over certain
tenants and expresses his will that all of them shall do liege homage to the
donee 'in mea salva fidelitate.' Thus the general duty to be faithful to the
king does not prevent homage to another being liege. Madox, Formulare,
No. 298 : William Bloet enfeoffs a tenant 'pro suo homagio et ligeantia, salva
fide Regis.'

[3] See the proceedings against the bishop of Exeter, Co. Lit. 65 a. As to the
similar measure of the Emperor Frederick I., see Waitz, D. V. G. vi. 46. The
kings of the French after a struggle had for a while abandoned the attempt to
insist on the insertion of these saving clauses; Luchaire, Institutions monarchiques, ii. 27. See also Somma, pp. 39, 94.

[4] Britton, i. 185; Fleta, 114. See Hale, P. C. i. 62–76. The idea that
allegiance (*ligeantia, ligeaunce*) is due only to the king slowly gains ground.
The same process went on in France; 'the progress of monarchical power gave
rise to the principle that liege homage can be done only to the sovereign';
Giraud, Bibl. de l'École des chartes, Sér. III., vol. iii. p. 4.

[5] Chron. Sax. ann. 1086; Florence, ii. 19, speaks only of an oath of fealty;
but we are hardly in a position to contradict the Peterborough chronicler.

the relation between king and subject look like a mere copy of
the relation between lord and vassal. This we can see even if
we look back to the first days of incipient feudalism: 'All shall
swear in the name of the Lord fealty to King Edmund as a
man ought to be faithful to his lord'[1]; the obligation of man to
lord is better known, more strongly felt, than the obligation of
subject to king. At the accession of Edward I. the danger
seems past, at least for a while; the feudal force seems to have
well-nigh spent itself; but obviously homage and fealty, liege
homage and liege fealty, have meant a great deal.

Vassalism in the Leges Henrici. In the *Leges Henrici* we may find the high-water-mark of
English vassalism. Every man owes faith to his lord of life
and limb and earthly worship, and must observe his lord's
command in all that is honourable and proper, saving the faith
due to God and the ruler of the land; but theft, treason, murder,
or anything that is against God and the catholic faith, such
things are to be commanded to none, and done by none. [p. 281]
Saving these, however, faith must be kept to lords, more
especially to a liege lord, and without his consent one may have
no other lord[2]. If the lord takes away his man's land or deserts
him in mortal peril, he forfeits his lordship; but the man must
be long suffering, he must bear with his lord's maltreatment of
him for thirty days in war, for year and day in peace[3]. Every
one may aid his lord when attacked and obey him in all things
lawful; and so too the lord is bound to help his man with aid
and counsel in all things, and may be his warrant—at least in
certain cases—if he attacks or molests another[4]. To kill one's
lord is compared to blasphemy against the Holy Ghost; it is a
crime to be punished by a death cruel enough to seem a fit
beginning for the torments of hell[5]. If, on the other hand, the
lord slays his man who has done no wrong, the offence can be
paid for with money[6].

---

[1] Laws of Edmund, III. § 1.

[2] Leg. Hen. 55, § 3, accepting the variant *Deum* for *dominum.*

[3] Ibid. 43, § 8.

[4] Ibid. 82, § 3-6. In what cases the lord can warrant violence, is left an open
question.

[5] Ibid. 75, § 1. Apparently the traitor is to be flayed alive.

[6] Ibid. 75, § 3. Compare the Norman law; Très ancien coutumier (Tardif),
c. 35: if a lord kills his man he shall be punished by death; if a man kills his
lord he shall be drawn and hanged, unless it be by misadventure, and even if it
be by misadventure he shall be punished with death.

Bracton defines homage thus:—Homage is a bond of law Bracton on homage. (*vinculum iuris*) by which one is holden and bound to warrant, defend and acquit the tenant in his seisin against all men, in return for a certain service (*per certum servitium*) named and expressed in the gift, and *vice versa* whereby the tenant is 'really' bound (*re obligatur*) to keep faith to his lord and do the due service; and such is the connexion by homage between lord and tenant that the lord owes as much to the tenant as the tenant to the lord, save only reverence[1]. Such a definition tends to bring the whole matter within the legitimate province of the law of contract: there is a bargain about a tenement; the lessee is to do certain services, the lessor is to warrant the title. Warranty is still an important matter, and the doing and receipt of homage still have important results in the law about warranty; but even here the courts are beginning to neglect homage and to lay stress merely on the relation which exists, [p. 282] whether homage has or has not been done, between a feoffor and his feoffee. And, as Bracton here hints, the feoffee's obligation to perform the services is beginning to be conceived rather as the outcome of a 'real' contract than as an outcome of the act of homage. To this point we may return hereafter, since it lies within the domain of private law. What had been the public, the political or anti-political, force of homage may best be seen by comparing passages in the text-books which deal with the problems which may arise when a man holds different tenements of different lords and those lords quarrel.

Such problems were possible even at the beginning of the Homage and private war. twelfth century, for a man might hold land of divers lords[2]. Glanvill, though he distinctly says that the tenant may have to fight against his lord at the king's command, says also that if a man has done divers homages for his divers fees to divers lords who 'infest' each other, and if his chief lord orders him to go in his proper person against another of his lords, he must obey the command, 'saving the service to that other lord from the fee that is held of him[3].' This can hardly be read otherwise than as a statement that private warfare may conceivably be lawful.

---

[1] Bracton, f. 78 b. This is based on Glanvill, ix. 4.

[2] Leg. Hen. 43, § 6: 'Quotcunque dominos aliquis habeat, vel quantumcunque de aliis tenet, ei magis obnoxius est, et eius residens esse debet, cuius ligius est.' Cf. 55, § 2; 82, § 5.

[3] Glanvill, ix. 1.

Bracton dealing with a like case uses more ambiguous words :—
If enmities arise between his different lords, the tenant must in
his proper person stand with him (*stabit cum eo*) to whom he has
done ligeance, while he must stand with his other lords by
attorney[1]. There is a great difference between Bracton's *stare
cum* and Glanvill's *ire contra*. Bracton's words may be satisfied
by supposing a tenant bound to do suit to the courts of two
lords who have quarrelled; he must go in person to the one
court, by attorney to the other. In Britton's book, however, or
at least in some manuscripts thereof, it is written that the
tenant may have to serve one lord 'against the other[2]'; and we
are hardly entitled to say that this doctrine, even as a legal [p. 283]
doctrine, was of no force. It is probable that even the king's
courts would have held that the man was justified, or at least
excused, in defending his lord and his lord's property against
hostile attacks, and such defence might easily become defensive
warfare. The great case which proves that Edward I. had the
will and the power to put down private war with a heavy hand,
even when it was levied between the most powerful men of his
realm, the case in which he sent an earl of Gloucester and an
earl of Hereford to prison, proves also that in the eyes of contemporaries the full enormity of their offence was found in their
having gone on with the war contrary to a royal prohibition, and
that the morality of the time would hardly suffer any severe
punishment to be inflicted upon those of their men who had
followed their banners in ignorance of the king's command.
Such persons, if guilty of homicide, robbery, arson or the like,
might doubtless be dealt with as common criminals; but for the
mere fact that they had gone out with banner displayed, it
would be hard to bring to bear upon them that prerogative
procedure which was set in motion in order to crush the
disobedient earls. At any rate, private war was an offence
which might be enormously exaggerated by breach of a royal
prohibition[3].

---

[1] Bracton, f. 79 b; Fleta, p. 207.

[2] Britton, ii. 41: 'Si deus seignurs soint en destaunce, si covendra al tenaunt
fere soen service a soen [seignur lige encountre soen autre] seignur en sa propre
person et de fere soen service a soen autre seignur par attourné.' The omission
in some MSS. of the words here printed within brackets is noteworthy.

[3] Rot. Parl. i. 70–77. See especially p. 77. But Edward was playing the
part of a king who is so strong that he can be merciful. Orderic, iv. 167, in an
important passage, points out the difference between England and Normandy.

The same feeling may be seen in another quarter. That a Sanctity of homage.
lord should make an attack on his man, or a man on his lord,
even under the forms of law, is scarcely to be tolerated. If the
man will bring an appeal, a criminal charge, against his lord, he
must first 'waive the tenement[1].' When a king is going to
[p. 284] declare war upon his barons he first defies them, for there
should be no attack while there is affiance. Henry III. in 1233
defied the Marshal, who then was no longer his man, but
'outside his homage'[2]; before the battle of Lewes he defied the
earls of Leicester and Gloucester, who thereupon renounced
homage and fealty[3]. We can hardly say that all this lies
outside the sphere of law, for rebellions and wars are conducted
on quasi-legal principles: that is a characteristic of the time.
Bracton fully admits that a man who holds land both in
England and in France may be bound to aid both kings when
they make war on each other; his liege lord he must serve in
person, but none the less he must discharge the service due to
his other lord[4].

But the most curious limitation to the force of vassalism Homage and felony.
will be found in the fact that a man can hardly 'go against'
any one at his lord's command without being guilty of the
distinctively feudal crime, without being guilty of 'felony.'
Common law, royal and national law, has, as it were, occupied
the very citadel of feudalism. Whatever may be the etymology
of *felony* (and of this we shall speak hereafter), there can be no
doubt that the word came to us from France, and that in
France and elsewhere it covered only the specifically feudal
crimes, those crimes which were breaches of the feudal nexus

Under Henry I., Ivo of Grandmesnil 'guerram in Anglia coeperat et vicinorum
rura suorum incendio combusserat, quod *in illa regione* crimen est inusitatum,
nec sine gravi ultione fit expiatum.' The ordinary English criminal law is
strong enough to suppress anything that we could fairly call private war; just
for this reason it is needless for Glanvill to say with his Norman contemporary,
'Nullus hominum audeat versus alium guerram facere'; Très ancien coutumier
(Tardif), c. 31. He can even indulge in a speculation as to the vassal's duty of
following one of his lords against another, for this must be read subject to the
rules of criminal law which forbid homicide and the like. In France there
arose a jurisprudence of private war, for which see Viollet, Établissements,
i. 180; Esmein, Histoire du droit français, 252.

[1] Bracton, f. 81 b, 141.

[2] Mat. Par. Chron. Maj. iii. 249, 258.

[3] Chron. T. Wykes, 149. Other chroniclers notice this incident as important.

[4] Bracton, f. 427 b.

and which would work a forfeiture or escheat of the fief, or, as the case might be, of the lordship; for the lord might be guilty of felony against his man just as the man might be guilty of felony against his lord. A mere common crime, however wicked and base, mere wilful homicide, or theft, is not a felony; there must be some breach of that faith and trust which ought to exist between lord and man. Now it would seem that for a while the word was used here as well as elsewhere in this restricted sense; in the Leges Henrici *felonia* is one among many crimes[1]. A little later it seems to cover every crime of any considerable gravity, and seems to have no reference whatever to the feudal bond, save in one respect, namely, that the felon's land escheats to his lord; nay, a charge of *felonia* has become an indispensable part of every charge of every [p. 285] crime that is to be punished by death or mutilation[2]. The details of this process are obscure. Possibly the lords saw no harm in a change which brought them abundant escheats; but an attack had been made upon vassalism at its very centre. To be true to your lord when there was any real strain on the feudal bond, to go out with him when he 'went against' some one else, would end, like enough, in your finding that you had committed a felony. This of course is no superficial change in the use of words; it bears witness to a deep change in thought and feeling. All the hatred and contempt which are behind the word *felon* are enlisted against the criminal, murderer, robber, thief, without reference to any breach of the bond of homage and fealty.

Feudal felony.

We can find traces of an older way of thinking. So late as 1225 William Blunt brought an action against Roger Gernon demanding homage, relief and scutage; Roger denied holding of the demandant and asserted that he held of William Briwere; the demandant replied 'with words of felony'—wickedly and in felony had Roger denied his service and done homage to another[3]. Such a use of the term *felonia* may have been belated, still felony in its more modern sense is not the only cause for an escheat. Glanvill speaks briefly:—the tenant will break the bond of homage if he does anything that may turn to the disherison of his lord or the disgrace of his lord's

---

[1] Leg. Hen. 43, § 7; 46, § 3; 53, § 4.

[2] Select Pleas of the Crown, pl. 67; Bracton, f. 141, last line.

[3] Note Book, pl. 1687.

person[1]. Bracton's phrase is 'anything that may turn to
'the disherison of the lord or any other atrocious injury.'
We can not prove from decided cases that any delict falling
short of a 'felony' in the modern sense of that term, and
unconnected with the tenure of the land, would have been
regarded by the king's courts of the thirteenth century as a
cause of escheat; but it would be rash to deny that the tenant
might lose the land by reviling his lord, particularly if the lord
[p. 286] kept a court and the tenant were duly forjudged the land by
his peers; and Bracton distinctly says that any violent laying
of hands upon the lord will cause a loss of the tenement[2]. As to
the dealings with the tenement which might work a disherison, lord or tenant might well lose his rights in the land by
disavowing the tenure. In Bracton's day this principle was
being degraded into a mere rule of property law, one of the
complicated mass of rules about warranty and so forth; but we
have just seen how in 1225 such a disavowal was still spoken
of as a felony[3].

In other quarters we may see that homage has been losing
its meaning. It has been connected with military tenure.
According to Bracton, it is due if the tenement is held by
knight's service, even though but one half-penny of scutage be
payable; it is due also if the tenure is a serjeanty, at all events
if the serjeanty be one that concerns the king; but it is not
due from tenants in socage, though as a matter of fact they
sometimes do it; if the tenure were villeinage, it would be
dangerous to take the tenant's homage, as this might imply an
enfranchisement[4]. Glanvill gives us an important clue when
he says that a woman can not do, though she may receive
homage[5]; in Bracton's day this is otherwise, a woman may well

Homage, by whom done and received.

---

[1] Glanv. ix. 1: 'Et generaliter nihil de iure facere poterit quis salva fide homagii quod vertat ad exheredationem domini sui vel ad dedecus corporis sui.'

[2] Bracton, f. 81 b. Compare Glanvill, ix. 1, who seems to demand an intent to do grievous harm. The lord's power to proceed in his own court against the tenant is fully admitted by Glanvill.

[3] Bracton, f. 81 b, gives a precedent of a writ of escheat grounded on a malicious disavowal by the tenant of the lord's title. The printed Registrum (see f. 164–5) does not contain any such writ, whence we may infer that it went out of use soon after Bracton's day.

[4] Bracton, f. 77 b, 78, 79 b.

[5] Glanvill, ix. 1, 2.

do homage[1]. Homage has implied a willingness to fight if need be, and even when it had become admitted that women might hold military fiefs—here in England they seem, as will be remarked hereafter, to have held such fiefs from the Conquest onwards—they could not say the words which imported an obligation to risk life itself in the lord's service[2]. But all this was passing away, and, despite what Bracton says, it seems to [p. 287] have been common for the socage tenant to do homage[3].

The lord's obligation. The contract was not one-sided. The lord was bound to defend and warrant his gift. When we hear of 'warranty,' we are wont to think of a mere institute of private law common enough at the present day, the obligation of a seller to compensate a buyer who is evicted by superior title, and the covenants for title expressed or implied in our modern purchase deeds appear as the representatives of the ancient warranty. But the primary obligation of the warrantor in old times was not that of making compensation. His obligation to give his tenant a tenement equal in value to that whence he had been ejected was but a secondary obligation arising upon the breach of the primary obligation, namely, the duty of defending the tenant in his possession 'against all men who can live and die.' If the tenant was attacked by process of law, he vouched his lord, he called upon his lord to defend the action, and the lord if he did his duty defended it. Now here we see a great force at work. Do what we may to make all men equal before the law, a rich man has and must always have advantages in litigation; he can command the best advice, the best advocacy. But in the middle ages the advantages of the rich and powerful must have been enormous. Happy then was the tenant who could say to any adverse claimant :—'Sue me if you will, but remember that behind me you will find the earl or the abbot.' Such an answer would often be final. We must understand this if we are to understand the history of commendation. The owner of land who gives it up to a great man and takes it

---

[1] Bracton, f. 78 b, § 4.

[2] In after days, according to Littleton, § 87, when an unmarried woman does homage, she is to say 'I do to you homage,' not 'Jeo devieng vostre feme.' But in the days of real vassalism there would have been no talk of the latter formula ; the question would have been as to 'Jeo devieng vostre homme.'

[3] This seems to have been so even in the twelfth century; see *e.g.* the Burton Cartulary, pp. 30–40.

back to hold by rent and services receives a 'valuable consideration' for the surrender and submission. This is so even
within the sphere of law and litigation; he has made his hold
upon the land secure, for he has at his back a warrantor whom
no one will rashly sue. We must add that he has a lord who
may use carnal weapons or let loose the thunders of the church
in defence of his tenant[1].

§ 7. *Relief and Primer Seisin.*

[p. 288] The lord's rights can not be summed up by saying that he The in-
cidents of
tenure.
is entitled to service of one kind or another from his tenant.
Blackstone in a well-known passage enumerates 'seven fruits
and consequences inseparably incident to the tenure in chivalry,
viz. aids, relief, primer seisin, wardship, marriage, fines for
alienation and escheat[1].' Of all of these we must speak, but we
shall speak of them in a somewhat different order, and in the
course of our discussion we must point out how far they were
peculiar to military tenure.

In the thirteenth century the rights of a person who holds Heritable
rights in
land.
land are usually heritable; when he dies the land will de-
scend to his heir. We must not here discuss the canons of
inheritance; it will be sufficient if we notice a few salient
points. In the first place, the 'heir' of English law is an
essentially different person from the Roman 'heres':—he never
claims under a will. With few exceptions, the broad rule holds
good that no one can give rights in land by his will, and even
in those cases in which such rights are thus given the person
who gets them does not get them as 'heir.' Only God, says
Glanvill, can make an heir, not man[3]. A distinction between
land and movables is thus established; even when the dead
man has not bequeathed his movables, the heir as such has
no claim to them. In the second place, one main rule of the
law of inheritance is the primogenitary rule:—among males
of equal degree only the eldest inherits. This rule has been

---

[1] Round, Ancient Charters, p. 69; Geoffrey Trussel gives an advowson to a
priory and adds 'and if any dispute arise about that church or the possession
thereof, I will come to the aid of the monks to deraign what the church ought
to hold, wheresoever it may be needful, to the best of my power, at their cost and
upon a horse of theirs if I have not got my own.'

[2] Comment. ii. 63.   [3] Glanvill, vii. 1.

gradually extending itself; once appropriate to the military tenures, it is becoming the common law for all. Women can inherit even though the tenure be military; they are postponed to males of equal degree; several women of equal degree will share the inheritance between them, will be coheiresses, *coheredes.* Lastly, though the rights of a tenant of land are usually heritable, this is not always the case; *A* may give land to *B* merely for his (*B*'s) life; on the death of this tenant for life there will be nothing for his heir; the land will 'return' or 'revert' to *A.* But more, to make the rights of the donee heritable rights, the giver must use words which make this [p. 289] plain; if he merely gives the land 'to *B*,' then *B* is only a tenant for life; he must give it 'to *B* and his heirs[1].'

Reliefs.
But the heir, whom we will suppose to be of full age, does not come to his inheritance without having to pay for it; he has to pay to his lord—and this is what concerns us here—a relief (*relevium*, or in earlier documents *relevatio* or *relevamen*). In Glanvill's day the relief for a knight's fee is fixed at 100*s.*; for socage land it is one year's rent; as to baronies and serjeanties, there is no settled rule; the heir must make the best bargain that he can[2]. The Dialogue on the Exchequer tells us that the relief for the knight's fee is 100*s.*; that for the barony is in the king's discretion[3]. Excessive reliefs stood foremost amongst the grievances alleged by the barons in 1215; they asked that the heir should have his inheritance by 'the ancient relief,' which relief was to be defined by the charter. And by the charter of 1215 it was defined; the heir of an earl's barony was to pay £100, the heir of a baron's barony £100, the heir to a knight's fee 100*s.*[4] This was repeated in the charters of 1216, 1217 and 1225; but at some time or another the relief for a baron's barony was reduced by one-third, namely, from £100 to 100 marks, and thus the notion that a barony consists of 13⅓ knights' fees was engendered. The change, however and whenever it was

---

[1] Note Book, pl. 964, 1235, 1811. In the more ancient charters the gift instead of being 'to X and his heirs' is often a gift 'in feudum et hereditatem' or 'hereditario iure possidendum.'

[2] Glanvill, ix. c. 4.   [3] Dial. ii. c. 10, 24.

[4] In 1229 on the death of Hugh Balliol his heir was charged with £150 for thirty fees; afterwards however the relief was reduced and he paid as for a barony; Excerpta e Rot. Fin. i. 183, 212.

introduced, was sanctioned by the charter of Edward I.[1]
Bracton states the law as to earldoms, baronies and knights' fees
in its final form; the relief for serjeants is still in the discretion
of the lords[2]. As to socage, he seems to doubt whether
anything that can properly be called a relief is payable; for
the lord has no wardship of the sokeman's heir, and in general
relief and wardship are connected rights. However, the heir
has to make a certain payment (*quaedam praestatio*), namely,
[p. 290] an additional year's rent. Then as to fee farm, Bracton says
that no fixed rule has been established; but a reasonable
payment should be made, regard being had to the needs of
the lord and the means of the tenant[3]. In Normandy the
relief seems to have had much the same history. In the
oldest statement of Norman law the reliefs of counts, barons
and knights are mentioned but their amount is not defined,
while tenements that are not held by military service are rated
at 5 shillings for the capital messuage and 12 pence per acre
for the land[4]. A little later we read that baronies pay £100
and knights' fees £15[5]. As in England, so in Normandy a
relief was payable by every heir, even though he were the direct
descendant of the dead tenant. This is noteworthy, for, according to a very common French custom, a relief was only exigible
when the land descended to a collateral heir; but in France, as
in England, we often find that one year's rent, or one year's
profit, of the land, is deemed the due relief[6].

[1] See the facsimiles of the various charters in Stat. of the Realm, vol. i.;
and Bémont, Chartes des libertés, pp. xxxi. 47.

[2] Bracton, f. 84 b.

[3] Bracton, f. 85 b, 86. In this passage fee farm is treated as distinct from
socage; by 'socage' Bracton seems here to mean the tenure of the sokemen.
See above p. 294. Britton, ii. 50, agrees that a relief is only due when the
tenure is knight's service or grand serjeanty. So does the apocryphal statute
De wardis et releviis; Statutes of the Realm, i. 228. See also Y.-B. 33–5 Edw. I.
p. 351. However, the additional year's rent payable for socage land was usually
called a relief. Thus on the Fine Rolls of Bracton's day it is common to find a
'relief' paid for socage land held of the king; see Excerpta e Rot. Fin. i. 78,
97, 126, 154; but these are not payments from the king's 'sokemen': the
sokemen would settle their affairs with the manorial bailiffs. Sometimes a
charter of feoffment fixes a conventional relief, and burgage reliefs are sometimes fixed by the borough charter; see *e.g.* Reg. Malmesb. ii. 34.

[4] Très ancien coutumier (ed. Tardif), c. 47.

[5] Ibid. c. 84; Somma, p. 107; Ancienne coutume, c. 34; Delisle, Bibliothèque de l'École des chartes, Sér. III. vol. ii. p. 99. The Norman pound is
worth much less than the English.

[6] D'Arbois de Jubainville, Biblioth. de l'École des chartes, Sér. III. vol. iii.

Rights of
the lord
on the
tenant's
death.

The amount of the due relief is not the only, perhaps not the most important, point that has been in debate. A tenant dies: his heir was living in the same house with him: or his heir was not living on the tenement but at once presents himself: or his heir has gone to the wars, or has gone on pilgrimage: or two claimants appear, each asserting that he is heir: or a stranger intrudes himself into the tenement, setting up a claim as heir, or relying on some title adverse to the ancestor, or on his strong right arm: what in all these [p. 291] cases are the rights of the lord? To simplify the question, What is the general notion of the lord's right—is he entitled to take the land and hold it until the true heir asks for it, does homage and pays relief, or is he only entitled to receive the relief having no concern with the land? There has been a conflict between inconsistent theories representing inconsistent interests. Already in Glanvill's day it is settled that if the heir is in seisin the lord may not turn him out; the heir may resist the lord. Still the lord is entitled to a certain recognition of the fact that, though the tenement belongs to the tenant, it belongs also to the lord; he may enter and go through the ceremony of taking seisin, but he must do no damage[1]. Bracton repeats this: in the case just put the lord may have 'a simple seisin' of the land which does not disturb the heir's seisin. But other cases must be discussed:—for example, at the ancestor's death the heir may be absent, the tenement left vacant. In this case the lord may enter, and then the heir when he appears must not oust the lord by force; if he does so, the lord will have an action against him and will be restored to possession. So again, if there are two rival claimants of the inheritance neither of whom is yet in possession, the lord may enter and hold the land until one of the two has proved his right[2]. We must remember that if no heir appears, the tenement will belong to the lord for good and all; also that if there is a dispute between several would-be heirs, the lord's court is, at least in theory, the proper tribunal for its decision, and the lord who takes homage from a pretender runs great risk in so doing: he may have to warrant that pretender's seisin, unless he has been careful to declare that the homage

pp. 139–142; Viollet, Établissements, i. 160–4; Esmein, Histoire du droit français, 203.

[1] Glanvill, vii. 9; ix. 4.   [2] Bracton, f. 252–3.

is received without prejudice to the rights of other claimants.
A conflict between two sets of proprietary rights, those of the
lord and those of the tenant, is thus complicated by the lord's
jurisdictional powers.   In the struggle which precedes the
Barons' War the grievances of the tenants who stand low in
the feudal scale become audible; and this is one chief
grievance—on the tenant's death the lord enters the tenement and wastes it; the heir can get no damages.   An
[p. 292] attempt to redress this grievance was made by the Provisions
of 1259; a more successful attempt by the Statute of 1267;
the heir is to have damages if the lord does any harm, for if
the heir is forthcoming and in possession of the land, the lord
is entitled to no more than 'a simple' or as we should say a
formal, 'seisin[1].'

But here, as in many other cases, the king is outside the Preroga-
common law.   This is fully recognized by the Statute of tive rights of the king.
Marlborough (1267)[2] and made yet clearer by the document
known as *Praerogativa Regis*[3].   When a tenant in chief of the
crown dies, the king's escheator seizes the land and inquires
who is next heir (*inquisitio post mortem*); not until the heir's
right has been established by inquest, not until he has done
homage, and paid, or given security for, his relief, will he be
put in seisin; and if, impatient of delay, he puts himself in
seisin, this will be a mere intrusion upon the king; for the
king is entitled to the primer seisin (*prima seisina*)[4].   The
machinery for enforcing this right seems to have been slowly
perfected under Henry III.; but there is no room for doubt
that the right itself had been enforced, though perhaps with
less regularity, at a much remoter time[5].   On the Pipe Roll of

[1] See the strikingly antifeudal passage in Bracton, f. 253 b; Note Book,
pl. 348, 1149; Petition of 1258 (Select Charters), cap. 1; Prov. Westm. c 9;
Stat. Marlb. c. 16; Britton, ii. 52 and note by Nichols.   For a picturesque case
of John's day, see Pleas of the Crown (Selden Soc.) pp. 67–75.

[2] Stat. Marl. c. 16.   [3] Statutes of the Realm, i. 226.

[4] In Bracton's day it was said by some that lords in general were entitled to
primer seisin; but Bracton, f. 252 b, thinks this an inaccurate phrase, for the
'simple seisin' to which the mesne lord is entitled is, not prior to, but concurrent with, the seisin of the heir.

[5] Glanvill, ix. 6: whenever the tenant of a barony dies the king seizes his
land.   For the history of the writ *Diem clausit extremum* see Roberts, Excerpta
e Rot. Fin. i. p. ix.   The escheators do not become prominent until the later
years of Henry III.'s reign.

1130 the reliefs that are mentioned are in some cases high[1], and the payment of relief is spoken of as though it were a condition precedent to the enjoyment of the land[2].

Earlier history of reliefs. We are thus brought within seventy years of the Conquest. [p. 293] As to what had happened in that interval, we have two emphatic declarations. Henry I. in his coronation charter said, 'When any of my barons, earls or others, who hold of me shall die, his heir shall not redeem, or buy back (*heres suus non redimet*) his land, as he used to do in the time of my brother, but shall relieve it with a just and lawful relief; and in like wise the men of my barons shall relieve their lands from their lords by a just and lawful relief[3].' In the second place, the chronicler when telling how Rufus kept bishoprics and abbeys vacant and made profit out of their temporalities, adds that he desired to be the heir of every man in England hallowed or lay[4]. We see then that there already was an idea of a just and lawful relief, that William Rufus had exceeded its measure, and had in effect required the heir to purchase his ancestor's land[5]. In order to discover what was the just and lawful relief, we naturally turn to the *Leges* of the time, and we find that the compilers of them consider that the modern relief is but the ancient English heriot under a new name.

Relief and heriot. We are told that the ancient heriot (*heregeatu*, military apparel) had at one time consisted of the horses and arms lent by the lord to his man which on the man's death were returned to the lord. In the laws of Cnut it is said that if by negligence or in consequence of sudden death any one quits this life intestate, the lord shall take no more of his property than his rightful heriot. The heriot of an earl is eight horses,

---

[1] Rot. Pip. p. 9, two hundred marks of silver and one mark of gold; p. 67, two hundred marks of silver.

[2] The phrase often is 'pro terra patris sui'; p. 36, 'ut sit saisitus de terra patris sui'; p. 36, 'ut filius suus hereditetur de terra W. avunculi sui'; p. 106, 'Agnes...reddit compotum de xl. s. ut filii sui hereditentur de terra patris eorum.' It is even allowable to speak of the lord as making the son the heir to his father; thus (temp. Hen. I.) the abbot of Abingdon 'fecit Henricum filium Oini heredem de omnibus quae fuerunt patris sui'; Hist. Abingd. ii. 138.

[3] Charter of Hen. I. c. 2.   [4] A. S. Chron. ann. 1100.

[5] See the curious story in Monast. i. 165. Under William II. the heirs of a man who has entered religion find that they cannot obtain his land without paying heavily, 'erant enim illis diebus consuetudines regis gravissimae'; so they commend themselves and their land to Bishop Gundulf of Rochester, who lends them money.

four saddled and four unsaddled, four helms, four hauberks, eight spears, as many shields, four swords and 200 mancusses of gold; that of a king's immediate thegn (*cyninges þegenes þe him nyhste syndon*) is four horses, two swords, four spears, as many shields, helm, hauberk and 50 mancusses of gold; that for a mesne thegn (*medemra þegna*) a horse and harness, his weapons, and a sum of money[1]. If a man falls before his lord in battle, no heriot is to be demanded[2]. We see from this and from other evidence that it was expected of the thegn that he [p. 294] would make provision for the heriot in his will. Now it is likely that for a long time before William's landing the old theory had ceased to describe the facts; the lord no longer provided armour for his dependent warriors; he gave them land instead, and very possibly the horses, arms and money rendered to the lord on his man's death were by this time considered as a due paid by the heir in respect of the land. At all events the Normans had no difficulty in regarding the heriot as a relief. On the first page of Domesday Book we read how, when a Kentish *alodiarius* dies, the king has the *relevationem terrae*, except on the lands of certain great lords[3]. In Berkshire when a king's own thegn or knight died he used to leave as a relief to the king all his arms and one saddled and one unsaddled horse[4]. In Nottinghamshire a thegn who has more than six manors pays £8 for the relief of his land to the king; if he has but six or fewer, he pays 3 marks to the sheriff[5]; a similar rule prevailed in Yorkshire[6]. But the most instructive entry is that which concerns the English (as opposed to the French) burgesses of Hereford. When a burgess who did service on horseback died, the king used to have his horse and arms; from one who had no horse the king had either 10 shillings or his land with the houses. If he died without a will, the king had all his movables (*pecuniam*)[7]. Probably if we could now unravel the knot of the old English land tenures, we should find that several different 'death duties'—to use a large phrase—proceeding from different principles were becoming intermixed and consolidated, and that this process was hastened by the Norman Conquest. However, it is on the basis of Cnut's law

---

[1] Cnut, II. 70, 71.   [2] Cnut, II. 78.
[3] D. B. i. 1.   [4] Ibid. i. 56 b.
[5] Ibid. i. 280 b.   [6] Ibid. i. 298 b.
[7] Ibid. i. 179; see the same page for the moneyer's *relevamentum.*

about heriots that the compilers of the *Leges* attempt to
construct a law of reliefs. The *Leges Henrici* define the
relevationes of the earl, the king's thegn and the mediate thegn
(*mediocris thayni*) by translating the words of Cnut[1]. The
Leis Williame follow the same model, but add that the relief
of the villein is his best beast, and that a year's rent is the
relief of one who holds land at a yearly rent[2]. Passing by for
the moment this mention of the agricultural classes, we seem
entitled to the inference that Cnut's law appeared as the only [p. 295]
measure by which the 'just and lawful relief' of Henry's
charter could be determined. Of any competing Norman
measure we hear nothing. In Normandy, as in England, the
relief sometimes consisted of the dead man's armour, and was
therefore, in the oldest sense of the word, a 'heriot'[3]. But that
Henry observed, or promised to observe Cnut's law, we may not
infer; its terms were fast becoming obsolete. Perhaps he
considered, and was justified by Norman law in considering,
that, at least in the case of earldoms and baronies, there was
no fixed rule. The reliefs mentioned in the one Pipe Roll of
his reign that has come down to us suggest that he allowed
himself a liberal discretion and paid little regard to the antique
rules about heriots.

Heritabi-
lity of fees
in the Con-
queror's
reign.

We are thus led to the question whether the followers
of the Conqueror who received great gifts of English lands held
those lands heritably. It is certain that they did; but this
answer may require qualification and the difficulty of the
question should be seen. As a matter of fact, their heirs in
some cases succeeded them, and we even find women succeeding
to baronies and military fees. But the number of tenures
existing at a later day that can be traced back to the Conqueror's reign by an unbroken thread of inheritance might easily
be exaggerated. The great honours were frequently falling
into the king's hand by way of escheat. True, that in all or
most cases the cause why the heir did not inherit may have
been the treason or felony of his ancestor, or something that

---

[1] Leg. Hen. c. 14.

[2] Leg. Will. I. c. 20.

[3] Lib. Rub. ii. 647 : of the knights of the bishop of Bayeux it is written :
'Et unusquisque miles debet feodum suum relevare de morte patris sui per xv.
libras Rothomagensis monetae vel per equum et loricam.' Cf. Bouquet, xxiii.
701.

the king chose to treat as such[1].   But this practical precariousness of tenure would check the formation of a law of inheritance
applicable to military fees, and we have to remember that new
canons of inheritance, primogenitary canons, were being evolved.
Primogeniture was new in England, perhaps it was not very
old in Normandy; near the end of the twelfth century both in
England and in Normandy some of the most elementary points
[p. 296] in the new system were still unsettled[2].   Any uncertainty
about the rules of descent would give an opening for the king's
interference[3].   Add to this that the line between office and
property is long an uncertain, fluctuating line.   Are the earldoms, the counties, *comitatus*, to be hereditary; are the sheriffdoms, the vice-counties, *vice-comitatus*, to be hereditary; is the
comes to be the successor of the ancient ealdorman; is the sheriff
to be like the Norman viscount[4]?   And what of the new
castles that the king has erected?   The very *caput honoris*, is
it not a royal fortress?   Any reminiscence of precarious *beneficia*
that was latent in Norman law would bear fruit when such
questions as these had to be answered by a conquering king
who was building up a kingdom for himself and his heirs.   No
doubt his followers believed that they obtained hereditary
estates, though we do not know that they had any warrant for
this belief on parchment.   But they knew that their heirs must
relieve their lands.   What would be the measure and conditions
of the relief, time would show.

And as with the king, so with the mesne lords.   The abbot
of Abingdon soon after the Conquest enfeoffed knights to fill
the places of the thegns who fell at Hastings, regardless of any

Mesne lords and heritable fees.

---

[1] In Normandy before the Conquest disherison seems to have been a common
event and to have given the duke much land of which he could dispose.   See
above p. 71.

[2] This point will be discussed in our chapter on Inheritance.

[3] Thus when the father had lands or 'honours' both in Normandy and
England and left several sons there was a problem to be solved.   It is thus
that Orderic, ii. 405, speaks of the death of William FitzOsbern: 'Guillelmus
Rex eius honorem filiis eius distribuit, Guillelmo Bretolium totamque patris
possessionem in Normannia, et Rogerio Herfordensem comitatum.'   See also
iii. 427 and 455 as to the Beaumont and Grandmesnil inheritances.   Even in
much later days any doubt about the rules of inheritance brought profit to the
king; see as to the Mandeville inheritance, Round, Ancient Charters, p. 97, and
as to the Buckland inheritance, Note Book, pl. 12.

[4] See Stubbs, Const. Hist. i. 295, 390.   Dr Stubbs takes Orderic to task for
not observing distinctions.   May we not infer that those distinctions were not
very obvious?

rights that the heirs of those thegns might have. Perhaps
they were disinherited on the score of what was accounted the
felony of their ancestors. This, however, is not the defence
relied on by the chronicler of the abbey, who was not without
patriotism; the thegns, he thinks, had little enough right to
the possession of lands that had been given to the church.
Then in the days of Rufus one of the new knights died leaving
three daughters; the abbot of the day stoutly denied that
there had been any hereditary feoffment, and at last would
only admit the heiresses and their husbands as tenants for [p. 297]
life on their abjuring all heritable rights[1]. Dare we say that
he was obviously in the wrong? A historian of law may easily
credit his characters with too much foresight; the truth is that
men gave lands and took lands and left the terms of the tenure
to be decided thereafter by the course of events and their own
strong wills[2]. And so the *feoda* of the Norman reigns are
indubitably hereditary: the very word is beginning to imply,
even if it does not already clearly denote, heritability; but
the lord has rights and to define them is difficult. The past
history of the *precaria* which became *beneficia*, the *beneficia*
which became *feoda*, the evolution of primogenitary rules,
the conquest of England and consequent clash of laws, the
ever renewed 'treasons' and 'felonies' perpetrated by the
barons, all tended to keep the matter in uncertainty, and
when finally the king's rights emerge into clear daylight,
they are large: the heir of the baron must make the best
bargain that he can. To ascribe the law of reliefs and
primer seisins to the covetousness of Rufus and the cunning
of Flambard is to look only at the surface.

History of
the heriot.　　The heriot was not suppressed by the relief, though in
course of time it underwent a transformation. Glanvill tells
us that the free man who makes a will is bound to 'recognize'
his lord with the best and principal thing that he has and then
to 'recognize' the church[3]. Bracton repeats this: the lord
should have the best chattel, the church the second best, or
the third best, or it may be the church is entitled to nothing,

---

[1] Hist. Abingd. ii. 35.

[2] Early in the twelfth century the abbot of Burton grants land to one Orm;
the charter provides that on Orm's death his son shall have the land on paying
' pro relevatione ipsius terrae tantum pecuniae quantum nobilis homo dare debet
pro tali terra'; Burton Cart. p. 30.

[3] Glanvill, vii. 5.

for customs vary[1]. This will remind us of the gifts of arms
and money made to the king by his thegns in the old days
with a request that their wills may be allowed 'to stand.'
Elsewhere Bracton calls these testamentary gifts to the lords
'heriots'; he tells us that the lord gets them by grace rather
than by right, that they are regulated by local customs, that
they do not touch the inheritance and that they must not
be compared to reliefs. Britton adds that in general they
are paid rather by villeins than by freemen[2]. Turning to
manorial surveys, we find it among the commonest of customs
that when a tenant in villeinage dies, the lord shall have the
best beast; sometimes a similar due is taken from the goods
of the dead freeholder, and it is to these customary dues that
the name 'heriot' permanently attaches itself. Occasionally
we still hear of the freeholder's horse and armour going to
his lord; but far more commonly the tenement that is burdened by a heriot is a peasant's holding, the lord gets the best
ox, and in this case the term *heriot* must in the eyes of the
etymologist be inappropriate[3]. We may guess that in the
heriot of the later middle ages no less than four ancient
elements have met :—(1) the warrior who has received arms
from his lord should on his death return them; (2) the peasant
who has received the stock on his farm from his lord should
return it, and if his representatives are allowed to keep it,
they must recognize the lord's right to the whole by yielding
up one article and that the best; (3) all the chattels of a
serf belong in strictness of law to his lord and the lord takes
the best of them to manifest his right; (4) in the infancy
of testamentary power it has been prudent, if not necessary,
that the would-be testator, however high his rank, should
purchase from the king or some other lord that favour and
warranty without which his bequests will hardly 'stand.' But
at any rate in course of time the heriot is separated from the
relief.

[p. 298]

If a relief is payable when the original tenant dies and
his heir takes up the inheritance, should not a similar payment be made when the original lord dies? We are told
that, in the early days of the vassalic *beneficium*, the death

Relief on
the lord's
death.

---

[1] Bracton, f. 60.

[2] Bracton, f. 86 ; Fleta, p. 212 ; Britton, ii. 51.

[3] Vinogradoff, Villainage, p. 161.

of either party to the contract put an end to the tenancy,
and on the continent the new lord on succeeding to his
ancestor could often exact a payment from the tenant[1]. A
remarkable document has come down to us in which William
Rufus fixes the *relevamen* which is to be paid to him by the
knights of the episcopal barony of Worcester; Hugh de Lacy
is to pay £20, Gilbert FitzTurold 100 shillings, the Abbot
of Evesham £30, and so forth. The occasion of the relief
seems this, that the bishop of Worcester is dead and Rufus [p. 299]
chooses to regard himself as the successor of St Wulfstan,
since the temporalities of the see are in his hand; 'for he
would be the heir of every man whether hallowed or lay'[2].
This we may regard as an act of oppression, but the legal
excuse for it probably is that a relief is due from the tenants
to their new lord. Of such payments we do not hear much
more under the name of reliefs; but in Normandy one of the
regular 'aids' payable to the lord was an aid towards helping
him to pay his own relief; half the relief that he had to pay
he might obtain from his tenants by way of aid[3]. In England
we do not reckon this among the regular aids, but Glanvill
distinctly sanctions the lord's claim[4], and we may see that
the new bishop or abbot often expected that his knights and
other tenants would 'recognize' him handsomely when he
entered into possession of his temporalities[5].

§ 8. *Wardship and Marriage.*

Wardship
and
marriage.

Of great and increasing importance as men grow wealthier
and begin to traffic in all manner of rights, are the rights of
the lord to wardship (*custodia, warda*) and marriage (*maritagium*), and these have been among the chief causes of
that classification of tenures which has come before us.

---

[1] Schröder, D. R. G., 392; German feudists distinguish the two cases as
Mannsfall and *Herrnfall*.

[2] Heming, Cart. p. 79; Round, Feudal England, 308.

[3] Très ancien coutumier, c. 47–8; Somma, p. 109.

[4] Glanvill, ix. 8.

[5] Thus in 1182 the newly-made abbot Samson demanded an aid from his
knights, and being dissatisfied with what they offered, took occasion to pay
them out for their illiberality; Jocelin of Brakelond, p. 20. The Bishop of
Ely in Edward I.'s day attempts to exact a recognition of this sort from his
freeholders: Y.-B. 33–5 Edw. I., pp. 135, 139.

In Bracton's day they had reached their full stature.   Their
nature may be illustrated by a simple case.   A tenant, who has
but one tenement, and who holds it by knight's service or
military serjeanty[1] of a mesne lord, dies leaving as heir a son
who is under the age of twenty-one years.   The lord will have
the wardship of the land until the heir attains that age or dies
without having attained it.   He will take the rents and profits
of the tenement for his own use, but ought thereout to pro-
[p. 300] vide for the youth's maintenance and pay the dead man's
debts[2]; he must not commit waste; if he does so, he forfeits
the wardship[3].   But, besides the wardship of the land, he
will be entitled to the wardship of the body of the heir; if
the heir escapes from his custody, if another takes the heir
from his custody, this is a wrong to him; by legal process he
can compel the restoration of the heir's body[4].   But further,
as guardian of the heir's body he is entitled to the boy's
'marriage'; he can sell him in marriage[5]; but the marriage
must not be of a disparaging kind[6].   The law does not go
so far as actively to constrain the ward to marry the mate
provided by the guardian, nor does it declare null a marriage
solemnized without the lord's consent, though we have a hint
that early in Henry III.'s reign such an union might not
have all those legal results that a marriage usually has[7].   The
maxim was admitted, strange as this may seem to us, that
'marriages should be free',[8] and the church would neither have
solemnized nor annulled a sacrament at the bidding of the lay
tribunals.   Still if the ward married without the lord's consent, he wronged the lord, and so did any one who took part
in procuring such a marriage[9].   Without making any great

---

[1] Bracton, f. 35 b; Note Book, pl. 758.

[2] Glanvill, vii. 9; Bracton, f. 87.   The duty of paying debts is gradually
shifted from the heir to the executor.

[3] Note Book, pl. 485, 717, 1840.

[4] Note Book, pl. 256, 349, 812, 1131, cases before Stat. Merton.   In pl. 1608
we find that it might be dangerous for an abbess to receive a young lady as a
nun.

[5] Sometimes, even in pleadings, this is frankly stated; 'Adam dicit...quod
vendidit ei predictam Emmam cum terra sua': Note Book, pl. 270.

[6] Charter of 1215, c. 6; Stat. Mert. c. 7; Petition of 1258, c. 6.

[7] In Note Book, pl. 965, it is suggested that a woman, who has married a
ward without his lord's consent, ought not to have dower.

[8] Bracton, f. 89, quotes this maxim, 'Libera debent esse coniugia.'

[9] Note Book, pl. 1286, *Quare permisit se maritari* after the Statute; pl. 1280.

change in the substantive law, the Statute of Merton (1236) defined the lord's right by giving him new and efficient remedies:—the current of legislation had in this instance set in his favour.

Wardship of female heirs.

If the heir was a woman, the lord's right of wardship was much the same; but whether the wardship of a woman was to endure until she attained the age of twenty-one, or was to cease when she attained the age of fourteen, seems to have been a moot point[1]. Marriage with her lord's consent put [p. 301] an end to the wardship of a woman. But according to old law, which Bracton regarded as still in force, no woman holding by military service could lawfully marry without her lord's consent, and even a father holding by military service could not in his lifetime lawfully give his daughter in marriage without his lord's consent[2]. This right the king rigorously enforces over widows who hold of him in chief; to marry such a widow without the king's licence is a grave offence[3]. The lord's rights, it will be understood, were proof against any claim on the part of even the nearest of kin; the heir fell into the lord's hands even though his mother were alive. An apparent exception existed when the heir inherited from his mother while his father was living; but this was hardly an exception, for in this case the father, according to an opinion that was gradually prevailing, continued in possession of his late wife's land, not as guardian of the heir, but in his own right[4].

Priority among lords.

If the dead man held by knight's service or military serjeanty of several mesne lords, each of them got the wardship of the tenement that was holden of him. As to which of them should have the wardship of the heir's body and with it the right of marriage, there was intricate law; the general rule traced back the titles under which the dead man held the various tenements and preferred that lord from whom, or from whose ancestors, the most ancient title was derived; that lord

Quare maritavit after the Statute; pl. 1090, 1596, *Quare duxit in uxorem* against husband of ward before the Statute; pl. 1278, the same after the Statute.

[1] Bracton, f. 86 b. As the text now stands we are left in some doubt about Bracton's own opinion. In later times the law was found in Stat. Westm. I. c. 22.

[2] Glanvill, vii. 12; Bracton, f. 88.

[3] See *e.g.* Excerpta e Rot. Fin. ii. 149.

[4] Note Book, pl. 266; Bracton, f. 89 b.

would usually have been, not merely the dead man's lord, but his liege lord[1].

If the dead man held his one tenement in socage, burgage, or fee farm, or by a non-military serjeanty, his lord had no right to wardship or marriage: such was the general rule. As a matter of fact, however, we find socage tenure subjected to these burdens. This seems to have been the case throughout the bishop of Winchester's barony[2]; the dean and chapter of Hereford claimed wardship of the heirs of all their freehold tenants[3]; the archbishop of Canterbury, the prior of Christ Church, the monks of Dover claimed the same right over the heirs of their gavelkinders[4]. This Bracton regarded as an abuse, though one that might be sanctioned by prescription[5]. The ordinary rule was that the guardianship both of the land and of the child should go to the nearest of those relations who could have no hope of inheriting the land. Thus, in the common case, when the dead tenant in socage left a son and a widow, the widow would have the wardship of her son and of his land; she would be 'guardian in socage,' for she never could be his heir. To state the main upshot of the rule—maternal kinsfolk have the wardship of a paternal inheritance, paternal kinsfolk of a maternal inheritance[6]. When the heir attained his fifteenth year, guardianship in socage came to an end[7]. If the dead man held one tenement by knight's service, another by socage, the wardship of the one would belong to its lord, that of the other to a kinsman of the heir; as to the wardship of the heir's body, this and his marriage would belong to the lord of whom he held by military tenure[8].

What tenures give wardship.

Once more we see the king above the common rules[9]. If the dead man held in chief of the crown by knight's service or by grand serjeanty, the king was entitled to the wardship of the heir's body and to his marriage, no matter how many other lords there might be, and no regard being had to the relative antiquity of the various titles by which the tenements were

Prerogative wardship.

[p. 302]

---

[1] Note Book, pl. 661, 868, 906; Bracton, f. 89 b.

[2] Bracton, f. 85 b, 88; 'in episcopatu Wintoniae' probably means not the diocese but the barony of the bishop.

[3] Note Book, pl. 990.　　　[4] Rot. Hund. i. 202-231.

[5] Bracton, f. 85 b.　　　[6] Bracton, f. 87 b.

[7] Glanvill, vii. 9; Bracton, f. 86 b.　　　[8] Bracton, f. 88.

[9] Glanvill, vii. 10; Bracton, f. 87 b; Note Book, pl. 743, 908, 1221, 1200.

holden : no one can compete with the king. But further, the king was entitled to the wardship of all the lands which this dead man held, no matter of whom he held them. Such was the right of 'prerogative wardship,' and a clause in the Great Charter had been necessary to keep it within these spacious bounds[1]. The king was thereby excluded from a prerogative wardship when the tenement holden in chief of the crown was holden in socage, burgage, fee farm or by a petty serjeanty. He was also excluded when the dead man, though a tenant in chief of the king, held not 'as of the crown' but 'as of an [p. 303] honour' which was temporarily or permanently in the king's hands. It is this last rule that chiefly serves to establish a difference between tenure *ut de corona* and tenure *ut de honore*[2].

The lord's rights vendible. The guardian's rights in the person, in the marriage, in the lands of the heir are regarded as property; they are saleable, assignable rights; large sums are paid for the wardships and marriages of wealthy heirs[3]; indeed so thoroughly proprietary and pecuniary are these rights that they can be disposed of by will; they pass like chattels to the guardian's executors[4]. In Bracton's day no distinction in this respect seems drawn between the guardian in chivalry and the guardian in socage. Neither one nor the other need account to the heir for the profits of the land; the one like the other can sell the ward's marriage[5]. This was so until the eve of the Barons' War, when one of the Provisions of Westminster, afterwards confirmed by the Statute of Marlborough, laid down the rule that the guardian in socage must, when the heir has attained majority, account to him or her for the profits of the land, and is not to give or sell the ward in marriage save to the profit of the ward[6]. This should be had in mind if we are to understand the rights of the guardian in chivalry. The morality of the twelfth century saw nothing shameful in the sale of a marriage;

---

[1] Charter of 1215, cc. 37, 43.   [2] See above, p. 281.

[3] Geoffrey de Mandeville promises John 20,000 marks for the Countess of Gloucester and her land : Rot. Obl. p. 520.

[4] The treatment of a wardship as a chattel can be traced to the early years of Henry III.; Excerpta e Rot. Fin. i. 163, 177, 230, 234.

[5] Bracton, f. 89 : 'Si autem cum heres infra aetatem extiterit et sub custodia parentum de sokagio, propinquior consanguineus eum maritare poterit sine alicuius iniuria vel aliis vendere maritagium.'

[6] Prov. Westm. (1259), c. 12 ; Stat. Marlb. (1267), c. 17.

the law of the time looked upon guardianship as a profitable right and would hardly have had the means of compelling a guardian to render accounts, even had it wished so to do[1].

One small point remains to be mentioned. It is the law Wardship and the serjeanties. [p. 304] about wardships and marriages that gradually divides the serjeanties into two classes, known as 'grand' and 'petty.' In the Great Charter, John was forced to say that he would claim no prerogative wardship in respect of 'any small serjeanty such as that of supplying us with knives or arrows or the like[2].' The term 'small serjeanty' seems one which is not yet technical, and the nature of those serjeanties which are too trivial to justify the royal claim is indicated in the rudest manner. In Bracton's day one opinion would have applied a merely pecuniary test; a great serjeanty is one that is worth 100 shillings[3]; but gradually a different line seems to have been drawn: the tenant by grand serjeanty must do his service in person, and his service must not consist of a mere render[4]. Another question was whether tenure by serjeanty of a mesne lord would give the lord wardship and marriage. Here also a line had to be drawn, but where it should be drawn was a question between Raleigh and Segrave. The 'rodknight's' serjeanty of riding with his lord, will this give wardship and marriage? Raleigh decided that it would; Segrave dissented. Bracton seems inclined to hold that the lord's rights only arise when the serjeanty is one which concerns the defence of the realm[5].

Looking back from Bracton to Glanvill we see but little The law in Glanvill. change. In his treatment of these matters Bracton has but revised and expanded his forerunner's text[6]. The Statute of Merton has at a few points given a sharper edge to the lord's rights; the Great Charter has suppressed some abuses which

---

[1] Coke, 2 Inst. 135, regards the chapter of the Statute of Marlborough touching guardianship in socage as a 'declaration of the common law'; but he did not know the Provisions of Westminster and has no warrant for his doctrine. An action of account was a very new action in 1259. Events seem to have taken the same course in Germany; the guardian is gradually made accountable; a profitable right, *tutela usufructuaria*, is turned into a trust; Schröder, D. R. G., 713.

[2] Charter of 1215, c. 37.

[3] Bracton, f. 87 b.

[4] Note Book, pl. 743, 1183, 1231, 1270, 1280.

[5] Bracton, f. 35 b, 87 b; Note Book, pl. 758.

[6] Reeves, Hist. Engl. Law, ed. 1814, i. 284, has noticed this.

had grown up under Richard and John, in the main abuses of
the prerogatival rights. To speak of the English lords as
groaning under the burdens of wardship and marriage is hardly
permissible[1]; we do not hear their groans. In the days of
their power, in 1215 and in 1258, they had little to suggest; it
was enough that the heir's land should not be wasted, that
wards should not be married below their station[2]. Certainly [p. 305]
there was at one time a tradition that in or about the year 1222
'the magnates of England granted to King Henry the wardship
of their heirs and of their lands, which was the beginning of
many evils in England[3].' This story, however, has not been
traced beyond chronicles which in this context must be styled
modern, and as it is absolutely certain that the king's right
to wardship was much older than Henry III.'s day, we may
well doubt whether there is even a grain of truth in the
tale[4]. More important is it for us to notice with many recent
writers that Glanvill says nothing about the lord's right to the
marriage of a male ward; he speaks only of the marriages of
women. This is remarkable, but we can not adopt the popular
opinion that this new right, if new we must call it, 'was based
simply on a strained construction of the general word *heredes*
in a section of Magna Carta[5].' We can trace the sale of the
marriages of boys back to a very few years after Glanvill's
death; in 1193 the bishop of Ely, William Longchamp, for 220
marks buys from the king the wardship of Stephen Beauchamp
and the right to marry him wherever he may please[6]. Such
transactions are common enough throughout the reigns of
Richard and John. Archbishop Hubert gives 4,000 marks for
the wardship and marriage of Robert Stuteville, though the
king reserves a certain veto on the choice of a bride[7]. If two
men who have filled the office of chief justiciar invest their

---

[1] Freeman, William Rufus, i. 335: 'burthens and exactions under which
Englishmen, and pre-eminently the rich and noble among Englishmen, groaned
for not much less than six hundred years after Flambard's day.'

[2] Articles of the Barons, c. 3, 27; Charter of 1215, c. 4, 5, 6, 37; Petition
of 1258, c. 2, 3.

[3] Higden, Polychron. viii 202; Chron. de Melsa, i. 443.

[4] Selden, Notes on Fortescue, cap. 44.

[5] Digby, Hist. of Real Property, ch. iii. sec. i. § 3; Blackstone, Comment.
ii. 71.

[6] Madox, Exch. i. 323–5.

[7] Rot. Cart. 108: see also ibid. 27, 48, 104, 116, 120. See Hardy's Introduction to the Oblate and Fine Rolls, p. xxxvi.

money thus, the security is fairly good.   We must suspect that under Henry II. the sale of the male ward's marriage was a growing practice.   As to earlier days, the one extant Pipe Roll of Henry I.'s reign shows us the king selling wardships[1], [p.306] and selling the marriages of women[2]; it seems to show that even the male ward could not lawfully marry without his lord's consent[3].

Then however in our backward progress we come to the declaration of Henry I. in his coronation charter:—'If any of my barons or other men wishes to give his daughter, or sister, or niece, or cousin in marriage, let him speak with me; but I will neither take anything of his for the licence, nor will I forbid him to give her away, unless it be to an enemy of mine. And if on the death of one of my barons or other men he leaves a daughter as heir, I will give her with her land by the counsel of my barons.   If he leaves a widow, who is without children, she shall have her dower and marriage portion, and I will not give her in marriage against her will.   If she has children, she shall have her dower and marriage portion while she remains chaste, and I will not give her unless with her consent.   And the wife or some other relative who has the best claim shall be guardian of the land and of the children.   And I bid my barons keep within the same bounds as regards the sons, daughters and wives of their men[4].'   That Henry made these promises is certain, that he broke them is equally certain; but here again, as in the matter of reliefs, the question arises whether his promises represent the old law as it stood before the tyranny of Rufus and Flambard, or whether he is buying

Earlier law.

---

[1] Pipe Roll, *e.g.* p. 37, 'pro custodia terrae W. donec heres suus possit terram tenere'; p. 66, 'Uxor Walteri filii Goduini et Robertus frater Goduini... ut habeant in custodia terram et pueros ipsius Walteri'; p. 83, 'pro custodia filii W. de D. cum terra sua.'   In 1121 Henry I. grants 'Sibilla daughter of Bernard of Neufmarché and her land' to Miles of Gloucester; Round, Ancient Charters, p. 8.

[2] Pipe Roll, *e.g.* p. 8, 'ut ducat in uxorem sororem Ilberti de Laci'; p. 43, 'pro Cecilia filia Alani...cum dote et maritagio suo'; p. 66, 'pro terra et filia R. de C. ad opus Hugonis nepotis sui'; p. 81, 'pro uxore Eduardi de Sar[isbiria] cum terra sua ad opus Pagani filii sui'; p. 92, 'ut mater sua duceret virum ad electum suum'; p. 136, 'pro uxore W. F. cum dote sua'; p. 96, 'ne capiat virum nisi quem voluerit.'

[3] Ibid. p. 8, 'ut Rex concedat ei ducere uxorem'; p. 26, 'ut ducat uxorem ad velle suum.'

[4] Charter of Hen. I. c. 3, 4.

support by relaxations of ancient rules. The question is
difficult, for of the Conqueror's practice we know little, and
of the Norman law of the eleventh century we know, if that
be possible, less.

Norman
law.　　　In later days, Norman law and English law agree; they
agree even in some of the minuter details of prerogative
wardship, for as in England no lord can compete with the
king, so in Normandy none can compete with the duke.
Perhaps under French dominion some of the worst characteristics of the Anglo-Norman law were mitigated. In Glanvill's [p. 307]
day the rule that a ward might not lawfully marry without
the lord's consent was applied in Normandy to male as well
as to female wards; in later statements of the rule we hear
only of female wards[1]. From a Norman lawyer, a contemporary
of Glanvill, we have, what no English lawyer gives us, namely,
a defence of the law, and a curious defence it is:—'A fatherless
heir must be in ward to some one. Who shall be his guardian?
His mother? No. Why not? She will take another husband
and have sons by him, and they, greedy of the heritage, will
slay their firstborn brother, or the step-father will slay his
step-son. Who then shall be the guardian? The child's blood
kinsmen? No. Why not? Lest, thirsting for his heritage,
they destroy him. For the prevention of such faithless cruelty,
it is established that the boy be in ward to one who was bound
to his father by the tie of homage. And who is such an one?
The lord of the land who never can inherit that land in
demesne; for heirs of a noble race always have many heirs.
Besides they should be brought up in good houses and honourably educated. Those who are brought up in their lords' houses
are the apter to serve their lords faithfully and love them in
truth ; and the lords can not look with hatred on those whom
they have reared, but will love them and faithfully guard their
woods and tenements and apply the profits of their land to
their advancement.' As to prerogative wardship, the duke,
who is bound to rule all his people, is more especially bound
to have a care for the orphan[2].

The
Norman
apology.　　　That this quaint apology is mere nonsense we are not
entitled to say. There was a strong feeling that to commit

---

[1] Très ancien coutumier, c. 11; Somma, p. 101 ff.; Ancienne coutume, c. 33;
Delisle, Bibl. de l'École des chartes, sér. III. vol. iii. p. 99.

[2] Très ancien coutumier, p. 10.

the care of a child to the custody of his expectant heir was to
set the wolf to guard the lamb.   Fortescue, when he sang the
lauds of the laws of England, made boast of the wisdom of
our rules about socage guardianship.   Some French customs
managed the matter yet more prudently, giving the custody
of the lands to those who might inherit, the custody of the
child's person to those who could not inherit from him.   Still
we can not regard the rights of English and Norman lords
[p. 308] as instituted for the protection of infant life, or for the
advancement of the ward by education in a 'good house,'
though here we may see some set-off for what we are wont to
regard as tyrannous exactions.   The real question is whether
we are entitled to find the explanation of the English and
Norman, and (it should be added) the Scottish, law of wardship
in the ancient history of the precarious *beneficium*.

The history of the law has been pictured thus:—Gradually Origin
of these
rights.
the 'benefice' lost its precarious character; it became a
usufruct for the tenant's life; the heirs male of his body,
if competent to perform the lord's service, acquired first a
claim, then a right to succeed him; female heirs, collateral
heirs, were slowly admitted; even an infant heir has a claim
to succeed, a claim to succeed hereafter when he shall be
able to serve the lord; meanwhile the lord will hold the
land and train the heir.   As to female heirs, if they are
to be admitted at all, it is certain that they must not
marry without their lord's consent.   Gradually tenants at
will are making themselves absolute owners.   The English
and Norman law of the twelfth century represent a particular
stage in this process.   In the duchy, in the island kingdom,
under pressure of strong government, customs have crystallized
at an early time, while the financial necessities of the king,
the wealth of his subjects, the early development of commercial
ideas, give to the law its most repulsive features:—if any
one has a right in England, that right must be a saleable
commodity.   When French and German law become definite
in the thirteenth century they represent a later stage in the
transformation of the *beneficium*; yet further encroachments
have been made upon the lord's rights, though of their once
wider compass there are many memorials.   The lord has a
certain influence on the choice of the heir's guardian; he
confers the fief upon the guardian and sees that his own

rights are not thereby impaired; if no kinsman is forthcoming, then he keeps the fief in his own hands; he has also a word to say about the marriage of his female tenants. These French and German phenomena find their best explanation in the law of England and Normandy[1].

The precarion *beneficium.* How far this hypothetical history can be verified in the [p. 309] scanty annals of the Norman duchy is a question about which we dare say no more than has been said above[2]. There seems however to be just enough evidence to show that the Conqueror both in Normandy and in England expected that he would be consulted before any of his female tenants in chief—he had but few—took to herself a husband, and, as already remarked, the inheritance of great fiefs, at least where an office was bound up with the land, was not altogether beyond his control[3]. There were cases in his own family which might support such a claim; had not Richard the Fearless been in ward to his lord King Louis: had not William himself been claimed by King Henry? Men said so[4]. If the kings of the French had been compelled to abandon all hopes of contesting the heritability of the great fiefs, they had yielded slowly and reluctantly, and perhaps had hardly yet brought themselves to acknowledge the full import of the unpleasant facts[5]. The king of the English was to be not less of a king than the king of the French, and rights of wardship and marriage were necessary to him if he

---

[1] Hallam, Middle Ages, ed. 1837, vol. i. pp. 189-191, and Freeman, William Rufus, i, 340, remark the peculiar severity of English and Norman law. As to Germany, see Schröder, D. R. G. 405. As to France, D'Arbois de Jubainville, Recherches sur la minorité et ses effets dans le droit féodal français, Bibl. de l'École des chartes, sér. iii. vol. ii. p. 415, vol. iii. 136, 533; Viollet, Histoire du droit civil français, 536; Luchaire, Manuel des institutions françaises, 209; Esmein, Histoire du droit français, 211.

[2] See above, p. 71.

[3] See Orderic, ii. 409: 'Praefatus Guillelmus [de Molinis] Gualterii de Talesia filius fuit et in militia nimium viguit; unde Guillelmus Princeps filiam Guidmundi cum toto ei honore Molinensi contulit.' Florence, an. 1074: 'Herefordensis comes Rogerus, filius Willelmi eiusdem pagae comitis, East-Anglorum comiti Radulfo, contra praeceptum regis Willelmi, sororem suam coniugem tradidit.' So of St Wulfstan we have this story: 'Hanc terram tenuit Sirof de episcopo [de Wirecestre] T. R. E. quo mortuo dedit episcopus filiam eius cum hac terra cuidam suo militi qui et matrem pasceret et episcopo inde serviret'; D. B. i. 173. [4] See above, p. 71.

[5] Luchaire, Institutions monarchiques, ii. 17, fixes on the date of the Norman Conquest of England as that at which the French kings may be said to have finally abandoned all hope of controlling the inheritance of the great fiefs.

was to keep any hold upon his feudatories. The use or abuse
of such rights for merely fiscal purposes may begin at a later
time; but there the rights were. As to the mesne lords, they
seem to have taken the first opportunity that occurred of
asserting similar rights; in the reign of Rufus the abbot
of Abingdon was already claiming the wardship of an infant
tenant[1]. On the whole it seems to us that the old is the true
[p. 310] story, and that the rights of wardship and marriage are, if we
look at Europe as a whole, the outcome of a process which is
benefiting the feudatory at the expense of his lord, though it
may also be reducing to the level of feudatories men whose
predecessors had no landlords above them. Unfortunately in
England feudalism itself becomes commercial.

§ 9. *Restraints on Alienation.*

In the middle of the thirteenth century the tenant enjoyed
a large power of disposing of his tenement by act *inter vivos*,
though this was subject to some restraints in favour of his
lord. About the history of these restraints different opinions
have been held. The old English tradition, represented by
Coke, regarded it as a process by which limits were gradually
set to ancient liberty[2]. On the other hand, the cosmopolitan
'learning of feuds,' which Blackstone made popular, assumed
the inalienability of the fief as a starting point:—gradually
the powers of the tenant grew at the expense of the lord[3]. Of
late years a renewed attention to the English authorities has
occasioned a reaction in favour of Coke's doctrine[4]. The
evidence deserves a patient examination, the result of which
may be that we shall see some truth in both of the rival
opinions, and come to the conclusion that the controversy has
been chiefly occasioned by an attempt, common to all parties,
to make the law of the Norman reigns more definite than really
it was.

Historical theories about the power of alienation.

---

[1] Hist. Abingd. ii. 23.
[2] Coke, 2nd Inst. 65; Co. Lit. 43 a.
[3] Wright, Tenures, 154; Gilbert, Tenures, 51–2; Blackstone, Com. ii. 71–2.
[4] Report on Dignity of a Peer, 398–401; Digby, Hist. Real Property, ch. iii.
sec. 2; Scrutton, Land in Fetters, 41; Challis, Real Property, 2nd ed. p. 13.
See however, Williams, Real Property, ed. 18, p. 65 ff.

Some distinctions must first be drawn. The tenant may desire to alienate the whole, or only some part of the tenement, by substituting for himself some new tenant who will hold the tenement, or the part so alienated, of his, the alienator's, lord; or again, he may desire to add a new rung to the bottom of the scale of tenure, to have a tenant who will hold the whole or part of the land of him, and in this case the services for which he stipulates may be different from those by which he himself holds of his lord;—we have to contrast 'substitution' and 'subinfeudation[1].' Now each of these two processes may harm [p. 311] the lord, but the harm done by the one will, to a lawyer's eye, be different from that done by the other. First, however, we have to notice that nothing that the tenant can do without his lord's concurrence will remove from the land the burden of that service which is due to his lord from him and from it. The tenement itself owes the service; the 'reality,' if we may so speak, of the burden can be brought home by means of distress to any one into whose hands the land may come. But though this be so, an alienation of any kind may make against the lord's interest. If a new is substituted for an old tenant, a poor may take the place of a rich, a dishonest that of an honest man, a foe that of a friend, and the solemn bond of homage will be feeble if the vassal has a free power of putting another man in his room. If the substitution affects part only of the tenement, the lord may suffer in another way, and it is hardly to be supposed that he can be bound by an apportionment of the service effected without his concurrence, so that instead of being able to look to one man and six hides for his scutage or rent, he can be compelled to look to one man and four hides for two-thirds of it, to another man and two hides for the residue[2]. The harm done by subinfeudation is of a different kind. There will still be the old tenant liable as before; on his death the lord will get a relief or possibly a wardship and marriage, on his death without heirs, an escheat. These rights will not be destroyed by the subinfeudation, but their value may be seriously lessened. Suppose that *A* enfeoffed *B* to hold by knight's service, and that *B* enfeoffed *C* to hold at a rent of a pound of pepper; *B* dies leaving an heir within age;

---

[1] In the course of this discussion it will be convenient to use the term *alienation* to cover both *alienation by way of substitution* and *subinfeudation*.

[2] Bracton, f. 395: 'particularis solutio multa habet incommoda.'

A is entitled to a wardship; but it will be worth very little: instead of being entitled to enjoy the land itself until the heir is of age, he will get a few annual pounds of pepper. And so in case of an escheat, instead of enjoying the land for ever he may have but a trifling rent[1]. Obviously the case is at its worst [p. 312] when the tenant makes a gift in frankalmoin; a wardship will now be of no value at all; an escheat will give but a nominal seignory over a corporation which pays no rent, which never dies, nor marries, nor commits felony. Still, it is plausible to say with Bracton, that the lord is not injured; his rights remain what they were, though their value is diminished; he suffers *damnum*, but there is no *iniuria*[2].

Also in our investigation we must keep our eyes open to differences between the various tenures. As just said, a gift in frankalmoin, though a very common, is yet an extreme case; it reduces the value of the feudal casualties to nothing. Tenure by serjeanty again may require special treatment, for is a servant to alienate the fund which should sustain him in his lord's service? Lastly, though pure feudal theory can draw no distinction between the king and other lords, still we have already seen that the English king has very exceptional rights within the feudal sphere. Even if no exceptional rules were applied to him, still his position would be unique. Too often in discussions of questions about feudal law we are wont to speak of lords and tenants as though they were two different classes of persons with conflicting interests. Therefore it is necessary to remember that the king was the only person who was always lord and never tenant; that his greatest feudatories had one interest as lords, another as tenants; that the baron, who did not like to see his vassals creating new sub-tenancies, could not forget that he himself had

Preliminary distinctions.

----

[1] Escheat of a mesne lordship gives rise to some pretty problems discussed by Bracton, f. 23 b (the passage is an 'addicio'):—*A* enfeoffs *B* at a rent of 10 shillings; *B* enfeoffs *C* at a rent of 5 shillings; *B* dies without an heir; is *A* entitled to 5, or 10, or 15 shillings a year? In favour of 15 it may be said that 10 are due to him under his feoffment of *B*, and 5 more because he now fills *B*'s place; but Bracton decides in favour of 10. Again, *A* enfeoffs *B* at a rent of 5; *B* enfeoffs *C* at a rent of 10; *B* dies without an heir; Bracton thinks that *A* is entitled to 10. On f. 48 he treats as an insoluble puzzle the question whether *A* is entitled to the wardship of *C*'s heir, if *C* held of *B* in socage, and *B*, whose rights have escheated to *A*, held of *A* by knight's service.

[2] Bracton, f. 45 b, 46.

a lord. The conflict of interests takes place within the mind of every magnate of the realm, and the result is that the development of definite law is slow.

This premised, we turn to our history, and first to that part of it which lies within legal memory; of the earlier time we shall be better able to speak when we have seen its outcome. Now the main facts of which account must be taken are as [p. 313] follows:

Glanvill.   (1) Glanvill nowhere says that the tenant can not alienate his land without his lord's consent, though, as he speaks at some length of the restraints on alienation that are set by the rights of expectant heirs, he has an excellent opportunity for saying that the rights of the lord also must be considered[1].

The Great Charter.   (2) The Great Charter of 1217 is the first document of a legislative kind that expressly mentions any restraint in favour of the lord. It says—'No free man shall henceforth give or sell so much of his land as that out of the residue he may not sufficiently do to the lord of the fee the service which pertains to that fee[2].' This has all the appearance of being a rule which imposes a new or defines a pre-existing restraint; to read it as mitigating a pre-existing restraint would do violence to its words. Coke speaks as though its only effect was to make the excessive gift voidable by the donor's heir[3]; but it certainly could be avoided by the donor's lord; this we learn both from Bracton and from a decision on which he relies[4].

Bracton.   (3) Throughout his work Bracton shows a strong leaning in favour of free alienation. As regards subinfeudation, he argues laboriously that it does no wrong, though it may do damage, to the lords[5]. The very earnestness of his argument shows that he has to combat a strong feeling, still we must take his opinion as that of the royal court. The rule laid down by the third edition of the Charter he mentions only in a very casual way, as though it were directed chiefly, if not solely, against gifts in frankalmoin[6]; collections of charters and collections of pleas from his time seem to show that it

---

[1] Glanv. vii. 1. As noticed by Dr Brunner, Pol. Science Quarterly, xi. 339, it is possible to find in Glanvill's text the assumption that, without the lord's consent, there can be no 'substitution.'

[2] Charter, 1217, c. 39; Coke, 2nd Inst. 65.

[3] 2nd Inst. 66.

[4] Bracton, f. 169 b; Note Book, pl. 1248.

[5] Bracton, f. 45 b–46 b.   [6] Bracton, f. 169 b, 305.

produced little effect[1]. The strength of Bracton's inclination in favour of subinfeudation may be shown by a passage in which he goes so far as to question the justice of the rule which treated service as a burden on land. He supposes that

[p. 314] A enfeoffs B to hold by a certain service, and that B enfeoffs C to hold the whole or part of the tenement by a less service; the rigour of the law, he says, permits A to distrain C for all the service due from B, but this is against equity[2]. Then as to substitutions, he holds that even when B has done homage to A, nevertheless B may give A a new tenant by enfeoffing C to hold of A, and C will then hold of A whether A likes it or no[3]. Bracton does not even expressly allow A to object that C is his personal enemy or too poor to do the service, which is very remarkable, since he does allow that the lord can not substitute for himself in the bond of homage a new lord who is the enemy of the tenant, or too needy to fulfil the duties of warranty[4]. He does not even say that the tenant can not give a fragment of the tenement to be holden of the lord by a proportional part of the service, though we may take it that in his opinion the inequitable rigour of the law[5] would prevent the tenant and his feoffee from making an apportionment which would bind the lord.

(4) Just in Bracton's time alienations in mortmain were beginning to cause murmurs. The charter of 1217 had struck at certain collusive practices to which the churches had been privy[6]. In 1258 at the Oxford parliament the barons prayed remedy, that men of religion may not enter the fees of earls and barons and others without their will, whereby they lose for ever their wardships, marriages, reliefs and escheats[7]. In 1259 the Provisions of Westminster ordained that it shall not be lawful for men of religion to enter the fee of any one without the licence of the lord of whom the land is holden[8]. These

Legislation as to mortmain.

---

[1] The only case in the Note Book in which it is mentioned is pl. 1248.

[2] Bracton, f. 21 b.   This passage is an 'addicio.'

[3] Bracton, f. 81.   [4] Bracton, f. 82.   [5] Bracton, f. 21 b.

[6] Charter, 1217, c. 43.   One is not to enfeoff a religious house and then take back the land as tenant of that house. The mischief to be prevented seems to be this :—Some favoured religious bodies, *e.g.* the Templars, have royal charters which by general words set free all the lands that they now have, or shall hereafter acquire, from many burdens. A man gives land to such a house, and then becomes that house's tenant, and as such he claims immunity under the charter.

[7] Petition of Barons, c. 10.   [8] Provisions, cap. 14.

Provisions were now law, now not law, as the barons or the
king obtained the mastery. Most of them were re-enacted by
the Statute of Marlborough in 1267, but not the provision now
in question; from which we may gather that the clergy were
influential enough with the king, who was enjoying his own [p. 315]
again, to put off the evil day. But not for long, for in 1279
the Statute *De Viris Religiosis*[1], after referring to the Provisions of Westminster as though they were or had been law[2],
put a check upon alienations in mortmain. No religious persons were to acquire land; if they did, the land was to be forfeited to the lord, and he had a brief term given him for taking
advantage of the forfeiture; if he failed to do so, the lord next
above him in the feudal scale had a similar opportunity; and
so on up to the king. The statute does not merely condemn
gifts in frankalmoin; the religious are not to acquire more
land, even though they are willing to pay a full rent for it.
However, the king and the other lords, if any, whose interests
were concerned could bind themselves to take no advantage of
the statute, and licences to acquire land in mortmain were
somewhat easily obtained.

Alienation of serjeanties. (5) From a comparatively early date we learn that serjeanties were inalienable. Already in 1198 the itinerant
justices were directed to make inquest touching the king's
serjeanties[3]. In 1205 John ordered an inquest as to the
serjeanties, thegnages, drengages and other services and lands
of the honour of Lancaster, which honour was then in his
hands; the sheriffs were to seize all such as had been alienated
since the coronation of Henry II. without licence from the
king or other good warrant[4]. This claim was steadily maintained by Henry III.[5] Towards the middle of his reign it was
enforced with retrospective rigour; Robert Passelew was sent
through England to ' arrent ' the alienated serjeanties, that is to
say, to change the tenure from serjeanty into knight's service

---

[1] Stat. 7 Edw. I. For the parallel French ordinance of 1275 see Langlois,
Le règne de Philippe le Hardi, 206 ff.; Esmein, Histoire du droit français, 278.

[2] The reference is not, as commonly supposed, to the Charter of 1217; it is
a recital of one of the Provisions of 1259. These Provisions were unknown to
our classical commentators.

[3] Hoveden, iv. 62.

[4] Rot. Cl. i. 55 ; Abbrev. Placit. p. 48 (Bedf.). See also Liber Rubeus, vol. ii.
p. cclxxxv.

[5] Rot. Cl. ii. 38 ; Note Book, pl. 1665 ; Bracton, f. 395.

or socage. One instance out of a very large number will serve
to show what was done. Walter Devenish held land by the
serjeanty of finding three arrows when the king should hunt
on Dartmoor; he had alienated parts of the tenement to sub-
tenants, his services were now changed into a rent of three
[p. 316] shillings, one-third of which was to be paid to him by his sub-
tenants[1]. That many of the king's tenants by serjeanty had
alienated parts of their tenements by way of subinfeudation
is instructive: we learn that a restraint on alienation might
exist in theory and yet be much disregarded in practice. Our
evidence chiefly concerns serjeanties held of the king; but we
may guess that other lords thought that a similar rule might
be applied to their serjeants; and the serjeants of the honour of
Lancaster, whose alienations John attacked, were not tenants
in chief of the crown.

(6) Bracton nowhere says that any special restriction is   Special law
imposed on the tenants in chief of the crown; the utmost that   for the
he does is to suggest, and this not very definitely, that the   king's
Charter of 1217 has been construed favourably to the king.   immediate
tenants.
The tenant in chief by knight's service of the king may not
make a gift in frankalmoin, or a feoffment which reserves a less
service than that due to the king[2]. But just about the time
when Bracton was writing Henry III. issued an important
ordinance. It takes the form of a writ dated the 15th of July,
in the fortieth year of the reign (1256). The king asserts
that it is an intolerable invasion of royal rights that men
should without his special consent enter by way of purchase
or otherwise the baronies and fees that are holden of him in
chief. He declares that for the future no one is to do this, and
bids the sheriff seize the land upon which any one enters in
contravention of this decree. This writ, however, remained
unknown to our historians until it was published in 1896, and,
as we shall see hereafter, even the lawyers of the fourteenth
century seem to have been ignorant of its existence[3]. Perhaps
the king did not wish or did not dare to enforce in all cases the

---

[1] Testa de Nevill, 197. The whole book is full of information about the
arrentation of serjeanties.

[2] Bracton, f. 169 b. The passage as it stands is not very plain. See also
f. 395.

[3] It was discovered on the Close Roll by Mr Turner and published by him in
L. Q. R. xii. 300. Equally important ordinances may yet be latent.

broad rule that he had laid down; the Barons' War was
at hand. The apocryphal Statute *Praerogativa Regis*, which
may represent the practice of the earlier years of Edward I.,
says that no one who holds of the king in chief by knight's
service may without the king's licence alienate the greater
part of his land so that the residue is not sufficient to do the
service, 'but this is not wont to be understood of members or
parcels of the said lands.' It adds that the king has been
accustomed to set to rent (*arrentare*) serjeanties that have
been alienated[1]. In 1290 a petitioner says that the king has
a prerogative that those who hold of him in chief can not give
or alienate their lands without his licence; certainly they can
not alienate all that they so hold[2]. Britton states that earls,
barons, knights and serjeants who hold of the king in chief can
not without his licence alienate their fees, but the king may
eject the purchasers, no matter how ancient the alienation,
since time does not run against the king[3]. Fleta states broadly
that no tenements holden of the king can be given without his
assent[4]. This becomes the law of after times. Before the end [p. 317]
of Edward's reign both theory and practice draw a marked
distinction between the king and other lords, and the king is
making a considerable revenue out of licences to alienate and
fines for alienations effected without licence[5].

Growth of
the pre-
rogative
right.

(7) The growth of the royal right may be traced also in
the articles delivered to the itinerant justices. Already in
Richard's reign they are to inquire 'of the king's serjeanties,
who has them, and through whom, and how much, and what
they are worth'[6]. A similar inquiry is found among the articles
of Henry III.'s reign; but, though there were divers other
inquiries about royal rights, wardships, escheats and the like,
there seems to have been none as yet into alienations of lands
not holden by serjeanty[7]. But in or about 1254 a special commission was issued[8], which was a forerunner of the more famous
Quo Waranto inquiry of Edward I.'s reign, and among the
articles, besides that about serjeanties, there seems to have

---

[1] As to the date of this document, see E. H. R. vi. 367.
[2] Calend. Geneal. 415.   [3] Britton, i. 222.   [4] Fleta, 178.
[5] See Rot. Orig. Abbrev. *e.g.* 126; see also Y.-B. 33-5 Edw. I. 306.
[6] Hoveden, iv. 62.
[7] Bracton, f. 116 b; Cart. Glouc. ii. 276; Ann. Burton. 330, A.D. 1254.
[8] Rot. Hund. i. Introduction and p. 20.

been one 'of knights, freeholders, men of religion or others, holding land on the king's demesne by gift or sale of the sokemen or by provision of the warden or bailiffs,' and another 'of men of religion who have entered the king's fee so that the king loses wards, reliefs and tallage[1].' The right asserted is growing more ample; and two years later the king issued the decisive writ. And so the inquiry becomes more extensive. In 1274 it runs thus:—'of the fees of the king and of his tenants, who now holds of him in chief, and how many fees each holds, and what fees were wont to be holden of the king in chief but now are held through a mesne lord (*per medium*), and what mesne lord, and when they were alienated, and how and by whom[2].' Thenceforth this is one of the usual articles of the eyre, and as such it is given by Fleta and Britton[3]; it formed one of the *Nova Capitula* which were distinguished from the more ancient articles.

[p. 318]   (8) The famous statute of 1290, the *Quia Emptores Terrarum*[4], lies outside our limits, but a word must be said of it.   It declared that every free man might sell his tenement or any part of it, but so that the feoffee should hold of the same lord and by the same services, of whom and by which the feoffor held.   In case only a part was sold, the services were to be apportioned between the part sold and the part retained according to their quantities; this apportionment was binding on the lord.   The statute is a compromise; the great lords had to concede to their tenants a full liberty of alienation by way of substitution—substitution even of many tenants for one tenant —and thus incur a danger of losing their services by the process of apportionment; on the other hand, subinfeudation with its consequent depreciation of escheats, wardships and marriages was stopped.   Nothing was said about the king's rights and no one seems to have imagined that the tenants in chief of the crown were set free to alienate without royal licence; on the contrary, it is just at the moment when all other tenants are gaining perfect freedom, that the king's claim to restrain any and every alienation by his tenants in chief attains its full amplitude[5].

Quia emptores

---

[1] Rot. Hund. i. 20–34.   [2] Rot. Hund. i.   Introduction.
[3] Fleta, pp. 25, 26 ; Britton, i. 71.   [4] Stat. 18 Edw. I.
[5] To treat this measure as having been passed in the interest of the great lords seems a mistake. The one person who had all to gain and nothing to lose by the new law was the king.

(9) What was the legal basis of this prerogative right? Already in the middle of the fourteenth century the lawyers had no certain answer for this question. The writ of 1256 they seem to have forgotten or but vaguely remembered and incorrectly dated; also their speculations are obscured and vitiated by the belief that the *Praerogativa Regis* was a statute. Already in Edward II.'s day it was clear that the royal claims were too extensive to be covered by the clause in the Charter of 1217. In 1325 complaint was made in parliament that the rule applicable to tenants in chief of the crown was being extended to tenants who held of honours which had fallen into the king's hands; the king acknowledged the distinction; as lord of an honour he had only such rights as were given to all lords by the Charter[1]. In 1327 a statute was required to settle that, on an alienation without licence, the king was entitled only to a reasonable fine and not to a forfeiture of the land[2]. In 1341 it [p. 319] was suggested in court that before the thirtieth year of Henry III. a tenant in chief might alienate without licence[3]. In 1346 it was asserted and denied by pleaders that before the twentieth year of Henry III. a tenant in chief of the crown could alienate like any other tenant. The reporter apparently has his doubts and tells us to consider the date of the *Praerogativa Regis*[4]. In 1352 the question was discussed whether in Henry III.'s reign the tenant in chief could subinfeudate without licence, and apparently the decision was to the effect that he could[5]. In 1355 the lawyers are once more debating whether something happened in the twentieth year of Henry III. to prevent the tenant in chief from subinfeudating[6]. Why do they single out the twentieth or thirtieth year (1235–6, 1245–6) of Henry III. as important? To say with Coke[7] that in the twentieth (or rather in the following) year Magna Carta was confirmed, is not satisfactory; the same might be said of so many years, and the Magna Carta of the lawyers' statute books was the charter of 9 Henry III. (1225), confirmed by Edward I. To say that they referred the *Praerogativa Regis* to the twentieth or thirtieth year of Henry seems impossible, since that enigmatical document mentions King

---

[1] Rot. Parl. i. 430.   [2] Stat. 1 Edw. III. c. 12.

[3] Y. B. Pasch. 15 Edw. III. (ed. Pike), pp. 157–8.

[4] Lib. Ass. f. 73, ann. 20, pl. 17; see also Fitz. Abr. *Avowre*, 126.

[5] Lib. Ass. f. 124, ann. 26, pl. 37.   [6] Lib. Ass. f. 160, ann. 29, pl. 19.

[7] 2nd Inst. 66; Co. Lit. 43 a.

Edward. Probably they were thinking of the writ of the fortieth year (1256). The discussion, however, was taken up in parliament, and there the king's right was treated as the outcome of the *Praerogativa Regis,* and was said to have had its beginning in the reign of King Edward I.[1] A declaration of the law was demanded; but the king desired further information. The question was of practical importance, for it came to this:—Could the king attack a possessor of land on the ground of an alienation made without licence in the days of King Henry—or, more generally, was there any limit of time that could be set to this prerogative right? In 1360 a statute confirmed all subinfeudations made by the tenants in chief under Henry III. and earlier kings[2]. As we can hardly [p. 320] believe that Edward III. gave up any right to which he considered himself justly entitled, we may infer that the result of repeated discussions in the courts and in parliament was to date the change in the law at the accession of Edward I. in 1272, about sixteen years after what we may now regard as the decisive ordinance[3].

On the whole then, we may be inclined to accept, with some modification, Coke's theory of this episode. We may believe that the only restraint on the alienation of tenements holden of mesne lords that existed after the year 1217 was the somewhat vague restraint imposed or defined by the charter of that year; that, apart from this, the tenant might alienate the whole or any part of the land by way of subinfeudation, and the whole, though perhaps not a part of it, by way of substitution; that the king's prerogative right gradually grew out of the right allowed to all lords by the charter, though it exceeded the words of that compact; that it was first asserted in all its breadth in the writ or ordinance of 1256, and may not have been stringently enforced until the accession of Edward I.[4]

Summary as to law after the date of the Charter.

---

[1] Rot. Parl. ii. 265.   [2] Stat. 34 Edw. III. c. 15.

[3] In 1412 Hankford J. said that in Henry III.'s time a tenant in chief of the crown might have alienated as freely as any other tenant; Y. B. 14 Hen. IV. f. 4 (Mich. pl. 6).

[4] While writs bidding the sheriffs seize lands which have been alienated without licence appear upon the very earliest Fine Rolls of Edward I., we have in vain sought for any similar writs upon some of the last Fine Rolls of Henry III. Fine Roll, 1 Edw. I. m. 9: the sheriff of Sussex is ordered to seize tenements which Franco de Bohun, a tenant in chief by barony, has sold without licence to Almaric de Lucy. For other instances see the same roll, m. 16, m. 22;

But as to an earlier period, there is much to be said on the other side; there are the once fashionable arguments drawn from 'the learning of feuds,' while more solid arguments may be derived from English and Norman deeds.

Older law.   As regards 'the original constitution of feuds' little need here be said: it was an old story long before the battle of Hastings. Very generally the continental vassal could not substitute a new vassal for himself without his lord's consent; but commonly he had some power of subinfeudation[1]. Wherever ᵢp. 321] we look in the twelfth century we see differences of practice, and in some cases the law is becoming more favourable to the lords, less favourable to the tenants[2]. In this instance however we have no need to look beyond England and Normandy. For the period between 1066 and 1217 we have hundreds of Anglo-Norman charters. English charters, and at first sight they seem to go the full length of proving that from the Conquest onward no tenant could alienate his land without his lord's consent. It so happens also that in Normandy we can trace this restraint on alienation back to the time when the duke of the Normans was not yet king of the English[3]. The chronicle of Orderic is full of gifts made to the Abbey of St Evroul, and in case after case the chronicler is careful to tell us how the gift was confirmed by the donor's lord or lords; in seeking confirmation the monks ascend the scale of tenure and do not stop until they reach the duke[4]. Then, after the Conquest, they acquire lands in England; for instance, they acquire lands from some of the men of the earl of Chester; they seek the earl's confirmation and the king's. The abbot journeys to England and obtains from the Conqueror a liberal charter confirming the gifts and confirmations of his barons[5]. This is no solitary phenomenon.

Roll of 3 Edw. I. m. 15, m. 21; Roll of 5 Edw. I. m. 5. See also the discussions in Y. B. 32-3 Edw. I. p. 38; 33-5 Edw. I. pp. 306, 470.

[1] Waitz, D. V. G. vi. 67-9.

[2] See the law ascribed to Conrad II. in M. G., Leges, ii. 38 and the Constitutio Lotharii, ibid. 84; Richter, Annalen, iii. 317. The Lombard feudists of the twelfth century seem to have held that in the past the vassal had enjoyed a greater liberty than was left to him by modern ordinances; Lib. Feud. i. xiii; ii. ix; ii. xxxiv, §§ 2, 3. For France, see Luchaire, Manuel des institutions françaises, 171; Esmein, Histoire du droit français, 213.

[3] See above, p. 69, note 2.

[4] Orderic, ii. 15 fol. See also Cartulaire de l'abbaye de la Sainte Trinité du Mont de Rouen, *passim.*

[5] Orderic, iii. 18, 26.

Every collection of monastic charters tells the same tale. No gift is considered safe until it has been confirmed by the king and all who stand between the king and the donor[1]. Often the donor's lord joins in the gift itself; it is made *annuente domino meo, concedente domino meo*; still more often he confirms it after it has been made. What is more, he sometimes confirms prospectively whatever gifts any of his men may make to the favoured monastery. For a while we do not hear much [p. 322] of money being paid for such confirmations; lands are plentiful and lords are pious; but already in Henry I.'s day men are paying for confirmations[2], and now and again we read stories which seem to show that a lord would sometimes call in question a feoffment to which he had not consented[3].

But considerable care is necessary in drawing inferences Discussion from these documents. Most of the very early charters that charters. we possess relate to gifts in frankalmoin, and, when examined, they will often appear to be confirmations and something more. In royal confirmations it is common to find words that are not merely confirmatory. Sometimes the king denounces a penalty, a forfeiture of £10, against any who shall disturb the donees; often he wills that the donees may enjoy 'sake and soke' and other liberties, which, at least in his opinion, none

[1] For Norman instances see Orderic's chronicle; English instances are to be found everywhere.

[2] Pipe Roll, 31 Hen. I.; fines are paid, p. 34, 'pro concessione terrae quam H. de L. ei dedit'; p. 45, 'pro concessione terrarum quas episcopus ei dedit'; p. 73, 'ut habeat terram quam abbas de B. ei dedit'; p. 91, 'pro concessione terrae quam tenet de H. filio E.'; p. 96, 'pro concessione terrae de qua R. de B. cum hereditavit'; p. 105, 'ut rex firmet in cartha ecclesiae suae de A. omnes res quas comes de Warwic ei dedit ad opus eiusdem ecclesiae'; p. 108, 'pro concessione terrae...quam comes de Warwic ei dedit.' To judge from the later Pipe Rolls, it would seem as if the king for a while abandoned the attempt to make a steady revenue out of his confirmations; but we may not be entitled to this inference. Chron. de Melsa, i. 221: the archbishop of York circ. 1190 takes 60 marks for confirming a tenant's gift.

[3] For very early cases see Hist. Abingd. ii. 7, 8, 9. The abbot gives land to Robert of Ouilly, but, repenting himself, is able to get back the land because the king has not confirmed the gift. Then he bought Nuneham from Leofwine and, since the Conqueror was in Normandy, procured and paid for the assent of Odo of Bayeux who was acting as regent; but he lost his money, for the king having quarrelled with Odo gave the land to another. Rufus peremptorily forbids the abbot of Ramsey to alienate any part of his demesne 'without my licence'; Cart. Rams. i. 234. In John's reign licences to mortgage become common; Rot. Pat. 1, 3, 4, 7, 59. See also the mandate in favour of the bishop of Ely, Rot. Pat. 47.

but he can grant. Then again, words which look merely
confirmatory, demand a careful criticism. For instance if *B*
holds of *A* by knight's service and enfeoffs the abbot of *C* in
free alms, then, when *A* confirms the gift, we must be diligent
to observe whether he reserves his right to exact the service
from the land, or uses words importing that the land is to be
frankalmoin, not merely as between *B* and the abbot, but even
as regards the confirmer himself. Thus, to take a real example,
when Robert earl of Gloucester confirms a gift which one of his
tenants has made to St Peter's Abbey, he adds ' I will that the [p. 323]
said monks hold the same freely, quietly and honourably in
frankalmoin for ever[1].' Such words, which are very commonly
found, will in all likelihood debar the earl and his heirs from
ever exacting any service from this land. Indeed in Bracton's
day a lord confirming a tenant's gift had to be extremely
cautious if he wished to retain the service due from the land;
if *B* who held of *A* at a rent of a hundred shillings enfeoffed *C*
at a rent of one shilling, the mere word *confirmo* used by *A*
might, if unexplained, deprive him of ninety-nine shillings a
year[2]. Again, at least in Norman documents, there is much
to suggest that a subinfeudation effected without the lord's
consent was neither void nor voidable by the lord so long as
the mesne seignory of the donor endured; the donee's danger
lay in this, that by the donor's felony or want of heirs this
seignory would escheat and the donor's lord would then be able
to avoid the gift[3]. Again, we must remark that in this context
little stress can be laid on confirmations when the confirmer is
the king, for, quite apart from all feudal theory, a royal charter
was a very efficient protection against litigation. When once
such a charter was produced by the person in possession, the
king's justices would stay their hands; they would proceed no
further *rege inconsulto*[4]. We find too that religious houses are

---

[1] Cart. Glouc. i. 319; ii. 89. See the confirmation by Earl Richard of
Chester in Hist. Abingd. ii. 69.

[2] Bracton, f. 21 b. The passage is an ' addicio.'

[3] See *e.g.* Orderic, ii. 449: a lord confirms his man's gift to the abbey and
adds that if the man by any crime shall lose his fee (*feudum*), the church is still
to keep the land that has been given to it. See also Très ancien coutumier
(Tardif), c. 89. This view of the matter seems to have become of great importance in the history of Scottish law; see Ross, Lectures on Conveyancing, ii.
251–3. See also Schröder, D. R. G. p. 399, note 58.

[4] Bracton, f. 382 b. In 1251 this had become a grievous obstacle to the
course of justice, and an ordinance was made to the effect that a royal charter of

[p. 324] not content with one royal confirmation; they obtain a fresh charter from each successive king, for, be the law what it may, no prudent man will trust to the king's respect for his ancestor's promises. Lastly, to complete the picture, we may add that the usual practice of the monasteries was, not to apply to the king whenever they received a gift, but to wait until they had a considerable number of gifts and then get all of them confirmed by one instrument.

In the teeth however of the long series of diplomata stretching back to the Conquest, and in Normandy beyond the Conquest, some of which deal with cases in which the donee is a layman and the confirming lord is not the king, it is quite impossible for us to hold that the restriction expressed in the charter of 1217 was a new thing, or that the free alienability of 'the fee simple' is the starting point of English law. We must be content with a laxer principle: with some such idea as this, that the tenant may lawfully do anything that does not seriously damage the interests of his lord. He may make reasonable gifts, but not unreasonable. The reasonableness of the gift would be a matter for the lord's court; the tenant would be entitled to the judgment of his peers. The charter of 1217 is a fair, though a vague compromise of conflicting claims. That it should have been so favourable to the tenants as it was, may fairly surprise us, if we have regard to other countries, and to the extreme severity of our English law about reliefs, primer seisins, wardships and marriages[1]. But the confirmation should not stay the action, unless the charter was so worded that the king would be bound to give an exchange to the donee in case of his being evicted. At least from John's reign onwards royal confirmations were usually so framed that the king was not bound to give an exchange. He would be so bound if he simply confirmed 'the gift of *A. B.*,' but he was not so bound if he confirmed 'the reasonable (*i.e.* lawful) gift of *A. B.*'; in the latter case he only confirmed the gift in so far as it was no wrong to any one. For this rule see Bract. f. 59 b; and see Rot. Cart. p. 79, where it is noted that by special order of King John the word *rationabiliter* was omitted from a charter of confirmation. As to the special value of royal charters even in the worst days of the French kingship, see Luchaire, Institutions monarchiques, i. 117.

Conclusions as to the law of the Norman time.

[1] The French seigneur, who did not usually get a relief from the heir, if the heir was a descendant of the dead man, did very generally receive a fine when the tenement was alienated, under such names as *lods et ventes, quint et requint*; also he had the *retrait féodal* or right of repurchasing within a certain limited time the land sold by his tenant at the price given for it. For Normandy, see Très ancien coutumier, c. 57, 89–91; Somma, p. 96; Ancienne coutume, c. 29; on the face of these texts, Norman law seems to grow more favourable to the lords during the thirteenth century.

Norman Conquest must for a while have favoured ' free trade
in land'. William, when he conferred the forfeited estates of
English earls and thegns on his French followers, must have
known and intended that there should be some reasonable
amount of subinfeudation. This was absolutely required by
the new military system; the count or baron was to have
knights to follow his banner, and the services of knights could
only be secured by feoffments. For a long time it would be
possible for the vassals to endow sub-vassals, for the sub-vassals [p. 325]
to endow other sub-vassals, without any loss being inflicted on
the great lords or on the king. We must add to this that for a
full century after the Conquest, despite occasional quarrels, the
king was in close league with the church; as against his too
rebellious barons he relied on the prelates, and the prelates of
course desired that men should be free to make gifts to pious
uses. And just when the interests of the church as an acquirer
of land were beginning to come into serious conflict with the
needs of the state, the function of declaring the law of England
was being committed to a group of professional lawyers who for
several reasons were likely to favour free alienation. Often
they were ecclesiastics; always they were the king's servants,
and as such inclined to loosen the feudal bond whenever this
could be done without prejudice to their master's rights. But,
besides all this, it seems clear that merely as jurists, and all
considerations of political expediency apart, they were disposed
to concede to every tenant the fullest possible power of dealing
with his land. Just when they were deciding that the common
law put no restriction on this power in favour of the lord, they
were rapidly and finally destroying the restrictions which had
existed in favour of the tenant's expectant heirs. This process
will come before us hereafter, but should be noticed in this
context. If the English lawyers are shutting their ears to the
claims of the lords, they are shutting their ears to the claims of
the kindred also, and this just at a time when in Normandy
and other countries the claims of the lord and the claims of
the expectant heir are finding a formal recognition in the new
jurisprudence. Whether we ascribe this result to the precocious maturity of our system of royal justice, or to some
cause deep-seated in our national character, we must look at
these two facts together:—if the English law knows no *retrait
féodal*, it knows no *retrait lignager*.

As regards the form that alienation took, subinfeudation Usual form was certainly much commoner than substitution. Still we find of aliena-
tion. the latter at an early date, if not in charters, at least in fines levied before the king's court. Not unfrequently in John's reign one party to the transaction grants a tenement to the [p. 326] other party to hold 'of the chief lords of the fee[1].' It is not always possible for us to discover the real meaning of such a transaction, as we can not always tell whether the fine is the settlement of a genuine dispute, or a mere piece of convey-ancing machinery; but it seems clear that fines were levied with little, if any, regard for the lord's interest, and that their effect often was to give him a new immediate tenant of the whole, or even (for so it would seem) of part only of the tenement. As regards modes of conveyance less solemn than a fine, had it not been for Bracton's distinct assertion, we should probably have come to the opinion that a new tenant, even of the whole tenement, could not be forced upon an unwilling lord. Whether we look to collections of charters or to collections of pleadings, we find the lord's consent frequently mentioned[2]; indeed sometimes the transaction takes the form of a surrender by the old tenant to the lord and a feoffment by the lord of the new tenant. When about the middle of the twelfth century Reginald Puer sells land to Whitby Abbey, he resigns all his right into the hand of Roger Mowbray to the use (*ad opus*) of the monks, to whom Roger gives it, putting them in seisin by the same rod (*lignum*) by which the resignation had been made[3]. When Alexander Buddicombe sells that fifth part of a knight's fee which he holds of Hawise Gurney to Thomas Fitz-William, he 'demises himself' in Hawise's court and renders the land to her by the branch of a tree, whereupon she gives seisin to Thomas by the same branch[4]. Still there are Bracton's plain words:—albeit the tenant has done homage (and this of course makes the case extreme) he may put a new tenant in his place, and the lord must accept him, will he, nill he[5].

To sum up the whole of a lengthy argument, the sound General
summary
as to
alienation
by the
tenant.

---

[1] Fines, ed. Hunter, i. 32, 54, 110, 115, 123, 188, 239; ii. 59.

[2] Note Book, pl. 627, 779, 947, 984, 1616, 1924.

[3] Whitby Cart. i. 203.

[4] Madox, Formulare, p. 54. So T. de G. and his wife having sold land to the abbot of Meaux surrender it by the rod to the count of Aumâle in his court (A.D. 1160–1182), Chron. de Melsa, i. 165, 224.

[5] Bracton, f. 81.

conclusion seems to be that, in treating the matter as one
of purely English history, we must start not from the absolute
inalienability of 'the fief,' nor from the absolute alienability of
'the fee simple,' but from something much less satisfactory,
an indeterminate right of the lord to prevent alienations which
would seriously impair his interests, a right which might
remain in abeyance so long as there was plenty of scope for [p. 327]
subinfeudation and the liberty of endowing churches was not
abused, a right on which the king's court was seldom if ever
called upon to pronounce, since the lord could enforce it in his
own court, a right which was at length defined, though in
loose terms, by the charter of 1217. But very probably the
king's legal position was from the first exceptional, and it
certainly became exceptional in the course of the thirteenth
century; with no text of law to rely upon but the charter, he
succeeded, under stress of pecuniary troubles, in gradually
establishing a right which could not be justified by the terms
of that instrument.

Gifts made by a lord with the consent of his court. That we may be right in taking as the starting point of our
law principles so vague as those just stated, may appear from
this, that if we often find a lord confirming his tenants' gifts,
we sometimes find a lord consulting or professing to consult
his tenants before he makes a feoffment. When Aubrey de
Vere gives land to the Abbey of Abingdon, 'all his knights'
are said to join in the grant[1]; Earl Hugh of Chester speaks
with 'his barons' before he makes a similar gift[2]; Roger de
Merlay when he endows Newminster does so with the consent
of 'his men'[3]; 'the knights' and the 'good men' of the abbot
of Abingdon give their consent to an exchange which he is
making with one of his tenants[4], and so the abbot of Ramsey
by the counsel of his barons retains the homage of Robert
Foliot at the cost of two thousand eels a year[5]. Each feudal
group strives to be a little state; its ruler and his subjects
alike have an interest in all that concerns its territory. Still
this notion, that the lord ought to hold a parliament before he
makes a feoffment, never hardens into law.

Alienation of a seignory. But now another question arises. Can a lord dispose of his
rights over a tenant and his tenement without that tenant's

---

[1] Hist. Abingd. ii. 59–60.　　　[2] Hist. Abingd. ii. 20.
[3] Newminster Cart. p. 2.　　　[4] Hist. Abingd. ii. 136.
[5] Cart. Rams. i. 153.

consent? We will suppose that A has enfeoffed B who has enfeoffed C, and ask whether B can, without C's concurrence, either put X in his (B's) place, so that C will hold of X who will hold of A, or place X between himself and C, so that C will hold of X, who will hold of B, who will hold of A. Now here we [p. 328] have to consider two different difficulties. First there is what we may call the feudal difficulty, that of giving C a new lord, of holding him bound to serve X when he has contracted to serve B. Secondly there is a difficulty that is quite unconnected with the nature of the feudal bond but may be thus stated :—Every gift, every transfer of rights, involves a transfer of seisin, of possession. When a tenant is to be enfeoffed as a tenant in demesne, then in order to complete the feoffment it is absolutely necessary that the feoffor should deliver possession of the land to the feoffee, and this act is performed on the land; the feoffor solemnly puts the feoffee in seisin and then quits the land. But there can be no such delivery of possession in the case that is under our notice ; C is tenant in demesne; it is not intended that X shall become tenant in demesne; B and X have no business to go onto the land and disturb C in his possession; what is to be given to X is not the right to take the fruits of the land but the right to C's services. We can not in this place discuss this notion that a gift or a transfer of rights involves a transfer of possession; but it is deeply engrained in the law of the thirteenth century. It would seem then, that the only mode in which B can complete his gift to X, is by persuading or compelling C to recognize X as his lord. When such a recognition has taken place, then we may say that X possesses the object of the transfer; he is seised of C's services, he is also seised of the land ' in service ' (*seisitus in servitio*). The two difficulties then, though in a given case they may conspire, are essentially different; the difference is brought out by the question: Has B any legal process for compelling C to accept X as his lord?

According to Bracton, we must distinguish. If C has done homage to B, then C may, for good cause, object to having his homage made over to X. He may object that X is his enemy —a light enmity says Bracton is not a sufficient cause—or that X is too poor to fulfil the duty of warranty, or again that homage is indivisible, and that he can not be bound to do homage to X for part of the tenement, while he still holds

Law of attorn-ment.

the other part of *B*; but unless such cause is shown, *C*'s homage can be transferred to *X*. As regards the service due from the tenement, as distinct from homage, this can always be transferred, even against the tenant's will; the court has a process for compelling the tenant to acknowledge that he holds of the new lord; it has a process for 'attorning', *i.e.* turning over, [p. 329] the tenant to the new lord[1]. He gives a case from 1223 :—*X* demanded homage from *C*, saying that *B* had attorned *C*'s homage and service to him, *X* ; thereupon *C* said that he held nothing of *X* and that he would not depart from *B* who was his lord; then *B* was summoned and stated that he had made the gift to *X* ; but *C* still objected that he held two tenements of *B* by a single homage and service, only one of which tenements had been given to *X*, and that he would not divide his homage ; whereupon the court adjudged that *X* should have seisin of *C*'s service, but that *C* could not be compelled to do homage to *X*. Service, says Bracton, can always, but homage can not always be attorned[2].

Objections to attornment.

It is somewhat curious, as noticed above, that Bracton should allow the tenant to object to his homage being transferred, for he does not allow, at least expressly, any similar objection on the part of a lord whose tenant desires to put a new tenant in his place. Possibly the necessity for an attornment, which really rested on quite other grounds, kept alive one side of an ancient rule while the other side had withered. But Bracton is very favourable to tenants. He holds, for example, that the tenant can always waive or resign his tenement and so free himself from the duties of service and homage, while the lord can not waive the homage or refuse the service, and so free himself from the duty of warranty ; and the tenant may object if any attempt be made to substitute an insolvent for a solvent warrantor[3].

Practice of alienating seignories.

On the whole we have little reason to suppose that the rights of the tenants had ever in this country been a serious

---

[1] In this age it is seldom said that the tenant attorns (*attornat seipsum*) to the new lord ; the old lord, or in some cases the court, attorns (*attornat*) the tenant to the new lord, or attorns the service and homage to the new lord.

[2] Bracton, f. 81 b–82 b. See also Y. B. 32–3 Edw. I. p. 43.

[3] Bracton, f. 80 b, 81 b, 382 § 5. However, if the lord was so poor that he was unable to warrant the tenant, he was allowed to disclaim the seignory and the tenant then held of the next lord in the ascending scale ; Note Book, pl. 563, 674.

obstacle to alienations by the lords[1]. In the charters we find
the lords apparently exercising the fullest power of giving away
the homages and the services of their tenants. If there was
[p. 330] any reason to suppose that the tenant would object to recognizing a new lord, then a fine would be levied, and the tenant
would be called on by a writ known as *Per quae servitia* to
show cause why he should not be attorned[2]. Fines transferring
services are quite common; the subject-matter of the transfer
is usually described as the service, or the homage and service
of such an one[3]. It would be a mistake to suppose that the
lofty feudal ladders that we find in the thirteenth century, had
been always, or even generally, manufactured only by the process
of adding new rungs at their nether ends; new rungs were
often inserted in their middles.

§ 10. *Aids.*

The duties implied in the relation between man and lord Duty of
are but slowly developed and made legal duties. There long aiding the lord.
remains a fringe of vague obligations. The man should come
to the aid of the lord in all his necessities; the man's purse
as well as his body should be at his lord's disposal if the lord
is in a strait. Gradually the occasions on which an aid of
money may be demanded are determined. Glanvill mentions
the aid which helps a lord to pay the relief due to his overlord,
the aid for knighting the lord's eldest son and marrying his
eldest daughter; also he raises the question whether the lord
may not demand an aid for the maintenance of a war in
which he is concerned; such a demand, he thinks, can not be
pressed[4]. From the Normandy of Glanvill's time we hear of

---

[1] In 1130 R. de C. fined to the king 'ut Symon de Belcampo dominus suus
non daret servitium suum nisi concessu suo': Pipe Roll, 31 Hen. I. p. 62.

[2] Note Book, pl. 236, 369, 593, 598, 627, 948, 1622. The tenant who will
not attorn can be sent to gaol: Y. B. 33–5 Edw. I. p. 317.

[3] Fines, ed. Hunter, *e.g.* 61, 65, 77, 109. When the tenant himself is spoken
of as the subject of the transfer, he generally is a tenant in villeinage; but it
would be rash to draw this inference in all cases. See *e.g.* Chron. de Melsa, i.
176 (A.D. 1160–72) a gift of a half-carucate and of Gilbert son of Richard, who
holds the land, with his wife and their children. Whalley Coucher, i. 6, 7: a gift
of Leving and Guy his brother and their heirs, who seem to be freehold tenants
of the donor.

[4] Glanv. ix. 8: 'Utrum vero ad guerram suam manutenendam possint

the aid for the lord's relief, for marrying his daughter and knighting his eldest son[1]. The charter of 1215 mentioned as [p. 331] the three aids, which the king might take without the common counsel of the realm, that for redeeming his body, that for marrying his daughter and that for knighting his son; and such aids were to be reasonable[2]. As is well known, the clause which dealt with this matter appeared in no later edition of the charter. During John's reign the prior of St Swithin's took an aid fron his freeholders, farmers and villeins for the payment of his debts[3]; the bishop of Winchester took an aid for the expenses to which he had been put in the maintenance of the king's honour and the dignity of the church[4]; the abbot of Peterborough took an aid to enable him to pay a fine to the king[5]; the earl of Salisbury to enable him to stock his land[6]. Nor do such aids cease with the year 1215; in Henry III.'s reign the bishop of Bath took an aid for the support of his knights in the king's service[7]. In 1217, after a Welsh war, the king's military tenants who had done their service received permission, not only to collect the scutage from their knights, but also to raise a reasonable aid from all their free men[8]. However, the clause expunged from the charter seems practically to have fixed the law. We learn also that it was next to impossible for the lords to collect aids without obtaining the king's writ and the sheriff's assistance. That writ would name no sum; the aid was to be 'reasonable.' So late as 1235 we see Henry Tracey, having first obtained the king's writ, holding a little parliament of his knights in Devonshire; they grant him an aid of 20 shillings on the knight's fee for the marriage of his eldest daughter[9]. Bracton speaks of these aids as due rather of grace than of right; they are the outcome of a personal not of a predial obligation; they are not to be reckoned as 'services'[10]. This is the ancient theory; but it must already have been obsolescent. A statute of 1275 fixed the rate of the aid to be taken for marrying the eldest

---

domini huiusmodi auxilia exigere quaero. Obtinet autem quod non possunt ad id tenentes distringere de iure, nisi quatenus facere velint.' In this passage *guerra sua* hardly means a national war.

[1] Très ancien coutumier, c. 47, 48; Somma, p. 110; Ancienne coutume, c. 35.
[2] Charter of 1215, c. 12.　　　　　　[3] Rot. Pat. p. 52.
[4] Rot. Pat. p. 61.　　　[5] Rot. Cl. i. 66.　　　[6] Rot. Cl. i. 127.
[7] Rot. Cl. i. 306.　　　[8] Rot. Cl. i. 570–1.　　[9] Note Book, pl. 1146.
[10] Bracton, f. 36 b.

daughter and knighting the eldest son at 20 shillings for the knight's fee and 20 shillings for 20 librates of socage land[1], and thus in effect destroyed the doctrine of the lord's need and [p. 332] the tenant's gracious help. This statute bound the mesne lords; a later statute was required to bind the king[2]. The constitutional side of the history of aids we need not here discuss, but the aid is one of the most widely distributed of the feudal phenomena[3].

§ 11. *Escheat and Forfeiture.*

In the background but ever ready to become prominent Escheat. stands the lord's right to escheats. This forms as it were a basis for all his other rights. The superiority which he always has over the land may at any time become once more a full ownership of it. Though he has given the land to the tenant and his heirs, still there may well be a failure of heirs, for the tenant can not institute an heir; only God makes heirs; and in this case the land falls to, escheats (*excadere*) to the lord. Already in Glanvill's day a lawyer may sometimes speak of the lord as the tenant's *ultimus heres*[4]; but such a phrase hardly expresses the law. When land escheats the lord's superiority swells into simple ownership; all along he has had rights in the land[5]. Nor is a failure of heirs the only cause of an escheat. If the tenant is outlawed or convicted of felony then, after the king has exercised the very ancient right of wasting the criminal's land for year and day, the tenement returns to its lord. A distinction is established between treason and felony; if a tenant commits treason all his lands, of whomsoever they were holden, are *forfeited* to the king, while the felon's lands *escheat* to his lord. How far back this distinction can be traced seems doubtful; but John and his successors apparently insisted upon it when they enriched themselves by seizing the *terrae*

[1] Stat. West. I. (3 Edw. I.) c. 36.

[2] Stat. 25 Edw. III. stat. 5, c. 11.   Stubbs, Const. Hist. ii. 521.

[3] See Ducange, s. v. *auxilium*; Madox, Exchequer, ch. xv. § 1; Viollet, Établissements, iv. 18–20; Luchaire, Manuel des institutions françaises, 206.

[4] Glanv. vii. 17: ' Ultimi heredes aliquorum sunt eorum domini.'

[5] Bracton, f. 297 b (last lines), distinguishes between cases in which the lord who comes to the land by escheat can be treated as filling the place of the tenant's heir from those in which such treatment is impossible.

Normannorum, the English lands of those who preferred to be
Frenchmen rather than Englishmen when the victories of
Philip Augustus forced upon them the choice between two
nationalities. As regards felony, we have seen that the idea
implied by that term had been changing; it now stood for [p. 333]
'serious crime,' it had once stood for 'breach of the feudal bond.'
On the one hand, the lords had gained; they got escheats if
their tenants committed such crimes as homicide or theft; on
the other hand they had lost. By openly disavowing his lord
the tenant might indeed lose his tenement; even in Bracton's
day such a disavowal was sometimes called felonious[1], and in
much later times a disavowal and a consequent forfeiture might
be found in the fact that the tenant had paid his rent, or done
his homage, to a wrongful, instead of to the rightful, claimant
of the seignory. But, on the other hand, the lord seems to
have had very little power of ejecting a tenant for the mere
non-performance, even the wilful and protracted non-performance of his services. This is a matter which requires some
examination.

Lord's remedies against defaulting tenant. In Bracton's day the lord when the services are in arrear
has three courses open to him. (1) We may mention first—
though this is not his readiest remedy—an action in the king's
court for the recovery of customs and services. This is a
laborious action. It is regarded as proprietary, not possessory.
Action in the king's court. A lord will hardly use it unless there is some dispute between
him and his tenant about the nature or quantity of the services.
In that case it will conclusively establish the lord's title, and
the victorious lord will have the sheriff's aid in distraining
for the arrears. But, unless there has been some disavowal
of the tenure on the tenant's part, there is no action in the
king's court that will give the lord the land in demesne.
Feoffors and feoffees are indeed free to make the express
bargain that if the services are in arrear the feoffor may enter
once more on the land and take it to himself; but we shall
see few such bargains made before the middle of the thirteenth century[2]. Such then is our common law, and it is well

---

[1] See above, p. 285.

[2] Hist. Abingd. ii. p. 168, gives from Henry I.'s day an instance of a re-entry
clause in a feoffment in fee; but such clauses seem quite uncommon, even in
leases for years, until about 1250. The lords may still be relying on the
efficiency of their courts.

worthy of remark; it does not turn out the tenant from the land because he can not or will not perform his services. Two statutes of Edward I. were required to give the lord an ampler remedy:—the action called *cessavit per biennium* was [p. 334] invented; if the tenant allowed his services to fall into arrear for two years, the lord might claim the land in demesne[1]. There can, we think, be little doubt that this new action was borrowed immediately from the canon law and mediately from the legislation of Justinian. It is one of the very few English actions that we can trace directly to a foreign model[2].

(2) The lord's handiest remedy is that of distraining his tenant to perform the services that are in arrear. This means Distress. that, carefully observing certain rules as to when and where and what he may seize, he takes the chattels that are found upon the tenement and keeps them until the tenant either tenders the arrears or finds security to contest in a court of law the justice of the seizure. The idea of distress (*districtio*) is that of bringing compulsion to bear upon a person who is thereby to be forced into doing something or leaving something undone; it is not a means whereby the distrainor can satisfy the debt that is due to him. He may not appropriate the *namium*, the thing that he has taken, nor may he sell it; he must keep it as a gage (*vadium*) so that the person from whom it has been taken may be constrained to perform his duty. This right to distrain for services in arrear is in the latter half of the thirteenth century a right that is freely exercised by every landlord, and he exercises it although he has as yet taken no judicial proceedings of any kind against his tenant. Nevertheless, we may see much to make us think that this power of extra-judicial distraint is not very old. Bracton speaks as though it were still usual for a lord to obtain a judgment in his own court before he distrains a tenant into

---

[1] Stat. Glouc. c. 4; Stat. Westm. II. c. 21; Second Institute, 295, 400. Coke says that he had 'read amongst ancient records' that a *cessavit* was brought in the reign of King John. We have found no trace of any such action before the statutes.

[2] Blackstone, Comment. iii. 232. In Cod. 4. 66. 2, Justinian lays down the rule that the *emphyteuta* whose rent is in arrear for three years may be ejected. In Nov. 7. 3. 2, the period of three years is cut down to two years where the landlord is a church. In this form the rule passes into the canon law; c. 4, X. 3. 18.

the performance of his services; and we may see that in his
day some lords were still taking this course[1].

Proceed-
ings in the
lord's own
court. (3) This leads us to speak of the possibility of proceedings [p. 335]
being taken in the lord's own court for the exaction of the rent
or the expulsion of the defaulting tenant. It is possible that
at one time the non-performance of services was regarded as a
sufficient cause of forfeiture. Against any disseising of the
tenant 'without a judgment,' there had for a long time past
been a strong feeling; it finds utterance in the most famous
words of the Great Charter. But probably the lord who
kept a court was entitled to demand of it a judgment 'ab-
judicating' from the tenement a tenant who, after sufficient
warnings, would not render his due service[2]. However, it seems
that our king's court will not sanction so strong a measure.
The most that it permits the lord to do is this:—after distraining the tenant by his chattels, the lord may obtain from his
seignorial tribunal a judgment authorizing him to distrain the
tenant by his land. This obtained, he can seize the land into
his own hand, but only by way of distress, only as a mere *gage*
(*simplex namium*), and as a mode of coercing the tenant into
the path of duty. He may take no fruits from the land, he
may make no profit of it, he must ever be ready to give it up if
the tenant will satisfy all just demands[3]. Even this is possible
only to the lord who is great enough to keep up an efficient
court for his freeholders. In England the aboriginal weakness
and rapid degeneration of the feudal tribunals, and the dominance of a royal court which does not love seignorial justice
secure to the freeholding tenant a very tight grip on the land.
At the end of Henry III.'s reign he is too well off. If he
chooses to let the land 'lie fresh,' to keep no distrainable chattels

---

[1] Leg. Henr. 51 § 3; Glanvill, ix. 8; Bracton, f. 157 b; Note Book, pl. 2, 78,
270, 348, 370, 1207; Bigelow, Hist. Procedure, 202–8. Distraint as a means of
compelling appearance in court is of course another matter.

[2] Hist. Abingd. ii. p. 128: in Henry I.'s time a tenant of the abbey is held
to have forfeited his land by default in military service; but the abbot does not
proceed to extremities. See also Bigelow, Placita, pp. 97, 166–173. The last of
these cases goes to show that even in the earliest years of Henry II. a tenant
could not be deprived of his land for non-payment of rent. In older times a
refusal to perform military service would have been a near approach to a felony.
Lib. Feud. ii. 24: 'Non est alia iustior causa beneficii auferendi, quam si id,
propter quod beneficium datum fuerit, servitium facere recusaverit.' But in
England 'feudal' tenure in becoming universal soon loses its 'conditionalness.'

[3] Glanvill, ix. c. 8; Bracton, f. 205 b; Note Book, pl. 2, 270, 348, 370.

on it, his lord is powerless. An action must be borrowed
from the canonists in order that he may be constrained to fulfil
his engagements or be turned out of his tenement[1].

[p. 336]   However, in the thirteenth century the possibility, never
very remote, that the land would escheat, was, when coupled
with the power of distress, a quite sufficient manifestation of
the idea that the land, though it was the tenant's, was also the
lord's. The tenant's interest in it might at any time expire
and leave the lord's interest subsisting.

We are now in a position to foresee that of the four great
free tenures one is destined to grow at the expense of the rest.
For a moment it might be thought that the trenchant statute
of 1290, the *Quia emptores terrarum*, would stereotype the
tenures for ever. To some extent this is true in law but
only to some extent. Even after the statute a new tenure
might sometimes be created. Every feoffment made by a tenant
in frankalmoin in favour of a layman would create a tenure
between the donee and the donor's lord which could not be
frankalmoin, since the donee was a layman, and which was
reckoned a tenure in socage; thus in a perfectly regular way
socage would grow at the expense of frankalmoin[2]. We have
seen also that in the course of the thirteenth century many of
the serjeanties were deliberately commuted for less archaic
tenures, in some cases by the consent of both parties, still more
often against the tenant's will: he had put himself into the
wrong by alienating without the king's licence, and the king
exercised the right of 'arrenting the serjeanty[3].' But we will
here speak of changes less definitely made. When once it was
established that the little serjeanties gave the king no prerogative wardship, 'petty serjeanty' came to be regarded as but
'socage in effect[4].' A similar cause gave rise to the doctrine
that tenure of a mesne lord is never tenure by serjeanty[5];

(marginal note: Survey of the various tenures.)

---

[1] The extreme reluctance of ancient law to deprive a tenant of his tenement
merely because he has not paid rent is shown by the *gavelet* procedure of the
Kentish custom; Statutes, i. p. 225. After a great deal of forbearance the land
is at last adjudged to the lord; but even then the tenant has a theoretical right
of redeeming it by paying the arrears nine (or is it eighteen?) times over and
adding a wergild of £5. The law does not like to say that he has lost the land
for good and all, though it imposes an impossible condition upon him if he
wishes to have it back again.

[2] Littleton, sec. 139.   [3] See above, p. 334.

[4] Littleton, sec. 160; see above, p. 323.   [5] Littleton, sec. 159.

the rights of a mesne lord to the wardship and marriage of his tenant by serjeanty seem to have become doubtful, and to have finally disappeared, and by this time the term *socage* [p. 337] already covered so heterogeneous a mass of tenures that it could be easily stretched yet a little further so as to include what Bracton would certainly have called serjeanties[1]. Again, there can be little doubt that a very large number of military tenures became tenures in socage, and this without anyone observing the change. In Bracton's day the test of military tenure is the liability to scutage, and, as already said, the peasant or yeoman very often had to pay it; if he had not to pay it, this was because his lord had consented to bear the burden. In Edward I.'s day scutage was becoming, under his grandson it became, obsolete. There was nothing then in actual fact to mark off the services of the yeoman who was liable to pay scutage as well as to pay rent, from those of the yeoman who was free even in law from this never collected tax. The one was theoretically a military tenant, the other was not; in the one case the lord might have claimed wardship and marriage, in the other he could not; but then we have to observe, that, if the tenant held at a full or even a substantial rent, wardship and marriage would be unprofitable rights. The lord wanted rent-paying tenants; he did not want land thrown on his hands together with a troop of girls and boys with claims for food and clothing. Thus, scutage being extinct, wardships and marriages unprofitable, mere oblivion would do the rest; many a tenure which had once been, at least in name, a military tenure would become socage. Thus socage begins to swallow up the other tenures, and preparation is already made for the day when all, or practically all, tenants will hold by the once humble tenure of the *sokemanni*.

§ 12. *Unfree Tenure.*

Freehold tenure.

The tenures of which we have hitherto spoken are free tenures. To free tenure is opposed villein tenure, to the free tenement the villein tenement, to the freeholder (*libere tenens*) the tenant in villeinage. This is the contrast suggested by the

[1] Britton, ii. 10, and the editor's note.

word 'free'; but the terms 'free tenement' and 'freeholder'
are becoming the centre of technical learning. We may well
[p. 338] find that a man holds land and that there is no taint of
villeinage or unfreedom in the case, and yet that he has no
freehold and is not a freeholder. These terms have begun to
imply that the tenant holds heritably, or for life. Perhaps
we shall be truer to history if we state this doctrine in a
negative form :—these terms imply that the tenant does not
hold merely at the will of another, and that he does not hold
for some definite space of time : a tenant at will is not a freeholder, a tenant for years is not a freeholder. Such tenancies
as these are becoming common in every zone of the social
system, and they imply no servility, nothing that is inconsistent with perfect freedom. Thus, for example, King John
will provide for his foreign captains by giving them lands 'for
their support in our service so long as we shall think fit,' and in
such a case this tenancy at will by a soldier is from some points
of view the best representative of the *beneficia* and *feoda* of past
centuries[1]. But now-a-days such tenancies are sharply contrasted with *feoda ;* the tenant has no fee and no free tenement.
And so again we may see a great man taking lands for a term
of years at a money rent ; he has done nothing in derogation of
his freedom ; the rent may be trifling ; still he is no freeholder.

A full explanation of this phenomenon, that a man should Technical meaning of 'freehold.'
hold land, and hold it not unfreely, and yet not hold it freely,
can not be given in this context since it would involve a discussion of the English theory of possession or seisin. But we
must not fail to notice that the term 'free tenement' has ever
since Henry II.'s day implied possessory protection by the
king's court. This is of great moment. From our statement
of the relation between the freehold tenant and his lord we
have as yet omitted the element of jurisdiction. The existence
of this element our law fully admitted and at one time it
threatened to become of vital importance. It was law that
the lord might hold a court of and for his tenants ; it was
law that if *A* was holding land of *M* and *X* desired to prove
that he and not *A* ought to be *M*'s tenant, *M*'s court (if he held
one) was the tribunal proper to decide upon the justice of this
claim ; only if *M* made default in justice, could *X* (perhaps
after recourse to all *M*'s superior lords) bring his case before

---

[1] See *e.g.* the provision for Engelard of Cigogné: Rot. Cl. i. 79.

the king's court. This principle of feudal justice is admitted, [p. 330] though its operation has been hampered and controlled; in particular, the king has given in his court a possessory remedy to every ejected freeholder. Every one who can say that he has been 'disseised unjustly and without a judgment of his free tenement' shall be restored to his seisin by the king's justices. Thus the term 'free tenement' becomes the pivot of a whole system of remedies. Clearly they are denied to one who has been holding 'unfreely,' who has been holding in villeinage; but a doctrine of possession now becomes necessary and has many problems before it   What if the ejected person was holding at the will of another? Perhaps it is natural to say that, albeit he occupied or 'detained' the tenement, still he was not possessed of it. At any rate this was said. The tenant at will *tenet nomine alieno; possidet cuius nomine possidetur;* eject the tenant at will, you disseise (dispossess) not him, but his lord, and his lord has the remedy. And what of the tenant for years? The same was said. He holds on behalf of another; eject him, you disseise that other. Such was the doctrine of the twelfth century; but already before the middle of the thirteenth the lawyers had discovered that they had made a mistake, that the 'termor' or tenant for years deserved possessory protection, and they invented a new action for him. The action however was new, and did not interfere with the older actions which protected the seisin of free tenement; it was too late to say that the termor had a free tenement or was a freeholder. This episode in our legal history had important consequences; it rules the terminology of our law even at the present day and hereafter we shall speak of it more at large: it is an episode in the history of private law. In the thirteenth century the main contrast suggested by the phrase 'free tenement' was still the villein tenement, and tenure in villeinage is intimately connected with some of the main principles of public law; indeed from one point of view it may be regarded as a creature of the law of jurisdiction, of the law which establishes courts of justice and assigns to each of them its proper sphere.

Villeinage as tenure and as status.

The name 'villeinage' at once tells us that we are approaching a region in which the law of tenure is as a matter of fact intertwined with the law of personal status: 'villeinage' is a tenure, it is also a status. On the one hand, the tenant in [p. 340] villeinage is normally a villein; the unfree tenements are held by unfree men; on the other hand, the villein usually has a villein tenement; the unfree man is an unfree tenant. Then again, the *villanus* gets his name from the *villa*, and this may well lead us to expect that his condition can not be adequately described if we isolate him from his fellows; he is a member of a community, a villein community. The law of tenure, the law of status, the law which regulates the communal life of vills or townships are knotted together. Still the knot may be unravelled. It is very possible, as Bracton often assures us, for a free man to hold in villeinage, and thus we may speak of villein tenure as something distinct from villein status. Again, as we shall hereafter see, the communal element which undoubtedly exists in villeinage, is much neglected by the king's courts, and is rather of social and economic than of legal importance.

We may suppose therefore that the tenant in villeinage is a free man. What then are the characteristics of his tenure[1]? Now in the first place we may notice that it is not protected in the king's courts. For a moment perhaps there was some little doubt about this, some chance that Pateshull and Raleigh would forestall by two long centuries the exploits ascribed to Brian and Danby, and would protect the predecessor of the copyholder even against his lord[2]. This would have been a bold stroke. The ready remedy for the ejected freeholder laid stress on the fact that he had been disseised of his 'free' tenement, and, however free the tenant in villeinage might be, his tenement was unfree. A quite new remedy would have been necessary for his protection; the opportunity for its invention was lost, and did not recur until the middle ages were expiring[3].

Villein tenure.

Unprotected by the king's courts.

---

[1] We need hardly say that the whole of this subject is admirably discussed in Vinogradoff's Villainage in England.

[2] The important cases are *Bestenover* v. *Montacute*, Note-Book, pl. 70, 88, and *William Henry's son* v. *Bartholomew Eustace's son*, Ibid. pl. 1103. As to the decisions of Brian and Danby under Edw. IV., see Littl. Tenures, sec. 77; it is doubtful whether Littleton wrote this passage.

[3] Vinogradoff, Villainage, 78–81. It is possible to regard these decisions of Pateshull and Raleigh as belated rather than premature; but the formula of the assize of novel disseisin lays stress on the freedom of the tenement, and therefore goes to prove that the lawyers of Henry II.'s reign had not intended to protect villein holding. The original version of Magna Carta might seem to give protection to the free man holding in villeinage; but in 1217 some words were

It was law then, that if the tenant in villeinage was ejected, [p. 341] either by his lord or by a third person, the king's court would not restore him to the land, nor would it give him damages against his lord in respect of the ejectment. He held the land *nomine alieno,* on his lord's behalf; if a third person ejected him, the lord was disseised. Before the end of the thirteenth century, the king's courts were beginning to state their doctrine in a more positive shape :—the tenant in villeinage is in our eyes a tenant at will of the lord[1].

Want of remedy and want of right. The shade of meaning which such words bear at any given moment is hard to catch, for this depends on the relation between the king's courts and other courts. At a time when the feudal courts have become insignificant, denial of remedy in the king's court will be equivalent to a denial of right, and to say that the tenant in villeinage is deemed by the king's court to hold at his lord's will is in effect to say that the lord will do nothing illegal in ejecting him. At an earlier time the royal tribunal was but one among many organs of the law, and the cause for our wonder should be that it has undertaken to protect in his possession every one who holds freely, not that it has stopped at this point and denied protection to those who, albeit free men, are doing what are deemed villein services. We have but to look abroad to see this. By its care for every freeholder, though he were but a socage tenant with many lords above him, our king's court would gradually propagate the notion that those whom it left uncared for were rightless. But this would be an affair of time. Even in the thirteenth century, the freeholder could not always bring a proprietary action before the royal tribunal without the help of some legal fiction, and in Bracton's day men had not yet forgotten that the royal remedies which were in daily use were new indulgences conceded by the prince to his people[2].

interpolated, apparently for the very purpose of showing that his case was outside the charter. The text of 1215 says, 'Nullus liber homo......dissaisietur... nisi per legale judicium etc.' That of 1217 says 'Nullus liber homo......dis-*saisietur de libero tenemento suo vel libertatibus vel liberis consuetudinibus suis...* nisi etc.'

[1] Britton, ii. 13: 'Villenage est tenement de demeynes de chescun seignur, baillé a tenir a sa volunté par vileins services de emprouwer al oes le seignur.'

[2] Bracton, f. 164 b: 'de beneficio principis succurritur ei per recognitionem assisae novae disseisinae multis vigiliis excogitatam et inventam.'

[p. 342] As a matter of fact, tenure in villeinage is protected, and if we choose to say that it is protected by 'positive morality' rather than by 'law properly so called,' we are bound to add that it is protected by a morality which keeps a court, which uses legal forms, which is conceived as law, or as something akin to law[1]. The lord has a court; in that court the tenant in villeinage, even though he be personally unfree, appears as no mere tenant at will, but as holding permanently, often heritably, on fairly definite terms. He is a customary tenant, *custumarius, consuetudinarius;* he holds according to the custom of the manor. Were we Germans, we might say that he holds under *Hofrecht,* the law of the manor, though his rights are not recognized by *Landrecht,* the general law of the realm. This we can not say; the manorial custom very rarely, if ever, dignifies itself with the name of law; but still it is a custom which has been and ought to be enforced by a court, enforced if need be by compulsory processes which will eject the wrongful in favour of the rightful occupant. The tenant in villeinage does not scruple to say that he is seised of the land *de iure* 'according to the custom of the manor[2],' though his lord may be seised of it according to the law of the king's courts. Such evidence as we have goes to show that, when his lord was not concerned, he was well enough protected in his holding. The rolls of manorial courts bear witness to a great deal of litigation concerning the villein tenements; it seems to be conducted with strict regularity; the procedure does not err on the side of formlessness; it is rigid, it is captious; the court is no court of equity which can overlook a pleader's blunder and do natural justice; it administers custom. No doubt there are cash transactions between the lord and the litigants; the lord has procedural advantages for sale; but then so has the king. There is nothing disgraceful, nothing illegal, in buying the right to have an inquest, a good inquest, nor even in promising an augmented price if the verdict be favourable. Then as to the case between lord and tenant, the tenant can not sue the lord in the lord's court; the tenant in villeinage ejected by the lord has no remedy anywhere. But is this, we may ask, a

---

[1] We are here dealing with normal cases. Sometimes, as will be explained in our chapter on Jurisdiction, the lord may have had so few tenants in villeinage that he did not keep a court for them.

[2] Select Pleas in Manorial Courts, *e.g.* p. 39.

denial of legal right? The king disseises the Earl of Glou- [p. 343]
cester; the earl has no remedy, no remedy anywhere; yet we
do not deny that the honour of Gloucester is the earl's by law
or that in disseising him the king will break the law.

Evidence of the 'extents.'   A good proof that the lords in general felt themselves
bound more or less conclusively by the terms of the customary
tenures is to be found in the care they took that those terms
should be recorded. From time to time an 'extent' was made
of the manor. A jury of tenants, often of unfree men, was
sworn to set forth the particulars of each tenancy and its
verdict condescended to the smallest details. Such extents
were made in the interest of the lords, who were anxious that
all due services should be done; but they imply that other and
greater services are not due, and that the customary tenants,
even though they be unfree men, owe these services for their
tenements, no less and no more. Statements to the effect that
the tenants are not bound to do services of a particular kind
are not very uncommon.

Attempt to define villein tenure.   As characteristics of villein tenure we have therefore these
two features:—it is not protected by the king's courts; in
general it is protected by another court, the court of the lord,
though even there it is not protected against the lord. Still as
a matter of legal theory we can not regard these features as the
essence of the tenure. We should invert the order of logic
were we to say that this tenure is villein because the king's
justices treat it as a mere tenure at will; rather they treat it as
a mere tenure at will because it is a villein, an unfree, tenure.
We must look therefore in this as in other cases to the services
which the tenant performs, if we are to define the nature of his
tenure. He holds in villeinage because he performs villein
services.

The manorial arrangement.   A brief digression into a domain which belongs rather to
economic than to legal history here becomes inevitable. The
phenomena of medieval agriculture are now attracting the
attention that they deserve: here we are only concerned with
them in so far as some knowledge of them must be presupposed
by any exposition of the law of the thirteenth century[1].
Postponing until a later time any debate as to whether the

---

[1] It will be almost needless to refer the reader to the works of Nasse,
Seebohm, Ashley, Cunningham and Vinogradoff. See also Maitland, Domesday
Book, 362 ff.

[p. 344] term *manor* bore a technical meaning, we observe that this term is constantly used to describe a proprietary unit of common occurrence :—the well-to-do landholder holds a manor or many manors. Now speaking very generally we may say that a man who holds a manor has in the first place a house or homestead which is occupied by himself, his bailiffs or servants. Along with this he holds cultivable land, which is in the fullest sense (so far as feudal theory permits) his own ; it is his demesne land. Then also, as part of the same complex of rights, he holds land which is holden of him by tenants, some of whom, it may be, are freeholders, holding in socage or by military service, while the remainder of them, usually the large majority of them, hold in villeinage, by a merely customary tenure. In the terms used to describe these various lands we notice a certain instructive ambiguity. The land that the lord himself occupies and of which he takes the fruits he indubitably holds 'in demesne'; the land holden of him by his freehold tenants he indubitably does not hold 'in demesne'; his freehold tenants hold it in demesne, unless indeed, as may well be the case, they have yet other freeholders below them. But as to the lands holden of him by villein tenure, the use of words seems to fluctuate ; at one moment he is said to hold and be seised of them in demesne, at the next they are sharply distinguished from his demesne lands, that term being reserved for those portions of the soil in which no tenant free or villein has any rights. In short, language reflects the dual nature of tenure in villeinage ; it is tenure and yet it is not tenure. The king's courts, giving no protection to the tenant, say that the lord is seised in demesne ; but the manorial custom must distinguish between the lands holden in villeinage and those lands which are occupied by the lord and which in a narrower sense of the word are his demesne[1].

---

[1] Thus Bracton, f. 75 b : 'tam dominica quam villenagia quae dici possunt dominica.' Ibid. f. 98 : 'tertia pars villenagii quod est quasi dominicum.' In the Hundred Rolls some jurors habitually reckon the villeinage to be part of the demesne, while others as habitually exclude the villeinage when they give the contents of the demesne. Thus (ii. 343) in the Bunstow Hundred of Essex their formula is—the lord has *x* acres in demesne of which *y* are in villeinage. On the other hand, in Huntingdonshire (*e.g.* ii. 656) the lands holden by villein tenants are not part of what the lord holds in demesne. The word *demesne,* which is the Anglo-French equivalent for the Latin *dominicum,* is very curious. Our spelling of it seems due to a false derivation from the French *mesnie* (household) ; the demesne lands supply the lord's household. Not improbably

The field
system.

We have usually therefore in the manor lands of three [p. 345] kinds, (1) the demesne strictly so called, (2) the land of the lord's freehold tenants, (3) the *villenagium*, the land holden of the lord by villein or customary tenure. Now in the common case all these lands are bound together into a single whole by two economic bonds. In the first place, the demesne lands are cultivated wholly or in part by the labour of the tenants of the other lands, labour which they are bound to supply by reason of their tenure. A little labour in the way of ploughing and reaping is got out of the freehold tenants; much labour of many various kinds is obtained from the tenants in villeinage, so much in many cases that the lord has but small, if any, need to hire labourers. Then in the second place, these various tenements lie intermingled; neither the lord's demesne nor the tenant's tenement can be surrounded by one ring-fence. The lord has his house and homestead; each tenant has his house with more or less curtilage surrounding it; but the arable portions of the demesne and of the various other tenements lie mixed up together in the great open fields. There will be two or three or perhaps more great fields, and each tenement will consist of a number of small strips, of an acre or half-acre apiece, dissipated about in each of these fields[1]. These fields are subjected to a common course of agriculture, a two-field system or a three-field system, so that a whole field will lie idle at one time, or be sown with winter seed or, as the case may be, with spring seed. After harvest and until the time for tilling comes, the lord and the tenants turn their beasts to graze over the whole field.

The
virgates.

Then we further notice that the various tenements, at least those held in villeinage, are supposed to be of equal extent and of equal value, or rather to fall into a few classes, the members of each class being equal among themselves. Thus it is usual to find a number of tenants in villeinage each of whom is said [p. 346]

---

another mistake confounded confusion. Bracton, f. 263, apparently believed that the word was connected with the Latin *mensa:* 'est autem dominicum quod quis habet ad mensam suam'; the demesne lands supply the lord's table, they are his 'board-lands.' Cf. Whitby Cart. i. 200: 'et ea conditione...illam ...terram ecclesiae reddidi ut nullus a dominica mensa illam auferret.' Spelman, Gloss. s.v. *dominicum*, long ago pointed out that the *s* in *demesne* is an intruder.

1 Thus a tenement containing in all but five acres may consist of no less than fourteen disconnected pieces; Fines, ed. Hunter, i. 42.

to hold a virgate or yard of land.   Each of them has his house
and the same number of strips of arable land; each of them
does precisely the same service to his lord.   Then there may
appear a class of half-virgaters, each of whom does about half
what is done by a virgater; and there may be classes which
have smaller tenements but which yet have some arable land.
Then, most likely, there will be a class of cottagers without
any arable; but the cottage and croft of one of them will be
regarded as equal to the cottage and croft of another and will
provide the lord with the same services.   And we sometimes
seem to see that the distribution of the arable strips is so
arranged as to equalize the value of the various tenements.   All
the virgates are to be equal in value as well as equal in acreage
so far as is possible.   One virgater must not have more than
his share of the best land.   The strips have been distributed
with some regularity, so that a strip of B's virgate will always
have a strip of A's to the right and a strip of C's to the left of
it.   Then again, the manor will probably comprise meadow land
and pasture land.   Each virgate may have a piece of meadow
annexed to it, the meadow being treated as an appurtenance of
the arable land; or again, some of the meadows may be divided
each year by lot between the various tenants, and the lord may
have certain strips thereof in one year and other strips in
another year[1]; but, when the grass has been mown, all the
strips will be thrown open to the cattle of the lord and his
tenants.   There is also land permanently devoted to pasturage;
a right to turn out beasts upon it is commonly annexed to
every tenement or to every considerable tenement.   Lastly, we
must just notice that in the lord's court the manor has an
organ capable of regulating all these matters, capable for
example of deciding how many beasts each tenement may send
to the pasture, and, when the rights of the freehold tenants
are not concerned, the decrees and judgments of this court will
be binding, for the king's courts will give no help to those who
hold in villeinage.

[p. 348]   Now speaking generally we may say that the services which *Villein*
the tenant in villeinage owes to his lord consist chiefly of the *services.*
duty of cultivating the lord's demesne.   Before the thirteenth
century is over we may indeed find numerous cases in which
the payment of a money rent forms a substantial part of his

[1] Vinogradoff, p. 259.

service and he is hardly bound to do more labour than is exacted from many of the freeholders, some ploughing and some
reaping. It is very possible that there are some classes of
tenants now reckoned to hold in villeinage, whose predecessors
were in this same position at a remote time; they are *gavel-
manni*, men who pay *gafol*, or they are *censuarii*, and such their
forefathers may have been all along[1]. To suppose that in all
cases the system of rents paid in money or in produce has
grown out of a system of labour services is to make an
unverified assumption. On the other hand, in very many
cases we can see that the money rent is new. We may see
the process of commutation in all its various stages, from the
stage in which the lord is beginning to take a penny or a
halfpenny instead of each 'work' that in that particular year he
does not happen to want, through the stage in which he
habitually takes each year the same sum in respect of the
same number of works but has expressly reserved to himself
the power of exacting the works in kind, to the ultimate stage
in which there is a distinct understanding that the tenant is
to pay rent instead of doing work. But we may for a moment
treat as typical the cases in which the tenant hardly pays anything. Of such cases there are plenty. The tenant may pay
some small sums, but these are not regarded as the rent of his
tenement. They bear English names; sometimes they seem to
have their origin in the lord's jurisdictional powers rather than
in his rights as a landowner, as when we read of *tithingpenny,
wardpenny, witepenny*; sometimes they look like a return made
to the lord, not for the tenement itself, but for rights over the
wastes and waters, as when we read of *fishsilver, woodsilver,
sedgesilver*. But in the main the tenant must work for his
tenement.

A typical
case of
villein
services.

Now the labour that he has to do is often minutely defined [p. 349]
by the manorial custom and described in the manorial 'extent.'
Let us take one out of a thousand examples. In the Abbot of
Ramsey's manor of Stukeley in Huntingdonshire the services of
a virgater are these[2]:—From the 29th of September until the
29th of June he must work two days a week, to wit on Monday
and Wednesday; and on Friday he must plough with all the
beasts of his team; but he has a holiday for a fortnight at

---

[1] Vinogradoff, Essay I. chap. vi.
[2] Cart. Rams. i. 393.

Christmas and for a week at Easter and at Whitsuntide. If one
of the Fridays on which he ought to plough is a festival or if
the weather is bad, he must do the ploughing on some other
day. Between the 29th of September and the 11th of November
he must also plough and harrow half an acre for wheat, and for
sowing that half-acre he must give of his own seed the eighth
part of a quarter: whether that quantity be more or less than
is necessary for sowing the half-acre he must give that quantity,
no more, no less: and on account of this seed he is excused
one day's work. At Christmas time he must make two quarters
of malt and for each quarter he is excused one day's work. At
Christmas he shall give three hens and a cock or four pence
and at Easter ten eggs. He must also do six carryings (*ave-
ragia*) in the year within the county between the 29th of June
and the end of harvest at whatever time the bailiff shall choose,
or, if the lord pleases, he shall between the 29th of June and
the 29th of September work five days a week, working the
whole day at whatever work is set him, besides carrying corn,
for he shall carry but four cartloads of corn for a day's work.
If at harvest time the lord shall have two or three 'boon works'
(*precationes*), he shall come to them with all the able-bodied
members of his family save his wife, so that he must send at
least three men to the work. He pays sheriff's aid, hundredpenny and ward-penny, namely 6¼*d.*

Now the main features of this arrangement we find repeated Week work
and boon
days.
in countless instances. The tenant has to do 'week work,' as it
has been called: to work two or three days in every week
during the greater part of the year, four or five during the busy
summer months. Then at harvest time there are also some
'boon days' (*precariae, precationes*); at the lord's petition or
boon the tenant must bring all his hands to reap and carry the
[p. 850] crops and on these days the lord often has to supply food; at
Stukeley it is bread, beer and cheese on the first day, meat on
the second, herrings on the third. But matters are yet more
minutely fixed. Our Stukeley tenant has to 'work' so many
days a week; the choice of work rests with the lord, but
custom has fixed the amount that shall be accounted a day's
work. For instance on the neighbouring manor of Warboys
gathering and carrying three bundles of thorns are regarded as
a day's work[1]. At Stukeley if the tenant has to fell timber, the

---

[1] Cart. Rams. i. 310.

day's work is over at noon, unless the lord provides dinner, and then the work lasts all day. Sometimes it is remarked that a task which counts as a day's work can really be done in half a day[1]. The exact distance that he must go with his lord's wagons in order that he may claim to have performed an *averagium* is well known, and, when the lord is bound to supply food or drink, the quantity and quality thereof are determined. On the Ramsey manors a sick tenant will be excused a whole year's work if his illness lasts so long; after the year he must get his work done for him as best he may. A half-virgater will do proportionately less work, a cottager still less; thus at Stukeley the cottager works on Mondays throughout the year and on Fridays also in harvest time.

Merchet and tallage.

There is more to be said. Our Stukeley virgater pays 'merchet' as best he may, that is to say, if he wishes to give his daughter in marriage he must pay money to the lord and the amount that he has to pay is not fixed. If he has a foal or calf born of his own mare or cow, he must not sell it without the lord's leave. If he has an oak, ash or pear-tree growing in his court, he must not fell it, except for the repair of his house, without the lord's leave. When he dies his widow shall pay a heriot of five shillings and be quit of work for thirty days. These are common features, and the merchet is of peculiar importance, as will be seen hereafter. Sometimes it is only paid if the girl is married outside the vill; sometimes the amount is fixed. And so as to selling beasts; occasionally the lord's right is but a right of preemption. And then in many cases the villein tenants are liable to be tallaged, sometimes once a year, sometimes twice in seven years; sometimes the [p. 351] amount of this tax is defined, sometimes they can be 'tallaged high and low' (*de haut en bas*). Often they are bound to 'suit of mill,' that is to say, they must not grind their corn elsewhere than at the lord's mill. About all these matters we sometimes find rules which set certain definite limits to the tenant's duty and the lord's right[2].

What is the essence of villein tenure.

Such were some of the commonest services due from the

---

[1] Cart. Rams. i. 315: 'opera ad taschum assignata, quae aliquando per dimidium diem poterunt adimpleri.'

[2] Thus Cart. Rams. i. 473: the tenant owes suit to the lord's mill; but between 1st Aug. and 29th Sept. he may grind elsewhere if the lord's mill is too busy, and corn that he has purchased may be ground anywhere.

holder of a villein tenement. As yet, however, we have attained to nothing that can be called a definition of the tenure.
To say that it is a tenure defined by custom but not protected
by the king's courts is no satisfactory definition, for this, as
already said, is to mistake the consequence for the cause. Now
Bracton constantly assumes that everyone will understand him
when he speaks of villein services, but he never undertakes
to tell us precisely what it is that makes them villein, and,
when we turn to the manorial extents, we not unfrequently
meet with tenures that we know not how to classify. Apart
from the tenants who certainly are freeholders and the tenants
who certainly hold in villeinage, we see here and there a few
men whose position seems very doubtful; we do not like to
predict either that they will or that they will not find protection in the royal courts. We have to remember that the
test which in later days will serve to mark off freehold from
copyhold tenure is as yet inapplicable. No one as yet holds
land 'by copy of court roll'; the lords are only just beginning
to keep court rolls and it is long ere the court roll becomes a
register of title. If alienations and descents are entered upon
it, this is done merely to show that the steward has received or
has yet to collect a fine or a heriot, and the terms on which a
new tenant takes land are seldom mentioned. If from a modern
conveyance of a copyhold tenement we abstract the copy of the
court roll and even the court roll itself, we still have left the
intermediation of the lord between the vendor and the purchaser: the land is supposed to pass through the lord's hand.
[p. 352] But when dealing with the thirteenth, to say nothing of the
twelfth, century, we can not make the lord's intervention a
proof of villein tenure. We may well find the conveyance of a
freehold taking in all essentials the form of 'surrender and
admittance'; the old tenant yields up the land to the lord, the
lord gives it to the new tenant; the transaction takes place in
court; the symbolical rod is employed; no charter is necessary[1].
Indeed when there was to be no subinfeudation but a substitution of a new for an old tenant, we may well be surprised that
this could ever be effected without a double conveyance. Moreover if we say that the lord can prevent the alienation of villein,
but can not prevent the alienation of free tenements we still
have not solved the question; to say that a tenement is villein

[1] See above, p. 345.

because it can not be alienated without the lord's consent, is to put the cart before the horse.

'The will of the lord.' Nor again can we find the solution in the phrase 'to hold at the will of the lord.' If for a moment we take this phrase merely to denote that the tenure is unprotected by the king's court, we are brought once more to the fruitless proposition that it is unprotected because it is unprotected. If, on the other hand, we take the phrase to imply that there is no court which protects the tenure, or that the lord can at any moment eject the tenant without breach of any custom, then, to say the least, the great mass of villein tenures will escape from our definition. Tenures which really are tenures 'at will,' unprotected by any custom, are to be found, and that too in high places, but then they are in general carefully distinguished from the villein tenures. In the extents and manorial rolls of the thirteenth century it is rare to find that the tenants in villeinage are said to hold at the will of the lord[1]. Still when we turn, as we now must, to find the element in villein services which makes them villein, this phrase 'at the lord's will' must again meet us.

Villeinage and labour. That a tenure which compels to agricultural labour is [p.353] unfree, this we certainly can not say. The philology of the time made ploughing service the characteristic feature of socage[2], and often enough a freeholder had to give his aid in ploughing and reaping his lord's demesne; nor can we say for certain that he could always do his work by deputy, for the duty cast upon him was sometimes such as could not well be delegated, in particular that of riding after the labourers 'with his rod' and keeping them up to their work[3]. There is nothing servile in having to do such a duty in person. In general, no doubt, the freeholder only aids his lord's agriculture

[1] In the Hundred Rolls the phrase 'at the will of the lord' occurs often enough in connexion with particular services, *e.g.* ii. 479, 'possunt talliari ad voluntatem domini'; and where rent is payable the same phrase is often used to show that the lord has a choice between rent and work, *e.g.* ii. 554, 'et valent consuetudines eiusdem per annum ad voluntatem domini vj. sol.'; but it is rare to find it said that the tenant in villeinage *holds* at the will of the lord. However the jurors of the Northstow hundred of Cambridgeshire say this plainly in some cases (ii. 461-2) as also do those of the Papworth hundred.

[2] See above, p. 293.

[3] Thus when it is said that a tenant must bring his servants to the boon works 'et ipse debet eos adducere et ibi interesse,' his presence in person seems required; Placit. Abbrev. p. 97 (Bedf.).

during a few weeks in the year; he helps at the 'boon works'
but does no 'week work'; still it is difficult to make the
distinction between freedom and unfreedom turn upon the
mere amount of work that has to be done. If there is no
villeinage in labouring ten days in the year why should there
be any villeinage in labouring three days a week? On the
whole our guides direct us not to the character, nor to the
amount of the work, but to its certainty or uncertainty[1].
The typical tenant in villeinage does not know in the evening
what he will have to do in the morning[2]. Now this, when
properly understood, is very generally true of the tenants who
are bound to do much labour, to do 'week work.' They
know a great deal about the amount of work that they will
have to do in each year, in each week, on each day; they know,
for example, that the custom exacts from them three and no
more 'works' in every week, that Tuesday is not a work day,
that if they are set to ditch they must ditch so many perches
before the 'work' will be accomplished, that to drive a cart to
one place is 'one work,' to another place 'two works'; they know
whether when set to thresh they can stop at nones or must
go on to vespers. Still there is a large element of real uncertainty; the lord's will counts for much; when they go to bed on
Sunday night they do not know what Monday's work will be: it
may be threshing, ditching, carrying; they can not tell. This
seems the point that is seized by law and that general opinion
[p. 354] of which law is the exponent: any considerable uncertainty as
to the amount or the kind of the agricultural services makes the
tenure unfree. The tenure is unfree, not because the tenant
'holds at the will of the lord,' in the sense of being removable
at a moment's notice, but because his services, though in many
respects minutely defined by custom, can not be altogether
defined without frequent reference to the lord's will. This
doctrine has good sense in it. The man who on going to bed
knows that he must spend the morrow in working for his lord
and does not know to what kind of work he may be put, though
he may be legally a free man, free to fling up his tenement and
go away, is in fact for the time being bound by his tenure
to live the same life that is led by the great mass of unfree
men. Custom sets many limits to his labours; custom sets
many limits to theirs; the idea of abandoning his home never

---

[1] Note Book, pl. 1210.   [2] Bracton, f. 26, 208 b.

enters his head; the lord's will plays a large part in shaping his life.

Definition of villein services. This then seems to have been the test usually applied by the king's court. If the labour services are 'uncertain,' the tenure is unfree; and it is a test which condemns as unfree the great bulk of the tenures which obliged men to perform any considerable amount of agricultural labour for their lord, because, however minutely some particulars of those services may be defined, there is generally a spacious room left for the play of the lord's will. Thus the test roughly coincides with another:— labour service is not necessarily unfree, but a service which consists of much labour, of labour to be done all the year round, is almost of necessity unfree; for almost of necessity the tenant will be bound to obey, within wide limits, whatever commands the lord or the lord's bailiff may give him. Thus to hold land by 'fork and flail,' by work done day by day, or week by week on the lord's demesne, is to hold in villeinage[1].

Tests of villein tenure. Other tests are in use. Any service which stamps the tenant as an unfree man, stamps his tenure as unfree; and in common opinion such services there are, notably the *merchetum.*

The merchet. Now among the thousands of entries in English documents relating to this payment, it would we believe be utterly impossible to find one which gave any sanction to the tales of a *ius primae noctis*[2]. The context in which this duty is usually mentioned [p. 355] explains at least one of the reasons which underlie it. The tenant may not give his daughter (in some cases his son or daughter) in marriage—at least not outside the manor,—and he may not have his son ordained, and he may not sell horse or ox, without the lord's leave:—the stock on the tenement is not to be diminished. No doubt a subjection to this restraint was regarded as very base, and sometimes it is described in vigorous words which express a free man's loathing for servility:—'he must buy, he must make ransom for, his flesh and blood.' This is intelligible; a payment for leave to give one's daughter in marriage or for leave to send one's son to school, naturally suggests bondage, personal bondage, bondage which is in one's blood. It is constantly used as a test of personal serfage

---

[1] Placit. Abbrev. p. 23 (Bucks.): 'tenet ad furcam et flagellum et in villenagio'; Ibid. p. 92 (North.): 'per consuetudines serviles ad furcam et flagellum.' See Vinogradoff, p. 170.

[2] These stories are examined by Karl Schmidt, Jus Primae Noctis.

and *a fortiori* of unfree tenure. Bracton will just allow that
the man who has to pay a merchet need not be a bondman;
it may in a given case be an incident of unfree tenure
rather than of personal servility. However, though this test
was commonly applied, we can not say that it was conclusive
even of the unfreedom of the tenure. In Northumberland
there certainly were lords of manors, lords of entire vills, who
paid merchet [1], and then we have to remember that in Scotland,
at least according to the *Regiam Maiestatem*, every woman,
were she noble, were she serf, paid 'merchet,' paid it in kine
(an earl's daughter paid twelve cows)[2], while in Wales a similar
payment was made on the marriage of every girl[3]. Very
possibly several different payments originating at different
times, perhaps among different races, and expressive of different
ideas have been fused together; but in England the merchet
is generally regarded as a base payment, a mark, though not
a conclusive mark, of personal unfreedom[4].

[1] See *e.g.* Testa de Neville, p. 393.

[2] Reg. Maj. lib. iv. c. 54.

[3] Ancient Laws of Wales; see Index s.v. *amobyr, amobragium.*

[4] In two places Bracton (f. 26, 208 b) speaks as though merchet could never
be exacted from a free man; in a third passage (f. 195) he allows that a free
man may be compelled to pay it by reason of an express agreement. Fleta,
p. 193, and Britton, i. 196, think that it is not conclusive of personal unfreedom. For the law of later days see Littleton, secs. 174 (an interpolation),
209 and Coke's comment thereon. Coke's doctrine is that the merchet may
be exacted from a free man by reason of special reservation, though not by
reason of general custom, and the positive half of this rule seems to be borne
out by Y. B. 43 Edw. III. f. 5 (Hil. pl. 13); as to the negative half, see Littleton's remark in Y. B. 34 Hen. VI. f. 15 (Mich. pl. 28). In 10 Edw. III. f. 22
(Pasch. pl. 41) a case came before the court illustrating the Northumbrian
tenures referred to in our text; the tenant, it is said, did homage, paid scutage
and merchet. It is chiefly in Northumbria, the home of drengage and thegnage
(see above, p. 279), that freeholders are to be found paying merchet; but
tenants bearing the distinctive name of Freeman and yet paying merchet are
met with elsewhere, *e.g.* Pleas in Manorial Courts, i. 94. Vinogradoff, p. 154,
argues from the Hundred Rolls that there were considerable parts of England
in which the villeins were not subject to this exaction, since the jurors of some
hundreds say nothing about it. But when we find it habitually mentioned
throughout some hundreds and never mentioned in others, the sounder
inference seems to be that it was almost universal. Some juries think fit to
mention it, others do not; just as some juries think fit to say that the villeins
hold at the will of the lord, while others do not. So again the jury for the
Langtree hundred of Oxfordshire (ii. 774) call all the tenants in villeinage
servi, while in some Cambridgeshire hundreds they are in general *custumarii.*
For a discussion of the derivation of the word *merchet* see Y. B. 15 Edw. III.,
ed. Pike, Introduction, pp. xv–xliii.

Other tests of villein tenure.

Other tests are at times suggested. The duty of serving as [p. 356] the lord's reeve whenever the lord pleases, the liability to be tallaged 'high and low,' these also are treated as implying personal bondage[1]. If the tenement descends to the youngest son instead of to the eldest son or to all the sons, the inference is sometimes drawn that it is not free. On the whole, however, our books constantly bring us back to the 'uncertainty' of the service as the best criterion of villein tenure. Certainty and uncertainty, however, are, as we have seen, matters of degree. In few, if any, cases is there no custom setting bounds to the tenant's duty of working for his lord; in most cases many bounds are set; the number of days in every week which he must spend on the demesne is ascertained; often the amount of any given kind of labour that will pass for a day's work is determined; but yet there is much uncertainty, for the tenant knows not in the evening whether in the morning he will be kept working in the fields or sent a long journey with a cart. We need not be surprised therefore if in the thirteenth century 'freehold' and 'villeinhold' are already becoming technical [p. 357] ideas, matters of law; jurors who can describe the services are unwilling to say whether they are free or unfree, but will leave this question for the justices[2]. And next we have to note that though labour service, indefinite or but partially defined labour service, seems to be the original essence of villein tenure, this does not remain so for long. When once it has been established

---

[1] Now and then in the extents a man who seems to be a freeholder is said to pay tallage; *e.g.* Cart. Rams. i. 322: 'dat talliagium cum villanis quotiens-cunque ipsi talliantur.' In Y. B. 8 Edw. III. f. 66 (Mich. pl. 31) it is said that the bishop of Ely held land by the service of being tallaged along with the villeins. Of course the bishop was free, but his tenement also seems to have been considered free.

[2] Thus, Placit. Abbrev. 90 (Mid.), in 1215 jurors say—We do not know whether the tenement is free; the tenant had to plough three acres for his lord, to mow three turns and carry to the lord's barn, receiving for this the best sheep in the lord's fold, to attend boon days and give an Easter egg; we never heard that he made fine for marrying his daughter or selling his oxen; but the lord used to seek an aid from him once in seven years. *Held* that the tenement was free. On p. 84 (Berk.) is another special verdict in an action for dower; there is no week work; the jurors however had never heard of a woman being endowed of such a tenement, but after her husband's death the widow used to hold the whole. *Held* that the tenement was not free, at least for the purpose of endowment. In 1228 (Note Book, pl. 281) we find another case in which, according to one story, the jurors doubted, because, though the tenant owed labour services, he knew 'quid debuit facere et quid non.'

that a tenement is unfree, that tenement will not become
free, at least in the eyes of lawyers, even though the services
are modified or transformed. Without any definite agreement,
a lord begins to take money instead of exacting labour, and
gradually it becomes the custom that he shall take money, and
a precisely fixed sum of money, in lieu of all the week-work.
This change does not give the tenant a freehold, a right in the
land which the king's courts will protect; something far more
definite would be required for that purpose, an enfranchisement,
a feoffment. Thus it falls out that a tenant who according
to the custom of the manor pays a money rent and does no
more labour for his lord than is owed by many a freeholder,
may still be no freeholder but a tenant in villeinage; he still is
protected only by custom and in the view of the royal justices
is but a tenant at will. Then gradually what has been called
'the conveyancing test' becomes applicable. Dealings with
villein tenements are set forth upon the rolls of the lord's
court; the villein tenement is conceived to be holden 'by roll
of court,' or even 'by copy of court roll,' and the mode of
conveyance serves to mark off the most beneficial of villein-
holds from the most onerous of freeholds; the one passes
by 'surrender and admittance,' the other by 'feoffment.' In
[p. 358] Henry III.'s time this process which secured for the tenant
in villeinage a written, a registered title, and gave him the
name of 'copyholder,' was but beginning, and it is possible
that in some cases the lord by taking money instead of labour
did as a matter of fact suffer his tenants to become freeholders;
but probably he was in general careful enough to prevent this,
for him undesirable, consequence, by retaining and enforcing a
right to some distinctively servile dues. But our definition of
villein tenure must be wide enough to include cases in which
there has been a commutation of labour service into rent, and
on the whole we may do well in saying that villein tenure
is the tenure of one who owes to his lord in respect of his
tenement 'uncertain' labour services, or who (by himself or his
predecessors) has owed such services in the past, or who is
subject to distinctively servile burdens such as merchet, arbitrary tallage, or the duty of serving as reeve. This we believe
to be the main idea; but we must receive it subject to two
remarks, namely, that, as so often said, 'uncertainty' is a
matter of degree, and that in some cases a tenure which all

along had been tenure at a money rent may have been brought
within the sphere of villeinage by some untrue, or at all events
unverified, theory as to its past history. Here as elsewhere law
has done its work of classification by means of types rather
than by means of definitions[1].

To fix in precise words the degree of binding force that the [p. 359]
lords in their thoughts and their deeds ascribed to the manorial
custom would be impossible. Generalizations about the moral
sentiments of a great and heterogeneous class of men are apt to
be fallacious, and, when a lord pays respect to a custom which
can not be enforced against him by any compulsory process, it
will be hard for us to choose between the many possible motives
by which he may have been urged; provident self-interest, a
desire for a quiet life, humane fellow-feeling for his dependants,
besides a respect for the custom as a custom may all have pulled
one way. There is some evidence to show that the mere reverence for the custom as a custom grew weaker during the thirteenth century. When early in that age the king's justices were
considering whether they would not protect the villein tenant
against his lord[2], they must have felt that the custom was very
like law. On the other hand, when they had definitely abandoned this enterprise, the lords must have been more and more

---

[1] It may be said that we contradict Bracton in making 'uncertainty' the
essence of villein service, for he not unfrequently (*e.g.* f. 7, 26) speaks of villein
services and servile works which are certain and determinate; such are the
services and works owed by some classes of tenants on the ancient demesne.
The truth is that the term 'certain' is used in two different but closely connected senses; the one takes the law of the king's court, the other takes the
custom of the manor as its criterion. Services may be accounted uncertain
either (1) because the custom can not define them without frequent reference to
the lord's will, or (2) because, if the lord chooses to break the custom, the
king's court will not help the tenants. In the ordinary case of villeinage the
services are uncertain in both senses, and uncertain in the second sense because
uncertain in the first. But there are cases on the ancient demesne in which
the services are uncertain in the first, but not in the second sense, and these
seem to be Bracton's 'servitia villana sed certa.' We can not fully define them
without speaking of the lord's will, nevertheless the definition is legally binding
on the lord. Suppose the terms of a tenure to be that *A* must work three days
a week for *B* at whatever kind of agricultural labour *B* may require; in one
sense these terms are very uncertain, but if courts of law enforce them, then in
another sense they are certain. Still it is not to be denied that the word
'villein' may sometimes have been applied to any hard work in the fields. In
the thirteenth century it was a word of abuse; a 'villein deed' is a base and
cowardly deed; 'villein words' are gross words, bad language.

[2] Above, p. 359.

tempted to regard the custom as but a revocable expression of their own wills[1]. Certainly the lawyers began to use language which must have suggested to the lords that they might eject their tenants whenever they pleased[2]. On the whole, however, the two clauses of the formula which is in after times to describe the position of the copyholder, grew into definiteness side by side :—the tenant in villeinage holds 'at the will of the lord,' but 'according to the custom of the manor.'

Our task is the more difficult because fully developed copy- *Treatment of villein tenure in practice.* hold tenure, even as it exists in the nineteenth century, allows that there are many acts and defaults by which a tenant may forfeit his tenement. Now a strict definition of these causes of forfeiture only appears late in the day; little of the kind is to be found in the 'extents' of the thirteenth century. Seldom, if ever, were the lords brought to acknowledge that the causes of forfeiture were definable. Many admissions against their own interests the 'extents' of their manors may contain; they suffer it to be recorded that 'a day's work' ends at noon, that in return [p. 360] for some works they must provide food, even that the work is not worth the food that has to be provided; but they do not admit that for certain causes and for certain causes only may they take the tenements into their own hands.

As a matter of fact, it is seldom of an actual ejectment that *Ejectment of villeins.* the peasant has to complain. If he makes default in his services, he in general suffers no more than a small amercement; seldom does it exceed six pence. Even if he commits waste, if, for example, he lets his house go out of repair, he generally has full warning and an opportunity for amending his conduct before the lord takes the extreme measure of ejecting him. An extreme measure it was, for tenants were valuable; then as now 'it paid to be a good landlord.' Two motives, and perhaps two only, might make a lord wish to clear the cultivators from his land; he might wish to fill their place with beasts of the chase or with monks. Happily for the peasantry, rights of sporting were franchises which had to be purchased from the king, while we may hope that the pious founder dealt generously with his tenants. One of the stories which best illustrates the nature of their customary rights tells how when Henry II. was founding

---

[1] Thus Bracton, f. 263: 'villenagium quod traditur villanis, quod quis tempestive et intempestive resumere possit pro voluntate sua et revocare.'

[2] See *e.g.* Britton's definition of the tenure as given above, p. 360.

the Carthusian priory of Witham in Somersetshire he cleared
the villeins off the land, but gave each of them the choice of
becoming free or receiving a tenement in any royal manor that
he might choose. But the holy Hugh was not content with this,
he made Henry pay compensation to the villeins for their houses;
nor did he stop there; they must be allowed to carry away the
materials, though for these they have already received a money
equivalent[1]. At an earlier date an Earl of Lincoln, clearing the
ground for Revesby Abbey, had given the dispossessed rustics
a choice between freedom and other tenements[2].

Increased
services.

What the tenant in villeinage had to fear was not so much
arbitrary ejectment as an attempt to raise his rent, or to exact
from him new and degrading services which would make him
an unfree man. We can not altogether acquit the lords of such
attempts. The fact that the services described in the later 'extents' seem heavier than those described in the earlier, the fact
that the debasing *merchetum* seems to become far commoner as
time goes on, these facts are not very cogent, for the extents [p. 361]
become more minute and particular and we seldom can be quite
sure that what is expressed in the later documents was not
implied in the earlier[3]. We can not so easily dispose of the
evidence that late in the thirteenth century large masses of the
tenants believed and sought to prove that their lords had broken
the custom and imposed new burdens upon them. They sought
to show in case after case that they were living on the ancient
demesne of the crown, and that therefore they were protected
against any increase of services. Generally they failed; Domesday Book was produced and proved that they had no right to
claim the king's help. The fact remains that they had hoped
to prove that the lords were breaking the custom. To this we
must add that in many of these cases the lord was a religious
house[4]. Now there is plenty of evidence that of all landlords

[1] Magna Vita S. Hugonis, p. 68; Somersetshire Pleas, pl. 1521.

[2] Monast. v. 454. See as to the foundation of Kirkstall, Ibid. v. 530–1,
'amotis habitatoribus.'

[3] However it seems clear that during the thirteenth century the bishop of
Ely increased the services of some of his Cambridgeshire tenants. He exacted
one more day's work in the week. This appears on a comparison of the two
unprinted registers mss. Cot. Tib. B. 2; Claud. C. 11.

[4] The Placitorum Abbreviatio for the first twenty years of Edward I.'s reign
gives at least twenty actions of this character, in ten of which the defendant
was a religious house. In fourteen out of the twenty it was shown that the

the religious houses were the most severe—not the most oppressive, but the most tenacious of their rights; they were bent
on the maintenance of pure villein tenure and personal villeinage. The immortal but soulless corporation with her wealth
of accurate records would yield no inch, would enfranchise no
serf, would enfranchise no tenement. In practice the secular
lord was more humane, because he was more human, because
he was careless, because he wanted ready money, because he
would die. Still it is to the professed in religion that we may
fairly look for a high theory of justice, and when we find that
it is against them that the peasants make their loudest complaints, we may be pretty sure that the religion of the time
saw nothing very wrong in the proceedings of a lord who without
any cruelty tried to get the most that he could out of his villein
tenements. We may well doubt whether the best morality of
the time required him to regard the villein services as fixed for
good and all, or as variable only by means of some formal agreement such as never could have been made had but one tenant
[p. 362] refused his consent. The process of commutation, which in the
end was to give the copyholder his valuable rights, was set
going by the lord's will; he chose to exact money instead of
labour, and, if he took but a fair sum, he was not to be condemned. We can not contend therefore that the lord's will was
fettered by rigid custom, or that any man conceived that it
ought to be so fettered. On the other hand, as we shall soon see,
there is in the king's treatment of his peasants, the men of ' the
ancient demesne,' a convincing proof that the just landlord was
expected to pay heed to the custom and not to break through
it save for good cause.

Had the tenant in villeinage heritable rights? Of rights *Heritable*
recognized by the king's courts we have not to speak; but the *rights in villein*
manorial court frequently admitted that his rights were herit- *tenements.*
able, at least as against all but the lord. Often a claimant
comes into court and declares in set terms how he is the rightful heir and how some one else is wrongfully withholding his
inheritance. Thus, for example: 'John of Bagmere demands
against John son of Walter of Wells one virgate of land with
the appurtenances in the vill of Combe as his right according to
the custom of the manor, and therefore as his right, for he says

manor in question was not on the ancient demesne, and only in two cases (if
we mistake not) did the tenants get a judgment.

that one John of Bagmere his grandfather died seised thereof as
his right according to the custom of the manor, and from that
John the right descended according to the custom of the manor
to his son William, the demandant's father, whose heir the
demandant is according to the custom of the manor[1].' This is
just the formula which a man would use in the king's court
were he claiming a freehold inheritance, save that at every turn
reference is made to the custom of the manor; according to the
custom inheritance is a matter of strict right as against all but
the lord. The documents are much more chary of admitting
that as against the lord the heir has any rights. On the death
of a tenant a heriot becomes due, usually the best beast or best
chattel or a fixed sum of money; but this is regarded less as a
'relief' to be paid by an heir than as a payment due out of the
dead man's estate, and if an 'extent' speaks of the heir at all,
this is in general to tell us that he must 'do the lord's will,' or
must 'redeem the land at the will of the lord[2].' The court rolls [p. 363]
seem to show that as a matter of fact heirs were admitted on
fairly easy terms, the lord taking an additional year's rent or the
like, and the pleadings in which hereditary right is asserted
against others than the lord testify to a strong feeling that the
villein tenements are heritable; still as against the lord the
heir has rather a claim to inherit than an inheritance. The
records of this age but rarely say that a tenant is admitted
'to hold to him and his heirs,' generally they say no more than
that the lord has given the land to *A.B.* When, as would
generally be the case, the tenants were personally unfree, the
lord would have run some danger in talking about their heirs,
for lawyers were saying that the serf could have no heir but his
lord and drawing thence the deduction that a serf might be
enfranchised by unguarded words[3]. This may be the reason
why early court rolls, when they do expressly allow that a new
tenant is to have transmissible rights, do so by speaking not of

---

[1] Proceedings of the court of the Abbot of Bec at Combe in Hampshire,
A.D. 1290; Select Pleas in Manorial Courts, i. 34; see also p. 39, where a man
counts upon the seisin of his great-grandmother.

[2] Cart. Glouc. iii. 148: 'et post decessum ipsius heres eius redimet terram
ad voluntatem domini.' Ibid. p. 182: 'et post decessum suum heres eius
antequam terram illam ingrediatur redimet illam ad voluntatem domini.' Rot.
Hund. ii. 874: 'et si filius eorum voluerit tenere eandem terram tunc facit
gratum dicti Abbatis.'

[3] Bracton, f. 192 b.

his heirs but of his *sequela*. This is not a pretty word to use of a man, for it is the word that one uses of pigs and the like; the tenant is to hold to him and his brood, his litter[1]. We shall better understand the nature of the heir's right against the lord, a right to inherit if the lord pleases, if we are persuaded that in many a case the inheritance was not very valuable. Certainly in the fourteenth century there were lords who would but too gladly have found heirs to take up the villein tenements at the accustomed services[2]. We may hardly argue thence to an earlier time; but no doubt the services were often as good a return for the land as could have been obtained. A strong man with strong sons might do them and thrive; the weak and needy could not, and were removed with the full

[p. 364] approbation of the other men of the vill, whose burdens had been increased by the impotence of their fellow-labourer.

Further the lord took care that the tenements should not be broken up among coheirs. Often the tenant's widow enjoyed the whole tenement during her life or until she married a second time without the lord's leave[3]. Often the customary rule of inheritance gave the land to the dead man's youngest son, and this was accounted a mark of villein tenure[4]. Perhaps in some cases the family kept together, and the son who was admitted as tenant was regarded as representing his brothers; but this must have been a matter of morals rather than of law or of enforceable custom. By one means or another the unity of the tenement was preserved and it is rare to find it held by a party of coheirs. Exceptions there doubtless were, but on the evidence afforded by the 'extents' and the Hundred Rolls it is hard to believe that in the thirteenth century the lords held themselves bound by custom to admit the heir on his tendering a fixed fine[5]. 'Precarious inheritance,' if we may use such a term, was

Unity of the tenement.

---

[1] 'Sequela, dicitur de pullis equinis, vitulinis, aliisque animalibus quae matrem sequuntur'; Du Cange, Glossarium. When King John is forced to promise that he will banish his foreign captains ' et totam sequelam eorundem ' (Charter, c. 50), this phrase expresses a bitter hatred and contempt. Gerard de Athée, the most famous of the band, was, it was said, of servile birth.

[2] Maitland, History of a Cambridgeshire Manor, E. H. R. ix. 423 ff.

[3] If a widow holds the whole of her husband's tenement, instead of enjoying but a third or a half, this is regarded as a sign that the tenement is villein; Placit. Abbrev. p. 84 (Berk.).

[4] Note Book, 794, 1005, 1062.

[5] The 'extent' of Holm in Norfolk, Cart. Rams. i. 401, is a rare example of a manor in which the tenements were allowed to descend to coheirs and

of common occurrence in all zones of society. The baronial relief had but lately been determined; the tenant by serjeanty still relieved his land 'at the will of the lord.' We know too that in later days the heir of a copyhold tenant very often had to pay an 'arbitrary' fine, while in other cases lords have succeeded in proving that the successors of the villein tenants were but tenants for life[1].

Alienation of villein tenements. Of the alienation, of the sale and purchase, of villein tene- [p. 365] ments we read little. We may be sure that this could not be effected without the lord's leave; the seller came into the lord's court and surrendered the land into the steward's hand, who thereupon admitted the new tenant and gave him seisin. The new tenant paid a fine; often it would be one year's value of the tenement. But in this region there seems to have been but little custom, and we may be fairly certain that the lords of this period did not allow that new tenants could be forced upon them against their will. If the tenant attempted to alienate the tenement without the lord's leave, this was a cause of forfeiture[2]; if he attempted to make a lease of it, this, if not a cause of forfeiture, subjected him to an amercement[3].

Villein tenure and villein status. Finally we must note that the tenant in villeinage was usually regarded as an unfree man, a bondman, *villanus, nativus, servus*. That a free man should hold in villeinage was possible, and up and down the country there may have been many free men with villein tenements; what is more, there likely enough were many men whose status was dubious. This is one of the most remarkable points in villeinage; villein tenure is of far greater practical importance than villein status. To prove that

coheiresses; thus three sons and coheirs hold twelve acres, six daughters and coheiresses hold thirty acres. But then the tenure is not villeinage of the common kind; probably it is not freehold, for merchet is paid, but there is no week work. The widow's right to hold the whole or a portion of the tenement is often much better settled than the heir's right. Thus at Brancaster, Cart. Rams. i. 416, the widow gives a heriot and for this becomes entitled to enjoy half the land: the son or daughter, if such there be, must make fine for the other half 'quoad melius poterit.' In the Domesday of St Paul's, p. 52, there is an often cited passage which seems to show that the Canons in 1222 admitted that some of their customary tenants had heritable rights. On the other hand, in 1327 the monks of Christchurch at Canterbury forbade the steward of a Devonshire manor to admit any heir or other person who demanded admittance as a right; Literae Cantuarienses, i. 229, 385.

[1] See Halmote Rolls of the Priory of Durham (Surtees Soc.), Introduction.

[2] See the very early (1239) specimen of a court roll in Cart. Rams. i. 423–9.

[3] Select Pleas in Manorial Courts, i. 91, 171.

a man was personally unfree was, as we shall see in the next chapter, a difficult matter, and a case in which a lord had in his own interest to undertake this proof was not very common. So long as the tenant did not make up his mind to quit hearth and home, leaving the means of his livelihood behind him, the lord had seldom to fall back upon an assertion of personal bondage in order to get what he wanted. If the tenant was refractory the lord could distrain him, could take the tenement away for a time or for good and all. For all this however, the 'extents' of the thirteenth century show that in the estimation of their lords—and, we must add, of their neighbours,—the holders of unfree tenements were as a general rule unfree men. This is apparent in 'extents' to which the tenants themselves pledge their oaths; it is plain upon the face of the Hundred Rolls. The juries of different hundreds may choose different phrases; but in one way or another, either by using such [p. 366] terms as *nativus* and *servus*, which imply personal unfreedom, or by laying stress on the payment of the merchet, they generally show that in their opinion the case of a free man holding in villeinage is uncommon and may fairly be neglected by those who are dealing with large masses of men.

§ 13. *The Ancient Demesne*[1].

The king is a great land-owner. Besides being the supreme lord of all land, he has many manors of his own; there is a constant flow of lands into and out of the royal hands; they come to him by escheat and forfeiture, they leave him by gifts and restorations. Now a distinction is drawn among the manors that he has. Some of them constitute, so to speak, the original endowment of the kingship, they are that ancient demesne of the crown which the Conqueror held when the great settlement of the Conquest was completed and was registered in Domesday Book[2]. What has fallen in since that time is not considered as so permanently annexed to the kingly office; it is not expected of the king that he will keep in his own hands the numerous honours, baronies and manors

[marginal note: The ancient demesne and the other royal estates.]

---

[1] See Vinogradoff, Villainage in England, p. 89 ff.

[2] See the Exon. Domesday, D. B. iv. 75: 'Dominicatus Regis *ad Regnum pertinens* in Deveniscira.'

with which felony and treason and want of heirs are constantly supplying him; rather it is expected that he will give these away again. On the other hand, he ought not to dissipate the old demesne manors. He does give them out, and that too to be held of him heritably, but often he reserves a substantial money rent; they are to be held of him in 'fee farm.' This is hardly a matter of law; all the king's manors are the king's to give upon what terms he pleases; still his ancient patrimony is regarded as more closely bound up with his office than are those mere windfalls which now and again come to his hands[1].

Immunities of the ancient demesne.

But in law also the distinction is important. We are [p. 367] accustomed to define a 'franchise' as a portion of royal power in the hands of a subject, so that to speak of the king as having franchises would be a contradiction in terms. Nevertheless in early history the king appears as the first of all franchise holders, the first in point of greatness and the first, it well may be, in point of time. The king's estates are (to borrow a word from abroad) 'immunities,' perhaps the oldest of all immunities; they stand outside the normal, national system of justice, police and finance. Inside them there prevails a royal, which is also a seignorial, justice, and which remains distinct from the ordinary justice of the realm, even when that is done in the king's name. The tenants on the ancient, the permanent, manors of the crown enjoy many 'liberties' which flow from the king's rights, they are to a very high degree exempt from all justice, save that which is done among them by a court which they constitute and which is presided over by a royal bailiff, exempt to a very high degree even from the justice of the king's 'courts of common law' when those courts have come into existence. They know little of the sheriff; they have not to attend the moots of the shire or the hundred; they need not serve as jurors; wherever they go they pay no toll; they are not taxed like other folk; on the other hand they are liable to be tallaged by the king. The king profits by these immunities; his manors are governed from within; the cultivators of his demesnes cannot be distracted from their duties

---

[1] See Fleta, p. 3: 'Antiqua maneria vel iura coronae annexa Regi non licebit alienare, sed omnis Rex coronae suae alienata revocare tenetur'; Britton, i. 221. A strong support for this doctrine is found in what seems to be the coronation oath of Edward I.; see Stubbs, Const. Hist. ii. 105.

to him[1]. He attracts men to his land; the serf who lives
there unclaimed for year and day is privileged against re-
capture.

When new manors come to the king's hands they do not
enjoy these immunities. On the other hand, when the king
gives away in fee farm or otherwise one of the ancient manors,
the donee takes it with all its privileges. This we may say is
an illustration of a general rule of law :—the escheat of a mesne
lordship should leave unaltered the rights and duties of those
who are the subjects of that lordship, and if a lord puts a
mesne between himself and his tenant, that tenant should
neither gain nor lose by the change. Thus, once ancient demesne, always ancient demesne. The tenants who have been
free of toll but liable to tallage should still be free of toll but
liable to tallage, though the king has ceased to be and the
Prior of Barnwell has become their immediate lord.

Once ancient demesne, always ancient demesne.

All this would make the ancient demesne of importance in
the history of political arrangements, in the history of the
franchises, of justice, police and finance, though here the franchises and immunities enjoyed by the king's estates would
have to take their place beside the very similar franchises and
immunities enjoyed by the estates of other privileged persons.
But we do not at once see why there should be any form of
land tenure peculiar to the ancient demesne. However, such a
form of land tenure there is.

Peculiar tenures on the ancient demesne.

Briefly stated, the phenomenon which deserves investigation
is this :—On the ancient demesne there is a large class of persons whose economic and social position is much the same, if
not quite the same, as that of the ordinary holders in villeinage,
but who are very adequately protected by law, or by custom
which has all the force of law, in the enjoyment of their tenements. This protection is given to them by two remedies specially adapted to meet their case; the one is 'the little writ of
right close according to the custom of the manor,' the other is
the writ of *Monstraverunt*. We will speak first of these remedies and then of the class for whose sake they exist.

The problem stated.

The 'little writ of right close' is not unlike the 'great writ
of right patent.' This latter is the ordinary proprietary

The little writ of right.

[p. 368]

---

[1] Britton, ii. p. 13, gives this as the reason for the little writ of right. The
sokemen who enjoy it are the tillers of the king's soil, and disputes about that
soil are to be decided within the manor by simple and rapid processes.

remedy for one who thinks that he ought to hold land by free
tenure of a mesne lord. The writ patent is directed by the
king to the mesne lord; it bids him 'hold full right' (*plenum
rectum teneas*) to the demandant and adds a threat that if he
is remiss, the king's sheriff will interfere[1]. The lord then, if
he has a court, holds a court, and justice can there be done to
the demandant, though there are several ways in which the
case can be withdrawn from his tribunal and removed first into
the county court and then into the king's court. Now the
little writ is a similar writ. It is directed by the king to the
bailiffs of the manor[2]—this will be so whether the king is
himself the immediate lord of the manor or whether it is in [p. 369]
the hands of a mesne—and it bids the bailiffs do full right to
the demandant 'according to the custom of the manor'[3]. It
contains no threat of the sheriff's interference, and this may
be the reason why it is a 'close writ' and not a 'patent writ,'
since no one but the recipient, who is not a public official,
is required to act upon it. Thereupon the court of the manor
proceeds to hear and is fully competent to determine the cause.
Still it acts under surveillance. If it is going wrong, the sheriff
can be sent with four knights of the county to watch its proceedings[4], and there are means by which the matter can be
brought before the king's central court[5]. This writ, we say, is
in use both when the manor is in the king's hand, so that the
demandant is claiming to hold immediately of him, and also
when the manor has been given to a mesne lord. In the latter
case the lord himself may be the defendant. So long as the
king is the immediate lord, there can be no writ against
the lord; of course not; but the would-be tenant of a few
acres on the ancient demesne is in this respect no worse off
than the mightiest of the barons; he who would get justice out
of the king must petition for it in humble wise. But when
the manor has been given to a subject, then the writ will
lie against him; he can be required to do justice in a case
in which, if the complaint be true, he himself is the evil

---

[1] Glanv. xii. c. 3; Bracton, f. 328; Reg. Brev. f. 1.

[2] When the lord himself is the deforciant, it is directed to him, in other
cases to his bailiffs, see Reg. Brev. f. 9 b.

[3] Reg. Brev. f. 9.

[4] By the writ *Accedas ad curiam*, Reg. Brev. f. 9 b.

[5] By the writ of *Recordari*, Reg. Brev. f. 10 b, 11.

doer. This is a remarkable point. The abbot of Ramsey holds the manor of King's Ripton, which is part of the ancient demesne. Joan of Alconbury thinks that she ought to hold eight acres which are in the abbot's hand. The abbot is summoned once, twice, thrice and then distrained once, twice, thrice, to appear in his own court and answer her demand[1].

Now so long as the manor is in the king's hand, the case of the persons of whom we are speaking may not seem to differ radically from the case of villein tenants. Any one who claims to hold in villeinage is likely to get good enough justice in the lord's court, provided that his opponent be not the lord. The difference may seem to be merely procedural. When a man claims villein land in an ordinary manor, he proceeds without [p. 370] any writ; ordinary lords do not keep chanceries; when he claims unfree land (for so we will for the moment suppose it to be) in a manor of which the king is the immediate lord, and which is regarded as part of the permanent endowment of the crown, he must use a writ. This is but a detail. For a moment we may even feel inclined to say that there is nothing in the distinction but that love for parchment and wax which is natural to a government office. Even when it is added that the court of a manor on the ancient demesne acts under the supervision of the courts of common law, we may find analogies for this on the estates of prelates and other great lords. Such a lord sometimes has a central court, an 'honorial' court, which controls the doings of his manorial courts; the so-called courts of common law, it may be said, are the king's central court, the court of the great honour of England. Still, though there may be some truth in these suggestions, they must not be suffered to conceal a really important distinction. In the case of the ancient demesne, even while the manor is immediately subject to the king, the *consuetudo manerii* is put on a level with the law of the realm; it is enforced by the highest of all tribunals; indeed it is *lex et consuetudo manerii*[2]. Nor is the mere use of a writ of no importance; it solemnly sanctions the custom. We have far more reason for saying that the distinction between 'great' and 'little,' between 'close' and

Meaning of the little writ.

---

[1] Select Pleas in Manorial Courts, i. pp. 114–121.

[2] Reg. Brev. 10 b: 'Cum secundum *legem* et consuetudinem infra maneria quae de huiusmodi antiquo dominico coronae existunt hactenus ut dicitur usitatas etc.'

'open' than that the distinction between 'writ' and 'no writ'
is trivial. But when the manor goes out of the king's hand,
then there is a truly abnormal state of affairs; the king
compels the lord to do justice to claimants of land who yet
claim no freehold. A climax is reached when the lord himself
has to answer in the manorial court and submit himself to
its process.

The *Mon-*
straverunt.   This is not all. The little writ serves the turn of a man
who claims land according to the custom of the manor; but
the tenants of whom we are speaking are protected, and protected collectively, against any increase of their services. This
is very plain when the manor is in the hands of a mesne lord.
If he attempts to increase the customary services, some of the [p. 371]
tenants, acting on behalf of all, will go to the royal chancery
and obtain a writ against him. Such a writ begins with the
word *Monstraverunt*[1]. The king addresses the lord:—'*A, B*
and *C*, men of your manor of *X*, which is of the ancient demesne
of the crown of England, have shown us that you exact from
them other customs and services than those which they owe,
and which their ancestors did in the time when that manor
was in the hands of our predecessors, kings of England; therefore we command you to cease from such exactions, otherwise
we shall order our sheriff to interfere.' The lord being deaf to
this command, another writ is sent compelling him to come
and answer for his disobedience before the king or before the
justices of the Bench. When the case comes before the royal
court, the complainants have in the first place to show that the
manor is part of the ancient demesne; Domesday Book is used
for this purpose as a conclusive test. Then, if this fact is
proved or admitted, there arises the question whether the lord
has exacted unaccustomed services, and if this is answered
against him, it is adjudged that he shall do so no more. Here
then we see a class of tenants who are not freeholders, but
who are fully protected in the king's court against their lord.
Of course if the manor is in the king's hand, there is no
place for this procedure[2]. Still if the tenants allege that they
are being oppressed by the king's bailiffs, they can present a

---

[1] Reg. Brev. f. 14.

[2] Fleta, p. 4: 'sed cum huiusmodi [sokemanni] per Regem vel suos ex-
pellantur ab huiusmodi tenemento, non habetur remedium nisi tantum suppli-
catio.'

petition to the king and the matter will be investigated in
the exchequer[1].

[p. 372]   And now we may ask, who are the persons for whose sake The classes
these remedies exist.   Bracton in a classical passage tells us of tenants. Bracton's
that on the king's demesne there are several kinds of men.   In statement.
the first place there are serfs or born bondmen who were (*i.e.* in
the persons of their ancestors) serfs before the Conquest, at the
Conquest and after the Conquest, and to this day they perform
villein services and uncertain services and they are bound to do
whatever is commanded to them, provided it be lawful and
right.   And at the Conquest there were free men who freely
held their tenements by free services or free customs, and, when
they were ejected by the mighty, they came back and received
the same tenements to hold in villeinage by doing servile works,
but certain and specified works; and they are called *glebae
ascriptitii* and none the less are they free men, for, albeit they
do servile works, still they do these, not by reason of personal
status, but by reason of their tenure; and for this reason they
cannot bring the assizes of novel disseisin or mort d'ancestor
[the freeholder's possessory remedies], for their tenement is
villeinage, though privileged villeinage; they can only bring
the little writ of right according to the custom of the manor;
and for this reason are they called *glebae ascriptitii*, for they

---

[1] As to this last point see Vinogradoff, p. 103.   It is very probable that the
Monstraverunt did not become a writ 'of course' until a comparatively late time.
It is not mentioned by Glanvill or Bracton, nor have we found it in any
Registrum Brevium of Henry III.'s reign.   There is some sign that the step of
making it a writ 'of course' was not taken until 1290.   In that year the men
of Grendon, asserting that they were on the ancient demesne, complained of
their lords to the king.   The petition is thus endorsed: 'Let the Chancellor
convene the justices and provide for this and similar cases a remedy to endure
for all time': Rot. Parl. i. 60.   But such writs were in use early in Henry III.'s
reign: see Note Book, pl. 1230, 1237, Placit. Abbrev. 113, 119; and were
extremely common in the early years of Edward I.   The comparatively late
appearance of this writ as a writ *de cursu* is no proof that the principle which
it enforced was new; but it is, as Vinogradoff has well argued, some proof that
the procedure against mesne lords grew out of a procedure against royal bailiffs.
Against the royal bailiffs there would naturally be no writ 'of course': if a man
would complain of the king's agents he must begin with a petition to the king.
As to the little writ of right, Glanvill does not, and has no occasion to mention
this; in his day 'original writs' of any kind were still somewhat new as normal
institutes of the law.   On the other hand the writ is found in a Registrum of
Henry III.'s time as a writ *de cursu* and is currently mentioned by Bracton as a
well-known thing; see Maitland, Register of Original Writs, Harvard Law
Review, iii. 170.

enjoy the privilege of not being removed from the soil so long as they do their right services—no matter to whose hands the king's demesne may come; nor can they be compelled to hold their tenements against their will. Then there is another set of men on the king's manors who hold of the demesne by the same customs and villein services as the above, and they do not hold in villeinage nor are they serfs, nor were they such at or before the Conquest, but they hold under covenant which they have made with the lord, and some of them have charters and some have not, and, if they are ejected from their tenements, they shall (according to some) have the assize of novel disseisin, and their heirs shall have the assize of mort d'ancestor. And there are other sorts of men in the king's manors and [p. 373] demesnes, who there, as might be the case elsewhere, hold freely in free socage or by military service under some modern feoffment made since the Conquest [1].

Bracton's statement discussed.

Whereas then on ordinary manors we have, according to legal theory, but two tenures that must for our present purpose be distinguished, on the ancient demesne we have at least three. There are freeholders of the common kind, holding in free socage or by military service, and they require no special remedies. There are serfs holding in absolute villeinage. But between them there is a class of tenants whom Bracton oddly enough calls *glebae ascriptitii* because they can not be ejected from their holdings; they are free men; they can leave their tenements when they will; they hold by villein services, but services which are certain; they use the little writ of right. Lastly there is a class to which we may be allowed to give the name of 'conventioners' [2]. They differ from the *ascriptitii* rather in the origin of their holding and in the nature of their remedies than in the substance of their rights and duties. The *ascriptitii* are supposed to trace the origin of their class back to the Conquest; they hold by customary tenure; the 'conventioners' hold under modern agreements, and it is arguable that, though they do villein services, they have the ordinary remedies of freeholders.

A second statement.

In another and equally well known passage we hear of the same four classes. Bracton is speaking now without special reference to the ancient demesne, and remarks that villeinage

---

[1] Bracton, f. 7 b ; Fleta, pp. 3, 4.
[2] These do not appear very clearly in Fleta, p. 4.

may be either absolute or privileged. Absolute villeinage is
the tenure of one who, be he free or be he serf, is bound to do
whatever is commanded him, and does not know in the evening
what he must do in the morning. Then there is a villeinage
which is not so absolute; as when land is granted by covenant
to a free man or a serf for fixed, though villein, customs and
services. If such a 'conventioner' is ejected, Bracton (dis-
allowing the opinion which would give him the freeholder's
assizes) holds that his proper remedy is an action on the
covenant. Then, says he, there is another kind of villeinage
[p. 374] which is held of the king from the Conquest of England, which
is called villein socage, and is villeinage though privileged
villeinage; for the tenants of the king's demesnes have this
privilege that they may not be removed from the soil so long
as they can and will do their due service, and these 'villein
sokemen' are properly called *glebae ascriptitii*; they do villein,
but fixed and specified, services. Lastly, he once more remarks
that in a royal manor there may be knights and freeholders,
holding by military service or by free socage[1].

These freeholders we may dismiss from our minds; they
have and they require no peculiar remedies; indeed, the term
'ancient demesne' having begun to imply peculiar remedies, we
find it contrasted with 'freehold,' and in a judgment of Edward
I.'s reign we are told that the lord of the manor, be he the king
or no, can change 'ancient demesne' into 'freehold' by enfeoffing
a tenant[2]; after such a feoffment the tenement is no longer
ancient demesne, but 'is at the common law[3].' The case also
of the 'conventioners' we may for a while postpone, for it is not
very important, though it is very curious. There remain two
classes of tenants: those who hold in absolute villeinage and
those who in Bracton's terms hold in privileged villeinage, or in
villein socage, and who are villein sokemen and 'ascript to [*i.e.*
irremovable from] the soil.' It is the men of this last class who
use the little writ of right.

Such is the legal doctrine, and at some points it corresponds well with what we can learn of actual arrangements.

The four classes of tenants.

The theory borne out by practice.

---

[1] Bracton, f. 208 b.

[2] Placit. Abbrev. p. 233 (Berks.): 'et cum licet cuilibet capitali domino
mutare antiquum dominicum in liberum tenementum et maxime dominus
Rex.'

[3] Ibid. p. 228 (Berks.); cf. ibid. p. 241 (Ebor.); Y. B. 20–1 Edw. I. 378.

On an ordinary manor we rarely find more than two classes
of tenants that can be called legal classes. We may find more
than two economic classes :—in the common case there will be
a class of virgaters, a class of half-virgaters, a class of crofters
and cotters, and there may well be a class of tenants who pay
rents and do but little labour, while other classes must do
'week work'—we find *censuarii* as well as *operarii*. Also,
as already said, we may find some tenants (but hardly classes
of tenants) about whose tenure we may doubt whether it be
freehold or no. Still in general there is a clear dichotomy;
there are freeholders and then there is one other great class.
The latter may be called by different names according to the [p. 375]
taste of the jurors; its members may be termed *servi, nativi,
bondi, villani, custumarii, consuetudinarii*; but legally their
tenure is always the same; they hold according to the custom
of the manor but their tenure is unrecognized by the king's
courts. When, however, in turning over the Hundred Rolls
we come upon a manor of the ancient demesne, we often see
a more elaborate stratification, and in particular we read of
sokemen; and conversely when we see this more elaborate
stratification and discover sokemen, we can usually learn that
we are on the ancient demesne. Thus at Soham in Cambridgeshire, besides ordinary freeholders, there are free sokemen, bond
sokemen, and *villani*, and at Fordham there are ordinary freeholders, sokemen and *villani*[1]. We hardly need the testimony
of Domesday Book: *Saham manerium Regis, Fordeham dominica villa Regis*[2]. In Huntingdonshire at Brampton there
are freeholders, free sokemen, and bond sokemen, at Alconbury
numerous sokemen[3]; the natural inference may be verified in
Domesday Book[4]. No one could look through the Oxfordshire surveys without singling out the manor of Bensington[5]
with its many *liberi sokemanni*, who are kept apart from its
libere tenentes, and inferring that it was a manor of no ordinary
kind. It is so with the court rolls. To say nothing of the
'little writs of right' which are stitched to their membranes,
the rolls of a manor on the ancient demesne are distinguished
by entries which show that land is freely bought and sold[6],
and if in the Hundred Rolls we are told that the *custumarii*

---

[1] R. H. ii. 501–2.   [2] D. B. i. 189.   [3] R. H. 607–13.
[4] D. B. i. 203 b.   [5] R. H. ii. 751.
[6] Select Pleas in Manorial Courts, p. 106–124.

of Chesterton have sold their half-virgates, we hardly need look
to see whether Chesterton be not *dominica villa Regis* [1].

We have, however, no little difficulty in marking off Bracton's
'absolute villeinage' from his 'privileged villeinage.' His test
is the 'certainty' or 'uncertainty' of the services due from the
tenant. But, as we have already seen, there lurks an ambiguity
in these simple terms. If by saying that a tenant owes *servitia certa et nominata*, we mean that the terms of his tenure
are defended by legal remedies, remedies the administration of
which either belongs to, or is at least supervised by, the highest
[p. 376] court in the land, then we are treading a vicious circle : the
remedies are given because the services are certain, the services
are certain because the remedies are given. If, on the other
hand, we look at the nature of the services, and say that they
are certain if they can be defined without any reference to the
lord's will, then we exact too much from those who are to claim
the law's protection. The men of King's Ripton in Huntingdonshire used the little writ of right, they used the *Monstraverunt*,
they distrained their lord, the abbot of Ramsey, to answer them
in the manorial court ; but, according to an 'extent' made by
their representatives, they were bound to work one day a week
all the year round 'at whatever work he commanded them' and
three days a week during August and September. Of them it
might well be said that when they went to bed on Sunday night
they did not know what they would have to do on Monday. In
short, here as when we were outside the ancient demesne we
come upon a matter of degree. There is hardly a tenant of
whom it can be said that no custom prevents him from having
to do just whatever services the lord may command ; on the
other hand, there is hardly a tenant doing any substantial
amount of agricultural labour, of whom it can be said that
he has never to attend to the lord's will ; even the true freeholder must do his boon works in autumn, and the very essence
of a boon work is that, within some spacious limit, described by
such a word as 'harvest-time,' it must be done when it is
asked for. How low down in the social and economic scale the
protection given by the little writ and the *Monstraverunt* would
go is excellently shown by the case of Ripton Regis. When
pressed in pleading, the tenants admitted that ever since
Henry I.'s day they had been paying arbitrary reliefs, arbitrary

[1] R. H. ii. 402-3.

tallages, arbitrary merchet; but still they used the little writ and the *Monstraverunt,* and, if the abbot sought to make them work two days a week instead of one, they had their remedy in the king's court[1].

Practical difficulties.

This being so, the lawyers never seem able to obtain any firm hold for their theory. They can repeat that there are three classes of tenants, free men, villeins and sokemen; but how to draw the line between mere villeinage and the socage tenure of ancient demesne is a difficult problem[2]. It is not as though we had merely to fix the distinction at some one point [p 377] in a single scale of degrees; there are many scales as well as many degrees. Besides the scale of agricultural labour with its infinite particulars, there are the scales of tallage, of relief, of heriot, of merchet. Even if, following Bracton, we say that the sokeman should at least be personally free and free to quit his tenement, the men of King's Ripton will appeal against our judgment, for at least they do all that free men ought not to do according to legal theories. They pay arbitrary tallage, arbitrary merchet, they can not have their sons ordained, they may not leave the manor without the lord's licence; and yet, when all this has been proved against them, they go on using the little writ of right and distraining their lord[3]. Our law never surmounted these difficulties until tenure in villeinage was protected by the king's court under the name of copyhold tenure, and the line between common copyhold and the privileged villeinage of the ancient demesne had become of little significance. Even then many a curious, if unimportant, problem was left for lawyers to fight over.

Sokemanry and socage.

On the other hand, to mark off the tenure of the sokeman, which is sometimes called 'sokemanry[4],' from the freehold tenure known as free socage was no easy task: the very words that we employ in stating the problem show that this was so.

[1] Cart. Rams. i. 397; Select Pleas in Manorial Courts, 99–129.

[2] Y. B. 21–2 Edw. I. p. 499; Y. B. 1 Edw. II. f. 19.

[3] See Seebohm, E. H. R. vii. 453, an able review of Vinogradoff's book. Mr Seebohm thinks that the men of Ripton failed to prove that they were 'privileged villeins,' and no doubt it is true that in one sense they were convicted of being very 'ordinary villeins'; they owed hard and degrading services and were in many respects subject to 'the will of the lord.' But, for all this, they have got the little writ and the *Monstraverunt* and the abbot can not make them work two days a week instead of one. So they are 'privileged villeins.'

[4] Y. B. 21–2 Edw. I. p. 250: 'son barun tint en sokemanerie.' Y. B. 33–5 Edw. I. p. 557: 'tyent en sokemanerie.'

The question whether 'the customary freeholders' who appear
in our later books were really freeholders and as such entitled
to vote in the election of knights of the shire, the question
which required for its solution, not merely the learning of a
Blackstone, but the authority of an act of parliament[1], was
a question prepared of old. The sokeman on the ancient
demesne can not usually be accounted a freeholder; the *liberi
sokemanni* are marked off in the 'extents' from the *libere
tenentes*; they use the little writ of right: they can not use
[p. 378] the great writ or the possessory assizes which speak of seisin
of free tenement. But is this so always? There is extant
an elaborate opinion given by a lawyer of Edward I.'s day,
one Aunger of Ripon, and it is found in so many manuscripts
that certainly it must have been considered very sound and
useful[2]. He says that, according to his masters, there are
three cases in which a tenant, who holds part of the soil of
the ancient demesne, may use the assize of novel disseisin.
The first is the case of a freeholder who holds in an ancient
demesne manor, and this we may pass by. The second is where
one of the sokemen has enfeoffed some free 'outsider' (*liber
homo extrinsecus*) and this feoffee has been left undisturbed for
a while by the lord; if after this he is ejected by the lord
or any other, he can bring the assize. This case is quite
intelligible because if my villein makes a feoffment, I must
eject the feoffee at once or not at all, since otherwise he will
be able to bring the assize against me[3]:—for the law of the
thirteenth century is rigorous against self-help. But thirdly,
if any 'outsider' ejects a sokeman, the latter can bring the
assize; this must be so (argues Aunger) for if someone ejects my
mere villein, that villein by my leave will be able to recover
in an assize; *a fortiori* we argue to the case of a sokeman
whose estate is superior to that of a villein[4]. Thus, according
to this remarkable opinion, the term 'free' when applied to a

---

[1] Stat. 31 Geo. II. c. 14.

[2] Printed by Horwood, Y. B. 20–1 Edw. I. p. xviii. The document is transcribed along with the apocryphal statutes and is sometimes entitled *Statutum
de Antiquo Dominico.*

[3] Note Book, pl. 1203.

[4] There seems to be a sad logical gap in this argument. The ejected villein,
if with his lord's permission he brought an assize, would have to bring it in his
lord's name, but Aunger seems certainly to suppose that the sokeman could
bring it in his own name.

tenement is a relative term—we shall see in the next chapter
that the term 'free' when applied to a person is a relative
term—for while as between himself and his lord the sokeman
is no freeholder, still as regards all 'outsiders' he can say that
he has a free tenement, and, if ejected by them, he can make
good the assertion that he has been disseised *de libero tenemento
suo.* Thus we see that the perplexing terminology of later
days which knows of 'customary freeholds' which are 'privileged copyholds,' has a very ancient root. Even the lawyers
of the thirteenth century, or some of them, maintained that
for certain purposes the sokeman had 'a free tenement[1].' Nor [p. 379]
is this strange, for the class which was using the little writ
of right was miscellaneous. If, on the one hand, it included
men like those of King's Ripton who were stamped with every
common mark of personal servility, it included on the other
hand men who had valuable interests in tenements, which
they sold and mortgaged and settled upon their families
without any interference on the part of their lord. Such men
are brought before us by a judgment of Edward I.'s day;
when they sell their lands they do not even surrender them
into the lord's hand, they make a feoffment as a freeholder
would; they make charters of feoffment, and then the alienation
is enrolled in the manorial court; for all this, however, 'no writ
runs among them but the little writ of right[2].'

**Later
theory and
practice.**
　　We must not here recount the subsequent fate of the
tenants on the ancient demesne, nor would this be easy, for
it is clear that, if the law itself did not undergo much change,
the terms in which it was expressed were unstable. But we
may note that an opinion grew up that the class protected by
the little writ of right was really a class of freeholders, and
then the inference was drawn that tenants who alienated
their tenements, not in the freeholder's method by feoffment,
but by a surrender into the hands of the lord, could not use the
little writ because they were not freeholders. This doctrine
comes to the front early in the fifteenth century, at a time, that

---

[1] So in later times we find the anomaly that if on the ancient demesne the
lord disseises the tenant, the tenant may elect between an action in the manorial
court and a (freeholder's) action in the king's court: Y. B. 41 Edw. III. f. 22
(Mich. pl. 13); 41 Lib. Ass. f. 253, pl. 7. See Stat. 9 Hen. IV. c. 5, which shows
that by naming the lord as a disseisor one could evade his jurisdiction and bring
a dispute about a tenement on the ancient demesne before the king's court.

[2] Placit. Abbrev. 246-7.

is, when it was no longer capable of doing much harm to those
'sokemen of base tenure' whom it excluded from the benefits
of the little writ, since under the name of copyholders they
were on the point of obtaining a perfectly adequate protection
under other writs. But, as already said, the difficulty was
prepared of old[1].

[p. 380]   And now two questions may occur to us. First, why should
there be a peculiar class of customary tenants on those manors
which have been in the king's hand ever since the Norman
Conquest? Secondly, why should the king interfere for the
protection of customary tenants even when those manors have
passed out of his own hand? The second question is the more
easily answered. There has been an application of a very
general rule of law which has come before us on more than one
occasion. It may be thus stated:—the transfer of a lordship
from one person to another should not affect the position of the
tenants; as regards them it is *res inter alios acta*. When an
honour escheats to the king, the tenants of that honour do
not become liable to the special burdens which lie on those
who are regarded as having held immediately of the crown
from all time; the honour has still a notional existence for
their benefit. Even so when the king parts with one of his
ancient manors and puts a mesne lord over it, the tenants are
neither to gain nor to lose by this transaction; as regards them,
their rights and duties, the manor is still conceived as part of
the royal demesne. A bye motive may secure the observance

Why is a special treatment of the ancient demesne necessary?

---

[1] The most important case from the later middle ages seems to be Y. B. 14
Hen. IV. f. 34 (Hil. pl. 51). Hankford there fixes the terminology of later
times; for compare Fitz. Nat. Brev. f. 12 b. On the ancient demesne there are
(*b*) sokemen of free tenure, who are free holders, who use the little writ and
who, as it seems, convey by feoffment, and (*c*) sokemen of base tenure who hold
by the rod, who surrender into the lord's hand, who are unprotected by the
little writ, but sue for their tenements by bill [*i.e.* petition] in the lord's court.
Of any (*a*) tenants by knight's service who may hold of an ancient demesne
manor, no mention is here made, since their tenure is hardly conceived as a
'tenure in ancient demesne.' The doctrine of the thirteenth century makes a
different distribution; there are (*a*) freeholders, who may hold either by knight's
service or in free socage and who have the ordinary freeholder's remedies;
(*b*) the tenants in privileged villeinage, who have the little writ and who usually
convey by surrender; (*c*) the tenants in absolute villeinage, who at least in
strict law have no protected tenant right. The question discussed in later
days, 'In whom is the freehold? Is it in the lord, or is it in the tenant?'
implies a conception of '*the* freehold' to which the lawyers of Henry III.'s
day had hardly come.

of this general rule in the case that is now before us. The king hardly regards these manors as having utterly ceased to be his, for, to say nothing of a possible act of resumption[1] and to say nothing of escheats and forfeitures, many of these manors are let out to the mesne lords at substantial rents; they are held at 'fee farm' and the king is concerned to see that the security for his rent is not impaired. It would be impaired were the tenants ill treated. This point, of importance in social history, is brought out by many actions for 'waste' sued [p. 381] by wards against their guardians; the guardian has not merely cut down trees and pulled down houses, but he has 'destroyed,' 'exiled' or impoverished the villeins[2]. Still the desire to keep well stocked and well managed the manors which supply the king with his fee farm rents, can serve but to give a little additional force to a general rule of law. It is a rule which cuts both ways. If we find tenants eagerly contending that they are on the privileged soil, we may also find, though hardly so often, a lord affirming that his manor is on the ancient demesne while the tenant denies this. The special law for the old patrimony of the king will profit now one and now the other party to the tenure[3].

The king preserves an old settlement. We come then to the main question. Why on those manors which have never left the king's hand is there a large class of tenants such as are hardly to be found elsewhere, a class of 'sokemen,' holding in 'privileged villeinage'? All the evidence that we have conspires to tell us that there has been less change on these manors than elsewhere, and that the phenomenon before us is an unusual degree of conservatism. In the first place, the very name of 'ancient demesne' shows us that the law supposes itself to be conservative. It is maintaining the Conquest settlement. To decide the question whether a manor be ancient demesne or no, it will go back far beyond all ordinary terms of

---

[1] Fleta, p. 3–4; Britton, i. 221–2.

[2] See Note Book, pl. 632: 'destruxit duos villanos divites ita quod pauperes effecti sunt'; pl. 691: 'talliavit quendam villanum etc. ita quod ipsum fugavit.'

[3] The lord distrains the tenant for services; the tenant brings a replevin; the lord pleads ancient demesne: Y. B. 12 Edw. II. 384; Y. B. 29 Edw. III. f. 9. If the question is between sokemanry and mere villeinage, the tenant will desire to show that the land is ancient demesne; but if the question is between sokemanry and ordinary freeholding, then this contention will come from the lord, for he would rather that a case in which he is concerned should come into the manorial court than that it should go before the king's justices.

limitation and prescription, far beyond 'the beginning of legal memory'; it will be content with no evidence save that of the great survey. Nay in theory the ancient demesne gained its specific quality before Domesday Book was made. The lawyers of the fourteenth century had some doubts as to the exact moment of time at which the manor must have been in the king's hand in order to make it ancient demesne for good and all, [p. 382] and the rule of evidence that they had adopted, namely that no testimony was admissible save that of Domesday Book, must have tended to cause some little confusion; still on the whole they think that the privileged manors are 'the manors of St Edward'[1]. In this, though hardly in any other, context they will go behind the Norman Conquest. In the second place, Bracton regards these sokemen as an ancient race; it holds its lands under a great concession made to it soon after the Conquest. If new settlers come onto the ancient demesne, whatever rights they may gain under agreements made with their lords, they are not sokemen nor entitled to the peculiar privileges of sokemen. This theory, however difficult of application two centuries after the Conquest, was no idle theory; we are constantly reminded that the special characteristics of the ancient demesne, if they inhere in certain tenements, inhere also in 'the blood of the sokemen.' Thus when the men of Tavistock have recourse to a *Monstraverunt*, it is objected that many of them are *adventitii*[2]. Thus the men of King's Ripton hold themselves to be a privileged race; even the ordinary rules of inheritance must yield when the choice is between a claimant who is not 'of the blood of the vill' and one who is[3]. Thus

---

[1] Y. B. 15 Edw. II. f. 455; Y. B. 13–4 Edw. III. (Pike), p. 102; Fitz. Abr. *Auncien Demesne*, pl. 15; Y. B. 49 Edw. III. f. 22–3; Vinogradoff, p. 90. The rule as to the exclusive use of Domesday may well be of comparatively late growth; in one of the earliest cases the sheriff is directed to inquire whether the land be ancient demesne or no; Placit. Abbrev. p. 119 (Staf.). In some cases the appeal to Domesday would have been misleading. No one, for example, could discover from that record that the manor of King's Ripton was ancient demesne; probably it is there reckoned as a member of an adjoining manor, still its lord when at war with his refractory tenants raised no question as to its quality; Select Pleas in Manorial Courts, i. p. 99.

[2] Placit. Abbrev. 270–1; Vinogradoff, 118–9. Vinogradoff's criticism of this decision seems unnecessarily severe. All that can be said against the judges is that they apparently gave one bad reason for a sound judgment. A jury had found that the men of Tavistock were of servile condition; this was foundation enough for the decision.

[3] Select Pleas in Manorial Courts, i. 105–6.

again, Aunger of Ripon treats the little writ of right as a
remedy which has place only where both parties are born
sokemen, or where one is a born sokeman and the other the
lord; against an *extrinsecus* or *forinsecus* there may be an assize[1].
Thirdly, without examining at any length the terminology of [p. 383]
Domesday Book, we can say at once that the ancient demesne
manors of the thirteenth century have preserved, while other
manors have lost, some features which in the Conqueror's survey
are by no means peculiar to the royal villages; it is on the
ancient demesne that we find more than one legal class of tenants
who are not freeholders; it is on the ancient demesne that we
find large groups of tenants still rejoicing in the ancient name
of sokemen.

Why the
king pro-
tects his
tenants.
　　　　　Why has the king here shown himself as a conservative?
Certainly we can not answer that it is in the nature of kings
to be conservative or solve the problem by an allusion to the
inertness of a government bureau. In matters of law the royal
power has been the great disturbing force, the king has been
the radical reformer. Of course it is well to observe that on
a royal manor there hardly can be any of those 'half-rights'
(if such a term may be invented) that may exist elsewhere.
The custom of a royal manor, if the king recognizes it at all,
must stand on much the same level as the law of the land; it
will be administered by royal officers, and in the last resort it
will be administered by royal officers who happen to be the
judges of the supreme court of law. Still the king suffers this,
and holds himself bound to suffer it, and his judges, for
example, Bracton, say that he is bound to suffer it, say that
the sokemen are irremovable so long as they do their services,
say that their services are *servitia certa et nominata*. What we
have to attribute to the king in a special degree is no mere
inertness, nor is it enlightened self interest (for this we should
look to the monastic rather than to the royal estates) but it is
a respect for custom, an acknowledgment that the rules administered in his manorial courts have all the force of law.
Perhaps it is no paradox that he keeps the custom best because

---

[1] Y. B. 20–21 Edw. I. p. xix. Cf. Fleta, p. 4: 'Provisum est etiam quod
huiusmodi tenentes *inter se* tantum unicum beneficium habeant recuperationis
tenementorum per quoddam breve de recto clausum.' Britton, ii. 13: 'le bref
de dreit clos pledable par baillif del maner de tort fet *del un sokeman al autre.*'
See also Y. B. 21–2 Edw. I. p. 501.

there can be no talk of his being forced to keep it. Another lord will draw a firm line between the rights of his freehold tenants, which he can be compelled to observe, and the rights, if such they are to be called, of his customary tenants, which he can ignore with impunity, and, as a remedy in the king's [p. 384] supreme court is more and more regarded as a touchstone of every would-be right, he will begin to reason that there is no right where there is no compulsion. It is otherwise with the king. If he ejects his sokeman, no action will lie against him; none will lie against him if he disseises the palatine earl. In either case the person wronged can but petition for right; in either case the wrongdoer must answer for his act before the one tribunal competent to try him; he must appear before the throne of God. Morally the king can never be as irresponsible as is another lord of a manor, just because legally no bounds, or no definite bounds, are set to his irresponsibility. Men will not easily distinguish between his two capacities. If a landlord, he is still the king, the supreme judge over all men, the fountain of justice; he has sworn to do justice; the abbot, the baron, the knight have taken no such oath. We may add that the king is bound to maintain the laws and customs of 'the glorious king St Edward his predecessor.' Should he not then begin at home? It is as the tenants of St Edward that the men of the ancient demesne claim his protection[1].

Speaking generally we have said that outside the ancient demesne all the tenures of the non-freeholding peasantry are in law one tenure, tenure in villeinage. This is the doctrine of the lawyers of the thirteenth century, and on the whole it is well borne out by the manorial 'extents.' Economically considered there are many modes of peasant tenure, for the tenement may be large or small, the agricultural services may be light or heavy, 'week work' may be exacted or money may be taken; but just as the modern lawyer makes 'leasehold tenure' cover such economically different things as a lease of a house in London and a lease of a farm, a lease for a year and a lease for a thousand years, beneficial leases and leases at rack rent, so all these modes of peasant tenure can be brought under one head. The legal quality which they have in common and which keeps them together, is, we may say, their customary quality; they are not protected by the law of the king's courts,

Customary freehold.

---

[1] See the coronation oath of Edward II., Stubbs, Const. Hist. ii. 317.

but they are protected, more or less perfectly, by the customs administered in the manorial courts. Legally they form one tenure, because in all cases the kind of protection that they receive is the same. In this quality there are no degrees, or none that can be fixed with legal precision. Of course there [p. 385] are good and bad landlords, landlords who respect the custom, landlords who break it, conservative landlords and improving landlords; but all this is no matter of law. What we do not see is that one and the same landlord in one and the same manor admits that he has divers classes of non-freeholding tenants, which differ from each other in the validity of their tenure; what we do not see is a 'privileged' beside an 'absolute' villeinage. Still there are exceptions, and perhaps, were they all collected, they would form a considerable mass: in particular if the documents concerning Kent, East Anglia and Northumbria were patiently examined. In a cartulary of the twelfth century, in the Black Book of Peterborough, we still find on one and the same manor various classes of tenants bearing the names which are familiar to all who read Domesday Book. There are large groups of *sochemanni* who are kept well apart from the *villani*, but who very probably could not have made good a claim to be considered as freeholders in the king's court[1]. Even in the Hundred Rolls we may, though as a rarity, find a class of sokemen marked off from the freeholders on the one hand and the tenants in villeinage on the other, though the manor is not on the ancient demesne. It is so at Swavesey in Cambridgeshire. When Domesday Book was made Count Alan held it, and it is still held by Ellen de la Zouche 'as of the honour of Britanny'. She has freehold tenants, a group of *villani* who hold *de villenagio*, a group of cotters; but besides these a group of *sokemanni* who hold *sokelond*[2]. In the north the 'tenants in drengage' are severed from the freeholders and from the 'tenants in bondage[3];' and, if the Kentish 'gavelmen' succeeded in making 'gavelkind' a freehold tenure, and in some respects a privileged freehold tenure, since peculiarly cheap and easy remedies for its protection were allowed them, their

[1] Chron. Petrob. p. 160: 'et xi. sochemanni . . . . in estate facient per **xv.** dies quicquid iusserit dominus.'

[2] R. H. ii. 469–470.

[3] Boldon Book, and Bp. Hatfield's Survey, *e.g.* pp. 29–30.

tenure was still spoken of as though it were not absolutely 'free'; it may be contrasted with 'frank fee' just as the tenure [p. 386] of the king's sokemen may be contrasted with 'frank fee [1].'

To this we must add that modern courts of law have from time to time been puzzled by the appearance before them of classes of tenants seeming to occupy a middle state between that of freeholders and that of copyholders. They are said to hold 'according to the custom of the manor,' but not 'at the will of the lord'; they convey their tenements sometimes by surrender and admittance in the lord's court, sometimes by a deed of bargain and sale followed by an admittance; often they are subject to some of the usual burdens of copyhold tenure. They have come sometimes from manors which formed part of the ancient demesne, sometimes from other manors; in particular they have often come from a part of England in which, if Domesday Book be the final test, there can be no ancient demesne, namely, from the northernmost counties. Now it would be foolish to argue that the ancestors in law of any given group of such tenants enjoyed in the thirteenth century a condition superior to that of the ordinary tenants in villeinage. The full formula which is supposed to describe the tenure of the copyholder—'to hold at the will of the lord according to the custom of the manor'—is seldom found on the earliest court rolls. Any set of early court rolls is likely to show many variations in the phrases used about one and the same set of tenements, and in any particular case the omission of all allusion to the will of the lord from the formula which became current in the manorial court or the steward's office, may be of recent origin and the outcome of an accident. An example may show how rash such inferences may be. The Dean and Chapter, successors of the Prior and Convent, of Durham have (it is said) no copyholders, having succeeded in proving that their peasant tenants held only for life and without any right of renewal. The Bishop of Durham has, or lately had, plenty of copyholders. But in all probability the explanation of this difference is to be found in what from our point of view are comparatively modern times. The convent, like many other

Customary freehold in modern times.

---

[1] Placit. Abbrev. p. 233: in 1298 the whole county [court] of Kent is asked the question how tenements held in gavelkind can be changed into *liberum feodum.* Spelman, Gloss. s. v. *Sokemanria* gives from a Register of Christ Church, Canterbury, a remarkable classification of tenures.

religious houses, took steps to prevent its villein or 'bondage' [p. 387]
tenements from being heritable in fact; the 'corporation sole'
was less far-sighted than the 'corporation aggregate[1].' And
again, the modern cases which introduce us to 'customary freeholders' seldom tell us of more than one class of customary
tenants on the manor that is in question:—on that manor
there are no tenants who are said to hold 'at the will of the
lord.' Still when all the modern evidence is taken in the mass,
it supports the inference that we should have drawn from
the state of the ancient demesne. That inference is that the
very general absence in the thirteenth century of any class of
tenants mediate between the freeholders, who enjoy full and
immediate royal protection, and the customary tenants, who (as
men are beginning to say) hold at the will of the lord, is of
late origin, the effect of legal rules and legal theories rather
than of ancient economic facts.

No place
for a
tenure
between
freehold
and
villeinage.

With its newly centralized royal justice, the law of the
thirteenth century has no place for the sokeman. Even when he
is preserved on the royal demesne, it hardly knows how to deal
with him, can hardly decide whether he is a freeholder, thinks
that he may be a freeholder as regards some and not as regards
others. Outside the ancient demesne it proposes the dilemma,
'Protected by the king or not protected by the king, and if not
protected by him, then held at the will of the lord.' But if we
strive to go behind the amazing activity of the king's court, as
behind a new thing, if we think of the freeholder as having to
go in the first instance to his lord's court and hardly able as a
matter of fact to get much further, then the edge of the
dilemma is blunted. That the application of this logical
weapon did some immediate harm to the higher classes of
peasants can hardly be doubted. Our legal terminology does
indeed suggest that not a few of them, in particular not a few
of the sokemen, fell at once on the right side of the line. How
else can it happen that 'free socage' became the name of a free
tenure, a tenure by which even in Bracton's day barons and
knights are well content to hold? But, on the whole, the
doctrine of the lawyers seems to have been that any considerable amount of labour service must be villein service, must make
the tenure unfree and unprotected, because it cannot but be
service which in many particulars will be done at the will of the [p. 388]

---

[1] Durham Halmote Rolls, Introduction, pp. xxxv.–xxxvii.

lord. Such a doctrine must have condemned many a sokeman of the twelfth century to hold in villeinage.

But of the past history of those tenures which are not The 'conventioners.' freehold we must not speak in this place, for, however sharply the lawyers may contrast the two, villein tenure is, as a matter of fact, closely connected with villein status, a topic which will come before us in the next chapter. We have, however, yet to say a few words about a class of tenants who passed under our notice when we were transcribing Bracton's account of the ancient demesne. Marked off from the 'privileged villeinage' of the sokeman stands the tenure of certain *adventitii*, who, though they perform services similar to those of the sokemen, do not belong to that privileged race. They are regarded as 'outsiders' who have recently come to the manor, who have taken tenements under agreements (*conventiones*), who must perform agricultural services and who are protected by law; but their title to protection is given them not by the custom of the manor, but by the terms of the agreement; we have called them 'conventioners[1].' Bracton's own opinion seems to be that their rights are not 'real' rights; on the contrary, they are personal, contractual rights, to be enforced not by possessory or proprietary actions but by an action on the covenant. However, he admits that others thought differently, would have allowed these men the possessory assizes and therefore, for this would follow, would have treated them as freeholders. Bracton's doctrine about this matter represents, so we may guess, rather a passing inclination than a settled practice. Two great causes made against its perdurance. In the first place, the theory that the sokemen were a privileged race, that the privilege ran, if we may so speak, rather in their blood than in their tenure, though we may find many traces of it, could not be permanently maintained. The day for racial laws was past, and as a matter of practice no barrier could be kept up between the natural progeny of the sokemen and these 'adventitious' conventioners. In the second place, the whole [p. 389] tendency of English land law was setting strongly in favour of the principle that any one who has a right to be in the

---

[1] Bracton, f. 7, says of them 'tenent de dominico.' This phrase here and in some other places seems to mean that they hold land which until lately was in the lord's hand, and had once been part of his demesne in the narrowest sense of that term.

occupation of land has a right in the land, and whilst in occupation has a true possession of the land. This is seen most clearly in the treatment of tenants for terms of years. For a short while an attempt had been made to treat them as having rights, but merely personal, contractual rights; but, before Bracton wrote, the attempt had broken down, and the termor was considered as possessing the land and as having rights in it. And so with these conventioners:—Bracton's suggestion is very interesting, especially because he thinks that even an unfree man may have a remedy upon a covenant against the covenantor; but we cannot find that it struck deep root[1]. On the whole, outside the ancient demesne, the law maintains the dilemma, 'Freehold, or unprotected by law;' while even on the ancient demesne, 'Freehold, Absolute Villeinage, Privileged Villeinage (Sokemanry)' exhaust all the possible cases.

Conclusion.

Thus at the end of this prolonged account of the law of tenure we are brought back to a remark with which we started. Everywhere we see at first sight a simplicity that is truly marvellous. All the variegated facts of landholdership have been brought under the sway of a single formula, 'the formula of dependent tenure,' and the only modes of tenure which the law distinguishes are very few. If the reader does not think that our law is simple, he should look abroad or he should look at the facts which our law has endeavoured to master. Has endeavoured to master, we say, for it has not succeeded at every point in its grand undertaking. It has dealt rudely with the facts, it has neglected many a distinction of great social and economic importance, it has driven its trenchant dilemmas through the middle of natural classes and athwart some lines of customary morality; but it has been bold and strong and therefore simple.

[1] Concanen's Report of *Rowe* v. *Brenton* (1830) gives us interesting glimpses of large classes of 'conventioners' on some of the Cornish manors. When they first appear they seem to be holding under *conventiones*, that is to say, leases for short terms of years. Bracton does not say whether the tenants whom he describes hold for terms of years. A lease for years is very often called a *conventio*, and in Bracton's day the writ of covenant existed chiefly for the benefit of termors.

CHAPTER II.

THE SORTS AND CONDITIONS OF MEN.

[p. 390] OF the divers sorts and conditions of men our law of the Law of personal condition. thirteenth century has much to say; there are many classes of persons which must be regarded as legally constituted classes. Among laymen the time has indeed already come when men of one sort, free and lawful men (*liberi et legales homines*) can be treated as men of the common, the ordinary, we may perhaps say the normal sort, while men of all other sorts enjoy privileges or are subject to disabilities which can be called exceptional. The lay Englishman, free but not noble, who is of full age and who has forfeited none of his rights by crime or sin, is the law's typical man, typical person. But besides such men there are within the secular order noble men and unfree men; then there are monks and nuns who are dead to the world; then there is the clergy constituting a separate 'estate'; there are Jews and there are aliens; there are excommunicates, outlaws and convicted felons who have lost some or all of their civil rights; also we may here make mention of infants and of women, both married and unmarried, even though their condition be better discussed in connexion with family law, and a word should perhaps be said of lunatics, idiots and lepers. Lastly, there are 'juristic persons' to be considered, for the law is beginning to know the corporation.

But if for a while we fix our attention on the lay order, it may seem to us that, when compared with the contemporary law of France or at any rate of Germany, our law of *status* is poor: in other words, it has little to say about estates or ranks of men. Men are either free men or serfs; there is not much more to be said. When compared with tenure, status is unimportant.

This much we might learn from the history of a technical [p. 391] term. Our modern English writers on jurisprudence are constantly put to shifts for a word which shall translate the Latin *status* and frequently have to leave it untranslated; *estate* would make us think of rights in land, and *condition* also has hard work to do in our law of property and of obligations. The fate in England of the word *status* or *estate* is very curious. Bracton could still sharply oppose it to rights in land. A favourite maxim of his is that a man's free or villein tenure of a tenement does not affect his free or villein estate[1]. But very soon after his death we hear of a man having a *status* in fee simple or a *status* for life, and though such a phrase as 'the three estates of the realm' may endure, and our church may bid us pray 'for all estates of men,' still the English lawyer when he hears of *estates* will think first of rights in land, while the English layman will, like enough, think of land itself, of fields and houses. This means that our land law has been vastly more important than our law of ranks. And so it is at an early time; we read much more in the law-books of tenants by knight's service, serjeanty, burgage, socage, than of knights, serjeants, burgesses and sokemen; nay, even the great distinction between bond and free is apt to appear in practice rather as a distinction between tenures than as a distinction between persons.

§ 1. *The Earls and Barons.*

Our law hardly knows anything of a noble or of a gentle class; all free men are in the main equal before the law. For a moment this may seem strange. A conquered country is hardly the place in which we should look for an equality, which, having regard to other lands, we must call exceptional. Yet in truth it is the result of the Conquest, though a result

---

[1] Bracton will occasionally use the word *status* to stand for the whole mass of a person's rights, even with special reference to his proprietary rights in land, as when (f. 423 b) he discusses the maxim that an infant's *status* is not to be changed; but he chiefly uses the word when discussing personal freedom and personal slavery; these are the two great *estates*. In one passage (f. 40 b, line 23) he seems to use the word *status* in its later meaning—'Si autem totum non habuerit statum transfert id quod habet'; but the MSS. show that he wrote not *statum*, but *statim*.

[p. 392] that was slowly evolved. The compiler of the *Leges Henrici* would willingly have given us a full law of ranks or estates of men; but the materials at his command were too heterogeneous: counts, barons, earls, thegns, Norman *milites*, English radknights, vidames, vavassors, sokemen, villeins, ceorls, serfs, two-hundred men, six-hundred men—a text writer can do little with this disorderly mass. But a strong king can do with it what he pleases; he can make his favour the measure of nobility; they are noble whom he treats as such. And he does not choose that there shall be much nobility. Gradually a small noble class is formed, an estate of temporal lords, of earls and barons. The principles which hold it together are far rather land tenure and the king's will than the transmission of noble blood. Its members have political privileges which are the counterpart of political duties; the king consults them, and is in some sort bound to consult them, and they are bound to attend his summons and give him counsel. They have hardly any other privileges. During the baron's life his children have no privileges; on his death only the new baron becomes noble.

The privileges of the earl or the baron are, we say, extremely few. Doubtless from of old every free man was entitled to be judged by his peers[1]: that is to say, he was entitled to insist that those who were to sit as his judges should not be of a legal rank lower than his own. Under the dominance of the law of tenure this rule would take the form that a vassal is not to be judged by sub-vassals. So long as the king's court was a court of tenants in chief any man would have found there those who were at least his equals, and even in a county court there would have been barons enough to judge any baron. As the administration of royal justice gradually became the function of professional lawyers, the cry for a *iudicium parium* was raised by the nobles, and in words this was conceded to them[2] For a long time, however, the concession had no very marked effect, because the court held *coram Rege*, though for every-day purposes but a bench of professional justices, might at any moment assume a shape to which no baron could have taken exception; even a parliament to which all the barons had been [p. 393] summoned might still be regarded as this same court taking

Privileges of the barons.

---

[1] Leg. Hen. c. 31, 32, 33.
[2] Magna Carta (1215), c. 39. See above, p. 173.

for the nonce a specially solemn form. And the meaning of the rule was not very plain. On the one hand, we hear the assertion that even in civil suits the earl or baron should have the judgment of his peers[1], on the other hand Peter des Roches, the king's minister, can say that the king's justices are the peers of any man[2], and the very title of the 'barons' of the exchequer forbids us to treat this as mere insolence. And so Bracton gives us no doctrine as to the privilege of the barons. He does recognize the distinction between the king's court of justices and the king's court of 'peers,' but for the sake of a quite other doctrine, which left but few traces in later law. When there is a charge of treason, the king himself is the accuser, and life, limb and inheritance are at stake; therefore it is not seemly that the king, either in person or by his justices, who represent his person, should be judge; so Bracton throws out the suggestion that the cause should come before the 'peers[3].' We have here no privilege of peerage, but a special rule for all cases of high treason, based on the maxim that no one should be judge in his own cause. Under the Edwards the privilege of peerage was gradually ascertained, as the court of law held *coram Rege*, which by this time was known as the King's Bench, became more utterly distinct from the assembly of the barons. But in the end the baron had gained very little. If charged with treason or felony, he was tried by his peers; if charged with a misdemeanour (*transgressio*), if sued in a civil suit by high or low, if the king challenged his choicest franchises, there was no special court for him; he had to abide the judgment of the king's justices[4]. A certain freedom from arrest in civil causes we may perhaps allow him; but in Bracton's age arrest in civil causes was as yet no common [p. 394] event. That the tenant in chief could not be excommunicated

---

[1] Note Book, pl. 1213 (A.D. 1236–7): the Earl of Chester in a civil suit claims the judgment of his peers, but abandons this claim in order to put forward another, namely, that the plea being a 'common plea' should not be heard *coram Rege*. Placit. Abbrev. p. 201 (A.D. 1281): the Earl of Gloucester, being sued for his franchises in Glamorgan, insists that he ought to have the judgment of his peers, namely, the lords marchers.

[2] A.D. 1233; Mat. Par. iii. 252, 257 ; vi. 73; Note Book, pl. 857.

[3] Bracton, f. 119.

[4] In the fourteenth century it was held that a peer in a civil suit was entitled to have at least one knight on the jury. But this can have nothing to do with the *iudicium parium*, for the knight is neither the peer's peer nor his judge. See Y. B. 12–3 Edw. III. (ed. Pike), p. 291.

without the king's leave was a privilege of the king rather than
of the baronage. One other privilege the baron had, but it was
of questionable value. When he was adjudged to be in the king's
mercy, the amount of the amercement was fixed, or 'affeered,'
not by his merely 'free and lawful' neighbours but by his
peers. For this purpose, however, his peers were found in the
'barons' of the exchequer[1] and these experts in finance were
not likely to spare him[2]. There are a few little rules of
procedure which distinguish the noble from the non-noble.
Thus we are told that a summons to court should allow an earl
one month, a baron three weeks, a free man a fortnight[3]; and
we may see some traces of a rule which exempts a baron from
the necessity of swearing[4]. Even the members of the king's
family are under the ordinary law, though in their 'personal'
actions they have the same benefit of expeditious procedure
that is enjoyed by merchants[5]. Very different is the case of
the king, who in all litigation 'is prerogative.'

§ 2. *The Knights.*

Below the barons stand the knights; the law honours them
by subjecting them to special burdens; but still knighthood can
hardly be accounted a legal *status*. In the administration of
royal justice there is a great deal of work that can be done
only by knights, at all events if there are knights to be had.
Four knights, twelve knights, are constantly required as representatives of the county court or as recognitors. For some
purposes mere free and lawful men will serve, for others knights
must be employed. On the whole we may say that knights
are required for the more solemn, the more ancient, the more
decisive processes. To swear to a question of possession, free
and lawful men are good enough; to give the final and con-
[p. 395] clusive verdict about a matter of right, knights are needed.
They are treated as an able, trustworthy class; but we no longer

The knights.

---

[1] Bracton, f. 116 b.

[2] Madox, Exch. i. 530–9: the Abbot of Croyland and Thomas de Furnival
protest that they are not barons in order to escape from heavy amercements.

[3] This from the thirteenth century version of Glanvill contained in MS.
Camb. Univ. Mm. i. 27, f. 30 b.

[4] Bracton, f. 337 b–338.   [5] Bracton, f. 444.

find any such rule as that the oath of one thegn is equivalent
to the oath of six ceorls. In administrative law therefore the
knight is liable to some special burdens; in no other respect
does he differ from the mere free man. Even military service
and scutage have become matters of tenure rather than matters
of rank, and, though the king may strive to force into knighthood all men of a certain degree of wealth, we have no such
rule as that none but a knight can hold a knight's fee. Still
less have we any such rule as that none but a knight or none
but a baron can keep a seignorial court.

§ 3. *The Unfree.*

The
unfree.

In the main, then, all free men are equal before the law.
Just because this is so the line between the free and the unfree
seems very sharp. And the line between freedom and unfreedom is the line between freedom and servitude[1]. Bracton
accepts to the full the Roman dilemma: *Omnes homines aut
liberi sunt aut servi*[2]. He will have no mere unfreedom, no
semi-servile class, no merely prædial serfage, nothing equivalent to the Roman *colonatus*[3]. All men are either free men or
serfs, and every serf is as much a serf as any other serf[4]. We
use the word *serf*, not the word *slave*; but it is to be remembered that Bracton had not got the word *slave*. He used
the worst word that he had got, the word which, as he well
knew, had described the Roman slave whom his owner might
kill. And the serf has a *dominus*; we may prefer to render
this by *lord* and not by *master* or *owner*, and it is worthy of
observation that medieval Latin can not express this distinction; if the serf has a *dominus*, the palatine earl, nay,
the king of England, so long as he is duke of Aquitaine, has a
dominus also, and this is somewhat in the serf's favour; but
still Bracton uses the only words by which he could have
described a slave and a slave-owner. True that *servus* is [p. 396]

---

[1] Here again we must refer to Vinogradoff's work for the discussion of many
details. See also Leadam, in Proceedings of Royal Hist. Soc. vi. 167, and in
L. Q. R. ix. 348.

[2] Bracton, f. 4 b.

[3] Bracton, f. 4 b; Bracton and Azo, p. 49.

[4] Bracton, f. 5; Fleta, pp. 1, 239, § 23; Britton, i. 197 and the editor's note.

neither the commonest nor yet the most technical name for the
unfree man; more commonly he is called *villanus* or *nativus*,
and these are the words used in legal pleadings; but for Bracton
these three terms are interchangeable, and though efforts, not
very consistent or successful efforts, might be made to distinguish between them[1], and some thought it wrong to call the
villeins serfs[2], still it is certain that *nativus* always implied
personal unfreedom, that *villanus* did the same when employed
by lawyers, and that Bracton was right in saying that the law
of his time knew no degrees of personal unfreedom. Even in
common practice and by men who were not jurists the word
servus was sometimes used as an equivalent for *nativus* or
villanus. The jurors of one hundred will call all the unfree
people *servi*, while in the next hundred they will be *villani*[3].
In French *villein* is the common word; but the feminine of
villein is *nieve* (*nativa*)[4].

There are no degrees of personal unfreedom; there is no
such thing as merely prædial serfage. A free man may hold
in villeinage; but that is an utterly different thing; he is
in no sort a serf; so far from being bound to the soil he can
fling up his tenement and go whithersoever he pleases[5]. In
later centuries certain niceties of pleading gave rise to the
terms 'villein in gross' and 'villein regardant,' and in yet later
times, when villeinage of any kind was obsolescent, these were
supposed to point to two different classes of men, the villein
regardant being inseverable from a particular manor, while
the villein in gross might bé detached from the soil and sold
[p. 397] as a chattel. The law of Bracton's time recognizes no such
distinction[6]. As a matter of fact and a matter of custom,

General
idea of
serfage.

---

[1] See the attempts of John of Longueville, Nichols's Britton, i. 195 note;
Vinogradoff, p. 45 note.

[2] Mirror, (Selden Soc.), pp. 79, 165.

[3] For example, in the Hundred Rolls for Oxfordshire (R. H. ii. 688 ff.)

[4] The English *bondman* may have been common, for we often read of *bondi*
or *bondes*; but this word covers an instructive ambiguity; a Scandinavian word,
meaning man and hence peasant, has been misunderstood to imply bondage, *i.e.*
servility. See Vinogradoff, p. 145. Britton writing in French frequently used
the word *serf*, and there is no sufficient reason for denying that this word was
used also in English speech. We shall use it as a translation of Bracton's
servus.

[5] See above p. 390 as to Bracton's odd use of the term *ascriptitius*.

[6] We hold this to have been fully proved by Hallam, Middle Ages, ed. 1837,
vol. iii. p. 256, and by Vinogradoff, pp. 48–56. But they are perhaps inclined

English serfage may well be called prædial. In the first place, it rarely if ever happens that the serfs are employed in other work than agriculture and its attendant processes; their function is to cultivate their lord's demesne. In the second place, the serf usually holds more or less land, at least a cottage, or else is the member of a household whose head holds land, and the services that he does to his lord are constantly regarded in practice as the return which is due from him in respect of this tenement or even as the return due from the tenement itself; such services, as we have already seen, are often minutely defined by custom. In the third place, his lord does not feed or clothe him; he makes his own living by cultivating his villein tenement, or, in case he is but a cottager, by earning wages at the hand of his wealthier neighbours. In the fourth place, he is seldom severed from his tenement; he is seldom sold as a chattel, though this happens now and again[1]; he passes from feoffor to feoffee, from ancestor to heir as annexed to the soil. For all this, the law as administered by the king's court permits his lord to remove him from the tenement. It could hardly have done otherwise, for he held in villeinage, and even a free man holding in villeinage could be ejected from his tenement whenever the lord pleased without finding a remedy before the king's justices. But as to the serf, not only could he be removed from one tenement, he could be placed in another; his lord might set him to work of any kind; the king's court would not interfere; for he was a *servus* and his person belonged [p. 398] to his lord; 'he was merely the chattel of his lord to give and 'sell at his pleasure[2].'

to give too late a date to the appearance of the idea that there are two classes of villeins. Thus in Y. B. 1 Hen. IV. f. 5 (Mich. pl. 11) a nieve brings an appeal for the death of her husband against her lord; it is argued that if the lord be convicted, the appellant will become free; to this it is replied, Not so, if she be regardant to a manor, for in that case she will be forfeited and become the king's nieve; but otherwise would it be if she were a villein in gross.

    [1] See *e.g.* Cart. Glouc. ii. 4: the Bishop of Hereford grants a villein to the Abbey of Gloucester. Cart. Burton, p. 75, grant of a *nativus* by the Abbot of Burton to the Abbess of Polesworth. Note Book, pl. 1103: a villein sold for 40 shillings; this price will hardly cover a tenement. Register of Abp. Gray (Surtees Soc.), p. 282: the Archbishop of York buys two *nativi* for 20 pounds. Selby Coucher Book, i. 278: a *nativus* is sold for four shillings and a *talentum*. Ninth Rep. Hist. MSS. Ap. 1, p. 32: a man and his sons are sold to the Chapter of St Paul's for 60 shillings, a mare, a cart and 28 sheep.

    [2] Britton, i. 197.

But, whatever terms the lawyers may use, their own first Relativity of serfage.
principles will forbid us to speak of the English 'serf' as a
slave: their own first principles, we say, for what we find is not
a general law of slavery humanely mitigated in some details,
but a conception of serfdom which at many points comes into
conflict with our notion of slavery. In his treatment of the
subject Bracton frequently insists on the relativity of serfdom.
Serfdom with him is hardly a status; it is but a relation
between two persons, serf and lord. As regards his lord the serf
has, at least as a rule, no rights; but as regards other persons
he has all or nearly all the rights of a free man; it is nothing
to them that he is a serf[1]. Now this relative serfdom we cannot call slavery. As regards mankind at large the serf so far
from being a mere thing is a free man. This seems to be the
main principle of the law of Bracton's day. We must now examine each of its two sides: the serf's rightlessness as regards
his lord, his freedom or 'quasi-freedom' as regards men in
general. It will then remain to speak of his relation to the
state.

In relation to his lord the general rule makes him rightless. (1) The serf in relation to his lord.
Criminal law indeed protects him in life and limb. Such
protection however need not be regarded as an exception to the
rule. Bracton can here fall back upon the Institutes:—the
state is concerned to see that no one shall make an ill use
of his property[2]. Our modern statutes which prohibit cruelty
to animals do not give rights to dogs and horses, and, though
it is certain that the lord could be punished for killing or
maiming his villein, it is not certain that the villein or his heir
could set the law in motion by means of an 'appeal[3].' The

---

[1] Bracton, f. 197 b, line 3, appeals to common opinion; 'dicitur enim
vulgariter quod quis potest esse servus unius et liber homo alterius.' He uses
the same phrase, f. 25, line 13, f. 196 b, line 36. On f. 198 b, he says, 'Cum quis
servus sit, non erit servus cuilibet de populo.' Britton, i. 199; Fleta, p. 111
(§ 15).

[2] Bracton, f. 6, § 3; f. 155 b, § 3. Britton, i. 195 and the Longueville note.

[3] Bracton, f. 141: the serf only has an 'appeal' in case of high treason.
For later law as to appeals by villeins see Y. B. 18 Edw. III. f. 32, Mich. pl. 4
(which appears also as 11 Hen. IV. f. 93, Trin. pl. 52); 1 Hen. IV. f. 5, Mich.
pl. 11; Fitz. Abr. *Corone*, pl. 17; Lit. sec. 189, 190, 194, and Coke's comment.
Littleton's doctrine is that a villein's heir has an appeal for the death of his
ancestor, that a nieve has an appeal for rape, but that a villein has no appeal
for mayhem, though for this crime the lord may be indicted. When a civil
action was brought for beating, wounding, imprisonment, etc. there seems to

protection afforded by criminal law seems to go no further than [p. 399]
the preservation of life and limb.   The lord may beat or imprison his serf, though of such doings we do not hear very
much[1].

Rightless-
ness of
the serf.

As against his lord the serf can have no proprietary rights.
If he holds in villeinage of his lord, of course he is not protected
in his holding by the king's courts; but then this want of
protection we need not regard as a consequence of his serfdom,
for, were he a free man, he still would be unprotected; and then,
just as the free man holding in villeinage is protected by
custom and manorial courts, so the serf is similarly protected[2].
His rightlessness appears more clearly as regards his chattels
and any land that he may have acquired from one who is
not his master.   As regards any movable goods that he has,
the lord may take these to himself.   We hear indeed hints
that his 'wainage,' his instruments of husbandry, are protected even against his lord[3], and that his lord can be guilty
against him of the crime of robbery[4]; but these hints are
either belated or premature; the lord has a right to seize his
chattels.   But it is a right to seize them and so become owner
of them: until seizure, the serf is their owner and others
can deal with him as such[5].   As a matter of fact we hear little
of arbitrary seizures, much of seizures which are not arbitrary
but are the enforcement of manorial customs.   The villeins
are constantly amerced and distrained; the lord in his court
habitually treats them as owners of chattels, he even permits [p. 400]
them to make wills, and when they die he contents himself with

have been some doubt as to how much of the charge the defendant should
formally deny before pleading that the plaintiff was his villein; see Y. B. 33–5
Edw. I. p. 296.

   [1] Select Pleas of the Crown, p. 3: a villein kept in chains because he wished
to run away.   For the imprisonment of a body of rebellious tenants in the 14th
century see Literae Cantuarienses, vol. ii. p. xxxvii.

   [2] A MS. of Bracton in the Phillipps Library, No. 3510, has a marginal note
written early in the fourteenth century which states the hereditary rights of the
villeins in forcible terms.   'Item usque ad tertium gradum inclusive illi de
parentela et sanguine villanorum, sive mares fuerint sive feminae, succedent iure
hereditario in terras et tenementa villanorum.   Et si per iniquum dominum
seu ballivum eiciantur, iniuriatur eis in hoc, quia legem suam habent ut liberi
homines suam.'

   [3] Bracton, f. 6, § 3; Bracton and Azo, pp. 67, 71; Vinogradoff, p. 74.

   [4] Bracton, f. 155 b, § 3.

   [5] See especially Bracton, f. 193 b, line 6.

a heriot[1]. So here again, when we look at the facts, the serf's
condition seems better described as unprotectedness than as
rightlessness, though doubtless a lord may from time to time
seize goods without being able to justify the seizure by reference
to custom. Then, if the serf acquires land from some third
person to hold by free tenure, he whose serf he is may seize it
and hold it; but until such seizure the serf is tenant and
others may and must treat him as such.

And then we find that all this rightlessness or unprotectedness exists only where serfdom exists *de facto*. The learning of
seisin or possession and the rigid prohibition of self-help have
come to the aid of the serfs. Serfdom and liberty are treated
as things of which there may be possession, legally protected
possession[2]. A fugitive serf may somewhat easily acquire a
'seisin' of liberty. When he is seised of liberty the lord's
power of self-help is gone; he can no longer capture the
fugitive without a writ; he can no longer take any lands or
chattels that the fugitive may have acquired since his flight[3].
He must have recourse to a writ, and the fugitive will have
an opportunity of asserting that by rights he is a free man,
and of asserting this in the king's court before justices who
openly profess a leaning in favour of liberty[4]. We need not
suppose that this curious extension of the idea of possession is
due to this leaning; it is part and parcel of one of the great
[p. 401] constructive exploits of medieval law:—relationships which
exist *de facto* are to be protected until it be proved that they
do not exist *de iure*. Still the doctrine, though it had a double

Serfdom de iure and de facto.

---

[1] But customs vary very much in this respect. The Abbey of Bec claims
the chattels of all villeins who die intestate; R. H. ii. 758 and an unprinted
custumal belonging to King's Coll. Camb. The Abbot of Ramsey makes a
similar claim at St Ives; Cart. Rams. i. 290. At Warboys and Caldicote if the
villein has no heir of his body the abbot takes a third of the goods. At
Hemingford the villein can make a will 'even in the absence of the reeve or
serjeant.' Often the best of the villein's chattels were regarded as annexed to
the tenement and could not be bequeathed; see Literae Cantuarienses, ii. 411–2.

[2] See in particular Bracton, f. 190 b, line 8: '...in possessione servitutis...in
possessione libertatis.' Bracton quaintly misappropriates the term *statu liber*
for the serf who is *de facto* free, while the free man who is *de facto* a serf is
statu servus. Bracton and Azo, 78.

[3] Bracton, f. 191.

[4] Bracton, f. 191 b, last lines: 'in statu dubio semper erit pro libertate
iudicandum'; f. 193, 'in hoc dubio erit pro libertate iudicandum ita quod in
benigniorem partem cadat interpretatio.'

edge, told against the lords. Apparently in Bracton's day a
serf who fled had to be captured within four days; otherwise
he could not be captured, unless within year and day he
returned to 'his villein nest'[1]: a parallel rule gave the ejected
landholder but four days for self-help[2]. Of course, however,
every absence from the lord's land was not a flight; the serf
might be living elsewhere and making some periodic payment,
chevagium, head-money, in recognition of his lord's rights: if so,
he was not in seisin of his liberty. What the Institutes say
about domesticated animals can be regarded as to the point[3].

Covenant
between
lord and
serf.   Yet another qualification of rightlessness is suggested.
More than once Bracton comes to the question whether the
lord may not be bound by an agreement, or covenant, made
with his serf. He is inclined to say Yes. His reasoning is
this:—the lord can manumit his serf, make him free for all
purposes; but the greater includes the less; therefore the serf
may be made a free man for a single purpose, namely that of
exacting some covenanted benefit, and yet for the rest may
remain a serf[4]. Such reasoning is natural if once we regard
serfdom as a mere relationship between two persons. It does
not, however, seem to have prevailed for any long time, for our
law came to a principle which was both more easily defensible
and more hostile to serfdom, namely that if the lord makes a
covenant with his serf, this implies a manumission; he becomes
free because his lord has treated him as free[5]. Bracton's
doctrine very possibly had facts behind it and was no empty
speculation, for we do find lords making formal agreements
with their serfs[6]; but it ran counter to a main current of [p. 402]
English land law. The agreements that Bracton had in view

[1] Bracton, f. 6 b, 7; Bracton and Azo, p. 77; Y. B. 21–2 Edw. I. p. 449;
33–5 Edw. I. p. 205.

[2] Bracton, f. 163. These strict possessory rules were being relaxed before
the end of the century. Year and day takes the place of the four days; Britton,
i. 199, 201.

[3] Bracton, f. 6 b: 'ad similitudinem cervorum domesticorum.' Cf. Britton,
i. 201; Y. B. 32–3 Edw. I. p. 56.

[4] Bracton, f. 24 b, 208 b; Vinogradoff, pp. 70–4.

[5] Littleton, sec. 205–7.

[6] See Vinogradoff, p. 73. Add to his illustrations, Cart. Glouc. ii. 87:
grant of land to G. our 'native' for life and to his wife during her viduity, at
a rent and in consideration of a gross sum; he is not to marry son or daughter
without our leave. Select Pleas in Manorial Courts, i. 172: elaborate agreement
between the abbot of Battle and his villeins. Note Book, pl. 784, 1814.

were in the main agreements relating to the tenure of land, and as we have already seen[1], our law was strongly disinclined to recognize any contract concerning the occupation of land which was merely a contract and not a bestowal of 'real' rights: it urged the dilemma—no right to occupy land or some one of the known forms of legal tenure.

The serf's position in relation to all men other than his lord is simple:—he is to be treated as a free man[2]. When the lord is not concerned, criminal law makes no difference between bond and free, and apparently the free man may have to do battle with the bond. A blow given to a serf is a wrong to the serf. It may also give his lord a cause of action against the striker; but here also the law makes no difference between bond and free. If my serf is assaulted so that I lose his services or so that I suffer contumely, I have an action for damages; but it would be no otherwise had the assaulted person been my free servant[3]. So also in defining the master's liability for wrongful acts done by his dependants, the same principles as regards authorization and ratification seem to be applied whether the dependants be free servants or serfs[4]. It is rather for the acts of members, free or bond, of his household (*manupastus, mainpast*) that a man can be held liable than for the acts of his serfs[5]. (2) The serf in relation to third persons.

Then in relation to men in general, the serf may have lands and goods, property and possession, and all appropriate remedies. Of course if he is ejected from a villein tenement, he has no action; the action belongs to the lord of whom he holds the tenement, who may or may not be his personal lord; were he a free man holding in villeinage he would be no better off[6]. But the serf can own and possess chattels and hold a tenement against all but his lord. This general proposition may require some qualifications or explanations in particular instances. [p. 403] We read in the Dialogue on the Exchequer that if the lord owes scutage to the crown his serf's chattels can be seized, but The serf's property.

---

[1] See above, pp. 405-6.   [2] Hengham Parva, c. 8.

[3] Bracton, f. 155 § 2, 155 b § 3.   [4] Bracton, f. 204, 204 b.

[5] A man's liability for the doings of his mainpast will deserve fuller discussion in another context.

[6] In Bracton's day the man who purchases and obtains possession of villein land from a villein is protected against the lord's self-help; Note Book, pl. 1203.

ought not to be seized until his own chattels have been exhausted[1]; we read in Bracton that when a lord is to be distrained his villein's chattels should be the very first object of attack[2]; but in these cases we may say that the serf, having no proprietary rights against his lord, is treated as having none against those who by virtue of legal process are enabled to claim what the lord himself could seize :—the general principle is hardly impaired by such qualifications, and it is a most important principle.

Relative serfdom.

Still it is not a natural principle.   This attempt to treat a man now as a chattel and now as a free and lawful person, or rather to treat him as being both at one and the same moment, must give rise to difficult problems such as no law of true slavery can ever have to meet. Suppose for example that a villein makes an agreement with one who is not his lord; it seems certain that the villein can enforce it; but can the other contractor enforce it? To this question we have a definite answer from Britton[3]:—a contract can not be enforced against a villein; if he is sued and pleads 'I was the villein of *X* when this agreement was made and all that I have belongs to him,' then the plaintiff, unless he will contradict this plea, must fail and his action will be dismissed; nor can he sue *X*, for (unless there is some agency in the case) the lord is not bound by his serf's contract. In later times this rule must have been altered; the plea 'I am the villein of *X* and hold this land of him in villeinage' was often urged in actions for land, but we do not find the plea 'I am the villein of *X*' set up in purely 'personal' actions, as assuredly it would have been had it been a good plea[4]. But, even if we admit that a villein may be sued upon a contract, the creditor's remedy is precarious, for the lord can seize all the lands and chattels of his serf, and an action against his serf is just what will [p. 404] arouse his usually dormant right. Thus the law, in trying to work out its curious principle of 'relative servitude,' is driven

---

[1] Dialogus de Scaccario, ii. c. 14.

[2] Bracton, f. 217, line 36. We seem to see here a change unfavourable to the villein.

[3] Britton, ii. 159, 168–9.

[4] See Broke, Abr. *Villenage*, pl. 33: in an assize of mort d'ancestor one of the defendants pleaded that he was the villein of *X* and the action was dismissed. Broke notes that he did not add that he held in villeinage and therefore treats the case as curious. Still this was an action for land.

to treat the serf as a privileged person, as one who can sue
but can not be sued upon a contract; and, even when it allows
that he can be sued, it can give the creditor but a poor chance
of getting paid and will hardly prevent collusion between
villeins and friendly lords. Again, we see the ecclesiastical
courts condemning the villein to pay money for his sins, fornication and the like, and then we see the villein getting into
trouble with his lord for having thus expended money which
in some sort was his lord's[1]. The law with its idea of relative
servitude seems to be fighting against the very nature of things
and the very nature of persons.

Lastly, we should notice the serf's position in public law.
It is highly probable that a serf could not sit as the judge
of a free man, though it may be much doubted whether this
rule was strictly observed in the manorial courts[2]. He could
not sit as a judge in the communal courts, though he often
had to go to them in the humbler capacity of a 'presenter.'
So too he could not be a juror in civil causes; this he probably
regarded as a blessed exemption from a duty which fell heavily
on free men. But in criminal matters and in fiscal matters
he had to make presentments. At least in the earlier part
of the century, the verdict or testimony which sends free
men to the gallows is commonly that of twelve free men
endorsed by that of the representatives of four townships, and
such representatives were very often, perhaps normally, born
villeins. Such representatives served on coroners' inquests, and
the king took their testimony when he wished to know the
extent of his royal rights[3]. In the 'halimoots' or manorial
courts the serfs are busy as presenters, jurors, affeerers of
amercements, if not as judges; they fill the manorial offices;
the reeve of the township is commonly a serf. What is more,
[p. 405] the state in its exactions pays little heed to the line between
free and bond; it expects all men, not merely all free men, to
have arms[4]; so soon as it begins to levy taxes on movables, the

(3) The serf in relation to the state.

---

[1] Select Pleas in Manorial Courts, i. 97, 98.

[2] On a very early roll of a Norfolk manor, for a sight of which we have to
thank Dr Jessopp, a villein is amerced for having essoined a free man, 'et
testatur per curiam quod non potest assoniare liberum hominem.'

[3] Thus the Hundred Rolls seem to be founded on the presentments made as
well by representatives of townships, who would often be unfree, as by free and
lawful jurors of the hundreds; see the rolls for Essex, R. H. i. 136 ff.

[4] The original Assize of Arms (1181) contemplates only the arming of free

serfs, if they have chattels enough, must pay for them[1]. It is but a small set-off for all this onerous freedom that a serf can not be produced as champion or as compurgator; and even this rule is made to operate in favour of liberty; if a lord produces a serf as champion or compurgator this is an implied manumission[2]. The serfs have to bear many of the burdens of liberty. The state has a direct claim upon their bodies, their goods, their time and their testimony, and if for a moment this seems to make their lot the less tolerable, it prevents our thinking of them as domestic animals, the chattels of their lords.

How men become serfs.

Having seen what serfdom means, we may ask how men become serfs. The answer is that almost always the serf is a born serf; *nativus* and *villanus* were commonly used as interchangeable terms[3]. But as to the course by which serfdom is transmitted from parent to child we find more doubts than we might have expected. If both parents are serfs, of course the child is a serf; but if one parent is free and the other a serf, then difficulties seem to arise. The writer of the *Leges Henrici* holds that the child follows the father; but he quotes the proverb, 'Vitulus matris est cuiuscunque taurus alluserit,' and seems to admit that in practice the child is treated as a serf if either of the parents is unfree[4]. Glanvill is clear that the child of an unfree woman is a serf and seems to think that the child of an unfree man is no better off[5]. Thus we should get the rule, which had been approved by the church, namely, that, whenever free and servile blood are mixed, the servile prevails[6]. Bracton, however, has a more elaborate scheme. A bastard [p. 406]

Servile birth.

men; but the writ of 1252 requires that the *villani*, if rich enough, shall be armed. It is plain also that already in 1225 *villani* were *iurati ad arma*. This appears from the writ of that year for the collection of a fifteenth. See these documents in Stubbs, Sel. Charters.

[1] Even the ordinance for the Saladin tithe draws no line between free and unfree. The fifteenth of 1225 was levied from *villani*; so apparently were the fortieth of 1232 and the thirtieth of 1237.

[2] Bracton, f. 194, last lines.

[3] Thus Britton, i. 197, says that the 'native' who is a native not by birth but by his own confession is more properly called a villein.

[4] Leg. Henr. c. 77.　　　　　[5] Glanvill, lib. v. c. 6.

[6] See c. 15, C. 32, qu. 4. This was altered by c. 8, X. 1, 18. Such a rule, expressed in the German proverb 'das Kind folgt der ärgeren Hand,' is by no means unnatural; see Heusler, Institutionen, i. 188. In France they say 'Le mauvais emporte le bon': Viollet, Histoire du droit civil, p. 319.

follows the mother; the child of a bondwoman, if born out of
wedlock, is a serf; if born in wedlock and of a free father, then
another distinction must be taken; if a free man takes a bondwoman to wife and they dwell in her villein tenement, then
their offspring will be born serfs, but if she follows him to 'a
free couch' then their children will be born free. So also when
a bondman marries a free woman, the character of the tenement
in which they dwell determines the character of their offspring[1].
The influence thus ascribed to the tenement is very curious;
it shows that to keep villein status and villein tenure apart
was in practice a difficult matter, even for a lawyer ever ready
to insist that in theory they had nothing to do with each other.
In later days the courts seem to have adopted the simple rule
that the condition of the father is the decisive fact, and to
have pressed this rule to the absurd, if humane, conclusion that
a bastard is always born free since he has no father[2].

'Mixed marriages' indeed gave a great deal of trouble **Mixed marriages.**
throughout the middle ages by raising questions as to the
rights and remedies of the husband and wife[3]. Ultimately
'the better opinion of our books' was that the marriage of a
female serf with a free man, other than her lord, did not
absolutely enfranchise her, but merely made her free during
the marriage[4]. In 1302, however, we find two justices denouncing this doctrine as false, 'and worse than false, for it is
heresy;' apparently they think that such a marriage has all the
effect of a manumission; but their opinion did not go undisputed[5]. Such a marriage would not at any rate drag down the
free man into personal servitude, though according to Bracton
the issue of it would be serfs if they were born in the villein
[p. 407] tenement. In the converse case in which a bondman marries a
free woman, he of course is not enfranchised, though Bracton's
doctrine would make their children free if born in her free
tenement. On the contrary, it might be thought that, at all

---

[1] Bracton, f. 5, 194 b; Bracton and Azo, p. 53; Note Book, pl. 1041, 1839.

[2] See Vinogradoff, pp. 59–63, also the note on Leg. Hen. c. 77 in Thorpe's
Ancient Laws and Institutes. The freedom of the bastard appears at least as
early as Y. B. 19 Edw. II. f. 651–2. It appears also in Beaumanoir (c. 45, sec.
16) where it is the more curious because the general rule is 'Servitude vient de
par les mères.'

[3] See the Abridgements, tit. *Villenage.*

[4] Co. Lit. 123 a, 136 b, 137 b.

[5] Y. B. 30–1 Edw. I. 164–8. Comp. Britton, i. 199; Y. B. 18 Edw. II. 604.

events if she went to live along with her villein husband in his villein tenement and to bear him villein children, she herself would be accounted a villein. But this was not the rule. How far during the marriage she could make good any rights against her husband's lord (and it will be remembered that as against all others her husband was a free man) was very doubtful; she could not sue without her husband, and if he joined in the action, the lord would say, 'You are my villein[1].' But on her husband's death she would be free once more, or rather her freedom would once more become apparent and operative[2].

Influence of place of birth. Faint traces may be found of an opinion that birth in a certain district or a certain tenement will make the child unfree, or as the case may be free, no matter the condition of its parents; but, except in the well-known privilege of Kentish soil, it seems to have found no legal sanction[3].

Villeins by confession. A person born free rarely becomes a serf. When Bracton speaks of prisoners of war being held as slaves and of a freedman being reduced to slavery on account of his ingratitude, this is but romanesque learning[4]. We do not in this age hear of servitude as a punishment, though the Welsh marchers claim the right of selling criminals as slaves[5], and King John can threaten all men with slavery if they do not take arms to resist [p. 408] an invasion[6]. Nor do we any longer hear of free men selling

---

[1] Bracton, f. 202, 202 b; Britton, i. 281. Bracton's own opinion seems this:—Free woman with free tenement marries a bondman; his lord ejects them from her free tenement; they can sue him. (See Bracton's Note Book, pl. 1837; it is not stated in this case that the disseisor was the villein's lord.) But apparently Bracton admits that this is not the prevailing opinion, at all events if the lord is in seisin of the husband. Observe the words 'secundum quosdam quod ego non approbo.' But at any rate during the marriage the wife can have no action against her husband's lord save one based on the disturbance of her possession.

[2] Bracton, f. 202, 428 b, 430 b; Britton, f. 198–9; Note Book, pl. 702, 1139. As to the whole of this subject, see Vinogradoff, pp. 61–3.

[3] Assize Roll, Lincoln, No. 481 (57 Hen. III.), m. 3: 'in villa de Bellesby sunt duo feoda, scilicet, feodum de Fauemer et feodum Peverel et... omnes illi qui nati sunt in feodo de Fauemer liberi sunt, omnes vero illi qui nati sunt in feodo Peverel villani sunt.'

[4] Bracton, f. 5. But as to the ingratitude of one who has become free by knighthood, or by orders, see Britton, i. 208; Fleta, p. 111.

[5] P. Q. W. 818–9.

[6] Rot. Pat. i. 55. If they make default they and their heirs shall be *servi* for ever, paying every year four pence per head. A chevage of four pence a head

themselves into slavery. But it is a principle of law that if a
person has once confessed himself the serf of another in a court
of record, he can never thereafter be heard to contradict this
assertion, and so 'confession' takes its place beside 'birth' as
one of the origins of servility. There are abundant cases in our
records which suggest that this talk about confession is not
idle[1]; a defendant sometimes seeks to evade a plaintiff's demand by confessing that he is the villein of a third person, and
thus, even in the later middle ages, men may sometimes have
purchased peace and protection at the cost of liberty[2].

Whether prolonged serfdom *de facto* will generate serfdom
de iure was in Edward I.'s day a moot point. Some justices
laid down as a maxim that no prescription can ever make
servile, blood that once was free. Others flatly denied this
rule, and apparently held that if from father to son a succession
of free men went on doing villein services, the time would come
when an unfree child would be born to a free father. One
opinion would have condemned to servitude the fifth generation
in a series of persons performing base services, while a Scottish
law-book mentions the fourth generation, and a common form
[p. 409] of pleading made a lord assert that he had been seised of the
grandfather and great-great-grandfather of the man whose
liberty was in dispute. Opinion might fluctuate about this
question, because procedural rules prevented it from being

Serfdom
by pre-
scription.

seems to have been common in France; hence the serf is *homo quatuor num-
morum.*

[1] Note Book, pl. 466, 591, 1411, 1885, 1887, 1894; Y. B. 30–1 Edw. I.
p. 454; Y. B. 32–3 Edw. I. p. 4; Y. B. 19 Edw. II. f. 651.

[2] But how could a defendant gain anything by saying untruly that he was
personally a villein? In an action for land was it not enough to say, 'I hold in
villeinage, or I hold at will, and therefore I am not the right person to be sued';
while is it not only in actions for land that we find defendants relying on
villeinage of any kind? The answer is given by a case of 1292; Y. B. 20–1
Edw. I. p. 41. If the defendant merely pleads tenure in villeinage, the plaintiff
may contradict him and the falsehood of the plea may be established; but if he
adds that he is a villein, then the plaintiff can make no reply and fails in his
suit. Perhaps it was considered improbable that any one would condemn
himself and his posterity to perpetual servitude unless he had good cause for so
doing. At any rate there was no reply to this confession of villein status until
in 1363 a Statute, 37 Edw. III. c. 17, permitted the plaintiff to contradict it.
In 15 Edw. III. Fitz. Abr. *Brief*, 322, the absurdity of the rule is shown :—'It
is hard; for a man may confess himself villein to his father or his cousin, and
then next day get a release from him.' 'Yes, it is hard,' is the reply, 'but it is
law.'

often brought to a decision. The general rule as to the means by which free or servile status could be conclusively proved was that it must be proved *per parentes*. If the burden of proof lay on the person whose status was in question, he had to produce free kinsmen; if it lay on the would-be lord, he had to produce kinsmen of the would-be free man who would confess themselves serfs. A mere verdict of the country might settle the question provisionally and, as we may say, for possessory purposes, but could not settle it conclusively except as against one who had voluntarily submitted to this test. The burden of the proof is thrown on one side or on the other by seisin; the man who is in *de facto* enjoyment of liberty continues to be free until his servility is proved; the man who is under the power of a lord must remain so until he has shown his right to liberty. On the whole the procedural rules seem favourable to freedom. In Bracton's day a four days' flight[1] might throw the burden of proof upon the lord, and he would have to make out his title, not by the testimony of free and lawful neighbours, who would naturally infer serfdom *de iure* from serfdom *de facto*, but by the testimony of the fugitive's own kinsfolk as to the fugitive's pedigree, and they must confess themselves serfs before their testimony can be of any avail[2]. On the other hand, if a man has been doing villein services, he may as a matter of fact easily fall into serfage, unless he is willing to run from hearth and home and risk all upon a successful flight and an action at law. If for generation after generation his stock has held a villein tenement and done villein services he will be reckoned a villein, that is, a serf; even his kinsfolk will not dare to swear that he is free. There is no form of service so distinctively servile that it must needs be ascribed to servile [p.410] status and not to villein tenure; even the merchet, which is regarded as the best test, may sometimes be paid *ratione*

---

[1] See above, p. 418.

[2] On the face of it this looks like an ancient procedure, which has been preserved in this case *in favorem libertatis*. The lord ends his count by offering 'suit,' to wit, *A*, *B*, *C*, kinsmen of the defendant. In most other cases the production of suit has in the king's court become a mere formality, but here it is still all important. A jury may be brought in to decide whether the 'suitors' are really of kin to the defendant. Cases illustrating this procedure are, Note Book, pl. 1005, 1041, 1167, 1812; Y. B. 32–3 Edw. I. p. 514; Northumberland Assize Rolls (Surtees Soc.) pp. 46, 159, 196.

tenementi and not *ratione personae*[1]; but a prolonged performance of villein services must put a family's free status in jeopardy. That this is not so as a matter of law seems the opinion of the highest authorities; but the fact that a contrary opinion was current both in England and in Scotland may well make us think that in common life there had been a close connexion between villein tenure and villein status[2].

And now as to manumission:—A lord can easily enfranchise his serf. He can do so expressly by a charter of manumission; he does so impliedly by a grant of land to be held freely by the serf and his heirs, for a serf can have no heir but his lord[3]; he does so impliedly by certain acts which treat the serf as free, by producing him in the king's court as his champion or his compurgator[4]; it is becoming dangerous for a lord to make any written agreement with his serf[5]. There has been a difficulty as to a direct purchase of liberty. If the serf paid money to the lord for the grant of freedom, the lord might, it would seem, revoke the grant on the ground that his serf's money was his own money. This technical difficulty, for perhaps it was no more, was evaded by the intervention of a third person [p. 411] who made the purchase nominally with his own but really with the serf's money, and the serf having been sold and delivered

How serfdom ceases.

Manumission.

---

[1] See above, p. 373, and Britton, i. 196. In Y. B. 8 Edw. III. f. 66 (Mich. pl. 31) it is said that the bishop of Ely held land by the service of being tallaged along with the villeins.

[2] The best illustration of this point is a case of 20 Edw. I. reported in the notes to Hale's Pleas of the Crown, ii. 298. Two justices of assize laid down the rule 'quod nulla praescriptio temporis potest liberum sanguinem in servitutem reducere.' The case was then brought before the auditors of complaints, who declared that this maxim ' omnino falsum est.' The case was then taken into the King's Bench, but with what result does not appear. Britton, i. 196, 206, denies that long performance of base services, *e.g.* payment of merchet, can make a free stock unfree. So does Hengham in Y. B. 33–5 Edw. I. p. 15 : 'praescriptio temporis non redigit sanguinem liberum in servitutem.' On the other hand, a gloss in the Longueville MS. at Cambridge, printed by Vinogradoff, p. 63, says that in the fifth generation villein services will make free blood servile. The Scottish *Quoniam Attachiamenta*, c. 39 (Acts of Parliament of Scotland, i. 655), makes the fourth generation servile. Then in Fitz. Abr. *Villenage*, pl. 24, we have an extract from an unprinted Year Book of Edward III., which seems to say that a stock may become servile by holding in villeinage from time immemorial.

[3] Bracton, f. 24 b, 194 b. Britton, i. 198.

[4] Bracton, f. 194.

[5] See above, p. 418.

(the ownership did not pass until delivery) was then set free by his new owner[1].

In Bracton's day every act of manumission by the lord seems to have conferred full and perfect freedom; the freed man was in all respects the equal of the free born. This could hardly have been otherwise since, as we have seen, serfdom was regarded for the more part as a mere relation between two persons. Glanvill seems to have held a different opinion. He speaks as though the liberation would make the serf free as regards his former lord but leave him a serf as regards all other men[2]. The chief, if not the only, point that Glanvill had before his mind when he wrote this, seems to have been that the freed villein could not be produced as champion or as compurgator. It is possible also that he had in view acts of enfranchisement which were merely private and would not have denied that there were solemner methods by which absolute freedom could be conferred. In the *Leges Henrici* the man who wishes to free his serf must do so in public, 'in a church or a market or a county court or a hundred court, openly and before witnesses'; lance and sword are bestowed on the new free man and a ceremony is enacted which shows him that all ways lie open to his feet[3]. Glanvill may have required some such public act if perfect liberty was to be conferred; but Bracton, who habitually regards serfdom as a mere relationship, sees no difficulty; the lord by destroying the relationship destroys serfdom. Here we seem to see a modern notion of relative serfdom growing at the expense of [p. 412] an older notion of true slavery. To turn a thing into a person

---

[1] Glanvill, v. 5. This passage is very difficult, but seems to be explained by Bracton, f. 194 b. We may doubt whether Glanvill means to deny that a lord can gratuitously liberate his serf. If however he liberates him in consideration of a sum of money then a difficulty arises; this is met by the intermediation of a third person who purchases the serf nominally with his own, though really with the serf's money. Bracton says 'eligat fidem alicuius qui eum emat *quasi* propriis denariis suis.' Still villeins are said to buy their own liberty; *e.g.* Note Book, pl. 31, 343. The books of conveyancing precedents of the thirteenth century, *e.g.* the Luffield and Carpenter MSS. at Cambridge (Ee. i. 1; Mm. i. 27), give forms of manumission by way of sale; the former shows how the transaction can be accomplished either by two deeds or by a single deed. But see Vinogradoff, p. 86, who deals somewhat differently with the difficult passage in Glanvill.

[2] Glanvill, v. 5.

[3] Leg. Henr. c. 78 § 1: 'et liberas ei vias et portas conscribat apertas.'

is a feat that can not be performed without the aid of the state
but to make free as against yourself one who is already free as
against all but you, this you can easily do, for it is hardly a
matter of public law[1].

A serf will also become free (1) by dwelling for year and
day on the king's demesne or in a privileged town—this is
an assertion of a prerogative right which peoples the king's
manors and boroughs[2]; (2) by being knighted—knighthood
confers but a provisional freedom, for the knighted serf can be
degraded when his servility is proved[3]; (3) by entering religion
or receiving holy orders; it is unlawful to ordain a serf—this is
forbidden by canon as well as by temporal law[4],—but, when
once ordained, he is free, though his serfdom revives if he
resumes a secular life[5]. The lord's right of action for the
recovery of a serf was subject to a prescriptive term; in 1236
the year 1210 was chosen as the limit, and this limit was not
altered until 1275[6]; we have already seen that his right of
self-help the lord lost somewhat easily, though less easily as
time went on[7].

Such briefly stated is the English law of villeinage or
serfage in the thirteenth century. Its central idea, that of the
relativity of serfage, is strange. It looks artificial: that is to
say, it seems to betray the handiwork of lawyers who have
forced ancient facts into a modern theory. Slavery is very
intelligible; so is slavery tempered by humane rules which will
forbid an owner to maltreat his human chattel; so again is a
prædial serfage, and the ancient laws of our race compel us to
[p. 413] admit that there may be a half-free class, men who are neither

Other modes of enfranchisement.

Summary.

---

[1] Note Book, pl. 1749. Here again Vinogradoff, pp. 86–8, gives a somewhat
different explanation.

[2] Glanvill, v. 5; Bracton, f. 190 b; Fleta, 111, 235; Britton, i. 200, 209;
Stubbs, Hoveden, vol. ii. (Introduction), p. xl.

[3] Bracton, f. 190 b, 198 b; Britton, i. 200, 208; Fleta, 111.

[4] See the whole of Dist. 54 and X. 1, 18. In 1270 Robert de Montalt at his
mother's request enfranchised by charter his 'beloved and faithful clerk' Roger
de Malberthorpe, who perhaps was not in holy orders: Assize Roll, Lincoln,
No. 494, m. 43 d.

[5] Bracton, f. 5,190 b; Britton, i. 200, 208; Fleta, 111. According to Fleta
the serf who has been ordained may be degraded by the bishop if he proves a
disobedient clerk, and thereupon he relapses into serfdom.

[6] Note Book, pl. 1217; Stat. Westm. I. (3 Edw. I.) c. 39.

[7] See above, p. 418.

liberi homines nor yet *servi*[1]; but a merely relative serfdom is a juristic curiosity[2]. In defining it we have ever to be using the phrases 'in relation to,' 'as regards,' 'as against,' phrases which would not easily occur to the unlettered, and law which allows my serf to sue any free man but me, even to sue my lord, does not look like a natural expression of any of those deep-seated sentiments which demand that divers classes of men shall be kept asunder. Then this idea of relative servitude has to be further qualified before it will square with facts and customs and current notions of right and wrong. When a lord allows it to be recorded that on the death of his servile tenant he is entitled to the best beast, he goes very far towards admitting that he is not entitled to seize the chattels of his serf without good cause. We hesitate before we describe the serf as rightless even as against his lord, and, if we infer want of right from want of remedy, we feel that we may be doing violence to the thoughts of a generation which saw little difference between law and custom. On the whole looking at the law of Bracton's day we might guess that here as elsewhere the king's court has been carrying out a great work of simplification; we might even guess that its 'serf-villein,' rightless against his lord, free against all but his lord, is as a matter of history a composite person, a serf and a villein rolled into one[3].

Retrospect. Fusion of villeins and slaves. That this simplifying process greatly improved the legal position of the serf can hardly be doubted. We need not indeed suppose that the *theow* or *servus* of earlier times had been subjected to a rigorously consistent conception of slavery. Still in the main he had been rightless, a chattel; and we may [p. 414]

---

[1] As to the *liti* and *aldiones* see Brunner, D. R. G. i. 101.

[2] A comparison between our medieval serfdom and the slavery of the ancient world might seem to some beside the point on the ground that the ancients were heathen. But a no less startling contrast might be drawn between our medieval serfdom and the law which Englishmen and men of English race evolved for their negro slaves. It was quite untroubled by any idea of 'relativity,' and reproduced, though it had hardly copied, the main features of Roman law. See T. R. Cobb, An Inquiry into the Law of Negro Slavery, Philadelphia, 1858.

[3] The contemporary law of France knew how to keep the *vilain* and the *serf* well apart. Sometimes the former word is used to describe the whole mass of peasants bond and free. 'Mais souvent aussi le même mot est employé avec une signification restreinte et s'applique au paysan libre, par opposition au serf, comme la tenure en villenage est opposée à la tenure en mainmorte': Luchaire, Manuel des institutions, p. 329. A contemporary French critic of Bracton's book would have accused him of mixing up two classes of men.

be sure that his rightlessness had not been the merely relative
rightlessness of the 'serf-villein' of later days, free against all
but his lord.   Indeed we may say that in the course of the
twelfth century slavery was abolished.   That on the other hand
the *villani* suffered in the process is very likely.   Certainly
they suffered in name.   A few of them, notably those on the
king's manors, may have fallen on the right side of the Roman
dilemma 'aut liberi aut servi,' and as free men holding by
unfree tenure may have become even more distinctively free
than they were before; but most of them fell on the wrong
side; they got a bad name and were brought within the range of
maxims which described the English *theow* or the Roman slave.

Probably we ought not to impute to the lawyers of this
age any conscious desire to raise the serf or to debase the
villein.   The great motive force which directs their doings in
this as in other instances is a desire for the utmost generality
and simplicity.   They will have as few distinctions as possible.
All rights in land can be expressed by the formula of dependent
tenure; all conceivable tenures can be brought under some
half-dozen heads; so also the lines which have divided men
into sorts and conditions may with advantage be obliterated,
save one great line.   All men are free or serfs; all free men are
equal; all serfs are equal:—no law of ranks can be simpler than
that.   In this instance they had Roman law to help them; but
even that was not simple enough for them; the notion of *coloni*
who are the serfs of a tenement rather than of a person, though
it might seem to have so many points of contact with the facts
of English villeinage, was rejected in the name of simplicity[1].
They will carry through all complexities a maxim of their
own:—the serf is his lord's chattel but is free against all save
his lord.   They reck little of the interests of any classes, high
or low; but the interests of the state, of peace and order and
royal justice are ever before them.

The levelling process.

We have spoken at some length of the 'serf-villeins' of the
thirteenth century, for they formed a very large class.   For
several reasons precise calculations are impossible.   In the first
place, tenure is so much more important than status, at least so
much more important as a matter of manorial economy, that
the 'extents' and surveys are not very careful to separate the
personally free from the personally unfree.   In the second place,

The number of the serfs

[p. 415]

---

[1] Bracton, f. 4 b.

it is highly probable that large numbers of men did not know on which side of the legal gulf they stood; they and their ancestors had been doing services that were accounted villein, paying merchet and so forth; but this was not conclusive, and if they escaped from their lord it might be very difficult for him to prove them his 'natives.' On the other hand, while they remained in his power, they could have little hope of proving themselves free, and if they fled they left their all behind them. In the third place, a great part of our information comes from the estates of the wealthiest abbeys, and while admitting to the full that the monks had no wish to ill-treat their peasantry, we can not but believe that of all lords they were the most active and most far-sighted. Lastly, we have as yet in print but little information about certain counties which we have reason to suppose were the least tainted with servitude, about Kent (already in Edward I.'s time it was said that no one could be born a villein in Kent[1]), about Norfolk and Suffolk, about the Northumbrian shires. Still, when all is said, there remain the Hundred Rolls for the counties of Bedford, Buckingham, Cambridge, Huntingdon and Oxford, and no one can read them without coming to the conclusion that the greater half of the rural population is unfree. The jurors of various hundreds may tell us this in different ways; but very commonly by some name such as *nativi* or *servi*, by some phrase about 'ransom of flesh and blood' or the like, they show their belief that taken in the lump those peasants, who are not freeholders and are not royal sokemen, are not free men.

Occasionally a man who was born a villein might find a grand career open to him. It was said that John's trusty captain Gerard de Athée, whose name is handed down to infamy by Magna Carta, was of servile birth[2]; in 1313 the bishop of Durham manumitted a scholar of Merton who was already a 'master'[3]; in 1308 Simon of Paris, mercer and alderman, who had been sheriff of London, was arrested as a fugitive villein, after being required to serve as reeve of his native manor[4].

Rise of
villeins.

---

[1] Kentish Custumal (Statutes, i. 222); Y. B. 30–1 Edw. I. p. 168. But see Note Book, pl. 1419.

[2] Maitland, Pleas of the Crown for Gloucestershire, p. xiii.

[3] Depositions and Ecclesiastical Proceedings from the Court of Durham (Surtees Soc.), p. 6.

[4] Y. B. 1 Edw. II. f. 4; Liber de Antiquis Legibus, p. 249.

[p. 416]

§ 4. *The Religious.*

Another large part of medieval society is made up of men Civil death. and women who have 'entered religion and become professed,' of monks, nuns, 'regular' canons and friars who have taken vows of poverty and obedience and quitted this world. Now a transition from the villein to the monk seems harsh. Bracton however makes it:—the villein being under the power of his lord may, like the monk, be considered as 'civilly dead[1].' From the lawyer's point of view the analogy that is thus suggested will not seem altogether fanciful and profitless. It is not as a specially holy person but as a property-less and a specially obedient person that law knows the monk. He has no will of his own (*non habet velle, neque nolle*[2]) because he is subject to the will of another, and, though as a matter of religion that will may be thought of as the divine will expressed in the rule of St Benet or St Bernard, still within the sphere of temporal law it is represented by the will of the abbot. It could not be suffered that by a mere declaration of his intention to live a holy life untroubled by mundane affairs a man should shuffle off not only the rights but the duties that the law has cast upon him; but a vow of obedience is a different matter; it is not very unlike a submission to slavery.

The fiction of 'civil death' seems called in to explain and Growth of the idea of civil death. define rules of law which have been gradually growing up[3]. By the dooms of Æthelred and of Cnut the cloister-monk is forbidden to pay or to receive the feud money, that is to say, the money payable by the kindred of a man-slayer to the kindred of the slain, 'for he leaves behind his kin-law when he submits to rule-law'; he ceases to be a member of a natural family when he puts himself under the monastic rule and enters a spiritual family[4]. Already Alfred had decreed that if I entrust goods to 'another man's monk' without the leave of

---

[1] Bracton, f. 421 b: 'Est etiam mors civilis in servo in servitute sub potestate domini constituto.'

[2] See *e.g.* Lyndwood, p. 163.

[3] For the parallel and closely similar French law, see Viollet, Histoire du droit civil, p. 283.

[4] Æthelr. viii. 25; Cnut, i. 5, § 2: 'He gǽð of his mǽg-lage, þonne he gebýhð tú regol-lage.'

that monk's 'lord' and the goods are lost, I must go without remedy[1]. At a later time we find the same principle applied [p. 417] if the monk to whom I have entrusted the goods denies the receipt of them, and the monk is here classed along with the slave, the wife, the infant child. These passages presuppose that we can not sue the monk without his prelate, his 'lord,' and they declare that the monk can not make his prelate liable for the safety, or the return, or the price of goods, unless he has been expressly authorized to do so[2]. But it is very doubtful whether in the days before the Conquest or even for some years afterwards the principle that is hinted at by the term 'civil death' was rigorously enforced. The older and laxer forms of monasticism could not be overcome by one blow. In Æthelred's day the cloisterless monk who recked not of the rule but was trying to make the best of both worlds was well known[3]. We find too in Domesday Book that a monk will sometimes hold land of his house, or of his abbot, and the state seems to regard him as being the responsible tenant of that land[4].

Meaning of civil death.

But stricter notions began to prevail and to find expression in the term 'civil death.' In one large department of law the fiction is elegantly maintained. A monk or nun can not acquire or have any proprietary rights. When a man becomes 'professed in religion,' his heir at once inherits from him any land that he has[5], and, if he has made a will, it takes effect at once as though he were naturally dead. If after this a kinsman of his dies leaving land which according to the ordinary rules of inheritance would descend to him, he is overlooked as though he were no longer in the land of the living; the inheritance misses him and passes to some more distant relative. The rule is not that what descends to him belongs to the house of which

[1] Alf. 20.

[2] Cnut, i. 5, § 2, Cod. Colbert; Leg. Henr. 23, § 3, 45, § 2, 3. On the other hand, the abbot has to answer for the acts of the obedientiaries of his house, *i.e.* of the sacrist, cellarer, almoner, vestiary and the like. They have a general power of binding him.

[3] Æthelr. v. 5; vi. 3.

[4] *e.g.* D. B. i. 90: 'Praeter hanc terram habet Abbas [Glastingberiensis] xx. carucatas quae numquam geldaverunt..... De terra quae non geldat tenet Alnodus monachus i. hidam liberaliter de Abbate concessu Regis.' But *Monachus* may be a layman's surname. So late as 1175 it is necessary to prohibit monks from taking land as *firmarii;* Johnson, Canons, ii. 62.

[5] This appears already in Glanvill, xiii. 5, 6.

[p. 418] he is an inmate; nothing descends to him for he is already dead[1]. In the eye of ecclesiastical law the monk who became a *proprietarius*, the monk, that is, who arrogated to himself any proprietary rights or the separate enjoyment of any wealth, committed about as bad an offence as he could commit[2].

A fiction, however, which would regard a living man as dead must find that limits are set to it by this material world. A monk does wrong or suffers wrong; we can not treat the case as though wrong had been done to a corpse or by a ghost. A monk of Ramsey assaults and beats a monk of Thorney; the law is not content that the injury should go unredressed. As regards those grave crimes which are known as felonies, the monk is dealt with as though he were an ordained clerk; he enjoys that 'benefit of clergy' of which we must speak hereafter. For smaller offences, the 'misdemeanours' of later law, monks, like secular clerks, could be tried by the temporal courts and imprisoned[3]. As to torts or civil wrongs, the rule was that the monk could neither sue nor be sued without his 'sovereign.' The man assaulted by a monk would bring his action against that monk and that monk's abbot, while, if a monk were assaulted, his abbot and he could bring the action[4]. The abbot seems to have been entitled to receive any compensation that became due for damage done to the monk, and to have been compelled to make amends for damage that the monk did. Our law did not say that a monk could not sue or be sued, it said that he could not sue or be sued without his sovereign. Nor did it say that a wrong done to a monk was the same as a wrong done to his abbot, or that a wrong done by a monk was the same as a wrong done by his abbot. It is not all one whether a monk of Ramsey has beaten a monk of Thorney, or the abbot of Ramsey has beaten the abbot of [p. 419] Thorney. The maxim *Actio personalis moritur cum persona*

Difficulties arising from civil death.

---

[1] Select Civil Pleas (Seld. Soc.), i. pl. 208 ; Note Book, pl. 455, 1057, 1139, 1586, 1594.

[2] See cc. 2, 4, 6, X. 3, 35. For proceedings against a *proprietarius*, see Lit. Cantuarienses, iii. 176–7.

[3] Edward I. kept ten of the Westminster monks in prison on the ground that they, if not cognizant of a robbery of the king's treasury, were guilty of negligence which made the robbery possible. Rishanger, 222, 225, 420; Flores Historiarum, 116 ; Pike, History of Crime, i. 198.

[4] See the writs in Reg. Brev. Orig. 107 b.

seems to have been applied as though the two monks were truly *personae*. The action died with the offending monk and with the offended. Often enough the analogy afforded by the law of husband and wife is brought into the debate. A blow given by John's wife to Peter's wife is not the same as a blow given by John to Peter; yet John may have to pay money because his wife is a striker and Peter may receive money because his wife has been stricken. If we may judge from the Year Books, a long time elapsed before accurate rules about this matter were evolved, and perhaps some questions were still open when the day came for the suppression of the monasteries. But the main principle that guides our lawyers in this region is, not that the monk is dead, but that, though he can do wrong and suffer wrong, he has not and can not have any property. Problems which in themselves were difficult were made yet more difficult by the slow growth of the idea that the head of the monastery, though he is a natural person, is also in a certain sense an immortal, non-natural person, or 'corporation sole,' and is likewise the head of a 'corporation aggregate[1].'

The monk as agent.

A monk could make no contract; but he was fully capable of acting as the agent of his sovereign, and even in litigation he would often appear as the abbot's attorney. A monk might be another man's executor, for the execution of testaments is a spiritual matter[2]. It would be a mistake to suppose that monks never took part in worldly affairs. The obedientiaries of a great abbey must often have been keen men of business, largely engaged in buying and selling, and the manorial courts of the abbey were frequently held by the cellarer or some other person who was civilly dead. Whatever the ecclesiastical law may do, the temporal law does not attempt to keep the monks out of courts and fairs and markets; it merely says that a monk has not and can not have any property of his own.

---

[1] Interesting discussions will be found in Y. B. 49 Edw. III. f. 25 (Mich. pl. 5); 20 Hen. VI. f. 21 (Hil. pl. 19).

[2] Y. B. 3 Hen. VI. f. 23 (Hil. pl. 2). In his character of executor he might even have an action of debt against his prelate. Hence a riddle:—When can a man sue his own executor? When owing money to a monastery, he becomes professed in it and afterwards abbot of it. But ecclesiastical law forbad the monk to become an executor without the leave of his abbot and (in England) the ordinary. See Lyndwood, p. 168.

[p. 420]   The manner in which the monks were treated by the Abbatial
monarchy. ecclesiastical law we shall not discuss; but the temporal law seems to have assumed that every monk was the absolute subject of some 'sovereign'—normally an abbot, but in some cases a prior or a bishop[1]. Whatever degree of 'constitutional government,' of government in accordance with 'the rule' or the statutes of the order, of government by an assembly, by a chapter, might prevail within the house, was no affair of the secular power. It treated the sovereign as an absolute monarch and would hardly be persuaded to step between him and his subjects. Against him they could urge no complaint. We may indeed suppose that he might have been indicted for slaying or maiming them; but even in this case he would have enjoyed the benefit of clergy and been sent for trial to an ecclesiastical court. So long as he did not deprive them of life or limb he committed no crime of which the lay tribunals would take any account, and undoubtedly the penances that were inflicted were sometimes extremely rigorous[2]. According to the common law of the church the monks might appeal from their abbot to the bishop of the diocese, but some of the great houses were exempt from the bishop's control and then there was no help to be had save from Rome. Occasionally the monks would unite to resist their abbot, and fierce and protracted litigation before the Roman curia would be the result[3]. But the individual monk was helpless; if he escaped from his cloister, the temporal power would come to the aid of the church and deliver up this 'apostate' to his ecclesiastical superiors[4].

Late in the day we hear discussions as to the possibility of Return to
civil life. the dead coming to life. In the fifteenth century lawyers said

---

[1] In our law French the term *sovereign* is technically used in this context: see *e.g.* Britton, i. 159.

[2] See the long statement as to the cruelties practised among the Dominican friars; Flores Historiarum, iii. 161.

[3] The great quarrel between the monks of Canterbury and the two archbishops Baldwin and Hubert, of which a long account is given by Dr Stubbs in the Introduction to the Epistolae Cantuarienses, is a classical example. But here the question, if regarded from the point of view of English temporal law, was this—Whether the archbishop was or was not the 'sovereign' of the cathedral monastery.

[4] See the writ *De apostata capiendo*, Reg. Brev. Orig. 71 b. A good story of an escape is told in Literae Cantuarienses, ii. p. xxxviii.

that, though the 'sovereign' might release the monk from his [p. 421]
obedience, none but the pope could restore him to the world of
civil rights[1].   Rules about such a point had not been very
necessary, for dispensations from monastic vows had been uncommon.   Of course in a manner the monk came back to legal
life if he became the sovereign of a religious house, still more
if, as well he might, he became a bishop; but it may be much
doubted whether the lawyers of the thirteenth century would
have seen in this the new birth of a natural person.   They had
not drawn any clear line between 'natural' and 'juristic' persons,
and the monk who was elected to an abbacy became thereby
persona ecclesiae, the human representative of a personified
institution.   Only by virtue of papal bull and royal charter
could an abbot make a valid will, for 'by the common law an
abbot can not have property or executors[2].'   We are not sure
that an abbot could have inherited from a kinsman.   The dual
personality of a bishop seems to have been more readily admitted, still, as we shall remark below, there had been much
controversy as to whether a bishop had anything to leave by
his will.   It is not easily that lawyers come to think of one
man as two persons, or to talk of 'official capacities' and
'corporations sole.'

Civil death
as a de-
velopment
of the
abbot's
mund.

We can not take leave of the monks without noticing that
in medieval law monasticism is no such isolated phenomenon
as it would be in modern law.   Of course the relationship that
exists between abbot and monk is not just that which exists
between lord and villein, still less is it that which we see
between husband and wife.   But to compare these three
relationships together is not the mere fetch of an advocate at
a loss for arguments nor the fancy of a too subtle jurist.   As
a matter of history they well may have a common element.
They all may be off-shoots of one radical idea, that of the
Germanic *mund*, a word which we feebly render by *guardianship* or *protection*.   Certain it is that our common law of
husband and wife curiously reproduces some features of the law
of abbot and monk, and we might understand the legal history
of villeinage and the legal history of monasticism the better if
we brought them into connexion with each other.

---

[1] Y. B. 3 Hen. VI. f. 23 (Hil. pl. 2).
[2] Y. B. 32–3 Edw. I. 356.

[p. 422] ## § 5.　*The Clergy.*

Collectively the clergy are an estate of the realm. With this constitutional doctrine we are not here concerned, nor are we called upon to describe the organization of the clerical body; but, taken individually, every ordained clerk has a peculiar legal status; he is subject to special rules of ecclesiastical law and to special rules of temporal law. We can not say that the clerk is subject only to ecclesiastical, while the layman is subject only to temporal law. Neither half of such a dogma would have been accepted by state or church. Every layman, unless he were a Jew, was subject to ecclesiastical law. It regulated many affairs of his life, marriages, divorces, testaments, intestate succession; it would try him and punish him for various offences, for adultery, fornication, defamation; it would constrain him to pay tithes and other similar dues; in the last resort it could excommunicate him and then the state would come to its aid. Even the Jews, though of course they were not members of the church, were (at least so the clergy contended) within the sphere of ecclesiastical legislation and subject to some of the processes of the spiritual courts[1]. In general terms we can say no more than that the ordained clerk was within many rules of ecclesiastical law which did not affect the layman, and that it had a tighter hold over him, since it could suspend him from office, deprive him of benefice and degrade him from his orders. So, on the other hand, the clerk was subject to temporal law. It had some special rules for him, but they were not many.

Legal position of the ordained clerk.

At the end of Henry III.'s reign, with one great and a few petty exceptions, the clerk was protected by and subject to the same rules of temporal law which guarded and governed the layman. If a clerk was slain, wounded, robbed or assaulted, the wrong-doer would be punished by the temporal law just as though the injured person had been of the laity. The clerk could own chattels, he could hold land by any tenure, he could [p. 423] make contracts; the temporal law protected his possession and

The clerk under temporal law.

---

[1] Langton's Constitutions, 1222, c. 51, 52 (adopting canons of the Fourth Lateran Council) in Johnson, Canons, ii. 120; Gravamina of 1257, Mat. Par. Chron. Maj. vi. 360–1; Boniface's Constitutions, 1261, c. 7, Johnson, Canons, ii. 197.

his proprietary rights, it enforced his contracts, without taking any note of his peculiar status. Even when he had to assert possessory or proprietary rights which belonged to him as the *rector* or *persona* of a church, he had to do this in the lay courts, usually by the very same actions that were competent to laymen, but sometimes by an action specially adapted to the needs of parsons[1]. We count it no real exception that a clerk who had attained to the subdiaconate could not marry, for the validity of any marriage was a matter for ecclesiastical law; and on the other hand, though the canons forbad the clergy to engage in trade, we are not aware that the lay courts attempted to enforce this rule by holding that their trading contracts were void. Then the clerk was subject to the temporal law. All the ordinary civil actions could be brought against him; he could be sued on a contract, he could be sued for a tort, he could be sued as a disseisor, he could be sued as one who held what did not belong to him, and this although he was holding it in the name of his church. Moreover, for any crime that fell short of felony he could be tried and punished in the common way.

Exceptional rules applied to the clerk. There are a few small exceptions. As a general rule the ecclesiastical courts may not take cognizance of an act of violence. If a layman is assaulted, they will be prohibited from inflicting punishment or penance upon the offender. But violence done to the person of a clerk is within their competence. As already said it is also within the competence of the temporal tribunals. He who has assaulted a clerk may be fined or imprisoned for his breach of the king's peace; he may be compelled to pay damages for the wrong that he has done; he may be put to penance for his sin[2]; indeed he is already excommunicate *lata sententia*, and, except at the hour of death, can only be absolved by the pope or one who wields papal authority[3]. In such a case the clergy do not care to urge their favourite maxim that no one is to be punished twice for the same offence. But this is a small matter. In civil causes a clerk enjoys a certain freedom from arrest[4], but this as yet is of

---

[1] See above, p. 247.

[2] Bracton's Note Book, pl. 444, 766; Circumspecte Agatis; Articuli Cleri (1315); Statutes of the Realm, i. 101, 171; Blackstone, Com. iv. 217.

[3] c. 29, C. 17, qu. 4; see Lyndwood, p. 329 *ad fin.*

[4] Bracton, f. 442 b, 443 b.

no great importance. On the other hand, the lay courts have invented a special machinery for compelling the appearance of clerks who are sued in personal actions. They direct the bishop of the diocese to produce such clerks, and will proceed against his barony if he is negligent in this matter. For this purpose the clergy are treated as forming part of his *familia*—as being within his *mund*, we might say,—and the episcopal barony is a material pledge for their appearance[1]. But this again is a small matter, and is far from being a privilege of the clergy; indeed they vigorously, but vainly, protest against this treatment[2].

[p. 424]

It remains for us to speak of the one great exception, namely, that which is to be known for centuries as the 'benefit of clergy[3]'. It comes to this, that an ordained clerk, who commits any of those grave crimes that are known as felonies, can be tried only in an ecclesiastical court, and can be punished only by such punishment as that court can inflict. But we must descend to particulars, for generalities may be misleading. A clerk is charged with a murder; it is the sheriff's duty to arrest him. Probably his bishop will demand him. If so, he will be delivered up; but the bishop will become bound in a heavy sum, a hundred pounds, to produce him before the justices in eyre. The bishop can keep him in prison and very possibly will do so, for, should he escape, the hundred pounds will be forfeited. In the middle of the thirteenth century it is matter of complaint among the clergy that owing to this procedure clerks may languish for five or six years in the episcopal gaol without being brought to trial[4]. At last the justices come, and this clerk is brought before them, or some other clerk, who has not yet been arrested, is indicted or appealed before them. In the end it comes about by one means or another that they have before them a clerk indicted or appealed of felony. And now we may follow the words of the enrolment that will be made :—'And the said *A. B.* comes and says that he is a clerk

Benefit of clergy.

---

[1] Bracton, f. 443 ; Note Book, pl. 143, 276, 407, 576, 802.

[2] Gravamina of 1257, Mat. Par. Chron. Maj. vi. 354–5.

[3] Hale's treatment of this matter in his Pleas of the Crown is full and good, but he says little of times so remote as those with which we are dealing. See Makower, Const. Hist., 399 ff.

[4] Grosseteste's protest, Ann. Burton, 424 ; Mat. Par. Chron. Maj. vi. 355–6; Ann. Burton, 417 ; Johnson, Canons, ii. 193 ; Court Baron (Selden Society), 19; Select Pleas of the Crown, pl. 160.

'and that he can not—*or*, that he will not—answer here. And
'the official of the bishop of X comes and demands him as a
'clerk—*or*, comes and craves the bishop's court.' In Bracton's
day the clerk will thereupon be delivered to the bishop or his [p. 425]
officer and no inquest will be made by the justices touching
guilt or innocence[1]. But before the end of Henry III.'s reign
the procedure will not be so simple[2]. The roll of the court
will go on to say—'Therefore let him be delivered; but in
'order that it may be known in what character (*qualis*) he is to
'be delivered [*or*, in order that the king's peace may be pre-
'served,] let the truth of the matter be inquired of the country.
'And the twelve jurors and the four neighbouring townships
'say upon their oath, that he is guilty, [*or*, not guilty] and
'therefore as such let him be delivered.' In other words the
justices proceed to take 'an inquest *ex officio*.' This is not a
trial; the clerk has not submitted to it; he has not pleaded;
but a verdict is taken. If this is favourable to the accused, he
is acquitted, at least in so far as a secular court can acquit him;
but if the jurors are against him, then he is delivered to the
bishop[3]. In the one case his lands and goods, if they have
been seized by the royal officers, are at once restored to him,
unless he has been guilty of flight and has thus forfeited his
chattels[4]; in the other case they will be retained until he has
been tried, and their fate will depend on the result of his trial[5].

---

[1] Bracton, f. 123 b. Early examples will be found in Select Pleas of the
Crown, *e.g.* pl. 49 (a subdeacon), 117 (a subdeacon), 123, 140, 160, 189 (an
acolyte), 197 and Note Book, *e.g.* pl. 548 (a prior).

[2] Coke, 2nd Inst. 164, rightly observes that the change takes place between
Bracton (f. 123 b) and Britton (vol. i. p. 27). He attributes it to Stat. West. I.
(1275) cap. 2. But as a matter of fact the eyre rolls of the last years of
Henry III. show that the change has already taken place. See, for example, the
roll of a Cambridgeshire eyre of 45 Hen. III. (Assize Rolls, No. 82) *passim*. We
know from Matthew Paris, Chron. Maj. iv. 614, that in 1247 some new rule was
made about criminous clerks and that the clergy disliked it, but we have not
got the text of this decree. Despite the commentaries of Coke and Hale, we may
doubt whether the Statute of Westminster made any definite change in the law.
The new king sanctions the clerical privilege, but tells the prelates that they
must be careful in the matter of purgation, and that otherwise he will be
obliged to make some change. Thereupon in 1279 Abp. Peckham made some
effort to improve the procedure in the spiritual court; Johnson, Canons, ii. 267.

[3] This account is based chiefly on the Assize Roll just mentioned. Sometimes if the verdict is favourable the judgment is *Ideo quietus*.

[4] Y. B. 33–5 Edw. I. p. 57.

[5] Hale, P. C. ii. 383. The clergy protested against the forfeiture, saying that

For tried he has not yet been. He will be tried in the bishop's court.

[p. 426] Of what went on in the bishop's court we unfortunately know very little; but we have reason to believe that before the end of the century its procedure in these cases was already becoming little better than a farce. In criminal cases the canon law had adopted the world-old process of compurgation, and here in England the ecclesiastical courts had never reformed away this ancient mode of proof. The blame for this should not fall wholly upon the prelates. Very possibly the lay courts would have prevented them from introducing in criminal cases any newer or more rational form of trial. Had any newer form been introduced, it would have been that 'inquisitorial' procedure which historians trace to the decretals of Innocent III.[1] In the twelfth century we find an archdeacon who is accused of poisoning his archbishop directed to purge himself with three archdeacons and four deacons[2]. Lucius III. told the bishop of Winchester that he was too severe in investigating the character of compurgators[3]. Bishop Jocelin of Salisbury cleared himself of complicity in the murder of Becket with four or five oath-helpers[4]. Hubert Walter, sitting as archbishop, forbad that more compurgators than the canonical twelve should be demanded[5]. Shortly before this we find the bishop of Ely offering to prove with a hundred swearers that he took no part in the arrest of the archbishop of York[6]. No doubt in theory the ecclesiastical judge was not in all cases strictly bound to send the clerk to 'his purgation.' If there was what was technically known as an *accusatio*, a definite written charge preferred by the person who was injured, the judge might hold that the accusation was fully proved by the accuser's witnesses and might convict the accused[7]. But the proof required of an accuser by the canon law was rigorous[8], and, from all we can

Trial in the courts of the church.

---

it was a second punishment for a single offence; Gravamina of 1257, Mat. Par. vi. 356.

[1] Fournier, Les officialités au moyen âge, 262–281. No doubt this procedure was used in the case of minor offences; but we are speaking of felonies.

[2] Letters of John of Salisbury, No. 122, ed. Giles, i. 170.

[3] c. 9, X. 5, 34. The whole of tit. 34 bears on this matter.

[4] Sarum Charters, 35.　　　　[5] Johnson, Canons, ii. 81, 91.

[6] Hoveden, iii. 250.　　　　[7] Fournier, *op. cit.* 235–256.

[8] Thus in the case of the archdeacon accused of poisoning the archbishop, the accuser could not make good the charge 'secundum subtilitatem legum et canonum'; see John of Salisbury's letter cited above.

hear, the common practice in England seems to have been to allow the clerk to purge himself. Archbishop Peckham at the instance of Edward I. vaguely ordered that this should not be done too readily[1]; in the middle of the fourteenth century [p. 427] Archbishop Islip made a not very earnest effort for the same end[2]; but the whole procedure was falling into contempt. Already in certain bad cases the lay courts were forbidding the bishops to admit the accused clerks to their purgation[3], that is, according to the old theory, were forbidding that these accused clerks should be tried at all. So early as 1238 we find the bishop of Exeter in trouble for having sent to purgation a subdeacon who had been outlawed on a charge of murder, and, though the clerk has purged himself, he is compelled to abjure the realm[4]. In Edward I.'s day the king's justices could treat a canonical purgation with the scorn that it deserved[5].

Punishment for felonious clerks. If he failed in his purgation the clerk was convicted and punished. At least in theory there were many punishments at the bishop's disposal. The chief limit to his power was set by the elementary rule that the church would never pronounce a judgment of blood. He could degrade the clerk from his orders, and, as an additional punishment, relegate him to a monastery or keep him in prison for life. A whipping might be inflicted[6], and Becket, it seems, had recourse even to the branding iron[7]. One of the minor questions in the quarrel between Thomas and Henry was whether an ecclesiastical court could exile a convicted clerk or compel him to abjure the realm[8]. Innocent III. told the bishop of London that clerks convicted of larceny or other great crimes were to be first degraded and then closely imprisoned in monasteries[9]. In 1222 a church council under Stephen Langton seems to have condemned two of the laity to that close imprisonment which was known as immuration; the

---

[1] Johnson, Canons, ii. 267; Stat. West. I. c. 2.

[2] Constitution of 1351, Johnson, Canons, ii. 413.

[3] *Berton's case*, Ryley, Plac. Parl. 56; Rolls of Parliament, i. 40; Hale, P. C. ii. 328.

[4] Rot. Cl. 22 Hen. III. m. 17 d; compare Bracton, f. 134 b.

[5] Rolls of Parl. i. 146. It is adjudged that two persons have committed adultery, though they have purged themselves in court Christian. The lady's compurgators were women.

[6] Herbert of Bosham, Materials for History of Becket, iii. 265.

[7] Fitz Stephen, Materials, iii. 45–6.

[8] Herbert of Bosham, Materials, iii. 267, 270.

[9] c. 6, X. 5, 37.

culprits had been guilty of fanatical blasphemy[1]. In 1261 the constitutions of Archbishop Boniface required that every bishop should keep a proper prison, and declared that every clerk convicted of a capital crime should be kept in gaol for the rest of his life[2]. This then was the punishment due to felonious clerks; we fear that but few of them suffered it.

[p. 428]

The privilege was not confined to clerks in orders, for it was shared with them by the monks, and there seems no reason for doubting that nuns were entitled to the same privilege, though, to their credit be it said, we have in our period found no cases which prove this[3]. On the other hand, it had not as yet become the privilege of every one who could read or pretend to read a verse in the bible. The justices insist that ordination must be proved by the bishop's letters. It is still regarded rather as the privilege of the church than of the accused clerk; if his bishop does not claim him he will be kept in prison, perhaps he will be compelled, as a layman would be compelled, to stand his trial[4]. We are not able, however, to indulge the hope that the bishop allowed the criminal law to take its course unless he had some reason for believing that the clerk was innocent[5]. The plea rolls seem to prove that his official sits day after day in the court of the justices in eyre and as mere matter of course 'demands' every clerk who is accused; and in every eyre many clerks will be accused of the worst crimes and their neighbours will swear that they are guilty. By marrying a second time, or by marrying a widow, the clerk, who thus became *bigamus*, forfeited his immunities:—this rule, promulgated by the council of Lyons under Gregory X., was at once received in England and a retrospective force was attributed to it by a statute of Edward I.[6]

What persons were entitled to the privilege.

---

[1] Maitland, The Deacon and the Jewess, L. Q. R., ii. 153, 165.

[2] Johnson, Canons, ii. 207–8.

[3] Hale, P. C. ii. 328, says, 'Nuns had the exemption from temporal jurisdiction, but the privilege of clergy was never allowed them by our law.' But elsewhere, P. C. ii. 371, 'Anciently nuns professed were admitted to the privilege of clergy.' He cites a case from 1348, Fitz. Abr. *Corone*, pl. 461, which speaks of a woman—she is not expressly called a nun—being claimed by and delivered to the ordinary.

[4] Select Pleas of the Crown, pl. 185. At a later date the judges would allow 'his clergy' to a man who could read, though the ordinary did not claim him; Hale, P. C. ii. 373.

[5] This hope is expressed by Dr Stubbs, Const. Hist. § 722.

[6] c. un. in vi°. 1. 12; Statute 4 Edw. I. *De Bigamis*. For an early case of

[p. 429]

What
offences
were
within the
privilege.

It is probable that already in the thirteenth century a clerk charged with high treason, at all events with one of the worst forms of high treason, such as imagining the king's death or levying war against him, would in vain have relied on the liberties of the church[1]. There seems even to have been some doubt as to whether counterfeiting the king's seal was not a crime so high as to exceed the limits of the clerical immunity[2]. At the other end of the scale the clerk charged with a mere *transgressio*, a misdemeanour we may say, enjoyed no exceptional privilege but could be fined or imprisoned like another man. Henry II. within a very few years after Becket's death and while the whole of Christendom was ringing with the fame of the new martyr, was able to insist with the assent of a papal legate that forest offences were not within the benefit of clergy[3], and before the end of the next century the lay courts were habitually punishing the clergy for their *transgressiones*. However, it should be understood that the full extent of the clerical claim had been and was that, not merely every criminal charge, but every personal action, against a clerk was a matter which lay outside the competence of the temporal tribunal. This claim died hard; it was asserted near the end of Henry III.'s reign by a constitution of Archbishop Boniface; Bracton had to treat it with respect, though he rejected it. His doctrine even as to the felonies of clerks is a curious and we may say a very unclerical one. The king's court does not try the accused clerk; but there is no sound principle which prevents its doing so. Still the appropriate punishment for the felonious clerk is degradation, and this the lay tribunal cannot inflict. The logical result of this would be that the king's court should try the clerk and, should he be convicted, hand him over to the ordinary, not for trial, but for punishment. However at present this is not the practice[4]. Probably it is in consequence of such reasoning as this that a few years later the king's justices will not deliver up a clerk until they have first

'bigamy' see Y. B. 30–1 Edw. I. p. 530. Fleta, p. 51, speaks as though the rule which excluded *bigami* from privilege had been revoked by the Council of Lyons. There must be some mistake here.

[1] Hale, P. C. ii. 330.

[2] *Berton's case*, Ryley, Plac. Parl. 56; Rolls of Parl. i. 40; Hale, P. C. ii. 331–2; Bracton, f. 413 b, allows the privilege in this case.

[3] Diceto, i. 410.

[4] Bracton, f. 401, 401 b, 407, 411.

taken an 'inquest of office' as to his guilt. Thereby they do
their best to lessen the harm that is done by an invidious and
[p. 430] mischievous immunity. The criminal will purge himself in the
court Christian, but a jury of his neighbours will have sworn
that he is guilty. Further we must remember that all along
the justices insist that, though the clerk is not tried by a
secular tribunal, none the less he can be and ought to be
accused before it, and that he can be outlawed if he does not
appear when he has been accused. In this way the criminal
law has some hold over the clerk, though for centuries yet to
come the benefit of clergy will breed crime and impede the
course of reasonable and impartial justice[1].

Here we might prudently leave 'the benefit of clergy,' for *The Constitutions
of Cla-
rendon.*
to speak of its earlier history is to meddle with the quarrel
between Henry II. and Becket. Protesting however that it is
not our part to criticize men or motives or policies, we are none
the less bound to state, and if possible to answer, certain purely
legal questions. These are in the main three :—(1) What was
the scheme for the treatment of criminous clerks that Henry
proposed in the most famous of the Constitutions of Clarendon ?
(2) What was the relation of that scheme to the practice of his
ancestors ? (3) What was its relation to the law of the catholic
church as understood in the year 1164 ?

(1) To the first question our answer will be brief[2]. We
must admit that historians have read the celebrated clause[3] in

---

[1] As regards the *transgressiones* (trespass and misdemeanour are but slowly
differentiated from each other) of clerks, the history of this matter may be
traced thus :—In 1176 Henry II. concedes that no clerk shall be drawn into the
lay court in any criminal cause or for any offence, except offences against
forest law ; Diceto, i. 410. Bracton, f. 401 b, says that every day clerks are
sued in the lay courts both on contracts and for trespasses. In 1237 the
clergy claim exemption in all personal actions ; Ann. Burton. 254. In 1257
they repeat the protest ; Mat. Par. vi. 357. In 1258 Grosseteste repeats it, and
about this time Robert de Marisco asserts it in large terms ; Ann. Burt. 424,
426. In 1261 it is asserted by the Constitutions of Abp. Boniface ; Johnson,
Canons, ii. 185. It covers contract and quasi-contract, delict and quasi-delict.
In 1263 the Pope, who has reasons for not quarrelling with Henry III., will not
confirm the constitutions, but implores the king to give way ; Bull of Urban IV.
Foedera i. 424. The conflict is now nearly over ; but even in 1279 a clerk is
still, though vainly, protesting that an action for assault and wounding can not
be brought against him in the king's court ; Hale, P. C. ii. 325. Maitland,
Canon Law in England, E. H. R. xi. 647 ; Makower, Const. Hist. 407 ff.

[2] Maitland, Henry II. and the Criminous Clerks, E. H. R. vii. 224.

[3] Const. Clar. c. 3 : 'Clerici rettati et accusati de quacunque re, summoniti

various ways; but for our own part we cannot doubt that it [p. 431]

Henry II.'s scheme. means this:—A clerk who is suspected of a crime is to be
brought before the temporal court and accused there; unless he
will admit the truth of the charge, he must in formal terms
plead his innocence; this done, he will be sent to the ecclesiastical court for trial; if found guilty he is to be deposed from
his orders and brought back to the temporal court; royal
officers will have been present at his trial and will see that he
does not make his escape; when they have brought him back
to the temporal court, he will then—perhaps without any
further trial, but this is not clear—be sentenced to the layman's punishment, to death or mutilation. Henry does not
claim a right to try or to pronounce judgment upon the
criminous clerk; on the contrary, he admits that the trial must
take place in the ecclesiastical court; but he does insist upon
three principles: (i) that the accusation must be made in the
lay court, which will thus obtain seisin of the cause and be
enabled to watch its further progress; (ii) that royal officers are
to be present at the trial; (iii) that the clerk—or rather the
layman, for such he will really be—who has been deposed
from his orders for a crime, can be punished for that crime by
the temporal power[1].

To this scheme Becket objected in the name of the church's
law, and it is certain that he objected, not merely to the first
two of these three rules, but also to the third, and this on the
ground that it would punish a man twice over for one offence
and thus infringe the maxim, *Nec enim Deus iudicat bis in
idipsum*[2].

---

a iustitia regis venient in curiam ipsius, responsuri ibidem de hoc unde
videbitur curiae regis quod ibidem sit respondendum, et in curia ecclesiastica
unde videbitur quod ibidem sit respondendum; ita quod iustitia regis mittet in
curiam sanctae ecclesiae ad videndum qua ratione res ibi tractabitur; et si
clericus convictus vel confessus fuerit, non debet de cetero eum ecclesia tueri.'

[1] The constitution was thus understood by Reuter, Geschichte Alexanders
des dritten, i. 372-3; Hefele, Conciliengeschichte, (ed. 2) v. 625; Makower,
Const. Hist. 402. Dr Stubbs, Const. Hist. i. 501, says that Henry proposed
that ' clerical criminals should be tried in the ordinary courts of the country.'
Henry may at one time have gone as far as this; but we can not believe that
this is the scheme defined by the constitutions.

[2] Materials for the History of Becket, ii. 28, iii. 281; iv. 39, 96, 202. No
point in the controversy seems better attested by Becket's own friends and
biographers than that he insisted on this argument. This seems fatal to that
interpretation of the constitutions which would make Henry propose that

[p. 432]   (2) We turn to our second question. Did this scheme Henry's scheme and past history. fairly represent the practice of Henry I.'s day? We note that it does not profess to represent the practice of Stephen's day. For legal purposes Stephen's reign is to be ignored, not because he was an usurper, but because it was a time of war and of 'unlaw.' Sixty years later this doctrine still prevails; a litigant can not rely on what happened in Stephen's reign, for it was not a time of peace[1]. Still, though the son of the Empress is but applying a general doctrine to a particular case, his pregnant assertion that the constitutions express his grandfather's customs seems an admission that those customs had in some particulars gone out of use under his immediate predecessor.

So sparse is the evidence directly bearing on this question *Henry's allegations not contested.* that we gladly catch at any admission made by either of the parties to the quarrel, and we may not unfairly urge that in this case judgment should go by default. Henry did assert repeatedly and emphatically with the concurrence of his barons and with the approval of many bishops that he was but restoring the old customs. Becket and his friends, so far as we can see, would not meet this allegation[2]. When one of the martyr's biographers reminds us that Christ said, not 'I am the custom,' but 'I am the truth,' we can not but infer that on the question of fact Henry was substantially in the right. The archbishop and his partizans are fond of speaking of 'the so-called customs,' as 'pravities' and 'abuses;' but they will not meet the king on his own ground[3].

This premised, we look for direct evidence to the reigns of *Earlier law. The Conqueror's ordinance.* the Norman kings. First we read how the Conqueror ordained that no bishop or archdeacon should administer the episcopal

---

criminous clerks shall be treated like criminous laymen. The famous *Nemo bis in idipsum* may be ultimately traced to some words of the prophet Nahum (i. 9) which in our Bibles appear as 'Affliction shall not rise up the second time.' Gratian has much to say of this maxim in D. 3 *de poen.* For the distinction that was gradually drawn between deposition and degradation, see Hinschius, Kirchenrecht, v. 51.

[1] Bracton's Note Book, pl. 251: 'non fuit seisitus in tempore illo nisi tantum in tempore Stephani Regis quod fuit werrinum.'

[2] See Pauli, Geschichte von England, iii. 44; Reuter, Geschichte Alexanders des dritten, i. 369–370.

[3] The strongest denial that the so-called customs were customs, is that which comes from Fitz Stephen, Materials, iii. 47: 'Sed scriptae nunquam prius fuerant, nec omnino fuerant in regno hae consuetudines.'

laws in the hundred court, nor bring to the judgment of secular men any cause relating to the rule of souls. Such causes the bishops are to decide, not according to hundred law, but according to the canons and the episcopal laws. The secular power is to aid the church against those whom she has [p. 433] excommunicated. The conduct of the ordeal as a specially ecclesiastical process is declared to be the bishop's business[1]. This tells us little that is to our point. William assumes that all men know what causes are spiritual, what secular. The only matter on which he speaks definitely is the ordeal, and here the two powers will cooperate harmoniously; the bishop will preside at the ceremony, but doubtless the order that sends a man to the fire or to the water will, at least in very many cases, be the order of the hundred court. Of any immunity of clerks from secular jurisdiction or temporal punishment there is no word.

The Leges Henrici.   The author of the Leges Henrici is already borrowing from foreign canonists and we can not tell how far he is stating customs that actually prevail in England. He says plainly enough that no accusation, be it for grave crime, be it for light offence, is to be brought against any ordained clerk save before his bishop[2]. This certainly is at variance with one part of Henry II.'s claim, for Henry insisted that the first step in a criminal cause should be taken in the king's court; but it does not touch the greater question of double punishment.

Precedents for the trial of clerks.   We turn from general statements to recorded cases. We can find very few. Most of them may be called 'state trials,' and it is not to state trials that we can trust for impartial applications of medieval law; but Domesday Book seems to tell of a clerk who was in peril of death or mutilation, for his body was in the king's mercy[3]. Lanfranc had no difficulty in advising the Conqueror that he might condemn his half-brother Odo to imprisonment and disherison on a charge of rebellion and treason, though Odo pleaded an immunity from secular

---

[1] Schmid, Gesetze, p. 357; Stubbs, Select Charters. There can we think be little doubt that in this ordinance *iudicium* is used in a technical sense for the ordeal, *iudicium Dei.*

[2] Leg. Hen. Prim. 57, § 9: 'De illis, qui ad sacros ordines pertinent, et eis, qui sacris ordinibus promoti sunt, coram praelatis suis est agendum de omnibus inculpationibus, maximis et minoribus.'

[3] D. B. ii. 7: 'Quidam clericus Comitis E[ustachii] .... iudicatus est esse in misericordia regis et de omni cessu suo et de corpore suo.'

justice[1]. The king, so the great lawyer thought, might distinguish between the Earl of Kent and the Bishop of Bayeux though these two persons happened to be one man. But the [p. 434] case is not decisive, for the punishment did not touch life or member, and very probably Lanfranc could have shown to the satisfaction of all canonists that the warlike Odo had forfeited every clerical privilege by his scandalously military life[2]. Of the trial of Bishop William of Durham for a treacherous rebellion against Rufus a long and lively report has come down to us[3]. The bishop repeatedly and in strong, clear terms asserted his exemption from temporal justice:—he should be tried according to the sacred canons in a canonically constituted court. It will not satisfy him that among his judges there are his own metropolitan and the archbishop of Canterbury and many bishops, for they are not clad in their episcopal vestments, they are mixed up with the lay nobles and are sitting under the king's presidency. Lanfranc baffles and defeats him; judgment is pronounced upon him and pronounced by a layman, Hugh of Beaumont. The bishop appealed to Rome, but never prosecuted his appeal. Here the sentence merely was that the bishop's fief was forfeited, and the severest canonist could not deny that a purely feudal cause was within the competence of the king's court, nor perhaps could he have refuted Lanfranc's opinion that if, after the judgment of forfeiture, the bishop would not surrender his fief, he might lawfully be arrested[4]. Still less can be made of King Stephen's proceedings against Bishop Roger of Salisbury, his nephews and his son. The king took advantage of an affray between the men of the bishops and the men of Earl Alan; he impleaded the bishops because their men had broken his peace, and by way of satisfaction demanded a surrender of their castles. This they refused. He then imprisoned them, maltreated them in gaol and went so far as to put a rope round the chancellor's neck; he thus

---

[1] Freeman, Norm. Conq. iv. 684.

[2] Thus in Leg. Hen. 57, § 9: 'Cum clerico qui uxorem habeat et firmam teneat laicorum et rebus extrinsecis seculariter deditus est, seculariter est disceptandum.'

[3] Simeon of Durham, i. 170. Freeman, William Rufus, i. 89, tells the story at length.

[4] The bishop relies less on the mere fact of his being a bishop than on this coupled with the fact that he has been and is dispossessed. 'Spoliatus episcopus ante omnia debet restitui' is the burden of his plea.

obtained the desired fortresses. An ecclesiastical council held by his brother, the legate, cited him; the immunity of clerks was strongly asserted; the king's proceedings were condemned, and it is even said that he did penance for them; also at one [p. 435] time or another he appealed to Rome; but he kept the castles[1]. However, before this Stephen had made a momentous concession: he had sworn that justice and power over ecclesiastical persons and over all clerks and their possessions should belong to the bishops; and by this oath he must, so we think, be taken to have admitted whatever claims of immunity could be fairly made in the name of canon law[2]. Then concerning the treatment of criminous clerks in his reign we have a valuable story, which John of Salisbury, writing in the name of Archbishop Theobald, reported to the Pope. Osbert, an archdeacon, was accused of having poisoned Archbishop William of York. The charge was preferred by a clerk who had been in the service of the dead prelate. It was made in the presence of King Stephen and the bishops and barons of England. The accuser was ready to prove his case by the hot iron or the boiling water, by battle, or by any other proof. Osbert relied on his clerical privilege and refused to be judged by laymen. Pledges were given on both sides for the further prosecution of the suit; they were given to the king, for the king insisted that, because of the atrocity of the crime and because it was in his presence that the accusation had been made, the case was within his jurisdiction. We and our brethren, says Theobald, protested. Now Stephen is dead and we have had the utmost difficulty in getting Osbert out of King Henry's hands. We ordered him to purge himself; but he has appealed to you[3].

Summary.   From such isolated instances as these it would be impossible to extract any definite results for the history of law; but, while they are not inconsistent with Henry's allegation about the customs of his grandfather, they seem to show that the canonical trial, which Henry was willing to grant, had not

---

[1] Will. Malmesb. Gesta Regum, ii. 548–554; Henr. Huntingd. 265; Gesta Stephani, 47; Will. Newb. i. 35; Gervase Cant. i. 104.

[2] Second Charter of Stephen; Statutes of the Realm, Charters p. 3; Will. Malmesb. Gesta Regum, ii. 541: 'Ecclesiasticarum personarum et omnium clericorum et rerum eorum, iustitiam et potestatem, et distributionem bonorum ecclesiasticorum, in manu episcoporum esse perhibeo et confirmo.'

[3] Letters of John of Salisbury (ed. Giles) No. 122. William of Newburgh, i. 80, treats the story of the poisoned chalice as untrue and absurd.

always been granted, even by Stephen[1]. As to the law that
[p. 436] prevailed in England before the Conquest little is known and
little could be profitably said in this context, for the Conqueror's ordinance must be treated as the beginning of a new
era[2]. However, when King Alfred ordains that the man-slaying
priest is to be unhallowed by his bishop and then delivered up
from the church, unless his lord will compound for the wergild,
he is laying down one of the main principles for which Henry
contended[3]. If we would pursue the question behind the
Norman Conquest, it is much rather the law of France than
the law of England that should be studied. At least in this
matter the Conqueror was an innovator, and the terms which
he made with those who were to be the rulers of the English
church were terms made by one who was not an Englishman with
those who were not Englishmen. The early history of clerical
privileges on the continent of Europe is a long and a dark tale
and one that we can not pretend to tell. Henry II.'s scheme
was not unlike that which Justinian had sanctioned[4]. In
Henry's day this resemblance was perceived by the learned and
was much in his favour:—he was offering the clergy what the
leges, the almost sacred *leges*, gave them[5]. But the practice
which had prevailed in Gaul was connected rather with the
Theodosian Code than with Justinian's legislation, and under
the Merovingian and Karlovingian kings the Frankish clergy
had not been able to obtain such liberal terms as Henry was
willing to concede at Clarendon[6]. During the age which saw

---

[1] Anselm had some difficulty in preventing Henry I. from enforcing by
pecuniary fines the canons against married priests. Eadmer, Hist. Nov.
172–5–6.

[2] See Stubbs, Const. Hist. § 87; Schmid, Glossar, s. v. *Geistliche*; Makower,
Const. Hist. 390.

[3] Alfred, 21. See Schmid's note. The Latin version is important: 'Si quis
presbyter hominem occidat, capiatur, et totum unde sibi mansionem emerat, et
exordinet eum episcopus, et tunc ab ecclesia reddatur.' Henry reading this in
the twelfth century might well say that he was fulfilling its spirit, if not its
letter.

[4] Nov. 83; Nov. 123. 21 § 1; Hinschius, Kirchenrecht, iv. 794–7.

[5] Summa Causae (Materials, iv. 202): 'Episcopi dicebant secundum *leges
seculi* clericos exauctoratos curiae tradendos, et post poenam spiritualem
corporaliter puniendos.'

[6] Löning, Kirchenrecht, i. 304, ii. 516; Hinschius, *op. cit.* iv. 849–64;
Nissl, Gerichtsstand des Clerus; Brunner, D. R. G. ii. 311–320. The story
is elaborate because it must distinguish between (1) bishops, (2) priests and
deacons, (3) the inferior clergy.

the Pseudo-Isidore and his fellows at their work, the age which leads up to the pontificate of Gregory VII., the clerical claims were advancing. We think it very possible that Lanfranc would have demanded and the Conqueror conceded the general principle that the trial of the accused clerk must take place [p 437] before the spiritual forum; but we may well doubt whether more than this would have been conceded or even demanded, whether as much as this could always be obtained. Of what happened during Stephen's troubled reign we know too little, but the clerical claims were still advancing, were taking an accurate shape in the *Decretum Gratiani*, and it is not unlikely that Stephen was forced to allow that only before a spiritual court can a clerk be accused, though from this rule he might hope to maintain some exceptions[1].

Henry's scheme and canon law.

(3) This leads us to our third question: Was Becket compelled by the law of the church, as it was understood in the year 1164, to reject Henry's constitution? We must distinguish. There were two particulars in the plan, to which a canonist bred in the school of Gratian was entitled and bound to refuse his assent[2]. A clerk in orders ought not to be accused of crime before the temporal judge, and the mission of royal officers to the church's court can be regarded as an insult to the church's justice. We can not say that these matters were matters of detail; Henry thought them of grave importance; but they become insignificant when set beside the question of double punishment. Now as regards this vital point, Becket propounded a doctrine which, so far as we are aware, had neither been tolerated by the state nor consecrated by the church. He asserted that the state must not punish the criminous clerk for that crime for which he has already suffered degradation. In 1164 a good deal had lately been written about this matter by the most renowned canonists of the age. We do not say that there was no room for doubt; there were obscure passages in the *Decretum* which needed comment; but we can say that two of the most famous masters of the canon law had considered and overruled the opinion of

---

[1] According to William of Newburgh, i. 140, it was said that a hundred murders had been perpetrated by clerks during Henry's reign before the king took action.

[2] The pope seems to have condemned this constitution as a whole; Materials, v. 74. He was not called upon to say how much of it was tolerable.

St Thomas, while we can name no writer who had maintained it. What is more, that opinion, though owing to his martyrdom it was suffered to do immeasurable mischief in England by fostering crime and crippling justice, was never consistently [p. 438] maintained by the canonists; had it been maintained, no deposed or degraded clerk would ever have been handed over to the lay power as a heretic or a forger of papal bulls. As a general principle of law, Becket's theory about double punishment was condemned by Innocent III.; the decree which condemns it is to this day part of the statute law of the catholic church[1].

---

[1] As to this matter of double punishment, Henry's canonists based his case on two passages of the Pseudo-Isidore which appear as cc. 18, 31, C. 11, qu. 1. These say in effect that in certain cases an offending clerk after being degraded is *curiae tradendus*. Does this mean that he is to be delivered to the lay court for further punishment? Henry's party said Yes; Becket's No. Our question ought to be, not what these words meant for the Pseudo-Isidore, still less what they meant for Arcadius and Honorius, from whom he stole them, but what they meant for the best ecclesiastical lawyers of the middle of the twelfth century. In 1164 five great canonists have lately had or are just having their say, namely, Gratian, Paucapalea, Roland (now Alexander III.), Rufinus and Stephanus Tornacensis. We can hardly bring ourselves to doubt that Gratian (see the dicta on cc. 26. 30. 47, e. qu.) would have agreed with Henry's contention. And the same must be said of Paucapalea (Summa, ed. Schulte, p. 78) and Roland (Summa, ed. Thaner, p. 25). Then Rufinus distinctly says that the clerk is to be degraded, 'et dimittetur post hoc iudici secundum leges publicas puniendus' (Summa, ed. Schulte, p. 274). Stephanus considers the opinion that Becket adopts and rejects it. Some say that the degraded clerk is not to be accused before the secular judge, since thus he will be tried twice for one offence. Others say that there is no occasion for a further accusation, but that he can be punished by the secular judge without a second trial. But the better opinion is, says Stephen, that the secular judge should try him; the Authenticum [=Nov. 123. 21 § 1] supports this doctrine (Summa, ed. Schulte, p. 212). An anonymous author of this period (Summa Rolandi, ed. Thaner, p. 293) has no doubt that the canon law sanctions it. Something may depend on the date of the decretal of Alexander III. which stands as c. 4, X. 2, 1. In later times the canonists admitted that there were various cases in which the degraded clerk was to be delivered to the lay power for further punishment. See the gloss on c. 18, C. 11, qu. 1; also Fournier, Officialités, 67–8. In 1222 Stephen Langton handed over to the lay power a deacon whom he had degraded for turning Jew and the lay power burnt him; see L. Q. R. ii. 153. Innocent III. (c. 7, X. 5, 20) ordained that the forgers of papal letters should be handed over, and further declared (c. 27, X. 5, 40) that this procedure was sanctioned by the doubtful passages in the Decretum. If once it be allowed that there is here no breach of that fundamental maxim which requires that a man be not punished twice for one offence, then there remains no more than a question about the relative gravity of offences:—is, for example, the forgery of a decretal a worse crime than a murder? Lastly, since Becket was willing to add imprisonment for life

Curiously enough that point in Henry's scheme which in [p.439] the eyes of the canonist must have seemed the least defensible, was successfully defended. As we have seen, his successors maintained the rule that clerks can be haled before the king's justices and accused of capital crimes. On the other hand, the not uncanonical principle which would have brought back the degraded clerk to hear a sentence in the royal court was abandoned. The result was lamentable.

The murderers of clerks.

One small matter remains to be noticed. It has sometimes been assumed by English writers that the clergy were willing to admit a certain measure of reciprocity, that they were willing that their own lives should be protected only by ecclesiastical law and ecclesiastical tribunals and that this is proved by the fate of the archbishop's murderers. Now it is true that a clerk was forbidden by the law of the church to go before a lay court and seek a judgment of blood; but to say this is one thing, to say that the lay murderer of a clerk is not to be punished by the lay prince is quite another thing, and we are not persuaded that any one ever said it except when he was in a logical strait. As we read the chronicles, Henry was blamed by his contemporaries for not having brought the murderers to justice and put them to death, though it was admitted by some that he was in a very awkward position :— he would be blamed if he let them escape, he would be blamed if he punished them, for this would be casting upon them the burden of a crime of which in common opinion he himself was not guiltless. He thought it best that they should go to the pope[1]. Afterwards he declared that he had been unable to

to degradation, provided that both punishments came from the ecclesiastical court, it is plain that the principle for which he contended was a highly technical principle condemning not two punishments but two judgments. This long note has seemed necessary, for in England it has been too readily assumed by both parties to the controversy that all Becket's claims were sanctioned by the law of the church. We dare not speak confidently of such a matter but have grave doubts about the truth of this assumption.

[1] Will. Newb. i. 163: 'Sive autem parceret homicidis illis, sive non, considerabat proclives esse homines ad male sentiendum de eo. Nam si parceret sceleratissimis, tanti mali ausum vel auctoritatem praestitisse videretur. Si vero in eis plecteret, quod absque eius mandato non attentasse putabantur, utrobique nequissimus diceretur. Idcirco parcendum eis duxit.' Another account, Materials, iv. 162, says that Henry knew that he could not make his peace with the church, unless he punished the murderers by death ('et traderet Sathanae in interitum carnis'), and yet was ashamed to punish them, because the crime had been committed for his sake. And again of the knights it is said

arrest them[1]. It would seem indeed that for a very few years
some English ecclesiastics were driven by the stress of Becket's
[p. 440] logic to say that they would be content if the murderers of
clerks were handed over to the mild judgments of the church;
or perhaps the true story is that this assertion was put into
their mouths as a *reductio ad absurdum* of their demands by
those who, though clerks and bishops, were the king's clerks.
At any rate very soon after the martyrdom Archbishop Richard,
the martyr's successor, wrote to three of the martyr's most
deadly foes, who were by this time three prelates of the
English church and the three principal justices of King Henry's
court, he wrote to Richard of Ilchester, John of Oxford and
Geoffrey Ridel, and told them that the doctrine which would
deal thus tenderly with lay offenders was a damnable opinion
and utterly at variance with canon law[2]. Repudiating the line
of argument favoured by his sainted predecessor, he assured
his three suffragans that a layman might be first excommunicated by the church and then hanged by the state
without being punished twice for one offence[3]. Henry could
now make terms; he had something to sell. In 1176 a papal
legate conceded that he might punish clerks for breaches of the
forest law, and in return the king granted that the lives of
clerks should be protected as well as, or even better than, the
lives of laymen[4].

(p. 163) that they sought the Pope when it had become clear that they must fall
into the hands either of God or of man.

[1] Gesta Henrici, i. 32; Hoveden, ii. 35 : 'malefactores illos, qui ... archi-
episcopum occiderunt habere non poterat.'

[2] He seems to have referred to cc. 39, 47, C. 23, qu. 5; c. 2, C. 15, qu. 6;
cc. 19. 20, C. 11, qu. 1.

[3] Trivet, an. 1176 (Eng. Hist. Soc.), p. 82 : 'In ecclesia Anglorum damnosa
omnibus et omnino damnanda consuetudo invaluit ... Si Judaeus aut laicorum
vilissimus occiditur statim supplicio mortis occisor addicitur. Si quis vero sacer-
dotem sive clericum minoris aut maioris status occiderit, sola excommunicatione
contenta, aut (ut verius loquar) contempta, ecclesia materialis opem gladii non
requirit.' This, the archbishop argues, is directly contrary to many canons.
He adds : 'Nec dicatur quod aliquis bis puniatur propter hoc in idipsum, nec
enim iteratum est quod ab uno incipitur et ab altero consummatur.' A neater
reply to Becket's talk of double punishment could not be given.

[4] Diceto, i. 410 : 'Concedo etiam quod interfectores clericorum, qui eos
scienter vel praemeditati interfecerint, convicti vel confessi coram iustitiario
meo, praesente episcopo vel eius officiali, praeter consuetam laicorum vindictam,
suam et suorum de hereditate quae eos contingit perpetuam sustineant exheredationem.' This seems to show that so late as 1176 the ordinary sentence
on a manslayer did not always involve disherison.

§ 6. *Aliens.*

[p. 411]

The
classical
common
law.

When our common law issues from the middle ages both its tests of nationality and its treatment of aliens are hardly such as we might have expected them to be.

Who are
aliens ?

1. As regards the definition of the two great classes of men which have to be distinguished from each other, the main rule is very simple. The place of birth is all-important. A child born within any territory that is subject to the king of England is a natural-born subject of the king of England, and is no alien in England. On the other hand, with some exceptions, every child born elsewhere is an alien, no matter the nationality of its parents.

The full extent of the first half of this rule was settled in 1608 by the famous decision in Calvin's case :—a child born in Scotland after the moment when King James the Sixth became King James the First is no alien in England[1]. The decision was one which pleased the king and displeased many of his subjects; but no other judgment could have been given, unless many precedents derived from times when our kings had large territories on the continent of Europe had been disregarded.

The other half of the rule takes us back to the middle of the fourteenth century. In 1343 a great debate has sprung up among men of the law and others as to the national character of the children born to English parents in foreign parts. The king seems to fear that this may touch even the succession to the throne; the prelates and barons reassure him; there never has been any doubt that the king's children wherever born are capable of inheriting from their ancestors. But as regards other children they hesitate. It is agreed in parliament that children ' born in the king's service,' no matter the place of their birth, can inherit; but time is short, this difficult matter requires further discussion, and so it is also agreed that no statute shall be made upon the present occasion[2]. Then in 1350 the debate is resumed. Once more there is a solemn protest that as to the king's children there is not and has never been any doubt at all. For the rest, it is ordained by statute

---

[1] *Calvin's case*, 7 Rep. 1.
[2] Rolls of Parliament, ii. 139.

[p. 442] that 'children born without the ligeance of the king, whose fathers and mothers at the time of their birth be and shall be at the faith and ligeance of the king of England, shall have and enjoy the same benefits and advantages to have and bear inheritance within the same ligeance as [certain children in whose favour this rule was being retrospectively applied], so always that the mothers of such children do pass the sea by the licence and wills of their husbands[1].' Certain children already born, were then declared capable of inheriting. The inference which we should draw from the proceedings of 1343 and 1350 is that the parliament thought that it was defining a somewhat debatable point in the common law, not that it was introducing a new rule. There is very little in the earlier Year Books that bears on this point: just enough, it may be, to suggest that the usual forms of pleading threw difficulties in the way of any one born 'out of the king's ligeance,' and that 'the king's ligeance' was regarded as a geographical tract[2].

2. An alien can not hold land in England. If the person to whom land would descend according to the common rules of inheritance is an alien, it misses him and passes to some remoter kinsman of the dead man. If, on the other hand, an alien obtains land by gift, sale, lease or the like, the transaction is not a nullity, but the king can seize the land and keep it for himself. Late in the middle ages we hear of a narrow exception:—an alien merchant may hire a house for the purposes of his trade[3]. Also it is said that an alien may have goods and chattels; he may make a will of them, and, should he die intestate, they will be administered for the benefit of his kinsfolk. But it is very noticeable that according to Littleton an alien can bring no action whether real or personal, and when his great commentator explains this to mean that no alien can bring a real action, that no alien enemy can bring a personal action, but that an alien whose sovereign is in league with our own may bring personal actions, we can not but feel that this is a bold treatment of a carefully worded text[4].

Disabilities of the alien.

---

[1] Rolls of Parliament, ii. 231; Statute 25 Edw. III. *de natis ultra mare.*

[2] Fitz. Abr. *Aiell.* pl. 8 (5 Edw. II.); Y. B. 6 Edw. III. f. 22 (Pasch. pl. 47); Y. B. 8 Edw. III. f. 51 (Trin. pl. 38); Fitz. Abr. *Briefe*, pl. 677 (Mich. 13 Edw. III.); compare Y. B. (ed. Pike), Mich. 13 Edw. III. pp. 76–8.

[3] So far as we are aware this appears first in Y. B. 32 Hen. VI. f. 23 (Hil. pl. 5). For the extent of the exception in Coke's day see Co. Lit. 2 b.

[4] Lit. sec. 198; Co. Lit. 129 b.

Naturaliza-
tion.

3. Nothing short of a statute can give to an alien all the [p. 413] rights of a natural born subject; but some of these can be conferred by the king's letters patent making the alien a 'denizen.' A denizen thus made can hold land, and he can acquire land by gift, sale or the like, but he can not inherit, and a child of his born before the act of denization can not inherit from him[1].

Law of
earlier
times.

Now there is room for serious doubt whether these rules can be traced far beyond the end of the thirteenth century. Very ancient law may regard every stranger as an enemy; but it will lay far more stress upon purity of blood than on place of birth; it will be tribal rather than territorial law. At a later time the friendly stranger will have no strict legal rights, no rights given him by the folk-law, but will live under the protection, the *mund*, of the ruler or some other great man. There is much in the treatment received by Jews and foreign merchants in the thirteenth century which suggests this doctrine. But feudalism is opposed to tribalism and even to nationalism : we become a lord's subjects by doing homage to him, and this done, the nationality of our ancestors and the place of our birth are insignificant. The law of feudal contract attempts for a while to swallow up all other law. In England, however, a yet mightier force than feudalism came into play. A foreigner at the head of an army recruited from many lands conquered England, became king of the English, endowed his followers with English lands. For a long time after this there could be little law against aliens, there could hardly be such a thing as English nationality. Even had the king claimed a right to seize the lands of aliens, he would not have exercised it. Again, the territory within which, according to later law, subjects would be born to the king of England, was large; under Henry II. it became vast. It comprehended Ireland ; at times (to say the least) it comprehended Scotland ; it stretched to the Pyrenees. Then again, the law even of Bracton's day acknowledged that a man might be a subject of the French king and hold land in France and yet be a subject of the English king and hold land in England. It was prepared to meet the case of a war between the two kings: the amphibious baron must fight in person for his liege lord, but he must also send

---

[1] Co. Lit. 8 a, 129 a.

[p. 444] his due contingent of knights to the opposite army[1]. In generation after generation a Robert Bruce holds land on both sides of the Scottish border; no one cares to remember on which side of it he was born[2]. Simon de Montfort obtained the Leicester inheritance; where he was born historians can not tell us; it matters not. He obtained the Leicester inheritance though his elder brother Almaric was living. Almaric was adhering to the French king, the enemy of our king, and that might be a good reason for passing him by; but Almaric must solemnly resign his claim before Simon's can be entertained[3].

It is, we believe, in the loss of Normandy that our law of aliens finds its starting point. In the first place, John seized the lands of those of his nobles who adhered to Philip, and preferred to be French rather than English. This was a forfeiture for treason. At the same time we see traces of that curious dislike of perpetual disherison which meets us in other quarters. Some of these lands, the *terrae Normannorum*, are given to new tenants in fee simple, but subject to a proviso that they may be taken away again if ever the Normans come back to their allegiance[4]. In the second place, a permanent relation of warfare is established between England and France. It endures from the beginning of John's reign until 1259 when Henry resigned his claim to Normandy. True that during this long half-century there was very little fighting and there were many truces; but all along the English theory was that Henry was by right Duke of Normandy and Count of Anjou, that the king of France was deforcing him of his inheritance, and that the day would come when the rebellious, or the invaded, provinces would obey their lawful lord. Thus a man who is living in obedience to the king of France is an enemy. If, says Bracton, such an one claims land against you, you may except against him; your exception however is not 'peremptory,' it is 'dilatory'; it may lose its force when our king enjoys his own

Growth of the law disabling aliens.

---

[1] Bracton, f. 427 b. He mentions as examples the Earl Marshal and M [Ingeram?] de Fiennes.

[2] Mackay, Lives of the Bruces in Dict. Nat. Biogr.

[3] Annals of Tewkesbury, 111; Mat. Par. Chron. Maj. iii. 524.

[4] Note Book, pl. 750. The king gave part of the lands of Ralph of Tankerville to Basset and his heirs 'donec eam reddiderit heredibus praedicti Radulfi per voluntatem suam vel per pacem.' There are many other examples.

again[1]. What he says is fully borne out by recorded cases [p. 445] from the early years of Henry III. A claimant of land is met, not by the simple 'You are an alien,' but by the far more elaborate 'You are within the power of the king of France and resident in France, and it has been provided by the council of our lord the king that no subject of the king of France is to be answered in England until Englishmen are answered in France[2].' Then Matthew Paris tells us how in 1244 Saint Louis, urging that 'no man may serve two masters,' insisted that all persons living in France must make choice between him and Henry, how Henry retorted by seizing the English lands of the Frenchmen, especially of the Normans, without giving them any chance of choosing an English nationality, and how Louis treated this retort as a breach of truce[3].

The king and the alien.   Blackstone is at no loss for reasons why an alien should not hold land in England, but when he has to explain why the king should seize the land which aliens acquire, we feel that he is in difficulties. He suggests that this forfeiture 'is intended by way of punishment for the alien's presumption in attempting to acquire any landed property[4].' The truth seems to be that in the course of the thirteenth century our kings acquired a habit of seizing the lands of Normans and other Frenchmen. The Normans are traitors; the Frenchmen are enemies. All this will be otherwise if a permanent peace is ever established. But that permanent peace never comes, and it is always difficult to obtain a restoration of lands which the king has seized. France is the one foreign country that has to be considered in this context; Germans and Italians come here as merchants, but they have no ancestral claims to urge and do not want English lands, while as to Scotland, owing to the English king's claim to an overlordship or to some other reason, Balliols and Bruces hold land on both sides of the border until a long war breaks out between the two countries. To us it seems that the king's claim to seize the lands of aliens is an

---

[1] Bracton, f. 298, 415 b, 427 b, 428 b. He is not quite certain what will happen if ever there be peace. His phrase 'donec terrae fuerint communes' seems to mean, not so much 'when there is peace between England and France,' as 'when Normandy, Anjou, etc. are once more under the ruler whom England obeys.'

[2] Note Book, pl. 110, 1396.

[3] Mat. Par. Chron. Maj. iv. 288.   [4] Comment. i. 372.

[p. 446] exaggerated generalization of his claim to seize the lands of his French enemies. Such an exaggerated generalization of a royal right will not seem strange to those who have studied the growth of the king's prerogatives[1].

And so too Bracton's 'dilatory exception' becomes per-emptory: 'You are an alien and your king is at war with our king' becomes 'You are an alien.' An English nation is gradually forming itself. Already there is a cry of 'England for the English.' The king's foreign favourites are detested; glad enough would Englishmen be if he would but seize their lands impartially and indiscriminately, and never endow another alien, be he Norman or Poitevin or Savoyard, with another inch of land. A trace of this feeling we may see when Bracton says that while the state of war endures the king cannot enable the alien to bring an action[2]. Probably in Edward I.'s day the law is, not merely that an alien enemy can not sue, but that an alien can not acquire land. A curious story comes to us which is worthy of repetition. A tenant in chief of the crown died leaving two co-heiresses; King Henry granted the wardship and marriage of these two young ladies to Elyas de Rabayn; Elyas took one of them to wife and sent the other to be married beyond the seas so that he might obtain the whole inheritance. In 1290 her son, though born abroad, claimed his mother's share; and claimed it successfully. The court defeated the scheme of the fraudulent guardian, but declared that its judgment was to form no precedent in favour of other aliens[3]. From Edward's day also we have letters of denization or of naturalization: the two would hardly as yet be distinguished. Though Elyas Daubeny was born beyond the seas, the king holds him for a pure Englishman and wills that he shall be

(margin: Growth of the king's claim to the alien's land.)

---

[1] See the apocryphal statute, *Praerogativa Regis*, c. 14 (Statutes, i. p. 226). Here we seem to see the king's claim growing. First we have an assertion of his right to the lands of the Normans, then we are told that this extends also to lands of certain persons born beyond the sea, and we have various readings of the clause which defines this class of persons. One version says, 'those whose ancestors were in the faith of the King of France in the reign of King John.' Another, 'those who were not in the king's faith.' In this context 'foreigner' and 'subject of the King of France' are for practical purposes synonymous terms. In France also the *droit d'aubaine* but slowly attains its full stature; Viollet, Histoire du droit civil, p. 365.

[2] Bracton, f. 427 b.

[3] Rolls of Parliament. i. 44.

held as such by all men and that he may sue in all courts [p. 447] notwithstanding any 'exception' of alienage[1].

The kinds of aliens.

The law of Henry III.'s reign has to deal as a matter of fact with two and only two great classes of aliens. The first consists of Frenchmen who have claims to English lands. Such claims are in some cases ancestral, and these, as we have seen, can not be heard while there is war or an abiding cause for war between France and England. In other cases the claimants are recipients of royal favours; they are the king's half-brothers, the queen's uncles or the attendants of these exalted persons; the king gives them lands and, except at a revolutionary moment, they hold their lands safely; some of them were born in provinces which *de iure* (so Englishmen think) belong to the king; all of them by doing homage to the king become his men, and this must be naturalization enough. The other great class consists of alien merchants; they do not come here to settle; they do not want land; they would be well content were they permitted to lodge where they pleased.

The alien merchant.

Mere common law has little to do with these foreign merchants. Their business takes them into the chartered towns. The law under which they live is a mesh of privileges and of privileges that are hardly consistent. They themselves will have charters derived from the king; but they will be living in boroughs which have charters derived from the king, and first and foremost among the rights for which the burghers long is the right of confining the activity of foreign merchants within narrow bounds. The conflict goes on with varying fortunes from century to century. On the whole the king, the prelates and barons support the merchants; they are useful, they lend money, they lower prices, they will pay for favours; but often a weak king must give way and yield to the complaints of the burghers. Already the Great Charter provides that merchants may freely enter and dwell in and leave the realm; but the same Great Charter confirms all the ancient liberties and customs of London and the other boroughs, and

---

[1] Rolls of Parliament, i. 135: 'Dominus Rex ipsum Elyam Anglicum purum tenet.' Coke, Co. Lit. 129 a, cites these letters as though they effected but a limited denization. 'The king may make a particular denization, quod in *quibusdam* curiis suis Angliae audiatur.' For *quibusdam* read *quibuscumque*. No one will now-a-days be misled by Coke's derivation of *denizen* from '*donaison* i.e. *donatio*.' The word originally means one who is within, *de intus, deinz, dans*, as opposed to one who is an outsider.

[p. 448] thus takes away with one hand what it gives with the other[1]. The burghers have a very strong opinion that their liberties and customs are infringed if a foreign merchant dwells within their walls for more than forty days, if he hires a house, if he fails to take up his abode with some reponsible burgher, if he sells in secret, if he sells to foreigners, if he sells in detail. In Henry III.'s day the struggle is but beginning. It reaches the first of its many climaxes in 1303 when Edward I. grants the great *Carta Mercatoria*[2]. It will interest rather the economist than the lawyer, and rather the student of the fourteenth and fifteenth centuries than the student of earlier times[3].

We may perhaps regard Coke's doctrine that the alien friend is protected by 'personal actions' as ancient common law. In Edward I.'s day we even find that an Italian merchant resident in England, who as a Ghibelline had been ejected from his house in Florence by victorious Guelfs, hoped to recover damages for this wrong in the courts of the king of England; he failed, because 'it is not the custom of England that any one should answer in England for a trespass committed in a foreign country in time of war or in any other manner[4].' The *Carta Mercatoria* of Edward I., the validity of which did not pass unquestioned, and statutes of Edward III. secured to aliens the benefit of a jury composed wholly or in part of aliens[5]. In 1454 it is said that a foreign merchant may hire a house and defend his possession of it by an action of trespass[6]. If we suppose this to have been ancient common law, still it must have been law which had but little chance of asserting itself; the burghers have steadily fought against it and very commonly have been successful[7]. Littleton's bold assertion that an alien can bring no action real or personal may be less open to exception than his commentator supposed[8], for in Littleton's day we hear that the proper court

The alien and common law.

---

[1] Charter of 1215, c. 13, 41.

[2] Munimenta Gildhallae, vol. i. pt. ii. pp. 205–8.

[3] The story is told at length by Schanz, Englische Handelspolitik, i. 379–433.

[4] Plac. Abbrev. p. 201.

[5] Carta Mercatoria, c. 3; Liber Rubeus, iii. 1063; Stat. 27 Edw. III. stat. 2. c. 8; 28 Edw. III. c. 13.

[6] Y. B. 32 Hen. VI. f. 23 (Hil. pl. 5).

[7] Indeed they had lately obtained two statutes declaring that alien merchants must dwell with English hosts and not elsewhere; 5 Hen. IV. c. 9; 4 Hen. V. c. 5.

[8] See above, p. 459.

for aliens who have come here under the king's safe conduct [p. 449] is the Court of Chancery; 'they are not bound to sue according to the law of the land, nor to abide the trial by twelve men and other solemnities of the law of the land, but shall sue in the Chancery and the matter shall be determined by the law of nature¹.' This is a doctrine characteristic of the fifteenth century. But all along it is as men privileged by the king, rather than as men subject to ordinary law, that the foreign merchants get a hearing. They can seldom make their way to the king's justices because the courts of the towns in which they live claim an exclusive cognizance of actions brought against the burgesses, and when the foreigners do get to the royal courts there is a contest between privilege and privilege. Probably the king can banish them at any time; his loyal subjects in the boroughs would not be sorry if he did, for these aliens are always taking the bread out of the mouths of honest folk. Then, at least in the thirteenth century, the common belief is that they are all usurers and therefore living in mortal sin. We are told that in 1240 Henry III. banished the so-called Caursini; but that they only lay hid for a time, the king conniving at their presence. A little while afterwards they are acquiring splendid palaces in London; no one dares attack them, for they call themselves the Pope's merchants; now and again the king will imprison a few, to the delight of their Jewish rivals; but he is half-hearted. And so there is little common law for these people².

Has the merchant a peculiar status? Ought we to reckon merchants of all kinds, English and foreign, as forming one of the sorts or conditions of men known to the law? Hardly, though as the historian of our constitution has shown, they nearly become for political purposes one of the estates of the realm³. Still they do not become this. Then in

---

¹ Y. B. 13 Edw. III. f. 9 (Pasch. pl. 5). This is the celebrated case of the carrier who 'broke bulk.'

² Mat. Par. iv. 8; v. 245. See Du Cange, s.v. *Caorcini*. The name has been derived from Cahors in France, from Caorsa in Piedmont, from a Florentine family of Corsini. Paris speaks of 'Caursini praecipue Senonenses.' Probably by *Senonenses* he means men of Siena, not of Sens. It seems fairly plain that already the origin of the name was unknown, and that at least in England *Caursin* was equivalent to foreign usurer. Had the word borne an obvious meaning, Paris would hardly have dared to perpetrate so bad a joke as (iii. 331) 'quasi causantes, vel capientes, et ursini.'

³ Stubbs, Const. Hist. § 195.

[p. 450] private law 'merchantship,' if we may make that word, seems
too indefinite and also seems to have too few legal consequences
to permit of our calling it a status. We might illustrate this
from modern law. Until lately no one but 'a trader' could
be made bankrupt; still we should hardly say that in 1860
'tradership' was a status. There was, so far as we are aware,
but this one rule which marked off the 'trader' from the 'non-
trader,' and a man became and ceased to be a trader without
any solemnity by a process that we may call indefinite, though
a court of law might have had to decide whether at a given
moment that process had been accomplished.

Before the end of the thirteenth century 'the law merchant' The law
was already conceived as a body of rules which stood apart   merchant
from the common law[1]. But it seems to have been rather
a special law for mercantile transactions than a special law
for merchants. It would we think have been found chiefly
to consist of what would now be called rules of evidence, rules
about the proof to be given of sales and other contracts, rules as
to the legal value of the tally and the God's penny; for example,
the law merchant took one view of the effect of an 'earnest,' the
common law another. These special mercantile rules were conceived as being specially known to merchants; in the courts
of fairs and markets the assembled merchants declare the law;
in Edward II.'s day twelve merchants are summoned from
each of four cities to testify before the king's bench about a
doubtful point in the 'lex mercatoria.' Also these rules are
not conceived to be purely English law; they are, we may say,
a *ius gentium* known to merchants throughout Christendom,
and could we now recover them we might find some which had
their origin on the coasts of the Mediterranean. But this is
not the place for their discussion, for we take the law merchant
to be not so much the law for a class of men as the law for a
class of transactions.

[1] Select Pleas in Manorial Courts (Seld. Soc.), i. 133.

§ 7.   *The Jews*[1].

General
idea of the
Jew's
position.

The Jew came to England in the wake of the Norman Conqueror.   That no Israelites had ever dwelt in this country before the year 1066 we dare not say ; but if so, they have left no traces of their presence that are of any importance to us[2]. They were brought hither from Normandy, brought hither as the king's dependants and (the word will hardly be too strong) the king's serfs.   In the first half of the twelfth century their condition was thus described by the author of the *Leges Edwardi* in a passage which suggests that among the regalia to which the Norman barons aspired was the privilege of keeping Jews of their own :—'It is to be known that all the Jews wheresoever they be in the realm are under the liege wardship and protection of the king ; nor may any of them without the king's licence subject himself to any rich man, for the Jews and all that they have are the king's, and should any one detain them or their chattels, the king may demand them as his own[3].'   This gives us one of the two main ideas that our law in later times has about the Jew :—he with all that he has belongs to the king.   Bracton puts the same thought in these words :—'The Jew can have nothing that is his own, for whatever he acquires, he acquires, not for himself, but for the king ; for the Jews live not for themselves but for others, and so they acquire not for themselves but for others[4].'   The other main idea is one which will not seem strange to us after what we have said of villeinage.   This servility is a relative servility ; in relation to all men, save the king, the Jew is free.   He will require some special treatment, for if he is to be here at all and do any good, he must be allowed to do things that are forbidden to Christians, notably to take interest on money lent. And courts of justice must pay some regard to his religion ;

---

[1] Three volumes of Publications of the Anglo-Jewish Historical Exhibition issuing from the office of the Jewish Chronicle (1888) contain valuable essays, documents, bibliographies, etc.   We shall make our references chiefly to these. Prynne's Demurrer, Tovey's Anglia Judaica, Madox's chapter on the Exchequer of the Jews, and the plea roll printed in Cole's Documents Illustrative of English History are among the most important sources of information.   See also Jacobs, The Jews of Angevin England.

[2] Liebermann, Zeitschrift für Geschichtswissenschaft, i. 182.

[3] Leges Edw. Conf. c. 25.   [4] Bracton, f. 386 b.

[p. 452] for example, they must suffer him to swear upon the roll of the law instead of the gospels; but in general, if his royal master's interests are not concerned, he is to be dealt with as though he were a Gentile. A third principle is accepted— the Jews themselves would desire its acceptance—namely, that when the interests of neither the king nor any other Christian are concerned, the Jews may arrange their own affairs and settle their own disputes in their own way and by their own Hebrew law[1].

For about a century and a half they were an important element in English history. In spite of the king's exactions and of occasional outbursts of popular fury, they throve. They were wealthy; they bore an enormous weight of taxation[2]. We may say that at times they 'financed' the kingdom; there were few great nobles who had not at one time or another borrowed money from the Israelite, and paid the two pence per pound per week that was charged by way of usury. What the great folk did, the smaller folk did also. This money-lending business required some governmental regulation. In the first place, the king had a deep interest in it, for whatever was owed to a Jew was potentially owed to the king, and he would naturally desire to have ready at hand written evidence that he could use against his debtors. In the second place, this matter could hardly be left to the ordinary English tribunals. For one thing, they would do but scant justice to the Jew, and therefore but scant justice to the king, who stood behind the Jew. For another thing, it is highly probable that the Jewish 'gage' was among Englishmen a novel and an alien institution, since it broke through the old law by giving rights in land to a creditor who did not take possession. In 1194 therefore an edict was issued about these Jewish loans[3]. In every town in which the Jews lived, an office, as we should say, was established for the registration of their deeds. All loans and payments of loans were to be made under the eye of

The exchequer of the Jews.

---

[1] There is a good deal of evidence which tends to show that in the first half of the twelfth century the Jew's legal position was not so bad as it afterwards became. The doctrine, not without supporters in England, which teaches that the disabilities of the Jew were due, not to the mere fact that he was a Jew, but to the fact, real or presumed, that he was a usurer and therefore living in mortal sin, seems to us groundless. Our law did not regard usury as any offence in a Jew; on the contrary, it enforced his usurious contracts for him.

[2] Gross, Publications, i. 195.   [3] Hoveden, iii. 266.

certain officers, some of them Christians, some of them Jews, and a copy or 'part' of every deed was to be deposited in an [p. 453] 'ark' or chest under official custody. A few years later a department of the royal exchequer—the exchequer of the Jews—was organized for the supervision of this business[1]. At its head were a few 'Justices of the Jews.' We hear for a while that some of these justices are themselves Jews, and all along Jews filled subordinate offices in the court; and this was necessary, for many of the documents that came before it were written in the Hebrew language. This exchequer of the Jews was, like the great exchequer, both a financial bureau and a judicial tribunal. It managed all the king's transactions —and they were many—with the Jews, saw to the exaction of tallages, reliefs, escheats and forfeitures, and also acted judicially, not merely as between king and Jew, but also as between king and Gentile when, as often happened, the king had for some cause or another 'seized into his hand' the debts due to one of his Jews by Christian debtors. Also it heard and determined all manner of disputes between Jew and Christian. Such disputes, it is true, generally related to loans of money, but the court seems to have aimed at and acquired a competence, and an exclusive competence, in all causes whether civil or criminal in which a Jew was implicated, unless it was some merely civil cause between two Hebrews which could be left to a purely Jewish tribunal. For this reason we can read very little of the Jews in the records of any other court, and until such rolls of the Jewish exchequer as exist have been published, we shall be more ignorant than we ought to be[2].

Vice of the law applied to Jews.   The system could not work well; it oppressed both Jew and Englishmen. Despised and disliked the once chosen people would always have been in a society of medieval Christians;

---

[1] Gross, Publications, i. 174.

[2] The earliest extant roll was printed in Cole's Documents; it is that for 3–4 Henry III. A list of the other rolls is given in Publications, iii. p. xiv. Occasionally cases in which Jews are concerned come onto the ordinary plea rolls and some are printed in the Placitorum Abbreviatio and in Bracton's Note Book. References to these are given in Publications, iii. 4, 24. Cases of small debts were heard by the constables of the royal castles; the court of the University of Oxford claimed pleas between Jew and scholar, and in London the civic court held plea touching land between Jew and Gentile; but on the whole the competence of the exchequer seems to have been exclusive.

perhaps they would have been accused of crucifying children and occasionally massacred; but they would not have been so persistently hated as they were, had they not been made the [p. 454] engines of royal indigence. From the middle of the thirteenth century onwards the king was compelled to rob them of their privileges, to forbid them to hold land, to forbid them even to take interest[1]. This last prohibition could not be carried into effect; there was little or nothing that the Jews could profitably do if they were cut off from lending money. Their expulsion in 1290 looks like the only possible solution of a difficult problem.

A few more words may be said about their legal condition for it was curious and may serve to illustrate some general principles of our medieval law.

The Jew's relation to the king is very much like the villein's relation to his lord. In strictness of law whatever the Jew has belongs to the king; he 'acquires for the king' as the villein 'acquires for his lord.' But, just as the lord rarely seizes his villein's chattels save for certain reasons, so the king rarely seizes the Jew's chattels save for certain reasons; until the seizure has been made, the villein or the Jew is treated as an owner and can behave as such. Again, as the lord is wont to be content with the customary services, heriots, merchets and so forth of his villeins and to tallage them only at regular intervals, so the king, unless he is in some unusual strait, will treat his Jews by customary rules; for example he will not exact from the heir by way of relief more than one-third of the inheritance[2]. The king respects the course and practice of his *Scaccarium Iudaeorum*, the custom of his Jewry, much as the lord respects the custom of the manor. Again, the king does justice upon and between his Jews, as the lord does justice upon and between his villeins. The maxim that what is the Jew's is the king's is not infringed when the king after a judicial hearing decides that for a certain offence a certain Jew must pay a certain sum, and just so the lord keeps in the background his right to seize all the goods of every villein while his court is condemning this or

Relation of the Jew to the king.

---

[1] Edict of 1271 forbidding them to hold land, Foed. i. 489; prohibition of usury, Statutes of the Realm, i. 221. See also the ordinance printed by Gross in Publications, i. 219.

[2] Gross, Publications, i. 192, 225.

that villein to a fine, a forfeiture or an amercement. Again, the king can grant privileges to his Jews—Henry II. gave them a charter and John a magnificent charter—without [p. 455] emancipating them or fundamentally changing their legal condition[1]. Lastly the lord when his own interests are not at stake is content that his villeins should settle their own disputes in their own way under the supervision of his steward, and so the king is content that, as between Jews, Jewish law shall be administered by Jewish judges.

The Jew's servility.

The analogy may not be perfect. It is but too possible that in his dealings with his Jews the king's rapacity was checked by few considerations that were not prudential, and that the course and practice of his Jewry extracted from them the utmost that a far-sighted selfishness could allow itself to demand. The villein was a Christian; the custom of the manor had ancient roots and was closely akin to the common law. The relation between king and Jew was new, at least in England, and it was in many respects unique; the Jew belonged to a despicable race and professed a detestable creed. For all this, the analogy holds good at the most important point: the Jew, though he is the king's serf, is a free man in relation to all other persons. We call him a serf. We have no direct authority for so doing, for we have seen no text in which he is called *servus*; but Bracton has gone very near this word when he said that what the Jew acquires he acquires for the king. Not only can the king mortgage or lease his Jewry, his *Iudaismum*, as a whole[2], but there is one known case in which an individual Jew was first given by the king to his son and afterwards enfranchised; *donavimus libertati* was the phrase used; hereafter in consideration of an honorary rent of a pair of gilt spurs he is to be free from all tallages, aids, loans and demands[3].

The Jew's freedom in relation to all others than his

---

[1] Rot. Cart. Joh. p. 93. The charter of Henry II. seems to be lost. For a charter granted by Richard, see Foedera, i. 51.

[2] In 1255 Henry III. mortgaged his Jewry to his brother Richard: Tovey, p. 135; Mat. Par. Chron. Maj. v. 488. Afterwards Henry assigned it to his son Edward, who assigned it for two years to two Caursin merchants: Tovey, pp. 157-9.

[3] Tovey, p. 185 (54 Hen. III.). In France the Jew seems to have been distinctly called *servus;* Viollet, Histoire du droit civil, p. 356; Luchaire, Manuel des institutions, p. 582.

master seems to have been amply protected by the exchequer. So far as we can see he found there a favourable audience. He could sue and be sued, accuse and be accused, and the [p. 456] rules of procedure, which in the main were the ordinary English rules, were not unduly favourable to his Christian adversary. He 'made his law' upon the books of Moses; he was not required to do battle; he might put himself upon a jury one half of which would consist of men of his own race and creed. He enjoyed a splendid monopoly; he might frankly bargain for interest on his loans and charge about forty-three per cent. per annum[1]. Unless we are mistaken, no law prevented him from holding lands[2], though it is not until late in the day that he appears as a landholder on a large scale, and when this happens it is a scandal that cries aloud for removal. He had a house, sometimes a fine house, in the town. His choice of a dwelling place seems to have been confined to those towns which had 'arks,' or as we might say 'loan registries'; he would hardly have wished to live elsewhere; but there were boroughs which had obtained royal charters enabling them to exclude him[3]. Many lands were gaged to him, but, though we do not fully understand the nature of these gages, it seems to us that the Hebrew creditor seldom took, or at all events kept, possession of the land, and that his gage was not conceived as giving him any place in the scale of lords and tenants. However, late in Henry III.'s reign it became apparent that the Jews were holding lands in fee and that they had military tenants below them; they were claiming the wardships and marriages of infant heirs, and were even daring to present Christian clerks to Christian bishops for induction into Christian churches[4]. This was not to be borne. In 1271 the edict went forth that they were no longer to hold free tenement, though they might keep their own houses[5]. Some galling restrictions had already been laid upon them at the instance of the church; they were to fast in Lent; they were to wear distinctive badges upon their garments; they were not

---

[1] Gross, Publications, i. 207.

[2] Bracton, f. 13. In feoffments made by certain convents it is common to find a stipulation that the land is not to be sold or gaged to Jews.

[3] Gross, Publications, i. 190.

[4] Gesta Abbatum, i. 401; Liber de Antiquis Legibus, 234.

[5] Foed. i. 489.

to keep Christian servants or have intercourse with Christian
women ; they were not to enter the churches; they were to
acquire no more schools or synagogues than they already
possessed.

Law be-
tween Jew
and Jew.   As between Jew and Jew, if the king's interests were in no [p. 457]
wise concerned, Jewish tribunals administered the Jewish law
(*lex Iudaica*). Questions of inheritance, for example, do not
come before the ordinary English tribunals, and come but rarely
and incidentally before the exchequer of the Jews. When
Hebrew dealt with Hebrew the document, the *shetar* (Lat.
starrum, Fr. *estarre*) which recorded the transaction was written
in the Hebrew language and the parties to it, instead of
affixing their seals (some Jews had seals), signed their names[1].
Often such a document was executed in the presence of official
witnesses and was sanctioned by an oath upon the law. The
precise nature of the tribunals which did justice between Jews
we can not here discuss; it is a matter for those who are
learned in Hebrew antiquities; but to all appearance they were
not mere boards of arbitrators but courts with coercive power[2].
Whether they aspired to execute their decrees by physical force
we do not know; but apparently, like our own ecclesiastical
courts, they could wield the weapon of excommunication, and
this spiritual sword may have been sufficient for the accomplishment of all their purposes[3]. To Gentiles at all events it
seemed that the Jews had 'priests' and 'bishops' (*presbyteri,
sacerdotes, episcopi*) who did justice among them. Over the
appointment of these officers the king exercised a control, not
very unlike that which he exercised over the appointment of
English bishops[4]. The Jews of each town, or of each synagogue,
and again all the Jews of England, constituted a *communa* with
which he could deal as a single whole. He could impose a tax
or a penalty upon it, and leave it to settle as between its
various members the final incidence of the impost.

[1] A collection of Shetaroth or 'stars' has been published by M. D. Davis :
Publications, vol. ii. As to the use of seals see p. 285. Tovey, p. 183, gives an
engraving of a seal appended to a charter of feoffment.

[2] See the volume of Shetaroth, pp. 4, 109, 136, 143, 178, 298, 336.

[3] Henry III. permits the 'masters of the law' to pronounce 'summam
excommunicationem' against those who will not pay their promised contributions to the London cemetery ; Tovey, p. 127; Jacobs, Publications, i. 46.

[4] In 1257 Henry III. deposed 'bishop' Elyas and declared that for the
future the Jews might elect their own *sacerdotes* : Madox, Exch. i. 261.

Whether the sojourn of the Jews in England left any Influence
of the Jew
on English
law. permanent marks upon the body of our law is a question that we dare not debate, though we may raise it. We can hardly [p. 458] suppose that from the *Lex Iudaica,* the Hebrew law which the Jews administered among themselves, anything passed into the code of the contemptuous Christian. But that the international *Lex Iudaismi*[1] perished in 1290 without leaving any memorial of itself is by no means so certain. We should not be surprised to learn that the practice of preserving in the treasury one 'part' (the *pes* or 'foot') of every indenture which recorded a fine levied in the royal court, was suggested by the practice of depositing in an official ark one copy of every bond given to a Jew. Both practices can be traced to the same year, the year 1194[2]. Again, very early in Edward I.'s day we hear that 'according to the assize and statutes of the king's Jewry, his Jews ought to have one moiety of the lands, rents and chattels of their Christian debtors until they shall have received their debts[3].' A few years afterwards, and just before the banishment of the Jews, a famous statute gave a Christian creditor a very similar remedy, the well-known writ of *elegit,* which therefore may be a lasting monument of the Hebrew money-lender[4]. But at any rate we ought to remember the Jew when we make our estimate of the thirteenth century. Landowners are borrowing large sums, and the enormous rate of interest that they contract to pay, if it shows the badness of the security that is offered for the loan—the Jew holds his all at the king's will and usury does not run against infants; the security therefore is very bad—shows also the intensity of the demand for money. Many an ancient tie between men,—the tie of kinship, the tie of homage—is being dissolved or transmuted by the touch of Jewish gold; land is being brought to market and feudal rights are being capitalized.

[1] Y. B. 32–3 Edw. I. p. 355: 'ley de Jwerye.'

[2] In our chapter on Ownership and Possession we shall trace the preservation of the *pedes finium* to this point. See vol. ii. p. 97.

[3] Madox, Exchequer, i. 247 from a roll of 3–4 Edw. I.; Statutes of the Realm, i. 221.

[4] Stat. West. II. 13 Edw. I. c. 18.

§ 8. *Outlaws and Convicted Felons.* [p. 459]

Outlawry.   We must now glance briefly at certain classes of men who for their offences or their contumacy are deprived of some of those rights which their 'lawful' neighbours enjoy. Among them we reckon outlaws, convicted felons and excommunicates.

The history of outlawry can be better told in connexion with the criminal law than in the present context. Outlawry is the last weapon of ancient law, but one that it must often use. As has been well said, it is the sentence of death pronounced by a community which has no police constables or professional hangmen[1]. To pursue the outlaw and knock him on the head as though he were a wild beast is the right and duty of every law-abiding man. 'Let him bear the wolf's head[2]:' this phrase is in use even in the thirteenth century. But as the power of the state and the number of its weapons increase, outlawry loses some of its gravity; instead of being a substantive punishment, it becomes mere 'criminal process,' a means of compelling accused persons to stand their trial. Just in Bracton's day it is undergoing a further degradation. In one place he says that recourse can be had to outlawry only when there is an accusation of one of those crimes which are punished by loss of life or member. This, no doubt, is the old doctrine, and his whole exposition of the effects of outlawry is in harmony with it. At a later time he has glossed his text:—there may, he says, be outlawry even when the offence is no felony but a mere *transgressio*, provided that it be a breach of the king's peace[3]. This is important. In course of time our law is going to know two kinds of outlawry; with allusion to the analogous process of excommunication we might call them the greater and the less. A man outlawed on a charge of felony is as one attainted of that felony; while if outlawed for a misdemeanour or in a civil action (for in the course of the fourteenth century the process of outlawry spreads

---

[1] Brunner, D. R. G. i. 173.

[2] Bracton, f. 125 b; Select Pleas of the Crown, pl. 47; Y. B. 20–1 Edw. I. p. 237.

[3] Bracton, f. 127 b. The passage 'Facta autem possunt esse plura...aliquantulum cum humana' is a marginal gloss. See Note Book, pl. 82, 85, 1263, 1267; Co. Lit. 128 b.

[p. 460] rapidly through many of the personal actions) he is in no such evil plight. But this distinction belongs to the future. The learning of outlawry as it is in Bracton is still the learning of outlawry for felony.

The outlaw's life is insecure. In Bracton's day he ought not to be slain unless he is resisting capture or fleeing from it; but it is every one's duty to capture him. And out in Gloucestershire and Herefordshire on the Welsh march custom allows that he may be killed at any time[1]. If knowing his condition we harbour him, this is a capital crime[2]. He is a 'lawless man' and a 'friendless man[3].' Of every proprietary, possessory, contractual right he is deprived; the king is entitled to lay waste his land and it then escheats to his lord; he forfeits his chattels to the king; every contract, every bond of homage or fealty in which he is engaged is dissolved. If the king inlaws him, he comes back into the world like a new-born babe, *quasi modo genitus*, capable indeed of acquiring new rights, but unable to assert any of those that he had before his outlawry. An annihilation of the outlawry would have a different operation, but the inlawed outlaw is not the old person restored to legal life; he is a new person[4]. The law of forfeiture and escheat for felony is taking an extremely severe form. It is held that the conviction or the outlawry 'relates back' to the moment at which the crime was perpetrated, so that acts done by the felon in the interim are avoided[5]. It is held that the felon's blood is corrupt and that a child born to him after the felony is incapable of inheriting, not merely from him, but from any one else[6]. Though we speak but briefly of outlawry, we

Condition of the outlaw.

---

[1] Bracton, f. 128 b. The printed book has *Hertford* instead of *Hereford*. The citation from the Digest should be, Dig. ad legem Corneliam de Sicariis et Veneficis (48. 8) 3 § 6, 'Transfugas licet ubicunque inventi fuerint quasi hostes interficere.' As to killing an outlaw, see Britton, i. 51. So late as 1328 it was argued that a plea of the dead man's outlawry was a sufficient answer to an indictment for slaying him; 2 Lib. Ass. pl. 3, f. 3; Y. B. 2 Edw. III. f. 6 (Hil. pl. 17); and it would even seem that the same assertion was made in 1353; 27 Lib. Ass. p. 41, f. 137.

[2] Bracton, f. 128 b.

[3] Bracton, f. 125, 128 b.   [4] Bracton, f. 132 b.

[5] Bracton, f. 30 b, citing Dig. de donationibus (39. 5) 15: 'Post contractum capitale crimen donationes factae non valent ex constitutione divorum Severi et Antonini, si condemnatio secuta sit.' See also Fleta, p. 43.

[6] Bracton, f. 130: 'cum sit progenitus talis ex testiculo et sanguine felonis.' Fleta, p. 43.

are speaking of no rarity; the number of men outlawed at [p. 461] every eyre is very large; ten men are outlawed for one who is hanged.

§ 9. *Excommunicates.*

Excommu-
nication. Closely allied to outlawry is excommunication; it is in fact an ecclesiastical outlawry[1], and, like temporal outlawry, though once it was the law's last and most terrible weapon against the obstinate offender, it is now regarded as a normal process for compelling the appearance in court of those who are accused. Indeed as regards the laity, since the spiritual courts can not direct a seizure of body, lands or goods, those courts must, if mere citations fail to produce an appearance, at once have recourse to their last weapon. Then, as ordained by William the Conqueror, the lay power comes to their aid[2]. If the excommunicate does not seek absolution within forty days (this period seems to be fixed already in the twelfth century[3]), the ordinary will signify this to the king; a writ for the arrest of the offender will be issued, and he will be kept in prison until he makes his submission[4].

The excommunicate is, says Bracton, a spiritual leper; he can do no valid act in the law; he can not sue; but he can be sued, for he must not take advantage by his own wrong-doing; one may not pray with him, talk with him, eat with him[5]. The clergy from time to time complain that this precept is not well observed and that the king is backward in the arrest of excommunicates[6]. In spite of the condemnation which had fallen on the Constitutions of Clarendon, our kings seem to have stedfastly asserted the Conqueror's principle that their tenants in chief, at all events their ministers, sheriffs and bailiffs, were not to be excommunicated without royal licence. Edward I. compelled Archbishop Peckham to withdraw a general sentence pronounced against those ministers who were

---

[1] Æthelr. viii. 42. The excommunicate is 'God's outlaw.'

[2] Schmid, Gesetze, p. 357; Leg. Edw. Conf. 2, § 9.

[3] Leg. Edw. Conf. 6.

[4] Bracton, f. 426 b, 427; Reg. Brev. Orig. f. 65.

[5] Bracton, f. 426 b : 'Excommunicato enim interdicitur omnis actus legitimus.' Note Book, pl. 552; Britton, i. 322; Lit. sec. 201.

[6] Gravamina of 1257, Mat. Par. Chron. Maj. vi. 355; Constitutions of 1261, Johnson, Canons, ii. 192.

[p. 462] remiss in their duty of capturing excommunicates[1] and in 1293 the Archbishop of York made fine with four thousand marks for having excommunicated the Bishop of Durham; he had failed to take the distinction between what was done by his suffragan bishop and what was done by a palatine earl[2]. A practice of the lay courts yet more objectionable to the clergy was that of directing a bishop to absolve an excommunicate. They did not treat the spiritual courts as inferior courts, they did not entertain appeals or evoke causes; but still they had to protect their own jurisdiction. A suit would be instituted in the bishop's court about some matter, which, according to the thinking of the king's justices, did not lie within its sphere; to those justices the defendant would come for a writ of prohibition; meanwhile he would be excommunicated, and then the plaintiff and the ecclesiastical judges, when called before the royal court, would refuse to answer one who was outside the pale of the church. In such a case it is not an unheard of thing that the lay court should command the bishop to pronounce an absolution[3]; but much the same end may be attained if the lay court simply ignores a sentence which in its opinion has been obtained in fraud of its rights[4]. On the whole, however, before the end of Henry III.'s reign the two sets of courts are working together harmoniously. There is always a brisk border warfare simmering between them, in which, as is natural, the tribunal which has the direct command of physical force is apt to gain the victory; but this is no longer a world-shaking conflict between church and state, it is rather a struggle between two professional classes, each of which likes power and business and has no dislike for fees and perquisites. In the eyes of the secular lawyers the baronies of the bishops are a pledge that the censures of the church will not be used so as to deprive the king of his rights[5]. Even an appeal to Rome

---

[1] Johnson, Canons, ii. 258; Rolls of Parliament, i. 224.

[2] Rolls of Parliament, i. 102. In 1194 Archbishop Geoffrey of York was in trouble for having contemned the king by excommunicating one of his ministers; Rolls of the King's Court (Pipe Roll Soc.) vol. i. p. xvii.

[3] Note Book, pl. 670. See Ann. Burton. 255, 413; Mat. Par. Chron. Maj. vi. 354; Articuli Cleri, c. 7 (Statutes i. 172).

[4] Bracton, f. 408, 426 b, 427; Co. Lit. 134 a.

[5] Bracton, f. 427: 'Nunquam capietur aliquis ad mandatum iudicum delegatorum vel archidiaconorum vel alterius iudicis inferioris, quia rex in episcopis coertionem habet propter baroniam.'

is duly respected by the lay power—more than duly respected, [p. 463] some English churchmen may have thought, for thereby the wealthy excommunicate is often enabled to postpone to an indefinite date the evil day when he must go to prison or submit himself[1].

Excommunication and civil rights.　We have compared excommunication to outlawry; but, at least in this world, the consequences of the temporal were far more severe than those of the spiritual ban. The excommunicate forfeited none of those rights which were sanctioned by lay tribunals. He became incapable of asserting them by action; but the 'exception of excommunication' was only a dilatory, not a peremptory, plea, and the plaintiff might go on with his action so soon as he had made his peace with the church[2]. Despite their adoption of the bold phrase 'The excommunicate can do no act in law,' our secular judges seem to have thought that they had given sufficient aid to the spiritual power when they had shut their ears to the *funesta vox* of the church's outlaw[3]. They stopped short of declaring that he could not acquire rights or dispose of his property, but those, who knowing of his condition had dealings with him, were guilty of an offence which the ecclesiastical courts might punish if they pleased.

§ 10.　*Lepers, Lunatics and Idiots.*

The leper.　This would not be the place in which to speak at any length of the legal disability of those who are suffering from mental or bodily disease; but a few words should be said of lepers and of idiots. Bracton compares the excommunicate to the leper, and the leper is excommunicate in a very real sense. He is put outside the community of mankind; the place for him is the lazar house[4]. Not only is he incapable of suing and of making gifts or contracts, but he is even incapable of inheriting. He still remains the owner of what was his before his 'segregation,' but he can not inherit[5].

---

　　[1] Bracton, f. 426 b; Reg. Brev. Orig. f. 68.

　　[2] Bracton, f. 426 b; Lit. sec. 201.

　　[3] Bracton, f. 426 b; 'funestam enim vocem interdici oportet.'

　　[4] The Court Baron (Seld. Soc.), p. 134.

　　[5] Bracton, f. 12, 421; Select Civil Pleas, pl. 157; Note Book, pl. 807, 1648. For parallel and similar French law, see Viollet, Histoire du droit civil, p. 375.

[p. 464]　Among the insane our law draws a marked distinction; it The idiot. separates the lunatic from the idiot or born fool[1]. About the latter there is a curious story to be told. In Edward I.'s day the king claims a wardship of the lands of all natural fools, no matter of whom such lands may be holden. He is morally bound to maintain the idiots out of the income of their estates, but still the right is a profitable right analogous to the lord's wardship of an infant tenant. But there is reason to believe that this is a new right, or that at any rate there has been a struggle for it between the lords and the king. If idiocy be treated as similar to infancy, this analogy is in favour of the lords; at all events if the idiot be a military tenant, feudal principles would give the custody of his land not to the king, but to the lord, while of socage land some kinsman of the fool might naturally claim a wardship. Edward I. was told that by the law of Scotland the lord had the wardship of an idiot's land[2]. But in England a different rule had been established, and this, as we think, by some statute or ordinance made in the last days of Henry III. If we have rightly read an obscure tale, Robert Walerand, a minister, justice and favourite of the king, procured this ordinance foreseeing that he must leave an idiot as his heir and desirous that his land should fall rather into the king's hand than into the hands of his lords[3]. The king's right is distinctly stated in the document known as *Praerogativa Regis*, which we believe to come from the early years of Edward I. The same document seems to be the oldest that gives us any clear information about a wardship of The lunatics. The king is to provide that the lunatic and his lunatic. family are properly maintained out of the income of his estate, and the residue is to be handed over to him upon his restoration to sanity, or, should he die without having recovered his wits, is to be administered by the ordinary for the good of his soul; but the king is to take nothing to his own use[4]. Once more we see prerogatival rights growing, while feudal claims fall into the background; and in the case of lunacy we see a guardianship, a *mund*, which is not profitable to the guardian, and this at present is a novel and a noteworthy thing[5].

---

[1] Blackstone, Comm. i. 302.

[2] Memoranda de Parliamento, 33 Edw. I. (Rolls Ser.), p. 228.

[3] Maitland, Praerogativa Regis, E. H. R. vi. 369.

[4] Praerogativa Regis, c. 11, 12 (Statutes, i. 226).　　[5] See above, p. 322.

§ 11. *Women.*

Legal
position of
women.

We have been rapidly diminishing the number of 'normal persons,' of free and lawful men. We have yet to speak of half the inhabitants of England. No text-writer, no statute, ever makes any general statement as to the position of women[1]. This is treated as obvious, and we believe that it can be defined with some accuracy by one brief phrase :—private law with few exceptions puts women on a par with men ; public law gives a woman no rights and exacts from her no duties, save that of paying taxes and performing such services as can be performed by deputy.

Women in
private
law.

A very different doctrine is suggested by one ancient rule. A woman can never be outlawed, for a woman is never in law. We may well suppose this to come from a very remote time. But in Bracton's day it means nothing, for a woman, though she can not be outlawed, can be 'waived,' declared a 'waif,' and 'waiver' seems to have all the effects of outlawry[2]. Women are now 'in' all private law, and are the equals of men. The law of inheritance, it is true, shows a preference for males over females ; but not a very strong preference, for a daughter will exclude a brother of the dead man, and the law of wardship and marriage, though it makes some difference between the male and the female ward, is almost equally severe for both. But the woman can hold land, even by military tenure, can own chattels, make a will, make a contract, can sue and be sued. She sues and is sued in person without the interposition of a guardian ; she can plead with her own voice if she pleases ; indeed—and this is a strong case—a married woman will sometimes appear as her husband's attorney[3]. A widow will often be the guardian of her own children ; a lady will often be the guardian of the children of her tenants.

---

[1] Bracton, f. 5: 'Et differunt feminae a masculis in multis, quia earum deterior est conditio quam masculorum.' This comes from Azo, who gives many examples, while Bracton gives none.

[2] Bracton, f. 125 b; Britton, i. 50. This doctrine is connected with the rule that a woman can not be in frankpledge, and this probably implies or has implied that every woman is the mainpast of some man.

[3] Note Book, pl. 342, 1361, 1507.

[p.466] The other half of our proposition, that which excludes women from all public functions, was subject to few if any real exceptions. In the thirteenth century the question whether a woman could inherit the crown of England must have been extremely doubtful, for the Empress had never been queen of England. Queens-consort and queens-dowager had acted as regents during the absence of their husbands or sons and presided in court and council[1]. The line between office and property can not always be exactly marked; it has been difficult to prevent the shrievalties from becoming hereditary; if a woman may be a *comitissa*, why not a *vice-comitissa*[2]? Ornamental offices, hereditary grand serjeanties, women are allowed to carry to their husbands and to transmit to their heirs. So also, when the constitution of the House of Lords takes shape, the husbands of peeresses are summoned to sit there as 'tenants by the curtesy[3],' but peeresses are not summoned. 'The nearest approach to such a summons,' says Dr Stubbs, 'is that of four abbesses, who in 1306 were cited to a great council held to grant an aid on the knighting of the prince of Wales[4].'

Women in public law.

In the nineteenth century our courts have more than once considered the question whether women did suit to the local moots, more especially to the county court, and have come to what we think the right conclusion[5]. Undoubtedly a woman might owe suit to the hundred or the county[6], or rather (for this we think to be the truer phrase) the land that she held might owe suit. Also it is certain that some sheriffs in the latter part of Henry III.'s reign had insisted on the personal attendance of women, not indeed at the county courts, but at

Women in court.

---

[1] Already in D. B. i. 238 b we read of pleas 'coram regina Mathilde.'

[2] For several years under Henry III. Ela, countess of Salisbury, was sheriff of Wiltshire; see list of sheriffs in 31st Rep. of Deputy-Keeper. But in this case there was a claim to an hereditary shrievalty; Note Book, pl. 1235. The wife of Ranulf Glanvill, sheriff of Yorkshire, is called *Berta Vicecomitissa* in a charter: Round, Geoffrey de Mandeville, 385.

[3] Hargrave's note to Co. Lit. 29 a.

[4] Stubbs, Const. Hist. § 751. Rolls of Parliament, iv. 270 (A.D. 1425): the earl of Norfolk had issue Margaret his heir, 'to whom no place in Parlement myght apperteyne, by cause she was a woman.'

[5] *Chorlton* v. *Lings*, L. R. 4 C. P. 374; *Beresford-Hope* v. *Sandhurst*, 23 Q. B. D. 79.

[6] Rot. Hund. ii. 62: 'Domina J. le E. tenet W. . . . et facit sectam ad comitatum et hundredum.' One example among many.

those plenary meetings of the hundred courts that were known as the sheriff's turns. But it is equally certain that this exaction was regarded as an abuse and forbidden[1]. We can [p. 467] not doubt, though the evidence on this point is rather tacit than express, that women did the suit due from their land by deputy. Again, we never find women as jurors, except when, as not unfrequently happened, some expectant heir alleged that there was a plot to supplant him by the production of a supposititious child, in which case a jury of matrons was employed[2]. To say that women could not be jurors is in this period almost equivalent to saying that they could not give evidence, but their names sometimes appear among the witnesses of charters[3]. In all actions a plaintiff had to produce a suit (*secta*) of persons who in theory were prepared to testify on his behalf; we can not find that he ever brought women. One of the actions in which such 'suitors' were of importance was the action for deciding whether a person was free or villein, and here Britton expressly tells us that a woman's testimony was not received, 'for the blood of a man shall not be tried by women'; the word of women, we are elsewhere told, can not be admitted as proof, 'because of their frailty[4].' In the ecclesiastical courts the rule seems to have been that a woman's compurgators

---

[1] The Provisions of 1259, c. 10 (Stat. i. 9), say that the prelates, barons, earls, 'nec [*al.* vel] aliqui religiosi [*al. ins.* viri] seu mulieres' need not attend the turn unless specially summoned. The reading of the Close differs slightly from that of the Patent Roll. The Statute of Marlborough, c. 10 (Stat. i. 22), repeats this with a small variation; the persons who need not attend are the prelates, earls, barons, 'nec aliqui *viri* religiosi seu mulieres.' The question has been raised whether in this last passage *mulieres* is governed by *religiosi*. In any case we should have answered this in the negative, but a comparison of the various texts seems to make this plain; in one version of the Provisions there is no *viri*. The term *religiosi* was often used as a substantive. The whole section has the air of dealing with a modern abuse, for the turn is to be held as in the time of the king's ancestors. The reference to a special summons means this, that the persons exempted from doing suit to the turn may none the less have to go to it for the purpose of defending actions that are pending in the hundred court, or of answering the accusations which the presenting jurors bring against them.

[2] Bracton, f. 69; Note Book, pl. 198.

[3] Cart. Rievaulx, p. 62: five men and six women, including Ranulf Glanvill and his wife, witness a widow's gift.

[4] Britton, i. 207: 'de sicum saunc de homme ne peut, ne deit, estre tryé par femmes'; Fleta, 111–2; Fitz. Abr. *Villenage*, pl. 37 (13 Edw. I.); Northumberland Assize Rolls (Surtees Soc.), p. 275.

ought to be women[1], just as a man's compurgators ought to be men, but apparently in the king's court a woman had to find [p 468] male oath-helpers[2]. In one respect a woman's capacity of suing was curtailed by her inability to fight. A rule older than, but sanctioned by, the Great Charter prevented her from bringing an appeal of felony unless the crime of which she complained was violence to her person or the slaughter of her husband[3]. In these excepted cases the accused must submit to trial by jury; at an earlier time one or other of the parties would have been sent to the ordeal[4]. In the thirteenth century this limitation of the right to make criminal charges was already becoming of little importance, since the procedure by way of appeal (that is, of private accusation) was giving place to the indictment.

On the whole we may say that, though it has no formulated *Summary.* theory about the position of women, a sure instinct has already guided the law to a general rule which will endure until our own time. As regards private rights women are on the same level as men, though postponed in the canons of inheritance; but public functions they have none. In the camp, at the council board, on the bench, in the jury box there is no place for them[5].

We have been speaking of women who are sole, who are *Married* spinsters or widows. Women who have husbands are in a *women.* different position. This, however, can be best discussed as part of family law, and under that title we shall also say what has to be said of infants. But here it may be well to observe that the main idea which governs the law of husband and wife is not that of an 'unity of person,' but that of the guardianship, the *mund*, the profitable guardianship, which the husband has over the wife and over her property.

---

[1] Rolls of Parliament, i. 146–7.

[2] Note Book, pl. 7: 'Lex de masculis si femina defendat.'

[3] Glanvill, lib. xiv. c. 1, 3. 6; Select Pleas of the Crown, i. pl. 32; Charter of 1215, c. 54; Bracton, f. 148. It is often said that the woman must allege that her husband was slain 'within her arms.' This seems to be only a picturesque 'common form.'

[4] Glanv. xiv. 3.

[5] In the version of Glanvill's treatise given by MS. Camb. Univ. Mm. i. 27, f. 31 b, it is remarked that women can never essoin themselves as being on the king's service, 'quia non possunt nec debent nec solent esse in servitio domini Regis in exercitu nec in aliis servitiis regalibus.'

§ 12.　*Corporations and Churches*[1].　　[p. 469]

The cor-
poration.

Every system of law that has attained a certain degree of
maturity seems compelled by the ever-increasing complexity
of human affairs to create persons who are not men, or rather
(for this may be a truer statement) to recognize that such
persons have come and are coming into existence, and to
regulate their rights and duties. In the history of medieval
Europe we have to watch on the one hand the evolution of
groups (in particular, religious groups and groups of burgesses)
which in our eyes seem to display all or many of the characteristics of corporations, and on the other hand the play of
thought around that idea of an *universitas* which was being
slowly discovered in the Roman law books.

Analysis
of the cor-
poration.

We have become so familiar with the idea of 'a corporation
aggregate of many' that we have ceased to wonder at it.
When we are told by statute that the word 'person' is to
include 'body politic,' that seems to us a very natural rule[2].
Nevertheless, this idea was gradually fashioned, and when
we attempt to analyze it we find that it is an elastic because
it is, if we may so say, a very contentless idea, a blank form
of legal thought. Little enough in common have the divers
corporations known to English law: for example, the Ecclesiastical Commissioners for England; the Dean and Chapter of
Ely; the Chancellor, Masters and Scholars of the University
of Oxford; the Mayor, Aldermen and Burgesses of the Borough
of Cambridge; the Governor and Company of the Bank of
England; the Great Northern Railway Company; Styles, Nokes
and Company (Limited). Among 'natural persons' the law
for a long time past has been able to single out one class as [p. 470]
being normal or typical and to treat other classes as exceptional; and to this we may add that in course of time some of
the exceptional classes disappear; the noble class disappears,
the unfree class disappears. Far otherwise is it with the

---

[1] A repeated perusal of Dr Gierke's great book, Das deutsche Genossenschaftsrecht, Berlin, 1868–81, has occasioned many changes in this section,
which in the first edition bore the title *Fictitious Persons*. See also Gierke,
Deutsches Privatrecht, vol. i.

[2] Interpretation Act 1889 (52 & 53 Vic. c. 63) sec. 2. 19.

'artificial persons' or 'group-persons'; we can hardly call one
corporation more normal than another and modern legislation
is constantly supplying us with new kinds. Thus we are not
likely to find the essence of a corporation in any one rule of
law. If, for example, an English lawyer would make all turn
on the common seal, he would be setting up a merely English
rule as a necessary maxim of jurisprudence; nor only so, for
he would be begging an important question about the early
history of corporations in England. Some again may feel
inclined to say that a corporation must have its origin in
a special act of the State, for example, in England a royal
charter; but they again will be in danger of begging a question about ancient history, while they will have difficulty in
squaring their opinion with the modern history of joint-stock
companies. Modern legislation enables a small group of private
men to engender a corporation by registration, and to urge
that this is the effect of 'statute' and not of 'common law'
is to insist upon a distinction which we hardly dare carry
beyond the four seas. Or, to come to a more vital point, shall
we demand that an individual corporator shall not be liable
for the debts of the corporation? 'Si quid universitati debetur singulis non debetur; nec quod debet universitas singuli
debent[1]'—is not this the very core of the matter? Once more
modern legislation bids us pause:—there is no reason why a
statute should not say that a judgment obtained against a
corporation can be enforced against all the lands and all the
goods of every single corporator, and this although the corporation still exists:—in ordering that this be so, the legislature does not contradict itself[2]. Nor again is it only from
modern statute, that we receive this warning; our ancient
[p. 471] common law gives us the same warning in unmistakable
terms. If we insist that common law can not hold the *singuli*
liable for the debt of the *universitas*, we shall find little to say
about corporations in any century earlier than the fifteenth.

Hitherto the lesson that we have been taking to ourselves **Beginnings**
is that we are not to deny the presence of the idea of a **of cor-**
porateness.
corporation merely because it is not producing all of what we

---

[1] Dig. 3. 4, 7.

[2] In the first half of this century our parliament tried many experiments of
this kind. See for example the Act for the Registration of Joint-Stock
Companies, 7 & 8 Vic. c. 110, sec. 25, 66.

consider its natural effects. The warning is equally necessary
that in remote times we may somewhat easily discover corporations that never existed. The history of the earlier part of
our own century proves that large commercial enterprises may
be conducted and much done in the way of subordinate government by aggregates of men that are not incorporated. The
law of tenancy in common and joint tenancy, the law of
partnership, these have been found equal to many heavy and
novel demands. And when we turn to a far-off past we may
be in great danger of too readily seeing a corporation in some
group of landholders, which, if modern distinctions are to be
applied at all, would be better classed as a group of joint
tenants than as a corporation.

Personality of the corporation.

The core of the matter seems to be that for more or less
numerous purposes some organized group of men[1] is treated as
an unit which has rights and duties other than the rights and
duties of all or any of its members. What is true of this
whole need not be true of the sum of its parts, and what is
true of the sum of the parts need not be true of the whole.
The corporation, for example, can own land and its land will
not be owned by the sum of the corporators; and, on the other
hand, if all the corporators are co-owners of a thing, then
that thing is not owned by the corporation. This being so,
lawyers from the thirteenth century onwards have been wont to
attribute to the corporation a 'personality' that is 'fictitious'
or 'artificial.' Now 'person' and 'personality' seem to be
appropriate words, and, if they were not at our disposal, we
should be driven to coin others of a similar import[2]. The
corporate unit has become a subject of rights and duties. On
the other hand, the adjectives which are often used to qualify
this personality are open to serious objection, since they seem
to speak to us of some trick or exploit performed by lawyers
and to suggest a wide departure of legal theory from fact and
common opinion. It may at least be plausibly maintained
that the subject of those rights and duties which we ascribe
to the corporation is no figment but the organized group of
men, though this group is treated as pure unit. Unless all
social and political organization deserves to be called fictitious,

---

[1] We neglect for a while that unhappy freak of English law the corporation
sole.

[2] Such as the German *Rechtssubject, Rechtssubjectivität.*

a contract between a municipal corporation and a joint-stock company is not a relationship between two fictions; it is a relationship between two groups, but between two groups each of which is so organized that for the purpose of the matter in hand, and for many other purposes, it can be treated as an indivisible unit and compared to a man.

One of the difficulties that beset us at this point is that we are tempted or compelled to seek the aid of those inadequate analogies that are supplied to us by the objects which we see and handle. First we picture to ourselves a body made up of men as a man's body is made up of members. Then we find ourselves rejecting some of the inferences which this similitude, this crude anthropomorphism[1], might suggest. For instance, we have to admit that every 'member' may be injured while the whole 'body' suffers no injury. And then perhaps we say in our haste that the corporation which has rights and duties can be no better than fiction or artifice. But all that is proved by the collapse of such analogical reasoning is that social organization differs from, if it also resembles, that organization which the biologist studies; and this should hardly need proof. *The anthropomorphic picture of a corporation.*

Were we to digress to modern times, we might be able to show that the theory which speaks of the corporation's personality as fictitious, a theory which English lawyers borrowed from medieval canonists, has never suited our English law very well. It should at all events be known that on the continent of Europe this doctrine no longer enjoys an undisputed orthodoxy either among the students of the Roman *universitas*[2] or among the students of medieval and modern corporations. But here we are dealing with a time when in our own country the need for any idea of a corporation, whether as *persona ficta* or as 'group-person,' has hardly become evident. *Is the personality fictitious?*

[p. 473] Now if for a moment we take our stand in Edward IV.'s reign, when the middle ages are nearing their end, we can say that the idea of a corporation is already in the minds of our lawyers; it may trouble them,—this is shown by their *The corporation at the end of the middle ages.*

[1] For some anthropomorphic vagaries of the middle ages, see Gierke, D. G. R. iii. 549.

[2] Gierke, D. G. R. iii. 132.

frequent discussions about its nature—but still it is there[1]. First we notice that they already have a term for it, namely, *corporacion*, for which *corps corporat* and *corps politik* are equivalents. Then under this term several entities which have little in common have been brought: in particular, abbot and convent, dean and chapter, mayor and commonalty. With such 'incorporated bodies' they contrast aggregates of men that are not incorporated, townships, parishes, gilds[2]. They demand that incorporatedness shall have some definite and authoritative commencement; the corporation does not grow by nature; it must be made, by the act of parliament, or of the king, or of the pope[3], though prescription may be equivalent to royal charter. The rule that the corporation can do no act save by a writing under its common seal they enforce with severity; it is an anomaly, a concession to practical necessities, that the commands of the corporation about petty affairs can come to its servants through less formal channels[4]. The corporation is invisible, incorporeal, immortal; it can not be assaulted, or beaten or imprisoned; it can not commit treason; a doubt has occurred as to whether it can commit a [p. 474] trespass[5], but this doubt (though it will give trouble so late as the year 1842[6]) has been rejected by practice, if not removed by any consistent theory[7]. We even find it said that the corporation is but a name[8]. On the other hand, it is a

---

[1] See the Year Books of Edward IV. in general, but especially the great case *Abbot of St Benet's (Hulme)* v. *Mayor and Commonalty of Norwich*, four times reported, Y. B. 21 Edw. IV. f. 7, 12, 27, 67.

[2] Y. B. 20 Edw. IV. f. 2 (Pasch. pl. 7): an unincorporated gild or fraternity. 12 Hen. VII. f. 27 (Trin. pl. 7): 'feffement fuit fait al oeps de paroissiens que n'est nule corporacion.'

[3] Y. B. 14 Hen. VIII. f. 3 (Mich. pl. 2); dean and chapter, mayor and commonalty are incorporated by the king; the mendicant friars by the pope; abbot and convent by both king and pope.

[4] Y. B. 4 Hen. VII. f. 6 (Pasch. pl. 2); 4 Hen. VII. f. 17 (Mich. pl. 7); 7 Hen. VII. f. 9 (Hil. pl. 2); 7 Hen. VII. f. 16 (Trin. pl. 3).

[5] Lib. Ass. ann. 22, f. 100, pl. 67.

[6] *Maund* v. *Monmouthshire Canal Company*, 4 Manning and Granger's Reports, 452.

[7] *Abp. of York* v. *Mayor etc. of Hull*, Y. B. 45 Edw. III. f. 2 (Hil. pl. 5); Y. B. 8 Hen. VI. f. 1 (Mich. pl. 2); Y. B. 18 Hen. VI. f. 11 (Trin. pl. 1); Y. B. 32 Hen. VI. f. 8 (Mich. pl. 13).

[8] Y. B. 21 Edw. IV. f. 13 (Mich. pl. 4): 'le corporacion de eux n'est que un nosme, que ne poit my estre vieu, et n'est my substance, e a ceo nosme ou corps est impossible de faire un tort.'

person[1]. It is at once a person and yet but a name; in short, it is *persona ficta*.

The main difficulty that the lawyers have in manipulating this idea is occasioned by the fact that almost every corporation has a 'head,' which head is separately and expressly designated by the formal title of the juristic person. It is regarded as an anomaly that at Ripon there should be a corporation of canons without a head[2]; normally there is a head; the ideal person is not the Convent of St Albans, the Chapter of Lincoln, the Commonalty of Norwich, but the Abbot and Convent of St Albans, the Dean and Chapter of Lincoln, the Mayor, Sheriffs and Commonalty of Norwich. This keeps alive the anthropomorphic idea. In 1481 a puzzling question arose as to whether when a dean and chapter brought an action, a juror might be challenged on the ground that he was brother to one of the canons. An advocate who urges that the juror is 'a stranger to the chapter, for it is a body of such a nature that it can have neither brother nor cousin,' none the less concedes that peradventure it might have been otherwise had the juror been brother to the dean[3]. Elsewhere the relation between dean and chapter is compared to that between husband and wife; 'the chapter is *covert* by the dean as the wife is *coverte* by her husband[4].' From the same year, 1481, we get one of [p. 475] the most interesting cases in all the Year Books[5]:—The Abbot of Holme sued the Mayor, Sheriffs and Commonalty of Norwich on a bond, and they pleaded that when the bond was made the then abbot had got the then mayor in prison and extorted the bond by duress[6]. The lawyers very generally admit that the corporation itself can not be in prison or suffer duress, and that it would be no defence to urge that when the bond was made some few of the citizens of Norwich were (as they generally would be) in gaol. But then in this case 'the head' of the corporation was incarcerated. 'I tell you, Sir,' says counsel

The corporation and its head. Anthropomorphism.

---

[1] Y. B. 32 Hen. VI. f. 9 (Mich. pl. 13): 'ils sont per cest nosme un person corporate'; Y. B. 21 Edw. IV. f. 32 (Pasch. pl. 28) per Catesby.

[2] Y. B. 18 Hen. VI. f. 16 (Trin. pl. 4); Y. B. 21 Edw. IV. f. 28 (Pasch. pl. 22). Compare what is said of the Canons of Southwell in *Sutton's Hospital Case*, 10 Coke's Reports, 30 b.

[3] Y. B. 21 Edw. IV. f. 31 (Pasch. pl. 28), f. 63 (Mich. pl. 33).

[4] Y. B. 2 Hen. VI. f. 9 (Pasch. pl. 6) per Rolf.

[5] Y. B. 21 Edw. IV. f. 7, 12, 27, 67.

[6] For the facts of this interesting case, see Green, Town Life, ii. 391.

for the city[1], 'that every body politic is made up of natural men. And as regards what has been said touching its inseverability, I do not admit that; for they allow that mayor, sheriffs and commonalty make up a single body; here then are members, namely, the mayor is one member...the sheriffs another member...the third is the commonalty...In this case there is an alleged imprisonment of one of the distinct members named in the title of the corporation, to wit, the mayor, who is the head and (as in a body natural) the principal member... and if one member of the body natural be restrained or beaten, that is a restraint or battery of the whole body.' This idea that a corporation consists of head and members, that every act of the corporation requires the assent of its head, that, if for a while it is headless, it is capable of no act save that of electing a new head, has given trouble in more recent times and is perhaps capable of giving trouble even at the present day[2]; it is a relic of what we have called anthropomorphism. In Edward IV.'s day we are told[3] that the Mayor and Commonalty of Newcastle gave a bond to the person who happened to be mayor, naming him by his personal name. It was held void, for a man can not be bound to himself. So long as such a decision for such a reason is possible, the modern idea of a corporation is not secure; at any rate it is hampered by an inconsistent and older idea. Still in the Year Books of Edward IV. that idea is present, nay, prominent, and some [p. 476] important rules of law in which it is implied have already been settled. In particular it is established that if the corporation becomes liable upon contract or for tort, this does not give a remedy against the persons, lands or goods of the corporators; the corporation itself is liable; execution will be done only on its lands and its goods.

The corporation vanishes as we pursue it.

We go back but a little way in the Year Books and the idea that we have been watching begins to disappear. The figure of the ideal person vanishes, or rather it seems at times to become a mere mass of natural persons. One instance will

[1] Y. B. 21 Edw. IV. f. 69.

[2] See Grant on Corporations, p. 110, where it is said that 'if the master of a college devise lands to the college, they cannot take, because at the moment of his death they are an incomplete body.' But in 1333 an abbot was successfully sued upon a bond given by prior and convent during a vacancy: Y. B. 7 Edw. III. f. 35 (Trin. pl. 35).

[3] Y. B. 21 Edw. IV. f. 15, f. 68, per Vivisour.

serve to illustrate this change. So late as 1429 an action of trespass was brought against the Mayor, Bailiffs and Commonalty of Ipswich and one J. Jabe[1]. The defendants pleaded the marvellous plea that Jabe was one of the commonalty and therefore was named twice over. If the defendants are found guilty, then (it was urged) Jabe will be charged twice over; besides he may be found not guilty and the commonalty guilty: that is to say, he may be found both guilty and not guilty. We do not know how the case was decided; but it was twice discussed. Incidentally a fundamental question of corporation law was raised. Suppose that judgment is given against the commonalty, can the goods of the members be taken in execution? On the whole the judges think that they can not, but are not very sure. They make an admission of great importance to us, namely, that it is the common course in the King's Bench that if a community be amerced, the amercement shall be levied from all the goods of the members of the community[2]. The obvious tendency of this admission they seek to avoid by saying that there is a great difference between the king and anyone else. As we shall hereafter see this admission was unavoidable; the goods of the members of municipal communities were constantly treated as liable to satisfy the king for debts due by the community as a whole. And a mere doubt about the general principle of corporate [p. 477] liability occurring at so late a date as 1429 is remarkable[3]. We have indeed observed before now that the non-liability of individual corporators for the debts of the corporation can not be regarded as of the essence of a corporation. Still unless such non-liability had been common, the modern idea of a corporation would hardly have been formed.

In all this there is nothing to surprise us. Surprising it would have been had the English lawyers of Bracton's day obtained a firm hold of the notion of an *universitas*. In that case they would have been ahead of their Italian contemporaries, who had Code and Digest to set them thinking. It

Gradual appearance of the group-person.

---

[1] Y. B. 8 Hen. VI. f. 1 (Mich. pl. 2); f. 14 (Mich. pl. 34).

[2] The words are ' sera levie de touts biens etc.'; it is clear from the context that this means 'shall be levied from all the goods of the members.'

[3] In 1437 it is said that if a man recovers debt or damages against a commonalty he shall only have execution against the goods that they have in common; Fitz. Abr. *Execution*, pl. 128, citing an unprinted Y. B. of Mich. 16 Hen. VI.

would be a mistake to suppose that what we are wont to consider the true theory of *universitates* lay so plainly written on the face of the Roman law-books that no one could read them attentively without grasping it. The glossators did not grasp it. Bracton's master Azo had not grasped it. They were by no means certain about the difference between the *universitas* and the *societas* or partnership. The canonists of the thirteenth century were just beginning to proclaim that the *universitas* is a *persona* and a *persona ficta*. Bracton's contemporary, Pope Innocent IV. (Sinibaldus Fliscus), has been called the father of the modern theory of corporations. We now begin to hear the dogma (of which all English lawyers know a vulgar version) that the *universitas* can be punished neither in this world nor in the next, for that it has nor soul nor body. And yet, when these steps had been taken, many an elementary question lay open for the civilians and canonists[1].

The law of Bracton's time

This premised, we turn to the law of Henry III.'s day, for [p. 478] the purpose of hearing what it has to say (1) of corporations in general, and (2) of the more important kinds into which corporations may be divided. But at once we discover that of corporations in general little is said, and the law is not dividing corporations into various kinds, thus proceeding from the abstract to the concrete; rather it is slowly coming to the idea of a corporation by dealing with corporations (if so we may call them) of very different kinds.

The communitas.

In the first place we can find in our law-books no such terms as *corporation, body corporate, body politic*, though we may read much of *convents, chapters*, and *communities*. The largest term in general use is *community, commonalty*, or *commune*, in Latin *communitas* or *communa*. It is a large, vague word; in the fourteenth century it is often applied to the English nation, 'the community' or 'the commune of the land'; it is applied to the Cistercian order[2]; it is applied to the University of Cambridge, for 'in the vill of Cambridge there are two communes, one of clerks and one of lay men[3]';

---

[1] See Gierke, D. G. R. especially vol. iii. pp. 202–6, 227–85. Innocent says, 'cum collegium in causa universitatis fingatur una persona.' Johannes Andreae says, 'universitas non est capax poenae capitalis, corporalis, spiritualis . . . . cum corpus animatum non habeat ad hoc aptum.' The amusing question was discussed whether a corporation could be a godmother.

[2] Rot. Parl. i. 420.   [3] Rot. Parl. ii. 47.

it can be applied to 'the community of merchants who hold the king's staple of wools[1]'; it was applied to the 'bachelors' of England who in 1259 had joined together to obtain concessions from the king[2]. But we dare not translate it by *corporation,* for if on the one hand it is describing cities and boroughs which already are, or at least are on their way to become, corporations, it will stand equally well for counties, hundreds and townships, which in the end have failed to acquire a corporate character, and we should be unwilling to suppose that the corporate character once definitely acquired was afterwards lost. One term there was (so it may seem to us) capable of binding together all the groups of men that were personified, namely, the word *universitas.* But its fate has been curious and instructive. In our modern languages the Roman term that most nearly answered to our *corporation* stands for the corporations of one small class, the learned corporations that were founded in the twelfth and thirteenth centuries and others that in later days were fashioned after [p. 479] their likeness. These were in the middle ages the corporations by preeminence, and if the universities of Oxford and Cambridge cared to assert that they are the oldest of English corporations something might be said in favour of their claim. For the rest, the word *universitas* is of common use in legal documents; but only in one context, and one which shows how vague a term it could be. The maker of a charter salutes 'All the faithful in Christ,' or 'All the sons of Holy Church,' and then requests their attention by *Noverit universitas vestra.* Now the idea of the Church as the mystical body of Christ has had an important influence on the growth of the law of corporations; it did much towards fashioning for us the anthropomorphic picture of the many members in one body. Still in days when the word *universitas* was put to its commonest use in describing a world-wide, divinely created organization, it could be of small service to lawyers as an accurate word of art.

Bracton has a little to say about *universitates*; it is meagre, it is vague, it is for the more part borrowed from Azo, but none the less it is instructive. In the first place, the cities and boroughs are the only examples of *universitates* which

Bracton and the universitas.

---

[1] Rot. Parl. ii. 191.

[2] Ann. Burton, 471: 'communitas bacheleriae Angliae.'

occur to him. In the second place, following the Institutes[1], he admits that there are *res universitatis* which are to be contrasted with *res singulorum*. Thirdly, no definite examples of *res universitatis* does he give save those that are given by the Institutes, namely, the *theatrum* and *stadium*. The inference is obvious that, though he allowed the possibility of an *universitas* holding land, he knew little of the English city or borough as a landowner; it is not in his manner to give Roman examples when he can give English, while as to our medieval boroughs having *stadia et theatra*, that is nonsense. Fourthly, he knows that if the English *universitas*, the city or borough, has but little land and few goods, it has magnificent *libertates*, franchises, governmental powers and immunities, and these are a common subject of litigation. Fifthly, when he speaks of such litigation he speaks vaguely, and hardly distinguishes between the *universitas* and the aggregate of *singuli*. Sixthly, he nowhere makes an act of royal or public power necessary to the existence of an *universitas*. Lastly, he does [p. 480] not bring any ecclesiastical bodies under this heading; they fall within another form of thought[2].

---

[1] Inst. 2. 1. 6: 'Universitatis sunt, non singulorum, veluti quae in civitatibus sunt, ut theatra, stadia et similia et si qua alia sunt communia civitatium.'

[2] Bracton, f. 8: 'Universitatis vero sunt, non singulorum, quae sunt in civitatibus, ut theatrum, stadia et huiusmodi et si qua sunt in civitatibus communia.' Ibid. f. 180 b: 'Item videre debent [iuratores in assisa novae disseisinae] utrum tenementum fuerit sacrum et deo dedicatum, vel quasi sacrum, sicut publicum, vel universitatis ut stadium, theatrum, muri et portae civitatum' (the *muri* and *portae* are from Inst. 2. 1. 10). Ibid. f. 207 b: 'Item tenementorum quoddam nec sacrum, nec sanctum, sed publicum alicuius, scilicet universitatis vel communionis vel omnium et non alicuius hominis privati vel singularis, sicut sunt theatra et stadia vel loca publica, sive sunt in civitatibus vel extra.' Ibid. f. 228 b: 'Item [servitus poterit esse] personalis tantum ... item localis et non certis personis sicut alicuius universitatis, burgensium et civium, et omnes conqueri possunt et unus sub nomine universitatis' (this concerning 'servitudes,' in particular common of pasture). Ibid. f. 56 b: 'Item esto quod dominus rex (here we come to something practical), duobus concesserit aliquam libertatem, ut si alicui universitati, sicut civibus vel burgensibus vel aliquibus aliis quod mercatum habeant vel feriam in villa sua, civitate, vel burgo ... si postmodum concedat consimilem libertatem aliquibus in regno suo ... secundum quod praedictum est videndum erit qui illorum praeferri debeant in tali libertate.' Ibid. f. 102: a real action may be brought 'nomine alicuius universitatis sicut in rem communem.' Ibid. f. 171 b, if the king errs the 'universitas regni et baronagium' may perhaps correct his errors 'in curia domini Regis.' The passage on f. 8 in which Bracton draws a

Being unable to find any theory about corporations in general, we are obliged to descend to the various kinds of corporations: to consider, that is, the manner in which the law of the thirteenth century treated those various groups of men which seem to us to have a more or less corporate existence. They are either ecclesiastical or temporal. No law as yet for cor- porations in general.

For many centuries before Bracton's day there have been in England what we may call 'church lands[1].' In some sort or another they have 'belonged' to 'churches.' But to fashion a satisfactory theory as to the ownership of these lands has been a task beset by practical and intellectual difficulties. The scheme of church-property-law which had prevailed in the Roman world before the German deluge had been a system of centralized and official administration. All the ecclesiastical property within a diocese was under the control and at the disposal of a single officer, the bishop of the *civitas*. His powers were very large; his subordinates, the diocesan clergy, received the stipends that he allowed them. Such a scheme was adapted only to an age that was far advanced in commerce and orderly government, and we may doubt whether it served even as an ideal in England where the thread of ecclesiastical tradition had been broken. It implies an easy transmission of wealth and messages from place to place; it was thoroughly civic and could not be maintained in a world of villages and manors inhabited by rude barbarians. If there is to be much Christianity in the land, not only must there be village churches, but the village church must be a proprietary centre, an economically self-sufficing institution. Church lands.

Then, as we are beginning to understand, the German has brought with him into the Roman and Christian world the notion that, if he builds a church upon his land, it is his church. If in the days of heathenry he had built a god-house on his land, it would have been his god-house, and he would have made profit out of it[2]. This is the origin of ecclesiastical The owned church.

distinction between two kinds of *res universitatis* is horribly mangled in the printed text (for *usualia* read *alia*). See Bracton and Azo, pp. 87, 90, 95.

[1] As to the whole of this matter, see Stutz, Geschichte des kirchlichen Benefizialwesens, Berlin, 1895, and the review by Hinschius of this important book in Zeitschrift d. Sav.-Stift., Germ. Abt. xvii. 135. Also see Dr Stutz's brilliant lecture Die Eigenkirche, Berlin, 1895.

[2] Stutz, Benefizialwesen, i. 89. Some information about this matter comes from Iceland.

patronage. The right which from the twelfth century onwards appears as a mere right of patronage, an *advocatio* or advowson, is in origin an ownership of the soil upon which the church stands and an ownership of any lands or goods that have been set apart for the sustenance of a priest who offers sacrifice at the shrine. By slow degrees, which are now being traced, this church-founder and his heirs have to be taught that they can not do just what they like with their own; and, for example, that they can not have their church worked for them by ordained slaves. The bishop will not consecrate the altar unless a sufficient provision of worldly goods is secured for the priest. The owner or patron, whichever we call him, must hand over the church and an appurtenant glebe to the priest by way of 'loan.' In modern England it is in this context and this context only that we still know, though only in name, the 'land-loan' of the old Frankish world: the parson still has a 'benefice,' a *beneficium*. It is long before the founder's ownership is whittled down to patronage. We may be fairly sure that the famous ceorl who throve to thegn-right by 'having' five hides of his own land, 'church and kitchen, bell-house and burhgeat,' was conceived to 'have' the church in no very different sense from that in which he 'had' the bell-house and the kitchen[1]. In Domesday Book the village church is apt to appear as an owned thing if also as an owning person: 'There are here a church and seven serfs and one mill': 'There are here a chapel and three serfs and one mill': 'There is one chapel which renders eight shillings[2]': 'Culling the burgess has a church of St Mary of 26 acres, Leofstan the priest has a church of St Augustin of 11 acres, Leoflet a free woman had a church of St Laurence of 12 acres[3].' Even Bracton must complain that the layman will talk of giving a church when he means that he is giving an advowson[4]. Hence the strongly proprietary element that there is in the right of patronage, an element of which the 'religious' take full advantage when they engulf the parish churches in the property of their minsters. Modern ecclesiastical reformers who would curtail such rights as the patron still enjoys may fairly say that they

---

[1] Schmid, Gesetze, p. 388.
[2] D. B. i. 34 b, 35.
[3] D. B. ii. 290 b.
[4] Bracton, f. 53.

are consummating the work of a thousand years; but they should not talk of 'restoration[1].'

The early history of church-property in England has never yet been written, and we can not aspire to write it. We do not, for example, know how the parish church became an owning unit with rights distinct from those of the bishop and his cathedral church on the one hand and from those of the founder or patron on the other. But there is a supernatural element in the story. Great changes take place behind a mystic veil. At least for the purposes of popular thought and speech, God and the saints become the subjects of legal rights, if not of legal duties. 'God's property and the church's twelve fold':—such were the first written words of English law. In the old land-books this notion is put before us in many striking phrases. In the oldest of them the newly converted Æthelbert says, 'To thee Saint Andrew and to thy [p. 481] church at Rochester where Justus the Bishop presides do I give a portion of my land[2].' The saint is the owner; his church at this place or that is mentioned because it is necessary to show of which of his many estates the gift is to form part. If a man will give land to the chief of the Apostles he should give it to St Peter and his church at Gloucester, or to St Peter and his church at Westminster; Justinian himself had been obliged to establish a rule for the interpretation of testaments by which the Saviour or some archangel or martyr was nominated heir and no church or monastery was named[3]. The Anglo-Saxon charters and Domesday Book seem to suppose even a physical connexion between the land given to a saint and the particular church with which it is, or is to be, legally connected; geography must yield to law; the acres may be remote from the hallowed spot, nevertheless they 'lie in the [p. 482] church[4].' Just as the earl or thegn may have many manors

---

[1] It is not contended that as regards every parish church this is the history of its advowson. The *Eigenkirche* (the owned church) begins to affect the whole system of law, and the bishop's power over churches that perhaps had never been owned now begins to look proprietary; they are 'his' churches. So too kings assert a patronage over ancient cathedrals, and the emperor may even wish to treat the church of Rome as 'his' church.

[2] Kemble, Cod. Dipl. No. 1; Stubbs and Haddan, iii. 52.

[3] Cod. 1. 2 (de SS. Ecclesiis), 26. The form came down from the pagan classical law; 'Deos heredes instituere non possumus praeter eos quos senatus-consulto constitutionibusve principum instituere concessum est, sicuti Iovem Tarpeium' etc. Ulp. Reg. xxii. § 6.

[4] Gierke, ii. pp. 542—5. See *e.g.* Kemble, Cod. Dipl. No. 847: 'ic wille ꝥæt

and a piece of land remote from the manorial centre may 'lie in' or 'be of' one of those manors, so the saint will have many churches each with land belonging to it. Gradually (if we may so speak) the saint retires behind his churches; the church rather than the saint is thought of as the holder of lands and chattels. When it comes to precise legal thinking the saint is an impracticable person, for if we ascribe rightful we may also have to ascribe wrongful possession to him, and from this we shrink, though Domesday Book courageously charges St Paul with an 'invasion' of land that is not his own[1]. But how is the church conceived? In the first instance very grossly as a structure of wood and stone. Land belongs to a church, is an appurtenance of a church, just as other land belongs to or is appurtenant to some hall or dwelling-house. But, as the saint retires, the idea of the church is spiritualized; it becomes a person and, we may say, an ideal, juristic person.

The saint's administrators.

All this while there are human beings who are directing the affairs of the saint and the church, receiving, distributing, enjoying the produce of the land. They are the saint's administrators; they are the *rectores* of his church. Some of them, notably the bishops, since their powers of administration are very large, may be spoken of as landholders; but still the land which the bishop has as bishop is hardly his own; when he demands it, he demands it not *ut ius suum*, but *ut ius ecclesiae suae*.

Illustrations from Domesday Book.

Very often in Domesday Book the saint is the landowner; Saint Paul holds land, Saint Constantine holds land, the Count of Mortain holds land of Saint Petroc[2]. Leofstan held land under 'the glorious king Edmund[3].' Often a particular *ecclesia*, or an *abbatia*, holds land. Sometimes the land is described as that of the saint, but the church is said to hold it[4]; sometimes this relation is reversed, the land is the land of

---

ðæt land æt Merseham . . . ligce into Cristes circean on Cantwarabyrig.' D. B. i. 91 b: 'in aecclesia Carentone iacet una hida et dimidia . . . in aecclesia de Curi est dimidia hida.' Ibid. 210 b: 'Haec terra fuit in aecclesia S. Benedicti.'

[1] D. B. ii. 13: 'Aliam Nessetocham tenuit Turstinus Ruffus . . . modo Sanctus Paulus invasit.' We might compare this to those phrases current at Oxford and Cambridge which tell how Magdalene has won a cricket match and the like; but there is less of conscious abbreviation in the one case than in the other.

[2] D. B. i. 121.   [3] D. B. ii. 416 b.

[4] D. B. i. 104: 'Terra S. Stefani de Cadomo: Ecclesia Cadomonensis tenet de Rege Northam.'

[p. 483] the church but the saint holds it[1]. Often, again, the land is spoken of as that of the ruler of the church; this is frequently the case when a bishop is concerned:—the land is the land of the Bishop of Exeter and the Bishop of Exeter holds it. Still this is no invariable rule; the church of Worcester, an episcopal church, has lands and St Mary of Worcester holds them[2]; and it is not the Bishop of Rome, but the Roman church of St Peter the Apostle who holds land in Somerset[3]. Sometimes the abbey holds land, sometimes the abbot; sometimes again a distinction is drawn between abbey and abbot; the demesne manors are held by the church itself, but the manors given to knights are held of the abbot[4]. There are cases (not very many) in which groups of canons are said to hold lands[5], to hold them in common[6].

We have said that the 'church' becomes a person. If, however, we ask how the 'church' is to be conceived, we obtain very various answers from canonists, divines and philosophers. Materialism and mysticism are closely allied. At one moment a theorist will maintain that between the death of a parish priest and the induction of his successor the possession of the glebe is being held and retained by the walls of the church[7]; at the next moment we hear of the body or the bride of the Redeemer. With the more exalted of such doctrines the lawyer has little concern; but he should notice that the *ecclesia particularis* which stands on a certain spot is conceived as a part and member of the *ecclesia universalis,* for this theory leaves a strong mark on that notion of a corporation, an *universitas,* which the canonist propagates. He is by the law of his being a centralizer, and perhaps will not shrink from the conclusion that, if analysis be carried to its logical limit, the *dominium*

The church as person.

---

[1] D. B. i. 165: 'Terra aecclesiae de Bade: S. Petrus de Bada tenuit Alvestone.'

[2] D. B. i. 164 b.   [3] D. B. i. 91.

[4] D. B. i. 103 b: 'Terra aecclesiae de Tavestoch ... Ipsa aecclesia tenet Middeltone ... Goisfridus tenet de abbate Lideltone ... Ipsa aecclesia tenet Adrelie ... Radulfus tenet de abbate Torneberie.'

[5] D. B. i. 136: 'Canonici Lundonienses tenent.' Ib. 146: 'Canonici de Oxeneford tenent.' Ib. 157: 'Canonici S. Fridesvidae tenent.' Ib. 247 b: 'Canonici de Hantone tenent.'

[6] D. B. i. 17: 'Canonici de Cicestre tenent communiter.'

[7] Gierke, D. G. R. iii. 195; 'parietes possessionem retineant.' Ibid. 252: 'bona ipsa sunt loci inclusi muro, ad instar vacantis hereditatis, quae vicem personae obtinet.'

of all church-property is in the pope.   At any rate the will of
the *ecclesia particularis*, the episcopal or parochial church, is
not to be found wholly within it.   It lives a life that is not
its own; the life of a 'member[1]'.

The church
as *univer-
sitas* and
*persona
ficta.*

Meanwhile the legists, exploring Code and Digest, were
slowly discovering the *universitas* and endeavouring to mark it
off from the partnership and the group of co-proprietors.   The
canonists seized this new learning and carried it further.
The greater churches had about them a certain collegiateness;
there was a group composed of bishop and canons, or abbot and
monks.   Here then was an idea that they wanted.   The
ecclesia is an *universitas*, and the *universitas* is a *persona*.
That they should go on to add (as Innocent IV. did) that it
is *persona ficta* was not unnatural.   The organized group was
distinct from the 'church'; its will might not be the church's
will.   To this we must add that the canonist's law aspired to
deal not only with wrong and crime, reparation and punishment,
but also with sin and damnation.   In his eyes a person who
can not sin and can not be damned can only be *persona ficta*.
So the *universitas* is not the organized group, but a feigned
substratum for rights.   This theory will easily lead to a denial
that a corporation can commit either crime or wrong, and
Innocent went this length; but both practice and theory
rejected his doctrine[2].   The relationship between the group
and the feigned substratum could never be fully explained.
The leading idea, however, was that the group was not, but
only represented, and at times (if we may so speak) mis-
represented, the corporation.   How little of corporateness, of
collegiateness, there is in the canonical idea of a corporation
is shown by the ease with which this same idea is extended
to a case in which there is no plurality, no group.   Our curious
phrase 'corporation sole' only appears late in the day and seems
to be exclusively English; but the canonists had come very
near to it in their treatment of the cases in which an *ecclesia*

---

[1] As to all this see Gierke, D. G. R. iii. § 8.

[2] Gierke, D. G. R. iii. 343, 402, 491.   Why the law should create 'fictions'
which commit torts and crimes, must always be a difficult question, though
when once breach of contract or wrongful possession has been attributed to a
corporation the plunge has been made.   If, however, wrong-doing was to be
ascribed to an *ecclesia*, there was convenience in the theory that *this* 'church'
was only *nomen iuris* or an intellectual device and not a member of the body
of Christ.

had but one cleric connected with it; the *dignitas* or the *sedes* or the like could be personified[1]. Here, as in the case of a 'corporation aggregate,' there is 'fictitious' personality. So the canonist's corporation is rather a personified institution than an unified group of men.

With the evolution of these ideas the English temporal courts of the thirteenth century were not concerned. The canonical theory of the *persona ficta* was to bear fruit, some good, some bad, in the English common law of later days; but the internal affairs of the ecclesiastical groups could seldom or never be brought before the lay tribunals, and at the time of which we speak municipal growth had hardly reached that stage at which there would be a crying need for some theory or another of a town's personality. As yet we hear nothing in the secular courts of corporations whether aggregate or sole, and though we hear much of 'churches' the lawyers at Westminster have no occasion to analyze the idea that they are employing.

The temporal courts and the churches.

From their point of view we may look at the churches, and first at the parish church. When the rector dies or resigns his post there is no breach in the ownership or even in the possession. It is common to find a rector pleading ' I found my church seised of that land.' The theory is well stated in a judgment of 1307 :—A church is always under age and is to be treated as an infant, and it is not according to law that infants should be disinherited by the negligence of their guardians or be barred of an action in case they would complain of things wrongfully done by their guardians while they are under age[2]. Here we

The parish church.

[p. 484]

---

[1] Gierke, D. G. R. iii. 271, says that this personification of the *sedes* or *dignitas* did not introduce a second and independent category of juristic persons beside the corporation; rather the canonist's idea of a corporation was already so much the idea of an institution [not of an organized body of men] that the corporate element in it might disappear altogether without any essential change becoming necessary. True, he continues, the personified *dignitas* was not directly subsumed under the title of a corporation, [this is just what did happen in England,] but it was regarded as a phenomenon analogous to a corporation, and to some extent as a variation on the same theme. So far as we are aware the ' corporation sole ' begins to appear *eo nomine* only in the later Year Books.

[2] Placit. Abbrev. 304 (Norff.). Y. B. 21-2 Edw. I. p. 33 : ' le eglise est dedeinz age.' Comp. Bract. f. 226 b : ' Et cum ecclesia fungatur vice minoris, acquiritur per rectorem et retinet per eundem, sicut minor per tutorem. Et quamvis moriatur rector, non tamen cadit ecclesia a seisina sua, de aliquo de quo rector seisitus moritur nomine ecclesiae suae, non magis quam minor si

have a juristic person, the church, with a natural person as its guardian, and with the patron and the ordinary to check that guardian in his administrative acts, for some things the rector can not do without the consent of patron and ordinary. Had this principle been held fast, our later law books would have been relieved of some cumbrous disputations about 'the kind of fee' that a parson has[1].

The abbatial church.
The case of an abbey was less simple in theory, though the monarchical character of abbatial rule deprived some speculative questions of their importance. The *ecclesia* or *abbatia* succeeded the saint as the subject of proprietary rights. But, at least in the view of the king's courts, the abbot's power was almost that of an absolute owner. Already in Domesday Book we see that it matters little whether one says that the land is held by the church of Ely, the abbey of Ely, or the abbot of Ely. True that when lands are given to an abbey it is rare to find no mention of 'the convent' or 'the monks' as well as of God, the saint and the abbot. True also that when the abbey lands are alienated the feoffment is usually said to be made either by the abbot and convent, or by the abbot with the consent of the convent. For all this, the temporal courts [p. 485] are apt to treat the abbot as the one and only natural person who has anything to do with the proprietary rights of the abbey. To the complete exclusion of convent or monks he fully represents the abbey before the law; he sues and is sued alone[2]. A rule of ecclesiastical law forbidding prelates to dissipate the lands of their churches[3] was so far enforced by the temporal courts that they would give to an abbot an action for recovering lands that had been alienated by his predecessor without the consent of the convent. But this action was given to the successor, not to the convent. Had the convent raised its voice, it would have been told that all its members were dead in law; and even the succeeding abbot could not get back the land without a law-suit; the alienation was voidable,

---

custos suus moriatur.' Thus it is to Bracton a matter of indifference whether the church be seised by the instrumentality of its rector, or the rector be seised on behalf of his church; the two phrases are equivalent.

[1] Co. Lit. 300 b, 301 a.

[2] The same is true of an independent priory; the prior is its representative before the law.

[3] See *e.g.* cc. 1, 2, 3, X. 3, 10; two of these three passages deal with English cases.

not void[1]. And so with obligations: the question commonly
takes the form 'when and how can an abbot bind his successors?'
rather than ' when and how can an abbot bind his church or the
convent ? ' In short, owing to the legal deadness of the monks,
the abbey property seems to be administered by, and represented by, (and we may easily pass thence to possessed by
and owned by) the series of successive abbots. In the hands
of the king's justices even this series is apt to break up into
a set of disconnected links, each of which is a man. Each
successive abbot might sue for lands of which the church had
been dispossessed during the abbacy of one of his predecessors;
but if a claim for compensation in respect of some unlawful act,
such as an abstraction of the church's goods, accrued to one abbot,
it died with him and was not competent to his successor. *Actio
personalis moritur cum persona*, and here the person wronged
is dead, for he was a natural person and could die. To make
the law otherwise, a clause in the statute of 1267 was necessary[2].
Thus, though even in the legal notion of an abbey there is an
element that we may call 'communal,' an element which is
[p. 486] recognized by the ordinary forms of conveyances and obligations, and sanctioned by the rule that alienations of land are
voidable if made without the consent of the convent, still this
element is by no means prominent, and the abbot's powers of
dealing with property and of binding the abbey (that is his
successors) by contract are limited much rather by the idea
of the church itself as the true subject of rights and duties,
than by any principle that would make him but one among
a number of corporators.

The case of a bishop is not essentially unlike that of an
abbot. True that the lands of the see are very often, from
Domesday Book downwards, spoken of simply as the lands of
the bishop; the fact that they constituted a barony made such
language the more natural[3]; none the less they were the lands
of his church[4]. And in the bishop's case it is at least necessary

The
episcopal
church.

---

[1] For the writs of entry 'sine assensu' see Bracton, f. 323; Note Book,
pl. 866, 1727; Reg. Brev. Orig. f. 230.

[2] Stat. Marlb. c. 28. This came of our having no 'real' action for movables.

[3] Placit. Abbrev. 49 (temp. Joh.) : 'Dominus episcopus Londoniensis ...
petit ... unam sokam ... ut ius suum quod pertinet ad baroniam suam quam
tenet de episcopatu suo.'

[4] The usual form of a royal charter makes this clear; the grant is 'to God
and the church of St Mary and the bishop of Salisbury and his successors;

to distinguish the man from the bishop[1]. All the abbot's lands
are the abbey lands, but a bishop may hold lands and goods
which in no wise belong to his see; he will have 'heirs' as well
as official 'successors' and may make a will; occasionally he
has a great private fortune. In recognizing the possibility oi
one man having, as we should say, two capacities, a natural and
a politic or official capacity, the law made an important step;
there are signs that it was not easily made[2]; but the idea of
the church as the true owner of the episcopal lands made this
step the easier, for in one of his two capacities the bishop was
no owner but merely a *rector* or *custos*. Again, there was a
communal element to be considered. The lands of the see, if
they were the lands of the bishop, were also in some sort the
lands of the cathedral convent or chapter, and this, though it
might be a group of monks dead to the law, might also be a
group of secular canons, each of whom was a fully competent
legal person. To a small extent the law recognized the interest [p. 487]
of this group; without its consent the bishop could make no
alienation of the church's lands that would not be voidable by
his successor. Still the members of the chapter had no action
if the bishop without their consent dissipated the wealth of the
see, and this shows us that the person wronged by such dissipa-
tion was not a community of which the bishop was the head,
but rather the church, an ideal person, whose guardian he was.
He might do nothing to the disherison of his ward without the
advice of his council, his constitutional advisers.

Disintegra-
tion of
ecclesiasti-
cal groups.

There is, however, within the ecclesiastical sphere a well
marked movement towards individualism; it goes on from
century to century. The clerical groups begin to divide their
property. As a first stage we may notice the permanent
allotment of lands to specific wants of the group; one manor
supplies the monks with food, another with clothing, one in
some sort belongs to the cellarer, another to the almoner,
sacrist, vestiary. Such arrangements, though they seem to
have been regarded as solemn and permanent, were matters

'to God and the church of SS. Mary and Ethelbert of Hereford and Giles
bishop of the said church and his successors'; Rot. Cart. 67, 106.

[1] D. B. i. 135: 'Terra Roberti Episcopi de Cestre. Episcopus de Cestre
tenet Mimmine ... Hoc manerium non est de episcopatu, sed fuit Raynerii
patris Roberti episcopi.'

[2] We shall return to this point in the next section.

of internal economy and, at least as regards the outside world, had no legal effect: the abbot still represented all the lands and all the affairs of the abbey before the law. But sometimes, even in a monastic society, the process went further; often when a bishop's church was monastic, as for example at Canterbury, Durham and Worcester, a partition of lands was made between the bishop and the monks, and even the temporal law took notice of such a partition; the Prior of Canterbury became the legal representative of one section, if we may so speak, of the now divided *ecclesia* of Canterbury[1]. Even in the case of an abbey such partitions were sometimes made, and the Prior of Westminster sued the Abbot[2]. When the group was not monastic but secular the process often went much further; prebends were created; the bishop held lands in right of his bishopric, the dean in right of his deanery, the [p. 488] prebendary in right of his prebend[3]. Though for ecclesiastical purposes the group might be organic, it as an unit had little to do within the sphere of lay justice, and, if we may use the terms of a later day, the 'corporation aggregate' was almost resolved into a mere collection of 'corporations sole.'

Still throughout the middle ages there were groups of ecclesiastics which, as we should say, were corporations aggregate and which, being composed of seculars, were not subject to the monarchical rule of an abbot. The number and wealth of such bodies, and therefore their importance in the history of our law, might easily be exaggerated, but still they existed, and took part in litigation; suits, for example, are said to be brought by and against the canons or the dean and canons of a church[4]. In these cases we seem to see all the elements of a corporation aggregate. In the first place, there is personality; the lands, the affairs, administered by dean and

Communal groups of secular clerks.

---

[1] The Epistolae Cantuarienses contain a long account from the twelfth century of the litigation between the Archbishop and the monks of Christ Church touching a partition of their territory. In this case even Domesday Book shows a partition; the Archbishop has land and 'the monks of the Archbishop' have other land.

[2] Y. B. 40 Edw. III. f. 28 per Finchden; Prynne, Records, ii. 764.

[3] Early cases of prebendaries suing are Placit. Abbrev. 62 (Dorset); Note Book, pl. 411. As to the division of land between bishop and chapter, see 25 Ass. f. 116, pl. 8.

[4] Placit. Abbrev. 53 (Hereford), action against the canons of Hereford; Note Book, pl. 482, 493, 654, 692, 886, actions by and against 'the dean and chapter' of St Paul's.

canons, master and brethren, are the lands, the affairs, of a
church or a hospital. In the second place, the administrators
for the time being are a legally organized body, a body which
perdures while its members come and go[1]. In the third place,
this body transacts business as a body by means of meetings
and votings and resolutions; the motive power is not (as [p. 489]
it is in the case of an abbey) the will of a single man.
Our lawyers, however, learnt from the ecclesiastical groups
fewer valuable lessons than we might have expected. The
groups which were compact were despotically ruled, and
the groups which were not despotically ruled were not very
numerous nor very wealthy and seldom came before the courts
as organized bodies.

Internal
affairs of
clerical
groups.

As regards the internal economy of the ecclesiastical groups, [p. 490]
our common law of the thirteenth century had little to say.
Not only was this a matter for ecclesiastical law, but a deep-
seated reverence for a seal served to adjourn some difficult
questions which otherwise must have come before the king's
courts. A natural person is bound by his seal; he has himself
to blame if some one else, at all events some one whom he has
trusted, puts his seal to a bad use[2]. So with the church. If
Brother Walter, the sacrist of St Edmunds, gets hold of the seal
which usually hangs beside the holy bier and therewith seals a
bond for forty marks to Benedict the Jew of Norwich, there is [p. 491]
nothing for an enraged abbot to do but to depose Brother
Walter[3]. It would seem that normally the abbot kept the seal
and thus could bind the house. In 1321 it was said that many

---

[1] Bracton's best passage about this matter (f. 374 b) runs as follows:—If an
abbot, prior, or other collegiate men demand land or an advowson or the like in
the name of their church on the seisin of their predecessors, they say 'And
whereof such an abbot was seised in his demesne etc.' They do not in their
count trace a descent from abbot to abbot, or prior to prior, nor do they
mention the abbots or priors intermediate [between themselves and him on
whose seisin they rely,] *for in colleges and chapters the same body endures for
ever*, although all may die one after the other, and others may be placed in
their stead; just as with flocks of sheep, the flock remains the same though the
sheep die; nor does one succeed to another by right of succession as when a
right descends heritably, *for the right always belongs to the church and the
church is permanent:* and this one sees in charters, where the gift is made first
and foremost to God and such a church, and only in a secondary way to the
monks or canons.

[2] Glanv. x. c. 12; Britton, i. 164–6.

[3] Chron. Jocelini de Brakelonda, pp. 2, 4, 22.

a priory in England had no common seal; the prior's seal served
all purposes[1]. A remarkable attempt was made by Edward I.
and his barons to protect the house against the abbot, not so
much in the interest of the monks, as in the interest of pious
founders, who saw their good intentions brought to naught and
the fruits of their donations sent across the sea to the profit
of the alien. The common seal, said the Statute of Carlisle
(1307), was to remain in the custody of the prior and four
discreet inmates of the house and be laid up in safety under
the privy seal of the abbot. This statute should be famous,
for it was one of the very few illustrations that Coke could give
of his doctrine that a statute may be void for unreasonable-
ness[2]; and certainly it would seem that in 1449 the court took
upon itself to call this statute void, partly because it was
self-contradictory (for how can one use a seal at all if it is
always locked up?) but also 'because if the statute were observed every common seal might be defeated by a mere surmise
which could not be the subject of a trial[3].' From this we
may gather that the statute had little effect.

The canonists had by this time much to say about the manner in which legal acts can be done by or on behalf of corporations aggregate. They had a theory of duly convened meetings, and a theory of the powers of majorities. The most noticeable point in their doctrine is that the will of the *universitas* was expressed, not necessarily by the *maior pars conventus*, but by the *maior et sanior pars*. Presumably the major was also the saner part, but an opening was given for dissentients to represent to the rulers of the church (for after all an *ecclesia particularis* was but a member of the *ecclesia universalis*) that the resolution of the majority was not the will of the church[4]. Much of this learning about corporate acts must have been fairly well known to many educated Englishmen, including some of the king's judges, and must have been frequently discussed in the chapterhouses, for chapters were quarrelsome and the last word about their quarrels could be said by Italian lawyers. But the influence of all this doctrine upon English temporal law was as yet

The power of majorities.

---

[1] Y. B. Mich. 15 Edw. II. f. 452.
[2] *Dr Bonham's Case*, 8 Rep. 118 a; 2nd Inst. 587–8.
[3] Fitz. Abr. *Annuitie*, pl. 41 (apparently from an unprinted Y. B.).
[4] Gierke, D. G. R. iii. 322, 392, 470.

indirect and subtle and we have not the knowledge that would enable us to trace it.

The ecclesiastical and the temporal communities.

It is in no wise strange that the English lawyers of this age [p. 492] had not as yet brought the ecclesiastical and the temporal corporations under one heading; so different were they. This we see at once when we have asked the question 'What temporal groups of men are there which can have any claim to be corporate?' and have answered it by saying 'Chiefly counties, hundreds, townships, manors, cities and boroughs, in a word (since we can coin no better term) *land communities.*' The church, the religious order, the hospital, exists for a definite purpose: for the honour of a patron saint, the defence of the Holy Land, the relief of lepers. The ideal person has a permanent ideal will expressed in the rule of St Benedict or in some foundation charter. But for what purpose do townships and boroughs exist? Where is the permanent will of a city to be found? Again, the group of monks or canons is a voluntary society; of their own free choice and by a definite act men become members of chapters or convents; but, at least normally, the member of a township can hardly be said to have chosen to be a member; it may be that he has inherited a tenement; it may be that he has bought one; but even in the latter case the main thing that he bought was a tenement, not a place in a community. In these respects the chapters and convents stood nearer to our modern joint-stock companies than to the medieval boroughs. The company is a voluntary society and has a definite aim expressed in its memorandum and articles. But the township or the borough has come into being no one knows when, and exists no one knows why.

The boroughs and other land communities.

Bracton seems to feel—to feel perhaps rather than to know —that among these communities a line should be drawn, that cities and boroughs display some phenomenon, some degree of organic unity, that is not to be found in the open country that the civic or burghal community is no mere community but an *universitas civium vel burgensium*[1]. But at this point we must for a while break off our discussion. The question whether and in what sense these land communities or some of them deserve to be called corporate units can only be approached after we have examined their structure and

[1] Bracton, f. 228 b.

functions, and to this examination we must devote another chapter. Only at its end and, it is to be feared, after many digressions, can we return to the person who is not a man. That person, if he exists, is implicated in a system of local self-government.

[p. 495]

§ 13. *The King and The Crown.*

The legal position of the king has been fully discussed by historians of our constitution, and on the province which they have made their own we do not intend to trespass. Nor do we think that a chapter on the law of persons is the proper place in which to collect all or nearly all that can be said of the king. Still there is a question concerning him to which we are naturally led by what we have recently said about 'fictitious' persons :—Is the king merely a natural person, or does the law see beside or behind the natural Henry or Edward some non-natural, ideal person, some 'corporation sole'[1]? *Is there a Crown?*

In the sixteenth century our lawyers will use mystical language of the king. At times they will seem bent on elaborating a creed of royalty which shall take no shame if set beside the Athanasian symbol. The king has a body corporate in a body natural and a body natural in a body corporate. They can dispute as to whether certain attributes which belong to the king belong to him in his natural or in his politic capacity. Some of their grandiose phrases may be due to nothing better than a desire to stand well with the reigning prince; some of their subtle distinctions may be due to that love of mystery which is natural to us all; nevertheless we must allow that there were real difficulties to be solved, and that the personification of the kingly office in the guise of a corporation sole was in the then state of the law an almost necessary expedient for the solution of those difficulties. Also we might show that if, on the one hand, this lawyerly doctrine was apt to flatter the vanity of kings, it was, on the other hand, a not very clumsy expression of those limits which had gradually *Sixteenth century theories of the king's two bodies.*

[p. 496]

---

[1] See Gierke, D. G. R. ii. 562–8.

been set to the king's lawful power and that it served to harmonize modern with ancient law. But we are now to deal with ancient times, in particular with the thirteenth century. The metaphysical king, the corporation sole, does not yet exist; the difficulties which are met by his creation are only beginning to arise.

Personification of the kingship not necessary,

In the first place, let us notice that a great deal can be done without any personification of the kingly office. The mere amount of the business that is performed in the king's name but without his knowledge does not demand any such feat of jurisprudence as the creation of a new person. The ordinary law of agency is equal to the occasion. To this we may add that the gulf between the king and the greatest of his subjects is by no means so wide as it will afterwards become. A great prelate or a palatine earl will like the king have many high placed officers, stewards, chancellors, treasurers and the like, who will do many acts in his name, judicial acts and governmental acts, of which in all probability he will hear no word.

The king's rights as intensified private rights.

Then again, the rights of the king are conceived as differing from the rights of other men rather in degree than in kind. At the beginning of Edward I.'s reign this is expressed by lawyers in their common saying, 'The king is prerogative.' As yet the term *prerogative* is hardly used except in this adjectival manner. It suggests to us that the king has the rights which are given to others by the ordinary law, but that we are likely to find that each particular right is intensified when it is the king's; the usual definition of it is exceeded, 'for the king is prerogative.' For example, he has the rights [p. 497] of a feudal lord to wardships and marriages, but in his case these rights are augmented. If the whole law were written down, we should not be sent to one great chapter of it to learn the law of the kingship; rather we should see at the end of every proposition of private law or procedural law some note to the effect that this proposition must be modified before it is applied to the king's case. 'Prerogativity' is exceptionality[1].

---

[1] Y. B. 20–21 Edw. I. p. 57: 'Mes yl ne tendy nul averement pur le Roy, pur coe ke le Roy sy est prerogatyf'; p. 69 'Le Roy est prerogatif; par quey nul prescripcion de tens ne court encontre ly'; p. 112 'You can not, in this writ of right, demand on the seisin of Kings Richard and John and Henry, in such wise that if one fail, you may hold to the others.' 'Sir, we can, for the king is

Such is the general conception ; and, turning to particulars, The king and other lords. we shall usually see that the king's rights can be brought under it. He has hardly a power for which an analogy can not be found elsewhere. If he holds a court of his tenants in chief, his barons will do the like; if he asks an aid from them, they will ask an aid from their knights; if he tallages his demesne land, they can exercise a similar right. It is with difficulty that they are restrained from declaring war. If he prosecutes criminals, this is because his peace has been broken, and other lords are often proceeding against offenders who have done them 'shame and damage' by breaking their peace. In pardoning a criminal, the king only waives his rights, and he can not waive the rights of others; he cannot prevent a private prosecutor from urging an appeal of felony[1].

The kingly power is a mode of *dominium*; the ownership The kingship as property. of a chattel, the lordship, the tenancy, of lands, these also are modes of *dominium*. We may argue backwards and forwards between the kingly right and the rights of private landholders. This is the more remarkable in the case of inheritance, for, as is well known, the notion that the kingship is in some sort elective is but slowly dying[2]. For all this, the king is conceived to hold his lands by a strict hereditary right, and [p. 498] between his lands and the kingship it would be hard to distinguish. This is the way in which King Edward asserts his title to land in Lincolnshire:—'Richard my ancestor was seised thereof in his demesne as of fee, and from the said Richard, because he died without an heir of his body, the right descended to a certain King John as his brother and heir, and from him to King Henry as his son and heir, and from the said Henry to me as his son and heir[3].' Such a declaration may seem strange, for nothing is said of Arthur, and in

prerogative.' Y. B. 33–35 Edw. I. p. 407 : 'Le roi est en sa terre si prerogatif qil ne voet aver nul sur luy'...'Pur sa prerogativeté ne serrioms mie oustez de nos services.'

[1] Bracton, f. 132 b : 'Non enim poterit rex gratiam facere cum iniuria et damno aliorum. Poterit quidem dare quod suum est, hoc est pacem suam,... quod autem alienum est dare non potest per suam gratiam.'

[2] Bracton, f. 107 : 'Ad hoc autem creatus est et electus, ut iustitiam faciat universis.'

[3] P. Q. W. 389. See also Note Book, pl. 199, where 'the young king,' Henry son of Henry II., is mentioned in the pedigree; 'et de ipso Henrico [secundo] descendit ius illius advocacionis Henrico Regi filio suo et de ipso Henrico Regi Ricardo fratri suo.'

Edward I.'s day the ordinary law of inheritance would have preferred Arthur to John. But this brings out another point :— We may argue from the whole kingdom to each acre of land. The problem which was opened by the death of Richard was at that time an unsolved question—primogenitary rules were as yet new—Glanvill did not know how it should be answered[1]. John obtained the crown. This was a precedent in favour of the uncle against the nephew, and as such it was treated by Bracton in the case of private inheritances. The nephew may have the better right, but if the uncle is the first to take possession, the nephew can not succeed in an action 'because of the king's case[2].' In Edward I.'s day lawyers know that there is something odd in the king's pedigree : we must not argue about it[3]. Still the descent of the crown was not so unique a phenomenon then as it is now-a-days. No one, it may be, would have proposed to divide England among several coheiresses, and we can not say with certainty that a woman could have inherited the crown; but the question whether the county of Chester was partible had lately been treated as open[4], while in Scotland not only was the crown claimed for the Maid of Norway, but Bruce and Hastings urged [p. 499] that the kingdom was divisible and should be divided between them and Balliol[5].

The king's rights can be exercised by him. Even if we find that the king has some unique rights, rights for which analogies will be sought in vain, still they are rights that a natural person can exercise. Thus the royal lawyers are bent on establishing the doctrine that all justiciary powers are derived from the king. In terms made familiar by

---

[1] Glanvill, vii. 3.

[2] Bracton, f. 267 b, 282, 327 b ; Note Book, pl. 230, 982. In the Très ancien coutumier, ed. Tardif, p. 13 we find 'Filius, licet postgenitus, heres propinquior est hereditatis patris sui quam nepotes, filii fratris sui primogeniti'; but a glossator adds 'sicut contingit de Johanne, rege Anglico, et de multis aliis, et hoc est falsissimum iudicium.'

[3] Y. B. 20-21 Edw. I. p. 73: 'Nota ke nul home ne put chalanger la descente encontre le Roy, tot seyt coe en un bref de dreit.'

[4] Note Book, pl. 1127, 1227, 1273.

[5] See the Processus Scotiae, Foedera, i. 762. Bruce at one turn in the argument asserted 'quod mulier regnare non debet, quia officium regiminis exercere non potest.' The theory that the kingdom was partible was but the second string to his bow. At another turn he asserted that the ordinary rules of inheritance were inapplicable and that the canons for the inheritance of a kingdom should be found in 'the law of nature.'

the canonists, they assert that the king is the 'judge ordinary' of the whole realm and that all others who administer justice are 'judges delegate[1].' They have difficulty enough in making good this assertion in the teeth of feudal claims; but, when it is made, it does not attribute justiciary powers to a fictitious person, it attributes them to a real Henry or Edward. Bracton is in earnest when he says that, were the king strong enough, he would do all justice in person[2]. Far distant is the thought that the king may not sit as the active president of his own court. King Henry sits there and important cases will be adjourned if he be not present[3]. Justices have been fined for proceeding in the king's absence[4]. There is something anomalous in the ascription to a king of powers that he may not lawfully exercise in person, something which may suggest that our 'king' is rather a figment of the law than a man; but that a man should be able to do by delegate what he may do himself if he pleases—there is nothing strange in that. Then again, the doctrine that the king's will can only be expressed by formal documents, sealed, or signed and countersigned, does not [p. 500] belong to the twelfth or thirteenth centuries. On the contrary, the king's will expressed by word of mouth is more potent than any writ[5].

The rule which in later times will be expressed by the phrase 'The king can do no wrong' causes no difficulty. That you can neither sue nor prosecute the king is a simple fact, which does not require that we shall invest the king with any non-natural attributes or make him other than the sinful man that he is. The king can do wrong; he can break the law; he is below the law, though he is below no man and below no

The king can do wrong, but no action lies against him.

---

[1] Bract. f. 108: 'Dictum est supra de ordinaria iurisdictione, quae pertinet ad regem: consequenter dicendum est de iurisdictione delegata.'

[2] Bract. f. 107.

[3] Plac. Abbrev. p. 107 (25 Hen. III.): 'Et quia dominus rex absens fuit, nec fuerunt ibi nisi pauci de consilio domini Regis, noluerunt illi qui praesentes fuerunt adiudicare duellum nec aliud in absentia ipsius domini Regis vel maioris consilii sui.'

[4] Rot. Cl. i. 114: writ pardoning Jacob of Poterne.

[5] Rot. Cur. Reg. (ed. Palgrave) i. 47 (A.D. 1194): 'Et dominus Cantuariensis [Hubert Walter, chief justiciar,] dicit quod ipse accepit ab ore domini Regis quod ipse redderet seisinam terrae...Consideratum est quod magis ratum habetur quod dominus Rex ore praecepit quam quod per litteras mandavit.' Note Book, pl. 239 (A.D. 1234): 'testificatio domini Regis per cartam vel viva voce omnem aliam probationem excedit.'

court of law. It is quite conceivable that he should be below
a court of law [1]. In the second half of the century some lawyers
are already arguing that this is or ought to be the case [2]. What
is more, a pious legend of Westminster Hall tells how 'in
ancient times every writ of right droiturel or possessory lay
against the king [3].' The lawyer who said this in Edward I.'s
day was careful to leave the ancient times indefinite; probably
he was referring to the good old days of the Confessor and,
like Blackstone after him, saw 'our Saxon ancestors' implead-
ing each other by writs of entry [4]. But the legend grew, and,
as legends will, became more definite. In the middle of the
fourteenth century the common belief was that down to the
time of Edward I. the king could be sued like a private person,
and a judge said that he had seen a writ beginning with
Praecipe Henrico Regi Angliae [5]. If he had seen anything of
the kind, it was some joke, some forgery, or possibly some relic
of the Barons' War. About this matter there should be no
doubt at all. Bracton, no mere text writer, but an experienced [p. 501]
judge of the highest court, says plainly that writs do not run
against the king [6]. 'Our lord the king can not be summoned
or receive a command from any one'—this comes from a judgment of the king's court in 1234 [7]. 'Our court is not above us
and can not summon nor compel us against our will'—this
comes from a writ tested by Hubert de Burgh in 1223 [8]. This
positive evidence is strong; the negative evidence is overwhelming. If Henry III. had been capable of being sued, he
would have passed his life as a defendant. In the opinion of

---

[1] See the cautious passage in Bracton, f. 171 b.

[2] See the violent passage in Bracton, f. 34 and Fleta, p. 17. For reasons
given in the Introduction to Bracton's Note Book, i. 29–33, we do not believe
that this was part of Bracton's original text and gravely doubt whether he
wrote it.

[3] Y. B. 33–5 Edw. I. p. 471: 'en auncien temps chescun bref e de dreit e de
possessioun girreit ben ver le roi.'

[4] Bl. Comm. iii. 184: 'In the times of our Saxon ancestors, the right of
possession seems only to have been recoverable by writ of entry.'

[5] Y. B. 22 Edw. III. f. 3 (Hil. pl. 25); 24 Edw. III. f. 55 (Trin. pl. 40); 43
Edw. III. f. 22 (Mich. pl. 12). The passages are given by Allen, Prerogative,
190.

[6] Bracton, f. 5 b: 'Si autem ab eo [sc. a rege] petatur, cum breve non currat
contra ipsum, locus erit supplicationi.' Again f. 382 b: 'summoneri non potest
per breve.' See also f. 52, 107, 171 b, 368, 412; also Note Book, i. pp. 26–33.

[7] Note Book, pl. 1108.

[8] Rot. Cl. i. 549.

many of his subjects he was for ever breaking the law. Plea
rolls from his reign there are plenty, and in the seventeenth
century they were jealously scanned by eyes which did not look
kindly upon kings. Where are the records of cases in which
King Henry issued writs against himself? We can not but
believe that *Praecipe Henrico Regi* is what Francis Bacon
called it, an old fable[1]. To this must be added that the king
has power to shield those who do unlawful acts in his name, and
can withdraw from the ordinary course of justice cases in which
he has any concern. If the king disseises *A* and transfers the
land to *X*, then *X* when he is sued will say that he can not
answer without the king, and the action will be stayed until
the king orders that it shall proceed. So if the king's bailiff is
charged with a disseisin done in the king's name, the justices
will indeed take a verdict about the facts, but they will give no
judgment *Rege inconsulto*[2]. Still all this 'prerogativity' is
compatible with humanity, and when the king appears as a
plaintiff or submits to be treated as a defendant the difference
between him and a private person is less marked in the thirteenth century than it is in later times. When he is a plaintiff
[p. 502] he will often employ one of the ordinary writs. A defendant,
instead of using what even in Bracton's day was becoming the
proper formula 'I can not answer without the king,' will sometimes boldly say 'I vouch the king to warranty[3].' 'In the
pleadings and proceedings of the king's suits,' exclaims Bacon,
'what a garland of prerogatives doth the law put upon them![4]'
This garland is not woven all at once and some of its flowers
were but buds in the days of Henry III. But our main point
must be that there is as yet little in the law of procedure to
suggest that the king is other than a natural person, nothing to
suggest that he has two capacities. He enjoys the same privileges whether the matter under discussion is what we should

---

[1] Bacon, Case *de Rege Inconsulto* (Works, ed. Spedding, vii. 694): 'for you
will not revive old fables (as Justinian calls things of that nature) *Praecipe
Henrico Regi etc.*'

[2] Bracton, f. 171 b. Note Book, pl. 401, 1106, 1108, 1133, 1141, 1236, 1593,
1766. Y. B. 30–31 Edw. I. p. 172; 33–35 Edw. I. p. 539. Reg. Brev. Orig.
221–2.

[3] Note Book, pl. 1183: 'vocat inde ad warantum dominum Regem.' Contrast pl. 393: 'Rex debet ei warentizare si ausus esset illum vocare ad warantum sicut alium hominem.' Bracton, f. 382 b; Y. B. 21–2 Edw. I. p. 287.

[4] Bacon, Works, ed. Spedding, vii. 693.

call 'an act of state' or whether it is a private bargain. And,
after all, the grandest of his immunities is no anomaly. He
can not be compelled to answer in his own court, but this is
true of every petty lord of every petty manor; that there
happens to be in this world no court above his court is, we may
say, an accident.

King's
lands and
crown
lands. Then again, no line is drawn, at least no marked line,
between those proprietary rights which the king has as king
and those which he has in his private capacity. The nation,
the state, is not personified; there are no lands which belong
to the nation or to the state. The king's lands are the king's
lands; the king's treasure is the king's treasure: there is no
more to be said. True that a distinction is made between 'the
ancient demesne of the crown' and lands that have come to
the king by modern title. The main import of this distinction
is to be found in the strong sentiment—it is rather a sentiment than a rule of law—that the ancient demesne should not
be given away, and that, if it be given away, some future king
may resume it[1]. But even here private law affords or has
afforded an analogy. It is only of late years, only since Glanvill
wrote, that a tenant in fee simple has been able utterly to
disappoint his expectant heirs by alienating his land; his power
over land which he himself has purchased has been greater than
his power over lands which have descended to him and which
constitute the ancient demesne of his family. The king, who [p. 503]
asserts a right to revoke the improvident grants of his ancestors,
is relying on an antique rule of family law, rather than upon
any such doctrine as that kings are trustees for the nation.
The idea that a man may hold land or goods in two different
capacities is not easily formed.

Slow
growth of
a law of
'capaci-
ties.' We may see this even in the ecclesiastical region. Though
here the personality of the saint or of the church makes the
distinction easier, still in age after age people find much difficulty in marking off office from property, and in separating
the lands and goods which a man enjoys or uses because he
is the ruler of a church from those which, as we should say,
belong to him in his private capacity. On the one hand, it
is hard to prevent the ecclesiastical benefice from becoming

---

[1] Britton, i. 221: 'Rois ausi ne porraint rien aliener des dreitz de lour
coroune ne de lour reauté, qe ne soit repellablu par lour successours.' See
above, p. 384.

hereditary. On the other hand, it is not readily admitted that a bishop or a parson can have property which is in no sense the property of his church. This difficulty it is which provides an excuse for that interference by the king with the goods of dead bishops, which historians are too apt to treat as sufficiently explained by mere rapacity. An abuse we are willing to call it, but there is an excuse for it. On the death of the bishop, the king is guardian of the temporalities of the church; the dead bishop's goods are the goods of the church[1]. This idea is well brought out by what is told of St Hugh of Lincoln. He did not approve the new custom that bishops should make wills. Still he consented to make one lest otherwise his goods should be seized by the king. Evidently the saintly bishop thought that his goods were his church's goods; he made a will in order to defeat, if possible, the all too logical, if impious, deduction which kings were ready to draw from this pious doctrine[2]. King Stephen had to promise that he would not interfere with the testaments of the bishops, and that, on the death of a bishop intestate, his goods should be distributed for the benefit of his soul by the counsel of the church; but then he was also making something very like a renunciation of his right to a profitable guardianship of the temporalities of the [p. 504] vacant see[3]. His successors seize the goods of intestate bishops and expect bishops to apply for a licence if they want to make wills. When Archbishop Roger of York died in 1182, Henry II. enjoyed a windfall of £11,000, to say nothing of the spoons and salt-cellars. A very just retribution, says the dean of St Paul's, and quotes from his Digest 'quod quisque iuris in alterum statuerit, uti debet eodem iure,' for this Roger had obtained a papal bull enabling him to seize the goods of any clerk in his diocese who, even though he made a testament, did not before his death distribute his goods with his own hands[4]. The pope was just as bad as the king in this matter. In 1246 he proclaimed that the goods of all intestate clerks belonged to him, though in the next year he retired from an indefensible position[5]. No doubt

---

[1] See Luchaire, Manuel des institutions, p. 49. This notion begets the *ius spolii*, *droit de dépouilles*, of continental law.

[2] Magna Vita S. Hugonis, p. 334.

[3] Second Charter of Stephen: Stubbs, Select Charters; Statutes, vol. i. (Charters) p. 3.

[4] Diceto, ii. 12. He cites the rubric of Dig. 2. 2.

[5] Mat. Par. Chron. Maj. iv. 522, 604.

the canonists could distinguish well enough between the property of the church and the property of the prelate; still we can see that this is a lawyerly distinction; a saintly bishop, like Hugh of Lincoln, will scout it in the interest of his church, a covetous bishop will make light of it in the interest of himself and his kinsfolk, a needy king will know how and when it can be profitably ignored.

No lay corpora-
tions sole
other than
the crown. If these things be done within the ecclesiastical sphere where dead saints still are active, where the canon law with its Roman traditions prevails, what may we not expect in the temporal sphere? Far easier for us is it to personify a church, which actually holds the body, and is guarded by the soul, of the saint, than to personify a nation, a state. No medieval king is tempted to say 'I am the state,' for '*Ego sum status*' would be nonsense. On the other hand, no one will say to him 'This land, though it may be called your land, is really the land of the state.' And so the king's land is the king's land and there is no more to be said about it. It should be remembered that in our fully developed common law the king, or crown, is the only corporation sole of a lay kind. The temporal law of the thirteenth century will aid us with no analogy if we would distinguish between the king's private property and his official property. Often enough has office become property, or rather (for this we believe to be nearer the truth) rights which older and vaguer law had regarded as half official, half proprietary, have become definitely proprietary. Earldoms and serjeanties belong to this category; but we can not distinguish between the lands which the earl has as earl and those which he has as [p. 505] man. On the other hand, those offices which have not fallen into this category do not comprise or carry with them any proprietary rights of any kind. The shrievalty is an office, but the sheriff as sheriff has no lands, no goods[1]. What is more, trusteeship, at all events a permanent trusteeship, is as yet unknown to the law and can supply us with no analogy. No form of legal thought that is at our disposal will enable us to separate the lands of the nation from the lands of the king.

---

[1] We make our nearest approach to the personification of a temporal office when some officer attempts to prescribe for fees or perquisites. In 7 Edw. I. a castellan of Bamborough is charged with holding certain pleas which, according to general law, belong to the sheriff. He replies, 'I found the said castle seised of this custom.' Here Bamborough castle is personified. But this is not a fruitful idea. Northumberland Assize Rolls, 353.

But at least, it will be urged, the king can not devise the
kingdom by his will. No, but the general law is that a landowner can not devise his land by his will: only God can make
an heir, not man. And, after all, this impotence of the king
has not been very clearly demonstrated. If standing in the
thirteenth century we ask why on the Conqueror's death Rufus
became king of the English, while Robert became duke of the
Normans, it is not plain that there is any better answer forthcoming than that the Conqueror, like other lords who had
lands on both sides of the sea, partitioned his estates among
his sons. But, as already said, the fact that land can not be
devised by testament is a sufficient reply to any who would
draw distinctions between kingdoms and other estates. Moreover in the middle of the thirteenth century it is by no means
so clear as a patriotic Englishman might wish it to be that the
king of England does not hold his kingdom of the pope at an
annual rent by virtue of John's surrender and Innocent's re-
grant[1]. And, as we saw above, if the king ought to consult his
barons before he grants away any large tract of his kingdom,
common opinion has expected that a great baron will consult
his men, or at least profess to consult them, before he makes
[p. 506] large grants out of his honour[2]. As to the king's treasure, it is
the king's treasure and he may do what he pleases with it,
though very likely his successor may find an excuse for dis-
regarding some or all of his bequests. Edward III. in his will,
draws a marked distinction between the debts that he owes as
a private person and the debts that he owes as a king; his
executors are to pay the former, while the latter will fall upon
his heir and successor. We shall hardly find such a distinction
in earlier times[3].

As yet no king has succeeded to another without there

[side note: Is the kingdom alienable?]

[side note: The king can die.]

---

[1] See the protests of 1301 and 1366; Foedera, i. 926; Rolls of Parliament,
ii. 290. Stubbs, Const. Hist. § 700: 'John's surrender and subsequent homage
first created the shadow of a feudal relation, which was respected by Henry III.,
but repudiated by the parliaments of Edward I. and Edward III.' As to
Richard's transactions with the Emperor, it was easy for an Englishman to
hold them 'void for duress'; they were 'contra leges, contra canones, contra
bonos mores'; Diceto, ii. 113.

[2] See above, p. 346.

[3] Will of Edward III., Nicolas, Royal Wills, p. 59. He distinguishes
between 'debita nostra contemplacione personae nostrae contracta' and 'debita
racione regni seu guerrarum nostrarum contracta.'

being an interregnum. In the case that is just happening when we make our survey this interregnum is very short. Edward I. far away in the Holy Land began to reign on the day, not of his father's death, but of his father's funeral[1]. But there is here no legal fiction, nothing that demands any mysterious phrase about the king's immortality. Edward I. really reigns, before he is crowned, and Edward II. will really reign so soon as his father has ceased to breathe. There is less excuse here for a fiction than there is in the case of a bishop; also there are fewer materials ready to the hand of the constructive lawyer. The bishop's throne must be vacant at least for a few days, and meanwhile the eternally infant church has other guardians, a guardian of its temporalities, a guardian of its spiritualities. But looking back a little way to cases in which there has been an interregnum of considerable duration, we see that lawyers have not been prepared to stop the gap with a metaphysical king, the personified kingship. When the king dies, his peace dies, and there is no king's peace until another king is crowned. The king then who has a peace is a mortal man. The evil consequences of this principle may have been somewhat lessened by a proclamation of the peace of one who, though he is not yet king of England, is by hereditary right lord of England. Still such a shift tells us that the only king known to the law is a natural person[2].

The king can be under age. A case has lately occurred which, so we may think, must [p. 507] have put the old theory of the kingship to a severe strain. A child but nine years old was crowned. The coronation of Henry III. was an important event. It was, if we may so speak, a two-edged event. On the one hand, it confirmed the doctrine of pure hereditary right; it applied to the kingship the common land law. On the other hand, it showed that a king capable of ruling was no necessity; all that a king could do might be done by a regent and a council in the name of an infant. How William Marshall became 'rector regis et regni' is in this context a question of no great interest. There was a

---

[1] Henry died late on Wednesday. Edward's peace was proclaimed in Westminster Hall early on Thursday. But he dates his reign from the next Sunday, on which day his father was buried and the magnates took the oath of fealty. Foedera, i. 497.

[2] Select Pleas of the Crown (Seld. Soc.), pl. 84. In John's day an appellor alleges a crime committed during the late interregnum but after 'the peace of the King then Duke of Normandy and Lord of England' had been sworn.

grave national crisis; there was civil war; a foreign enemy was
in the land. Those barons who had not rejected John did the
obvious thing, chose the obvious man as their leader. It was
not a time for constitutional dissertations. What happened
during Henry's minority is of greater significance. In litigation
which touches royal rights the ordinary rule of private law is
applied. An action for land is brought; the person in possession alleges that the king is his warrantor; the action must
remain in suspense until the king is of full age[1]. Then, when
Henry was of full age, he insisted that all charters granted in
his name during his minority required confirmation, even the
Great Charter and the Forest Charter. He did this we are
told by the advice of Hubert de Burgh[2]. To exclaim against
his faithlessness, his greed, his imprudence, is far easier than
to discover any then admitted principle of law which would
condemn him. Suppose that his guardians have improvidently
alienated some piece of his demesne land, is he not to have
the ordinary right which every infant enjoys on attaining his
majority[3]? Donations, we might say, are one thing, laws
another, and Magna Carta is a code of laws. But where and
[p. 508] how could the line be drawn? In form the Great Charter was
a charter, and between it and the mere gift of single knight's
fee there was a long and gently graduated series of charters
granting 'liberties' of various kinds to individuals and to
larger or smaller classes of men[4]. A claim to revoke what is in
fact a body of general laws is one which will set men thinking,
and may lead them in the end to some mystical dogma such as
that the king is never under age; but no such dogma has as
yet been fashioned. The king of the thirteenth century is a
natural person and may be 'under disability.'

In course of time we see the beginnings of a doctrine of
public or official capacities. Lanfranc hints at it when he

Germs of a doctrine of 'capaci- ties.'

[1] Note Book, pl. 1500 (A.D. 1221): 'Loquela ista remaneat ad aetatem domini
Regis ut tunc faciat inde voluntatem suam.' Ibid. pl. 1639 (A.D. 1223): 'Iudicium ponitur in respectum usque ad aetatem domini Regis.'

[2] Mat. Par. (from Wendover) iii. 75–6, 91, 122.

[3] Note Book, pl. 1221. The king of Scots petitions for a wardship, urging
in his favour something that happened during the minority. Henry's council
replies that this happened 'tempore Huberti de Burgo Comitis Kantiae qui
amicus fuit et familiaris ipsi Regi Scotiae et qui regnum Angliae habuit in
manu sua.' Therefore it is of no avail.

[4] This point will be further discussed in our next chapter where we deal
with borough charters.

suggests that the Conqueror, though he may not arrest the bishop of Bayeux, may lawfully arrest the earl of Kent[1]. Some progress has been made before the end of the thirteenth century. In a carefully worded judgment our king's court declares that the bishop of Durham 'has a double status, to wit, a temporal and a spiritual status.' The archbishop of York has excommunicated the bishop for imprisoning some of his metropolitan's men. But to imprison men belongs to the bishop's temporal status. Therefore the archbishop has excommunicated not his suffragan bishop but the king's tenant in chief and must pay a fine[2]. A still more interesting case concerns King Edward himself. He in his father's life time was holding the vill of Stamford and was exercising in it the franchise known as the return of writs. He granted the vill to the earl of Warenne. Having become king, he demanded by what warrant the earl claimed the franchise. The earl replied 'By your own gift; you gave me all that you had in Stamford.' The king's counsel then pleads that Edward himself had no title to the franchise, and that, being king, he is bound to resume all rights unlawfully detached from the crown, even though he himself, while as yet no king, was the guilty person. 'He is now of another estate than he was then and is *quasi* another person.' The earl combats this theory—'He is one and the same person [p. 509] that he was when he made the gift.' Judgment is given for the king[3]. Thus the idea of dual personality may already prevail when the king relies upon it. To enforce it when it would tell against his interests would be a harder task. And as yet this idea looks very new. If there is to be a personification, something material, something as visible as a church, must be personified.

Personi-
fication of
the crown. We can see the beginnings, but only the beginnings, of a process which personifies the king's 'crown.' And here it may be remarked that even in our own day this process has never

---

[1] See above, p. 451.

[2] Rolls of Parliament, i. 102–5: 'Episcopus Dunelmensis dupplicem habet statum, scilicet, temporalem et spiritualem, et ad statum illum temporalem incarcerationes et imprisonamenta per ministros eiusdem Episcopi pertinent facienda.'

[3] P. Q. W. 429–30. Thornton the king's counsel pleads that the king 'est alterius condicionis quam prius fuit et quasi altera persona.' The earl replies, 'Una et eadem persona est tam in statu regio quam in statu quo vocabatur communiter Dominus Edwardus'—King Edward is the same person as the Lord Edward of former times.

gone so far as to modify the formal language of our law. Of course lawyers and judges and even statutes have now for a long time spoken of the rights of the Crown, have spoken of the Crown as doing this, that, and the other act. Still in the strictest language of the law, the language of pleading, the Crown does nothing; it does not sue, it does not prosecute; the king or queen does it all. A personification of the crown has been required, not so much by any purely 'juristic necessities,' as by constitutional doctrines which, though they may now-a-days be as well observed as any laws could be, are none the less no laws. Under the cover of the crown—that 'metaphor kept in the Tower,' as Tom Paine called it—our slow revolution is accomplishing itself. In the thirteenth century this golden circlet is beginning to be useful. We first hear talk of it when crimes are committed, not only against the king's peace, but also against 'his crown and dignity.' Then we hear of rights which are inseverably annexed to the crown; they indeed make the crown, for the king's crown is to do justice and keep the peace[1]. This is pleasant doctrine for the king, if it is also a sound doctrine for the state; it enables him to resume 'liberties' which have been alienated from the crown and check the growth of seignorial justice. In the fourteenth century it is possible to say that the crown, like a church, is always under age and that no lapse of time will bar the demands of this [p. 510] *quasi* infant[2]. But as yet to distinguish between the crown and the king, between the king and the man, is to teach a treasonable doctrine. In Edward II.'s day that doctrine becomes prominent and charges of holding it are bandied to and fro. The barons who are leagued against one of the king's favourites, Piers Gaveston, are said to hold that allegiance is due rather to the crown than to the person of the king. A few years afterwards the barons who are leagued against another of the king's favourites, the younger Despenser, accuse him of having held this very doctrine, and, owing to their success, it becomes for all time, to use Coke's phrase, 'a damnable and damned opinion.' But all this lies in the future[3].

---

[1] Bracton, f. 55 b: 'Est enim corona regis facere iusticiam et iudicium et tenere pacem, et sine quibus corona consistere non potest, nec tenere.'

[2] Placit. Abbrev. p. 339 (15 Edw. II.): 'de iure coronae suae etc., quae semper est quasi minoris aetatis.'

[3] Chronicles of Edward I. and Edward II. ed. Stubbs, i. p. 153, ii. p. 33, 65;

We are not contending that the proprietary theory of the kingship—if we may give that name to the doctrine which we have been endeavouring to expound—is the most ancient theory, or that it ever fully expresses all the facts and thoughts and feelings which determine what a king shall be and what a king shall do. Probably there has been a one-sided development of those elements in the ancient ideas which have been found capable of legal treatment, while other elements have been forgotten or extruded from the sphere of law. The Conquest of England, the strong monarchy, the tyranny (if we please to call it so) which was founded by the Norman kings, have favoured those and only those notions which exalt the king and give him a property in his kingdom. Still the phenomenon in question is not purely English and can not be explained without reference to the history of jurisprudence[1]. The elements in the old tribal kingship which survived in the struggle for existence were those which in the then state of legal thought were capable of being accurately expressed and defined. For vague thoughts, for half thoughts, the lawyer can find no place. What, for example, is he to make of a title to the crown which is partly hereditary, partly elective? The elective element can not be developed, for no one can define who are the electors, no one as yet has rules about the powers [p. 511] of majorities. Therefore the elective element must perish or become a mere form. And so with the king's lands. Either they belong to him or they belong to some other person or persons. Say for a moment that they belong to the nation, how can such a doctrine be enforced when as yet we have no idea, or but the vaguest idea of official capacities, of trusteeship, of corporations aggregate and corporations sole? We do not wish to prejudge any debatable questions of early English history, but that men had clear ideas about these matters in the tenth century and lost them during the twelfth and thirteenth, those ages of brilliant intellectual progress, is not easily to be believed. The one general result to which we come at the end of this long and variegated chapter is that even in Bracton's day the number of legal ideas is very small and public law has hardly an idea of its own.

Statutes of the Realm, i. 182; *Calvin's Case*, 7 Coke's Rep. 11; see also *In re Stepney Election Petition*, 17 Q. B. D. 54.

[1] Gierke, D. G. R. ii. 564–8.

CHAPTER III.

JURISDICTION AND THE COMMUNITIES OF THE LAND.

[p. 512] IN an exposition of any system of law, ancient or modern, a large space must be given to the composition and competence of courts. In a statement of modern law, however, we should hardly place this topic in the forefront. Courts exist for the purpose of defining and enforcing the rules of substantive law. But when we are dealing with the middle ages, we can not thus regard what we may call the 'law of jurisdiction' as merely subsidiary or 'adjective.' It is intertwined with the law of property and the law of personal status and this in many different ways. In the first place, jurisdiction is a proprietary right, or the subject matter of proprietary rights, profitable, alienable, inheritable rights, which are often bound up with the tenure of land. In the second place, jurisdiction is one of the main ties which keeps society together; the man is bound to his lord by this as well as other bonds; he is not merely his lord's man and his lord's tenant, but he is also his lord's 'justiciable'; his lord is his 'sovereign'; he owes to his lord not merely service but also suit; and thus once more the law of jurisdiction is implicated with the land law[1]. Turning again to the masses of unfree men, we see another connexion between jurisdiction and ownership. If we examine the rights of the lord over his villein we find it difficult to decide where ownership leaves off and where jurisdiction begins; we may have to say, either that the idea of ownership, the master's ownership of the slave, has been tem-
[p. 513] pered by the idea of jurisdiction, or that rights of jurisdiction

Place of the law of jurisdiction in the medieval scheme.

---

[1] Y. B. 18 Edw. II. f. 571: 'le Priour fuit son justisable.' Stat. 28 Edw. III. c. 11: 'celui qe est sovereign de la ville.'

are being converted into rights of ownership. Again, we have
to form the notion of different spheres of jurisdiction, and this
must colour our treatment of important private rights. It is
not enough to say that a man has a right in land: we must
add that it is, or is not, a right protected by the king's courts,
for although it may be ignored there, still it may be protected
by other courts, for example by the court of the manor. Nor
is this the result of a mere division of labour such as at
the present day may send petty cases to petty tribunals. The
various courts have their roots in various principles, in various
rights, the rights of the king, of the church, of feudal lords,
of ancient communities. Lastly, we have been compelled to
break off our discussion of the 'land communities,' as we have
called them, because we could not describe their organization
without speaking at some length of courts, their constitution and
competence. In the main the organization of these communities is justiciary; the shire has a court, the hundred a court,
the manor a court, the borough a court, and in a large measure
it is this that makes the shire, the hundred, the manor, the
borough into a *communitas*. Thus in speaking of jurisdiction
we shall naturally be led to describe the nature of these communities and to consider why some of them are, while others
of them are not, attaining personality.

The
principle
that all
temporal
justice
proceeds
from the
king.

If we leave out of sight the courts of the church and con-
centrate our attention upon secular justice, we see at first
sight a certain theoretical unity. Who, asks Bracton, ought
to be judge in temporal causes? The king; no one else:—
this is the meaning of the kingship, that the king should do
justice to all. It is want of time and strength that authorizes
and compels him to depute his duties to others. All temporal
judges are his delegates[1]. But Bracton was a royal justice,
and, though he could easily show that he and his fellows
derived their authority from the king, he does not attempt
to prove, and could hardly have succeeded in proving, that,
even in legal theory, all the jurisdictional powers of the feudal [p. 514]
lords were delegated to them by the king. The law of his time
is obliged to distinguish the 'regalities' that are delegated
from the powers that have another origin. Easier would it
have been to show that as a mere matter of fact, despite all
theories, despite the words of the Great Charter, the king's

[1] Bracton, f. 107-8.

court was mastering all the justice of the land, was subordinating to itself the feudal courts, was making them insignificant; but in so doing some startling contrasts between facts and theories would have been disclosed. Even the ancient courts of the shire and the hundred, courts which had no lords, courts which were presided over by royal officers, might have occasioned doubts:—could the suitors who made the judgments in these courts be called the king's deputies? Bracton takes the easiest of courses, that of ignoring difficulties; he asserts the broad principle that all temporal jurisdiction is the king's, and leaves us to discover how far either facts or legal theories can be brought under this principle. Still the assertion is important; the principle is not the mere speculation of a lawyer; it has been making itself good as against other principles which in part were older, in part were newer, making itself good against tribalism, communalism, feudalism.

It is not, however, with a discussion of this dogma that all 'ordinary,' *i.e.* non-delegated, jurisdiction is in the king[1] that we can begin our investigation. We must look at the courts as they exist at the close of Henry III.'s reign, prefacing any further remarks by a summary statement, which may show the main outlines of the system, though it will neglect exceptional cases. Scheme of the courts.

For the purposes of temporal justice England is divided into counties; the county is divided into hundreds; the hundred is divided into vills or townships[2]. The county has a court, the hundred has a court, the vill or township as such, has no court; but the vill is an important unit in the administration of the law. Again, the vill is very often coincident with a manor and the manor has a court. Division of the land.

[p. 515] The county court meets once a month. It is presided over by a royal officer, the sheriff, who in some matters is assisted and checked by elective officers, the coroners. It is attended by suitors (*sectatores*), certain freeholders of the shire who are bound to attend it, to do suit (*facere sectam*) to it. They are The county court.

---

[1] Bracton, f. 108: 'Dictum est in proximo de ordinaria iurisdictione quae pertinet ad regem, consequenter dicendum est de iurisdictione delegata.'

[2] This is not strictly true, for the vill may well extend into two or three hundreds and into two counties. For some examples see Committee on Parish Boundaries, Parl. Pap. 1873, vol. 8, p. 225.

the judges or doomsmen (*iudicatores*) of the court. It enter-
tains some of the initial proceedings in criminal cases, but for
the more part it is a civil, non-criminal court ; it has an original
jurisdiction in personal actions ; real actions come to it when
the feudal courts make default in justice ; cases are sent down
to it for trial by jury from the king's court.

The hundred court.   The hundred court meets once in three weeks. Normally
its president should be the sheriff or a bailiff to whom the
sheriff has committed the hundred ; but many of the hundred
courts are in private hands, and, when this is so, the lord's
steward presides. Freeholders of the hundred owe suit to it ;
these suitors are the doomsmen. Its competence seems much
the same as that of the county court, though its powers are
confined within narrower geographical limits ; but real actions
do not come to it, nor do we hear of actions being transmitted
to it by the king's court.

The sheriff's turn.   Twice a year the sheriff makes a tour or turn (*turnus vicecomitis*) through all the hundreds of the county. He holds
each of the hundred courts and on these occasions many
persons besides the ordinary suitors ought to be present. One
of his objects is to hold a view of frank-pledge (*visus franci-
plegii*), to see that all persons who ought to be, are in a
tithing. For this purpose strict law might require that all
such persons should be present, but often they seem to be
sufficiently represented by the chief pledges (*capitales plegii*),
the heads of their tithings, the tithingmen (*decennarii*). The
curious organization of frank-pledge is interlaced with the
organization of townships and of manors, and the townships
also have to be represented at the sheriff's turn, each by
its reeve and four of its men ; for another object of the turn
is that the sheriff may hold what we may call a 'police court.'
Presentments respecting crimes and minor offences are there
made by the representatives of the townships and a jury of
freeholders. The presentments of minor offences are disposed
of on the spot ; presentments of crimes merely serve to initiate
proceedings against the accused who will be tried by the [p. 516]
king's justices. In his 'turn' the sheriff acts as a judge with
powers delegated from the king, and seemingly the suitors of
the hundred have nothing to do with the judgments.

Seignorial courts.   This we may say is the national system of local courts, and
these courts for want of a better title we may call 'communal'

—thereby meaning that the court represents, though it is not elected by, a *communitas*. From them we must distinguish courts which in a wide sense of the word we might call feudal, but which it may be better to call seignorial; they are courts which have lords. These seignorial courts do not form a system comprising the whole land, but are dotted about sporadically. We must divide their powers into two classes. It would seem that the mere fact that a man had tenants gave him a right to hold a court of and for them. A court authorized by this principle, which we may call the feudal principle, would have, at least over the freehold tenants, but a purely civil, that is, non-criminal, non-penal, jurisdiction; it would be competent for personal actions and also for real actions in which freehold lands were demanded; but the latter could only be begun by a royal writ (*breve de recto tenendo*) and might easily be removed from it by a similar mandate. Over unfree persons and unfree tenements its authority would be more ample; about the title to lands held in villeinage it would be able to say the last word, it could enforce the manorial custom and inflict minor punishments upon the villeins. Probably there was nothing in law to prevent a lord standing high in the feudal scale from holding a single court for all his tenants, and occasionally we read of the court of a wide-spread honour. Usually, however, the lord's court is the court of a single manor and very frequently the manor is a single vill. The legal theory of later times distinguished between the court for freeholders and the court for customary tenants, calling the former a *court baron*, the latter a *customary court*; in the court baron, it is said, the freehold suitors (*sectatores*) were the judges; in the customary court the lord's steward was the only judge; but it is very doubtful whether we can carry back this distinction into the age of which we are now speaking.

Feudal courts.

Contrasted with the jurisdictional powers which a lord has merely because he is a lord with tenants, stand the franchises, liberties, royalties (*libertates, regalia*), powers and immunities which can only be possessed by those to whom the king has granted them. These franchises were of the most various orders, ranging from the powers of the palatine earl to those of the lord of a petty manor who had merely the view of frankpledge and the police jurisdiction that was incident to it. This last franchise was common, and the court in which the lord

Franchise courts.

[p. 517]

Leets.

exercised it twice a year was acquiring the name of a *leet* (*leta*); it was a police court for the presentment of offences and for the punishment of minor offences; it was co-ordinate with the sheriff's turn. Sometimes the lord had yet higher justice in his hands and might hang thieves taken in the act of theft; and thus gradually we ascend the scale of 'royalties' which leads up to the palatine earldoms.

Borough
courts.

The cities and boroughs—vills, that is, which have attained a certain degree of organization and independence—have courts of their own. But of these municipal courts very little can be said in general terms; they are the outcome not of laws but of privileges.

The king's
court.

Above all other courts rises the king's court, which has gradually been dividing itself into three permanent courts, the King's Bench, the Common Bench, the Exchequer. But, besides these permanent and central, it assumes temporary and local forms. Royal justices are sent into the counties under divers commissions; it may be to take the assizes (possessory actions) of the county, it may be to deliver the gaol, it may be as justices in eyre (*in itinere*) to hold all the pleas of the county, civil and criminal. In this last case the justices preside over a very full, solemn and prolonged meeting of the county court. In one way and another, now by the evocation of causes, now by the invention of new actions, the king's courts are not merely reducing all other courts into subordination, but are making them petty courts, courts for the smaller affairs of the smaller folk.

Such being the main outlines, we may endeavour to fill in certain parts of the picture, avoiding much repetition of those matters which have been sufficiently discussed by historians of the English constitution.

§ 1.　*The County.*　[p. 518]

The
county.

Of the origin of the various counties we shall therefore say nothing[1]; but there is one phenomenon which deserves a few words, namely, the 'detached part of a county.' The map of England has never shown such striking examples of dissipated counties as those displayed by the map of Scotland; still the

---

[1] See Stubbs, Const. Hist. i. 122.

total number of cases in which a county has had outlying members is by no means small[1]. It seems certain that many of these anomalies are due to very ancient causes; possibly in a few cases they take us back to the days of intertribal warfare; more probably they illustrate the connexion between property and jurisdiction. The lord of a hundred in one had an estate lying in another shire; he obliged all his men to attend his hundred court; such a proceeding may or may not have been warranted by some royal charter. Thus Domesday Book includes in Worcestershire islands which are surrounded by other counties. These islands belong to the hundred of Oswaldslaw, which belongs to the church of Worcester; but then these islands themselves belong, in a somewhat different sense, to the same church; the church is lord of the land, lord also of the hundredal jurisdiction. These 'detached portions of counties' seem to bring before our eyes the struggle between national and private justice; their small significance in English history and their rapid descent into the category of petty nuisances show how that struggle was decided[2].

Of the county officers, again, we need say but little since constitutional history has taken them under her protection. The earl, except in the case of the palatine earldoms, has little to do with the government of the county which gives him his title; even before the beginning of legal memory he has, we may say, nothing to do with the county, save to be girt with its sword and to receive a third of its pleas, 'the third penny of the county[3].' On the other hand, the sheriff, who, despite the fact that in Latin he is *vicecomes* and in French *le viscount*, has never been the vice-gerent of the earl, is the governor of the shire, the captain of its forces, the president of its court, a distinctively royal officer, appointed by the king, dismissible at a moment's notice, strictly accountable to the Exchequer[4].

[p. 519] *marginal note:* The county officers.

---

[1] A great deal of information may be gained from Schedule M to the Statute 2–3 Will. IV. c. 64.

[2] In 1269 the under-sheriff of Staffordshire is charged with taking a vill out of one hundred to put it in another which he farmed in fee; Staffordshire Collections (Salt Soc.), iv. 170.

[3] Stubbs, Const. Hist. i. 389–394; Round, Geoffrey de Mandeville, 287.

[4] The continued use of the English title *sheriff* might be sufficiently proved by its reappearance on the surface of legal history in later days; but even in the thirteenth century we hear of local exactions which are known as *shirreves welcome, scirrewescot, chiryveschot,* i.e. *auxilium vicecomitis;* R. H. i. 157, 454, 484.

A danger that sheriffdoms would become hereditary offices has been surmounted; at the end of the thirteenth century a danger (if such we think it) that sheriffdoms will become elective offices is being surmounted in spite of popular demands which gradually die out, and pious forgeries which long trouble the stream of legal history[1].   Already before the beginning of the thirteenth century the sheriff is losing some of his powers; before the end we see the first germs of an institution which is destined to grow at his expense, the knights assigned to keep the peace of the county whose successors will be justices of the peace.   But the sheriff of this century, still more the sheriff of the twelfth, is a great man with miscellaneous functions, military and financial, executive and judicial.   Below him in rank and of more recent origin stand the coroners, or, to give them their full title, the keepers of the pleas of the crown (*custodes placitorum coronae*).   Normally the county has four coroners who are elected by the county in the county court.   Their origin is traced to an ordinance of 1194.   The function implied by their title is that of keeping (*custodire*) as distinguished from that of holding [p. 520] (*tenere*) the pleas of the crown; they are not to hear and determine causes, but are to keep record of all that goes on in the county and concerns the administration of criminal justice, and more particularly must they guard the revenues which will come to the king if such justice be duly done[2].

The county community

The 'county' is not a mere stretch of land, a governmental district; it is an organized body of men; it is a *communitas*. We must stop short of saying that it is a corporation.   The idea of a corporation is being evolved but slowly, and our shires never become corporations, so that in later days the term 'county corporate' is employed to distinguish certain municipal boroughs, which have been endowed with the organization of counties, from the ordinary shires or 'counties at large.'   With such 'counties corporate' we have not to deal; they belong to

[1] Reference is here made to the chapter *De heretochiis* (Schmid, cap. 32 *a*) interpolated into some copies of the Leges Edwardi Confessoris.   As to hereditary sheriffs, see Stubbs, Const. Hist. i. 295; as to elective sheriffs, ibid. ii. 206–8.

[2] Stubbs, Const. Hist. i. 505.   Though we see no reason to reject the common doctrine that the general institution of coroners is due to the measure of 1194, still the office of keeping the pleas of the crown may have been known at an earlier time.   See Gross, Coroners' Rolls (Seld. Soc.) Introduction.

another age.   But attending only to the 'counties at large,' we
notice that the law and the language of our period seem at
first sight to treat them much as though they were corporations,
and in this respect to draw no hard line between them and
the chartered towns; the borough is a *communitas,* so is the
county.   It would even seem that under Edward I. the county
of Devon had a common seal[1].   This may have been an exceptional manifestation of unity; but John had granted to
Cornwall and to Devonshire charters which in form differed
little from those that he granted to boroughs:—if a grant of
liberties might be made to the men of a town and their heirs,
so also a grant of liberties, a grant of freedom from forestal
exactions, a grant of the right to elect a sheriff, might be
made to the men of a county and their heirs[2].   But the county
[p. 521] was apt to find its unity brought home to it in the form of
liabilities rather than in the form of rights.   The county was
punished for the mistakes and misdoings of its assembly, the
county court[3].

In the language of the time this proposition that the county must answer for the acts and defaults of the county court appears as a truism, for it can only be expressed by saying that the county must answer for the acts and defaults of the county.   County and county court are so thoroughly one that the same word stands for both.   Rarely, if ever, do we meet with any such term as *curia comitatus* or *curia de comitatu*; the assembly is the *comitatus*, and every session of the assembly is a *comitatus*; for example, when a man is to be outlawed, a proclamation commanding him to present himself must be made in 'five successive counties,' that is at five

The county court.

---

[1] Calendarium Genealogicum, p. 487; a lady ends a document with these
words 'In cuius rei testimonium sigillum meum praesentibus apposui, et quia
sigillum meum est incognitum sigillum comitatus Devoniae apponi procuravi.'
At a later time the hundreds have seals, but these are the outcome of a statute
relating to the transmission of vagrants.

[2] Rot. Cart. 122, 132.   Rot. Cl. i. 457; ii. 25, 169.   Henry II. by charter
granted to the men of Derbyshire that their county court should be held at
Derby instead of at Nottingham.

[3] It will be remembered that to this day the county is an indictable unit,
though no corporation.   The difficulty occasioned by the fact that the county
could not hold land was met by a statute of 1858 (21 and 22 Vic. c. 92), which
provided for lands being held by the clerk of the peace.   At a much earlier
time we find the judges puzzled by the question how damages under the Statute
of Winchester can be recovered from the county; Y. B. Pasch. 17 Edw. II.
f. 539.

successive sessions of the county court. The actual assembly
of men sitting at a certain time and place is the county; the
permanent institution of which that particular assembly is,
as it were, a fleeting representation, is the county; the county
again is a tract of ground; the county is the whole body of
persons who hold lands or reside within that tract, whether
they participate in the doings of the assembly or no. And so
with the word *shire*, which is maintaining its ground alongside
county; if an abbot and his tenants are to be freed from the
duty of attending the county court, it is quite enough to say
that they are to be 'quit of all shires' (*quieti ab omnibus
schiris*). What we say of the county is true also of the
hundred; our law Latin has no such term as 'the court of
the hundred'; the 'hundred' is a district, a body of landholders and residents, a court, the session of a court.

Identity of county and county court.

This absolute identity of the county and its court might be
abundantly illustrated from the rolls which describe the proceedings of the justices in eyre. They come into the county; [p. 522]
the whole county is convened to meet them; the county gives
evidence, answers questions, records its customs, expresses its
suspicions, is believed or disbelieved, is punished. Thus the
justices visit Lincolnshire in 1202; the county gives one account
of proceedings which took place in the county, the coroners'
rolls give another account; the testimony of the latter is
treated as conclusive; the justices therefore are on the point
of fining or amercing the county, but the county forestalls
their judgment by offering a sum of £200 to be paid by the
county[1]. But not merely is the county thus visited in its
home; it has often to appear at Westminster and answer
touching its misdeeds, in particular the miscarriages of justice
which have taken place in its court. A writ of false judgment
(*de falso iudicio*) is brought against the county; thereby the
sheriff is directed to 'record' the proceedings that have taken
place in the county, that is, to cause those proceedings to be
recited or recapitulated in the county court, and then to send
four knights to bear the 'record,' written or unwritten, to
Westminster. The knights come there; they bear record, or
rather the county bears record through their mouths, for what
they say the county says. The complainant disputes this record

---

[1] Select Pleas of the Crown, i. pl. 38. This volume contains many other
illustrations of the same principle. See also Madox, Exch. i. 567.

and offers battle; the county maintains the truth of its record and offers to prove it by the body of a free man of the county, who—so we fear—is no better than a hired champion[1]. The county must pay for its false judgments[2].

The constitution of the body which thus represented, and indeed was, the county has been the theme of sharp controversies[3]; but it has usually been discussed in its relation to the history of parliament. Two opinions have prevailed; some would make the county court an assembly of all the freeholders of the shire, others would make it an assembly of the tenants in chief. Both of these theories have the merit of being simple, but the demerit of being too simple to meet the facts disclosed by documents of the thirteenth century. Of the county court as it was at that time we will first speak, and, this done, we may be the better able to understand the sparse evidence that comes to us from an earlier age[4]. Constitution of the county court.

[p. 523]

And first we must notice that of any right of attending the county court we read no word. Of the duty of attending it we read much, and obviously this duty was irksome. Men seek for charters which shall absolve them from it. In the twelfth century immunities of this kind were frequently granted to religious houses and occasionally to laymen, and, at least in some cases, not merely the grantees themselves but all their tenants were delivered from the burden of doing suit to the communal courts[5]. Precise calculations about such a matter are impossible; it must suffice therefore to say that before the beginning of Edward I.'s reign large tracts of England enjoyed a chartered liberty from this burden. To chartered we must add prescriptive liberties; to immunities that were legally valid we must add others that were actually enjoyed. Prelates and barons 'subtracted the suit'—such was the phrase—due from themselves and their tenants whenever they saw a chance Suit of court no right but a burden.

---

[1] Note Book, pl. 40, 212, 243, 445, 955, 1019, 1130, 1412, 1436, 1672, 1730. Observe in pl. 1019 'Et comitatus hoc defendit praecise,' and in pl. 1412 'Et comitatus dicit quod tale fuit recordum.'

[2] Madox, Exch. i. 556 (31 Hen. III.); the whole county of Norfolk owes £11 for a false judgment.

[3] See Stubbs, Const. Hist. ii. 208–232.

[4] Maitland, The Suitors of the County Court, E. H. R. iii. 418.

[5] In some cases it is quite clear that the immunity excuses not only the grantee himself but also his tenants from suit of court; in other cases this is left in some doubt. See our first edition, i. 523.

of doing this with impunity, and a long continued subtraction would ripen into a lawful franchise.

Suit of court is laborious. Nor is this cause for surprise. Let us try to picture to ourselves the position of some petty freeholder whose lands lie on the north coast of Devon. Once a month he must attend the county court; once a month, that is, he must toil to Exeter, and we can not always allow him a horse. Even if the court gets through its business in one day, he will be [p. 524] away from home for a week at least and his journeyings and sojournings will be at his own cost. When he returns he will have to remember that the hundred court meets once in three weeks, the manorial court once in three weeks, and that he owes suit to both of them. Is it credible that all freeholders discharge these duties?

Sessions of the court. In Henry III.'s reign the county court is usually holden once a month. The third edition of Magna Carta, that of 1217, says that it is not to be holden oftener, but adds that in counties in which it has not sat so frequently the old rule is to prevail[1]. The Lincolnshire court met every forty days[2]; but monthly sessions seem to have been usual elsewhere; in 1219 the county of Surrey was amerced for holding more frequent sessions[3]. As to the hundred court, an ordinance of 1234 declared that it was to meet but once in three weeks[4]. We thus learn that before 1217 the county courts had sometimes been holden at intervals of less than a month, while the ordinance of 1234 expressly tells us that in Henry II.'s day the hundred courts and baronial courts had sat once a fortnight. It is difficult to make these tidings fit into a consistent story with our earlier evidence. A law of Edward the Elder had said in general terms that every reeve is to have a moot in every four weeks[5]. Edgar commanded that the hundreds were to meet once a month[6]; elsewhere he adds that the burghmoot shall be held thrice a year, the shiremoot twice[7]. This last rule is repeated by Cnut with the qualification that the moots are to be held oftener if need be[8]. Henry I. ordains that the

---

[1] Charter of 1217, cap. 42: 'Nullus comitatus de cetero teneatur nisi de mense in mensem, et ubi maior terminus esse solebat, maior sit.'

[2] Note Book, pl. 1730: 'Comitatus Lincolniae semper solet sedere de xl. diebus in xl. dies.'

[3] Note Book, pl. 40.

[4] Statutes, i. 118; Ann. Dunstap. p. 139.

[5] Edward II. 8.

[6] Edgar I. 1.

[7] Edgar III. 5.

[8] Cnut II. 18.

counties and hundreds are to sit as they did in the Confessor's day and not otherwise; if more frequent sessions are required for any royal business they will be summoned[1].   An exposition of this ordinance, which seems to be the work of a contemporary, declares it to mean that the shiremoot and burghmoot [p. 525] are to be holden twice, the hundredmoot twelve times a year, seven days' notice being given unless royal business demands a departure from this rule.   To these assemblies are to come all the lords of lands.   Twice a year, however, a specially full hundred court (the sheriff's turn of later days) is to be holden, at which all the free men (*liberi*) are to be present, whether they be householders or dependants, in order that the tithings may be examined and found full[2].   To this exposition we must return; for the moment we have only to notice that the county court is to all seeming held but twice in the year.   How to reconcile this with the state of things existing a century later and presupposed by the Charter of 1217 is a difficult question. Has the burden of suit been multiplied six fold?

Now that a court with much judicial business will sit but twice a year we can hardly believe.   Medieval procedure required that a suit should come before the court on many occasions before a judgment could be given.   The parties must appear in person, not by attorney; roads are bad; simple justice requires that a defendant should have ample opportunity of appearing before he is treated as contumacious[3].   According to the law of the thirteenth century no man could be outlawed until he was *quinto exactus,* that is until his appearance had been demanded in five successive county courts.   If we suppose that the court sat but once in six months, then the process of outlawry, which we may well suppose to be very ancient, could not be accomplished in less than two years and a half[4].   We

Full courts and intermediate courts.

---

[1] Writ in Select Charters; Liebermann, Quadripartitus, 165.

[2] Leg. Henr. 7, 8, 51, § 2.

[3] In an action for land in a local court, the person in possession was often allowed 'three summonses, three defaults and three essoins before appearance' (Select Pleas in Manorial Courts, i. 107, 112—120) so that if the court sat but twice a year he would have some four years before the day for answering the demandant would arrive.   The MS. Book of Cerne in Camb. Univ. Libr. tells of a suit between the Abbot of Cerne and the Prior of St Swithin's which has come before ten successive county courts and yet seems far from a judgment.

[4] Bracton, f. 125 b.   This rule which required that the outlawry should not take place until the fifth, or according to another mode of reckoning the fourth,

can hardly avoid one of two suppositions and perhaps both should be combined, namely, that in the days before the Con- [p. 526] quest the shire-moot had done little of the ordinary judicial work, this being usually disposed of by the hundred courts, and secondly that between the solemn half-yearly meetings of the county court, at which all the suitors were required to be present, there intervened less solemn meetings attended only by a smaller group of suitors before whom the formal and preliminary steps in litigation, the 'interlocutory proceedings' as we should call them, could be taken. This latter theory is supported by numerous entries upon the Hundred Rolls. Just as there are many men who owe suit to the two half-yearly meetings of the hundred court which are known as the sheriff's turns but owe no suit to the intervening sessions, so, at least in certain shires, the suitors of the county court fall into two classes; many are bound to go month by month, while others are bound to go but twice a year; they go to two meetings which are distinguished as 'the great counties' or 'the general counties[1].' The suitors of the manorial courts fall into two similar classes; some must appear every three weeks, others twice a year[2].

The suitors. But whichever of these two classes we examine, we can not say that it is constituted either by all the freeholders of the shire or merely by the tenants in chief. A more complex idea must be introduced, but one which will not be unfamiliar to us after what we have seen of scutage. Suit to the county and hundred is a burden incumbent on land. It has taken

county court, is recognized in a case of 1221 : Select Pleas of the Crown, vol. i. pl. 129. So also there is constant mention in the A.-S. dooms of the voucher of successive warrantors, and each voucher must have involved at least one adjournment.

[1] See *e.g.* the account of Oxfordshire, R. H. ii. 835–877; of many of the landowners it is said 'facit duos adventus ad magnos comitatus Oxoniae,' or 'facit bis sectam ad duos magnos comitatus Oxoniae.' So in Yorkshire; 'facere solebant unum adventum singulis annis ad generalem comitatum Eboraci'; P. Q. W. 217.

[2] The difficulty noticed in this paragraph is discussed by Stubbs, Const. Hist. i. 649. All that we can add to his explanations is the fact that long after 1217 two half-yearly meetings of the county court are distinguished as 'the great counties' from the ordinary monthly meetings, and the suggestion that, though the Leges Henrici speak only of the great half-yearly meetings, there may also have been monthly meetings attended only by a small body of suitors. The history of the Frankish courts supplies analogies.

root in particular acres. Feoffments and private bargains can
not shift that burden from the land, nor will they increase
[p. 527] the number of suits that are due; but, as between the various
persons interested in that land, they can and will determine
who is to do the suit. We will suppose that *A* holds a tract
of land for which he owes a suit to the county; he enfeoffs
B, C and *D* with parcels of that land. One suit and no more
is due. Probably as regards the king and his sheriff all four
persons are liable for that suit; all or any of them can be
attacked if the suit be not done; but, as between themselves,
the terms of the feoffments decide which of them ought to
do it.

We may be pardoned for spending some little time over this Suit is a
doctrine, for it illustrates the complicated texture of medieval 'real' burden.
society and the large liberty that men enjoyed of regulating
by private bargains what we might deem matters of public
law.

And in the first place we notice that suit to the communal
courts is often spoken of as the whole or part of the service
by which a man holds his land; it is mentioned in the same
breath with suit to the lord's court, rent and scutage[1]. A
man may hold his land by the service of finding one doomsman
for the hundred court, or may hold it for 9*s.* 2½*d.* and half a
doomsman[2]. Then again we find such cases as the following.
In the vill of Bottisham the Earl of Gloucester has some forty
freehold tenants; two of them do suit to the hundred and
county courts for the earl and the whole township[3]. The Abbot
of Ramsey has a manor at Burwell: the jurors do not know
that he does any service for it except two suits to every county
court; but these two are actually done by two tenants of his;
J. A. holds a hide and does one suit, B. B. holds ninety acres
and does the other. Any number of similar instances might

---

[1] R. H. ii. 483: 'W. G. holds two virgates of the Abbot of Ramsey. For one
virgate he does suit to the county of Cambridge and the hundred and pays 12*d.*
towards the sheriff's aid. For the other virgate he pays 5*s.* a year to the Abbot
and does suit to the Abbot's court at Broughton.' Y. B. Trin. 7 Edw. II. f. 243:
'Your predecessor enfeoffed William of the one virgate to hold by homage,
fealty, three shillings a year and suit to his court, and for the other virgate, to
do suit to the hundred of A. and the county of Hertford for the vill of L.'

[2] Testa de Nevill, 404–5. The word translated as doomsman is *iudex*,
instead of which *index* is too frequently printed.

[3] R. H. ii. 488.

be found. As regards suit to the hundred court, we have [p. 528] yet more explicit tidings. The opinion of the jurors from whose verdicts the Hundred Rolls were compiled was distinctly this, that suit was a burden on particular tenements, a burden not to be increased by any subdivision of those tenements. They complain that the Earl of Surrey who holds the hundred of Gallow has not observed this rule. There was, for instance, a tenement in South Creake containing 100 acres; it owed a single suit; it has been divided into 40 tenements and 40 suits are exacted[1]. And so, again, if the tenement becomes partible among coheiresses, the number of suits, at least in the jurors' opinion, should not be increased; the burden should lie on the share of the eldest sister[2].

'Reality' of suit.

Once more, the king sets the law in motion against someone who has 'subtracted his suit.' Now were this duty incumbent on all freeholders, nothing would be simpler than the king's case; he would merely have to say 'You are a freeholder of the county and you are not doing suit.' But the king's advocates do not adopt this easy course; they make it a matter of seisin. The king demands a suit because he has, or his ancestors have, been seised of a suit done by the defendant or his predecessors in title. King Edward I. demands a suit to the hundred court from the Earl of Norfolk and relies on the seisin of King Henry III. The Earl comes and denies the king's right and the seisin of King Henry. A jury gives the Earl a verdict and he goes quit[3]. If the mere fact that the Earl was a freeholder would have made him liable to do suit, the king's counsel sadly mismanaged their case. This is but one example from among many.

The vill as a suit-owing unit.

Now all this seems inconsistent with the notion that a [p. 529] freeholder as such owes suit. Somehow or another the court, or the king—for it is in the king's name that the duty must be enforced—has become entitled to a fixed number of suits, each of which is incumbent on a certain tract of land. Of the size and nature of these suit-owing tracts our evidence only permits us to say that there is no uniformity, but that often a whole vill or manor is represented by a single suitor. It would seem that even 'the great counties' or 'general counties' were not

---

[1] R. H. i. 455. See also the hundred of Humbleyard, ibid. 471.
[2] R. H. i. 498.
[3] P. Q. W. 730.

very large assemblies, while the court which met once a month
was, at least in some shires, much smaller. Possibly different
opinions as to the nature of the duty prevailed in different
counties. In Yorkshire, for example, where suits exigible from
all freeholders would have been an intolerable burden, the usual
attendants at the county court seem to be the stewards of the
tenants in chief[1]. But in general the assembly was formed out
of miscellaneous elements; there were tenants by military
service and socage tenants, tenants in chief of the king and
tenants of mesne lords, great men and small men. Many of
them were knights, the predecessors of the country gentlemen
who for centuries to come will do justice and manage the
county business because they like the work; but there were
also yeomen, holders of but a virgate or so apiece, who went
there because they were bound to go by their tenure; they pay
little or no rent because they discharge a duty which otherwise would fall upon their lords.

At the same time we must not credit the men of the
thirteenth century with a thoroughly consistent doctrine as
to the 'real' character of the duty[2]. There is a conflict of
[p. 530] interests and therefore a clash of theories. In 1258, when the
Barons' War was at hand, there was an outcry about suit of
court; new-fangled suits are exacted as well to counties and
hundreds as to franchise courts[3]. The provision made in
answer to this outcry spoke only of suits due to the courts of
the lords and does not seem to touch the county courts or such
of the hundred courts as were not in private hands[4]. Among
other points it decides that, when a tenement which owes a
suit descends to coheirs or is divided by feoffment, no more
than one suit is due. This may be the decision of a question

Inconsistent theories of suit.

---

[1] Thus Baldwin Wake holds a manor of Nicholas de Meynill who holds of
Peter de Maulay; Peter does suit to the county of York by his steward for all
his tenants; therefore none is due from Baldwin; P. Q. W. 199. In the
fifteenth century the stewards of the great lords seem to have been the electors
for the county of York. See Stubbs, Const. Hist., iii. 424, as to the peculiar
character of the Yorkshire elections.

[2] It may be necessary to warn the reader that the 'suit real' of old books,
which is contrasted with 'suit service,' suggests a falsehood to us moderns.
The word 'real' in this context means 'royal,' and an attempt was made at
times to prevent this 'suit royal' from becoming 'real' in the sense in which
we use that word. See Y. B. 33-5 Edw. I. p. 91.

[3] Petition of the Barons, c. 24.

[4] Provisions of Westminster, c. 1, 2, 3; Stat. Marlb. c. 9.

that had been open, and we find that the converse case had been debatable. If a division of the tenement does not increase the number of suits, the union of several tenements, we might argue, ought not to decrease that number. But we find it otherwise decided, 'for it is not consonant to law that when two inheritances descend to one heir, or when one person acquires divers tenements, more suits than one should be due for these several inheritances or tenements to one and the same court[1].' 'Reality' and 'personality,' if we may so speak, are contending for the mastery, and the result which emerges after the days of Lewes and Evesham seems favourable to the freeholders. When a tenement is divided, the suit is considered as annexed to the land; when two tenements meet, it is deemed a personal duty. It is not impossible that early in the fourteenth century the attempt to compel reluctant suitors to attend the county court was already being abandoned. In the other local courts it was usual to receive and enrol the 'essoins,' that is the excuses for non-attendance, of the suitors who did not appear. But this, we are told, was not done in the county courts, whence we may infer that those who did not attend were not at pains to excuse themselves[2]. There is much in the later history of parliamentary elections to make us believe that little trouble was taken to enforce the appearance of those who were bound to come, and that no trouble was taken to exclude the presence of others[3].

The court in its fullest form.

Besides the shape that it took once in every four weeks and [p. 531] the fuller shape that it took once in every six months, the county court may have taken a yet ampler shape upon great occasions, in particular when it was summoned to meet the justices in eyre, an event which, according to the opinion of the suitors of Henry III.'s day, was not to occur more than once in seven years and which as a matter of fact did not occur much oftener. That the common immunity 'from shires and hundreds' did not discharge its possessors from having to appear at these grand meetings is clear. It may even be argued that on these rare occasions all the freeholders of the county

---

[1] Writ of 43 Hen. III. found in a MS. Registrum Brevium; Camb. Univ. Lib. Kk. v. 33.

[2] The Court Baron (Selden Soc.) pp. 80-1.

[3] See Riess, *Geschichte des Wahlrechts*, cap. 3; but Riess, to our thinking, passes too lightly by the duty of suit of court.

had to present themselves. But the writs which summon these meetings hardly prove this[1]; we find some traces of persons bound by tenure to discharge the suit due from vills and manors even when that suit is to be done before the justices in eyre[2], and the lists of persons who either sent excuses for not coming or were amerced for being absent without excuse do not point to assemblages so large as those which must have come together had every freeholder of the shire been bound to attend them.

[p. 532] From a time remoter than the thirteenth century we have little evidence; indeed the passage in the *Leges Henrici* to which reference has already been made[3] seems to tell us all that we can learn. It gives us a list of the persons who are to attend the shiremoot—*episcopi, comites, vicedomini, vicarii, centenarii, aldermanni, praefecti, praepositi, barones, vavassores, tungrevii, et ceteri terrarum domini.* Of some of the titles here mentioned an explanation is to be sought rather in France than in England; we may doubt whether to the writer's mind they conveyed any precise meaning, whether he meant much more than that all persons of distinction, all the great, ought to come[4]. But who are the *terrarum domini?* That they are not

The communal courts in earlier times.

---

[1] For the form of the summons see Rot. Cl. i. 380, 473, 476; ii. 151, 213; Bracton, f. 109 b. It runs thus:—'Summone per bonos summonitores omnes archiepiscopos, episcopos, comites, et barones, milites et libere tenentes de tota bailliva tua et de qualibet villa iiij. legales homines et praepositum et de quolibet burgo xij. legales burgenses per totam ballivam tuam et omnes alios de bailliva tua qui coram iusticiariis nostris itinerantibus venire solent et debent.' Now to say 'Summon all the archbishops, bishops, earls, barons, knights and freeholders of your bailiwick and all others of your bailiwick who are wont and ought to attend the justices' is to use a phrase which is not too precise. May it not mean 'Summon those (freeholders and others) who are wont and ought to come'?

[2] Thus a tenant of the Abbot of Gloucester is bound to acquit the whole vill from suit to all courts of the hundred or of the county or of justices and all other suits which pertain to the said vill; Cart. Glouc. i. 386. At Northleach a tenant of the Abbot is bound to do suit for his lord to the county and the hundred and must remain before the justices in eyre during the whole of their session; Ibid. iii. 180.

[3] Leg. Hen. 7, § 2.

[4] The *vicedomini* may possibly be the *vicecomites*, the sheriffs, who, if this be not so, are omitted from the list; but the three titles *vicedomini, vicarii, centenarii* coming together suggest that the writer is using up all the titles that he knows, whether French or English. Neither the *vidame* nor the *viguier* took root in England; the *centenarii* may be the bailiffs of the hundreds, but the conjunction of these three titles is rather French or Frankish than English.

merely the tenants in chief may fairly be argued from the fact
that vavassors as well as barons are among them, though we
can not be certain that either of a baron or of a vavassor any
exact definition could have been given[1].   Whether the term
'lords of lands' or 'owners of lands' was intended to comprise   [p. 533]
the humbler freeholders (for example, the considerable class of
persons who appear in Domesday Book as *liberi homines*), may
be doubtful; *dominus* is a flexible word; but we have some
proof that in Henry I.'s time 'small men,' *minuti homines*, owed
suit to the county court and served as doomsmen[2].   Altogether
the words of our text are vague; they point to no one clearly
established rule, but rather to a struggle between various
principles[3].

A struggle
between
various
principles.

One principle might be found in personal rank : the rank
of a baron, knight, vavassor, thegn.   Another in the characters
of the various tenures : military and non-military, serjeanty
and socage.   A third in the grades of tenure, tenancy in chief
of the king being contrasted with mesne tenures.   Probably
a fourth was already being found in what we take leave to call
mere ·realism' and private bargainings; suit is becoming a
debt owed by manors and acres, and those who represent the
burdened land may adjust the burden as seems to them best.
If a lord attends, we are told, he thereby discharges all the land

Stapleton, Norman Exchequer Rolls, i. xxxv., says that the titles *vicarius* and
centenarius are not met with in Norman diplomas of a later date than the
eleventh century.

[1] Neither the theory that the *vavassor* must needs be a vassal's vassal, nor
the derivation of his name from *vassi vassorum* can be regarded as certain.   In
England the word is rare.   We said somewhat more of it in our first edition,
i. 532.   It is very remarkable that in the list of titles now under discussion
milites does not occur.

[2] Thus in the Pipe Roll of 31 Hen. I., p. 28, there is mention of the 'minuti
iudices et iuratores,' whose misdoings have rendered them liable for a sum of
more than 300 marks.   Elsewhere the same document uses the terms 'minuti
homines' and 'smalemanni' as though they represent a well-recognized class :
thus p. 103, 'iuratores et minuti homines'; p. 132, 'de tainis et dreinnis [thegns
and drengs] et smalemannis inter Tinam et Teodam.'

[3] The difficulty is increased by Leg. Hen. Prim. 29, § 1, where it is said that
the king's judges are to be the barons of the county who have free lands, while
villeins, cotsets, farthinglanders (*ferdingi*) and other unsubstantial folk (*viles vel
inopes personae*) are not to act as judges.   This passage seems to contemplate
the existence of no class intermediate between *barones* and *villani* ; but, unless
both of these terms are used with enormous licence, such a class there certainly
was,

that he holds in demesne[1]. Suppose him to make a feoffment
of part of this land; why should a second suit become due?
The court is entitled only to such suits as it has been seised
of in the past.

The privilege of doing his suit by attorney to the courts of Suit by
the county, the trithing, the hundred and to the seignorial attorney.
courts was conceded to every free man by the Statute of
[p. 534] Merton in 1236[2]. This general concession we may treat as
new, though for a long time past the greater men were privileged to send their stewards or a deputation of villagers from
their villages[3], and sometimes the tenant who was bound by
his tenure to discharge the suit due from the land was spoken
of as the enfeoffed attorney or attorned feoffee of his lord[4].
As to the deputation of villagers, we read nothing of this in
documents later than the *Leges Henrici*, though, as will be
seen hereafter, the reeve and four men of the township have
to attend the sheriff's turn and the coroner's inquests, and
they must go to the county court if they have a crime to
present. Nor do the *Leges Henrici* contemplate their appearance as normal:—if neither the lord nor his steward can be
present, then the reeve, priest and four men may appear and
acquit the vill of its suit. Still this draws our attention to yet
another principle that has been at work: the county court
represents not merely all the lands, but also all the vills of the
shire, and it is quite in conformity with this that in the thirteenth century the suit-owing unit of land should frequently
be a vill[5].

Perhaps it is this heterogeneous character of the county and Represen-
hundred courts which makes it possible for men to regard them character
as thoroughly representative assemblies and to speak of them of county
as being the counties and hundreds. They do not represent court.
one well-defined class or condition of men, and they do represent all the lands of the shire, franchises excepted. Every

---

[1] Leg. Hen. 7, § 7.   [2] Stat. Mert. c. 10.   [3] Leg. Hen. c. 7, § 7.

[4] Thus the Prior of Deerhurst owes a single suit to the county of Oxford for
his manor of Taynton; this is done for him by J. S., his attorney enfeoffed for
this purpose in ancient times; R. H. ii. 733.

[5] In one of the Phillipps MSS. of Bracton, No. 3510, f. 36 d., a note from the
early years of cent. xiv. says that when the county is fined for false judgment,
'tunc soli liberi homines per quos iudicia talia redduntur divites et pauperes
pro aequalibus portionibus contribuunt, nullo modo disenarii, i.e. custumarii';
but 'soli custumarii et non liberi homines' pay the murder fine.

landholder who holds his land freely may be deemed to be present there, if not in person then by someone who represents his land, it may be by his lord, or it may be by his tenant. At any rate the whole shire, franchises excepted, seems responsible for the misdoings and defaults of its court, even for those which take place in the thinly attended meetings that are holden month by month.

The suitors as doomsmen.

The suitors were the doomsmen of the court. The evidence [p. 535] that they bore this English title is indeed slight, but some such term we must use[1]. Occasionally in Latin documents they are spoken of as *iudices*, more commonly as *iudicatores*[2]; *iusticiarii* they are not; *iudicatores* is a word which serves to distinguish them from ecclesiastical *iudices* and royal *iusticiarii*[3]. But whatever may have been their English title, their function is put before us as that of 'making the judgments.' If for a moment we adopt German terms, we can say that they are *die Urteilfinder*, while the sheriff or (as the case may be) the bailiff of the hundred, or the steward of the franchise is *der Richter*. He is, we may say, the presiding magistrate; he summons the court, he 'holds the court,' he 'holds the pleas,' he regulates the whole procedure, he issues the mandates; but he does not make the judgments: when the time for a judgment has come he demands it from the suitors. During the Norman period this seems the constitution of all courts, high and low. When there is a trial in the king's court, the king demands a judgment from the assembled prelates and barons[4]. But the gradual intrusion of the sworn inquest, of the nascent trial by jury, soon begins to transfigure those courts in which the king presides by himself or his commissioners; justices and jurors begin to take the place of president and doomsmen, and

---

[1] See Hazlitt's edition of Blount's Tenures, p. 174, citing the Hundred Roll of Hereford; 'solebat facere sectam ad hundredum praedictum et esse unus doomsman de eodem hundredo.' But this has not been found in the printed Hundred Roll.

[2] Hazlitt's Blount, pp. 46, 152, 'per servitium inveniendi unum iudicatorem'; Select Pleas in Manorial Courts, i. p. lxv, 'pro defectu iudicatorum.' In the Pipe Roll of 31 Hen. I. we find p. 27, 'iudicatores comitatus,' p. 28 'minuti iudices,' p. 34 'iudices et iuratores de Eborascira,' p. 97 'de iudicibus comitatus et hundretorum.'

[3] In Normandy the contrast is between the *iusticiarius* and the *iudiciarii*. See Somma, pp. 31–2.

[4] When a peccant vicar choral of Salisbury is brought before the dean and chapter, the dean asks the canons for a judgment: Reg. St Osmund, ii. 24.

this process is so rapid that we have now-a-days some difficulty in describing the ancient courts without using foreign or archaic terms. Still the communal courts preserve their ancient form. Under Edward I. Hengham says that if a false judgment is given in the county court, the sheriff ought not to be punished;
[p. 536] 'the county, that is, the commune of the county' is to be punished; therefore, he adds, let the suitors beware. Perhaps in his day some explanation of this state of things was thought necessary, at any rate he gives one :—sheriffs might err from partiality or from ignorance; besides sheriffs are sometimes men of little substance and would be unable to pay an amercement if convicted of a false judgment. Therefore, says he, it is ordained that the judgment be given by the whole county[1].

That even in the thirteenth century the participation of the suitors in the judgments was no mere formality we may learn from records which give us valuable glimpses of the county courts and their procedure. In 1226 there was a quarrel between the sheriff of Lincolnshire and the suitors. The version of the story favourable to the sheriff is this :—One day he held pleas in the county court from early morn to vespertide and then, since many pleas remained unheard for lack of daylight, he told the 'stewards and knights and others of the county' that they must come again next morning, hear the plaints and make the judgments. On the following morning the sheriff took his seat; the knights and stewards remained outside the house; he bade them come in, hear the plaints and make the judgments. They refused, and even those who had entered the house left it saying that the county court should only be holden for one day at a time. Therefore the sheriff, since he alone could not make the judgments, adjourned the plaintiffs and defendants to the wapentake courts; seven score cases were left unheard. Then he held a court for the ten wapentakes of Ancaster, to which came many, both knights and others;
[p. 537] among them Theobald Hauteyn and Hugh of Humby; and, the pleadings having been heard, the sheriff told the knights to make the judgments. Then Theobald arose and said that they ought not to make the judgments there nor elsewhere outside the county court, for he had lately been in the king's court talking with the Archbishop and the Earl of Chester and other magnates and he was certain that before three weeks were out

A session of the county court.

---

[1] Hengham Magna, cap. iv.

they would have the king's writ freeing them from these exactions. Thereupon the sheriff answered that for all this he
should not stay his hand from doing justice to the poor until
he received some command to the contrary; and once more he
bade the knights and others make the judgments. They then
asked leave to talk the matter over by themselves and went
out. While they were in conference, Theobald and Hugh came
to them, and protested that the sheriff was infringing Magna
Carta and the franchises of the magnates, and advised them
to make no judgments. Then they entered the house, and
Theobald as their spokesman said that they were not bound to
make any judgments, and abused the sheriff and demanded
his warrant for holding pleas in the wapentake. The sheriff
answered that he thought that he as sheriff and bailiff of the
king had warrant enough, and then departed, his business
undone. Then arose Thomas Fitz Simon, the steward of John
Marshall, and said that Hugh was wrong in demanding the
sheriff's warrant and that it was rather for Hugh to show why
the sheriff should not hold pleas. And then Thomas deemed a
doom (*et unum iudicium fecit idem Thomas*). 'That's your
doom,' was the scornful answer; 'we shall have your lord here
presently and will tell him how you behave yourself in this
county[1].'

The suitors and the dooms. We have told this curious story at length because it illustrates several points, the constitution of the court by 'the
stewards, knights and others,' the amount of business that it
has to do, such that after a long day's work a hundred and
forty causes must stand adjourned, the unwillingness of the
suitors to do anything that may increase the burden of the
suit, the position of the sheriff as the presiding officer, his
incompetence to make judgments. Over and over again the
function of the suitors is defined as that of making judgments.
And it is much rather as 'judges of law' than as 'judges of [p. 538]
fact'—if into such a context we may introduce these modern
terms—that the suitors are expected to be active. In the
seventeenth century John Smyth could boast of the good
justice done by the free suitors of the hundred of Berkeley
where 'there had not been in any age any trials by jury[2].' A
collection of precedents designed for the use of the stewards of

---

[1] Note Book, pl. 1730. See also pl. 212.
[2] Smyth, Lives of the Berkeleys, iii. 12.

the manorial courts has come down to us. In most of the hypothetical cases all is supposed to go smoothly; the plaintiff pleads, the defendant pleads, and then the steward as a matter of course gives the judgment of the court, to the effect that there must be an inquest or that the defendant is to bring compurgators to prove his case. We may indeed read through almost the whole tract without discovering that the steward has assessors. But in one case the defendant does not deny the plaintiff's plaint with adequate particularity. Thereupon the steward bids the parties retire and addresses the dooms-men :—'Fair sirs, ye who are of this court, how seemeth it to you that the defendant hath defended this?' A spokesman answers that the defence was insufficient. The parties are then recalled and the steward informs them of the judgment of the court[1]. Probably in a manorial court the steward would often have his own way; but a sheriff might find that some of the suitors of the county knew more law than he did, and our story from Lincolnshire will show that they might have opinions of their own about the meaning of Magna Carta. To give one more example :—In Edward I.'s day the palatinate of Chester had fallen into the king's hand; the justiciar of Chester was the king's officer. On one occasion he was presiding in the palatine court and Ralph Hengham, one of the royal justices of England, had been sent thither to act as his assessor. An assize of last presentation came before them; certain usual words were missing from the writ. Thereupon arose one John of Whetenhall, who was sitting among the doomsmen of the county, and asserted that the Earl of Chester had delivered to them a register of original writs and that the writ in the present case conformed to that register. The doomsmen then demanded an adjournment until the morrow, and then one of them pronounced the judgment. Hengham declared that the judgment was against law and departed. Thus, even in the presence of a royal justice, the doomsmen of Chester decided questions of law[2]. On other occasions we find these 'doomsmen and suitors' asserting that before a judgment of their court is evoked to the king's court, all the barons and [p. 539] their stewards and all the doomsmen of the county must be

---

[1] The Court Baron (Selden Soc.) p. 48.
[2] Placit. Abbrev. 268–9.

summoned to decide whether they will stand by the judgment
or amend it[1].

Powers of
a majority.

We learn from one passage in the *Leges Henrici* that if the
judges disagreed the opinion of the majority prevailed[2]; in
another passage we are told that the opinion which is to prevail
is that of the better men and that which is most acceptable to
the justice. The latter text, though not unambiguous, seems
to mean that, if the doomsmen differ about the doom, the sheriff
or other president of the court may adopt the ruling that he
thinks best, but should have regard to the rank and repute of
those who have offered their opinions[3]. A case would not
necessarily be heard by the whole body of suitors. In the first
place, some might be rejected from the judgment-seat for
divers reasons, in particular as not being the 'peers' of the
parties; for it is in this context that we first hear the phrase
that became famous at a later time, *iudicium parium suorum.*
Every one is to be judged by his peers and by men of the same
district; there are to be no 'foreign judgments,' that is to say,
judgments by strangers; the great man is not to perish by the
judgment of those of lower degree[4]. How far this dangerously
aristocratic principle was carried we can not say; to all appearance the old scheme of estates of men, which recognized
such equations as 1 thegn = 6 ceorls, gave way before feudal
influences, while those influences were not powerful enough to
substitute in its stead a classification based on the various
kinds or the various grades of tenure. The small are not to
judge the great:—no more accurate principle can be stated.
In the second place, it seems to have been a common practice,
at least in certain districts, for the parties to elect from among
the suitors a few judges to decide their dispute; both parties [p. 540]

---

1 Placit. Abbrev. 229, 287.

2 Leg. Henr. c. 5, § 6.

3 Leg. Henr. c. 31, § 2: 'vincat sententia meliorum et cui iustitia magis
acquieverit.' Even if *iustitia* here means 'justice' and not 'the justice,' still it
would be for the justice to decide on which side justice lay. In these *Leges* the
title *iustitia* seems to be often given to the sheriff or other president of the
court. The general theory of the time demands that the prevailing opinion
shall be that of the *maior et sanior pars.* See above p. 509. Also see the
Norman Somma, p. 33: if the discreter folk are in the minority, judgment shall
be deferred to another session.

4 Leg. Henr. c. 31 § 7: 'Unusquisque per pares suos est iudicandus, et
eiusdem provinciae; peregrina vero iudicia modis omnibus submovemus.' Ibid.
c. 32, § 1: 'nec summorum quispiam minorum iudicatione dispereat.'

might agree in choosing the same men, or the one party would choose half of the whole number, the other party the other half[1].

We may well suppose that the ordinary business of the court was transacted by a small group of active men. Of such a group we hear something, and the members of it seem to bear the strange name *busones* or *buzones*. Bracton tells us that, when the king's justices in eyre come into the county and have proclaimed the object of their mission, they shall go apart, taking with them some four or six or more of the great folk of the county, who are called the *busones* of the county and whose opinions carry weight with the rest, and shall have a colloquy with them[2]. To suggest that in the place of this curious word we should read *barones* is easy; but the same word occurs elsewhere. In John's reign the county of Gloucester was amerced for a false judgment; the roll which records this adds, 'And let the knights of the county who are wont to take part in false judgments and are *buzones iudiciorum*, be arrested[3].' Neither passage would suggest that this title was official, or more than a cant name for the active doomsmen of the shire-moot; but the context into which Bracton introduces it may serve to show how the way was paved for the justices of the peace of a later time.

The buzones.

To what we have said above concerning the competence of this court little can here be added. Seemingly its jurisdiction in actions for land had become of small importance in the course of the thirteenth century. It formed a stepping-stone between the feudal court and the royal court, and he who brought his case thus far meant to carry it further. As regards personal actions, in Edward I.'s day its competence was restricted within a limit of forty shillings[4]. When, how and why this limit was imposed is a difficult question. Possibly we may trace it to an exposition which the king's justices had given of the Statute of Gloucester (1278), though this statute

Business of the court.

[p. 541]

---

[1] Leg. Henr. c. 31, § 8: 'In quibusdam locis utrumque eligitur iudicium, medietas ab eis quorum est negotium.' The history of Ramsey Abbey, c. xlvii. p. 79, describes an action brought in the days before the Conquest: 'xxxvi barones de amicis utriusque partis pari numero electos ipsi iudices constituerunt.'

[2] Bracton, f. 115 b.

[3] Placit. Abbrev. p. 85. The word occurs twice in the record.

[4] Britton, i. 155; Fleta, 133.

on the face of it seems to favour the local tribunals, for it merely says that none shall have a writ of trespass in the king's court unless he will affirm that the goods taken away were worth forty shillings at the least[1]. But the sum of forty shillings is mentioned at a much earlier time. In the Irish Register of Writs of John's day a writ directing the sheriff to hold a plea of debt (in technical language 'a *Justicies* for debt') is given with the remark that if the debt be less than forty shillings this writ can be obtained without gift, that is without payment to the king, while if the debt is greater the plaintiff must find security to pay the king a third of the sum that he recovers[2]. In a treatise of somewhat later date[3] we find the same rule, but the limiting sum has been raised from forty shillings to thirty marks. In general a plaintiff who went to the county court to recover a debt did not want any writ at all, though the royal missive might be useful, since it would urge a dilatory and not impartial sheriff to do his duty. Perhaps some combination between a rule about the fees to be paid for writs and the rule laid down by the Statute of Gloucester produced that limitation of the competence of our local courts which in the end was their ruin. However, in Edward I.'s day ruin was a long way off; forty shillings was as yet a good round sum.

Outlawry in the county court.

One act of jurisdiction, one supreme and solemn act, could be performed only in the county courts and in the folk-moot of London, the act of outlawry. Even the king's court did not perform it. The king's justices could order that a man should be 'exacted,' that is, that proclamation should be made bidding him come in to the king's peace, and could further order that in case of his not appearing he should be outlawed; but the ceremony of exaction and outlawry could take place only in a shire-moot or folk-moot. And so it is even in our own day, or rather so it would be, had not outlawry become a mere [p. 542] name[4].

Governmental functions.

In the main the county court is a court of law; but in the middle ages jurisdiction is never very clearly separated

[1] Stat. 6 Edw. I. c. 8.

[2] Maitland, History of the Register, Harv. L. R., iii. 112.

[3] Maitland, Glanvill Revised, Harv. L. R. vol. vi.

[4] John Wilkes was outlawed in the county court of Middlesex 'at the Three Tons in Brook Street near Holborne in the county of Middlesex': Burrow's Reports, p. 2530.

from government, and, as has been sufficiently shown elsewhere[1], the assembly of the shire sometimes has fiscal, military and administrative business before it. It can even treat with the king about the grant of a tax, and ultimately, as all know, it sends chosen knights to represent it in the parliaments. Still we should have but little warrant for calling it a governmental assembly. It can declare the custom of the county, but we do not often hear of its issuing ordinances or by-laws, though, with the sanction of the justices in eyre, the county of Northumberland, all the free men thereof unanimously consenting, institutes a close time for the precious salmon[2]. Nor must we endow this assembly with any inherent power of imposing taxes, though the liability of the county for the repair of certain bridges appears at an early time and may occasionally have necessitated a vote and resolution. Thus in John's reign the Abbot of Lilleshall says that the sheriff and other magnates provided that he should build a bridge at Atcham and in return might take certain tolls[3]. Still in Edward II.'s reign the communities of Shropshire and Cheshire go to the king for leave to levy a pavage for the improvement of a ford[4], and, as we shall see below, even the boroughs did not at this time aspire to much liberty of self-taxation.

Hengham speaks as though the county court was sometimes held in the open air and in out-of-the-way places[5]. Usually it was held in the county town; but in Edward II.'s day the sheriff of Sussex had been holding it at divers places, and to fix it at Chichester required a royal ordinance[6]. In Henry II.'s reign the county court of Derbyshire was held at Nottingham until the king established it at Derby on the petition of the Derbyshire folk[7]. Some moots may still have assembled in the open air; the Lincolnshire court sat in doors[8]; Earl Edmund built a great hall at Lostwithiel for the county court of Cornwall[9]; but we still hear of 'a green place' in which the court of Essex was holden[10]. Apparently in old times the

Place of session.

[p. 543]

[1] Stubbs, Const. Hist. ii. 208–216.

[2] Northumberland Assize Rolls, p. 208.

[3] Select Pleas of the Crown, pl. 176.   [4] Rot. Parl. i. 397.

[5] Hengham Magna, cap. 4: 'quia frequenter evenit quod comitatus tenentur in silvis et campestribus foris villis et alibi.'

[6] Rot. Parl. i. 379; see also Stat. 19 Hen. VII. c. 24.

[7] P. Q. W. 159.   [8] See above, p. 549.

[9] Rot. Parl. i. 296.   [10] R. H. i. 142.

doomsmen of the court sat upon four benches arranged in a square; what was done in court was done 'within the four benches[1].'

§ 2.   *The Hundred.*

The hundred as a district.
The county is divided into hundreds or into wapentakes or into wards, the term 'wapentake' appearing in Yorkshire, Lincolnshire, Derbyshire, Nottinghamshire, the term 'ward' in the northernmost counties. It is well known that the size of the hundred varies very greatly, but that it varies according to a certain general rule. 'Thus Kent and Sussex at the time when Domesday Book was compiled, each contained more than sixty hundreds, as they do at present; and in the counties which composed the ancient kingdom of Wessex, the hundreds are almost as numerous, while the irregularity of size, and the scattered confusion of the component parts of these ancient hundreds must have been the result of usurpation or of improvident grants......On the contrary, Norfolk and Suffolk (the East-Anglian counties) maintain a regularity of division still applicable in many instances to the administration of justice. In the midland counties the hundreds increase in size, but are not deficient in regularity. In Lancashire (a county of greater extent than any of the Wessex counties) there are no more than six hundreds—in Cheshire, seven:—and upon the whole so irregular is this distribution of territory, that while some of the southern hundreds do not exceed two square miles...... ......the hundreds of Lancashire average at three hundred square miles in area[2].' If we consider not acreage but a more significant fact, namely, the number of vills in the hundred, we [p. 544] are brought to similar results. A Kentish hundred will often contain but two, three or four vills; there seem to be instances in which vill and hundred are coterminous[3]. A 'detached part'

---

[1] Northumberland Assize Rolls (Surtees Soc.) p. 196: 'infra quatuor bancos.' In the borough court at Totnes proceedings take place 'inter quatuor scamna gildhallae'; Third Rep. Hist. MSS. Ap. 342. In later days the suitors of a court baron are sometimes called its 'benchers.'

[2] Population Abstract, 1831, vol. i. pp. xiv–xv.

[3] Thus the hundred of Barclay seems to consist of the parish of Biddenden: Ibid. i. 266.

of a hundred is commoner than a 'detached part' of a county; some hundreds have from a remote time been extremely discrete.

The hundred had a court. According to the *Leges Henrici* it was held twelve times a year[1]; but in 1234, an ordinance states that in Henry II.'s time it was held at fortnightly intervals and declares that for the future it is to sit but once in every three weeks[2]. It seems to have been supplied with suitors in the same way that the county court was supplied:— the duty of suit had taken root in the soil. In some cases the number of suitors was small. We read that in the wapentake of Bingham in Nottinghamshire there were but twelve persons who owed suit; each of them had been enfeoffed to do the suit due from a barony; the baronies of Tutbury, Peverel, Lovetot, Paynel, Dover, Richmond, Gaunt and Byron were represented each by a suitor, the baronies of Basset and Deyncourt by two suitors apiece[3]. On the other hand so late as the reign of Charles I. the court of the hundred of Berkeley in Gloucestershire had four hundred suitors, of whom 'seldom or never less than twenty and commonly many more attended[4].' It was a court for civil, that is non-criminal, causes; but, unlike the county court, it did not hold plea of lands; thus the actions which came before it were chiefly actions of debt and trespass. It does not seem to have been in any accurate sense inferior to the county court: that is to say, no appeal or complaint for default of justice could be taken from the one to the other.

The hundred court

Those hundreds which had not fallen into other hands were 'in the king's hands.' The sheriff seems usually to have let them at farm to bailiffs; the bailiff presided in the court and after paying his rent made what gain he could from fees and amercements. Complaints are frequent that the sheriffs have raised the old rents; the bailiffs who have to pay advanced rents indemnify themselves by new exactions. In Sussex each hundred seems to have had a beadle, that is a summoner, who was called an alderman. We are told in Edward I.'s day that in time past these officers had been elected by those who paid [p. 545] the hundred-scot; but now, at least in one case, they buy their

Hundreds in the king's hands.

---

[1] Leg. Hen. 7, § 4.   [2] See above, p. 538.
[3] R. H. ii. 318.
[4] Smyth, Lives of the Berkeleys, iii. 13.

offices and make a profit by extortion[1]. We hear further that
such of the tenants of the barony of L'Aigle as owed suit to the
hundred court paid the sheriff £9. 17s. 6d. a year in order that
their suit to the county court might be done for them by the
aldermen of the hundreds, and this new hint as to the actual
composition of a shire-moot is welcome[2].

Hundreds
in private
hands.

But many of the hundreds had been granted to private
persons. From 1255 we have an account of the thirty-nine
hundreds of Wiltshire; sixteen and a half were in the king's
hand; twenty-two and a half were in the hands of others. What
is more, in thirteen cases the lord of the hundred claimed to
exclude the sheriff from holding a turn; he himself had the
view of frankpledge throughout the hundred save where this
was in the hands of the lords of manors[3]. In 1320 the men
of Devon said that almost all the hundreds of their shire
belonged to the magnates[4]. In this sense a 'hundred' is an
'incorporeal thing'; the lord of a hundred need not be lord
or tenant of a single acre of land within the precinct.

Duties of
the
hundred.

The hundred, like the county, was conceived to be fully
represented by its court. If the court gave a false judgment,
the hundred had to pay for it. And the hundred, like the
county, had communal duties and could be fined for neglect
of them. The chief example is the famous murder fine. If
a person was slain and the slayer was not produced, then the
hundred was fined, unless the kinsfolk of the dead man would
come and 'present his Englishry,' that is to say, prove him to
be an Englishman by birth. The Statute of Winchester (1285)
made the hundred liable for robberies committed within its
borders in case the robbers were not produced[5]. On the other [p. 546]
hand, we do not in this age hear of the hundred as having
any communal property, though a pasture that was 'common'
to a whole hundred may still have existed[6].

The
sheriff's
turn.

Twice a year the sheriff makes a progress or 'turn' through
the hundreds, or rather through those which are not in the
hands of such lords as have the right to exclude him. The
Leges Henrici tell us how twice a year a specially full hundred
court is to be held for the purpose of seeing that the tithings

[1] R. H. ii. 214, 217.   [2] R. H. ii. 204–5.
[3] R. H. ii. 230–238.   [4] Rot. Parl. i. 381.
[5] Stat. Wint. 13 Edw. I.
[6] Maitland, Domesday Book and Beyond, p. 355.

are full and that all men are in frankpledge[1]. Henry II. by
the Assize of Clarendon ordered the sheriffs to inquire of
robbers, murderers and thieves by the oath of twelve men
of each hundred and of four men of each vill, and at the same
time he directed that the sheriffs should hold the view of
frankpledge as well within the franchises of the magnates as
without.   These purposes are answered by the sheriff's 'turn'
(the word occurs in the charter of 1217[2])—the object of the
turn is 'quod pax nostra teneatur et quod tethinga integra
sit.' The procedure of the turn at the end of the thirteenth
century was this:—Each vill in the hundred was represented
by its reeve and four men, or each tithing was represented by
its tithing-man, or perhaps in some places both systems of
representation prevailed concurrently:—the representatives
would for the more part be *villani.* Then besides them a
jury of freeholders was wanted. It is probable that in strict
theory every freeholder should have been present, but twelve
there had to be. Then the sheriff set before the representatives of the vills or tithings a set of inquiries known as
'the articles of the view.' The list seems to have varied
from place to place and time to time. Its object was threefold,
(1) to see that the system of frankpledge (of which we shall
speak below) was in proper working order, (2) to obtain accusations against those suspected of grave crimes, in order that
the sheriff might capture them and keep them imprisoned or
on bail until the king's justices should come to hold an eyre
or deliver the gaol (for by this time the sheriff had lost the
power of holding pleas of the crown), and (3) to obtain accu-
[p. 547] sations against those suspected of minor offences in order that
they might be amerced by the sheriff. With this last object
in sight the articles specified many petty misdeeds: hue and
cry wrongfully raised, watercourses impeded, roads diverted,
brawls and affrays, breaches of the assize of bread and beer,
and so forth. The representatives of the vills or tithings in
answer to these articles made presentments which were laid
before the twelve freeholders, who had power to reject or
supply omissions in them. Upon the presentments thus endorsed by the freeholders, the sheriff took action, issuing orders
for the arrest of those charged with felony and declaring those
charged with pettier misdeeds to be in the king's mercy. He

---

[1] Leg. Henr. c. 8.   [2] Charter of 1217, c. 42.

seems to have been the only judge in this court[1], but the amercements were 'affeered'—that is to say, the amount to be paid by each person who had fallen into the king's mercy was fixed—by two or more of the suitors who were sworn to do the work justly[2].

§ 3.   *The Vill and The Township.*

England mapped out into vills.

It seems nearly true, though not quite true, to say that the whole of England is divided into vills: nearly true, for it is commonly assumed that every spot of land must lie within some vill: not quite true, for it may be that there are spots so highly endowed with immunities, so much outside the ordinary rules of police law and fiscal law, that they are not accounted to form part of any vill, while in all probability there are some tracts, which are deemed to belong to two, three, or more vills in common.   Even a city or borough is a vill, or perhaps in some cases a group of vills[3].

Vill and parish.

Of the varying size of the vills it is needless to speak, for [p. 548] in general the vill of the thirteenth century is the 'civil parish' of the nineteenth.   The parish is originally a purely ecclesiastical district, and during the middle ages it is no unit in the geography of our temporal law, though from time to time the secular courts must notice it when disputes arise about tithes and the like[4].   In southern England the parish normally coincided with the vill; in the northern counties the

---

[1] So in the court leet the bailiff is sole judge—'judge for the day': Y. B. 21–2 Edw. I. p. 25: 'le baylif en ceo jor ad le regal e dorra jugement.'

[2] Select Pleas in Manorial Courts, pp. xxvii–xxxviii.

[3] Fortescue, De Laudibus, cap. 24: 'Hundreda vero dividuntur per villas, sub quarum appellatione continentur et burgi atque civitates....... Vix in Anglia est locus aliquis qui non infra villarum ambitus contineatur, licet privilegiati loci infra villas de eisdem villis pars esse non censeatur.'   The general theory appears in the rule which expects that everyone who brings an action for land will be able to name the vill or vills in which the land lies.   The law about this matter, however, was elaborate; in some actions it was enough to name a hamlet, not so in others; see Y. B. Mich. 15 Edw. II. f. 450.   We hear of a spot in which the sheriff held his turn which was in no vill but was common to several vills, Y. B. Pasch. 17 Edw. II. f. 536 (a folio so numbered which seemingly ought to be numbered 544).

[4] That the Saladin tithe of 1188 was collected from the parishes is no real exception; payment of it was enforced as a religious duty by excommunication.

parishes were large; often a parish consisted of a group of
vills. In our modern law the parish has, at least in name,
supplanted the vill or township; but this is due to causes
which did not come into play until the Tudor time when the
rate for the relief of the poor was imposed. The law then
began to enforce a duty which had theretofore been enforced
by religion and naturally it adopted for this purpose the
geography of the church. Then in course of time other rates
were imposed, and the poor's rate was taken as their model.
Thus the parish became the important district for most of the
purposes of local government. But this victory of the parish
over the township was hardly more than a change of name.
The townships of northern England insisted that, albeit they
were not parishes, they ought to be treated as units in the
poor law system, as parishes for the purposes of the poor law,
and then by force of statutory interpretations the old vill got
a new name and appeared as the 'civil parish[1].'

As the county or hundred may be discrete, so also the
vill may be discrete and apparently some of our vills were
composed of scattered fragments. In certain parts of Gloucestershire, for example, until scientific frontiers were established
by a modern commission, a parish consisted of a large number
[p. 549] of small strips of land lying intermingled with the lands of
other parishes, in such a way as forcibly to suggest that at
some remote time some one agricultural community split up
into several communities, each of which was given a share of
land of every quality[2]. A detached portion of a parish lying
ten miles away from the main body is by no means an unknown
phenomenon, while of certain parts of the north of England
we are told that the townships are intermixed 'so that there

Discrete vills.

---

[1] This process begins with Stat. 14 Car. II. c. 12, sec. 21. At length in
1889 the rule is laid down that in statutes the word 'parish' is to mean prima
facie 'a place for which a separate poor rate is or can be made, or for which
a separate overseer is or can be appointed'; Stat. 52 and 53 Vic. c. 63, sec. 5;
see also 29 and 30 Vic. c. 113, sec. 18. We could wish our newly invented
'parish councils' a better name.

[2] See the very interesting map of Donisthorpe given in Gomme, Village
Community, p. 288, and at the end of the Report of the Committee on Commons'
Inclosure, Parl. Pap. 1844, vol. 5. See also Report of Committee on
Boundaries of Parishes, Parl. Pap. 1873, vol. 8, Minutes of Evidence, p. 85,
where Col. Leach mentions a case in Gloucestershire, of which the present
writer has some knowledge:—some ten parishes were intermixed in the most
intricate fashion.

is the most complete jumble which it is possible to conceive[1].'
The 'extra-parochial place' finds its explanation in the history
of the church; in many cases that explanation need go back no
further than some papal bull of recent date; but when, lying
outside any known ecclesiastical division we find a single acre
known as No Man's Land, and then another small patch
bearing the same name which has but two inhabitants, and
then a No Man's Heath of nine acres[2], we shall be strongly
tempted to believe that as there were extra-parochial places,
so also (if we may coin a new term) there were 'extra-villar'
places, odds and ends which no township would acknowledge
as its own.   So also in our own day some large moors in the
north of England are, or have lately been, deemed to be
territory common to several different townships[3].

Hamlets.   Besides vills there were hamlets; but the hamlet seems
always to have lain within the boundaries of a vill, and, though
the law might for some purposes take note of its existence[4],
still it seems to have been but rarely treated as more than
a mere geographical tract.   On the other hand, the vill or
township was no mere part of the earth's surface, it was a
community[5].

Vill and
village.
We have little reason for believing that all our English vills
conformed to a single type, or that their histories had been
approximately identical.   But there is a type to which many
conformed and which we must keep before our minds.   It is
that of the nucleated village with open fields.   All the houses
of the vill are collected into one cluster.   Around and inside
this cluster there may be many little 'closes,' crofts and
paddocks; but by far the larger part of the territory of the
vill lies uninclosed by any permanent fences.   The arable lies
in two, three or more great 'fields,' each of which is cut up
into multitudinous strips.   These strips are reckoned to be
acres, half-acres and roods.   A villager who has in all but
thirty arable acres will have perhaps some forty or fifty strips

---

[1] Col. Leach, *loc. cit.* p. 85.

[2] Report of Committee on Parish Boundaries, Appendix, pp. 217–219.

[3] Ibid. App. p. 242.   [4] Y. B. 15 Edw. II. f. 450.

[5] The so-called Statute of Exeter, Statutes of the Realm, vol. i. p. 210,
ordains an inquiry which is to be made by vills, demi-vills and hamlets, a vill
being represented by eight men, a demi-vill by six, a hamlet by four.   But this
seems exceptional.   The meaning of a demi-vill will become plainer hereafter.

scattered about in all parts of the territory. A rude rotation of crop and fallow, the two-course or the three-course system, is observed, and, so soon as a crop has been garnered, the whole of the 'field' which has borne it is depastured by the cattle of the villagers. Often the meadows are similarly treated : that is to say, for the purpose of growing a hay-crop they are enjoyed in severalty, but after the hay-harvest they become pasture for the beasts of many 'commoners.' Then there are permanent pastures which are never inclosed or enjoyed in severalty but lie open at all seasons. Villages of this kind were numerous in southern and eastern England. Others there were which did not widely depart from the same type though they already contained some large closes and some severed pastures. In the west there was more ring-fenced property, and sometimes the vill looks like a group of small hamlets which is being kept together merely by legal and governmental bonds. The questions of remote history that are suggested by the maps of our villages we must not here discuss or even raise ; but in many, perhaps in most, cases the township or community of the vill can not but be compacter and in some sort more communal than is the community of a hundred or a county. Even if there is no corporate and no common property, there is at least a great deal of common enjoyment, and the economic affairs of every villager are closely intertwined with those of his neighbours[1].

[p. 550] Modern usage may treat the two words *vill* and *township* as though they were synonymous ; but in this respect medieval Latin was a more accurate language than our own; it distinguished between the *villa* and the *villata*, between the tract of land and the organized body of inhabitants. Doubtless the English word which answered to the Latin *villa* was *tún, ton, town,* a word which in comparatively modern times we have allowed the larger towns to appropriate to themselves. We can not say that the distinction between *villa* and *villata* was always, still it was very generally, observed. If a crime takes place in the *villa*, the town of Trumpington, the *villata*, the township of Trumpington, may get into trouble. And so in what follows we shall use *vill* as an equivalent for *villa*, and *township* as an equivalent for *villata*, thus

Vill and township.

---

[1] Domesday and Beyond, pp. 10 ff.

distinguishing the plot of ground from the community that inhabits it[1].

Duties of township.   For the township is a *communitas*[2], which, even if it has not rights, certainly has duties. We may reckon up the most important of them. It ought to attend the court held by the justices in eyre[3]. It ought to attend the sheriff's turn. It ought to attend the hundred and county courts whenever it has any crime to present[4]. It must come at the coroner's call to make inquest when a dead man's body is found[5]. It is bound to see that all its members who ought to be in frankpledge are in frankpledge. In some parts of the country the township is itself a frankpledge, a tithing, a *borgh*, and in this case it is responsible for the production of any of its [p. 551] members who is accused of crime[6]. Apart from this, it was bound to arrest malefactors; at all events if a person was slain within its boundaries during the daytime and the slayer was not arrested, it was liable to an amercement. In the thirteenth century this liability was frequently enforced by the justices in their eyres; it must be distinguished from the liability of the hundred for the murder fine and seems to flow from no known act of legislation but to be based on immemorial custom[7]. Again, from of old it was the duty of the township to raise the hue and cry and follow the trail of stolen cattle. In 1221 the jurors of Bridgnorth complained to the justices that the sheriff required of them the impossible

---

[1] The notion that *villata* is a diminutive of *villa* is groundless. North Riding Records, vol. iv. [N.S.] p. 174: 'et si villate villarum predictarum non veniant....'

[2] Thus P. Q. W. 293, the *communitas* of a vill goes to the sheriff's turn by its tithing-man; R. H. i. 275, the coroner's clerk exacted money from the *communa* of the vill of Sutton.

[3] Summons of the Eyre, Stubbs, Select Charters, ann. 1231; Maitland, Pleas of the Crown for the County of Gloucester, *passim*.

[4] See writ of 1234, Ann. Dunstap. p. 139; R. H. ii. 29, presentments of the crown are made in the county court by the four neighbouring vills (i.e. neighbouring the scene of the crime) and if they do not come they are amerced; they are amerced once more when the justices in eyre come round; this is matter of complaint.

[5] Bracton, f. 121 b. Gross, Coroners' Rolls, *passim*.

[6] See below, p. 568.

[7] See Statute 3 Hen. VII. c. 1; Coke, 3rd Institute, 53; Hale, Pleas of the Crown, i. 448. The rule seems to be an ancient one; see Gloucestershire Pleas of the Crown, pp. 60, 147.

task of following the trail through the middle of the town[1].
Moreover, it was a common practice to commit prisoners to
the charge of the *villata*, and then, if the prisoners escaped,
the *villata* was amerced. So if a malefactor took sanctuary, the
neighbouring townships had to watch the church and prevent
his escape[2].

Most of these liabilities can be traced back into the reign *Early*
examples
of Henry II. A few examples of amercements may be given *of its*
from among the many collected by Madox[3]. The men of *duties.*
Tixover are amerced for refusing to swear the king's assize,
the township of Isle for not making suit after a murderer, the
township of Rock for doing nothing when a man was slain
in their vill, the township of Midwinter for receiving a man
who was not in frankpledge, and the township of Newbold for
a concealment and for burying a dead man without the view
of the sheriff's serjeant.

During the thirteenth century the activity of the township *Statutory*
duties of
[p. 552] was further developed by legislation. An ordinance of 1233 *township*
provided that in every *villa* watch should be kept throughout
the night by four men at the least. This was repeated in
1252 and at the same time new provision was made for enforcing the assize of arms. The original assize of 1181 had
not treated the *villata* as an organized entity; it had required
that individuals should have the armour suitable to their
station. The ordinance of 1252 decreed that in every township a constable or two constables should be appointed, and a
chief constable in each hundred to convene the *iurati ad arma*.
In 1253 this is supplemented by a provision that arms necessary for the pursuit of malefactors are to be provided at the
cost of the township and are to remain to the use of the township[4]. The whole system of the assize of arms and of watch
and ward was consolidated in 1285 by the Statute of Winchester; the constabulary and the militia took the form that
they were to keep during the rest of the middle ages[5].

---

[1] Select Pleas of the Crown, pl. 173. [2] Ibid. pl. 135.
[3] Madox, Hist. Exch. i. 541–568.
[4] Stubbs, Select Charters: 'cum arcubus et sagittis et aliis levibus armis
quae debent provideri ad custum totius villae et quae semper remaneant ad
opus praedictae villae.'
[5] The documents of 1181, 1233, 1252, 1253, 1285 are all printed in the Select
Charters.

Contribu-
tion of
township
to general
fines.
Again, we see the vill as a district bound to contribute to
the fines and amercements which are imposed upon the county
and the hundred, for instance, the murder fines for which the
hundred is liable.   In the Hundred Rolls we read numerous
complaints about vills and parts of vills which have been
'subtracted' from these duties by lords, who have or pretend
to have immunities.   The effect of such subtraction was to
increase the burden that fell on the neighbouring vills.   Every
extension of the 'franchises' damaged 'the geldable,' that is
to say, the lands and vills which enjoyed no privilege.

Unjust
exactions
from
townships.
The township again is constantly brought before us as
having had to bear all manner of unlawful exactions.   The
Hundred Rolls teem with complaints.   Not only have the townships been amerced, according to their own account unjustly
amerced, for the neglect of their police duties, but the royal
officers have refused to do their own duties without being paid
by the townships.   Sheriffs will not take prisoners off their
hands and coroners will not suffer them to bury their dead [p. 553]
until there had been payment.   One typical instance will be
enough.   A criminal took sanctuary in the church at Fosdike;
the township was bound to watch the church until the coroner
came; the coroner would not come for less than a mark; so
the township had to watch the church forty days to its great
damage[1].

'Miscellane-
ous
offences
of the
township.
The practice of amercing the township for neglect of its
police duties may have begotten the practice, which certainly
prevailed in the thirteenth century, of treating the township
as an amerciable unit capable of committing misdeeds of many
kinds.   Already in Henry II.'s day the township of Maltby
owes four marks for having ploughed up the king's highway[2].
In 1235 certain townships are to be amerced for having helped
a man to put himself in seisin without waiting for the presence
of the sheriff's officer; their amercement is to be affeered by
other townships[3].   On the Hundred Rolls we may find such
entries as the following;—the township of Godmanchester has
made a purpresture upon the king's highway and has appropriated therefrom the third of a rod; the whole township of
Eynesbury has dug in the king's highway and obstructed it to
the nuisance of the country[4].   In one part of Cambridgeshire

---

[1] R. H. i. 308.   [2] Pipe Roll, 12 Hen. II. p. 49.
[3] Note Book, pl. 1170.   [4] R. H. ii. 666.

the hundredors speak of the townships as communes (*communae*) and accuse them of sundry transgressions; the commune of Ely has occupied a fishery which used to belong to the manor of Soham; the commune of Reach has broken through the big dike (the Devil's Ditch), so has the commune of Swaffham Bulbeck, which also neglects to repair its bridge; the commune of Exning has ploughed up the waste of Burwell, has obstructed the highway and diverted a watercourse. On the other hand, Thomas of Bodenham has appropriated land from the commune of Burwell[1]. Even an assault and battery may be attributed to a township, for the whole township of Kennet has beaten and wounded two bailiffs[2].

[p. 554] All this seems to set before us the township as a legal entity which has, if not rights, at all events many and multifarious duties, and we might naturally suppose that in order to perform these duties it must have had some permanent organization: for example, some court or assembly in which the incidence of these duties could be apportioned among its members. When however we search for such organization we fail; at least for a while we seem to fail. Organization we find, but it is manorial; courts we find in plenty, but they are courts of manors. The township as such has no court, no assembly. And so with the officers of the township:—the constable is a new officer, his importance lies in the future, while as to the reeve we only know him in real life as the reeve of a lord, the reeve of a manor, usually a villein elected by his fellows in the lord's court, presented to and accepted by the lord's steward, compelled to serve the office because he is not a free man. We must turn therefore from the township to the manor, but before that can be reached we must traverse the whole field of seignorial justice. The facts that we have to study are intricate; the legal principles have tied themselves into knots; we must pull out the threads one by one.

Organization of the township.

---

[1] R. H. ii. 497–498: 'Thomas de Bodeham appropriavit sibi de communa de Borewelle.' This is a little ambiguous and perhaps should be translated by 'T. de B. has appropriated part of Burwell common.'

[2] R. H. i. 54.

§ 4. *The Tithing.*

Frank-
pledge.

A good example of this intricacy is afforded by the system of frankpledge. We have had to mention it when speaking of the sheriff's turn, and again when speaking of the township's duties. But also it is closely connected in many ways with manorial affairs, with the relation between lord and men. Taken by itself it is a remarkable institution and one that suggests difficult questions.

The system in century xiii.

And first we may look at the law as stated by Bracton[1]. Every male of the age of twelve years, be he free, be he serf, ought to be in a frankpledge and a tithing (*in franco plegio et in decenna*). To this rule there are numerous exceptions according to the varying customs of different districts. The magnates, knights and their kinsmen, clerks and the like need not be in frankpledge; the freeholder (in one passage Bracton even says the free man[2]) need not be in frankpledge, nor need [p. 555] the citizen who has fixed property:—his land is equivalent to a frankpledge. Again, instead of being in frankpledge one may be in the mainpast of another. The head of a household answers for the appearance in court of the members of his household, his servants, his retainers, those whom his hand feeds, his *manupastus* or *mainpast*—we may use a very old English word and say his *loaf-eaters*[3]. They are in his *frith-lorgh* and need no other pledge[4]. But, these exceptions being made, a male of the age of twelve years or upwards ought to be, and it is the duty of the township in which he dwells to see that he is, in frankpledge and tithing. If he is accused of a crime and not forthcoming and the township has failed in this duty, then it will be amerced. If on the other hand he was in a tithing, then the amercement will fall upon the tithing.

Township and tithing.

The strict enforcement of these rules is abundantly proved by the rolls of the itinerant justices. When an accused person is not produced, his township is amerced if he was not in a

---

[1] Bracton, f. 124–5.

[2] Bracton, f. 124 b; 'clericus, liber homo et huiusmodi.'

[3] Du Cange's examples s. v. *manupastus* are almost exclusively from England or Normandy.

[4] Bracton, f. 121 b. He is here making use of Leg. Edw. Conf. 20 (19).

tithing (*decenna, theothinga, thuthinga* etc.), and, if he was in a tithing, then that tithing is amerced. But to all seeming the 'tithing' meant different things in different parts of the country. There can be no doubt that over a large part of England the persons subject to the law of frankpledge were distributed into groups, each consisting of ten, or in some cases of twelve or more, persons; each group was known as a 'tithing'; each was presided over by one of the associated persons who was known as the chief-pledge, tithing-man, head-borough, borsholder, head or elder, that is, of the *borh* or pledge[1]. The township discharged its duty by seeing that all who were resident within its boundaries were in these groups. On the other hand, in the southernmost and some western counties there seems to be a different arrangement:—the vill is a tithing, or in some cases a group of geographically separated tithings; the tithing is a district, even the *borgha* [p. 556] or pledge is a district[2]; the tithingman is the tithingman of a place, of a vill or hamlet; the personal groups of ten or a dozen men are not found. In this part of the country the two duties, which elsewhere we see as two, seem fused into one: the township discharges its duty of having all its members in frankpledge and tithing by being itself a tithing and a frankpledge[3]. But further, there were large parts of England in which there was no frankpledge. In the middle of the thirteenth century the men of Shropshire asserted that within their boundaries no one was in a tithing; at the end of the century the jurors of Westmoreland declared that the law of Englishry, of murder fines, of tithing, of frankpledge, of mainpast, did not prevail and never had prevailed north of the Trent; at any rate it did not prevail in their county. Probably they drew the line at too southerly a point; but it is, to say the least, doubtful whether the system of frankpledge extended to any part of the ancient kingdom of Northumbria[4].

---

[1] See the facsimile of a part of a Norwich frankpledge roll in Leet Jurisdiction in Norwich (Selden Soc.) p. xlvii.

[2] See the Hundred Roll for Kent, where the *borgha* seems often to be a tract of land. Thus, p. 202, a murder has been committed 'in borgha de Patrichesburn.'

[3] Palgrave, Engl. Commonwealth, vol. ii. pp. cxx–cxxvi; Stubbs, Const. Hist. i. 91–5; Maitland, Pleas of the Crown for Gloucester, p. xxxi.

[4] Palgrave, Engl. Commonwealth, vol. i. pp. cxxiii–iv; Stubbs, Const.

The view
of frank-
pledge.
The maintenance of this system is enforced, not merely by amercements inflicted when the township or the tithing has failed in its duty and a criminal has escaped from justice, but also by periodical inspections and what we might call 'field-days' of the frankpledges. Twice a year the sheriff holds in each hundred a specially full hundred court to see that all men who ought to be are in frankpledge. These half-yearly meetings we can trace back to the reign of Henry I.; they may be much older; in course of time they acquire the name [p. 557] of the sheriff's 'turn.' But though Henry II. in the Assize of Clarendon (1166) had strictly decreed that this business was to be in the sheriff's hands[1], we find in the thirteenth century that there are large masses of men who never go near the sheriff's turn. They are the men of lords who rightfully or wrongfully exercise the franchise that is known as 'view of frankpledge': that is to say, of lords who in their own courts see that their tenants are in frankpledge and take the profits which arise from the exercise of this jurisdiction; sometimes they allow the sheriff to be present, very often they exclude him altogether. Of all the franchises, the royal rights in private hands, view of frankpledge is perhaps the commonest.

Attendance
at the
view.
The strict theory of the law seems to have required that all the frankpledges should attend the view; but as a matter of fact it was usual for none but the chief pledges to attend; often however they had to bring with them a sum of money which was accepted in lieu of the production of their tithings. Thus a system of representation of the tithing arose and very naturally it became bound up in intricate combinations with the representation of the township by its reeve and four men. Especially when the 'view' is in private hands, we often find that the duty of presenting offenders is performed by the chief

Hist. i. 95. In Leg. Edw. Conf. 20 (19), it is said that what the English (*Angli*) call *frithborgas* the Yorkshiremen (*Eboracenses*) call *tenmannetale*. But whatever may be the origin of this latter word, we only find it elsewhere as the name of a money payment. Thus Hoveden, iii. 242 : in 1194 Richard imposed a tax of two shillings on the carucate 'quod ab antiquis nominatur Temantale.' See Rievaulx Cartulary, p. 142 : 'Danegeld id est Themanetele'; compare Whitby Cartulary, i. 196–7. In northern charters the word occurs commonly enough in the list of immunities.

[1] Ass. Clarend. c. 9. There is to be no one within castle or without, no, not even in the honour of Wallingford, who shall deny the sheriff's right to enter his court or his land to view the frankpledges; all are to be under pledges and are to be placed in free pledge before the sheriff.

pledges, who thus form themselves into a jury. Under the influence of the Assize of Clarendon, the duty of producing one's fellow-pledges to answer accusations seems to have been enlarged into a duty of reporting their offences and making presentments of all that went wrong in the tithing.

Of the means by which men were 'brought into tithings,' into the groups of ten or a dozen, we know very little. Could a youth choose his tithing? Could a tithing expel or refuse to admit a member whose bad character would make him burdensome? The answer to these and to similar questions seems to be that the men who had to be in tithings were generally unfree men. They were brought into tithings by the lord or his steward and they could not resist[1]. We may find a chief pledge paying a few pence to his lord in order that a certain man, presumably a bad subject, may be removed from his tithing. The chief pledge seems to have exercised a certain authority over his subordinate pledges; they owed him some obedience[2], and probably in the southern counties the tithingman of the tithing, the borhsealdor of the borh, was also normally the reeve of the vill; but it is only in legal legends that he has any judicial powers[3].

Constitution of tithings.

[p. 558]

§ 5. *Seignorial Jurisdiction.*

According to the legal theory of the thirteenth century seignorial jurisdiction has two roots—(1) the delegation of royal powers, (2) the relation between lord and tenants. Jurisdictional rights are divided into two classes. On the one hand, there are the franchises and regalities (*libertates, regalia*) which, at least according to the opinion of the king's lawyers, can only exist in the hands of a subject by virtue of a grant from the crown. On the other hand, there is jurisdiction involved

Regalities and feudal rights.

---

[1] Sometimes the tithingman was elected by the men of the tithing. Rot. Hund. i. 212 (Kent): 'J. B. distrinxit J. de E. ut esset borgesaldre sine electione borgae suae.' In some boroughs, *e.g.* Norwich, men who were in every sense free men were in frankpledge, see Hudson, Leet Jurisdiction in Norwich (Selden Soc.) p. lxvii. But on the plea rolls of some counties, *e.g.* Staffordshire, we find entries which state that a man is not in frankpledge ' quia liber.'

[2] Select Pleas in Manorial Courts, p. 169.

[3] Leg. Edw. Conf. 26 (28). This in all probability is mere fable.

in the mere possession of a manor or in the mere fact of having tenants; we may briefly characterize it as being of a civil, non-criminal kind[1]. Bracton in the statement of his general theory of temporal justice seems to neglect it. In this we can not follow him. As to the franchises he speaks [p. 559] very positively. Who can bestow them? The king, and only he, for all justice and judgment, all that concerns the peace, all coercive power are his. Those things therefore that concern jurisdiction or that concern the peace belong to no one, but only to the king's crown and dignity, and they can not be separated from the crown, since they make the crown, for the king's crown is to do judgment and justice and keep the peace. Such jurisdictional rights can not be held by a private person 'unless it be given him from above.' Then he lays down two maxims:—'Iurisdictio delegata non potest delegari':—'Nullum tempus occurrit regi[2].'

Acquisition of the regalities. Two very wholesome maxims; but it is clear that they have not been observed and we may doubt whether the kings themselves have made strenuous efforts to maintain them. Our information about the franchises must be drawn for the more part from pleadings of Edward I.'s reign; but these, despite their wealth of detail, are not very satisfactory, or rather disclose a state of things that is not easily described. Early in his reign Edward began a vigorous attack upon the franchises. First by means of inquests, the results of which are recorded on the Hundred Rolls, he ascertained what franchises were actually exercised, and then he sent out his judges and pleaders to demand by what warrant (*quo waranto*) the lords were wielding these powers. His advocates took the highest ground, propounded extreme doctrines, doctrines which would have destroyed a large half of the existing 'liberties.' But the king did not proceed to extremities; few judgments were given; he had gained his main object; any further growth of the franchises was stopped; in 1290 he consented to a compromise. A continuous seisin for the last hundred years—the coronation of Richard I. was chosen as a limiting date—was to be a sufficient answer to the inquiry *quo waranto*[3].

---

[1] A similar distinction is drawn for France by Esmein, Histoire du droit français, ed. 2, p. 259.

[2] Bracton, f. 55 b.

[3] Select Pleas in Manorial Courts, pp. xviii–xxii, lxxvii.

Thus we hear no statements of the law which can claim to be impartial. On the one hand, we have the doctrines of the king's law officers, on the other hand, a mass of facts which prove that these doctrines, if they are not new, have been ignored. Let us see how far the royal advocates can go. The [p. 560] bishop of Ely is defending his egregious liberties by charters of Edgar, the Confessor, the Conqueror, and Henry III. Gilbert Thornton to all his other objections adds this—'Allow for one moment that all these liberties are expressly mentioned in the charters, still the king has an action for revoking them, since he has never confirmed them. As regards the franchises of his crown each successive king is to be deemed an infant. His case is like that of a church. Each successive rector can revoke the lands of the church if they have been alienated by his predecessor[1].' That the franchises are inalienable is constantly asserted. Robert FitzNicholas took upon himself to grant the view of frankpledge of two-thirds of a vill to John Giffard ; this, says Thornton, is a cause of forfeiture ; he was bound to exercise the jurisdiction in person and not to give it to another[2]. If you urge long seisin, you aggravate your offence[3]. Your usurpation can not have had an innocent beginning ; every one, says Bracton, must know that these things belong to the crown[4]. It is plain to all, says Thornton, that upon the conquest of England every jurisdiction was united to the crown[5] :—this historical theory is of great use when Anglo-Saxon charters are propounded. Even if it be allowed that there are cases in which user can beget title, this concession can only be made in favour of those whose ancestors came in with the Conqueror ; no churchman can take advantage of it[6]. And, if it comes to charters, the king is entitled to

---

[1] P. Q. W. 308. Thornton makes the same point against the abbot of Ramsey ; P. Q. W. 305.

[2] P. Q. W. 86 ; see also 10, 87, 88, 105, 242.

[3] P. Q. W. 4.   [4] Bracton, f. 56.

[5] P. Q. W. 4, 259, 303.

[6] This curious argument is used by William Inge against the abbot of St Mary's, York ; P. Q. W. 122 : by Gilbert Thornton, Ibid. 671 : and more than once by Hugh Lowther, Ibid. 676–7. Thus against the bishop of Coventry, Lowther says, ' The bishop can not show that any of his predecessors came with the Conqueror and obtained these liberties by [the] conquest (*per conquestum*), for the bishop and all his predecessors were, as one may say, men of religion (*quasi religiosi, i.e.* in the same category as professed monks) and they and their church were enfeoffed by others, and therefore they cannot claim

the benefit of every doubt; he is not to be ousted of his rights by 'obscure and general words[1].' He is the giver and it is [p. 561] for him to interpret his gift[2]. 'Liberties' are easily forfeited by abuse or by mere non-use. The grantee must take the first opportunity that occurs of getting seisin of the franchise and must maintain his seisin. In Edward I.'s day he loses his right unless he claims it before the justices in eyre whenever they come round. Unfortunately the forfeited liberties are easily restored in consideration of a sum of money. It is this that prevents a modern reader from heartily taking the king's side in the controversy. Despite all that is said about the inseparability of justice from the crown, the king sells liberties and compels the purchasers to buy them over and over again.

Various kinds of franchises. We may now glance at the franchises, first mentioning briefly those which have least to do with justice and then speaking more at length of the jurisdictional powers.

Fiscal immunities. (i) *Fiscal Immunities.* The grantees, their men, and their lands are freed from every imaginable form of taxation, 'imperial and local'—if we may use such modern terms:—from all scots and gelds, danegelds, neatgelds, horngelds, footgelds, woodgelds, felgelds, scutage, carucage, hidage, tallage, aids for the king, aids for the sheriff and his bailiffs, wardpenny, averpenny, hundredpenny, tithingpenny, borghhalfpenny, chevage, headpenny[3]; further, from all indirect taxes:—from passage, pontage, peage, lastage, stallage, vinage, weitage, toll; further from all fines and amercements imposed upon the shires and the hundreds, in particular from the murder fine.

Immunities from personal service. (ii) *Immunities from personal service.* They are freed from military service, 'from hosts and summonses to the host,' from suit of court, from all shires, trithings, lathes, wapentakes and hundreds, from jury service, from tithings and frankpledge, from the duty of repairing castles, parks,

these franchises from time immemorial.' These arguments about liberties obtained by conquest afforded some ground for the earl of Warenne's famous assertion that the sword was his *warantus.*

[1] P. Q. W. 305.

[2] Bracton, f. 34, § 3.

[3] Thus the charter of 1199 for the Templars (Rot. Cart. p. 1) specially mentions, besides the minor local dues, aids of the king and of the sheriffs, hidage, carucage, danegeld, horngeld, scutage, and tallage. See also the charter of the Hospitallers, ibid. p. 15, and that for Sempringham, p. 18.

roads and bridges, from the duty of carrying the king's treasure and victuals, from carriage and summage and navige.

(iii) *Immunities from forest law.* These are usually the subject of special bargains and are not thrown about with a [p. 562] lavish hand; but sometimes the grantees succeed in freeing themselves, their lands, men and dogs from some or all of the forestal regulations, from the swainmotes, regards of the forest, amercements of the forest, 'waste and assart[1].' The immunities shade off into licences, such as that of keeping eight brachets and a pair of greyhounds and hunting the fox, the hare and the wild cat in the king's forest of Essex[2].

Immunities from forest law.

(iv) *Fiscal powers.* The king, it will be remembered, from time to time grants to his tenants the power of taking an aid or a scutage from their tenants, and, though these imposts may be regarded as feudal services, yet in practice they can not be collected without a royal writ, and in course of time even theory seems to require that the king should have granted his tenants 'their scutages' and given them leave to levy their aids[3]. Again, the king can make a permanent grant of the produce of a tax and of the right to collect it; thus John gave to the bishop of Ely and his successors the patronage over the abbot of Thorney and 'the aid of sheriffs and their bailiffs from all the men and tenements belonging to the said abbey,' so that the bishops became entitled to the due known as the sheriff's aid[4]. It is by no means improbable that a similar result was sometimes produced by mere words of immunity. When the king frees an abbey from scots and gelds, do the tenants, free and villein, of the abbey get the benefit of this exemption purchased by their lord's money, or do they not now have to pay to the abbot what formerly they paid to the royal officers? John had granted that the monks of Ramsey and their de-[p. 563] mesnes and all the men of their demesnes should be free of all aids and demands of sheriffs and reeves and bailiffs[5]; but at a later time we find the tenants of the abbey paying 'sheriff's aid'; doubtless they pay it to the abbot, and thus a tax becomes something very like a feudal service[6]. If we may infer

Fiscal powers.

---

[1] See the charters of the Templars and Hospitallers and the Peterborough charter, Rot. Cart. 82.

[2] Rot. Cart. 49.   [3] See above, pp. 274, 350.

[4] Rot. Cart. 204 (A.D. 1215).

[5] Cart. Rams. ii. 62 (A.D. 1202).

[6] Cart. Rams. *passim*, *e.g.* i. 456: 'et sciendum quod omnes terrae hydatae

that the same process had been at work ior a long time past, one of the sources of feudalism is here laid bare[1].

(v) *Jurisdictional Powers.* A royal charter of the thirteenth century very often, though by no means always, declares that the donee and his heirs are to hold the land with certain rights or powers which are described by English words. Of such words the commonest are 'cum saca et soca et toll et theam'; often 'infangenethef' is added; more rarely 'utfangenethef' also; while in some cases there is a long list[2]. The less usual of the words are the more intelligible; primarily they denote certain crimes, certain punishments, certain modes of procedure; in the charters they mean that the donee is to have jurisdiction over these crimes, power to inflict these punishments, power to use these modes of procedure. Thus he is to have housebreaking, breach of a special peace, waylaying, receipt of outlaws, the wites for bloodshed, for fighting, for flying from battle, for neglect of military service, for fornication, for suffering an escape from prison, he is to have the ordeal and the judicial combat. The list is careful to include just those crimes which Cnut had declared to be reserved pleas of the crown, those jurisdictional rights which the king has over all men unless he has seen fit to grant them away by express words[3]. Under the old law a grant accompanied by these words would seemingly have stripped the king of all jurisdiction, except, it may be, a certain justice of last resort. And the Norman Conquest made no sudden change; the criminal law revealed by Domesday Book is of the old type and the pleas of the crown are just those which are included in the lists [p. 564] that are before us. But during the latter half of the twelfth century criminal law rapidly took a new shape; the doctrine of felony was developed, capital punishment supplanted the old wites, and the specially royal processes of indictment and inquest were introduced. The result seems to have been that the powers conferred by these old words became antiquated, the very meaning of the terms became disputable and those

praeter dominicum et terras liberorum dant ad auxilium vicecomitis; terris autem liberorum remisit . . Hugo Abbas . . . praedictum auxilium.'

[1] Maitland, Domesday Book and Beyond, 278 ff.

[2] Charter of the Hospitallers (1199), Rot. Cart. p. 15: 'et hamsoka et grithbrige et blodwita et ficthwita et flictwita et fredwita et hengwita et leirwita et flemenesfrith et murdro et latrocinio et ordel et oreste.'

[3] Cnut, II. 12–15.

who wished for grants of high justice were compelled to purchase less dubious phrases.   The most liberal grants were not
unfrequently qualified by reservations the meaning of which
grew ampler as time went on.   The king declares that he
reserves nothing for himself 'except those things which belong
to the king's crown,' 'except justice of life and member,' 'except murder, treasure trove, rape, and breach of the peace[1].'
As the king's peace extends itself, as all serious crimes become
felonies and deserve punishment of life and member, the reservation grows at the expense of the grant.   Little in the
thirteenth century was to be got out of these ancient words
beyond the proceeds of a few minor offences, scuffles, affrays,
fornication.   Thus *infangenethef* might give one power to hang
one's own thief if caught within one's own territory, and *utfangenethef* the power to hang him wherever caught; but it
seems essential that he should be caught 'handhaving or back-
bearing,' that is, with the stolen goods upon him and that he
should be prosecuted by the loser of the goods.   The manorial
gallows was a common object of the country, but under these
restrictions it can not have been very useful[2].

[p. 565]   Now these antique words occur in two different contexts. *Contrast between immunities and powers.*
At first sight we may even say that two formulas which seem
to us contradictory are used as though they were equivalent.
Sometimes the charter says that the donee is to hold his land
with bloodwite, fightwite and so forth; more often that he is to
hold it free and quit of bloodwite, fightwite and so forth; yet
we can hardly doubt that the two phrases mean the same

---

[1] Rot. Cart. 2, 20, 22, 32, 33.

[2] A comparison of the *Exposiciones Vocabulorum* or glossaries of Anglo-
Saxon law terms will be found in the Red Book of the Exchequer iii. 1032.
It is clear that in the thirteenth century there was but little agreement as
to the meaning of these terms, whence we may draw the inference that they
had become of small value.   Thus Henry III. granted a charter to the
Abbot of Colchester for the purpose of explaining the words *frithsokne*,
infangenethef and *flemenefremth* contained in a charter of Richard I.; see Rot.
Cart. Introduction p. xxxvii.   There was much doubt as to what was meant by
hengwite and as to the exact limits of the right of *utfangenethef*.   In cases of
quo waranto the king's advocates are fond of puzzling their adversaries by
asking them to explain what they mean by these old words.   Thus the Prior of
Drax is asked to construe *sak sok tol et them*; 'et Prior nichil dicit'; P. Q. W.
211.   Still on examination of the Charter Rolls it will appear that these words
were not thrown about quite at haphazard; thus *utfangenethef* was much rarer
than *infangenethef*.   William Marshall makes a liberal grant of jurisdiction to
Tintern Abbey, but expressly reserves *utfangenethef* to himself; Monast. v. 269.

thing. To declare that a lord is to hold his lands free of
bloodwite is to declare that if blood be shed by his tenants
the king will not be entitled to the wite or fine; this, however,
seems regarded as implying as matter of course that the lord
will get the wite, for crimes are not to go unpunished. The
principle thus brought out is one that is of service to us when
we are dealing with a time the charters of which are couched
in yet vaguer terms:—to free a lord's land from royal jurisdiction or from the exactions which are appurtenant to the
exercise of royal jurisdiction is to create a seignorial jurisdiction.
The king's lawyers sometimes protest against this principle,
protest that a grant of immunity from frankpledge is not
equivalent to a grant of view of frankpledge; but the lords
refuse to recognize the distinction and may have history upon
their side[1].

Sake and soke; toll and team. But the four commonest words are the most interesting. [p. 566]
In the thirteenth century there is already much doubt as to
their meaning, and among the lawyers we see a strong tendency
to make them mean as little as possible. Thus *toll* is sometimes the right to take toll, sometimes the right to be free
of toll; but often it is merely the right to tallage one's villeins,
a right which every lord of villeins enjoys without the need
of a royal grant[2]. Then *team* is taken to mean the brood,

---

[1] Thus compare in Rot. Cart. the charters for the Temple (p. 1), the
Hospital (p. 15), Christ Church, Canterbury (p. 24), St Edmunds (p. 38), which
convey *grithbrice etc.*, with those for Dereham (p. 22), Fontevraud (p. 72),
Norwich (p. 81), which declare that the land is to be free of these things.
Sometimes we find an intermediate formula, *e.g.* in the charter for Sempringham
(p. 18); the land is to be held free of *gritbriche, blodwite etc.*, and the monks
are to have *flemenesfrit etc.* The point to which attention is drawn is well
illustrated by the charter for the bishop of Salisbury (p. 66); the land is to be
exempt from *blodwite etc.* and frankpledge; but on this follows the qualification
'but so that the view of frankpledge be made in the bishop's court before our
serjeant.' The natural result of declaring the bishop's land to be free of frankpledge would be to give the bishop the right of holding the view without the
interference of any royal official. The bishop of Winchester is asked by what
warrant he claims view of frankpledge; he produces a charter acquitting his
lands of frankpledge; the king's advocate insists that this does not give him the
view and craves judgment: judgment is reserved; P. Q. W. 83. The same
point is taken against the Hospitallers, Ibid. 92: and against the Prior of
Coventry, Ibid. 242: but in each case judgment is reserved.

[2] Leg. Edw. Conf. 22: '*Tol*, quod nos vocamus theloneum, scilicet libertatem emendi et vendendi in terra sua'; P. Q. W. 275: '*Thol*, quite de toun
doner'; P. Q. W. 511: '*Tol* . . . . pro voluntate sua tallagium de villanis suis.'

the offspring, the 'sequela' of one's villeins[1]; but this we
may be sure is a mistake.   Apparently it ought to mean the
right to hold a court into which outsiders may be vouched
as warrantors, or, to use a more technical term, the right to
enforce a 'foreign voucher.'   The word *sac* (or, as we had better
spell it, *sake*), the Anglo-Saxon *sácu*, the modern German *Sache*,
means thing, cause, matter; the glossarists of the thirteenth
century have not forgotten this and refer to the English phrase
'for which sake'; in legal language it means a cause, a matter,
an action, or as the Germans say *Rechtssache*; a grant then
of *sake* should be a grant—by a very general term—of jurisdiction[2].   Most important of all is *soke* or *soken*, which is used
as a very large word to denote justiciary rights and the area
within which they are exercised.

The remote history of these terms has been discussed elsewhere[3].   Here we have only to observe that in the thirteenth
century the words *sake* and *soke* are regarded as describing
jurisdiction, but jurisdiction of a kind that every lord has
although he has no such words in his charter and although he
[p. 567] has no charter from the king.   Like the 'general words'
common in conveyances of a later date ('together with all
easements, commons' and the like) they only serve to describe
rights which the donee would have though no such words were
employed; they give no franchise, they merely point to the
feudal or manorial jurisdiction which every one may have if
he holds a manor, or which every one may have if he has
tenants[4].   On the whole the prevailing doctrine seems to have
been that *sake* and *soke* did nothing, that *toll* and *theam* did
nothing, that *infangenethef* and *utfangenethef* merely gave the
right to hang 'hand-having' thieves, thieves taken 'with the
mainour' (*cum manuopere*), while the other old words could

*Sake and
soke in
cent. xiii.*

---

[1] P. Q. W. 275: '*Them*, aver progeny de vos humes'; Fleta, f. 62: '*Them*
acquietantiam amerciamentorum sequelae propriorum suorum.'

[2] Hoveden, ii. 242: 'Sackke, interpretatur iurisdictio, id est, curt et justise.'
Camb. Univ. Lib. MS. Dd. vii. 6. f. 63 b: 'quia sake anglice encheson gallice,
et dicitur for wych sake pur quele encheson.'   At Manchester we find a
payment called *sakfe* (sake-fee): 'debet ei sakfe et sectam ad curiam'; Roll for
Pasch. 34 Hen. III. (No. 140) m. 7.

[3] Maitland, Domesday Book and Beyond, pp. 80, 258.

[4] P. Q. W. 245: 'sak, sok, toll et theam quae quidem verba habent referri
ad cur[iam] baron[is] et non ad visum franciplegii.'   Keilway's Reports, 150 b:
'chescun seignior de commen droit avera tiels choses.'

not be trusted to do much, though they might serve to define and possibly to increase the ordinary powers of a feudal court[1].

The serious franchises of a jurisdictional kind were claimed under other words, or still more frequently were claimed by prescription. As the most serious, though the least exalted, we must reckon 'view of frankpledge and all that to view of frankpledge doth belong'—as the most serious, because it was extremely common. Occasionally we find a clear grant of 'view of frankpledge,' occasionally a grant of immunity from frankpledge which may or may not have amounted to the same thing[2], and perhaps a grant of *frithsoken*,—the word is not very common—would have the same operation[3]. Far more commonly a lord prescribed for the 'view,' and prescribed for it successfully. The right thus named comprised not merely the right to execute the law of frankpledge and take the profits thence arising, but also the right to hold twice a year [p. 568] a court coordinate with the sheriff's turn, a police court, a court for the presentment of offences and the punishment of offences that fell short of felony. Towards the end of the

thirteenth century the word *leet* (*leta*)—which seems to have spread outwards from the East Anglian counties—was becoming a common name for such a court, but to the last *visus franciplegii* remained the most formal and correct of titles. The lord who had this franchise claimed to swear in a body of jurors—often they were the chief pledges or heads of the tithings—and to put before them those same 'articles of the view' (*capitula visus*) which the sheriff employed in his 'turn.' The minor offences were punished on the spot by amercements which went to swell the lord's revenue. But

[1] The use that could be made of such a word as *bloodwite* is shown by a case in P. Q. W. 381-2. The Earl of Lincoln claims to hold plea of all trespasses committed within his fee, and to proceed either at the suit of a plaintiff or *ex officio*, provided that the word *bloodwite* be not mentioned: if it is mentioned, then his court does not meddle with the case any more, but leaves it for the county court. Thereupon he is asked whether he claims to punish a trespasser for wounds or bloodshed. Yes, he answers, provided that the plaintiff makes no mention of *bloodwite*. This from Edward I.'s day.

[2] See above p. 578. An early instance is found in Henry II.'s charter for Hurley, Monast. iii. 434: 'Praeterea praecipio et firmiter defendo ne francos suos plegios prior et homines sui alibi annuatim recenseant nisi in eadem curia S. Mariae et sua.'

[3] P. Q. W. 235 (Abbot of Colchester), 275 (Abbot of Westminster); Rot. Cart. Introd. p. xxxvii.

probably the pecuniary profit was in the eyes of the lords a small matter when compared with the power that was thus secured to them.   Twice a year the villagers, bond and free, had to report themselves and tell tales one of another, while no tale went outside the manor to the ears of jealous neighbours or rapacious officials.   Probably the tenants also were gainers by the franchise; they could manage their own affairs without the interference of 'foreigners[1].'

The king's advocates at times protested that only the tenant of a whole vill could enjoy this regality; the view, they say, must be a view for a vill, a view for a manor will not do, nor may a lord collect in his tithings tenants from divers vills[2]; again, he ought to have at least twelve whole tithings, twelve chief pledges, so that none may be punished without the oath of twelve[3].   These contentions were sometimes successfully urged, and the theory which connects the view of frankpledge with the organization of a perfect township (*villa integra*) may be a clue to past history; but as a matter of fact the franchise had been subinfeudated and was sometimes exercised over collections of men resident on various pieces of land geographically detached from each other and connected only by the fact that they were all holden of the same lord.   Thus the view is sometimes divided between immediate lord and overlord; John Engaine holds manors at Gidding and Dillington of the Abbot of Ramsey; when the day for the view comes, the Abbot's bailiff appears, hands to John's steward the articles of the view, and takes two shillings out of the proceeds of the day, while John keeps the rest[4].   In Rutland the Prior of the Hospitallers holds the whole vill of Whitwell, he has twelve tenants in Dreystoke, one in Gunthorpe, two in Martinstoke, one in Barnardshill and twelve in Uppingham, for these he holds a view twice a year at Whitwell and Uppingham[5]; tenants from several Bedfordshire villages go to the view held by Humphrey de Bohun at Kimbolton in Huntingdonshire[6].

The lord who has the view of frankpledge usually has also 'the assize of beer,' that is, the power of enforcing the general

The vill and the view.

[p. 569]

The assize of bread and beer.

---

[1] Rot. Cart. 80; John grants to the monks of Norwich 'quod visus franci-plegii fiat in curia eorum coram serviente nostro sine admixtione hominum alieni homagii.'

[2] P. Q. W. 85, 89, 90, 91, 293–4–5.   [3] P. Q. W. 5, 6, 7, 293.

[4] P. Q. W. 297.   [5] P. Q. W. 672.

[6] P. Q. W. 12.

ordinances which from time to time fix the prices at which
beer may be sold; sometimes, but much more rarely, he claims
the assize of bread. Out of beer the lords made some considerable profit. It is common to find manorial jurors presenting as a matter of course that all the brewers, or rather
alewives, of the village have 'brewed against the assize'; whereupon all of them are amerced; and it is common to find the
king's advocates complaining that the lords inflict pecuniary
amercements upon those hardened offenders who ought by
rights to suffer in their persons by means of pillory and tumbrell. Pillory and tumbrell are the outward and visible signs
of this jurisdiction, just as a gallows is the manifestation of
'infangenethef'; the lord who does not keep proper instruments of justice, proper *iudicialia*, is liable to lose his franchise.
Express grants of the assize of beer are uncommon; on the
other hand many lords claim it by prescription, while the
lords of Northumberland, Cumberland, Yorkshire and Lincolnshire assert that they are not even bound to prescribe for
it, since it is theirs by the common custom of their counties[1]. [p. 570]
We have therefore come upon the line which divides those
seignorial powers which are deemed regalities from those which
have their justification in the mere relation between lord and
tenants, and we find it a vague, fluctuating line settled in some
cases by local customs.

High
justice.

Many were the lords who held the view of frankpledge,
(the *leet* of later days) and the assize of beer; comparatively
few were the lords who had more exalted jurisdictional powers.
Still of such powers we find a gradually ascending scale. At
the top are the two palatinates, the county of Chester, the
bishopric of Durham; but below them stand lordships which
are almost palatine and which leave their mark on the map
of England for many centuries. When in 1888 the day has
come for remodelling the government of our shires, the liberties
of St Edmund, of St Etheldreda of Ely, of St Peter of
Medeshamstead are still respected[2]. These together with the
marcherships on the Welsh border are the most splendid instances. Sometimes the lord exercised the highest justice only

---

[1] P. Q. W. 125–6, 189, 191–2–3–6, 220, 226, 417, 599.

[2] Local Government Act 1888, sec. 46; the eastern division of Suffolk
(which represents the liberty of St Edmund), the isle of Ely, the soke of
Peterborough, are still 'administrative counties.'

within a small territory immediately surrounding his castle or monastery, a *leugata, banlieu, lowy.* Among these powers we may notice the following:

(*a*) *Amerciamenta hominum.* The lord has a right to the amercements of his men, even though those amercements are inflicted in the king's court. The amercements are paid into the royal exchequer, and then the lord petitions that they may be paid out to him.

(*b*) *Catalla felonum et fugitivorum.* The lord, though he does not try felons, unless they be handhaving thieves, gets the forfeited chattels of condemned felons and outlaws which ordinarily would belong to the king. With this is sometimes coupled the right to hang felons sentenced by the king's justices.

[p. 571] (*c*) *Returnus*[1] *brevium.* This is a highly valued right. Within the lord's territory the 'return of writs' belongs to him: that is to say, if the sheriff receives a writ ('original' or 'judicial') bidding him summon, attach or distrain one resident within that territory, or seize lands or goods, he must deliver that writ to the bailiff of the liberty who will execute the precept. Only in case the lord or his bailiff has been guilty of default and a second writ comes to the sheriff containing the clause '*quod non omittas propter aliquam libertatem*,' will he be justified in entering the privileged precinct.

(*d*) Some lords have, and prescribe to have, coroners of their own—a remarkable fact, since to the best of our knowledge coroners were first instituted on this side of the limit of legal memory.

(*e*) Some lords compel the king's justices in eyre to come and sit within their precincts and even to occupy a secondary position. They come there—such at least is the lord's theory—merely to see that the lord's court makes no default in justice; but the business of the court, even though it consist of pleas of the crown, is conducted by the lord himself, his bailiffs or justices. Sometimes the lord claims that for the time being he himself is *iustitiarius domini Regis*[2].

(*f*) Some lords have a civil jurisdiction within their territories which excludes the jurisdiction of the king's courts.

---

[1] In old documents *returnus* is certainly commoner than *returna.*

[2] Select Pleas in Manorial Courts, pp. xxv–xxvi; but it was the Abbot of Byland, not of Kirkstall, who required the king's justices to sit at Clifton.

If an action concerning anything within the precinct is begun before the Bench at Westminster, the lord sends a bailiff to 'crave cognizance' of the cause and he is allowed it (*petit curiam suam et habet*).

High franchises claimed by prescription. Some of the highest powers were claimed by prescription; for example, the Archbishop of York declared that he and his predecessors had wielded them from time immemorial; not one scrap of parchment did he deign to produce. He even claimed to coin money by prescription[1]. And we may state as a general rule that just the very highest jurisdictional powers were seldom claimed by any other title. Occasionally a bishop or an abbot would rely on the vague, large words of some Anglo-Saxon land-book. But this was a false move; the king's [p. 572] lawyers were not astute palaeographers or diplomatists, but any charter couched in terms sufficiently loose to pass for one moment as belonging to the age before the Conquest could be met by the doctrine that the king was not to be deprived of his rights by 'obscure and general words.' For their markets and fairs, their chases and warrens, for *amerciamenta hominum* and *catalla felonum* the lords have charters; but when they hold all the pleas of the crown, when they appoint justices and coroners, when they coin money, when they treat the king's justices as distinguished visitors to be 'accommodated with a seat upon the bench,' then they prescribe:—they and all their predecessors have done the like; so they say and so the country says.

The properly feudal jurisdiction. But apart from all franchises, a lord has jurisdiction over his tenants. This he does not claim by royal grant, nor does he prescribe for it; in its exercise we can not call him the king's delegate. English law of the thirteenth century seems to have admitted the broad rule that every lord with tenants enough to form a court may, so far as the king is concerned, hold a court of and for his tenants. We say 'so far as the king is concerned.' Whether a lord enfeoffing a tenant had to stipulate for suit of court if he wished to oblige the feoffee to serve as a doomsman is a different question. Only late in the day was that question brought before the royal justices. Some seem to have held that an express stipulation was necessary if more suit was to be exacted than such as was necessary to enable the lord to exercise any regal jurisdiction with which

[1] P. Q. W. 198.

he had been entrusted.   Others were of a different opinion.
The matter was settled by the Statute of Marlborough (1267)[1]:
—the lord who exacts suit to his feudal court must rely
upon express stipulation or upon a somewhat brief prescriptive
title[2].   This, however, is a matter of comparatively little importance; the greater matter is that mere tenure gives to every
lord, who has the means of exercising it, a jurisdiction over his
tenant; his tenant is his justiciable.

This jurisdiction, if the tenant is a freeholder, is not of a
high order, nor is it very lucrative.   It is but a civil juris-
[p. 573] diction, and it is hampered and controlled by royal justice.
What is more, the feudal court is generally a manorial court,
a court for a small district.   Even though we can not at the
moment explain the full import of this proposition, we may
dwell on it for a moment.   We shall beg no question by
saying that the manor usually is but a small space of ground:
small, that is, when we compare it with the total amount of
land which a great noble will hold 'either in demesne or in
service.'   A rich religious house may have twenty manors
in demesne; a lay noble will not have so many in demesne,
but he will have some few in demesne and many more in
service; his honour will consist of a large number of manors
scattered about in divers parts of England; of some few he
will be the immediate lord, while others will be holden of
him by his knights.   Now the simple principle of feudal
justice that we have lately stated would authorize such a lord
to hold a court for his honour, to hold one court for all his immediate tenants; or, again, if his tenants were widely scattered,
he might hold several honorial courts, one, let us say, for his
Kentish tenants, another in Gloucestershire, another in Yorkshire.   And thus between the actual occupant of a tenement
and the king there might stand a whole hierarchy of courts.
We have seen above how between Roger of St German who
held land in Huntingdonshire and the king there were no less
than seven mesne lords[3].   The principle which is now before
us would in such a case permit the existence of seven feudal
courts.   That such was the law we can hardly doubt; no
narrower principle will explain the facts.   Very often the lord

The feudal court is usually a manorial court.

---

[1] Stat. Marlb. c. 9.

[2] Select Pleas in Manorial Courts, p. xlviii.

[3] See above, p. 233.

of a manor who had a court of his own was himself bound to do suit at his lord's court.   The petition which the barons presented at the Oxford parliament of 1258 assumes that not seldom three feudal courts tower one above the other.   Complaint is made that the Abbot of Peterborough does not allow his freeholders to hold courts for their tenants, whereas this is sanctioned by law and custom throughout the realm.   The Prior of Dunstable was compelled to concede that his burgesses might hold courts for their tenants.   Furthermore, it seems to have been a common practice for a wealthy abbey to keep a court, known as a *halimoot*, on each of its manors, while in [p. 574] addition to these manorial courts it kept a central court, a *libera curia* for all its greater freehold tenants.   And we may now and again meet with courts which are distinctly called courts of honours.   The rule then was, not merely that the lord of a manor may hold a court for the manor, but that a lord may hold a court for his tenants.

Nevertheless it must be allowed that in the thirteenth century full advantage was not taken of the principle.   Subinfeudation had gone far indeed and, as said above, the jurisdiction over freeholders was no longer very valuable; it brought the lord little money and did not add much to his power.   The feudal courts that we see in active work are for the more part manorial courts, and the affairs with which they are concerned are mainly the affairs of tenants in villeinage, even the affairs of villeins.   As a matter of fact, feudal jurisdiction seems intimately connected with the entities known as manors and these manors again seem to be intimately connected with townships.   Still these links exist rather in the world of fact than in the world of law; the legal principle is the simple principle that tenure implies jurisdiction.   The Abbot of Ramsey may bring to his court at Broughton his freehold tenants from seven counties; the burgess of Dunstable may hold a court for his tenants[1].

Juris-
diction of
feudal
court.

Of these feudal,—they will in general be manorial—courts we may now give a brief account; first we will speak of their competence and then of their constitution.

[1] As to all this matter, see Select Pleas in Manorial Courts, Introduction. A good instance of the abandonment of a honorial court is given in Winchcombe Landboc, i. 13: 'Aliquando autem omnes liberi maneriorum solebant sequi curiam Winchecombe de tribus septimanis in tres.   Et Abbas Johannes concessit quod facerent sectam illam in maneriis.'

I. *Civil Litigation.* (i) *Personal Actions.* They entertain personal actions, at least when the amount at stake is less than forty shillings; in particular, actions of debt, detinue, trespass and covenant. This jurisdiction seems to be considered as arising out of the relationship between man and lord. On the other hand, the action of replevin (*de vetito namii*) is royal and few lords claim to entertain it. Perhaps in theory the defendant ought to be an immediate tenant of the lord, but it is very likely that a lord often compelled any resident on his land to answer in his court, at all events when there was between them no lower lord with a court of his own. That the plaintiff also should be the lord's man would not be necessary. This jurisdiction was a useful, thriving reality. We may well find a manorial court which generally has some ten to twenty personal actions depending before it, and, as we shall see later on, these humble courts seem to have recognized certain causes of action for which the king's courts offered no remedy; they gave damages in cases of slander and libel and possibly they enforced some agreements to which the king's courts would have paid no heed.

[p. 575]

(ii) *Actions for the recovery of freehold land.* Since the days of Henry II. the rule had been that no one could be compelled to answer for his freehold without the king's writ[1]. On the other hand stood the rule, sanctioned by Magna Carta, that for a true proprietary action for land admittedly held of a certain lord, that lord's court was the proper tribunal, and, though the king's judges and chancellors gradually impaired the force of this rule by the invention of new actions which were in effect proprietary, though they may have been nominally possessory, still throughout the thirteenth century and even in the fourteenth we hear of a good many actions begun in the feudal courts by ' writ of right.' Very seldom however, unless our books mislead us, were such actions finally disposed of in those courts; to get them removed first into the county courts and then into the king's court was easy, and if the tenant (the passive party in the litigation) chose to reject the duel and put himself upon the grand assize, the competence of the lord's court was at an end. Hengham tells us that in his day the lords rarely asserted this jurisdiction over

---

[1] See above, p. 147.

freehold land, for they could get little or no profit out of it[1].

(iii) *Actions relating to customary or villein tenements.* [p. 576] In all matters which concerned a merely customary title to land the lord's court was the only competent tribunal, for of such a title the king's judges would know nothing. No royal writ was necessary. Still we see the lord's court doing strict justice in due form of law; there is no formless arbitration, there are formal pleadings which are strictly construed. Before the end of the century pleaders in manorial courts are making use of phrases which seem to have their origin at Westminster[2]; but all along they have been using technical phrases, tracing the descent of the customary tenement from heir to heir, alleging 'seisin as of right,' alleging the taking of 'esplees,' adding however at every turn 'according to the custom of the manor[3].' The justice which the customary tenants got was strict justice; it was not 'equity' on the one hand, but on the other it was not 'the will of the lord.'

. (iv) *Litigation between lord and man.* That the lord could sue his tenant seems plain; the entries on a court roll largely consist of such as show how the lord's bailiff made accusations against the tenants and how the lord recovered damages

---

[1] See Hengham Magna, cap. 3. See also Note Book, *e.g.* pl. 26, proceedings in the court of the Earl of Warenne carried as far as the first blows of the duel when a concord was made; pl. 40, proceedings in the court of Margery de Sumery irregularly removed into the county court; pl. 212, proceedings in the court of the Earl of Warenne removed into the county court; pl. 1436, lengthy and repeated litigation in the court of the Bp. of Bath; in one instance the first blows of the duel were struck; pl. 1847, proceedings in the court of the Constable of Chester stayed by a forged writ. Then see Y. B. Edw. II., f. 263 (*Droit*), 524 (*Droit*), 633 (*Faux jugement*), and 244 (*Droit*); in this last case a judgment was given in the lord's court. Though the process of removing a writ of right from the feudal court was easily accomplished, it involved an assertion that the lord had made default in justice, and to this the demandant pledged his oath. A Registrum Brevium in the Cambridge Library, Mm. i. 27, describes the process thus—The demandant shall come with the bailiff of the hundred to the lord's court and bring in his hand his writ and a book [presumably the gospels] and shall stand on the threshold of the court and swear on the book that he will plead no further in that court by the writ which he holds in his hand, since the court has failed to do him justice; and then he shall have a writ to the bailiffs and the sheriff stating that he has abjured the court and proved its default.

[2] See The Court Baron (Selden Soc.) p. 119 where the form of a writ of entry *ad terminum qui praeteriit* is adopted.

[3] Select Pleas in Manorial Courts, pp. 17, 34, 39, 123, 173.

from them; the tenants are charged with trespasses, or with breaches of the manorial custom[1]. It is late in the day before we hear any suggestion that such a course of procedure is inequitable since it makes the lord a judge in his own cause, and even then it is admitted to be 'the common course throughout the land[2].' There is much to show that in the past one of the main uses of a feudal court had been that it enabled the lord [p. 577] to compel his tenants to perform their services; this will appear from what has been said about the law of distress[3]. As to the objection that the lord is both judge and party, that fails, for the lord is not judge; the defendant has the judgment of his peers. On the other hand, the lord can not be sued in his court; this is true of him as it is true of the king. The proper feudal course for one who claims to hold land of X but can not get that land is to demand justice from X, and if this demand fails, to go to the court of X's lord. A lord distrained to answer in his own court is the most startling anomaly of the ancient demesne.

II. *Presentments.* Even though the lord does not aspire to, or on this particular day is not exercising, the franchise of view of frankpledge, he often makes use of a procedure which involves presentment. Jurors are sworn in, sometimes twelve, but often less than twelve, to present offences. Perhaps in theory they have no business to present any offences which touch the king's peace, such as assaults, since in adjudicating on these the lord would be usurping a franchise, and ought to confine themselves to breaches of the manorial custom and invasions of the lord's proprietary rights. But it is difficult to maintain or even to draw the line, difficult to prevent a lord from making his feudal court a police court. Especially is this so when the tenants are unfree; if the lord amerces a serf for drawing his knife, pilfering his neighbour's goods, using bad words, he is after all but demanding money which already is his own; even if he puts the man in the stocks or turns him out of the vill, this, if it can be regarded as an act of justice, can also be regarded as an act of ownership. And so we find that the presentments are miscellaneous:—A has assaulted B;

---

[1] See the precedents in The Court Baron.

[2] Y. B. 44 Edw. III. f. 19 (Trin. pl. 14). The same suggestion is made in Y. B. 21–2 Edw. I. p. 157. The answer is 'The court is judge.'

[3] See above, p. 353.

C has abused *D*; *E* is a scolding wife; *F*'s daughter has been guilty of fornication and so he owes a leyrwite; *G*, a freeholder, is dead and his son owes a relief; *H* is the lord's *nativus* and has left the manor; *J* came late to the boon works; *K* keeps his dung-heap before his door; *L* has fished in the lord's pond; *M* sells sour beer; *N* puts more beasts on the pasture than the by-law allows him; *O* rescued his impounded beasts; and so forth. As a rule when there is no question touching free-hold the accused seems to get little chance of denying these [p. 578] charges, but is at once amerced; sixpenny and threepenny amercements are common.

III. *Governmental Power and By-laws.* Within narrow limits a feudal court might be, not merely a court of justice, but also an assembly capable of discussing and arranging the affairs of the tenurial group. To such an assembly the lord would in old times appeal when he wanted an aid from his military tenants[1], or when he wanted them, or some of them on behalf of all, to go to the war[2]. But among the knights of an honour there was little communalism; each individual had his rights and duties; the one could not be impaired, the other could not be aggravated by any resolution of his peers. As to manorial by-laws we must speak hereafter. Over unfree men, even over the free men who hold unfree lands, such by-laws, being made with the lord's approval, would have great power; a breach of them might be punished by a forfeiture of the tenement; a recalcitrant bondman might be set in the stocks; but to enforce by-laws against a free-holding free man was a more difficult matter.

IV. *Appellate Jurisdiction.* When a great lord had many halimoots and one *libera curia*, difficult cases which arose in the former were sometimes reserved for the latter. But the magnates had aimed at more than this. They had wished for an appellate jurisdiction, or rather a 'jurisdiction in error' over the courts of their tenants. Had the first principle of feudal justice been allowed free play, their demand must have been conceded. But it failed. If the court of the lower lord made default in justice, the case could be removed at once into the county court and thence to the king's court, and none

---

[1] See above, p. 350.
[2] Select Pleas in Manorial Courts, i. 49, 50; Mat. Par. Chron. Maj. vi. 438.

but the king's court could hear a charge of false judgment[1]. After a severe struggle these rules were established; to their operation it is due that in England we hear little of exalted feudal courts, courts of baronies and honours.

V. *Conveyancing Business.* In later ages the work of a manorial court will chiefly consist in witnessing transfers of copyhold land; the court roll will become a register of title for the copyholders. At the accession of Edward I., however, [p. 579] the practice of keeping court rolls was still new, and, though from time to time we may hear how a tenant in villeinage 'puts himself upon the roll' by way of proving his title[2], still on such rolls as we have seen entries of 'surrenders and admittances' are so few and so irregular that we can not believe that they were of much importance. However, such power of alienation as the custom of the manor gives to the tenant in villeinage is often exercised in court. He can only alienate his tenement by surrendering it to the lord, and, if this is done in open court, the lord's acceptance of a new tenant will be witnessed by the men of the court, and their testimony will be useful at a future time. We have no reason, however, for saying that only in court could a lord give villein land to a new tenant or concede to a dead tenant's heir the tenement of his ancestor, for, according to the law of the king's court, the land was the lord's to do what he liked with. From an ancient demesne manor we may already hear how a tenant who was too ill to come to court made a surrender to the bailiff out of court to the intent that the bailiff might make the surrender in court[3]. With the transfer of freehold land the court had in general little to do; the tenants subinfeudated their tenements without going to the court, and in the thirteenth century they already thrust new immediate tenants upon their lord without asking for his cooperation[4]; still a careful lord would oblige the manorial jury to present deaths and descents which took place among his freeholders, in order that he might secure his reliefs, wardships and marriages. As homage had to be done to the lord in his proper person, it

---

[1] Select Pleas in Manorial Courts, Introduction, p. lviij.   See also Rot. Cur. Regis, i. 357.

[2] The Court Baron, pp. 121, 134.

[3] Select Pleas in Manorial Courts, i. 126 (A.D. 1301).

[4] See above, p. 345.

was more usually done in his house than in the manorial court.

Constitution of the feudal court. The president.
And now as to the constitution of the court. There seems no reason why the lord should not preside over it in person, and occasionally an abbot or prior would do this[1]. Often the cellarer of the abbey, himself a monk, would hold the courts; but generally they were held by the lord's steward. Some abbots and other lords had allowed the stewardship to become hereditary; they had enfeoffed knights who were to hold their lands by the serjeanty of stewardship. But before the end of the thirteenth century the work was falling into the hands [p. 580] of lawyers. Very great lawyers did not scorn it. A little later, in 1335, we find the prior of Christ Church offering the office of steward to no less a person than Sir John Stonor, who had been for some years one of the king's justices[2]; he would not accept, but he was in no wise offended by, the proposal. And then, when a weighty cause is to be heard in the court of Merstham, the prior sends down one of his counsel to afforce the court[3]. At an earlier time, when the abbot of St Alban's had quarrelled with his knights, he induced one of the king's justices, who had come to deliver the gaol, to preside over the feudal assembly under the ash tree[4]. And, as we have said before, men were beginning to write books which should teach stewards how to hold plea, and very technical books they are[5].

The suitors.
As in the communal so in the feudal courts, the president has doomsmen at his side. When he is making the view of frankpledge, when (to use the terms of a later day) the court is acting as a 'court leet,' he—like the sheriff in his 'turn'—seems to be the only judge: the procedure by way of presentment is not easily compatible with the action of a body of doomsmen; the view of frankpledge is a royal franchise, and for the time being the steward is *quasi* a royal justice[6]. But 'in the court baron the suitors are the judges'—this rule is well maintained throughout the middle ages. At their end it is said that two suitors will suffice; we may well doubt whether so small a number would have been adequate at an

---

[1] Durham Halmotes, i. pp. xi, xii.
[2] Lit. Cantuar. ii. 84, 86, 98, 108.   [3] Ibid. 272.
[4] Mat. Par. Chron. Maj. vi. 438.
[5] See The Court Baron (Selden Soc.).   [6] Bracton, f. 98.

earlier time[1]. Heriet, a justice of John's reign, seems to have demanded twelve[2]. How far any distinction was drawn in practice between cases which affected free men and those which affected unfree men is a doubtful question[3]. In Coke's day it was said that the lord of a manor had one court, 'a court baron,' for his freeholders and another court, 'a customary court,' for his [p.581] copyholders, and that in the latter the lord or his steward was the judge. Now over his unfree men the lord had, according to the law of the king's court, almost unlimited power; short of maiming them he might do what he liked with them; and every tenant of an unfree tenement was a tenant at will. Nevertheless in the court rolls and the manuals for stewards which come to us from the thirteenth and fourteenth centuries we cannot discover two courts or two methods of constituting the court. Freeholders and serfs are said to owe suit to the same halimoot, and, so far as we can see, the *curia* which pronounces judgment is always the same body. Occasionally distinctions of status are noticed. When the lord is holding a view of frankpledge, if he has many tenants, he will sometimes copy the procedure of the sheriff's turn; the presentments will be made in the first instance by *villani*, and will then be revised by a jury of freeholders[4]. Sometimes two bondmen will be appointed to affeer the amercements of the bond, while two free men will affeer the amercements of the free[5]. No doubt, again, a free man might have objected if among his doomsmen he saw a serf. No doubt, again, the theory that the villein tenements were held at the will of the lord was by no means idle; the lord could not be compelled to accept a new tenant against his will. Still, so far as we can see, when the lord's interests were not being actively asserted, the serf who sued or was sued in the manorial court got the same justice as that which the free man got; he got in theory the judgment, not of his lord, but of a body of doomsmen who were at least his peers. We say that such a judgment he got in theory; in practice the question became of less and less moment, for trial by jury

---

[1] Select Pleas in Manorial Courts, vol. i. p. lxii.; add to the references Y. B. 7 Edw. II. f. 238: six suitors are not enough for a little writ of right in a manor on the ancient demesne.

[2] Munimenta Gildhallae, i. 116.

[3] Select Pleas in Manorial Courts, vol. i. pp. lx–lxxiii.

[4] The Court Baron, pp. 100, 110.   [5] Ibid. p. 101.

gradually forced its way into the manorial courts. In strictness
of law the lord could not compel his free men to serve as jurors
in civil causes; they and the king were agreed that none but
the king should make them swear; but the lord could force
his bondmen to swear, and many a small freeholder would
serve rather than quarrel with his lord. At any rate trial by
jury made its way into these courts, and it hardly leaves a
place for the doomsman; indeed in course of time the cry
for a *iudicium parium* is (to the great distortion of history)
supposed to find its satisfaction in trial by jury. Very late [p. 582]
in the day (for we can not trace this further back than a Star
Chamber case of Henry VIII.'s reign) we hear a doctrine
which, if it has any historical warrant at all, suggests that
no lord could hold a court even for his bondmen unless he had
free doomsmen, for it is said that there can be no manor without at least two freeholders owing suit of court. Interpret this
doctrine how we may, we can not believe it ancient. As to
the question about the use of words we shall speak below; but
we do not believe that all the *maneria* of the twelfth and
thirteenth centuries comprised freeholders. As to the questions
of law, we can not find that a lord's jurisdiction over free men
was in any wise dependent upon his having villein tenants, or
that his jurisdiction over his villeins demanded the existence
of freeholders. Very little weight should be ascribed to the
unreasoned, unexplained dictum of the Star Chamber delivered
at a time when the feudal courts were senile and villeinage
was all but dead, and yet this dictum seems to be the only
source of the famous doctrine that a manor can not exist
without two freeholders[1].

§ 6.   *The Manor.*

The
manor.

And now at length we may go up against the manor. We
may make our task the easier if we observe that 'the manor' is
more prominent in modern theories than in medieval texts.
Bracton rarely uses the term *manerium*. Only in one context
does he give anything that can be called an explanation of that
word and it explains very little. A person who brings an

---

[1] Select Pleas in Manorial Courts, vol. i. pp. lx–lxxiii.

action for land must specify the land that he claims. In so doing, he will perhaps use the word *manerium*, and therefore it is necessary to note that manors and vills are not all one, that sometimes a manor and a vill bear the same name, that sometimes a manor contains several vills, and again that a manor is not the same thing as a mansion[1]. But what is the essence of a *manerium* we are never told. Such records of litigation as [p. 583] we have in print give us no further help. Sometimes, though not very often, the object demanded in an action is a manor, and we may find disputes as to whether a particular tenement is or is not a part, or 'a member' of a particular manor. The word is used in conveyances, and doubts may arise as to what has passed to the donee by a gift of 'the manor of Dale.' But in conveyances the term is much less common than we with our theories of 'a manorial system' might expect. Even when we turn to the Hundred Rolls and read the detailed descriptions of tenures and tenements, of the groups formed by lords and tenants, though we may well think that we are reading of manors, still we may often read through many pages without seeing the word *manerium*. May we hope that we have shown, as Bracton showed, that much may be said of the law of tenure, of status, of jurisdiction, though that word be never employed?

In a sense therefore we must deny that in the thirteenth century the word *manerium* was a technical term, that it could be placed in the same category with *villa, feodum unius militis, liberum tenementum, villenagium*. There are reasons for thinking that in a remoter past and especially in Domesday Book, this term had borne a definite legal sense which was concerned with the levy of the danegeld[2]. Be that as it may, we believe that in the thirteenth century no strict definition of a manor could have been fashioned. Any word that is commonly used in the transaction of business is likely to come before the law-courts and to be discussed by pleaders and judges. A modern court may be called upon to decide whether a four-roomed cottage was fairly described as 'a country house'; but still, 'country house' is not a technical term. In our own day the term 'estate' is used by Englishmen to describe tracts of land; but who can accurately define its meaning? If we

Manor not a technical word.

---

[1] Bracton, f. 212, 434 b.

[2] Maitland, Domesday Book and Beyond, 107 ff; and, to the contrary, Tait, E. H. R. xii. 768.

read in a biography that the hero had 'an estate in Kent' we should expect him to have had more than a rood of cabbage-garden; but how much more? Must there have been a house and some fields? must he have had land 'in hand'? must he [p. 584] have had tenant farmers and cottagers? And what of 'a country seat'?

Indefinite-
ness of the
term
manor.
In the thirteenth century the term *manerium* seems to have been no more precise than the term 'estate' (as commonly used by laymen) is at the present day. It implied, for example, a certain geographical extent, neither too small, nor too large, and a certain geographical continuity; but the requisite size, the requisite continuity could not be defined. A manor in Cambridgeshire might have a member in Suffolk; a manor in Kent could not have a member in Northumberland; but the exact degree of discontinuity that would have rendered the term inappropriate could not be fixed. Modern attempts to define a manor break down before this difficulty. Most, if not all, of them would suffer or even compel us to describe many a vast honour scattered about over all England as being a single manor[1].

A typical
manor.
Therefore to ask for a definition of a manor is to ask for what can not be given. We may however draw a picture of a typical manor, and, this done, we may discuss the deviations from this type.

(1) The typical manor is geographically coincident with a vill; the lord of the manor is also the lord of the vill; manor and vill have one name; the group of men, which, when regarded from one point, appears as the *villata* or township, if regarded from another point appears as a group of tenants; all persons who have lands in the vill hold of one and the same lord. This gives unity to the manor, for the township has many public duties, and the question whether a given acre is part of the vill or whether a given person is a member of the township is, we may say, a question of public law.

---

[1] Thus Scriven, Copyholds, i. 1:—'A manor . . . . is the district . . . granted by the ancient kings of this realm to the lords or barons, with liberty to parcel the land out to inferior tenants, reserving such duties and services as they thought convenient, and with power to hold a court (from thence called a court baron), for redressing misdemeanours, punishing the offences of their tenants and settling any disputes of property between them.' With such a definition as this we can not face the question—Why is it said of some tenant in chief that he has fifteen manors, no more and no less?

(2) The inhabited and cultivated lands of the manor are divisible into three portions; the lord holds land in demesne (in the narrowest sense of that term[1]) and on this stand his [p. 585] house and homestead, and these are sometimes called pre-eminently the *manerium*; then there are lands held of him by freehold tenure, and there are lands held of him by unfree or customary tenure. The arable portion of the manor usually lies in two or three great open fields, and the strips which are held by the lord, by the freeholders, by the customary tenants lie intermingled. There is also pasture land; much of it is held by the lord in demesne, but over it the tenants have rights of common. The manor is an economic unit; the lord's demesne lands in that manor are to a considerable extent cultivated by means of the labour services which are due from the tenants. (3) If the lord is a great man with several manors, even though these be contiguous, the accounts of each are separately kept; very generally each manor will have its bailiff and its reeve. (4) Lastly, the lord holds a court for the manor; if he is a great man, besides having a court for each manor, he may hold a central court for all his principal freeholders, but each manor will usually have a court of its own.

Thus we may regard the typical manor (1) as being, *qua* vill, an unit of public law, of police and fiscal law, (2) as being an unit in the system of agriculture, (3) as being an unit in the management of property, (4) as being a jurisdictional unit. But we have now to see that hardly one of these traits can be considered as absolutely essential. The most important is the connexion between the manor and the vill; a consideration of this we must for a while postpone; but this much may be premised that in very many instances the manor is not geographically coincident with a vill nor yet with any group of vills.

We may begin by saying that the manor comprises a house, or at all events a homestead, occupied by the lord, his servants or lessees. This from the etymologist's point of view appears as the essence of the manor. The term manor (*manerium*) is one of the many words which have their origin in the Latin verb *manere*; *mansus, mansa* (common in the Anglo-Saxon land-books), *mansio, mansura* or *masura, messuagium*

The manor house

---

[1] See above, p. 363.

are other examples, and it would seem that each of these has
but slowly acquired a shade of meaning peculiar to itself.   In
our thirteenth century 'manor,' 'mansion' and 'messuage' are
no longer convertible terms, though 'manor' is still occasionally [p. 586]
used to signify just the lord's house or homestead and no
more: the *porta manerii* is the door of the house or of the
court-yard; the *situs manerii* is the site of the house together
with its curtilage[1]; indeed in France the word *manoir* seems
seldom, if ever, to bear a more extended meaning.   Still the
word is commonly used so as to include much more than a
house, as, for example, when Bracton tells us that a chief
manor may contain several sub-manors, that a *manerium* may
be composed of several vills[2].

Sometimes a phrase seems to halt between the narrower
and the wider meaning and shows us the relation between the
two.   When it is written that certain lands 'belong to' such
a manor, a connexion legal and economic between them and a
certain building is, or may be, in the writer's mind.   Occasionally the word 'hall,' which may have been common in
English speech, is used in the same way—'he owes suit to
the hall (*aula*) of Horningsheath,' 'it is customary land of the
hall (*aula*) of Packenham[3].'

Occupation
of the
manor
house.

However, we dare not say that it is indispensably necessary
that the manor should include a house occupied by the lord.
On a strictly personal occupation of course we can not insist.
Many manors were in the hands of the religious, and neither
did the monks live on the manors, nor was it usual for a
bishop or abbot to reside on all his manors in turn; if he had
three or four residences, this was enough; but he might have

---

[1] See the instances given by Blakesley in L. Q. R. v. 114–5.   Select Pleas in
Manorial Courts, p. 44: 'et insuper ad portam manerii dicti domini . . . . hute-
sium levavit.'   Durham Halmote Rolls, p. 11: 'homines de Dalton solebant
habere communam cum animalibus suis a porta manerii versus viam de
Hesilden.'   Ibid. p. 36: 'et portas eiusdem manerii fregerunt.'   R. H. ii. 578;
the Abbot of *G* holds a manor in the vill of *S* which contains 5 acres, and he has
in the same vill a garden which contains 3 acres, and he has there in demesne
8 score acres of land, 20 acres of pasture, and 4 acres of meadow, and he holds
the said manor in almoin; he has also freehold and servile tenants.   At the
present day such a name as Dale Manor is often enough the name of a house.

[2] Bracton, f. 212, 434 b.

[3] Bodleian, Suffolk Court Rolls, No. 3.   It is not here implied that the Eng.
hall, A.-S. *heal*, has any etymological connexion with Lat. *aula*; nevertheless
the two words seem to have been treated as exactly equivalent.

thirty or forty manors. The centre of the typical manor is often a homestead or farmyard with but humble buildings placed under the charge of a bailiff, rather than a fine dwelling [p. 587] for the lord and his family. But it is doubtful whether we can even insist upon the homestead. Often we may find that the *situs manerii* has been let to a tenant at a rent; we can not be certain that there are any longer any buildings upon it, and if there are, they are no longer occupied by the lord or his servants.

A similar doubt must be suggested as to the necessity of land held in demesne. Undoubtedly it is a normal feature of a manor that there should be land the fruits (not the rents but the actual fruits) of which come to the lord's garners; the unfree, and often the free, tenants assist in the cultivation of this land, the raising of these fruits; the economist is apt to consider this as the essence of the manorial arrangement. But suppose that the lord, more or less permanently, parts with this land in exchange for a rent; has he ceased to hold a manor, to be lord of a manor, to have the right to hold a court for all the tenants of the manor? To all these questions we must answer, No, at least if the supposed alienation be no more than a lease for years. Towards the end of the century it was becoming common for the lord to let the land that he had held in demesne; but the farmer (*firmarius*) of the demesne land did not become lord of the manor, the lessor did not cease to be lord, the tenants still held immediately of him, he still kept a court for them and took its profits. As to the effect of more permanent alienations, there may be more doubt, and we must distinguish a question about the use of words from a question about the existence of rights. If the lord of a manor enfeoffed another person with all the demesne lands, this gift, we may be sure, did not necessarily carry with it a lordship over the tenants of the free and unfree tenements, a right to all their rents and services, a jurisdiction over them. Men were very free to make what arrangements they pleased. We have, for example, an instructive verdict concerning the history of a Cambridgeshire vill. The earl of Gloucester holds Bottisham of the king. But his predecessors gave 'the whole manor of Bottisham with all lands, demesnes and tenements, villeinages, [p. 588] coterells, pastures, meadows, mills, franchise of bull and ram and all appurtenances and easements to two houses of religion,

Demesne land.

to wit, a moiety to Anglesey Priory and a moiety to Tonbridge
Priory, saving to himself and his successors the free rents of
the free tenants in the same vill, and saving suit of court
from three weeks to three weeks, and saving the homages and
reliefs of the free tenants and wardships and escheats and all
pleas.' The result is that the prior of Anglesey has 200 acres
and 6 villeins and 5 coterells, the prior of Tonbridge has a
like holding, while the earl has some 40 freehold tenants for
whom he holds a court; the view of frankpledge for the whole
vill is in his hand[1]. Here we have the lord of a manor giving
half his demesnes and half his villein tenements to one priory,
half to another, but retaining to himself an immediate lordship
over the freeholders, his right to receive their rents and to hold
a court for them. An endless variety of such arrangements was
possible, the only legal limit being that which would have
protected freehold tenants against any aggravation of their
services. Probably, while the labour services of the villeins
remained uncommuted, a lord did not often part with the
whole, or nearly the whole, of his demesne land without giving
along with this a right to those services which his villeins had
been accustomed to do on that land; to have done so would
have been to lighten or even to abolish the services; but when
those services were commuted into money dues, there was
nothing to prevent the lord conveying away his demesne and
retaining his immediate lordship over the villeins and his
right to their rents.

The
freehold
tenants.
　　To give positive proof that no freehold tenants were necessary to constitute a *manerium* is difficult, for, as already said,
we may turn many pages of the Hundred Rolls without seeing
that word, and certain it seems that towards the end of the
thirteenth century a lord seldom had many villein tenants
without having just a few freeholders intermingled with them.
Still instances may be found in which a lord has a considerable
group of villein tenants with whom no freeholder is associated.
Thus, on the abbot of Gloucester's estates we find that in
village after village, in which he has demesne land and many
tenants in villeinage and in which he holds a court with villein
suitors, he has no freeholders, or but one freeholder; yet in [p. 589]
these villages he has *maneria*[2]. Again, a comparison between

---

[1] R. H. ii. 487.

[2] Cart. Glouc. iii. 103, *et passim*. See also in R. H. ii. 695, the Templars'

the surveys of the thirteenth century and the earlier documents seems to show that many of the freehold tenancies are of modern origin. As regards two of the abbot of Peterborough's manors we may compare the Hundred Roll with the ancient Black Book. On the 'manor' of Alwalton, according to the younger of these documents, there are two *libere tenentes*, the one is the parish parson, the other holds but a messuage with a rood and three acres; the Black Book tells of no freeholders. It is so also on the 'manor' of Fletton; the Black Book mentions no freeholders; the Hundred Roll mentions two, one of whom gets his land from his grandfather, who was steward in the abbot's hall[1]. Indeed in the Black Book we come across vill after vill in which the abbot has many villeins and no freehold tenant. The theory that freehold tenants are necessary to constitute a manor will allow to some mighty lords of the twelfth century very few manors indeed.

One limit may perhaps be set to our scepticism:—there must be villein tenements, there must at all events be some tenants holding 'of' the manor. As a matter of fact this probably was so. In the then state of agriculture a tract of any considerable size held in demesne almost of necessity implied a group of persons whose tenure of other lands obliged them to aid their lord in his husbandry. Still when we find the word 'manor' used, as sometimes it is, to denote just the lord's house and homestead, and when we consider the close connexion that there is between 'manor,' 'manse,' 'mansion,' 'messuage,' we may doubt whether there is any severe rule of fashion, to say nothing of law, about the use of these terms. Again, we are not able to produce any example from the thirteenth century of an estate which is called a manor but which has no villein or customary tenements bound up in it or with it; still we should not be surprised to find that if [p. 590] a lord enfranchised all his villein tenements he still was said to hold a manor; he might get a good deal of occasional labour out of his freeholders, so that their lands would still be knotted to his demesne lands so as to form an economic

Tenants in villeinage.

---

estate at Bradwell; Ibid. 714, Sampson Foliot holds the manor (expressly so called) of Albury but has no free tenant; Ibid. 715, the Templars' estate at Merton; Ibid. 723, the Templars' estate at Littlemore, they have no freeholder, the customary tenants attend their court.

[1] R. H. ii. 638–9; Chron. Petrob. (Camden Soc.), 160, 165.

unit. Nor have we any warrant for supposing that this state of things could be produced only by enfranchisement. In the account of eastern England given in Domesday Book it is possible to find *maneria* which have no tenants who are below the rank of sokemen, and some of these manors may still have been 'manors' in the thirteenth century, manors with freehold tenants, but without tenants of a baser kind.

The manor court.

Again, to turn to another point, we hardly dare say that a person who has villein or customary tenants must have a manor or must have a court. What can we make of the numerous cases in which a man has but three or four such tenants? Does he hold a court for them? Let us examine the vill of Upton in Huntingdonshire:—*A* has a messuage and half a carucate in demesne and the sixth part of a wood and 'the sixth part of one free tenant,' John the Freeman, who pays him 8*d.* and holds one carucate; and *A* has also one virgate and a half in villeinage which three villeins hold of him, each of whom pays him 10*s.* and merchet, and he has 'the sixth part of two villeins,' and each of them pays him 19*d.* for the sixth part of one carucate; and he has two coterells each of whom pays him 3*s.* 8*d.*, and 'half one coterell' who pays him 10*d.*, and 'the sixth part of two coterells' each of whom pays him 6*d.* :—*B* and *C* and *D* have estates similar to *A*'s and there are some other holdings[1]. Whether *A* would have said that he had a manor we do not know, but we can hardly believe that he kept a court for his tenants and fractional parts of tenants. Obviously in this case there has been a descent among coheiresses: part of the estate that descended to them has been partitioned, part remains unpartitioned.

But similar results might be caused by subinfeudation. Once upon a time the king held Great Wilbraham: he gave [p. 591] half of it to Nigel the Chamberlain, who gave half that half as his daughter's marriage portion; this quarter of the vill is now held by Robert de l'Isle, who has 10 customary tenants. Nigel gave away another piece to the Abbot of Warden; the residue of his moiety descended to his five daughters. Then the king gave a quarter of the other moiety to one Picot, and the remaining three-eighths to Hubert de Burgh, who gave them to the Templars. The consequence is that the *custumarii* of Wilbraham are divided among many lords, one of whom has

---

[1] R. H. ii. 620.

but three[1]. A case may be found in which a man has a few freehold tenants and just one customary tenant (a *servus*)[2], many cases in which he has two or three villeins and two or three cottagers. In these cases we can not easily believe that the villeins are protected by any court or by any custom. When a great lord detaches a few of his customary tenants to form an endowment for some retainer, they can hardly keep their old condition; in course of time they must rise or they must fall: their services being commuted into money, they may make good their claim to be freeholders, or on the other hand they may become tenants at will in the strictest sense of the term.

To the size of the manor we can set neither an inferior nor a superior limit. Occasionally diminutive words are coined to indicate manors which are of less than the normal size; thus Domesday Book tells us how the Bishop had a *maneriolum* in Lincoln with one carucate of land and sake and soke and toll and team[3]; and the Hundred Rolls tell us of a *manerettum* in Devonshire[4]. In Domesday Book the word *manerium* often covers an exceedingly small quantity of land; the so-called [p. 592] manor is only a peasant's tenement[5]. In the thirteenth century we shall hardly find the word given to such little estates. On the other hand, the very largest manors which then meet us have all the appearance of being old.

Size of the manor.

Four cases may be mentioned. The ancient demesne manor of Bensington in Oxfordshire has according to the jurors been vast; Henley-on-Thames, Nettlebed, Wyfold, Huntercombe, Warborough, Shillingford, Holcombe and Crowmarsh have been its hamlets, and four hundreds and a half have been appurtenant to it[6]. In Domesday Book Bensington pays the king the large sum of £80 and 100 shillings 'and the soke of four and a half hundreds pertains to this manor[7].' In Suffolk lies the huge royal 'manor' of Lothingland, containing the towns of Gorleston and Lowestoft, which lie some nine miles apart[8]; this represents a great estate held by Earl Gurth in the time of the Confessor[9]. In Lincolnshire the king's manor

---

[1] R. H. ii. 491.   [2] R. H. ii. 875.
[3] D. B. i. 336.   [4] R. H. i. 66.
[5] Maitland, Domesday Book and Beyond, 116.
[6] R. H. ii. 751.   [7] D. B. i. 154.
[8] R. H. ii. 160–9.   [9] D. B. ii. 283.

of Castor includes many adjacent villages or parts of them[1];
this had been a great estate of Earl Morcar with 240 sokemen,
24 villani, 28 bordarii[2]. The manor of Taunton Dean covered
numerous villages; in the Conqueror's day it brought the
bishop of Winchester £154 a year[3]; it has become the classical
example of manors abnormally large.

Administrative unity.

We may probably insist that the unity of the manor implies
a certain unity in its administration. A lord may have many
manors lying side by side, and yet they are separate manors,
because he treats them as separate. It may, no doubt, be
true that the manor generally had one set of open fields
to itself, one set and no more; but exceptions on both sides
of this rule must have been common. Each of the vast
maneria of Domesday Book can not have had just one set of
fields and no more, and some of these vast *maneria* still [p. 593]
existed in the thirteenth century. On the other hand, when
in Cambridgeshire we find several manors in almost every
vill and then look at maps that were made before the inclosure
of the open fields, we shall learn to doubt whether in this
part of England the lands of the manor could, even normally,
be brought within a ring fence; they seem to have lain intermixed in the common fields with the lands of the other manors
of the same vill. The delimitation of one manor from other
manors of the same lord seems to be a matter of convenience:
one may become two, two may become one, as the lord chooses
to have his accounts kept, his rents collected, his produce
garnered in this way or in that. At least with the consent
of his freehold tenants, a lord may 'attorn' a piece of land
to this manor or that, decide that the tenants shall pay their
rents at this house or at that, while as to his villeins,
their consent need not be asked[4].

Summary.

On the whole therefore we come to the conclusion that in
the thirteenth century the word 'manor,' like the 'estate' of
our own day, was a vague, though common and useful word.
Applied to a given instance it might be definite enough; no
one would doubt that certain acres belonged to the manor of
Dale, just as now-a-days it may be notorious throughout the
countryside that certain acres are part of the Dale estate; but
to have inquired what it was that gave the manor of Dale its

---

[1] R. H. i. 265.   [2] D. B. i. 338 b.   [3] D. B. i. 87 b.
[4] See Note Book, pl. 695.

unity, what made it one manor not two manors (to be called perhaps Upper Dale and Lower Dale), what were the characteristics a loss of which would have been fatal to its existence as a single manor, would have been to ask questions no clear answer to which could have been had, because they would seldom have been useful questions.   They could only arise in a practical form when there was a dispute as to how much land had passed by some feoffment or lease, and on such occasions they would be settled by general repute:—the jurors would say that the plot in question had always, or had never, been accounted part of the manor.   In other words, we are inclined to think that the mere fact that a certain tract of land or a certain complex of rights was a *manerium* had no immediate [p. 594] legal consequences.   In particular, it seems to us that the men of the time would generally have argued from the court to the manor, rather than from the manor to the court, and would have said 'A single court is held for it, therefore it is a manor,' rather than 'It is a manor and therefore it has a court.'

§ 7.   *The Manor and The Township.*

In a famous passage Ordericus Vitalis asserts the identity of the *manerium* and the *villa*:—the Bishop of Coutances held by the Conqueror's gift two hundred and eighty 'villas quas a manendo manerios vulgo vocamus[1].' An assumption to the same effect seems to be made by the writ which ordered the Domesday Inquest; the priest, the reeve and six *villani* of every *villa* are to swear, in the first place how the *mansio* is called, who held it under the Confessor, who holds it now, how many ploughs there are in demesne, how many the men have— and so forth.   It is assumed that England is, and has been, held in *villae*, that each *villa* has its *mansio*.   The answering verdicts do not altogether bear out this assumption.   The local names which are used (when they are not names of counties or hundreds) seem to be with few, if any, exceptions the names of places which were accounted *villae*; they are names of villages, and generally there is no difficulty about finding them as names of villages upon the modern map.   Now

Coincidence of manor and vill.

---

[1] Ord. Vital. ii. 223.

very commonly it is true that a single lord holds the whole place which bears one of these names. The formula used is '*A* (name of a tenant in chief) *tenet X* (place name),' and we do not find that any person, other than *A* and tenants of his, holds anything in *X*. But this rule is subject to so many exceptions that in some parts of the country it ceases to be the rule. Such is the case in the neighbourhood of Cambridge. For example, there are five tenancies in chief in Trumpington and six in Grantchester; no one therefore could call himself the lord of Trumpington or of Grantchester, save the king, and he only in the sense in which he was lord of every vill in England. In documents that are later than Domesday Book we some- [p. 595] times find the same assumption, which in French we might express thus: *Nulle ville sans seigneur*. In the *Leges Henrici*[1] the priest, reeve and four of the best men of the vill appear as representatives of the lord. Of what lord? The lord of the vill. The Saladin tithe of 1188 is to be assessed in each parish in the presence of the serjeant and clerk of the baron. Of what baron? The lord of the parish. For the assessment of the tax of 1198 the presence is required of the lord of each vill or the bailiff of the vill[2]. Even the statute book of the fourteenth century seems sometimes to assume that every vill will have its lord[3].

Coinci-
dence
assumed
as normal.

All this is significant, for it seems to testify to a common belief that normally vill and manor are but two names for one thing: the *villa* of public law is the *manerium* of property law. In favour of the assumption that this is the common and typical, we may add that it is the simple and explicable case. When vill and manor coincide, then we see an organization which will enable the township to discharge its public duties. It now has a court, in which a reeve and constable may be appointed and in which all questions relating to the apportionment of public duties can be decided. We can also see how in this case the township can have 'common' rights, the right for example to turn out beasts on a common pasture; the soil of that pasture belongs to the lord of the vill and regu-

---

[1] Leg. Hen. c. 7, § 7.

[2] See the documents of 1188 and 1198 in Stubbs, Select Charters.

[3] Stat. 28 Edw. III. c. 11: 'et enquestes soient auxint prises en villes . . . . par celui qe est sovereign de la ville.' Compare Stat. 23 Edw. III. (of Labourers) c. 4: 'et si domini villarum vel maneriorum.'

lations concerning its use can be made in his court. All will
go smoothly, for the *communitas* or *communa* of the township
has a governing body, a representative assembly which meets
periodically. Very frequently this case is put before us in the
rolls of manorial courts :—the body of persons who attend
the court represent the township and indeed are the township,
and so we read how the *villata* gives evidence, gives judgments,
makes presentments, makes by-laws[1]. The lord's court in such
[p. 596] a case was not merely the court of a manor, it was the court
of a vill, of a township; in English speech it may often have
been called the town-moot or township-moot[2].

Such was the simple, and we have seen some reason for
calling it the typical, case. But in many parts of the country
it can not have been the common case. In the thirteenth
century the terms 'manor' and 'vill' were not equivalent.
The legal principles which shape the manor are not those
which shape the vill. For a moment we may even be tempted
to say that the vill is an unit of public, the manor an unit
of private law; the one an unit for police purposes and fiscal
purposes, the other a complex of proprietary rights and of
the mutual obligations which bind lord to tenants and tenants
to lord. And there is truth here. To all appearance the
boundaries of the vills are matters of public law, not to be
disturbed by conveyance or contract. New townships can not
be created or old townships abolished by the lord of the soil,
for in so doing he would disarrange the fiscal, administrative,
justiciary scheme of the hundred, the county, the kingdom,
and might aggravate the burdens incumbent on his neighbours[3]. The power of making new vills without licence from
above must cease as the centralization of government and
justice becomes more perfect, probably had ceased before the

*This coin-
cidence not
always
found.*

---

[1] Bodleian, Suffolk Court Rolls No. 3 :—'Villata dicit quod P. S. et E. C.
fodierunt communam de H. . . . . . et quia consuetudo villae non est talis,
consideratum est quod P. et E. distringantur.' Duchy of Lancaster Court
Rolls, Bundle 62, No. 750 :—'Consideratum est per totam villatam.' Select
Pleas in Manorial Courts, i. 11 : 'Villata presentat.'

[2] As a matter of fact the title of the court on its roll will seldom use any of
these terms. The court is simply the court of Mickleton or of Littleton.

[3] Bracton, f. 211, speaks of the formation of new vills. Seemingly if in the
vill of *A* a new group of houses is formed, this may come to be known as the
vill of *B* ; but these houses will be also in the vill of *A*. In pleading one may
describe them indifferently as in *A* or in *B*.

end of the twelfth century. But the next century was near
its end before landowners had lost the power of creating
new manors. The process of subinfeudation went on rapidly;
it was governed by rules of private law; it created new
manors. Partition among coheiresses was another source of
new manors; even in later centuries when legal doctrines had
collected round the word 'manor,' and the general theory was
that a manor must have existed from before the beginning
of legal memory, it was still admitted that a partition among
co-parceners might make two manors out of one[1]. But ser- [p.597]
viceable though this general idea may be, this contrast between
the units of public and of private law, we can not press it
home. At least according to our modern ideas, a court is an
institute of public not of private law; but it is rather the
manor than the township that has a court; the township as
such has none. Still, though it may be impossible for us to
explain the distinction by any general terms of modern jurisprudence, it existed[2].

Non-
manorial
vills.

Bracton expressly tells us that a manor may contain several
vills[3]. The bishop of Durham seems to have held sixty-seven
vills distributed into ten manors, so that on an average each
manor contained more than six vills[4]. Such cases, common in
the north, we may at the moment pass by as raising no great
difficulty; the lord may keep but one court for several vills,
still there is a court which can act as a governing body for
every vill. Far more perplexing is the case in which there was
no court with authority over the whole vill. Yet such a case
was common. If we may trust our county histories, there are

[1] *Sir Moyle Finch's Case*, 6 Co. Rep. 64. The Statute *Quia Emptores* had
the effect of preventing the creation (otherwise than by 'act of law') of new
manors. But, in laying down the rule that even the king could not create a
new manor, lawyers, being in this case unable to rely on the statute, invented
the wholesome, if unhistorical, principle that a manor can only come to
perfection by continuance of time.

[2] The differentiation of the two terms is marked by a case in Y. B. Edw. II.
f. 65. Counsel says that in ancient times a man might levy a fine of a
vill. This remark, which is true (for see *e.g.* Fines, ed. Hunter, i. 259), seems
to imply that a vill was no longer regarded as a subject for conveyance. In the
case before the court Henry Percy pleaded that the Abp. of Canterbury held of
him four vills. This was rejected, and he tried to amend his plea by substituting
for the four vills a manor to which three vills are appurtenant.

[3] Bracton, f. 434.

[4] Durham Halmote Rolls, Introd. p. viii.

often, at least in the south of England, two, three or four manors in the same vill. When we have made large allowances for the vanity of modern landowners, who have liked the sound of the word 'manor,' the case remains common, and, at least in Cambridgeshire, the Hundred Rolls show that it was common in the reign of Edward I., while Domesday Book shows that it had been common ever since the Conquest. When there are several manors in a vill, the names that they bear are often not true local names but family names, the names of the [p. 598] persons who held them in the thirteenth or some later century.

There is, however, a difficulty before us when we attempt to define the cases that are under discussion. We must in the first place mark off the instances in which there is a chief manor with several sub-manors, for in these instances the whole vill may be subject mediately or immediately to one and the same court, the court of the chief manor. That court will be attended by the lords of the sub-manors or their representatives and may be able to act as a governing assembly for a whole vill or for a group of vills[1]. But, though it is hard to fix the limit, we come upon cases which we can no longer describe as presenting the phenomenon of manor and sub-manor. The difficulty is occasioned by the vagueness of the term 'manor' and the fact that in a certain sense every vill in England must have a lord who is lord of the whole vill; at all events the king will be lord of the vill; all the titles of all the landholders may meet at some point short of the king; the whole vill may belong to the honour of Gloucester; but at any rate they will meet in the king. Now when in a single vill we find three or four lords each with land in desmesne, freehold tenants and villeins, and each lord holds immediately of the king, or traces his title from the king through a different series of mesne lords, and when we find that the king himself has no demesne land and no villein tenants in or near the vill, we feel that any talk of chief manor and sub-manors will be out of place :—the king has no manor there, and no one has a manor which contains the whole vill. The case is much the same if the titles of the various lords meet in the Earl of Gloucester; the whole vill forms part of the honour of Gloucester; the lords

Manor and sub-manor.

---

[1] Thus the tenants of the manor of Bampton Pogeys which is held by Robert Pogeys must once a year appear in the court of Robert's lord William of Valence; R. H. ii. 689.

may be bound to attend the court, or one of the courts of that honour; but if the Earl has no demesne land and no villein tenants in the neighbourhood, we shall not say that any of the Earl's manors comprises this vill. But we have to use vague phrases such as 'in the neighbourhood.' In Oxfordshire Robert Danvers has a considerable estate at Tetsworth, John Clifford at Milton, Henry de Bruyli at Waterstoke, Jordan Forester at Ascot, the abbot of Thame at Affington, Nicholas Segrave at Moreton, William Quatermains at Weston; each of them has [p. 599] many tenants; most of them have what according to any definition must be manors; their holdings lie in various vills, some lying more than five miles from Thame; yet each of them holds 'of the manor of Thame,' which belongs to the Bishop of Lincoln[1]. However, we have already said our say about the verbal question; the point now of importance is that to all appearance there were many cases in which there was no feudal court that could in any sense claim authority over the whole vill and many other cases in which the only feudal unity of the whole vill was due to the fact that every part of it was remotely held of some great lord and was, or might be, represented in the court of some wide-spread honour. England was not composed of manors. In many a vill we may find a few tenements which in the feudal or tenurial system stand far apart from the tenements with which they are intermixed. Their holders are small people who are the immediate tenants of the king, or of some magnate who has no other land in that vill or in its neighbourhood.

The affairs of the non-manorial vill.

How then were the internal affairs of the vill regulated? It may seem to us that here we ought to detect some organization of the vill that is not manorial, not feudal, some 'townshipmoot,' or some intermanorial organization. The township must have a reeve, the township must send four good men to court, the township must capture felons and keep them in custody, the township must make all manner of payments, periodic and occasional. How can these duties be apportioned if there be no court, assembly, governing body of the vill?

Permanent apportionment of the township's duties.

We have looked for such organization in our documents without finding it. To say that it must have existed is an expedient from which at present we shrink. Such evidence as we have points, not to any village assembly, but to permanent [p. 600]

[1] R. H. ii. 821.

arrangements made once for all, arrangements under which, at least as between the various manors, lords of manors and extra-manorial freeholders, the communal burdens of the township have become 'real' burdens. Once more we come upon the 'realism' of the time; one manor owes an aliquot share of all imposts exacted from the vill, another manor another share. The duty of sending representatives to the courts has been permanently apportioned. To represent Dodford in Bucking-hamshire one lord supplies three men, another the fourth man and the reeve[1]. The vill of Thurlby and Morton used to appear before the justices as an entire vill; but now the Templars 'subtract' one man whereby the king's business is impeded[2]. The fourth part of the vill of Willingham, namely the fee of Cantilupe, does not make its accustomed suit, to the king's damage of 2*d.* per annum[3]. The township of Abingdon Parva used to come to the eyre and the sheriff's turn by four men and the reeve, but now John of Girund withdraws one man and the Prioress of St Radegund another, so that but three come[4]. Such entries as these seem to show that the burden of providing the five representatives, like every similar burden, tended to become a permanent charge on particular acres of land.

And so with the duty of contributing to fines and amerce-ments. The aliquot share that each hundred must contribute towards a fine imposed on the county is known, and the aliquot share that each vill must pay to a fine imposed on the hundred is known. Thus it is known that if a fine is imposed on the hundred of Hoo in Kent, the abbot of Reading ought to pay one third of it, 'for he stands for a third in the said hundred as the third lord of the said hundred[5].' What is to happen if he procures a charter exempting his lands from these fines is not very clear; the men of the hundred hold one opinion, the officers of the exchequer another. So again it is not certain how far these apportionments are unalterable:—the men of Marshland declare that they ought to bear one third of the charges cast upon the hundred of Freebridge, while the other men of Freebridge assert that new assessments should be made from time to time[6]. And so it is within the vill. In an ancient survey of the lands of St Edmund we read that the vill

Allotment of financial burdens.

[p. 601]

---

[1] R. H. i. 33.
[2] R. H. i. 286.
[3] R. H. i. 364.
[4] R. H. i. 52.
[5] R. H. i. 220.
[6] Rot. Parl. i. 428.

of Risby is divided into four parts; the hall of the convent with its men is one fourth, the land of Ralph Breton another, the land of Norman another, the land of William and of the sokemen another[1]. Thus when we are told that a township contributes this or that amount to some ancient impost, towards the danegeld, the sheriff's aid, the hundred-scot or the like, we must not at once assume that any organization of the township was requisite for the assessment of this due. These taxes seem to be radicated in the soil. In the Lincolnshire Hundred Rolls we often read how '*A. B.* has subtracted service due to the king, to wit, the sheriff's aid from one carucate, or from six bovates, or from a half-bovate of land, to the king's damage 20*d.*, or to the king's damage 1¼*d.*[2]' In the case of some of these dues the men of the township may have been jointly and severally liable for the whole amount which is said to be paid by or due from it; still, as between the various parts of the vill, there was a permanent apportionment. We often hear complaints that the financial affairs of the township have been disordered by claims of immunity from taxation, and they show that, if one lord shuffles off his burden, he increases, at least for a time, the burden of his neighbours. Hugh de Gornay gave one carucate out of his manor of Houghton to the prior of Dunstable; the tenants of this carucate used to contribute to the amercements of the township of Houghton; but now they claim franchise under the king's charter; the township has been amerced for an escape to the amount of 100*s.*; the sum was to be collected rateably according to the extents of lands (*per porciones et extentas terrarum*); the prior's share was 20*s.*; he will not pay; but the vill has to pay instead[3]. But, though a gross sum is charged on the vill and the men of the vill may be jointly and severally liable for the whole sum, still within [p. 602] the vill the shares of the several tenements have been fixed once and for all.

The church rate.

Such was, we suspect, or in the past had been, the case with the church-rate or its precursor. We here tread on

---

[1] Gage, History of Suffolk, p. xii. ff.   [2] R. H. i. 255–6.

[3] R. H. i. 8. Entries which seem to imply that if a lord withdraws his land or his men from the scot and lot of the vill, the rest of the vill suffers, are common enough; thus *e.g.* R. H. i. 18, the whole of Eton from Baldwin's bridge to Windsor bridge used to be at scot and lot with Windsor, but now it is 'subtracted' by the King of Almain.

ground every inch of which has been undermined by bitter
controversy; we will traverse it rapidly[1]. Whether or no the
church-rate has a remote origin, whether it is connected with
ancient church-scots and light-scots, whether, on the other
hand, the clergy have shuffled off a burden which once fell on
them, we do not inquire. We think it however quite plain
that in the thirteenth century the general custom of the
church of England, swerving in this from the *ius commune* of
the catholic church, cast the burden of repairing the nave of
the parish church and providing the main part of the ecclesiastical apparatus, not upon the parson, but upon the parishioners,
and that the lay power left the spiritual tribunals free to
enforce this custom by spiritual censures. But we are by no
means satisfied that this custom demanded any permanent
organization of the parishioners, any 'vestry' that would meet
and grant a rate. So far as we can see, the burden is a 'real
burden,' incumbent on land. The ecclesiastical power can, we
take it, deal directly with each individual landowner, can
excommunicate him and procure his imprisonment if he will
not contribute his proper share to whatever expenditure has
become necessary for the due repair of the fabric, and the
question of necessity is decided by the ecclesiastical court.
The duty of repairing the parish church is analogous to the
duty of repairing the county bridges; it is planted in the soil
and to the soil it has ceded; it is apportioned according to
hidage or acreage. No doubt, the occasional nature of the
charge almost compels the rector or the archdeacon to deal
with the parishioners as a body, to call them together and
endeavour to persuade them that a wall is crumbling or that a
[p. 603] new missal is wanted. The parishioners will make terms with
him; they may vote him a rate to be assessed in this way or
in that; and very likely, as they will have to pay, they will
hire the workmen and buy the materials. The splendour and
costliness of the churches and their furniture increase very
rapidly; the parson's demands grow heavier and more frequent.
What goes on in the kingdom at large is going on in each
parish. Money-voting vestries became as indispensable to the
rector as money-voting parliaments are to the king. Movable

---

[1] Among the best of the many pamphlets on this subject are, W. H. Hale,
The Antiquity of the Church Rate System (1837); W. Goode, A Brief History
of Church Rates (1838); Robert Swan, The Principle of Church Rates (1837).

wealth must be brought within the sphere of taxation.   To our minds it would be as rash to argue from the 'vestries' or parishioners' meetings of the fourteenth and fifteenth centuries to similar assemblies of an earlier time, as it would be to argue that the commons of the realm were represented in the councils of Henry II. because they were represented in the parliaments of Edward I.   And so with the church-wardens.   We are not persuaded that as a general rule there were church-wardens in the thirteenth century.   They and their legal powers are, to our thinking, the outcome of two movements, one in the world of fact, the other in the world of legal thought.   If the parishioners are compelled to provide precious books, robes, vessels, they will naturally desire to have their say about the custody of these articles; parsons have been known to sell the church plate.   Secondly, as we have seen, in the later middle ages a dead saint or a personified *ecclesia* would no longer serve as a *persona* capable of proprietary and possessory rights.   The lawyers are beginning to hold that the rector is in some sort the owner or tenant of the church-yard and the glebe; they have to find an owner, at all events a possessor, for what in the past had been the chattels owned and possessed by a saint or a personified *ecclesia*; the church-wardens present themselves as claimants for property and possession[1].

[1] The first clear tidings that we get as to the incidence of the duty that is cast upon the parishioners tell us that they contribute 'secundum portionem terrae quam possident in eadem parochia'; Synod of Exeter (1287), Wilkins, Concilia, ii. 138.   John de Athona, Const. Othoboni, can. *improbam*, gloss. ad v. *peragendam*, doubts whether the burden is 'real' or 'personal,' decides in favour of reality, but on either side alleges nothing beyond ineptitudes out of Cole and Digest.   In 1275 the township of Graveley contracts with a mason for the repair of a wall of the church; he is to have 3*s*. 2*d*. for the work and a garb of wheat from every house; 'the attorney of the township' sued him in the fair of St Ives; Select Pleas in Manorial Courts, p. 150.   In 1370 we see parishioners assembled, making a regular rate and distraining for it; but it seems exceedingly doubtful whether their resolution binds one who has not assented to it; Y. B. 44 Edw. III. f. 18 (Trin. pl. 13).   This case does not look as if a 'vestry' had an old and well-established power of granting, assessing and enforcing a rate.   As to the church-wardens, they become prominent enough in the Year Books of the fifteenth century; but even then some elementary principles seem to be in dispute; see *e.g.* Y. B. 11 Hen. IV. f. 12 (Mich. pl. 23); 8 Hen. V. f. 4 (Hil. pl. 15); 37 Hen. VI. f. 30 (Trin. pl. 11).   The Synod of Exeter in 1287 (see above) had said, 'Ornamenta ecclesiae securae custodiae committantur, *non tamen sub custodia laicorum*, nisi id necessitas maior expostulaverit.'   The Church-wardens' Accounts edited by Bishop Hobhouse in 1890 for the Somerset Record Society point to the conclusion that in the

[p. 604]   A curious glimpse into medieval habits and thoughts is given us by the history of those royal taxes upon movable goods which are becoming common at the end of our period. Upon the face of the documents which prescribe how the tax is to be levied we see little enough of 'realism.' Every man in England is to pay a fifteenth of his movables and therefore every man of Littleton must do so. In order to reveal the amount of his wealth, some of his neighbours must be examined, and for the purpose of the requisite assessment ̇the vill will be taken as its unit. Four or six men must come from each vill to meet the chief taxers whom the king has appointed. It is possible that in some of the early instances these representatives were chosen by their fellow villagers—even this would not entitle us to imagine any standing assembly of the township—but so soon as the procedure becomes perfectly clear, the villar representatives are not elected by their neighbours[1]. The king appoints 'chief taxers' for the county; they are to

[p. 605] cause to come before them so many men from each vill that they, the chief taxers, may be able to choose out four or six, who are thereupon to appraise the goods of every man of their vill[2]. Of any sum of money cast upon the vill as a whole we read no word; each individual man of the kingdom is to pay a fifteenth of his movables. However, in Edward III.'s reign the effect of repeated taxations is that certain quotas have already struck root in the soil of the vills. Frequently a township complains that it is assessed too highly, for it is not so

Apportionment of taxes on movables.

fourteenth and fifteenth centuries the making and enforcement of a compulsory church-rate was a rare event; indeed the learned editor (p. 231) says that he knows of but one case before the reign of Elizabeth. The church-wardens seem to have got the money that they needed by means of voluntary gifts and legacies and of 'church-ales' which opened the purses of the parishioners.

[1] The very fact that the mode of assessment was often changed points to the conclusion that there was no permanent organization apt for the purpose. In 1188 the individual taxpayer assesses himself but is liable to be checked by the lord's steward and the parish priest; if they dispute the correctness of his estimate, four or six of his fellow parishioners are sworn to assess him. In 1198 the vill is represented by the lord of the vill or his bailiff, the reeve and four men. In 1207 the taxpayers declare their own liability. So in 1225 the taxpayer swears as to his own goods and those of two of his next neighbours, differences being referred to a jury of twelve. In 1232 four men are to be chosen (*eligantur*) in each vill, and they with the reeve are to make the assessment. In 1237 four men are to be chosen (*eligi*) in each vill to make the assessment. See the writs in Stubbs, Select Charters.

[2] Rot. Parl. i. 239, 240, 269, 442, 445, 450, 457; ii. 447.

rich as once it was.   Arundel has suffered by fire, Frismark
by water; in Bradway there used to live a rich man who paid
two-thirds of the taxes, but now he is dead; men are leaving
Derby to live at Nottingham because the burden of tenths
and fifteenths lies heavy on the former town; the men of
Newport complain that the pressure of the fifteenth upon them
is increased because the Prior of Newport has acquired lands in
their vill and is free from taxation[1].   Now all this means that
a given vill is rated at a certain sum, and that, whenever a
fifteenth or a tenth of movables is payable, the chief taxers
insist that a fifteenth or a tenth of that sum must come from
that vill.   There is in this case nothing that we can with
accuracy call communal or common liability.   The sub-taxers
have to apportion this fixed sum among the men of their vill,
and the individual man will be liable only for the amount
which they cast upon him.   Still there is a localized allotment
of the tax among the vills.   The case is the more instructive
because the growth of this system seems but half recognized.
If a township is impoverished by flood or fire or the death of
a wealthy member, it demands a new taxation and seems to
regard this as matter of right.   This is a remarkable example
of the 'realism' of medieval law.   Even a tax on movables
can not live without roots; it must attach itself to the land.
We see this happening in the full light of the fourteenth century to the detriment of the royal exchequer, which is forced
to regard the wealth of England as a fixed quantity.   We may
be fairly sure that in earlier days this realism was yet stronger,
and where it prevailed no permanent communal machinery
was required for the apportionment of public burdens.

Actions
against the
hundred.
The student of the middle ages will at first sight see [p. 603]
communalism everywhere.   It seems to be an all pervading
principle.   Communities rather than individual men appear
as the chief units in the governmental system.   A little experience will make him distrust this communalism; he will
begin to regard it as the thin cloak of a rough and rude individualism.   He reads of an action for damages given against
a hundred which has neglected its police duties[2].   At first he
may think that the hundred as an *universitas* has property
out of which the damages can be paid.   He will soon be

---

[1] Rot. Parl. ii. 184–9, 213.

[2] Statute of Winchester, 13 Edw. I.

persuaded that this is not so. He next imagines the hundred-moot levying a rate for the payment of a sum that has been adjudged to be due from the hundred. But, turning to his books, he finds that there is nothing in the case that ought to be called communal liability; there is merely a joint and several liability. The person who has been injured picks out two or three wealthy inhabitants of the district, sues them for the whole sum and recovers it from them. But at all events (so he may think) these men will be able to claim a contribution from their fellow inhabitants. No, the burden lies where it originally falls. This is so until Elizabeth's day, when for the first time a more equitable and a more communal principle is introduced, and all the inhabitants are rated for the relief of those who have suffered for the sins of the hundred[1]. What we begin by calling the permanent charges on the community turn out to be 'real' burdens apportioned for good and all upon manors and virgates and acres of land, while, at least in some cases, as we have just seen, the occasional charges are distributed by chance.

But (to return to the township) the unity which public law demands from it is not the only unity that it displays. Having read, for example, in the Hundred Rolls, how in Cambridgeshire the vill contained two, three, four manors, having verified this in Domesday Book, having seen for instance how ever since the Conquest there have been five tenancies in chief in Trumpington, six in Grantchester, we turn to maps which [p. 607] show that very often these manors were not continuous tracts of land. Each village has its great open fields; the fields take their names from the villages, not from the manors; the lands of the various manors lie intermixed in the fields. Now this we can not treat as a mere geographical fact. Cultivation of the common fields implies a system of agriculture which must in some degree be communal. To this we must add that in the thirteenth century rights of pasture are far more commonly attributed to the men or the community of a vill

Economic affairs of the non-manorial vill.

---

[1] Stat. 27 Eliz. c. 13. sec. 4: 'And although the whole hundred where such robberies and felonies are committed . . . are by the said statutes . . . charged with the answering to the party robbed his damages; yet nevertheless the recovery and execution . . . is had against one or a very few persons of the said inhabitants, and he and they . . . have not heretofore by law had any mean or way to have any contribution of or from the residue of the said hundred.'

than to the tenants of a manor. In some cases it must have
been difficult enough to say to whom belonged the soil of the
waste land over which these rights were exercised. If a manor
coincides with the vill, there is no difficulty; the lord of the
manor owns the waste land; and again if there is a chief manor
coincident with the vill, then the lord of the chief manor owns
the waste, or such parts of it as have not been allotted in
severalty to the various sub-manors. But, as we have seen,
these cases do not exhaust all possibilities or all realities.
There might be four or five manors in the vill between which
there was no subordination : each lord might trace his title up
to the king along a different feudal thread. We may take as
an instance the vill of Gamlingay in Cambridgeshire, not because it is abnormally elaborate, but because it attracted
Nasse's attention[1]. 'The whole township (*villata* not *villa*) of
Gamlingay has twelve score acres of common pasture and
heath.' According to the jurors the whole township came to
King Stephen by way of escheat, and out of it he enfeoffed
three men, namely the predecessor of John Avenel, the predecessor of William of Leicester, and the predecessor of Hugh
of Babington, besides which he gave a certain tenement to
his steward Walkelin which has now come to the abbot of
Sawtrey. John Avenel has a well-marked manor with demesne,
customary tenants and many freeholders, who have other freeholders under them. The same is true of Hugh of Babington.
William of Leicester sold his part to Walter of Merton, and
it has gone to endow his house of scholars at Oxford; they
have demesne land and many freehold tenants. All these
tenements are accounted to belong to the honour of Boulogne;
but there is yet another tenement with a hide of land which
Richard of Edensore holds of the honour of Gloucester[1]. Who [p. 603]
then owned those twelve score acres of pasture and heath
over which 'the whole township of Gamlingay' had rights
of common ? Perhaps this question has never yet been considered by the lords or tenants of Gamlingay. So long as
certain land is regarded as doomed for ever to be pasture land,
and so long as every one knows how many beasts he may
turn out on it, the question as to the ownership of the soil
does not arise. We must not be quick to say that in the past

---

[1] Agricultural Community (transl. Ouvry), p. 60.
[2] R. H. ii. 529–534.

the township of Gamlingay has owned this soil; far truer may
it be to say that the idea of ownership had never been applied
to it. But we are now dealing with the thirteenth century,
and our present point must be that in Gamlingay we see
no court, no assembly, capable of dealing with this waste. We
do not see it in our documents. Shall we say that none the
less it must be there?

Before we give an affirmative answer we ought to observe *Intercom-moning vills.*
that there were many cases in which two, three, or more vills
intercommoned. Of such cases we read much in the thirteenth
century, but they grow ever rarer as time goes on[1]. Sometimes the boundaries of vills were uncertain; between lay a
waste over which the cattle roamed indiscriminately and no
one could fix the spot where the territory of one vill left off
and that of another began[2]. Now, when we see this, we do
not feel compelled to suppose that there was some permanent
'intervillar' organization, some assembly in which the several
townships met each other to regulate the affairs of the common.
So when there are several manors in one vill; the rights of
the various lords in 'the common of the vill' seem regarded
as having been determined once for all by the terms of their
feoffments, and, if there is to be any new regulation of them,
this is accomplished, not by the action of any court or assembly,
[p. 609] but by a treaty. Each lord can represent himself and his
villeins; his freeholders give their consent. Such treaties were
not unknown. The Abbot of Malmesbury wished to enclose
part of a great moor called Corsgrave. Twelve deeds were
necessary for this purpose. By one the lord of Foxley 'on
behalf of himself and all his men of servile condition' released
his right of common; by the others various freehold tenants
of Foxley released their rights[3]. As to the customary course
of agriculture, that needs no regulation; it maintains itself,

---

[1] Note Book, pl. 174, 330, 628, 839, 971, 1721; Year Book, Edw. II. f. 170,
183, 314, 327, 330. In Somersham the Bp of Ely had a great wood of 300 acres
in which the men of the townships of Warboys, Woodhurst, Waldhurst, St Ives,
Needingworth and Holywell, all of which belonged to the abbot of Ramsey, had
common together with the men of the bishop's large soke of Somersham;
R. H. ii. 605; Cart. Rams. i. 283. See also Domesday Book and Beyond, 355.

[2] Note Book, pl. 174. The jurors can not tell the limits of Billinghay and
North Kyme in Lincolnshire, for there are marshes in which the men of these
two vills intercommon.

[3] Reg. Malmesb. ii. 153–165. For another instance see Ibid. ii. 185.

as it will maintain itself in the eighteenth century when the manorial courts are perishing. As yet men do not wish to break through it. What could one do with one's scattered strips of land if one set the custom at naught? They must lie profitless[1].

Return to the manorial vill.

But that the township had and needed little permanent organization we shall better understand if we return to the case in which a vill and a manor are coincident. Here at first sight we may seem to see an effective organization; the vill is no mere administrative district; the township is a 'village community.' Certainly this is so; the township is a *communa*, a *communitas*, and this village community has a moot, a court and assembly of its own; the *communitas villae* is the *communitas halimoti*. Still under the influence of modern theories about 'archaic' facts we might exaggerate the amount of communalism or even of self-government which exists in the township.

Rights of common.

This will become apparent if we examine the rights that are known as rights of common. Here if anywhere we ought to see the communalism of the township at its strongest. The houses and arable acres, it may be said, are by this time owned in severalty, though a man's ownership of his arable is still subject to the rights of the township which are expressed in the programme of agriculture, the two-course system, or the three-course system; but the waste land with its pastures and woods and waters belongs to the township as a whole. True, it may be added, a lord has now assumed to himself the rights or many of the rights of the village corporation; legal theory supposes that the waste belongs to him; but then the members of the township, free and unfree, still enjoy this waste in [p. 610] common and regulate its enjoyment in their moot. Remove the lord, who is an aftergrowth, the township appears as a landowning community.

Rights of common and communal rights.

But does our evidence point this way? Let us take the case of the freeholders, which should be comparatively undisturbed by the effects of seignorial dominion. Are their rights 'of common' in any sense communal rights? Of course there is just this element of community about them:—they are

---

[1] In general a man could not get to a strip in the middle of an open field without crossing the strips of his neighbours. Only as a rare exception was the strip bounded by a cart-track.

rights to be enjoyed in common. A right of common is a right to enjoy something along with someone else, to turn out one's beasts on a pasture where the beasts of the lord and of one's fellow-tenants feed, to take sticks from a wood, turf from a moor, fish from a pond in which others are entitled to do similar acts. But, for all this, the right may be an individual's several right, a right that he has acquired by a several title, a right that he can enforce against his fellow-commoners, a right that he without aid from his fellow-commoners can enforce against strangers, a right over which his fellow-commoners have little or no control.

Such really are the freeholder's rights. At a later time our law definitely laid down the rule that the freehold tenant of a manor is entitled to 'common appendant,' which is defined as 'the right which every freehold tenant of a manor possesses, to depasture his commonable cattle, levant and couchant on his freehold tenement anciently arable, in the wastes of the manor[1].' To entitle himself to this right, a man merely has to show that he is a freehold tenant of the manor; he has not to show that this right has been granted by the lord to him or to his predecessors, nor has he to show that he has gained it by long-continued use. With common appendant is contrasted 'common appurtenant.' If a man claims some right which exceeds or swerves from the definition of common appendant, then he must make a title to it by grant or prescription. Such is the case, for example, if he would turn onto the waste beasts that are not commonable, donkeys, goats, swine or geese, if he would turn onto the waste more oxen or horses than are 'levant and couchant' on his tenement, or if he would claim common in respect of land that is not 'ancient arable.' Now, it has, so we think, been sufficiently shown that the terms in which this distinction is expressed are pretty modern; an accurate discrimination between 'appendancy' and 'appurtenancy' belongs rather to Littleton's day than to Bracton's[2]. Also it must be confessed that the substance of the distinction hardly appears in Bracton's text. His doctrine is that these rights of common are *iura in re aliena* and are to be gained either by grant or by adverse user, though he seems to admit a class of cases, not very easily

The freeholder's rights.

[p. 611]

---

[1] Williams, Rights of Common, p. 31.

[2] Scrutton, Commons and Common Fields, ch. 2.

definable, in which it is unnecessary for a claimant to prove any such title[1]. On the whole, however, a comparison of charters of feoffment with manorial surveys will bring us to the conclusion that in substance the distinction between appendancy and appurtenancy, between rights of common which require specific description and rights of common which arise whenever a tenement is given, unless they be excluded by negative words, is very old[2].

The freeholder and the community.

But, be this as it may, the freeholder's right of common is his several right, as much his several right as is his tenancy of his house. His 'seisin' of this right is fully protected by the king's court, protected by a similar action to that which guards his seisin of his house ; the assize of novel disseisin is supplemented by an assize of common. It seems fairly clear that before the Statute of Merton (1236) any single freeholder who had a right of common could prevent his lord from subtracting from that right any part of the land over which it had been exercisable[3]. That statute gave the lord a right to [p. 612]

[1] Bracton, f. 230, 230 b; Note Book, pl. 561. Bracton says that if in the same vill there are two neighbours who hold of the same barony and the same fee, then there is common between them, or rather not common, but a right which he prefers to call *vicinitas, vicinage.* Strictly construed this will mean that if in the same vill there are two freehold tenements held of the same manor there will be this 'vicinage-right' between them, for if the two tenements are of the same manor then they must be of the same barony and the same [great] fee, unless indeed there is no barony or honour in the case at all. Also strictly construed it will mean that a freehold tenant of a manor will always have common or 'vicinage-right' over any waste of his lord that lies in the same vill, and that the lord will have a similar right over his tenant's waste, for lord and tenant will be neighbours holding of the same barony or honour, though they stand on different degrees of the feudal scale. Thus we should get the rule that in any usual case the freeholder has a right to turn out beasts on his lord's waste without proving grant or prescription. It may be doubted, however, whether Bracton meant so much as this. The case that he had in view seems to have been that of two peers of the same tenure each of whom has a manor in one and the same vill. But his doctrine is not very plain.

[2] Vinogradoff, Villainage, 265–272.

[3] It is true that the often-discussed case Fitz. Abr. *Comen,* 26 (now printed in Bracton's Note Book, pl. 1975), may look the other way; but the language of the Statute, of Bracton's text, of the note in Note Book, pl. 1881, and the following extract from a plea roll of 1221, are in favour of what is here said. 'De illis qui habent magnas terras et non possunt essartare de terra sua vel pastura pro illis qui habent unam virgatam terrae cum sufficienter habere poterunt communam.' This is found on a roll which was formerly numbered as Coram Rege Roll, Hen. III. No. 14, m. 31. It seems to be a note made by justices in eyre of a matter that requires reform.

'approve,' that is, to make his profit of[1], and hence to enclose, to subtract, the waste land, provided that he left sufficient pasture for the commoners. How did matters stand before the statute? The individual freeholder addresses his lord and his fellows :—'True it is that the waste is superabundant; true that I am only entitled to turn out four oxen on it; true that if half of it were enclosed I should be none the worse off; true that all of you wish the enclosure made; true that I am selfish:—nevertheless I defy you to enclose one square yard; I defy you severally; I defy you jointly; you may meet in your court; you may pass what resolutions you please; I shall contemn them; for I have a right to put my beasts on this land and on every part of it; the law gives me this right and the king protects it.' This is not communalism; it is individualism *in excelsis*.

Over the freeholder the manorial court has little power; for him it is a court of law (though very generally he can evade its action and go straight to the king's court), but it is hardly a governmental assembly. He is very free of custom, he is very free of by-laws. The following brief record tells us much :—In 1223 Richard of Beseville and Joan his wife brought an assize of novel disseisin against Peter of Goldington and [p.613] thirty-six others for land in Ravensthorpe. 'And all of them come and confess that the tenement is the free tenement of Richard and Joan, but they [Richard and Joan] were not able to cultivate that tenement that year, for in that year the field lay fallow, and because contrary to the custom of the vill the plaintiffs cultivated that tenement, these defendants pastured the corn when it had sprouted.' Richard and Joan are not at pains to deny the custom; they abide the judgment of the court. 'And therefore it is considered that the said Richard and Joan remain in their seisin and that Peter and the others be in mercy[2].' We would willingly know more of this case; but on the face of it we seem to read that a freeholder can not be compelled by mere custom to allow his neighbours to pasture their beasts on his land, and that, to say the least, 'there cannot be a custom for inhabitants as such to have a profit *a prendre* in the soil of another[3].' To justify his act each of the defendants should have prescribed for a right of

Freedom of the freeholder.

---

[1] Oxford English Dictionary. [2] Note Book, pl. 1662.
[3] *Gateward's Case*, 6 Co. Rep. 59 b.

pasture, and prepared himself to prove that he and his predecessors had enjoyed such right time out of mind. But to require this is to deny the title of the community, to make each member of it plead and prove his own title; what is more, it is to require of him a difficult task. And so with the force of by-laws; what we read will make us think that against the freeholder they are weak. In the name of a custom or by-law the 'community' of a Nottinghamshire township turn their beasts onto the land where the parson has grown a crop; they are told that this is manifestly wrongful and not to be supported by any by-law; they must pay damages[1]. Some small power of regulating the rights of common belonging to the freeholders we may allow to the manorial court and its by-laws, but to all seeming it was small[2].

Commun-
alism
among the
villeins.

But the cases of freeholders holding land within a manor if they are important, and by no means uncommon, are (it may [p. 614] be said) not sufficiently numerous to disturb the reign of communalism. The freeholder, though he is in the township, is hardly of the township; he does not share all the communal burdens; he is not 'at scot and lot' with the township[3]. The 'community of the vill' is generally a body of men whom the lawyers call serfs, who have been reduced to something that is very like serfage by the action of their lords, and these men, who must be treated as the normal shareholders in the village, form a community, a commune, something that might not unfairly be called a corporation.

The villein
commu-
nity.

Certainly there is truth in this. Between the various members of the village community which is also a villein community there is a strong bond of economic interdependance. Not only do they cooperate when they are tilling the lord's demesne, but in all probability there is cooperation in the

---

[1] We gave an account of this case in our first edition, vol. i. p. 623.

[2] See Fitz. Abridg. *Assise*, pl. 413, an extremely ill-printed case, seemingly of Edward I.'s time. Apparently however a freeholder was held bound by a by-law to which he had not assented, directing that trenches in the fen in which he had a right of cutting turf should be filled up. See also Y. B. 44 Edw. III. f. 18, 19 (Trin. pl. 13), where it is asserted and denied that commoners would be bound by a by-law to the effect that no one should turn out his beasts before a certain day.

[3] This point is brought out by some of the manorial extents, *e.g.* those in Cart. Rams., where it is specially noted of some freeholder that he participates wholly or in part 'cum villata.'

culture of their own holdings. Very seldom will the peasant be able to plough his strips without the aid of his neighbours; he will not have oxen enough[1]. In some manors a tenant is bound by the express terms of his tenure as entered upon the court rolls to discharge, not only the duties which he will owe to the lord, but also the duties which he will owe to his neighbours[2]; and we may find a man forfeiting a tenement because he will neither dwell in it nor cultivate it nor 'do any neighbourliness to his neighbours[3]:' that is to say, he will take no share in the communal duties. In accordance with this idea we find that the lord treats the community of the vill as an entity that has duties towards him. It is constantly falling into his mercy for breach of duty; it is amerced for coming late to court, for committing waste, for damaging his crops, for not cleansing the [p. 615] pond, for not selling him poultry, for not having a common pinder, for not repairing the sheepfold, the mill, the smithy, when commanded to do so[4]. All the tenants of the vill owe one mark for an axletree delivered to them and lost by their default[5]. The lord sells the herbage of his land to the tenants of the vill, he leases the demesne land to them as a body. The community contracts with him and with others. The community of the vill of Monkton, except T. T. and W. T., is compelled to pay damages to W. S. for damage done in his corn[6]. On the other hand, Fair John has broken a covenant with the community of the vill of Wolviston by not paying the shepherd his salary, to the damage of the community, 6s. 8d.[7]. All manner of commands are given to the community, and the community itself makes all manner of by-laws (*byrlawes, bileges*)[8]. To mark off the sphere of the commands issued by the lord or his steward from that of the by-laws made by the

---

[1] Nasse, Agricultural Community (transl. Ouvry), pp. 42—45. But we can not find any evidence of oxen that belonged to the community. As to the 'common boat' of Newton, which Nasse mentions, doubtless the lord was the owner of it.

[2] Durham Halmotes, pp. 23, 29, 34 etc.:—'reddendo antiquam firmam et faciendo domino et vicinis quae incumbunt.' In this paragraph we shall cite these interesting rolls, though they belong to the fourteenth century.

[3] Ibid. pp. 56, 63:—'nec aliqua vicinitas inde fit vicinis'; 'nec invenire unum tenentem qui potest tenere vicinitatem.'

[4] Durham Halmotes, *passim.*   [5] Ibid. p. 83.   [6] Ibid. p. 20.   [7] Ibid. p. 22.

[8] See Skeat, Dict. s. v. *by-law*. There seems no doubt that the word *bylaw* means *townshiplaw*; it often occurs in the form *byrlawe*.

community would be hard : as hard as to mark off the sphere of
royal ordinances from that of parliamentary statutes[1]. The
lord is a constitutional king, and, when there is to be drastic
and permanent legislation, he acts with the counsel and consent
of his court; but still over the villeins and the villein tenements
he is every inch a king. If the common is to be stinted, the
consent of the court will be obtained; but a simple injunc-
tion will serve to tell all the tenants that they are not to keep
geese in the vill[2], not to buy beer save at the lord's brewhouse[3],
not to sell growing crops[4], that they must offer their fish and
poultry to the lord before they look for other purchasers[5], that
they must find beds for his officers[6], that they must not
associate with John Lollis, who has made too free with his
knife[7], that they must not sue in other courts[8], that they must
not throw about such words as *nativi* or *rustici*, though *nativi*
and *rustici* they assuredly are[9]. Indeed here lies the legal [p. 616]
possibility of all this communal organization of the township's
economy. When the freeholders are left out of sight, it appears
as a mass of villeins, or at any rate as a mass of men holding
their lands by villein tenure. Let one of them rebel against
the community, its customs or its by-laws, his body, it may be,
is safe against imprisonment or exile (exile from the vill is by
no means uncommon)[10], but his land is at the lord's mercy
and will be taken from him, the community sanctioning and
applauding the punishment[11].

The free-
holders
and the
village.

In dealing with freeholders one must be careful, otherwise
they will be off to the king's court, which shows little favour
to restrictive customs and by-laws, which will not open its doors
to the community as such, but will make each individual
asserter of communal rights answer why he has entered on

---

[1] See *e.g.* Durham Halmotes, where two formulas are constantly repeated,
'Iniunctum est omnibus tenentibus villae,' 'Ordinatum est ex communi
assensu.'

[2] Durham Halmotes, p. 45. [3] Ibid. p. 45. [4] Ibid. p. 90.
[5] Ibid. pp. 39, 49. [6] Ibid. p. 35. [7] Ibid. pp. 49, 50.
[8] Ibid. pp. 35, 39.

[9] Ibid. pp. 33, 40. Two men have just been proved to be *nativi* when a
command against the use of this word is issued.

[10] There are many cases on the Littleport rolls in which offenders are
'removed from the vill.'

[11] Durham Halmotes, p. 46: *G. F.* is ordered to manure his land and to
remove the crops that are growing on it without the lord's licence and to behave
like his neighbours on pain of losing the land.

another man's soil or impounded another man's cattle. Of
course there can be no talk of enforcing against freeholders the
mere commands of the lord, even though they be backed by
the common assent of the township, at all events when such
commands have nothing to do with the tenement. The freeholder may sell fish and poultry to whom he pleases; he may
associate with John Lollis if he pleases, provided that John be
a lawful man; it will be difficult to make him take his corn to
the common mill[1], impossible to make him lend the steward
his bed. But further, as we have already seen, it will be by no
means easy to diminish his right of pasture or to prevent him
from cultivating his land when and how he chooses if he can do
this without trespass. When injunctions are laid upon the vill,
when by-laws are made for the vill, the freeholders must be
treated as exceptions. It is ordained that no tenant of the vill
of Ferry Hill shall put horses in the oxen's pasture, save the
four *liberi*, each of whom may put there the horse on which he
rides[2]. All the tenants of the same vill, except the four *liberi*,
are amerced because they refused to have a common reaper
[p. 617] appointed for them by the lord's officer[3]. The mill fell into
disrepair. In 1366 order was given to distrain the free tenants
to repair it, while all the other tenants were ordered to repair
it by the next court day. In 1368 the freeholders, despite all
orders for distraining them, had not done their share of the
work; the customary tenants had done theirs[4]. But of the
exceptional position of the freeholders we have said enough;
over the customary tenants, especially if they are unfree men,
the village court has great power, for it is the lord's court. The
lord can treat them as a community because he can treat them
as villeins.

Still it would be easy for us to overestimate the communalism that there is in the vill, even when there are no
freeholders to be considered. In the first place, we must notice
that mere collective liability for transgressions implies little
communalism, little permanent organization, while it certainly
does not imply, though it does not exclude, the idea of corporate
unity. If the vill can be fined and amerced for neglect of
duties owed to the state or to the lord, so also the county and

Communalism and collective liability.

---

[1] Note Book, pl. 161: 'Nota quod liber homo non tenetur sequi molendinum
domini sui nisi gratis velit.'

[2] Durham Halmotes, p. 69.   [3] Ibid. p. 109.   [4] Ibid. pp. 51, 73, 75.

the hundred can be fined and amerced for false judgments, for murders, for robberies; but yet it has no common purse, no property. The county community has no property; the hundred community has no property. So likewise the township normally has no property. When a judgment for damages, fine or amercement is given against it, this 'it' at once becomes a mere mass of individuals who are jointly and severally liable for the whole amount, while, as between themselves, their proper shares are settled by the system of commensurable tenements; all virgaters pay equally, all cottagers equally.

The community as farmer.
Even when the manor is farmed by the villeins, as is sometimes the case, we may overstate the degree of communalism that there is in the arrangement. Sometimes the king lets one of his manors to the men of that manor[1]; sometimes other lords do the same. The lease in such a case seems generally to have been a lease at will; but there may have been some places with no pretensions to be called boroughs where the men of the vill farmed the vill in fee. Sometimes the lease, [p. 618] if such we must call it, seems to have comprised all the sources of revenue that the lord had in the manor, sometimes some of these were excepted out of it. Thus the Prior and Convent of Worcester have a manor at Hallow; 'the court' with the appurtenances, and two carucates of the demesne have been let to the villeins at a corn rent together with the meadows and casualties and heriots and the villeinage[2], though the convent still retains in its hand a barn, a moor, some meadow and some arable land. But we must not jump to the conclusion that the *villani* are carrying on the cultivation of the demesne land as 'a joint stock affair' by means of beasts and implements which belong to them in common or to a corporation of which they are the members. At Hallow the arable part of the demesne which has been handed over to them seems to be broken up into physically distinct shares, each of which is held by an individual *villanus* at a several rent. The upshot of the arrangement seems to be this:—the villagers, instead of being placed under a bailiff of the lord's choosing, are given the right to elect their own *firmarius*, and to him each pays the rent

---

[1] Madox, Firma Burgi, 54–56.

[2] Worcester Register, p. 47 a: 'Curia cum pertinenciis et duae carucatae terrae de dominico cum pratis et proventibus et heriatis et vilenagio traditae sunt villanis ad firmam.'

due from his ancient villein tenement and also the rent due
in respect of any part of the quondam demesne that he has
taken, and out of these rents, the profits of the court, and such
casualties as heriots, the elected farmer must pay 'the farm' of
the manor[1]. The lord obtains the joint and several guarantees
(if we may use so definite a term) of all his tenants for the
whole 'farm.' If the farmer can not pay the rent, the lord can
attack all or any of the tenants; if on the contrary the farmer
occasionally makes more than the 'farm,' very likely he keeps
the surplus to himself or possibly it is expended in festivity;
if a surplus becomes normal, then the rents of the individual
tenants will perhaps be reduced. But the lords, we may be
sure, took good care that these ventures should not be very
profitable.

But, to return to the usual case in which there is no farming, The manorial custom gives several rights not communal rights.
[p. 619] we see that the rights given by the manorial custom are, at
least for the more part, several rights given to individuals.
The tenant in villeinage holds his house and his virgate by a
title that is in no sense communal, and to this tenement are
annexed rights of pasture, customary rights of pasture; he
enjoys them, not because he is an inhabitant of the vill, but
because they are annexed as appurtenances to the tenement
that he holds. He transmits an inheritance to his heir as the
freeholder does, nor, so far as we can learn, does custom give
the court much power to regulate these rights. When a
statement of them is made and enrolled, it generally professes
to be, not a new ordinance, but an ancient custom, and the
function of the by-laws that are made is, at least in theory,
rather that of confirming and sanctioning old, than that of
introducing new rules, though new rules can be made from
time to time about minor matters.

Looking at the vill from the outside, contrasting it with Rights of the township disappear when examined.
other vills, men naturally use phrases which seem to attribute
rights to the community as a whole. The township of Sutton,
or the community of the vill of Norton, is said to pasture its or
their cattle (often enough the verb that follows *villata* is in the
plural number) over a particular moor. But just so a sheriff's
bailiff will be charged by jurors with taking the beasts of the
vill of Weston. The township as a community has no beasts;
the beasts that have been taken belonged in severalty to

---

[1] See the survey of Hallow; on p. 40 b the *firmarius* is mentioned.

certain individual men[1]. Even so with the rights of pasture; on analysis they are found to be the rights of certain individual men; they are exercised in common, but they are several rights.

Co-owner-
ship and
corporate
property.

Lastly, when, as may sometimes happen, the ownership of a tract of land seems to be attributed to a community, we have still to face that difficult question which has of late been exercising the minds of continental historians:—Have we before us a corporate unit or have we merely a group of co-owners[2]? England affords but few materials for an answer to this important question, for anything that even by a stretch of [p.620] language could be called a communal ownership of land, if it had ever existed, had become rare and anomalous before the stream of accurate documents begins to flow. But what we see will tend to make us believe that it was rather as a group of co-owning individuals than as a corporation that the members of the vill thought of themselves when they had a chance of applying either the one idea or the other.

An illus-
tration.

The manner in which the 'quasi-corporateness' of the township was dissolved at the touch of law may be illustrated by a story from Dunstable Priory. In 1293 the Prior brought an assize of novel disseisin against seventeen defendants concerning land at Toddington. Some of the defendants confessed themselves the villeins of John Peivere; others, who were freeholders, sought to justify what they had done. Thereupon the Prior pleaded that the lands in question, which seem to have consisted of many disconnected strips, had been in the seisin of the men of the township of Toddington, and that they by their unanimous will and assent enfeoffed his predecessor, Prior Simon, to hold to him and his successors for ever. The jurors endorsed this statement, adding that all the persons who had any right in the said land were congregated in one place at a court held at Toddington, and with one consent granted the land to Prior Simon and his successors, at a rent of six pence

---

[1] R. H. ii. 307: 'ballivi de Tychill nunquam cessaverunt occasionare villatam de Blida, gravando illam villatam per plures districtiones iniustas sibi factas.'

[2] What is the legal nature of the old German community (*Genossenschaft*)? Is it a group of co-owners? Is it an *universitas*? Is it *tertium quid*? This question raised by Beseler (Volksrecht und Juristenrecht, Leipzig, 1843, pp. 158 ff.) has of late found many answers. See Gierke, Deutsche Genossenschaftsrecht; Heusler, Institutionen, i. 253 ff.; Sohm, Die deutsche Genossenschaft, Leipzig, 1889.

a year payable to the said men of Toddington.   Prior Simon
(the jurors say) held the land and paid the rent; the present
Prior for several years held the land and paid the rent; the
defendants have dispossessed him[1].   The Prior recovered his
seisin.   Now this was a possessory action; the Prior had only
to prove (and he did prove) his seisin and disseisin; the sound-
ness of his title was not in question.   Still his title was a
feoffment by the men of the township made in the court of
Toddington.   But then we also learn that when this feoffment
was made the lord of Toddington, John Peivere, was an infant
in ward to the queen.   The men of Toddington who were
defendants in the assize relied on this; their case was that the
Prior obtained the land, not from them, but from the queen's
bailiff.   Then the Prior by expending a considerable sum
obtained from John Peivere a confirmation of the land 'into
[p. 621] which we had entry by the community of the men of Toddington,' and for the future the Prior 'by the attornment of the
men of Toddington' paid the rent of six pence, not to them,
but to their lord[2].   We see therefore the men of Toddington
making a feoffment, the Prior dealing with them as capable of
making a feoffment, of receiving rent, and then we see this title
melting away before the claims of the lord.   But further, we
see the defendants endeavouring to avoid a feoffment made by
the community in its court, and one of the reasons that they
urge is this:—When the feoffment was made, some of us were
under age.   Such a plea gives us an instructive glimpse into
their minds.   The men of Toddington suppose that they have
land; they ignore their lord.   Let us do the same; let us
suppose that John Peivere's rights have been gained by
modern usurpations.   What then, we may ask, is the men of
Toddington's theory of their own title?   That they form a
corporation?   That 'the community' in its court can alienate
its land?   No, but that they hold this land as co-owners, and
that unless every tenant is of full age and joins in the act there
can be no alienation[3].

[1] Ann. Dunstap. 378.

[2] Ibid. 392.

[3] See also Madox, Firma Burgi, 41.   Under Edward III. it was alleged that
the community of the vill of Tetsworth, in Oxfordshire, had given a house and
garden to the church of that vill; but the bishop of Lincoln proved that this
was untrue; he and his predecessors had always been seised of the premises.

However, except by way of rare exception, the men of the vill do not hold any property as joint tenants or tenants in common. Each of them has his house, his virgate or croft; each of them has or may have certain rights of pasture, of turbary, of fishing or the like in the lord's wastes or waters; but that is all. The consequence is that they rarely come before the courts as co-plaintiffs. This is not due to any speculative doctrine about the way in which corporations ought to sue. It is not due to the rule that an unincorporated group of persons can not sue under a general name. At present there is no such rule. As we shall see below when the boroughs come before us, the courts are ready to listen to complaints preferred in the name of classes of men who have some common interest to assert; the lawyers do not yet demand the appointment of an attorney under a common seal. 'The citizens' of *A*, 'the burgesses' of *B* can sue; their mayor or their bailiffs attend the court on their behalf; and even so 'the men' of *C*—which is a mere rural township, or which is [p. 622] a hundred—can sue and be sued, their bailiff or their reeve with four men will represent them. They can sue and be sued under a general name, if there is anything for them to sue and be sued about. But then this rarely happens. They hold no lands, they own no franchises, they, taken as a group, have no rights to assert or to defend. The great exception to this rule is that the practice of assessing taxes and imposing fines upon communities may give rights to a community. Thus we may read how certain named men of the hamlet of Bordesdon had to answer in the Exchequer to 'the men of the vill of Little Hormead' for not contributing to a fifteenth; it was a disputed question whether this hamlet should contribute towards the amount assessed on Little Hormead or to the amount assessed on Braughing[1]. Such disputes the exchequer must often have had to decide, and in so doing it considered that 'the men' of a vill were sufficiently represented by a few of their number. So also one township in the fens would sue its neighbour for a contribution towards the cost of maintaining and repairing the sewers, and would base its claim on the custom and use of the marsh[2]. But within the sphere of private law we seldom

---

[1] *Firma Burgi*, 110.

[2] Assize Roll, Lincoln, No. 481 (57 Hen. III.): '*A. B.* et *C. D.* pro se et tota communitate villatae de Helpingham optulerunt se versus *E. F.* et

see the men of the vill joining to bring an action under the general name which covers them. Some exceptional cases may be found upon the plea rolls. The line which divides the men of a vill from the burgesses of a borough is being drawn not by speculative theories but by practical needs. There is great need for actions by 'the burgesses,' for the burgesses have valuable franchises to assert, franchises which can hardly be regarded as the sum of the rights of individuals; but with the mere township it is otherwise. The community of the township is not incapable of suing, but it rarely sues, for it has nothing [p. 623] to sue about; it is not incapable of rights, but generally it is rightless. No lawyer's theory keeps it out of the courts. What is lacking is not a common seal but common property[1].

It is difficult to discuss these matters at length without making some disputable assumptions touching the origin of 'the English village community' and its history in centuries much earlier than the thirteenth. Some see in those centuries free communities that are becoming servile, while others see servile communities whose servility is being alleviated. We incline, for reasons that have been elsewhere given, to think that the former is the truer view[2]. But we do not regard the

Transition to the boroughs.

totam communitatem villae de Donyngton, et *G. H., J. K.* de Bykere et totam communitatem eiusdem villae de placito, quare cum mariscus de Helpingham exaquari vel assewari debeat et soleat per cursum cuiusdam aquae in mariscum in Donington et Bykere secundum consuetudinem et usum marisci quem cursum praedicti *A. B.* et alii et praedictae communitates reparare et sustinere debent et solebant etc.' The necessity of maintaining sewers, sluices, and water-gates sometimes gave rise to elaborate treaties between the freeholders of a large district. See, *e.g.* Selby Coucher, ii. 286.·

[1] Actions by or against 'the men' of places that are not boroughs will be found in Placit. Abbrev. pp. 2, 3, 24, 32, 95, 133, 140. The case on p. 95 is instructive:—' The men of Thanet' complain that the Abbot of St Augustine's has exacted undue services, and they put in their place thirty named men to sue for them; their claim fails and they are adjudged to be in mercy, ' save the other men of Thanet who took the abbot's part.' Thus, after all, the plaintiffs are not all the men of Thanet, nor do they represent all. Then on p. 140 there is an action of trespass by the Abbot of Faversham against ' the alderman and the whole community of that vill.' Judgment for damages is given against ' all the men of Faversham ' except four named persons. Here again, each individual ' man ' is acquitted or convicted on his own merits. See also Madox, Firma Burgi, 65 : the king and ' the king's men of Headington ' complain in the Exchequer that the Prior of St Frideswide has withheld from the said men a customary dinner. No doubt many other instances might be found; but, having regard to the number of vills in England and to the frequency of actions in which the boroughs take part, such instances seem very rare.

[2] Domesday Book and Beyond, pp. 221 ff.

old community as a landowning corporation. That peculiar kind and degree of union which permits or begets a distinction between what is owned by many men *ut singuli* and what is owned by them *ut universi* is not primitive, nor native in our villages. It is slowly developed in our boroughs.

§ 8. *The Borough.* [p. 625]

The city. Certain vills are more than vills; they are boroughs (*burgi*); certain boroughs are more than boroughs; they are cities (*civitates*). The latter of these two distinctions has little or no meaning in law. A habit, which seems to have its roots in the remote history of Gaul, will give the name *city* to none but a cathedral town[1]. This usage is in general well observed. In 1302 the sheriff of Cornwall, returning the names of the burgesses of Launceston and Bodmin who are to appear in parliament, says that there are no cities in his bailiwick; the sheriff of Essex and Hertfordshire says the like when he announces the result of elections at Colchester and Hertford[2]. However, the usage was not very rigid; Shrewsbury is called a city in a judicial record of Edward I.'s reign[3]; at an earlier date Cambridge was called a city[4]; and in Domesday Book the name *city* is given rather to county towns than to cathedral towns. But at any rate the *civitas* was also a *burgus*, the *cives* might be called *burgenses*, and the *communitas civium* or *communitas burgensium* was a *villata* and *communitas villae*[5].

The vill and the borough. Now, at least from the early years of the thirteenth century onwards, the distinction between the mere *villa* and the *burgus* was a familiar, if not a very precise, outline of public law. At recurring intervals the justices in eyre came into the county; each vill was to be represented by its reeve and four men, while each city or borough was to be represented by a jury of twelve. Thus when at a later day the sheriffs were bidden to cause every city and borough to send representatives to parliament, they knew what the command meant. If, however, we

---

[1] E. A. Freeman, Macmillan's Magazine, 1889, p. 20.
[2] Parl. Writs, i. 119, 120.
[3] Madox, Firma Burgi, p. 128.
[4] Placit. Abbrev. p. 98; Co. Lit. 109 b.
[5] Firma Burgi, chap. vi.

could bring one of these sheriffs to life and cross-question him over the definition of a borough, very possibly his answers would disappoint us; very possibly we should get little more from him than—'This place is a borough, for it has always been treated as such; that place is not a borough, for I can not [p. 626] remember its having ever sent twelve representatives to meet the justices in their eyres.' If we could induce our sheriff to go behind practice, and tell us what in his opinion it was that made a borough to be a borough, he would probably refer us, not to just one attribute, but to many attributes. In particular, if we talked to him of incorporation or artificial personality, unless he were an unusually learned sheriff, he would be puzzled. He would tell us that the boroughs had franchises (*libertates*), some more, some fewer, and he would in the end refuse to consecrate any particular *libertas* or any combination of *libertates* as at once the necessary and the sufficient essence of a borough.

We have not to write a history of the English boroughs[1]. That task, even if accomplished only in outline, would be long, so various from first to last have been the fortunes of our towns. We shall merely attempt to detect the more important of the legal elements which make a borough something other than a mere rural township and to raise some of those questions which the coming historian must answer. He will, so we think, consider the borough from two different points of view, and indeed, were this possible, he should occupy both at the same time; for the borough is both organ and organism. On the one hand, we have here a piece of England which is governed in a somewhat peculiar way. To use our modern terms, there is within it a 'local authority' of a somewhat unusual type and there is more 'local self-government' here than elsewhere. On the other hand, we have here a community which differs from the other communities of the land in that it is attaining the degree and kind of organization which we call corporate, so that, for example, it will be capable of appearing as an individual landowner among individual landowners, as a single contractor and as a single wrong-doer. Neither point of view should be neglected. In a still recent past various causes have induced Englishmen to think of the borough much rather

The borough and its community.

---

[1] See Gross, Bibliography of Municipal History (Harvard Historical Studies, 1897).

as a piece of the constitutional machinery of the English state than as an organism and a person that has life and property. Also it must be confessed that throughout the middle ages the central power was stronger in England than elsewhere and the boroughs served the state as its organs and its instruments. Still, if we ignore the peculiarly corporate character of the burgensic community, we fail to record one of the greatest moral and legal achievements of the middle ages, an achievement which made possible the countless and variegated corporations of modern days[1].

Preliminary sketch of early history.

In order that we may find a starting-point for what we have to say of the boroughs of the thirteenth century, we are compelled to premise a slight sketch of the boroughs of an older time. That it will be an imaginary sketch we fully admit; but some reasons have been given elsewhere for the belief that it is founded upon fact, and may be roughly true of those towns which set an example for others[2].

Borough and shire.

For at least a century and a half before the Norman Conquest, English law has known the borough as something different from the ordinary *tún* or vill. The typical borough has been (i) the *burh*, (ii) the *port*, and (iii) the moot-stow of a shire[3]. (i) It has been a fastness and place of refuge whose earth-works have, at least in some cases, been maintained by the men of the shire. It may even have been in some sort a garrison town: the great people of the shire may have been bound to keep in it houses or 'haws,' as they were called, and 'knights' of the old English kind[4]. (ii) A market has been held in it: that is to say, it has been one of the few places in which men might buy cattle and other goods without putting their necks in jeopardy; their bargains were attested by official witnesses and toll was taken from them. (iii) It has been the meeting-place,

---

[1] In Gierke's *Genossenschaftsrecht* the student will find an admirable model for the work that has yet to be done for England; it has induced us to recast this section of our book. Many sides of the subject have been excellently treated by Madox, Dr Stubbs, Dr Gross and Mrs Green; but just the legal side has received too little attention. The History of Boroughs by Merewether and Stephens seems to us, for all its industry, to be a long mistake.

[2] See Maitland, Domesday Book, p. 172; also Maitland, Township and Borough, Cambridge, 1898.

[3] Not necessarily of one of the counties of a later time.

[4] For these knights, see Gross, Gild Merchant, i. 183. For arguments against this theory see Tait, E. H. R. xii. 773.

the moot-stow of the shire, and perhaps because it was the county's town, it was in no hundred, but had a court of its own, a burh-moot or port-moot, which was co-ordinate with the hundred-moots. Moreover, a severe and exalted peace, the king's *burhgrið*, had reigned within it. This seems to be in origin the peace of the king's own palisaded homestead, and has been extended to those towns which are the military, commercial and political centres of national life[1].

But the borough has been a *tún*, and we may believe that in many cases its soil has been laid out in the old rural fashion : there have been wide open fields, meadows and pastures; there have been intermixed hides and yardlands. The borough community is a township, and, if in its moot it has the organization of a hundred, it none the less has for its territory several square miles of land on which corn is grown and beasts are depastured. The borough as vill.

The texture of this community is unusually heterogeneous. We suspect that there are within it the knights or other dependants of the shire-thegns. As the military element becomes less prominent, these thegns will let their houses to chapmen and craftsmen at money rents, but will endeavour to maintain as long as possible a jurisdictional control (sake and soke) over their tenants. Also there may be free and lordless house-owners and land-owners in the borough who increase this heterogeneity by commending themselves, their houses and their lands to the king or some other magnate : in particular, many will pay a little haw-gavel or land-gavel (house-rent or land-rent) to the king in return for his patronage. Thus it is likely that the borough, if it flourishes, will escape the fate that awaits many a common village : it will not as a whole become the king's or any one else's manor. On the other hand, strips of its arable fields may be worked into manors whose centres lie either within or without the town-ditch. At this point numerous variations are possible ; but, whatever happens to the arable, it is probable that the town community will retain some control over and use of the green pasture, and also that just in these vills the claims upon the pasture will begin to take a new shape. The 'men' of important people will be turning out their The borough's heterogeneity.

---

[1] It is not implied that all of these characteristics would be found in every borough. It is highly improbable that strict definition was possible in the tenth and impossible in the thirteenth century.

horses to graze and yet have no interest in the arable, and the opportunity for sale and purchase of corn and hay which the market offers may cause a rapid disintegration of the old self-sufficing hides and yardlands. Then in having a moot of its own, a moot established by national law, whose profits are received by king and earl, the borough has an organ capable of deeming dooms about this pasture, and, at least in some instances about the arable land also, and this power of 'right-speaking' can not be sharply distinguished from a power of regulation.

The borough and the king.

Thus to the eyes of the Conqueror's officers, whose heads are full of the formula of dependent tenure, the old borough presents itself as a knot that can not be untied. Unit it is; but they scruple to describe it as being *Terra Regis*, and clearly it is not any one else's land. It is not part of any one's fief, and yet it is not like one of the king's demesne manors, for (since commendation is hardening into tenure) there are in it pieces of many fiefs. The king is not its landlord, except in that wide and lordly, rather than landlordly, sense in which he is landlord of all England. On the other hand, the king, though some-times in conjunction with the earl, is the immediate lord of those institutions which give the borough its specific character: lord of its court and lord of its market, with a large fund of liberties to bestow upon its burgesses. As time goes on, the burgesses, who are coalescing in a new type of community, will be treated as an unit which has no lord but the king, and will pay tallages when the king's demesne manors are tallaged: but they will make their profit of their communal 'immediacy' by depriving all landlordship of its lordly character and reducing it to the level of a mere right to rent[1].

The borough court.

As an organ, the borough has its moot, which is held by the sheriff or some port-reeve who is his farmer. Perhaps all the free men or the house-holders are entitled and bound to sit as doomsmen. On the other hand, in some boroughs which have been Danish, there seems to be a group of hereditary law-men or doomsmen. Also we must reckon with the possibility that the military organization of the borough has caused the forma-tion of wards (*custodiae*), at the head of each of which stands an

---

[1] The king can convey away his lordship; but in England it is not common to find a borough of high rank that has been mediatized. Leicester is the great example.

alderman whose office, like every other office, is apt to pass to his son. But the little evidence that we have suggests that a close and definite college of doomsmen was exceptional, and we have small warrant for supposing the existence of any legally constituted 'patriciate.'

The burghal community being heterogeneous, voluntary societies are formed within it. Gilds spring up in the town. The festive and religious gild may be very old, may even be traced back to the days of heathenry[1]; it is likely to flourish in the soil of a borough. In particular, the 'knights' (of the old English type) who are in the borough form gilds, and the knights' gild may become an important factor in the life and even in the government of the town. The sphere of association and private enterprise can not at this time be marked off from the sphere of government and public power. The contractual or associative principle when it first manifests itself is unruly ; we see how the vassalic contract threatens for a while to make itself the one bond between men ; and even so a club of thegns or knights, or at a later day of merchants, may aspire (the phrase must be pardoned, for it seems apt) to 'boss' the town[2]. But at any rate gilds and gild-like structure have a great future before them in the boroughs.

The borough and the gilds.

It is probable that some of these traits of the old English borough were vanishing or ceasing to be distinctive even before the Norman Conquest. In the new age that then opened many changes tended to produce this effect. Castle-guard was substituted for the older *burh-bót*; markets were established in many places; the ordinary village had a court, a manorial court; the old *burh-griö* was merged in an ubiquitous and homogeneous royal peace. Another class of boroughs was coming into existence, the enfranchised manors. Perhaps the free-tenure of houses at fixed and light rents which was to be found in the old shire-towns, served as a model and generated the idea that, where such tenure is, there is a *liber burgus*; but just in this quarter a French strain may be sought and perhaps

Transition to cent. xiii.

---

[1] See Liebermann, Das englische Gilde im achten Jahrhundert, Archiv für das Studium der neueren Sprachen, xcvi. 333; also Gross, Gild Merchant, i. 174 ff.

[2] In very recent days Ipswich was 'bossed' by a Wellington Club and Cambridge by a Rutland Club. See also the story of Coventry as told by Mrs Green, Town Life, ii. 205 ff.

detected[1]. Be this as it may, the number of so-called *burgi*
increased rapidly. A lord created a *liber burgus* if he abolished
villein services, heriot and merchet, and instead thereof took
money-rents, as, for example, twelve pence from each house.
Moreover, he might allow his tenants, his *burgenses*, to farm the
court, to farm a market bestowed on him by the king, and to
elect a bailiff. It was difficult or impossible to mark the
lowest degree of privilege or exceptionality which would make
a township no mere township but a borough.

The
inferior
limit of
burgality.
We may dwell upon this difficulty for a short while since
it illustrates the slow growth of that new type of community
which we call municipal and corporate. We can not define
a borough as a vill in which burgage tenure prevails, for of
this we hear in places which were not called boroughs[2]. We
can not say that a borough is a vill which is held in farm
by the men of the vill, for this 'self-farming' may be found in
some little villages. Nor again can we say that the borough
is a township exempt from the jurisdiction of the hundred
court; many a mere rural township was quite as extra-
hundredal as was the normal borough, indeed it might well
be more exempt from the interference of the county officers
than was many a small borough, for its lord (let us say the
abbot of Westminster) had 'the return of writs' in all his
manors. Nor again can the test afforded by the practice of [p. 654]
the eyres have been applied except in a one-sided way. Probably a place which had never sent twelve, instead of four,
men to meet the justices would have had to show some recent
grant of new liberties before it could pretend to be more than
a township; but there seem to have been in some counties
many places which sent twelve men to the eyre and which
yet were not called boroughs or summoned to send burgesses
to parliament[3]. And when the parliamentary test became

[1] See Flach, Les origines de l'ancienne France, ii. 213 ff., especially 348.
Also the entry touching Rhuddlan in D. B. i. 269, and Somma, p. 98. At this
point Les Coutumes de Lorris, ed. Prou, 1884, are full of instructive matter.

[2] Thus the abbot of Bec has burgage tenants at Atherstone in Warwickshire:
Select Pleas in Manorial Courts, i. 40–1. So the abbot of Malmesbury had
burgage tenants at Pilton in Devonshire, Reg. Malmesb. ii. 34.

[3] In Edward III.'s reign the men of Bakewell in Derbyshire successfully
prove their right to appear by twelve men; P. Q. W. 138. The eyre and
hundred rolls show a good many 'manors,' especially ancient demesne manors,
appearing in this way, and it must be remembered that the manors of the
ancient demesne were in some respects taxed like cities and boroughs.

applicable the line that was drawn was irregular. It has been calculated that under the first two Edwards 166 boroughs were summoned once or more often; that on an average under Edward I. no more than 75, under Edward II. no more than 60 boroughs were actually represented[1]. At any rate the number rapidly decreased. That the sheriffs had an immense power in this matter is certain. In 1320 the sheriff of Bedford and Buckingham said that Bedford was the one borough in his bailiwick, though in 1316 five others had been summoned, namely, Amersham, Wendover, Aylesbury, Wycombe and Marlow[2].

The truth seems to be that the summons to parliament engendered a force which diminished the number of the would-be boroughs. Theretofore it had been well to be a borough; the townsfolk when they went before the justices in eyre had enjoyed the privilege of 'swearing by themselves,' of not being mixed up with 'foreigners'; but now they were called on to send to parliament representatives whom they would have to pay:—at such a price they would no longer be burgesses. Another force was making in the same direction; abbots and other far-sighted lords were beginning to discover that it was not well to have burgesses. Long ago the men of Bury St Edmund's had been freed from all servile works; the vill had received *nomen et libertatem burgi* from the abbot; a portmanmoot was held in it; Abbot Sampson had chartered it[3]. In 1302 the sheriff of Suffolk bade it return members, sending the mandate, as he was bound to do, to the abbot's steward. The steward made no answer[4]. Then from 1304 we hear how the men of Bury have been making a 'conspiracy' and holding 'conventicles' among themselves; they have been pretending to have an alderman and a merchant gild and to be 'free burgesses.' They must pay heavy damages to the abbot, and those who are too poor to pay must go to prison for a month[5]. They have not a gild merchant, nor a community, nor a common seal, nor a mayor. Thus Bury soon drops out from the list of English boroughs, though long before this,

Represen-
tation in
parliament.

---

[1] Riess, Geschichte des Wahlrechts zum englischen Parlament, 19, 20.

[2] Riess, *op. cit.* p. 23.

[3] Jocelin of Brakeland, p. 73. The charter is given in a Bury Register; Camb. Univ. Lib. Ff. ii. 33, f. 64 b.

[4] Parl. Writs, i. 123.   [5] Gross, Gild Merchant, ii. 33–5.

Jocelin of Brakeland, no friend of the townsfolk, had allowed it 'the title and franchise of a borough[1].' The short-sightedness of some burgesses who would not pay representatives, the far-sightedness of some lords who just at the critical moment perceived that burgesses would not be good tenants, the inertness of sheriffs who did not care to enter, for no gain to themselves, upon an arduous struggle, the indifference of the king who had no need of the men of little towns, all made for the same result. Before the end of the fourteenth century the number of towns represented in parliament had fallen to a hundred, and these were most unevenly distributed among the various counties. We are not called upon to explain this phenomenon, for it belongs to the fourteenth century; but it forcibly suggests that in the thirteenth no strict definition of a borough was possible. And in the end what is the legal definition? The effect is put in place of the cause :—'A burgh is an ancient towne, holden of the king or any other lord, which sendeth burgesses to the parliament...and it is called a burgh because it sendeth members to parliament[2].'

The typical boroughs and their franchises.

Every note in the gamut whose two extremes are the mere rural township and the great community of London might be found and sounded by the patient historian, and some of the small boroughs, whose inhabitants never attain to a truly urban life, are of great interest as archaeological museums; but we must here glance only at the towns which lead the van, and on the whole we shall find that those old English shire-boroughs, of whose early days we have spoken, remain in the front rank throughout the middle ages, though a few other towns, especially some seaports, become prominent. We may first look at the 'liberties' or 'franchises' which are bestowed by the charters of the twelfth and thirteenth centuries, and then we may say a little of the corporate character of the borough community[3].

[1] See Pike, Introduction to Y. B. 16 Edw. III., Vol. 1, for an interesting discussion of the case of Wells.

[2] Co. Lit. 108 b. See Stubbs, Const. Hist. iii. 448–450 ; Riess, Geschichte des Wahlrechts.

[3] Besides the various borough charters we shall rely on the Munimenta Gildhallae, the Domesday of Ipswich (Black Book of the Admiralty, vol. ii.), the Records of Nottingham (ed. Stevenson), the Records of Northampton (ed. 1898), the Records of Leicester, of which by Miss Bateson's permission we have seen proof-sheets, the Leet Jurisdiction in Norwich (Selden Soc.), a Norwich

[p. 627]　　(I) *Jurisdictional privileges.* Usually there is no need for the charter to grant the right to hold a court, for the court exists already either in the form of an ancient borough-moot or in that of a manorial court. Indeed one of the 'liberties' that the burghers sometimes seek is that their court, their port-moot, or borough-moot, shall not be held too often—not more frequently than once a week. On the other hand, a common clause provides that the burgesses, except the king's moneyers and servants, 'shall not plead beyond the walls' of the town, unless it be for tenements which lie elsewhere. Then sometimes a further attempt is made to define the competence of the court in a manner advantageous to the burgesses:—if a debt is incurred in the town, the plea upon it is to belong to the borough court. Franchises of this kind are of importance in the history of the boroughs because they give occasion for communal action. If a burgess is impleaded in the king's court, it behoves the officers of the borough to appear there and 'claim their court,' and any negligence in this matter is likely to be prejudicial to the borough as showing that it is not 'seised' of its franchises. Not unfrequently the burgesses enjoyed in their court a procedure differing from that of the royal tribunal; they were protected against innovations and reforms. When we find that trial by battle is excluded, we may think that civic is in advance of royal justice; when on the other hand we find that trial by jury is excluded, and that the accused burgess of the thirteenth century even in criminal cases will wage his law, while the non-burgess must abide the verdict of burgesses, we know that from Henry II.'s day onwards civic has been falling

[p. 628] behind royal justice, has been becoming antiquated and selfish[1]. This may not always be its own fault; it has not been permitted to improve itself; it is a chartered justice and must carefully keep within the limits of its charter.

Custumal, a manuscript copy of which has been kindly lent to us by the Rev. W. Hudson, the Winchester Custumal (the French version of which is given by Smirke, Archaeol. Journal, ix. 69, and the English version by Toulmin Smith, English Gilds, 349), the Custumals of the Cinque Ports printed at the end of Lyon's History of Dover, vol. ii., and the Custumal of Preston, printed in Dobson and Harland, History of Preston Guild. Dr Gross's Bibliography of Municipal History, New York, 1897, is an admirable guide.

[1] Munimenta Gildhallae, i. 102–112. Mr Riley in his marginal notes misses the distinction between compurgation and trial by jury. Select Pleas of the Crown, i. pl. 82.

Civil juris-
diction. Valuable though these courts may have been to the townsfolk, they were not suffered to do much harm to the cause of
common law. Some of the boroughs developed a possessory
procedure of their own; an 'assize of fresh force' took the
place of the king's assize of novel disseisin[1]; but even in
London a proprietary action for a burgage was begun by the
king's writ of right, and when that writ was sent to less
favoured towns it contained the usual threat of the sheriff's
interference[2]. The party dissatisfied by the judgment of the
borough court could bring the matter before the king's tribunal by a writ of false judgment. From time to time justices
commissioned by the king held a session at St Martin's le
Grand to correct the errors of the London husting. The
Londoners held their privilege so high that they would refuse
to answer even in the court of a fair that they frequented:
burgesses of other boroughs, though they had the same words
in their charters, were less haughty or more politic[3].

Criminal
jurisdic-
tion. The criminal justice of the boroughs seldom stretched to
any higher point than that of infangthief and utfangthief, or,
in other words, the punishment of criminals caught in the
act. The boroughs had to appear before the king's justices
in eyre. It was privilege enough for them that they should
appear there by twelve of their own men as though they
were hundreds, and that thus no foreigners should make pre- [p. 629]
sentments about what had happened within the walls. Even
the city of London underwent visitations; the gaol of Newgate
was delivered by royal commissioners, and an occasional eyre
held at the Tower would serve to bring the citizens to reason,
for they were like to find that in the eyes of the king's
advocates their choicest liberties had been endangered by
abuse[4].

Return of
writs. Some of the more important boroughs had also acquired
the franchise known as 'the return of writs.' It was valuable
to them, for, so long as they had it not, the sheriff's officers
were constantly entering the town in order to serve writs

---

[1] Munim. Gild. i. 114, 195; Ipswich Domesday, p. 66; Norwich Custumal,
c. 17; Records of Northampton, i. 234, 477.

[2] Reg. Brev. Orig. f. 2 b.

[3] Riley, Chronicle, p. 51. Select Pleas in Manorial Courts, i. 138–160.

[4] See the account of the eyre of Edward II.'s day at the Tower of London
which lasted for twenty-four weeks; Munimenta Gildhallae, vol. ii. pp. lxxxiv–c.,
285–432.

and execute the processes of the king's court. Nevertheless it
was not acquired until late in the day. John was, to say the
least, chary of granting it[1].

(II) *Tenurial Privileges.* When the period of charters begins, burgage tenure already prevails in many of the large towns; the townsfolk already hold their lands and houses at money rents, and merely as tenants they require no further favours. Otherwise is it when what has hitherto been but a rural manor is to become a *liber burgus*. In such a case there will be a commutation of services, a release from agricultural labour. Sometimes a free power of alienating his tenement is conceded to every burgess, sometimes it is distinctly said that he may make a will or make an heir; but in general the power, very commonly assumed, of bequeathing burgage tenements 'like chattels' seems to have been ascribed to custom rather than to express grant. Privileged tenure.

In the great towns the existence of a court enjoying royal franchises seems to have reduced the mesne tenures to political insignificance. At the time of the Conquest the burgesses of a county town were in many cases a heterogeneous mass; [p. 630] some of them held directly of the king, but others were the tenants, the justiciables and the burgesses of this prelate or of that baron. Seldom were the men of such a town 'peers of a tenure'; seldom was the soil an unbroken stretch of royal demesne. Not only might its bounds comprise many a private soke, but some of the townsfolk were accounted to belong to the rural manors of their lords. When therefore the king under pain of his full forfeiture ordains that none of them need answer in any court outside the borough for any tenement within the borough, he is practically detaching these burgesses from the manors to which they have belonged and is defying the principle of feudal justice. The men who have settled round his *burh* and his market are his burgesses, whosesoever tenants they may be. Here and there a lord who held some considerable quarter of a borough might keep a court for his tenants, and, as he had acquired for himself and them some immunity from taxation, they would refuse to mix with, to be at scot and lot with, their fellow townsmen. But a small Mesne tenure in the boroughs.

---

[1] Records of Nottingham, i. 40. Only in 1255 did Nottingham acquire it.
Northampton in 1257: Records of Northampton, i. 46. Cambridge in 1256:
Cooper, Annals, i. 46.

group of men who formerly were reckoned to belong to some distant manor would soon be merged in the general mass of burgesses.　They would still pay rent, not to the king, nor to the king's farmers, but as of old to their lord; still no other connexion would bind them to him, and he would soon sink into the position of a mere recipient of rent[1].　Where tenements can be devised by will escheats are rare; the rights of the mesne lords are forgotten, and then it is said that if any tenement in the borough escheats, it escheats to the king.　Such in Edward II.'s day was the rule in the city of London where many 'barons' had once had sake and soke[2].

Seignorial rights in the boroughs.　The rapidity of this process varied from borough to borough. In some of the smaller towns that were chartered by mesne lords it never took place at all.　The burghal court was a seignorial court, which assumed now the form of 'court leet' and now that of 'court baron'; and such it continued to be until the end.　But even in some great boroughs seignorial justice was a hardy plant.　In Stamford, which was an old royal borough, though it had come to the hands of the Earl [p. 631] of Warenne, four prelates and five other lords claimed to have court of all their tenants; and this in the year 1275[3]. In London nearer the beginning of the century there were many sokes, and it seems to have been usual that an action for land should be begun in a feudal court, and should only come before the civic husting after a default in justice had been made[4].　Even in Edward II.'s reign many lords have to say by what warrant they claim franchises in London.　The Bishop, Dean and Chapter of St Paul's have three sokes in Cornhill, Bishopsgate and Holborn where they exercise the right of infangthief, though the actual hanging is done outside the city at Finsbury and Stepney[5].　The Prior of Trinity Church, as representing the estate of the old English Knight-gild, holds the Portsoken and is an alderman by tenure; even civic jurors admit that his men and tenants sue and are sued in his courts[6].　There is feudalism in the gildhall itself. Robert FitzWalter still represents the lords of Baynard's castle, though the castle itself has been sold to the Archbishop of

---

[1] Maitland, Township and Borough, p. 71.
[2] Placit. Abbrev. 310 (London).
[3] R. H. i. 354.　　　[4] Munim. Gild. i. 64–5.　　　[5] P. Q. W. 456.
[6] P. Q. W. 472.

Canterbury. He must be summoned to every meeting of the
common council; when he enters the gildhall, the mayor must
rise to do him honour, and while he is there all the judgments
that are to be delivered shall be delivered by his mouth. Such
at all events is his opinion[1].

At a few points of private law the borough custom would Customary
swerve from the ordinary rules. Often the tenant of a burgage law.
could give it by last will, at least if he had not inherited it, for
some customs drew a distinction between inherited and purchased tenements. Then the customary rules of inheritance
might differ from those of the common law. A custom which
gives the whole tenement to the youngest son has gotten the
name 'borough English,' and has therefore been supposed to
be peculiarly appropriate to the circumstances of townsfolk.
Really, however, this name seems due to a single instance.
At Nottingham in the days of the Conquest a new French
[p. 632] borough grew up beside the old English borough, and the
customs of the *Burgus Franciscus* as to dower, inheritance
and the like had to be distinguished from those of the *Burgus
Anglicus*[2]. Among the customs of the 'borough English' was
the rule in question, and after the 'borough English' of
Nottingham the lawyers baptized it. As a matter of fact,
there is no reason for supposing that it had a burghal origin.
It is not very often found in the boroughs, while it was
common in rural manors. Nottingham supplies us also with a
rarer custom, namely (we must borrow a term from France),
the *retrait lignager*, the right of the heir apparent (or perhaps
of any kinsman) of one who sells his tenement to come forward
within year and day after the sale and buy back the tenement
at the price given for it[3]. At Dover the expectant heir had to
pay no more than nineteen shillings for every pound that the
stranger had paid[4]. On the continent of Europe such a right
was common; a mitigation it was of old law which required
the heir's consent to an alienation made by his ancestor. The
English common law seems to have leapt over this stage of
development, and to have passed at once from the rules laid
down by Glanvill, who in many cases requires the heir's

[1] P. Q. W. 472. Munim. Gild. ii. 149–151.
[2] Records of Nottingham, i. 124, 186.
[3] Records of Nottingham, i. 70, 100.
[4] Lyon, Dover, ii. 274.

consent, to the state of things described by Bracton in which
such consent is never necessary.   Now in a borough we should
look for a greater and not for a less power of selling lands than
prevailed elsewhere, and it is not impossible that the custom
of some boroughs fell behind just because at an earlier time it
had been in advance of the common law.   The borough obtains
from the king a charter saying that if any one holds a tenement in the town for year and day, the claims of every person
to that tenement shall be barred, unless he was in prison,
under age or beyond the seas[1].   The main object of this is to
preclude the claims of expectant heirs.   This puts the custom
in advance of the common law of Glanvill's day.   But some
boroughs stop here; Nottingham at least stops here for a   [p. 633]
while; its custom falls behind the common law and develops
a *retrait lignager.*   At Northampton we find not only the
retrait lignager, but also the *retrait féodal*[2].   Then, again, the
custom sometimes provided for a landlord, whose rent was in
arrear for year and day, a readier mode of ejecting his tenant
than the common law would have given[3].   But we do not find
many peculiarities of this sort.

Freedom
of serfs.

In this context we may mention another privilege that was
sometimes granted to a borough :—the serf who dwells in it for
a year and a day, at all events if he has become a burgess or a
member of the merchant gild, becomes free, or at least can not
be claimed by his lord so long as he remains within the
borough.   In its origin this seems an assertion of royal right.
The king treats his borough, the whole of his borough, as
though it were one of his ancient manors.   If a serf comes to

    [1] Maitland, Possession for Year and Day, Law Quarterly Review, v. 253.
This privilege was granted to Bury by the Abbot; the person protected must
have 'legally acquired' the tenement; Registrum Sacristae, Camb. Univ. Libr.
Ff. ii. 33. f. 64 b.   See also Customs of Winchester, Archaeol. Journal, ix. 74;
apparently when a citizen of Winchester wishes to make a conveyance of land
he presents the charter to the aldermen; thereupon 'the ban' is cried; then
after three days the charter is sealed with the city's seal; then after quiet
possession for year and day the purchaser is safe.   See also as to the custom of
Northampton, a note by Mr Green in L. Q. R. xiii. 116, and Records of
Northampton, i. 459 ff.

    [2] Records of Northampton, i. 214.

    [3] As to the London 'gavelet' see Muniment. Gildh. i. 62; see also the
Winchester custom, Archaeol. Journal, ix. 76, and the Reading custom,
Cunningham, Growth of English Industry, ed. 3, i. 618, and the Northampton
custom, Records of Northampton, i. 218.

dwell there, his lord must claim him at once or not at all, for
the king will not allow the lords to interfere with his lands.
As regards a borough, an express declaration of this principle is
necessary, for, as we have seen above, the land within the walls
of one of the greater towns was seldom an unbroken stretch
of royal demesne land.   Nevertheless 'the borough' as a whole
is the king's, and he announces that those who come there and
form part of the burghal community, although they may not
be holding their burgage tenements immediately of him, are to
enjoy the security that is conferred by the soil of the ancient
demesne[1].   The first declarations of this right are pitched in a
royal key.   Henry II. in his charter for Nottingham declares
that 'if any one, whencesoever he be, shall dwell in the
borough a year and a day in time of peace, no one, except the
king, shall have any right in him[2].'   We are not told that the
serf is to be free; but what remains in the king's hands for
year and day becomes the king's.   As the borough grows more
independent of the king, the rule begins to take the shape of a
[p. 634] privilege conceded to the burgesses instead of being a royal
prerogative.   The burgesses are glad of the concession; it
keeps their town free from the interference of foreigners, and
someone thought fit to add to the Conqueror's laws a clause
stating in the widest terms that, if a serf lives for year and day
in a city, borough or walled town, he shall become free[3].
Nevertheless, it would be a mistake to think that the townsfolk wished to obliterate the distinction between free and
bond; on the contrary, they were careful to prevent men of
servile birth from becoming citizens[4].

(III)   *Mercantile Privileges.*   The borough is not merely   Freedom
from toll.

---

[1] See above, p. 429.   [2] Records of Nottingham, i. 1.

[3] Leg. Will. Conq. III. c. 13 (Schmid, p. 356.)

[4] On this subject see Stubbs, Hoveden, vol. ii. p. xxxviii.   It is true that we
read in Glanvill and a few charters of the privilege as existing in certain
boroughs before we hear of it as existing on the royal demesne lands; but in
general the peculiarities of the ancient demesne are regarded as very ancient;
they are supposed to represent the conquest settlement.   In 1313 the would-be
law or charter of the Conqueror was pleaded by persons who were living in
Norwich: Placit. Abbrev. p. 316.   In 1308 Simon of Paris was imprisoned as a
villein; he brought an action and the plea that he was a citizen and alderman
of London was not received: Y. B. 1 Edw. II. f. 4.   At Norwich no one could
become a citizen unless he was already a free man: Norwich Custumal, cap. 36.
This was true of London also: Munim. Gildh. i. 33.   See Gross, Gild
Merchant, i. 30.

a governmental and in a certain measure a self-governing district, it is a possessor of mercantile privileges, and, as will be remarked below, it is chiefly in this character that it becomes a person in the eye of the law.   When a borough had obtained the right to farm itself, one of the most important sources of its revenue was toll.   Of this we must speak hereafter when we discuss the *firma burgi*.   Sometimes this fount of income was protected not merely by a rule of common law, which would have prevented even the king from setting up a new to the damage of an old market, but also by a royal ban which compelled the folk of the neighbourhood to do their buying and selling in the borough[1].   But those who took toll were anxious to be quit of toll, and perhaps the burgesses regarded freedom from toll as the most vital of all their rights.   Already in Domesday Book we read how the man who was domiciled in Dover and there paid the king's dues was quit of toll throughout all England[2].   Subsequent charters threw about such favours with a liberal hand; sometimes the burgesses were to be immune [p. 635] throughout all England, sometimes they carried their immunity into all the king's lands beyond the sea.   In our eyes, it may be, the best outcome of this privilege was that it provided an ever-recurring theme for inter-municipal litigation and aroused in the boroughs a consciousness of their personality.

The *Firma Burgi*.   (IV)   *The Firma Burgi.*   Often the borough farmed itself, or perhaps we had better say for the present that the burgesses farmed the borough.   They might hold their town under a lease for years or during the lessor's pleasure; they might hold it in fee farm: that is, under a perpetual lease.   Important as this step towards independence might be, it was not taken by some towns of high rank until late in the day; it would seem, for example, that the citizens of Winchester did not obtain a perpetual lease or grant of their city until the reign of Edward III.[3], while on the other hand at a much earlier date many a rural manor was being farmed by 'the men of the manor,' though hardly farmed in fee.

What was farmed?   Now in these cases the charter says that the king has granted the *burgus* or the *villa* to the burgesses[4].   What was

---

[1] Maitland, Township and Borough, p. 213.   [2] D. B. i. 1.

[3] Firma Burgi, 18–20; Gross, Gild Merchant, i. 6.

[4] The transaction is sometimes called a feoffment; *e.g.* R. H. i. 61: King John enfeoffed the burgesses of Derby.

the effect of such a grant? As we understand it, 'the burgesses', taken in some collective fashion, were to step into the shoes of the sheriff. They were to be entitled to certain revenues which he had previously collected. These would be chiefly the tolls, the profits of the court and such house-rents as had therefore been paid to the sheriff as the king's farmer; and there might also be the profits of a royal mill or the like. On the other hand, the king had not parted with all his landlordly rights. The burgesses, taken collectively, had not obtained a place in the scale of land-tenure. They had not become collectively or corporatively the *domini* or the *tenentes* of the soil that lay within the boundary of the town. This seems to be proved by the law of escheat. Each burgess still holds his tenement either of the king in chief or of some other man; he does not hold of the community, and, if there is an escheat, the community will not profit by it[1]. This is the situation that is set before us by that minute description of Cambridge which appears upon the Hundred Rolls. 'The burgesses of Cambridge hold the vill of Cambridge with all its appurtenances in fee farm of the king in chief, as in meadows, pastures, mills, waters and mill-pools with all franchises and free customs belonging to the said vill.' Nevertheless the burgesses, taken collectively, are not conceived as being the

[p. 656] lord of the individual burgess or of his tenement. If he pays rent to them, or rather to their bailiffs, the phrase used with wearisome iteration is—not 'he holds of the borough,' nor 'he holds of the burgesses,' but—'he pays to the bailiffs of Cambridge, who hold the said vill at fee farm of our lord the king, so many pence for haw-gavel, or so many for land-gavel towards their farm[2].' Bonenfant the Jew held an open place in the town of Cambridge; but he has lately been hanged for clipping coin, and that place has escheated, not to the burgesses, but to

[p. 637] the king[3]. The general theory of the law seems to be that, in becoming a farmer, the burgesses become rather a bailiff than a tenant, though a bailiff who, like many other medieval bailiffs, has to account each year for a fixed sum and may make a profit or a loss out of his office. In short, when a 'borough' is granted to the burgesses, this 'borough' belongs to the category of 'things incorporeal,' a category which comprises 'counties'

---

[1] As to the escheat of lands in London, see above, p. 646.
[2] R. H. ii. 356 ff.   [3] R. H. ii. 392.

and 'hundreds.' When a man is appointed sheriff, the king commits to him 'our county of X'; and so the king will grant to a baron 'the hundred of Y.' The sheriff will not own the soil of the county; the lord of the hundred need not be tenant or lord of the soil of the hundred; in each case what is given is not an ownership or tenancy of any land but a complex of royal rights and powers to be exercised within the limits of a certain tract.

The farm of the vill and the soil of the vill.

This question is of some importance; we have heard of its being raised in these last times between a municipal corporation and a telephone company—Did the *firma burgi* comprise any ownership, any tenancy of the soil? Therefore we will add one further argument. The citizens of London farmed not only the city of London but also the county of Middlesex. Now, not only does no one suppose that the civic corporation has a place in the scale of tenure between every Middlesex freeholder and the king, but no one supposes that the civic corporation became the tenant of all the roads and open spaces within the boundary of the shire[1]. So again, the citizens of York farmed the wapentake of Ainsty, and, if what was said be true, very [p. 638] ill they treated it. They sub-let it at an advanced rent to a bailiff, who used his subjects so vilely that they talked of selling their tenements and leaving the country[2]. But, as we understand the matter, the citizens of York held the wapentake in the same sense that the archbishop might have held it without being owner, lord or tenant of a rood of land. Should a question arise about these matters in our own day, great weight would very properly be ascribed to acts of user[3], and (to say nothing of modern statutes) many boroughs now have ampler charters than those that were granted in the thirteenth century. But as to the historical question, we can not think that the grant which made the burgesses *firmarii* of the *burgus*, made them *domini* or *tenentes* of the land that lay within the *burgus*.

The lands of the borough.

(v) *Property of the Borough.* But the 'borough' or 'vill' which the king 'granted' to the burgesses often comprised in some sense or another a large tract of arable and pasture

---

[1] The doctrine which gives the soil of high-ways to the owners of the adjoining lands is not, we are persuaded, of very ancient origin; but this matter can not be discussed here.

[2] R. H. i. 124–6.   [3] See *Beckett* v. *Corporation of Leeds*, L. R. 7 Ch. 421.

lying without the wall or the ditch, for the borough occupied
the shell of an old agrarian community.   The charter will
purport to concede the whole vill 'with all meadows, pastures
and waters thereto pertaining.'   Now as regards the arable, this
was holden by individuals and the most that the king could
give away was his seignory.   Apparently he did not give
away even that; the escheats were still to come to him, though
the burgesses might now receive such rents as had formerly
been paid to the sheriff.   As to the pastures, which were often
of wide extent, it is very probable that no exact idea of
ownership was yet applied to them.   On the one hand, rights
of common were being exercised over this land, and we may
believe that such rights were no longer so closely connected
with the arable as once they were, but were being more and
more regarded as annexed to membership of the feudally
heterogeneous burgensic community which in its moot had
an organ for their regulation.   On the other hand, the king
was lord of the vill, and the right to 'approve,' or make profit
of, its waste was rather in him than in the community.   This
continued to be so even when 'the burgesses' had become the
farmers of their town, for the right of approvement was not
one which the sheriff could have exercised for his own behoof
while he farmed the royal revenues.

The same seems to have been true of the intramural
'waste,' and of this there was often a goodly supply which
would be profitable at a later day.   The walls, ditches, streets
and open spaces of the borough were not as yet conceived
to be 'holden by' the community.   They were still the king's,
and he who encroached upon them committed a 'purpresture'
against the king[1].   The grant of the vill has not entitled the
burgesses to approve this 'waste'; a more explicit licence is
requisite, and such a licence they will sooner or later obtain.
The men of Bristol acquired it early; on the other hand we
may find Edward I. specially authorizing the citizens of
London to let certain vacant spots within the walls in order
that the rents may be applied to the maintenance of the
bridge[2], and other towns were asking for a similar permission
at a much later time[3].

The intramural waste.

---

[1] See the account of Lincoln, R. H. i. 397–8.   Ibid. i. 203, Canterbury.

[2] Munimenta Gildhallae, ii. 95, 274.

[3] As to all this matter see Maitland, Township and Borough, 185 ff.

None the less, subject to this royal lordship, the waste, both intramural and extramural, had from the first belonged in some vague sort to the community, and there are instances in which the community dealt with it. Thus, for example, in 1200 the community of Ipswich granted that their twelve chief portmen might have a certain meadow for the support of their horses[1]; and at an earlier time the men of Oxford gave an island to the alderman of their gild who gave it to Oseney Abbey[2]; also we may find the men of Cambridge erecting a hospital on a piece of common land in the middle of their town[3]. But before there could be much freely proprietary dealing with the pasture land on the part of the burgensic *universitas,* the rights of the commoners had to take the form of a mere usage which the corporator is permitted to make of the land which the *universitas* owns. So long as the rights of pasture are conceived to be rooted in the possession of arable strips or burgage houses, they are an impediment to those transactions, leases or sales, which would demonstrate that a corporation is owner of the soil[4]. On the whole we believe that in the thirteenth century the burgensic community, taken as unit, was rarely drawing any pecuniary revenue[5] out of the land which in this vague sort belonged to it, and seldom was there any land which belonged to it in any other sort: the community was but rarely a purchaser of land, and burgesses were not as yet devising land to a municipal corporation. A statute of Richard II. forbids the borough corporations to acquire land without licence, and proclaims the discovery that they are 'as perpetual as men of religion[6].' When we consider that ever since 1279, and indeed at an earlier time, the churches had been debarred by law

---

[1] Gross, Gild Merchant, ii. 122.

[2] Ibid. ii. 192.

[3] Maitland, Township and Borough, 161.

[4] It is in this quarter that Bracton, f. 228 b, already sees some specific peculiarity of the cities and boroughs, 'Item [servitus poterit esse] personalis tantum ... item localis et non certis personis, sicut alicuius universitatis burgensium et civium.' The context shows that he is thinking of pasture rights. In the case of a borough you have a right of pasture that is not 'real', nor 'personal,' but 'local.' It is not annexed to a house, nor granted to specific persons, but is exercised by all members of an *universitas.*

[5] Small fees taken from those who turned out beasts might go toward the provision of a town bull.

[6] Stat. 15 Ric. II. c. 5.

from augmenting their territories[1], we may draw the inference
that only in the course of the fourteenth century was the
attention of the king and magnates drawn to any diminution
of their feudal revenues occasioned by the 'perpetuity' of
municipal corporations[2].

Moreover, it appears to us that the community or corporation of the thirteenth century rarely had any considerable
revenue of which it could freely dispose.   The farming of the
vill was a more individualistic arrangement than we are wont
to suppose.   The burgesses were jointly and severally answerable to the king for the whole fee-farm rent; but, as between
themselves, the plan was that their annually elected bailiffs
should collect what the sheriffs had theretofore collected and
should be solely liable if this sum fell short of that which
was due to the king[3].   Perhaps too the bailiffs were entitled
to any profit that they could make; but we fancy that a
normal surplus of income over expenditure was not to be
looked for.   In order to get rid of the sheriff from their court,
the burgesses had promised a heavy rent[4].   Thus the old
revenue consisting of the haw-gavel rents, and the profits of
the court and market, was no free revenue, but was appropriated to the satisfaction of a chief-rent which it would
hardly meet.   In course of time other sources of income reveal
themselves; fees are paid by those who acquire the freedom
of the borough; mercantile privileges are sold; bits of waste
land are let to tenants; a treasurer or chamberlain begins to
appear beside the bailiffs and to keep an account with the
community; there is a common chest.   But all this is the work
of time[5], and even at the end of the middle ages the freely

The borough's revenue.

---

[1] See above, p. 334.

[2] In our first edition too little notice was taken of the right which the burgensic community (*ut universitas*) may have in the 'waste' or 'common' land of the vill. See Green, Town Life, ii. 237. An attempt has been made to repair the default elsewhere: Maitland, Township and Borough.

[3] Maitland, Township and Borough, pp. 77-9. See also Records of Northampton, i. 96.

[4] At a later time many of the rents were reduced on the score of the poverty of the towns, and, though we must not believe all the plaintive tales that the burgesses tell about the 'destruction' of their bailiffs, it seems fairly plain that the rents were heavy. See *e.g.* the story of Bedford, where the rent was reduced from £46 to £20; Munic. Com. Rep. 1835, iv. 2104; also Maitland, Township and Borough, 77; Hist. MS. Com. xi. 3, p. 4, Southampton.

[5] The Records of Leicester are especially valuable at this point.

disposable annual income of a great borough was not very large[1]. The growth of such an income, though it has as yet been little studied, is of much importance in legal history, for the town's personality only begins to stand out clearly when 'the town' has a revenue which is not going to be divided among the townsfolk[2].

Chattels of the borough.

If the community owned chattels, these must have been few [p. 640] and of no great value.   Perhaps already some sword, some staff, some chain of office was handed on from mayor to mayor, and there may have been drinking horns and casks of wine and beer for which it would have been hard to find an owner in the world of natural persons.   There was a muniment chest and there was a common seal.   But it is not for the sake of such trifles as these that law will undergo the pain of giving birth to the juristic person.   Sometimes, again, there would be a box with money in it; but, had a thief stolen box or money, we suspect that he would have been charged with stealing the proper goods and chattels of some natural man, the mayor or the chamberlain of the borough.   That those who collect rents and taxes should misappropriate the monies that they receive is, if we believe the jurors, a common event; but no one, so [p. 641] far as we know, ever speaks in this context of theft or felony. We shall see in another chapter that the question whether the treasurer (1) owned the money and owed a debt to the community, or (2) merely possessed money that was owned by the community might long be shrouded from view[3].

Elective officers.

(VI) *Election of Officers and Government of the Borough.* Already Henry I. had promised the Londoners that they might elect a sheriff and a justiciar from among themselves[4].   But London was in advance of other towns.   Gradually some of the greater boroughs obtain the right of electing their reeve or their bailiffs, who however do not enter on their offices until they have been presented to and approved by the king's justiciar.   Sometimes this step is taken before the burgesses have obtained the right of farming the borough in fee.   In

[1] Maitland, Township and Borough, 205 ff.; for Lynn, Hist. MS. Com. xi. 3, p. 213 ff.

[2] See Gierke, D. G. R. ii. 754.

[3] See the section on Movable Goods in our second volume.   The quasi-corporateness of our modern clubs etc. is rendered possible by a law of trusts which is not medieval.

[4] Schmid, Gesetze, p. 434.   See Round, Geoffrey de Mandeville, p. 347.

such a case the bailiffs, though elected by the townsfolk, are
still much rather the officers of the sheriff than the officers of
the community. They begin to look more like the officers
of the burgesses when the burgesses themselves have become
answerable for the *firma*; but even then, as we have lately said,
it is the bailiffs who, as between themselves and their fellow
townsmen, bear the loss if the farmed revenues fall short of
the king's rent. Some towns stop here for a long time; many
following the example of London buy the right to have an
elected mayor. No doubt this step also was important. No
doubt the Londoners, influenced by what was happening
abroad, set great store by the election of a *maior* who should
be the head of their *communa*; 'come what might they would
have no king but the mayor[1].' Even if we take no account
of such aspirations as were never fulfilled, it was important
that the town should have some one man as its chief; the
anthropomorphic picture of a body corporate required that
there should be a 'head[2].' Still it seems clear that a large
and wealthy city might get on well enough without a mayor;
until 1403 the citizens of Norwich were content with their
four bailiffs[3].

Beyond conceding the liberty to elect mayor and bailiffs Borough
and the liberty to elect coroners 'who shall see that the bailiffs leets.
of the borough deal justly and lawfully with rich and poor,'
the charters of this age seldom define any constitution for the
borough. They make no class of councillors, aldermen, chief
burgesses; they do not say how or by whom the dooms of
the burghal court shall be rendered. As we might expect, the
[p. 642] active organ of the borough is rather a court than a council.
The frankpledge system prevails in the boroughs. A view
of frankpledge is sometimes held for the whole borough (a
'mickletorn' it is called in some towns), whereat the mayor
or the bailiffs preside[4], or else the borough is divided into
wards or into 'leets,' each of which has its separate court[5].
The business of viewing the tithings and presenting offences

---

[1] Stubbs, Const. Hist. i. 674.   [2] See above, p. 491.

[3] Hudson, Archaeological Journal, vol. xlvi. p. 293.

[4] See the extracts from the Mickletorn rolls in Records of Nottingham,
vol. i.

[5] Norwich was divided into four leets. See Leet Jurisdiction in Norwich
(Selden Soc.).

seems to have been conducted within borough walls much as it was conducted in the open country. Naturally, however, the system of tithings sometimes took a territorial form; each small district of the town or each street had its tithingman[1]. Occasionally in boroughs which have little other organization a 'court leet' will in course of time assume the character of a regulative and governmental organ of a humble kind[2], and in some large towns the lower orders will give voice in 'presentments' to complaints against their rulers[3]; but in its origin the leet or view of frankpledge is much rather a royal police court than a communal assembly.

The borough court.

Then there is the old borough court holding frequent sessions. Often it sat once a week, and when 'foreigners' were concerned it would sit from day to day. Often it had no other name than 'the court of the borough (*curia burgi*)'; sometimes it was the 'husting,' the 'burwaremote,' 'portmote' or 'portmanmote.' Over it the mayor or the bailiffs presided, and perhaps in some places any burgess was capable of sitting in it as a doomsman. But the amount of business that it had to do would inevitably deprive it sooner or later of its popular character; the miscellaneous mass of burgesses would not easily be brought to do weekly suit of court. Already in Henry I.'s day there was in London a 'husting' distinct from the 'folkmoot.' Already before the Conquest there were twelve lawmen, twelve *iudices*, in some of the boroughs.

Court and council.

In 1200 John granted to the men of Ipswich a liberal charter. In pursuance of its terms they forthwith elected two bailiffs and four coroners. But they did not stop there. They decided that there should be in the borough twelve chief portmen 'as there are in the other free boroughs of England,' who should have full power to govern and maintain the borough and render the judgments of the town. Thereupon they chose twelve men,—among them were the four coroners, two of whom were also the two bailiffs—and these twelve were sworn to guard and govern the borough, to maintain its liberties and to render the judgments of its courts. Thereupon all the men [p. 643]

---

[1] See Nottingham Records, *e.g.* vol. i. p. 315, and compare Hudson's Introduction to Leet Jurisdiction in Norwich.

[2] Manchester Court Leet Records; Leader, Records of Sheffield, p. xl.

[3] Green, Town Life, ii. 341 (Nottingham); Dormer Harris, Life in an Old English Town (Coventry).

of the town swore to be obedient to them and to every of
them, save as against the king and the king's power[1]. We
discover at a little later time that the twelve chief portmen
hold their offices for life, though they may be removed for
misbehaviour by the judgment of their fellows. Vacancies
again are filled, not by popular election, but by co-optation[2].
Now certainly it would be rash to draw any wide inferences
from the few clear cases that come before us; nevertheless it
would seem that very commonly some select body was formed,
some body of twelve or twenty-four chief citizens, chief burgesses, chief portmen; formed by definite act as at Ipswich
or formed by a practice of summoning to the court only 'the
more discreet and more legal men.' This body at first is
rather a judicial than a governing body, for the powers entrusted to the burgesses by their charter are much rather
justiciary than governmental. But municipal life grows intenser and more complex; the court has to ordain and to tax
as well as to adjudge, and it is apt to become a council, the
governing body of the borough. Then, as trial by jury pene-
trates the boroughs, it sets up an important change. The old
pattern of a court with doomsmen who are there to declare
the law gives way before the new pattern with jurors who
bear witness to facts. In the town, as in the realm at
large, 'court' and 'council' are slowly differentiated; the
borough court becomes a mere tribunal, and by its side a
distinctly conciliar organ is developed. This, however, except
perhaps in exceptional London and a few other towns[3], seems
to be rather the work of the fourteenth than of the thirteenth
century[4]. The power of acting in the name of the borough
passed little by little from a general assembly of burgesses to
a council or 'select body'; but even until 1835 there were
towns, and towns with long histories, in which all the most
important business of the corporation had to be brought before
a meeting in which every corporator, every burgess or freeman,

---

[1] Gross, Gild Merchant, ii. 115.

[2] Ipswich Domesday, p. 167.

[3] For London, see Stubbs, Const. Hist. iii. § 809.

[4] Perhaps we may have to distinguish cases in which an old body of
doomsmen or lawmen develops into a council from others in which a council is
newly and deliberately instituted. In Germany the relation of the *Stadtrat* to
an older *Schöffenkolleg* has been much discussed. See Keutgen, Ursprung der
deutschen Stadtverfassung, 218 ff.

had a vote: such was the case at Winchester, Maidstone, Cambridge, Ipswich[1]. In the thirteenth century we may sometimes suspect that grants, ordinances and agreements to which 'the burgesses' or 'the community' are said to be parties may not have been sanctioned by any general assembly; but this should be no more than a suspicion until it can be verified in the history of the town that is in question[2].

Powers of self-government.   (VII) *By-laws and Self-government.* The charters do not [p. 644] expressly grant any power of legislation; but no doubt such power in varying degrees was often exercised:—in varying degrees, for however little distinction the law might make in this respect between borough and borough, there must have been a marked difference in fact between the city of London and some small market-town which had just attained to burghal rank. Not that we can at once ascribe greater powers to the wealthiest towns. On the contrary, in the petty borough whose governing court was still the court of its lord, the lord with the assent of his court would still be able to make ordinances almost as easily as, with the assent of his court, he could make ordinances for his rural manors, and the validity of such edicts would often pass unquestioned. But as an enfranchised town grew in trade, in wealth and in population, its folk would be tempted or compelled to enter on the regulation of affairs which had no existence in less busy places. Its 'customs' had been guaranteed to it, and the function of declaring custom could not always be marked off from that of imposing new rules. In London definite legislation begins at an early time. In 1189 Fitz-Alwyne's Assize was issued. It has been well called the earliest English 'Building Act[3]'; it contains stringent provisions about the houses that men may erect. A somewhat similar ordinance was issued in 1212 after a great fire, and it did not scruple to fix the rate of wages for masons, carpenters, tilers and the like[4]. Thenceforward ambitious attempts were

---

[1] Munic. Corp. Rep. 1835, vol. ii. p. 899 (Winchester); p. 760 (Maidstone, where the general assembly bears the name of Burghmote); vol. iv. p. 2188 (Cambridge); p. 2306 (Ipswich).

[2] We must carefully distinguish between (*a*) the development of a council within the burgensic body, and (*b*) the differentiation of a definite, and it may be small, burgensic body from the mass of inhabitants. Of the latter change we shall speak below. Though both processes may result in 'oligarchy,' they are very different. For the town councils of cent. xv., see Green, Town Life, ii. 268 ff.

[3] Munim. Gildh. i. pp. xxx. 319.   [4] Ibid. ii. 86.

[p. 645] made to regulate the price of commodities and the business of the various crafts. Now it is the poulterers who require attention, and now a code must be issued for the saddlers or the cordwainers; and then again exceptional privileges are conceded to foreign merchants; such a grant, for example, is made to the men of Amiens, Corbie and Nesle, for which they are to pay an annual sum of fifty marks towards the farm of the city[1]. The mayor and aldermen of London seem to conceive themselves to be endowed with almost unlimited legislative power over the whole province of trade and handicraft. And no doubt their ordinances were obeyed. The individual citizen, the individual 'foreigner,' dared not quarrel with them.

For all this, however, many doubts may occur to us touching the limits set by common law to their powers. Over against their wide claims we must set the wide claims of the king. Now and again some knot of traders, which thought itself oppressed, would be rich enough to stir the king to action, and when the king takes action even the City of London is apt to look powerless. In Edward II.'s day a dispute broke out between the civic authorities and the body of fishmongers on the one hand and certain fishmongers who did business at the Fish Wharf on the other[2]. Ordinances had been made prohibiting the sale of fish by retail at the wharf. The king was induced to dispute their validity. Much was said about their good and bad effects; but the king's counsel took high ground:—'The city of London is the city of our lord the king, and of his demesne, and it is not lawful for the mayor and commonalty, nor for any other, to make any ordinances in the said city without consulting the king[3].' So, again, at an earlier time Walter Hervey, mayor of London, had issued ordinances regulating the affairs of various crafts and affecting to confer on the craftsmen power to make yet other rules for their trade; but the validity of these ordinances was disputed, not only on the ground that the aldermen had not been consulted, but also because the regulations favoured unduly the richer men of the crafts[4].

Limits to legislative powers.

During the period now before us the common law does not come to close quarters with municipal by-laws; it is rarely, if [p. 646] ever, called upon to uphold them, for they are enforced in the

Enforcement of by-laws.

---

[1] Munim. Gild. ii. 64. [2] Ibid. ii. 385–407. [3] Ibid. ii. 405.
[4] Riley, Chronicles of Old London, p. 171.

municipal courts by those who made them[1]; it is rarely called upon to condemn them, for he must be both a bold and a rich citizen who will call in the king against the city. And so we obtain no jurisprudence of by-laws, no established tests for their validity.

The one thing that we can say with some certainty is that in theory no one in England can claim to legislate unless that power has been given him by the king—to say nothing of parliament. Those who claim to make by-laws must show that such power has been given to them by royal charter, or else they must show (and this they will hardly prove to the satisfaction of the king's justices) that they have been exercising it from time immemorial. On the whole, we may doubt whether in the majority of English towns much was done by way of legislation that might not be represented as being no more than a necessary definition and development of ancient customs. No decent person would consider himself aggrieved if a sharper edge was given to old rules directed against the wickedness of the 'forestaller' who enhanced the price of victuals[2].

Rates and taxes.

(VIII) *Self-taxing powers.* Powers of taxation are not expressly conceded by the charters of this age, and they must have been confined within narrow limits. If the burgesses wished to repair their walls, their bridges, their streets, they had to apply to the king for a grant of murage, pontage or pavage; and such grants were not to be had as matters of course[3]. In Edward I.'s day the petition came before the royal council in parliament, and the 'local rate,' we may say, [p. 647] was frequently a 'parliamentary tax'; but as the king had not

---

[1] Munim. Gildh. ii. 386. The fishmongers of the Fish Wharf say that they can get no redress in the city courts for their adversaries 'sount mestres et menours de la dite cité.'

[2] See Select Pleas of the Crown, pl. 137, for an early instance. In 1221 the men of Worcester confess to having 'provided' that no one shall sell victuals before the hour of prime. At Norwich there might be no buying or selling until the bell had rung for the mass of our Lady: Norwich Custumal, c. 37. The Ipswich Domesday contains a good many rules which are said to be ordained by the commonalty, though as a whole it was regarded as a statement of ancient customs. It was to contain (p. 18) 'the laws and usages of the town beforetime used so near as the same could be set forth (*a plus pres que hom les peot par bon avisement estimer*).'

[3] R. H. i. 108: the citizens of Scarborough have taken murage for two years beyond the time for which it was granted to them. In 1325 a request for murage preferred by the same burgesses is refused by the king; Rot. Parl. i. 423.

yet lost the right to tallage his boroughs, he could permit them
to tallage themselves.   The royal nature of the power to tax is
well illustrated by the loud complaints which come to our ears
from almost every ward in the city of London :—The great men
of the city have purchased charters exempting them from
tallages and thus the burden is thrown upon the smaller folk.
'Not just once, twice, thrice or four times have the mayor and
aldermen set tallages upon us without the special command
of the king or the assent and consent of the whole community;
they have spared the rich and distrained the poor, to the
disherison of the king and the destruction of his city[1].'   A
certain power in 'the whole community' to tallage its members,
these London citizens are willing to admit, but how far they
would have allowed a majority to tax a dissentient minority is
doubtful.   The heavy imposts to which they had recently been
compelled to submit were occasioned by the fines to which the
city had been subjected owing to the share which its citizens
had taken in the Barons' War.   Speaking generally we may say
that tallages, fines and amercements imposed upon the borough
from without, were (together with the murages, pontages and
pavages which, if not imposed from without, were at least
licensed from above) the main causes for municipal taxes.

The borough community had few other expenses to meet, Borough
it was not an 'improving corporation' with hosts of paid expenditure.
servants[2].   The individual burghers had to serve as officers, as
constables, ale-conners and the like, or find and pay fit substitutes, while small fees taken from suitors in the borough
court, or from the youths admitted into frankpledge, would
serve as a remuneration for the town clerk.   On the whole, the
burgher's duty of paying 'scot and lot' with his fellows came
home to him chiefly, if not solely, as a duty of contributing
towards sums exacted from the borough by a 'not-itself,' and
the question as to the legality of rates made for other purposes
[p. 648] was seldom raised[3].   Had it been raised, the recalcitrant

[1] R. H. i. 403 ff. especially 411.   There is a great deal about this matter in
the Liber de Antiquis Legibus.   See also the complaint from Northampton,
R. H. ii. 2.

[2] However in 1237 the Londoners had already been engaged in making a
conduit to bring the Tyburn water to the city; Munimenta Gildhallae, vol. ii.
p. 66.

[3] See the passages descriptive of scot and lot in Gross, Gild Merchant, i.
53–59.

burgher would have found no favour in the borough court, while an appeal to the king's court was only open to one who could afford to begin a small civil war against his neighbours. But even the city of London thought fit to obtain from Edward II. an express power of imposing tallages for its own use[1].

Tolls.

A large part of the borough's revenue was derived from tolls, if we use that term in its largest sense to include 'passage, pontage, lastage, stallage, bothage, ewage, tronage, scavage' and the like. Naturally a borough community intrusted with the farm of tolls was tempted to impose a stringent and protective tariff: its ideal of a perfectly 'free' trade was an unlimited power to tax other people. Nevertheless we may doubt whether it had any right to create new tolls. The charge of levying new tolls is extremely common; and those against whom it is brought seem always concerned to deny that there has been innovation. The land, it must be remembered, was full of private lords who were toll-takers, and there hardly could be one rule for them and another for the boroughs.

The Gild Merchant.

(IX)   *The Gild Merchant.*   In a large number of towns one of the privileges that has been granted to the burgesses and their heirs is that of having their gild merchant or market gild. If we attempt to expand the brief phrase used in the charter, we seem brought to some such result as the following:—The king gives to the burgesses a right to form or retain an association for the purpose of employing to the best advantage those mercantile immunities which by other words of his charter he has conferred upon them. They are to be toll free; they may organize themselves for the purpose of maintaining this freedom.

The formation of a gild.

A detailed story comes to us from Ipswich. In 1200 King John granted a charter to the burgesses; they were to hold the borough in fee farm; they were to be quit of toll and all similar dues throughout the king's lands; they were not to be impleaded outside their town; they were to have their gild merchant and their hanse; they were to elect two fit men to [p. 649] keep the reeveship of the borough; they were to elect four coroners. Thereupon the whole community met in the church-yard and elected two bailiffs and four coroners, and ordained, as we have said before, that there should be twelve chief

[1] Munim. Gildh. vol. ii. p. 273.

portmen who should guard and govern their borough and give its judgments. Then on a later day the chief portmen were elected and sworn. Then the bailiffs, coroners and chief portmen held a meeting and resolved that an alderman of the gild merchant should be elected by the community and that four men should be associated with him and that they should swear to maintain the said gild and all that appertained to it. Then the whole community met again and elected an alderman and four associates, who swore faithfully to govern the gild merchant and faithfully to deal with all the brethren. Then the alderman and his four associates in the presence of the people proclaimed that all who were of the liberty of the town should come before them and put themselves in the gild and give their hanse to the gild. Then the bailiffs, coroners, portmen and the whole community took counsel how the gild might best be maintained, and they decreed that the alderman and his successors should have a monopoly of gravestones, pavingstones and the like, and that of the proceeds of this monopoly he should render account to the bailiffs and coroners[1].

Thus, having got their charter, the burgesses of Ipswich proceed to form two different organizations; there is the governmental and justiciary organization with its bailiffs, coroners, twelve chief portmen; there is the gild organization with its alderman and his four associates. Certainly the two are closely connected. The gild is to be no mere private club. Every burgess is to place himself in the gild and pay his hanse, his entrance fee, to the gild, or otherwise, as we gather, he will lose some at least of the advantages, notably the mercantile advantages, that the words of the charter give to the burgesses of Ipswich and their heirs. No doubt it would be imprudent were we to base any large generalities upon a few cases. Not all the charters of even date are exactly like the Ipswich charter. Thus in the same year the same king granted a charter to the men of Gloucester. In this the privilege of not being impleaded without the walls and the privilege of being free of toll were expressly confined to 'the burgesses of Gloucester who are of the merchant gild[2].' In one place the merchant gild may have been of more, in another of less importance; in one place it may have become in practice, though hardly in theory, the governing body of the borough,

The gild and the government of the borough.

[p. 650]

---

[1] Gross, Gild Merchant, ii. 115–123.   [2] Rot. Cart. 56.

while in another place there was no such gild at all.   In
London itself traces of a merchant gild are, to say the least,
very faint, while Norwich stands out as an example of the
flourishing cities which to all seeming never had a merchant
gild[1].   The mercantile privileges granted to the burgesses
could be maintained and enforced without any such organization, while with the public justice and police of the borough
the gild as a general rule had nothing to do.   In boroughs
which had a gild merchant the burgess was not necessarily a
gildsman, the gildsman was not necessarily a burgess.

Objects of
the gild.
  The main object that the gild merchant has in view is
the maintenance of the mercantile privileges that have been
granted by charter.   This is an important and a difficult
matter.   A few merchants of the town go to some distant fair
or market; toll is taken from them; the lord of the fair, the
bailiffs of the rival city to which they have gone, scoff at their
charters, or temperately and reasonably set charter against
charter and seisin against seisin.   In such a case a solitary
trader far from home needs all the help that his fellows can
give.   And they are interested in his cause, for once let it be
established that the burgesses of X are in seisin of taking toll
from the burgesses of Y, then only by litigation, if at all, will
the burgesses of Y recover seisin of their immunity.   If the
privilege is to be preserved intact, the individual merchant
must be backed by a community of merchants which will take
immediate action, which will complain to the king and support
its complaint with a handsome gift, or which will forthwith [p. 651]
make reprisals against the aggressors.   To make reprisals they
are encouraged by their charters.   It is thus for example that
the king speaks in his charter to the men of Gloucester—and
similar clauses are not uncommon—'And if any one in our
whole land takes toll from the men of Gloucester of the gild
merchant, and shall refuse justice, the sheriff of Gloucestershire or the reeve of Gloucester shall for this take a *nam* at
Gloucester[2].'   If a gildsman of Gloucester be subjected to toll in
another town, the men of that other town had better not bring

---

[1] Gross, Gild Merchant, i. 22; Hudson, Constitution of Norwich, Archaeol.
Journ. vol. xlvi. p. 324.   See also Mr Stevenson's remark in Records of
Nottingham, i. 183.   The Ipswich Domesday seems to show that in that town
the gild had nothing to do with governmental affairs.
 [2] Rot. Cart. 57.

their wares to Gloucester. The merchants of the borough must
be organized in order that this inter-municipal warfare may be
conducted vigorously and prudently. Both vigour and prudence
are needful ; all those who are not exempt from toll should be
forced to pay it, while it is perilous to touch those who are
exempt. In order that their action may be both prompt and
deliberate, the merchants must be organized, must constantly
meet, must have executive officers and a common purse.

Still these mercantile privileges are not of equal importance *The gild
and the
burgesses.* to all the burgesses. Many of them are not traders ; but few
of them will carry goods to distant markets, though those few
are likely to be rich and powerful. Thus the gild organization
may remain quite distinct from the governmental organization ;
men may be burgesses who are not gildsmen. On the other
hand, it would certainly seem that rightly or wrongly the
gildsmen take upon themselves to receive as brethren men who
are not burgesses, men who do not live in, who do not hold
property in, the town, but who desire to share the immunities
which the traders of the town enjoy[1]. Thus, though according
to the terms of the charters 'the gild merchant' is a liberty,
a franchise, conceded to the burgesses, the gild comes to be a
body of persons which does not include all the burgesses and
does not exclude all who are not burgesses.

Further, at least in some cases, the gild merchant evolves *The gild
court.* out of itself a court of justice which exists beside the law
court of the borough. This can hardly be prevented ; the
craft gilds of London evolve courts of justice, the French and
[p. 652] German merchants in London evolve courts of justice, the
learned universities evolve courts of justice ; there can hardly
exist a body of men permanently united by any common
interest that will not make for itself a court of justice if it be
left for a few years to its own devices. The gild-brethren at
their 'morning-speeches' do not merely take counsel for the
maintenance of their privileges and the regulation of their
trade, but they assume to do justice. In the first place, they
decide questions of inheritance and succession. A person's
gilda, that is, his right as a member of the gild, is treated as
an object of ownership. With the consent of the court a man

---

[1] See the complaint against the community of Lynn; R. H. i. 461; also the
complaint against the men of Bedford; P. Q. W. 18.

may give it or sell it. If he dies possessed of it, then it will descend to his heir. And so at the morning-speech one person will come and demand against another the 'gild' of a dead ancestor 'as his right and inheritance,' using the very form of words by which he would have demanded ancestral lands. Such disputes, such actions we must call them, the gildsmen hear and determine at their morning-speeches. But besides this they entertain actions of debt and covenant and trespass, and hardly dare we call such assemblies mere courts of arbitration, for they can enforce their own decrees; if it comes to extremities, the contumacious brother can be expelled. The right of each gildsman to claim a share in any bargain that he sees one of his fellows making is another cause for litigation[1].

The borough as a franchise holder. Such in brief were the main franchises that the boroughs enjoyed, and these franchises, some or all of them, made the borough to be a borough. This gave the king a tight hold upon the townsfolk. The group of burgesses was a franchise-holder in a land full of franchise-holders, and had to submit to the rules which governed the other possessors of royal rights. It might lose its privileges by abuse or non-use; it might lose them by not claiming them before the justices in eyre, though in this case a moderate fine would procure their restoration. Four times at least within eleven years did Henry III. seize the city of London into his hands, once 'for receiving Walter Buriler without warrant for so doing,' once because of a false [p. 653] judgment in the hustings, once because the citizens prevented the mayor and aldermen from discussing certain matters with the king's justices, and once because the assize of bread and ale was not kept[2]. No doubt Henry was tyrannical and greedy, but these seizures show how weak was the most powerful of all the English cities. Then Edward I. kept London for many years without a mayor, and during this time he legislated for it in royal fashion :—'*le Roy voet*,' such is the formula by which by-laws are made[3]. And the king's inquests searched out the secrets of the borough; he was not to be put off with the story told by the rulers of the community. If he desired to know

---

[1] See in Gross, Gild Merchant, vol. ii. under Andover, Guildford, Leicester, Totnes ; also Records of Leicester (ed. Bateson) *passim, e.g.* p. 180.

[2] Riley, Chronicles, pp. 11, 15, 18, 22.

[3] Munim. Gildh. i. 251 ff. ; see especially pp. 280–298.

what had passed at Lincoln, he heard one jury of the great, another of the 'secondary,' a third of the 'lesser' folk[1].

We ought now to inquire whether the borough community differs from the other 'land communities' in exhibiting all or any of those peculiar characteristics to which we make reference when we speak of corporateness or personality. And at once it must be confessed that in the scale of 'towns' which begins with the common village and ends with London no break can be found. This does not, however, absolve us from the inquiry: black and white are different, though nature displays every shade of grey.

Corporate character of the borough community.

The doctrine that some act of public power is necessary if a corporation is to come into being had not as yet been accepted. Probably we must wait for the fourteenth century to hear a king's advocate proclaim that the burgesses can not have a *communitas* unless this be granted to them by the king[2]. As yet the charters contain no creative words. Nothing is said, as in the charters of the fifteenth century, about the erection of a 'corporation' or 'body politic'; nothing, as in the charters of the fourteenth, about the formation or confirmation of a *communitas*[3]. The *communitas* is already there; it may want privileges, but it exists. The notion that there is some 'feigning' to be done, some artifice to be applied, has not as yet been received from the canonists[4], and perhaps we ought to regret its reception; the corporation which exists 'by prescription' seems to defy it or to require that one fiction be explained by another[5]. The foundation, however, is being laid for a rule which will require a royal licence when a new corporation is to be formed. This work is being done partly by legists and decretists, who are discussing the *collegia illicita* of Roman law, partly by English statesmen. The king had begun to interfere with the creation of new *communitates*, with the creation of voluntary associations or gilds. Such intervention was dictated

Corporateness not bestowed by the king.

---

[1] R. H. i. 309–15–22.

[2] P. Q. W. 18. See the assertion of the Abbot of Bury, Gross, Gild Merchant, ii. 34.

[3] See Gross, Gild Merchant, i. 93.   [4] See above, p. 502.

[5] Must we say, for example, that the University of Cambridge (which is a corporation by prescription) is feigned by the law to be a person, because the law first feigns that by some charter granted before the time of Richard I. some king said in effect that there was to be this fiction? That this story would contradict some known facts in the history of the University seems the least of its demerits.

not by any 'juristic necessity,' any theory of personality, but by political expedience and financial needs. Gilds may give trouble; they may become aggressive *communae* of the French type. The Londoners from of old are a community, but they must not form a sworn *communa* unless the king consents. 'Adulterine gilds[1]' must be suppressed for much the same reason as that which decrees the destruction of 'adulterine castles.' Besides, here lies a not disreputable source of income. Men will pay for leave to form clubs; and it is to be remembered that the medieval gild is never content with the purely private position of a modern club, but aspires to exercise some jurisdiction and coercive power over its members, and perhaps over outsiders. Thus the notion is propagated that gild-like structure must not exist without royal licence, and this at a time when the structure of the burgensic community is assuming a gild-like shape[2].

Gild-like traits of the borough community.

For that was happening. The idea of voluntary association was moulding the community. In the great boroughs large sums of money were subscribed in order that privileges might be bought from the king, and the subscribing townsfolk naturally conceived that they purchased those privileges for themselves. Some definition of the privileged, the franchised, body was necessary, and yet in the great boroughs that body could not assume any of the old accustomed forms. The hide or the yardland could no longer be the groundwork of membership. Even the freehold tenure of a house would not serve to mark the line, for leases for years were becoming fashionable in the big towns. The gilds, especially perhaps the gilds of merchants, set an example. The community of burgesses is a voluntary association. Some men, it may be, have a right to join it, while others have no such right; but every member of it has joined it by a definite act. He has entered the

---

[1] Stubbs, Const. Hist. i. 454.

[2] Even the Italian lawyers, whose doctrines at a later time affect our English law, are inclined to admit that there are certain kinds of corporations which are permitted by the general law, and which therefore can and may be formed without any special licence from the ruler. The *universitas* requires at his hands approbation, rather than creation, and this approbation may be considered as given in advance and by general law to corporations formed for certain laudable objects. See Gierke, D. G. R. iii. 206, 288, 368, 436. Many legists admitted that the corporate character can be acquired by prescription. Ibid. 36C.

community, been admitted to it, paid an entrance-fee, 'sued out' or 'taken up' his liberty.

A step is being made towards corporateness. The borough Admission of burgesses. begins to look somewhat like a religious house or an order of knights. Just as the monk or the templar becomes professed of his own free will and is solemnly received into the order, so the new burgess enters 'the borough' (not the physical borough, but an ideal borough) of his own free will and is solemnly received into the community. If the monk took vows, so did the burgess: at Ipswich he swore upon his father's sword to maintain the freedom and conceal the secrets of the town[1]. This process of transformation is still exceedingly obscure[2]. Besides the influence of the gild, the influence of the sworn *communa* of the French town may be suspected[3]. But also the freedom from toll which has been granted to the burgesses may have played an important part at this crisis. The townsfolk perceived that they had enviable 'liberties' which were communicable to others, that they could, at least for some intents, make burgesses out of non-burgesses, that by so doing they could raise money, and that within limits which were not precisely ascertained they could themselves define the class which should enjoy the chartered liberties[4]. The task of tracing this change must be left to those who can afford to treat each borough separately, for doubtless it went further in some towns than in others; but it helps to transmute the idea of burgherhood.

In course of time a definite right to burgherhood is estab- The title to burgherhood. lished. Though there were many small variations, there was ultimately among our greater boroughs a remarkably unanimous agreement that this right was communicated by a father to his sons, or at least to his firstborn son, and by a master to his apprentices. We have not here a case of inheritance, for the son may claim 'his freedom' in his father's lifetime; but

[1] Ipswich Domesday, p. 129.

[2] For the parallel process in Germany, see Gierke, D. G. R. ii. 692. King John had licensed the sworn commune in many French towns; see Giry, Établissements de Rouen, *passim*.

[3] It seems highly improbable that the oath to maintain the liberties of the town was developed out of the oath of allegiance.

[4] See the early instances from Ipswich in Gross, Gild Merchant, ii. 123 ff. See also Ipswich Domesday, p. 153; Norwich Customal, c. 36. For a complaint of the sale of citizenship in London, see R. H. i. 405.

the community continues its existence by virtue of an individualistic communication of right by an old to a new member.
The right seems to flow downwards in blood and craft. It is a
curious idea and has not been subjected to the careful exploration that it deserves. Despite its universality, we may, at
least as regards the apprentices, doubt its great antiquity, and
should not be surprised if it had its origin in a practice which
exacted from the son of a burgess a smaller entrance-fee than
was demanded from other applicants[1]. When and where this
right to burgherhood was established, the privileged body
might become by degrees very different from and much smaller
than the sum of the substantial men of the town; but we have
little reason to suppose that during the age of which we are
here speaking this effect had become prominent. No doubt
from the first there were in the town many people who were
not deemed to be 'burgesses' or active and fully qualified
members of the community of the vill. There were women,
sons living with fathers, menial servants, apprentices: in a
word the 'mainpast' of the burgesses. Persons of this sort
there were in every community, in every township. Nor is it
impossible that some others were left out on the score of their
poverty: they had contributed nothing to those heavy sums
which were the price of the charters, and could pay no entrance-
fee to the common chest. It is likely that from the remotest
period our ancestors were familiar with the idea that a class of
men may be within a community and yet have no right to
share in the conduct of its affairs. Such probably was the
position of the *bordarii* and *cotarii* in the villages of old time[2].
This idea bore new fruit in the borough; many men might be
within the community of the town and yet have no vote in any
burgensic assembly.

The 'subject' in the borough charters.

These changes take place in a darkness which is unillumi-
nated by legal theory. Legal thought and legal phrases seem
to be lagging behind the facts. If we examine the form of a

---

[1] Sometimes a charter bestows privileges on the son of a burgess in his
father's lifetime; see for Newcastle, Acts of Parl. of Scotland, i. 33, 34; Records
of Chesterfield, 33. Compare Gierke, D. G. R. ii. 694; and Records of Leicester,
p. 219.

[2] They were *Schutzgenossen*, but not *Vollgenossen*. So in the German towns
there will be 'passive burghers,' *Bürger ohne Bürgerrecht*. See Gierke, D. G. R.
ii. 299, 702. The position of the Scholars in the *universitas* of Masters and
Scholars is similar.

borough charter we see that the king or some other lord is conceived as making a gift of franchises to 'the burgesses' or 'the men' of a certain town 'and their heirs.'   But in what mode, we may ask, does this gift operate?   (1) It may possibly give to each person, who at this moment is a burgess of the town, a several right which he will enjoy in severalty and transmit to his heirs.   Or (2) it may confer on all the now burgesses of the town a right of which they are to be joint tenants or tenants in common, and may thus institute some kind of co-proprietorship.   Or (3) it may be placing the right in some corporation or group-person in which the burgesses of the town are organized and unified.   And if we have to consider [p. 657] rights we have also to consider duties. 'The burgesses and their heirs' become liable for the farm of their borough.   What does this mean?   Who is liable to pay what?   What goods or lands can the king seize if the rent of the borough be not duly paid to him?

The difficulty of these questions will best be seen if beside a borough charter we place three other instruments, very similar to it in form, however different they may be from it and from each other in substance.   The Abbot and Convent of Malmesbury declare that they have granted a certain piece of ground at Pilton near Barnstaple 'to the men who have taken it of our house—our cell—of Pilton for the purpose of building houses, to have and to hold to them and their heirs of our said house of Pilton by rendering to the said church twelve pence yearly from each burgage[1].'   Now in this case we can hardly doubt that the rights given by the charter are rights given to each tenant severally, and rights that he is to enjoy in severalty.   He has taken a plot of building land and is to hold it heritably on the terms of burgage tenure, though Pilton is not, and is not to be, a borough.   There is to be no corporation; nor only so, there is to be (so far as we can see) no co-ownership, no common enjoyment.   We turn to another case.   King John would have it known that he has granted to his men of Cornwall that certain moors shall be disafforested and that the said men may hunt thereon; also that without their consent their serfs shall not be received into the liberties of the king's boroughs; also that the fees of the honour of Mortain (which are small[2]) shall not pay the full rate of scutage. 'Therefore,'

Discussion of the charters.

---

[1] Registr. Malmesbur. ii. 34.   [2] See above, p. 257.

he says, 'we will that the said men of Cornwall and their heirs
shall hold all the premises of us and our heirs with all liberties
and free customs[1].' The third charter to which we would ask
attention is one by which this same King John made a grant
to all the free men of England and their heirs; it is no other
than what will be known for all time as the Great Charter.
At the end of its famous clauses we read how all the men of
England are to have and to hold certain liberties to them and
their heirs of King John and his heirs for ever.

Charters for the borough, the county, the whole land.

Now these last two instruments, the Cornish charter and [p. 658]
the Great Charter, are in form just like an ordinary borough
charter. The king grants *libertates* to the men of Nottingham,
the men of Cornwall, the men of England and their heirs. In
what mode do the grantees hold the liberties? Does each
'man' acquire a several right to be enjoyed in severalty? Do
all the 'men' become tenants in common or joint tenants; or
again. is the true recipient of the grant a group-person, a
corporation? The form of the Great Charter and the charter
for the men of Cornwall compel us to say that these questions
have not been faced. If we take the Great Charter and work
out any theory as to its grantees and the mode in which they
received the boon, we are brought to absurdities. The modern
Englishman who would take advantage of its provisions must
show himself heir of some one who lived in 1215; or, if a clause
of the charter be broken, then either all Englishmen must join
in an action against the offender, or the corporation of England
must appear by its attorney. There remains the possibility
that this is a gift to uncertain persons, to all and singular who
at any time shall answer the description 'men of the realm of
England':—but is such a gift conceivable?

Charters and laws.

It may be replied that Magna Carta, whatever its form, is
in substance no deed of grant but a code of law. That is true;
but the fact remains that the form of this solemn instrument
is that of a deed of grant. That was the form which to the
prelates, clerks and lawyers of the time seemed the most apt
for the purpose. The king was to grant liberties to the men of
England as he had granted them to the men of Cornwall and
the men of London. Or let us look at the other side of this
similitude:—Henry III., if he grants liberties to the men of
Nottingham, will execute an instrument whose jural form will

---

[1] Rot. Cart. 206.

be exactly the same as that of the charters which he seals in favour of the men of England. This makes the borough of Nottingham look, not like a corporation, but merely like a portion of the earth's surface within which certain laws are to prevail.

Now it can hardly be doubted that certain clauses in the borough charters should be read as grants made to individuals of rights that are to be enjoyed by them in severalty. Such, for example, would be a clause declaring that the burgesses and their heirs shall hold their tenements in free burgage. It is like the Abbot of Malmesbury's charter for the men of Pilton. Each burgess gets a right to hold his tenement heritably at a burgage rent. 'The burgesses of X and their heirs' is here but a compendious phrase which saves us the trouble of naming many men by their proper names. And may this not also be true of other clauses: for instance, of the clause which declares how the burgesses and their heirs are to be free of toll throughout all England? Suppose the grant made to the burgesses of X; a certain burgess of X goes into the town of Y; toll is demanded from him; he refuses to pay; his chattels are seized. Now who is wronged, who can bring an action against the offender? Has this injury been done to the individual merchant, or to the mass of the men of X as co-owners of a franchise, or to the corporation known as 'the borough of X'; or again, have there been several wrongs? There is good cause for doubting whether the lawyers of this age were ready with an answer to these questions. On the one hand, we may find two citizens of Lincoln, who have been distrained in the town of Lynn, bringing their action against the bailiff of Lynn and relying on a charter granted to the citizens of Lincoln[1]. On the other hand, the plaintiffs who take action for such a cause will often be described as 'the citizens,' or 'the burgesses,' or 'the bailiffs,' or 'the mayor and commonalty' of the town whose charter has been infringed[2]; and yet we can not be certain that the courts would have given one action to the individual trader and another to the community, and compelled the offenders to pay first for unlawfully seizing a merchant's chattels and then for infringing a city's charter. Modern lawyers may be inclined

Criticism of the borough charters.

[p. 659]

---

[1] Y. B. 49 Edw. III. f. 6 (Hil. pl. 10); Gross, Gild Merchant, ii. 177 ff.
[2] Note Book, pl. 16, 145.

to say that when such a clause is treated as conferring rights on each individual burgess it is treated as an act of legislation, not as an act of donation; that the burgess who brings the action is not required to prove (very possibly he could not prove) that he was heir to one of the original donees; that in reality a law or an ordinance has been made declaring that any person who at any time shall be a citizen of Lincoln shall [p. 660] be quit of toll; but then this distinction between laws and grants is not one that we find in our records.

Rights conferred on the burgesses jointly.

There are, however, other clauses in the borough charters which can not be thus treated. For example, there is the clause relating to the fee farm of the 'borough,' which certainly does not mean that each burgess is to hold a certain share of the 'borough,' paying for that share a certain rent to the king. Again, so far as we have observed, the important clause which declares that the burgesses shall not be impleaded outside the borough is rarely, if ever, construed to mean that a right of refusing to answer in foreign courts is conferred on each burgess. On the contrary, when a burgess is impleaded in the king's court, the regular practice is that the officers or 'the burgesses' of the borough should intervene and claim cognizance of the cause, or (to use the language of the time) 'crave their court and obtain it[1].' Once more, if we take such a franchise as the return of writs, we can not possibly treat this as having been conferred on individuals to be enjoyed by them in severalty. In some sense or another it must belong to the community as a whole. But then in what sense?

The community as bearer of rights.

This brings us to the great problem. Is the right conceived as inhering in many men or in an organized group which is for this purpose an indivisible unit? The best answer that we can suggest for this difficult question is that the lawyers are trying to retain old forms of speech and thought and to regard the burgesses as a set of co-proprietors, while at the same time they are beginning to know that the borough community differs in kind from all other 'land communities' and that Bracton has got hold of the right idea when he calls it an *universitas*.

[1] Note Book, 294, 314, 489, 577, 589, 952, 1429. The Norwich Custumal c. 13 provides that when cognizance is claimed for the civic court the costs of the proceeding shall be paid by the defendant, but, if he can not pay, then the chamberlain of the city must pay. The claim of cognizance is treated as a matter which is of great importance to all the citizens.

In the first place, they are beginning to recognize the fact that the idea of inheritance will no longer serve to describe the means by which the existence of 'the burgesses' is perpetuated. The words 'and their successors' begin to supplant the old formula 'and their heirs[1].' This is a step in advance, for on the one hand the burgensic community is separated from the set of co-proprietors, and on the other hand it is brought into line with religious bodies. Even this novel phrase, however, is not very good, for the new burgess or new monk does not of necessity 'succeed' any other burgess or other monk. Our forefathers found it hard to conceive that one and the same community can continue to exist unless each new member steps into the place of some departed member. We have seen how in modern times there was within our boroughs an individualistic communication of right by father to son or master to apprentice, and this can be vaguely pictured as a kind of succession or perhaps of inheritance[2]. Down even to the present day the formal language of our law but ill expresses what has long ago become our thought. A transaction which would be commonly and aptly described as a contract between the University and the Town of Cambridge will become upon parchment a contract between Chancellor, Master and Scholars of the one part and Mayor, Aldermen and Burgesses of the other[3]. This retention by legal documents of a style or title which seems to lay stress rather on the plurality than on the unity of the group has set snares for those who would penetrate beneath style and title to the thought that is struggling to express itself[4].

Inheritance, succession and organization.

---

[1] An early example, from 1225, will be found in Nottingham Records, i. 18–20: the burgesses of Retford and their successors are to hold of the burgesses of Nottingham and their successors. See Gross, Gild Merchant, i. 95. The new phrase makes its way but slowly into royal charters; the chancery was conservative. However, for an early example of 'heirs and successors' in a royal document see John's charter for Waterford: Chartae, Privilegia et Immunitates, Irish Record Commission, p. 13.

[2] The phrase which tells us how a corporation may 'hold land in succession' is a misdescription of what really happens. Littleton and Choke make some good remarks about the use of the words 'and their successors' in Y. B. 39 Hen. VI. f. 13 (Mich. pl. 17).

[3] Apparently in Germany the style which purports to grant liberties 'to the citizens, their heirs and successors' yielded at what Englishmen must call a very early date to the style which treats 'the city' as the recipient of the chartered rights. See Gierke, D. G. R. ii. 627 ff.

[4] Thus, in spite of Mrs Green's able arguments (Town Life, ii. 231), we are

But we must pass from form to substance. Our law felt no difficulty about attributing misdeeds of many sorts and kinds to communities. The counties, hundreds and townships are always being fined and amerced for wrongful acts and defaults. So too the boroughs can be punished. Every borough in England from the city of London downwards lives in daily [p. 661] peril of forfeiting its charters, of seeing its mercantile privileges annulled, of seeing its elected magistrates displaced and itself handed over to the mercies of some royal *custos* or *firmarius*. If Londoners insult the queen or take the wrong side in the Barons' War, the city will have to redeem its privileges with an immense sum[1]. If in the town of Derby 'superfluous' tolls are taken and the members of the gild merchant are unduly favoured, the liberties of the borough will be seized[2]. The city of York claimed to farm the Ainsty; in support of this claim the mayor produced a charter which purported to be of the fourth year of King John; but the word *quarto* was [p. 662] written over an erasure. Judgment was given that the mayor should go to prison, that the charter should be quashed, and that the citizens should lose all that they claimed thereunder[3]. The mayor of Sandwich was found guilty of asserting by acts of violence certain supposed franchises of his town; 'and because he is convicted of the said trespass, and because whatever is done by the mayor in matters affecting the community is the act of the community itself, it is adjudged that the community of Sandwich lose its liberty[4].' Now between the punishment of a borough and the punishment of a county or village little difference would at first be seen. The one can be fined; the other can be fined. The fact that the burden of the impost will distribute itself much more automatically in the rural district than in the borough, where movable wealth will probably be assessed, is a fact of which no account need be taken by the court which inflicts the penalty. Still

inclined to think that in early documents the same thought can be and is expressed by (1) *Nos maior et burgenses*, (2) *Nos maior et communitas villae*, (3) *Nos maior et burgenses et tota communitas villae*. The last of these phrases aims at showing that the mayor and burgesses are not to be taken *ut singuli*, but are, as we should say, 'acting in their corporate capacity.'

[1] Riley, Chronicles, p. 84: the Londoners prayed that only the guilty might be punished.

[2] P. Q. W. 160.

[3] Placit. Abbrev. 199.

[4] Placit. Abbrev. 273.

it must become evident sooner or later that the borough
community can be punished in a peculiar fashion; it has
liberties and it can forfeit them. It can be equated with
other franchise-holders and punished as one of them would
be punished if he abused his franchise. Taken merely as unit
it can be punished, and the punishment may continue to
operate while old members are yielding place to new, whereas
a fine inflicted on a hundred divides itself immediately into
punishments inflicted upon certain men who are now living.
Sharp distinctions are not to be looked for in this quarter.
Even in the nineteenth century a county may be indicted for
non-repair of highways and until the other day a hundred
might be sued if rioters did damage[1]. But still the 'liberties'
of the borough give the law an opportunity of enforcing here
more clearly than elsewhere the thought that if the organized
community acting organically breaks the law, it in its unity
can be and should be punished[2].

In the region of civil liability little advance was possible. Civil
The burgesses may 'farm' the borough; but an ordinary township may farm its vill[3]. When the king accepted the burgesses
as farmers in place of the sheriff, he certainly did not mean to
exchange the liability of a well-to-do man for that of an unit
which had few, if any, chattels. On the contrary, instead of
looking to the wealth of one man, he now looked to the wealth
[p. 663] of many. If the rent of the borough fell into arrear, he could
proceed against all the burgesses or any burgess. A common
practice of the exchequer was to attack the rich. The sheriff
would be ordered to summon six of the richer burgesses to
answer for the rent[4]. This was for the king a convenient
procedure. He could exact payment of his rent, his fines and

---

[1] Stat. 49 & 50 Vic. c. 38. The claim for compensation is now made to 'the
police authority' and paid out of the police rate.

[2] The talk about 'fictitious' personality did not prevent the legists nor, with
some exceptions, the canonists from holding that an *universitas* can commit a
crime and be punished for it. On the contrary, they went great lengths in the
punishment of corporations; some of them were prepared to say that if a *civitas*
commits a capital crime, such as treason, *aratro decapitetur*. See Gierke,
D. G. R. iii. 234, 342, 402, 491, 738. In modern America the old doctrines
which would deprive a corporation of corporate existence if it abused its power
have borne new fruit, and joint-stock companies have learned the meaning of
quo waranto.

[3] Firma Burgi, c. 3. See above, p. 623.

[4] Firma Burgi, p. 157.

amercements from those who had money, and then could say
to the burgesses at large—'Now you can settle the ultimate
incidence of this impost among yourselves; the settlement is
your concern, not mine; at all events, it is not my concern so
long as I am acting, not as judge, but as creditor; for all of you
are, and each of you is, liable to me for the whole sum.'   Then
inside the borough, or the manor, there would be a settlement.
To meet the annual rent there were funds which normally
would be sufficient; the burgage rents, the tolls, the profits of
the court should be applied for this purpose, and the elected [p. 664]
bailiffs might be bound to make good the deficiency[1].   If a fine
or amercement had been inflicted, then a rate might become
necessary.   The men of a rural manor would probably be
charged according to the scheme of commensurable tenements;
the burgesses would be assessed according to their wealth in
goods and chattels.   If really there were any lands or goods
which we could properly describe as belonging to the borough
corporation, these also might be taken, but they would be only
a part, and usually a very small part, of the property of the
community; for the property of the community comprised, at
least for this purpose, all the lands and all the goods of every
burgess.   Development was especially slow in this quarter, for
not until 1285[2] could land, as distinct from the profits of land,
be regarded as an 'available asset' for the satisfaction of debts,
and the nascent municipal corporation had few, if any, chattels,
and little, if any, land that bore crops[3].

The com-
munities in
litigation.

Nor as yet can we find any marked distinction between the
various communities when they take part in litigation.   The
doctrine that a community can appear in court only by
attorney, that it can not possibly appear in person, has certainly
not been grasped.   'The citizens of X' or 'the burgesses of Y'
are said to appear, and they are not said to appear by attorney.
Or again, the mayor, or the bailiffs, or the mayor and bailiffs
appear to urge the claims and defend the rights of the community.   It is so with communities to which we can not

---

[1] See above, p. 655.

[2] Stat. West. ii. c. 18, which introduces the writ of *elegit*.

[3] In cent. xv. the notion of pure corporate liability was being grasped; see
above, p. 493.   For the growth of Italian doctrine, see Gierke, D. G. R. iii. 214,
379.   A subsidiary liability of the *singuli* for the debt of the *universitas* was
maintained by many writers.

ascribe incorporation[1]. In the exchequer 'the men' of this hundred, 'the men' of that township, are sued for fines, taxes and amercements. 'The fullers and dyers of Lincoln' sue 'the aldermen and reeves of Lincoln[2].' In Edward II.'s time Emery Gegge and Robert Wawayn 'on behalf of themselves and the other poor and middling burgesses of Scarborough' sue Roger
[p. 665] atte Cross, John Hugh's son, Warin Draper 'and the other rich burgesses of the said town[3].' John Abel is attached to answer Betino Frescobaldi 'and his companions merchants of the firm (*societas*) of the Frescobaldi of Florence[4].' At a later time when an action was brought against 'the Fellowship of the Lombard Merchants of Florence in London' and the sheriff, by way of making that society appear, distrained two of its members, the argument was advanced that this was an illegal act[5]; but in the thirteenth century we hear no such arguments; no one seems to think that they can be used. Much rather we are inclined to say that if there is any group of men having a permanent common interest, and if an unlawful act is done which can be regarded as a lesion of that interest, even though it does actual damage only to some one member of the group, then the members of it may join in an action, or one of them may sue on behalf of himself and all the other members:—as Bracton says 'Omnes conqueri possunt et unus sub nomine universitatis[6].' This is so within wide and indefinite limits. In the case of a borough attacked from without, it is natural that the complaint should be lodged by the chief officers of the community. The burghers compose a body, and what the head does in matters concerning the community, the whole body does[7]. But this is hardly more than a special instance of a

---

[1] Note Book, pl. 16: the burgesses of Scarborough complain of the bailiffs of York; the complaint is answered by the mayor, reeve and bailiffs; pl. 145: the burgesses of Beverley complain of the bailiffs of Lincoln; the complaint is answered by the mayor and bailiffs. Placit. Abbrev. p. 148: the whole county of Huntingdonshire sues the burgesses of Huntingdon. See Firma Burgi, ch. 7. For cases in which the *homines* of places that are not boroughs appear, see above, p. 633. In 1275 the little township of Graveley 'by its attorney' brings an action in the court of the Fair of St Ives; Select Pleas in Manorial Courts, p. 150.

[2] Placit. Abbrev. 65 (temp. Joh.).

[3] Firma Burgi, p. 96.   [4] Firma Burgi, p. 97 (temp. Edw. II.).

[5] Y. B. 19 Hen. VI. f. 80 (Trin. pl. 11).   [6] Bracton, f. 228 b.

[7] Placit. Abbrev. 273 (temp. Edw. I.): 'et factum maioris in hiis que tangunt communitatem est factum ipsius communitatis.'

general rule. Instead of being attacked from without, the borough may be divided within. If so, then *A* and *B* 'on behalf of the poor burgesses' can sue *C* and *D* 'and all other the rich burgesses.'

Debts owed to communities. Everywhere we find the same uncertain grasp of principles which we are wont to regard as elementary. Henry III., when he died, owed £400 to the community of Northampton:—so say the jurors of Northampton. Here at last, we may say, is a distinct case of a debt due to a corporation. But how was it incurred? Thus, say the jurors:—during the twenty last years of his reign the king's purveyors (*captores*) took to his use peltry to that value in the fairs of Northampton, Stamford, [p. 666] St Ives, Boston, Winchester and St Edmunds; what is more he owes the drapers of Northampton £100 for goods taken in the same fairs. The story, if true, is sad, for 'many of the townsfolk are dying of hunger and begging their bread and have abandoned their tenements in the town and the town itself[1].' But King Henry has not been taking the goods of a corporation; we much doubt whether there has been any joint-stock trading by all the burgesses or all the drapers of Northampton; he has taken the goods of individual traders. Nevertheless, in popular estimation he has incurred a debt to the community by taking goods from the stalls of Northampton merchants who were exercising 'liberties' of trading which were granted to all the men of Northampton and their heirs. Again, if a merchant of *X* owes a trading debt to a merchant of *Y*, then if other merchants of *X* go to the town of *Y*, or to some fair where the creditor finds them, they will like enough be held answerable for the debt—at all events if he proves that he has made a fruitless effort to obtain justice in the court of *X*:—they are the *communares* of the principal debtor, they are 'his peers and parceners,' they are 'in scot and lot' with him, and they, and each of them, must answer for his trading debts: for debts, that is, incurred in the exercise of trading privileges which they all enjoy in common[2]. And should a bailiff of *X* take

---

[1] R. H. ii. 5.

[2] Select Pleas in Manorial Courts, pp. 134–5; but the remarks there made about the gild merchant are withdrawn. This is the point of a clause common in borough charters to the effect that a burgess shall not be distrained for a debt for which he is neither principal debtor nor pledge. See in particular Records of Nottingham, i. 40. In 1275 (Stat. West. I. c. 23) this was made a general

unlawful toll from a merchant of Y, then woe betide the merchant of X who enters the town of Y. 'Collective liability'—this seems the best phrase—we may see everywhere, in so much that we are tempted to say, not merely *Quod communitas debet, debent singuli,* but also *Quod singulus debet, debet communitas.* In all seriousness we are driven to some such proposition as the following:—If several men have some permanent common [p. 667] interest, and in any matter relating to the prosecution of that interest one of them commits a wrong or incurs a debt, all and each of them will be liable. This is not the outcome of any doctrine of 'implied agency,' it expresses the nature of a *communitas.* But pure corporate liability—that we shall not easily find[1].

Nevertheless (and here we must turn to the other side of *The common seal.* the picture) the burgensic community is attaining that kind of unity which is personality. When in 1200 the community of Ipswich received its charter from King John, one of their first acts was to obtain a common seal and commit it to the care of the two bailiffs and one other of the chief portmen; they were sworn to set it to no letter or instrument save for the common honour and profit of the burgesses of the town, and only to use it with the assent of their peers, that is, of the other chief portmen[2]. No doubt by this time the greater boroughs were getting themselves seals[3]. Now we would not exaggerate the importance of this step—and we have seen how in Edward I.'s day the county of Devon had a seal[4]—still it was important. In the first place, it was a step towards the co-ordination of the boroughs with the religious houses, which in their turn were being co-ordinated with individual men. In

---

statutory rule so far as Englishmen were concerned. Not until 1353 was the benefit of the new rule extended to alien merchants. See Stat. 27 Edw. III. st. 2, c. 17 ; Fleta, p. 136 ; Coke, Second Institute, 204.

[1] Madox, Firma Burgi, c. 8: 'Anciently a corporate community might be answerable for the trespass or debt of particular persons members thereof; and particular members for the trespass or debt of the community.' Sohm, Die deutsche Genossenschaft, p. 19 : 'Die Genossenschaft haftet für die Schulden der Genossen, und der Genosse haftet für die Schulden der Genossenschaft. Beide Sätze gehen durch das ganze Mittelalter.'

[2] Gross, Gild Merchant, ii. 119, 121.

[3] An impression of the common seal used at Nottingham in 1225 may be seen in the frontispiece of Nottingham Records, vol. i.

[4] See above, p. 535.

the second place, there was now an outward and visible sign of the borough's unity[1]. A mode of conveying rights and creating obligations is established which goes far to confute the notion that the *communitas* is a mere sum of men with joint rights and joint liabilities. If the *communitas* be this, then the act by which it conveys away its rights or subjects itself to an obligation should, so we naturally suppose, be some act done by all its members. And so we have seen how the men of [p. 668] Toddington, thinking that they had land to give to the Priory of Dunstable, met in one place at a court holden for Toddington and there by their unanimous consent made the grant. And then we have seen how afterwards they asserted that the transaction did not bind them because some of them were infants when the grant was made[2]. This is not the way in which corporators behave; it is the way in which co-owners behave. No doubt there are other fashions in which a corporation can become bound beside the apposition of a common seal; we must not make our English formalism a measure for all mankind; still a formality which somewhat distinctly marks off some *communitates* from others, and a formality which is never used by co-owners who have come to co-ownership by the operation of merely private law, which is never used by co-heirs, is important. What is more the seal is intrusted to the guardianship of a few. The community at Ipswich which has just received its charter, which has just exercised its new right of electing bailiffs, which is in the act of establishing a council of chief portmen and a gild merchant, seems to feel that not only is it passing from a lower to a higher rank among the communities of the land, but that some new degree or even kind of unity has been attained: it must have a seal that is its, for it may now come before the law as pure unit and live as a person among persons. Rules as to when and by whom this seal may be affixed will be developed in course of time, and a definite theory about the power of majorities will take the

---

[1] Merewether and Stephens, History of Boroughs, p. 443, mention fifteen places which had seals, but 'which have never been incorporated.' But most, if not all, of them had at one time or another a claim to be called boroughs, and many of them were told to send members to Parliament in Edward I.'s reign. As early as 1296 the parishioners of St Mary Magdalen at Oxford had a common seal. See Blakiston, Durham College Rolls, Oxford Hist. Soc. Collectanea, iii. pp. vi, 26.

[2] See above, p. 630.

place of some loose notion which demands unanimity but is content if the voices of a dissentient few are overwhelmed by the shout of the assentient many. The unanimity of ancient moots is wonderful. Unconscious fiction begins its work at an early time. With one voice all the people say 'Yea, yea' or 'Nay, nay.' But now there is to be a small deliberative assembly 'to govern and maintain the borough' and the votes of the twelve will be counted[1].

What now is necessary is that the community, acting as a unit, should begin to develop its property. As regards rights in land, critically decisive acts are hardly to be expected at this early time. In some sort the 'waste' land, intramural and extramural, may belong to the community. But on the one hand this community must come to terms with the king about the right of 'approvement,' which is rather in him than in it[2], and, on the other hand, it must come to terms with the *singuli* about their rights of 'common'; and this may be a long process. The early examples in which a community disposes of land have a strong tinge of co-proprietorship about them[3]. Apparently the fourteenth century had come before there was any considerable quantity of land that was paying rent into municipal chests; and until this was happening, the notion of a true corporate ownership of town lands was insecure.

The borough's property.

Unless we are mistaken, the property that was most important in the evolution of corporate unity was the property that the borough had in its franchises, but more especially in [p.675] its tolls. Already in 1225 'the burgesses' of Nottingham under their common seal had demised to 'the burgesses' of Retford the tolls 'belonging to the borough of Nottingham' and arising within certain geographical limits—'to have and to hold at

The borough's property in its tolls.

---

[1] For the development of practice and theory touching the power of majorities, see Gierke, D. G. R. ii. 478; iii. 220, 322, 392, 470.

[2] See above, p. 653.

[3] Take for instance the transaction chronicled in Reg. Malmesb. ii. 150–5. The abbot and convent quit-claim 'to the burgesses who are of the gild merchant of Malmesbury their heirs and assigns' all right of pasture in certain land. On the other hand, *A. B*, alderman of the gild, *C. D* and *E. F*, stewards of the gild, seventeen other named persons, 'and the whole intrinsic community of the said vill and of the gild merchant,' declare that 'they' have quit-claimed to the abbey part of 'their' heath called Portmanneshethe, and that none of the said community nor any of their successors or heirs will claim any right therein, and thereto they set their common seal.

farm to the said burgesses of Retford and their successors of us and our successors for ever' at a rent of twenty marks[1]. Now this we can hardly regard otherwise than as a transaction between two persons. It can scarcely be thought that the now burgesses of Nottingham are in any tolerable sense co-owners of the right of taking toll. No one of them is entitled to an aliquot share of the tolls; no one of them has anything that he could demise to a burgess of Derby or of Retford; nay, if the Retford folk took a separate deed from each man of Nottingham they would get nothing thereby. What is wanted is not joint action but constitutional action; a common seal must be affixed by those who according to the constitution of the borough are entitled to affix it. Very possibly no man of Nottingham had yet said to himself 'Our borough is a person.' Had he done so he would have been in advance of the acutest English lawyers of his time, for Bracton and his master Azo were not very clear that the *res civitatis* were not the *res omnium civium*. But had he heard how a pope was ascribing a 'fictitious personality' to the *universitas*, he would perhaps have said: 'Yes, the Holy Father is right; our borough of Nottingham is a person.'

The ideal will of the borough.

It is in this region that we may find 'the ideal will' of the borough, a permanent purpose that keeps it together just as a religious house is kept together by the purpose of glorifying God according to the Benedictine or Cistercian rule. The borough wills to maintain and profit by its franchises, notably to take toll and be quit of toll. 'The franchises and liberties of the City of Norwich I will maintain and sustain with my body and goods'—such is the oath which the freeman of Norwich will take from century to century. The county, the hundred, the township, has no such will, no such definite, abiding purpose. It has no franchises, or, if it has a few, not such as must be vigorously 'maintained and sustained' by the bodies and goods of its members and anxiously guarded and administered by its rulers.

Last words on the borough's corporateness.

We may now sum up the whole of a long discussion which has strayed into regions that are insufficiently explored. The question, When did our English boroughs become incorporate? is one to which no precise answer can be given. It is a question about the evolution of a theory on the one hand and

---

[1] *Records of Nottingham*, i. 19.

the appearance of certain political, social and economic facts on
the other, and then it is a question about the application of the
theory to the facts.   The process was slow, and those who were
concerned in it were unconscious of it.   But this we may say,
that before the end of the thirteenth century the organization
that was to be found in our greater towns was of a kind which
imperatively demanded (so it will seem to us) some new idea.
Such old categories of legal thought as the vague *communitas*
were no longer adequate to express the relationships and habits
that were being formed, and a new line had to be drawn
between the boroughs and the other *communitates*.   We may
add too that Bracton saw this, though he saw it dimly[1].   And
if the facts were ready for the theory, a theory was being
fashioned for the facts, though those who were preparing it
were Italian lawyers.   But as yet there had been no junction
between English life and Italian thought.   'Church' and
'borough' are still standing far apart from each other; the
English courts are not yet co-ordinating 'mayor, aldermen
and burgesses' with 'abbot and monks' under the rubric of
Corporations.   What happened in the fourteenth and fifteenth
centuries must some day be told us by one who is adequately
learned.   If we may venture a guess, he will say that, along
with some ideas which were of the highest value, there stole
into our temporal law others which should have been left in that
ecclesiastical sphere which was their native home[2].   But for us
at the moment all this lies in the future.   At present we have
not heard those negative propositions which will give a keen
edge to the law of corporations.   We listen in vain for any one
to say that the lands of the city are not simply the lands of
the citizens, or that a debt owed by the borough is not a
debt owed by the burgesses.   So long as such sayings are not
said, the personality of the group-person is latent and insecure.

At the present time there is perhaps some danger that a
little too much stress will be laid on the communal traits of
medieval history.   It is a hard task to see old times just as
they were.   To a school which could only perceive individual
men and a 'sovereign one or many' succeeds another which, at

*The com-
munities
and the
nation.*

---

[1] See above, pp. 496, 654.

[2] We are not hinting at any formal or thorough reception of the Italian
doctrine, but certain of its phrases became part of the common inheritance of
educated mankind.   Every one knew that a corporation is *persona ficta*, or even
nomen iuris, that it can not sin, will not be damned, and so forth.

least when dealing with medieval history, exalts the independence and autonomy of some or all of those communities which lie within a nation. Certainly it was high time that this reaction should be felt; but it must not carry us beyond the truth, and in this chapter we may have seen enough to give us pause before we assent to any grand dogma which would make [p. 677] 'communalism' older than 'individualism.' The apparent communalism of old law covers an individualism which has deep and ancient roots. Every right, every duty, however communal its character, spontaneously becomes the right, the duty, of an individual by attaching itself to the land that he holds. Because he holds a certain messuage he may turn out two oxen on 'the common of the vill': because he holds a certain messuage he is a doomsman of the county court. And then again in the twelfth and thirteenth centuries we have seen [p. 678] some mighty forces, making not against, but for communalism of a certain sort. In many quarters we have seen their play. The county is amerced for false judgments, the hundred is fined for murders, the townships are compelled to attend the justices, men are forced into frankpledge, the burghers are jointly and severally liable for the *firma burgi*, the manorial lord treats his villeins as one responsible group. Men are drilled and regimented into communities in order that the state may be strong and the land may be at peace. Much of the communal life that we see is not spontaneous. The community is a community, not because it is a self-sufficient organism, but because it is a subordinate member of a greater community, of a nation. The nation is not a system of federated communities; the king is above all and has a direct hold on every individual. The communities are far more often the bearers of duties than of rights; they appear before the courts chiefly as punishable units; the proudest city will lose its liberties if it exceeds or abuses those powers that are given to it from above. But above the king himself—thus even a royal justice may think—is the greatest of all communities, 'the university of the realm[1].' The England that saw the birth of English law, the England of Magna Carta and the first parliaments, was a much governed and a little England.

[1] Bracton, f. 171 b.

END OF VOL. I.